AMERICAN COUNCIL OF LEARNED SOCIETIES

Dictionary
of Scientific
Biography

cSs

DICTIONARY
OF
SCIENTIFIC BIOGRAPHY

PUBLISHED UNDER THE AUSPICES OF
THE AMERICAN COUNCIL OF LEARNED SOCIETIES

The American Council of Learned Societies, organized in 1919 for the purpose of advancing the study of the humanities and of the humanistic aspects of the social sciences, is a nonprofit federation comprising forty national scholarly groups. The Council represents the humanities in the United States in the International Union of Academies, provides fellowships and grants-in-aid, supports research-and-planning conferences and symposia, and sponsors special projects and scholarly publications.

MEMBER ORGANIZATIONS

AMERICAN PHILOSOPHICAL SOCIETY, 1743
AMERICAN ACADEMY OF ARTS AND SCIENCES, 1780
AMERICAN ANTIQUARIAN SOCIETY, 1812
AMERICAN ORIENTAL SOCIETY, 1842
AMERICAN NUMISMATIC SOCIETY, 1858
AMERICAN PHILOLOGICAL ASSOCIATION, 1869
ARCHAEOLOGICAL INSTITUTE OF AMERICA, 1879
SOCIETY OF BIBLICAL LITERATURE, 1880
MODERN LANGUAGE ASSOCIATION OF AMERICA, 1883
AMERICAN HISTORICAL ASSOCIATION, 1884
AMERICAN ECONOMIC ASSOCIATION, 1885
AMERICAN FOLKLORE SOCIETY, 1888
AMERICAN DIALECT SOCIETY, 1889
AMERICAN PSYCHOLOGICAL ASSOCIATION, 1892
ASSOCIATION OF AMERICAN LAW SCHOOLS, 1900
AMERICAN PHILOSOPHICAL ASSOCIATION, 1901
AMERICAN ANTHROPOLOGICAL ASSOCIATION, 1902
AMERICAN POLITICAL SCIENCE ASSOCIATION, 1903
BIBLIOGRAPHICAL SOCIETY OF AMERICA, 1904
ASSOCIATION OF AMERICAN GEOGRAPHERS, 1904
HISPANIC SOCIETY OF AMERICA, 1904
AMERICAN SOCIOLOGICAL ASSOCIATION, 1905
AMERICAN SOCIETY OF INTERNATIONAL LAW, 1906
ORGANIZATION OF AMERICAN HISTORIANS, 1907
COLLEGE ART ASSOCIATION OF AMERICA, 1912
HISTORY OF SCIENCE SOCIETY, 1924
LINGUISTIC SOCIETY OF AMERICA, 1924
MEDIAEVAL ACADEMY OF AMERICA, 1925
AMERICAN MUSICOLOGICAL SOCIETY, 1934
SOCIETY OF ARCHITECTURAL HISTORIANS, 1940
ECONOMIC HISTORY ASSOCIATION, 1940
ASSOCIATION FOR ASIAN STUDIES, 1941
AMERICAN SOCIETY FOR AESTHETICS, 1942
METAPHYSICAL SOCIETY OF AMERICA, 1950
AMERICAN STUDIES ASSOCIATION, 1950
RENAISSANCE SOCIETY OF AMERICA, 1954
SOCIETY FOR ETHNOMUSICOLOGY, 1955
AMERICAN SOCIETY FOR LEGAL HISTORY, 1956
SOCIETY FOR THE HISTORY OF TECHNOLOGY, 1958
AMERICAN COMPARATIVE LITERATURE ASSOCIATION, 1960

DICTIONARY
OF
SCIENTIFIC BIOGRAPHY

CHARLES COULSTON GILLISPIE

Princeton University

EDITOR IN CHIEF

Volume IX

A. T. MACROBIUS – K. F. NAUMANN

CHARLES SCRIBNER'S SONS · NEW YORK

Editorial Board

Editorial Staff

Panel of Consultants

Contributors to Volume IX

The following are the contributors to Volume IX. Each author's name is followed by the institutional affiliation at the time of publication and the names of articles written for this volume. The symbol † indicates that an author is deceased.

S. MAQBUL AHMAD
Aligarh Muslim University
IBN MĀJID; AL-MAQDISĪ; AL-MASʿŪDĪ

GARLAND E. ALLEN
Washington University
T. H. MORGAN

FEDERICO ALLODI †
MASCAGNI

EDOARDO AMALDI
University of Rome
MAJORANA

JEAN ANTHONY
Muséum National d'Histoire Naturelle
MILNE-EDWARDS

WILLIAM H. AUSTIN
University of Houston
MORE

MARGARET E. BARON
NAPIER

ISABELLA G. BASHMAKOVA
Academy of Sciences of the U.S.S.R.
MOLIN

IRINA V. BATYUSHKOVA
Academy of Sciences of the U.S.S.R.
MUSHKETOV

ROBERT P. BECKINSALE
University of Oxford
MARTONNE

JOHN J. BEER
University of Delaware
MITTASCH

WHITFIELD J. BELL, JR.
American Philosophical Society Library
S. G. MORTON

LUIGI BELLONI
University of Milan
MALPIGHI; MARCHI; MENGHINI; MORGAGNI; MORICHINI

ENRIQUE BELTRÁN
Instituto Mexicano de Recursos Naturales
MAST

OTTO THEODOR BENFEY
Guilford College
J. L. MEYER

ALEX BERMAN
University of Cincinnati
MILLON; MOISSAN

PHILIP W. BISHOP
Smithsonian Institution
MUSHET

BRUNO A. BOLEY
Northwestern University
MENABREA

GERT H. BRIEGER
Duke University
METCHNIKOFF

T. A. A. BROADBENT †
MATHEWS

W. H. BROCK
University of Leicester
MARCHAND; MARIGNAC

THEODORE M. BROWN
City College, City University of New York
MAYOW

JED ZACHARY BUCHWALD
Harvard University
MELLONI; MOSSOTTI

K. E. BULLEN
University of Sidney
J. MILNE; MOHOROVIČIĆ

VERN L. BULLOUGH
California State University, Northridge
MONDINO DE' LUZZI

IVOR BULMER-THOMAS
MENAECHMUS; MENELAUS OF ALEXANDRIA

W. BURAU
University of Hamburg
W. F. MEYER

JOHN G. BURKE
University of California, Los Angeles
MICHEL-LÉVY; MOHS; K. F. NAUMANN

HAROLD L. BURSTYN
William Paterson College of New Jersey
M. F. MAURY; J. MURRAY

G. V. BYKOV
Academy of Sciences of the U.S.S.R.
MARKOVNIKOV

WILLIAM F. BYNUM
University College London
S. W. MITCHELL

RONALD S. CALINGER
Rensselaer Polytechnic Institute
E. H. MOORE

W. A. CAMPBELL
University of Newcastle upon Tyne
MOND

LUIGI CAMPEDELLI
University of Florence
MAGALOTTI; MAGINI

JULES CARLES
Institut Catholique de Toulouse
MOLIARD

ELOF AXEL CARLSON
State University of New York, Stony Brook
H. J. MULLER

ALBERT CAROZZI
University of Illinois
MAILLET; MUNIER-CHALMAS

CARLO CASTELLANI
MANTEGAZZA; MARCHIAFAVA; MOSSO

W. B. CASTLE
Harvard University
G. R. MINOT

JOHN CHALLINOR
University College of Wales
MANTELL

ROBERT A. CHIPMAN
University of Toledo
MARCONI

EDWIN CLARKE
University College London
C. L. MORGAN

M. J. CLARKSON
Liverpool School of Tropical Medicine
MANSON

I. B. COHEN
Harvard University
A. M. MAYER

WILLIAM COLEMAN
Johns Hopkins University
MENURET DE CHAMBAUD; NAUDIN

GEORGE W. CORNER
American Philosophical Society
MALL; C. S. MINOT

DAVID W. CORSON
University of Arizona
MASSON

ALBERT B. COSTA
Duquesne University
V. MEYER; MICHAEL

PIERRE COSTABEL
École Pratique des Hautes Études
MALEBRANCHE; MILHAUD; MORIN; MYLON

JULIANA HILL COTTON
MANARDO

MAURICE CRANSTON
London School of Economics
MILL

CONTRIBUTORS TO VOLUME IX

A. C. CROMBIE
University of Oxford
MERCENNE

MICHAEL J. CROWE
University of Notre Dame
A. F. MÖBIUS

GLYN DANIEL
University of Cambridge
MONTELIUS; MORTILLET

ROBERT DARNTON
Princeton University
MESMER

AUDREY B. DAVIS
Smithsonian Institution
MOSS; MURPHY

SUZANNE DELORME
Centre International de Synthèse
METZGER; MONTMOR

SALLY H. DIEKE
Johns Hopkins University
G. MOLL

J. DIEUDONNÉ
MINKOWSKI

YVONNE DOLD-SAMPLONIUS
AL-MĀHĀNĪ

J. DORFMAN
Academy of Sciences of the U.S.S.R.
MANDELSHTAM

SIGALIA C. DOSTROVSKY
Barnard College
MAIRAN

RAYNOR L. DUNCOMBE
Nautical Almanac Office, U.S. Naval Observatory
H. R. MORGAN

CAROLYN EISELE
Hunter College, City University of New York
G. A. MILLER

C. W. F. EVERITT
Stanford University
MAXWELL

JOSEPH EWAN
Tulane University
MICHAUX

W. V. FARRAR
University of Manchester
K. H. MEYER

I. A. FEDOSEYEV
Academy of Sciences of the U.S.S.R.
MAKAROV

MARTIN FICHMAN
York University
MAGNENUS; MALOUIN

C. P. FINLAYSON
University of Edinburgh Library
MONRO (PRIMUS); MONRO (SECUNDUS)

WALTHER FISCHER
MALLET

PIETRO FRANCESCHINI
MENEGHETTI

ERIC G. FORBES
University of Edinburgh
MASKELYNE; J. T. MAYER

H.-CHRIST. FREIESLEBEN
C. MAYER; MOLLWEIDE

O. R. FRISCH
University of Cambridge
MEITNER

JOSEPH S. FRUTON
Yale University
MEYERHOF

A. M. GEIST-HOFMAN
MOLESCHOTT

PATSY A. GERSTNER
Howard Dittrick Museum of Historical Medicine
J. MORTON

OWEN GINGERICH
Smithsonian Astrophysical Observatory
A. C. MAURY; MÉCHAIN; MESSIER

BENTLEY GLASS
State University of New York, Stony Brook
MAUPERTUIS

THOMAS F. GLICK
Boston University
MARKHAM; MARTÍNEZ

NORMAN T. GRIDGEMAN
National Research Council of Canada
VON MISES

A. T. GRIGORIAN
Academy of Sciences of the U.S.S.R.
MESHCHERSKY

M. D. GRMEK
Archives Internationales d'Histoire des Sciences
MAGENDIE

MICHAEL GROSS
Hampshire College
MAREY; MORAT

I. GRATTAN-GUINNESS
Middlesex Polytechnic of Enfield
MATHIEU

JACOB W. GRUBER
Temple University
MIVART

FRANCISCO GUERRA
Laboratorios Abelló
MOLINA; MONARDES

IAN HACKING
University of Cambridge
DE MOIVRE; MONTMOR

SAMI HAMARNEH
Smithsonian Institution
AL-MAJŪSĪ

J. L. HEILBRON
University of California, Berkeley
MOSELY

ROGER HEIM
Muséum National d'Histoire Naturelle
MAIRE

DIETER B. HERRMANN
Archenhold Observatory, Berlin
MADLER; G. MÜLLER

MAURICE HOCQUETTE
MAIGE; MANGIN

DORRIT HOFFLEIT
Maria Mitchell Observatory
M. MITCHELL

WILLIAM T. HOLSER
University of Oregon
MALLARD; MIERS

WŁODZIMIERZ HUBICKI
Marie Curie-Skłodowska University
MAIER; MARCHLEWSKI

THOMAS PARKE HUGHES
University of Pennsylvania
MIDGLEY

ALBERT Z. ISKANDAR
University of California, Los Angeles
IBN AL-NAFĪS

C. DE JAGER
Astronomical Institute at Utrecht
MINNAERT

JULIAN JAYNES
Princeton University
G. E. MÜLLER

DANIEL P. JONES
Oregon State University
MATTHIESSEN

PAUL JOVET
Centre National de Floristique
MAGNOL

HANS KANGRO
University of Hamburg
J. H. J. MÜLLER

ROBERT H. KARGON
Johns Hopkins University
W. MOLYNEAUX

GEORGE B. KAUFFMAN
California State University, Fresno
H. G. MAGNUS

B. M. KEDROV
Academy of Sciences of the U.S.S.R.
MENDELEEV

DANIEL J. KEVLES
California Institute of Technology
D. C. MILLER; MILLIKAN

GEORGE KISH
University of Michigan
MAURO; G. MERCATOR; MÜNSTER

MARC KLEIN
Faculté de Médecine, Strasbourg
MOHL

X

CONTRIBUTORS TO VOLUME IX

B. KNASTER
Mazurkiewicz

ZDENĚK KOPAL
University of Manchester
Michell

ELAINE KOPPELMAN
Goucher College
Mannheim; Moutard

SHELDON J. KOPPERL
Grand Valley State College
Mosander

V. KRUTA
Purkyne University, Brno
J. G. Mendel

P. G. KULIKOVSKY
Academy of Sciences of the U.S.S.R.
Maksutov; Moiseev

NAOITI KUMAGAI
Matuyama

GISELA KUTZBACH
University of Wisconsin
Margules

YVES LAISSUS
Bibliothèque Centrale du Muséum National d'Histoire Naturelle
J. Marchant; N. Marchant

WILLIAM LeFANU
Royal College of Surgeons, London
Mayo

HENRY M. LEICESTER
University of the Pacific
Muir; P. Müller

DONALD J. LE ROY
National Research Council of Canada
W. L. Miller

JACQUES R. LÉVY
Paris Observatory
Mineur

J. M. LÓPEZ DE AZCONA
Comisión Nacional de Geología, Madrid
Medina

EDWARD LURIE
University of Delaware
Marcou

DUNCAN McKIE
University of Cambridge
W. H. Miller

H. LEWIS McKINNEY
University of Kansas
F. Müller

ROGERS McVAUGH
University of Michigan
Mociño

MICHAEL S. MAHONEY
Princeton University
Mariotte

J. C. MALLET
Centre National de Floristique
Magnol

FREDERICK G. MANN
University Chemical Laboratory, Cambridge
Mills

F. MARKGRAF
University of Zurich Botanical Garden
Markgraf

BRIAN G. MARSDEN
Smithsonian Astrophysical Observatory
J. H. Moore

A. HUGHLETT MASON
University of Virginia
Mason

ARNALDO MASOTTI
Polytechnic of Milan
Maurolico

KIRTLEY F. MATHER
Harvard University
Merrill

KURT MAUEL
Verein Deutscher Ingenieure
F. R. H. C. Moll

OTTO MAYR
Smithsonian Institution
C. O. Mohr; Mollier; Müller-Breslau

JAGDISH MEHRA
University of Texas
Mie

S. R. MIKULINSKY
Academy of Sciences of the U.S.S.R.
Morozov

LORENZO MINIO-PALUELLO
University of Oxford
Michael Scot; Moerbeke

CHARLOTTE E. MOORE
National Bureau of Standards
Meggers

ELLEN J. MOORE
Natural History Museum, San Diego
E. Mitchell

GIUSEPPE MORUZZI
University of Pisa
Matteucci

ALIDA M. MUNTENDAM
Marum

A. NATUCCI
University of Genoa
Malfatti; Mengoli

G. NAUMOV
Academy of Sciences of the U.S.S.R.
Middendorf

J. D. NORTH
University of Oxford
Melvill; W. A. Miller; Nasmyth

A. NOUGARÈDE
University of Paris VI
Mirbel

LUBŎS NOVÝ
Czechoslovak Academy of Sciences
Marci de Kronland

ROBERT OLBY
University of Leeds
Miescher; Naegeli

C. D. O'MALLEY †
Massa

V. OREL
Mendelianum, Moravian Museum
J. G. Mendel

JOHN PARASCANDOLA
University of Wisconsin
Meltzer

LEONARD M. PAYNE
Royal College of Physicians, London
Merrett

KURT MØLLER PEDERSEN
University of Aarhus
Malus

OLAF PEDERSEN
University of Aarhus
Mohn

J. PELSENEER
Mansion

G. PETIT
University of Paris
Marion

STUART PIERSON
Memorial University of Newfoundland
Magellan; J. F. Meyer

SHLOMO PINES
The Hebrew University
Maimonides

DAVID PINGREE
Brown University
Mahādeva; Mahāvīra; Mahendra Sūri; Makaranda; Manilius; Māshā'allāh; Mathurānātha Śarman; Muniśvara Viśvarūpa; Muñjāla; Nāgésa; Nārāyana

A. F. PLAKHOTNIK
Academy of Sciences of the U.S.S.R.
Mesyatsev

A. F. PLATÉ
Academy of Sciences of the U.S.S.R.
Nametkin

HOWARD PLOTKIN
University of Western Ontario
S. Molyneaux

S. PLOTKIN
Academy of Sciences of the U.S.S.R.
Magnitsky

DENISE MADELEINE PLOUX, S.N.J.M.
College of the Holy Names
Matruchot

ARTHUR W. POLLISTER
Columbia University
T. H. Montgomery

CONTRIBUTORS TO VOLUME IX

LORIS PREMUDA
University of Padua
MAGATI; MAGGI; MERCATI

CARROLL PURSELL
University of California, Santa Barbara
J. C. MERRIAM

HANS QUERNER
University of Heidelberg
MEYEN; K. A. MÖBIUS

RHODA RAPPAPORT
Vassar College
MALESHERBES; MONNET

GERHARD REGNÉLL
University of Lund
NATHORST

LADISLAO RETI †
MARTINI

MARIA LUISA RIGHINI BONELLI
Istituto e Museo di Storia della Scienza, Florence
MIELI

GUENTER B. RISSE
University of Wisconsin, Madison
MECKEL

ABRAHAM ROBINSON
Yale University
MÉRAY; MITTAG-LEFFLER

FRANCESCO RODOLICO
University of Florence
MARSILI; MICHELI

JACQUES ROGER
University of Paris
MONTESQUIEU

PAUL LAWRENCE ROSE
New York University
MAGIOTTI; MAGNI; MARLIANI; MONTE

EDWARD ROSEN
City College, City University of New York
MÄSTLIN; MAYR

CHARLES E. ROSENBERG
University of Pennsylvania
H. N. MARTIN

B. A. ROSENFELD
Academy of Sciences of the U.S.S.R.
MALTSEV

BARBARA ROSS
University of Massachusetts
MORAY

K. D. ROTHSCHUH
Universität Münster/Westphalia
MEISSNER

M. J. S. RUDWICK
University of Cambridge
H. MILLER; MURCHISON

A. S. SAIDAN
University of Jordan
AL-NASAWĪ

JULIO SAMSÓ
Universidad Autonoma de Barcelona
MANṢŪR IBN 'ALĪ IBN 'IRĀQ

A. P. M. SANDERS
Biohistorisch Instituut der Rijksuniversität, Utrecht
MARTIUS

WILLIAM L. SCHAAF
Florida Atlantic University
MASERES

H. SCHADEWALDT
University of Düsseldorf
R. MARTIN

C. SCHALÉN
University of Lund
MÖLLER

F. SCHMEIDLER
University of Munich
MAURER

CHARLES B. SCHMITT
Warburg Institute
MAIGNAN

A. SEIDENBERG
University of California, Berkeley
MASCHERONI; G. MOHR

E. M. SENCHENKOVA
Academy of Sciences of the U.S.S.R.
MAKSIMOV

ELIZABETH NOBLE SHOR
Scripps Institution of Oceanography
MARSH; C. H. MERRIAM; E. S. MORSE

DIANA M. SIMPKINS
Polytechnic of North London
MALTHUS; MOFFETT; MOTTRAM; G. R. M. MURRAY

W. A. SMEATON
University College London
MONTGOLFIER BROTHERS

CYRIL STANLEY SMITH
Massachusetts Institute of Technology
MERICA

H. A. M. SNELDERS
State University of Utrecht
MULDER; MUNCKE

E. SNORRASON
Rigshospitalet, Copenhagen
O. F. MÜLLER

Y. I. SOLOVIEV
Academy of Sciences of the U.S.S.R.
MENSHUTKIN

LARRY T. SPENCER
Plymouth State College
E. D. MONTGOMERY

PIERRE SPEZIALI
University of Geneva
MOUTON; MYDORGE

ERNEST G. SPITTLER
John Carroll University
MORLEY

FRANS A. STAFLEU
University of Utrecht
MIQUEL

WILLIAM H. STAHL †
MACROBIUS; MARTIANUS CAPELLA

MARTIN S. STAUM
University of Calgary
MARGGRAF

WILLIAM T. STEARN
British Museum (Natural History)
MEDICUS; METTENIUS; P. MILLER; MOENCH

JOHANNES STEUDEL †
J. P. MÜLLER

V. T. STRINGFIELD
U. S. Geological Survey
MEINZER

D. J. STRUIK
Massachusetts Institute of Technology
METIUS FAMILY; MEUSNIER DE LA PLACE; MUSSCHENBROEK

ROGER H. STUEWER
University of Minnesota
MASCART

JUDITH P. SWAZEY
Boston University Medical School
R. MAGNUS; MARIE

LOYD S. SWENSON, JR.
University of Houston
MICHELSON

FERENC SZABADVÁRY
Technical University, Budapest
MARTINOVICS; MITSCHERLICH; C. F. MOHR; F. MÜLLER; A. NAUMANN

GEORGIO TABARRONI
University of Bologna–University of Modena
MANFREDI; MICHELINI; MONTANARI

JULIETTE TATON
MOUCHEZ

RENÉ TATON
École Pratique des Hautes Études
MARALDI FAMILY; MONGE

S. TEKELI
Ankara University
MUḤYI 'L-DĪN AL-MAGHRIBĪ

ANDRZEJ A. TESKE†
NATANSON

ANDRÉE TÉTRY
Faculté des Sciences
MESNIL

JEAN THÉODORIDÈS
Centre National de la Recherche Scientifique
MAUPAS

ROSE THOMASIAN
University of New Hampshire
MORO

CONTRIBUTORS TO VOLUME IX

HEINZ TOBIEN
University of Mainz
MARGERIE; MAYER-EYMAR; C. E. H.
VON MEYER

G. J. TOOMER
Brown University
METON

HENRY S. TROPP
Humboldt State University
MOULTON

A. J. TURNER
MILLINGTON

G. L'E. TURNER
University of Oxford
B. MARTIN; MORLAND

R. STEVEN TURNER
University of New Brunswick
J. R. MAYER

JUAN VERNET
University of Barcelona
AL-MAJRĪṬĪ; MARTÍ FRANQUÉS; MELLO

**GRAZIELLA FEDERICI
VESCOVINI**
University of Turin
MARSILIUS OF INGHEN

H. B. VICKERY
*Connecticut Agricultural Experiment
Station*
L. B. MENDEL

KURT VOGEL
University of Munich
MONTUCLA

WILLIAM A. WALLACE, O. P.
Catholic University of America
MAIOR

R. WALZER
University of Oxford
MARINUS

DEBORAH JEAN WARNER
Smithsonian Institution
MAUNDER

J. B. WATERHOUSE
University of Toronto
MAWSON

CHARLES WEBSTER
University of Oxford
MORISON

RODERICK WEBSTER
Adler Planetarium
NAIRNE

JOHN W. WELLS
Cornell University
MATHER

FRANZ WEVER
*Max-Planck-Institut für Eisenforschung,
Düsseldorf*
MARTENS

GEORGE W. WHITE
University of Illinois
J. MORSE

D. T. WHITESIDE
Whipple Science Museum
N. MERCATOR

G. J. WHITROW
*Imperial College of Science and
Technology*
E. A. MILNE

WESLEY C. WILLIAMS
Case Western Reserve University
MÉRY

FRANK H. WINTER
Smithsonian Institution
MONTGÉRY; W. MOORE

JÖRN HENNING WOLF
University of Munich
MOLDENHAWER

H. WUSSING
Karl Marx University
C. G. A. MAYER

JEAN WYART
University of Paris
MAUGUIN

ERI YAGI
Toyo University
NAGAOKA

ELLIS L. YOCHELSON
MEEK

**ALEXANDER A.
YOUSCHKEVITCH**
Academy of Sciences of the U.S.S.R.
MARKOV

A. YOUSCHKEVITCH
Academy of Sciences of the U.S.S.R.
MINDING

BRUNO ZANOBIO
University of Pavia
MATTIOLI

DICTIONARY
OF
SCIENTIFIC BIOGRAPHY

DICTIONARY OF SCIENTIFIC BIOGRAPHY

MACROBIUS — NAUMANN

MACROBIUS, AMBROSIUS THEODOSIUS (*b.* North Africa [?], *fl.* early fifth century A.D.), *Neoplatonic commentary.*

Macrobius bore the title *vir clarissimus et illustris*, indicating that he held high government positions. It has been customary to identify him with one of three officials by that name mentioned in the Codex Theodosianus as serving in 399/400, 410, and 422. A serious objection to these identifications is that Macrobius would thus have been known by the name Theodosius, and not as Macrobius. Moreover internal evidence in the *Saturnalia*, his larger extant work, suggests a date of composition in the 430's, rather than at the close of the fourth century. The only official named Theodosius recorded as holding office during this period was a prefect of Italy in 430, and this identification is therefore accordingly proposed.

The title of Macrobius' other extant work, his commentary on Cicero's *Somnium Scipionis*, thinly disguises its actual contents. Macrobius uses passages of Cicero's work as mere suggestions to construct a treatise on Neoplatonic philosophy—the most satisfactory and widely read Latin compendium on Neoplatonism that existed during the Middle Ages. Like *Somnium Scipionis*, Macrobius' *Commentarii* is in the tradition of Plato's *Timaeus*. Macrobius' main source appears to have been Porphyry's lost commentary on the *Timaeus*; and Cicero himself was probably inspired by Posidonius' lost commentary on the *Timaeus*.

Macrobius' lengthy excursuses on Pythagorean number lore, cosmography, world geography, and the harmony of the spheres established him as one of the leading popularizers of science in the Latin West. His chapters on numbers consist largely of conventional statements about the virtues of the numbers within the sacred Pythagorean decade, but include a fine explanation of the Pythagorean doctrine that numbers underlie all physical objects (*Commentarii*, 1.5.5–13).

Macrobius' excursus on the heavens (1.14.21–1.22.13) presents the stock features of popular hand-

books on astronomy. A spherical earth at the center of a spherical universe is encircled by seven planetary spheres and a celestial sphere which rotates diurnally from east to west. The planets have proper motions from west to east in addition to their more apparent motions from east to west, the result of their being "dragged along" by the rotation of the celestial sphere, The celestial circles are defined, with particular attention to the Milky Way, the dramatic setting of Scipio's dream. When Macrobius discusses the order of the planets (1.19.1–10), he is purposely ambiguous because his two infallible authorities, Plato and Cicero, differ about the position of the sun. Macrobius' vague statement about the upper and lower courses of Venus and Mercury has been misinterpreted since the Middle Ages as an exposition of Heraclides' geoheliocentric theory.

Macrobius and Martianus Capella were largely responsible for preserving Crates of Mallos' theory of an equatorial and meridional ocean dividing the earth into four quarters, each of which was assumed to be inhabited, and for the wide adoption of Eratosthenes' figure of 252,000 stades for the circumference of the earth. These concepts dominated scientific thinking on world geography in the Middle Ages.

BIBLIOGRAPHY

I. ORIGINAL WORKS. See the new critical ed. of Macrobius by J. Willis, 2 vols. (Leipzig, 1963; 2nd ed., 1970). W. Stahl's *Macrobius' Commentary on the Dream of Scipio* (New York, 1952; 2nd printing with supp. bibliography, New York–London, 1966) is an English trans. See also P. W. Davies' English trans. of the *Saturnalia* (New York, 1968) and N. Marinone's Italian trans. (Turin, 1967).

II. SECONDARY LITERATURE. In addition to the bibliography in the 2nd printing of Stahl's trans., the following more recent items are pertinent: A. Cameron, "The Date and Identity of Macrobius," in *Journal of Roman Studies*, **56** (1966), 25–38; M. A. Elferink, *La descente de l'âme d'après Macrobe* (Leiden, 1968); J. Flamant, "La technique du banquet dans les Saturnales de Macrobe," in *Revue des études latines*, **46** (1968) [1969], 303–319; H. Görgemanns,

"Die Bedeutung der Traumeinkleidung in *Somnium Scipionis*," in *Wiener Studien*, **81**, n.s. **2** (1968), 46–69; and E. Jeauneau, *Lectio philosophorum* (Amsterdam, 1973); M. H. de Ley, *Macrobius and Numenius* (Brussels, 1972); and "Le traité sur l'emplacement des enfers chez Macrobe," in *L'antiquité classique*, **36** (1967), 190–208. Also see N. Marinone, "Replica Macrobiana," in *Rivista di filologia e di istruzione classica*, **99**, n.s. **59** (1971), 1–4, 367–371; A. R. Sodano, "Porfirio commentatore di Platone," in *Entretiens sur l'antiquité classique*, **12** (1966), 193–228, on Macrobius, 198–211; E. Tuerk, "A propos de la bibliothèque de Macrobe," in *Latomus*, **27** (1968), 433–435; "Macrobe et les *Nuits Attiques*," ibid., **24** (1965), 381–406; J. Willis, "Macrobius," in *Altertum*, **12** (1966), 155–161; and C. Zintzen, "Römisches und neuplatonisches bei Macrobius," in *Palingenesia*, **4** (1969), 357–376.

WILLIAM H. STAHL

MÄDLER, JOHANN HEINRICH (*b*. Berlin, Germany, 29 May 1794; *d*. Hannover, Germany, 14 March 1874), *astronomy*.

After graduating from the Gymnasium, Mädler became, at the age of twenty-three, a seminary teacher in Berlin. His interest in astronomy had been awakened by the appearance of the comet of 1811, but he did not have an opportunity to make extensive astronomical observations until he met the rich Berlin banker Wilhelm Beer, half-brother of the composer Giacomo Meyerbeer. Beer maintained a private observatory in Berlin; and he and Mädler worked there together, mainly on lunar topography. In making their observations they used a Fraunhofer telescope with an aperture of 95 millimeters. Their joint publications gave such a favorable impression of Mädler's abilities that, beginning in 1836, he was an observer at the Berlin observatory, then directed by Encke. Here too he worked on the topography of the moon and the planets, chiefly Mars. The most important achievement from his collaboration with Beer was undoubtedly a map of the moon and accompanying two-volume text: *Der Mond nach seinen kosmischen und individuellen Verhältnissen* (1837). The lunar map (with a diameter of 97.5 centimeters) is in many respects the equal of Lohrmann's representation.

In 1840 Mädler accepted an offer from the observatory at Dorpat; he also obtained a professorship and began to publish his considerable body of work. The observatory possessed an excellent observational instrument, the celebrated Fraunhofer refractor with which Struve had determined the parallax of α Lyrae (1838). Mädler was thus led to undertake a new program of work in Dorpat and thereby to follow the tradition begun by Struve: the observation of

double stars. In his *Die Centralsonne*, Mädler sought to provide evidence that the Milky Way possesses a central constellation. He thought the latter, represented by a center of gravity, was formed by Alcyone in the Pleiades. Mädler vigorously defended this idea, but without success, for further research disproved his views.

Mädler was also a pioneer popularizer of astronomy. After giving popular scientific lectures, in 1841 he published *Populäre Astronomie*, which went through six editions during his lifetime. The book was distinguished by its author's thorough command of the material and pedagogically effective presentation of it. In contrast with most popularizers of science, who believed that "to instruct the public one needs only a superficial knowledge of the subject in question" (preface to the first edition), Mädler incorporated in his book the whole wealth of his knowledge, including that of the most recent literature. He also contributed to the dissemination of astronomical knowledge through articles in journals and newspapers. In 1888–1889—with the active cooperation of Wilhelm Foerster—the popular astronomy movement established its own institution in Berlin (the Urania Observatory); and today there is a large network of popular astronomy journals published throughout the world.

In *Populäre Astronomie*, Mädler had briefly sketched the history of astronomy. Following his departure from Dorpat (1865) and return to Germany, he devoted himself to this subject. The result of his labor, the two-volume *Geschichte der Himmelskunde* (1873), contains an extraordinary treasure of valuable historical data that Mädler had been gathering for decades. It left much to be desired, however, with regard to order and conception—probably a consequence of the author's advanced age, as was pointed out several years later by R. Wolf (1877).

Mädler was an argumentative scientist and thus acquired many enemies. Although he had a knowledge of history, he was often skeptical of new theories. For example, he rejected the progressive developmental ideas introduced into astronomy by Kant, Laplace, and Herschel and, twenty years before the discovery of the first spectroscopic double star, he disputed the validity of the Doppler principle.

BIBLIOGRAPHY

Mädler's writings include *Lehrbuch der Schönschreibekunst* (Berlin, 1825); *Physikalische Beobachtungen des Mars* (Berlin, 1830); *Mappa selenographica*, 4 vols. (Berlin, 1834–1836), prepared with Wilhelm Beer; *Der Mond nach seinen kosmischen und individuellen Verhältnissen oder allgemeine vergleichende Selenographie* (Berlin, 1837), written with Wilhelm Beer; *Populäre Astronomie* (Berlin, 1841 and later); *Astronomische Briefe* (Mitau, Latvia, 1846); *Die Centralsonne* (Dorpat, 1846); *Untersuchungen über die Fixstern-Systeme* (Mitau–Leipzig, 1847–1848). A bibliography of Mädler's scientific papers, which number more than 150 in the period 1829–1851, is in H. Kobold, ed., *Generalregister der Bände 1–40 der Astronomischen Nachrichten Nr. 1–960* (Kiel, 1936), cols. 72–74.

There are 17 letters to J. F. Encke and 8 letters to F. W. Bessel, in the Zentralarchiv der Akademie der Wissenschaften der DDR, Berlin, Bessel Nachlass; and 46 letters to H. C. Schumacher, in the Deutsche Staatsbibliothek, Berlin, Handschriftenabteilung, Schumacher Nachlass, and other MS material in the Staats- und Universitätsbibliothek Göttingen.

Biographical material is in S. Günther, *Allgemeine deutsche Biographie*, XX (1884), 37–39.

Dieter B. Herrmann

MAESTLIN, MICHAEL. See **Mästlin, Michael.**

MAGALHÃES. See **Magellan.**

MAGALOTTI, LORENZO (*b.* Rome, Italy, 13 December 1637; *d.* Florence, Italy, 4 March 1712), *dissemination of science.*

Born to an old and distinguished Florentine family, Magalotti lived during a period of marked contrasts arising from political upheavals, religious wars, and the influence of colonialism. In Italy there flourished, on the one hand, post-Galilean scientific progress, most significantly expressed in the Florentine Accademia del Cimento; on the other, however, was the decline of the Renaissance, which had been characterized by freedom of thought.

Magalotti was one of the first ten members of the Accademia del Cimento, which was founded in Florence in 1657 by Ferdinando II de' Medici and his brother Prince Leopoldo and which lasted only until 1667. Magalotti was the secretary of the Academy and reported its activity in the *Saggi di naturali esperienze fatte nell'Accademia del Cimento* (Florence, 1667), essays on natural experiments mainly carried out by Borelli, Redi, and Vincenzio Viviani. The volume immediately attracted considerable interest and was translated into English and Latin.

Magalotti acquired his scientific skill from studying

with Viviani, one of the last pupils of Galileo, and from attending at Pisa, then the major Italian university, the lectures of other scientists, notably Marcello Malpighi, Carlo Renaldini, and Giovanni Alfonso Borelli (1656). In 1667, however, he abandoned scientific studies and embarked on a series of travels as a diplomat in the service of the Medicis, which enabled him to become familiar with much of Europe and inspired many of his writings.

In his time Magalotti acquired considerable fame, but today his work appears not quite worthy of his many gifts and complex personality. He has the distinction, though, of having written the best scientific prose in Italian after that of Galileo; his descriptions of experiments in physics are written in colorful, almost dramatic, language. His contacts with different cultures enriched and gave freedom to his expression, which led his contemporaries to believe that his style showed too much foreign influence.

Magalotti published very little during his lifetime; his writings, which were much in demand, were circulated mostly in manuscript form and were not published until after his death. The most notable were the then celebrated *Lettere contro l'ateismo*, his short stories and poetic works, his many letters on scientific and other scholarly topics, and the singular essays on odors.

Magalotti became so interested in linguistics that he became involved in the Italian dictionary that was being prepared by the Accademia della Crusca. His literary style is characterized by lively prose and brilliant witticisms, which express his character as a man of the world but also may serve to disguise the spiritual disquiet which led him to enter a monastery for a few months in 1691. Magalotti seems in some ways a very modern figure, with acute critical abilities and a questioning mind, characterized also by a certain world-weariness.

BIBLIOGRAPHY

I. Original Works. Among Magalotti's writings are *Saggi di naturali esperienze fatte nell'Accademia del Cimento* (Florence, 1667), translated into English by R. Walter (London, 1684) and into Latin by Petrus van Musschenbroek (Leiden, 1731), photocopy ed. issued by Museum of the History of Science, Florence, and Domus Galileiana, Pisa (Florence–Pisa, 1957); *Notizie varie dell'imperio della China e di qualche altro paese adiacente* (Florence, 1697); the *Lettere familiari del Conte Lorenzo Magalotti gentiluomo fiorentino e accademico della Crusca,* known as *Lettere contro l'ateismo,* 2 pts. (Venice, 1719); *Lettere scientifiche ed erudite del Conte Lorenzo Magalotti gentiluomo . . .* (Florence, 1721); *Delle lettere familiari del*

Conte Lorenzo Magalotti e di altri insigni uomini a lui scritte (Florence, 1769); and *Varie operette del Conte Lorenzo Magalotti, con otto lettere su le terre odorose d'Europa e d'America dette volgarmente buccheri, ora pubblicate per la prima volta* (Milan, 1825).

II. SECONDARY LITERATURE. See Angelo Fabroni, *Vitae italorum doctrina excellentium, qui saec. XVII et XVIII floruerunt* (Rome, 1769), an Italian trans. of which by Cianfrogni is found in the *Lettere familiari* of 1769 (see above); Stefano Fermi, *Lorenzo Magalotti, scienziato e letterato, studio biografico-bibliografico critico* (Florence, 1903); and *Bibliografia magalottiana* (Piacenza, 1904); Cesare Guasti, "Lorenzo Magalotti, diplomatico," in *Giornale storico degli archivi Toscani* (1860–1861); Lorenzo Montano, *Le più belle pagine di Lorenzo Magalotti* (Milan, 1924); and Pompilio Pozzetti, *Lorenzo Magalotti. Elogium, habitum nonis Ianuarii 1787* (Florence, 1787).

LUIGI CAMPEDELLI

MAGATI, CESARE (*b*. Scandiano, Modena, Italy, 1579; *d*. Bologna, Italy, 9 September 1647), *surgery*.

Magati was the son of Giorgio Magati and of the former Claudia Mattacoda; his parents were of modest condition. One of his brothers, Giovanni Battista, was a doctor; his sister Laura was the grandmother of Antonio Vallisnieri. Magati obtained a doctorate in philosophy and medicine at Bologna in 1597. He was a pupil of the military surgeon Flaminio Rota and of Giulio Cesare Claudini, teacher of logic, philosophy, and practical medicine. Magati practiced the treatment of head wounds under Giovanni Battista Cortese, an expert in this field. He later moved to Rome, where he learned the methods of treating wounds used by surgeons there.

When he returned to Scandiano, Magati built up a successful practice and gained the patronage of the Marquis Enzio Bentivoglio, who recognized the earnestness and ability of the young surgeon and took him to Ferrara. There the established physicians received him with hostility, but he overcame their jealousy and in 1613 became a lecturer in surgery. This post became the focal point for the diffusion of his method of treating wounds and at the same time gave Magati useful opportunities to experiment.

In 1616, at the age of thirty-seven, Magati published, in Venice, the book for which he is particularly remembered, the collection of lectures *De rara medicatione vulnerum, seu de vulneribus raro tractandis, libri duo*. A few years later he became seriously ill and decided to join the Capuchin order. The investiture took place on 11 April 1618; he took his final vows a year later at Ravenna as Friar Liberato of Scandiano. But there was little peace for Magati in the monastery,

for he was assailed from all sides with requests for his help and his cures. His superiors granted him permission to practice, and he treated well-known patients throughout the territory of the house of Este.

For years Magati suffered from gallstones, and in 1647 he went to Bologna for an operation. The surgeon very neatly extracted three stones the size of an egg, but failed in the more difficult attempt to extract a fourth one covered with sharp projections; the bladder wall tore and Magati died three days later in great pain.

Magati was one of the forerunners of modern surgery. He was among the first to prescribe a rational treatment of wounds, quite different from contemporary methods, which advocated the frequent replacement of dressings and repeated local applications, on the same day, of various ointments.

Magati's major work, *De rara medicatione vulnerum*, was published in three editions. The book is divided into two parts, general and specialized. The style is prolix, with frequent mentions of Hippocrates and Galen. But the essence of Magati's new ideas is clearly expressed, and may be summarized thus; It is nature, not the doctor and his medicine, that heals wounds, because it is nature that eliminates pus, regenerates the flesh, repairs broken bones with callus, coagulates blood, and expels secretions. Therefore the best method of healing wounds is to give nature the means to do her work in the best way, by eliminating or avoiding obstacles. The frequent exposure of wounds to air is damaging, as is the introduction of probes and bandages, which encourage putrefaction. Magati denied the need to clean and anoint wounds; they should merely be bound with a linen cloth folded several times and left in place for five or six days. The bandage must not be heavy or unevenly distributed, and neither too tight nor too loose.

The validity of Magati's care of wounds was confirmed by Ludovico Settala, a doctor in the hospital at Milan. In the early part of the eighteenth century Dionisio Andrea Sancassani, also from Scandiano, tried to revive Magati's therapeutic methods and wrote three short works on the subject: *Chirone in campo, Lume all'occhio*, and *Magati redivivo*. But the time was not ripe, and minds accustomed to centuries-old methods could not quickly be persuaded to accept such innovations.

Two other works are attributed to Magati: *Tractatus quo raro vulnerum curatio defenditur contra Sennertum*, which was printed at the end of *De rara medicatione*, in the second (1676) edition, of which his brother Giovanni Battista appears as the author; and the *De Re Medica*, which appears to have been printed at the expense of the Este family.

4

BIBLIOGRAPHY

On Magati or his work, see W. von Brunn, *Kurze Geschichte der Chirurgie* (Berlin, 1928), pp. 219, 225, 265, 276; P. Capparoni, "Cesare Magati (Padre Liberato da Scandiano dei Minori Cappuccini)," in *Profili bio-bibliografici di medici e naturalisti celebri italiani dal secolo XV al secolo XVIII* (Rome, 1932), pp. 70–75; D. Giordano, "Medicazioni strane e medicazioni semplici," in *Scritti e discorsi pertinenti alla storia della medicina e ad argomenti diversi* (Milan, 1930), pp. 25–45; W. von Haberling, F. Hübotter, and H. Vierordt, eds., *Lexicon der hervorragenden Ärzte aller Zeiten und Völker*, 2nd ed., IV (Berlin-Vienna, 1932), 27–28; V. Putti, "Cesare Magati (1579–1647)," in *Biografie di chirurghi dal XVI a XIX secolo* (Bologna, 1941), pp. 9–16; and S. de Renzi, *Storia della medicina in Italia*, IV (Naples, 1845), 484–495.

LORIS PREMUDA

MAGELLAN, JEAN-HYACINTHE (Magalhães, João Jacinto de) (*b.* Aveiro, Portugal, 4 November 1722; *d.* Islington, England, 7 February 1790), *chemistry, physics, scientific instrumentation.*

Little is known about Magellan's youth and early manhood. His family, who made an unproven claim to be descended from Ferdinand Magellan, sent him to an Augustinian monastery in Coimbra when he was eleven years old, and there he lived and studied for about twenty years, first as a novice and then as a monk. There was a scientific tradition among the Coimbra Augustinians (it is reported that they studied the works of Newton), and as a consequence Magellan became well enough versed in astronomy to serve as a guide for, and to gain the friendship of, Gabriel de Bory during the latter's visit to Portugal in 1751 to observe a solar eclipse. A few years later Magellan sought and received permission from Pope Benedict XIV to leave the order. From 1755 to about 1764, Magellan traveled through Europe, finally settling in England, where he resided for the rest of his life. At some point he was converted to Protestantism. He never married.

Magellan produced no scientific work of serious consequence. He did, however, find ways to meet or to write to everyone whose activities interested him, and, as a result, is known chiefly for his wide circle of acquaintances and for acting as an intermediary in disseminating new information. He introduced English scientific instruments into France, edited Cronstedt's *Mineralogy*, and informed the French chemists of Priestley's work. He was a fellow of the Royal Society and a member of several European academies of science. Industrial spy, indefatigable learner of languages, shameless borrower from others' writings, Magellan nevertheless showed little of that malice usually associated with the gossip or the hanger-on. A curious mixture of unoriginality and independence, he had no great ambitions for himself.

Magellan wrote more about scientific instruments than about any other subject. His first work (1775), a description of English octants and sextants of the reflecting or Hadleyan type, was clearly written, detailed, and useful. He also wrote on barometers and other meteorological instruments (although not always with full understanding),[1] and on Atwood's machine. These works were all in French, in keeping with Magellan's role as correspondent of the Academy of Sciences, as agent of Trudaine de Montigny (*intendant* of finances), and as bearer of good news to the Continent from the land of the artisan-scientist coalition.[2]

Through his reading, correspondence, and acquaintances, Magellan kept up with the latest developments in English, Scottish, and Swedish chemistry and experimental physics. His work on "elementary fire" helped to disseminate the new theories of heat being worked out by Black, Irvine, and Crawford, and introduced the term "specific heat" (*chaleur spécifique*) into the language. It also gave the first published table of specific heats, although these were derived from determinations by Richard Kirwan.[3] Magellan early saw how important were the investigations of Priestley, whose good friend he became, and his characteristic response to Priestley's fundamental research was twofold: he told the French about it, and he produced a pamphlet describing some small improvements in the apparatus for making carbonated water and some refinements in the construction of nitric oxide eudiometers.[4]

Gustav von Engestrom, who had studied mineralogy with Cronstedt, was Magellan's link with Swedish chemistry. Engestrom translated into English, at Magellan's behest, the *Mineralogy* of Cronstedt (1770). Magellan undertook to publish a second edition, which was to have notes by Giovanni Fabbroni and Kirwan; but by the time he was ready, Kirwan's own *Mineralogy* had appeared (1784). Magellan went ahead, and, to Kirwan's great annoyance,[5] borrowed from him where appropriate, and also incorporated recently published findings of Bergman, Scheele, A. Mongez, and M. T. Brünnich. Although he "rearranged" the text to include new developments, Magellan was convinced that much in Cronstedt's system was still valuable. He especially endorsed the latter's combination of chemical analysis with the observation of the external characteristics of minerals.[6]

In his notes to Cronstedt, Magellan gave a good picture of conventional contemporary thinking about the foundations of chemistry. Thus various bodies, he said, although suspected of being compound, "may and even ought to be considered as primitive substances with respect to our knowledge of them, till they shall be experimentally decomposed."[7] Acid and alkaline substances act on other bodies in virtue of an "attraction," about which Magellan says:

> We may complain indeed of the deficiency of our knowledge in regard to the essential cause of this phenomenon which we mean to explain by the word *attraction*; but it being the ultimate effect our knowledge can reach to, after our observation has been driven from cause to cause of all that we can discern in nature, we must rest contented with the simple deductions from such an evident and general principle, whatever may be its original cause.[8]

Magellan also shared the widespread belief that the smallest bit of a chemically reacting substance is some sort of basic unit, and asserted at one and the same time that these smallest parts probably possess polarity, and that we know nothing whatever about them.[9] As Magellan's editing proceeded, the notes on Lavoisier's new theory of combustion and calcination increased,[10] until finally Magellan conceded to the arguments in the *Nomenclature* (1787). He retained the old language of the phlogiston theory for the remainder of the work, however, remarking, "*ut pes et caput uni reddantur formae*, according to the old adage of Horace."

NOTES

1. See W. E. K. Middleton, *A History of the Barometer* (Baltimore, 1964), 102–104, 114, 122–123, 259–260, 377; and *Invention of the Meteorological Instruments* (Baltimore, 1969), 79, 146.
2. See Birembaut, cited below, and M. Daumas, *Les instruments scientifiques aux xviie et xviiie siècles* (Paris, 1953), 138 ff.
3. Robert Fox, *The Caloric Theory of Gases* (Oxford, 1971), 26–29.
4. The story of Magellan's role in the introduction to France of Priestley's discoveries has been masterfully reconstructed in ch. 2 of Guerlac, cited below.
5. See the summary of Kirwan's letter (1788) to Banks in W. R. Dawson, ed., *The Banks Letters* (London, 1958), 493.
6. Cronstedt's *Mineralogy*, I, v–x.
7. *Ibid.*, p. 263 n; the work is continuously paginated.
8. *Ibid.*, p. 328 n.
9. *Ibid.*, pp. 428–431 n.
10. *Ibid.*, notes on pp. 285, 435 ff., 431–432, 444–445, 447, and 491–493, for example.

BIBLIOGRAPHY

I. ORIGINAL WORKS. Among Magellan's works are *Description des octants et sextants anglois ...* (Paris–London, 1775); *Description of a Glass Apparatus, for Making Mineral Waters Like Those of Pyrmont, Spa, Seltzer ... Together With the Description of Some New Eudiometers ... in a Letter to the Rev. Dr. Priestley* (London, 1777; 2nd ed., rev., 1779; 3rd ed., enl., 1783), German trans. by G. T. Wenzel (Dresden, 1780); *Description des nouveaux instruments à reflection pour observer avec plus de précision les distances angulaires sur mer ...* (London, 1779); *Collection de différents traités sur des instruments d'astronomie, physique ...* (Paris–London, 1775–1780); *Description et usages des nouveaux baromètres, pour mésurer la hauteur des montagnes et la profondeur des mines ...* (London, 1779); *Description et usages des instrumens d'astronomie et de physique faits à Londres, par ordre de la cour de Portugal en 1778 et 1779 ...* (London, 1779); *Notice des instrumens d'astronomie, de géodésie, de physique, etc., faits dernièrement à Londres par ordre de la cour d'Espagne ...* (London, 1780); *Description d'une machine nouvelle de dynamique inventée par M. G. Atwood, au moyen de laquelle on rend très aisement sensible les loix du mouvement des corps en ligne droite, et en rotation ...* (London, 1780); and *Essai sur la nouvelle théorie du feu élémentaire, et de la chaleur des corps ...* (London, 1780).

Magellan contributed to A. G. Lebègue de Presle, *Rélation ou notice des derniers jours de J. J. Rousseau ... avec une addition relative au même sujet, par J. H. Magellan* (London–Paris, 1778). He edited A. F. Cronstedt, *An Essay Towards a System of Mineralogy*, 2 vols. (London, 1781; 2nd ed., 1788); and *Voyages et mémoires de Maurice-Auguste, Comte de Benyowski sur la Pologne*, 2 vols. (Paris, 1791). He also published a number of articles in the *Journal de physique* between 1778 and 1783.

II. SECONDARY LITERATURE. For works about Magellan, see Arthur Birembaut, "Sur les lettres du physicien Magellan conservées aux Archives Nationales," in *Revue d'histoire des sciences et de leurs applications*, 9 (1956), 150–161; J.-P. Brissot, "Mémoires (1754–1793)," in C. Perroud, ed., *Mémoires et documents relatifs aux XVIIIe et XIXe siècles*, I (Paris, 1911), 362–363; Joaquim de Carvalho, "Correspondência científica dirigida a João Jacinto de Magalhães," in *Revista da Faculdade de ciências, Universidade de Coimbra*, 20 (1951), 93–283 and also published separately (Coimbra, 1952); Henry Guerlac, *Lavoisier: The Crucial Year* (Ithaca, N. Y., 1961), esp. ch. 2; John Nichols, *Literary Anecdotes of the Eighteenth Century*, VIII (London, 1814), 48–51n, and Alexandre Alberto de Sousa Pinto, *A vida e a obra de João Jacinto de Magalhães* (Pôrto, 1931).

STUART PIERSON

MAGENDIE, FRANÇOIS (*b.* Bordeaux, France, 6 October 1783; *d.* Sannois, Seine-et-Oise, France, 7 October 1855), *physiology, medicine.*

Magendie was a son of Antoine Magendie, a surgeon, and Marie Nicole de Perey. He had a younger brother, Jean-Jacques, whose name testifies to the admiration their father, an ardent republican, had for the ideas of Rousseau. The two boys were brought up in accord with Rousseau's pedagogical precepts: the emphasis was on their personal independence and not the instruction they received. As Pierre Flourens wrote in his *éloge* of François Magendie: "The new Émile, absolutely given over to himself, went about as he pleased in a liberty that very closely resembled abandonment." In 1791, swept along by the Revolution, the Magendie family moved to Paris, where the father devoted himself more to politics than to medicine. The death of his mother in 1792 and his father's activities on Revolutionary committees threw Magendie still further upon his own intellectual resources. Having reached the age of ten without having attended school or having learned to read and write, at his own wish he entered elementary school, where he made very rapid progress. At the age of fourteen he won the grand prize in a national contest for an essay on knowledge of the rights of man.

At sixteen, too young to be admitted to the École de Santé, Magendie became an apprentice at a Paris hospital, where the surgeon Alexis Boyer, a friend of his father's, accepted him as a pupil and entrusted him with the anatomical dissections. In 1803 Magendie passed the examination required for an *interne des hôpitaux* and entered the Hôpital Saint-Louis as a medical student. In 1807 he became an assistant in anatomy at the École de Médecine and gave courses in anatomy and physiology. He received his medical degree in Paris on 24 March 1808 after defending a dissertation entitled *Essai sur les usages du voile de palais avec quelques propositions sur la fracture du cartilage des côtes*. Magendie's studies reflect the chaotic situation of teaching in France during the period. A liberal education in his childhood, a practically oriented apprenticeship in medicine, the astonishing experience of the successive collapses of academic and doctrinal systems—all these combined to strengthen in Magendie a love of facts and a contempt for words, theories, and social conventions, as well as a rude frankness and a truly exceptional independence of judgment.

After his thesis Magendie's first publication was an article of a theoretical, not to say doctrinal, character. It appeared in the *Bulletin des sciences médicales*, which, published by the Société Médicale d'Émulation, did its utmost to glorify the memory of Bichat; yet Magendie's memoir was a harsh attack on the fundamental ideas of this intellectual master of French physicians. Magendie asserted: "[The] majority of physiological facts must be verified by new experiments and this is the only means of bringing the physics of living bodies out of the state of imperfection in which it lies at present" (*Bulletin des sciences médicales*, **4**

[1809], 147). According to Magendie, the biological sciences had remained behind the physical sciences because they utilized complicated ideas and pre-conceptions to explain facts which very often were not themselves established with certainty. Magendie still accepted the concept of a vital force (considering it a supposition that served merely to bring together in a single term all the characteristics proper to life), but he proposed "to abolish the two vital properties known under the names of animal sensibility and animal contractility and to consider them as functions" (*op. cit.* p. 166).

Further, he condemned Bichat's attempt to increase the number of vital properties by distinguishing them according to the organic tissues. In Magendie's view, physiology should explain the two phenomena essential to life—nutrition and movement—through reducing them to the organization of living beings and of their parts. Magendie's profession of faith is, in fact, the fundamental dogma of modern biology: "Two living bodies having the same organization will display the same vital phenomena; two living bodies having different organizations will display vital phenomena the diversity of which will always be in direct proportion to the difference in organization" (*op. cit.*, p. 159).

The gnoseological optimism of this youthful piece was rapidly replaced by a certain skepticism and a growing distrust of all theoretical generalization. Although he later honored Bichat by preparing his two major works for publication, Magendie furnished these editions with ample commentaries praising Bichat the experimenter but treating with irony all attempts at a systematic explanation of vital phenomena. The influence of the philosophy of the Idéologues had prevailed over the vitalist doctrines of the Montpellier school; and Magendie, having taken an aversion to all theories, made an extraordinary effort during most of his life to discover and collect the "facts" and refused, to the extent this was possible, to interpret them. "I compare myself," he said to Claude Bernard, "to a ragpicker: with my spiked stick in my hand and my basket on my back, I traverse the field of science and I gather what I find" (C. Bernard, *Magendie*, p. 13). This was, of course, an illusion: Magendie made his discoveries on the basis of certain theoretical considerations and within the framework of a rather well defined philosophy of biology. But this illusion was particularly important at a moment in the history of physiology when it was necessary to replace excessive speculation with recourse to the "facts"—that is, with recourse to the experimental method. In this sense Bernard was perfectly right when he stressed that "M. Magendie is not one of those men concerning whom one can give a sufficient idea simply by enumerating their works or by pointing out the discoveries with which they have enriched science" and that, for the historian of science, Magendie's principal merit consisted in the influence he exerted in orienting physiology toward experimental investigations.

In 1809 Magendie presented to the Académie des Sciences and to the Société Philomatique the results of his first experimental work, which he carried out in collaboration with the botanist and physician A. Raffeneau-Delile. In a series of ingenious experiments on various animals, the two investigators studied the toxic action of several drugs of vegetable origin, particularly of upas, nux vomica, and St.-Ignatius's bean. As Olmsted observes, these experiments mark the beginning of modern pharmacology. For the first time an experimental comparison was made of the similar effects produced by drugs of different botanical origin. Magendie held that the toxic or medicinal action of natural drugs depends on the chemical substances they contain, and it should be possible to obtain these substances in the pure state. As early as 1809 he suspected the existence of strychnine, later isolated, in accord with his predictions, by P. J. Pelletier (1819). Moreover, in 1817, in collaboration with Pelletier, Magendie discovered emetine, the active principle of ipecac. Immediately after the isolation of strychnine he demonstrated that it produces exactly the same type of poisoning as do certain vegetable drugs.

The experiments of 1809 enabled Magendie and Raffeneau-Delile to affirm that upas and nux vomica, which produce generalized convulsions and tetanus, must act on the spinal marrow and, in fact, must stimulate it very strongly. Sectioning the medulla— separating it from the brain—does not suppress the symptoms of the poisoning, whereas destruction of the medulla eliminates them completely. The character of the symptoms was found to be independent of the way in which the poison entered the organism, but the latter circumstance did influence the rapidity with which the first spasms began. Magendie thus formulated the principle of local action: A toxic or medicinal substance acts solely in terms of its direct contact with an effector organ. This principle obliged physiologists to accord great importance to the study of the absorption and transport of poisons and medicines in the organism.

At the beginning of the nineteenth century the generally accepted view was that absorption takes place exclusively through lymphatic vessels. This theory, elaborated by John Hunter and reinforced by Bichat's teaching, had replaced Haller's opinion,

according to which food and all other substances are absorbed through the veins. Magendie, however, demonstrated the existence of two absorption paths. He conducted a classic experiment in which a dog was poisoned following the introduction of the toxic substance into a limb that was connected to the body only by a blood vessel, or even only by a quill. Magendie concluded that the absorption of liquids and semiliquids is not a vital and physically inexplicable function of the lymphatics but a simple physicochemical phenomenon of the imbibition of tissues and of passage through vascular walls.

In 1811 Magendie was appointed anatomy demonstrator at the Faculté de Médecine of Paris, and for three years he taught anatomy and surgery. He displayed unusual skill during his operations at the École Pratique. Meanwhile, his rude behavior precipitated a conflict with the professor of anatomy, François Chaussier. The professor of surgery, Guillaume Dupuytren, saw Magendie as a dangerous rival and created difficulties for him at the Faculté de Médecine. In 1813 Magendie resigned from his post as demonstrator, opened an office as a practicing physician, and organized a private course in physiology. In his *éloge* Flourens speaks of a veritable "volte-face": in his opinion, Magendie suddenly buried all his ambitions as an anatomist and surgeon in order to devote himself to experimental physiology. Whether it was a long-considered project or simply an impulsive act cannot be known; in any case his private courses, featuring experiments on living animals, aroused the curiosity of the medical public and soon enjoyed a large success. It is from this moment that Claude Bernard dated the beginning of the "new physiology." "Magendie," he wrote, "joined example to precept. He undertook private courses of experimental physiology based on vivisections. He attracted numerous students, among whom were a great many foreigners. It was from this center that the young physiologists carried the seeds of the new experimental physiology into the neighboring schools, where it then developed with such prodigious rapidity" (*Rapport sur le progrès et la marche de la physiologie en France*, p. 7).

Magendie's teaching was not only oral. The interest evoked by his courses led him to write *Précis élémentaire de physiologie*, in which, just as in his lectures, experimental demonstration replaced theoretical discussion as much as possible. He thus created a new type of physiology textbook: philosophical deductions founded on anatomy and on doctrinal suppositions were greatly reduced in favor of simple and precise descriptions of experimental facts. The first volume of the *Précis* was published in 1816, the second in 1817.

This work, which went through four French editions and was translated into several other languages, including English and German, exerted a very profound influence on physicians and biologists during the first half of the nineteenth century.

In the introduction to his *Précis*, Magendie explained and justified his methods of investigating vital phenomena. Without abandoning his vitalist position (that is, he still accepted that "corps vivants" differ from "corps bruts" both in their form and composition and in certain supplementary laws that govern them), Magendie criticized the ontological interpretations of soul and of vital principle. He rejected as a dangerous illusion the methodological analogy between the vital force and Newtonian gravitation. For him, vital force would remain an empty term as long as it was impossible to link it, on the example of universal attraction, to a precise law. According to Magendie, the laws of life, even if they possess their own character, cannot be in contradiction with the physicochemical laws. The first task of physiology was to push the physical analysis of vital phenomena as far as possible. In theory and in practice, therefore, Magendie preached an empirical reductionism.

Between 1813 and 1821 Magendie made a great many discoveries in almost all the fields of research that then constituted physiology. Among these were proof of the passive role of the stomach in vomiting; explanation of the mechanism of deglutition; experiments on alimentation with nonnitrogenous substances (demonstration of the mammals' need for a protein supply and the first experimental production of an avitaminosis); experiments on digestive properties of pancreatic juice; proof of the liver's decisive role in detoxification processes; demonstration of the hemodynamic importance of the elasticity of the arteries; discovery of emetine and experiments on the toxic action of hydrocyanic acid; comparative anatomical investigations clarifying the mechanism of absorption; and new observations following vivisections of cranial nerves. Magendie was also the first to make comparative nutrition experiments with chemically pure substances.

Although Magendie was interested primarily in experimental physiology, he did not neglect medical practice. For many years he suffered from not being on a hospital staff, which would have facilitated the clinical study of new medicines. In 1818, following a competitive examination, he was named to the Bureau Central des Hôpitaux Parisiens; but until 1826 he had no official hospital assignment and had to rely on the understanding of his friend Henri Husson in order to observe treatments and to give a clinical

course at the Hôtel-Dieu. In 1819 he was requested to give a course at the Athénée Royal. In 1821 he published the first edition of his *Formulaire pour la préparation et l'emploi de plusieurs nouveaux médicaments*, a therapeutical manual much used by physicians. Magendie introduced into medical practice a series of recently discovered alkaloids: strychnine, morphine, brucine, codeine, quinine, and veratrine. He also generalized the therapeutic use of iodine and bromine salts. Contrary to the dominant opinion among the older physicians, Magendie favored the use of chemical substances over that of natural drugs and, in addition, had great confidence in pharmacological experiments on animals. He did not hesitate to test on himself all the substances that were shown to be harmless in the animal experiments.

In 1821 Magendie was elected to the Académie des Sciences and the Académie Royale de Médecine. In the same year he founded the *Journal de physiologie expérimentale*, the first periodical devoted exclusively to physiology. Starting with the second volume he added the words *et pathologie* to the title. Convinced that pathology is essentially "the physiology of the sick organism," Magendie already envisaged a complete reform of medicine by establishing it upon the experimental study of the vital functions; the idea of this project was later brilliantly defended and developed by his disciple Claude Bernard.

It was in his *Journal* that Magendie published the results of his investigations on the physiology of the nervous system and on the cerebrospinal fluid. The discovery of the Bell-Magendie law (1822) was the source of a distressing dispute over the parts played by Charles Bell and by Magendie in distinguishing the motor and sensory roots of the medulla. The historical documents relating to this subject do not appear to contradict Magendie's final claims:

> In sum, Charles Bell had had, before me, but unknown to me, the idea of separately cutting the spinal roots; he likewise discovered that the anterior influences muscular contractility more than the posterior does. This is a question of priority in which I have, from the beginning, honored him. Now, as for having established that these roots have distinct properties, distinct functions, that the anterior ones control movement, and the posterior ones sensation, this discovery belongs to me [*Comptes rendus ... des séances de l'Académie des sciences*, **24** (1847), 320].

Although it is possible that, from the start of his research on the spinal nerves, Magendie knew of Bell's general idea through the latter's assistant, John Shaw, it is nonetheless certain that the clear statement and the experimental verification of the law in question belongs to him. This discovery, of fundamental importance for neurophysiology, was completed by Magendie and Claude Bernard with the experimental explanation of an apparent exception known as *sensibilité récurrente* (1847).

In 1823 Magendie produced experimentally and described the rigidity that follows decerebration; he provided the first proof of the cerebellum's role in maintaining the equilibrium of the organism; and he cut the fifth pair of cranial nerves within the cranium itself, demonstrating the direct responsibility of these nerve structures for the sense of touch and their indirect trophic role in the maintenance of the function of the other senses. In 1824 he observed the circular movement ("mouvement de manège") that occurs in the rabbit following the section of the cerebellar peduncle. This experiment was the point of departure for Bernard's discovery of the "piqûre sucrée" and, later, of Jacques Loeb's experiments on the rotary movements of animals. During the period 1824–1828 Magendie made many discoveries concerning the origin, composition, and circulation of the cerebrospinal fluid. He showed that the brain cavities communicate freely with the spinal subarachnoid space and described the medial foramen in the roof of the fourth ventricle *(foramen Magendie)*. Through severing the various branches of the facial nerve, Magendie succeeded in definitively banishing the ancient hypothesis of the "nervous fluid."

During a trip to England in 1824, when he was a guest of William Hyde Wollaston's, Magendie gave several public demonstrations of his method of the experimental section of cranial nerves of living dogs. The cruel side of his experiments provoked an antivivisectionist campaign. Although powerful in Great Britain, this struggle for the protection of animals found no echo in France. Some colleagues, however, reproached Magendie for having experimented on sick people—that is, for having performed operations the goal of which was essentially scientific and not therapeutic. Such proceedings are described in Magendie's publications, but they were never really dangerous or mutilating. Particularly noteworthy are his experiments on the human retina, which could have led him, if he had had a taste for theoretical generalization, to the discovery of the law of the specific energy of the senses.

In 1830 Magendie finally obtained the directorship of a hospital department, the women's ward at the Hôtel-Dieu. Despite everything that one could say concerning his gruff manners toward his colleagues and his cruelty to animals, contemporary testimony agrees on the gentleness, patience, and understanding with which he treated his hospital patients. On 4 April 1831 he replaced J. C. A. Récamier in the chair of

medicine at the Collège de France. It was not without some difficulty that the medical instruction there was changed in style and in substance. Instead of expounding doctrines, Magendie gave public demonstrations of the experimental method; instead of teaching clinical medicine as it was practiced at the patient's bedside, he concentrated on the presentation of physiological and pathological knowledge derived from studies made on animals. Nevertheless, his initial lectures at the Collège de France were devoted to a medical problem of current concern: cholera. Magendie had just made a trip to England, to Sunderland, where he had been able to follow closely an epidemic of this disease. After his return to Paris, cholera broke out there. Magendie fought it courageously and devised a good symptomatic treatment, but he was seriously mistaken in asserting that it was not contagious. He also denied the contagiousness of yellow fever and opposed quarantine.

This error had dire consequences, in particular after 1848, when Magendie was appointed head of the Advisory Committee on Public Hygiene. Even though he belonged to the anticontagionist camp, Magendie had made a positive contribution to the study of infection: he had demonstrated experimentally that the saliva of rabid dogs contains a contagious principle. He also observed the effects of intravenous injections of putrid blood and led B. Gaspard to study the phases of sepsis by the experimental method (1822–1823). Another serious error of Magendie's was his impassioned activity against surgical anesthesia induced by ether (1847).

From 1832 to 1838 Magendie delivered his famous lectures on the physical phenomena of life at the Collège de France. These lectures were dominated by two main ideas: to extend as far as possible the purely physical explanation of vital phenomena and to base medical practice on the certain knowledge of normal and pathological physiology. Among the discoveries belonging to this period, the most interesting is that concerning the phenomenon later called anaphylaxis: Magendie ascertained that a second injection of egg white results in the death of rabbits that had tolerated perfectly well the first injection of the substance.

Beginning in 1838 Magendie's lectures dealt successively with the physiology of the nervous system, the dynamics of the circulation of the blood, the cerebrospinal fluid, and nutrition. In collaboration with Poiseuille, he carried out fundamental studies on arterial pressure and demonstrated the hemodynamic role of the elasticity of the major arteries. He also showed the very poor nutritive value of gelatin, until then utilized in the hospitals as an inexpensive food. In 1846 Magendie demonstrated that the presence of sugar in the blood is not necessarily a pathological phenomenon. These experiments on glycemia served Claude Bernard as the starting point of the research that culminated in his discovery of the glycogenic function of the liver.

Through his marriage to Henriette Bastienne de Puisaye in 1830, Magendie had acquired an estate in Sannois, Seine-et-Oise. There he led a very happy family life. Yielding to the fatigue brought on by approaching old age, he withdrew more and more to his country house, left the Hôtel-Dieu (1845), and had Bernard substitute for him at the Collège de France (1847). At Sannois he undertook experiments in plant physiology with a view to improving agricultural yield. He died probably of a heart ailment.

Balzac masterfully characterized Magendie, under the barely disguised name "docteur Maugredie," in *La peau de chagrin* (1831): "a distinguished intellect, but skeptical and contemptuous, who believed only in the scalpel" and who "claimed that the best medical system was to have none at all and to stick to the facts."

BIBLIOGRAPHY

I. ORIGINAL WORKS. Magendie's principal publications are "Quelques idées générales sur les phénomènes particuliers aux corps vivants," in *Bulletin des sciences médicales*, **4** (1809), 145–170; "Examen de l'action de quelques végétaux sur la moelle épinière," in *Nouveau bulletin scientifique de la Société philomatique*, **1** (1809), 368–405; *Mémoire sur le vomissement* (Paris, 1813); *Précis élémentaire de physiologie*, 2 vols. (Paris, 1816–1817; 2nd ed., rev., 1825; 3rd ed., rev., 1834; 4th ed., 1836); "Mémoire sur les propriétés nutritives des substances qui ne contiennent pas d'azote," in *Bulletin de la Société philomatique*, **4** (1816), 137; "Mémoire sur l'émétine et sur les trois espèces d'ipécacuanha," in *Journal général de médecine, de chirurgie et de pharmacie*, **59** (1817), 223–231, written with P. J. Pelletier; *Formulaire pour la préparation et l'emploi de plusieurs nouveaux médicaments, tels que la noix vomique, la morphine, etc.* (Paris, 1821); "Expériences sur les fonctions des racines des nerfs rachidiens," in *Journal de physiologie expérimentale et de pathologie*, **2** (1822), 276–279; "Expériences sur les fonctions des racines des nerfs que naissent de la moelle épinière," *ibid.*, pp. 366–371; "Mémoire sur les fonctions de quelques parties du système nerveux," *ibid.*, **4** (1824), 399–407; "Mémoire sur un liquide qui se trouve dans le crâne et le canal vertébral de l'homme et des animaux mammifères," *ibid.*, **5** (1825), 27–37, and **7** (1827), 1–29, 66–82; *Lectures on the Blood* (Philadelphia, 1839); *Leçons sur les fonctions et les maladies du système nerveux*, 2 vols. (Paris, 1839–1841); *Phénomènes physiques de la vie*, 4 vols. (Paris, 1842); and *Recherches physiologiques et cliniques sur le liquide céphalo-rachidien ou cérébrospinal* (Paris, 1842).

II. SECONDARY LITERATURE. Among the obituary notices containing information on Magendie's life and work, of special interest are F. Dubois, "Éloge de M. Magendie," in *Mémoires de l'Académie impériale de médecine de Paris*, **22** (1858), 1–36; and P. Flourens, *Éloge historique de François Magendie* (Paris, 1858), see also E. Littré, "Magendie," in *Journal des débats* (30 May and 28 June 1856); and A. E. Serres, *Funérailles de Magendie* (Paris, 1855). In a lecture at the Collège de France, Claude Bernard analyzed the historical influence, philosophical position, and character of his teacher: *François Magendie* (Paris, 1856).

For biographies of Magendie, see M. Genty, "François Magendie," in *Les biographies médicales*, IV (1935), 113–144; P. Menetrier, "Documents inédits concernant Magendie," in *Bulletin de la Société française d'histoire de la médecine*, **20** (1926), 251–258; the best modern biographical study is undoubtedly J. M. D. Olmsted, *François Magendie: Pioneer in Experimental Physiology and Scientific Medicine in XIX Century France* (New York, 1944).

Concerning Magendie's epistemological views and general ideas one should consult T. S. Hall, *Ideas of Life and Matter* (Chicago, 1969), II, 245–251; and O. Temkin, "The Philosophical Background of Magendie's Physiology," in *Bulletin of the History of Medicine*, **20** (1946), 10–35. On the pharmacological experiments see M. P. Earles, "Early Theories of Mode of Action of Drugs and Poisons," in *Annals of Science*, **17** (1961), 97–110. The controversy between Bell and Magendie over the discovery of the properties of the spinal nerves was well analyzed by C. Bernard, *Rapport sur le progrès et la marche de la physiologie en France* (Paris, 1867), pp. 10–14, 154–158; and by A. Flint, Jr., "Considérations historiques sur les propriétés des racines rachidiennes," in *Journal de l'anatomie et de la physiologie . . .*, **5** (1868), 520–538, 577–592. A recent restatement of the issue can be found in E. Clarke and C. D. O'Malley, *The Human Brain and Spinal Cord* (Berkeley–Los Angeles, 1968), pp. 296–303.

M. D. GRMEK

MAGGI, BARTOLOMEO (*b.* Bologna, Italy, 1477; *d.* 1552), *surgery*.

Maggi was professor of surgery at the University of Bologna and was the private physician of Pope Julius III. He did not become internationally renowned until 1550, when, because of his skill in treating wounds, he was summoned to Modena to tend the nephew of Pope Paul III, who had suffered a gunshot wound. Before this, Henry II of France had rewarded him with honors and gifts for his curative treatment of wounded French soldiers. He also had already created a school whose pupils supported and defended him in his controversy with Francesco Rota on the treatment of wounds.

Maggi's great ability is illustrated by his book on the treatment of wounds, which, while reflecting his valuable personal experiences and observations, also recalls a method of treatment already adopted in Italy. This method was also discussed by Paré, who acknowledged his debt to Maggi in the introduction to his own treatise on the subject. Maggi's book, published posthumously at Bologna in 1552 by his brother Giovanni Battista, is entitled *De vulnerum bombardorum et sclopetorum, globulis illatorum, et de eorum symptomatum curatione, tractatus.* This work, which in some ways was avant-garde, was of considerable benefit in the treatment of the war-wounded. Its main thesis can be summarized as follows: The wounds inflicted by firearms neither burn nor poison but are first-degree contusions. The shells propelled by firearms do not burn or scald on touch; do not set clothing on fire; do not produce blisters in the areas hit; do not burn gunpowder, hay, sulfur, straw, or tow; and do not give the wounded a burning sensation. A wax ball produces the same effect as a lead one and, like the lead ball, bounces. Shells, moreover, are not poisonous; the components of gunpowder—charcoal, sulfur, and niter—neither have the characteristics of poisons individually nor become poisonous in combination, since such a mixture can be tasted without ill effects. Wounds are contusions, and the gravity of the contusion determines the symptoms of the victim, who may reach a state of general shock. Maggi's theory became accepted, although it took several years. Shortly after its presentation it was defended by Leonardo Botallo in *De curandis vulneribus sclopetorum* (Lyons, 1560) and argued against by Francesco Rota in *De bellicorum tormentorum vulneribus eorumque curatione liber* (Venice, 1555).

A century before Magati's expounding of strange hemostatic practices (the application of boiled ass's or horse's dung, for example), Maggi, although he knew of other valid hemostatic cures, was treating amputation stumps with clay mixed with vinegar. He recommended the same remedy for those bitten by vipers, because clay is cold and the bite is warm *(contraria contrariis)*, and because earth, from which animals derive their poison, is a healthy medicament. Maggi is further remembered for his method of layered amputation.

Maggi was among the first to teach a rational method of treating gunshot wounds, and therefore his name has a deserved place in the history of surgery.

BIBLIOGRAPHY

On Maggi and his work, see C. Burci, *Storia compendiata della chirurgia italiana dal suo principio fino al secolo XIX*

(Florence, 1876), pp. 43–44; D. Giordano, "Medicazioni strane e medicazioni semplici," in *Scritti e discorsi pertinenti alla storia della medicina e ad argomenti diversi* (Milan, 1930), pp. 25–45; A. von Haller, *Bibliotheca chirurgica*, I (Bern–Basel, 1774), 206–207; and S. de Renzi, *Storia della medicina in Italia*, III (Naples, 1845), 660–666.

LORIS PREMUDA

MAGINI, GIOVANNI ANTONIO (*b.* Padua, Italy, 13 June 1555; *d.* Bologna, Italy, 11 February 1617), *mathematics, astronomy, geography, cartography.*

Magini graduated with a degree in philosophy from the University of Bologna in 1579; in 1588 he was appointed to one of the two chairs of mathematics there, having been preferred for that post to his younger contemporary Galileo. (The other chair was held by Pietro Cataldi, a mathematician of great prestige.) Magini alternated lectures on Euclid with classes in astronomy, which, stimulated by his passion for astrology, was actually his chief scholarly interest. Astrology itself had been taught at Bologna since 1125. Its study produced results occasionally useful to astronomers, as, for example, the more accurate calculation of celestial movements. Magini wrote several astrological works that were admired in their time, and also served the Gonzaga prince of Mantua as judicial astrologer (with varying results). For this reason he spent long periods of time in that city.

Like his astrological works, Magini's writings on astronomy remain of only historical interest, due in large part to his adherence to Ptolemaic principles. He rejected the Copernican theory, which was then being vindicated by Galileo; the conservatism of his thought indeed made him Galileo's enemy, and Magini more or less openly lent his support to libels against the younger man. Within the boundaries of his Ptolemaicism, Magini drew up complex theories, among them the multiplication of Ptolemaic spheres and orbits, and also performed some useful calculations. He was, in fact, much more skilled in calculation than in theory, and his ephemerides remained valid for a long time.

Magini's mathematical work was essentially practical. In 1592 he published his *Tabula tetragonica*, a table of the squares of natural numbers which was designed to permit the determination of the products of two factors as the difference between two squares. In 1609 he brought out extremely accurate trigonometric tables, in which he introduced new terms for what are now called cosines, cotangents, and cosecants. Magini's nomenclature enjoyed some currency, and was later adopted by Cavalieri, who succeeded him at Bologna. Magini made further contributions to practical geometry, including works on the geometry of the sphere and the applications of trigonometry, for which he invented certain calculating devices that may be reconstructed from his texts. Of his lectures on Euclid, some notes relating to the third book are extant in the Ambrosian Library in Milan.

Although Magini's fame in his own century rested upon these and other accomplishments (including his studies on mirrors and especially the concave spherical mirrors that he fabricated, one of which he presented to the emperor Rudolf II), he is today remembered chiefly as a geographer and cartographer. One of his earliest works was a commentary on Ptolemaic geography, in which he took up the problem of the topographical representation of the earth. He then embarked upon the ambitious project that, with interruptions, occupied him the rest of his life—an atlas of Italy, providing maps of each region (showing the borders of each state) with exact nomenclature and historical notes. The most complete edition of this atlas was published by his son, Fabio, in 1620, three years after Magini's death. Unfortunately, even this edition represents only a small part of Magini's actual work, since his notes for a greater volume, together with much of his library (particularly astrological works), were confiscated by the Roman Inquisition and apparently lost or destroyed.

BIBLIOGRAPHY

I. ORIGINAL WORKS. Magini wrote in Latin and most of his works were then translated into Italian. The major works are *Ephemerides coelestium motuum* (Venice, 1582); *Novae coelestium orbium Theoricae congruentes cum observationibus N. Copernici* (Venice, 1589); *De planis triangulis liber unicus et de dimitiendi ratione per quadrentem et geometricum quadratum libri quinque* (Venice, 1592); *Tabula tetragonica, seu quadratorum numerorum cum suis radicibus* (Venice, 1592); *Geographiae universae* (Venice, 1596); *Tabulae primi mobilis, quas directionum vulgo dicunt* (Venice, 1604). His later works include *Continuatio Ephemeridum coelestium motuum* (Venice, 1607); *Ephemeridum coelestium motuum, ab anno Domini 1608 usque ad annum 1630* (Frankfurt, 1608); *Tabulae generales ad Primum Mobile spectantes, et primo quidem sequitur magnus canon mathematicus* (Bologna, 1609); *Breve instruttione sopra l'apparenze et mirabili effetti dello specchio concavo sferico* (Bologna, 1611); *Geographiae universae* (Venice, 1616); *Tabulae novae iuxta Tychonis rationes elaboratae* (Bologna, 1619); and his atlas, *Italia* (Bologna, 1620).

II. SECONDARY LITERATURE. The best biography of Magini is A. Favaro, *Carteggio inedito di Ticone Brahe, Giovanni Keplero e di altri celebri astronomi e matematici dei secoli XVI e XVII con Giovanni Antonio Magini* (Bologna, 1886). Other works are R. Almagia, *L'Italia di G. A. Magini e la cartografia dell'Italia nei secoli XVI e XVII* (Naples, 1922); and G. Loria, *Storia delle matematiche* (Milan, 1950), pp. 380, 400, 422–425.

LUIGI CAMPEDELLI

MAGIOTTI, RAFFAELLO (*b.* Montevarchi, Italy, 1597; *d.* Rome, Italy, 1656), *physics, hydrostatics, hydrodynamics.*

Raffaello Magiotti studied in Florence and was one of the three favored pupils, along with Castelli and Torricelli, whom Galileo referred to as his Roman "triumvirate." After becoming a priest in the order of Santa Lucia della Chiavica, he was invited to accompany Cardinal Sacchetti to Rome around 1630 as his houseguest. At Rome Magiotti became well known as a scholar in mathematics, law, medicine, theology, and letters. His wide culture secured for him an appointment as *scrittore* in May 1636 on the scholarly staff of the Vatican Library with a salary of 200 scudi a year. Although Galileo, with whom he maintained a lively correspondence, and Castelli wished to nominate him (1638–1640) for the chair of mathematics at Pisa, Magiotti refused to leave the congenial intellectual life of Rome, where he died in 1656 of the plague.

It was probably Magiotti who, stimulated by Galileo's treatment of siphons in the *Two New Sciences* (1638), encouraged acquaintances at Rome to experiment further on siphons and the vacuum. At any rate, Magiotti was present at an experiment that was devised and staged at Rome by Berti, probably in 1640, but definitely at some time between December 1638 and 2 January 1644. From the description thereof left by Magiotti and other eyewitnesses, this experiment resembled the later "barometric" experiment performed by Torricelli in 1643–1644, although it is not clear whether Berti was trying to demonstrate air pressure. In a letter addressed to Marin Mersenne some years later (12 March 1648) Magiotti says that he had earlier forwarded news of the Berti experiment to Torricelli and had suggested that the use of a liquid such as seawater, which would be heavier than the plain water used by Berti, would make a significant difference in the result. "They [Torricelli and Viviani] then carried out experiments and eventually arrived at [the use of] mercury."

In the field of hydrodynamics, Torricelli openly acknowledged the aid of Magiotti. According to Torricelli's theory of flow (1643), the mean velocities of a liquid flowing out of the bottom outlet of a vessel are proportional to the square root of the head pressure, that is, the column of liquid above the outlet. This hypothesis was borne out experimentally by Magiotti who then determined the rate of flow through various sizes of openings. Magiotti thus anticipated by nearly thirty years the similar experiments of Edme Mariotte (1673). (Not surprisingly Torricelli greatly admired Magiotti and sought the priest's approval of his work on solid cycloids.)

Only one work by Magiotti was printed during his lifetime, the *Renitenza dell'Acqua alla Compressione* (1648). This work, in the form of a letter to Lorenzo de' Medici, embodies the first published announcement of the near incompressibility of water at a constant temperature—although Magiotti errs by insisting that water is absolutely incompressible—and the expansion and contraction of water and air according to changes in temperature. Several thermometers and other devices are mentioned, the most interesting being a "Cartesian devil" or "diver." In Magiotti's description, a stoppered cylinder containing an empty inverted jug is filled with water. As the stopper at the top is pushed into or withdrawn from the cylinder, the varying compression makes the jug fall or rise. The effect is caused by the incompressibility of the water. When the stopper is pushed into the cylinder, touching the water directly with no air space in between, the water forces itself into the jug, compressing the air therein and forcing the jug to descend. When the pressure is relaxed, the decompressed air forces the water out of the jug, which, again being lighter than water, rises to the surface. Although a related effect had been described earlier by Beeckman, Magiotti's is the first thorough—and the first printed—description of the Cartesian devil.

After Magiotti died, Leopold de' Medici commissioned Borelli in 1658 to seek out the late priest's manuscripts in Rome. Borelli reported that the writings had been destroyed by looters two years before. Despite this loss, however, Magiotti holds an important place in the history of science because of his probable connection with the first experiment to produce the vacuum, his experiments on hydrodynamics, and his announcement of the incompressibility of water.

BIBLIOGRAPHY

I. ORIGINAL WORKS. Magiotti's *Renitenza certissima dell'acqua alla compressione* (Rome, 1648) was reprinted in G. Targioni-Tozzetti, *Atti e memorie inedite dell'Accademia del Cimento e Notizie aneddote dei progressi delle scienze in Toscana*, II (Florence, 1780), 182–191; and in

L. Belloni, "Schemi e modelli della macchina vivente nel Seicento, con ristampa della lettera di R. Magiotti ...," in *Physis*, 5 (1963), 259–298. A MS version of the work is among the Galilean MSS at the Biblioteca Nazionale Centrale in Florence. The autograph of Magiotti's letter to Mersenne on the Berti vacuum experiment is in the Nationalbibliothek, Vienna, MS 7049, no. 127; it was printed in C. De Waard, *L'expérience barométrique; ses antécédents et ses explications* (Thouars, 1936), 178–181. The correspondence with Galileo is in A. Favaro, ed., *Opere di Galileo Galilei*, XVIII (Florence, 1890–1909), 525. Correspondence with Torricelli is in G. Loria and G. Loria, eds., *Opere di Evangelista Torricelli*, III (Faenza, 1919), 75 (cf. 37, 43, 102, 109, 150, 165, 204). A letter to Candido del Buono on the comet of December 1652 appears in A. Fabroni, ed., *Lettere inedite di uomini illustri*, II (Florence, 1775), 259–263 (cf. I, 151–152).

II. SECONDARY LITERATURE. A life of Magiotti is in G. Targioni-Tozzetti, *op. cit.*, I, 171–172. Also see *Opere di Galileo*, XX, 472–473. For Magiotti's role in the vacuum experiment and his other work see De Waard, *op. cit.*, 101–117, 132–137; W. E. K. Middleton, *The History of the Barometer* (Baltimore, 1964), 10–18; and *Invention of the Meteorological Instruments* (Baltimore, 1969), 3–18. For Torricelli's opinion of Magiotti, see *Opere di Galileo*, XVIII, 327, 331–332; and *Opere di Evangelista Torricelli*, I, 174, which also cites Magiotti's experimental verification of the theory of flow, II, 190.

Descriptions of the Berti experiment by Zucchi, Kircher, Maignan and K. Schott are reprinted by De Waard, *op. cit.*, 145 ff.

For the Cartesian devil, see G. Govi, "In che tempo e da chi siano inventati i ludioni, detti ordinariamente 'Diavoletti Cartesiani,'" in *Rendiconti dell'Accademia delle scienze fisiche e matematiche*, 18 (1879), 291–296.

PAUL LAWRENCE ROSE

MAGNENUS, JOHANN CHRYSOSTOM (*b.* Luxeuil-les-bains, France, *ca.* 1590; *d.* 1679[?]), *natural philosophy, medicine.*

Little is known of Magnenus' family and early life other than that he received the M.D. from the University of Dôle. He traveled for a period in Italy, becoming well-known as a doctor, and was subsequently appointed professor of medicine at the University of Pavia, where several years later he also secured the chair of philosophy. In 1660 Magnenus was chosen personal physician to the count of Fuensaldagne, ambassador to the French court, whom he accompanied to Paris.

Magnenus' importance in the history of science derives from his attempt to reinstate the Democritean theory of atomism as a respectable part of seventeenth-century natural philosophy. His *Democritus reviviscens* (1646), though marking less of a break with tradition than Gassendi's contemporaneous revival of Epicureanism, was typically regarded (for example, by Boyle) as instrumental in establishing a comprehensive alternative to Aristotelianism. Magnenus adopted Democritus' view that matter is composed of physically indivisible atoms which differ in size and shape for each element. He rejected the concept of *materia prima*, asserting that the elements are not interconvertible but preserve their atomic identity and properties when combined chemically.

Eight fundamental propositions for the existence of atoms were advanced by Magnenus, based on mathematical as well as chemical and other experimental considerations. Much of the experimental evidence was drawn from Daniel Sennert's *Hypomnemata physica* (Frankfurt, 1636) and Jacques Gaffarel's *Curiositez inouyes* (Paris, 1629), although he also cited the work of more prominent scientists of the period, including Galileo. Magnenus countered mathematical objections to the atomic theory by arguing that the continuum could not be built up from mathematical points, whether their number be finite, indeterminate, or infinite. Matter, he averred, consisted of atoms having definite dimensions (unlike mathematical points) which represent the physical limit to material division. There were three elementary atoms: fire, water, and earth. Each possessed specific properties and gave rise, by their various combinations, to all other natural substances. Air, because it had no characteristic properties but could assume, at different times, all primary properties, was not an element. It functioned as the neutral medium for propagating the specific properties of the elements during interaction and served to prevent a vacuum by filling the pores of compound bodies.

Magnenus' restoration of Democritean atomism was limited, to be sure. Unlike Democritus, he denied the existence of a void; his retention of Aristotelian substantial forms (now inherent in individual atoms) and his explanation of combination by an innate tendency to union further separates his system from classical atomism. Moreover, while the widespread reading and citation of his work facilitated the acceptance of atomistic ideas in general, his theory must be distinguished from those corpuscular philosophies, like Gassendi's and Boyle's, which sought to explicate natural phenomena solely on the basis of the size, shape, and movement of imperceptible particles. Magnenus accepted certain of the tenets of seventeenth-century mechanical philosophy but amalgamated them into a broader system incorporating traditional modes of qualitative chemical explanation. Thus he is representative of that atomist school which, during the seventeenth and eighteenth centuries, posed an alternative to strict mechanism in science.

BIBLIOGRAPHY

I. ORIGINAL WORKS. Magnenus' major scientific publication is *Democritus reviviscens sive de atomis. Addita est Democriti vita* (Pavia, 1646; Leiden, 1648; London–The Hague, 1658). Other writings include: *De tabaco exercitationes quatuordecim* (Pavia, 1648; Pavia–The Hague, 1658), which treats of the medical usage and effects of tobacco; and *De manna liber singularis* (Pavia, 1648; 2nd ed., Pavia–The Hague, 1658).

II. SECONDARY LITERATURE. For Magnenus' life and work, see J. Güsgens, *Die Naturphilosophie des Joannes Chrysostomus Magnenus* (Bonn, 1910). F. Ueberweg, *Grundriss der Geschichte der Philosophie*, rev. ed., III (Berlin, 1924), 171–174, places Magnenus among the French natural philosophers of the first half of the seventeenth century. Other assessments of his atomic theory include G. B. Stones, "The Atomic View of Matter in the XVth, XVIth, and XVIIth Centuries," in *Isis*, **10** (1928), 458–459; and J. R. Partington, *A History of Chemistry*, II (London, 1961), 455–458.

MARTIN FICHMAN

MAGNI, VALERIANO (*b.* Milan, Italy, 15 October 1586; *d.* Salzburg, Austria, 29 July 1661), *physics.*

At the age of two, Magni was taken by his parents, Constantino and Ottavia Magni, from Italy to Prague; he was to spend much of the rest of his life in central Europe. Magni entered the Capuchin order on 25 March 1602, adopting the name Valeriano in place of his original Christian name, Maximilian. After he had gained a reputation as a preacher and instructor at Prague, Linz, and Vienna, he was appointed in 1613 to a chair of philosophy in the Austrian capital. Three years later Magni helped to establish the Franciscan order in Poland at the request of Sigismund III; the king later tried to obtain a cardinal's hat for Magni. During the 1620's Magni was active in various roles: as Hapsburg envoy to Paris (1622–1623); novice-master at Linz; professor of philosophy at Prague; Franciscan provincial of Bohemia (1624); and Hapsburg emissary to Italy (1625). Following the death of his patron, Sigismund III, Magni played a decisive part in the selection of a successor (1632), and later worked in Poland to consolidate the position of the Catholic church. In 1642–1643, and again in 1645, Magni was in Italy, then in Poland (1646–1648), and subsequently in Vienna and Cologne. In 1655 the combative Magni's long-standing feud with the Jesuits (he had incited Urban VIII, a close friend, against them in 1631) led to his being accused of heresy; while trying to reconcile Protestants to the Catholic church, he had admitted the supremacy of the pope to be founded on tradition. Pleading that he was too ill to obey a summons to Rome, Magni was arrested in Vienna at the end of 1655. The emperor's intervention, however, secured his release the following February, whereupon he was sent to Salzburg. There he remained for the rest of his life.

In philosophy Magni was a vehement anti-Aristotelian and an admirer of Galileo and Descartes. In his fight with the Aristotelians, Magni made great use of an experiment designed to demonstrate the existence of the vacuum. Although this was practically identical with the barometric experiment described by Torricelli in 1643–1644, Magni claimed that this idea was conceived independently after reading of Galileo's work on siphons. There is no firm reason for doubting Magni's word on this, although at the time his claim aroused great controversy.

In mid-1647 Magni demonstrated his experiment at Warsaw in the presence of Wenceslas VII, and in July of that year he published an account of it *(Demonstratio ocularis)* which made much of the fact that light could traverse a vacuum, so proving, against Aristotle, that motion was possible in a void. News of the experiment was communicated by a French eyewitness, Des Noyers, to Mersenne at Paris in a letter dated 24 July 1647. Unfortunately for Magni, the French were then pursuing research on the vacuum, and Roberval, who replied on Mersenne's behalf to Des Noyers's letter, implicitly accused Magni of plagiarism. In his reply of 20 September 1647 (apparently printed in Paris in the same year) Roberval stated that the Torricelli experiment had been performed years before and that Magni, who was in Italy in 1645, must have heard of it there; in any case, the experiment had been repeated by Petit and Pascal at Rouen in 1646.

Magni quickly wrote a defense of his work, the "Narratio apologetica," dated 5 November 1647. This he had printed in a collection entitled *Admirando de vacuo,* which also contained reprints of the *Demonstratio ocularis* and of Roberval's letter to Des Noyers. Magni conceded that Torricelli now had the priority, but he strongly denied having heard anything of the Torricelli experiment before the arrival of Roberval's letter. Torricelli's work, he said, was not known to any of his (Magni's) friends at Rome. Rather, it was Galileo's writings that had stimulated him to devise the experiment.

Magni's forthright publication of the damaging letter of Roberval suggests strongly that he was telling the truth. In any event, the *Demonstratio ocularis* of

Magni is certainly important as the first printed account of the barometric experiment, Torricelli having left his description in manuscript. Although it was printed at Warsaw, Magni's treatise became quite well known following its reprinting at Paris in 1647 as part of an edition that also included Petit's account of the Rouen vacuum experiments. Interestingly, it was Magni who acquainted Guericke with the Torricellian barometric experiment when the two men met at Regensburg in 1654. The several editions of Magni's writings, and the controversy that surrounded them, undoubtedly helped to disseminate widely the news of the barometric experiment.

BIBLIOGRAPHY

I. ORIGINAL WORKS. Magni's main work on the vacuum is *Demonstratio ocularis; loci sine locato; corporis successive moti in vacuo; luminis nulli corpori inhaerentis* (Warsaw, 1647); repr. by M. Dominicy as *Observation touchant le vuide faite pour la première fois en France, contenue en une lettre écrite . . . par Monsieur Petit . . . le 10 Novembre 1646. Avec le discours qui en a esté imprimé en Pologne sur le mesme sujet, en Ieuillet 1647* (Paris, 1647). This work is also in *Admirando de vacuo* (Warsaw, 1647), which contains the critical letter of Roberval to Des Noyers as well as the "Narratio apologetica." The treatise also was published in Bologna (1648) and Venice (1649). Magni published a further treatise entitled *Vacuum pleno supletum* (Venice, 1650). His *Principia et specimen philosophiae* (Cologne, 1642) contains the *opuscula* on the vacuum.

Magni's main philosophical work is the *Opus philosophicum: I. Synopsis philosophiae Aristotelis. II. Philosophia Valeriani* (Lithomifflii, 1660). His main attack on the Jesuits is the *Apologia . . . contra imposturas Jesuitarum* (n.d. [1655?], n.p.).

Some of the vacuum materials are reprinted in Pascal, *Oeuvres,* Leon Brunschvicg, ed., II (Paris, 1908–1914), including Des Noyers's letter to Mersenne (15–18); Roberval's critique (21–35); and Magni's defense (503–506).

II. SECONDARY LITERATURE. German Abgottspon, *P. Valerianus Magni, Kapuziner* (Olten, 1939), deals mainly with Magni's political and religious life. Documents and an account of Magni as a scientist are given in Cornelis De Waard, *L'expérience barométrique, ses antécédents et ses explications* (Thouars, 1936); also see W. E. K. Middleton, *The History of the Barometer* (Baltimore, 1964), ch. 3. For the bibliography of Magni's writings on the vacuum see G. Hellmann, "Beiträge zur Erfindungsgeschichte meteorologischer Instrumente," in *Abhandlungen der Preussischen Akademie der Wissenschaften,* Phys.-Math. Kl., no. 1 (1920), 33–34.

An Aristotelian reply to Magni is Jacobus Pierius, *Ad experientiam nuper circa vacuum R. P. Valeriani Magni demonstrationem ocularem . . . responsio ex peripateticae philosophiae principiis desumpta* (Paris, 1648).

Contemporary references to Magni and the experiment are in Otto von Guericke, *Experimenta nova . . . Magde-*

burgica de vacuo spatio (Amsterdam, 1672), 117–118; Honoré Fabri, *Dialogi physici . . .* (Lyons, 1665), 182–183; and Jakub Dobrzenski, *Nova et amaenior . . . fontium . . . philosophia* (Ferrara, 1659), 27–28. Other references are cited in Lynn Thorndike, *A History of Magic and Experimental Science*, VII (New York, 1923–1958), 654, 659.

PAUL LAWRENCE ROSE

MAGNITSKY, LEONTY FILIPPOVICH (*b*. Ostashkov, Russia, 19 June 1669; *d*. Moscow, Russia, 30 October 1739), *mathematics.*

No precise information exists on Magnitsky's origins and early years. It is possible that he studied in Moscow at the Slavonic, Greek, and Latin Academy founded in 1687. It is also possible that he acquired his broad knowledge, which included many foreign languages, independently. In 1701 Peter the Great founded the Navigation School in Moscow, and it soon became the breeding ground for the technical intelligentsia. Peter brought Magnitsky there to teach in 1702. Magnitsky worked there for the rest of his life, and was named director in 1715.

Magnitsky's *Arithmetic* (1703) was the first guide to mathematics published in Russia. Its first edition of 2,400 copies was extraordinarily large for that time and it served as the basic textbook of mathematics in Russia for half a century. The founder of Russian science, Lomonosov, called it, along with one grammar book, "our gateways to learning." Magnitsky's textbook successfully combined the tradition of Russian mathematical literature of the seventeenth century with that of the western European mathematical schools. In the first section a detailed exposition of mathematical problems is given. The second section, almost an encyclopedia of the natural sciences of the time, contains information on algebra and its geometrical applications, the computation of trigonometric tables of sines, tangents, and secants, and information on navigational astronomy, geodesy, and navigation. There are also tables of magnetic declination, tables of latitude of the points of rising and setting of the sun and moon, and coordinates of the most important ports with their times of high and low tide.

Magnitsky also participated in the preparation of a Russian edition (1703) of the logarithmic tables of Vlacq (1628).

BIBLIOGRAPHY

Magnitsky's one published work was *Arifmetika, sirech nauka chislitelnaya. Tablitsy sinusov, tangensov i sekansov i logarifma sinusov i tangensov* ("Arithmetic, Called the Computational Science. Tables of Sines, Tangents, and Secants and Logarithms of Sines and Tangents"; Moscow, 1703).

Works about Magnitsky are: A. P. Denisov, *Leonty Filippovich Magnitsky* (Moscow, 1967); D. D. Galanin, *Leonty Filippovich Magnitsky i yego "Arifmetika"* ("Leonty Filippovich Magnitsky and his 'Arithmetic' "), 3 vols. (Moscow, 1914); and A. P. Youschkevitch, *Istoria matematika v Rossii do 1917 goda* ("History of Mathematics in Russia Until 1917"; Moscow, 1968).

S. PLOTKIN

MAGNOL, PIERRE (*b*. Montpellier, France, 8 June 1638; *d*. Montpellier, 21 May 1715), *botany.*

Magnol's father was an apothecary, and his mother came from a family of physicians. He was interested in botany from his youth; and in 1659, after receiving his medical degree, he decided that (as his son reports) "it would be very advantageous to him to make a serious study of plants" before practicing medicine. He then began to botanize in the area around Montpellier, in Provence, and in the neighboring islands. He was aided by Laugier, a professor of medicine who was the friend of Gaston, duke of Orleans, and who possessed a great knowledge of plants. Magnol's reputation grew rapidly, and people soon competed to join the excursions he led. He established contacts with many French and foreign botanists: John Ray, William Sherard, and James Petiver in London; Herman and Hotton in Leiden; Commelin in Amsterdam; the Rivinuses (Bachmanns) in Leipzig; Breyn in Danzig; Johann Heinrich Lavater in Zurich; Lelio and Giovanni Battista Triumpheti in Rome; Giovanni Ciassi in Venice; Boccone in Palermo; Nappus in Strasbourg; J. Salvador in Barcelona; Jacob Spon in Lyons; and Gui C. Fagon in Paris. In 1663 Magnol obtained, through J. P. de Tournefort, a *brevet de médecin ordinaire du roi*. In 1667 the king opposed his nomination as professor of medicine at the University of Montpellier (he was not appointed until 1694, but in the meantime he renounced Protestantism). Magnol was not disturbed by this rejection, which permitted him to devote his time to botany.

Magnol's *Botanicum Monspeliense*, containing, it is said, the description of 1,354 species, appeared in 1676; it was intended for his students, among whom were Antoine and Bernard de Jussieu. Out of love for botany Magnol agreed in 1687 to substitute for François Chicoyneau, whose sight was starting to fail, as demonstrator of plants at the botanical garden of Montpellier. In 1697 Magnol was named director of the botanical garden. He was called to Paris in 1709 to replace Tournefort at the Académie Royale des Sciences and was particularly warmly received there by Fontenelle. But he soon wished to return to his native city, where, in "his" garden, he cultivated rare plants. In 1697 he had published a catalog of this garden (*Hortus regius Monspeliensis*) in which several new species were described, including *Lonicera pyrenaica* and *Xanthium spinosum*.

An innovator in classification, Magnol was one of the first, in his *Prodromus historiae generalis plantarum* (1689), to classify plants in tables that made possible rapid identifications. In his *Novus caracter plantarum*, posthumously published by his son Antoine in 1720, "he proposed a new classification based on the calyx (a name that he gives even to the unique floral envelope of certain plants)." He demonstrated that the fig contains many flowers but was unable to interpret the fructification of the ferns. He recognized that the coral is a "living body" but thought it was a plant. Magnol also established that desiccation causes the tuber of the arum to lose its "burning acridity." He observed the underground components of the *Bryonia*, the cyclamen, the Jerusalem artichoke, turnips, and other plants and concluded that by drying them, kneading them with wheat or rye flour, and baking them a quite nourishing food could be obtained; it is the root of the creeping wheat-grass that gives bread the most agreeable taste. These observations were published in the *Histoire de la Société des sciences de Montpellier*.

Magnol helped to promote interest in botany, which he thought was excessively neglected by educated people, and attracted attention to the possibility of employing natural classifications. Moreover, he was undoubtedly the first to use the term "family" in the sense of a natural group. The family Magnoliaceae is represented by the genus *Magnolia*, which was dedicated to him by Plumier.

BIBLIOGRAPHY

I. ORIGINAL WORKS. Magnol's works are *Botanicum Monspeliense* (Lyons, 1676); *Prodromus historiae generalis plantarum in quo familiae plantarum per tabulas disponuntur* (Montpellier, 1689); *Hortus regius Monspeliensis* (Montpellier, 1697); and the posthumously published *Novus caracter plantarum, in duos tractatus divisus* (Montpellier, 1720). He also contributed various memoirs to the *Histoire de la Société royale des sciences de Montpellier*.

II. SECONDARY LITERATURE. The principal source is the biography by Magnol's son Antoine, in J. E. Planchon, ed., *La botanique à Montpellier. Notes et documents . . .* (Montpellier, 1884). See also L. Dulieu, "Les Magnol," in *Revue d'histoire des sciences et de leurs applications*, **12** (1959), 209–224; and Robert Zander, "Pierre Magnol," in *Das Gartenamt* (Nov. 1959), 245–246, with portrait.

PAUL JOVET
J. C. MALLET

MAGNUS, HEINRICH GUSTAV (*b.* Berlin, Germany, 2 May 1802; *d.* Berlin, 4 April 1870), *physics, chemistry.*

Magnus' father, Johann Matthias Magnus, the prosperous founder of a large trading firm, was able to provide his son with private instruction in mathematics and natural science. Magnus entered the University of Berlin in 1822; and in 1825 he published his first paper, an investigation of pyrophoric iron, cobalt, and nickel carried out under the direction of Eilhard Mitscherlich, discoverer of the law of isomorphism. After receiving his doctorate in September 1827 with a dissertation on tellurium, Magnus took the advice of Mitscherlich, Heinrich and Gustav Rose, and Friedrich Wöhler, all former students of Berzelius, and in October 1827 went to Stockholm to study with the great Swedish chemist, who became his lifelong friend and adviser.

It was in Berzelius' laboratory that Magnus not only discovered the first platinum-ammine compound (Magnus' green salt $[Pt(NH_3)_4][PtCl_4]$) and its related potassium salt $(K_2[PtCl_4])$ but also worked on the addition compound of ethylene and platinous chloride later described by the Danish chemist W. C. Zeise (Zeise's salt, $K[Pt(C_2H_4)Cl_3]$). In the summer of 1828 Magnus returned to Berlin, where, with the exception of a visit to Paris during 1828 and 1829, he remained until his death. His *Habilitationsschrift* on mineral analysis (1831) permitted him to begin lecturing on technology at the university and on chemistry at the municipal trade school but led to a break with his teacher Mitscherlich, who regarded the young *Privatdozent* as a dangerous competitor. In 1833 Magnus was appointed associate professor and in 1845 professor of technology and physics at the University of Berlin, where he also served as rector during 1861 and 1862. He married Bertha Humblot in 1840. Magnus became a member of the Berlin Academy of Sciences in 1840 and was one of the founding members of the German Chemical Society (1868). A number of his students became famous physicists.

As was true of most chemists of the time, Magnus' research interests were varied. From an initial interest in mineral analysis, he turned to inorganic chemistry, discovering periodic acid and its salts in 1833; organic chemistry, discovering ethionic and isethionic acids in 1833–1839 and the polymerization of hydrocarbons on heating in 1853; physiological chemistry, studying the oxygen and carbon dioxide content of blood in 1837–1845; and agricultural chemistry in 1849. Magnus gradually turned to physicochemical and eventually purely physical investigations, which constitute his most important scientific achievements.

18

Among these are his contributions to the theory of heat, thermal expansion of gases, boiling of liquids, vapor formation, electrolysis (Magnus' rule), induced and thermoelectric currents, optics, hydrodynamics, magnetism, and mechanics. Although his most important work was in physics, he never ceased investigating chemical problems in his private laboratory. These later chemical works, however, never led to results of general significance but served merely for his own instruction.

Neither a theoretician nor an original thinker, Magnus was, however, an acute, conscientious, and diligent experimenter who uncovered much valuable physical and chemical information—notably the Magnus effect.

BIBLIOGRAPHY

I. ORIGINAL WORKS. Magnus' papers are listed in the Royal Society Catalogue of Scientific Papers, IV, 182–184; VIII, 306. See esp. "Ueber die Eigenschaft metallischer Pulver, sich bei der gewöhnlichen Temperatur von selbst in der atmosphärischen Luft zu entzünden," in Annalen der Physik und Chemie, 3 (1825), 81–88; "Ueber einige neue Verbindungen des Platinchlorürs," ibid., 14 (1828), 239–242, with English trans. in G. B. Kauffman, ed., Classics in Coordination Chemistry, Part II. Selected Papers (1798–1935) (New York, in press); and "Ueber die Weinschwefel-säure, ihren Einfluss auf die Aetherbildung, und über zwei neue Säuren ähnlicher Zusammensetzung," ibid., 27 (1833), 367–387.

II. SECONDARY LITERATURE. See the notices by A. W. Hofmann, in Berichte der Deutschen Chemischen Gesellschaft, 3 (1870), 993; and A. W. Williamson, in Journal of the Chemical Society, 24 (1871), 610–615.

See also J. J. Berzelius, Aus Jac. Berzelius und Gustav Magnus' Briefwechsel in den Jahren 1828–1847, E. Hjelt, ed. (Brunswick, 1900); and W. Prandtl, Deutsche Chemiker in der ersten Hälfte des neunzehnten Jahrhunderts (Weinheim, 1956), 303–314.

GEORGE B. KAUFFMAN

MAGNUS, OLAUS. See **Olaus Magnus.**

MAGNUS, RUDOLF (*b.* Brunswick, Germany, 2 September 1873; *d.* Pontresina, Switzerland, 25 July 1927), *neurophysiology, pharmacology.*

Magnus was raised in a rich intellectual environment that embraced medicine, the law, and the humanities. His father practiced law in Brunswick, one grandfather was director of the Hamburg library, and the other was a physician. Magnus' initial career interests lay in literature and philosophy. Partly through the advice of a family friend, the chemist Richard Meyer, however, he decided to study medicine at Heidelberg. There his career was molded by such influential figures as Willy Kühne, the noted physiologist, and the chemist David Meyer; and he began lasting friendships with certain scientific figures, notably Jakob von Uexküll and Otto Cohnheim. In 1895, while still a medical student, Magnus showed his aptitude for original research in a paper presented at the Third International Congress of Physiology at Bern, dealing with a method for measuring blood pressure in an exposed artery. The further development and application of this technique was the subject of his doctoral thesis in 1898.

Magnus began his career in pharmacology, working first at Heidelberg as an assistant in 1898 and as a *Privatdozent* in 1900. At Heidelberg he continued investigations that he had begun as an undergraduate on the cardiovascular, renal, and intestinal systems, earning rapid and wide recognition for studies on the action of arsenic and of various pharmacologic agents in the gut, and on water balance in tissues.

In 1904 Magnus devised a now-standard technique in pharmacology for studying the responses of isolated muscle, suspending a loop of small intestine in warmed, oxygenated Locke-Ringer solution. Using the method to make a series of important observations on responses to alkaloid agents, on local reflexes, and on automatic rhythmicity, he discovered that the degree of stretching of the intestinal muscle determines the direction of stimulus conduction.

During his years at Heidelberg, Magnus made a series of visits to British research laboratories, beginning with a trip to work with E. A. Sharpey-Schafer at Edinburgh in 1900. Together they discovered the diuretic action of pituitary gland extracts. In 1905 Magnus went to Cambridge to learn surgical techniques for studying the autonomic nervous system from J. N. Langley, in order to continue his analysis of the relations between drug effects and nerve supply on the motility of intestinal muscle. The critical event that shaped the direction of his future neurophysiological investigations was his 1908 visit to Charles Sherrington at Liverpool.

Magnus accepted the professorship of pharmacology at the University of Utrecht in 1908, since there was then no vacant chair of pharmacology in Germany. During the next two decades his Utrecht group issued over 300 papers. The major corpus of Magnus' work, and that for which he is best known, deals with the reflex control of posture. He also continued an active program of teaching and research in pure pharmacology.

Magnus was noted as a teacher and speaker as well as a gifted investigator. The lectures he delivered in his pharmacology courses, published as *Pharmakologisches Praktikum*, reported on the latest research projects of his institute, particularly the pharmacology of the pulmonary circulation, and the isolation and identification of choline as the hormonal regulatory agent for intestinal muscle. The wide range of his interests, embracing history, philosophy, and botany, was demonstrated by a lecture series on Goethe as a natural scientist (1906).

Although present concepts of the body's equilibratory system are principally an outgrowth of Magnus' work, data on the role of the cerebellum in maintaining body attitudes had been accumulating slowly since experiments by François Magendie in the 1820's. Toward the end of the nineteenth century, David Ferrier's experiments on various animals led him to the idea of a cerebellovestibular connection, a germinal idea that helped launch the modern period of study of equilibratory functions.

The postural reflex studies by Magnus and his colleagues, particularly A. de Kleijn, were a model of the integrative neurophysiology being pioneered by Sherrington at Liverpool and Oxford. While Magnus was working with him in 1908, one of Sherrington's research interests was muscle tonus in mammals. Analyzing the reflex pathways involved in the production and maintenance of tonus, Sherrington concluded that tone in mammals is due to postural reflexes, as P. Q. Brondgeest in 1860 had shown it to be for frogs and rabbits. In 1910, drawing in part upon his observations of the "reflexe figures" assumed by decerebrate animals, Sherrington published a detailed analysis of the reflex control of stepping and standing.

Under Sherrington's guidance, Magnus in 1908 had begun experiments on mammalian muscle tonus, drawing in part upon Uexküll's work on the changing responses of the muscle bands in a marine worm to varying tensions. Encouraged by Sherrington to continue the investigation of equilibratory phenomena, Magnus and Kleijn published the first of their classic papers on the influence of head position on the tonus of extremities in 1912. The depth of Magnus' subsequent studies is suggested by the fact that one observation he and Sherrington had made independently—that rotation of the head in the decerebrate animal changes the muscle tonus of the limbs—generated a series of eighty-two publications by the Utrecht group.

The investigations of Magnus and his colleagues showed the many automatic reflex actions through which an animal assumes and maintains body postures, by sequences of coordinated reflexes and by the types of static "figures" demonstrated so clearly in the decerebrate preparation. Their fundamental analysis of equilibratory functions involved, first, a detailed study of tonic neck muscle and labyrinth reflexes and of labyrinth righting reflexes, by which body postures change in response to various stimuli as an animal constantly adjusts to its needs and environment. They then restudied the various reflexes they had cataloged after ablating the cerebellum, cerebrum, brain stem, or cervical spinal cord, in order to localize the brain and spinal cord areas controlling posture.

Their study of the labyrinth organs, which was inspired in part by the work of J. R. Ewald, led Magnus and Kleijn to a fundamental analysis of the responses of the ear's vestibular organs to natural stimuli. In one classic experiment they differentiated between the functions of the otolith organs and the semicircular canals by centrifuging anesthetized guinea pigs at high speed. The otolith membranes were detached by the procedure; but the canals, ampullae, and cristae remained intact. Magnus and Kleijn then found that reflexes resulting from static posture were abolished in the absence of the otolith mechanism but that the animals retained all the labyrinth reactions produced by rectilinear acceleration.

Through such studies Magnus' research group founded our knowledge of the complex integrative reflex system by which the brain stem and cervical spinal cord control musculature. Step by step they documented the functions of the vestibular apparatus, tonic neck and labyrinth reflexes, and other postural and righting reflexes and their neural pathways and control mechanisms. Magnus summarized the work of his Utrecht laboratory, and surveyed the work of others in his field, in *Die Körperstellung* (1924), a monograph justly cited as a classic work in reflex physiology. At the time of his sudden death in 1927, at age fifty-three, he and Kleijn were under consideration for the Nobel Prize in physiology or medicine for their fundamental contributions to neurophysiology.

BIBLIOGRAPHY

I. ORIGINAL WORKS. Magnus' writings include *Goethe als Naturforscher* (Leipzig, 1906); "Welche Teile des Zentralnervensystems müssen für das Zustandekommen der tonischen Hals- und Labyrinthereflexe auf die Körpermuskulatur vorhanden sein," in *Pflügers Archiv für die gesamte Physiologie des Menschen und der Tiere*, **159** (1914), 224–249; *Körperstellung experimentell-physiologische Untersuchungen über die einzelnen beider Körperstellung in Tätigkeit tretenden Reflexe, über ihr Zusammenwirken und ihre Störungen* (Berlin, 1924); and "Animal Posture," in *Pro-*

ceedings of the Royal Society, **98B** (1925), 339–353, the Croonian lecture.

II. SECONDARY LITERATURE. See H. H. Dale, "In Memoriam Rudolf Magnus (1873–1927)," in *Stanford University Publications, Medical Sciences*, **2** (1930), 241–247; J. F. Fulton, "Rudolf Magnus 1873–1927," in *Boston Medical and Surgical Journal*, **197** (1927–1928), 323–324; and I. N. W. Olninck, "Rudolf Magnus," in E. W. Haymaker, ed., *The Founders of Neurology* (Springfield, Ill., 1953), pp. 149–152.

JUDITH P. SWAZEY

MAGNUS, VALERIANUS. See **Magni, Valeriano.**

MAHĀDEVA (*fl.* western India, 1316), *astronomy.*

The scion of a Brahman family of astronomers and astrologers belonging to the Gautamagotra, a family that began with Bhogadeva and extended through successive generations represented by Mādhava, Padmanābha, and his father, Paraśurāma, Mahādeva resided on the banks of the Godāvarī River—probably near its source in Mahārāshtra. He wrote a lengthy set of astronomical tables, the *Mahādevī* (see essay in Supplement), employing the "true linear" arrangement (see D. Pingree, "On the Classification of Indian Planetary Tables," in *Journal for the History of Astronomy*, 1 [1970], 95–108, esp. 103–104) and the parameters of the *Brāhmapakṣa* (see essay in Supplement); their epoch is 28 March 1316. The extreme popularity of these tables in western India is indicated by the fact that over 100 manuscripts of them originating in that area have been identified. They have also been commented on by Nṛsiṃha of Nandipura in Gujarat (1528) and by Dhanarāja of Padmāvatī in Mārwār (Jodhpur) (1635) and have often been imitated by the astronomers of Gujarat and Rajasthan.

BIBLIOGRAPHY

The tables are discussed in detail by O. Neugebauer and D. Pingree, "The Astronomical Tables of Mahādeva," in *Proceedings of the American Philosophical Society*, **111** (1967), 69–92. See also D. Pingree, "Sanskrit Astronomical Tables in the United States," in *Transactions of the American Philosophical Society*, n.s. **58**, no. 3 (1968), 37a–39a; and "Sanskrit Astronomical Tables in England," in *Journal of Oriental Research* (Madras).

DAVID PINGREE

AL-MĀHĀNĪ, ABŪ 'ABD ALLĀH MUḤAMMAD IBN 'ĪSĀ (*b.* Mahān, Kerman, Persia; *fl.* Baghdad, *ca.* 860; *d. ca.* 880), *mathematics, astronomy.*

Our main source of information on al-Māhānī's life consists of quotations from an unspecified work by al-Māhānī in Ibn Yūnus' *Ḥākimite Tables*. Here Ibn Yūnus cites observations of conjunctions and lunar and solar eclipses made by al-Māhānī between 853 and 866. Al-Māhānī remarked, in connection with the lunar eclipses, that he calculated their beginnings with an astrolabe and that the beginnings of three consecutive eclipses were about half an hour later than calculated.

Al-Māhānī's main accomplishments lie in mathematics; in the *Fihrist* he is mentioned only as geometer and arithmetician. Al-Khayyāmī states that al-Māhānī was the first to attempt an algebraic solution of the Archimedean problem of dividing a sphere by a plane into segments the volumes of which are in a given ratio (*On the Sphere and the Cylinder* II, 4). Al-Māhānī expressed this problem in a cubic equation of the form $x^3 + a = cx^2$, but he could not proceed further. According to al-Khayyāmī, the problem was thought unsolvable until al-Khāzin succeeded by using conic sections. In Leiden there exists a manuscript copy of a commentary to al-Māhānī's treatise, probably by al-Qūhī.

Al-Māhānī wrote commentaries to books I, V, X, and XIII of Euclid's *Elements*. Of these, the treatise on the twenty-six propositions of book I that can be proved without a *reductio ad absurdum* has been lost. Part of a commentary on book X, on irrational ratios; an explanation of obscure passages in book XIII; and three (different?) treatises on ratio (book V) are extant. Since book V, on the theory of proportion, was presented in a synthetic form which did not reveal how the doctrine of proportions had come into being, Arabic mathematicians were dissatisfied with definition 5, the fundamental one. They did not deny its correctness, however, and accepted it as a principle. Gradually they replaced the Euclidean "equimultiple" definition by the pre-Eudoxian "anthyphairetic" definition, which compared magnitudes by comparing their expansion in continued fractions. The "anthyphairetic" conception appears in explicit form in al-Māhānī's treatise, in which he referred to Thābit ibn Qurra. Al-Māhānī regarded ratio as "the mutual behavior of two magnitudes when compared with one another by means of the Euclidean process of finding the greatest common measure." Two pairs of magnitudes were for him proportional when "the two series of quotients appearing in that process are identical." Essentially the same theory was worked out later by al-Nayrīzī. Neither established a connection with

Euclid's definition, which was first done by Ibn al-Haytham.

At the request of some geometers al-Māhānī wrote an improved edition of the *Sphaerica* of Menelaus—of book I and part of book II—which has been lost. His improvements consisted of inserting explanatory remarks, modernizing the language (with special consideration given to technical terms), and remodeling or replacing obscure proofs. This edition was revised and finished by Aḥmad ibn Abī Saʿīd al-Harawī in the tenth century. Al-Ṭūsī, who wrote the most widely known Arabic edition, considered al-Māhānī's and al-Harawī's improvements valueless and used the edition by Abū Naṣr Manṣūr ibn ʿIrāq.

BIBLIOGRAPHY

I. ORIGINAL WORKS. C. Brockelmann, *Geschichte der arabischen Literatur*, supp. I (Leiden, 1937), 383, lists the available MSS of al-Māhānī. Information on al-Māhānī is also given in H. Suter's translation of the *Fihrist* in *Das Mathematiker-Verzeichniss im Fihrist des Ibn abī Jaʿkūb al-Nadim*, in *Abhandlungen zur Geschichte der Mathematik*, VI (Leipzig, 1892), 25, 58. Partial translations and discussions of al-Māhānī's work are in M. Krause, *Die Sphärik von Menelaos aus Alexandrien* (Berlin, 1936), 1, 13, 23–26; G. P. Matvievskaya, *Uchenie o chisle na srednevekovom Blizhnem i Srednem Vostoke* ("Studies on Number in the Medieval Near and Middle East"; Tashkent, 1967), ch. 6, which deals with commentaries on Euclid X; and E. B. Plooij, *Euclid's Conception of Ratio* (Rotterdam, 1950), 4, 50, 61.

II. SECONDARY LITERATURE. On al-Māhānī's observations, see "Ibn Yūnus, *Le livre de la grande Table Hakémite*, trans. by J. J. A. Caussin de Perceval in *Notices et extraits de la Bibliothèque nationale*, 7 (1804), 58, 80, 102–112, 164. Information on al-Māhānī as a mathematician, especially his treatment of the Archimedean problem, is in F. Woepcke, *L'algèbre d'Omar Alkhayyāmī* (Paris, 1851), 2, 40–44, 96. On the anthyphairetic theory, see O. Becker, "*Eudoxos Studien I*," in *Quellen und Studien zur Geschichte der Mathematik, Astronomie und Physik*, Abt. B, **2** (1933), 311–333.

YVONNE DOLD-SAMPLONIUS

MAHĀVĪRA (*fl.* Mysore, India, ninth century), *mathematics.*

Mahāvīra, a Jain, wrote during the reign of Amoghavarṣa, the Rāṣṭrakūṭa monarch of Karṇāṭaka and Mahārāṣṭra between 814/815 and about 880. Nothing else of his life is known. His sole work was a major treatise on mathematics, the *Gaṇitasārasaṅgraha* (see essay in Supplement), in nine chapters:

1. Terminology.
2. Arithmetical operations.
3. Operations involving fractions.
4. Miscellaneous operations.
5. Operations involving the rule of three.
6. Mixed operations.
7. Operations relating to the calculations of areas.
8. Operations relating to excavations.
9. Operations relating to shadows.

There is one commentary on this work by a certain Varadarāja, and another in Kannaḍa, entitled *Daivajñavallabha.*

BIBLIOGRAPHY

The *Gaṇitasārasaṅgraha* was edited, with an English trans. and notes, by M. Raṅgācārya (Madras, 1912); and with a Hindi *anuvāda* by Lakṣmīcandra Jaina as *Jīvarāma Jaina Granthamālā* 12 (Solāpura, 1963). There are discussions of various aspects of this work (listed chronologically) by D. E. Smith, "The Ganita-Sara-Sangraha of Mahāvīrācārya," in *Bibliotheca mathematica*, 3, no. 9 (1908–1909), 106–110; B. Datta, "On Mahāvīra's Solution of Rational Triangles and Quadrilaterals," in *Bulletin of the Calcutta Mathematical Society*, **20** (1932), 267–294; B. Datta, "On the Relation of Mahāvīra to Śrīdhara," in *Isis*, **17** (1932), 25–33; B. Datta and A. N. Singh, *History of Hindu Mathematics*, 2 vols. (Lahore, 1935–1938; repr. in 1 vol., Bombay, 1962), *passim;* E. T. Bell, "Mahavira's Diophantine System," in *Bulletin of the Calcutta Mathematical Society*, **38** (1946), 121–122; and A. Volodarsky, "O traktate Magaviry 'Kratky kurs matematiki,'" in *Fiziko-matematicheskie nauki v stranakh vostoka*, II (Moscow, 1969), 98–130.

DAVID PINGREE

MAHENDRA SŪRI (*fl.* western India, 1370), *astronomy.*

A Jain and a pupil of Madana Sūri of Bhṛgupura (Broach, Gujarat), Mahendra Sūri wrote the first Sanskrit treatise on the astrolabe, the *Yantrarāja* (1370). He evidently used an Islamic source (see essay in Supplement); in it, for instance, $R = 3600' = 60$ parts; $\varepsilon = 1415' = 23;35°$. Furthermore, the commentary by his pupil, Malayendu Sūri, lists the latitudes of Ādane (Aden), Makkā (Mecca), Badaṣasāna (Badakhshan), Balaṣa (Balkh), Nayasāpura (Nīshāpūr), Samarakanda (Samarkand), Kāsagāra (Kashgar), and other Islamic cities, as well as "Hiṃsārapirojāvāda which is inhabited by the king Pīroja" (the king is Fīrūz Shāh Tughlaq [1351–1388], and the place the Hiṣar palace begun by Fīrūz at Firozabad, near Delhi, in 1354), and both the Persian and the Indian (Sanskrit) names of thirty-two stars.

There is another commentary on the *Yantrarāja* by Gopīrāja (1540) and a set of examples for the year 1512.

BIBLIOGRAPHY

The *Yantrarāja* was edited, with Malayendu's commentary, by Sudhākara Dvivedin (Benares, 1882) and by K. K. Raikva (Bombay, 1936). There are notices on Mahendra in S. Dvivedin, *Gaṇakataraṅgiṇi* (Benares, 1933), pp. 48–49, repr. from *The Pandit*, n.s. **14** (1892); and in Ś. B. Dīkṣita, *Bhāratīya Jyotiḥśāstra* (Poona, 1896; repr. Poona, 1931), p. 351 in repr. See also S. L. Katre, "Sultān Fīrūz Shāh Tughluk: Royal Patron of a Contemporary Sanskrit Work," in *Journal of Indian History*, **45** (1967), 357–367.

DAVID PINGREE

MAḤMŪD IBN MASʿŪD AL-SHĪRĀZĪ. See **Quṭb al-Dīn al-Shīrāzī.**

MAIER, MICHAEL (*b.* Rensburg, Holstein, Germany, *ca.* 1568; *d.* Magdeburg, Germany, 1662), *alchemy*.

Maier was probably the son of Johann Maier, an official of the duchy of Holstein. He studied first in either Rensburg or Kiel, and in 1587 he was studying at the University of Rostock. He owed his career to a relation of his mother's, Severin Goebel, a well-known physician of Gdańsk and Königsberg, who financed his studies. In 1589 Maier was in Nuremberg, and he was in Padua with the son of Goebel from 1589 to 1591. He began practicing surgery in 1590 without an academic degree. In 1592 he was at the University of Frankfurt an der Oder, where he had the title of *poeta laureatus caesareus*. He wrote elegant Latin verse, under the anagram "Hermes Malavici."

Next, Maier practiced at Königsberg under the supervision of Severin Goebel. On 24 May 1596 he was enrolled in the University of Bologna as *magister*, and in the same year enrolled himself at the University of Basel and received the doctorate in medicine after presenting his "Theses de epilepsia." It is not known where Maier took his doctorate in philosophy. It seems that before 1600 he was a courtier of Rudolf II and a writer in the German chancellery.

In 1601 Maier was in Königsberg, and on 11 September entered his name on the university rolls as "Michael Meierus Philosophiae et Medicinae Doctor Honoris Gratia," apparently in an attempt to obtain the status of professor or *extraneus* at this university. Obviously this did not occur, for in December 1601 he went to Gdańsk, where in the White Horse Inn he started medical practice, advertising his own remedies, such as frogs dried and then soaked in vinegar.

Before 1612 Maier had returned to Prague as a doctor. He became physician-in-ordinary to Rudolf II, although probably only in an honorary capacity, since his name does not figure in the court accounts. His family coat of arms was augmented, by the grace of the emperor, to include on one half a tree trunk with three branches, and on the other a toad bound by a chain to a flying eagle. The latter symbolized volatile and nonvolatile substances and in all likelihood was taken from an alchemical treatise ascribed to Ibn Sīnā, as can be gathered from Maier's *Symbola aureae mensae*. He was also named *comes palatinus* by the emperor. (A count palatine was an imperial official who exercised a sort of supervision over the universities and had the right to grant doctorates and the title of poet laureate.)

In 1611 Maier was in various cities of Saxony— Torgau, Leipzig, and Mühlhausen—where he met the landgraves Maurice of Hesse and Christian of Anhalt, both of whom shared his passionate devotion to music. During the period 1612–1614 Maier was in England, where he met Robert Fludd, William Paddy, Thomas Smith, and Francis Anthony and translated into Latin a treatise by Thomas Norton under the title of *Crede mihi seu ordinale*. Maier was not favorably impressed by England, as he stated in *Symbola aureae mensae*.

After his return to Germany, Maier helped to organize the publication of the works of Fludd in Frankfurt am Main. He became court physician to Landgrave Maurice, without, however, giving up his private practice. In 1618 he traveled to Stockhausen, where he attended a wealthy nobleman named von Eriedesel. Maier had a house in Frankfurt am Main, where his wife lived, and he bought alchemical works for the landgrave's library at the Frankfurt book fairs. In 1618 Maier moved to Magdeburg to become the physician of Duke Christian Wilhelm. He died there four years later.

Maier is an extremely puzzling figure, both in his works and in his very unsettled life. Without question, as a count palatine he was a political agent of the emperor. Maier was an ardent alchemist, a follower of Paracelsus and neo-Hermetic ideas. He was an implacable enemy of the Roman Catholic church, a defender of the Rosicrucian movement, and probably had a hand in the publication of the *Fama fraternitatis* (1616). Many of his works are written in a very Rosicrucian spirit.

All of Maier's treatises are written with great erudition and display substantial knowledge of mythology and ancient history. They are classic examples of the neo-Hermetic manner, having no clear chemical sense. Yet there appear in his writings sentences and considerations that are sometimes astonishing, as in *Viatorum . . . de montibus planetarium*, in which he deliberates why lead and copper weigh more after being roasted (as Lazarus Ercker had observed). In *Examen fucorum pseudochymiorum* Maier gives examples of the possibility of alchemical fraud and states that it is possible to estimate transmutation truly only by means of docimasy, that is, chemical analysis.

The writings of Maier were highly valued and popular among alchemists. In the history of chemistry they represent a certain regression, however, for Maier was a fervent believer in the transmutation of metals, which was for him a synonym of the word "chymia."

BIBLIOGRAPHY

I. ORIGINAL WORKS. Incomplete bibliographies of Maier's writings are in D. J. Duveen, *Bibliotheca alchemica et chemica* (London, 1965), p. 380; J. Ferguson, *Bibliotheca chimica* (Glasgow, 1906), II, 66; and N. Lenglet du Fresnoy, *Histoire de la philosophie hermétique* (The Hague, 1742), III, 225–230.

Among his works are *Arcana arcanissima* (n.p., n.d. [London, 1614?]); *De circulo physico quadrato* (Oppenheim, 1616); *Apologeticus quo causae clamorum seu revelatiorum Fratrum Rosae Crucis* (Frankfurt, 1617); *Atalanta fugiens* (Oppenheim, 1617); *Examen fucorum pseudochymiorum* (Frankfurt, 1617); *Jocus severus* (Frankfurt, 1617); *Lusus serius* (Frankfurt, 1617); *Silentium post clamores* (Frankfurt, 1617); *Symbola aureae mensae* (Frankfurt, 1617); *Themis aurea* (Frankfurt, 1618); *Tripus aureus* (Frankfurt, 1618), repr. in *Musaeum Hermeticum* (Frankfurt, 1749); *Viatorum hoc est de montibus planetarium* (Frankfurt, 1618); *Verum invectum* (Frankfurt, 1619); *De volucri arboreum* (Frankfurt, 1619); *Septimena philosophia* (Frankfurt, 1620); *Civitas corporis humani* (Frankfurt, 1621); *Cantilenae intellectuales de Phoenice redidivo* (Rostock, 1622); *Tractatus posthumus sive Ulysses* (Frankfurt, 1624); and *Viridarium chymicum* (Frankfurt, 1688).

II. SECONDARY LITERATURE. The literature on Maier's life is scanty. Most of the data in this article are the result of the author's research in various European libraries and archives. The best biography is considered to be J. B. Craven, *Count Michael Maier* (Kirkwall, Scotland, 1910; London, 1968), which really describes the contents of Maier's writings. H. M. E. De Jong, in the new ed. of *Atalanta fugiens* (London, 1969), elucidates the sources of the emblems and allegories in Maier's books. See also L. Thorndike, *A History of Magic and Experimental Science* (New York, 1958), VII, 167, 171–173, 213, and VIII, 113, 194.

A list of older literature on Maier's life and work is in Ferguson (see above), *loc. cit.*

WŁODZIMIERZ HUBICKI

MAIGE, ALBERT (*b.* Auxonne, France, 26 November 1872; *d.* Lille, France, 29 November 1943), *botany.*

Professor at Algiers (1900–1910), Poitiers (1911–1919), and Lille (1920–1943), Maige was a corresponding member of the Institut de France. Having determined the general adaptive characteristics of creeping plants, he determined the tendencies of a tapering evolution toward the morphology and anatomy of either rhizomes or climbing plants for which direct light discourages creeping and diffused light encourages creeping.

Maige's *Flore forestière de l'Algérie* begins with general botanical concepts applied to phytogeography, to silviculture, and to the natural history of the woody plants of Algeria. It also includes four keys designed to assist in the identification of specimens: the reproductive organs and the characteristics of leafy branches, of the bare branches of trees with caducous leaves, and of the principal native woods.

Besides the description of new galls and various anomalies, Maige's works in pathology and teratology include the study of the potato blight (*brunissure*), a physiological disorder caused by a progressive dehydration of the tissues, and, especially, the study of the disease of the cork oak known as "yellow spot," which gives wine the taste of cork.

In physiology, Maige determined that the respiratory rate of the plant decreases regularly from the earliest stages to the time of blooming and that it falls steeply as the flower fades. The respiratory physiology of the flower thus resembles that of the leaf. He found that the influence of variations in turgescence on the respiration of the cell is shown by a notable simultaneous elevation of turgescence and respiration. The diminution of turgescence produces the same effects up to an optimum concentration of the cellular juice, beyond which there occurs a diminution of the respiratory coefficients. Sugar solutions of various concentrations affect the respiration, the turgescence, and the growth of the cell.

Maige conducted research in cytology, the study of pollinic karyokinesis among the Nymphaeaceae. In cytophysiology he used the cytophysiological method of nuclear variations, which consists of depriving cells of nourishment, thus producing a decrease in nuclear volume, and observing whether or not the nucleus grows under the influence of various substances. Combined with the analogous method of plastid variations, it can contribute valuable data concerning the nutritive values of the substances being examined. In particular, these methods enabled Maige to show that the formation of starch causes the different sugars to pass through the same stages as does the breakdown of starch but in the opposite direction—notably through stages of the dextrins and the erythrodextrins. The several enzymes involved in these processes can be arrested at certain stages.

The formation and the digestion of starch in the cells are two distinct phenomena produced by different enzymes, or at least by enzymes localized in different cellular regions. That which governs starch formation is localized, Maige proved, in the leucoplast; that which provokes amylolysis, in the cytoplasm. In addition, the former inhibits the latter during starch formation.

BIBLIOGRAPHY

Maige's works include "Recherches biologiques sur les plantes rampantes," in *Annales des sciences naturelles (Botanique)* (1900), 249–364; *Flore forestière de l'Algérie* (Paris, 1914); and various works on cytophysiology in *Comptes rendus hebdomadaires de l'Académie des sciences* and *Comptes rendus de la Société de biologie.*

MAURICE HOCQUETTE

MAIGNAN, EMANUEL (*b.* Toulouse, France, 17 July 1601[?]; *d.* Toulouse, 29 October 1676), *physics.*

Born of a prominent Armagnac family, Maignan spent his boyhood in Toulouse and entered the order of Minims at an early age, taking his vows in 1619. He first studied philosophy with an Aristotelian named Ruffat but soon rebelled against the Peripatetic system, showing a strong interest and aptitude for mathematical studies. He taught philosophy and theology at the Minim convent of Monte Pincio in Rome from 1636 to 1650, during which time he became interested in the experimental approach to knowledge, coming into contact with Gasparo Berti, Raffaello Magiotti, and Athanasius Kircher. In this group he participated in the important experiments which helped to establish the possibility of artificially creating a void space in nature and which influenced the work of Torricelli and others. His *Cursus philosophicus* (1653), of which more than four-fifths is devoted to natural philosophy, provides one of the fullest accounts of these researches. In 1650 he returned to Toulouse, where he spent most of the remainder of his life. There he continued his experimental work but devoted much of his energy to the administrative and religious work of his order.

Once described by Pierre Bayle as "one of the greatest philosophers of the seventeenth century," Maignan has largely been forgotten, although he was an original and individualistic thinker of no small merit. His work in optics, instrument making and design, and various branches of physics is in need of reevaluation. His *Perspectiva horaria* (1648) is an extremely detailed and almost exhaustive discussion of sundials, both from a practical and from a theoretical point of view. In this work many optical topics such as sciagraphy are also treated.

Maignan is responsible for introducing a strongly experimental emphasis into the scholastic textbook, turning aside from the bookish Aristotelian tradition, while at the same time remaining critical of Descartes and other contemporary authors. His work, perhaps as well as any of the seventeenth century, shows the marked influence of experimentalism on scholastic thought. After Maignan's death a systematic textbook of his teachings meant for use in the schools was prepared by his follower and biographer, Jean Saguens (*Philosophia Magnani scholastica . . .*, 4 vols. [Toulouse, 1703]).

BIBLIOGRAPHY

I. ORIGINAL WORKS. Maignan's most important works are *Perspectiva horaria sive de horographia gnomonica tum theoretica tum pratica libri quatuor* (Rome, 1648); *Cursus philosophicus* (Toulouse, 1653; 2nd ed., enl., Lyons, 1673); *Philosophia sacra*, 2 pts. (Toulouse, 1661–Lyons, 1672). For more complete lists see Whitmore, listed below; and the catalog of the Bibliothèque Nationale, Paris, CIII, 786–787.

II. SECONDARY LITERATURE. The basic work on Maignan's life is apparently J. Saguens, *De vita . . . Emanuel Maignani* (Toulouse, 1703), not seen. See also (listed chronologically) Pierre Bayle, *Dictionnaire historique et critique*, X (Paris, 1820), 125–133; F. Sander, *Die Auffassung des Raumes bei Emanuel Maignan und Johannes Baptiste Morin* (Paderborn, 1934); C. de Waard, *L'expérience barométrique* (Thouars, 1936), *passim;* R. Ceñal, "Emmanuel Maignan: su vida, su obra, su influencia," in *Revista de estudios politicos* (Madrid), no. 66 (1952), 111–149; and "La filosofía de Emmanuel Maignan," in *Revista de filosofía* (Madrid), 13 (1954), 15–68; J. S. Spink, *French Free-Thought from Gassendi to Voltaire* (London, 1960), 75–84; W. E. K. Middleton, *The History of the Barometer* (Baltimore, 1964), *passim;* and P. J. S. Whitmore, *The Order of Minims in Seventeenth-Century France* (The Hague, 1967), 163–186, with additional bibliography, including MSS sources.

CHARLES B. SCHMITT

MAILLET, BENOÎT DE (*b*. St. Mihiel, France, 12 April 1656; *d*. Marseilles, France, 30 January 1738), *geology, oceanography, cosmogony.*

Maillet belonged to a noble family of Lorraine and received an excellent classical education. Through the favors of his protector, the chancellor Pontchartrain, he was appointed general consul of the king of France at Cairo in 1692, a position he held until 1708. During that time he was chosen by the king as his personal envoy to Ethiopia. Although political circumstances prevented him from accomplishing his mission, Maillet wrote a compilation entitled "Mémoires d'Éthiopie" that was included in Jeronymo Lobo's account of that country (1728).

Between 1708 and 1714 Maillet was consul in Leghorn. He ended his diplomatic career in 1720 as inspector of French establishments in the Levant and the Barbary States. After having spent two years in Paris while the plague was raging at Marseilles, he retired to that city on a handsome pension.

While in Egypt, Maillet completed an important historical and sociological volume entitled *Description de l'Égypte* (1735) and wrote most of his system on the diminution of the sea, *Telliamed ou entretiens d'un philosophe indien avec un missionaire françois sur la diminution de la mer, la formation de la terre, l'origine de l'homme, etc....* This fundamental work, in essence an ultraneptunian theory of the earth, was based largely on his geological field observations made during extensive travels throughout Egypt and other Mediterranean countries. Maillet must have taken full advantage of his fluency in Arabic to gain access to the manuscripts of many ancient Arabic authors, such as al-Khayyāmī, from whom he may have borrowed the original idea of the diminution of the sea.

For the publication of his system Maillet relied on the Abbé J. B. Le Mascrier, who had previously edited the *Description de l'Égypte*. Only ten years after Maillet's death did Le Mascrier reluctantly agree to the publication of the first edition (Amsterdam, 1738), which was followed by a second and third. Two English translations were also published. This unusual delay in publication resulted from the failure of Le Mascrier's editorial work to reduce the dangerous nature of the system; actually, he was willing to be acknowledged only as editor of the third edition. Indeed, even when presented under the name of a fictitious Indian philosopher (his own name spelled backward), Maillet's concepts were unorthodox and highly materialistic.

The proposed system did not admit God as an omnificent ruler, postulating instead an eternal universe undergoing natural changes at random. This universe was based on the Cartesian theory of vortices combined with Fontenelle's concept of the plurality of inhabited worlds. Heavenly bodies were believed to be eternally renovated through a mechanism of alternating luminous phases, during which they were similar to suns, and dark phases, when they were comparable with planets. At present the earth was in a dark phase, and the level of the universal ocean was being lowered by evaporation into outer space, at the rate of three inches per century, until total depletion would occur. This general regression had taken place for at least the past two billion years, an estimate indicating Maillet's acute perception of geological time (as stated in the manuscripts).

The first part of Maillet's system consisted of a study of shoreline features combined with the submarine exploration of the continental shelf by means of a diving machine, the ancestor of modern bathyscaphes. In this survey the sedimentary processes characteristic of rocky coasts, beaches, and deltas were discussed in great detail as a function of the pattern of waves, tides, and bottom currents. This analysis of present-day marine mechanisms was then applied to the geological past, following essentially uniformitarian principles. Maillet used all the aspects of his oceanographical knowledge to explain, by the action of the sea, all the physiographic, lithologic, paleontologic, and structural features of the geological record.

When the sea was in the stage of a universal ocean, its bottom currents' distribution of the sands, silts, and calcinated stones which were the remains of the previous luminous phase built the so-called primitive or primordial mountains, analogous to gigantic submarine bars. They represented the highest mountains, which consisted of a "uniform substance," occasionally displaying horizontal bedding. This description certainly referred to metamorphic rocks, since Maillet stressed the almost complete absence of fossils in them, claiming that at the time of their deposition the universal ocean was too deep to allow the existence of any form of life.

Following a certain amount of evaporation, the summits of the primitive mountains emerged; and in the surrounding shallow waters life appeared. Maillet explained this appearance of life on earth by assuming that the entire universe was filled with the seeds of all living beings. Invisible and imperishable, these seeds were always available for fecundation and the creation of new species whenever the waters of the globes, at certain times and under certain circumstances, became proper for such processes to occur.

The diminution of the sea and the related expansion of the continents compelled all forms of life to undergo a generalized transformism in order to adapt themselves to the new environmental conditions. Marine plants gave rise to land types; sea animals acquired flight and walking capacities and changed into birds and land animals; and mermen and mermaids emerged from the sea, developing into terrestrial human beings. Obviously transformism, but not evolution, was postulated in Maillet's system; and the very early appearance (one billion years ago, as stated in the manuscripts) of mankind, with its "petrified ships," earthenware, weapons, and tools allegedly found with human skeletons in rocks, did not present any particular difficulty of chronology.

Further lowering of the sea level led to the generation of the secondary mountains, or "daughters of the primitive ones." They consisted of fossiliferous and horizontally bedded sands and muds (sedimentary rocks) derived from the erosion of the primitive mountains by waves acting along coastlines. As a consequence of this process, the secondary mountains were younger and less high, and within any geological section of such mountains the beds were superposed from bottom to top in agreement with the law of superposition. This situation was also true with respect to the enclosed fossils, which were assumed to become more abundant at higher levels since the shallowing sea provided an increasingly favorable environment. Consequently, fossils showed important changes through time. This was an early expression of the modern concept of faunal successions.

In Maillet's system all the features of the primitive and secondary mountains dated back to the time of deposition of the soft materials. These were gradually cemented by marine salt and finally exposed through the diminution of the sea as a finished or "congealed" scenery which would remain essentially unaffected by weathering agents. Indeed, in Maillet's system, stream valleys represented ancient channels of marine currents used after emergence by streams only to funnel rainwater to the ocean. In his negation of stream erosion Maillet considered that these channels could be modified by tidal currents only during the gradual retreat of the sea, as shown today by estuaries.

The proposed system was also devoid of any mountain-building mechanism capable of uplifting, tilting, or folding strata. Since Maillet's geological knowledge was limited to essentially undisturbed sedimentary rock areas, he considered tilted and folded beds to be accidental features of mountains. He explained them as well through the action of marine bottom currents and waves he had observed along present coasts. Small-scale folds were interpreted as ripple marks, whereas large-scale tilting and folding of beds were explained by the action of currents which deposit regular layers of sediments over supposed irregularities of an "indurated substratum." Following the same line of reasoning, complicated folds were considered the results of violent storms during which currents flowed in complex patterns around rocky obstacles, eroding and depositing sediments in the shape of highly contorted beds.

Maillet's ideas unquestionably influenced many leading naturalists for almost a century, notably Buffon and Cuvier. The latter, although not in favor of Maillet's system, considered it to be the first systematic presentation of a theory of general transformism. Although Maillet was certainly a forerunner of Lamarck, this position should not obscure his major contribution, which is geological. His ultraneptunian theory of the earth, in which everything was explained by the action of a retreating sea, makes him a marine geologist of the eighteenth century.

BIBLIOGRAPHY

Maillet's "Mémoires d'Éthiopie" is in R. P. Jeronymo Lobo, *Relation historique d'Abissinie, traduite du portugais, continuée et augmentée de plusieurs dissertations, lettres et mémoires par M. Le Grand* (Paris, 1728). His work on Egypt is *Description de l'Égypte contenant plusieurs remarques curieuses sur la géographie ancienne et moderne de ce païs* (Paris, 1735). His major work is *Telliamed . . .* (Amsterdam, 1748; Basel, 1749; new ed., rev., corr., and enl., The Hague–Paris, 1755). English versions of the latter are *Telliamed: Or Discourses Between an Indian Philosopher and a French Missionary on the Diminution of the Sea . . .* (London, 1750); *Telliamed: Or the World Explained Containing Discourses Between an Indian Philosopher and a Missionary on the Diminution of the Sea . . .* (Baltimore, 1797); and *Telliamed: Or Conversations Between an Indian Philosopher and a French Missionary on the Diminution of the Sea,* edited and translated by A. V. Carozzi (Urbana, Ill., 1968), trans. of a 1728 MS and comparison with the final ed. of 1755.

Secondary literature is Fritz Neubert, *Einleitung in eine kritische Ausgabe von B. de Maillets Telliamed. Ein Beitrag zur Geschichte der französischen Aufklärungsliteratur,* Romanische Studien, no. 19 (Berlin, 1920).

ALBERT CAROZZI

MAIMONIDES, RABBI MOSES BEN MAIMON, also known by the acronym **RaMBaM** (*b.* Córdoba, Spain, 1135 or 1138; *d.* Cairo [or Fuṣṭāṭ], Egypt, 1204), *medicine, codification of the Jewish law, philosophy.*

Maimonides was the foremost representative of the school of thought that is designated as Jewish Aristotelianism. In consequence of the invasion of Muslim Spain by the Almohads, his family left Córdoba while he was a child and after an interval settled in 1159/1160 in Fez, Morocco, a country which, like Andalusia, was ruled by the Almohads. He lived there until 1165. Maimonides received his philosophical, scientific, and legal training in Spain and the Maghreb and prided himself on belonging to the Andalusian (rather than the Oriental) school of philosophy. It is also probable that the dogmas of the Almohad creed had some influence on his formulation of the thirteen fundamental Jewish religious principles. In 1166 Maimonides settled in Egypt, at first in Alexandria and then in Fuṣṭāṭ, near Cairo. In Egypt he was court physician and (either official or unofficial) head of the Jewish community. His works, with very few exceptions, were written in that country, where he spent the rest of his life.

Maimonides' writings may be classed according to their genres:

1. The legal works, the most important of which are his commentary on the Mishnah, written when he was still young, and his codification of the Talmudic law, known as *Mishnah Torah* or *Yad Hazaqa* ("A Strong Hand"). Certain portions of both these works treat of philosophical doctrine.

2. Popular or semipopular theological works destined for the general Jewish reader, such as the "Treatise on Resurrection."

3. A systematic philosophical text, the *Maqāla fī ṣināʿat al-manṭiq*, the only one written by Maimonides; it is a treatise on logic, and perhaps his earliest work.

4. *The Guide of the Perplexed*, completed a short time before Maimonides' death, which is in a class by itself. It deals in an unsystematic way with physics and metaphysics but also is concerned with the presuppositions and the imperatives of politics, religious belief and the religious commandments, and the final end of man. It is intended for the perplexed, that is, for those versed in Jewish lore who also have a smattering of and a capacity for philosophical knowledge and are thus in danger of abandoning the observance of the religious law.

5. A number of medical treatises, written in the last period of his life.

6. A very extensive correspondence, consisting of letters and rabbinical *responsa* addressed to notables of Jewish communities in various countries of the Islamic world and outside it—for instance, in the south of France.

All the main works of Maimonides, except *Mishnah Torah*, which is in Hebrew, were written in Arabic.

Maimonides affirmed that he did not intend to expound novel philosophical views; he attempted to show, *inter alia*, (1) that the teaching of philosophy need not, if the necessary precautions are taken, result in the disruption of society and the destruction of the Jewish religion and (2) that philosophy enables man to attain his final end, which is the perfection of his intellect.

We have firsthand evidence of the esteem in which Maimonides held various philosophers. In a letter to Samuel ibn Tibbon, the translator of the *Guide* into Hebrew, he had very high praise for Aristotle—who should, however, according to him, be read together with his commentators. It may be noted in this connection that Alexander of Aphrodisias appears to have had a significant influence on Maimonides.

The most trustworthy Muslim philosophers were, in Maimonides' opinion, al-Fārābī and Ibn Bājja. Ibn Sīnā was regarded as less reliable, although Maimonides used him freely; Ibn Sīnā sometimes provided him with the theological or semitheological terminology necessary for his purposes. According to the letter to Samuel ibn Tibbon, the study of Plato is much less useful than that of Aristotle; but, like that of al-Fārābī, Maimonides' political philosophy derived to a considerable extent from Plato's writings. The precautions taken by Maimonides in the *Guide* to avoid troubling the religious readers who lacked the capacity for philosophical thought entailed, as he explicitly states, unsystematic exposition and deliberate recourse to self-contradiction. To cite an important example, he set forth three conceptions of God which appear to be mutually incompatible.

The first of these conceptions is the God of Maimonides' brand of negative theology. This theology is different in an important respect from that of most Neoplatonists because, contrary to most of them, Maimonides did not admit mystic union, that is, an ecstatic experience of God which transcends the intellect but which man is able to achieve. Maimonides' negative theology stressed the impossibility of making a correct positive statement about the essence of God. Apparently, positive assertions can be regarded as true only if they are given a negative meaning. For instance, the statement "God is wise" signifies that He is not unwise. Maimonides denied—and was, because of this, taken to task in the fourteenth century by the Jewish philosopher Levi ben Gershon (Gersonides)—that this assertion may, when applied to God, have a positive content. Maimonides' conception of the unknowability of God, of there being nothing in the created world that is similar to or has a trace of Him, and the doctrine of negative attributes that fits in with these other points result in the recognition that it is impossible to transform God into an object of science. Metaphysics is thus deprived of its main object (or, according to another opinion, of one of its main objects).

A philosopher can, nevertheless, acquire the only knowledge of God of which man is capable: a knowledge of His activity. This is tantamount to a knowledge of the natural order of events, the expressions "divine actions" and "natural actions" being interchangeable. It appears to follow that it is in studying natural science and metaphysics that man achieves the only knowledge of God granted to him. It is admittedly a very limited knowledge, for an examination of the "divine actions" or "natural actions" does not legitimate any inference with regard to the divine essence. This impossibility is veiled by a generally accepted linguistic convention, in virtue of which "natural" or "divine" events are regarded as proceeding from certain dispositions in God; for instance, the care of parents for their offspring is said to be due to God's beneficence or mercifulness, and earthquakes and floods to His vengefulness.

Maimonides—who in this matter followed, at least as far as terminology is concerned, a well-established tradition—designated mercifulness, vengefulness, and other terms of this kind, when applied to God, as attributes of action. Such attributes represent an evaluation of the impact of natural (and perhaps also of historical) events on man or human society; they should not be taken as referring to God's essence.

A second conception of God expounded by Maimonides is the Aristotelian one. God is an intellect, that is, the subject, the object, and the act of intellection. Like other Aristotelian philosophers, Maimonides considered that these three form a unity. He follows such predecessors in considering, in disagreement with the tenor of Aristotle's text, that God's knowledge is not confined to Himself only. He may be held to know the specific forms and the natural order—or, in other words, the system of sciences. Since Maimonides adopted the Aristotelian view that the knower and the object of his knowledge are identical, this means that in his view (as in that of other medieval Aristotelian philosophers) God may be equated with a self-cognizant system of sciences, a conception which has a striking similarity to Hegel's interpretation of Aristotle's God (in the concluding portion of his *Encyclopedia*). It may be noted that according to Maimonides, God does not know individuals as such, that is, in their separate existence, but only in virtue of being their cause. It seems probable that this formula, like other theological traits in Maimonides' writings, may be derived from Ibn Sīnā (see Ibn Sīnā's *Kitāb al-Shifāʾ*, in *al-Ilāhīyāt*, II, M. Y. Moussa, S. Dunya, and S. Zayed, eds. [Cairo, 1960], p. 359).

In contradistinction to his Aristotelian predecessors, Maimonides appears to have set store by a comparison which indicates a similarity between God conceived as an intellect and the human intellect. This comparison contrasts—perhaps intentionally—with the extreme negative theology of what has been designated as his first conception of God; the extremism of this theology goes much beyond the analogous views expressed by the Muslim Aristotelian philosophers.

A third conception affirms the existence of a divine will, a notion that had been elaborated by al-Ghazālī and some earlier Mutakallimūn. Hence Maimonides may have been influenced to some extent by these thinkers. As we shall see, however, his views were markedly different from theirs.

A God not endowed with will is, according to Maimonides, an altogether powerless God, who is not able to lengthen the wings of a fly. This idea is wholly unacceptable for religion. In this context the question of whether the world has or has not been created in time becomes crucial. Temporal creation would mean an intervention of God in the course of events or, in other words, a miracle, the greatest of miracles; if this were admitted as possible, there would be no difficulty in accepting lesser ones.

No problem would arise if Maimonides were prepared to follow the example of the Mutakallimūn in denying the existence of a natural order and causality; this would mean complete rejection of Aristotelian physics. This he refused to do, and instead found another solution. He argued that the natural sciences are absolutely correct within certain limits but ought not to go beyond these limits. For there are spheres of knowledge the investigation of which transcends the powers of man; as far as science is concerned, certain questions are insoluble, the question of whether the world has been created in time being one of them. Given this fact, Maimonides chose the hypothesis of temporal creation, for the reason that the religious tradition, including the belief that Israel was chosen by God, can be explained and justified only in the light of this hypothesis. Thus the latter may be considered as a practical postulate required for the preservation of religion, and not as a theoretical truth.

Maimonides' emphasis on the limitations of human science is perhaps his most significant contribution to general—as distinct from Jewish—philosophical thought. Like Kant, he pointed out these limitations in order to make room for belief. He accepted Aristotelian physics insofar as it is concerned with the sublunar world; in his view it provides an example of a perfect scientific theory. It may be noted that in this connection he apparently preferred a mechanistic explanation. He certainly played down the role of final, as compared with efficient, causes in natural science.

Human science cannot, however, provide a satisfactory theory for the world of the heavenly spheres. Following his Muslim predecessors (see, for instance,

Ibn Sīnā, *Risāla fi'l-Ajrām al-'ulwiyya*, in *Tis' Rasā'il* [Cairo, 1908], p. 49), Maimonides posed some questions concerning this celestial world which, according to him, may be insoluble. For instance, he asked whether, given the difference between the stars and the spheres, one should not admit, in opposition to Aristotle's views, the existence of more than one kind of matter in the celestial world. A much more intractable problem was constituted by the flagrant contradiction between the Ptolemaic system, with its recourse to epicycles and eccentrics, and Aristotelian physics.

Unlike his contemporary Ibn Rushd, Maimonides did not believe that a correct system of astronomy was known in Aristotle's time and had since been forgotten, for he considered that at that time knowledge of mathematics was still very imperfect. Nor did he accept any of the attempts made by Muslim philosophers and astronomers to work out an astronomical system compatible with Aristotle's physics. The contradiction between astronomy and physics served his purpose. It proves, according to him, the limitation of human knowledge: man is unable to give a satisfactory scientific account of the world of the spheres.

This line of argument (insofar as it shows that the claim of science to propound an all-embracing, coherent, and true system of nature is untrue) concerns the problem of temporal creation only indirectly. The following reasoning, on the other hand, impinges directly upon this question. Maimonides argued that one should not extrapolate beyond certain limits from the knowledge of the natural order obtaining now, for there may have been a beginning prior to which another order may have existed. In this context Maimonides cited the example of a person who, not knowing the facts of birth, denies the possibility of human beings having first existed as embryos. According to him, the Aristotelian affirmation of the eternity of the world is based on a similar extrapolation.

Maimonides held no brief for Ibn Sīnā's opinion that the individual human soul survives the death of the body and is immortal. Like Alexander of Aphrodisias and other Aristotelians, he considered that in man only the actual intellect—which lacks all individual particularity—is capable of survival. In adopting this view, Maimonides clearly showed that, at least on this point, he preferred the philosophical truth as he saw it, however opposed it may seem to be to the current religious conception, to the sort of halfway house between theology and philosophy, which—in the severe judgment of certain Spanish Aristotelians—Ibn Sīnā, who was the dominant philosophical influence in the Muslim East, sought to establish.

Maimonides did, however, adopt certain conceptions of Ibn Sīnā. Thus, his view that existence is an accident derives from Ibn Sīnā's fundamental tenet that essences per se are neutral with respect to existence, which supervenes on them as an accident.

According to Maimonides, all prophets are philosophers, that is, men whose intellect is actualized. But in contradistinction to other philosophers, prophets have a highly developed imaginative faculty. Prophecy is a natural phenomenon.

This description of prophets does not, according to Maimonides' statement, apply to Moses, whose status is higher. In a popular treatise Maimonides refers to Moses' achieving union with the active intellect; such a union (or, to be more precise, a near union) is, according to Ibn Sīnā, a result of the prophetic faculty (see Ibn Sīnā's *De anima*, F. Rahman, ed. [Oxford, 1959], pp. 248–250), whereas, according to Ibn Bājja, it is attained by the great philosophers without the stimulation of such a faculty.

Religious revelation does not procure any knowledge of the highest truth that cannot be achieved by the human intellect; it does, however, have an educative role—as well as a political one. In Maimonides' words, "The Law as a whole aims at two things: the welfare of the soul and the welfare of the body" (*Guide of the Perplexed*, pt. III, ch. 27).

Because of the great diversity of human character, a common framework for the individuals belonging to one society can be provided only by a special category of men endowed with a capacity for government and for legislation. Those who have only a strong imagination, unaccompanied by proportionate intellectual powers, are not interested in the intellectual education of the members of the state which they found or govern. Moses, on the other hand, is the ideal lawgiver.

The law instituted by Moses had to take into account the historical circumstances—such as the influence of ancient Oriental paganism—and had to avoid too great a break with universal religious usage. To cite one example, sacrifices could not be abolished, because this would have been an excessively violent shock. In spite of these difficulties, Moses succeeded in establishing a polity to which Maimonides in the "Epistle to Yemen" (a popular work) applied the expression *al-madīnā al-fāḍila* ("the virtuous city"), used by the Muslim philosophers to designate the ideal state of Plato's *Republic*.

Not only does the Mosaic polity regulate men's actions in the best possible way, but the Scriptures by which this polity is ruled also contain hints toward philosophical truth that may guide such men as are capable of understanding them. Some of these truths are to be discovered in the beliefs taught to all who profess Judaism; these dogmas are, for evident reasons, formulated in language adapted to the understanding of ordinary, unphilosophical people. There are, however, other religious beliefs that, although they are not true, are necessary for the majority of the people, in order to safeguard a tolerable public order and to further morality. Such are the belief that God is angry with those who act in an unjust manner and the belief that He responds instantaneously to the prayers of someone wronged or deceived (*Guide of the Perplexed*, pt. III, ch. 28). The morality suited to men of the common run aims at their exercising a proper restraint over the passions or the appetites; it is an Aristotelian middle-of-the-road morality, not an ascetic one. The ascetic overtones which are occasionally encountered in the *Guide* concern the philosopher rather than the ordinary man.

There is a separate morality for the elite, which rules or should rule (see the *Guide*, pt. I, ch. 54; pt. III, chs. 51, 54). This ethical doctrine is connected with his interpretation of what ought to be man's superior goal, which is to love God and, as far as possible, to resemble Him.

From the point of view of negative theology, love of God can be achieved only through knowledge of divine activity in the world. This appears to signify that the highest perfection can be attained only by a man who leads the theoretical life. Maimonides was at pains, however, to show that the theoretical life can be combined with a life of action, as proved by the examples of the patriarchs and Moses. Moreover, a life of action can constitute an imitation of God. For the prophetic legislators and statesmen endeavor to imitate the operation of nature and God (the two being equivalent). Maimonides emphasized two characteristics that belong to both the actions of God-nature and the actions of the superior statesman. First, however beneficent or destructive—or, in ordinary human parlance, however merciful or vengeful—the actions in question appear to be, neither God nor the prophetic statesman is activated by passions. Second, the activity of nature (or God) tends to preserve the cosmic order, which includes the perpetuity of the species of living beings; but it has no consideration for the individual. In the same way, the prophetic lawgivers and statesmen, who in founding or governing a polity imitate this activity, must have in mind first and foremost the commonweal, the welfare of the majority, and must not be deterred from following a political course of action by the fact that it hurts individuals.

On the whole, Maimonides' medical treatises have been less thoroughly studied than his speculative and legal work. Like other medieval physicians he recognizes Galen as his master. Nevertheless, in a medical treatise entitled *Moses' Chapters on Medicine* he charged Galen with forty contradictions and also taxed him with ignorance in philosophical and theological matters. According to Maimonides, his criticism of Galen was independent of that of al-Rāzī, who wrote a work polemizing against Galen.

Two Hebrew versions of the *Guide* (by Samuel ibn Tibbon and al-Ḥarizi) were prepared a short time after the work was written. It had many Hebrew commentators of various and sometimes conflicting views; and because of its impact, it is certainly the most important work of Jewish medieval philosophy. In the period from 1200 to 1500 it provided most Jewish philosophers with a scheme of reference in relation to which they could formulate their own positions. In the thirteenth and fourteenth centuries it was vehemently denounced as antireligious—and was as vehemently defended.

Spinoza knew Maimonides well, polemizing against him but influenced by him particularly in the *Tractatus theologico-politicus*. Solomon Maimon wrote a commentary on the *Guide*. The *Guide* was translated from Hebrew into Latin in the thirteenth century and exerted, especially with regard to the problem of the eternity of the world but also on many other points, a considerable influence on Scholastic philosophers. This influence is very much in evidence in the works of Thomas Aquinas. In the postmedieval period, Maimonides influenced Jean Bodin and impressed Leibniz.

BIBLIOGRAPHY

I. ORIGINAL WORKS. Bibliographies of Maimonides' works are in J. I. Gorfinkle, "A Bibliography of Maimonides," in *Moses Maimonides 1135–1204*, I. Epstein, ed. (London, 1935), 231–248; L. G. Levy, *Maimonides* (Paris, 1911), supp. in *Cahiers juifs*, **2** (1935), 142–151; and G. Vajda, *Jüdische Philosophie* (Bern, 1950), pp. 20–24. See also M. Steinschneider, *Die arabische Literatur der Juden* (Frankfurt, 1902), pp. 199–221.

Works by Maimonides are *Guide of the Perplexed: Le guide des égarés*, Salomon Munk, ed., 3 vols. (Paris, 1856–1866), Arabic text and French trans. with many detailed notes, French trans. also re-ed. (Paris, 1960), also available in English as *The Guide of the Perplexed*, trans. with intro. and notes by Shlomo Pines (Chicago, 1963), intro. essay by Leo Strauss; "Maqāla fī ṣināʾat al-manṭiq" (Maimonides' treatise on logic), an incomplete Arabic text and the Hebrew versions edited, with an English trans., by I. Efros, in *Proceedings of the American Academy for Jewish Research*, **8** (1937–1938)—the complete text of the Arabic original of his treatise was found and edited, with a Turkish trans., by Mubahat Türker, in *Ankara Üniversitesi Dil ve tarih-coğrafya Fakültesi Dergisi*, **18** (1960), 14–64; "Treatise on Resurrection," original Arabic and Samuel ibn Tibbon's Hebrew trans. edited by J. Finkel, in

Proceedings of the American Academy for Jewish Research, **9** (1939), 1–42, 60–105; "Thamāniyat Fuṣūl," an exposition of ethics, Arabic text edited, with a German trans. by M. Wolff (Leiden, 1903); *Responsen und Briefe des Maimonides*, A. Lichtenberg, ed. (Leipzig, 1859); and *Teshubhot Ha-Rambam* ("Responsa of Maimonides"), 3 vols., J. Blau, ed. (Jerusalem, 1957–1961).

II. Secondary Literature. Works on Maimonides are Alexander Altmann, "Das Verhältnis Maimunis zur jüdischen Mystik," in *Monatsschrift für Geschichte und Wissenschaft des Judentums*, **80** (1936), 305–330; Salo Baron, ed., *Essays on Maimonides: An Octocentennial Volume* (New York, 1941); H. Davidson, "Maimonides Shemonah Perakim and Alfarabi's Fuṣūl Al-Madanī," in *Proceedings of the American Academy for Jewish Research*, **31** (1963), 33–50; Z. Diesendruck, "Maimonides' Lehre von der Prophetie," in G. A. Kohut, ed., *Jewish Studies in Memory of Israel Abrahams* (New York, 1927), pp. 74–134; and "Die Teleologie bei Maimonides," in *Hebrew Union College Annual*, **5** (1928), 415–534; I. Epstein, ed., *Moses Maimonides: 1135–1204* (London, 1935); Jakob Guttmann, *Der Einfluss der Maimonideschen Philosophie auf das christliche Abendland* (Leipzig, 1908); S. Pines, "Spinoza's Tractatus Theologica Politicus. Maimonides and Kant," in *Scripta universitatis atque bibliothecae hierosolymitanarum*, **10** (1968), 3–5; A. Rohner, *Das Schöfungsproblem bei Moses Maimonides, Albertus Magnus, und Thomas von Aquin* (Münster, 1913); Leon Roth, *The Guide for the Perplexed, Moses Maimonides* (London, 1948); and Leo Strauss, *Philosophie und Gesetz* (Berlin, 1935); "Quelques remarques sur la science politique de Maimonide et de Farabi," in *Revue des études juives*, **100** (1936), 1–37; and *Persecution and the Art of Writing* (Chicago, 1952), which includes "The Literary Character of *The Guide for the Perplexed*" (pp. 37–94), also in Baron's *Essays on Maimonides* (see above), 37–91.

See also the following works by H. A. Wolfson: "Maimonides and Halevi," in *Jewish Quarterly Review*, **2** (1911–1912), 297–337; "Maimonides on the Internal Senses," *ibid.*, **25** (1934–1935), 441–467; "Hallevi and Maimonides on Design, Chance, and Necessity," in *Proceedings of the American Academy for Jewish Research*, **11** (1941), 105–163; "Hallevi and Maimonides on Prophecy," in *Jewish Quarterly Review*, n.s. **32** (1941–1942), 345–370, and n.s. **33** (1942–1943), 49–82; "The Platonic, Aristotelian, and Stoic Theories of Creation in Hallevi and Maimonides," in I. Epstein, E. Levine, and C. Roth, eds., *Essays in Honor of the Very Rev. Dr. J. H. Hertz* (London, 1942), pp. 427–442; and "Maimonides on Negative Attributes," in A. Marx *et al.*, eds., *Louis Ginzberg Jubilee Volume* (New York, 1945), pp. 419–446.

Shlomo Pines

MAIOR (or MAIORIS), JOHN (frequently cited as **JEAN MAIR**) (*b.* Gleghornie, near Haddington, Scotland, 1469; *d.* St. Andrews, Scotland, 1550), *logic, mathematics, natural philosophy, history.*

Maior received his early education in Haddington, whence he passed to God's House (later Christ's College), Cambridge, and then to the University of Paris, where he enrolled at the Collège Ste. Barbe about 1492; he completed his education at the Collège de Montaigu. He received the licentiate in arts in 1495 and the licentiate and doctorate in theology in 1506. In 1518 Maior returned to Scotland, where he occupied the first chair of philosophy and theology at Glasgow; in 1522 he was invited to the University of St. Andrews to teach logic and theology. Attracted back to Paris in 1525, he taught there until 1531, when he returned again to St. Andrews. He became provost of St. Salvator's College in 1533 and, as dean of the theological faculty, was invited to the provincial council of 1549, although he could not attend because of advanced age.

Maior spent most of his productive life in Paris, where he formed a school of philosophers and theologians whose influence was unparalleled in its time. Himself taught by nominalists such as Thomas Bricot and Geronymo Pardo and by the Scotist Peter Tartaret, Maior showed a special predilection for nominalism while remaining open to realism, especially that of his *conterraneus* (countryman) John Duns Scotus. To this eclecticism Maior brought a great concern for positive sources, researching and editing with his students many terminist and Scholastic treatises and even contributing to history with his impressive *Historiae Majoris Britanniae, tam Angliae quam Scotiae* (Paris, 1521). His students included the Spaniards Luis Coronel and his brother Antonio and Gaspar Lax; the Scots Robert Caubraith, David Cranston, and George Lokert; and Peter Crokart of Brussels and John Dullaert of Ghent. They and their students quickly diffused Maior's ideals of scholarship through the universities of Spain, Britain, and France, and ultimately throughout Europe. In theology Maior was unsympathetic to the Reformers (he taught the young John Knox while at Glasgow) and remained faithful to the Church of Rome until his death.

Maior's importance for physical science derives from his interest in logic and mathematics and their application to the problems of natural philosophy. He became an important avenue through which the writings of the fourteenth-century Mertonians, especially Bradwardine, Heytesbury, and Swineshead, exerted an influence in the schools of the sixteenth century, including those at Padua and Pisa, where the young Galileo received his education. Among Maior's logical writings the treatise *Propositum de infinito* (1506) is important for its anticipation of modern mathematical treatments of infinity; in it he argues in favor of the existence of actual infinities (*infinita actu)* and discusses the possibilities of motion of an infinite body.

Maior also composed series of questions on all of Aristotle's physical works (Paris, 1526), based on "an exemplar sent to me from Britain" and thus probably written between 1518 and 1525; it is a balanced, if somewhat eclectic, exposition of the main positions that were then being argued by the nominalists and realists. Maior's commentaries on the *Sentences* are significant for their treatment of scientific questions in a theological context; they were used and cited, generally favorably, until the end of the sixteenth century.

BIBLIOGRAPHY

I. ORIGINAL WORKS. Hubert Élie, ed., *Le traité "De l'infini" de Jean Mair* (Paris, 1938), is a Latin ed. of the *Propositum de infinito* with French trans., intro., and notes. Some of Maior's works are listed in the *Dictionary of National Biography*, XII (1921–1922), 830–832. That list has been emended by R. G. Villoslada, S.J., "La universidad de Paris durante los estudios de Francisco de Vitoria, O.P. (1507–1522)," in *Analecta Gregoriana*, **14** (1938), 127–164; and by Élie, *op. cit.*, pp. v–xix. Villoslada also analyzes Maior's philosophical and theological writings and provides a guide to bibliography.

II. SECONDARY LITERATURE. See Hubert Élie, "Quelques maîtres de l'université de Paris vers l'an 1500," in *Archives d'histoire doctrinale et littéraire du moyen âge*, **18** (1950–1951), 193–243, esp. 205–212; and William A. Wallace, O.P., "The Concept of Motion in the Sixteenth Century," in *Proceedings of the American Catholic Philosophical Association*, **41** (1967), 184–195; also A. B. Emden, *A Biographical Register of The University of Cambridge to 1500* (Cambridge, 1963), 384–385.

WILLIAM A. WALLACE, O.P.

MAIR, SIMON. See **Mayr, Simon.**

MAIRAN, JEAN JACQUES D'ORTOUS DE (*b.* Béziers, France, 26 November 1678; *d.* Paris, France, 20 February 1771), *physics.*

Mairan was concerned with a wide variety of subjects, including heat, light, sound, motion, the shape of the earth, and the aurora. He wanted to find physical mechanisms (in the Cartesian sense) to explain phenomena. His theories were generally ingenious descriptions, which were sometimes mathematical and sometimes based on experiment. Despite his enthusiasm and diligence, Mairan often failed to perceive what was trivial and what was crucial about a theory or phenomenon. Nevertheless, Mairan was an important and sometimes controversial figure in the scientific community of his day. Working in the decades during which Newtonian ideas were becoming known in France, Mairan incorporated some of them in his theories; but he remained basically Cartesian.

Mairan's family came from the minor nobility. His parents were François d'Ortous de Mairan and Magdaleine d'Ortous. After studying classics at Toulouse, Mairan studied physics and mathematics in Paris, where Malebranche was one of his teachers. On returning to Béziers in 1704, Mairan continued to be interested in science, and in the years 1715 to 1717 he published his first major works, which received prizes from the Bordeaux Academy. In 1718 Mairan went to Paris and became a member of the Academy of Sciences. (He was made an associate member right away, an unusual procedure.) He later received official lodging in the Louvre. Mairan was secretary of the Academy from 1741 to 1743, succeeding Fontenelle, and he was made *pensionnaire géomètre* in 1746. He also belonged to the Royal Societies of London, Edinburgh, and Uppsala, the Petersburg Academy, and the Institute of Bologna. Mairan was an amateur pianist, he had a serious interest in Chinese culture, and he attended the Paris salons.

Like most of his other work, Mairan's work on heat continued over a long period and was ambitiously conceived. Mairan tried to explain temperature variations and changes of state. His theory of heat was essentially kinetic, but he felt that a subtle matter was necessary to account for the motions of the ultimate particles of ordinary matter and for the changes in these motions. On the basis of observations, experiments, and ingenious estimates, Mairan concluded that the earth has a "central fire" which is an important source of its heat.

Mairan tried to construct a theory of light which would be a Cartesian modification of Newton's theory. In analogy with light, he attempted to understand sound in terms of particles rather than waves. This theory was inspired by the fact that one can distinguish different pitches even when they are all produced together. Mairan postulated different species of particles to carry the different pitches in the propagation of sound.

Mairan's most intense controversies were associated with his ideas in mechanics. He became involved in the notorious *vis viva* controversy, arguing that the "force of a body" depends on its velocity rather than the square of its velocity. Contrary to some, Mairan was aware that velocity should be treated as a vector quantity, but his arguments in general did not provide any special clarification of the problem.

In connection with the shape of the earth, another controversial topic, Mairan tried to reconcile pendulum measurements (indicating that the force of gravity is weaker at the equator) with the Cassinis' (erroneous) measurements of the length of a degree along the meridian (indicating that the earth is elongated at the poles). Mairan proposed that attraction at a point on the earth varies, not according to Newton's law, but inversely as the product of the two principal radii of curvature!

BIBLIOGRAPHY

I. Original Works. Mairan's works include *Dissertation sur les variations du baromètre* (Bordeaux, 1715); *Dissertation sur la glace* (Bordeaux, 1716; Paris, 1749); *Dissertation sur la cause de la lumière des phosphores et des noctiluques* (Bordeaux, 1717); "Recherches géométriques sur la diminution des degrés terrestres en allant de l'equateur vers les poles," in *Mémoires de l'Académie royale des sciences* (1720); "Dissertation sur l'estimation et la mesure des forces motrices des corps," *ibid.* (1728); "Discours sur la propagation du son dans les différens tons qui le modifient," *ibid.* (1737).

More of Mairan's works are listed in J. C. Poggendorff, *Biographisch-Literarisches Handwörterbuch*, II (Leipzig, 1863), 18, and in the study by Kleinbaum mentioned below.

II. Secondary Works. Abby R. Kleinbaum, *Jean Jacques Dortous de Mairan (1678–1771): A Study of an Enlightenment Scientist* (Columbia Univ. Ph.D. diss., 1970), is an excellent study of Mairan's scientific work. The *éloge* of Mairan, by Grandjean de Fouchy, is in the *Histoire de l'Académie royale des sciences*, 1771 (Paris, 1774), 89–104. There is a discussion of Mairan's work with respect to Newtonianism and Cartesianism in Pierre Brunet, *L'introduction des théories de Newton en France au XVIII siècle* (Paris, 1928); Mairan's work on the shape of the earth is discussed in I. Todhunter, *A History of the Mathematical Theories of Attraction and the Figure of the Earth* (New York, 1962), I, 59–61; Mairan's role in the *vis viva* controversy is discussed in René Dugas, *A History of Mechanics* (Neuchâtel, 1955); Mairan's work on the aurora is discussed in J. Morton Briggs, "Aurora and Enlightenment," in *Isis*, **58** (1967), 491–503.

Sigalia C. Dostrovsky

MAIRE, RENÉ-CHARLES-JOSEPH-ERNEST (*b.* Lons-le-Saunier, France, 29 May 1878; *d.* Algiers, Algeria, 24 November 1949), *botany.*

The son of a forest ranger, Maire displayed a precocious interest in botany and at the age of fifteen published his first observations on the vegetation of the Jura. A student at the Faculties of Science and Medicine at Nancy, he was encouraged by the botanists Georges Le Monnier and Paul Vuillemin. By the age of twenty he had published about twenty papers. His interests led him to fieldwork as well as to laboratory observations. His favorite objects of study apart from the phanerogams were the fungi.

His doctoral dissertation on the cytology of the Basidiomycetes, which he defended in Paris at the age of twenty-four, is still a basic work. In it he explained why previous authors believed, wrongly, in the existence of acaryotic stages and he specified the nature of the metachromatic corpuscles. In addition he outlined the nuclear evolution of the Ustilaginales (smuts) and the Uredinales and defined the synkaryon. The latter, which is found among the fleshy Basidiomycetes, is a caryologic unit formed from two morphologically distinct but intimately related nuclei. Finally, he demonstrated that among the Ustilaginales the budding basidiospores or sporidia have a structure identical to that of the true blastosporous fungi, such as the *Saccharomyces.*

Maire supported the observations of Pierre-Auguste Dangeard on the cytological characteristics that originate in the spores and the mycelium of these Ascomycetes, and he agreed with Dangeard that among the fungi, fertilization, which is proper to the higher plants, is replaced by the fusion of two nuclei in the mother cell of the basidium and of the ascus.

At age thirty-three, after serving as a *maître de conférences* at the Faculty of Sciences of Caen, Maire was named to the chair of botany at Algiers. He held this post at the French University of North Africa for nearly forty years.

On several voyages in the Mediterranean basin, Maire studied the phanerogams and fungi of Corsica (1902–1904), the Balearic Islands (1905), the Olympus Mountains, and the Taurus Mountains. He demonstrated the phytogeographical heterogeneity of Thessaly and Epirus and identified six stages of vegetation in that region. Maire first went to Africa in 1902. From Tangier he traversed the area south of Oran and the mountains of Tlemcen, visiting Tunisia in 1909. Permanently settled in Algiers, he explored the Djuradjura and Babor mountains, South Oran, Mount Daya and the Tlemcen Mountains. Stationed in Thessaloniki during World War I, he spent his leaves on the island of Skíros and in Pilos. With Braun-Blanquet, who influenced his work, he published a phytogeographical sketch of Morocco (1925), after having climbed the High and Middle Atlas in 1921.

From 1931 to 1936 Maire made twenty-seven trips to Morocco. He described in detail the Mediterranean character of the Sous and examined the flora of the Moroccan coast, the Rif, Mount Zaian, Mount Tichchoukt, the summits of the High Atlas, the fir and oak forests of Tauzin, Ceuta and the Anti-Atlas, the high Dra River, the Tafilalet, and the plateau of the Lakes District. Maire held that the origins of the Moroccan flora and its autonomous evolution since the Pliocene, in conjunction with the penetration of the arcto-Tertiary floral element, explain the Iberian character of this vegetation. Maire was also active in these years in Algeria, notably in the Aurès Mountains, the phytogeographical map of which he helped to establish. From 1932 to 1935 he explored the Western Sahara as far as Tindouf, as well as the Tefedest, the Hoggar, and the Tassili N' Ajjer Mountains; he described three stages of tropical and Mediterranean vegetation in this region. The results of these gigantic botanical labors were set forth in *Contributions à l'étude de la flore de l'Afrique du Nord*; three volumes were prepared before Maire's death, the remaining were completed by his successors.

A first-rate mycologist endowed with an exceptional memory, Maire studied various fungi of Europe and the Maghreb: Laboulbeniales, rusts, Pezizales, Gasteromycetes, and especially the fleshy agarics. In 1908, while traveling in Sweden, Maire encountered the work of Elias Fries, which left a lasting impression on his own work. In his study of the *Russula*, Maire introduced the Ariadne's thread that permitted the discovery of the exact value of the characteristics of this difficult genus. His contributions to the mycology of the cedars of the Atlas Mountains and of Catalonia as well as to toxicology and to phytopathology are also important, and his account of the biology of the Uredinales is a model of clarity.

Maire became correspondent of the Paris Academy of Sciences in 1923 and nonresident member in 1946. He was also honorary president of the Société Mycologique de France, an organization in which he retained a lively interest.

A scientist whose devotion to work consumed all his energy, Maire was egocentric and severe about keeping to a regular schedule. There was no room in his life for anything besides his research. His personality bore the mark of his native Lorraine; he was even-tempered, rigorous, objective, easy to approach, indulgent, and accommodating—traits that made him universally popular.

BIBLIOGRAPHY

I. ORIGINAL WORKS. Maire's writings include his diss., "Recherches cytologiques et taxonomiques sur les basidiomycètes," in *Bulletin de la Société mycologique de France*, **18** (1902), 1–209, with 8 plates; "Les bases de la classification dans le genre *Russula*," *ibid.*, **26** (1910), 49–125, with figures; "La biologie des urédinales," in *Progressus rei botanicae*, **4** (1911), 109–162; "Études sur la végétation et la flore du Grand Atlas et du Moyen Atlas Marocains," which is *Mémoires de la Société des sciences naturelles et physique du Maroc*, no. 7 (1924), with 16 plates; and "Études sur la végétation et la flore marocaines," *ibid.*, no. 8 (1925), with map, plates, and figures.

II. SECONDARY LITERATURE. Articles devoted to Maire include L. Emberger, G. Malençon, and C. Sauvage, "Hommage à René Maire. I. L'Homme. II. Le Mycologue. III. Le Phanérogamiste," in *Bulletin de la Société des sciences naturelles du Maroc*, **1** (1950), 9; J. Feldmann, "René Maire," in *Revue générale de botanique*, **58** (1951), 65; "René Maire. Sa vie et son oeuvre," written with P. Guinier, in *Bulletin de la Société d'histoire naturelle de l'Afrique du Nord*, **41** (1952), contains a complete bibliography; B. P. G. Hochreutiner, "Un grand systématicien et mycologue français, René Maire," in *Mémoires de la Société botanique de France* (1950–1951), 132–136; F. Jelenc, "René Maire (1878–1949)," in *Revue bryologique et lichénologique*, n.s. **19** (1950), 5; and R. Kuhner, "René Maire (1878–1949)," in *Bulletin de la Société mycologique de France*, **49** (1953), 1–49.

ROGER HEIM

IBN MĀJID, SHIHĀB AL-DĪN AḤMAD IBN MĀJID (*fl.* Najd, Saudi Arabia, fifteenth century A.D.), *navigation*.

Ibn Mājid inherited his profession; both his father and grandfather were *mu'allim*, "masters of navigation," and both were known as experts in the navigation of the Red Sea, dreaded by sailors. Of the Arab navigators of the Middle Ages, none surpassed Ibn Mājid himself in the intimate knowledge and experience of both the Red Sea and the Indian Ocean. He knew almost all the sea routes from the Red Sea to East Africa, and from East Africa to China; proud of his achievements, he styled himself "The Successor of the Lions," or "The Lion of the Sea in Fury" (in his *Ḥāwiyat al-ikhtiṣār fī uṣūl 'ilm al-biḥār*, dated A.H. 866, or A.D. 1462, fol. 88b). He became a legend among pious mariners, who called him "Shaykh Mājid" and recited the *Fātiḥa*, the first chapter of the Koran, in his memory before embarking on certain seas.[1]

Ibn Mājid was well versed in the works of a number of both Muslim and Greek geographers, astronomers, and navigators. He considered the study of these sources to be essential to Arab navigators, and is known to have read books by Ptolemy, Abu'l-Ḥasan al-Marrākushī, al-Ṣūfī, al-Ṭūsī, Yāqūt al-Ḥamawī,

Ibn Saʿīd, al-Battānī, Ibn Ḥawqal, and Ulūgh Bēg—as well as the the works of three ʿAbbāsid sailors, Muḥammad ibn Shādān, Sahl ibn Abān, and Layth ibn Kahlān, whom he dismissed as mere compilers.[2]

Ibn Mājid himself wrote at least thirty-eight works, in both prose and poetry, of which twenty-five are extant. In these he took up a wide variety of astronomical and nautical subjects, including the lunar mansions; the stars that correspond to the thirty-eight rhumbs *(khanns)* of the mariner's compass; sea routes of the Indian Ocean and the latitude of harbors; birds as landmarks; coastlines; the "ten large islands" of the Indian Ocean (Arabia, Madagascar, Sumatra, Java, Taiwan, Ceylon, Zanzibar, Bahrein, Ibn Gāwān, and Socotra); a systematic survey of the coastal regions of Asia and Africa (in which he revealed a more detailed knowledge of the coasts of the Indian Ocean than those of the Mediterranean or Caspian Sea); the Red Sea; Arabian, Coptic, Byzantine, and Persian years; *bāshī*, the computation of the elevation of the polestar from its minimum height above the horizon; the proper direction of the Kaaba; landfalls, in particular landfalls on capes during monsoons; certain northern stars; months of the Byzantine calendar; general instructions for navigators; reefs and deeps; signs indicating land; observations of both constellations (Aquarius) and individual stars (Canopus, Arcturus); *majrās* (a course of a journey by sea); and European, especially Portuguese, navigators of the Indian Ocean. Ibn Mājid is, in addition, known to have revised and enlarged a book, called *al-Ḥijāziyya* and written in verse of the *rajaz* form, originally composed by his father.[3]

Of all his works, however, Ibn Mājid's *Kitāb al-Fawāʾid*, dated A.H. 895 (A.D. 1490), was the one most valuable to navigators. Indeed, the Turkish navigator Sīdī ʿAlī Reʾīs (who died in 1562) had, during a stay in Basra, acquired a copy of this book, together with Ibn Mājid's *Ḥāwiya* and some more nearly contemporary works of Sulaymān al-Mahrī, because, according to him, it was extremely difficult to navigate the Indian Ocean without them.[4] A modern scholar, Gabriel Ferrand, correctly described the *Kitāb al-Fawāʾid* as a "compendium of the known knowledge of theoretical and practical navigation" and as "a kind of synthesis of nautical science of the latter years of the Middle Ages." Ferrand described Ibn Mājid himself as the first writer on nautical science in its modern sense, adding that, apart from the inevitable errors in latitudes, his description of the Red Sea for navigational purposes had never been equaled.[5]

The *Kitāb al-Fawāʾid* also makes it clear that Ibn Mājid did not actually invent the mariner's compass,

although others have claimed that invention for him. Indeed, in folio 46b, he specified only that he fixed the needle (*al-maghnāṭīs*, or "magnet") to the case of the instrument. He did boast, however, that the compass used by the Arab navigators of the Indian Ocean was much superior to that employed by their Egyptian or Maghribi (North African) counterparts, since the Arab compass was divided into thirty-two, rather than only sixteen, sections. He further claimed that the Egyptians and Maghribis were unable to sail Arab ships, while Arabs could handle Egyptian and Maghribi vessels with great ease.[6]

Ibn Mājid's *Al-sufāliyya* is also of particular interest, since in it he records (folio 94a) the expeditions of the "Franks," or Portuguese (although the term was also used for Europeans in general). He was aware of the Portuguese circumnavigation of the Cape of Good Hope, an event that took place near the end of his life, and further aware of Portuguese navigation in the Indian Ocean. He wrote that the Franks, having passed through *al-madkhal* ("the place of entry") that lay between the Maghrib and Sofala (Mozambique), reached the latter coast in A.H. 900 (A.D. 1495), and proceeded to India. He gave a further account of their return to Portugal, by way of Zanzibar and through the same "passage of the Franks," and of their second voyage, in A.H. 906 (A.D. 1501) to India, where they purchased houses and settled down, having been befriended by the Sāmrī rulers (the zamorin kings of Kerala).

Al-madkhal was an object of much concern to Arab mariners, who believed it to be a sea channel that lay south of the Mountains of the Moon (the source of the Nile) and connected the Indian Ocean with the Atlantic. According to Ptolemaic tradition, the whole of the southern hemisphere was terra incognita, an extension of the southern coast of Africa; Arab maps of the period show the Indian Ocean as a lake, connected by a sea passage to the Pacific, and lacking any communication with the Atlantic. Al-Bīrūnī, however, had posited a channel between the Indian Ocean and the "Sea of Darkness"—the Atlantic—and had placed it somewhere south of the source of the Nile, between Sofala and the cape al-Raʾsūn (probably in the region of the Agulhas currents on modern maps). Abu ʾl-Fidāʾ quoted him in his own *Taqwīm al-Buldān*, a work known to Ibn Mājid, who considered his predecessor's theory to be proved by the accomplishments of "the experienced ones," the Portuguese.

Camoëns mentioned Ibn Mājid in *The Lusiads*, while a later Arab historian, Quṭb al-Dīn al-Nahrwālī, accused him of having drunkenly confided to the chief of the Franks *(al-amilandī)*, Vasco da Gama, the navigational information that allowed him to sail from East Africa to India.

NOTES

1. Ferrand, *Instructions nautiques*, III, 227–228.
2. *Kitāb al-Fawā'id*, fols. 3b–4a; *cf.* Ferrand, *op. cit.*, 229–233.
3. *Ibid.*, fol. 78a–b.
4. See Ferrand, in *Encyclopaedia of Islam*, 1st ed., IV, 363.
5. *Ibid.*, 365.
6. *Ibid.* and ff.

BIBLIOGRAPHY

I. ORIGINAL WORKS. Twenty-two of Ibn Mājid's works have been published in facsimile by G. Ferrand, *Instructions nautiques et routiers arabes et portugais des XVᵉ et XVIᵉ siècles*, 3 vols. (Paris, 1921–1928). These include both prose and poetical works (*urjūza*): *Kitāb al-Fawā'id fī uṣūl 'ilm al-baḥr wa 'l-qawā'id* (A.H. 895, A.D. 1490); *Ḥāwiyat al-ikhtiṣār fī uṣūl 'ilm al-biḥār* (A.H. 866, A.D. 1462); *Al-Mu'arraba* (A.H. 890, A.D. 1485); *Kiblat al-Islām fī jamī' al-dunyā* (A.H. 893, A.D. 1488); *Urjūza Barr al-'Arab fī Khalīj Fārs; Urjūza fī qismat al-jamma 'alā Banāt Na'sh* (A.H. 900, A.D. 1494–1495); *Kanz al-Ma'ālima wa dhakhīratihim fī 'ilm al-najhūlāt fī'l-baḥr wa 'l-nujūm wa 'l-burūj* (not dated, but probably written before A.H. 894, A.D. 1489); *Urjūza fī 'l-natakhāt li-Barr al-Hind wa Barr al-'Arab; Mīmiyyāt al-abdāl; Urjūza Mukhammasa; Urjūza* on the Byzantine months, rhyming in *nūn* (not dated, but probably written before 1475 or 1489); *Ḍarībat al-ḍarā'ib; Urjūza* dedicated to the caliph 'Alī ibn Abī Ṭālib (not dated, but written before 1475 or 1489); *Al-Qaṣīda al-Makkiyya; Nādirat al-abdāl; Al-Qaṣīda al-Bā'iyya*, called *Al-Dhahabiyya* (dated 16 Dhu 1-Ḥijja 882, or 21 March 1478); *Al-Fā'iqa* (not dated, but written before 1475); *Al-Balīgha*; nine short prose sections (*faṣl*); *Urjūza* called *Al-Sab'iyya*; untitled *Qaṣīda* (not dated, but written before 1475, 1478, or 1489); and *Qaṣīda* called *Al-Hādiya* (not dated, written before 1475, 1478, or 1489).

Three further *urjūzas*, *Al-Sufāliyya, Al-Ma'laqiyya*, and *Al-Tā'iyya*, have been published, with Russian translations and notes, by T. A. Shumovsky, *Thalāth rāhmānajāt al-majhūla li Aḥmad ibn Mājid: Tri nyeizvyestnioye lotsii Akhmada ibn Madzida arabskogo lotsmana Vasko da Gami* (Moscow–Leningrad, 1957).

Thirteen other works, specifically mentioned by Ibn Mājid in *Kitāb al-Fawā'id*, are no longer known.

II. SECONDARY LITERATURE. See S. Maqbul Ahmad, "The Arabs and the Rounding of the Cape of Good Hope," in *Dr. Zakir Husain Presentation Volume* (New Delhi, 1968), 90–100; M. Reinaud, *Géographie d'Aboulféda*, vol. I of *Introduction générale à la géographie des orientaux* (Paris, 1848); and *Encyclopaedia of Islam*, 2nd ed., III (Leiden, 1968), 856–859.

S. MAQBUL AHMAD

MAJORANA, ETTORE (*b.* Catania, Sicily, 5 August 1906; *d.* at sea, near Naples, 25/26 March 1938), *physics.*

Majorana was the fourth of the five children of Fabio Massimo Majorana, an engineer and inspector general of the Italian ministry of communications, and Dorina Corso. At the age of four he revealed the first signs of a gift for arithmetic. After schooling at home he entered the Jesuit Istituto Massimo in Rome and completed his secondary school education at the Liceo Torquato Tasso, passing his *maturità classica* in the summer of 1923. That fall he entered the School of Engineering of the University of Rome, where his fellow students included his older brother Luciano, Emilio Segrè, and Enrico Volterra, later professor of civil engineering at the University of Houston. Majorana was persuaded by Segrè to take up physics at the beginning of 1928. His lively mind, insight, and the range of his interests immediately impressed the new circle of physicists that had formed around Fermi. He was nicknamed "the Grand Inquisitor" for his exceptionally penetrating and inexorable capacity for scientific criticism, even of his own person and work. He received the doctorate in physics on 6 July 1929 with a thesis on the mechanics of radioactive nuclei sponsored by Fermi.

Fermi convinced Majorana to go abroad financed by a grant from the Consiglio Nazionale delle Ricerche; and Majorana began his journey at the end of January 1933, traveling first to Leipzig and then to Copenhagen. In Leipzig, Heisenberg persuaded Majorana to publish his paper on nuclear forces. He returned to Rome in the autumn of 1933 in poor health aggravated by gastritis, which he had developed in Germany and which was attributed by some to nervous exhaustion. He attended the Istituto di Fisica at intervals but stopped after a few months, despite his friends' attempts to lead him back to a normal life.

Appointed professor of theoretical physics at Naples in November 1937, Majorana soon discovered that his course was too advanced for the majority of students. On 25 March 1938 he wrote from Palermo to his colleague and friend Antonio Carrelli that he found life in general, and his own in particular, useless and had decided to commit suicide. A few hours later he sent a telegram to Carrelli asking him to disregard the letter and boarded a steamer for Naples that evening. Although he was seen at daybreak as the ship entered the Bay of Naples, no trace was ever found of him, despite an inquiry continued for several months and repeated appeals of his family published in the Italian press.

Majorana's total scientific production consists of nine papers, which can be divided into two parts:

six papers on problems of atomic and molecular physics, and three on nuclear physics or the properties of elementary particles. The first group of papers deals with the splitting of Roentgen terms of heavy elements induced by electron spin, the interpretation of recently observed spectral lines in terms of atomic states with two excited electrons, the formation of the molecular ion of helium, the binding of molecular hydrogen through a mechanism different from that of Walter Heitler and Heinz London, and the probability of reversing the magnetic moment of the atoms in a beam of polarized vapor moving through a rapidly varying magnetic field. The last paper remains a classic on nonadiabatic moment-inversion processes. Often quoted, it provides the basis for interpreting the experimental method of flipping neutron spin with a radio-frequency field. The other papers of this period (1928–1932) reveal a thorough knowledge of experimental data and an ease—particularly unusual at the time—in using the symmetry properties of the states to simplify problems or to choose the most suitable approximation for solving each problem quantitatively. The latter ability was at least partly due to Majorana's exceptional gift for calculation.

Majorana's major scientific contribution, however, is found in the last three papers. "Sulla teoria dei nuclei" (1932) concerns the theory of light nuclei under the assumption that they consist solely of protons and neutrons that interact through exchange forces acting only on the space coordinates (and not on the spin), so that the alpha particle—rather than the deuteron—is shown to be, as it is, the system with greatest binding energy per nucleon. The essential work on this paper was completed in the spring of 1932, only two months after the appearance of J. Chadwick's letter to the editor of *Nature* announcing the discovery of the neutron. Fermi and his friends tried in vain to persuade Majorana to publish, but he did not consider his work good enough and even forbade Fermi to mention his results at an international conference that was to take place in July 1932 in Paris. The July 1932 issue of *Zeitschrift für Physik* contains the first of Heisenberg's three famous papers on the same subject. They are based on Heisenberg's exchange forces, which differ from Majorana's forces in that not only the space coordinates but also the spin of the two particles are exchanged.

"Teoria relativistica di particelle con momento intrinseco arbitrario" (1932), the first paper of Majorana's second phase, concerns the relativistic theory of particles with arbitrary intrinsic angular momentum. Although in some ways outside the mainstream of the development of elementary-particle physics, it represents the first attempt to construct a relativistically invariant theory of arbitrary half-integer or integer-spin particles. Majorana's mathematically correct theory contains the first recognition, and the simplest development and application, of the infinite dimensional unitary representations of the Lorentz group. This theory lies outside the mainstream of successive development primarily because, from the outset, Majorana set himself the task of constructing a relativistically invariant linear theory of which the eigenvalues of the mass were all positive. This viewpoint was justified at the time the paper was written (summer 1932), since news of C. D. Anderson's discovery of the positron had not yet reached Rome.

Majorana's last paper was written in 1937 on Fermi's urging, after four years of not publishing because of poor health. It contains a symmetrical theory of the electron and the positron based on the Dirac equation but in which the states of negative energy are avoided and a neutral particle is identical to its antiparticle. The most characteristic point is the discovery of a representation of the Dirac matrices γ_k ($k = 1, 2, 3, 4$), in which the first three components are real, the fourth imaginary, like the vector $x \equiv \vec{r}$, ict (Majorana representation).

At present no neutral particle of the type suggested by Majorana is known, since it has been experimentally established that the neutron, lambda particle, and neutrino differ from their corresponding antiparticles. Nevertheless, Majorana's neutrino, ν_M, characterized by the equality $\nu_M = \bar{\nu}_M$ (the bar indicates the antiparticle), has played an important part in the physics of weak interactions, especially since the discovery by T. D. Lee and C. N. Yang of the nonconservation of parity and the development of the two-component theory of the neutrino. This theory is related to that of Majorana, to which, in certain aspects, it is equivalent. Contrary to the two-component theory, Majorana's does not require the neutrino to have a mass exactly equal to zero, and a small neutrino mass cannot at present be excluded on the basis of available experimental data.

Majorana had an extraordinary gift for mathematics, an exceptionally keen analytic mind, and an acute critical sense. It was perhaps the latter, together with a certain lack of balance on the human side, that interfered with his capacity for creative synthesis and prevented him from reaching a level of scientific productivity comparable to that attained at the same age by major contemporary physicists. Yet his choice of problems and his way—especially his mathematical methods—of attacking them showed that he was naturally in advance of his times and, in some cases, almost prophetic.

BIBLIOGRAPHY

I. ORIGINAL WORKS. Majorana's papers on atomic and molecular physics are "Sullo sdoppiamento dei termini Roentgen e ottici a causa dell'elettrone rotante . . .," in *Atti dell'Accademia nazionale dei Lincei. Rendiconti*, 6th ser., **8** (1928), 229–233, written with G. Gentile; "Sulla formazione dello ione molecolare di Elio," in *Nuovo cimento*, 8th ser., **8** (1931), 22–28; "I presunti termini anomali dell'Elio," ibid., 78–83; "Reazione pseudopolare fra atomi di idrogeno," in *Atti dell'Accademia nazionale dei Lincei. Rendiconti*, **13** (1931), 58–61; "Teoria dei tripletti P' incompleti," in *Nuovo cimento*, **8** (1931), 107–113; and "Atomi orientati in campo magnetico variabile," ibid., **9** (1932), 43–50.

His papers on elementary particles are "Teoria relativistica di particelle con momento intrinseco arbitrario," ibid., 335–344; "Sulla teoria dei nuclei," in *Ricerca scientifica*, **4** (1933), 559–565; and "Teoria simmetrica dell' elettrone e del positrone," in *Nuovo cimento*, **14** (1937), 171–184. See also the posthumously published "Il valore delle leggi statistiche nella fisica e nelle scienze sociali," in *Scientia* (Bologna), **71** (1942), 58–66.

II. SECONDARY LITERATURE. On Majorana's life and work, see E. Amaldi, *La vita e l'opera di Ettore Majorana* (Rome, 1966); an English trans. of the biographical note in this work is in A. Zichichi, ed., *Strong and Weak Interactions—Present Problems* (New York, 1966), 10–77, which also contains a list of Majorana's MSS at the Domus Galileiana, Pisa.

EDOARDO AMALDI

AL-MAJRĪṬĪ, ABU 'L-QĀSIM MASLAMA IBN AḤMAD AL-FARAḌĪ (*b.* Madrid, Spain, second half of the tenth century; *d.* Córdoba, Spain, *ca.* 1007), *astronomy.*

Little is known of al-Majrīṭī's life. He must have been quite an important personality, for Ibn Ḥazm (*d.* 1064) mentions him in his *Ṭawq al-ḥamāma* ("The Ring of the Dove"). It would appear that he early settled in Córdoba where, as a very young man, he studied with a geometrician named ʿAbd al-Ghāfir ibn Muḥammad; it may also be assumed that he was connected with the group of hellenizing scholars patronized by the Umayyad caliph ʿAbd al-Raḥmān III (A.D. 912–961). It is known that he was engaged in making astronomical observations in about A.D. 979; in this period he must have revised the astronomical tables of al-Khwārizmī. At some later date he also was responsible for making the *Rasāʾil* of the Ikhwān al-Ṣafāʾ known to Andalusian astronomers. He may in addition have served as court astrologer.

Al-Majrīṭī had several important disciples, whose later dispersion into all the provinces of Spain made his work known throughout the peninsula. One of these, al-Kirmānī (*d.* 1066), continued al-Majrīṭī's work in carrying Ikhwān al-Ṣafāʾ's *Rasāʾil* into Zaragoza and to the northern frontier. Another, Abu 'l-Qāsim Aṣbagh, better known as Ibn al-Samḥ (*d.* 1035), published a two-part treatise of 130 chapters on the construction and use of the astrolabe, as well as some astronomical tables constructed by the Indian methods, and a book, *Libro de las láminas de los siete planetas*, that was translated into Spanish and incorporated into the *Libros del saber de astronomía*. Others of al-Majrīṭī's followers were Abū 'l-Qāsim Aḥmad, nicknamed Ibn al-Ṣaffār (*d.* 1034), whose work on the astrolabe is, in its Latin version, attributed to al-Majrīṭī; the astrologer Ibn al-Khayyāṭ (*d.* 1055), much praised in the *Memoirs* of the zirī king ʿAbd Allāh; al-Zahrāwī; and Abū Muslim ibn Khaldūn of Seville. Through these men al-Majrīṭī exercised a considerable influence on the work of later scientists.

Of al-Majrīṭī's own works, the actual number is in some dispute. In general, it may be assumed that the magical and alchemical works attributed to him are spurious, especially since Ibn Ṣāʿid does not refer to them in his *Ṭabaqāt*. The works that may be considered genuine are the *Commercial Arithmetic (Muʿāmalāt)*, which, according to Ibn Khaldūn, dealt with sales, cadaster, and taxes, using arithmetical, geometrical, and algebraic operations, all of which were apparently used without much distinction; the very brief *Treatise on the Astrolabe* (not to be confused with the longer work by Ibn al-Ṣaffār), which treated both the construction and use of that instrument; his adaptation of al-Khwārizmī's astronomical tables to the longitude of Córdoba and to the Hijra calendar; his revision of some tables by al-Battānī; some notes on the theorem of Menelaus; and the lost *Tasṭīḥ basīṭ al-kura*, an Arabic translation of Ptolemy's *Planisphaerium*, which survives in a Latin version drawn from the Arabic by Hermann of Dalmatia (1143) and in a Hebrew recension (al-Majrīṭī's annotations to the original are also still extant).

Of the works often—but probably wrongly—attributed to al-Majrīṭī, the *Rutbat al-ḥakīm* ("The Rank of the Sage") was composed after 1009; it is alchemical in nature, and gives formulas and instructions for the purification of precious metals and describes the preparation of mercuric oxide on a quantitative basis. *Ghāyat al-ḥakīm* ("The Aim of the Wise") was translated into Spanish in 1256 by order of Alfonso el Sabio; it was widely distributed throughout Europe under the title *Picatrix* (a corruption of Buqrāṭis = Hippocrates), and is a compendium of magic, cosmology, astrological practice, and esoteric wisdom in general. As such, it provides the most complete picture of superstitions current in eleventh-century Islam. Also attributed to al-Majrīṭī are various opuscules which are in fact extracts, including passages on zoology and alchemy, from the *Rasā'il* of the Ikhwān al-Ṣafā', or have a certain relationship with these *Rasā'il* (like the *Risālat al jāmī'a*).

BIBLIOGRAPHY

I. ORIGINAL WORKS. Al-Majrīṭī's writings and those spurious works attributed to him are catalogued in Brockelmann, *Geschichte der arabischen Litteratur*, I (Weimar, 1898), 243, and supp. I (Leiden, 1937), 431.

Of the genuine works, the *Treatise on the Astrolabe* is edited and translated, with commentary, in J. Vernet and M. A. Catalá, "Las obras matemáticas de Maslama de Madrid," in *Al-Andalus*, **30** (1965), 15–45; see *ibid.*, pp. 46–47, an analysis of the position of the fixed stars by M. A. Catalá. Recent publications of the spurious works include Hellmut Ritter, ed., *Ghāyat al-ḥakīm* (Leipzig, 1933), and German trans. with Martin Plessner as "*Picatrix.*" *Das Ziehl des Weisen von Pseudo-Maǧriti* (London, 1962); and Jamil Saliba, ed., *Risāla al-jami'a* (Damascus, 1948), which provides a good illustration of eleventh-century Ismā'īlī propaganda.

II. SECONDARY LITERATURE. On al-Majrīṭī's revision of al-Kwārizmī's tables, see G. J. Toomer, in *Dictionary of Scientific Biography*, VII, 360–361; see also Axel Björnbo and H. Suter, *Thabits Werke über den Transversalensatz (liber de figura sectore)* (Erlangen, 1924), 23, 79, and 83. On the works probably falsely attributed to him, see E. J. Holmyard, "Maslama al-Majrīṭī and the Rutbat al-ḥakīm," in *Isis*, **6** (1924), 239–305; also on the *Picatrix* and bibliography related to it, see the index by Willy Hartner, *Oriens, Occidens* (Hildesheim, 1968).

Supplementary material may be found in J. A. Sánchez Pérez, *Biografías de matemáticos árabes que florecieron en España* (Madrid, 1921), no.84; George Sarton, *Introduction to the History of Science*, I (Baltimore, 1927), 668–669; and H. Suter, *Die Mathematiker und Astronomen der Araber und ihre Werke* (Leipzig, 1900), 176.

JUAN VERNET

AL-MAJŪSĪ, ABU'L-ḤASAN 'ALĪ IBN 'ABBĀS (latinized as **Haly Abbas**) (*b.* al-Ahwāz-Khūzistān, near Shiraz, Persia, first quarter of the tenth century; *d.* Shiraz, A.D. 994), *medicine, pharmacology, natural science.*

Nothing is known of al-Majūsī's ancestry except that the nickname Majūsī suggests that he, or most probably his father, was originally a Zoroastrian and that he does not seem to have traveled much outside his native country. Al-Majūsī received his medical training under the physician Abū Māhir Mūsā ibn Sayyār, author of a commentary on phlebotomy. Al-Majūsī served King 'Aḍud al-Dawla (*d.* 983), to whom he dedicated his only medical compendium, *Kāmil al-Ṣinā'ah al-Ṭibbiyyah*, called *al-Malikī (Liber regius)* in honor of his patron, who bore the title *Shāhanshāh* ("king of kings").

The *Kāmil* consists of twenty treatises on the theory and practice of medicine (ten on each). In it the author referred to how he has studied and used indigenous medicinal plants, as well as animal and mineral products, as therapeutics. Although several important physicians and natural scientists appeared in tenth-century Iraq and Persia, only a few seem to have been known to or acknowledged by al-Majūsī. For example, he referred to the two books of al-Rāzī (865–925), the most prolific and original medical author in tenth-century Persia and the leading clinician, social scientist, and alchemist of his time. Yet al-Majūsī did not mention his countryman and contemporary al-Ḥusayn ibn Nūḥ al-Qumrī, author of the famous book *Ghanā wa-Manā* ("On Life and Death"), or Aḥmad ibn Abī al-Ash'ath of Mosul, author of a praiseworthy text on the powers and utility of the materia medica entitled *Quwa 'l-Adwiya 'l-Mufrada* and one of the best medical educators of his time. From the introductory remarks in the *Kāmil*, al-Majūsī seems to have been critical of his predecessors, even those whom he quoted and whose writings influenced him, such as Hippocrates, Galen, Oribasius (fourth century), Ahrun the Priest (sixth century), and Yūḥannā ibn Sirābiyūn (ninth century). He did, however, praise Ḥunayn ibn Isḥāq (*d.* 873) as a reliable translator and fine scholar.

Al-Majūsī gave the following interesting, surprisingly accurate, and almost modern description of pleurisy: "Pleurisy is an inflammation of the pleura, with exudation which pours materials over the pleura from the head or chest .... Following are the four symptoms that always accompany pleurisy: fever, coughing, pricking in the side, and difficult breathing (dyspnea)." In defining theoretical medicine, he recognized three areas:

1. Knowledge of natural (instinctive) matters, such as the elements, temperaments, humors, actions, faculties (or powers), and parts.

2. Knowledge of things not part of human (instinctive) nature. This he apparently copied from Ḥunayn ibn Isḥāq's *Ars medica (al-Masā'il fi 'l-Ṭibb)*, which defined them as the six essential principles: the air we breathe and how to be free from pollution, work and rest, diet, wakefulness and slumber, use of vomit-inducing drugs and laxatives, and psychological impulses.

3. Knowledge of things outside the realm of natural

conditions of the human body and which are concerned with diseases, their causes, and their symptoms.

In describing the arteries and veins, al-Majūsī spoke of their divisions into numerous thin tubules spreading like hairs and of the connection between arteries and veins through tiny pores. He also described the function of the three valves in each of the pulmonary arteries, the aorta, and the two in what he called the veinal artery (most probably referring to the atrioventricular valves).

Al-Majūsī also propagated health measures to preserve normal conditions of body and mind, such as diet, rest and work, bathing, and physical exercises. For example, he cited three advantages of exercise:

1. It awakens and increases innate heat to enable the attraction and digestion of foods for assimilation by body organs (metabolism).

2. It helps relieve the body of its superfluities and cleans and expands its pores.

3. It solidifies and strengthens the body's organs by inducing contacts among them so that the body functions harmoniously and is able to resist disease.

Furthermore, he said of sleep that it helps to relax and refresh the brain and the senses, as well as assisting in digestion and normalizing humors.

Long before Ibn Sīnā, al-Majūsī emphasized the importance of psychotherapy and the relationship between psychology and medicine. Emotional reactions (manifestations, a'rāḍ nafsāniyya), he explained, may cause sickness or promote good health, depending on how they are controlled. He also spoke of passionate love and how it can cause illness if it has no fulfillment.

In addition, al-Majūsī discussed meteorology, hygiene, human behavior, and surgery, recommending frequent use of phlebotomy. In the section on embryology he clearly explained the presently accepted fact that the fetus is pushed out in parturition. His discussion of poisons, their symptoms, and their antidotes is an important chapter in the history of medieval toxicology. Furthermore, al-Majūsī elaborated on the effects of the use of opiates in a manner which is of interest to the history of drug addiction and abuse. His general discussions of materia medica and the therapeutics of crude and compound drugs are based on Dioscorides and Galen, with additions of indigenous, familiar drugs. Like his predecessor al-Rāzī, he used and promoted chemotherapy.

Regarding medical deontology, al-Majūsī emphasized the highest ethical standards and asked his colleagues, as well as all practitioners and medical students, to observe them as ordered and upheld in the Hippocratic writings. He also opposed the use of contraception, or of drugs that cause abortion, except in cases involving the physical or mental health of the mother, attitudes still heard and commended today.

Al-Majūsī boasted that in his Kāmil he covered the three most important points of a medical text: dealing with the most needed and highly honored art of healing; presentation of a much-improved medical compendium; and comprehensive coverage of the topic. In several areas, however, he seems to have fallen short of his objectives. Nonetheless, his diligent studies, personal observations, and detailed coverage of medical matters won al-Majūsī's book the high prestige it deserved in Islam. It was translated more than once into Latin and incunabula copies exist in many libraries, a proof of its wide acceptance and circulation in East and West for almost five centuries.

BIBLIOGRAPHY

I. ORIGINAL WORKS. Al-Majūsī's Kāmil al-Ṣinā'ah 'l-Ṭibbiyya in 20 treatises is believed to be his only medical contribution. Numerous Arabic MSS (complete or fragmentary) exist in many libraries. It was published in 2 vols., one on medical theory and one on medical practice (Cairo, 1877). The ninth treatise was also published on its own (Lucknow, 1906). The Kāmil was rendered in part into Latin in the Pantegni of Constantine the African (d. ca. 1085). In 1127 Stephen of Antioch translated the entire work into Latin, with annotations by Michael de Capella. This trans. was edited by Antonius Vitalis Pyrranensis and was first published under the title Liber regalis dispositio nominatus ex arabico venetiis (Venice, 1492), repr. under the title Liber totius medicinae necessariae continens, quem Haly filius Abbas edidit regique inscripsit (Lyons–Leiden, 1523).

II. SECONDARY LITERATURE. In Arabic the earliest and best biographies of al-Majūsī and accounts of his work are Jamāl al-Dīn 'Alī al-Qifṭī, Tārīkh al-Ḥukamā', Julius Lippert, ed. (Leipzig, 1903), p. 232; and Aḥmad ibn Abī Uṣaybi'a, 'Uyūn al-Anbā', I (Cairo, 1882), 236–237. In the West during the nineteenth century many historians of medicine wrote on al-Majūsī. See (in chronological order) K. P. J. Sprengel, Versuch einer pragmatische Geschichte der Arzneykunde, II (Halle, 1823), 412–418; Ferdinand Wüstenfeld, Geschichte der arabischen Aerzte und Naturforscher (Göttingen, 1840), p. 59; E. H. F. Meyer, Geschichte der Botanik, III (Königsberg, 1856), 176–178; Lucien Leclerc, Histoire de la médecine arabe, I (Paris, 1876), 381–388; George J. Fisher, "Biography of Haly Abbas," in Annals of Anatomy and Surgery, 7 (1883), 208, 255; and Ernst J. Gurlt, Geschichte der Chirurgie, I (Berlin, 1898), 615–618. Twentieth-century works include P. de Koning, Traité sur le calcul dans les reins (Leiden, 1898), pp. 124–185; and Trois traités d'anatomie arabes (Leiden, 1903), pp. 90–431; Max Neuburger, Geschichte der Medizin, II, pt. 1 (Stuttgart, 1911), 210; and Paul Richter,

"Über die spezielle Dermatologie des Ali b. Abbas aus de 10. Jahrhunderts," in *Archiv für Dermatologie und Syphilis*, **113** (1912), 849–864; after the earlier twentieth-century studies, the investigations of Edward G. Browne, *Arabian Medicine* (Cambridge, 1921), pp. 51–57, 123–124, added significant weight to the importance of al-Majūsī's work.

Special studies, besides those of Koning and Richter, include an important comparison and evaluation, by J. Wiberg, "The Anatomy of the Brain in the Works of Galen and 'Alī 'Abbās," in *Janus*, **19** (1914), 17–32, 84–104. For further discussions on al-Majūsī and his compendium see also (in chronological order) George Sarton, *Introduction to the History of Science*, I (Baltimore, 1927), 677–678; Carl Brockelmann, *Geschichte der arabischen Literatur*, I (Leiden, 1943), 273, and supp., I, 423; A. A. Khairallah, *Outline of Arabic Contributions to Medicine* (Beirut, 1946), pp. 116–117; Cyril Elgood, *A Medical History of Persia* (Cambridge, 1951), pp. 99–100, 153–157, 199, 279; A. Z. Iskandar, *Arabic MSS. on Medicine and Sciences* (London, 1967), pp. 119–124; and Sami Hamarneh, *Fihris Makhṭūṭāṭ al-Ẓāhiriyah* (Damascus, 1969), pp. 248–254.

SAMI HAMARNEH

MAKARANDA (*fl.* Benares, India, 1478), *astronomy.*

Makaranda wrote at Kāśī (Benares) an extremely influential set of astronomical tables, entitled *Makaranda* (see essay in Supplement), based on the *Saurapakṣa*. These tables are calendaric (for *tithis*, *nakṣatras*, and *yogas*), planetary, and for eclipses; their epoch is 1478. Their extreme popularity is indicated by the facts that there are almost 100 extant manuscripts (mostly from northern India) and that some twenty commentaries are known; the dated commentaries are by Harikarṇa of Hisāranagara (1610), Viśvanātha of Benares (1612–1630), Divākara (1627), Puruṣottama (1631), Kṛpārāma Miśra of Ahmadabad (1815), Jīvanātha of Patna (1823), and Nīlāmbara Jhā of Koilakh, Mithilā (nineteenth century). The continued popularity of the *Makaranda* at the end of the last century is proven by the several editions.

BIBLIOGRAPHY

The *Makaranda* was published at Benares in 1869 with the commentaries of Gokulanātha, Divākara, and Viśvanātha; the text with the first two commentaries was repub. in *Aruṇodaya*, I, pt. 15 (Calcutta, 1891). The *Makaranda* appeared alone also at Benares in 1880 and again in 1884. The tables in a number of MSS have been analyzed by D. Pingree, "Sanskrit Astronomical Tables in the United States," in *Transactions of the American Philosophical Society*, n.s. **58**, no. 3 (1968), 39b–46b; and in his "Sanskrit Astronomical Tables in England," in *Journal of Oriental Research* (Madras).

DAVID PINGREE

MAKAROV, STEPAN OSIPOVICH (*b.* Nikolayev, Russia, 8 March 1849; *d.* aboard the battleship *Petropavlovsk*, Port Arthur, Russia, 13 April 1904), *oceanography.*

His father, Osip Fyodorovich Makarov, retired from the navy in 1873 with the rank of junior captain. His mother came from a simple family and had no education; she died in 1857, leaving two daughters and three sons, of whom Stepan was the youngest. His officer's rank enabled Makarov's father to enroll his son at the age of ten at the naval school at Nikolayevsk-na-Amure, to which his father had been transferred. The five-month voyage from St. Petersburg instilled in him a love for the ocean and for sea voyages: Makarov often said, "At sea means at home."

Makarov graduated from the naval school in 1865. He served as a cadet and in May 1869 he was commissioned a warrant officer. Assigned to the Black Sea fleet in 1876 as commander of a steamer, he conducted successful military actions during the Russo-Turkish War.

In 1881–1882 as commander of the ambassadorial station ship *Taman* in Constantinople, Makarov conducted hydrological research in the Bosporus. In 1886–1889 he commanded the corvette *Vityaz* on its round-the-world voyage, and in 1896 he became vice-admiral. From the beginning of 1897 Makarov was actively involved in research on icebreakers in the North Atlantic. While planning the icebreaker *Ermak* Makarov studied previous voyages through ice, particularly on the Great Lakes. He supervised the building of the *Ermak* in England and in 1899–1901 completed the first voyages on it in polar latitudes. In December 1899 Makarov was named commander in chief of the Kronshtadt port and military governor of Kronshtadt. Makarov died during the Russo-Japanese War, when his battleship, the *Petropavlovsk*, was sunk by a Japanese mine.

Makarov began his oceanographic studies in 1881–1882 on currents in the Bosporus. In his first experiment Makarov proved the existence of a deep current running counter to the surface current. In the middle of the channel, he let down a barrel which was borne by the surface current toward the Sea of Marmara. At a certain depth the line began to pull in the opposite direction. The force of the deep current was so great that the barrel dragged the boat against the surface current. Makarov organized systematic observations of the water density and temperature at various depths, and of the velocity of the current throughout the strait. The velocity of the current was measured by a rotator, which Makarov invented and which he called a fluctometer. The velocity of the surface current varied from 6 to 3.22 feet per second, and of the lower from 3.22 to 1.84 feet per second. The density of the upper water was 1.015; the lower, 1.028. This difference in density between the less saline Black Sea and the more saline Sea of Marmara appears to be the reason for the existence of contrary currents in the Bosporus. Makarov estimated that the ratio of the volume of inflow to outflow in the Black Sea is 1 : 1.85; the difference is accounted for by fresh water flowing into the Black Sea. The results of Makarov's Bosporus research were published in *Ob obmene vod Chernogo i Sredi-zemnogo morey* ("On the Exchange of Water of the Black and Mediterranean Seas," 1885), which was a major contribution to oceanography.

In his main oceanographic work, *Vityaz i Tikhy okean* ("The *Vityaz* and the Pacific Ocean," 1894), he explained the hydrological observations carried out under his direction aboard the corvette *Vityaz* on its thirty-three-month round-the-world voyage. Although it was undertaken mainly for purposes of military instruction, Makarov began oceanographic observation at the outset. Makarov made more than 250 individual measurements of water density and temperature at depths from twenty-five to 800 meters. After careful analysis of the results of these observations and also descriptions in logs of other voyages, Makarov compiled the first water temperature tables for the North Pacific Ocean. He also considered the origin of the deep waters of the North Pacific, the reason for the homogeneous temperature and density of the water at every depth of the English Channel, the reason for the rising of deep waters near the mouths of large rivers, and the general pattern of ocean currents, with an indication of the primary significance of the action of the Coriolis force on sea currents. This main work of Makarov's, published simultaneously in Russian and French and awarded prizes by the St. Petersburg Academy of Sciences and the Russian Geographical Society, brought Makarov international recognition as a scientific oceanographer.

Makarov conceived the idea of opening up navigation along the northern borders of Siberia with the aid of icebreakers. "Straight Through to the North Pole!" was the expressive title of his report in 1897 to the Russian Geographical Society. On two voyages on the icebreaker *Ermak* to Spitsbergen and to Novaya Zemlya (1899–1901), Makarov gathered data on the Arctic ice and on the temperatures and salinity of the Arctic basin.

Although the *Ermak*, constructed on Makarov's initiative, did not achieve all the results for which its creator hoped, research in the Arctic Ocean with icebreakers has subsequently been widely realized in the Soviet Union.

Makarov must be credited with a great number of different inventions pertaining to oceanographic research and naval construction. He published several works on naval tactics, the chief of which was *Rassuzhdenia po voprosam morskoy taktiki* ("Considerations on Questions of Naval Tactics"). Several geographical areas including an island in the Nordenskjöld Archipelago and in the Kara Sea were named for him.

BIBLIOGRAPHY

I. ORIGINAL WORKS. Makarov's oceanographic works were published as *Okeanograficheskie raboty* (Moscow, 1950). See also *Ob issledovanii Severnogo Ledovitogo Okeana* ("Research in the Northern Arctic Ocean"; St. Petersburg, 1897), written with F. Vrangel; *Ermak vo ldakh* ("Ermak in the Ice"), 2 pts. (St. Petersburg, 1901); and *Rassuzhdenia po voprosam morskoy taktiki* ("Considerations on Questions of Naval Tactics"; Moscow, 1943).

II. SECONDARY LITERATURE. On Makarov and his work, see D. N. Anuchin, *O lyudyakh russkoy nauki i kultury* ("People of Russian Science and Culture"; Moscow, 1952), 318–328; A. D. Dobrovolsky, *Admiral S. O. Makarov, puteshestvennik i okeanograf* ("Admiral S. O. Makarov, Traveler and Oceanographer"; Moscow, 1948); A. N. Krylov, *Vitse-Admiral Makarov* ("Vice-Admiral Makarov"; Moscow–Leningrad, 1944); B. G. Ostrovsky, *Admiral Makarov* (Moscow, 1954); F. F. Vrangel, *Vitse-Admiral Stepan Osipovich Makarov*, 2 pts. (St. Petersburg, 1911–1913), a biographical sketch.

I. A. FEDOSEYEV

MAKSIMOV, NIKOLAY ALEKSANDROVICH (*b.* St. Petersburg [now Leningrad], Russia, 21 March 1880; *d.* Moscow, U.S.S.R., 9 May 1952), *plant physiology.*

After graduating from the Gymnasium in 1897, Maksimov entered the natural sciences section of the department of physics and mathematics of St. Petersburg University. He graduated in 1902, then remained to prepare for a professorship. In 1905 he became an assistant in the department of botany of the St. Petersburg Forestry Institute. In 1910 Maksimov traveled to Java, where he worked in the Buitenzorg (now Bogor) Botanical Garden. In 1913 he defended his master's thesis, "O vymerzanii i kholodostoykosti rasteny" ("On the Frost Kill and Cold Resistance of Plants"), at St. Petersburg University. The following year he transferred to the Tiflis Botanical Garden, where he organized a laboratory of plant physiology.

Maksimov moved to Leningrad in 1921 and began to work in the main botanical garden of the Academy of Sciences of the U.S.S.R., where he organized a laboratory of experimental plant ecology, which he directed until 1927. From 1925 to 1933 he was also director of the laboratory of plant physiology which he organized in the All-Union Research Institute of Plant Growing. At the same time (1922–1931) he carried out major work in teaching and management of the department of botany at the A. I. Herzen Peda-gogical Institute in Leningrad. From 1933 to 1939 Maksimov was in Saratov, at the All-Union Institute of Grain Economy, where he headed the section of plant physiology, and at Saratov University, in the department of plant physiology (1935–1939). In 1936 Maksimov began his work at the Institute of Plant Physiology of the Soviet Academy of Sciences, first as manager of the laboratory for growth and develop-ment of plants and, from 1939, as director of the institute. His teaching continued as part of his duties as head of the department of plant physiology of the Timiryazev Agricultural Academy in Moscow (1943–1951).

Maksimov's basic scientific research was connected with the study of frost resistance and drought resis-tance of plants. He was one of the most important pioneers in the study of the ecological physiology of plants. Maksimov's scientific work began with the study of respiration in fungi and the influence of injury on the respiration coefficient. His results were stated in the article "K voprosu o dykhanii" ("On the Ques-tion of Respiration"; 1904), one of the first investiga-tions in which the fermentative nature of respiration was established. In a later study of the respiration of woody plants during the winter, Maksimov became interested in why coniferous needles and winter buds do not die at low temperatures which other plants cannot endure. Studying cold resistance, he spoke against the current idea that this property does not depend on the external environment but is defined only by the plant's inner qualities. Maksimov con-sidered that the damage to or killing of the plant at low temperatures was caused by the formation and accumulation of ice crystals between the cells, which dehydrate and mechanically damage the protoplasm, leading to the coagulation of plasma colloids. He showed that the resistance of the cell to low tempera-

tures can be increased by the use of sugar and mineral salts and by an increase in the cell juice of the amount of other osmotically active substances that decrease the quantity of ice crystals formed. Thus he formulated the first theory of the "chemical defense of the plant against death by frost," which he presented in his master's thesis.

In 1914 Maksimov began a new and more fruitful stage of research—the study of the water system and drought resistance of plants. His first experiments showed that xerophyte plants with enough water supply transpire no less moisture than mesophytes and demonstrated the inadequacy of Schimper's then widely recognized theory. This theory explained the drought resistance of xerophytes as an ability to use water economically because of certain peculiarities in their anatomical-morphological structure that sup-posedly result in a level of transpiration much cur-tailed in comparison with that of mesophytes. Maksi-mov suggested that the basis of drought resistance of xerophytes lies not in their structure but in the bio-chemical capacity of their protoplasm to bear a pro-longed water shortage without harmful consequences. He saw the plant's capacity to sustain prolonged dehydration as a complex of the traits characterizing xerophytes: the peculiarities of their protoplasm, its specific structure at a comparatively high osmotic pres-sure, and the anatomical-morphological peculiarities of the plant's structure. Maksimov also recognized the variety of adaptations to the conditions of existence in various ecological groups of xerophytes, explaining their origin in nature from an evolutionary position. His works on the water system and drought resistance of plants laid the foundation for a new area in botany —the ecological physiology of plants.

Maksimov also conducted research on photosynthe-sis, growth, development, photoperiodism, and the natural and artificial stimulators of plant growth. All these investigations were carried out under laboratory conditions and also in a natural situation for wild plants and in the field for cultivated plants. Taken as a whole, this work had great significance for the theory as well as the practice of agriculture: Maksimov devel-oped a series of recommendations for obtaining higher yields in arid regions and in hothouses by the creation of a new regimen of artificial light, for directing the growth and development of plants by means of photoperiodic effects, and for rooting cuttings of culti-vated and wild plants under the influence of growth activators.

Besides his research, Maksimov paid much attention to scientific organization and set up laboratories of plant physiology in several institutions. He also devoted a substantial part of his time to teaching. His *Kratky* kurs fiziologii rasteny ("Short Course in Plant Physiology"), which went through nine editions between 1927 and 1958, greatly influenced the development of plant physiology in the Soviet Union. The seventh edition of this text was awarded the K. A. Timiryazev Prize in 1944. Maksimov also wrote *Vvedenie v botaniku* ("Introduction to Botany"; 1915), which went through two editions; a popular book, *Ot chego byvayut zasukhi i mozhno li s nimi borotsya* ("What Causes Droughts and How We Can Fight Them"; 1951); and *Kak zhivet rastenie* ("How a Plant Lives"; 1951). He also published about 250 scientific articles and notes.

For his teaching and research work in scientific organizations Maksimov was elected a corresponding member (1939) and an academician (1946) of the Academy of Sciences of the U.S.S.R. In 1945 he received the Order of the Red Banner of Labor and was elected a vice-president of the All-Union Botanical Society, of which he became an honorary member in 1947. Maksimov was also a corresponding member of the Czechoslovakian Agricultural Academy (1934) and a corresponding member of the Royal Netherlands Botanical Society (1936).

BIBLIOGRAPHY

I. Original Works. Maksimov's writings include "O vymerzanii i kholodostoykosti rasteny. Eksperimentalnye i kriticheskie issledovania" ("On the Frost Resistance and Cold Resistance of Plants. Experimental and Critical Research"), in *Izvestiya Lesnogo instituta*, no. 25 (1913), 1–330, his master's diss.; "Zasukhoustoychivost rasteny s fiziologicheskoy tochki zrenia" ("Drought Resistance of Plants From the Physiological Point of View"), in *Zhurnal opytnoi agronomii*, **22** (1921–1923), 173–186; "Znachenie v zhizni rastenia sootnoshenia mezhdu prodolzhitelnostyu dnya i nochi (fotoperiodizm)" ("The Significance of the Relation Between the Length of Day and of Night in the Life of the Plant [Photoperiodism]"), in *Trudy po prikladnoi botanike, genetike i selektsii*, **14**, no. 5 (1924–1925), 65–90; *Fiziologicheskie osnovy zasukhoustoychivosti rasteny* ("Physiological Bases of Drought Resistance in Plants"; Leningrad, 1936); "Rostovye veshchestva, priroda ikh deystvia i prakticheskoe primenenie" ("Growth Substances, the Nature of Their Effects and Practical Application"), in *Uspekhi sovremennoi biologii*, **22**, no. 2 (1946), 161–180; and *Izbrannye raboty po zasukhoustoychivosti i zimostoykosti rasteny* ("Selected Works in Drought Resistance and Winter Resistance of Plants"), 2 vols. (Moscow, 1952).

II. Secondary Literature. See P. A. Genkel, "Nauchnaya deyatelnost Nikolaya Aleksandrovicha Maksimova i ego rol v sozdanii ekologicheskoy fiziologii rasteny" ("The Scientific Career of N. A. Maksimov and His Role in the Creation of the Ecological Physiology of Plants"), in *Problemy fiziologii rasteny. Istoricheskie ocherki* ("Problems of Plant Physiology. Historical Sketches"; Moscow, 1969), pp. 306–331, literature about Maksimov on p. 326; *Nikolay Aleksandrovich Maksimov, materialy k biobibliografii uchenykh SSSR*, Ser. biol. nauk, fiziol. rast. ("Materials for a Biobibliography of Soviet Scientists, Biological Science Series, plant physiology"), no. 2 (Moscow–Leningrad, 1949), with intro. article by P. A. Genkel and bibliography of Maksimov's works and literature on him compiled by O. V. Isakova; and I. I. Tumanov, "Osnovnye cherty nauchnoy deyatelnosti N. A. Maksimova" ("Basic Outlines of the Scientific Work of N. A. Maksimov"), in *Pamyati akademika N. A. Maksimova* ("Recollections of Academician N. A. Maksimov"; Moscow, 1957), pp. 3–9.

E. M. Senchenkova

MAKSUTOV, DMITRY DMITRIEVICH (*b.* Odessa, Russia, 23 April 1896; *d.* Pulkovo [near Leningrad], U.S.S.R., 12 August 1964), *optics, astronomy.*

Maksutov's father, a seaman, aroused his son's early interest in astronomy; and Maksutov made his first observations with his father's two-inch spyglass, to which he fitted a set of eyepieces. When he was about twelve or thirteen he constructed his first reflector, 180 mm. in diameter. Acquainted with the articles of the well-known Russian optician A. A. Chikin, Maksutov made a Newtonian reflecting telescope of 210 mm. with which he began serious observations. Recognizing his enthusiasm and skill, the Russian Astronomical Society elected the fifteen-year-old optician a member. Before he graduated from the Odessa cadet corps, Maksutov was directing the astronomical observatory from 1909 to 1913 and conducting studies in cosmography with the students of the advanced classes. In 1914 he graduated from the military engineering school and, in 1915, completed courses in radiotelephony at the electrotechnical school. He served briefly in World War I in the Caucasus, and in 1916 transferred to the military aviation school in Tiflis. Having sustained a concussion in an accident he was demobilized and returned to Odessa. In 1917, he decided to go to the United States, hoping to meet the eminent optician G. W. Ritchey, who was then working at the Mount Wilson observatory. He got only as far as Harbin, China, where he lived for a while doing odd jobs. In 1919 he was sent to the radiotelegraph base at Tomsk. In 1920 he transferred together with the base personnel to the side of the Red Army. In Tomsk, Maksutov entered the Polytechnic Institute, where he simultaneously organized an optical workshop and repaired microscopes and telescopes. In 1920 Maksutov was invited to the recently formed Petrograd Optical

Institute, but the following year he returned to Odessa and began serious work in the theory of astronomical optics.

In 1923 Maksutov developed a general theory of aplanatic optical systems. In 1928 he obtained the first of his eighteen patents, for the invention of a photogastrograph, an ingenious instrument for examining the stomach. In 1930 Maksutov was again at the Leningrad Optical Institute, where he organized a laboratory of astronomical optics. Until 1952, when Maksutov transferred all his activities to the Pulkovo observatory, he worked tirelessly on developing a theory of astronomical optics and on manufacturing the optical systems of a series of astronomical instruments. At Pulkovo, where from 1944 he headed the section of astronomical instrument construction, Maksutov devised new methods of construction, improved the meniscus systems that he had invented in 1941 and that are now universally known, and originated new methods of calculating optical systems.

In 1941 Maksutov received the degree of doctor of technical sciences and the State prize; in 1944 he received the title of professor; and in 1946 he was elected corresponding member of the U.S.S.R. Academy of Sciences and received a second State prize. Maksutov was twice awarded the Order of Lenin and the order "Badge of Honor."

Maksutov was surrounded by both Soviet and foreign students, many of whom became eminent opticians. His monographs *Astronomicheskaya optika* ("Astronomical Optics") and *Izgotovlenie i issledovanie astronomicheskoy optiki* ("Preparation and Testing of Astronomical Optics") are basic references for all astronomical instrument makers and have been translated into several languages.

Maksutov's scientific career began in 1923 with his invention of aplanatic optical systems, in which the independently developed systems of H. Chrétien, K. Schwarzschild, and A. Couder proved to be specific cases of his more general solution. In 1932 he published a substantial summary monograph, *"Anaberratsionnye otrazhatelnye poverkhrosti i sistemy i novye metody ikh ispytania"* ("Anaberrational Reflecting Surfaces and Systems and New Methods of Testing Them"). Maksutov significantly improved the shadow method for qualitative verification of optical surfaces and extended it to quantitative applications, as described in the monograph *Tenevye metody issledovania opticheskikh sistem* ("Shadow Methods of Verification of Optical Systems"; 1934). He substantially improved the compensation method of testing the mirrors that he had proposed as far back as 1924 and described it in 1957 in "Novaya metodika issle-

dovania formy zerkal krupnykh teleskopov" ("A New Method for Examining the Forms of Mirrors of Large Telescopes").

As first-class master, Maksutov himself prepared at the Optical Institute the optics of such large instruments as the 381-mm. Schmidt telescope for the Engelhardt observatory, near Kazan, the Pulkovo solar telescope, the 820-mm. Pulkovo refractor, which the firm of Grubb-Parsons declined to make, and certain others. Being interested in replacing glass for the reflector with metal, Maksutov made a number of silvered metal mirrors, of which the largest was a 720-mm. parabolic mirror of high optical efficiency. In 1941 during the war, in dramatic circumstances of which he wrote brilliantly in his monograph *Astronomicheskaya optika* ("Astronomical optics"), Maksutov developed his meniscus system, now used in many photographic as well as optical instruments. Among the numerous instruments produced by Maksutov, the unique dual-meniscus 700-mm. astrometric astrograph of high optical efficiency, constructed for the expedition of the Pulkovo observatory to Chile, occupies a special place. His unfinished monograph "Meniskovye sistemy" ("Meniscus Systems") is the result of his work in this area.

BIBLIOGRAPHY

I. ORIGINAL WORKS. Maksutov's early works include: "Anaberratsionnye otrazhatelnye poverkhnosti i sistemy i novye sposoby ikh ispytania" ("Anaberrational Reflecting Surfaces and Systems and New Methods of Testing Them"), in *Trudy Gosudarstvennogo opticheskogo instituta*, no. 86 (1932), 3–120; "Issledovanie neskolkikh obektivov i zerkal po metodu fokogramm" ("Research on Some Objectives and Mirrors With the Focogram Method"), in *Optiko-Mekhanicheskaya Promyshlennost*, no. 2 (1932), 8–10; *Tenevye metody issledovania opticheskikh sistem* ("Shadow Methods of Research on Optical Systems"; Leningrad–Moscow, 1934); "On the Temperature Coefficient of the Focal Distance of an Object Glass," in *Tsirkulyar Glavnoi astronomicheskoi observatorii v Pulkove*, no. 20 (1936), 37–41; and "Sotovye zerkala iz splavov alyuminia" ("Honeycomb Mirrors From Alloys of Aluminum"), in *Optiko-Mekhanicheskaya Promyshlennost*, no. 3 (1937), 1–3.

Subsequent works are "Novye katadioptricheskie meniskovye sistemy" ("New Catadioptric Meniscus Systems"), in *Doklady Akademii nauk SSSR*, **37**, no. 4 (1942), 147–152, and in *Zhurnal Tekhnicheskoi Fiziki*, **13**, no. 3 (1943), 87–108, translated in *Journal of the Optical Society of America*, **34**, no. 5 (1944), 270–281; "Aplanaticheskie meniskovye teleobektivy" ("Aplanatic Meniscus Teleobjectives"), in *Doklady Akademii nauk SSSR*, Novaja Ser. tekhn. fiz., no. 7 (1945), 504–507; *Astronomicheskaya optika* ("Astronomical Optics"; Moscow, 1946); *Izgotovle-*

nie i issledovanie astronomicheskoy optiki ("Preparation and Testing of Astronomical Optics"; Moscow, 1948); and "Novaya metodika issledovania formy zerkal krupnykh teleskopov" ("A New Method for Examining the Forms of Mirrors of Large Telescopes"), in *Izvestiya glavnoi astronomicheskoi observatorii v Pulkove*, no. 160 (1957), 5–29.

II. SECONDARY LITERATURE. On Maksutov and his work, see the biographies by O. A. Melnikov, in *Astronomichesky kalendar na 1966 god* ("Astronomical Calendar for 1966"; Moscow, 1965), 231–236; N. N. Mikhelson, in *Izvestiya glavnoi astronomicheskoi observatorii v Pulkove*, **24**, no. 178 (1965), 2–7, with portrait and bibliography; and S. A. Shorygin, in *Astronomichesky kalendar na 1944 god* (Moscow, 1943), 125–129.

See also *Sky and Telescope*, **25**, no. 4 (1963), 228, for a list of twenty-two articles on Maksutov telescope constructions published in *Sky and Telescope* after 1956, including Maksutov's "New Catadioptric Meniscus Systems" (see above); and R. Riecker, *Fernrohre und ihre Meister* (Berlin, 1957), pp. 504–507.

P. G. KULIKOVSKY

MALEBRANCHE, NICOLAS (*b.* Paris, France, 5 August 1638; *d.* Paris, 13 October 1715), *philosophy, science.*

Malebranche's life spanned the same years as Louis XIV's, and a famous contemporary, Antoine Arnauld, termed his philosophy *"grand et magnifique,"* adjectives historians often apply to that monarch's reign. The grandeur of his philosophy consists in the way he assimilated the whole of the Cartesian heritage and attempted to elaborate, on theological foundations, an original, rationalist-oriented speculative system. The passage of time and the recently concluded publication of his works have restored to Malebranche the stature of a remarkable intellect, for whom the polemics in which he ceaselessly engaged were merely occasions to buttress his "search for truth." Yet, while his personality can be understood in terms of the profound—and religious—unity of his thought and life, the influence of his work is not free from paradox: Voltaire honored him as one of the greatest speculative thinkers, and d'Alembert placed his portrait above his writing table. A discussion of Malebranche would be incomplete without an attempt to comprehend why Enlightenment philosophers accorded him this praise, suspect as it was in the eyes of theologians.

The youngest son of a large family, Malebranche was born with a delicate constitution. Through his father, a royal counsellor, he was linked to the rural bourgeoisie. His mother, Catherine de Lauson, be-

longed to the minor nobility; her brother, Jean de Lauson, was governor of Canada. His family's modest wealth allowed him to pursue a special program of studies adapted to his physical disability. It was not until age sixteen that he entered the Collège de la Marche of the University of Paris. He received the master of arts degree there in 1656 after having attended the lectures of the renowned Peripatetic M. Rouillard. His piety inclined him toward the priesthood, and for three years he studied theology at the Sorbonne. It seems, however, that he was no more satisfied with this instruction than he had been with commentaries on Aristotle. He entered the Congregation of the Oratory on 20 January 1660, no doubt attracted by its reputation for liberty and culture in the service of the inner life. The impression he made on his new teachers was not altogether favorable. Although he was judged to be suited for the religious life and endowed with the virtues required in communal life, his was considered an "undistinguished intellect."

The explanation of this judgment may well be that, during his four years of Oratorian training, Malebranche, who was ordained priest on 20 September 1664, does not seem to have been sympathetic to the newest elements of the curriculum: an interest in history and erudition, and a passion for positive theology founded on critical study of the Scriptures. Malebranche was taught by the leaders of this tendency, Richard Simon and Charles Lecointe, but did not adopt their views. However that may be, he did become acquainted at the Oratory with the ideas of St. Augustine and Plato.

The stimulus for Malebranche's independent intellectual development came from Descartes, during the first year of his priesthood. It was said that this change resulted from his reading of the newly published *Traité de l'homme,* whose editors had sought to emphasize the broad area of agreement between Descartes and Augustine that was revealed by this posthumous work. Whatever the event that decided Malebranche in favor of this disputed book, it is certain that within three or four years he had completely redone his studies and had made the Cartesian legacy an integral part of his thought. Evidence for this assertion is to be found in *De la recherche de la vérité,* begun as early as 1668. The title itself reveals the inspiration he drew from the manuscripts generously made available to him by the circle around Claude Clerselier. Indeed, the content of the first volume exhibits this inspiration so clearly that Malebranche became involved in difficulties with the censors and had to postpone publication until 1674.

The following year, 1675, saw the publication of a

revised edition of the first volume, the second volume, and Jean Prestet's *Élémens des mathématiques*. The simultaneous appearance of these three books is significant. Prestet, a young man with no resources, owed everything to Malebranche and was evidently his pupil even before the Congregation decided officially in 1674 to recognize Malebranche as professor of mathematics at the seminary. The extremely gifted Prestet rapidly accomplished what Malebranche himself was unable to achieve while he was embroiled in difficulties over his philosophical writings. It was Malebranche, however, who was responsible for the simultaneous publication of 1675, for he wished to place before the public an original philosophical and mathematical synthesis attesting the vitality of Cartesianism.

The general impression given by this synthesis—an impression that accounts for its success—was not deceptive. It was indeed from Descartes that Malebranche attempted to discover a science and a method of reasoning founded on clear and distinct ideas. Later he himself declared that what Augustine lacked was the opportunity to learn from Descartes that bodies are not seen in themselves. From the beginning of his philosophical career Malebranche let it be known that he considered this a fundamental lesson. Rejecting sensible qualities, he held, like Descartes, that things are to be judged solely by the ideas that represent them to us according to their intelligible essence.

All the same the *Recherche de la vérité* touches on various subjects that are not at all Cartesian: primacy of religious goals, refutation of the doctrine of innate ideas, negation of composite substance, union of the problems of error and sin, explanation of the creation by God's love for himself, and affirmation that God acts in the most simple ways, that he is the sole efficient cause, and that natural causes are only "occasional" causes. The list of new branches that Malebranche grafted onto the Cartesian trunk and that corresponded to his hope of establishing a truly Christian philosophy could be expanded; but at this stage of his career it was a matter of possible materials for a new doctrine rather than such a doctrine itself.

Progress toward this goal is represented by *Conversations chrétiennes* (1677) and the third volume of the *Recherche* (1678), "containing several elucidations concerning the principal difficulties of the preceding volumes." But it was with the *Traité de la nature et de la grâce* (Amsterdam, 1680) that Malebranche emerged as the creator of a new system of the world. Inspired by a discussion with Arnauld in 1679, the book's immediate goal was to refute Jansenist ideas concerning grace and predestination. But in order to untangle this essentially religious problem, he transferred the debate to the philosophical plane, thus demonstrating

to what extent he disagreed with Descartes on the value of extending rational reflection to questions of theology.

In examining this book one grasps the essential difference between the two thinkers. A believer and a philosopher, Malebranche did not experience the hyperbolic doubt expressed in the first Cartesian *Méditation;* he did not confront the "Cogito" as the initial indubitable existence; he did not have to seek to escape from a structure of thought closed in upon itself by discovering a God who could guarantee the universality and immutability of truth. For Malebranche, as for Descartes, God was undoubtedly the keystone and foundation of all truth, but for the former he was not the God reached by philosophical speculation whose essence is demonstrated by his existence. Rather, he is Augustine's God *intimior intimo meo*, whose presence in man is the source of the believer's daily meditation and from whom all light descends. He is also the God of wisdom, creator of a universe ordered according to laws that are both perfectly simple and perfectly intelligible—the God who, acting uniquely for his own glory, created man that he might live in union with him and participate in his reason, in his word itself.

Thus, whereas Descartes refused as a vain undertaking any speculation on divine motivations, Malebranche found in this realm something on which he could base the exercise of human reason. In his doctrine the union of man and God is not only the goal of the religious life, it is also the means of attaining a vision, in God, in which there occurs the fullest possible communication of wisdom and intelligibility. Of course, Malebranche does not claim that this communication, the supreme guarantee against error, is a blessing easily obtained or permanently assured. But he does assert that in making the effort to discern the coherence of rational discourse, sinful man, whether Christian or atheist, always obtains some reflection of the universal reason, even if he is unaware of or actually denies its divine nature. Indeed Malebranche contends that attention is a *natural prayer* that God has established as the occasional cause of our knowledge.

The term and the notion of occasional cause are not due to Malebranche, but his use of them and the importance he gave to them were incontestably original. Assigning the source of all effective action to God, he took causality in the strict sense out of the created world. This world is indeed regulated by divine wisdom, but as a function of relationships that carry in themselves no necessity whatever. Moreover, the means that man has received to make it intelligible could only be indirect, that is, occasional. Malebranche thus arrived at a philosophical system that goes far beyond the theological problem that was, so to say, the occasion for its own complete formulation.

When the *Traité* appeared, it was already several years since Malebranche had been assigned any specific duties. Starting in 1680 he devoted all his time to writing and to his role as mediator between theology and Cartesian natural philosophy. He was assailed by polemics that obliged him to review, correct, and improve his system. It is impossible to recount this highly complicated story in a few lines or to discuss in detail the modifications he made in response to a flood of objections and difficulties. However interesting the debates in which Malebranche found himself involved (for example, over the coordination of the two different perfections represented by the divine laws and the divine work) and whatever accusations he was forced to counter (destroying Providence, excluding miracles, minimizing grace to the advantage of liberty), he did not need to modify for the scientific public the basic positions of his philosophy as outlined above.

It should be merely noted in passing that Malebranche, who was more skillful in the art of revising his texts than in that of controversy, rapidly alienated a number of people, even in the Oratory. In Arnauld's opinion he was incapable of maintaining a suitable degree of detachment, and Bossuet judged him severely. Most important, he failed to escape papal censure: the *Traité* was placed on the Index in 1690 while he was in the midst of preparing the third edition. He was sincerely troubled by the decision of the hierarchy, but it did not stop him. The seventh and last edition appeared in 1712, along with the sixth edition of the *Recherche*.

These figures are revealing. Malebranche was read in his own time as much by admirers as by opponents. So much is evident. What most clearly appears in this record of publication, however, is a tireless capacity for modifying his positions and a mind always receptive to suggestions, two rare qualities that testify to his character and intelligence. Malebranche owed his position in the scientific movement of his time to this harmony of his personal qualities with his doctrine of occasionalism.

It is not difficult to understand why occasionalism was a conception particularly conducive to the advance of experimental science. To the degree that nature appeared, to Malebranche, as simply a sphere of relations, the dialogue between reason and experience became for him, inevitably, the fundamental stimulus in the pursuit of knowledge. For when reason was supported by metaphysics, as it was in Descartes, it had much too great a tendency to declare what should be, a priori, and to call upon experience solely for confirmation. In his view, however, the only means of discovery available to the human mind are occasional causes, that is, causes which could have been totally different and which are the reflection not of some ontological necessity but only of the Creator's will. Consequently, experience is indispensable. Of course, it must be intimately conjoined with the exercise of reason in order to attain knowledge of the relations that God has established in his Creation in fact, and not involuntarily, as it were, to comply with some metaphysical imperative. While Malebranche's philosophy provided, above all, a rationale for the study of physics, what is striking is the way in which he was led to grasp this fact himself and to work simultaneously in very different disciplines.

As noted above, the simultaneous publication of Prestet's *Élémens* and the first edition of the *Recherche* suggests that Malebranche was sufficiently well-versed in Cartesian mathematics to have been capable of inspiring a highly talented disciple and to have worked with him on an up-to-date textbook. John Wallis in his *Treatise of Algebra* (1684) did not hesitate to attribute to Malebranche the authorship of the *Élémens* and to reproach the work for being merely a compilation, one that failed to cite its sources other than Descartes and Viète. In replying to this accusation, Prestet clearly implied that he was not annoyed at the attribution of his book to "a person more skillful than he," but he ironically asserted his astonishment that anyone could have supposed he had read so many specialized works. Dating his own initiation in mathematics to 1671, he artlessly stated that Descartes was virtually his only source and that, moreover, he was completely dissatisfied with the few other books that had come to his attention. These remarks would be as true of Malebranche as of Prestet himself.

It is likely that Malebranche's duties as a professor of mathematics lasted only a short while. In any case they have left no further trace. Moreover, when Leibniz met Prestet at Malebranche's residence during his stay in Paris, he was well aware of their respective roles, as is evident from his later correspondence with Malebranche. The disciple, who clearly surpassed his master in the technical realm, was entrusted with the actual mathematical portion of the work; but the master directed the research, and his orientation of it consisted in giving the greatest possible development to Cartesian mathematics.

The *Élémens* consisted of two parts. The first was devoted to arithmetic and algebra, the second to analysis, that is, the application of the two former disciplines to the resolution of all problems concerned with magnitude *(grandeur)*. By magnitude, the author specified that he meant not only what is susceptible of extension in various dimensions but, more generally, everything "susceptible of more and less" *(de plus et de moins)*—in other words, everything that could enter, according to Archimedean logic, into the formal rules of relations. The plan of the work corresponded to one of the aspects of the intelligibility that Malebranche promised to the exercise of the human mind. Prestet added: "We do not attempt to understand or even to reason about the infinite," a point of view which was in accord with Descartes's thinking and to which he always remained faithful. The authors cited in the section on analysis were Diophantus, Viète, and Descartes. In his view, however, Descartes's method was "the most general, the most fruitful, and the most simple of all." In utilizing this method he completed Descartes's effort, notably with regard to equations of the fourth and fifth degree, an area in which he fancied that he had made a theoretical advance.

As to that, he deluded himself a bit, but he did at least provoke Leibniz' curiosity and interest in the subject. Leibniz was disappointed to learn from Malebranche in 1679 that Prestet, who had entered the Oratory and was busy preparing for the priesthood, had not pursued his investigations. This circumstance explains why the theory of equations and the analytic expression of roots constituted the grounds on which Leibniz chose to attack Malebranche. In telling Malebranche that this was the area that most clearly demonstrated the insufficiency and limitations of the Cartesian method, Leibniz was on the right track. Between 1680 and 1690 Malebranche progressively detached himself from Prestet, whose teaching at the University of Angers during these years was marked by painful conflicts with the Jesuits.

True, a new person in Malebranche's immediate entourage, the Abbé Catelan, lent Prestet a hand in assimilating English mathematics and in attempting to attach Barrow's method and Wallis' arithmetic of the infinitesimals to Cartesian mathematics. But Malebranche also became acquainted with a young gentleman, the Marquis de L'Hospital, whom he considered more receptive to the changes that he suspected might be necessary. Prestet died in 1691 after having published two volumes of *Nouveaux élémens* (1689), leaving in manuscript a third volume on geometry that was never published because of Malebranche's unfavorable opinion. For a few months Catelan sought to continue Prestet's work, but the cause was already lost. From 1690 to 1691 Malebranche devoted all his attention to the compromise that L'Hospital had worked out and then ardently followed what the latter was learning from Johann I Bernoulli in 1692. The arrival in Paris of this messenger of Leibniz' new calculus was the "occasion" that completely rearranged the mathematical landscape. Malebranche left to his Oratorian collaborators the task of completing the fair copy of the manuscript recording the mathematical reform elaborated by L'Hospital the preceding year, and the two of them became converts to the movement emanating from Hannover.

This rapid sequence of events within the space of only two or three years undoubtedly reproduced, in a certain way, the situation of 1671–1675. Malebranche assimilated the innovations, pen in hand, and convinced himself of the necessity of encouraging research in the new direction. L'Hospital was the real mathematician, the one who mastered the material and proceeded faster. He soon asserted his own independence from Malebranche; in 1696 he published his *Analyse des infiniment petits* virtually without consulting him. This independence, moreover, was the sign of a new reality. The rapidity with which mathematics was developing reflected the fruitfulness of analysis, which combined consideration of the infinite with the operational procedures of the differential and integral calculus. And the rapid pace accentuated the distinction between those who truly deserved to be considered mathematicians, and the partisans who could only follow, more or less closely, with greater or less difficulty. Malebranche henceforth belonged in the second category.

All the same, he possessed the valuable assets of freshness and enthusiasm. In this regard Leibniz said he had to laugh to see how Malebranche was so enamored of algebra, so enchanted with its operational effectiveness. The enchantment that Malebranche found in the mathematics of the infinitesimal analysis attests to the same naïveté. He failed to distinguish clearly between the respective roles of logic and calculation. Believing that the new mathematics was within striking distance of perfection, he could not understand what restrained the great masters from placing their discoveries before the public. What diminishes Malebranche's standing as a mathematician in the eyes of the specialists, his naïveté, was the same quality that made his advocacy more effective.

In the fifth edition of the *Recherche de la vérité* (1700), Malebranche replaced all the mathematical references he had previously given with L'Hospital's *Analyse* and a work on integral calculus that his former secretary, Louis Carré, had just compiled from material in the archives of the Oratory. Fully aware of its deficiencies, Malebranche expressed the hope that a better work would shortly appear and hinted that the required effort was under way. He had good reason for doing so, because in 1698 he had, in effect, assigned this task to the Oratorian Charles-René Reyneau, Prestet's successor at Angers. And to the extent that this outstanding teacher encountered great difficulties in absorbing the infinitesimal methods, there were grounds for thinking that the result of his labor would correspond to the conditions required for the dissemination of the new ideas in the schools and would, in short, constitute a good textbook.

The enterprise was marked by many vicissitudes and was not completed until 1708, after the happy conclusion at the Académie des Sciences of the polemic provoked by Michel Rolle against the infinitesimals. (Malebranche played the most active role in bringing about this happy ending.) Although Reyneau's *Analyse démontrée* appeared in 1708, later than expected, it answered all the more fully to the hopes placed in it. The first textbook of the new mathematics, it fulfilled the important social function indispensable to all reform. It was from one of this work's posthumous editions that d'Alembert learned the subject.

It is evident that Malebranche holds no place in the history of mathematics by virtue of any specific discovery, nor any claim to be considered a true mathematician. Nevertheless, the history of mathematics at the end of the seventeenth century—at least in France —cannot be described without referring to his activity. The mainspring of the spread and development of Cartesian mathematics, Malebranche successively insisted on the need for reform and fostered the introduction of Leibnizian mathematics. Throughout these changes, moreover, he was concerned with their implications for teaching.

While the importance of intelligibility in his philosophy accounts for his special interest in mathematics, it was, rather, toward physics and the natural sciences that Malebranche turned his attention. The first edition of the *Recherche* clearly demonstrates that this vast subject attracted Malebranche's interest from the start and that he had already read extensively in it. In the realm of physics, Rohault's recent publication seemed to Malebranche both adequate and faithful to the Cartesian method. The only topic in which Malebranche felt obliged to make a personal contribution was that of the laws of collision. It is also the question to which he returned in 1692 in publishing a small volume entitled *Des loix de la communication des mouvements.*

The date 1692 in itself is significant, but to understand fully Malebranche's statement that this short treatise was written in order to meet Leibniz' criticisms, it is not sufficient to consider only the mathematical developments outlined above. It must also be recalled that in 1686–1687 Leibniz had launched an attack in the *Acta eruditorum* against the Cartesian identification of force with the quantity of motion and had thereby provoked a bitter controversy with Cate-

lan, who was then friendly with Malebranche. Moreover, in 1692 Malebranche was the recipient of a manuscript copy of Leibniz' *Essay de dynamique.* The brief work that he brought out almost simultaneously shows that Malebranche was able to assimilate criticism without capitulating to it.

Although Malebranche agreed to revise the whole of his presentation of the subject, he did not consent to abandon any more of the Cartesian legacy than he had already done in dropping the principle that a force inheres in the state of rest. Further, he assumed that he had answered Leibniz' objections by distinguishing three types of laws, corresponding to the "different suppositions that may be held relating to colliding bodies and to the surrounding medium." On this occasion, moreover, he gave greater importance to the notion of elasticity. Nevertheless, his conclusion, presented with highly interesting remarks on the respective roles of theoretical speculation and experiment, makes clear that he was not satisfied with his work and was ready for a more radical revision. He undertook such a revision in several steps in the years 1698 to 1700, characterizing his own publication of 1692 as a "wretched little treatise."

In the course of this tumultuous development of his ideas Malebranche made his most original contribution to the scientific movement—and did so in his capacity as speculative philosopher. In his exposition of the third law of impact, he invested collision theory with a clarity that was lacking in Mariotte's *Traité de la percussion ou chocq des corps* (1673). After concisely expressing the principles of research, he judiciously chose numerical examples and then stated a position that he firmly maintained in the following years: the scientist's duty is to begin with the diversity of observations and then to establish laws. These laws, when submitted to mathematical operations, should reflect natural effects step by step. It was in this connection that Malebranche was dissatisfied with Mariotte's propositions. The latter had, it is true, clearly distinguished between two operations. First, he disregarded elasticity and treated the bodies as if they were soft. Second, he superimposed the effect of elasticity, which consisted in assigning the respective velocities in inverse ratio to the masses. But in Malebranche's view the first operation was unintelligible, since bodies without elasticity were, he supposed, necessarily hard. And the second operation ran into serious logical difficulties, for taking the force to be the absolute quantity of motion led to paradoxical results. Malebranche satisfied himself with regard to the first point in 1698–1699 by means of a modification of the concept of matter, the subject of his "Mémoire sur la lumière, les couleurs etc." He attempted to overcome the second problem by considering the property of reciprocity, which Mariotte's laws assumed, to be a "revelation" of the experiment, the sort of principle of intelligibility to which all rational effort must be subject. While correcting the proofs for the fifth edition of the *Recherche*, he was rewarded by the discovery that the whole question became clarified if the absolute quantity of motion were replaced by the algebraic quantity, that is, if the sign were taken into account.

This discovery led to the final corrections, which now furnished an original way of demonstrating, without paralogism or *petitio principii*, the laws of elastic collision. Moreover, this method of improving Mariotte's presentation avoided adopting Leibniz' point of view and preserved as much as possible of Descartes's conception.

Convinced that he had found a solution, Malebranche turned his attention all the more resolutely toward other problems. The memoir alluded to above won him membership in the Académie des Sciences at the time of its reorganization in 1699. Henceforth, Malebranche actively participated in scientific life, while gathering the material he was to incorporate in the sixth edition of the *Recherche* (1712), in which he made the necessary revisions, corrections, and additions in those sections devoted to all the topics in which he thought science bore on his philosophy.

It is most important to note that certain authors have erred in ridiculing the patching up of the Cartesian vortices that Malebranche is supposed to have begun. To be sure, he speaks of subtle matter and vortices, but his system arises from a syncretism that borrowed much from recent advances in physics and especially from the work of Huygens. Malebranche's subtle matter is a unique primary substance that, forced to move at high speed in a closed universe, is obliged to whirl in vortices the dimensions of which can decrease without limit, a property predicated on the supposition that no vacuum can exist. The formula for centrifugal force then requires that these small vortices, which are actually the universal material of all physical entities, be not only perfectly elastic but capable, as well, of releasing a "fearful" force upon breaking up. A theoretical model of this sort is not a trivial invention.

Nor is there anything trivial about the manner in which Malebranche utilized this model to study luminous phenomena and to provide an account of universal gravitation, of planetary motion, and of gravity. This model, considered in itself as the seat of action in the universe, inspired his idea that light consists of vibration in a medium under pressure. And considered in all its ramifications, it led him to conceive of the gross matter accessible to our senses as the result of a condensation in the neighborhood of a vortical center. This picture was imposed by the inapplicability to the case of large vortices of a homogeneous mechanical model centered on a point with invariant properties for distances near to or far from the center.

Although all this theoretical effort must be granted a certain originality, none of it was adopted by eighteenth-century science. It was not until much later that scientists again took up the idea that frequency is characteristic of colors or the idea that orthography can help establish the laws of central systems of small diameter—and when they did they were unaware that Malebranche had advocated such views.

Nor did anything come either of the hours that Malebranche spent at the microscope or of his botanical observations. Despite the importance he accorded to the experimental method after 1700, he never considered himself more than an amateur, concerned simply to grasp what it was that the specialization of others was accomplishing. The only experiment that we can confidently attribute to his own efforts—before his reading of Newton's *Opticks*—concerned the virtual equivalence of air and of the vacuum produced in the air pump as mediums for the propagation of light. It was a perfect example of the ambiguity of so-called crucial experiments. Malebranche's improvements in methods for observing generation in eggs in the hatchery were trivial and presupposed confirmation of the ovist theory. Even though the science of life seemed to him a realm apart, incomprehensible without the idea of finality, he applied to it what is now known as the notion of structure, deriving from his mathematical critique of being and extension. That is why he advocated the doctrine of the *emboîtement des germes*.

It has to be admitted that Malebranche came to a scientific career, in the broad sense, too late in life. It was unusual enough that at age sixty he was able to carry out experimental research which showed a greater command of the subject than he could have won from books alone; and more should not be asked of him. Faithful to his speculative temperament, he was ardently concerned to preserve from his Cartesian past those values he thought enduring and to bequeath a system reconciling this past with the science of his day. This arduous enterprise condemned him to be a follower, not a leader, and it is not surprising that his work failed to exhibit intimate knowledge of the most advanced developments of contemporary science. The reformulation of results that have become common knowledge always requires the discovery of new results, if it is to incite interest. Malebranche failed to go beyond the reexpression of either the sine law of refraction of light or the inverse-square law of gravitation, and he left his vibratory theory of colors in only a rudimentary state.

Still, the high level of reflection he demanded from his readers exerted an influence on the most diverse thinkers both in France and abroad. As in the case of mathematics, Malebranche has a claim to be remembered in the history of physics, a science the autonomy of which was scarcely recognized in the last years of the seventeenth century and which had to formulate a charter for itself. In this respect Malebranche indisputably answered to the needs of his time, and his efforts were not in vain.

Thus, to the extent that Malebranche enriched theoretical speculation and worked to fashion a suitable basis for the union of the rational and the experimental, he made a genuine contribution to the autonomy of science. His activity was always inspired by his religious philosophy and, reciprocally, his results appeared to him to provide support for it. Others could complete the separation, retaining the autonomy and discarding the philosophy.

In preparing this account the author has sought to adhere to the facts available to him. This same fidelity, however, obliges him to restore to Malebranche something beyong the authorship of a body of thought that advanced an enlightened rationalism. The restitution concerns the virtues that Malebranche constantly displayed during his life: a capacity to correct himself, a sensitivity to the difficulties of the ordinary reader and to the needs of his time, and a perseverance in educating himself in many fields. In Malebranche, the man is inseparable from the thinker, and the man was wholly imbued with Christian faith. One may, of course, not share this faith, and then the separation of science from belief is easy to effect. But whoever accepts the lesson to be learned in contemplating the total, integrated image of a life will no less easily perceive the violence of such an act. This is why, after several centuries, the message offered by Malebranche endures.

BIBLIOGRAPHY

I. ORIGINAL WORKS. The complete works of Malebranche, published under the direction of André Robinet as *Oeuvres complètes*, 20 vols. (Paris, 1958–1968), include correspondence and MSS. For his scientific work, see esp. vol. III, *Éclaircissements de la recherche de la vérité* (1678–1712); and vol. XVII, pt. 1, *Lois du mouvement* (1675–1712); and pt. 2, *Mathematica,* containing unpublished mathematical and other works, with critical annotations by P. Costabel.

Six eds. of *De la recherche de la vérité* were published, at Paris, during Malebranche's lifetime: the first three, in 2 vols. (1674–1675, 1675, 1677–1678); the 4th and 5th, in 3 vols. (1678–1679, 1700); and the 6th, in 4 vols. (1712). The *Traité de la nature et de la grâce* (Amsterdam, 1680) was followed in 1681 by *Éclaircissement, ou la suite du Traité ....*

II. SECONDARY LITERATURE. Works on Malebranche and his work include V. Delbos, *Étude de la philosophie de Malebranche* (Paris, 1924); G. Dreyfus, *La volonté selon Malebranche* (Paris, 1958); H. Gouhier, *La vocation de Malebranche* (Paris, 1926); and *La philosophie de Malebranche et son expérience religieuse* (Paris, 1926); M. Gueroult, *Malebranche*, 3 vols. (Paris, 1955–1959); A. Robinet, *Malebranche, de l'Académie des sciences* (Paris, 1970); and G. Rodis-Lewis, *Nicolas Malebranche* (Paris, 1963). See also *Malebranche—l'homme et l'oeuvre* (Paris, 1966), published by the Centre International de Synthèse.

PIERRE COSTABEL

MALESHERBES, CHRÉTIEN-GUILLAUME DE LAMOIGNON DE (*b.* Paris, France, 6 December 1721; *d.* Paris, 22 April 1794), *agronomy, botany.*

Member of a distinguished family of the *noblesse de robe*, Malesherbes was the son of Guillaume de Lamoignon, chancellor of France (1750–1768), and was related by marriage to the families of Chateaubriand, La Luzerne, Rosanbo, and Tocqueville. A magistrate by profession, he was one of the most enlightened officials of the *ancien régime*, holding at various times the posts of director general of the Librairie, first president of the Cour des Aides, and minister under Turgot (1774–1776) and under Loménie de Brienne (1787–1788). He was an influential spokesman for freedom of the press, religious toleration, and tax reform. A member of the Académie Française and the Société Royale d'Agriculture, he was also honorary member of the Académie des Inscriptions et Belles-Lettres and the Académie Royale des Sciences. Late in 1792 he volunteered to serve as defense counsel at the forthcoming trial of Louis XVI. Subsequently accused of having defended the king and of other "acts of treason," he was tried by the Revolutionary Tribunal and guillotined.

Malesherbes studied botany with Bernard de Jussieu (1746–1749) and chemistry with G.-F. Rouelle, and maintained a lifelong interest in natural history. He wrote little for publication, and accounts of his scientific activities, ideas, and influence must be sought principally in his correspondence and in memoirs often intended for circulation among his friends. These sources show him to have had some competence in botany and especially in agronomy, and reveal his role in supplying scientists with information and patronage.

Among Malesherbes's earliest works, although

published posthumously (1798), was a critique of the first volumes of Buffon's *Histoire naturelle* (1749). Here he not only disagreed with specific details but also replied effectively to Buffon's attack on naturalists who emphasized the accumulation of data and on botanists who believed it possible to discover a natural system of classification.

Malesherbes was concerned with the improvement of breeds of livestock, the cultivation of wastes, and the naturalization in France of such crops as wild rice. From about 1760 his estate at Malesherbes (Loiret) was essentially an experimental farm devoted largely to the cultivation and acclimatization of "exotic" trees. Rather than purely ornamental trees or botanical rarities, useful trees, and especially conifers, were of particular interest to Malesherbes. Varieties of pine, for example, were important for shipbuilding; and he tried to discover the soil and climate most suitable for naturalizing in France the pines of Corsica and the Baltic. While some agronomists advocated a national program of marsh drainage, Malesherbes pointed out that such soil was often sterile for staple crops; instead, he proposed broadening existing afforestation attempts by the introduction of the swamp cypresses of Virginia. These and other trees, he argued, would provide rot-resistant naval timber, alleviate the national fuel shortage, and turn marshes to efficient use. He was able to test some of his ideas during the exceptionally harsh winter of 1788–1789, when he made detailed observations of the survival capabilities of his own forest trees.

Malesherbes's interest in trees came increasingly to center on those of North America when, during the American Revolution, he shared the hope that France could establish close commercial and cultural ties with an independent United States. Although some North American plants had long been available to French naturalists, collection was not systematic and tended to be done through English intermediaries. Malesherbes's own contacts in America were strengthened after 1779 when his nephew, the Marquis de La Luzerne, was sent there as minister plenipotentiary; his American correspondents also came to include Thomas Jefferson and Benjamin Franklin and French diplomats F. Barbé de Marbois, L.-G. Otto, and H. St. Jean de Crèvecoeur. He arranged to have shipments of seeds and seedlings sent to the Paris firm of Vilmorin-Andrieux so that American plants could be widely distributed in France.

Malesherbes's interest in the dissemination of new ideas is apparent in the two agricultural pamphlets published during his lifetime. In the first he emphasized the need for organized communication among agronomists so that experimental results could be verified and made widely known. In the second he attempted to direct the attention of the National Assembly to problems of landholding that were intimately connected with legal, social, and agricultural change.

Malesherbes often contributed to the work of other scientists and served as their patron. He transmitted the results of his own experiments to agronomists H.-L. Duhamel du Monceau and P. Varenne de Fenille for use in their publications, and he did the same for chemist P.-J. Macquer, stipulating that Macquer refrain from publicly acknowledging his aid. During his travels he gathered information useful for the geological maps of J.-E. Guettard, and he donated his collection of minerals to the École des Mines soon after its founding in 1783. It was his patronage that enabled mineralogist A.-G. Monnet to obtain a post with the Bureau du Commerce.

Recognizing the limits of his own training and ability, Malesherbes tried to recruit professional translators and scientists to work on such projects as the translation of English agricultural writings and of Pehr Kalm's *Travels in North America* (first published in Swedish, 1753–1761, and soon afterward in German and English). His role, as he saw it, was that of the scientific amateur, possessed of enough training to understand the work of the professionals and enough ability, wealth, and influence to aid them. The agronomists who knew him best disagreed with part of this evaluation and looked upon Malesherbes as their colleague.

BIBLIOGRAPHY

I. ORIGINAL WORKS. Malesherbes's publications are *Mémoire sur les moyens d'accélérer les progrès de l'économie rurale en France. Lu à la Société royale d'agriculture* (Paris, 1790), also published in *Mémoires de la Société nationale d'agriculture de France* (spring trimester 1790); *Idées d'un agriculteur patriote sur le défrichement des terres incultes* (Paris, 1791), repr. in *Annales de l'agriculture françoise*, **10** (an X), 9–26; and *Observations de Lamoignon-Malesherbes sur l'histoire naturelle générale et particulière de Buffon et Daubenton*, with intro. and notes by L.-P. Abeille, 2 vols. (Paris, 1798). There are also several works on nonscientific subjects.

Large collections of MSS are extant, some in private hands; see the first work by Grosclaude (below). Also Bibliothèque de l'Institut de France, Paris, MS 997; and Bibliothèque Centrale du Muséum National d'Histoire Naturelle, Paris, MSS 238, 239, 949, 1765. Relevant documents in the possession of the American Philosophical Society, Philadelphia, are described by Gilbert Chinard, "Recently Acquired Botanical Documents," in *Proceedings of the American Philosophical Society*, **101** (1957), 508–522.

II. SECONDARY LITERATURE. Biographies are numerous and began to appear soon after Malesherbes's death, but these works have in most respects been superseded. See Pierre Grosclaude, *Malesherbes, témoin et interprète de son temps* (Paris, 1961), and *Malesherbes et son temps: Nouveaux documents inédits* (Paris, 1964); J. M. S. Allison, *Lamoignon de Malesherbes, Defender and Reformer of the French Monarchy, 1721–1794* (New Haven, 1938); J. Sabrazès, "Malesherbes, l'homme de bien, le réformateur, le savant," in *Gazette hebdomadaire des sciences médicales de Bordeaux*, no. 39 (25 Sept. 1932); André J. Bourde, *Agronomie et agronomes en France au XVIIIe siècle*, 3 vols. (Paris, 1967); and Joseph Laissus, "Monsieur de Malesherbes et 'la montagne qui cogne' (1782–1783)," in *Comptes rendus du quatre-vingt-douzième Congrès national des sociétés savantes, Strasbourg et Colmar, 1967: Section des sciences*, I (Paris, 1969), 233–254.

RHODA RAPPAPORT

MALFATTI, GIAN FRANCESCO (*b.* Ala, Trento, Italy, 1731; *d.* Ferrara, Italy, 9 October 1807), *mathematics.*

After completing his studies in Bologna under the guidance of Francesco Maria Zanotti, Gabriele Manfredi, and Vincenzo Riccati, Malfatti went to Ferrara in 1754, where he founded a school of mathematics and physics. In 1771, when the University of Ferrara was reestablished, he was appointed professor of mathematics. He held this post for about thirty years, teaching all phases of mathematics from Euclidean geometry to calculus.

Malfatti became famous for his paper "De aequationibus quadrato-cubicis disquisitio analytica" (1770), in which, given an equation of the fifth degree, he constructed a resolvent of the equation of the sixth degree, that is, the well-known Malfatti resolvent. If the root is known, the complete resolution of the given equation may be deduced. The latter, however, cannot be obtained by means of rational root expressions; rather, as Brioschi later demonstrated, it is obtained by means of elliptical transcendents.

Malfatti also demonstrated that a memoir on the theory of probability, published by Lagrange in 1774 and proclaimed by Poisson as "one of Lagrange's most beautiful works," nevertheless required explanation at one point.

In a brief treatise entitled *Della curva cassiniana* (1781), Malfatti demonstrated that a special case of Cassini's curve, the lemniscate, has the property that a mass point moving on it under gravity goes along any arc of the curve in the same time as it traverses the subtending chord.

In 1802 Malfatti gave the first, brilliant solution of the problem that bears his name: "Describe in a triangle three circumferences that are mutually tangent, each of which touches two sides of the triangle." Many illustrious mathematicians had dealt with this problem. Jacques Bernoulli (1654–1705) had earlier dealt with the special case in which the triangle is isosceles. An elegant geometric solution was supplied by Steiner (*Crelle's Journal*, vol. 1, 1826), while Clebsch, dealing with the same problem in 1857, made an excellent application of the elliptical functions (*Crelle's Journal*, vol. 53, 1857).

In a letter to A. M. Lorgna (27 April 1783), Malfatti gave the polar equation concerning the squaring of the circle.

BIBLIOGRAPHY

I. ORIGINAL WORKS. Among Malfatti's works are "De aequationibus quadrato-cubicis disquisitio analytica," in *Atti dell'Accademia dei Fisiocritici di Siena* (1770); *Memorie della Società italiana delle scienze detta dei XL*, 3; *Della curva cassiniana* (Pavia, 1781); *Memorie della Società italiana delle scienze detta dei XL*, **10** (1802); and his letter to Lorgna, in *Bullettino di bibliografia e di storia delle scienze matematiche e fisiche*, **9** (1876), 438.

II. SECONDARY LITERATURE. For further information on Malfatti and his work, see G. B. Biadego, "Intorno alla vita e agli scritti di Gianfrancesco Malfatti, matematico del sec. XVIII°," in *Bullettino di bibliografia e storia delle matematiche del Boncompagni*, **9** (1876); E. Bortolotti, "Sulla risolvente di Malfatti," in *Atti dell'Accademia di Modena*, 3rd ser., **7** (1906); "Commemorazione di G. F. Malfatti," in *Atti della XIX riunione della Società italiana per il progresso delle scienze* (1930). Also see article on Malfatti in *Enciclopedia italiana* (Milan, 1934), XXII, 16; F. Brioschi, "Sulla risolvente di Malfatti," in *Memorie dell'Istituto lombardo di scienze e lettere*, **9** (1863); Gino Loria, *Curve piane speciali: Teoria e storia* (Milan, 1930), I, 265, and II, 23; and *Storia delle matematiche*, 2nd ed. (Milan, 1950), *passim*; A. Procissi, "Questioni connesse al problema di Malfatti e bibliografia," in *Periodico di matematiche*, 4th ser., **12** (1932); and A. Wittstein, *Geschichte des Malfatti'schen Problems* (Munich, 1871).

A. NATUCCI

IBN MALKĀ. See **Abu'l Barakāt.**

MALL, FRANKLIN PAINE (*b.* Belle Plaine, Iowa, 28 September 1862; *d.* Baltimore, Maryland, 17 November 1917), *anatomy, embryology, physiology.*

Mall was the only son of Franz Mall, a farmer born at Solingen, Germany; his mother, the former Louise Christine Miller, was also a native of Germany and died when he was ten years old. He attended a local academy, where an able teacher awakened his interest in science. In 1880, at the age of eighteen, Mall began medical studies at the University of Michigan, where he had three stimulating teachers: Corydon L. Ford, professor of anatomy, a superb lecturer but not an original investigator; Victor C. Vaughan, biochemist and bacteriologist; and Henry Sewall, physiologist. William J. Mayo, later a famous surgeon, was a classmate.

Influenced, no doubt, by Vaughan and Sewall, who had gone to Germany for scientific training, Mall, after taking the M.D. degree in 1883, went to Heidelberg with the intention of becoming a specialist in ophthalmology. Finding himself more interested in anatomical research than in the practice of medicine, he went in 1884 to Leipzig, where he became a student of Wilhelm His, the greatest embryologist of the time, who admitted him to close association in the laboratory and became a lifelong friend and adviser. During the same year Mall met another American postgraduate student, William H. Welch, who later, as dean of the Johns Hopkins University School of Medicine, invited Mall to be its first professor of anatomy. After completing a study of the development of the thymus gland (which, incidentally, contradicted earlier work by His), Mall moved, on the advice of His, to the laboratory of Carl Ludwig at Leipzig. Ludwig set for the young Mall a study of the structure of the small intestine, which he accomplished with such skill and breadth of view as to win the admiration of Ludwig, who personally saw Mall's monograph through the press after the latter left for America in 1886.

Welch, who had returned to America some years earlier, had organized a department of pathology at the Johns Hopkins Hospital preliminary to the creation of a school of medicine. Mall applied to him for a post and was given the first fellowship in the new laboratory. He remained there for three years, studying the structure of the stomach and intestines from both the anatomical and the physiological standpoints, partly in collaboration with the surgeon William S. Halsted. He also studied the microscopic structure of connective tissue by highly original methods. On the basis of his description Halsted developed the method of suturing the intestine in surgical operations that is known by his name.

Because Mall's position with Welch was not permanent, he was much concerned about his future, opportunities for full-time medical research and teaching being very limited at that time; but in 1889 he was offered an adjunct professorship of anatomy at Clark University, Worcester, Massachusetts, then being organized by the psychologist G. Stanley Hall.

The appointment seemed to offer Mall an opportunity to develop anatomical research and to put the teaching of that subject on as high a scientific basis as in Germany; the prevalent approach in American schools was that of didactic instruction, serving only as preparation for surgery. He remained at Clark University for three years, until the faculty's growing dissatisfaction with Hall's administration led to the departure of several young professors, Mall going to the University of Chicago as professor of anatomy at its school of medicine. While at Clark, however, his research led to an important discovery, that of the vasomotor nerves of the portal vein. At this time also Mall constructed a model of an early human embryo by the Born wax-plate method, the first to be made in America, and thus began the program of embryological research on which his reputation is chiefly based.

Mall remained in Chicago only one year, for in 1893, when Johns Hopkins University opened its long-planned school of medicine with Welch as dean, Mall was called to head its department of anatomy. Free to plan instruction without constraint of tradition, Mall at once began to reform the teaching of anatomy in the United States by giving few lectures while providing his students full opportunity to learn for themselves by dissection, with the aid of textbooks and atlases and the advice of instructors engaged in research. Mall designed and maintained quiet and scrupulously clean small laboratory rooms in place of the large dissecting halls of the older schools; he also insisted on accurate work, familiarity with the literature of the field, and scientific rather than purely practical aims. The same principles were applied to the teaching of microscopic anatomy and neurology, conducted largely by his staff. The members of his staff were given full freedom to direct their own researches under his lightly imposed leadership, that of an older, more experienced fellow student rather than a taskmaster. The success of Mall's methods is demonstrated by the fact that they were carried to a score of other universities by those of his pupils and assistants who became professors of anatomy, and many physicians and medical teachers found in his laboratory an intellectual awakening and a stimulus to become independent scientific investigators. Outstanding researchers who worked with him were Ross G. Harrison, Florence R. Sabin, George L. Streeter, Warren H. Lewis, and Herbert M. Evans.

In 1894 Mall married Mabel Glover of Washington, D.C., one of the three women students in his first class at Johns Hopkins. They had two daughters.

Mall's own investigations during the early years in Baltimore dealt chiefly with the structure of the spleen and the liver. His study of the very peculiar arrangement of blood vessels in the spleen underlies the current conception that this organ serves as a storage place for the blood. His work on the liver gave rise to two important generalizations with which he extended ideas of his teacher Wilhelm His. One of these states that the extremely thin tubular tissue (endothelium) of which the capillary blood vessels consist, and which forms the lining of the veins and arteries, is the primary structure of the vascular system and in the larger vessels is reinforced by muscle and connective-tissue cells. Studying the liver, Mall showed that organ to be made up of small structural units each of which contains all the essential tissue elements—hepatic cells, blood vessels, and bile ducts, systematically arranged within the unit; and he demonstrated that the blood vessels supplying the units are so arranged as to distribute the blood equally to each of them. This concept of structural units was extended, by him and by some of his students, to other organs.

While a postgraduate student in Leipzig with Wilhelm His, Mall had begun to collect human embryos; and in Baltimore he continued to build up his collection. With this material he made valuable studies of the development of the intestinal canal, the body cavities, the diaphragm, and the abdominal walls. In 1910–1912 Mall collaborated with Franz Keibel of Freiburg in editing *Handbook of Human Embryology*, written by American and German experts. The two-volume work has not yet been superseded.

The growth of Mall's collection of human embryos and their preparation for research use made so large a demand on the resources of his university department that in 1913 he appealed to the Carnegie Institution of Washington to create a department of embryology at the Johns Hopkins Medical School, to which he gave his collection, by that time the largest in the world. He led this laboratory until his death in 1917, holding its directorship as well as the Johns Hopkins chair of anatomy. The first six volumes of the Carnegie *Contributions to Embryology* were edited by Mall with the highest standards of textual perfection and illustration. A comprehensive program of research laid down by him was continued and largely completed under his successor, George L. Streeter.

Mall's service to anatomy and embryology beyond his own laboratory began in 1900, when, with Charles S. Minot of Harvard and George S. Huntington of Columbia University, he founded the *American Journal of Anatomy* and for eight years, with sound financial judgment, published it from his laboratory with one of his staff, Henry McElderry Knower, as managing editor. Mall and Minot also joined in 1900 in a successful effort to rejuvenate the American

Association of Anatomists, which since its foundation in 1888 had represented the older, relatively unoriginal phase of anatomical study in the United States. Never putting himself forward in its organization, Mall was strongly influential in placing and keeping it on a high scientific level. As its president in 1906–1908 he overcame his reluctance, or inability, to speak in public and made the only formal address of his career, under the characteristically modest title "Some Points of Interest to Anatomists."

As in the councils of his profession, so also in the Johns Hopkins University, Mall exerted a quiet but profound influence. His close friendship since his student days in Germany with William H. Welch, dean of the school of medicine and eloquent, magnetic leader of American medical education, gave Mall a channel for his ideas and a spokesman for the ideals they both cherished. Mall was the chief proponent of the so-called concentration system, under which the medical student's time was no longer divided between several concurrently taught subjects but was allotted to not more than two subjects at a time, which were taken up for long periods, up to two trimesters. Thus the student received a thorough, uninterrupted conspectus of each subject. This system, begun at Johns Hopkins, was generally adopted by the American medical schools.

Mall was also a leader, in his inconspicuous way, in the highly controversial movement for full-time teachers of the clinical subjects, as opposed to use of medical practitioners devoting only part of their time to teaching. Full-time teaching of the preclinical sciences—anatomy, physiology, biochemistry and pathology—was well under way in the American schools by the turn of the century, as Mall's appointment to the Johns Hopkins chair of anatomy shows; but the radical move for which he worked was to put the teaching of internal medicine, surgery, and the major specialties into the hands of able men freed from the necessity of earning their living by private practice and, as salaried professors, devoting their full time to teaching, research, and the care of patients in university hospitals. Mall had gotten the germ of this idea from Carl Ludwig at Leipzig and had discussed it during the early years of the Johns Hopkins Medical School. A former member of his staff, Lewellys F. Barker, first presented the plan publicly in an address at Chicago in 1903. Through Welch, who was at first lukewarm, a program for full-time clinical teaching at Johns Hopkins was drawn up in 1913 and implemented by a grant from the General Education Board of New York.

As the foregoing record has indicated, Mall possessed an unusual combination of far-reaching originality with shy reticence, of scientific detachment with shrewd business sense. He never overran his budget and always had a reserve on hand. He was wise in his selection of young men for his staff and highly successful in placing them, when they matured, in important positions. Admirably fair-minded, he was, however, intolerant of stupidity.

Mall's disapproval of excessive lecturing in anatomical teaching was based not only on his pedagogical ideas but also on lack of talent for formal speaking before classes and scientific societies. When he did, rarely, speak to such groups, he was not outstandingly clear. On the other hand, he always had time for private discussions with students and staff members, in or out of classroom and laboratory. His remarks, however, were not always directly related to the topic of the conversation; they were often very whimsical and seemingly farfetched, but they always included a serious idea which the hearer might miss until after days or months he suddenly perceived what Mall had intended subtly to convey. Without the mediation of his ideas by Minot in the American Association of Anatomists, and in the larger affairs of medical education by Welch and by Abraham Flexner of the General Education Board and the Rockefeller Foundation, Mall would never have seen his reform projects carried out; but indirectly he influenced many pupils and associates to whom he addressed himself privately.

BIBLIOGRAPHY

I. ORIGINAL WORKS. The author of many scientific articles, Mall also was joint editor, with Franz Keibel, of *Handbook of Human Embryology*, 2 vols. (Philadelphia, 1910–1912), to which he contributed 3 chapters.

II. SECONDARY LITERATURE. See "Memorial Services in Honor of Franklin Paine Mall, Professor of Anatomy, Johns Hopkins University, 1893 to 1917," in *Johns Hopkins Hospital Bulletin*, **29** (1918), 109–123, with portrait and complete bibliography; and the following works by Florence R. Sabin: "Franklin Paine Mall, a Review of His Scientific Achievement," in *Science*, n.s. **47** (1918), 254–261; *Franklin Paine Mall, the Story of a Mind* (Baltimore, 1934), with portraits and selected bibliography; and "Franklin Paine Mall, 1862–1917," in *Biographical Memoirs. National Academy of Sciences*, **16** (1936), 65–122, with portrait and complete bibliography.

GEORGE W. CORNER

MALLARD, (FRANÇOIS) ERNEST (*b.* Châteauneuf-sur-Cher, France, 4 February 1833; *d.* Paris, France, 6 July 1894), *mineralogy, mining engineering.*

The son of a lawyer, Mallard was brought up in St.-Amand-Montrond. He studied at the Collège de Bourges, the École Polytechnique, and the École des Mines, from which he graduated in 1853 as *ingénieur des mines.* He began his career as a geologist for the Corps des Mines but in 1859 was transferred to fill the chair of mineralogy at its École des Mineurs at Saint-Étienne. He continued his work for the Corps, first in geological mapping and after 1868 on problems of mining engineering. His work attracted favorable notice from G. A. Daubrée, professor of mineralogy at the École des Mines; and when Daubrée became director of the school in 1872, he chose Mallard to fill the vacated chair of mineralogy. The new post was a decisive change for Mallard, involving a new concentration on more directly mineralogical problems, the area in which he found greatest satisfaction and made his most important contributions. He continued as a member of investigative commissions in the Corps des Mines, for which he was promoted in 1867 to engineer first class and in 1886 to inspector general. In 1869 he received the *croix de chevalier* and in 1888 became an officer of the Legion of Honor. He was proposed, unsuccessfully, for several vacancies in the mineralogy section of the Académie des Sciences and finally was elected in 1890. In 1879 he was the second president of the Société minéralogique de France.

Mallard had great personal modesty but did not hesitate to put into print his thoughtful objections to publications of other scientists. He never wished to marry; he followed his vocations single-mindedly. Termier poignantly describes Mallard's camaraderie with students during field excursions.

Mallard's contributions in crystallography began in 1876, not long after he had assumed the chair of mineralogy at Paris. He took as his starting point the *Études cristallographiques*[1] of Auguste Bravais, who had been professor of physics there from 1845 to 1855. While Sohncke[2] and later A. Schönflies[3] were developing Bravais's concept of a lattice of translationally equivalent points into a complete mathematical description of symmetry of crystals (the 230 space groups), Mallard independently developed other aspects of Bravais's theories. This work had its notable beginning in the memoir *Explication des phénomènes optiques anomaux*, on optically "anomalous" crystals (that is, those crystals the morphology of which seems to be of greater symmetry than their optics), in which the powerful new polarizing microscope showed the importance of twinning in these "crystalline edifices" and of pseudosymmetry as an explanatory concept.

A summary of Mallard's ideas was offered in a two-volume work with atlas entitled *Traité de cristal-*

lographie géométrique et physique, published in 1879 (geometrical crystallography, lattice theory, and morphology) and 1884 (crystal physics). Here, for the first time, the convoluted mathematical apparatus of Bravais was stripped away to reveal in a didactic but complete fashion the essential contributions of the lattice theory. Mallard recognized the way in which this theory corresponded to a special case of Haüy's *molécules intégrantes* while admitting that the unsupportable remainder of Haüy's theories of crystal structure had led to its being completely discredited by the German school of geometrical crystallographers. Wherever possible, he applied Bravais's theory to an understanding of the wide range of physical properties of crystals that had been investigated in the thirty intervening years; and he found in a strict definition of homogeneity a common basis for both the lattice theory and the newer macroscopic description of physical properties of anisotropic crystals by characteristic ellipsoids. The detailed and generally favorable reviews of these volumes in Germany,[4] where a divergent direction of theory had been followed since the time of C. S. Weiss, attests to their persuasive completeness.

A third volume of the *Traité*, in which Mallard planned to discuss isomorphism, polymorphism, twinning, pseudosymmetry, and crystal growth, was never completed. Some of his original work on these subjects was published separately.[5] In this respect his most important contribution was his theory of twins based on the continuation or pseudo-continuation of a lattice between the twinned crystals. Mallard's development and extension of Bravais's lattice theory, especially to the explanation of the importance of crystal faces ("law of Bravais") and of twins, was further developed by observations and refined by Georges Friedel,[6] who was Mallard's student at the École des Mines; Friedel's exposition on these subjects remained the definitive statement until very recent direct structural theories. On the other hand, Mallard's theory of circular polarization in crystals as equivalent to a stack of thin, linearly polarized sheets has not stood the test of time.[7]

Mallard also made notable scientific contributions in his capacity as a mining engineer. In 1878, soon after it was formed, he was appointed to an official commission investigating methods of preventing methane explosions in mines. A series of laboratory and field investigations in collaboration with H. Le Chatelier, then professor of general chemistry at the École des Mines, resulted in a series of joint papers on the design of safety lamps, on combustion temperature, on velocity of flame propagation, and on the importance of mixtures of coal dust. They instituted the use of ammonium nitrate as an explosive; its low temperature of detonation made it safer (less likely to propagate in mixtures of air with gas or coal), and it has remained the preferred explosive to this day. Mallard continued his collaboration with Le Chatelier in experiments on the thermal properties of crystals.

A key figure in the French school of crystallography and a bridge from Bravais to Friedel, Mallard was described as having ... "definitively displaced the center of gravity of crystallography that, thereafter, could not be cultivated as a descriptive science, but was elevated to the rank of a rational science."[8]

NOTES

1. *Études cristallographiques* (Paris, 1866), reprinting papers published during 1850 and 1851.
2. *Entwickelung einer Theorie der Krystallstruktur* (Leipzig, 1879) and "Erweiterung der Theorie der Krystallstruktur," in *Zeitschrift für Krystallographie und Mineralogie*, **14** (1888), 426–446.
3. The importance of the Mallard-Bravais viewpoint on symmetry is acknowledged by Arthur Schönflies in "Bemerkungen über Theorien der Krystallstruktur," in *Zeitschrift für physikalische Chemie*, **9** (1892), 158–170.
4. C. Klein, in *Neues Jahrbuch für Mineralogie, Geologie und Paläontologie* (1880), **2**, 1–5; *ibid.* (1886), **1**, 1–5.
5. E.g., in Edmond Fremy, *Encyclopédie chimique*, I (Paris, 1882), 610–774; and *Revue scientifique*, **24** (1887), 129–138, 165–171.
6. Summarized in *Leçons de cristallographie* (Paris, 1926).
7. Mallard, *Traité*, II, chs. 8–9; refuted in J. R. Partington, *Advanced Treatise on Physical Chemistry*, IV (London, 1953), p. 355.
8. Translated from Wrybouff's memorial, p. 249.

BIBLIOGRAPHY

I. ORIGINAL WORKS. A complete bibliography is given in Lapparent's memorial (see below). In addition to *Explication des phénomènes optiques anomaux* (Paris, 1877), repr. from *Annales des mines et des carburants*, 7th ser., **10** (1876), 60–196; and *Traité de cristallographie géométrique et physique*, 2 vols. and atlas (Paris, 1879–1884), the most important later crystallographic papers may be "Les groupements cristallins," in *Revue scientifique*, **24** (1887), 129–138, 165–171; "Sur l'isomorphisme des chlorates et des azotates et sur la vraisemblance de la quasi-identité de l'arrangement moléculaire dans toutes les substances cristallisées," in *Bulletin de la Société française de minéralogie*, **7** (1884), 349–401; and "Sur la théorie des macles," *ibid.*, **8** (1885), 452–469. The work with Le Chatelier on mine safety is given in a series of papers in *Annales des mines* (many of which are summarized in short notes in the *Comptes rendus de l'Académie des sciences* [1879–1889]), notably three memoirs in *Annales des mines*, 8th ser., **4** (1883), 276–568; and in a series of commission reports published by the government and listed in the catalog of the *Bibliothèque nationale*, CIV (Paris, 1930), 593–594. One notable paper not listed in Lapparent's bibliography is "De la définition de la température dans la théorie mécanique de la chaleur et de l'interprétation physique du second principle fondamental de cette théorie," in *Comptes rendus de l'Académie des sciences*, **75** (1872), 1479–1484.

II. SECONDARY LITERATURE. Mallard's life and works were well covered from diverse viewpoints in a dozen contemporary memorials, most of which are listed in the Royal Society *Catalogue of Scientific Papers*, XVI, 1028. The most informative are those by A. de Lapparent, in *Annales des mines*, 9th ser., **7** (1895), 267–303, with bibliography; G. Wrybouff, in *Bulletin de la Société française de minéralogie*, **7** (1894), 241–266, with bibliography and portrait; and P. Termier, in *Bulletin de la Société géologique de France*, **23** (1895), 179–191. Mallard is barely mentioned by his contemporary Paul Groth in the latter's *Entwicklungsgeschichte der mineralogischen Wissenschaften* (Berlin, 1926; repr. 1970), and his contributions do not seem to have been reviewed elsewhere.

WILLIAM T. HOLSER

MALLET, ROBERT (*b*. Dublin, Ireland, 3 June 1810; *d*. London, England, 5 November 1881), *technology, seismology*.

Mallet's father, John Mallet, of Devonshire, owned a plumbing business and copper and brass foundry in Dublin, from which he made a large fortune. He married a cousin, also named Mallet. Robert, their only son, was educated at Bective House in Dublin; he entered Trinity College, Dublin, in December 1826, graduating with a B.A. in 1830. After joining his father's company, he built it up into one of the most important engineering works in Ireland; he himself became an inventive designer-engineer and versatile researcher.

In November 1831 Mallet married Cordelia Watson, who died in 1854. He remarried in 1861. He left two daughters and three sons. Mallet's eyesight deteriorated seriously after the winter of 1871–1872.

In 1861 Mallet settled in London as a consulting engineer. He edited four volumes of the *Practical Mechanic's Journal* (1865–1869), for which he prepared the *Journal Record of the Great Exhibition* (London, 1862), and, in collaboration with R. F. Fairlie, *The Safes' Challenge Contest at the International Exhibition of Paris in 1867* (1868).

Mallet was a member of many organizations, including the Royal Irish Academy (1832), the British Association (1835), the Institution of Civil Engineers of Ireland (1839, associate; 1842, member; 1866, president), and the Royal Geological Society of Ireland (1847, president). He became a fellow of the Royal Society of London in 1854 and later served as a member of its council. Mallet also received an honorary doctor of laws degree from Trinity College and was awarded numerous scientific medals.

Among Mallet's notable technical accomplishments were the erection of the roof of St. George's Church in Dublin with hoists of his own design; his "manumotive" for baggage transport, which, with eight men driving it, covered the five miles from Dublin to Kingstown in twenty minutes (1834); his procedure for the electromagnetic separation of brass and iron filings; and his method of bleaching turf for the manufacture of paper (1835). His multifarious engineering projects also involved work on steam-driven printing plants, bridges, hydraulic presses, ventilators and heaters, brewery machinery, railroads, dock gates, viaducts, lighthouses, and coal mines. Mallet worked out a plan to supply Dublin with water from six reservoirs on the Dodder, for which he carried out the surveying at his own expense in 1841. His name is associated with the "buckled plates," which he patented in 1852, used for flooring and later for railroad ties.

From 1850 to 1856 Mallet worked on the design of heavy guns. With his comprehensive account entitled *The Physical Conditions Involved in the Construction of Artillery, With an Investigation of the Relative and Absolute Values of the Materials Principally Employed, and of Some Hitherto Unexplained Causes of the Destruction of Cannon in Service* (Dublin, 1856), he created a basis for later books on ordnance and on casting and founding.

In view of these many technical achievements and the demands of running such a large business, it is remarkable that Mallet still found time for scientific research in the most varied fields. Among his scientific papers are investigations of the "seed-dispersing apparatus" of *Erodium moschatum* (1836); the blackening of photographic paper due to the radiation of glowing cinders (1837); the photochemical bleaching of caustic potash; the effect of boiling on organic and inorganic substances (1838); the improvement of the manufacture of optical glasses; and the application of the "electrotype process in conducting organic analysis" (1843).

The author of fundamental works on the effect of air and water—especially pure and polluted seawater—on wrought and cast iron and also on steel (1836–1873), Mallet is one of the founders of research on corrosion. In this way and through his studies dealing with the physical properties and electrochemical relationships of copper and tin alloys with tin and zinc, he made important early contributions to the science of materials. He also dealt with the state of aggregation of alloys (1840–1844), with the coefficients of elasticity and with failure in wrought iron (1859), and with the expansion of cast iron (1875).

Completely aside from his profession as an engineer, Mallet was interested in the structure of County Galway trap and the columnar structure of basalts, and in glacier movement, the plasticity of glacial ice, and the lamination of Irish slates.

Stimulated by Charles Lyell's description of the earthquake in Calabria in 1783, Mallet explained its "vorticose movement" by the position of the center of gravity, adhesion, or—as the case may be—friction, and the inertia of the squared stone affected by the tremor (1846). In the same year he presented to the Royal Irish Academy his *On the Dynamics of Earthquakes*. In this work he differentiated the so-called earth wave, great sea wave, forced sea wave, and aerial or sound wave. Mallet considered local elevations of portions of the earth's solid crust to be the cause of earthquakes. He produced an experimental seismograph in 1846. Important elements of his model, which was never actually used, were incorporated in the seismograph that Luigi Palmieri made in 1855. Between 1850 and 1861 Mallet set off explosions in different locations to determine the rate of travel of seismic waves in sand (825 feet per second), solid granite (1,665 feet per second), and quartzite (1,162 feet per second). According to A. Sieberg (1924), Mallet should be considered the founder of the physics of earthquakes. The term "seismology" we owe to Mallet, as well as "seismic focus," "angle of emergence," "isoseismal line," and "meizoseismal area."

Mallet presented his most important seismic results in four *Report[s] to the British Association* (1850, 1851, 1852–1854, 1858) and in four editions of the *Admiralty Manual of Scientific Enquiry* (1849, 1851, 1859, 1871). Between them, they contain an extensive catalog—which he prepared and debated with his son, John W. Mallet—of 6,831 earthquakes reported between 1606 B.C. and A.D. 1858 and his seismic map of the world. In February 1858 he visited the region of the Neapolitan earthquake of 16 December 1857. In 1869, with Oldham, he developed a spherical projection seismograph.

Through his work in seismology, Mallet encountered possible connections with vulcanicity. He eventually studied the problem of the emergence of volcanic foci in particular. In 1862 he published "Proposed Measurement of the Temperatures of Active Volcanic Foci to the Greatest Attainable Depth . . ." (*Report of the British Association for the Advancement of Science* for 1862). In 1872 he submitted his principal paper on vulcanicity, "Volcanic Energy; an Attempt to Develop Its True Origin and Cosmical Relations" (*Philosophical Transactions of the Royal Society*, **163**, no. 1 [1873], 147–227).

In 1870 Mallet made exhaustive analyses of sixteen different types of rock. Through computation he concluded that (1) "the crushing of the earth's solid crust affords a supply of energy sufficient to account for terrestrial vulcanicity"; and (2) that "the necessary amount of crushing falls within the limits that may be admitted as due to terrestrial contraction by secular refrigeration" (*ibid.*, p. 214). Although this theory received little attention in the following years, it nevertheless contained some ingenious conceptions that were taken over by later researchers. In any case, it deserves recognition as an early example of the mathematical utilization of experimental findings in the service of geological speculation.

BIBLIOGRAPHY

I. ORIGINAL WORKS. A list of eighty-five (incorrectly numbered ninety-one) papers by Mallet is in Royal Society *Catalogue of Scientific Papers*, IV, 205–208; VIII, 314; X, 703–704. See also Poggendorff, III, pt. 2, 861–862.

In addition to works cited in the text, Mallet wrote *Great Neapolitan Earthquake of 1857: The First Principles of Observational Seismology*, 2 vols. (London, 1862). Works which he translated and to which he contributed include H. Law, *Civil Engineering* (London, 1869), with Mallet's notes and illustrations; G. Field, *The Rudiments of Colours and of Colouring* (London, 1870), revised and partly rewritten by Mallet; L. L. de Koninck, *A Practical Manual of Chemical Analysis and Assaying* (London, 1872), which he edited and to which he contributed notes; and L. Palmieri, *The Eruption of Vesuvius in 1872* (London, 1873), with notes and intro. by Mallet.

II. SECONDARY LITERATURE. For obituaries of Mallet, see *Engineer*, **52** (1881), 352–353, 371–372, 389–390; *Minutes of Proceedings of the Institution of Civil Engineers*, **68** (1882), 297–304; *Proceedings of the Royal Society*, **33** (1882), 19–20; and *Quarterly Journal of the Geological Society of London*, **38** (1882), 54–56.

See also (listed chronologically) *Dictionary of National Biography*, XXXV (1893), 429–430, which gives Mallet's place of death as Enmore, Surrey; R. Ehlert, "Zusammenstellung, Erläuterung und kritische Beurtheilung der wichtigsten Seismometer," in *Beiträge zur Geophysik*, **3** (1898), 350–475; K. A. von Zittel, *Geschichte der Geologie und Paläontologie bis Ende des 19. Jahrhunderts* (Munich, 1899); Charles Davison, *The Founders of Seismology* (Cambridge, 1927); and L. Mintrop, "100 Jahre physikalische Erdbebenforschung und Sprengtechnik," in *Naturwissenschaften*, **34** (1947), 257–262, 289–295.

WALTHER FISCHER

MALOUIN, PAUL-JACQUES (*b*. Caen, France, 29 June 1701; *d*. Versailles, France, 3 January 1778), *medicine, chemistry*.

Malouin was born into a venerable Caen family. His parents, N. Malouin and N. Poupart, wanted him to pursue a legal career. He was sent to Paris to study law, but turned instead to scientific pursuits and, after a brief return to his native city from 1730 to 1733, settled in the French capital to teach and practice medicine. A relative of Fontenelle, permanent secretary of the Académie Royale des Sciences, Malouin quickly attracted a prominent clientele, which included members of the royal family. He emphasized the importance of hygiene and the comprehensive application of chemical remedies and theory to medicine, presenting his findings formally as professor of medicine at the Collège Royal from 1767 to 1775. In his will he provided for the establishment of an annual public meeting at the Faculty of Medicine in Paris to apprise the nation of the most recent medical discoveries and advances.

Malouin complemented his medical career with an active interest in the developing science of chemistry. Elected to the Academy as *adjoint chimiste* in 1742, he became *pensionnaire chimiste* in 1766 and director of the Academy for 1772; he was made a fellow of the Royal Society of London in 1753. Malouin's chemical studies are relatively unimportant, although several memoirs read in 1742 and 1743 on zinc and tin were then useful. A contributor to the early volumes of Diderot's *Encyclopédie*, Malouin wrote a number of competent articles on various chemical topics: "Alchimie," "Antimoine," "Acide," and "Alkali." He worked frequently with Bourdelin, professor of chemistry at the Jardin du Roi, and often lectured in his stead. He also contributed important articles on milling and baking in the Academy's series *Description des Arts et Métiers,* applying chemical theory and method to those two trades, vital in the economic and social life of the *ancien régime*. Malouin's methods for grinding wheat and mixing flour yielded bread of higher quality.

BIBLIOGRAPHY

I. ORIGINAL WORKS. Malouin's major works are *Traité de chimie, contenant la manière de préparer les remèdes qui sont les plus en usage dans la pratique de la médecine* (Paris, 1734); and *Chimie médicinale, contenant la manière de préparer les remèdes les plus usités, et la méthode pour la guérison des maladies*, 2 vols. (Paris, 1750; 2nd ed., 1755). His work on milling and baking, entitled *Description et détails des arts du meunier, du vermicelier et du boulanger, avec une histoire abrégée de la boulangerie et un dictionnaire*

de ces arts (Paris, 1767), appeared as a volume in the series *Description des Arts et Métiers, faites ou approuvées par Messieurs de l'Académie Royale des Sciences.*

II. SECONDARY LITERATURE. The best biographical source for Malouin is M. Condorcet, "Éloge de M. Malouin," in A. Condorcet O'Connor and M. F. Arago, eds., *Oeuvres de Condorcet*, II (Paris, 1847), 320–332. Consult also Jean-Charles Des Essartz, *Éloge de Malouin* (Paris, 1778); and F. Hoefer, ed., *Nouvelle biographie générale*, XXXIII (Paris, 1860), 97–98. A brief assessment of Malouin's chemical work is in J. R. Partington, *A History of Chemistry*, III (London, 1961), 72.

MARTIN FICHMAN

MALPIGHI, MARCELLO (*b*. Crevalcore, Bologna, Italy, baptized 10 March 1628; *d*. Rome, Italy, 29 November 1694), *medicine, microscopic and comparative anatomy, embryology*.

Malpighi was the son of Marcantonio Malpighi and Maria Cremonini. In 1646 he entered the University of Bologna, where his tutor was the Peripatetic philosopher Francesco Natali. On Natali's advice Malpighi in 1649 began to study medicine. He first attended the school conducted by Bartolomeo Massari, then that of Andrea Mariani; with Carlo Fracassati he was among the nine students allowed to attend the dissections and vivisections that Massari conducted in his own house.

Malpighi graduated as doctor of medicine and philosophy in 1653; three years later, still in Bologna, he began teaching as a lecturer in logic, but toward the end of the year he was called to the chair of theoretical medicine at the University of Pisa. The three years that he spent in Pisa were fundamental to the formation of Malpighi's science. Influenced by Giovanni Alfonso Borelli, who was then professor of mathematics in the same university, Malpighi turned from Peripateticism to a "free and Democritean philosophy." He also participated in animal dissections in Borelli's home laboratory and, through Borelli, entered the scientific orbit of the school of Galileo, which was at that time best represented in Tuscany itself, in the Accademia del Cimento (1657–1667).

By 1659, however, Malpighi was no longer able to tolerate the Pisan climate. He therefore returned to Bologna to become extraordinary lecturer in theoretical medicine. Toward the end of 1660 he assumed the ordinary lectureship at the university in practical medicine. In 1662 he went to the University of Messina, where he held the principal chair of medicine; four years later he returned to Bologna to lecture in practical medicine again. A letter of 28 December 1667 asked him to undertake scientific correspondence with the Royal Society of London; Malpighi agreed, and the society subsequently supervised the printing of all his later works. In 1691 Malpighi was called to Rome as chief physician to Pope Innocent XII. He died there, in his apartments in the Quirinal Palace.

Malpighi's first—and fundamental—work is the *De pulmonibus*, two short letters which he sent to Borelli in Pisa and which were published in Bologna in 1661. After his return to Bologna in 1659 Malpighi, together with Carlo Fracassati, continued to conduct dissections and vivisections. In the course of these he used the microscope to make fundamental discoveries about the lungs, which he quickly announced in the letters to Borelli.

According to the traditional quaternary system, the lungs were fleshy viscera, endowed with a sanguine nature and hot-humid temperament. Having subjected them to microscopical examination, Malpighi found them to be an aggregate of membranous alveoli opening into the ultimate tracheobronchial ramifications and surrounded by a capillary network. He had thus discovered the connections, until then sought in vain, between the arteries and the veins. His observations were of basic significance for two reasons—the pulmonary parenchyma (and subsequently the other parenchymas) for the first time could be seen to have a structure, and the observation of the capillaries confirmed the theory of the circulation of the blood and assured its general acceptance.

Malpighi's mastery of microscopic technique was apparent even in *De pulmonibus*. He used instruments of different magnifying powers and made observations with both reflected and transmitted light. He prepared specimens in a number of ways, including drying, boiling, insufflation (of the tracheobronchial tree or of systems of blood vessels), vascular perfusion, deaeration (by crushing), corrosion, or a combination of these methods. In choosing to examine the frog, Malpighi was able to avail himself of the so-called "microscope of nature." He was able to visualize, with a relatively small magnification, so minute a feature as the capillary (the capillary network itself is so fine in mammals that Malpighi was never able to observe it with the microscopes available to him). Malpighi acutely remarked that nature is accustomed "to undertake its great works only after a series of attempts at lower levels, and to outline in imperfect animals the plan of perfect animals."

Malpighi saw the structure of the lung as air cells surrounded by a network of blood vessels; he interpreted this structure as a well-devised mechanism to insure the mixing of particles of chyle with particles of blood—in other words, for the conversion of chyle to blood (then called hematosis), a function that the Galenists attributed to the liver. Jean Pecquet had shown in 1647 that the chyle, instead of being conveyed to the liver, was introduced into the blood in the superior vena cava, at a point shortly before that vessel reached the heart, and was then distributed to the lungs through the pulmonary artery.

In the four years, 1662–1666, that he spent at the University of Messina, Malpighi enthusiastically continued his researches on fundamental structures, making use also of marine animals from the Strait of Messina. He published the results of these researches in a series of treatises in 1665–1666. These were devoted mainly to three major topics—neurology, adenology, and hematology.

The short works *De lingua* (Bologna, 1665) and *De externo tactus organo* (Naples, 1665) are closely linked to each other. In *De lingua*, Malpighi reported peeling two layers from the surface of the tongue—the horny layer and the reticular (or mucous) layer that is now named for him—and thus exposing the papillary body, in which he distinguished three orders of papillae. He speculated that these papillae could be reached through pores in the epithelium and thereby stimulated by "sapid" particles dissolved in the saliva, the organismal liquid the significance of which had been recognized just a few years previously by Nicholas Steno. It is easy here to recognize the influence of Galileo, who in *Il saggiatore* (1623) had suggested that the very small taste particles, when "placed on the upper surface of the tongue and, mixed with its moisture, penetrate it and carry the tastes, pleasant or otherwise, according to the differences in the touching of the different shapes of these tiny corpuscles, and according to whether they are few or many, faster or slower."

Malpighi's discovery of the sensory receptors—the papillae of the tongue were followed by the cutaneous (or tactile) papillae—formed part of a wider neuroanatomical research. In the treatise *De cerebro*, which was published in 1665 with *De lingua*, he dealt mainly with the white substance of the central nervous system, which he found to be composed of the same fibers that form the nerves. Malpighi conceived of these fibers as long, fine channels filled with a liquid—the nerve fluid—which was secreted by the cortical gray matter, or, more precisely, by the cortical glands. In his later treatise *De cerebri cortice* (1666), Malpighi claimed to have demonstrated these glands, but his results were in fact due to an artifact.

On the basis of his observations, whether true or false, Malpighi in any event succeeded in constructing a mechanism to encompass the entire neural course from the cortex of the brain to the peripheral endings of the nerves: the neuron, in which the transmission of the nervous impulse could be equated with the transmission of a mechanical impulse through a liquid mass in accordance with Pascal's principle.

During his years in Messina, Malpighi made further investigations into the structure of another mechanism fundamental to his iatromechanical atomism: the gland, or secretion machine. The function of this mechanism was to select specific particles of blood brought by an afferent artery, to separate them from others flowing back through an efferent vein, and to introduce them, as an independent liquid, into an excretory duct. The sieve may thus be used as a convenient model ("cribrum" and "secretio" are even etymologically the same); it offers an a priori explanation of the operation of the secreting mechanism by postulating a proportionality of form and dimension between the pores and the particles to be separated. Malpighi certainly recognized that he could not investigate this "minima simplexque meatuum structura" directly, but he did not abandon his search for the mechanism that might contain the pores. This he localized, a priori, at the point at which the smallest ramifications of the artery, vein, and duct are joined together.

Malpighi continued to search for ever finer and more minute structures within the glandular parenchyma. These investigations were stimulated by the discovery of the pancreatic duct (by Wirsüng in 1642), the testicular duct (by Highmore in 1651), the submandibular duct (by Wharton in 1656), and the parotid duct (by Steno in 1660).

The secreting mechanism devised by Malpighi was based on a follicle that, on one hand, is continuous into the secretory tubule, and, on the other, is surrounded by the ultimate ramifications of the arteries, veins, and nerves. In passing from the artery to the vein, the blood channel and the contiguous glandular follicle are permeable to the particles that must be eliminated and impermeable to the particles of venous blood. By analogy with the sieve, and without invoking vitalistic arguments, secretion can thus be explained in purely mechanical terms. In *De renibus* Malpighi set down a series of convincing observations in support of his system. He skillfully made use of staining techniques by affusion to show the renal tubules, both straight and twisted, while by injecting coloring into the arteries he was able to demonstrate the tufts of vessels attached to the branches of the interlobular arteries. He believed, however, that the ampullar extremities of the renal tubules (the Malpighi corpuscles) were enclosed within the vascular tufts.

Malpighi reiterated and developed his theory of glandular structure in the epistolary dissertation *De structura glandularum conglobatarum consimiliumque*

partium, dated June 1688 and published in London the following year. Although the "conglobate" glands of Sylvius—that is, the lymph nodes—are emphasized in the title, less than half the treatise is devoted to them. For the rest, Malpighi reported additional observations on glands that were already known and considerably expanded his earlier work on the secretory mechanism. He also included remarks on the glandular membranes (later classified by Bichat as serous and mucous).

Having established the capillary circulation and devised a mechanism to explain hematosis; having defined and systematized a nervous mechanism endowed with highly acute sensory receptors; and having postulated a secreting mechanism, Malpighi turned to an analysis of the blood—the universal fluid necessary to all these machines. His chief hematological treatise, *De polypo cordis*, appeared in 1666 (or 1668?) as an appendix to *De viscerum structura*.

"Heart polyps" had been identified for some time and with a certain frequency, especially in patients who had died from severe cardiorespiratory insufficiency. Previous researchers had explained such polyps in various ways, even invoking traditional humoral theory. Malpighi, however, considered these lesions to be the result of an intravitam process of coagulation, which had as its model the coagulation of blood extracted from the organism. The study of coagulum was thus fundamental, and culminated in Malpighi's demonstration that the "phlogistic crust" was, despite its whitish color, derived from the whole blood that "confuses our poor eyes with its purple [color]." To this end he broke the blood down into its component parts (a method that he had successfully employed in his studies of viscera and organs) by continuing artificially in the coagulum the separation (into coagulum and serum) that occurs naturally when blood is extracted from an organism. Malpighi found that the coagulum, after repeated washings, "from being intensely red and black becomes white, while the water is reddened by the extracted particles of color." The phlogistic crust thus corresponds in large part to the bleached-out coagulum; the difference between them is only quantitative (that is, it lies in the amount of coloring material that each contains) and not qualitative, as supposed by the humoral theory.

Microscopic examination of a clot of coagulum also enabled Malpighi to observe, as separate components, the interlacing white fibers that arise from the conglutination of much smaller but similarly shaped filaments (a process similar to that which occurs in the crystallization of salts) and the red fluid that fills the interstices of these meshes of fibers. With the microscope Malpighi could perceive that the red fluid was composed of a host of red "atoms"; it is thus clear that the discovery of the red corpuscles—although variously attributed by a number of authors who would seem to be unaware of their unmistakable description in the *De polypo cordis*—is surely Malpighi's.

Malpighi was able to utilize even a morbid deviation such as the heart polyp toward an investigation of a normal phenomenon. He studied aberrations to cast light upon normal organisms. In the same way, he studied simple animals to understand more complex ones, writing that the

> study of insects, fish, and the first unelaborated outlines of animals has been used in this century . . . to discover much more than was achieved by previous ages, which limited their investigations to the bodies of perfect animals only.

Having stated this methodological formulation, Malpighi applied it in his work on the silkworm, *De bombyce* (London, 1669), and in the later embryological and botanical works that were edited by the Royal Society for publication in London in the 1670's.

Malpighi was led to do embryological research through an analogy with the artisan who "in building machines must first manufacture the individual parts, so that the pieces are first seen separately, which must then be fitted together," as he asserted in *De formatione pulli in ovo* (1673). In *De bombyce*, he had carefully observed the artisan nature construct each of the three stages—larva, chrysalis, and moth—through which the silkworm is formed. He further remarked on the specific apparatuses with which the silkworm is provided, among them the air ducts (tracheae) and the blood duct with a number of pulsating centers (corcula).

With the *De formatione* and the subsequent appendix to it (1675), Malpighi brought a fine structural content to embryology, which became a valuable aid to illustrating the morphology of the adult. So, too, the study of lower forms of life clarifies the morphology of more highly developed ones. Malpighi noted that the study "of the first unelaborated outlines of animals in the course of development" is particularly fruitful because the artisan nature forms them separately before combining them with one another. In the embryo, for example, the miliary glands, which will merge to form the liver, are still distinguishable as the cecal sacs (which in crustaceans remain distinct). From this point on, the paths of embryogenesis and phylogenesis were destined to cross.

The chick fetus develops in a manner similar to that of the plant embryo contained within a plant seed: from being enveloped at the start, it simultaneously "evolves" and grows in size as a result of the influx of food (yolk and albumen) liquefied by the warmth of the nest or by the fermentation process set in motion by fecundation. This notion, that embryogenesis consists of the development of constituents that in some sense existed prior to incubation, but which are nevertheless secondary to fecundation (see Adelmann), since they are induced by the "colliquamentum" of the pellucid area by the aura—or spiritous emanation—of the male seed, gave fuel to the doctrine of preformation, which then became a strong alternative to the traditional doctrine of epigenesis.

Malpighi's chief embryological discoveries were the vascular area embraced by the terminal sinus, the cardiac tube and its segmentation, the aortic arches, the somites, the neural folds and the neural tube, the cerebral vesicles, the optic vesicles, the protoliver, the glands of the prestomach, and the feather follicles.

Malpighi clearly stated his comparative method in the introduction to *Anatomes plantarum idea* (1675):

> The nature of things, enveloped in shadows, is revealed only by the analogical method ["cum solo analogismo pateat"]. Hence the necessity to follow it entirely, so as to be able to analyze the most complex mechanisms by means of simpler ones that are more easily accessible to the experience of the senses. It is the most important and most perfect things, however, that are the most immediately attractive to human genius, since they are the most necessary to human utility and therefore most worthy of consideration.

This had been true in the early work of even Malpighi himself. With youthful ardor, he had flung himself into the investigation of higher animals,

> . . . but these, enveloped in their own shadows, remain in obscurity; hence it is necessary to study them through the analogues provided by simple animals ["simplicium analogismo egent"]. I was therefore attracted to the investigation of insects; but this too has its difficulties. So, in the end, I turned to the investigation of plants, so that by an extensive study of this kingdom I might find a way to return to early studies, beginning with vegetant nature. But perhaps not even this will be enough, since the yet simpler kingdom of minerals and elements should take precedence. At this point the undertaking becomes immense, and absolutely out of all proportion to my strength.

If Malpighi retreated before the demands of making a systematic study of minerals, he nonetheless undertook the study of plants with extraordinary success. *Anatome plantarum*, which appeared in London in two parts (1675 and 1679), earned him acclaim (along with Nehemiah Grew) as the founder of the microscopic study of plant anatomy. In his investigation Malpighi found that plants also have a mechanical structure: he described their ducts (some of which he compared to the tracheae of insects) and their basic "cellular" structure (an aggregate of "utricles"), which Hooke had already described (as "cellulae") in the *Micrographia*.

In his later studies Malpighi used the "microscope of nature" as it was manifest in natural anomalies, and in particular in monstrosities and pathological aberrations. For example, he investigated warts and found the dermic papillae to be strikingly enlarged. Anomalous structures may be not only enlarged but also so arranged as to clarify individual components in the normal state. Thus, in onychogryphosis the lamellar structure of the normal nail is apparent; while in the jugular horn of a calf the reinforced projections of the papillae stand out, whereas in the normal horn they are concealed.

The correspondence between normal and anomalous horn is not only structural, but also morphogenetic, since the metamorphosis of the cutaneous strata into the horn is caused by mechanical stimulation. Under normal conditions this stimulation is exerted by the bony excrescence of the frontal bone: in the jugular horn it is the result of the irritation of the yoke and of the resulting saccate accumulation of fluid in the subcutaneous tissue. Malpighi adduced a similar mechanical morphogenesis in the polycystic kidney: the glandular follicles (Malpighi's corpuscles) appear enlarged and distinct in this condition because they have been dilated by urostasis secondary to a blockage of the outflow channels. Similarly, in the nodules of the cirrhotic liver, the hepatic follicles are enlarged by the "microscope of nature," as are lymphatic follicles that have been altered by disease (usually tuberculosis).

In *De polypo cordis* and subsequent treatises it is possible to identify explicit references to pathological material obtained during autopsy. Malpighi recognized the importance of local lesions, and his pathological investigations were considerably enhanced by the microscopic anatomy of the 1660's, of which he himself was the most important investigator. The discovery of minute functional mechanisms, which in the aggregate give rise to the vital event, gave abnormal structures an added significance. The anatomical investigation of the breakdown of any of these mechanisms—even if only in such macroscopic equivalents as the lesions visible in the dissecting room—demonstrated the effect of such disturbances on the economy of the organism as a whole. Such clinical manifestations are proportional to the place and nature of the lesion; subtle anatomy thus gave rise to the anatomical investigation of the causes and localizations of disease (to paraphrase the title of the later work of Morgagni).

In his medical anatomy (or practical anatomy, as it was then called), in his emphasis on those aspects of anatomy proper to medical practice, and above all, in his use of anatomoclinical parallelism, Malpighi shaped the work of at least two generations. His pupils included Albertini and Valsalva; the *De sedibus et causis morborum per anatomen indagatis* of their pupil Morgagni represents a most important continuation of Malpighi's work.

Malpighi also made considerable contributions to vegetable pathology. In particular he made a study of plant galls, which he found to be a morbid alteration of the structural plan of the infested plant. Finally, Malpighi wrote an important methodological work, *De recentiorum medicorum studio*, in which he supported rational medicine against the empiricists. Rational medicine was also the basis for his many *Consultationes*, which attest to the medical practice that he carried out concurrently with his biological researches.

BIBLIOGRAPHY

I. ORIGINAL WORKS. Malpighi's most important works are *De pulmonibus observationes anatomicae* (Bologna, 1661); *De pulmonibus epistola altera* (Bologna, 1661); *Epistolae anatomicae de cerebro, ac lingua … Quibus Anonymi accessit exercitatio de omento, pinguedine, et adiposis ductibus* (Bologna, 1665); *De externo tactus organo anatomica observatio* (Naples, 1665); *De viscerum structura exercitatio anatomica … Accedit dissertatio eiusdem de polypo cordis* (Bologna, 1666); *Dissertatio epistolica de bombyce* (London, 1669); *Dissertatio epistolica de formatione pulli in ovo* (London, 1673); *Anatomes plantarum pars prima. Cui subjungitur appendix iteratas et auctas de ovo incubato observationes continens* (London, 1675), which is prefaced by *Anatomes plantarum idea*, dated November 1671; *Anatomes plantarum pars altera* (London, 1679); "Dissertatio epistolica varii argumenti" [addressed to Jacob Spon], in *Philosophical Transactions of the Royal Society of London*, **14** (1684), 601–608, 630–646; *Opera omnia* (London, 1686; repr. Leiden, 1687); *De structura glandularum conglobatarum consimiliumque partium epistola* (London, 1689); *Opera posthuma* (London, 1697; repr. Amsterdam, 1698); *Consultationum medicinalium centuria prima* (Padua, 1713); and *Consultationum medicarum nonnullarumque dissertationum collectio* (Venice, 1747), written with J. M. Lancisi.

A recent selection is Luigi Belloni, ed., *Opere scelte* (Turin, 1967), with an introduction containing a useful synopsis of Malpighi's work.

II. SECONDARY LITERATURE. A definitive biography is Howard B. Adelmann, *Marcello Malpighi and the Evolution of Embryology* (Ithaca, N. Y., 1966).

LUIGI BELLONI

MALTHUS, THOMAS ROBERT (*b.* near Guildford, Surrey, England, 13 February 1766; *d.* near Bath, England, 23 December 1834), *political economy.*

Malthus is known in the history of science almost exclusively for his influence on Charles Darwin, exerted almost accidentally. His life, work, and friends were mainly centered on social conditions and political economy, and his work on population was part of these. He did have early training in mathematics, however, and based his arguments on the careful analysis of observed data.

Robert Malthus (he appears never to have been called Thomas) was the sixth child of seven born to Daniel Malthus and his wife, the former Henrietta Catherine Graham. Daniel Malthus, a scholar and a friend and admirer of Rousseau, provided a stimulating home life and education for the boy, and later sent him to study with Richard Graves at Claverton and at the Dissenting Academy of Warrington under Gilbert Wakefield.

In 1784 Malthus went up to Jesus College, Cambridge, where his tutor was William Frend. He read for the mathematical tripos and graduated in 1788, being ninth wrangler; but he also read widely in French and English history and literature and in Newtonian physics. He had already shown his interest in the practical rather than the abstract. He played games and lived a full social life, apparently unaffected by his cleft palate and harelip. The friends he made at Cambridge influenced the rest of his life; the most important was William Otter (1768–1840), later bishop of Chichester. Malthus and Otter traveled extensively in Europe and maintained the relationship after their marriages. Malthus' son, Henry, married Otter's daughter Sophia. Otter probably wrote the memorial to Malthus in Bath Abbey, and he certainly wrote the "Memoir" published with the second edition of the *Principles of Political Economy.*

Malthus followed graduation with ordination, but more in the tradition of the younger sons of English gentry entering the Church than as a step consistent with his intellectual development. For some years he held a curacy at Okewood Chapel in Surrey, near the home of his parents at Albury, and was active in his pastoral functions from 1792 to 1794. He showed a genuine interest in and concern for the local people and an understanding of their problems, a sympathy which makes surprising his later references to the laboring class almost as though they were a community apart. From 1803 until his death he held a sinecure as rector of Walesbury in Lincolnshire.

In 1799 Malthus and Otter, together with friends from Jesus College, E. D. Clarke and J. M. Cripps, traveled through northern Germany and Norway. Afterward Malthus and Otter went on to Sweden, Finland, and Russia. Malthus' detailed diaries of these journeys provided some of the evidence he needed to develop his theory of population growth. Clarke also published a record of his travels. In 1800 Malthus' parents died; by 1802 he was traveling again, this time in France and Switzerland, in a party that included his cousin Harriet Eckersall.

Jesus College elected Malthus to a fellowship in 1793, and he was resident intermittently until he had to resign upon his marriage to Harriet Eckersall in 1804. They had one son, Henry, who followed his father into the ministry, and two daughters: Emily, who married, and Lucy, who died before her father. About the time of Malthus' marriage, the East India Company founded a new college, first at Hertford and then at Haileybury, to give a general education to staff members before they went on service overseas. The first known professorship of history and political economy was established there, and Malthus was invited to fill the post. He took it up in 1805, and it gave him the security of a home and an income that enabled him to spend the rest of his life writing and lecturing.

In order to teach political economy, Malthus needed to extend his knowledge. He wrote two pamphlets on the Corn Laws (1814, 1815); a short, unexceptional tract on rent (1815); statements on Haileybury (1813, 1817); and a major work, *Principles of Political Economy* (1820). This included an analogy of his population theory with the quantity of funds designed for the maintenance of labor and the prudential habits of the laboring classes.

In 1819 the Royal Society elected Malthus to a fellowship. He was also a member of the French Institute and the Berlin Academy, and a founding member of the Statistical Society (1834). In 1827 he was called upon to give evidence on emigration before a committee of the House of Commons.

Although their life was quiet, Robert and Henrietta Malthus traveled and entertained their many friends, including David Ricardo, Harriet Martineau, Otter, and William Empson, who was also at Haileybury. Malthus managed, in spite of the controversy flowing around him, to keep a reputation as a warm, charming, and lively companion.

Principle of Population. Malthus' first writing was an unpublished pamphlet, *The Crisis* (extracts are quoted by Otter). Stimulated by Pitt's Poor Law Bill of 1796, he supported the proposal for children's allowances, but was already expressing unease at the current idea that an increase in population was desirable.

He was not the first to propound the theory that population tends to increase proportionately faster than the supply of food—and he freely acknowledged that he was not—nor was the first edition of his *Essay on the Principle of Population*, published anonymously in 1798, a fully worked-out thesis. He wrote: "I had for some time been aware that population and food increased in different ratios; and a vague opinion had been floating in my mind that they could only be kept equal by some species of misery or vice."

Stimulated by doubts about Pitt's policy and by publications of William Godwin, Condorcet, and others, Malthus hammered out the *Essay* in discussions with his father, who accepted Godwin's belief in the potential immortality and perfectibility of man. Countering apparently rosy visions, Malthus swung to pessimism about the inevitability of poverty and the irresponsibility of the poor, an attitude which his opponents called inhuman. These observations were based at least partially on experience, for he had, as a curate, seen how in the country many births were registered but few deaths, yet, as he said, "sons of labourers are very apt to be stunted in their growth, and are a long while arriving at maturity."

The central argument of the *Essay* lies in two postulates:

"That food is necessary to the existence of man";

"That the passion between the sexes is necessary, and will remain nearly in its present state" [p. 11]; and four conclusions:

> ... that the power of population is indefinitely greater than the power in the earth to produce subsistence for man.
>
> Population, when unchecked, increases in a geometrical ratio. Subsistence increases only in arithmetical ratio. A slight acquaintance with numbers will shew the immensity of the first power in comparison with the second.
>
> By that law of our nature which makes food necessary to the life of man, the effects of those two unequal powers must be kept equal.
>
> This implies a strong and constantly operating check on population from the difficulty of subsistence [p. 13].

The postulates are taken as self-evident; the deduced consequences are examined in more detail, including the various checks on population, such as postponed marriage, infant mortality, epidemics, and famine. He presented no numerical data to support either the tendency to geometrical rate of growth of the population or the arithmetical rate of growth of food supply; these suppositions are reasonable but largely intuitive. Malthus seems also to have failed to realize that although the existence of checks is a firm deduction, there is no reason to suppose that they operate constantly.

The style of the essay—short paragraphs, pungent sentences, and an elegant but matter-of-fact air—undoubtedly contributed to the impact of the work on a community already deeply concerned with the social problems of the Industrial Revolution. It was also brief—only some 50,000 words—and the edition seems to have been small, since the work is now rare.

Malthus realized that he needed more evidence to support his views and that he had not taken sufficient account of the effects of rising standards of living. He therefore listened to criticisms and used information gathered on his travels in Europe, information which tended to be observational rather than numerical. For example, he correlated the poverty of fishermen in Drontheim with their earlier marriages and larger families—in contrast with the people of the interior parts of the country—without considering other possible variables.

Malthus' next publication, *The Present High Price of Provisions* (1800), again published anonymously, returned to the problems of poor relief. In it he made the case that linking poor relief to the cost of grain resulted in driving the price even higher. He also pointed out that whereas previously grain had been exported, there was no longer enough to go round; and therefore, assuming that agricultural production had increased or at least not declined, the population must have increased. The first census in Great Britain (1801) tended to confirm this assertion.

The second and greatly expanded edition of the *Principle of Population* was published in 1803 and carried the author's name. It provided the theoretical framework to the conclusions of the first *Essay*, with several additional chapters, including information from China and Japan as well as from countries he had visited. The argument was rewritten in terms more academic if less immediate. He explained that "everything depends on the relative proportions between population and food, and not on the absolute number of people," and that when the absolute quantity of provisions is increased, the number of consumers more than keeps up with it. If, therefore, he argued, it is not possible to maintain the production of food to satisfy the population, then the population must be kept down to the level of food; failure will result in deprivation and misery. He then went on to reexamine positive and preventive checks, introducing the new idea of voluntary "natural restraint" by late marriage and sexual abstinence before marriage. He does not seem to have considered abstinence after marriage and was strongly opposed to both abortion and contraception.

Later editions of the *Essay* were rewritten and included new appendixes of evidence, until the sixth edition (1826) required three volumes and contained some 250,000 words. Malthus' last statement on population was his *Summary View of the Principle of Population* (1830), rewritten from an article he had done for the 1824 supplement to the *Encyclopaedia Britannica*. It was condensed again to some 20,000 words, but by now it contained a greater element of social comment. There is not only the observation of tendencies but also reference to the bad structure of society and the unfavorable distribution of wealth. There have been numerous reprints and translations. Malthus has been widely read, but he has also been widely misquoted or quoted out of context. His observations have been interpreted by both his supposed followers and his enemies with overtones which suggest that his work is prescriptive rather than descriptive.

Influence on the Theory of Evolution. Malthus' *Essay* was a crucial contribution to Darwin's thinking about natural selection when he returned in 1836 from the *Beagle* voyage. In July 1837 Darwin began his "Notebook on Transmutation of Species," in which he wrote:

> In October 1838, that is, fifteen months after I had begun my systematic enquiry, I happened to read for amusement "Malthus on Population," and being well prepared to appreciate the struggle for existence ... it at once struck me that under these circumstances favourable variations would tend to be preserved and unfavourable ones to be destroyed. The result would be the formation of a new species [*Life and Letters*, I, 83].

Later, in the *Origin of Species*, he wrote that the struggle for existence "is the doctrine of Malthus applied with manifold force to the whole animal and vegetable kingdoms; for in this case there can be no artificial increase of food, and no prudential restraint from marriage" [p. 63].

Alfred Russel Wallace, who arrived at a worked-out formulation of the theory of evolution at almost precisely the same time as Darwin, acknowledged that "perhaps the most important book I read was Malthus's *Principles of Population*" (*My Life*, p. 232).

Although there were four decennial censuses before Malthus' death, he did not himself analyze the data, although he did influence Lambert Quetelet and Pierre Verhulst, who made precise statistical studies on growth of populations in developed countries and showed how the early exponential growth changed to an S curve.

Influence on Social Theory. Notwithstanding the anonymity of the first *Essay*, the authorship soon became known. Godwin wrote to Malthus immediately, and the book loosed a storm of controversy that is still rumbling. It has influenced all demographers since, as well as many students of economic theory and genetic inheritance. The early controversy is described concisely by Leslie Stephen and more fully by Bonar and McCleary. Besides Godwin, Ricardo corresponded lengthily and critically but accepted much of his theory, as did Francis Place. Ricardo and Malthus did not meet until 1811 but formed a valuable friendship. Hazlitt, Cobbett, and Coleridge attacked him for real or supposed views.

The current attitude around the end of the eighteenth century, when need for industrial workers was increasing, was that population growth was desirable in itself and that welfare provisions should encourage large families. Malthus' principle, that population tends to increase up to the limits of the means of subsistence, could be extended to suggest that if the level of subsistence were lowered by reducing state welfare provisions, then the population would naturally settle at a lower level and the working classes could avoid checks due to both misery and vice by planning and observing "prudential restraint." Malthus himself believed that the effects of the Poor Laws were harmful, but he never recommended the withdrawal of benefits and believed it to be "the duty of every individual, to use his utmost efforts to remove evil from himself, and from as large a circle as he can influence."

In 1807 Samuel Whitbread, M.P., introduced a bill to reform the Poor Laws, attempting to reduce misery and vice by a series of proposals which included a national system of education, encouragement of saving, and equalization of county taxes from which the welfare benefits were paid. Malthus wrote him an open letter, published as a pamphlet, in which he supported the plan for general education (he made it clear that the poor should be able to understand both the reason for their condition and the means of alleviating it), but he opposed vigorously the building of tenement cottages on the ground that the rents would increase the number of dependent poor except where there was a high demand for labor. If it were possible, the Poor Laws should be restricted to maintaining only the average number of children that might have been expected from each marriage, and he hoped that "the poor would be deterred from early and improvident marriages more by the fear of dependent poverty than by the contemplation of positive distress."

Malthus appears to have ignored the point that any average must have many examples above the average. Visualizing a progressive increase in the proportion of the dependent population under the laws then in effect, he admitted to being "really unable to suggest any provision which would effectually secure us against an approach to the evils here contemplated, and not be open to the objection of violating our promises to the poor." Probably this pamphlet was widely read and was a main source of the image of Malthus as a pessimist and supporter of laissez-faire political economy. He was an analyst, not a creator of imaginative legislation; and the problems he dealt with are still with us in one form or another. He was at least more clear than some politicians about "our promises to the poor." Nothing came of Whitbread's bill in its original form, and Malthus had produced no constructive amendments, so the law remained unchanged until the Poor Law Amendment Act (1834), which abolished relief outside the workhouses that were to be set up under boards of guardians for those qualified and willing to live there.

More cheerfully and positively, in his *Principles of Political Economy* (1820) Malthus was proposing investment in public works and private luxury as a means of increasing effective demand, and hence as a palliative to economic distress. The nation, he thought, must balance the power to produce and the will to consume.

After all the accretions on Malthusian principles, it was perhaps natural that Marx and Engels should have seen Malthus as an advocate of repressive treatment of the working class, rather than appreciating his anticipation of their own belief that the demand for labor regulates population.

However bitter and distorted the controversy has been, Malthus' achievement was to show that population studies, although overlaid with emotional and often irrational influences, can be examined and analyzed empirically, discussed on a rational basis, and ultimately can form the subject of positive policy making.

BIBLIOGRAPHY

I. ORIGINAL WORKS. Malthus' first major work, published anonymously, was *An Essay on the Principle of Population, as It Affects the Future Improvement of Society, With Remarks on the Speculations of Mr. Godwin, M. Condorcet, and Other Writers* (London, 1798). The 2nd ed., *An Essay on the Principle of Population, or a View of Its Past and Present Effects on Human Happiness, With an Enquiry Into Our Prospects Respecting the Future Removal or Mitigation of the Evils Which It Occasions. . . .* (London, 1803), was signed T. R. Malthus. There was a 3rd ed., with appendixes (1806); a 4th ed. (1807), reprinted with additions, 2 vols. (1817); a 5th ed., with appendixes, 3 vols. (1817); a 6th ed., with appendixes (1826); and the 7th and posthumous ed. (1872). There have been numerous other eds. and trans. It is worth mentioning the facs. repr. of the 1st ed., with notes comparing it with the 2nd, by J. Bonar (London, 1926), and a modern repr. of the

7th ed. (New York, 1969). Extracts from the 1798 and 1803 eds. were reprinted in *Parallel Chapters From the First and Second Editions of "An Essay on the Principle of Population,"* D. Ricardo, ed. (New York, 1895). The last statement was *A Summary View of the Principle of Population* (London, 1830). There was also a repr. of the first *Essay* and *Summary View*, edited, with an intro., by A. Flew (London, 1970).

Malthus' other major work is *Principles of Political Economy Considered With a View to Their Practical Applications* (London, 1820); 2nd ed. (London, 1836), with considerable alterations from the author's own MS, also contains an original memoir by Otter that includes extracts from *The Crisis*; there is also a modern repr. (New York, 1964).

Malthus' journal of his travels is P. James, ed., *The Travel Diaries of Thomas Robert Malthus* (Cambridge, 1966).

Malthus' library of 2,300 volumes is in Jesus College, Cambridge. There have clearly been many letters and other MSS available to students of Malthus, but few can be located now. The travel diaries are in Cambridge University Library. In her introduction James refers briefly to other manuscripts, including the unpublished *Recollections* of Malthus' niece, Louisa Bray.

II. SECONDARY LITERATURE. The most comprehensive bibliography is Library of Congress, *List of References on Malthus and Malthusianism* (Washington, D.C., 1920). Later eds. of Malthus' works, translations, and works on him may be traced through the national bibliographies, and particularly through the *General Catalogue of Printed Books in the British Museum*, CLI (1962), cols. 313–314, and supps. There is also an extensive bibliography for 1793–1880 in Glass (see below).

The best source for Malthus' personal life is P. James, "Biographical Sketch," in *The Travel Diaries* (see above), in which she gives full details of all her sources. Otter's "Memoir," added to the 2nd ed. of *Principles of Political Economy*, and W. Empson's review of this ed. in *Edinburgh Review*, **64** (1837), 469–506, contain much personal information. The standard biography is J. Bonar, *Malthus and His Work* (London, 1885; 2nd ed., 1924). There are also C. R. Drysdale, *The Life and Writings of Thomas R. Malthus*, 2nd ed. (London, 1892); and a short biographical sketch by G. T. Bettany in his ed. of *Principle of Population* (London, 1890). L. Stephen's article in the *Dictionary of National Biography*, XXXVI (1893), 886–890, summarizes the early controversy; and there is an evaluation by J. M. Keynes in his *Essays in Biography*, new ed. (London, 1951), 81–124.

The three works which provoked Malthus' *Essay* are W. Godwin, *An Enquiry Concerning Political Justice, and Its Influence on General Virtue and Happiness* (London, 1793); and *The Enquirer: Reflections on Education, Manners and Literature* (Dublin–London, 1797); and Condorcet, ed., *Outlines of an Historical View of the Progress of the Human Mind* (London, 1795), translated from the French.

Works on Malthus' theories, their influence, and their place in theories of population are numerous. D. V. Glass, ed., *Introduction to Malthus* (London, 1953), contains three essays, reprs. of the *Summary View*, and the letter to Whitbread. A general and appreciative account is G. F. McCleary, *The Malthusian Population Theory* (London, 1953). Ricardo's reactions are published in *The Works and Correspondence of David Ricardo*, P. Staffa, ed., II (London, 1951). One of the most vigorous attacks was W. Hazlitt, *The Spirit of the Age* (London, 1825), 251–276. A detailed study of Malthus' influence on social history is D. Eversley, *Social Theories of Fertility and the Malthusian Debate* (Oxford, 1959). There is an account of the relationship of Malthus' and Darwin's theories in M. T. Ghiselin, *The Triumph of the Darwinian Method* (Berkeley–Los Angeles, 1969), 46–77, which gives further references.

Diana M. Simpkins

MALTSEV (or **Malcev**), **ANATOLY IVANOVICH** (*b*. Misheronsky, near Moscow, Russia, 27 November 1909; *d*. Novosibirsk, U.S.S.R., 7 July 1967), *mathematics.*

The son of a glassblower, Maltsev graduated in 1931 from Moscow University and completed his graduate work there under A. N. Kolmogorov. He received his M.S. in 1937 and the D.S. in 1941 and became professor of mathematics in 1944. He was a corresponding member of the Academy of Sciences of the U.S.S.R. from 1953 and was elected a member in 1958.

From 1932 to 1960 Maltsev taught mathematics at the Ivanovo Pedagogical Institute in Moscow, rising from assistant to head of the department of algebra. He worked at the Mathematical Institute of the Academy in Moscow from 1941 to 1960, when he became head of the department of algebra at the Mathematical Institute of the Siberian branch of the Academy in Novosibirsk as well as head of the chair of algebra and mathematical logic at the University of Novosibirsk. He received the State Prize in 1946 for his work in algebra and, in 1964, the Lenin Prize for his work in the application of mathematical logic to algebra and in the theory of algebraic systems. In 1956 he was named Honored Scientist of the Russian Federation and in 1963 was elected president of the Siberian Mathematical Society.

Maltsev's most important work was in algebra and mathematical logic. In his first publication (1936), which dealt with a general method for obtaining local theorems in mathematical logic, he provided such a theorem for the limited calculus of predicates of arbitrary signature. By means of this theorem an arbitrary set of formulas of this calculus is noncontradictory when—and only when—any finite subset of this set is noncontradictory. In this work the theorem of the extension of infinite models was also proved. Both theorems are important in mathematical logic and in the theory of models, the creation of which Maltsev himself was largely responsible for. His local method enabled him to prove (1941) a series of important theorems of the theory of groups and other algebraic systems. In 1956 he generalized his local theorems to cover many classes of models. Ideas similar to those presented in the last of these works led A. Robinson to formulate his nonstandard analysis, in which actual infinitesimally small and great magnitudes obtained an original substantiation.

Maltsev's most important works in algebra dealt with the theory of Lie groups. He proved (1940, 1943) that for a Lie group to have an exact linear representation, linear representability of the radical of this Lie group and the corresponding factor group constitutes a necessary and sufficient condition. In 1941 he proved that Cartan's theorem of the inclusion of an arbitrary local Lie group into a full Lie group cannot be generalized for local general topological groups. In 1944 he described all semisimple subgroups of simple Lie groups of infinite classes and exceptional classes G and F, and proved the conjugateness of semisimple factors in Levi's decomposition of Lie groups and algebras.

The following year Maltsev defined the rational submodulus of Lie algebra, characterizing the Lie group by the finite-leaved covering; and he discovered the criteria for a subgroup of a Lie group, corresponding to a given subalgebra of Lie algebra, to be closed. He also proved that maximal compact subgroups of a connected Lie group are conjugate (Cartan's problem) and that a Lie group is homeomorphic to a direct product of such a subgroup by Euclidean space. In 1948 he obtained important results in the theory of nilpotent manifolds, i.e. homogeneous manifolds the fundamental groups of which are nilpotent Lie groups. In 1951 he proved the so-called Maltsev-Kolchin theorem of solvable linear groups and studied properties of solvable groups of integer matrices and new classes of solvable groups. In 1955 he constructed an alternative analogue of Lie groups and a corresponding analogue of Lie algebras that are now called Maltsev algebras. In 1957 he constructed the general theory of free topological algebras as being a generalization of topological groups.

In the last ten years of his life Maltsev obtained important results in the theory of algebraic systems and models and in the synthesis of algebra and mathematical logic, which he described in a series of papers and in the posthumous *Algebraicheskie sistemy* ("Algebraic Systems," 1970). His results in the theory of algorithms are presented in the monograph *Algoritmy i rekursivnye funktsii* ("Algorithms and Recursive Functions," 1965). Maltsev was the author of an important textbook of algebra, *Osnovy lineynoy algebry* ("Foundations of Linear Algebra," 1948), founded the journal *Algebra i logika. Seminar*, and was editor-in-chief of *Sibirskii matematicheskii zhurnal*.

BIBLIOGRAPHY

A bibliography of 96 works follows the obituary of Maltsev by P. S. Aleksandrov *et al.*, in *Uspekhi matematicheskikh nauk*, **23**, no. 3 (1968), 159–170. Works referred to above are "Untersuchungen aus dem Gebiete der mathematischen Logik," in *Matematicheskii sbornik*, **1** (1936), 323–326; "Ob izomorfnom predstavlenii beskonechnykh grupp matritsami" ("On the Isomorphic Representation of Infinite Groups by Means of Matrices"), *ibid.*, **8** (1940), 405–422; "Ob odnom obshchem metode polucheniya lokalnykh teorem teorii grupp" ("On a General Method for Obtaining Local Theorems of the Theory of Groups"), in *Uchenye zapiski Ivanovskogo pedagogicheskogo instituta*, Fiz.-mat. fak., **1**, no. 1 (1941), 3–9; "O lokalnykh i polnykh topologicheskikh gruppakh" ("On Local and Full Topological Groups"), in *Doklady Akademii nauk SSSR*, **32**, no. 9 (1941), 606–608; "O lineyno svyaznykh lokalno zamknutykh gruppakh" ("On Linearly Connected Locally Closed Groups"), *ibid.*, **41**, no. 8 (1943), 108–110; "O poluprostykh podgruppakh grupp Li" ("On Semisimple Subgroups of Lie Groups"), in *Izvestiya Akademii nauk SSSR*, Ser. mat., **8** (1944), 143–174; "On the Theory of the Lie Groups in the Large," in *Matematicheskii sbornik*, **16** (1945), 163–190; **19** (1946), 523–524; *Osnovy lineynoy algebry* ("Foundations of Linear Algebra"; Moscow–Leningrad, 1948; 2nd ed., Moscow, 1956; 3rd ed., Moscow, 1970); "Ob odnom klasse odnorodnykh prostranstv" ("On One Class of Homogenous Spaces"), in *Izvestiya Akademii nauk SSSR*, Ser. mat., **13** (1949), 9–32; "O nekotorykh klassakh beskonechnykh razreshimykh grupp" ("On Certain Classes of Infinite Solvable Groups"), in *Matematicheskii sbornik*, **28** (1951), 567–588; "Analiticheskie lupy" ("Analytical Loops"), *ibid.*, **36** (1955), 569–576; "O predstavleniyakh modeley" ("On Representations of Models"), in *Doklady Akademii nauk SSSR*, **108**, no. 1 (1956), 27–29; "Svobodnye topologicheskie algebry" ("Free Topological Algebras"), in *Izvestiya Akademii nauk SSSR*, Ser. mat., **21** (1957), 171–198; "Modelnye sootvetstviya" ("Model Correspondences"), *ibid.*, **23** (1959), 313–336; "Regulyarnye proizvedeniya modeley" ("Regular Products of Models"), *ibid.*, 489–502; "Konstruktivnye algebry" ("Constructive Algebras"), in *Uspekhi matematicheskikh nauk*, **16**, no. 3 (1961), 3–60; *Algoritmy i rekursivnye funktsii* ("Algorithms and Recursive Functions"; Moscow, 1965); and *Algebraicheskie sistemy* ("Algebraic Systems"; Moscow, 1970).

B. A. ROSENFELD

MALUS, ÉTIENNE LOUIS (*b*. Paris, France, 23 July 1775; *d*. Paris, 24 February 1812), *optics*.

The son of Anne-Louis Malus du Mitry and Louise-Charlotte Desboves, Malus was privately educated, mainly in Greek, Latin, and mathematics. He revealed his mathematical skill in 1793 at the entrance examination to the military school in Mézières. His father's position as treasurer of France compromised the family during the Revolution; so Malus served as a simple soldier until 1794, when he was sent to the École Polytechnique. He became sublieutenant of engineers on 20 February 1796 and captain of engineers on 19 June 1796, and he took part in Napoleon's expedition to Egypt and Syria (1798–1801). Malus survived an infection and landed in Marseilles on 14 October 1801. In 1802–1803 he was at Lille; he was subdirector for the fortifications of Anvers (1804–1806) and Strasbourg (1806–1808). In 1808 Malus was called to Paris, where he became major of engineers on 5 December 1810.

Malus was among the first students to enter the École Polytechnique, where he received his basic scientific education (1794–1796). Interested primarily in optics, he composed a memoir in Cairo stating that the constituent principle of light was a particular combination of caloric and oxygen. In September 1802 the Société des Sciences, de l'Agriculture et des Arts de Lille began regular meetings; Malus became vice-president on 11 February 1803 and president the following January. From 1805 he was examiner in geometry and analysis at the École Polytechnique and, from 1806, in physics as well. This post gave Malus the opportunity of long stays in Paris and contacts with other physicists. On 20 April 1807 he presented his first memoir, "Traité d'optique," to the first class of the Institute. He received the mathematical prize of the Institute on 2 January 1810. The greatest event in Malus's career was undoubtedly his election to membership of the first class of the Institute (18 August 1810). Malus was also a member of the Institut d'Égypte (22 August 1798), the Société d'Arcueil (1809), and the Société Philomatique (April 1810). On 22 March 1811 Thomas Young informed Malus that the Royal Society of London had awarded him the Rumford Medal. His last memoir was read to the Institute on 19 August 1811.

At Giessen, just before he was ordered to Egypt, he planned to marry Wilhelmine-Louise Koch, the eldest daughter of the university chancellor, but they were not married until after his return. She died on 18 August 1813. Malus's influential friends included Monge, whom he first met as director of the École Polytechnique; Berthollet, who also was with Napoleon on the Egyptian expedition; and Laplace, who at the beginning of the nineteenth century was particularly interested in optics.

In "Traité d'optique" Malus considered mathematically the properties of a system of contiguous rays of light in three dimensions. He found the equation of the caustic surfaces, and the Malus theorem: Light rays emanating from a point source, after being reflected or refracted from a surface, are all normal to a common surface, but after a second reflection or refraction they will no longer have this property. If the perpendicular surface is identified with a wavefront, it is obvious that this result is false, which Malus did not realize because he adhered to the Newtonian emission theory of light, and the Malus theorem was not proved in its full generality until W. R. Hamilton (1824) and Quetelet and Gergonne (1825). The line of thought and the results of the "Traité d'optique" were continued and generalized by Hamilton in his "Theory of Systems of Rays" (1827).

Double refraction had first been observed in Iceland spar by Erasmus Bartholin. The laws governing it were found by Huygens from the assumption that the wavelets of the extraordinary rays were ellipsoids of revolution with major axes parallel to the axis of the crystal. If one crystal of Iceland spar is placed over another in such a way that the principal sections of the crystals are parallel, then the ordinary rays produced in the upper crystal undergo ordinary refraction only in the lower crystal, while the extraordinary rays undergo only an extraordinary refraction. If the principal sections are perpendicular to each other, the ordinary rays undergo an extraordinary refraction and vice versa. Huygens could not account for these observations, and Newton used them to refute Huygens' wave theory. Newton considered light as particles, and the above-mentioned polarization phenomenon indicated to him that these particles had sides. In Query 25 of the *Optics* he announced his own (false) rule for double refraction, which was adopted for the next century. In 1788 Haüy found experimentally that Huygens' law was true only in certain special cases, but in 1802 Wollaston found experimental evidence for the Huygenian construction. In "Mémoire sur la mesure du pouvoir réfringent" Malus showed that Wollaston's experiments were incomplete, and so the French corpuscularian physicists did not trust Wollaston's results. They thought, moreover, that Wollaston was associated with Thomas Young and therefore with the wave hypothesis.

In this situation the Institute on 4 January 1808 proposed a prize which required an experimental and theoretical explanation of double refraction. The French "Newtonian" scientists hoped that Malus would find a precise and general law for double refraction within the framework of an emission theory of light. Malus was a skilled mathematician and during 1807 he had carried out experiments on double refraction. By December 1808 Malus had finished his experimental investigations, which verified the Huygenian law. What remained was a theoretical deduction of the law. In January 1809, Laplace published a memoir in which he deduced Huygens' law within the framework of Newtonian mechanics, using the principle of least action, and Malus considered this an insolence which deprived him of the priority. In 1810 Malus won the prize for his "Théorie de la double réfraction," published in 1811. Here he deduced the law following the same method as Laplace, by means of the principle of least action. Malus won the prize therefore mainly because of his original experimental researches and his discussion of the short-range forces that produce double refraction. Also of great importance was his law for the relative intensities of the ordinary and extraordinary rays.

While working on double refraction Malus discovered that a ray of sunlight reflected at a certain angle from a transparent medium behaves in exactly the same manner as if it had been ordinarily refracted by a double refracting medium. He found that each medium had a characteristic angle of reflection for which this happened, 52°45′ for water and 35°25′ for glass. Malus did not postpone publishing his discovery until the end of the competition, but announced it to the Institute on 12 December 1808. He also showed that if the two rays emanating from a crystal are reflected from a water surface at an angle less than 52°45′ and if the principal section of the crystal is parallel to the plane of reflection then the ordinary ray is totally refracted; and if the principal section is perpendicular to the plane of reflection the extraordinary ray is totally refracted. He concluded that these phenomena could be accounted for only by supposing that light consisted of particles which were lined up by reflection and refraction and remained mutually parallel afterward. In "Mémoire sur de nouveaux phénomènes d'optique" Malus said that light particles have sides or poles and used for the first time the word "polarization" to characterize the phenomenon.

All transparent and opaque bodies polarize light more or less by reflection, and for each medium a characteristic angle of reflection will totally polarize the reflected ray in the plane of reflection. The refracted rays will contain light that is polarized perpendicular to the reflected light and light that is not polarized. Malus carried out numerous experiments to determine characteristic angles and relative intensities. If the intensity of the incident, polarized ray is unity, then the intensity I of ray reflected at the characteristic angle will be $I = \cos^2 \alpha$, where α is the angle between the planes of polarization of the incident and the reflected rays. He also found the relative intensities of reflected and ordinarily and extraordinarily refracted light. For instance Malus found that if two double refracting crystals are placed one above the other with parallel refracting surfaces, the relative intensities I_{oo}, I_{oe}, I_{eo}, and I_{ee} of the rays subject to ordinary-ordinary, ordinary-extraordinary, extraordinary-ordinary, and extraordinary-extraordinary refraction will be

$$I_{oo} = I_{ee} = \cos^2 i$$
$$I_{oe} = I_{eo} = \sin^2 i,$$

where i is the angle between the two principal sections. He also found that the ordinary and extraordinary rays are polarized perpendicularly to each other.

All material bodies will, to a certain extent, polarize rays of light by reflection. At first Malus thought that this was not true of metallic surfaces, but he later found that rays reflected from such a surface contain two kinds of mutual perpendicularly polarized light together with light not polarized. By reflection at a certain angle, later called the principal angle of incidence, all the reflected light was circularly polarized (Malus did not use this term). The theory of metallic reflection was developed by Brewster, MacCullagh, and Cauchy.

Malus did not indicate whether his results were found experimentally or theoretically. After his death his researches on polarization were followed up by Arago and Biot in France and Brewster in England. In the wave theory of light polarization was explained from the assumption of the transversality of light waves. This was proposed both by Fresnel and Young (1816), but it was not until 1821 that Fresnel succeeded in laying a mechanical foundation for the theory of transverse waves in an elastic medium.

BIBLIOGRAPHY

I. ORIGINAL WORKS. A bibliography of sixteen memoirs by Malus is in Royal Society *Catalogue of Scientific Papers*, IV, 210–211. Those cited in the text are "Mémoire sur la mesure du pouvoir réfringent des corps opaques," in *Nouveau bulletin des sciences de la Société philomatique de Paris*, **1** (1807), 77–81; "Mémoire sur de nouveaux phénomènes d'optique," *ibid.*, **2** (1811), 291–295; "Traité d'optique," in *Mémoires présentés à l'Institut des sciences par divers savants*, **2** (1811), 214–302; and "Théorie de la double réfraction de la lumière dans les substances cristallines," *ibid.*, 303–508. Malus recorded his activities on scientific expeditions to various parts of Egypt in his diary, published posthumously as *L'agenda de Malus. Souvenirs de l'expédition d'Égypte 1798–1801* (Paris, 1892). Collec-

tions of MSS are at the Bibliothèque de l'Institut and the Archives de l'Académie des Sciences in Paris.

II. SECONDARY LITERATURE. On his life, see the biographies by Jean-Baptiste Biot, in Michaud, ed., *Biographie universelle*, XXVI (Paris, 1820), 410 ff.; and by François Arago in his *Oeuvres*, III (Paris, 1855), 113–155. Much valuable information can be found in M. Crosland, *The Society of Arcueil* (London, 1967). See also Anatole de Norguet, "Malus, fondateur de la Société des sciences de Lille," in *Mémoires de la Société des sciences, de l'agriculture et des arts de Lille*, 3rd ser., **10** (1872), 225–232. The history of the Malus theorem is presented in *The Mathematical Papers of Sir William Rowan Hamilton*, I (Cambridge, 1931), 463 ff. Laplace's paper on double refraction, "Mémoire sur les mouvements de la lumière dans les milieux diaphanes," is in *Oeuvres complètes de Laplace*, XII (Paris, 1898), 267–298.

KURT MØLLER PEDERSEN

MANARDO, GIOVANNI (*b*. Ferrara, Italy, 24 July 1462; *d*. Ferrara, 7 March 1536), *medicine, botany*.

Manardo belonged to a distinguished Ferrarese family; his father, Francesco Manardo, was a notary —as were many of his other relatives—while his great-uncle, Antonio Manardo, was an apothecary. Manardo studied at the University of Ferrara, where his teachers included Battista Guarini, Niccolò Leoniceno, and Francesco Benzi, son of the physician Ugo Benzi. He received his doctorate in arts and medicine on 17 October 1482; that same year he was appointed lecturer at the university. Although Manardo remained at Ferrara for the next ten years, his academic promotion, or a career at court, may have been obviated by his unwillingness to accept the prevalent theoretical and astrological basis assigned to medicine.

From 1493 to 1502 Manardo and his wife, Samaritana da Monte, lived in Mirandola, where he served as tutor and physician to Giovanni Francesco Pico and also assisted him in editing the works of his famous uncle, Pico della Mirandola. In spite of the French invasion of Italy, and under the influence of Pico della Mirandola's theories, Manardo began to concentrate more heavily on separating medicine from astrology, while recognizing astronomy as a discrete science.

It was probably during these years also that Manardo's studies led to his scientific travels in Italy and the brief lectureships attributed to him at Perugia, Padua, and Pavia. In 1507 and 1509 he returned to Ferrara, and again in 1512 when his son Timoteo was included among his pupils. In 1513 Manardo went to Hungary, where, through the influence of Celio Calcagnini and on the recommendation of Cardinal Ippolito d'Este, he was appointed royal physician to Ladislaus Jagellon and to his successor, Louis II. From Hungary Manardo was able to journey to Croatia, Austria, and Poland. Subsequently his son (who had on 31 January 1514 qualified in medicine at Ferrara, under Leoniceno's sponsorship) joined Manardo. The younger man wrote an account of his travels, *Odoiporicon Germanicum et Pannonicum*, which was praised by Calcagnini but is now lost.

In 1518 both Manardo and his son returned to Ferrara; there is no further record of Timoteo Manardo's career, although he may have become a monk. Manardo himself succeeded Leoniceno as professor of medicine at the university in 1524 and also became personal physician to Alfonso I d'Este, duke of Ferrara. He remained in Ferrara for the rest of his life; when he was seventy-three, he married Giulia dei Sassoli da Bergamo, a widow with two children, who survived him, with their daughter, Marietta.

Manardo brought to his science new methods of interpretation, analysis, and classification. He had learned a Galenic, anti-Arabic medicine from Leoniceno; to this he added an empirical, intuitive methodology, firmly based on clinical observation, and a broad knowledge of Greek, Latin, Arabic, and biblical sources. He was thus able to resolve some of the linguistic confusion that surrounded his disciplines, and to devise a consistent nomenclature for his work in both pathology and botany.

In medicine, Manardo divided diseases into groups, according to their natures and cures. In dermatology he distinguished among psoriasis, filariasis, scabies, and syphilis, which he established as a specifically venereal entity. (Leoniceno and others had attributed the spread of syphilis to climatic conditions—humidity, rain, and flood—operating under the influence of the planets.) As an alternative to the widely used and dangerous mercuric treatment of the disease, Manardo proposed the West Indian remedy, *Guaiacum sanctum*, dissolved in wine. In ophthalmology he made a distinction between cataract and glaucoma; he further recognized the relationship between systemic—or internal—health and vision.

Manardo's major medical work, *Epistolae medicinales*, is divided into twenty books which consist of 103 letters based on case histories, professional discussions, and personal observations. Among the epistles is one on external diseases, addressed to the Ferrarese surgeon Santanna, which was followed by a long letter on internal diseases, written in the last years of Manardo's life at the request of A. M. Canano (Manardo lived to complete the discussion of phthisis). In sum, the letters represent a development of Ugo Benzi's *Consilia;* in substance they anticipate the scientific dissertations of the seventeenth century.

As a botanist, Manardo drew upon observations made in the course of his travels to distinguish among the properties of the variants that occur within a single species growing in differing locations. These variations are of practical importance in both pharmacy and dietetics; Manardo made further mention of them in his commentary on the *Simplicia et composita* (sometimes called the *Grabadin*) attributed to Johannes Mesue the Younger and in his criticism of V. M. Adriani's translation of Dioscorides.

Manardo enjoyed considerable contemporary fame. He attended the last illnesses of Cardinal Ippolito d'Este, his early patron, and of Ariosto, who had praised him by name in *Orlando Furioso* (canto XLVI, stanza 14). His pupil L. G. Giraldi wrote a moving poem on the occasion of his departure for Hungary, and G. P. Valeriano dedicated to him book twenty-four of his fifty-eight-book *Geroglifici*. Erasmus owned Manardo's works, S. Champier corresponded with him, and Rabelais (himself a physician) wrote a preface to the 1532 edition of the *Epistolae*. Manardo's writings were plagiarized by Leonhard Fuchs and cited by Vesalius.

BIBLIOGRAPHY

I. ORIGINAL WORKS. Manardo's *Epistolae medicinales* were published in a number of editions: books I–VI (Ferrara, 1521; Paris, 1528; Strasbourg, 1529); books VII–XII, with a preface by Rabelais (Lyons, 1532); books I–XVIII (Basel, 1535); and the complete 20-book work (eight eds., Basel, 1540–Hannover, 1611). Manardo also published a partial translation and commentary on Galen's *Ars medicinalis* (Rome, 1525; Basel, 1529, 1536, 1540, 1541; Padua, 1553, 1564), and a commentary on the *Simplicia et composita*, attributed to Johannes Mesue the Younger (Venice, 1558, 1561, 1581, 1589, 1623).

II. SECONDARY LITERATURE. There is no comprehensive biobibliographical work on Manardo, but three recent publications provide essential references to earlier works about him. See Árpád Herczeg, "Johannes Manardus Hofarzt in Ungarn und Ferrara im Zeitalter der Renaissance," *Janus*, 33 (1929), 52–78, 85–130, with portraits, separately published in Hungarian as *Manardus János, 1462–1536, magyar udvari föorvos élete és müvei* (Budapest, 1929); *Atti del Convegno internazionale per le celebrazione della nascità di Giovanni Manardo, 1462–1536* (Ferrara, 1963); and L. Münster, "Ferrara e Bologna sotto i rapporti delle loro scuole medico—naturalistiche nell' epoca umanistica—rinascimentale," in *Rivista di storia della medicina* (1966), 11–12, 17–18, assesses the value of Manardo's contribution.

JULIANA HILL COTTON

MANASSEH. See **Māshā'llāh.**

MANDELSHTAM, LEONID ISAAKOVICH (*b.* Mogilev, Russia, 5 May 1879; *d.* Moscow, U.S.S.R., 27 November 1944), *physics.*

Mandelshtam's father, Isaak Grigorievich Mandelshtam, was a physician widely known in southern Russia. His mother, Minna Lvovna Kahn, was her husband's second cousin, knew several foreign languages, and was an outstanding pianist. Mandelshtam's uncles, the biologist A. G. Gurvich and the distinguished specialist in petroleum chemistry L. G. Gurvich, greatly influenced his upbringing. Soon after his birth the family moved to Odessa, where Mandelshtam passed his childhood and youth. After graduating from the Gymnasium with honors in 1897, he entered the mathematical section of the Faculty of Physics and Mathematics of Novorossysk University in Odessa; two years later he was expelled for having participated in antigovernment student riots.

He continued his education at the Faculty of Physics and Mathematics of Strasbourg University, where Ferdinand Braun soon attracted him to scientific research in his own laboratory—primarily questions of electromagnetic vibration and their application to radiotelegraphy. In 1902 Mandelshtam defended his dissertation for the doctorate of natural philosophy at Strasbourg University, with highest distinction. He then became Braun's extra-staff personal assistant and, in 1903, his second staff assistant at the Strasbourg Physical Institute. Mandelshtam's friendship and collaboration with the distinguished Russian radiophysicist Nikolay Dmitrievich Papaleksi, which continued until his death, began at this time.

In 1907 Mandelshtam married Lidya Solomonovna Isakovich, the first Russian woman architect. In 1914, just before the beginning of World War I, Mandelshtam returned to Russia with his family and Papaleksi. After working as privatdocent in physics at Novorossysk University, in 1915 he became scientific consultant at the Petrograd radiotelegraph factory and, in 1917, professor of physics at the Polytechnical Institute in Tiflis. From 1918 to 1921 he was scientific consultant of the Central Radio Laboratory in Moscow and later in Petrograd. In 1925 he was appointed professor of theoretical physics at Moscow State University. He settled in Moscow, where he began his long collaboration with the prominent Soviet physicist G. S. Landsberg. In 1928 Mandelshtam was elected a corresponding member of the Academy of Sciences of the U.S.S.R. and in 1929 an active member. From the fall of 1934 Mandelshtam took an active part in the work of the P. N. Lebedev Physical Institute of the Academy of Sciences in Moscow, in addition to his work at the university.

Because of serious heart disease Mandelshtam was evacuated during World War II to Borovoye in Kazakhstan, where he continued his theoretical work. After the war he returned to Moscow and spent the rest of his life at Moscow State University and the Lebedev Physical Institute.

Mandelshtam's scientific research, which embraced extremely varied areas of physics and its practical applications, centered fundamentally on optics and radiophysics. His accomplishments in optics include the discovery of the phenomenon of combination scattering, the study of the effect of the fluctuation scattering of light in a uniform medium, and the theory of the microscope. In an early work (1907) Mandelshtam was the first to show that the scattering of light observed in a uniform medium was caused not by the presence of movement among the molecules, as Rayleigh had asserted, but by the occurrence of irregularities connected, according to Smoluchowski's idea, with the fluctuations of density caused by random heat motion.

In 1918 Mandelshtam proposed the idea that the Rayleigh lines must reveal a fine structure, caused by the scattering of light on adiabatic fluctuations. His work on this question did not appear until 1926, after the publication of an analogous idea of Brillouin. The Mandelshtam-Brillouin effect was first experimentally demonstrated by Mandelshtam and Landsberg in 1930 in crystals and by E. F. Gross in liquids. During this research Mandelshtam and Landsberg discovered in 1928 an essentially new effect in crystals, combination scattering, which consists of a regular variation in the frequency of light scattering. An analogous effect was discovered at the same time in liquids by the Indian physicists C. V. Raman and K. S. Krishnan. A preliminary communication of the discovery of the Indian scientists appeared in print a few months before the communication of Mandelshtam and Landsberg. The effect, known in the Soviet Union as combination scattering, is elsewhere called the Raman effect. The study of these phenomena led Mandelshtam to the discovery and investigation of light scattering in fluctuations originating on the surface of a liquid.

In radiophysics and its applications Mandelshtam's research with Papaleksi on nonlinear vibrations and the creation of radiogeodesy is of especially great significance. Begun in 1918, their research on nonlinear vibrations led to results obtained in the 1930's in the formulation of so-called conditions of discontinuity, which are the basis of "explosive" vibrations and led to the development of the theory of multivibrators. The subsequent discovery of the conditions of appearance of n-type resonance made it possible to stimulate vibrations in a circuit, the frequencies of which are precisely *n* times lower than the frequencies of external electromotive forces. Associated with this work is the research on vibrations in linear systems with parameters changing through time. In 1931 Mandelshtam and Papaleksi constructed the first alternating-current parametrical generator with periodically changing inductivity. One of their most distinguished achievements was the radio-interference method of precise measurement invented in 1938 (radiogeodesy), which was also the most precise method of measuring the velocity of propagation of radio waves. In conjunction with studies in optics and radiophysics, Mandelshtam also conducted theoretical research on the basic problems of quantum mechanics. An outstanding lecturer who loved teaching, Mandelshtam taught a large school of physicists, including a number of distinguished scientists (I. E. Tamm, M. A. Leontovich, A. A. Andronov, S. E. Khaikin, among others).

BIBLIOGRAPHY

Mandelshtam's complete collected works were published as *Polnoe sobranie trudov*, S. M. Rytov and M. A. Leontovich, eds., 5 vols. (Leningrad, 1947–1955). A biographical sketch by N. D. Papaleksi is in I, 7–66. See also N. D. Papaleksi, "Kratky ocherk zhizni i nauchnoy deyatelnosti Leonida Isaakovicha Mandelshtama," in *Uspekhi fizicheskikh nauk*, **27**, no. 2 (1945), 143–158, a short sketch of Mandelshtam's life and scientific work.

J. DORFMAN

MANFREDI, EUSTACHIO (*b.* Bologna, Italy, 20 September 1674; *d.* Bologna, 15 February 1739), *astronomy, hydraulics.*

A well-known poet as well as scientist, Manfredi was the eldest son of Alfonso Manfredi, a notary originally from Lugo (near Ravenna), and Anna Maria Fiorini. Encouraged by his father to study philosophy while attending Jesuit schools, he took a degree in law in 1692 but never practiced it. Having shown an early preference for science, he studied mathematics and hydraulics with Domenico Guglielmini and began to study astronomy by himself. By 1690 he had founded his own scientific academy, the Inquieti, a private institution that in 1714 became the Academy of Sciences of the Institute of Bologna. In 1699 Manfredi became lecturer in mathematics at the University of Bologna; but obliged by family financial difficulties to accept two positions, in 1704 he became head of a pontifical college in Bologna and then superintendent of waters for the region, a post he retained until his death. He was relieved from the first post in 1711 by his appointment as astronomer of the recently founded Institute of Sciences.

In 1715 Manfredi completed his two-volume *Ephemerides motuum coelestium* for 1715–1725, based on the still unpublished tables of Cassini in Paris, his predecessor in the chair of astronomy at Bologna. Intended, unlike most of its predecessors, not for astrological use but for practical astronomy, the ephemerides were of unusual extent and practicality. They included tables of the meridian crossing of the planets, tables of the eclipses of the satellites of Jupiter and of the conjunction of the moon and the principal stars, as well as maps of the regions of the earth affected by solar eclipses. The ephemerides were preceded by a volume of instructions including tables that were reprinted by Eustachio Zanotti in 1750. In 1725 Manfredi published a similar, highly successful work for the period 1726–1750 that in some ways anticipated the *Nautical Almanac* (1766).

Soon after his appointment as astronomer, Manfredi calculated the latitude and longitude of the new observatory at Bologna by following the polar star with two mobile quadrants and an eight-foot wall semicircle; the three series of observations confirmed his results obtained in other parts of the city. With a team of assistants that included Francesco Algarotti he carefully measured the annual motion of several fixed stars chosen at various ecliptical latitudes, in order to confirm and identify precisely their apparently elliptical orbits. Although he recognized that the phenomenon could not be a parallactic effect—a conclusion he had apparently reached in 1719—he did not publish on it until 1729, the year in which Bradley gave the exact explanation: the first astronomical evidence of the earth's revolution and a confirmation that the value of the velocity of light, although extremely great, is finite. Manfredi regarded these explanations as insufficiently tested hypotheses and remained, like Cassini and certain other contemporary astronomers, a lifelong adherent of the geocentric and geostatic conception of the world. The phenomenon is still known as the annual aberration of fixed stars, the name Manfredi gave it in the title of *De annuis inerrantium stellarum aberrationibus* (1729).

In 1736 Manfredi published *De gnomone meridiano Bononiensi ad Divi Petronii* [*templum*], for which he had been collecting material since his youth. The work also included a history and description of Cassini's meridian and observations made on the solar "species" since the instrument had been introduced in 1655. These observations are of meteorological as well as astronomical interest. The following year Manfredi published *Astronomicae ac geographicae observationes selectae* by Francesco Bianchini of Verona, after patiently organizing and completing his notes.

Most of Manfredi's many publications appeared in Latin in the proceedings of the Academy of Sciences of Bologna and in French in the *Mémoires* of the Académie des Sciences, in which he published his observations and descriptions of solar and lunar eclipses, comets, transits of Mercury, and an aurora borealis. Other works appeared posthumously in Italian and considerably updated older treatises in Latin, which was always less used.

Manfredi had ordered for his observatory the latest astronomical instruments from England, but they did not arrive until two years after his death from kidney and bladder stones. Manfredi was a foreign member of the Académie des Sciences (1726) and a member of the Royal Society of London (1729). Recognition of his mastery of the Italian language was expressed by his membership in the Accademia della Crusca of Florence (1706), an honor then reserved almost entirely for Tuscans.

BIBLIOGRAPHY

I. ORIGINAL WORKS. Manfredi's scientific works include *Ephemerides motuum coelestium*, 2 vols. (Bologna, 1715); *Novissimae ephemerides motuum coelestium*, 2 vols. (Bologna, 1725); *De annuis inerrantium stellarum aberrationibus* (Bologna, 1729); *De gnomone meridiano Bononiensi ad Divi Petronii* (Bologna, 1736); and Francesco Bianchini, *Astronomicae ac geographicae observationes selectae* (Verona, 1737), which Manfredi edited.

Posthumously published works are Domenico Guglielmini, *Della natura de' fiumi* (Bologna, 1739), with Manfredi's annotations; *Elementi della cronologia* (Bologna, 1744); *Istituzioni astronomiche* (Bologna, 1749); and *Elementi della geometria* (Bologna, 1755).

II. SECONDARY LITERATURE. On Manfredi and his work, see Henri Bédaride, "Eustachio Manfredi," in *Études italiennes 1928–1929* (Paris, 1930), 75–124; Paolo Dore, "Origine e funzione dell'Istituto e della Accademia delle scienze di Bologna," in *L'archiginnasio*, **35** (1940), 201, 206; Angelo Fabroni, *Vitae Italorum*, V (Pisa, 1779), 140–225; Fontenelle, "Éloge de M. Manfredi," in *Histoires de l'Académie royale des sciences* for 1739 (Amsterdam, 1743), 80–99; Guido Horn D'Arturo, "Chi fu il primo a parlare di aberrazione?" in *Coelum*, **3** (1933), 279; and *Piccola enciclopedia astronomica*, II (Bologna, 1960), 294–295; D. Provenzal, *I riformatori della bella letteratura italiana* (Rocca S. Casciano, 1900), p. 251–311; P. Riccardi, *Biblioteca matematica italiana*, II (Modena, 1873–1876), cols. 79–88; F. M. Zanotti, *Elogio del dottor Eustachio Manfredi* (Verona, 1739); G. P. Zanotti, *Vita di Eustachio Manfredi* (Bologna, 1745), with portrait.

GIORGIO TABARRONI

MANGIN, LOUIS ALEXANDRE (*b.* Paris, France, 8 September 1852; *d.* Grignon, France, 27 January 1937), *botany*.

Mangin was professor of cryptogamy at the Muséum National d'Histoire Naturelle in Paris from 1906 to 1932; he served as director of that institution concurrently from 1920. He was a member of the Académie des Sciences, its vice-president in 1928, and its president in 1929. His researches were not limited to the cryptogams, although he did write on micromycetes, species of *Penicillium*, and the phylogeny of *Atichiales*, as well as studying the composition and seasonal and geographical variations of the phytoplankton collected on the Antarctic expedition of the *Pourquoi-Pas?* (directed by J.-B. Charcot) and on the North Sea expedition of the *Scotia*. He also did significant work in plant anatomy and physiology and phytopathology, and made important contributions to plant histology.

Mangin's work in plant anatomy included a study of the vascular system of the monocotyledons. He also established that adventitious roots arise from a special meristem (which he called "souche dictogène") which is seated in the pericycle; he thought, however, that only the central core and the bark of the adventitious root are formed by this apical meristem, the root cap being constituted from the internal layers of the bark.

In plant physiology Mangin observed the waxy cuticle and determined thereby the importance and function in respiration of the stomata. In collaboration with Gaston Bonnier he published a series of papers on their joint researches into plant respiration within various experimental environments. Mangin and Bonnier also devised an apparatus—consisting of a gas bubble imprisoned between two columns of mercury and subjected successively to the actions of caustic potash and pyrogallic acid—for the purpose of rapidly analyzing the atmosphere surrounding plants. They were particularly concerned with the ratio that existed between the oxygen absorbed and the carbon dioxide discharged by each species (which they found to be constant).

Mangin may be considered one of the founders of phytopathology; he furthered its study as the guiding spirit of the Société de Pathologie Végétale et d'Entomologie Agricole de France. He published studies on mycorrhiza of fruit trees (1889); on wheat foot-rot (which he showed to be a consequence of the association of the grain with several species of fungus, including *Ophiobolus graminis* and *Leptosphaeria herpotrichoides*); and, with P. Viala, on vine diseases, especially "phtyriose," which they found to be due to a cochineal insect associated with a polypore, *Bornetia corium.* He also did research on root rot in chestnut trees and needle-shedding disease in firs.

As a histologist, Mangin pioneered in the use of color reactives for microscopic investigation. In 1890 to 1910 he employed a whole series of azoic dyes in the work on the composition of plant membranes whereby he established the characteristics of cellulose and pectin materials and showed that the young membranes of vascular plants always contain these compounds. In 1890 he reported his discovery of callose to the Academy, and went on to describe its microchemical properties and to define its diverse forms according to the condensation of the molecule. He showed callose to exist in all membranes and in such special calcified formations as cystoliths; demonstrated gums and mucilages to be the end products of the jellification of cellular membranes; and recorded important observations on the constitution of the membranes of pollen grains. In his final investigations on the subject Mangin ascertained the essentially variable constitution of the cellular membranes in mushrooms—cellulose and callose in Peronosporaceae, cellulose and pectin compounds in Mucoraceae, and various combinations of callose in other groups.

BIBLIOGRAPHY

I. ORIGINAL WORKS. Mangin's report on callose is "Sur la callose, nouvelle substance fondamentale existant dans la membrane," in *Comptes rendus hebdomadaires de l'Académie des sciences*, **110** (1890), 644–647. His collaborative work with Bonnier is summarized in "La fonction respiratoire chez les végétaux," in *Annales des sciences naturelles (botanique)*, 7th series, **2** (1885), 365–380, which draws upon the papers that appeared in *Annales*, 6th series, **17** (1884); **18** (1884), 293–381; and **19** (1885), 217–255.

Mangin was the author of several textbooks, including *Botanique élémentaire* (1883); *Éléments de botanique* (1884); *Cours élémentaire de botanique* (1885); and *Anatomie et physiologie végétale* (1895).

II. SECONDARY LITERATURE. Mangin's work with Bonnier is discussed in M. H. Jumelle, "L'oeuvre scientifique de Gaston Bonnier," in *Revue générale de botanique*, **36** (1924), 289–307.

MAURICE HOCQUETTE

MANILIUS, MARCUS (*fl.* Rome, beginning of the first century A.D.), *astrology.*

Manilius' life is a mystery to us. Even his name is variously presented in the somewhat restricted manuscript tradition of his one surviving work as Manlius or Mallius, to which is often added Boenius or Boevius; this probably reflects some confusion with the philosopher Anicius Manlius Boethius. The fact is that Manilius is known to us only through an incomplete Latin poem on astrology, the *Astronomicôn libri V*.[1] The composition of this poem began while Augustus was still reigning, and book I was written later than A.D. 9; but it has been much debated whether the work as we have it was completed before Augustus' death in A.D. 14[2] or only under his successor, Tiberius.[3] In either case, Manilius intended to write more than the five books preserved in our manuscripts. Not only does he promise to expound the nature of the planets in book II and fail to accomplish this before the end of book V, but the poem as it stands is not adequate for its purpose—the instruction of students in the science of astrology. In fact, its astrological content, while important because of its antiquity (Manilius' is our oldest connected treatise on astrology), is quite rudimentary.

Roughly, the scheme of the *Astronomica* is as follows. Book I treats the sphere, zodiacal and other constellations, great circles, and comets; book II, the zodiacal signs, their classifications, interrelations, and subdivisions, and the *dodecatopus;* book III, the twelve astrological places (here called *athla*), the Lot of Fortune, the rising times of the signs at Alexandria,[4] the lord of the year, and the length of life; book IV, the decans, the *monomoria*, and an astrological geography; and book V, the fixed stars that rise simultaneously with points on the ecliptic. The possessor of only this poem could not hope to cast or to read a horoscope; he would have several thousand Latin hexameters, some of which are very fine, and a curious congeries of strange doctrines, many of which are found in no other extant text in either Greek or Latin.

The sources of Manilius' doctrines are not often evident. Housman has cited those that are in his edition, and also a large number of parallel passages. An attempt at a survey of the sources in book I was made by R. Blum.[5] The evidence which points to his use of Hermetic astrological writings is strong,[6] and the relation of book V to Germanicus' version of Aratus' *Phaenomena* has been studied by H. Wempe.[7] But the fragmentary state of our knowledge of the early stages of the development of astrology in Hellenistic Egypt makes it impossible to pursue the search for Manilius' sources much further. It is even more difficult (though not because of a lack of texts) to discern any influence exercised by Manilius over later astrologers. If he was read at all in antiquity, it was not by the profession.

NOTES

1. But see P. Thielscher, "Ist 'M. Manilii Astronomicon libri V' richtig?" in *Hermes*, **84** (1956), 353–372.

2. See E. Flores, "Augusto nella visione astrologica di Manilio ed il problema della cronologia degli Astronomicon libri," in *Annali della Facoltà di Lettere e Filosofia della Università di Napoli*, **9** (1960–1961), 5–66.
3. See E. Gebhardt, "Zur Datierungsfrage des Manilius," in *Rheinisches Museum für Philologie*, **104** (1961), 278–286.
4. See O. Neugebauer, "On Some Astronomical Papyri and Related Problems of Ancient Geography," in *Transactions of the American Philosophical Society*, n. s. **32** (1942), 251–263.
5. *Manilius' Quelle im ersten Buche der Astronomica* (Berlin, 1934).
6. See G. Villauri, "Gli *Astronomica* di Manilio e le fonti ermetiche," in *Rivista di Filologia e di Istruzione Classica*, n.s. **32** (1954), 133–167; and M. Valvo, "Considerazioni su Manilio e l'ermetismo," in *Siculorum Gymnasium*, **9** (1956), 108–117.
7. "Die literarischen Beziehungen und das chronologischen Verhältnis zwischen Germanicus und Manilius," in *Rheinisches Museum für Philologie*, **84** (1935), 89–96.

BIBLIOGRAPHY

The standard ed. of Manilius is that by A. E. Housman, 2nd ed., 5 vols. (Cambridge, 1937). Numerous articles on the text tradition and certain difficult passages have appeared since 1937; among the most impressive of these are by G. P. Goold, "De fonte codicum Manilianorum," in *Rheinisches Museum für Philologie*, **97** (1954), 359–372, and "Adversaria Maniliana," in *Phoenix*, **13** (Toronto, 1959), 93–112, from whom a new critical ed. is expected. See also E. Flores, *Contributi di filologia maniliana* (Naples, 1966).

DAVID PINGREE

MANNHEIM, VICTOR MAYER AMÉDÉE (*b.* Paris, France, 17 July 1831; *d.* Paris, 11 December 1906), *geometry*.

A follower of the geometric tradition of Poncelet and Chasles, Amédée Mannheim, like his predecessors, spent most of his professional career associated with the École Polytechnique, which he entered in 1848. In 1850 he went to the École d'Application at Metz. While still a student he invented a type of slide rule, a modified version of which is still in use. After graduation as a lieutenant, he spent several years at various provincial garrisons. In 1859 he was appointed *répétiteur* at the École Polytechnique; in 1863, examiner; and in 1864, professor of descriptive geometry. He attained the rank of colonel in the engineering corps, retiring from the army in 1890 and from his teaching post in 1901. He was a dedicated and popular teacher, strongly devoted to the École Polytechnique, and was one of the founders of the Société Amicale des Anciens Élèves de l'École.

Mannheim worked in many branches of geometry. His primary interest was in projective geometry, and he was influenced by Chasles's work on the polar

reciprocal transformation, which he further investigated with respect to metric properties. He applied these studies in his work in kinematic geometry, which he defined as the study of motion, independent of force, time, and any elements outside the moving figure. He also made significant contributions to the theory of surfaces, primarily in regard to Fresnel's wave surfaces. Most of his results can be found in his texts, *Cours de géométrie descriptive de l'École Polytechnique* (1880) and *Principes et développements de la géométrie cinématique* (1894), which, although he was an enthusiast for the synthetic method in geometry, contained much differential geometry, as well as a good summary of that subject. In recognition of his contributions to the field of geometry Mannheim was awarded the Poncelet Prize in 1872.

BIBLIOGRAPHY

I. ORIGINAL WORKS. Mannheim's early works on the polar reciprocal transformation include his *Théorie des polaires réciproques* (Metz, 1851); and *Transformation de propriétés métriques des figures à l'aide de la théorie des polaires réciproques* (Paris, 1857). His work in kinematic geometry is found primarily in *Cours de géométrie descriptive de l'École Polytechnique comprenant les éléments de la géométrie cinématique* (Paris, 1880; 2nd ed. 1886); and *Principes et développements de la géométrie cinématique; ouvrage contenant de nombreuses applications à la théorie des surfaces* (Paris, 1894). A complete list of his works is in Poggendorff, III, 865–866; IV, 952; and V, 801; and in the article by Loria cited below. For a list of his important papers in the theory of surfaces, see G. Loria, *Il passato ed il presente delle principali teorie geometriche*, 2nd ed. (Turin, 1896), 115.

II. SECONDARY LITERATURE. For an account of Mannheim's life, see C. A. Laisant, "La vie et les travaux d'Amédée Mannheim," in *L'enseignement mathématique*, **9** (1907), 169–179. A much fuller account of his work is G. Loria, "L'opera geometrica di A. Mannheim," in *Rendiconti de Circolo matematico di Palermo*, **26** (1908), 1–63, and "A. Mannheim—Soldier and Mathematician," in *Scripta Mathematica*, **2** (1934), 337–342. Mannheim's works on the wave surface is considered in C. Niven, "On M. Mannheim's Researches on the Wave Surface," in *Quarterly Journal of Pure and Applied Mathematics*, **15** (1878), 242–257.

ELAINE KOPPELMAN

MANSION, PAUL (*b.* Marchin, near Huy, Belgium, 3 June 1844; *d.* Ghent, Belgium, 16 April 1919), *mathematics, history and philosophy of science*.

Mansion was a professor at the University of Ghent, member of the Royal Academy of Belgium, and director of the Journal *Mathesis*. He entered the École Normale des Sciences at Ghent in 1862; and by the age of twenty-three he was teaching advanced courses. He held an eminent position in the scientific world of Belgium despite his extreme narrow-mindedness. In 1874 he founded, with Eugène-Charles Catalan and J. Neuberg, the *Nouvelle correspondance mathématique*; this title was chosen in memory of the *Correspondance mathématique et physique*, edited by Garnier and Adolphe Quetelet. Through the efforts of Mansion and Neuberg, who were encouraged by Catalan himself, the *Nouvelle correspondance* was succeeded in 1881 by *Mathesis*. Mansion retired in 1910.

Alphonse Demoulin's notice on Mansion (1929) includes a bibliography of 349 items, some of which were published in important foreign compendia. Several others appeared in German translation. Mansion's own French translations of works by Riemann, Julius Plücker, Clebsch, Dante, and even Cardinal Manning attest to the extent of his interests. Among other subjects, he taught the history of mathematics and of the physical sciences, in which field he wrote in particular on Greek astronomy, Copernicus, Galileo, and Kepler. His desire to justify the positions of Catholic orthodoxy is evident.

BIBLIOGRAPHY

A bibliography of Mansion's works is in the notice by A. Demoulin, in *Annuaire de l'Académie royale de Belgique*, **95** (1929), 77–147. On Mansion's life and work see L. Godeaux, in *Biographie nationale publiée par l'Académie royale de Belgique*, XXX (Brussels, 1959), 540–542; and in *Florilège des sciences en Belgique pendant le 19ᵉ siècle et le début du 20ᵉ siècle* (Brussels, 1968), 129–132.

J. PELSENEER

MANSON, PATRICK (*b*. Old Meldrum, Aberdeen, Scotland, 3 October 1844; *d*. London, England, 9 April 1922), *tropical medicine*.

Manson was born at Cromlet Hill, Old Meldrum, in Aberdeenshire, the second son of a family of five sons and four daughters. His father, John Manson, was a bank manager and a local laird. His mother, who exercised a profound influence upon him up to the time of her death at the age of eighty-eight, was Elizabeth Livingstone, a distant cousin of David Livingstone the explorer, and a member of a well-known local family named Blaikie.

In his youth Manson was considered rather dull by his teacher, who complained that he spent too much of his time shooting partridges and rabbits and too little on classical education. At the age of eleven he shot a savage cat and "extracted from its innards a long tapeworm," his first practical exercise in parasitology.

In 1857 the family moved to Aberdeen, where Patrick attended the Gymnasium and the West End Academy. His mother's family owned a large engineering works in the city, to which, at the age of fourteen, Manson became apprenticed. He undertook the heavy work so enthusiastically that he developed curvature of the spine and a partial paresis of the right arm, which for the next six months forced him to spend most of each day lying on his back. Nevertheless, for two hours daily he contrived to study natural history at Marischal College, which so stimulated his interest in science that, upon learning that his work would count as part of the medical curriculum, he decided not to return to engineering but to devote his life to medicine.

He became a student at the Aberdeen Medical School in 1860, graduated M.B., C.M., in 1865, M.D. in 1866, and as his first appointment became assistant medical officer at the Durham County Mental Asylum. He remained in Durham for only a year. Persuaded by his elder brother, then working in Shanghai, to travel overseas, he obtained the post of medical officer for Formosa in the Chinese Imperial Maritime Customs, where his official duties were to inspect ships calling at the port of Takao (now Kaohsiung) and to treat their crews. Of this work he kept a careful diary now preserved at Manson House in London, in which he made detailed descriptions of cases of elephantiasis, leprosy, and "heart disease"— which he later recognized as beriberi. At the end of 1870 he unwittingly became involved in the political struggle between China and Japan, to escape from which, on the advice of the British consul, he left Formosa early in 1871 and settled at Amoy on the mainland of China.

His private practice there and his post at the Baptist Missionary Hospital provided him with an immense number of cases that added greatly to his experience. His special interest in elephantiasis led him to devise surgical procedures for removing the masses of tissue associated with the disease, of which, it is recorded, he removed over a ton in a period of three years.

At the end of 1874 Manson returned to Great Britain on a year's leave, during which he was married to Henrietta Isabella Thurburn on 21 December 1875. He spent much of his leave searching the libraries for literature on elephantiasis, in the course of which, on 25 March 1875, while working in the British Museum, he came across the work of Timothy Lewis, a surgeon in the Indian Army Medical Service, on *Filaria sanguinis hominis* (F.S.H.). Lewis was convinced that F.S.H. was the immature form of a much larger adult worm, which he eventually discovered in 1877, some nine months after its discovery by Thomas Lane Bancroft in Australia. He also believed that the microfilariae or the adult worms were the causative agents of disease, although nothing was known of the method of transmission. Manson pondered long on these discoveries of Lewis, and from them he formulated his theory of mosquito transmission. So great was his interest that upon his return to Amoy he devoted all his spare time to investigating the correctness of his theory.

To this end he enlisted the assistance of two medical students to examine blood for the presence of F.S.H. One of the students could work only at night, and Manson noticed that a significantly higher proportion of positives was obtained by this "night observer" than by the day worker. From this observation he stumbled upon the hitherto unsuspected phenomenon of microfilarial periodicity. By training two men whose blood contained microfilariae to examine each other every three hours for six weeks, he was able conclusively to demonstrate that microfilariae were present in the blood in larger numbers at night than during the day. (The resulting graphs of microfilarial numbers are now preserved in the London School of Hygiene and Tropical Medicine.) He also demonstrated that the microfilariae were surrounded by a sheath, from which they could escape when the blood was cooled in ice. This observation led him to postulate that F.S.H. was an embryo worm that could continue its development outside the human body in the common brown mosquito of Amoy (now identified as *Culex fatigans*). He then persuaded his gardener, who was infected with microfilariae, to allow large numbers of mosquitoes to feed upon him; and by dissecting the fed mosquitoes he was able to trace the development of the worm through the intestine and into the thoracic musculature. In his publications of 1877 and 1878 Manson referred to the mosquitoes as "nurses."

His work, however, was greatly hampered by the absence of literature on the life cycle of mosquitoes. He mistakenly believed that mosquitoes took only a single meal of blood, with the result that most of his mosquitoes died within five days. He also erroneously believed that man became infected by ingesting the larvae in water, into which they were released when the mosquitoes laid their eggs.

Nevertheless, these early experiments provided the first proof of the obligatory involvement of an arthropod vector in the life cycle of a parasite. The almost unending list of parasites now known to require an arthropod as a necessary alternate host is testimony of the fundamental nature of Manson's concept. Yet, when his work on periodicity and on development in the mosquito was presented to the Linnean Society of London by the president, Spencer Cobbold, on 7 March 1878, the only recognition that it received was incredulity and ridicule.

Manson's part in the elucidation of the transmission of malaria by mosquitoes took place some sixteen years later. In 1890, under financial pressure caused by depreciation of the Chinese dollar, he set up practice in London and was appointed physician to the Seamen's Hospital, where he had access to many cases of tropical disease. He carried out prolonged observations on the "exflagellation" of malaria and, in a paper published in 1894, postulated that the process was a normal part of the life cycle of the parasite in the stomach of the mosquito. In the same year he met Ronald Ross, with whom, after showing him the malaria parasite, he spent long hours discussing the mosquito-malaria theory. Largely as a result of pressure on the India Office brought to bear by Manson, Ross was dispatched to India the following year to investigate the theory. Manson's advice was to "follow the flagellum," and Ross soon succeeded in observing exflagellation in the stomach of the mosquito. But the problem of following the parasite into the tissues of the mosquito, of which only one species is suitable for development, proved to be a Herculean task. Throughout the months of investigation that followed, Manson maintained a continuous correspondence with Ross, much of which has now been published. In August 1897 Ross dissected a new type of mosquito (*Anopheles*) that had fed on a malaria patient, and in it he found pigmented round bodies on the stomach wall. The pigmented bodies were sent to Manson, who confirmed their significance. Soon afterward Ross was removed to an area where human malaria was absent, and there he applied himself to the study of *Proteosoma*, a malaria parasite of sparrows. From this study he was able in 1898 to describe its complete life cycle in the mosquito. The discovery was announced by Manson at a meeting of the British Medical Association in Edinburgh. Ross fully acknowledged the part played by Manson; but Manson, with characteristic modesty, disclaimed any credit save that of having "discovered" Ross. Meanwhile, in Italy, Grassi in 1898 transmitted human malaria by the bite of a mosquito and in 1901 described the complete life cycle of the parasite.

Manson was responsible not only for the concept of the mosquito-transmission theory but also for bringing the findings of Ross and Grassi to the attention of the public and thus for spreading the knowledge that eventually led to the practical control of malaria. In 1900, from a consignment of infected mosquitoes sent by Grassi to London, Manson succeeded in infecting his son and a laboratory technician by mosquito bite. In the same year Manson sent two of his pupils, Low and Sambon, to live for three months in a highly malarious area of Italy. By the simple expedient of spending each night in a mosquito-proof hut, they remained healthy and uninfected, while their neighbors lay sick and dying of the disease. Manson was involved in the whole field of tropical medicine, as well as in the discovery of many other pathogenic parasites and in the elucidation of their life cycles, including *Paragonimus westermanni*, *Sparganum mansoni*, *Schistosoma mansoni* and *S. japonicum*, *Oxyspirura mansoni*, *Loa loa*, and *Filaria perstans*.

Manson was a man of deep penetrative mind, original in thought, creative in imagination, careful and patient in experimentation. He was possessed of an overwhelming desire to communicate his knowledge to others, and so stimulating was his enthusiasm that wherever he went he invariably gathered about him a group of eager students. He played a significant part in the foundation of the College of Medicine at Hong Kong (later to form the basis of the University of Hong Kong) and became the first dean. In a letter to *Lancet* published in 1897 he stressed the need for special training of doctors destined for work in the tropics. Despite the disapproval of many of his colleagues, his recommendations led to the foundation of the London School of Tropical Medicine in 1899, some six months after the opening of the world's first tropical school in Liverpool. On many subsequent occasions Manson pleaded for funds for "our tropical schools," which became the models for similar institutions throughout the world. *Tropical Diseases. A Manual of the Diseases of Warm Climates* (1898), his principal work, is now in its seventeenth edition and has become a classic textbook of tropical medicine. He taught continually at the London School of Tropical Medicine and its nearby hospital until his retirement in 1914. He was elected a fellow of the Royal Society in 1900, received a knighthood in 1903, and was medical adviser to the Colonial Office for nearly twenty years. In 1907 he was one of the founders of the Royal Society of Tropical Medicine and was elected its first president. After his retirement he spent most of his time fishing in Ireland, interspersed with visits to Ceylon, Rhodesia, and South Africa. The last of his frequent visits to the London School took place only two weeks before his death at the age of seventy-seven. He is buried in Aberdeen.

BIBLIOGRAPHY

A series of articles in commemoration of Manson's life and work, including a short autobiography, appeared in *Journal of Tropical Medicine and Hygiene*, **25** (1922), 155–206; see also the bibliography of his writings compiled by S. Honeyman, *ibid.*, 206–208. See also the obituaries in *Lancet* (1922), 767–769; *Proceedings of the Royal Society*, **94** (1922), xliii–xlviii; and *Transactions of the Royal Society of Tropical Medicine and Hygiene*, **16** (1922), 1–15; and the article by J. W. W. Stephens in *Dictionary of National Biography 1922–1930* (London, 1937), 560–562.

Full-length studies of Manson's life and work are Philip Manson-Bahr, *Patrick Manson, the Father of Tropical Medicine* (London–New York, 1962); P. Manson-Bahr and A. Alcock, *The Life and Work of Sir Patrick Manson* (London, 1927); and Ronald Ross, *Memories of Sir Patrick Manson* (London, 1930).

M. J. CLARKSON

MANṢŪR IBN ʿALĪ IBN ʿIRĀQ, ABŪ NAṢR (*fl.* Khwarizm [now Kara-Kalpakskaya, A.S.S.R.]; *d.* Ghazna [?] [now Ghazni, Afghanistan], *ca.* 1036), *mathematics, astronomy.*

Abū Naṣr was probably a native of Gīlān (Persia); it is likely that he belonged to the family of Banū ʿIrāq who ruled Khwarizm until it fell to the Maʾmūnī dynasty in A.D. 995. He was a disciple of Abuʾl Wafāʾ al-Būzjānī and the teacher of al-Bīrūnī. Abū Naṣr passed most of his life in the court of the monarchs ʿAlī ibn Maʾmūn and Abuʾl-ʿAbbās Maʾmūn, who extended their patronage to a number of scientists, including al-Bīrūnī and Ibn Sīnā. About 1016, the year in which Abuʾl-ʿAbbās Maʾmūn died, both Abū Naṣr and al-Bīrūnī left Khwarizm and went to the court of Sultan Maḥmūd al-Ghaznawī in Ghazna, where Abū Naṣr spent the rest of his life.

Abū Naṣr's fame is due in large part to his collaboration with al-Bīrūnī. Although this collaboration is generally considered to have begun in about 1008, the year in which al-Bīrūnī returned to Khwarizm from the court of Jurjān (now Kunya-Urgench, Turkmen S.S.R.), there is ample evidence for an earlier date. For example, in his *Al-Āthār al-bāqiya* ("Chronology"), finished in the year 1000, al-Bīrūnī refers to Abū Naṣr as *Ustādhī*—"my master," while Abū Naṣr dedicated his book on the azimuth, written sometime before 998, to his pupil.

This collaboration also presents grave difficulties in assigning the authorship of specific works. A case in point is some twelve works that al-Bīrūnī lists as being written "in my name" *(bismī)*, a phrase that has led scholars to consider them to be of his own composition. Nallino has, however, pointed out that *bismī* might also mean "addressed to me" or "dedicated to me"—by Abū Naṣr—and there is considerable evidence in support of this interpretation. For instance, the phrase is used in this sense in both medieval texts (the *Mafātīḥ al-ʿulūm* of Muḥammad ibn Aḥmad al-Khwārizmī of 977) and modern ones of which there is no doubt of the authorship. The incipits and explicits of the works in question make it clear, moreover, that they were written by Abū Naṣr in response to al-Bīrūnī's request for solutions to specific problems that had arisen in the course of his more general researches. Indeed, in some of al-Bīrūnī's own books he mentioned Abū Naṣr by name and stated that his book incorporates the results of some investigations that the older man carried out at his request. Al-Bīrūnī gave Abū Naṣr full credit for his discoveries—as, indeed, he gave full credit to each of his several collaborators, including Abū Sahl al-Masīḥī, a certain Abū ʿAlī al-Ḥasan ibn al-Jīlī (otherwise unidentified) and Ibn Sīnā, who wrote answers to philosophical questions submitted to him by al-Bīrūnī.

The extent of the collaboration between Abū Naṣr and al-Bīrūnī may be demonstrated by the latter's work on the determination of the obliquity of the ecliptic. Al-Bīrūnī carried out observations in Khwarizm in 997, and in Ghazna in 1016, 1019, and 1020. Employing the classical method of measuring the meridian height of the sun at the time of the solstices, he computed the angle of inclination as 23°35′. On the other hand, however, al-Bīrūnī became acquainted with a work by Muḥammad ibn al-Ṣabbāḥ, in which the latter described a method for determining the position, ortive amplitude, and maximum declination of the sun. Since al-Bīrūnī's copy was full of apparent errors, he gave it to Abū Naṣr and asked him to correct it and to prepare a critical report of Ibn al-Ṣabbāḥ's techniques.

Abū Naṣr thus came to write his *Risāla fī 'l-barāhīn ʿalā ʿamal Muḥammad ibn al-Ṣabbāḥ* ("A Treatise on the Demonstration of the Construction Devised by Muḥammad Ibn al-Ṣabbāḥ"), in which he took up Ibn al-Ṣabbāḥ's method in detail and demonstrated that it must be in error to the extent that it depended on the hypothesis of the uniform movement of the sun on the ecliptic. According to Ibn al-Ṣabbāḥ, the ortive amplitude of the sun at solstice (a_t) may be obtained by making three observations of the solar ortive amplitude (a_1, a_2, a_3) at thirty-day intervals within a single season of the year. He thus reached the formula:

$$2 \sin a_t = \frac{2 \sin a_2 \sqrt{(2 \sin a_2)^2 - 2 \sin a_1 2 \sin a_3}}{\sqrt{(2 \sin a_2)^2 - (\sin a + \sin a_3)^2}}.$$

The same result may also be obtained from only two observations (a_1, a_2) if the distance (d) covered by the sun on the ecliptic over the period between the two observations is known:

$$2 \sin a_t = \frac{R \sqrt{\dfrac{R^2(\sin a_1 + \sin a_2)^2}{\cos^2 \dfrac{d}{2}} - 4 \sin a_1 \sin a_2}}{\sin \dfrac{d}{2}}.$$

The value of a_t is thus extractable in two ways, and the value of the maximum declination can then be discovered by applying the formula of al-Battānī and Ḥabash:

$$\sin \text{ort. ampl.} = \frac{\sin \partial x R}{\cos \varphi}.$$

Al-Bīrūnī then took up Abū Naṣr's clarification of Ibn al-Ṣabbāḥ's work, citing it in his own *Al-Qānūn al-Masʿūdī* and *Taḥdīd*. He remained, however, primarily interested in obtaining the angle of inclination, and simplified Ibn al-Ṣabbāḥ's methods to that end. He thus, within the two formulas, substituted three and two, respectively, observations of the declination of the sun for the three and two observations of solar ortive amplitude. By this method he obtained values for the angle of inclination of 23°25′19″ and 23°24′16″, respectively. These values are clearly at odds with that then commonly held (23°35′) and confirmed by al-Bīrūnī's own observations. Al-Bīrūnī then returned to Abū Naṣr's work, and explained the discrepancy as being due to Ibn al-Ṣabbāḥ's supposition of the uniform motion of the sun on the ecliptic, as well as to the continuous use of sines and square roots.

Abū Naṣr's contributions to trigonometry are more direct. He is one of the three authors (the others being Abu'l Wafāʾ and Abū Maḥmūd al-Khujandī) to whom al-Ṭūsī attributed the discovery of the sine law whereby in a spherical triangle the sines of the sides are in relationship to the sines of the opposite angles as

$$\frac{\sin a}{\sin A} = \frac{\sin b}{\sin B} = \frac{\sin c}{\sin C},$$

or, in a plane triangle, the sides are in relationship to the sines of the opposite angles as

$$\frac{a}{\sin A} = \frac{b}{\sin B} = \frac{c}{\sin C}.$$

The question of which of these three mathematicians was actually the first to discover this law remains unresolved, however. Luckey has convincingly argued against al-Khujandī, pointing out that he was essentially a practical astronomer, unconcerned with theoretical problems. Both Abū Naṣr and Abu'l Wafāʾ, on the other hand, claimed discovery of the law, and while it is impossible to determine who has the better right, two considerations would seem to corroborate Abū Naṣr's contention. First, he employed the law a number of times throughout his astronomical and geometrical writings; whether or not it was his own finding, he nevertheless dealt with it as a significant novelty. Second, Abū Naṣr treated the demonstration of this law in two of his most important works, the *Al-Majisṭī al-Shāhī* ("Almagest of the Shah") and the *Kitāb fi 'l-sumūt* ("Book of the Azimuth"), as well as in two lesser ones, *Risāla fī maʿrifat al-qisiyy al-falakiyya* ("Treatise on the Determination of Spherical Arcs") and *Risāla fi 'l-jawāb ʿan masāʾil handasiyya suʾila ʿanhā* ("Treatise in Which Some Geometrical Questions Addressed to Him are Answered").

The *Al-Majisṭī al-Shāhī* and the *Kitāb fi 'l-sumūt* have both been lost. It is known that the latter was written at the request of al-Bīrūnī, as well as dedicated to him, and that it was concerned with various procedures for calculating the direction of the *qibla*. Abū Naṣr's other significant work, the most complete Arabic version of the *Spherics* of Menelaus, is, however, still extant (although the original Greek text is lost). Of the twenty-two works that are known to have been written by Abū Naṣr, a total of seventeen remain, of which sixteen have been published.

In addition to the books cited above, the remainder of Abū Naṣr's work consisted of short monographs on specific problems of geometry or astronomy. These lesser writings include *Risāla fī ḥall shubha ʿaraḍat fi 'l-thālitha ʿashar min Kitāb al-Uṣūl* ("Treatise in Which a Difficulty in the Thirteenth Book of the *Elements* is Solved"); *Maqāla fī iṣlāḥ shakl min kitāb Mānālāwus fi 'l-kuriyyāt ʿadala fīhi muṣalliḥū hādha 'l-kitāb* ("On the Correction of a Proposition in the *Spherics* of Menelaus, in Which the Emendators of This Book Have Erred"); *Risāla fī ṣanʿat al-asṭurlāb bi 'l-ṭarīq al-ṣināʿī* ("Treatise on the Construction of the Astrolabe in the Artisan's Manner"); *Risāla fi 'l-asṭurlāb al-sarṭānī al-muŷannaḥ fī ḥaqīqatihi bi 'l-ṭarīq al-sināʿi* ("Treatise on the True Winged Crab Astrolabe, According to the Artisan's Method"); and *Faṣl min kitāb fī kuriyyat al-samāʾ* ("A Chapter From a Book on the Sphericity of the Heavens").

BIBLIOGRAPHY

I. ORIGINAL WORKS. Abū Naṣr's version of the *Spherics* of Menelaus exists in an excellent critical edition, with German trans., by Max Krause, "Die Sphärik von Menelaos aus Alexandrien in der Verbesserung von Abū Naṣr Manṣūr ibn ʿAlī ibn ʿIrāq. Mit Untersuchungen zur Geschichte des Textes bei den islamischen Mathematikern," in *Abhandlungen der K. Gesellschaft der Wissenschaften zu Göttingen*, Phil.-hist. Kl., no. 17 (Berlin, 1936). Most of the rest of his extant work has been badly edited as *Rasāʾil Abī Naṣr Manṣūr ilā 'l-Bīrūnī. Dāʾirat al-Maʿārif al-ʿUthmāniyya* (Hyderabad, 1948); six of the same treatises are trans. into Spanish in Julio Samsó, *Estudios sobre Abū Naṣr Manṣūr* (Barcelona, 1969).

II. SECONDARY LITERATURE. On Abū Naṣr and his work, see D. J. Boilot, "L'oeuvre d'al-Beruni: essai bibliographique," in *Mélanges de l'Institut dominicain d'études orientales*, **2** (1955), 161–256; "Bibliographie d'al-Beruni. Corrigenda et addenda," *ibid.*, **3** (1956), 391–396; E. S. Kennedy and H. Sharkas, "Two Medieval Methods for Determining the Obliquity of the Ecliptic," in *Mathematical Teacher*, **55** (1962), 286–290; Julio Samsó, *Estudios sobre Abū Naṣr Manṣūr b. ʿAlī b. ʿIrāq* (Barcelona, 1969); "Contribución a un análisis de la terminología matemático-astronómica de Abū Naṣr Manṣūr b. ʿAlī b. ʿIrāq," in *Pensamiento*, **25** (1969), 235–248; Paul Luckey, "Zur Entstehung der Kugeldreiectsrechnung," in *Deutsche Mathematik*, **5** (1940–1941), 405–446; Muḥammad Shafī, "Abū Naṣr ibn ʿIrāq aur us kā sanah wafāt" ("Abū Naṣr ibn ʿIrāq and the Date of his Death"), in Urdu with English summary, in *60 doğum münasebetyle Zeki Velidi Togan'a armağan. Symbolae in honorem Z. V. Togan* (Istanbul, 1954–1955), 484–492; Heinrich Suter, "Zur Trigonometrie der Araber," in *Bibliotheca Mathematica*, 3rd ser., X (1910), 156–160; and K. Vogel and Max Krause, "Die Sphärik von Menelaus aus Alexandrien in der Verbesserung von Abū Naṣr b. ʿAlī ibn ʿIrāq," in *Gnomon*, **15** (1939), 343–395.

JULIO SAMSÓ

MANTEGAZZA, PAOLO (*b.* Monza, Italy, 31 December 1831; *d.* San Terenzo di Lerici, Italy, 17 August 1910), *medicine, anthropology.*

Mantegazza was born into a rich family who gave him a liberal and sophisticated education. His mother, to whom he dedicated one of his books, was Laura Solari, herself notably well-educated, and famous for her ardent patriotism. Under her inspiration Mantegazza took part in the "Cinque Giornate" of 1848, in which the Milanese were able, after furious street fighting, to repel the Austrian occupying forces. Since he was sixteen, Mantegazza was allowed to serve only as a courier in the insurrection, but it nevertheless marked his baptism of fire.

Mantegazza attended the universities of Pisa and Pavia, graduating from the latter in 1853 with honors in medicine. He began scientific experimentation while he was still a student, and when he was nineteen presented to the Istituto Lombardo Accademia di Scienze e Lettere a memoir on spontaneous generation—a still somewhat controversial topic—that aroused considerable interest.

After his graduation Mantegazza traveled extensively in Europe (he knew seven languages), then moved to South America. In 1856 he established a medical practice in Salto, Argentina, where he was engaged in founding an agricultural colony and where he married an Argentinian. He shortly thereafter abandoned the colonization project and returned with his wife to Italy; in 1858 he became an assistant at the Ospedale Maggiore in Milan. The following year, in spite of his numerous professional commitments, he requested that he be allowed to take part in a competition for the unsalaried post of honorary assistant in the same institution. In 1860 Mantegazza was appointed to the chair of general pathology at the University of Pavia, where he subsequently established the first laboratory of experimental pathology in Europe. Ten years later, in 1870, he went to Florence to fill the first Italian chair of anthropology. Here he built up an important museum of anthropology and ethnology and founded the journal *Archivio per l'antropologia e la etnografia*. Following the death of his first wife, Mantegazza married Maria Fantoni, the daughter of a Florentine aristocrat.

Mantegazza published a great number of books, both popular and scientific. Among the latter, those that record his researches on the physiology of reproduction and on what are today called opotherapy and endocrinology are particularly important. Taking up Spallanzani's work of the preceding century, Mantegazza conducted a series of experiments in which he subjected frog sperm to low temperatures to determine its viability. From the data that he compiled he was able to conclude that it should be possible to preserve sperm by this method; and he went on to speculate on the feasibility of artificial insemination, writing that it might be a practice applicable to man. He also made experiments designed to demonstrate that tuberculosis is contagious, and was the first to show that bacteria reproduce by means of spores. He conducted researches on transplanting amphibian testicles, and did work on animal organ transplants in general.

The abundance and variety of Mantegazza's works written for the layman quite overshadowed his scientific works, however. He was an active popularizer, at a time when science was considered to be the preserve of the initiated few. His works on hygiene are particularly significant; he courageously dealt with a number of then-proscribed topics, including sex education. Indeed, there was almost no medical or social problem to which he did not devote a book, pamphlet, or lecture; his books were highly successful, and a few have had modern editions. (He also wrote several novels in the lachrymose and romantic style popular at the time.)

Mantegazza lived to be nearly eighty. He was much honored for his scientific achievements. He was a member of a number of scientific academies and institutes, and was awarded decorations by his own and foreign governments.

BIBLIOGRAPHY

I. ORIGINAL WORKS. Among Mantegazza's original works are *Della vitalità dei zoospermi della rana e del trapiantamento dei testicoli da un animale all' altro* (Milan, 1860); *Della temperatura delle orine in diverse ore del giorno e in diversi climi* (Milan, 1862); *Sugli innesti animali e sulla organizzazione artificiale della fibrina* (Milan, 1864); *Sulla congestione: ricerche di patologia sperimentale* (Milan, 1864); *Degli innesti animali e della produzione artificiale delle cellule: ricerche sperimentali* (Milan, 1865); *Delle alterazioni istologiche prodotte dal taglio dei nervi* (Milan, 1867). Two works on other scientists are *Maurizio Bufalini: biografia* (Turin, 1863); and *Carlo Darwin e il suo ultimo libro* (Milan, 1868). His later scientific books include *Fisiologia dell' amore* (Milan, 1873); *Fisiologia del dolore* (Milan, 1880); and *Fisiologia della donna* (Milan, 1893).

II. SECONDARY LITERATURE. Works about Mantegazza include F. Bazzi, "Paolo Mantegazza nel cinquantenario della morte," in *Castalia*, **3** (1960), 126; and E. V. Ferrario, "Una lettera inedita di Paolo Mantegazza sulla fecondazione artificiale," *ibid.* (1962), 134.

CARLO CASTELLANI

MANTELL, GIDEON ALGERNON (*b.* Lewes, Sussex, England, 3 February 1790; *d.* London, England, 10 November 1852), *geology.*

The son of a shoemaker in Lewes, Mantell studied medicine in London and in 1811 returned to Lewes, where he became a busy and successful surgeon. Geology was, however, an overmastering passion, and while at Lewes he made great discoveries and amassed an important collection. In 1833 he moved to Brighton, where his practice became largely eclipsed by his interest in geology. His house with his collection of fossils was turned into a public museum, and his distracted wife and children were forced to seek shelter elsewhere. In 1838 he sold the "Mantellian collection" for £5,000 to the British Museum and bought a practice at Clapham, moving to London in 1844. A prolific writer of books and memoirs (as well as letters and verse), he had enormous energy and enthusiasm but in later life suffered from a painful spinal disease. He was a conspicuous member of the Geological Society of London, of which he became a vice-president in 1848.

In 1835 he was the second recipient of its high honor, the Wollaston Medal (the first was William Smith). Mantell was elected a fellow of the Royal Society in 1825 and he received a Royal Medal in 1849.

Mantell's first and most important book was *The Fossils of the South Downs, or Illustrations of the Geology of Sussex* (1822), a large quarto volume with forty-two lithographic plates. It is now known chiefly for the large number of fossils (nearly all invertebrates) from the Cretaceous and Tertiary strata, but particularly from the Chalk, that Mantell described and illustrated. Many were new species, named by him and now familiar. The most notable fossil here fully described for the first time and named by him is the sponge *Ventriculites*. He wrote various papers on other Chalk fossils, particularly on belemnites and the microscopic organisms found in flint nodules. Mantell included a colored geological map that is on a larger scale and is more detailed and accurate than existing maps of the district (the parts of the general maps of England and Wales by William Smith, 1815, and Greenough, 1819), although the succession of the Cretaceous strata below the Chalk was not satisfactorily settled until 1824, by W. H. Fitton and T. Webster.

An important advance in the knowledge of the geology of northwestern Europe was the recognition of the freshwater origin of the Wealden series of the Cretaceous together with the uppermost series of the Jurassic (Purbeckian). This suggestion was first made by Conybeare in *Outlines of the Geology of England and Wales* (1822), in which he looks forward to support by the forthcoming "work of Mr. Mantell on the fossils of Sussex." Mantell, however, following a warning by George Sowerby on some of his fossil shells from the Wealden, deprecates rather than confirms the inference of a freshwater origin. In a letter to Webster of November 1822 Fitton gave his opinion that the whole of the Purbeck-Wealden series was freshwater, and he published this opinion in *Annals of Philosophy* (1824). Thus, it cannot be said that Mantell was the first to establish the freshwater origin of the Wealden beds, as has been stated, although the evidence he had already obtained (1822), and particularly the evidence he later obtained, did in fact support it, as he came to realize.

Mantell is best known for his discovery of the first dinosaur ever to be described properly—a momentous event. During the second and third decades of the nineteenth century remains of aquatic saurians had been found and described in Britain by several leading geologists, particularly by Conybeare and Buckland, and in France by Cuvier, the founder of vertebrate paleontology. But the existence of the great land saurians (named Dinosauria by Richard Owen in 1842) had not even been suspected. Their enormous diversity is now known in great detail, and the extent of their dominance of life during the entire Mesozoic is fully realized. Fossils that were clearly teeth but unlike any known fossil teeth were found in 1822 by Mantell (it was Mrs. Mantell who first noticed them in a pile of stones along the roadside) together with some loosely scattered bones. In 1825 he was shown teeth of the modern lizard iguana, and he saw that his fossil teeth were similar but much larger. Mantell described the fossil teeth in a paper to the Royal Society in that year and called the large herbivorous reptile to which they must have belonged *Iguanodon*. Although bones that could definitely be shown to have belonged to the same animal had not been found, such associations came to light in 1835 in various parts of the Wealden formation of southern England. The fossils were studied by Richard Owen, and *Iguanodon* was reconstructed in a life-size model (together with models of other dinosaurs) in the grounds of the Crystal Palace in south London in 1854. By a curious mistake the reptile was reconstructed with a horned nose, but the bone thus placed was later found to be a large spike at the end of this biped's "thumb."

In 1832 Mantell discovered the first strongly armored group of dinosaurs. He described this fossil, which he named *Hylaeosaurus*, in *The Geology of the South-east of England* (1833). Like the *Iguanodon*, *Hylaeosaurus* was discovered in the Tilgate Forest region of northern Sussex. Meanwhile, Buckland in 1824 had described the remains of the large carnivorous dinosaur *Megalosaurus* from the Jurassic near Oxford. Thus the first three dinosaurs to be known, the *Iguanodon*, the *Megalosaurus*, and the *Hylaeosaurus*, each belonged to a quite distinct group, later called Ornithopoda, Theropoda, and Ankylosauria, respectively. Although Mantell may be said to have been essentially an amateur collector and expounder—although a very expert and extraordinarily industrious one—he was professionally qualified to examine and report on matters of vertebrate paleontology by reason of his anatomical knowledge as a surgeon.

BIBLIOGRAPHY

I. ORIGINAL WORKS. Mantell's papers are listed in Royal Society *Catalogue of Scientific Papers*, IV, 219–220. His chief works are *The Fossils of the South Downs, or Illustrations of the Geology of Sussex* (London, 1822); "On the Teeth of the *Iguanodon*, a Newly-discovered Fossil Herbivorous Reptile," in *Philosophical Transactions of the Royal Society*, **115** (1825), 179–186; *Illustrations of the Geology of Sussex* (London, 1827); *The Geology of the South-east of England* (London, 1833); *The Wonders of*

Geology (London, 1838); *The Medals of Creation* (London, 1844); and *Geological Excursions Round the Isle of Wight and the Adjoining Coast of Dorsetshire* (London, 1847).

II. SECONDARY LITERATURE. Obituary notices include Lord Rosse, in *Proceedings of the Royal Society*, **6** (1852), 252–256; *Gentleman's Magazine*, n.s. **38** (1852), 644–647, unsigned; W. Hopkins, in *Proceedings of the Geological Society*, **9** (1853), xxii–xxv; B. Silliman, *American Journal of Science*, **15** (1853), 147–149; *A Reminiscence of G. A. Mantell. By a Member of the Council of the Clapham Museum. To Which is Appended an Obituary by Professor Silliman* (London, 1853); and T. R. Jones, notice prefaced to his edition (7th) of Mantell's *Wonders of Geology* (London, 1857).

See also M. A. Lower, *The Worthies of Sussex* (Lewes, 1865); W. Topley, *The Geology of the Weald*, Memoirs of the Geological Survey of England and Wales (1875), *passim*; T. G. Bonney, in *Dictionary of National Biography*, XXXVI (1893), 99–100; H. B. Woodward, *The History of the Geological Society of London* (London, 1908), 122; S. Spokes, *Gideon Algernon Mantell* (London, 1927); E. C. Curwen, ed., *The Journal of Gideon Mantell, Surgeon and Geologist* (Oxford, 1940); E. H. Colbert, *Dinosaurs: Their Discovery and Their World* (London, 1962), 33–35; W. A. S. Sarjeant, "The Xanthidia," in *Mercian Geologist*, **2** (1967), 249; E. H. Colbert, *Men and Dinosaurs* (London, 1970), *passim;* W. E. Swinton, *The Dinosaurs* (London, 1970), 28–34, 201–208; A. D. Morris, "Gideon Algernon Mantell (1790–1852)," in *Proceedings of the Royal Society of Medicine*, **65** (1971), 215–221; and L. G. Wilson, *Charles Lyell: the Years to 1841* (New Haven–London, 1972), *passim*.

JOHN CHALLINOR

AL-MAQDISĪ (or **Muqaddasī**), **SHAMS AL-DĪN ABŪ 'ABDALLĀH MUHAMMAD IBN AHMAD IBN ABĪ BAKR AL-BANNĀ' AL-SHĀMĪ AL-MAQDISĪ AL-BASHSHĀRĪ** (*b*. Bayt al-Maqdis [Jerusalem], *ca*. A.D. 946; *d. ca*. the end of the tenth century), *geography, cartography*.

Al-Maqdisī spent most of his youth in Jerusalem, then traveled throughout the *Mamlakat al-Islām* (the "Kingdom of Islam"), excepting only al-Andalus (southern Spain), Sind, and Sijistān (southern Afghanistan). He also visited Sicily. His great geographical compendium, the *Kitāb ahsan al-taqāsīm fī ma'rifat al-aqālīm*, which he completed in Shīrāz in A.D. 985, would indicate, among other things, that he was knowledgeable in Islamic jurisprudence and a follower of the Hanafī school of Islamic law.

The geographical writers of the Middle Ages—both western and Arab—had mainly dealt in narrow segments of the subject, producing individual works on mathematical, physical, or descriptive geography, or writing of trade routes and kingdoms or toponymy.

Al-Maqdisī was not satisfied with such works; he criticized those of al-Jayhānī, Abū Zayd Ahmad ibn Sahl al-Balkhī, Ibn al-Faqīh al-Hamadhānī, and Ibn Khurradādhbih, for example, for being directed to the specific needs of specific rulers, or for simply being too brief to be of practical use. He himself therefore planned a work of wider scope, designed to meet the needs and requirements of a wider audience—merchants, travelers, and people of culture. Of geography, he wrote that "It is a science in which kings and nobles take a keen interest, [while] the judges and the jurists seek it and the common people and the leaders love it." Al-Maqdisī's view of the subject embraced a variety of topics, including various sects and schisms, trade and commerce, weights and measures, customs and traditions, coinage and monetary systems, and languages and dialects; to all of these subjects he brought a critical mind and narrative and investigative skills.

Although al-Maqdisī brought a new aim to geography, his method was that of the Balkhī school, of whom the chief adherents were, besides al-Balkhī himself, al-Istakhrī (who lived in the first half of the tenth century) and Ibn Hawqal (who completed his geographical work in A.D. 977). The Balkhī geographers limited their descriptive writings to the *Mamlakat al-Islām* and attempted to align their geographical concepts with those of the Koran and the *Hadīth* ("Traditions of the Prophet"). An example of al-Maqdisī's use of the holy books may be found in his discourse on the seas, in which he argued that the Koranic verse describing the "confluence of the two seas between which was situated *al-barzakh* [the interstice]" actually referred to the meeting of the Mediterranean Sea and the Indian Ocean (which most Arab geographers thought to be a lake) at the Isthmus of Suez, since *al-barzakh* was the land between the al-Faramā and al-Qulzum of the Koran. Like the Balkhī geographers, al-Maqdisī also confined himself to the *Mamlakat al-Islām* and began his account with the description of the "Island of Arabia," which must take precedence since it contained both the holy cities of Mecca and Medina. As he noted in the *Kitāb ahsan al-taqāsīm*, he neither visited the countries of the infidels nor saw any point in describing them.

Al-Maqdisī nonetheless held independent views and differed from the Balkhī geographers on a number of points. He tried to judge every geographical problem independently and in a scholarly manner; he observed, regarding the authenticity of his own work:

Know that many scholars and ministers have written on the subject [of geography] but most [of their writing], nay, all of it, is based upon hearsay, while we have entered every region and have acquired knowledge through experience. Moreover, we did not cease investigation, enquiry, and [attempts to gain] insight into the unknown [al-ghayb]. Thus, our book is arranged in three parts: first, what we have observed; second, what we have heard from trustworthy sources; and third, what we have found in books written on this subject and others.

Al-Maqdisī began his *Kitāb aḥsan al-taqāsīm* with general remarks on a number of subjects, among them seas and rivers; place names and their variants (including names common to more than one place); the special characteristics of various regions; the sects of Islam and the non-Muslim inhabitants of the Islamic world; personal travel narratives; and sections entitled "Places About Which There are Differences of Opinion," "Epitome for the Jurists," and "World *Aqālīm* [regions or administrative districts] and the Position of the *Qibla*." These introductory passages embody some of al-Maqdisī's innovations; he was, for example, the first Arab geographer to determine and standardize the meanings and connotations of Arabic geographical terms, and the first to provide a list of towns and other features for quick reference.

According to al-Maqdisī, the Islamic world was not symmetrical, but rather irregular in shape. He divided this world into fourteen regions *(aqālīm)*, of which he designated six—the "Island of Arabia," 'Irāq (southern Mesopotamia), Aqūr (al-Jazīra, or northern Mesopotamia), al-Shām (Syria), Miṣr (Egypt), and al-Maghrib—as *'Arab*. The remaining eight—al-Mashriq (the kingdom of the Samanids), al-Daylam (Gilan and the mountainous regions east of the Caspian Sea), al-Riḥāb (Azerbaydzhan, Arran, and Armenia), al-Jibāl (ancient Media), Khūzistān (the area south of Media and east of Mesopotamia), Fārs (ancient Persia), Kirmān (the region to the south of Fārs), and al-Sind—he called *'Ajam*, Persian. Each of these districts, it may be noted, is demarcated by well-defined physical boundaries, which al-Maqdisī undoubtedly took into account. In commenting upon them, he further divided his remarks on each region into two sections, of which one was dedicated to physical features, toponymy, and political subdivisions, while the other contained a discussion of general features.

Al-Maqdisī drew a map of each *iqlīm*, indicating regional boundaries and trade routes in red, sandy areas in yellow, salt seas in green, rivers in blue, and mountains in ochre. Although most of the maps have been lost, it is possible to reconstruct them to some degree by considering those made by other geographers of the Balkhī school, the conventions of which al-Maqdisī again followed (although his book suggests

that he specifically disagreed with some of the maps drawn by al-Balkhī). The world maps of this school are round, showing the land mass encircled by an ocean from which the Mediterranean Sea and the Indian Ocean flow, almost meeting at the Isthmus of Suez. The boundaries of the various *aqālīm* are then shown within the land mass. Because of this high degree of stylization, these maps are less accurate than the more detailed maps of specific regions, which conform more closely to the geographers' descriptions; since the maps that al-Maqdisī drew for the *Kitāb aḥsan al-taqāsīm* were of the latter type, some fair amount of accuracy may be assumed.

Al-Maqdisī's book is also notable for its literary style. He wrote in an ornamental and varied manner, occasionally framing his comments in rhymed prose *(saj')*. He used the local dialect of each region in describing it, or, when he did not do so, he explained, he used the Syrian dialect that was native to him. Through this imitation, the language of his section on al-Mashriq is the most rhetorical, since the people of this area were perfect in Arabic; but because the language of the people of Egypt and al-Maghrib was weak and unadorned, and that of the inhabitants of al-Baṭā'ih (the swamps of Iraq) ugly, so, too, is the language in which al-Maqdisī wrote of them.

BIBLIOGRAPHY

Al-Maqdisī's geographical work, *Kitāb aḥsan al-taqāsim fī ma'rifat al-aqālīm* ("The Best Division for Knowledge of Regions"), is in M. J. de Goeje, ed., *Bibliotheca geographorum arabicorum*, 2nd ed., III (Leiden, 1906). An English trans. up to the *iqlīm* of Egypt is G. Ranking and R. Azoo, *Aḥsanu-t-taqāsim fī ma'rifat-i-l-aqālīm*, in *Bibliotheca indica*, n.s. (Calcutta, 1897–1910); a French trans. is A. Miquel, *Al-Muqaddasī, Aḥsan al-Taqāsim fī Ma'rifat al-Aqālīm, La meilleure répartition pour la connaissance des provinces* (Damascus, 1963); and an Urdu trans. is Khurshīd Aḥmad Fārīq, *Islāmī dunyā daswīn ṣadī 'iswī mēn* (Delhi, 1962).

See I. I. Krakovsky, *Istoria arabskoy geograficheskoy literatury* (Moscow–Leningrad, 1957); translated into Arabic by Salāḥ al-Dīn 'Uthmān Hāshim as *Ta'rikh al-adab al-jughrāfī al-'Arabī* (Cairo, 1963).

S. MAQBUL AHMAD

MARALDI, GIACOMO FILIPPO (MARALDI I) (*b.* Perinaldo, Imperia, Italy, 21 August 1665; *d.* Paris, France, 1 December 1729), *astronomy, geodesy.*
MARALDI, GIOVANNI DOMENICO (MARALDI II) (*b.* Perinaldo, Imperia, Italy, 17 April 1709; *d.* Perinaldo, 14 November 1788), *astronomy, geodesy.*

Maraldi I was the son of Francesco Maraldi and Angela Cassini, sister of Cassini I, who had helped found the Paris observatory. After finishing his studies of the classics and of mathematics, he was called to Paris in 1687 by his uncle Cassini I. He soon became his devoted collaborator, and eventually assisted his son, Cassini II, as well. He participated in the observatory's work for thirty years.

Upon arriving in France, Maraldi I started producing a new catalog of the fixed stars, a project he continued throughout his career. This important work, which he almost succeeded in completing, unfortunately was never published, with the exception of certain stellar positions utilized by Deslisle, Manfredi, and Brouckner. An active participant in the daily observations made at the observatory, Maraldi I left behind several unpublished journals. He published many notes in the annual volumes of the *Histoire de l'Académie royale des sciences* concerning the planets, their satellites, eclipses and variable stars, as well as some more theoretical memoirs. In one of the latter, "Considérations sur la seconde inégalité du mouvement des satellites de Jupiter et l'hypothèse du mouvement successif de la lumière" (*Histoire de l'Académie pour l'année 1707* [Paris, 1708], 25–32), he defended the point of view of Cassini I, opposing the hypothesis of the finite velocity of light, conceived by Ole Römer to account for certain irregularities in the movement of Jupiter's satellites.

In 1700 and 1701 Maraldi I participated with Cassini II, J. M. de Chazelles and Pierre Couplet in the operations directed by Cassini I to extend the meridian of Paris to France's southern frontier. He then spent two years in Rome, making various astronomical observations—including one on the zodiacal light—and sharing in the determination and construction of the meridian of the Church of the Carthusians. He returned to Paris in 1703 and resumed his observations, interrupting them for several months in 1718, to take part, with Cassini II and G. de La Hire, in the extension as far as Dunkirk of the Paris–Amiens meridian measured by Jean Picard in 1670.

Maraldi I's personal work was overly influenced by the conservative ideas of Cassini I and was only of the second rank. But as a steady and scrupulously careful observer he contributed significantly to the smooth operation of the observatory and to the realization of important programs of astronomical and geodesic research. He was successively student (1694), associate (1699), and pensioner (1702) of the Academy of Sciences of Paris.

In 1726 Maraldi brought his nephew Giovanni Domenico (Maraldi II), the son of his brother Gian Domenico and Angela Francesca Mavena, to Paris. Maraldi II, who had studied in San Remo and Pisa, worked first under Cassini II and then under Cassini

de Thury (Cassini III), until 1771, when he returned to Italy. He carried out regular astronomical and meteorological observations until 1787 and published many notes drawn from them in the *Histoire de l'Académie*. He likewise participated in various geodesic operations directed by Cassini II and Cassini III: the triangulation of the west perpendicular to the meridian of Paris (1733); the partial survey of the Atlantic coast (1735); the verification of the Paris meridian (1739–1740); and also an experiment designed to measure the speed of sound in the air (1738). Lastly, he shared in the fundamental work carried out to establish the map of France. The greater part of Maraldi II's activity, however, was concerned with positional astronomy. Although he published no books of his own, he edited the *Connaissance des temps* from 1735 to 1759 and also the posthumous work of his friend Lacaille: *Coelum australe stelliferum* (Paris, 1763). Among the numerous memoirs which he published, the most important were devoted to the observation and theory of the movements of the satellites of Jupiter, in which he made many improvements. We may note that in 1740 he finally accepted Römer's theory of a finite value of the speed of light.

Named *adjoint* of the Academy of Sciences in 1731, he was promoted to associate in 1733, to pensioner in 1758, and finally to veteran pensioner in 1772. "An industrious and worthy astronomer" and "an assiduous observer of all the phenomena," Maraldi II "was not content to calculate them; he sought to make them serve the development of his theories." This judgment of Delambre, an author who generally had little good to say for the Cassini family and its allies, is sufficient testimony to the quality of his work, especially regarding the improvement of the tables of Jupiter's satellites.

BIBLIOGRAPHY

I. Original Works. The works of the Maraldis were almost all published in *Histoire de l'Académie royale des sciences;* the list of their works is given in successive vols. of *Table générale des matières contenues dans l'Histoire et dans les Mémoires de l'Académie royale des sciences*, I–IV (1729–1734) for Maraldi I and IV–X (1734–1809) for Maraldi II. The most important of these works are also in Poggendorff, II, cols. 37–38 for Maraldi I and col. 38 for Maraldi II; P. Riccardi, *Biblioteca matematica italiana*, I (Bologna, 1870; repr. Milan, 1952), cols. 98–102 for Maraldi I, cols. 102–105 for Maraldi II; and J. Houzeau and A. Lancaster, *Bibliographie générale de l'astronomie*, 3 vols. (Brussels, 1882–1889; repr. London, 1964), see index.

II. Secondary Literature. For studies dealing with both Maraldis see the following (in chronological order): A. Fabroni, *Vitae italorum doctrina excellentium*, VIII (Pisa, 1781), 293–320; J. J. Bailly, *Histoire de l'astronomie moderne*, 3 vols. (Paris, 1779–1782), see III index; J. D. Cassini IV, *Mémoires pour servir à l'histoire des sciences et à celle de l'Observatoire de Paris* (Paris, 1810), 348–357; J. J. Weiss, *Biographie universelle*, new ed., XXVI (Paris, 1861), 410–411; J. B. Delambre, *Histoire de l'astronomie au XVIIIe siècle* (Paris, 1827), 239–250; F. Hoefer, ed., *Nouvelle biographie générale*, XXXIII (Paris, 1860), cols. 348–350; C. Wolf, *Histoire de l'Observatoire de Paris . . .* (Paris, 1902), see index; F. Boquet, *Histoire de l'astronomie* (Paris, 1925), 403–404 and 425–426; and N. Nielsen, *Géomètres français du XVIIIe siècle* (Copenhagen–Paris, 1935), 297–300.

On Maraldi I, see B. Fontenelle, "Éloge de Jacques-Philippe Maraldi," in *Histoire de l'Académie royale des sciences pour l'année 1729* (Paris, 1731), 116–120; and C. G. Jöcher in *Allgemeines Gelehrtenlexikon*, III (Leipzig, 1751), col. 130.

On Maraldi II see J. D. Cassini IV, "Éloge de J. D. Maraldi," in *Magasin encyclopédique*, **1** (1810), 268–282; and J. de Lalande, in *Bibliographie astronomique* (Paris, 1803), see index.

RENÉ TATON

MARCGRAF, GEORG. See **Markgraf, Georg.**

MARCHAND, RICHARD FELIX (*b*. Berlin, Germany, 25 August 1813; *d*. Halle, Germany, 2 August 1850), *chemistry.*

The son of a Berlin lawyer, Marchand had already published a substantial amount of original research on organic chemistry while a medical student at the University of Halle, before he graduated in 1837. This work brought him the friendship of Otto Erdmann, professor of technical chemistry at the neighboring University of Leipzig. In 1838 he became lecturer in chemistry at the Royal Prussian Artillery and Engineering School in Berlin, but not until 1840 was he recognized as privatdocent by the University of Berlin. In 1843 he became extraordinary professor of chemistry at the University of Halle (where he had been licensed to teach since 1838), and in 1846 he succeeded to the permanent chair.

Wöhler, writing in 1839, describes Marchand as a tall, elegant youth with "negroid Mephistopheles features, very free and easy in manner almost to a level of impertinence, full of sudden ideas, wisecracks and satirical remarks; all, however, combined with a sure amiability and genius, so that one cannot help liking him."[1] Nicknamed "Dr. Méchant" by Berlin society, during his short life (ended by cholera) he

accomplished an impressive amount of experimental research and popular lecturing. In 1844 he married Marianne Baerensprung. One of their three children, Jacob Felix, became a distinguished physiologist.

Marchand's publications, which are primarily descriptive and analytical, encompass biochemistry, in which he was greatly inspired by Liebig's *Die Thier-Chemie*, organic chemistry, and determinations of atomic weights. In 1837 Marchand published an important analytical paper on the controversial subject of the constitution of ethyl sulfuric acid; in this he supported the view of Serullas that it was a bisulfate of ordinary ether.[2] Although this challenged the interpretation held by Liebig at this time, Liebig soon saw that Marchand's work supported the ethyl-radical concept which had been introduced in 1834. Following Dumas, in 1838, Marchand and Erdmann developed a technique for the estimation of nitrogen in organic compounds by using copper oxide in an inert atmosphere of carbon dioxide. In 1842 they extended Hess's technique for organic analyses, using as oxidizing agents copper oxide and streams of air and oxygen controlled from gasometers. From 1841, following the dramatic reduction of the atomic weight of carbon from 76.43 to 75.08 (O = 100), Marchand and Erdmann devoted their attentions to the accurate redetermination of atomic weights. Their drastic modifications of Berzelian values and their enthusiastic support for Prout's hypothesis that atomic weights were whole numbers on the hydrogen scale, infuriated Berzelius. He dismissed them unkindly—and erroneously—as careless "apes" and bunglers who always echoed Dumas.[3]

NOTES

1. Wöhler to Berzelius, 12 Oct. 1839. See Wallach, p. 138.
2. R. F. Marchand, "Ueber die ätherschwefelsauren Salze," in *Annalen der Physik und Chemie*, **41** (1837), 596–634.
3. Berzelius to Wöhler, 28 Feb. 1843 and 25 Mar. 1845. See Wallach, pp. 393, 530.

BIBLIOGRAPHY

I. ORIGINAL WORKS. A list of Marchand's 132 papers (17 written with Erdmann) is in the Royal Society *Catalogue of Scientific Papers,* IV, 229–233. Marchand also published *Acidium sulphuricum quam vim in alcoholem exerceat quaeque et hinc prodeuntium et similium compositionum natura sit et constitutio* (Leipzig, 1838), his diss.; *Lehrbuch der organischen Chemie* (Leipzig, 1838); *Grundriss der organischen Chemie* (Leipzig, 1839; Berlin, 1838), also in Dutch trans. (Amsterdam, 1840); *Lehrbuch der physiologischen Chemie* (Berlin, 1844); *Chemische Tafeln zur Berechnung der Analysen* (Leipzig, 1847); *Ueber die Alchemie. Ein Vortrag im wissenschaftlichen Vereine zu Berlin am 20 Februar 1847* (Halle, 1847); *Ueber die Luftschifffahrt. Ein Vortrag im wissenschaftlichen Vereine zu Berlin am 12 Januar 1850* (Leipzig, 1850); and *Das Geld* (Leipzig, 1852).

With Erdmann he edited the *Journal für praktische Chemie*, **16–50** (1839–1850).

II. SECONDARY LITERATURE. There are no formal obituaries. Existing biographical information is based entirely on a vague eulogy in B. F. Voigt, ed., *Neuer Nekrolog der Deutschen*, no. 28 (1850), (Weimar, 1852), 452. But note J. Jordan and O. Kern, *Die Universitäten Wittenberg und Halle vor und bei ihrer Vereinigung* (Halle, 1917); and J. Asen, *Gesamtverzeichnis des Lehrkörpers der Universität Berlin* (Leipzig, 1955), 124.

For contemporary references to Marchand, see J. J. Berzelius, *Jahres-Bericht über die Fortschritte der physischen Wissenschaften*, XIV–XXIV (Tübingen, 1835–1845), and *Vollständiges Sach-und-Namen Register zum Jahres-Bericht* (Tübingen, 1847); O. Wallach, *Briefwechsel zwischen J. Berzelius und F. Wöhler*, 2 vols. (Leipzig, 1901), esp. vol. II; and H. G. Söderbaum, ed., *Jac. Berzelius Bref* (Uppsala, 1912–1935), II, 227–231 (V, to Mulder); III, 212 (VII, to Marignac).

For the joint papers with Erdmann on atomic weights, see *Dictionary of Scientific Biography*, IV, 395, notes 7–9.

Marchand's Berlin career may be traced in *Acta der Königlichen Friederich-Wilhelms-Universität zu Berlin betreffend die Habilitationen der Privatdocenten* (1838–1843), 65–67, 77–82 (Archives of Humboldt-Universität zu Berlin, Philos. Fak. Littr. H, Nro. 1, vol. VI [1203]). See also the lecture registers and faculty records in the archives of Martin Luther-Universität, Halle–Wittenberg. A few letters to Berzelius are preserved at the Royal Swedish Academy of Sciences, Stockholm.

For the context of Marchand's contributions to biochemistry see F. Holmes, ed., *Liebig's Animal Chemistry*, repr. ed. (New York–London, 1964), vii–cxvi; for his atomic weight research see the secondary literature cited for his collaborator O. L. Erdmann in *Dictionary of Scientific Biography*.

W. H. BROCK

MARCHANT, JEAN (*b.* 1650; *d.* Paris, France, 11 November 1738); **MARCHANT, NICOLAS** (*d.* Paris, June 1678), *botany.*

Jean Marchant was the son and successor of Nicolas Marchant. The botanical concerns of father and son were so similar that the works of one have often been attributed to the other. In particular, both men devoted much of their effort—Nicolas, the last ten years of his life, and Jean, almost all his life's work—to the preparation of the *Histoire des plantes*, undertaken in

1667 by the Académie Royale des Sciences at the urging of Claude Perrault. Each prepared a large number of botanical descriptions for this project which was, however, never published, being abandoned by the Academy in 1694.

Nicolas Marchant held a degree in medicine from the University of Padua, and he appears to have become interested in botany at quite an early date. Following his university training he became apothecary to Gaston, duc d'Orléans, the brother of Louis XIII. In this capacity he was often resident at the château of Blois, where Gaston had established a botanical garden. The garden was under the management of Abel Brunyer, who was also first physician to the duke, and of Robert Morison and Jean Laugier. Nicolas Marchant certainly collaborated with all three of these men, and perhaps accompanied Morison on a botanical excursion to the area around La Rochelle in 1657. The duke died on 2 February 1660 and Nicolas Marchant entered the service of the king late in that year, although it is not known what his title or function in the royal household was. (Of the others, the Protestants Brunyer and Laugier received no official reemployment, while Morison rejected an offer made by Nicolas Fouquet, the minister of finance, and returned to his native England.)

The elder Marchant was one of the founding members of the Académie Royale des Sciences, and remained the only botanist in the organization until the election of Denis Dodart in 1673. In addition to his work toward the *Histoire des plantes*, he collaborated in editing the *Mémoires pour servir à l'histoire des plantes*, which Dodart published in 1676. On 9 November 1674 Colbert named Nicolas Marchant "concierge et directeur de la culture des plantes du Jardin Royal," and in this post Marchant had a garden at his disposal for the experimental cultivation of exotic species. He was also one of the first botanists to take up the study of the lower plants; following his death his son named the common liverwort *Marchantia* in his honor.

Jean Marchant was elected to his father's place in the Academy on 18 June 1678 and also succeeded him immediately in his post at the Jardin du Roi. He continued his father's work on the *Histoire* and increased the specimens in the experimental garden until, in the year 1680 alone, he received more than 500 species of seeds and plants sent to him from abroad. The Academy's decision to give up the *Histoire* cost Jean Marchant the royal pension that the government had granted him for this work, and in the same year, 1694, his position at the royal garden was abolished.

Deprived of royal subsidies, of the official support of the Academy, and of his experimental garden, Jean

Marchant nevertheless continued to prepare botanical descriptions, which he now intended to publish as a work of his own. Although the greater part of this work also remained unpublished, some fifteen of his notices did appear in the Academy's *Mémoires*. Among these, his "Observations sur la nature des plantes" is particularly interesting, since in it Jean Marchant dealt with the notion of partial transformism among plants, thus foreshadowing one of the tenets of evolution.

BIBLIOGRAPHY

I. ORIGINAL WORKS. The greater number of the known manuscripts of both Jean and Nicolas Marchant are in the Bibliothèque Centrale du Muséum National d'Histoire Naturelle, Paris, *cotes* MSS 89, 447–451, 1155, 1356, and 2253. Compare *Catalogue général des manuscrits des bibliothèques publiques de France, Paris*, II, *Muséum d'histoire naturelle* by Amédée Boinet (Paris, 1914), 16, 90–91, 192, 226, and LV, *Muséum d'histoire naturelle. Supplément*, by Yves Laissus (Paris, 1965), 53.

The published works of Jean Marchant comprise fifteen memoirs that appeared in *Mémoires de l'Académie royale des sciences depuis 1666 jusqu'à 1699*, **10** (1730), and in *Histoire de l'Académie royale des sciences . . . avec les mémoires de mathématiques et physiques . . .* (1701, 1706, 1707, 1709, 1711, 1713, 1718, 1719, 1723, 1727, 1733, 1735); the complete list is in Abbé Rozier, *Nouvelle table des articles contenus dans les volumes de l'Académie royale de Paris, depuis 1666 jusqu'à 1770 . . .*, IV (Paris, 1776), 245. Two of these fifteen memoirs are erroneously attributed to Nicolas Marchant; see B. de Fontenelle, *Histoire de l'Académie royale des sciences*, 2 vols. (Paris, 1733).

Jean Marchant, "Observations sur la nature des plantes," is in the *Mémoires* for 1719, 59–66; see also *Histoire*, 57–58. "Liste des plantes citées dans les mémoires de l'Académie, dont les descriptions, données par M. Marchant, ont été réservées pour un ouvrage particulier," is in Godin, *Table alphabétique des matières contenues dans l'Histoire et les Mémoires de l'Académie royale des sciences . . .*, 4 vols. (Paris, 1729–1734), II, *années* 1699–1710, 391–392; III, *années* 1711–1720, 216–217; and IV, *années* 1721–1730, 210–211.

II. SECONDARY LITERATURE. On Nicolas Marchant, see Edmond Bonnet, "Gaston de France, duc d'Orléans, considéré comme botaniste," in *Comptes rendus de l'Association française pour l'avancement des sciences, 19ème session, Limoges 1890* (1891), 416–421; and Nicolas-François-Joseph Eloy, *Dictionnaire historique de la médecine ancienne et moderne . . .*, III (Mons, 1778), 159–160.

On both Jean and Nicolas Marchant, see Yves Laissus and Anne-Marie Monseigny, "Les plantes du roi. Note sur un grand ouvrage de botanique préparé au XVIIe siècle par l'Académie royale des sciences," in *Revue d'histoire des sciences*, **22** (1969), 193–236.

YVES LAISSUS

MARCHI, VITTORIO (*b.* Novellara, Reggio nell' Emilia, Italy, 30 May 1851; *d.* Iesi, Ancona, Italy, 12 May 1908), *pathology*.

Marchi studied at the University of Modena, from which he received a degree in chemistry and pharmacy in 1873. He took a further degree in medicine and surgery in 1882; by then he had already conducted significant research, particularly in demonstrating Golgi tendon organs, including those of the motor muscles of the eye. Soon after his second graduation Marchi became a lecturer in anatomy at the university; he simultaneously served as an anatomist and pathologist at the Reggio nell'Emilia lunatic asylum.

In 1883 a government grant allowed Marchi to continue his studies in Golgi's own general pathology laboratory at the University of Pavia. Here he investigated the fine structure of the corpus striatum and optic thalamus by means of Golgi's "black reaction." By this method, nerve fragments are subjected to three processes—being treated with potassium bichromate, osmium chloride and potassium bichromate, and finally silver nitrate—whereby a black precipitate that demonstrates the nerve elements is formed. Marchi refined Golgi's method, omitting a step. By subjecting nerve fragments to only the potassium bichromate and osmium chloride and potassium bichromate, he was able to demonstrate recently degenerated nerve fibers. The destruction of a cell or the interruption of a nerve fiber is followed by the degeneration of the part of the fiber distal to the lesion; one of the concomitant results of such degeneration is the conversion of myelin to droplets of fat, and it is these fat globules ("Marchi's globules") that are stained black by osmium bichlorate in Marchi's method. (Normal fiber remains unstained.)

Marchi described this staining technique in a series of reports that appeared in 1885. These included notes on lesions of the annular protuberance, on the double crossing of the pyramidal fasciculi, and particularly the preliminary note on the descending degeneration secondary to cortical lesions. In the last of these Marchi fully expounded the significance of his method.

More important than these papers, however, was Marchi's experimental work on the descending degeneration that results from entire or partial extirpation of the cerebellum. From 1885 Marchi was in Florence, where he conducted researches at the physiology laboratory of the Istituto di Studi Superiori Clinici e di Perfezionamento, then under the direction of Luciani. His work served to clarify the structure of the cerebellar pedunculi; this in turn led to the recognition of the efferent fibers that run from the cerebellum to the spinal cord. The tractus tectospinalis is known as "Marchi's tract."

Marchi's scientific contributions were not rewarded with the university chair that he sought. He gave up research and in 1888 began to practice medicine at San Benedetto del Tronto. From 1890 until his death he was head physician of the hospital of Iesi.

BIBLIOGRAPHY

I. ORIGINAL WORKS. Among Marchi's works published in journals are "Sulla terminazione della fibra muscolare nella fibra tendinea," in *Lo Spallanzani*, **9** (1880), 194–197; "Sulle terminazioni periferiche dei nervi," in *Rivista sperimentale di freniatria e di medicina legale*, **8** (1882), 477–489, esp. 485–486; "Sugli organi terminali nervosi nei tendini dei muscoli motori dell'occhio," in *Atti della Reale Accademia delle scienze di Torino*, **16** (1880–1881), 206–207; "Sugli organi terminali nervosi (corpi di Golgi) nei tendini dei muscoli motori del bulbo oculare," in *Archivio per le scienze mediche*, **5** (1882), 273–282; and "Ueber di Terminalorgane der Nerven (Golgi's Nervenkörperchen) in den Sehnen der Augenmuskeln," in *Albrecht v. Graefes Archiv für Ophthalmologie*, **28**, pt. 1 (1882), 203–213.

See also "Un caso di sarcoma cerebrale in un alienato," in *Rivista sperimentale di freniatria*, **9** (1883), 114–117; "Sulla fina anatomia dei corpi striati," *ibid.*, 331–334; "Sull'istologia patologica della paralisi progressiva," *ibid.*, 220–221; "Sulla struttura dei talami ottici," *ibid.*, **10** (1884), 329–332; "Sopra un caso di doppio incrociamento dei fasci piramidali," in *Archivio italiano per le malattie nervose*, **22** (1885), 255–266; "Contributo allo studio delle lesioni della protuberanza anulare," in *Rivista sperimentale di freniatria*, **11** (1885), 254–278, written with Giovanni Algeri; "Sulle degenerazioni discendenti consecutive a lesioni della corteccia cerebrale," *ibid.*, 492–494, written with Algeri; "Sulle degenerazioni discendenti consecutive a lesioni sperimentali in diverse zone della corteccia cerebrale," *ibid.*, **12** (1886), 208–252, written with Algeri; "Sulle degenerazioni consecutive all'estirpazione totale e parziale del cervelletto," *ibid.*, 50–56; "Sulla fine struttura dei corpi striati e dei talami ottici," *ibid.*, 285–306; "Sulle degenerazioni consecutive a estirpazione totale e parziale del cervelletto," *ibid.*, 224, and **13** (1887), 446–452; "Sul decorso dei cordoni posteriori nel midollo spinale," *ibid.*, **13** (1887), 206–207; "Ricerche anatomo-patologiche e bacteriologiche sul tifo pellagroso," *ibid.*, **14** (1888), 341–348; and "Sull'origine e decorso dei peduncoli cerebellari e sui loro rapporti cogli altri centri nervosi," *ibid.*, **17** (1891), 357–368.

A separate publication is *Sull'origine e decorso dei peduncoli cerebellari e sui loro rapporti cogli altri centri nervosi* (Florence, 1891).

II. SECONDARY LITERATURE. Works about Marchi include [Arturo Donaggio], *Onoranze nella R. Università di Modena a Vittorio Marchi nel 25° anniversario della sua morte* (Reggio nell'Emilia, 1933); Battista Grassi, *I progressi della biologia e delle sue applicazioni pratiche conseguiti in Italia nell'ultimo cinquantennio* (Rome, 1911), 170; Luigi Luciani, "Vittorio Marchi," in *Archives italiennes de biologie*, **49** (1908), 149–152; Manfredo Manfredi, "Vittorio Marchi e il suo 'metodo,' " in Luigi Barchi, ed., *Medici e naturalisti Reggiani* (Reggio nell'Emilia, 1935), 159–169; P. Petrazzani, "Prof. Vittorio Marchi," in *Rivista sperimentale di freniatria*, **34** (1908), 319–320; and Antonio A. Rizzoli, "An Unusual Case of Meningioma With the Involvement of Russell's Hook Bundle as Described by Vittorio Marchi (1851–1908)," in *Medical History*, **17** (1973), 95–97.

LUIGI BELLONI

MARCHIAFAVA, ETTORE (*b.* Rome, Italy, 3 January 1847; *d.* Rome, 23 October 1935), *pathology, anatomy.*

Marchiafava was the son of Anna Vercelli and Francesco Marchiafava. He began his career at a time of great social and political upheaval. In the scientific world polemics raged—such as those between Bufalini and Tommasini on the ultimate cause of disease—over the direction that science should take in light of the many major discoveries then being made.

The great prevalence of communicable diseases, especially malaria and tuberculosis, exerted a strong influence in determining Marchiafava's line of research. After obtaining a degree at the University of Rome in 1869, he went for a short period to Berlin, where Koch was making progress in the study of tuberculosis. The young scientist returned to Italy with a strong interest in bacteriology and parasitology.

In 1872 Marchiafava was nominated assistant to the professor of pathological anatomy at the University of Rome; he became associate professor in 1881 and full professor in 1883. After his official retirement in 1922 he continued his research and writing in the department he had helped organize.

Marchiafava was not only a great pathological anatomist but also an outstanding clinician and a faithful follower of Morgagni, so that from pathological anatomy and from the data he obtained in studying corpses, he was able to make his clinical interpretations.

Marchiafava's first research was essentially in parasitology. He spent many years studying the morphology and the biological cycle of the malarial parasite. He showed the modifications that the presence of amoeboid bodies causes in the erythrocytes, and demonstrated that these changes were closely related to the growth and multiplication of the parasite. This demonstration derived from the parallel study of microscopic blood data and the clinical pattern of fever peaks. The most important result of the research was Marchiafava's discovery that malarial infection is transmitted through the blood. He spent the entire period from 1880 to 1891 in this intensive study, which enabled him to distinguish between the agent of the estivo-autumnal fever and that of the tertian and quartan fevers. As a senator, elected in 1913, and later as hygiene assessor of Rome (1918), he urged the adoption of antimalarial measures.

In 1884 Marchiafava, in collaboration with A. Celli, identified meningococcus as the etiological agent of epidemic cerebral and spinal meningitis. Another of his findings, which bears his name, was Marchiafava's postpneumonic triad, characterized by the simultaneous presence of a meningitis infection and an endocardial ulcer, which he related to septicemia in the lungs.

His name is also remembered in the Marchiafava-Bignami syndrome, which is a special primitive alteration of nerve fibers caused by chronic alcoholism, affecting in particular the corpus callosum and the frontal commissure.

In 1911 Marchiafava described a form of chronic acquired hemolitic jaundice characterized by a hemoglobinemia with hemoglobinuria and progressive anemia, the Marchiafava-Micheli syndrome. He later conducted more detailed studies on this form of the disease, which he named hemolitic anemia with perpetual hemosiderinuria.

A pioneer in the field of cardiac pathology, Marchiafava showed the importance of coronary sclerosis in the pathogenesis of cardiac infarction and suggested the use of theobromine as a treatment for this disease. Early in his career he made other important studies that showed the bacterial nature of endocardial ulcers. He also did research in angiotic obliteration in interstitial inflammations and particularly in tuberculosis. Marchiafava was especially interested in tuberculosis and examined in detail the structural modifications occurring where the bronchi join the lungs, as well as the clinical epidemiology of the disease. On kidney pathology he studied and described glomerulonephritis related to infections such as scarlet fever.

BIBLIOGRAPHY

I. ORIGINAL WORKS. The main works of Marchiafava are *Sul parasita delle febbri gravi estivo-autunnali* (Rome, 1889); *Sulle febbri malariche estivo-autunnali* (Rome, 1892); *La infezione malarica* (Milan, 1903); *La perniciosità della malaria* (Rome, 1928); and *La eredità in patologia* (Turin, 1930).

II. SECONDARY LITERATURE. Works about Marchiafava include G. Bompiani, "Ettore Marchiafava," in *Patholo-gica*, **28** (1936), 93–99; L. W. Hackett, "Prof. Ettore Marchiafava," in *Transactions of the Royal Society of Tropical Medicine and Hygiene*, **29** (1936); L. Stroppiana, "Ettore Marchiafava a cento anni dalla nascità," in *Castalia*, **1** (1948), 17–18; and P. Verga, "Ettore Marchiafava," in *Riforma medica*, **51** (1935), 1736–1737.

CARLO CASTELLANI

MARCHLEWSKI, LEON PAWEŁ TEODOR (*b.* Włocławek, Poland, 15 December 1869; *d.* Cracow, Poland, 16 January 1946), *chemistry*.

Marchlewski was the son of Józef Marchlewski, a grain merchant, and Augusta Riksreerend. Having finished his secondary education in Warsaw, he worked there for a year in a chemistry laboratory of the Museum of Agriculture and Industry; then, in 1888, enrolled in the Polytechnical School in Zurich. From 1890 until 1892, the year in which he received the doctorate from the University of Zurich, Marchlewski served as an assistant to Georg Lunge. While working with Lunge he published his first scientific papers; these were largely analytical and technological in nature, and were concerned with inorganic chemistry, the determination of iodine and sulfur in compounds, and the gas-volumetric determination of carbon dioxide. He also drew up tables of the density of hydrochloric and nitric acids that continue to be consulted.

From 1892 until 1898, Marchlewski worked in England in the private laboratory of Edward Schunck at Kersal, near Manchester. Schunck had been Liebig's pupil, and his own area of research was plant pigments. With him, Marchlewski published papers on natural glucosides, including arbutin, phlorizin, and datiscin. Marchlewski offered a new interpretation of the structure of these compounds, which brought him into conflict with E. Fischer; Marchlewski was eventually proved to be right. He also explained the structure of rubiadin and of indican, a compound which had been discovered by Schunck and which Marchlewski showed to be a glucoside of indoxyl. Most important, he began to make his own investigations of plant pigments, including isatin and chlorophyll and its derivatives, a subject upon which he first reported in a paper written with Schunk in 1897.

In 1898 Marchlewski became director of the research laboratory attached to the Claus and Ree factory at Clayton. He was at the same time a lecturer in technology at the Institute of Science and Technology in Manchester. During his stay in England he married Fanny Hargreaves; they had three sons. In 1900 Marchlewski returned with his family to Poland, where he had been appointed to the Food Examination Research Institute in Cracow. He became lecturer in chemical technology at Jagiellonian University there in the same year.

Marchlewski again took up the studies of chlorophyll that he had begun in England. He had already experimentally obtained phylloporphyrin and compared its absorption spectra with those of hematoporphyrin, concluding that the two compounds are closely related, as are chlorophyll and hemoglobin. In Cracow, he obtained phyllocyanin from chlorophyll; he then demonstrated that hemopyrrole could be derived from this compound as well as from hemin. He further obtained phyllophylin, a substance similar to hemin itself, from phylloporphyrin and ferrous salts. Marchlewski published the results of some of these researches with Nencki. His own monograph *Die Chemie der Chlorophylle*, published in 1903, established his authority in this field.

In 1904 Marchlewski declined the offer of a chair of chemistry at the University of Lvov; two years later, he was appointed professor of medical chemistry at Jagiellonian University. He had by then published eighty-four papers—almost half of his life's work—in chemical journals. He received another appointment almost immediately, and left Cracow to become director of the Research Institute in Puławy, where he remained until 1923. He then returned to occupy the chair of medical chemistry at Jagiellonian University, where he remained (except for an interruption during World War II) for the rest of his life. He twice served the university as dean of the medical faculty, and was rector of it in 1932.

Marchlewski's work on chlorophyll involved him in a series of controversies with the German chemist Willstätter. Although Marchlewski was not always correct (it is difficult, for example, to understand how he, an outstanding analyst, could have overlooked the presence of magnesium in chlorophyll), the debates themselves contributed to the growth of chlorophyll research. Marchlewski was also highly critical of the work of the botanist Tsvet, who had devised a technique for separating chlorophyll into its component parts by dissolving it in alcohol, then passing it through a column filled with calcium carbonate, sugar, and inulin. Marchlewski considered Tsvet to be ignorant of chemistry, and Tsvet, as a direct result of Marchlewski's criticism, suspended his researches. Marchlewski fully understood Tsvet's method a few years later, and greatly regretted his interference.

Marchlewski's last important achievement was the discovery of phylloerythrin, a compound that results from the breakdown of chlorophyll during digestion by herbivores. In his last years he devoted himself exclusively to spectral analysis, which he saw as the chief means toward explaining the structure of organic compounds.

BIBLIOGRAPHY

I. ORIGINAL WORKS. Marchlewski wrote 201 papers, of which a complete list is given by his student H. Malarski, "Leon Marchlewski. 1869–1946," in *Pamiętniki państwowego naukowego instytutu gospodarstwa wiejskiego*, **18E** (1948), 1–27. His most important books are *Die Chemie der Chlorophylle* (Brunswick, 1903); *Teorye i metody badania współczesnej chemii organicznej* ("Theories and Methods of Contemporary Organic Chemistry"; Lvov, 1905); *Chemia organiczna* ("Organic Chemistry"; Cracow, 1910; repr. 1924); and *Podręcznik do badań fizjologiczno-chemicznych* ("Handbook of Physiological and Chemical Research"; Cracow, 1916). Marchlewski's personal acta are preserved in the archives of Jagiellonian University, Cracow, S. II, 619; some of his letters may be found in the archives of the Polish Academy of Sciences, Cracow, the Jagiellonian Library, and the Ossolineum, Wrocław.

II. SECONDARY LITERATURE. See A. Gałecki, "Udział Polaków w uprawianiu i rozwoju chemii" ("Poles Who Participated in the Development of Chemistry"), in *Polska w kulturze powszechnej*, II (Cracow, 1918), 336–337; W. Lampe, "Śp. Leon Marchlewski," in *Rocznik towarzystwa naukowego Warszawskiego*, **39** (1946), 131–134; and B. Skarzyński, "Leon Marchlewski," in *Roczniki Chemii*, **22** (1948), 1–18, repr. in *Polscy badacze przyrody* (Warsaw, 1959), 289–312. On Marchlewski's controversy with Tsvet, see T. Robinson, "Michael Tswett," in *Chymia*, **6** (1960), 146–161.

WŁODZIMIERZ HUBICKI

MARCI OF KRONLAND, JOHANNES MARCUS

(*b.* Lanškroun, Bohemia [now Czechoslovakia], 13 June 1595; *d.* Prague, Bohemia [now Czechoslovakia], 10 April 1667), *physics, mathematics, medicine.*

Marci, whose father was clerk to an aristocrat, received his early education at the Jesuit college in Jindřichův Hradec, then studied philosophy and theology in Olomouc and, from 1618 on, medicine in Prague. He took the M.D. in 1625, then began to lecture at the Prague Faculty of Medicine. He achieved considerable renown as a physician, becoming physician to the Kingdom of Bohemia and personal attendant to two emperors, Ferdinand III and Leopold I.

Although it is recorded that Marci wished to become a priest and a Jesuit, and although he took a staunchly Catholic position during the forced civil re-Catholicization of Bohemia and Moravia (1625–1626), he nevertheless represented the anti-Jesuit party in the affairs of Prague University. To gain support at the Vatican for his party's purpose, which was to prevent the Jesuits from gaining control of the medical and legal faculties (since they already held the faculties of philosophy and theology), Marci undertook a diplomatic trip to Italy, which had important results in his scientific life. During this trip, which he made in 1639, Marci met Paul Guldin and Athanasius Kircher, with whom he corresponded for a long time, and also read Galileo's *Discorsi*, although he did not meet Galileo.

Marci's political activities did not injure his career. He was professor of medicine at Prague University from about 1620 to 1660. In 1648 he took active part in defending the city against the Swedes; he was knighted for merit in 1654. He retained his academic position even after the Prague Charles University merged with the Jesuit institution to become Charles-Ferdinand University, a unification that greatly favored Jesuit pretensions. Marci became rector of the university in 1662; according to Jesuit sources he was admitted to the Society shortly before his death.

As a scientist, Marci worked in considerable isolation. The Catholic Counter-Reformation, exploited by the Hapsburg rulers, had gradually strangled scientific life in Bohemia, and access to the works of foreign scientists was severely limited. Marci's knowledge of the researches of his contemporaries was therefore at best random, and his own work shows evidences of the ideological pressures of his own Prague environment. Marci studied many scientific subjects, including astronomy and mathematics; in the latter he was probably stimulated by the work of the Jesuit Grégoire de Saint-Vincent, who taught at Prague.

Marci's most important work was, however, accomplished in medicine and physics. His 1639 book, *De proportione motus*, contained his theory of the collision of bodies (particularly elastic bodies) and gave an account of the experiments whereby he reached it. Although these experiments are described precisely, Marci was unable to formulate general quantitative laws from them, since his results were not drawn from exact measurements of either of the sizes and weights of the spheres that he employed or of the direction and velocity of their motion. Rather, he was content with simple comparisons of the properties that he investigated, characterizing them as being "smaller," "bigger," or "the same" as each other; his allegations of their proportionalities are thus unproven. Some of his concepts, too (for example that of impulse), lack exact definition, but despite these shortcomings, his observations and conclusions are generally right. He was able to distinguish different qualities of spheres and to state the concepts of solid bodies and of quantity of motion.

The section on the collision of bodies in *De proportione motus* is only one of those in which Marci dealt in problems of mechanics. He also stated the correct relationship between the duration of the oscillation of a pendulum and its length and proposed using a pendulum for measuring short periods of time (for example, for taking the pulse of a patient). He further described the properties of free fall. Here the question of the influence on Marci of Galileo's *Discorsi* must arise. The *Discorsi* was published a year before *De proportione motus*, and Marci certainly read it before publishing his own book, but the exact extent to which he drew upon it remains unknown. Certainly Marci had less skill than Galileo in reducing mechanics to mathematical forms; but if, in later years, he chose to emphasize the divergence of his opinions from Galileo's, he may well have been influenced by the attitude of the church toward the latter's writings.

Marci also carried out research in optics, setting down most of his results in *Thaumantias liber de arcu coelesti* (1648). In his optical experiments, designed to explain the phenomenon of the rainbow, Marci placed himself in the line of such Bohemian and Moravian investigators as Kepler, Christophe Scheiner, Baltasar Konrád, and Melchior Haněl. In his experiments on the decomposition of white light, for which he employed prisms, Marci described the spectral colors and recorded that each color corresponded to a specific refraction angle. He also stated that the color of a ray is constant when it is again refracted through another prism (*Thaumantias liber de arcu coelesti*, pp. 99–100). He did not mention the reconstitution of the spectrum into white light (a result that is first to be found in the work of Newton), although he did study the "mixture" of colored rays. He also made inconclusive experiments on light phenomena on thin films. In general, Marci's optical works are not successful in speculation, since his attempts to deduce the properties of light and to explain the causes of observed phenomena on the basis of his optical knowledge become entangled in the philosophical notions of his time.

Marci's medical works also become involved in philosophical as well as theoretical problems. It is interesting to note that he devoted particular attention to questions of what would now be termed neurology, psychology, and psychophysiology, in treatises that have not yet been fully evaluated. His work on epilepsy is, however, worthy of special note, since in it Marci tried to adopt a purely medical approach to the disease and to analyze critically both previous descriptions of epileptic fits and existing theories of their origin. From these data he drew, in obscure and symbolic terms, the conclusion that epilepsy is, in fact, a nervous disease; this result is in keeping with his theories of perception, memory, and imagination, in which his method was observational and his guiding principle that later formulated by Locke as "nihil est in intellectu quod non prius fuerit in sensu."

It is thus apparent that philosophical considerations figured importantly in Marci's scientific work; it is perhaps less obvious that his philosophy was in turn colored by developments in the natural sciences. Marci's philosophy represented a sometimes incoherent fusion of Aristotelian and Platonic ideas with Catholic mysticism. From these elements he derived a speculative pantheism, based on a "world soul"—uniting the macrocosmos and the microcosmos—and a "virtus plastica sive seminalis," or an "active idea." He attempted to confirm his mystical beliefs by means of then newly established and often subjectively interpreted tenets of natural science; he further called upon these new discoveries to answer such philosophical questions as the relationship between mind and body and to elaborate a general view of the world and nature. (In so doing he drew close to the later systems of *Naturphilosophie*.) Marci's philosophical ideas probably had some influence on such Prague philosophers as Hirnheim (and perhaps even on the young Spinoza), while some of his ideas were taken up by the Cambridge Platonists, among them Ralph Cudworth and, in particular, Francis Glisson.

BIBLIOGRAPHY

Marci's principal works are *De proportione motus figurarum rectilinearum et circuli quadratura ex motu* (Prague, 1639), repr. in *Acta historiae rerum naturalium necnon technicarum*, special issue 3 (1967), 131–258; *Thaumantias liber de arcu coelesti deque colorum apparentium natura, ortu et causis, in quo pellucidi opticae fontes a sua scaturigine, ab his vero colorigeni rivi derivantur* (Prague, 1648; repr. 1968); *Lithurgia mentis seu disceptatio medico-philosophica et optica de natura epilepsiae ...* (Regensburg, 1678); and *Ortho-Sophia seu philosophia impulsus universalis* (Prague, 1683).

Bibliographies of writings by and about Marci are Dagmar Ledrerová, "Bibliographie de Johannes Marcus Marci," in *Acta historiae rerum naturalium necnon technicarum*, special issue 3 (1967), 39–50; and "Bibliografie Jana Marka Marci," in *Zprávy Čs. společnosti pro dějiny věd a techniky*, nos. 9–10 (1968), 107–119.

LUBOŠ NOVÝ

MARCONI, GUGLIELMO (*b.* Bologna, Italy, 25 April 1874; *d.* Rome, Italy, 20 July 1937), *engineering, physics.*

Marconi was the second son of Giuseppe Marconi, a wealthy landowner, and his second wife, Annie Jameson, the daughter of an Irish whiskey distiller. His limited formal education, of early private tutoring followed by several years at the Leghorn lyceum, included special instruction in physics. His first wife, Beatrice O'Brien, was of an aristocratic Irish family; his second, Maria Bezzi-Scali, belonged to the papal nobility. Marconi was always a devoted citizen of Italy, and frequently acted in an official capacity for his government. Chief among the many honors awarded him was the Nobel Prize for physics, which he shared with K. F. Braun in 1909.

Marconi seems to have first learned in 1894 of Hertz's laboratory experiments with electromagnetic waves. He was immediately curious as to how far the waves might travel, and began to experiment, with the assistance of Prof. A. Righi of Bologna. His initial apparatus resembled Hertz's in its use of a Ruhmkorff-coil spark gap oscillator and dipole antennas with parabolic reflectors, but it replaced Hertz's sparking-ring detector with the coherer that had been employed earlier by Branly and Lodge. Marconi quickly discovered that increased transmission distance could be obtained with larger antennas, and his first important invention was the use of sizable elevated antenna structures and ground connections at both transmitter and receiver, in place of Hertz's dipoles. With this change he achieved in 1895 a transmission distance of 1.5 miles (the length of the family estate), and at about the same time conceived of "wireless telegraph" communication through keying the transmitter in telegraph code.

Marconi was unable to interest the Italian government in the practical potentialities of his work, however. In February 1896 he moved to London, where one of his Irish cousins, Henry Jameson Davis, helped him prepare a patent application. Davis also arranged demonstrations of the wireless telegraph for government officials and in 1897 helped to form and finance the Wireless Telegraph and Signal Co., Ltd., which in 1900 became Marconi's Wireless Telegraph Co., Ltd. By the latter year Marconi had experimentally increased his signaling distance to 150 miles, and had decided to attempt transatlantic transmission. A powerful transmitter was built at Poldhu, Cornwall, England, and a large receiving antenna placed on Cape Cod, Massachusetts. When the latter blew down in 1901, Marconi, who was anxious to forestall any competitors, sailed for Newfoundland where, using a kiteborne antenna and Solari's carbon-on-steel detector with a telephone receiver, on 12 December he received the first transatlantic wireless communication, the three code dots signifying the letter "S." Already well known, Marconi, at twenty-seven, became world famous overnight.

From 1902 Marconi devoted more of his time to managing his companies, which by 1914 held a commanding position in British and American maritime radio service. (The Radio Corporation of America was formed in 1919, partly to acquire his United States interests.) Throughout his career Marconi was exceptionally fortunate in his ability to attract highly qualified employees and consultants; among them J. A. Fleming, inventor of the thermionic diode; H. J. Round, who developed the triode as a radio-frequency oscillator and amplifier independently of De Forest; R. M. Vyvyan, who installed many of the early spark stations; and C. S. Franklin, designer of directional antennas. It was Franklin who—drawing upon Marconi's earlier notion of exploring the communication potentialities of shortwaves by employing dipole antennas with highly directional reflectors—in 1920 developed such dipole antennas into a beamed radio-telephone circuit between London and Birmingham, operating at 20 MHz. Following a series of discoveries (made by radio amateurs, among others) that indicated the feasibility of establishing a 10,000-mile shortwave communication network, operable by both day and night, Marconi's company completed a globe-girdling system of shortwave beam stations in 1927.

From 1921 on Marconi had used his steam yacht *Elettra* as home, laboratory, and mobile receiving station in propagation experiments. In 1932 he discovered that still higher frequency waves (microwaves) could be received at a point much farther below the optical horizon than had been predicted by any theory. This phenomenon was exploited in later "scatter propagation" circuits, which added new reliability to communications in arctic regions.

BIBLIOGRAPHY

I. ORIGINAL WORKS. Papers by Marconi are "Wireless Telegraphy," in *Proceedings of the Institution of Electrical Engineers*, **28** (1899), 273; "Wireless Telegraphy," in *Proceedings of the Royal Institution of Great Britain*, **16** (1899–1901), 247–256; "Syntonic Wireless Telegraphy," in *Royal Society of Arts. Journal*, **49** (1901), 505; "The Progress of Electric Space Telegraphy," in *Proceedings of the Royal Institution of Great Britain*, **17** (1902–1904), 195–210; "A Note on the Effect of Daylight Upon the Propagation of Electromagnetic Impulses over Long Distances," in *Proceedings of the Royal Society*, **70** (1902), 344; and "Address on Wireless Telegraphy to Annual Dinner," in *Transactions of the American Institute of Electrical Engineers*, **19** (1902), 93–121.

See also "Recent Advances in Wireless Telegraphy," in *Proceedings of the Royal Institution of Great Britain*, **18** (1905–1907), 31–45; "Transatlantic Wireless Telegraphy," *ibid.*, **19** (1908–1910), 107–130; "Radiotelegraphy," *ibid.*, **20** (1911–1913), 193–209; "Radio Telegraphy," in *Proceedings of the Institute of Radio Engineers*, **10** (1922), 215–238; "Results Obtained Over Very Long Distance by Short Wave Directional Wireless Telegraphy, More Generally Referred to as the Beam System," in *Royal Society of Arts. Journal*, **72** (1924), 607; "Radio Communication," in *Proceedings of the Institute of Radio Engineers*, **16** (1928), 40–69; and "Radio Communication by Means of Very Short Electric Waves," in *Proceedings of the Royal Institution of Great Britain*, **27** (1931–1933), 509–544.

II. SECONDARY LITERATURE. For information on Marconi's life and work, see B. L. Jacot de Boinod and D. M. B. Collier, *Marconi—Master of Space* (London, 1935); Douglas Coe, *Marconi, Pioneer of Radio* (New York, 1943); O. E. Dunlap, Jr., *Marconi, The Man and His Wireless* (New York, 1937); Degna Marconi, *My Father, Marconi* (New York, 1962); and W. P. Jolly, *Marconi* (New York, 1972).

ROBERT A. CHIPMAN

MARCOU, JULES (*b*. Salins, France, 20 April 1824; *d*. Cambridge, Massachusetts, 17 April 1898), *geology, paleontology, topography*.

Marcou was born in the Jura, and the natural history of the area had much to do with determining the course of his work in science. Educated in his native Salins and the lycée at Besançon, Marcou went to Paris to study at the Collège Saint-Louis. Ill health caused an interruption in his education, and after returning to Salins he began to explore the geology and paleontology of his native Jura. Marcou's first published work was in mathematics, but his growing knowledge of natural history had become so extensive that by 1845 he was able to publish a highly original analysis of Jurassic fossils ("Recherches géologiques sur le Jura Salinois") in the *Mémoires de la Société d'histoire naturelle de Neuchâtel*. Louis Agassiz, editor of the journal, was impressed by the young man's grasp of a complex subject. The Swiss paleontologist encouraged the young man to do further work in the field, an ambition buttressed by Marcou's appointment as professor of mineralogy at the Sorbonne in 1846 and curator of fossil conchology at the Jardin des Plantes in 1847. With the support of Agassiz, in 1848 Marcou was awarded a traveling fellowship under the auspices of the Jardin des Plantes. He chose to spend this time under the guidance of Agassiz, who had gone to the United States. Thus in a short time, Marcou had established himself as a rising figure in geology and paleontology.

Marcou's outstanding contributions were in stratigraphical geology and geological mapping, most notably a "Geological Map of the World" published in two European editions in 1862 and in 1875, a work one biographer classified as "the point of departure for all subsequent maps of this class." The majority of his more than 180 publications—books, collections of maps, and articles—were in French.

In 1850 Marcou married Jane Belknap, daughter of the historian Jeremy Belknap, and this association with New England lineage and wealth made him independent of material concerns, and he was able to carry on explorations and publish his findings. Marcou did not consider America or its scientists in the light of any permanent physical or intellectual association. After exploring Lake Superior with Agassiz during 1848–1849, he returned to Europe in 1850. He came to the United States again in 1853 as an explorer of the trans-Mississippi West but left the following year. He remained in Europe, chiefly as a professor at the École Polytechnique of Zurich, until 1859, when he returned to the United States to aid Agassiz in the organization and teaching activities of the newly established Museum of Comparative Zoology at Harvard College. After 1864 he returned to France on several occasions but considered Cambridge, Massachusetts, his primary residence. Marcou was physically prepossessing and intellectually dogmatic, with a high opinion of his own abilities— which were significant in areas other than science. His *Derivation of the Name America* (Washington, 1890) remains a highly original piece of scholarship, and his two-volume study of the life of Agassiz was a particularly modern appraisal for its time, especially for its dispassionate presentation of Agassiz's scientific work. In 1867 Marcou was awarded the grand cross of the Legion of Honor, and in 1875 he undertook his last scientific exploration, in the employ of the United States Geographical Surveys West of the One Hundredth Meridian, wherein he did original work in the topography and stratigraphy of southern California.

Marcou did not support the theory of organic evolution. Three years before his death he wrote that Charles Darwin had "failed to give a doctrine well based and acceptable," insisting that natural history progressed through reliance on new facts rather than hypotheses and theories.

This position was in some contrast to Marcou's career in American science. As a field geologist, his experience was limited. Nevertheless, beginning in 1853 he became a party to a series of controversies that demonstrated his disdain for the work of Americans, and at the same time were a witness to the rise of modern American geology. Marcou's role in these disputes took the form of insistence on the correctness of his identification of American stratigraphic topology. This certainty was grounded on little direct knowledge or experience, a condition that infuriated men of the caliber of William P. Blake, James Dwight Dana, James Hall, and William Barton Rogers, who were establishing the character of American professional geology. Early in his American career, Marcou stoutly defended the veracity and general utility of Ebenezer Emmons' so-called Taconic system of New York stratigraphy, pitting himself against Dana and Hall in a matter not fully resolved for nearly fifty years. The *Geology of North America* (Zurich, 1858) contained an entire chapter castigating the scientific work and methods of Blake, Hall, and Dana, as well as "criticisms of the *American Journal of Science and Arts.*" Marcou's controversies with American geologists of established reputation were epitomized in his attack on John Wesley Powell and the research orientation of the United States Geological Survey in his *The Geological Map of the United States and the United States Geological Survey* (Cambridge, Mass., 1892).

In 1853 Agassiz's influence had gained Marcou a position as geologist with the United States Army Topographical Corps surveying a Pacific railroad route along the thirty-fifth parallel. Marcou's field experience, extending from Arkansas into California, was sufficient to embolden him to publish a geological map of the United States. This map (published in enlarged editions in 1855 and 1858) was an epitome of the argumentations surrounding the professionalization of American geology. The 1858 edition was especially offensive to American naturalists. Each edition of the map was criticized first by Hall, then by Blake, and finally by Dana, and each condemnation was met by Marcou with greater insistence on his veracity. The points at issue were matters of stratigraphic identification. Marcou was criticized for identifying large portions of the United States as belonging to the Jurassic and Triassic periods, rather than the conventional Cretaceous classification. The matter was made even less agreeable by Marcou's retention of important fossil evidence which belonged to the government; and upon its ultimate return, it was plain that these materials were of European rather than American Jurassic origin. Marcou had identified large portions of the continent as belonging to a period younger than the Jurassic, and, in the view of men such as Blake, all such analyses had been done without benefit of field experience and were of little service to American geology.

Subsequent investigations demonstrated that Marcou was at least partially correct in his nonempirical support of the Taconic system and his definition of the American Jurassic. It is significant that this European geologist, working in the tradition of Georges Cuvier, Jules Thurmann, and Agassiz, was consistent with an earlier period of universalist ambitions to define natural history. It is also noteworthy that his critics demonstrated, by the nature of their disputation, that it was impossible, on the basis of limited knowledge, to construct an American geological map of sufficient detail. By the late 1880's, the work of the early railroad surveys and post-Civil War government geographical and geological efforts had made such contributions possible. Marcou's independence was not unusual in the annals of other aspects of American natural history.

Marcou, whose career began as a promising fieldworker, was at his best as a teacher and descriptive stratigraphic geologist whose observations stimulated Americans to be more critical of their physical history. In this respect, his work served an important purpose in that it helped persuade both Americans and Europeans of the need for careful, comparative research methods and publications.

BIBLIOGRAPHY

I. ORIGINAL WORKS. A bibliography of Marcou's publications in invertebrate paleontology is in John Belknap Marcou, "Bibliography of Publications Relating to the Collection of Fossil Invertebrates in the United States National Museum," *Bulletin. United States National Museum*, no. 30 (Washington, 1885–1886), 241–244. Marcou's works published in the United States are listed in Max Meisel, *A Bibliography of American Natural History*, 3 vols. (New York, 1924–1929), II–III.

Among his significant works are *A Geological Map of the United States and the British Provinces of North America* ... (Boston, 1853); *Carte géologique des États Unis* ... (Paris, 1855); *Geology of North America* ... (Zurich, 1858); *Letter to M. Joachim Barrande on the Taconic Rocks of Vermont and Canada* (Cambridge, Mass., 1862); *Carte géologique de la terre* (Zurich, 1875); *American Geological Classification and Nomenclature* (Cambridge, Mass., 1888); and *Life, Letters and Works of Louis Agassiz*, 2 vols. (New York–London, 1895).

II. SECONDARY LITERATURE. Alpheus Hyatt, "Jules Marcou," in *Proceedings of the American Academy of Arts and Sciences*, **34** (1899), 651–656; Hubert Lyman Clark, "Marcou, Jules," in *Dictionary of American Biography*; William Goetzmann, *Army Exploration in the American West: 1803–1863* (New Haven, 1959), *passim*; Edward Lurie, *Louis Agassiz: A Life in Science* (Chicago, 1960), *passim*; George P. Merrill, *The First One Hundred Years of American Geology* (New Haven, 1924), *passim*.

EDWARD LURIE

MARCUS, JOHANNES. See **Marci of Kronland.**

MAREY, ÉTIENNE-JULES (*b*. Beaune, France, 5 March 1830; *d*. Paris, France, 15 May 1904), *physiology.*

Marey's central significance for the development of physiology in France lies in his adoption and advocacy of two fundamental techniques in experimental physiology: graphical recording and cinematography.

Marey studied medicine at the Faculty of Medicine of Paris and then was an intern at the Hôpital Cochin. His doctoral dissertation (1857) on the circulation of the blood utilized recording instruments that were modified versions of those developed by German physiologists, particularly Karl Ludwig. By installing these instruments in his lodgings on the Rue Cuvier, he established the first private laboratory in Paris for the study of experimental physiology. In 1868 he succeeded Pierre Flourens in the chair of "natural history of organized bodies" at the Collège de France.

During the first decade of his research career (1857–1867) Marey applied the technique of graphical recording to the study of the mechanics and hydraulics of the circulatory system, the heartbeat, respiration, and muscle contraction in general. He analyzed the circulatory and muscular systems in terms of the physical variables, elasticity, resistance, and tonicity. With the graphical trace he established the relationship of heart rate and blood pressure, thus supplementing previous studies of the value of blood pressure in a vessel with traces of its waveform.

After having identified the actions of parts of the organ or system under investigation by means of particular motions of the recording stylus, Marey constructed an artificial model of the organ or system. By manipulating these constructions to obtain wave forms identical to those produced in the living subject, he demonstrated the accuracy of his analyses of the characteristics of his graphical traces.

In this early work Marey sought to apply his methods and results to pathology and to clinical diagnosis. His concern with the greatest possible accuracy in graphical records was matched by his concern for simplifying instruments so that they could be easily used by the clinical diagnostician.

During this first decade Marey's accomplishments depended more upon technical achievement than upon innovative choice of problems. His research topics were in fact fairly straightforward extensions of investigations begun by Bernard, Helmholtz, and Vierordt. Emil du Bois-Reymond, Fick, and Weber were also important influences. After 1868, however, he turned to what was then a more novel area for the application of recording devices—the study of human and animal locomotion. Using traces of the motions of bird and insect wings, Marey showed that changes in the form of the wing modify its air-resistance properties; rather than contracting the wing flexor and extensor muscles, this surface change accounts for much of the upward and forward motion of the flying animal. By this means Marey determined the mechanical requirements for the physiological apparatus of flight. As with his deductions drawn from his circulatory studies, here too he sought to verify his deductions by constructing models that would display the same properties as those of the living specimen. He examined the structure of the muscle and skeletal systems in the light of these mechanical requirements to learn how the size and insertion of muscles, bone length, and joint angles combined to fulfill those requirements.

Marey also studied the length and frequency of steps taken by human beings and quadrupeds under various environmental conditions. Again, he sought the clinical application of his results—in this case to elucidate different locomotor pathologies. This work depended upon the invention of "Marey's tambour," a device for the transmission and recording of subtle motions without seriously limiting the subject's freedom of movement. The tambour is an air-filled metal capsule covered by a rubber membrane. When compression distorts the membrane, air is forced through an opening from the capsule into a fine, flexible tube; at the opposite end of the tube a similar capsule receives these variations in air pressure and its membrane activates the movable lever on the graphical recorder. Marey's tambour was still being used in 1955.

When Marey saw that the pattern of leg motions and hoofbeats of a trotting horse could be depicted clearly by photographs taken in rapid succession, he turned to the perfection of a photographic device that could be used to improve his studies of animal locomotion. Beginning in 1881, his modifications of a camera that had been used by Janssen to record the transit of Venus in 1874 made an important contribution to the development of cinematographic techniques. Also in 1881 he persuaded the municipal council of Paris to annex to his professorial chair land at the Parc-des-Princes, where he constructed a physiological station for the photographic study of animal motion outdoors under the most natural conditions possible. For almost the whole of the following two decades he devoted himself to the application of cinematography to physiology, extending its use to such subjects as photographing water currents produced by the motions of fish and microscopic organisms.

In Marey's view, physiology "is itself but the study of organic movements," and the graph best represents all the variations that such phenomena undergo. Marey believed, however, that these motions ultimately were to be explained by laws of physics and chemistry. Furthermore, while he accepted the application of physiological research to medical problems, he subordinated this utilitarian purpose to a more abstract goal: "analyzing the conditions which modify the functions of life and . . . better determining the laws which regulate these functions." Toward this end medicine served only as one further means of analysis.

Marey's strong desire to see the graph become the language of physiological description led him to fear that confusion and repetition would increase without some standardization of the equipment and parameters used in recording. He therefore proposed to the fourth International Physiological Congress in 1898 that a committee be formed to suggest uniform standards and to perfect the technology of recording devices. When his suggestion was accepted, he solicited and obtained donations from the French government, the municipality of Paris, the Royal Society of London, and other scientific academies for construction at the Parc-des-Princes of an institute where the committee members could work. This institute has since been called the Institut Marey.

In 1895 he became president of the Académie des Sciences, to which he had been elected in 1878.

BIBLIOGRAPHY

I. ORIGINAL WORKS. Marey published more than 150 papers, which are indexed in the Royal Society *Catalogue of Scientific Papers*, IV, 237; VIII, 327–328; X, 719–720; XII, 484; XVII, 16–17. Among his major papers are "Recherches hydrauliques sur la circulation du sang," in *Annales des sciences naturelles. Zoologie* . . ., 4th ser., **8** (1857), 329–364; "Études physiologiques sur les caractères du battement du coeur et les conditions qui le modifient," in *Journal de l'anatomie et de la physiologie*, **2** (1865), 276–301, 416–425; "Étude graphique des mouvements respiratoires et des influences qui les modifient," *ibid.*, 425–453; "Études graphiques sur la nature de la contraction musculaire," *ibid.*, **3** (1866), 225–242, 403–416; "Mémoire sur le vol des insectes et des oiseaux," in *Annales des sciences naturelles. Zoologie* . . ., 5th ser., **12** (1869), 49–150, and **15** (1872), art. 13; "De la locomotion terrestre chez les bipèdes et les quadrupèdes," in Robin's *Journal anatomique*, **9** (1873), 42–80; "Emploi de la photographie instantanée pour l'analyse des mouvements chez les animaux," in *Comptes rendus . . . de l'Académie des sciences*, **94** (1882), 1013–1020; "La photochronographie et ses applications à l'analyse des phénomènes physiologiques," in *Archives de physiologie normale et pathologique*, **1** (1889), 508–517; and

"Mesures à prendre pour l'uniformisation des méthodes et le contrôle des instruments employés en physiologie," in *Comptes rendus ... de l'Académie des sciences*, **127** (1899), 375–381.

Among Marey's books are *Physiologie médicale de la circulation du sang* (Paris, 1863); *Du mouvement dans les fonctions de la vie* (Paris, 1868); *La machine animale, locomotion terrestre et aérienne* (Paris, 1873); *La méthode graphique dans les sciences expérimentales* (Paris, 1878); and *Le mouvement* (Paris, 1894).

II. SECONDARY LITERATURE. See Association Internationale de l'Institut Marey, *Travaux de l'Institut Marey* (Paris, 1905–1910), which contain summaries of laboratory work at the institute; A. Chauveau, H. Poincaré, and C. Richet, "Inauguration du monument élevé à la mémoire de Étienne-Jules Marey," in *Mémoires de l'Académie des sciences de l'Institut de France*, 2nd ser., **52** (1915), separately paginated; A. R. Michaelis, *Research Films* (New York, 1955), 4–6, 118–119, and *passim*; "E. J. Marey—Physiologist and First Cinematographer," in *Medical History*, **10** (1966), 2; and "Marey, Étienne-Jules," in Trevor I. Williams, ed., *A Biographical Dictionary of Scientists* (London, 1969), 352–353; "Obituary, É.-J. Marey," in *Lancet* (1904), **1**, 1530–1533; Henri de Parville *et al.*, *Hommage à M. Marey* (Paris, 1902); and C. J. Wiggers, "Some Significant Advances in Cardiac Physiology," in *Bulletin of the History of Medicine*, **34** (1960), 1–15, esp. 9–10.

Background to the development of graphical recording techniques in physiology is in H. E. Hoff and L. A. Geddes, "The Technological Background of Physiological Discovery: Ballistics and the Graphic Method," in *Journal of the History of Medicine and Allied Sciences*, **15** (1960), 345–363.

MICHAEL GROSS

MARGERIE, EMMANUEL MARIE PIERRE MARTIN JACQUIN DE (*b.* Paris, France, 11 November 1862; *d.* Paris, 21 December 1953), *geology, physical geography.*

Margerie came from a cultured Paris family that included several diplomats. He and his brother and sister received an excellent private education, and his childhood vacation travels awakened his interest in geology and geography. At fifteen he attended the lectures of Lapparent at the Institut Catholique in Paris and became a member of the French Geological Society. He took part, in 1878, in the first International Geological Congress in Paris. He did not complete any university training or take any examinations. While very young he began his study of foreign languages, especially German and English, and eventually he was able to read most other European languages as well. This ability was an important factor in his later scientific achievements.

Until the end of World War I, Margerie lived in Paris on an independent income. From 1918 to 1933 he was director of the Service Géologique de la carte d'Alsace et de Lorraine in Strasbourg. After his retirement, he returned to Paris, where he remained until his death. In 1903 Margerie married Renée Ferrer, who survived him. He was sympathetic, with a probing, analytic mind, and he unreservedly made available to his colleagues, especially the younger ones, his extensive knowledge of the international literature on geology and geography. He was a member—and often president—of more than fifty academies and learned societies throughout the world, and received numerous medals, distinctions, and prizes.

Margerie published 265 scientific works, primarily in regional geology, tectonics, and physical geography, as well as geographic and geologic cartography. Most of his publications were designed to make known the work of foreign researchers, to comment upon it, and to synthesize the results; and this was his forte. By virtue of the critical analyses and broad range of subjects, many of these publications were and continue to be of outstanding importance for the study of geology.

Among these works belongs *Les dislocations de l'écorce terrestre* (1888), which Margerie edited with Albert Heim. In this trilingual work (English, French, and German) the editors collected the technical terms, expressions, and concepts employed in geological tectonics, compared them with one another, and listed the corresponding words in the other languages. The lasting importance of this publication for tectonics was reflected in the decision of the 1948 International Geological Congress that the appropriate committee complete the work and bring it up to date.

Also in 1888 Margerie published a work on geomorphology, *Les formes du terrain*, written with General de La Noë, director of the Service Géographique de l'Armée. This book sets forth, for the first time, the causal relationship between the morphology of the earth's surface, and its geological structure and historical development.

In 1896 Margerie published a reference work that is still of value, the *Catalogue des bibliographies géologiques*. But his great reputation among scientists stemmed from his six-volume French translation of Suess's *Das Antlitz der Erde* (1897–1918). Executed with great empathy, and enlarged through many additional illustrations and bibliographical references, this edition enabled scientists who were not proficient in German to study Suess's epochal work.

Margerie was also the author of many specialized geological and geomorphological studies. At the start of his career he published reports (1892, 1893), in collaboration with F. Schrader, on the geomorphological structure of the Pyrenees, which were a combination of his own fieldwork and a critical evaluation of older works. Soon afterward he studied the Swiss and French Jura and the result was the voluminous publication *Le Jura* (1922–1936). This work, which he himself held in especially high regard, is still indispensable for all studies of the Jura.

Margerie devoted a large number of individual studies to the geology and morphology of North America, made from observations gathered in the course of several trips. His last major work, *Études américaines. Géologie et géographie* (1952), is a critical survey of the most important geological works, the topographic and geologic maps, and the history of the United States Geological Survey, as well as a compendium of knowledge about the geological structure of the continent.

Margerie never visited Asia, but through a series of bibliographical analyses he brought the most important publications on Asia to the attention of an international audience. Notable among these was the analysis of the works of the Swedish explorer Hedin on the orography of Tibet (1928).

The 1922 International Geological Congress appointed a committee to prepare a geological map of Africa. Margerie was appointed director of the project because of his wide experience in cartography. The first sheet appeared in 1937, and the publication was concluded in 1952. Margerie was associated with the publication of another cartographic undertaking of international importance—the *Carte générale bathymétrique des océans* (completed in 1931).

Among Margerie's last major publications were the four volumes of *Critique et géologie* (1943–1948). These, together with *Études américaines*, provide a retrospect of the author's career, scientific goals, and accomplishments. Many colleagues and contemporaries, and their correspondence with him, are described in these volumes, which offer a deep insight into the history of geology and geography, and especially into the emergence and development of the leading ideas in these subjects in the late nineteenth and early twentieth centuries.

BIBLIOGRAPHY

I. Original Works. Margerie's works include *Les dislocations de l'écorce terrestre* (Zurich, 1888), written with A. Heim; and *Les formes du terrain* (Paris, 1888), written with G. de La Noë. With F. Schrader he wrote "Aperçu de la structure géologique des Pyrénées," in *Annuaire du Club alpin français*, **18** (1892), 557–619; and "Aperçu de la forme et du relief des Pyrénées," *ibid.*, **19**

(1893), 432–453. He also wrote *Catalogue des bibliographies géologiques* (Paris, 1896); and, with several collaborators, *La face de la terre*, 6 vols. (Paris, 1897–1918), the trans. of Suess's *Das Antlitz der Erde*. Other works include "Le Jura," in *Mémoires pour servir à l'explication de la carte géologique de la France*, 2 vols. (Paris, 1922–1936); "L'oeuvre de Sven Hedin et l'orographie du Tibet," in *Bulletin de la Section de géographie des travaux historiques et scientifiques*, **43** (1928), 1–139; "Les dernières feuilles de la carte générale bathymétrique des océans (panneau du pôle nord)," in *Comptes rendus hebdomadaires des séances de l'Académie des Sciences*, **192** (1931), 1689–1694, and in *Bulletin de l'Institut océanographique*, **580** (1931), 1–6; *Critique et géologie. Contribution à l'histoire des sciences de la terre*, 4 vols. (Paris, 1943–1948); "Carte géologique internationale de l'Afrique," in *Comptes rendus . . . de l'Académie des Sciences*, **235** (1952), 591–592; and *Études américaines. Géologie et géographie*, I (Paris, 1952).

II. Secondary Literature. On Margerie and his work, see the anonymous article in *Comptes rendus du Comité national français de géodésie et géophysique* (1955), 32–34; H. Badoux in *Actes de la société helvétique des sciences naturelles*, **134** (1954), 347–348; P. Fourmarier, in *Bulletin de la Société géologique de France*, 6th ser., **4** (1954), 281–302, with a complete bibliography and portrait; S. Gillet, in *Bulletin du Service de la carte géologique d'Alsace et de Lorraine*, **7** (1954), 5–7, with portrait; C. Jacob, in *Comptes rendus . . . de l'Académie des Sciences*, **238** (1954), 20–23; E. Paréjas, in *Archives des Sciences*, **8** (1955), 69–70; and C. E. Wegmann, in *Geologische Rundschau*, **42** (1954), 314–316.

Heinz Tobien

MARGGRAF, ANDREAS SIGISMUND (*b.* Berlin, Prussia, 3 March 1709; *d.* Berlin, 7 August 1782), *chemistry.*

The few recorded accounts of Marggraf's personal life portray a modest, even-tempered man of precarious health but of single-minded devotion to study and laboratory experimentation. The influence of his mother, Anne Kellner, remains obscure; but it is known that his father, Henning Christian Marggraf, apothecary to the royal court at Berlin and assessor (assistant) at the Collegium Medico-Chirurgicum, introduced him to a circle of pharmacists and chemists. Marggraf's professional apprenticeship comprised several stages: from 1725 to 1730 he was a pupil of Caspar Neumann, his father's colleague at the court pharmacy and medical school and a disciple of Stahl; from 1730 to 1733, he assisted the apothecary Rossler in Frankfurt-am-Main and studied with the chemist Spielmann the elder at the University of Strasbourg; in 1733 at Halle he heard the lectures of Friedrich Hoffmann in medicine and of Johann Juncker in chemistry; in 1734 he traveled to Freiberg, Saxony, to study metallurgy with Henckel. After two years with his father in the Berlin court pharmacy, Marggraf visited Wolfenbüttel, Brunswick, in 1737 but refused an offer of the post of ducal apothecary. He chose to return to Berlin, where he was admitted the following year to the Königlich Preussischen Societät der Wissenschaften (reorganized in 1744–1746 as the Académie Royale des Sciences et Belles-Lettres). Despite the recriminations of a senior academician, J.-H. Pott, Frederick II selected Marggraf as director of the Academy's chemical laboratory in 1753 and as director of its Class of Experimental Philosophy in 1760. Marggraf was also a member of the Kurakademie der Nützlichen Wissenschaften of Mainz and a foreign associate of the Paris Academy of Sciences (1777). Although unable to write after suffering a stroke in 1774, Marggraf confounded attempts to replace him and prepared studies for publication until 1781.

Contemporaries recognized Marggraf as a masterful experimental chemist because of the extraordinary range of his interests and the painstaking nature of his procedures. As an adherent of the Stahl-Juncker phlogiston theory of combustion and calcination, he remained a figure of the "Chemical Ancien Regime." But just as eighteenth-century statecraft sometimes prefigured Revolutionary politics, so Marggraf's interest in chemistry for its own sake, his refinement of analytical tools, and his use of the balance anticipated some facets of the Chemical Revolution.

Marggraf's innovations in analytical methods included an emphasis on "wet methods," or solvent extraction, with careful attention to washing and recrystallization of the end product. His work with certain organic substances, for example the acid extracted from ants (1749) and the "essential oil" of cedar shavings (1753), combined traditional destructive distillation with the sophisticated use of solvents later practiced by G. F. Rouelle. Marggraf's most significant contribution to applied chemistry was his extraction and crystallization of sugar from plants commonly grown in Europe. In 1747 he used boiling rectified alcohol to extract the juice from the dried roots of *Beta alba* (white mangel-wurzel), *Sium sisarum* (skirret), and *Beta radicae rapae* (red mangel-wurzel). When crystals appeared several weeks later, he confirmed their identity with those of cane sugar by microscopic observation—perhaps the first such use of the microscope in the chemical laboratory.

Marggraf also developed a less costly process involving the maceration of roots to obtain the juice and the use of limewater to aid sugar crystallization. Although he envisaged a kind of household industry to assure the poor farmer a new source of sugar, half a century elapsed before any technological application of the laboratory procedures. Achard, Marggraf's successor as director of the Class of Experimental Philosophy, began experiments on sugar refining in 1786; his first factory became operational under royal patronage in 1802 at Kunern, Silesia. Napoleon's Continental System aroused even greater interest in France and Prussia in a substitute for overseas sugarcane.

On several other occasions Marggraf applied tests significant for modern analytical chemistry. In 1759, to distinguish "cubic niter" (sodium nitrate) from "prismatic niter" (potassium nitrate) crystals, he used, besides the microscope, the flame test—forerunner of modern emission spectroscopy—which differentiated the violet flash of ignition of saltpeter from the yellowish flash of the sodium nitrate. The blowpipe, a tube designed to intensify the flame by directing air upon it, refined this test to reveal characteristic colors and products upon the fusion of a metal. In 1745 Marggraf pioneered the use of the reagent Prussian blue, "fixed alkali ignited with dried cattle blood," as an indicator for the iron content of limestone.

The most notable of Marggraf's isolations of mineral substances were his production of the "acid of phosphorus" and his improved preparation of phosphorus itself. In 1740 he obtained white "flowers" (oxide of phosphorus) from the combustion of phosphorus and recorded, without explanation, the phenomenon so crucial to Lavoisier in 1772, that the calx showed an increase in weight. More remarkable to Marggraf was the hydration of the product in air to form the previously unknown oily phosphoric acid. When heated with coal this acid yielded, in Marggraf's terms, phlogiston and phosphorus.

The preparation of phosphorus had remained a highly prized monopoly of a few German and English chemists (notably Boyle's assistant Hanckwitz) until the French government purchased rights to Kunckel's process in 1737 and permitted Hellot to publish his experiments the same year in the *Mémoires* of the Paris Academy. In 1725 Marggraf had observed Neumann's preparation of phosphorus "with extreme difficulty" from urine and sand. Applying suggestions recorded in Henckel's *Pyritologia* (1725), Marggraf in 1743 evaporated stale urine to obtain a crystallizable "microcosmic salt" that, when heated to redness, yielded a clear glass (sodium metaphosphate), ammonia, and water. A lead calx–sal ammoniac mixture then reduced the "glass" to phosphorus. This method superseded Hellot's preparation, but in 1774 and 1777 Scheele developed a more economical method of obtaining phosphorus from bone ash.

Marggraf attempted to confirm the contention of Stahl and Hellot that phosphorus is a mixture of "acid of sea salt" (hydrochloric acid) and phlogiston. When his efforts to produce phosphorus from hydrochloric acid without urine failed, he cautiously concluded that the acid of phosphorus is distinct and related to the "peculiar salt" in urine necessary for the synthesis of phosphorus. In 1746 he distinguished this salt from Haupt's "sal mirabile perlato" (dodecahydrate of sodium phosphate) by the reducible product it yielded upon heating. Marggraf also substantiated Pott's observation that phosphorus is contained in vegetable matter, and reasoned that the higher yields of phosphorus from urine in the summer are proportional to increased consumption of vegetable foods.

In 1750 Marggraf noted that the earth contained in "Bologna stone" (barium sulfide), another phosphorescent substance, is heavier and more soluble than lime. In the same memoir he anticipated Lavoisier's conclusions by identifying the constituents of gypsum as water, lime, and vitriolic acid.

Until the invention of the Leblanc process, many chemists unsuccessfully sought an inexpensive means of converting common salt into soda for soap manufacture. With that motive Marggraf investigated (1758) the reasoning of H.-L. Duhamel du Monceau that the "alkali" of potash differs from that of rock salt. Besides using microscopic and flame tests, Marggraf recorded the difference in solubility or tendency to deliquescence of the sulfates, chlorides, and carbonates of sodium and potassium. He designated sodium salts as "mineral fixed alkali" and potassium compounds as "vegetable fixed alkali." In 1764 he treated plant parts with acids to establish that the vegetable alkali is an essential plant constituent and not merely a product of distillation.

On at least two occasions Marggraf followed Hoffmann's suggestions concerning the distinctiveness of particular "earths." He showed in 1754 that alumina is a peculiar alkaline earth soluble in acids. Moreover, he refuted the notion of Stahl, Neumann, and Pott that lime is a constituent of alum and, like Lavoisier in 1777, insisted that potash or ammonia is indispensable for alum crystallization. Despite his ignorance of Black's experiments, Marggraf recognized that magnesia, the "bitter earth" related to Epsom salt, is a "genuine and true alkaline earth."

Even Marggraf's less enduring achievements were sometimes remarkable challenges to existing assumptions. His assertion in 1747 that even "pure" commercially available tin contains up to 1/8 arsenic by weight raised doubts about the use of tin in food containers or kitchen utensils until the Bayen commission of the Paris School of Pharmacy concluded in 1781 that the arsenic impurities in various tin samples averaged 1/480 by weight (one grain per ounce). In 1768 Marggraf contradicted the assumption that earths

are never volatile by alleging that a distillation of fluorspar with sulfuric acid partially "volatilized" the stone. Only in 1786 did Scheele identify the volatile substance as a mixture of a new acid (prepared by the action of concentrated sulfuric acid on solid fluorite) and glass (now recognized as silicon fluorite).

Marggraf sometimes retained an alchemical outlook—specifically in his memoirs of 1751 and 1756, in which he supported the conviction that water can be transformed into earth. In a 1743 discussion of the crystallization of "microcosmic salt" he had noted his expectation that silver in nitric acid, with phlogiston and a "fine vitrifiable earth," would be subject to "partial transformation"; but he found no trace of a "nobler metal."

Several of Marggraf's pupils were also distinguished analytical chemists. Valentin Rose the elder (1736–1771), a Berlin apothecary, invented a fusible alloy of bismuth, tin, and lead; his son Valentin Rose the younger (1762–1807) was assessor (assistant) at the Berlin Ober-Collegium-Medicum; and their associate Martin Klaproth discovered uranium oxide and became first professor of chemistry at the University of Berlin.

Even without the technical achievements of Achard, Marggraf's work would remain a valuable illustration of the eighteenth-century search for precision in laboratory techniques and for purity in chemical reagents, as well as of the refusal to construct grand theory.

BIBLIOGRAPHY

I. ORIGINAL WORKS. A full list of Marggraf's memoirs was compiled by O. Köhnke in Adolf von Harnack, *Geschichte der Königlich Preussischen Akademie der Wissenschaften zu Berlin*, III (Berlin, 1900), 179–181. The originals appear in the publications of the Berlin Royal Society of Sciences and Royal Academy of Sciences (1740–1781): *Miscellanea Berolinensia ad incrementum scientiarum . . .*, 7 vols. (Berlin, 1710–1743); *Histoires de l'Académie royale des sciences et des belles-lettres de Berlin, . . . avec les mémoires . . .*, 25 vols. (Berlin, 1746–1771); and *Nouveaux mémoires de l'Académie royale des sciences et belles-lettres. . .*, 17 vols. (1772–1788). With the editorial assistance of J.-G. Lehmann, Marggraf collected his memoirs and added four MS dissertations in *Chymische Schriften*, 2 vols. (Berlin, 1761–1767), rev. ed. of vol. I appeared in 1768. Formey's French trans. of vol. I was published by J. F. Demachy as *Opuscules chymiques*, 2 vols. (Paris, 1762). An annotated German text of three memoirs is available in Ostwalds Klassiker: *Einige neue Methoden, den Phosphor im festen Zustande sowohl leichter als bisher aus dem Urin darzustellen . . .*, G. Mielke, ed. (Leipzig, 1913), which includes "Chemische Untersuchungen eines sehr bemerkenswerten Salzes, welches die Säure des Phosphors enthält" (1746). See also *Versuche einen wahren Zucker aus verschiedenen Pflanzen, die in unseren Ländern wachsen, zu ziehen,* Edmund O. von Lippmann, ed. (Leipzig, 1907).

II. SECONDARY LITERATURE. See Condorcet, "Éloge," in *Histoire de l'Académie* for 1782 (Paris, 1785), 122–131, repr. in Condorcet's *Oeuvres,* A. Condorcet O'Connor, ed. (Paris, 1847), II, 598–610; Formey, in *Histoire de l'Académie . . . de Berlin, année 1783* (Berlin, 1785), 63–72; A. de L., in *Nouvelle biographie générale,* XXXIII (Paris, 1860), cols. 549–553; Edmund O. von Lippmann, "Andreas Sigismund Marggraf," in Eduard Farber, ed., *Great Chemists* (New York–London, 1961), 193–200; Max Speter, "Marggraf," in Gunther Bugge, ed., *Das Buch der grossen Chemiker,* I (Berlin, 1929), 231–234; and John Ferguson, *Bibliotheca chemica,* II (Glasgow, 1906), 76–77.

The best single summary is in J. R. Partington, *A History of Chemistry,* II (London, 1961), 723–729. See also Frederic L. Holmes, "Analysis by Fire and Solvent Extractions: The Metamorphosis of a Tradition," in *Isis,* **62** (1971), 129–148; Hermann Kopp, *Geschichte der Chemie,* I (Brunswick, 1843), 208–211; Max Speter, "Zur Geschichte des Marggrafschen Urin-Phosphors," in *Chemisch-technische Rundschau,* **44** (13 Aug. 1929), 1049–1051; Ferenc Szabadváry, *History of Analytical Chemistry,* G. Svehla, trans. (Oxford, 1966), 51–52, 55–59; and Mary Elvira Weeks, *Discovery of the Elements,* 7th ed. (Easton, Pa., 1968), 497–498, 560–561, 861–864.

MARTIN S. STAUM

MARGULES, MAX (*b.* Brody, Galicia [now Ukrainian S.S.R.], 23 April 1856; *d.* Perchtoldsdorf, near Vienna, Austria, 4 October 1920), *meteorology, physics.*

One of the most important meteorologists of the early twentieth century, Margules provided the first thorough, theoretical analyses of atmospheric energy processes and deeply influenced the evolution of present concepts of such processes. He studied mathematics and physics at Vienna and in 1877 joined the staff of the Zentralanstalt für Meteorologie in Vienna. From 1879 to 1880 he continued his studies at Berlin and then returned to Vienna as *Privatdozent* in physics. In 1882 he resigned from this post, thus terminating his career at the university. He was then reemployed by the Zentralanstalt until 1906. During this time Margules produced a small number of highly important papers in meteorology. In 1906, at the age of fifty, he retired and gave up meteorology, again concentrating on physical chemistry, apparently because of embitterment at the lack of recognition for his work. Lonely, unmarried and without close friends, he literally starved to death during the austere postwar period.

After returning to the Zentralanstalt in 1882, Margules continued to pursue physical and physical-chemical investigations in his free time. His publications dealt with electrodynamics, the physical chemistry of gases, and hydrodynamics. Independently of Gibbs and Duhem, he developed in 1895 a formula for the relation between the partial vapor pressures and the composition of a binary liquid mixture, now known as the Duhem-Margules equation. In 1881–1882 he furnished a theoretical analysis of the rotational oscillations of viscous fluids in a cylinder.

From 1890 to 1893 Margules produced a series of papers related to meteorology that dealt with oscillation periods of the earth's atmosphere and the solar semidiurnal barometric pressure oscillation, the universal character of which had been established by his colleague Hann. William Thomson had suggested that the magnitude of this oscillation could be explained by a resonance oscillation of the entire atmosphere. Margules substantiated this hypothesis theoretically by computing free and forced oscillations of the atmosphere on the basis of Laplace's tidal theory. He never considered his results to be a rigorous proof, however, because of several unrealistic assumptions and the lack of a physical explanation for the semidiurnal temperature variation. Margules also investigated the oscillations of a periodically heated atmosphere, using various heating models, and gave a general classification of these motions.

While these studies still tended toward theoretical physics, Margules' next investigations dealt in a novel manner with problems fundamental to meteorology. In 1901 he demonstrated that the kinetic energy displayed in storms was far too great to be derived from the potential energy of the pressure field. He reduced the pressure field, which meteorologists had previously regarded as an explanation for the genesis of atmospheric motions, to a mere "cog-wheel in the storm's machinery."

In a famous 1905 paper Margules proposed a new source for the production of kinetic energy by studying models of energy transformations in the atmosphere that involved the isentropic redistribution of warm and cold air masses from a state of instability to one of stability. He showed that the realizable kinetic energy of these closed systems was the difference between the sums of internal energy and gravitational potential energy at the beginning and the end of the redistribution process. Margules considered this quantity, which is now called available potential energy, as the source of kinetic energy in storms. His theoretical analyses supported F. H. Bigelow's view that the coexistence of warm and cold air masses is the precondition for the development of storms. The cyclone model subsequently developed by J. Bjerknes was based energetically largely on Margules' work. Margules' results formed the basis for F. M. Exner's and A. Refsdal's investigations and have continued to influence meteorological thought. The work of E. Lorenz is an example.

In his discussion of idealized situations in which there is a large store of available potential energy (1906), Margules demonstrated that on the rotating earth two air masses of different temperatures, separated by an inclined surface of discontinuity, can exist in equilibrium under certain conditions. He developed a formula for the slope of this surface, using methods developed by Helmholtz. Bjerknes and his group later applied Margules' formula to their cyclone model, in which such frontal surfaces were the salient feature.

Margules considered the study of detailed observations, distributed three-dimensionally, to be of utmost importance for progress in meteorological theory. For this reason in 1895 he began to install a small network of stations around Vienna. Observations from these and nearby mountain stations allowed him to study the progression of cold and warm air masses and sudden variations in barometric pressure and wind during the passage of storms; these observations influenced his theoretical considerations and vice versa.

Margules also attempted to determine the frictional dissipation of kinetic energy and made the first estimate of the efficiency of the general circulation of the atmosphere as a thermodynamic engine. One of his last meteorological investigations, which dealt with the development of temperature inversions by descending motion and divergence, contributed to the understanding of anticyclones.

BIBLIOGRAPHY

I. ORIGINAL WORKS. Most of Margules' papers are listed in Poggendorff, III, 870–871; IV, 960; V, 807. Many of his important publications are in *Sitzungsberichte der Akademie der Wissenschaften in Wien*, Math.-naturwiss. Kl., Abt. IIa: "Über die Bestimmung des Reibungs- und Gleitcoefficienten aus ebenen Bewegungen einer Flüssigkeit," **83** (1881), 588–602; "Die Rotationsschwingungen flüssiger Zylinder," **85** (1882), 343–368; "Über die Schwingungen periodisch erwärmter Luft," **99** (1890), 204–227, English trans. by C. Abbe in "The Mechanics of the Earth's Atmosphere," 2nd collection, *Smithsonian Miscellaneous Collection*, **34** (1893), 296–318; "Luftbewegungen in einer rotierenden Sphäroidschale," pt. 1, **101** (1892), 597–626; pt. 2, **102** (1893), 11–56; pt. 3, *ibid.*, 1369–1421; and "Über die Zusammensetzung der gesättigten Dämpfe von Mischungen," **104** (1895), 1243–1278.

See also "Über den Arbeitswert einer Luftdruckverteilung und über die Erhaltung der Druckunterschiede," in *Denkschriften der Akademie der Wissenschaften*, Math.-naturwiss. Kl., **73** (1901), 329–345, English trans. by C. Abbe in "The Mechanics of the Earth's Atmosphere," 3rd collection, *Smithsonian Miscellaneous Collection*, **51** (1910), 501–532; "Über die Beziehung zwischen Barometerschwankungen und Kontinuitätsgleichung," in *Boltzmann-Festschrift* (Leipzig, 1904), 585–589; "Über die Energie der Stürme," in *Jahrbuch der Zentralanstalt für Meteorologie und Erdmagnetismus*, **40** (1905), 1–26, English trans. by C. Abbe in "The Mechanics of the Earth's Atmosphere," 3rd collection (see above), 533–595; "Über die Änderung des vertikalen Temperaturgefälles durch Zusammendrückung oder Ausbreitung einer Luftmasse," in *Meteorologische Zeitschrift*, **23** (1906), 241–244; "Über die Temperaturschichtung in stationär bewegter und in ruhender Luft," *ibid.* (1906), 243–254; and "Zur Sturmtheorie," *ibid.*, **23** (1906), 481–497.

II. SECONDARY LITERATURE. Some information on Margules' personal life may be found in the obituaries in *Meteorologische Zeitschrift*, **37** (1920), 322–324; and *Das Wetter*, **37** (1920), 161–165. See also F. Knoll, ed., *Österreichische Naturforscher, Ärzte und Techniker* (Vienna, 1957), 40–42.

GISELA KUTZBACH

MARIANO, JACOPO. See **Taccola, Jacopo Mariano.**

MARIE, PIERRE (*b.* Paris, France, 9 September 1853; *d.* Normandy, France, 13 April 1940), *neurology*.

Marie, the son of an upper-middle-class French family, studied law before deciding to enter medicine. After completing medical school, he was named *interne des hôpitaux* in 1878 and began his work in neurology under the tutelage of J.-M. Charcot at the Salpêtrière and Bicêtre. He soon became one of Charcot's most outstanding students and served as his laboratory and clinic chief and special assistant. Promoted to *médecin des hôpitaux* in Paris (1888), he was appointed agrégé at the Paris Faculty of Medicine (1889). As part of his work for this position, he presented to the faculty a series of lectures on diseases of the spinal cord, which were published in 1892.

From 1897 to 1907, Marie worked at the Bicêtre, where he created a neurological service that gained worldwide repute. In 1907 he successfully applied for the vacant chair of pathological anatomy in the Faculty of Medicine, and during his ten years there dedicated himself to that profession. With the aid of Gustave Roussy, his successor, Marie completely modernized the teaching of pathological anatomy in medical schools.

Marie resumed his work in clinical neurology in 1918 when he was named to the chair of clinical neurology at the Salpêtrière upon Dejerine's death. During the war, Marie and his colleagues in "Charcot's clinic" devoted most of their time to the study and treatment of neurological traumas in the wounded.

A brilliant clinician in the tradition of Charcot, Marie was an outstanding, demanding teacher. Between 1885 and 1910, the most productive period of his career, he wrote numerous articles and books and developed an international school of neurology which was to produce many distinguished pupils. He possessed a keen intuition which was sharpened by a rigorous approach to the study and practice of neurology. Capable of making shrewd clinical judgments, Marie successfully identified and described a series of disorders with which his name is linked. In one of his earliest and most significant works (1886–1891), he provided the first description and study of acromegaly. Marie's analysis of this pituitary gland disorder was a fundamental contribution to the nascent field of endocrinology. He also was the first to define muscular atrophy type Charcot-Marie (1886); pulmonary hypertrophic osteoarthropathy (1890); cerebellar heredoataxia (1893); cleidocranial dysostosis (1897); and rhizomelic spondylosis (1898).

During this early period of the neurosciences, Marie's views sometimes involved him in great controversy. After a ten-year study, his three papers on aphasia appeared in *Semaine médicale* (1906). They generated much discussion, and three special sessions of the Société Française de Neurologie de Paris convened in 1908 to compare Marie's views on language disorders, which differed from Broca's widely accepted doctrine that aphasia is caused by a lesion in the cerebral hemisphere's "speech center."

Marie led a quiet, private life with his wife and only child, André, who also became a physician. He received few visitors and avoided public appearances although he was awarded numerous honors. His abiding interests were art, the *Revue neurologique*, which he and E. Brissaud founded in 1893, and the Société Française de Neurologie, which he served as its first general secretary.

Marie resigned from his chair at the Salpêtrière and retired at the age of seventy-two, first to the Côte d'Azur and then to Normandy. Grieved by the death of his wife and son, he lived as a virtual recluse there and was increasingly troubled by ill health until his death.

BIBLIOGRAPHY

I. Original Works. Marie's writings include *Essays on Acromegaly*, with bibliography and appendix of cases by other authors (London, 1891); *Exposé des titres et travaux scientifiques* (Paris, n.d.); *Leçons sur les maladies de la moelle épinière* (Paris, 1892); *Leçons de clinique médicale (Hôtel Dieu 1894–1895)* (Paris, 1896); *Lectures on Diseases of the Spinal Cord*, trans. by M. Lubbock (London, 1895); *Neurologie*, 2 vols. (Paris, 1923); and *Travaux et mémoires* (Paris, 1926).

II. Secondary Literature. See Georges Guillain, "Nécrologie. Pierre Marie (1853–1940)," in *Bulletin de l'Académie de médecine*, **123** (1940), 524–535; "Pierre Marie (1853–1940)," in *Revue neurologique*, **72** (1940), 533–543; and Gustave Roussy, "Pierre Marie (1853–1940), Nécrologie," in *Presse médicale*, **48** (1940), 481–483.

JUDITH P. SWAZEY

MARIGNAC, JEAN CHARLES GALISSARD DE (*b.* Geneva, Switzerland, 24 April 1817; *d.* Geneva, 15 April 1894), *inorganic chemistry, physical chemistry.*

Descended from a distinguished Huguenot family, Marignac was the son of Jacob de Marignac, a judge and *conseiller d'état.* His mother was the sister of the pharmacist and physiologist Augustin Le Royer, whose house and laboratory adjoining the Marignac home was a center of Genevan scientific life. In 1835, after education at the Académie de Genève, Marignac entered the École Polytechnique in Paris, where he attended the chemistry lectures of Le Royer's former pupil J. B. Dumas. From 1837 to 1839 he studied engineering and mineralogy at the École des Mines. During 1840 Marignac traveled extensively through Europe, and for a short time he studied the derivatives of naphthalene in Liebig's laboratory at Giessen—his only research on organic chemistry. Through the influence of Dumas, he spent six months during 1841 at the porcelain factory at Sèvres; but, eager for an academic career, in the same year he succeeded Benjamin Delaplanche in the chair of chemistry at the Académie de Genève, taking on in addition the chair of mineralogy in 1845. He resigned in 1878, five years after the Academy became the University of Geneva. From 1884 on, chronic heart disease rendered Marignac a stoic but helpless invalid.

Marignac married Marie Dominicé in 1845. They had five children, one of whom, Édouard, died while a student at the École Polytechnique. Marignac worked unassisted in a damp cellar laboratory for most of his life; and this, together with his reticence and modesty, helped to create the erroneous impression that he was a recluse. From 1846 to 1857 he was a joint editor of the Swiss journal *Archives des sciences.* He commanded great respect from his students and, with the aged Berzelius' enthusiastic approval, a worldwide renown for his analytical accuracy. Always modern in outlook, he supported the work on mass action of Guldberg and Waage; he switched to two-volume formulas (such as H_2O) in 1858; and he attended the important Karlsruhe conference in 1860. In the French controversy over equivalent weights versus atomic weights in 1877, he gave statesmanlike support for the modern school.[1]

Although Marignac completed a large amount of research on mineralogy (showing, for example, that silica should be represented by the formula SiO_2, not SiO_3, because of the isomorphism between fluorstannates and fluorsilicates) and physical chemistry (where he explored the thermal effects of adding variable concentrations of different solutions together, and the alteration of the specific heats of solutions with dilution), only his contributions to inorganic chemistry will be mentioned here. In this field he accurately determined the atomic weights of nearly thirty elements and helped to unravel the tortuous chemistry of niobium and tantalum, the silicates, the tungstates, and the rare earths.

In 1842, inspired by a wave of criticism of Berzelius' atomic weights and by the plausibility of Prout's hypothesis that atomic weights were whole-number multiples of that of hydrogen, Marignac determined the atomic weights of chlorine, potassium, and silver by various methods accurate to $\pm 10^{-3}$. Although his results did not confirm "Prout's law" (as he termed it), he suggested in 1843 that the real multiple might possess only half the atomic weight of hydrogen—a suggestion not approved by Berzelius.[2]

When, in 1860, Stas dismissed Prout's law as an "illusion," Marignac cautioned that deviations from the law of definite proportions might sometimes occur —a possibility suggested by an erroneous view of the composition of acids which he then held. More speculatively, he suggested that Prout's law might be an "ideal" law (like Boyle's law) which was subject to perturbing influences such that the weights of the subatomic particles of the primordial matter (from which ordinary chemical atoms were composed) did not add up to exactly the experimentally determined "atomic" weights. This daring speculation was revived in 1915 by W. D. Harkins and E. D. Wilson, and from it the concept of the packing fraction was developed by F. W. Aston in 1920. Marignac was full of praise for Stas's reply to his challenge in 1865, but unlike Stas he was never able to accept that chance alone was the reason why atomic weights were so close to integers on the $O = 16$ scale (which he urged chemists to adopt in 1883). Unlike Crookes, Marignac did not speculate concerning the genesis of elements; although obviously sympathetic toward Crookes's hypothesis of 1887, he found it wanting for its dubious arguments drawn from rare-earth separations and spectroscopy.[3]

Marignac's groundwork with the rare earths (in which he was frequently helped spectroscopically by his physicist colleague J. L. Soret) began in the 1840's with the separation of the three cerium oxides from cerite. In 1878 he showed, after exacting fractionations based on differing solubilities, that the erbia extracted from gadolinite contained a colorless earth, ytterbia, which he correctly supposed was an oxide of a new metal, ytterbium. His ytterbia was in fact impure, for L. F. Nilson was able to extract scandia from it in 1879; and in 1907 Urbain separated it into (neo)ytterbia and lutecia (now called lutetia). In 1880 Marignac isolated white and yellow oxides from samarskite, which he uncommittedly labeled $Y\alpha$ and $Y\beta$ (samaria). In 1886, at Boisbaudran's request, he named the former gadolinia, and the element "gadolinium." Marignac is usually regarded as the discoverer of ytterbium and gadolinium. In general, his separations were a strategic and indispensable part of chemists' success in understanding the elements of the rare-earth series.

NOTES

1. For the debates at the French Academy of Sciences, see *Comptes rendus . . . de l'Académie des sciences*, **84** (1877), *passim*; and Marignac's comments, in his *Oeuvres*, II, 649–667.
2. J. J. Berzelius, in the Swedish Academy's *Jahres-Bericht*, **24** (1845), 60–62. In 1858 Marignac pointed out that a quarter-unit would preserve Prout's law. *Oeuvres*, I, 571.
3. For Crookes's reply, see *Chemical News . . .*, **56** (1887), 39–40.

BIBLIOGRAPHY

I. ORIGINAL WORKS. Marignac's 111 published papers were handsomely repr. as *Oeuvres complètes de J. C. Galissard de Marignac*, E. Ador, ed., 2 vols. (Geneva, 1902–1903), with portrait and a complete list of Marignac's atomic weights. From 1846 to 1857 Marignac was joint editor with A. de La Rive of *Archives des sciences physiques et naturelles*, **1–36** (a supp. of the *Bibliothèque universelle de Genève*). Marignac's criticism of J. S. Stas is translated in [L. Dobbin and J. Kendall,] *Prout's Hypothesis*, Alembic Club Reprints, no. 20 (Edinburgh, 1932), which also contains the relevant portions of Stas's memoir of 1860; for Stas's "answer" of 1865, see "Nouvelles recherches sur les lois des proportions chimiques, sur les poids atomiques et leurs rapports mutuels," in *Mémoires de l'Académie royale de Belgique*, **35** (1865), 3–311. For Kekulé's critique of Marignac's criticism, see his "Considérations d'un mémoire de M. Stas sur les lois des proportions chimiques," in *Bulletin de l'Académie royale de Belgique*, **19** (1865), 411–420, repr. in R. Anschütz, *August Kekulé* (Berlin, 1929), II, 357–364. For a view of Marignac's mineralogy by a lifelong friend, see A. L. O. Le Grand des Cloizeaux, *Manuel de minéralogie*, 2 vols. (Paris, 1862–1874). Two letters from the Berzelius-Marignac correspondence are in H. G. Söderbaum, ed., *Jac. Berzelius Bref*, III, pt. 7 (Uppsala, 1920), 210–216; note also 253–254.

MSS held by the Bibliothèque Publique et Universitaire de Genève include travel diaries (1839, 1840), analytical notebooks (1844 on), Swiss correspondence, and lecture notes of Marignac's students.

II. SECONDARY LITERATURE. The basic life of Marignac is by Ador in the *Oeuvres*, I, i–lv, repr. from the *Archives des sciences*, **32** (1894), 183–215, and partly repr. with portrait and bibliography in *Bulletin de la Société chimique de Paris*, **17** (1894), 233–239 and *Berichte der Deutschen chemischen Gesellschaft*, **27** (1894), 979–1021. Other useful notices are P. T. Cleve, "Marignac Memorial Lecture," in *Journal of the Chemical Society*, **67** (1895), 468–489, with portrait and bibliography, repr. in *Memorial Lectures Delivered Before the Chemical Society, 1893–1900* (London, 1901); and "De Marignac," in Société des Amis de l'École, *L'École polytechnique* (Paris, 1932), pp. 194–196.

Information on Marignac's atomic weights is in *Prout's Hypothesis* (see above); I. Freund, *The Study of Chemical Composition* (Cambridge, 1904; repr. New York, 1968), pp. 599–603; and W. V. Farrar, "Nineteenth-Century Speculations on the Complexity of the Chemical Elements," in *British Journal for the History of Science*, **2** (1965), 307–308. For Marignac's contribution to rare-earth chemistry, see the obituary by Cleve (above); O. I. Deineka, "Issledovania Mariniaka po khimii redkozemelnykh elementov" ("The Research of Marignac in the Chemistry of the Rare-Earth Elements"), in *Trudy Instituta istorii estestvoznaniya i tekhniki*, **39** (1962), 87–94; and M. E. Weeks, *Discovery of the Elements*, 7th ed. (Easton, Pa., 1968), ch. 16, *passim*.

W. H. BROCK

MARINUS (*b.* Neapolis [the Biblical Shechem, now Nablus], Palestine; *fl.* second half of fifth century A.D.; *d.* Athens[?]), *philosophy*.

Marinus, probably a Samaritan (perhaps also a Jew), became a convert to the Hellenic-pagan way of life.[1] He joined the Platonic Academy when Proclus, who dedicated his commentary on the Myth of Er in Plato's *Republic* to him, was its head.[2] After Proclus' death in A.D. 485 Marinus became the president of the Academy; he was evidently—and, as far as one can judge, rightly—considered the best representative of the views of Proclus, whom he praised and eulogized in an extant biography.

If one wants to assess the change in the philosophical climate since Plotinus' death in A.D. 270, it is very instructive to compare Porphyry's *Life of Plotinus* with Marinus' *Life of Proclus*, written two centuries later. Marinus, however, does not seem to have been merely a dogmatic follower of his systematizing predecessor; he did not hesitate to adopt an independent

and more realistic, down-to-earth attitude wherever he deemed it necessary. In his exegesis of Plato he rightly maintained, for instance, that Plato, when writing the *Parmenides*, had not, as Proclus' other disciples thought, been concerned with gods but with εἴδη, "Forms." Like other late Neoplatonists, he appreciated mathematics very highly: "I wished everything were mathematics."[3]

Marinus proposed a new solution to the Peripatetic-Academic problem of the Active Intelligence (νοῦς ποιητικός) by localizing it, as did the great Aristotelian Alexander of Aphrodisias (*ca.* A.D. 200), in the superlunary world but no longer identifying it with the First Cause. He placed it below the First Cause, as an "angelic, spiritual" being, making it a kind of intermediary between the highest stage of man's intellect and the unchanging superior world.[4] His view became, in due course, important for Islamic Arabic philosophers and was, with slight modifications, adopted by two of the most outstanding among them, al-Fārābī and Ibn Sīnā.[5]

NOTES

1. Damascius, *Vita Isidori*, R. Asmus, ed., ch. 141: τὸ Ἑλληνικὸν ἠγάπησεν.
2. See Proclus, *In rem publicam*, W. Kroll, ed., II, pp. 96, 200.
3. Elias, *Prolegomena*, A. Busse, ed., in *Commentaria in Aristotelem Graeca*, XVIII, pp. 28, 29: εἴθε πάντα μαθήματα ἦν.
4. See Pseudo-Philoponus, *De Anima*, M. Hayduck, ed., in *Commentaria in Aristotelem Graeca*, p. 535.
5. See R. Walzer in "Aristotle's Active Intellect (νοῦς ποιητικός) in Greek and Early Islamic Philosophy," in *Potino e il Neoplatonismo in Oriente e in Occidente* (Rome, 1974).

BIBLIOGRAPHY

I. ORIGINAL WORKS. The only extant philosophical work by Marinus is the biography of Proclus, J. Boissonade, ed. (Leipzig, 1814), repr. in *Procli opera inedita*, V. Cousin, ed., 2nd ed. (Paris, 1864), and in Diogenes Laërtius, C. G. Cobet, ed. (Paris, 1878). There is an English trans. from the Greek in L. G. Rosan, *The Philosophy of Proclus* (New York, 1949).

II. SECONDARY LITERATURE. The best account of Marinus is in F. Ueberweg and K. Praechter, *Die Philosophie des Altertums*, XIII (Tübingen, 1953), pp. 631 ff. His influence on Islamic Arabic philosophers is discussed by R. Walzer, in *Le néoplatonisme* (Paris, 1971), pp. 319 ff.

R. WALZER

MARION, ANTOINE FORTUNÉ (*b.* Aix-en-Provence, France, 10 October 1846; *d.* Marseilles, France, 22 January 1900), *zoology, geology, botany, plant paleontology*.

Marion came from a family of modest means. He attended the *lycée* at Aix, where he was a classmate of the novelist Émile Zola. His intelligence and inclination toward the natural sciences attracted the attention of Henri Coquand, professor of geology at the Faculté des Sciences of Marseilles, who had him appointed an assistant in natural history in 1862, a few days before he received his *baccalauréat ès lettres* and two years before his *baccalauréat ès sciences*. In 1868 he earned his *licence ès sciences naturelles*, and in 1869 he shared the Bordin Prize of the Academy of Sciences for his "Recherches anatomiques et zoologiques sur des nématoïdes non parasites marins." This work formed the basis of his doctoral thesis (1870).

In 1858 Marion had presented to the Marquis Gaston de Saporta a fossil leaf of *Magnolia*, a new variety, which he had discovered in the gypsum of Aix. This incident marked the beginning of a long collaboration and friendship, which remained, according to Saporta, "free from any disturbance or element of discord."

Marion's first publications (1867), which dealt with geology and paleontology, were followed by memoirs on plant paleontology published either alone or in collaboration with Saporta. Marion continued to publish works in this field until 1888, interspersing them with others on zoology, embryology, and marine biology. One of the most noteworthy is *L'évolution du règne végétal*, in three volumes (1881–1885). This synthesis, long a classic in the field, is not, properly speaking, a theoretical work but an attempt to apply transformist ideas to the history of plant life.

In 1871 as *chargé de cours* Marion gave a free course on the geology of Provence at the Faculté des Sciences of Marseilles. From October 1871 to November 1872 he took over the teaching of the natural sciences at the *lycée* of Marseilles. The Faculty of Sciences nominated him to fill the chair of geology left vacant by the death of Lespès—which, if Marion had obtained it, would have given his career a very different pattern. In 1872 he gave a course *(cours complémentaire)* on zoology for the École Pratique des Hautes Études and directed a laboratory of marine zoology established in the Allée de Meilhan, where the Faculté des Sciences had been. Numerous French and foreign researchers soon came to the laboratory, including Bobretsky, Weismann, O. Schmidt, and especially A. Kovalevsky, with whom Marion became quite friendly; he was also visited by Alexander Agassiz.

In 1876 a chair of zoology was established at Marseilles; Marion had to wait until he was thirty to assume it. This post helped him to gain acceptance for his plan to build a large marine laboratory on the coast at Endoume, a project initiated in 1878 with the support of the city of Marseilles. A source of hardship and disappointment for Marion, the project was finally accomplished after the city council of Marseilles at long last approved the necessary legislation on 16 December 1887.

In 1880 Marion succeeded the botanist E. M. Heckel as director of the Museum of Natural History of Marseilles. In 1883 he founded the museum's *Annales*, which until his death were subtitled *Travaux du Laboratoire de zoologie marine*. Indeed, Marion considered this publication to be essentially the organ of the laboratory; his wish was to coordinate the activities of the laboratory of marine zoology, the Endoume station, and the museum. In his goal of enriching the Marseilles museum with regional collections he amassed most of the material in the Salle de Provence.

A very special aspect of Marion's scientific activity was his involvement in the struggle against phylloxera from 1876 to 1878. Recognizing the inadequacy of sulfocarbonate and the efficacy of carbon disulfide, he devised methods of injecting the latter substance into the soil. These methods were of considerable value until the studies on American vines had been completed and had shown that the grafting of stock from California produced immunity. These efforts brought Marion considerable recognition as well as French and foreign honors. He received the Grande Médaille of the French National Society of Agriculture (1881) and was made Knight of the Crown of Italy (1879), Commander of Christ (Portugal, 1880), and Commander of Saint Anne (Russia, 1893). The Russian government invited him to be a member of a Commission on Vineyards, which visited Bessarabia, the Crimea, and the Caucasus. He was a member of a similar mission in the vineyards of Hungary.

Marion's extremely important zoological work dealt with marine invertebrates. After his thesis (1870), he returned to his research on the free-living nematodes (roundworms) of the Gulf of Marseilles (1870). Several of his publications are entitled "Recherches sur les animaux inférieurs du golfe de Marseille" (1873–1874). His studies in the field include memoirs on the parasitic Rotifera (1872), the nemerteans (1869–1875), the echinoderms (1873), the zoantharians (1882), the Alcyonarians (1877, 1882, 1884), the parasitic crustaceans (1882), the annelids (1874), the enteropneusts (1885, 1886), and the mollusks (1885, 1886). Two works were awarded the Grand Prize in Physical Sciences by the Academy of Sciences in 1885: "Esquisse d'une topographie zoologique du golfe de Marseille" (1883) and "Considérations sur les faunes profondes de la Méditerranée étudiées d'après les dragages opérés sur les côtes méridionales de France" (1883).

Marion constantly sought practical applications of marine zoology. He was ahead of his time in advocating the establishment of "maritime fields" where marine animals could be raised, studied, and experimented on in isolated reserves. He was a man of seductive charm and simplicity, of extremely varied talents and an open mind, and an exceptional teacher. In 1887 he was elected a corresponding member of the Institut de France. Although not cautious about his health, he dreaded long trips; before leaving for Russia, he wondered whether he would return, lamenting his "rather prematurely impaired health" (unpublished letter to Lacaze-Duthiers). Deeply grieved by the sudden death of his only daughter, he died a few months later.

BIBLIOGRAPHY

I. ORIGINAL WORKS. Marion's writings on botany and plant paleontology include "Description des plantes fossiles de Ronzon (Haute-Loire)," in Comptes rendus . . . de l'Académie des sciences, 74 (1872), 62–64; "Essai sur l'état de la végétation à l'époque des marnes heersiennes de Gelinden," in Mémoires de l'Académie royale des sciences, des lettres et des beaux-arts, de Belgique, 37, no. 6 (1873), written with Saporta; "Recherches sur les végétaux fossiles de Meximieux (Ain), précédées d'une introduction stratigraphique par A. Falsan," in Archives du Muséum d'histoire naturelle de Lyon, 1 (1875–1876), 131–324, written with Saporta; "Sur les genres Williamsonia et Goniolina," in Comptes rendus . . . de l'Académie des sciences, 92 (1881), 1185–1188, 1268–1270, written with Saporta; L'évolution du règne végétal. Les cryptogames, in Bibliothèque des Sciences Internationales (Paris, 1881), written with Saporta; L'évolution du règne végétal. Les phanérogames, 2 vols. (Paris, 1885), written with Saporta; and "Sur les Gomphostrobus heterophylla, conifères prototypiques du Permien de Lodève," in Comptes rendus . . . de l'Académie des sciences, 110 (1890), 892–894.

On zoology and marine biology, see "Note sur l'histologie du système nerveux des némertes," in Comptes rendus . . . de l'Académie des sciences, 68 (1869), 1474–1475; "Recherches anatomiques et zoologiques sur des nématoïdes non parasites marins," in Annales des sciences naturelles (zoologie), 13 (1870), 1–90; "Recherches sur les animaux inférieurs du golfe de Marseille. Sur un nouveau némertien hermaphrodite. Observations sur Borlasia Kefersteini," ibid., 17 (1873), 1–21; "Recherches sur les animaux inférieurs du golfe de Marseille. II. Description de crustacés amphipodes parasites des salpes," ibid., n.s. 1 (1874), 1–20; "Sur les espèces méditerranéennes du genre Eusyllis," in Comptes rendus . . . de l'Académie des sciences, 80 (1875), 498–499; "Étude des annélides du golfe de Marseille," in Annales des sciences naturelles, n.s. 2 (1875), 1–106, written with N. Bobretsky; "Révision des nématoïdes du golfe de Marseille," in Comptes rendus . . . de l'Académie des sciences, 80 (1875), 499–501; and "Dragages au large de Marseille (juillet–septembre 1875)," in Annales des sciences naturelles, n.s. 8 (1879).

See also "Études sur les Neomenia," in Zoologischer Anzeiger, 5 (1882), 61–64, written with Kovalevsky; "Considérations sur les faunes profondes de la Méditerranée étudiées d'après les dragages opérés sur les côtes méridionales de la France," in Annales du Musée d'histoire naturelle de Marseille, 1,2 (1883), 1–40, which won the Academy's Grand Prize in Physical Sciences in 1885; "Documents pour l'histoire embryogénique des alcyonnaires," ibid., 1,4 (1883), 1–50, written with Kovalevsky; "Esquisse d'une topographie zoologique du golfe de Marseille," ibid., 1,1 (1883), 1–120; "Organisation du Lepidomenia hystrix, nouveau type de solénogastre," in Comptes rendus . . . de l'Académie des sciences, 103 (1886), 757–759, written with Kovalevsky; "Documents ichthyologiques. Énumération des espèces rares de poissons capturés sur les côtes de Provence," in Zoologischer Anzeiger, 9 (1886), 375–380; "Contribution à l'histoire naturelle des solénogastres ou aplacophores," in Annales du Musée d'histoire naturelle de Marseille, 3 (1887), 1–76, written with Kovalevsky; and "Sur les espèces de Proneomenia des côtes de Provence," in Comptes rendus . . . de l'Académie des sciences, 106 (1888), 529–532, written with Kovalevsky.

Works on applied marine zoology appeared in the Annales du Musée d'histoire naturelle de Marseille (Travaux du Laboratoire de zoologie marine). In vol. 3 (1886–1889) are articles on the anchovy and remarks on the mackerel of the Provençal coast. In vol. 4 (1890–1894) are memoirs on the fishing and the reproduction of the Atherina hepsetus, on floating eggs and young fish observed in the Gulf of Marseilles in 1890, and on the raising of some young fish, as well as remarks on the systematic exploitation of the shore land. Also included are climatic observations made at the zoological station at Endoume for the study of the regional fishing industry. Vol. 5 (1897–1899) contains mainly articles on climatic conditions during 1893, 1894, and 1895 designed "to aid in the statistical study of the fishing industry on the Marseilles coast."

On Marion's efforts to combat phylloxera, see "Sur l'emploi du sulfure de carbone contre le Phylloxera," in Comptes rendus . . . de l'Académie des sciences, 82 (1876), 1381; and "Remarques sur l'emploi du sulfure de carbone au traitement des vignes phylloxérées," ibid., 112 (1891), 1113–1117, written with G. Gastine. There are various articles on agricultural techniques and applied zoology in Revue générale d'agriculture et de viticulture méridionales (May–Oct. 1898).

II. SECONDARY LITERATURE. See G. Gastine, "Antoine-Fortuné Marion," in Bulletin mensuel de la Société départementale d'agriculture des Bouches-du-Rhône, no. 2 (Feb. 1900), 33–43; Jourdan, A. Vayssière, and G. Gastine, "Notice sur la vie et les travaux de A. F. Marion," in Annales de la Faculté des sciences de Marseille, 11 (1901), 1–26; G. Petit, "F. A. [sic] Marion (1846–1900)," in Bulletin du Muséum d'histoire naturelle de Marseille, 1, no. 1 (1941), 5–12; Marquis de Saporta, "Notice sur les travaux scientifiques de M. A. F. Marion," in Mémoires de l'Académie des sciences, agriculture, arts et belles-lettres d'Aix, **13** (1885), 241–284; and A. Vayssière, "Notice bibliographique sur A. F. Marion," in *Annales du Musée d'histoire naturelle de Marseille*, **6** (1901), 7–9.

G. PETIT

MARIOTTE, EDME (*d.* Paris, France, 12 May 1684), *experimental physics, mechanics, hydraulics, optics, plant physiology, meteorology, surveying, methodology.*

Honored as the man who introduced experimental physics into France,[1] Mariotte played a central role in the work of the Paris Academy of Sciences from shortly after its formation in 1666 until his death in 1684. He became, in fact, so identified with the Academy that no trace remains of his life outside of it or before joining it. There is no documentation to support the tentative claim of most sources that he was born around 1620 in Dijon. His date of birth is entirely unknown, and his title of *seigneur de Chaseüil* makes the present-day Chazeuil in Burgundy (Côte-d'Or) the more likely site of his birth and childhood; several families of Mariottes are recorded for the immediate area in the early seventeenth century. Indirect evidence places him as titular abbot and prior of St.-Martin-de-Beaumont-sur-Vingeanne (Côte-d'Or), but his precise ecclesiastical standing is uncertain; contemporary sources generally do not refer to him by a clerical title.[2]

If not born in Dijon, Mariotte appears to have been residing there when he was named to the Academy. His letter announcing the discovery of the blind spot in the eye was sent from Dijon in 1668, as was the one extant (and perhaps only) letter he wrote to Christiaan Huygens. A letter from one Oded Louis Mathion to Huygens in 1669 suggests that Mariotte was then still in Dijon or at least that he had been there long enough to establish personal contacts.[3] By the 1670's, however, Mariotte had moved to Paris, where he spent the rest of his life.

Lack of biographical information makes it impossible to determine what drew Mariotte to the study of science and when or where he learned what he knew when named to the Academy. Seldom citing the names of others in his works, all written after joining the Academy, he left no clues about his scientific education. The circumstances surrounding his nomination, the letter to Huygens in 1668, and the nature of his scientific work combine to suggest that he was self-taught in relative isolation.[4]

It was as a plant physiologist that Mariotte first attracted the attention of the Academy shortly after its founding. Engaged in discussion of Claude Perrault's theory of the vegetation of plants, the original academicians apparently invited a contribution by Mariotte, who held the "singular doctrine"[5] that sap circulated through plants in a manner analogous to the circulation of blood in animals. Mariotte's verbal presentation of his theory and of the experiments on which it was based drew a rejoinder from Perrault, and the Academy charged the two men to return with written accounts and further experiments. At the same time, apparently, Mariotte was elected to membership as *physicien*. He carried out his charge on 27 July 1667, presenting the first draft of what was published in 1679 as *De la végétation des plantes*. His detailed argument from plant anatomy and from a series of ingenious experiments failed to resolve the controversy completely, and only in the early 1670's did accumulated evidence provided by others vindicate his position.

Whatever the advanced state of his botanical learning in 1666, Mariotte's education in other realms of science seems to have taken place in the Academy. When, for example, late in 1667 or early in 1668, he presented some of his findings on "the motion of pendulums and of heavy things that fall toward the center [of the earth]" and an account of "why the strings of the lute impress their motion on those in unison or in [the ratio of an] octave with them," he learned from Huygens that Galileo had already achieved similar results and only then, on Huygens' advice, read Galileo's *Two New Sciences*.[6] All of Mariotte's works have two basic characteristics: they treat subjects discussed at length in the Academy, and they rest in large part on fundamental results achieved by others. His own strength lay in his talent for recognizing the importance of those results, for confirming them by new and careful experiments, and for drawing out their implications.

Mariotte's career was an Academy career, which embodied the pattern of research envisaged by the founders of the institution. Although named as *physicien*, he soon shared in the work of the *mathématiciens* as well. In 1668, while continuing the debate on plant circulation, he took active part in a discussion of the comparative mechanical advantages of small and large wheels on a rocky road, read a paper containing twenty-nine propositions on the motive force of water and air (a subject to which he repeatedly returned during his career), read another paper on perspective (geometrical optics), and reviewed two recently published mathematical works.

Also in 1668 Mariotte published his first work, *Nouvelle découverte touchant la veüe*, which immediately embroiled him in a controversy that lasted until his death, although no one denied the discovery itself. Curious about what happened to light rays striking the base of the optic nerve, Mariotte devised a simple experiment: placing two small white spots on a dark background, one in the center and the other two feet to the right and slightly below the center line, he covered his left eye and focused his right eye on the center spot. When he backed away about nine feet, he found that the second spot disappeared completely, leaving a single spot on a completely dark surface; the slightest motion of his eye or head brought the second spot back into view. By experiments with black spots on a white background and with the spots reversed for the left eye, he determined that the spot disappeared when the light from it directly struck the base of the optic nerve, which therefore constituted a blind spot or, as he called it, defect of vision in the eye.

The discovery, confirmed by Mariotte's colleagues in both Paris and London, startled him into abandoning the traditional (and correct) view that images in the eye are formed on the retina (a continuous layer of tissue) and adopting the choroid coat behind the retina (discontinuous precisely where the optic nerve passes through it to attach to the retina) as the seat of vision. Mariotte's fellow academician, the anatomist Jean Pecquet, who with others had been investigating the eye since 1667, immediately disputed this conclusion and wrote to defend the traditional view. A series of experiments carried out before the Academy in August 1669 only widened the area of disagreement between the two men, as did Perrault's support of Pecquet. Mariotte published a rebuttal of Pecquet's critique in 1671, but by then the issue had become moot.[7] As the *Lettres écrites par MM. Mariotte, Pecquet et Perrault . . .* (1676) reveals, Pecquet and Perrault could not provide a convincing explanation for a blind spot on the retina (partly because they disagreed with Mariotte over the action of nerves), and Mariotte rested part of his argument on phenomena now known to be irrelevant (such as the reflection of light from the choroid of certain animals).

Although the controversy over the seat of vision dominated Mariotte's attention in 1669 and 1670, he continued his research in other areas. In 1669 he took part in discussions of the cause of weight (in which he supported some form of action at a distance against Huygens' mechanical explanation) and of the nature of coagulation of liquids. The latter issue seems to lie behind a series of experiments on freezing, carried out and presented jointly with Perrault in 1670. The experiments, which concerned the pattern of formation of ice and the trapping of air bubbles in it, enabled Mariotte to construct a burning glass of ice.

In 1671 Mariotte read a portion of his *Traité du nivellement* (published in 1672) describing a new form of level which used the surface of free-standing water as a horizontal reference and employed reflection of a mark on the sighting stick to gain greater accuracy in sighting. In the treatise itself he gave full instructions for the instrument's use in the field and a detailed analysis of its accuracy in comparison with that of traditional levels, in particular the *chorobates* of Vitruvius. In 1672 Mariotte's activities in the Academy were restricted largely to confirmation of G. D. Cassini's discoveries of a spot on Jupiter and a new satellite (Rhea) of Saturn.

As early as 1670 Mariotte had announced his intention to compose a major work on the impact of bodies. Completed and read to the Academy in 1671, it was published in 1673 as *Traité de la percussion ou choc des corps*. The first comprehensive treatment of the laws of inelastic and elastic impact and of their application to various physical problems, it long served as the standard work on the subject and went through three editions in Mariotte's lifetime.

Part I of the two-part treatise begins with the definitions of "inelastic body," "elastic body," and "relative velocity" and then makes four "suppositions": (1) the law of inertia; (2) Galileo's theorem linking the speeds of free-falling bodies to the heights from which they fall from rest ($v^2 \propto h$); (3) the independence of the speed acquired from the path taken in falling; and (4) the tautochronism of simple pendulums for small oscillations. The suppositions form the basis for an experimental apparatus consisting of two simple pendulums of equal length, the replaceable bobs (the impacting bodies) of which meet at dead center. To facilitate measurement, Mariotte makes the further assumption that for small arcs the velocity of the bob varies as the arc length (rather than the versine). Repeated experiments on inelastic clay bobs of varying sizes confirm a series of propositions, most of them termed by Mariotte "principles of experience": the additivity of motion (both directly and obliquely), the dependence of impact only on the relative velocity of the bodies (confirmed by the extent of flattening on impact), the quantity of motion (weight times speed) as the effective parameter of impact (also measured by flattening), and the laws of inelastic collision linking initial and final speeds through the conservation of quantity of motion.

The laws governing elastic collisions then follow from those of inelastic collision by means of the principle that a perfectly elastic body deformed by the impact of a "hard and inelastic" body regains its original shape and, in doing so, imparts to the impacting body its original speed. Confirmed by experiments involving the striking of a stretched string by a pendulum bob, the principle leads Mariotte to another series of experiments designed to show that such apparently "hard" bodies as ivory or glass balls in fact deform upon impact. In one test he lets ivory balls fall from varying heights onto a steel anvil coated lightly with dust; circles of varying widths show that the degree of flattening is dependent on the speed of the ball at impact, and the return of the balls to their initial heights confirms his principle of full restoration. By treating elastic bodies at the point of maximum deformation as inelastic ones, and by then distributing the added speeds acquired by restoration inversely as the weights of the bodies, Mariotte succeeds in determining the laws of elastic collision, applying them in one instance to the recoil of a cannon and directly testing the results experimentally. Part I closes with the transmission of an impulse through a chain of contiguous elastic bodies, a problem first posed by Descartes's theory of light.

Part II opens with a treatment of oblique collision, in which Mariotte employs (without citing his source) Huygens' model of impact in a moving boat. In Mariotte's use of the model, the boat is traveling at right angles to the plane of the impacting pendulums, allowing the application of the parallelogram of motion to derive the laws of oblique collision from those of direct impact. Mariotte then turns to some problems in hydrodynamics, in which he combines the hydrostatic paradox and the results thus far obtained to argue that the speed of efflux of water from a filled tank varies as the square root of the height of the surface above the opening. Examining next the force of that efflux, he determines by use of a balance beam that the force is to the weight of the water in the reservoir as the cross-sectional area of the tube (or opening) is to that of the reservoir. Combining these results, he concludes that the force of impact of a moving stream against a quiescent body varies as the cross-sectional area of the stream and the square of its speed. In a particularly suggestive passage Mariotte argues that a body moved by a steady stream of fluid striking it (that is, by a succession of uniform impulses) accelerates in the same manner as a falling body, that is, according to Galileo's law of $S \propto t^2$. In contradiction to Galileo, however, he insists that bodies falling through air must have a finite first speed of motion.

The use of a balance beam as apparatus and model leads to a treatment of the center of percussion, or center of agitation, of a compound pendulum, that is, the point on the pendulum that strikes an object with the greatest force. In one of the earliest published applications of algebraic analysis to physical problems, Mariotte obtains a solution by determining the point

that divides a rigid bar rotating about one endpoint into two segments having equal quantities of motion. His attempt then to equate the center of percussion with the center of oscillation (he calls it the center of vibration) makes his treatment of the latter far less successful than that of Huygens in his *Horologium oscillatorium*, also published in 1673. A few experiments on the fall of bodies through various media, performed in 1682 with Philippe de La Hire, bring the final version of the *Traité de la percussion* to a close.

Taken as a whole, the treatise reveals Mariotte as a gifted experimenter, learned enough in mathematics to link experiment and theory and to draw the theoretical implications of his work. He made full use of the results obtained by his predecessors and contemporaries, but his experimental mode of analysis and presentation differed markedly from their approaches to the problem. Clearly he knew of the work of Wallis, Wren, and Huygens published in the *Philosophical Transactions of the Royal Society* in 1668; and there are enough striking similarities between Mariotte's treatise and Huygens' then unpublished paper on impact (*De motu corporum ex percussione,* in *Oeuvres*, XVI) to suggest that he knew the content of the latter, perhaps verbally from Huygens himself. Certainly his colleagues in the Academy recognized Mariotte's debt to others while they praised the clarity of his presentation. And yet Galileo's name alone appears in the treatise; Huygens' in particular is conspicuously absent.

Some seventeen years later, in 1690, when Mariotte was dead, Huygens responded to this slight (whether intentional or not) by accusing Mariotte of plagiarism. "Mariotte took everything from me," he protested in a sketch of an introduction to a treatise on impact never completed,

> ... as can attest those of the Academy, M. du Hamel, M. Gallois, and the registers. [He took] the machine, the experiment on the rebound of glass balls, the experiment of one or more balls pushed together against a line of equal balls, the theorems that I had published [in the *Philosophical Transactions* (1668) and the *Journal des sçavans* (1669)]. He should have mentioned me. I told him that one day, and he could not respond.[8]

Except for the published theorems, if Mariotte took the other ideas from Huygens, he could have done so only when Huygens offered them in the course of Academy discussions. Mariotte may well have considered the content of those discussions the common property of all academicians and have felt no need to record their specific sources when publishing them under his own name.

Certainly in 1671 and 1673 Huygens made no proprietary claims in the Academy. His response to Mariotte's treatise consisted of a critique of the theory of elasticity on which parts of it were based. His commitment on cosmological grounds to the existence in nature of perfectly hard bodies that rebound from one another and transmit impulses placed him at odds with Mariotte's empirically based rejection of them.[9] Later that same theory of elastic rebound formed an integral part of Huygens' *Traité de la lumière* (1690). Huygens also later denied Mariotte any role in the determination of the center of oscillation, claiming (despite the evidence of Mariotte's treatise) that he had discussed only the center of percussion and had failed to demonstrate that it was the same as the center of oscillation.

Following the presentation of the *Traité de la percussion*, Mariotte seems largely to have withdrawn from Academy activities until 1675. Scattered evidence, particularly a striking demonstration of the hydrostatic paradox performed before a large audience at the Collège de Bourgogne in Paris in 1674 and reported in the *Journal des sçavans* in 1678 (p. 214), suggests that he was at work on the pneumatic experiments that form the basis of his *De la nature de l'air* (1679). Like his other works, *Nature de l'air* combines a review and reconfirmation of what was already known about its subject with some original contributions. Like the *Traité de la percussion*, it also omits the name of the author on whom Mariotte clearly had relied most heavily, in this case Robert Boyle, while acknowledging its debt to a more distant source, Blaise Pascal's *Équilibre des liqueurs*.

Nature de l'air focuses on three main properties of air: its weight, its elasticity, and its solubility in water. To show that air has weight, Mariotte points out the behavior of the mercury barometer and the common interpretation that the weight of the column of mercury counterbalances the weight of the column of air standing on the reservoir. Turning to the elasticity of air, he presents a series of experiments in which air is trapped in the mercury tube before it is immersed in the reservoir, thus depressing the height at which the mercury settles. He thereby establishes that

> ... the ratio of the expanded air to the volume of that left above the mercury before the experiment is the same as that of twenty-eight inches of mercury, which is the whole weight of the atmosphere, to the excess of twenty-eight inches over the height at which [the mercury] remains after the experiment. This makes known sufficiently for one to take it as a certain rule of nature that air is condensed in proportion to the weight with which it is charged.[10]

This last statement, further confirmed by experiments with a double-column barometer and extended to the expansion of air through experiments in a vacuum receiver, has gained Mariotte a share of Boyle's credit for the discovery and formulation of the volume-pressure law; indeed, it is called "Mariotte's law" in France. If, however, in the essay Mariotte gives no credit to Boyle, neither does he make any claims of originality; rather, he treats the law as one of a series of well-known properties of air.

Interested in the barometer more as a meteorological tool than as an experimental apparatus, Mariotte turns next to a discussion of the relation between barometric pressure and winds and weather (a subject to which he returned at greater length in his *Traité du mouvement des eaux*), and then to the solubility of air in water. The determination through experiment that water does absorb air in amounts dependent on pressure and temperature leads him, in one of his rare excursions into the theory of matter, to posit the existence of a *matière aérienne*, a highly condensed form of matter into which air is forced under high pressure and low temperature. His discussion, which includes the work on freezing done with Perrault in 1670, rests in part, however, on a lack of distinction between the air dissolved in water and the water vapor produced by high temperature and low pressure.

Despite his commitment to a special form of matter to explain solubility, Mariotte rejects any attempt to reduce the elasticity of air to a more fundamental mechanism. Explicitly denying the existence of an expansive subtle matter among the particles of air, he prefers to rely heuristically on Boyle's analogy (without citing the source) of a ball of cotton or wool fibers. A similar analogy of sponges piled on top of one another, together with the volume-pressure law, suggests to him a means for determining the height of the atmosphere. On the initial assumption that a given volume of air at sea level would expand some 4,000 times without the pressure of the air above it and that the pressure drops uniformly with increasing altitude, he divides the atmosphere into 4,032 strata, each stratum corresponding to a drop of 1/12 line (1/144 inch) in pressure from a height of twenty-eight inches of mercury at sea level. Comparing measurements made by Toinard and Rohault with ones made by himself with Cassini and Picard, he estimates that at sea level a rise of five feet in altitude corresponds to a drop of 1/12 line in pressure; hence the first stratum is five feet in height. By the volume-pressure law, the 2,016th stratum is ten feet thick, the 3,024th is twenty feet thick, and so on.

As a simplifying arithmetical approximation to the resulting geometric progression, Mariotte assumes an average stratum of 7.5 feet for the first 2,016 strata, an average of fifteen feet for the next 1,008, and so on. Each group of strata then has a thickness of 15,120 feet, or 5/4 league, and a total of twelve groups has a total height of fifteen leagues (sixty kilometers). As Mariotte notes, varying estimates of the full expansibility of air lead to different values for the height of the atmosphere; but even a factor of 8 million produces a height of less than thirty leagues by his method, which he further confirms by theoretical calculation of the known heights of mountains.

Mariotte's essay closes with some random observations, one of which, an assertion that air is not colorless but blue, forecasts his next major investigation. Involved in 1675–1676 in the Academy's (never completed) project to meet Louis XIV's request for a complete inventory of the machines in use in France, which was to be prefaced by a short theoretical introduction,[11] and in 1677 in a series of varied experiments, by 1678 he had begun a fairly continuous series of reports to the Academy on the rainbow and the refraction of light by lenses and small apertures. A proposal by Carcavi in March 1679 for a complete treatise on optics by Mariotte, Picard, and La Hire resulted in Mariotte's presentation in July and August of his *De la nature des couleurs*. He worked further on the essay over the next two years, reporting frequently to the Academy. In 1681 he read the final version, which then appeared as the fourth of the *Essays de physique*.

Perhaps the best example of Mariotte's experimental finesse, the essay on colors also illustrates well his scientific eclecticism, combining Cartesian epistemology, Baconian methodology, and Aristotelian modes of explanation. He begins:

> Among our sensations it is difficult not to confuse what comes from the part of objects with what comes from the part of our senses. . . . Supposing this, one clearly sees that it is not easy to say much about colors, . . . and that all one can expect in such a difficult subject is to give some general rules and to derive from them consequences that can be of some use in the arts and satisfy somewhat the natural desire we have to render account of everything that appears to us.[12]

On the basis, then, of four suppositions (the geometric structure of the light cone and of a sunbeam passing through an aperture; the gross phenomenon of refraction, including partial reflection; the refraction of light toward the normal in the denser medium, and conversely; and the focusing of the human eye),[13] Mariotte presents a comprehensive catalog of experimental results concerning refraction, emphasizing the precise order and intensity of the colors produced and the angles of the rays producing them.

Mariotte's review of various mechanisms proposed for explaining these results finds fundamental weaknesses in all of them. In particular Descartes's notion of a rotatory tendency to motion, besides being inherently unclear, implies constantly alternating patterns of color contrary to observation; and Newton's proposal of white light as a composite of monochromatic colors, although it explains much, fails on the crucial test. That is, repeating Newton's refraction of violet rays through a prism, Mariotte finds further separation in the form of red and yellow fringes about the image.[14] In the absence of an adequate theory, he retreats in the essay to eight "principles of experience," which are essentially generalizations of the behavior of refracted light as observed in the preceding experiments. Using these principles, Mariotte then undertakes to explain a long series of observed phenomena, including the chromaticism of lenses, the shape of the spectrum, and diffraction about thin objects. The explanations are merely a prelude, however, to his main concern, a complete account of the rainbow.

Reviewing previous accounts from Aristotle to Descartes, Mariotte states his basic agreement with that of Descartes but points to its lack of complete correspondence with observation. In particular Descartes failed to explain the upper and lower boundaries (40° and 44°) of the primary rainbow. Mariotte's own full account applies to Descartes's basic mechanism the precise measurements made in the preceding experiments but ends with a small divergence between the calculated and the observed height of the rainbow. The divergence, a matter of forty-six minutes of arc, led Mariotte to carry out with La Hire a protracted series of refraction experiments using water-filled glass spheres. Employing the techniques established in his essay on air, he made adjustments for the different densities of air (and hence different indexes of refraction) at sea level and at 500 feet, where the rainbow is formed, and for the heating effects of the sun on the water in the spheres. This work brings theory and observation into closer alignment. Similar but less extensive use of the "principles" offers satisfying explanations of stellar coronas (explained by refraction through water vapor in the clouds), solar and lunar coronas, and parhelia and false moons (all explained by refraction through small filaments of snow in the shape of equilateral prisms).

In contrast with the precision and clarity of the treatment of refraction in part I of the essay, Mariotte's attempt in part II to explain the color of directly observed bodies seems vague and undirected, perhaps because there was little for him to build on. A mass of undigested empirical phenomena forces him ultimately to retreat to an essentialist stance and to argue, for example, that "the weak and discontinuous light of the ignited fumes of brandy, sulfur, and other subtle and rarefied exhalations is disposed with respect to the organs of vision in a manner suited to make blue appear."[15]

For all its apparent diversity, Mariotte's research reflects a continuing concern with the motion of bodies in a resisting medium. The subject forms the core of the letter to Huygens in 1668 and of part II of the *Traité de la percussion* in 1673. Moreover, it was the subject of a full Academy investigation in 1669. A report in 1676 on the reflection and refraction of cannon balls striking water, and one in 1677 on the resistance of air to projectile motion, pursued the issue further. It was, however, only in 1678 that Mariotte broached the topic that would unite this research in a common theme: natural springs, artificial fountains, and the flow of water through pipes. His long report formed the basis for his *Traité du mouvement des eaux et des autres corps fluides*, published posthumously by La Hire in 1686. Mariotte was still working on the treatise at his death; his last two reports to the Academy dealt with the dispersion of water fired from a cannon and with the origin of the winds.

The *Mouvement des eaux*, a treatise in five parts, represents Mariotte's grand synthesis. Part I, section 1, reviews the basic properties of air and water as presented in the *Nature de l'air* and the paper on freezing. Section 2 uses these properties, together with meteorological and geological data, to argue that natural springs and rivers derive their water exclusively from rainfall (an extension of a theory first proposed by Pierre Perrault in 1674); the discussion includes an original estimate of the average total rainfall in France and of the content of its major rivers. Section 3 carries the meteorological discussion into the topic of the winds and their origin. Having met with some success in establishing a chain of weather stations across Europe,[16] Mariotte uses their reports and those of others to give a full account of the world's and Europe's major winds, basing it on the daily eastward rotation of the earth, the rarefaction and condensation of air due to heating and cooling, and changes in the distance of the moon from apogee to perigee. The account is particularly striking for the extent of detailed geographical and meteorological information from around the world.

Part II deals with the balancing forces of fluids due to weight, elasticity, and impact. Beginning with a treatment of statics based on a "universal principle of mechanics" akin to that of virtual velocities and

illustrated by the solution of what is known as "Mariotte's paradox,"[17] the treatise moves to experimental and theoretical demonstrations of the hydrostatic paradox and the Archimedean principle of floating bodies. Turning from the force of weight to that of elasticity, it recapitulates in some detail the discussion of the volume-pressure law in the *Nature de l'air*, asserting of water only that it is practically incompressible and hence has no elastic force. It does, however, have a force of impact, which Mariotte had already begun to explore in part II of the *Traité de la percussion* and which he continues to study here in the form of the speed of efflux of water through a small hole at the base of a reservoir. Five "rules of jets of water" relate the speed and force of the flow to the height of the reservoir and the cross-sectional area of the opening. The rules are then adapted to the impact of flowing water against the paddles of mills; direct measurement tends to confirm the applicability of the laws of inelastic collision to the situation.

Part III derives directly from Mariotte's work at the fountains of Chantilly in 1678 and is devoted to the experimental determination of the constants required for applying his theoretical rules to actual fountains. Of particular interest here is his report on the variation of the period of a pendulum with respect to latitude, a consideration made necessary by the use of the pendulum as a timing device for measuring rate of flow. Part IV continues in a practical vein, discussing the deviation from the ideal in real fountains. The discussion provides an opportunity to introduce Mariotte's findings on the effect of air resistance on the path and speed of projectiles, both solid and fluid, and leads directly to the subject of friction in conduit pipes, the opening topic of part V, again treated with reference to experiments performed at Chantilly.

Part V and the treatise conclude with a study of the strength of materials, in which Mariotte disputes Galileo's analysis and solution of the problem of the breaking strength of a loaded beam.[18] His solution, based largely on experimental results, is then applied to water pipes, relating the height of the reservoir to the necessary cross-sectional thickness of the pipes.

Mariotte's treatise attracted widespread attention and was the only one of his major works to be translated into English (by J. T. Desaguliers in 1718). Although eventually superseded in its theoretical portions by Daniel Bernoulli's *Hydrodynamica* (1738), it remained a standard practical guide to the construction of fountains for some time thereafter.

According to the testimony of La Hire and his colleagues, Mariotte was also the author of an unsigned *Essay de logique* that appeared in 1678. B. Rochot has shown that this work closely resembles in content and structure, and frequently quotes verbatim, an unpublished manuscript by Roberval.[19] According to Rochot, however, Mariotte did not plagiarize Roberval but, rather, succeeded him at his death in 1675 as recording secretary for an Academy project on scientific method, whence the absence of an author's name upon publication. The work bears Mariotte's unmistakable stamp, however, both in the fit between its proposed methodology and his actual research procedures and in the use of his own research as examples (in particular the argument for the choroid as the seat of vision).

Like all treatises on method in the seventeenth century, Mariotte's rests on the conviction that divergence of scientific opinion derives from faults in procedure—that is, from faulty deduction or induction, from inadequate experimentation, or from failure to observe procedure arising out of ulterior motives. Because the last is beyond his control, and because the rules of proper deduction are well known, Mariotte concentrates on the rules of induction, especially induction based on experiment. Following Descartes, he accepts both a distinction between reality and perception and also the existence of self-evident propositions that are true of reality. For the most part, however, those propositions are of a mathematical nature, abstracted from the contingencies of the natural world, which are known only through sense data. Since those data do not allow the distinction between the perception and what is perceived, they make extremely difficult, perhaps even impossible, any reliable transition from knowing the world as it appears to us to knowing the world as it really is. Hence, for Mariotte induction and analysis must stop at general principles that are directly verifiable by the senses. Although hypothetical systems that go beyond this point can have immense heuristic and organizational value (he gives as examples both the Ptolemaic and the Copernican systems), they generally can claim no epistemological status other than convenience.

In general Mariotte brought to his *Essay de logique* the precepts and procedures that characterize his actual research. Concerned more with the articulation and application of experimentally determined generalizations than with their reduction to more fundamental (and unverifiable) mechanisms or principles, Mariotte treated subjects in piecemeal fashion, relying on common sense and good judgment based on intimate familiarity with the physical situation to guide his reasoning. His essay seldom delves beyond this level of analysis, and his fifty-three general principles do little more than recapitulate what had been the common methodological stock of experimentalists since Aristotle. His distrust of theoretical systems extended to methodology itself and led him at one point in the essay to assert that there are no sure rules of method, other than constant experimentation in the study of nature.

As an active member of the Academy for over twenty-five years, Mariotte exerted influence over scientific colleagues both within and without that institution. His closest associate seems to have been La Hire, but during his tenure he carried out joint investigations with most of the other members, including Huygens. His work was known to the Royal Society and was cited by Newton in the *Principia*. Mariotte conducted an extensive correspondence (as yet unpublished) with Leibniz, for whom he was a source of information about the work of the Academy in the early and mid-1670's and who in turn cooperated with Mariotte's meteorological survey. Huygens' accusation of plagiarism in 1690 seems to have done little to dim the reputation Mariotte had earned during his career. In speaking of his death in 1684, J.-B. du Hamel summed up that career as follows:

> The mind of this man was highly capable of all learning, and the works published by him attest to the highest erudition. In 1667, on the strength of a singular doctrine, he was elected to the Academy. In him, sharp inventiveness always shone forth combined with the industry to carry through, as the works referred to in the course of this treatise will testify. His cleverness in the design of experiments was almost incredible, and he carried them out with minimal expense.[20]

NOTES

1. Condorcet, "Éloge de Mariotte," in *Éloges des académiciens de l'Académie royale des sciences, morts depuis 1666, jusqu'en 1699* (Paris, 1773), 49; *Oeuvres complètes de Christiaan Huygens*, VI (Amsterdam, 1895), 177, n. 1.
2. C. Oursel reviews previous accounts and the available documentation regarding Mariotte's birthdate and birthplace in *Annales de Bourgogne*, III (1931), 72–74.
3. Huygens, *Oeuvres*, VI, 536.
4. According to J. A. Vollgraf in Huygens, *Oeuvres*, XXII (1950), 631, Huygens knew nothing of Mariotte until the latter joined the Academy in 1666.
5. J.-B. du Hamel, *Regiae scientiarum academiae historia*, 2nd ed. (Paris, 1701), 233. For the full context of the remark, see the quotation at the end of the present article.
6. Huygens, *Oeuvres*, VI, 177–178.
7. Huygens, for one, thought Mariotte's to be the stronger argument; see Huygens, *Oeuvres*, XIII (1916), 795. William Molyneux in his *Dioptrica nova* (London, 1692) opted for the retina but acknowledged the strength of Mariotte's argument and felt the choice was immaterial.
8. Huygens, *Oeuvres*, XVI (1929), 209.

9. Mariotte's theory of elastic bodies is also a major theme of the review of the *Traité de la percussion* that appeared in the *Journal des sçavans*, **4** (1676), 122–125.
10. Mariotte, *Oeuvres* (1717), 152.
11. On this project see the full account in du Hamel, *Historia*, 150–155.
12. Mariotte, *Oeuvres*, 196–197.
13. Interestingly, Mariotte mentions the sine law of refraction only in passing and nowhere treats it as a phenomenon to be explained.
14. See in this regard the letter from Leibniz to Huygens, 26 Apr. 1694, in Huygens, *Oeuvres*, X (1905), 602. In it Leibniz refers to Mariotte's experiment and asks if Huygens has had the opportunity to investigate it further.
15. Mariotte, *Oeuvres*, 285.
16. According to Wolf, *History of Science, Technology, and Philosophy in the 16th and 17th Centuries*, 2nd ed. (New York, 1950), I, 312–314, Mariotte's effort was not the first, having been preceded most notably by that of the Accademia del Cimento in 1667.
17. The paradox is the reversal of the normal law of a bent-arm balance in the following situation: one arm of the balance is parallel to the horizon, the other inclined downward, the weights are placed at equal distances from the fulcrum along the arms, and the free-rolling weight on the inclined arm is held in place by a frictionless vertical wall. See Pierre Costabel, "Le paradox de Mariotte," in *Archives internationales de l'histoire des sciences*, **2** (1949), 864–881.
18. For details see Wolf, II, 474–477.
19. B. Rochot, "Roberval, Mariotte et la logique," in *Archives internationales de l'histoire des sciences*, **6** (1953), 38–43.
20. Du Hamel, *Historia*, p. 233.

BIBLIOGRAPHY

I. ORIGINAL WORKS. *Oeuvres de Mariotte*, 2 vols. in one (Leiden, 1717; 2nd ed., The Hague, 1740), contains all of Mariotte's published works and one unpublished paper; most of the articles that appeared under his name in vols. I, II, and X of the *Histoire de l'Académie depuis 1666 jusqu'en 1699* (Paris, 1733) are reports made to the Academy prior to their inclusion in the published works. The 1717 *Oeuvres* includes the following:

1. (I, 1–116) *Traité de la percussion ou choc des corps*, 3rd ed. (Paris, 1684)—(the *Oeuvres* dates it 1679, but the concluding experiments were not carried out until 1682); 1st ed., Paris, 1673; 2nd ed. in *Recueil de plusieurs traitez de mathématique de l'Académie royale des sciences* (Paris, 1676). Reviewed in *Journal des sçavans*, **4** (1676), 122–125.

2. (I, 117–320) *Essays de physique, pour servir à la science des choses naturelles*:

a. (I, 119–147) *De la végétation des plantes* (Paris, 1679); reviewed in *Journal des sçavans*, **7** (1679), 245–250. G. Bugler, in *Revue d'histoire des sciences . . .*, **3** (1950), 242–250, reports a 1676 version under the title *Lettre sur le sujet des plantes;* the report is confirmed by the "Avis" of the *Oeuvres* but not by other sources.

b. (I, 148–182) *De la nature de l'air* (Paris, 1679); reviewed in *Journal des sçavans*, **7** (1679), 300–304.

c. (I, 183–194) *Du chaud et du froid* (Paris, 1679); reviewed in *Journal des sçavans*, **7** (1679), 297–299.

d. (I, 195–320) *De la nature des couleurs* (Paris, 1681); reviewed in *Journal des sçavans*, **9** (1681), 369–374.

3. (II, 321–481) *Traité du mouvement des eaux et des autres corps fluides* (Paris, 1686; 2nd ed., Paris, 1690; 3rd ed., Paris, 1700), trans. into English by J. T. Desaguliers as *The Motion of Water and Other Fluids, Being a Treatise of Hydrostaticks . . .* (London, 1718).

4. (II, 482–494) "Règles pour les jets d'eau," in *Divers ouvrages de mathématique et physique par MM. de l'Académie royale des sciences* (Paris, 1693), English trans. by Desaguliers as addendum to *Traité . . . des eaux.*

5. (II, 495–534) "Lettres écrites par MM. Mariotte, Pecquet et Perrault sur le sujet d'une nouvelle découverte touchant la veüe par M. Mariotte," in *Recueil de plusieurs traitez de mathématique . . .* (Paris, 1676), and then separately (Paris, 1682). Mariotte's first letter was originally published, along with Pecquet's response, as *Nouvelle découverte touchant la veüe* (Paris, 1668) and was reviewed in *Journal des sçavans*, **2** (1668), 401–409. Mariotte's reply was published as *Seconde lettre de M. Mariotte à M. Pecquet pour montrer que la choroïde est le principal organe de la veüe* (Paris, 1671).

6. (II, 535–556) *Traité du nivellement, avec la description de quelques niveaux nouvellement inventez* (Paris, 1672), repub. in *Recueil . . .* (Paris, 1676); reviewed in *Journal des sçavans*, **3** (1672), 130–131.

7. (II, 557–566) "Traité du mouvement des pendules," from MS letter to Huygens repub. from Leiden MS in Huygens, *Oeuvres*, VI, 178–186.

[The pagination of the 1717 *Oeuvres* jumps from 566 to 600; the table of contents and the index show no work omitted.]

8. (II, 600–608) *Expériences touchant les couleurs et la congélation de l'eau*. Both taken from Academy records as later published in the *Histoire de l'Académie depuis 1666 jusqu'en 1699*, X, 507–513; the paper on freezing appeared earlier in *Journal des sçavans*, **3** (1672), 28–32.

9. (II, 609–701) *Essay de logique, contenant les principes des sciences et la manière de s'en servir pour faire des bons raisonnemens* (Paris, 1678), unsigned.

Of these works only three have been republished in a modern ed.: *Discours de la nature de l'air, de la végétation des plantes. Nouvelle découverte touchant la vue*, in the series *Maîtres de la Pensée Scientifique* (Paris, 1923).

Few original papers remain, the most important of which are 28 letters from Mariotte to Leibniz and 10 from Leibniz to Mariotte. According to P. Costabel, *Archives internationales d'histoire des sciences*, **2** (1949), 882, n. 1, they are among the Leibniz papers in Hannover.

II. SECONDARY LITERATURE. There is no biography or secondary account of Mariotte's work. The above account has been culled largely from references to him in Huygens' correspondence and papers (Huygens, *Oeuvres*, passim) and in J.-B. du Hamel's *Historia*, passim. Condorcet's *éloge* gives only the broadest outline of Mariotte's career, as do other general French biographical reference works. The fullest catalog of his positive achievements remains Abraham Wolf's scattered references in the 2 vols. of his *History of Science, Technology and Philosophy in the 16th and 17th Centuries*, 2nd ed. (New York, 1950), which have the added virtue of placing those achievements in their contemporary context. For specific aspects of Mariotte's career, see Pierre Brunet, "La méthodologie de Mariotte," in *Archives internationales d'histoire des sciences*, **1** (1947), 26–59; G. Bugler, "Un précurseur de la biologie expérimentale: Edme Mariotte," in *Revue d'histoire des sciences* . . ., **3** (1950), 242–250; Pierre Costabel, "Le paradoxe de Mariotte," in *Archives internationales d'histoire des sciences*, **2** (1949), 864–881; and "Mariotte et le phénomène élastique," in *84e Congrès des sociétés savantes* (Paris, 1960), 67–69; Douglas McKie, "Boyle's Law," in *Endeavour*, **7** (1948), 148–151; Jean Pelseneer, "Petite contribution à la connaissance de Mariotte," in *Isis*, **42** (1951), 299–301; Bernard Rochot, "Roberval, Mariotte et la logique," in *Archives internationales d'histoire des sciences*, **6** (1953), 38–43; Maurice Solovine, "À propos d'un tricentenaire oublié: Edme Mariotte (1620–1920)," in *Revue scientifique* (24 Dec. 1921), 708–709; and E. Williams, "Some Observations of Leonardo, Galileo, Mariotte, and Others Relative to Size Effect," in *Annals of Science*, **13** (1957), 23–29.

On the blind-spot controversy, see John M. Hirschfield, "The Académie Royale des Sciences (1666–1683): Inauguration and Initial Problems of Method" (diss., University of Chicago, 1957), ch. 8.

MICHAEL S. MAHONEY

MARIUS, SIMON. See **Mayr, Simon.**

MARKGRAF (or **Marcgraf**), **GEORG** (*b.* Liebstadt, Meissen, Germany, 20 September 1610; *d.* Luanda, Angola, August 1644), *astronomy, botany, zoology.*

Markgraf was the son of Georg Markgraf, headmaster of the Liebstadt school, and Elisabeth Simon, daughter of the pastor there. He was educated at home, where he became proficient in Greek, Latin, music, and drawing; in 1627 he began to travel and to study with scientists throughout Germany. He matriculated at the University of Leiden on 11 September 1636, already well versed in all applications of mathematics and in both the natural sciences and medicine.

Markgraf had long been interested in observing the stars of the southern hemisphere; the opportunity to do so arose when he was invited to participate in a military and exploratory expedition to the Dutch settlements in Brazil. The expedition was under the leadership of Count Maurice of Nassau, who was at that time laying siege to the Portuguese settlement of São Salvador (now Bahía). The research staff, under the direction of Willem Pies (William Piso), left Leiden to join the count on 1 January 1638. Markgraf began his scientific work—making maps and assembling botanical and zoological collections—amid the difficult and often gravely dangerous circumstances of war.

At the end of the siege, the expedition sailed for Pernambuco. They founded the town of Mauritzstad (now part of Recife) and built the castle of Vrijburg on the island of Antonio Vaz. Markgraf drew up the plans for the new town and its fortifications, and Maurice installed an observatory for him in a tower of the castle. Markgraf determined the exact position of his site and began to make observations, including those of the planet Mercury and of the solar eclipse of 13 November 1640. He introduced into the island specimens of plants and animals that he had collected on his journeys; the park of Vrijburg Castle was subsequently made a botanical and zoological garden. With an escort of soldiers, to protect him against attack by Indians or by the Portuguese, Markgraf also mapped the region from Rio São Francisco to Ceará and Maranhão and made watercolor depictions, from nature, of flora and fauna. His methods of observing and painting were pioneering, analogous to those of Konrad Gesner in Europe.

Although Markgraf wished to return to Holland in 1644 to compile the results of his researches, he sailed to the Dutch settlements of East Africa to do further fieldwork. He died of a fever in Luanda; he had previously given all his collections and manuscripts into the keeping of Maurice of Nassau.

BIBLIOGRAPHY

I. ORIGINAL WORKS. The best evidence of Markgraf's work is in "Historiae rerum naturalium Brasiliae libri octo," in Jan De Laet, ed., *Historia naturalis Brasiliae* (Leiden–Amsterdam, 1648); Willem Pies, *De Indiae utriusque re naturali et medica libri quatuordecim*, 2nd ed. (Amsterdam, 1658), jumbles Markgraf's and Pies's observations. The printer states that he added the paper on the solar eclipse but, at the suggestion of competent astronomers, did not publish other astronomical notes. Casparis Barlaei (van Baerle), *Rerum per octennium in Brasilia et alibi gestarum sub praefectura illustrissimi comitis J. Mauritii Nassaviae &c. historia* (Amsterdam, 1657), contains Markgraf's geographical maps, which are much praised by specialists.

The dried plants introduced by Markgraf to the botanical garden of the island of Antonio Vaz and blocks for his woodcuts are at the Botanical Museum, Copenhagen. *Liber principis*, the collection of Markgraf's watercolors, was at the Preussische Staatsbibliothek, Berlin, until 1945.

II. SECONDARY LITERATURE. The first account of Markgraf's life, with important details, was written by his brother Christian and appeared in J. J. Manget, *Bibliotheca scriptorum medicorum*, XII (Geneva, 1731), 262–264. Part of it is a defense against Pies.

An early and comprehensive paper is H. Lichtenstein, "Die Werke von Marcgrave und Piso über die Naturgeschichte Brasiliens, erläutert aus den wiederaufgefundenen Originalzeichnungen," in *Abhandlungen der Preussischen Akademie der Wissenschaften*, Physikalische Abhandlungen, for 1814–1815 (1818), 201–222; for 1817 (1819), 155–178; for 1820–1821 (1823), 237–254, 267–288; and for 1826 (1829), 49–65.

An appreciation of Markgraf's significance as a pioneer of Brazilian botany is C. von Martius, "Versuch eines Commentars über die Pflanzen in den Werken von Marcgrav und Piso über Brasilien," in *Abhandlungen der Bayerischen Akademie der Wissenschaften*, Math.-phys. Kl., **7** (1853), 179–238.

Some important corrections derived from archival studies are presented by J. Moreira, "Marcgrave e Piso," in *Revista do Museu paulista*, **14** (1926), 649–673. Corresponding notes on the relationship of Markgraf and Pies are given by R. von Ihering, "George Marcgrave," *ibid.*, **9** (1914), 307–315.

The outstanding value of Markgraf's geographical maps is judged by V. Hantzsch, "Georg Marggraf," in *Berichte über die Verhandlungen der K. Sächsischen Gesellschaft der Wissenschaften zu Leipzig*, Phil.-hist. Kl., **48** (1896), 199–227.

Markgraf's plants in his books of 1648 and 1658 were identified most successfully by Dom Bento Pickel, "Piso e Marcgrave na botânica brasileira," in *Revista da flora medicinal* (Rio), **16** (1949), 155.

Markgraf's model herbarium is evaluated briefly by F. Liebmann in N. Wallich's trans. of Martius' paper in *Hooker's Journal of Botany and Kew Garden Miscellany*, **5** (1853), 167–168, note.

A recent reference of Markgraf's herbarium is given by B. MacBryde, "Rediscovery of G. Marcgrave's Brazilian Collections (1638–1644)," in *Taxon*, **19** (1970), 349.

F. MARKGRAF

MARKHAM, CLEMENTS ROBERT (*b*. Stillingfleet, Yorkshire, England, 20 July 1830; *d*. London, England, 30 January 1916), *geography*.

The second son of David F. Markham and the former Catherine Milner, Markham attended Westminster School for two years before joining the Royal Navy as a cadet in 1844. By the time he left the service in December 1851, he had acquired various technical, nautical, and geographical skills, which were the extent of his formal education. After a year in Peru (1852–1853) studying Inca ruins, he spent most of the next two decades in the service of the India Office. In 1860 Markham planned and executed a project for the acclimatization of Peruvian cinchona in India, an enterprise which had immense significance for public health and for the Indian economy. During this period he wrote extensively on topics in geography, economic botany, and technology related to the development of the British Empire. Combining these pursuits with a historical interest in the diffusion of Islamic technology, he studied the irrigation systems of southeastern Spain with an eye toward the agricultural development of the Madura district of India.

Markham left the India Office in 1877 and devoted the rest of his life to the promotion of geographical research, exploration, and education. He considered himself a comparative and historical geographer and stressed the value of historical records for the study of physical geography. Markham was secretary of the Hakluyt Society (1858–1886) and then president (1889–1909). Under his direction the society published a series of historical accounts of exploration. Markham edited twenty volumes of the series himself and was responsible for editions of several important treatises in the history of science, including a reedition of Edward Grimston's translation (1604) of José de Acosta's *Natural and Moral History of the Indies*; Robert Hues's *Tractatus de globis coelesti et terrestri ac eorem usu conscriptus* (1594); and Garcia da Orta's *Colloquies on the Simples and Drugs of India*, the latter in Markham's translation.

Markham's major work took place in the Royal Geographical Society, which he had joined in 1854. As a secretary from 1863 to 1888 and as president from 1893 to 1905, Markham helped to found a school of geography at Oxford; and it was under his aegis that the *Geographical Journal* became "the chief repository of geographical information from all parts of the world" ("Presidential Address," in *Geographical Journal*, **22** [1903], 1).

As president he enjoined both the Geographical Society and the nation to embark upon what he called an "Antarctic crusade" (*Geographical Journal*, **14** [1899], 479). He believed that the polar regions, particularly the southern one, comprised the single great geographical problem left for England to solve. Markham's program for polar exploration was carefully conceived. His chief arctic canons were that progress should always be made along the coastlines and that in order to be successful, an expedition had to remain over at least one winter in order to collect significant meteorological and magnetic data. Polar research should have two principal focuses: work conducted on the shore and that carried out aboard ship along the coasts. Research on shore would include (1) geographical exploration, (2) geology, (3) studies of glaciation, (4) magnetic observations, (5) meteorological observations, (6) pendulum observations, (7) studies of tides, and (8) inshore and land biology. Shipboard tasks would comprise (1) surveying coastlines,

(2) magnetic observations, (3) meteorological studies, (4) deep-sea soundings, and (5) marine biology (see *Geographical Journal*, **18** [1901], 13–25). As president of the Geographical Society, he established a research committee for polar exploration designed to ensure the maximum preparation and planning toward the accomplishment of these goals.

Not interested in promoting a mere race to the poles, Markham frequently stressed that the aim of such expeditions was to "secure useful scientific results" ("Presidential Address," in *Geographical Journal*, **4** [1894], 7). Although he worked closely with the Royal Society in the planning of polar expeditions, Markham always favored navy men over scientists to lead expeditions.

The last part of Markham's career was linked to the fortunes of Commander Robert F. Scott, whose first Antarctic expedition (voyage of the *Discovery*, 1901–1904) was the crowning achievement of Markham's exploration program. He continued writing on the subject and played an active role in the planning of Scott's fatal expedition on the *Terra Nova* (1910–1912). Described by a navy colleague as a "peripatetic encyclopedia," Markham's scholarship suffered from overextended interests and hasty research. His organizational and promotional talents, however, sufficed to make him the leading figure of Victorian geography.

BIBLIOGRAPHY

I. ORIGINAL WORKS. Markham's main scientific work divides into three primary categories: writings relating to Indian problems, those describing or promoting polar exploration, and essays concerning the nature and history of geographical research.

On the acclimatization of cinchona, see *Travels in Peru and India While Superintending the Collection of Chinchona Plants and Seeds in South America, and Their Introduction Into India* (London, 1862); and *Peruvian Bark* (London, 1880). See also his treatise on the diffusion of irrigation practices, *Report on the Irrigation of Eastern Spain* (London, 1867).

Of the Arctic literature, the important titles are *Franklin's Footsteps* (London, 1853); *The Threshold of the Unknown Region* (London, 1873); *Arctic and Antarctic Exploration* (Liverpool, 1895); *Antarctic Exploration: A Plea for a National Expedition* (London, 1898); "The Antarctic Expeditions," in *Geographical Journal*, **14** (1899), 473–481; "Considerations Respecting Routes for an Antarctic Expedition," *ibid.*, **18** (1901), 13–25; "The First Year's Work of the National Antarctic Expedition," *ibid.*, **22** (1903), 13–20; and his posthumous book, *Lands of Silence* (Cambridge, 1921).

For geographical history and theory, see "The Limits Between Geology and Physical Geography," in *Geographical Journal*, **2** (1893), 518–525; *Major James Rennell and*

the Rise of Modern English Geography (London, 1895); "The Field of Geography," in *Geographical Journal*, **11** (1898), 1–15; "View of the Progress of Geographical Discovery," in *Encyclopaedia Britannica*, 9th ed. (1875), under "Geography"; and "The History of the Gradual Development of the Groundwork of Geographical Science," in *Geographical Journal*, **46** (1915), 173–185.

On Markham's role as a geographical entrepreneur, see *The Fifty Years' Work of the Royal Geographical Society* (London, 1881); "The Present Standpoint of Geography," in *Geographical Journal*, **2** (1893), 481–504; *Hakluyt: His Life and Work. With a Short Account of the Aims and Achievements of the Hakluyt Society* (London, 1896); *Address on the Fiftieth Anniversary of the Foundation of the [Hakluyt] Society* (London, 1911); and his presidential addresses to the Royal Geographical Society, all pub. in *Geographical Journal*, esp. those of 1894 (**4**, 1–25), 1899 (**14**, 1–14), 1901 (**18**, 1–13), and 1903 (**22**, 1–13).

II. SECONDARY LITERATURE. Antonio Olivas, "Contribución a la bibliografía de Sir Clements Robert Markham," in *Boletín bibliográfico* (Lima), **12** (1942), 69–91, is adequate for secondary literature about Markham emanating from Latin America but is deficient otherwise. The standard biographical source is Albert H. Markham, *The Life of Sir Clements R. Markham* (London, 1917). On Markham's role in the Antarctic expeditions, see Robert F. Scott, *The Voyage of the "Discovery"* (dedicated to Markham as "the father of the expedition"), 2 vols. (London, 1905; repr. New York, 1969); Margery and James Fisher, *Shackleton and the Antarctic* (Boston, 1958); and L. B. Quartermain, *South to the Pole* (London, 1967), which cites the relevant earlier bibliography. On Markham's deficiencies as a translator, see Harry Bernstein and Bailey W. Diffie, "Sir Clements R. Markham as a Translator," in *Hispanic American Historical Review*, **17** (1937), 546–557.

THOMAS F. GLICK

MARKOV, ANDREI ANDREEVICH (*b.* Ryazan, Russia, 14 June 1856; *d.* Petrograd [now Leningrad], U.S.S.R., 20 May 1922), *mathematics*.

Markov's father, Andrei Grigorievich Markov, a member of the gentry, served in St. Petersburg in the Forestry Department and managed a private estate. His mother, Nadezhda Petrovna, was the daughter of a state employee. Markov was in poor health and used crutches until he was ten years old. He early manifested a talent for mathematics in high school but was not diligent in other courses. In 1874 Markov entered the mathematics department of St. Petersburg University and enrolled in a seminar for superior students, led by A. N. Korkin and E. I. Zolotarev. He had met them in his high school days after presenting a paper on integration of linear differential equations (which contained results already known). He also attended lectures by the head of the St. Petersburg mathematical school, P. L. Chebyshev, and afterward became a consistent follower of his ideas.

In 1878 Markov graduated from the university with a gold medal for his thesis, "Ob integrirovanii differentsialnykh uravnenii pri pomoshchi nepreryvnykh drobei" ("On the Integration of Differential Equations by Means of Continued Fractions") and remained at the university to prepare for a professorship. In 1880 he defended his master's thesis, "O binarnykh kvadratichnykh formakh polozhitelnogo opredelitelia" ("On the Binary Quadratic Forms With Positive Determinant"; *Izbrannye trudy*, pp. 9–83), and began teaching in the university as a docent. In 1884 he defended his doctoral dissertation, devoted to continued fractions and the problem of moments. In 1883 he married Maria Ivanovna Valvatyeva, the daughter of the proprietress of the estate managed by his father. They had been childhood friends, and Markov had helped her to learn mathematics. Later he proposed to her, but her mother agreed to the marriage only after Markov strengthened his social position.

For twenty-five years Markov combined research with intensive teaching at St. Petersburg University. In 1886 he was named extraordinary professor and in 1893, full professor. In this period he studied many questions: number theory, continued fractions, functions least deviating from zero, approximate quadrature formulas, integration in elementary functions, the problem of moments, probability theory, and differential equations. His lectures were distinguished by an irreproachable strictness of argument, and he developed in his students that mathematical cast of mind that takes nothing for granted. He included in his courses many recent results of investigations, while often omitting traditional questions. The lectures were difficult, and only serious students could understand them. He stated his opinions in a peremptory manner and was extremely exacting with his associates. During his lectures he did not bother about the order of equations on the blackboard, nor about his personal appearance. He was also a faculty adviser for a student mathematical circle. Nominated by Chebyshev, Markov was elected in 1886 an adjunct of the St. Petersburg Academy of Sciences; in 1890 he became an extraordinary academician and in 1896 an ordinary academician. In 1905, after twenty-five years of teaching, Markov retired to make room for younger mathematicians. He was named professor emeritus, but still taught the probability course at the university, by his right as an academician. At this time his scientific interests concentrated on probability theory and in particular on the chains later named for him.

A man of firm opinions, Markov participated in the liberal movement in Russia at the beginning of the twentieth century. In a series of caustic letters to academic and state authorities, he protested against the overruling, at the czar's order, of the election in 1902 of Maxim Gorky to the St. Petersburg Academy, he refused to receive decorations (1903), and he repudiated his membership in the electorate after the illegal dissolution of the Second State Duma by the government (1907). The authorities preferred not to respond to these declarations, considering them the extravagances of an academician. In 1913, when officials pompously celebrated the three-hundredth anniversary of the House of Romanov, Markov organized a celebration of the two-hundredth anniversary of the law of large numbers (in 1713 Jakob I Bernoulli's *Ars conjectandi* was posthumously published).

In September 1917 Markov asked the Academy to send him to the interior of Russia, and he spent the famine winter in Zaraisk, a little country town. There he voluntarily taught mathematics in a secondary school without pay. Soon after his return to Petrograd, his health declined sharply and he had an eye operation. In 1921 he continued lecturing, scarcely able to stand. He died after several months of intense suffering.

Markov belonged to Chebyshev's scientific school and, more than others, was faithful to the creed and the principles of his master. He inherited from Chebyshev an interest in concrete problems; a simplicity of mathematical procedures; a need to solve problems effectively, whether simple or algorithmic; and a desire to obtain exact limits for asymptotic results. These views coexisted with an underestimation of the role of some new general concepts in contemporary mathematics, namely of the axiomatic method and of the theory of functions of complex variables. Characteristic of Markov was the adherence to a chosen method of investigation and maintenance of his own view of what is valuable in science. He once said, "Mathematics is that which Gauss, Chebyshev, Lyapunov, Steklov, and I study" (N. M. Guenter, "O pedagogicheskoi deyatelnosti A. A. Markov," p. 37).

The principal aim of most of Markov's works in number theory and function theory was to evaluate the exact upper or lower bounds for various quantities (quadratic forms, integrals, derivatives). In probability theory it was at first to apply the bounds for integrals to the proof of the central limit theorem outlined by Chebyshev; later it was to discover new phenomena satisfying this theorem. Markov's work in various branches of mathematics is also united by systematic use of Chebyshev's favorite method of continued fractions, which became the principal instrument in Markov's investigations.

Markov's work in number theory was devoted mostly to the problem of arithmetical minima of indefinite quadratic forms studied previously in Russia by Korkin and Zolotarev (the topic goes back to Gauss and Hermite). These two authors had shown that if one excludes the form $f(x, y) = x^2 - xy - y^2$ (and the forms equivalent to it) for which $\min |f| = \sqrt{\frac{4}{5}d}$, then for the remaining binary forms $f(x, y) = ax^2 + 2bxy + cy^2$ with $d = b^2 - ac > 0$, one has $\min |f| \leqslant \sqrt{\frac{1}{2}d}$. By means of continued fractions Markov showed in his master's thesis (*Izbrannye trudy*, pp. 9–83) that 4/5 and 1/2 are the first two terms of an infinite decreasing sequence $\{N_k\}$ converging to 4/9, such that (1) for every N_k there exists a finite number of nonequivalent binary forms whose minimum is equal to $\sqrt{N_k d}$ and (2) if the minimum of any indefinite binary form is more than $\sqrt{\frac{4}{9}d}$, then it is equal to one of the values of $\sqrt{N_k d}$. To the limiting value $\sqrt{\frac{4}{9}d}$ there correspond infinitely many nonequivalent forms. Following the traditions of the Petersburg mathematical school, Markov also computed the first twenty numbers of $\{N_k\}$ and the forms corresponding to them. In 1901–1909 he returned to the problem of extrema of indefinite quadratic forms. He found the first four extremal forms of three variables (one of them was known to Korkin) and two extremal forms of four variables, and published a long list of ternary forms with $d \leqslant 50$. Markov's works on indefinite forms were continued both in the Soviet Union and in the West. Another problem of number theory was considered by Markov in his paper "Sur les nombres entiers dépendents d'une racine cubique d'un nombre entier ordinaire" (*Izbrannye trudy*, pp. 85–133). Following Zolotarev's ideas, Markov here obtained the final result for decomposition into ideal prime factors in the field generated by $\sqrt[3]{A}$ and calculated the units of these fields for all $A \leqslant 70$.

The next area of Markov's work concerned the evaluation of limits of functions, integrals, and derivatives. The problem of moments was the most notable among these topics. From a work of J. Bienaymé presented to the Paris Academy of Sciences in 1833 (republished in Liouville's *Journal de mathématiques pures et appliquées* in 1867), Chebyshev borrowed the problem of finding the upper and lower bounds of an integral

$$(1) \qquad \int_a^x f(x)\, dx$$

of a nonnegative function f with given values of its moments

$$(2) \quad m_k = \int_A^B x^k f(x)\, dx \qquad (k = 0, 1, \cdots, N)$$

and the idea of applying the solution of this problem

of moments to prove limit laws in probability theory. In 1874 Chebyshev published, without proofs, inequalities providing upper and lower bounds for integral (1) for some special values of a and $x(A < a < x < B)$. These bounds were expressed through the convergents of the continued fraction into which the series $\sum m_k/Z^{k+1}$ formally decomposes. The proofs of Chebyshev's inequalities appeared in 1884 in Markov's memoir "Démonstration de certaines inégalités de M. Tchebycheff" (*Izbrannye trudy po teorii nepreryvnykh drovei ...*, pp. 15–24). The same inequalities with the same proofs were published at almost the same time by the Dutch mathematician Stieltjes. Markov claimed priority, to which Stieltjes replied that he could not have known of Markov's paper and that Chebyshev's work had indeed escaped his attention. Later Markov and Stieltjes studied the problem of moments largely side by side and sometimes one would find new proofs of the other's already published results. Both used continued fractions in their investigations and developed their theory further; but a difference in their methodological approaches manifested itself: Markov was mostly interested in the case of finite numbers of given moments and he studied the problem entirely within the limits of classical calculus; Stieltjes paid more attention to the problem of given infinite sequences of moments, and, seeking the most adequate formulation of the problem, introduced a generalization of the classical integral—the so-called Stieltjes integral.

In his doctoral dissertation Markov solved the question of the upper and lower bounds of integral (1) in the case when the first N moments are known. In subsequent papers he generalized the problem by allowing the appearance of an additional factor $\Omega(x)$ under integral (1); allowing, instead of power moments (2), moments relative to arbitrary functions $\lambda_k(x)$; and substituting the condition $c \leqslant f(x) \leqslant C$ for $f(x) \geqslant 0$. In other papers he investigated the distribution of the roots of the denominators of the convergents of the continued fraction mentioned above and the convergence of this fraction. The last question is closely related to the uniqueness of the solution of the Stieltjes problem of moments (finding a function, given its infinite sequence of power moments). In 1895, in his memoir "Deux démonstrations de la convergence de certaines fractions continues" (*Izbrannye trudy po teorii nepreryvnykh drovei ...*, pp. 106–119), Markov obtained the following sufficient condition for the convergence, and therefore for the uniqueness of the Stieltjes problem, of functions defined on $[0, \infty)$: $\overline{\lim}_{k\to\infty} \sqrt[k]{m_k} < \infty$. Further results were obtained by O. Perron, H. Hamburger, F. Riesz, and T. G. Carleman.

Markov solved in 1889 another problem on extremal values which arose from the needs of chemistry in "Ob odnom voprose D. I. Mendeleeva" ("On a Question of D. I. Mendeleev"; *Izbrannye trudy po teorii nepreryvnykh drovei . . .*, pp. 51–75). Here Markov found the maximum possible value of the derivative $f'(z)$ of a polynomial $f(z)$ of degree $\leqslant n$ on an interval $[a, b]$, provided that $|f(z)| \leqslant L$ on $[a, b]$. (This maximum value is equal to $2n^2 L/(b - a)$.) Markov's result was generalized in 1892 by his younger brother Vladimir (who died five years afterward), and it was later extended for other cases by S. N. Bernstein and N. I. Akhiezer. Markov also worked on some other, practical extremal problems, namely the mapping of a part of a surface of revolution onto a plane with minimal deformations and the joining of two straight lines with a smooth curve having minimal curvature. The question of Mendeleev can be reformulated as a question about the maximum deviation of the polynomial $f(z)$ from zero, and it is therefore closely related to Chebyshev's theory of polynomials deviating least from zero and to some other topics connected with this theory, such as orthogonal polynomials (particularly Hermite and Legendre polynomials and the distribution of their roots), interpolation, and approximate quadrature formulas.

Markov obtained new results in all these areas; but unlike Chebyshev, who also studied quadrature formulas, Markov found in his formulas the expression of the remainder term. For example, in his doctoral dissertation he derived the remainder term of a quadrature formula originating with Gauss. Among other topics related to approximation calculus, Markov considered summation and improving the convergence of series. Evidence of Markov's liking for computation are his tables of the integral of probabilities calculated to eleven decimal places. Markov paid much attention to interpolation, summation, transformations of series, approximate calculation of integrals, and calculation of tables in his *Ischislenie konechnykh raznostei* ("Calculus of Finite Differences"). The difference equations themselves occupy a modest place in this book, which contains characteristic connections with the work of Briggs, Gauss, and Euler and many carefully calculated examples. Markov also obtained some results in the theory of differential equations— on Lamé's equation and the equation of the hypergeometric series—partly overlapping results of Felix Klein, and results concerning the possibility of expressing integrals in terms of elementary functions.

Markov's work in probability theory produced the greatest effect on the development of science. The basic achievements in probability theory by the middle of the nineteenth century were the law of large num-

bers, presented in its simplest version by Jakob I Bernoulli, and the central limit theorem (as it is now called) of de Moivre and Laplace. Satisfactory proofs under sufficiently wide assumptions had not been found, however, nor had the limits of their applicability. Through their closely interrelated works on these two laws Chebyshev, Markov, and Lyapunov created the foundation for the modernization of probability theory. In 1867 Chebyshev had found an elementary proof of the law of large numbers and turned to demonstrating the central limit theorem, using the solution of the problem of moments. The Bienaymé–Chebyshev problem mentioned above, translated into probability language, becomes a problem about the exact limits for the distribution function $F_\xi(x)$ of a random variable ξ with N given first moments $m_k = E\xi^k$. Let $\xi_1, \xi_2, \cdots, \xi_n, \cdots$ be a sequence of independent random variables with zero means (the case of nonzero $E\xi_n$ can be easily reduced to the considered one). According to Chebyshev's approach, one must show (a) that for every k the kth moment m_k of the normalized sum

$$\zeta_n = \frac{\xi_1 + \cdots + \xi_n}{\mathrm{var}(\xi_1 + \cdots + \xi_n)}$$

tends to the corresponding moment μ_k of the standard Gaussian distribution

$$\Phi(x) = \frac{1}{\sqrt{2\pi}} \int_{-\infty}^{x} e^{-\frac{y^2}{2}} \, dy$$

if $n \to \infty$, and (b) that if $m_k \to \mu_k$ for all k, then $F_{\zeta n}(x) \to \Phi(x)$. When Markov published (1884) the proofs of Chebyshev's inequalities concerning the moments, Chebyshev began to work faster. In 1886 he showed that if $m_k = \mu_k$, then $F(x) = \Phi(x)$ (for him, but not for Markov, it was equivalent to assertion [b]); and in 1887 he published a demonstration of point (a) based on incorrect manipulations with divergent series.

Markov decided to turn Chebyshev's argument into a correct one and fulfilled this aim in 1898 in the paper "Sur les racines de l'équation $e^{x^2}(d^n e^{-x^2}/dx^n) = 0$" (*Izbrannye trudy po teorii nepreryvnykh drovei . . .*, pp. 231–243; *Izbrannye trudy*, pp. 253–269) and in his letters to Professor A. V. Vassilyev at Kazan University, entitled "Zakon bolshikh chisel i sposob naimenshikh kvadratov" ("The Law of Large Numbers and the Method of Least Squares"; *Izbrannye trudy*, pp. 231–251). In the first of his letters Markov defined his aim thus:

The theorem which Chebyshev is proving . . . has been regarded as true for a long time, but is established by an extremely inaccurate procedure. I do not say proved because I do not recognize inaccurate proofs. . . . The known derivation of the theorem is inaccurate but simple. The derivation by Chebyshev on the contrary is very complicated, for it is based on preliminary investigations. . . . Therefore the question arises as to whether Chebyshev's derivation differs from the previous one only by its intricacy but is analogous to it in essentials, or whether one can make this derivation accurate. Your essay on Chebyshev's works strengthened my long-standing desire to simplify and at the same time to make quite accurate Chebyshev's analysis" [*Izbrannye trudy*, p. 231].

In his letters to Vassilyev, Markov established an arithmetical proof of convergence $m_k \to \mu_k$ (assertion [a]) under the following conditions: (1) for every k the sequence $E\xi_1^k, E\xi_2^k, \cdots$ is bounded and (2) $\text{var}(\xi_1 + \cdots + \xi_n) \geqslant cn$ for all n and some fixed $c > 0$. The corresponding calculation based on the expansion of the polynomial $(x_1 + \cdots + x_n)^k$ is maintained in all subsequent works by Markov on the limit theorem. In the article "Sur les racines . . ." Markov proved that $F(x) \to \Phi(x)$ if $m_k \to \mu_k$ (assertion [b]) by means of further analysis of Chebyshev's inequalities and continued fractions. He showed by examples that assumption (2), the need for which was unnoticed by Chebyshev, cannot be omitted.

In 1900 Markov published *Ischislenie veroyatnostei* ("Probability Calculus"). This book played an important role in modernizing probability theory. Characteristic features of the book are the inclusion of recent results obtained by Markov, rigorous proofs, elaborate references to classical works of the eighteenth century which for Markov had contemporary as well as historical importance, many numerical examples, and a polemical tone (Markov never missed an opportunity to mention an incorrectly solved example from another author and to correct the error).

But the triumph of the method of moments lasted only a short time. In 1901 Lyapunov, who was less influenced by their master, Chebyshev, and prized more highly the "transcendental" means (in Chebyshev's words) of the complex variable, played on Markov what he termed "a great dirty trick" (V. A. Steklov, "A. A. Markov," p. 178). Lyapunov discovered a new way to obtain and prove the limit theorems —the method of characteristic functions. The principal idea of this much more flexible method consists in assigning to the distribution of a random variable ξ not the sequence of moments $\{m_k\}$ but the characteristic function $\varphi(t) = Ee^{it\xi}$ and deducing the convergence of distributions from convergence of characteristic functions. Lyapunov proved the central limit theorem (for independent summands with zero means)

by his method under the conditions that (1) all moments $d_n = E \mid \xi_n \mid^{2+\delta}$ are finite for some $\delta > 0$, and

$$(2) \qquad \lim_{n \to \infty} \frac{[\text{var}(\xi_1 + \cdots + \xi_n)]^{2+\delta}}{(d_1 + \cdots + d_n)^2} = \infty,$$

which are near to necessary and sufficient ones. Although the second conditions of Markov and Lyapunov are of a similar character (both require rapid growth of the variance of the sum), the first condition of Lyapunov is incomparably wider than Chebyshev-Markov's, because it does not require even the existence of moments of the third and subsequent orders.

Markov struggled for eight years to rehabilitate the method of moments and was at last successful. In the memoir "Teorema o predele veroyatnosti dlya sluchaev akademika A. M. Lyapunova" ("Theorem About the Limit of Probability for the Cases of Academician A. M. Lyapunov"; *Izbrannye trudy*, pp. 319–337), included in the third edition of his *Ischislenie veroyatnostei*, Markov proved Lyapunov's result by using the new procedure of truncating the distributions, thus permitting one to reduce the general case to the case of bounded moments of every order. This procedure is still a useful device, but the method of moments could not stand the competition of the simpler and more universal method of characteristic functions. Also in the third edition of *Ischislenie veroyatnostei*, Markov showed, by means of truncating, that the law of large numbers is true for a sequence $\xi_1, \xi_2, \cdots, \xi_n, \cdots$ of independent random variables if for any $p > 1$ the moments $E \mid \xi_n \mid^p$ are bounded. (Chebyshev had proved the case $p = 2$.) Markov also deduced here the convergence of distributions from the convergence of moments for the cases when the limiting distribution is not Gaussian but has the density $Ae^{-x^2} \mid x \mid^\nu$ or $Ae^{-x}x^\delta$ ($x \geqslant 0$). (The theorem was demonstrated for other continuous limiting distributions in 1920 by M. Pólya.)

In his efforts to establish the limiting laws of probability in the most general situation and to enlarge the applications of the method of moments, Markov began a systematic study of sequences of mutually dependent variables, and selected from among them an important class later named for him. A sequence $\{\xi_n\}$ of random variables (or random phenomena of some other kind) is called a Markov chain if, given the value of the present variable ξ_n, the future ξ_{n+1} becomes independent of the past $\xi_1, \xi_2, \cdots, \xi_{n-1}$. If the conditional distribution of ξ_{n+1} given ξ_n (defined by transition probabilities at time n) does not depend on n, then the chain is called homogeneous. The possible values of ξ_n are the states of the chain. Such chains appeared for the first time in 1906 in Markov's paper "Rasprostranenie zakona bolshikh chisel na velichiny, zavisyashchie drug ot druga" ("The Extension of the Law of Large Numbers on Mutually Dependent Variables"; *Izbrannye trudy*, pp. 339–361). Markov started with the statement that if the variance of the sum $(\xi_1 + \cdots + \xi_n)$ grows more slowly than n^2, then the law of large numbers is true for the sequence $\{\xi_n\}$, no matter how the random variables depend on each other. He also gave examples of dependent variables satisfying this condition, among them a homogeneous chain with a finite number of states. Markov obtained the necessary estimation of the variance from the convergence as $n \to \infty$ of the distribution of ξ_n to some final distribution independent of the values of ξ_1 (the "ergodic" property of the chain).

In his next paper, "Issledovanie zamechatelnogo sluchaya zavisimykh ispytanii" ("Investigation of a Remarkable Case of Dependent Trials"; in *Izvestiya Peterburgskoi akademii nauk*, 6th ser., **1**, no. 3 [1907], 61–80), Markov proved the central limit theorem for the sums $\xi_1 + \cdots + \xi_n$, where $\{\xi_n\}$ is a homogeneous chain with two states, 0 and 1. In 1908, in the article "Rasprostranenie predelnykh theorem ischislenia veroyatnostei na summu velichin, svyazannykh v tsep" ("The Extension of the Limit Theorems of Probability Calculus to Sums of Variables Connected in a Chain"; *Izbrannye trudy*, pp. 365–397), he generalized this result to arbitrary homogeneous chains with finite numbers of states, whose transition probabilities satisfy some restrictions. The proof, as in all of Markov's works, was obtained by the method of moments. In "Issledovanie obshchego sluchaya ispytanii svyazannykh v tsep" ("Investigation of the General Case of Trials Connected in a Chain"; *Izbrannye trudy* [1910], pp. 467–507), Markov demonstrated the central limit theorem for nonhomogeneous chains with two states under the condition that all four transition probabilities remain in a fixed interval (c_1, c_2) $(0 < c_1 < c_2 < 1)$. In other articles, published in 1911–1912, he studied various generalizations of his chains (compound chains where ξ_n depends on several previous variables, so-called Markov-Bruns chains, partly observed chains) and deduced for them the central limit theorem under some restrictions.

Markov arrived at his chains starting from the internal needs of probability theory, and he never wrote about their applications to physical science. For him the only real examples of the chains were literary texts, where the two states denoted the vowels and the consonants (in order to illustrate his results he statistically worked up the alternation of vowels and consonants in Pushkin's *Eugene Onegin* (*Ischislenie veroyatnostei*, 4th ed., pp. 566–577). Nevertheless, the mathematical scheme offered by Markov and extended

later to families of random variables $\{\xi_t\}$ depending on continuous time t (which are called Markov processes, as suggested by Khinchin) has proved very fruitful and has found many applications. The development of molecular and statistical physics, quantum theory, and genetics showed that a deterministic approach is insufficient in natural sciences, and forced physicists to turn to probabilistic concepts. Through this evolution of scientific views, the Markov principle of statistical independence of future from past if the present is known, appeared to be the necessary probabilistic generalization of Huygens' principle of "absence of after effect." The far-reaching importance of such a generalization is shown by the fact that although Markov was the first to study the chains as a new, independent mathematical object, a number of random phenomena providing examples of Markov chains or processes were considered by other scientists before his work or concurrently with it. In 1889 the biologist Francis Galton studied the problem of survival of a family by means of a model reducing to a Markov chain with a denumerable number of states. An example of a Markov chain was considered in 1907 by Paul and T. Ehrenfest as a model of diffusion. In 1912 Poincaré, in the second edition of his *Calcul des probabilités*, in connection with the problem of card shuffling, proved the ergodic property for a chain defined on a permutation group and mentioned the possibility of an analogous approach to problems of statistical physics. An important example of a continuous Markov process was studied on a heuristic level in 1900–1901 by L. Bachelier in the theory of speculation. The same process appeared in 1905–1907 in works of Einstein and M. Smoluchowski on Brownian motion.

Markov's studies on chains were continued by S. N. Bernstein, M. Fréchet, V. I. Romanovsky, A. N. Kolmogorov, W. Doeblin, and many others. The first rigorous treatment of a continuous Markov process, the process of Brownian motion, was provided in 1923 by Wiener. The foundations of the general theory of Markov processes were laid down in the 1930's by Kolmogorov. The modern aspect of the theory of Markov processes, which became an intensively developing autonomous branch of mathematics, resulted from work by W. Feller, P. Lévy, J. Doob, E. B. Dynkin, K. Ito, and other contemporary probabilists.

Markov also studied other topics in probability: the method of least squares, the coefficient of variance, and some urn schemes.

BIBLIOGRAPHY

I. ORIGINAL WORKS. The most significant of Markov's papers are republished in *Izbrannye trudy po teorii nepre-*

ryvnykh drovei . . . and *Izbrannye trudy*, with modern commentaries; the latter contains a complete bibliography of original and secondary works to 1951. The earlier collection of his writings is *Izbrannye trudy po teorii nepreryvnykh drovei i teorii funktsii naimenee uklonyaiushchikhsya ot nulya*, N. I. Akhiezer, ed. ("Selected Works on Continued Fractions Theory and Theory of Functions Least Deviating From Zero"; Moscow, 1948), with comments by the ed. One of the memoirs was translated into English: "Functions Generated by Developing Power Series in Continued Fractions," in *Duke Mathematical Journal*, **7** (1940), 85–96. The later collection is *Izbrannye trudy. Teoria chisel. Teoria veroyatnostei*, Y. V. Linnik, ed. ("Selected Works. Number Theory. Probability Theory"; Moscow–Leningrad, 1951), which contains an essay on the papers in the volume and comments by the editor, and N. A. Sapogov, O. V. Sarmanov, and V. N. Timofeev; the most detailed biography of Markov, by his son A. A. Markov; and a full bibliography.

Individual works by Markov are *O nekotorykh prilozheniakh algebraicheskikh nepreryvnykh drobei* ("On Some Applications of Algebraic Continued Fractions"; St. Petersburg, 1884), his doctoral dissertation; *Tables des valeurs de l'intégrale $\int_x^\infty e^{-t^2} dt$* (St. Petersburg, 1888); *Ischislenie konechnykh raznostei* ("Differential Calculus"), 2 vols. (St. Petersburg, 1889–1891; 2nd ed., Odessa, 1910), also translated into German as *Differenzenrechnung* (Leipzig, 1896); and *Ischislenie veroyatnostei* ("Probability Calculus"; St. Petersburg, 1900; 2nd ed., 1908; 3rd ed., 1913; 4th ed., Moscow, 1924), posthumous 4th ed. with biographical note by A. S. Bezikovich, also translated into German as *Wahrscheinlichkeitsrechnung* (Leipzig–Berlin, 1912).

II. SECONDARY LITERATURE. Besides the biography in *Izbrannye trudy*, there is basic information in V. A. Steklov, "Andrei Andreevich Markov," in *Izvestiya Rossiiskoi akademii nauk*, **16** (1922), 169–184. See also *ibid.*, **17** (1923), 19–52; Y. V. Uspensky, "Ocherk nauchnoi deyatelnosti A. A. Markova" ("An Essay on the Scientific Work of A. A. Markov"); N. M. Guenter, "O pedagogicheskoi deyatelnosti A. A. Markova" ("On the Pedagogical Activity of A. A. Markov"); and A. Bezikovich, "Raboty A. A. Markova po teorii veroyatnostei" ("Markov's Works in Probability").

Various aspects of Markov's work are discussed in *Nauchnoe nasledie P. L. Chebysheva* ("The Scientific Heritage of P. L. Chebyshev"), I (Moscow–Leningrad, 1945), which compares Chebyshev's results in various fields with those of Markov, Lyapunov, and their followers in papers by N. I. Akhiezer (pp. 22–39), S. N. Bernstein (pp. 53–66), and V. L. Goncharov (pp. 154–155); and B. N. Delone, *Peterburgskaya shkola teorii chisel* ("The Petersburg School of Number Theory"; Moscow–Leningrad, 1947), which has a detailed exposition of Markov's master's thesis and a summary of further development of associated topics, pp. 141–193.

General surveys of Markov's life and work include B. V. Gnedenko, *Ocherki po istorii matematiki v Rossii* ("Essays on the History of Mathematics in Russia"; Moscow, 1946), pp. 125–133; *Istoria otechestvennoi mate-*

matiki ("History of Russian Mathematics"), II (Kiev, 1967), with an essay on Markov by I. B. Pogrebyssky, pp. 328–340; and A. P. Youschkevitch, *Istoria matematiki v Rossii do 1917 goda* ("History of Mathematics in Russia Until 1917"; Moscow, 1968), pp. 357–363, 395–403.

Post-Markov development of the theory of his chains is discussed by M. Fréchet, *Théorie des événements en chaine dans le cas d'un nombre fini d'états possible*, in *Recherches théoriques modernes sur le calcul des probabilités*, II (Paris, 1938); J. G. Kemeny and J. L. Snell, *Finite Markov Chains* (Princeton, 1960); and V. I. Romanovski, *Diskretnye tsepi Markova* ("Discrete Markov Chains"; Moscow, 1949).

An introduction to the modern theory of Markov processes is M. Loève, *Probability Theory* (Princeton, 1955), ch. 12.

ALEXANDER A. YOUSCHKEVITCH

MARKOVNIKOV, VLADIMIR VASILEVICH (*b.* Knyaginino, Nizhegorodskaya [now Gorki Region], Russia, 25 December 1837 [or 22 December 1838]; *d.* Moscow, Russia, 11 February 1904), *chemistry*.

Markovnikov was the son of an officer. In 1856 he entered Kazan University, where he was attracted to chemistry, which was taught by Butlerov. After graduating from the university in 1860 he became Butlerov's assistant in teaching inorganic and analytical chemistry. In his master's thesis, "Ob izomerii organicheskikh soedineny" ("On the Isomerism of Organic Compounds"; Kazan, 1865); in a number of other works; and especially in his doctoral thesis, "Materialy po voprosu o vzaimnom vlianii atomov v khimicheskikh soedineniakh" ("Materials on the Question of the Mutual Influence of Atoms in Chemical Compounds"; Kazan, 1869), he developed the theory of chemical structure experimentally and theoretically. From 1865 to 1867 he was in Germany, spending most of his time in the laboratories of Erlenmeyer at Heidelberg and of Kolbe at Leipzig. After his return he became assistant to, and then succeeded, Butlerov in the chair of chemistry at Kazan University. In 1871, however, protesting the arbitrariness of the administration, he resigned. Markovnikov was immediately invited to the University of Odessa, and in 1873 to Moscow University. There he improved the teaching of chemistry, set up a new chemical laboratory according to his own plans, and created his own school of chemists. His students included I. A. Kablukov, M. I. Konovalov, N. Y. Demyanov, D. N. Pryanishnikov, A. E. Chichibabin, A. A. Yakovkin, and N. M. Kizhner. In 1893, after Markovnikov had served his term in the chair of chemistry, he yielded it to N. D. Zelinsky but retained a part of the laboratory.

An important turning point in Markovnikov's

scientific career occurred in Moscow: he shifted his attention mainly to practical chemical research, and thus was reproached for betraying pure science. He devoted almost twenty-five years to the study of the hydrocarbons of Caucasian petroleum and to the chemistry of alicyclic hydrocarbons—"naphthenes," as he called them. But the range of Markovnikov's research also included the composition of the salts of the southern Russian bitter-salt lakes and the Caucasian sources of mineral waters, and methods and materials for testing railroad ties.

Markovnikov also studied the history of chemistry. He took the initiative in the publication of the Lomonosovskogo sbornika ("Lomonosov Collection"; Moscow, 1901), which included material on the history of Russian chemical laboratories; and he himself wrote a detailed sketch of the laboratories of Moscow University.

The most important results which Markovnikov obtained in his work on the theory of structure and the chemistry of petroleum and alicyclic compounds were the following. He tested certain conclusions, important in the first stage of structural theory, concerning the existence of isomers in a series of fatty acids (for example, butyric and isobutyric acid, the identity of "acetone" acid, obtained by G. Städeler in 1859 from "the mixture of acetone, hydrogen cyanide, and diluted hydrochloric acid," with isobutyric acid). Developing Butlerov's theory of the mutual influence of atoms, Markovnikov introduced certain "rules."

The rule for the substitution reaction in its general form states that with an unsymmetrical olefin, where two possible modes of addition are open, the reaction ordinarily follows a course such that the hydrogen becomes attached to the carbon atom of the olefin that already has the greater number of hydrogen atoms. Thus:

$$CH_3CH = CH_2 + HBr \rightarrow CH_3CHBrCH_3.$$

Markovnikov recognized that tertiary hydrogen atoms and hydrogen atoms in the α position to a carboxyl group are more active than hydrogen atoms in other positions. This also indicated to him at what point in a molecule destructive oxidation would take place. Markovnikov also first stated the rule that when molecules of water or hydrogen halide are obtained from alcohols or alkylhalides, the separation occurs between them and the two neighboring atoms of hydrogen.

An example from Markovnikov's doctoral thesis is:

$$\begin{array}{ll} CH_2OH \\ CH_2 \\ CH \\ \overline{CH_3CH_3} \end{array} \Big\rangle H_2O = \begin{array}{l} CH_2{}' \\ CH' \\ CH \\ \overline{CH_3CH_3}\, . \end{array}$$

This rule, as Markovnikov showed, can be used to determine the structure of unsaturated compounds. The formation of compounds of the hydrogen halides or water with an unsymmetrical olefin occurs so that the halogen or hydroxyl radical adds to the carbon of the ethylenic bond with the lesser number of hydrogen atoms while the hydrogen adds to the carbon with the larger number of hydrogen atoms. This is known in textbooks as the Markovnikov rule. Markovnikov explained the mechanism of the reactions of isomerization, similar to the transition of isobutyl alcohol to tertiary isobutyl alcohol by reference to such reactions of separation and addition. He also stated rules relating to monomolecular isomerization and certain other reactions, stressing their dependence on the conditions.

In 1872, two years before van't Hoff's stereochemical representation (tetrahedral) of the carbon atom, Markovnikov showed the necessity of developing a theory of chemical structure by studying the relation between chemical interaction and the "physical position" of atoms in space; and in 1876 he stated that "the relative distribution of atoms in a molecule should be expressed by chemical formulas."

Markovnikov was one of the first to understand the importance of studying the composition of petroleum hydrocarbons for practical uses. For example, he and his colleagues showed, contrary to the current opinion, that oil from the Caucasus contained derivatives of cyclopentane and aromatic hydrocarbons along with derivatives of cyclohexane. He discovered the existence of azeotropic mixtures of both these types of hydrocarbons. Markovnikov proposed a method for obtaining aromatic nitro derivatives by means of direct nitration of petroleum fractions.

Markovnikov's contribution to the chemistry of alicyclic compounds consists, first, in his experimental refutation of the prevailing opinion that the carbocyclic compounds could have only six-atom nuclei. In 1879 he synthesized the derivative of a four-membered cycle, and ten years later (at the same time as W. H. Perkin, Jr.) the derivative of a seven-membered cycle. In 1892 Markovnikov proposed the isomerization of a seven-membered cycle into the six-membered one and laid the basis for the study of mutual transformations of alicycles. Markovnikov also made the first classifications of alicyclic compounds in 1892.

BIBLIOGRAPHY

I. ORIGINAL WORKS. Many of Markovnikov's writings are in *Izbrannye trudy* ("Selected Works"), A. F. Platé and G. V. Bykov, eds., in the series Klassiki Nauki ("Classics of Science"; Moscow, 1955), with a 448-title biblio. of Markovnikov's works in the appendix, pp. 835–889.

Among his articles are "Zur Geschichte der Lehre über die chemische Structur," in *Zeitschrift für Chemie*, n.s. **1** (1865), 280–287; "Ueber die Acetonsäure," in *Annalen der Chemie und Pharmacie*, **146** (1868), 339–352; "Ueber die Abhängigkeit der verschiedenen Vertretbarkeit des Radicalwasserstoffs in den isomeren Buttersäuren," *ibid.*, **153** (1870), 228–259; "Tetrylendicarbonsäure (Homoitakonsäure)," *ibid.*, **208** (1881), 333–349, written with G. Krestovnikov; "Recherches sur le pétrole caucase," in *Annales de chimie et de physique*, 6th ser., **2** (1884), 372–484, written with V. Ogloblin; "Die aromatischen Kohlenwasserstoffe des Kaukasischen Erdöhls," in *Justus Liebig's Annalen der Chemie*, **234** (1886), 89–115; and "Die Naphtene und deren Derivate in dem allgemeinen System der organischen Verbindungen," in *Journal für praktische Chemie*, 2nd ser., **45** (1892), 561–580, and **46** (1892), 86–106.

Some of Markovnikov's correspondence is in "Pisma V. V. Markovnikova k A. M. Butlerovu" ("Letters of V. V. Markovnikov to A. M. Butlerov"), in *Pisma russkikh khimikov k A. M. Butlerovu* ("Letters of Russian Chemists to A. M. Butlerov"), vol. IV in the series Nauchnoe Nasledstvo ("Scientific Heritage"; Moscow, 1961), pp. 212–289.

II. SECONDARY LITERATURE. There is a collection entitled *Pamyati Vladimira Vasilevicha Markovnikova* ("In Memory of Vladimir Vasilevich Markovnikov"; Moscow, 1905).

See also H. Decker, "Wladimir Wasiliewitsch Markownikow," in *Berichte der Deutschen chemischen Gesellschaft*, **38** (1906), 4249–4259; H. M. Leicester, "Vladimir Vasil'evich Markovnikov," in *Journal of Chemical Education*, **18** (1941), 53–57; and "Kekulé, Butlerov, Markovnikov. Controversies on Chemical Structure From 1860 to 1870," in *Kekulé Centennial*, no. 61 in the series Advances in Chemistry (Washington, D.C., 1966), pp. 13–23; A. F. Platé and G. V. Bykov, "Ocherk zhizni i deyatelnosti V. V. Markovnikova" ("A Sketch of the Life and Work of V. V. Markovnikov"), in Markovnikov's *Izbrannye trudy*, pp. 719–777; and A. F. Platé, G. V. Bykov, and M. S. Eventova, *Vladimir Vasilevich Markovnikov. Ocherk zhizni i deyatelnosti. 1837–1904* ("Vladimir Vasilevich Markovnikov. A Sketch of His Life and Work"; Moscow, 1962).

G. V. BYKOV

MARLIANI, GIOVANNI (*b.* Milan, Italy, early fifteenth century; *d.* Milan, late 1483), *physics, mechanics, medicine.*

There is little information on Marliani's early life. Born into a patrician family, he probably studied arts and medicine at Pavia University. In 1440 he was elected to the College of Physicians at Milan: it seems that he had received his doctorate by then, or certainly before 1442. From 1441 to 1447 Marliani taught nat-

ural philosophy and "astrologia" at Pavia, and lectured on the physics of Bradwardine and Albert of Saxony. Under the short-lived Ambrosian Republic, he left Pavia for the University of Milan (1447–1450), where he taught medicine. He was also appointed to civic office. Following the collapse of the Ambrosian Republic, Marliani returned to Pavia, where he added medicine to his previous lectureships, eventually acquiring (1469) the chair of medical theory. His salaries testify to a successful career: in 1441 Marliani earned 40 florins a year; in 1447, 200 florins; in 1463, 500 florins, plus, by secret arrangement with Duke Francesco I Sforza, an additional 150 florins. Later a special chair was set up for the Marliani family, to be held first by Giovanni's son, Paolo, in 1483. Two other sons, Girolamo and Pietro, also lectured at the university. The fortune of the family was sealed with Marliani's appointment (probably in 1472) as court physician to Galeazzo Maria Sforza. He also enjoyed the favor of the latter's successor, Gian Galeazzo.

Despite his strongly Scholastic views, Marliani was well regarded by humanists of the time. Pico della Mirandola called him the greatest mathematician of the age, and Francesco Filelfo and Marliani corresponded on medical and Scholastic matters. Giorgio Valla, who studied medicine and mathematics under Marliani at Pavia, translated the *Problemata* of Alexander of Aphrodisias at the urging of his teacher. Valla stated that Marliani owned a copy of Jacobus Cremonensis' translation of Archimedes, but the sole extant mathematical work by Marliani is on common fractions and shows little originality or knowledge of Greek mathematics. Valla's later work, however, abandoned the Scholastic physics of his teacher in favor of classical mathematics. Most Renaissance humanists and mathematicians shared Valla's preference.

Three works by Marliani deal with heat in a strongly Aristotelian fashion. The heating or cooling action is regarded as a special case of motion and thus subject to Aristotle's mistaken law of motion. In the early treatise *De reactione*, for instance, reaction (meaning the capacity of an agent to be affected by its patient) is analyzed in terms of active and resistive powers, as though it were motion. Although Marliani admits his debt to Jacopo da Forlì and others, he systematically rejects many of these predecessors' arguments in favor of some rather tortuous arguments of his own. (His criticisms soon involved Marliani in a polemic with Gaetano da Thiene.) Two main points of interest appear in the *De reactione*, although neither is original. These are Marliani's distinction between intensity of heat (temperature) and its extension (quantity of heat) and his use of a numerical scale to represent the intensity. This scale consists of eight degrees of calidity and its coextensive frigidity ($F° = 8 - C°$). The Marliani scale should not, perhaps, be taken as a forerunner of the thermometric scale, since it depends conceptually upon an Aristotelian qualitative distinction between heat and cold.

The *Disputatio cum Joanne de Arculis* discusses the reduction of hot water (that is, whether hot water is cooled by an intrinsic tendency or an extrinsic agent, such as its container). Marliani again applies his Aristotelian principle relating action and resistance to the quantity of heat and cold present. In contrast with his Avicennist opponent Giovanni Arcolani of Verona, who argues for intrinsic reduction, Marliani maintains that at any temperature, hot and cold components of the water are in equilibrium and thus cannot act upon one another. Hence, the cooling agent must be external. He also concludes that the shapes of the agent and the patient, and their distance apart, are factors in a heat action.

De caliditate corporum humanorum combines Marliani's knowledge of medicine and physics. Distinguishing between heat intensity (temperature) and its extension (the quantity of "natural" heat produced by the body), Marliani concludes that the human body, while increasing its natural heat in the winter, maintains a more or less constant temperature through most of its parts. Nevertheless, he still feels obliged (despite a youthful repudiation) to accept the notion of antiperistasis (the increase of intensity when a body is suddenly surrounded by its contrary quality), which underlay the arguments for a varying body temperature.

Marliani's writings on mechanics center on two main problems of Scholastic physics. In the *Probatio calculatoris* the kinematic mean-speed theorem of accelerated motion is outlined with some clear proofs. Of more significance is the *De proportione motuum*, designed to solve a paradox in Aristotle's law of motion. The Aristotelian law held velocity to be proportional to the ratio of the moving power to the resistance. A paradox arose when the moving power was equal to the resistance. Obviously no motion should then occur, but the ratio in the law gave a positive value to the velocity in this case. Bradwardine's law tried to eliminate the paradox by stating that the "proportions of velocities in motions follow the proportion of the power of the motor, to the power of the thing moved." Using the proportion of proportions calls for a geometrical increase in the ratio of force to resistance. Bradwardine, however, used terms which can denote either an arithmetical or a geometrical increase—for instance, "dupla," to mean "double" or "squared." Misled by this ambiguous terminology to assume that Bradwardine had fallen into the same

trap as Aristotle, Marliani severely condemned the former and advanced his own law that velocity is proportional to the excess of the motor power over the resistance. Nevertheless, Bradwardine's law remained acceptable to most Renaissance Aristotelian philosophers.

Marliani's career and works suggest that he was a competent Scholastic physicist and an adept publicist of the *calculatores* and French Scholastics in Italy. Influential among philosophers (his *De reactione* was later discussed by Pietro Pomponazzi), Marliani seems to have stayed largely outside the mainstream of Italian Renaissance mathematics. Much of his great reputation seems also to have rested on his position as physician to the Sforzas.

BIBLIOGRAPHY

I. ORIGINAL WORKS. Unless otherwise noted, Marliani's works were printed at Pavia in 2 vols. in 1482. The dates of composition are in parentheses. The writings are *Tractatus de reactione* (1448); *In defensionem Tractatus de reactione* (against Gaetano da Thiene, 1454–1456); "Annotationes in librum de instanti Petri Mantuani," unpub. work in Biblioteca Vaticana, MS Vat. Lat. 2225 (see Thorndike, below); *Probatio cuiusdam sententiae calculatoris de motu locali* (1460); *Disputatio cum Joanne de Arculis* (1461); *Difficultates missae Philippo Adiute Veneto* (before 1464); "Algorismus de minutiis" (before 1464), unpub. MSS in Bibliothèque Nationale, Paris, MS N.A.L. 761, and Biblioteca Ambrosiana, Milan, MS A.203 infra; *Questio de proportione motuum in velocitate* (1464); and *Questio de caliditate corporum humanorum* (1472).

II. SECONDARY LITERATURE. For mentions of Marliani, see Pico della Mirandola, *Disputationes adversus astrologiam divinatricem*, E. Garin, ed. (Florence, 1946), pp. 632–633; and J. L. Heiberg, "Beiträge zur Geschichte Georg Valla's und seiner Bibliothek," in *Zentralblatt für Bibliothekswesen*, supp. **16** (1896), 11–12, 85. An excellent treatment is Marshall Clagett, *Giovanni Marliani and Late Medieval Physics* (New York, 1941); see also his "Note on the *Tractatus physici* Falsely Attributed to Giovanni Marliani," in *Isis*, **34** (1942), 168, appended to D. B. Durand's review of the book. See also A. Maier, *Die Vorläufer Galileis im 14. Jahrhundert* (Rome, 1949), pp. 107–110; and the inaccurate pages in P. Duhem, *Études sur Léonard de Vinci*, III (Paris, 1913), 497–500. Two letters to Marliani are in Francesco Filelfo, *Epistolarum* (Venice, 1502), fols. 152v, 184v.

For MSS see Lynn Thorndike, "Some Medieval and Renaissance Manuscripts on Physics," in *Proceedings of the American Philosophical Society*, **104** (1960), 188–201, esp. 195; and Lynn Thorndike and Pearl Kibre, *A Catalogue of Incipits of Medieval Scientific Writings in Latin*, 2nd ed. (London, 1963), index, under "Marliani."

For Scholastic science in fifteenth-century Italy, see

Carlo Dionisotti, "Ermolao Barbaro e la fortuna di Suiseth," in *Medioevo e Rinascimento. Studi in onore di Bruno Nardi* (Florence, 1955), I, 217–253, esp. 230–231.

PAUL LAWRENCE ROSE

MARSH, OTHNIEL CHARLES (*b.* Lockport, New York, 29 October 1831; *d.* New Haven, Connecticut, 18 March 1899), *vertebrate paleontology.*

Marsh was the oldest son of a farmer and shoe manufacturer of modest means, Caleb Marsh, and Mary Gaines Peabody Marsh; his mother died before he was three years old. Aided financially by his uncle George Peabody, Marsh graduated from Phillips Academy at Andover, Massachusetts, from Yale College (1860), and from its Sheffield Scientific School (1862). After three years of study in Europe, Marsh became professor of paleontology at Yale from 1866 until his death. From 1882 to 1892 he was also the first vertebrate paleontologist of the U.S. Geological Survey. A bachelor, he lived in solitary grandeur near Yale.

Marsh was elected to the National Academy of Sciences in 1874 and served as its president from 1883 to 1895. He was the recipient of many awards and honorary degrees, among them the Bigsby Medal (1877) and the Cuvier Prize (1897).

Marsh's scientific interests began in childhood with minerals and invertebrate fossils, chiefly from formations exposed by the nearby Erie Canal. He pursued mineralogy in his education but gradually turned toward paleontology. A marked characteristic was his keen acquisitiveness, which resulted in vast collections of fossils for the Peabody Museum at Yale, a gift of his generous uncle.

Through his many scientific descriptions and his popularization of extinct animals, Marsh established the infant field of vertebrate paleontology in the United States. Accompanied by Yale students and alumni, he led four expeditions from 1870 to 1873 through the western territories, from the White River badlands of South Dakota and Nebraska, to the Bridger, Uinta, and Green River basins of Wyoming, Utah, and Colorado, to the John Day fossil fields in Oregon, and back to the Cretaceous chalk region of western Kansas. The startling fossil discoveries of these trips led Marsh into keen and bitter competition with Edward Drinker Cope for a quarter of a century. After his early collecting years, Marsh only rarely and briefly returned to the fossil fields, but he hired many amateur and professional collectors to seek specimens throughout the western United States. He urged his collectors to search out all fragments of each find, and

so was able to describe remarkably complete specimens.

In his work on fossil mammals Marsh established the evolution of the horse as North American, with a series of specimens from Eocene to Pleistocene; he presented the earliest mammals then known, from Jurassic and Cretaceous beds; in competition with Cope, he described some of the extinct horned mammals called uintatheres and some of the massive brontotheres; and he established the existence of early primates on the North American continent. On the reptiles, Marsh enlarged the classification of the dinosaurs, and described eighty new forms, both giant and tiny, and he described Cretaceous winged reptiles and marine mosasaurs. He also presented the first known toothed birds, which proved the reptile ancestry of that class. He demonstrated the gradual enlargement of the vertebrate brain from the Paleozoic era forward. Marsh's classifications and descriptions of extinct vertebrates were major contributions to knowledge of evolution.

BIBLIOGRAPHY

Marsh published about 300 papers on vertebrate fossils but left much to be completed by his successors. His work on horses was summarized in "Fossil Horses in America," in *American Naturalist,* **8** (1874), 288–294. His magnum opus was *Odontornithes: A Monograph on the Extinct Toothed Birds of North America,* vol. VII of *U.S. Geological Exploration 40th Parallel* (Washington, D.C., 1880). Dinosaurs were summarized in "The Dinosaurs of North America," in *Report of the U.S. Geological Survey,* **16,** pt. 1 (1896), 133–414; and "Vertebrate Fossils [of the Denver Basin]," in *Monographs of the U.S. Geological Survey,* **27** (1896), 473–550. Marsh's material on mammals appeared in many single papers; and much of the Mesozoic material was later synthesized by G. G. Simpson in "American Mesozoic Mammalia," in *Memoirs of the Peabody Museum of Yale University,* **3,** pt. 1 (1929).

Marsh's life, accomplishments, and bibliography are well presented in Charles Schuchert and Clara M. LeVene, *O. C. Marsh: Pioneer in Paleontology* (New Haven, 1940).

ELIZABETH NOBLE SHOR

MARSILI (or **Marsigli**), **LUIGI FERDINANDO** (*b.* Bologna, Italy, 20 July 1658; *d.* Bologna, 1 November 1730), *natural history.*

Marsili was the son of a nobleman, Carlo Marsili, and the former Margherita Ercolani. He served in the army of Emperor Leopold I from 1682 to 1704, attained high rank, and participated in the negotiations for the peace of Karlowitz—but also was wounded, imprisoned, and even suffered the humiliation of demotion. Although he did not complete his formal schooling, Marsili accumulated a vast knowledge of history, politics, geography, and the natural sciences. He traveled widely throughout Italy and the rest of Europe, particularly in the regions around the Danube, and made several long sea voyages (from Venice to Constantinople, from Leghorn to Amsterdam). While much of his work dealt with the military sciences, history, and geography, he also made a name for himself as a naturalist. He combined a love of travel with the sharp eye of an observer imbued with the Galilean method. In his scientific activity he was always guided by a prudent sagacity that once prompted this advice: "The modern method of observation is the right one, but it is still in its infancy, and we must not be so rash as to expect instantly to deduce systems from these observations; that is something which only our successors, after centuries of study by this method, will be able to do" (letter from Marsili to the astronomer F. Bianchini, 24 December 1726, in *Lettere di vari illustri italiani e stranieri* [Reggio nell'Emilia, 1841], II, 91).

As a naturalist, with that same prudent sagacity, Marsili undertook the exploration of two basic subjects: the structure of the mountains and the natural condition of the sea, lakes, and rivers. He left many local observations concerning the structure of the mountains (noteworthy among them being those on the continuity of the *linea gypsea*, the gypsum-bearing strata in the hills of the Adriatic slope of the Apennines); accurate sketches of stratigraphic profiles; and even cartographic representations of particular geologic conditions, although he was far from grasping the geologic significance of the strata. Realizing this later, he gave up systematically elaborating his many "schedae pro structura orbis terraquei."

The sea had fascinated Marsili since childhood. In 1681 he published a study of the Bosporus, the result of observations that he had made at age twenty. It contained valid findings, notably the discovery of a countercurrent with waters of different density beneath the surface current of the strait. He later traveled around the Mediterranean, doing research mainly along the coasts of the Romagna and Provence. The keenness of his mind often made up for the crudeness of his instruments during these travels. In 1724 he published the first treatise on oceanography, *Histoire physique de la mer*. In it he treated problems which until then had been veiled by error and legend. Marsili examined every aspect of the subject: the morphology of the basin and relationships between the lands under and above water; the water's properties (color, temperature, salinity) and its motion (waves, currents,

tides); and the biology of the sea, which foretold the advent of marine botany. Among the plants he numbered animals like corals, which before his time had been regarded as inorganic matter.

Finally, Marsili was the precursor of the systematic oceanographic exploration that was to begin half a century later with the famous voyage of the *Endeavour*. Using the same methods, he studied Lake Garda, the largest lake in Italy, discussing its physical and biological aspects in a very valuable report, which remained unpublished until 1930. Marsili wrote a basic work on one of Europe's greatest rivers, *Danubius . . . observationibus geographicis, historicis, physicis perlustratus . . .* (1726), in which he devoted much space to a study of the riverbed and of the waters, as well as to the flora and fauna, and the mineralogy and geology of the adjacent land.

Marsili was also a skilled organizer of scientific work. In 1712 he founded the Accademia delle Scienze dell'Istituto di Bologna, which, under his influence, immediately became an active center of scientific research, consisting mainly of natural history exploration of the area around Bologna. With Domenico Galeazzi, Marsili set an example in 1719 by climbing and studying Mount Cimone, highest peak of the northern Apennines. When Marsili went to London in 1722, to be made a member of the Royal Society, Sir Isaac Newton insisted on presenting him personally and praised him in his speech as both an already famous scientist and a founder of the new Academy of Bologna.

BIBLIOGRAPHY

I. ORIGINAL WORKS. Marsili's writings include *Osservazioni intorno al Bosforo tracio ovvero canale di Constantinopoli . . .* (Rome, 1681), a booklet repr. in *Bollettino di pesca, piscicoltura e idrobiologia*, **11** (1935), 734–758; *Histoire physique de la mer* (Amsterdam, 1725); and *Danubius-Pannonicus-Mysicus observationibus geographicis, historicis, physicis perlustratus et in sex tomos digestus* (The Hague–Amsterdam, 1726), also trans. into French (The Hague, 1744). The volume *Scritti inediti di L. F. Marsili* (Bologna, 1930) includes "Osservazioni fisiche intorno al Lago di Garda," M. Longhena and A. Forti, eds., and "Storia naturale de' gessi e solfi nelle miniere di Romagna," T. Lipparini, ed. There is also Marsili's *Autobiografia* (Bologna, 1930).

The University of Bologna library has 176 vols. of Marsili's autograph letters and cartographic sketches: see L. Frati, *Catalogo dei manoscritti di L. F. Marsili* (Florence, 1928); and M. Longhena, *L'opera cartografica di L. F. Marsili* (Rome, 1933).

II. SECONDARY LITERATURE. For information on Marsili's life and work, see G. Fantuzzi, *Memorie della vita del generale conte L. F. Marsili* (Bologna, 1770), for the period up to 1711 drawn from Marsili's *Autobiografia.* See also two works by M. Longhena: *Il conte L. F. Marsili* (Milan, 1930) and "Il conte L. F. Marsili," in *Bollettino della Società geografica italiana,* **95** (1958), 539–573, with a complete list of Marsili's published writings and an extensive bibliography on Marsili the geographer and naturalist; and *Memorie intorno a L. F. Marsili* (Bologna, 1930).

FRANCESCO RODOLICO

MARSILIUS OF INGHEN (or Inguem or de Novimagio) (*b.* near Nijmegen, Netherlands; *d.* Heidelberg, Germany, 20 August 1396), *natural philosophy.*

Almost nothing is known of Marsilius' early life. Although his name would suggest that he was born in the village of Inghen (now Lienden in de Betuwej, in the diocese of Utrecht),[1] his biographers are not all in agreement on this point; Gustav Toepke and Gerhard Ritter, for example, hold that "Inghen" is a family name, and not derived from that of a place.[2] The first document that mentions Marsilius is the register of the University of Paris, which gives 27 September 1362 as the date of his inaugural lecture as master of arts.[3]

Marsilius remained at the University of Paris for twenty years. As a *magister regens* of the arts he had a large student following. He served as rector of the university in 1367 and again in 1371; in 1362 and from 1373 until 1375 he was procurator of the English nation;[4] and in 1368 and 1376 he represented the university at the papal court in Avignon. In the latter year Marsilius accompanied the pope, Gregory XI, to Rome; he was present there in 1378 when Urban VI—whom he strongly supported—was elected pope. He was thus present at the beginning of the Great Schism.

The University of Paris was rent by the schism. It is not known exactly when Marsilius left it for the University of Heidelberg, recently founded by Urban VI, but it is certain that he was rector of that institution for the first time in 1386 (he served six other terms in the post). In 1389 he made another journey to Rome, this time to pay homage to a new pope, Boniface IX, and to ask his aid for the university as well as his personal patronage. Marsilius died in Heidelberg seven years later.

In his writings Marsilius employed the traditional medieval method of composing commentaries and questions on the works of earlier authors. He wrote on the scientific works of Aristotle—particularly the *Physica,* the *Parva naturalia,* and *De generatione et corruptione*—and on the logical works of Aristotle, including the *Posterior Analytics* and *Topics,* which he dealt with in the manner prescribed by the nominal-

istic school of his time. He also wrote on theology, including a commentary on the four books of *Sentences* of Peter Lombard. His chief contributions to science lay in the field of physics, but even here his thought was always shaped by theological considerations.

Although Marsilius was born in the Netherlands and ended his life in Heidelberg, his work places him among the Parisian masters who may be considered to be the precursors of Leonardo and Galileo and the formers of the new physics of the fifteenth and sixteenth centuries. The leader of this group was Jean Buridan, of whom Marsilius declared himself a disciple, and their gift to science was the formulation of the concept of impetus—an impressed force—which they applied to the theory of gravity, acceleration, and the motion of projectiles. This was the *via moderna,* and these were the "new physicists."

Marsilius occupied a moderate and traditional position among these men, one much closer to the philosophical inquiries of Aristotle and Ibn Rushd (Averroës) than to the empiricism of Buridan. Evidence of his views may be found not only in his own writings, but also in those of his contemporaries. Blasius of Parma, for example, probably attended Marsilius' lectures during his sojourn in Paris, and in his *quaestio disputata* on the physical problem of the contact of bodies—in which he discussed whether or not the void exists and whether the action between bodies occurs directly or at a distance—he supported the traditional Aristotelian theory of the *horror vacui,* which position he attributed also to Marsilius.[5] Marsilius himself, as is clear in his works, never accepted the really novel implications for dynamics inherent in the doctrine of impetus.

Marsilius' concept of motion served him as a basis for an explanation of the entire physical world, both celestial and terrestrial. He avoided mechanical interpretation, and held that the motions of the heavens and the astronomical spheres are spiritual, eternal, incorruptible, and ungenerable; the bodies are moved in a "natural" motion that is circular and perfect and impressed upon them by angelic intelligences.[6] The initial source of this *virtus impressa* is, of course, God, the Creator and First Mover, the prime immobile mover who put into movement the whole *caelum* or the entire astrological universe. The perfect circular motion of the universe has since been maintained by the moving intelligences within the spheres.[7] Marsilius defined such motion as perfect "local" motion because it has no contrary and remains in its rightful place by nature—that is, within the order willed by God.[8]

The God-moved *caelum* in its turn moves the terrestrial world, which is not eternal but rather perpetual, beginning with time and lasting without end. The terrestrial world is not only generable but also corruptible and inferior, and moved almost exclusively by "unnatural" motions—or rather, by violent motions and "alterations" that provoke the birth and death of beings. In fact, according to Marsilius, all motion of natural, inferior, terrestrial things presupposes the action of a violent cause, whether such motion be "de loco naturale," away from the natural place, or "ad locum naturale," toward it.[9] Motion "de loco naturale" is acting against the natural order, while in the case of motion "ad locum naturale," it must already have so acted.[10] Typical violent motions are embodied in projectiles, tops, and smiths' wheels; the terrestrial world is moved by a plurality of moving causes which come from the heavens and are subordinate one to the other. These causes produce various effects by their concurrence. The destiny of an individual, for example, is shaped by concurrences among the Father, the heavens, God, and the moving intelligences;[11] God and the heavens influence human actions.

Marsilius thus appears to have accepted the doctrine of astrological determination on a philosophical level. He cited as an example the hungry dog that starves because it cannot decide which of two pieces of bread, placed at equal distances from it, to seize.[12] In reality, however, Marsilius maintained that man is free because the stars influence only the dog, but not the man, and that not everything in the world necessarily happens under absolutely determinate influences; chance or contingency can also play a part. Indeed, since he held that almost all motions of the inferior world are either violent or a mixture of local and violent movement, caused by a plurality of coincident agents, he also believed that it is possible to ascertain casual and fortuitous effects of which the primary cause is one among those that are concurrent and subordinate. Marsilius was thus able to admit the possibility of such extraordinary natural phenomena as eclipses, comets, and monsters.[13]

His system thus enabled Marsilius to explain physical mutations as instances of qualitative and violent alterations of bodies; the study of modifications of such essential physical qualities as heat and cold therefore assumed great importance.[14] Although he drew upon Buridan's doctrine of impetus to explain the special case of arrows and projectiles—or violent motion in its strictest sense—he moderated it in such a way that it might be reconciled with Aristotle's basic physical principle that every motion in the terrestrial world is caused by an agent outside the mobile. In other words, Marsilius did not fully accept Buridan's actual principle of impetus, whereby the mobile is permitted a permanent intrinsic moving force[15] which is impeded by the medium through which it moves. In Marsilius' view, the violent motion of a projectile is not impeded by the air through which it moves; rather, it is aided by it. The impetus that moves the projectile is a disposition given it by the first mover, which sets it into motion. The impetus is initially confined to that part of the mobile that is in contact with the mover, then diffused through the whole.[16] Such impetus does not last long; it becomes corrupt in the absence of intervention from the surrounding medium. The medium may, however, receive the impetus of the mobile to reinforce the speed of the moving body.[17]

Marsilius regarded the world as a plenum. He believed that no void could exist in the physical universe and that all heavy bodies tend to the center of the earth, which is the only center as God is the only prime mover. Were the universe sustained by many prime movers, there would be many worlds and many centers, but this, too, is impossible.[18] He therefore could not admit Ockham's thesis concerning the possibility of other worlds. Here again, as in all traditional problems of physics, Marsilius stood for a reconciliation of the *via antiqua* of Aristotle with the *via moderna* of the Parisian masters.[19]

NOTES

1. J. Fruytier, *Nieuw nederlandsch biografisch woordenboek*, VIII, 908–909.
2. G. Toepke, *Die Matrikel der Universität Heidelberg von 1386 bis 1662* (Heidelberg, 1884), I, 678–685; G. Ritter, "Marsilius von Inghen und die okkamistische Schule in Deutschland," p. 210.
3. H. Denifle and E. Chatelain, *Chartularium universitatis parisiensis*, III (Paris, 1897), see index.
4. H. Denifle and E. Chatelain, *Auctarium chartularium universitatis parisiensis. Liber procuratorum nationis Anglicanae* (Paris, 1897), I, cols. 272, 559, *passim*.
5. "Quaestio magistri Blasii de Parma utrum duo corpora," MS Bologna, Biblioteca Universitaria 2567, 198 (Frati 1332), fol. 59 r-a; see G. Federici Vescovini, "Problemi di fisica," pp. 192, 209.
6. *Quaestiones subtilissimae super octo libros physicorum* (Lyons, 1518), II, qu. 4, fols. 25v-a, b ff.
7. *Quaestiones super quattuor libros Sententiarum*, II, qu. II, ad. 2, fols. 208v-a–209v-a, ff.; qu. X, ads. 2 and 3, fols. 243v-b–245r-a, b (Strasbourg, 1501).
8. . . . *Physicorum*, II, qu. 4, fols. 25v-a, b; . . . *Sententiarum*, II, qu. 10, ad. 2, fol. 244r-b; ad. 3, fols. 245r-a, b.
9. . . . *Physicorum*, VIII, qu. 1, fols. 79r-b–v-a; VIII, qu. 2, fol. 80v-a.
10. *Ibid.*, II, qu. 4, fol. 26r-a, 2a conc.
11. *Ibid.*, II, qu. 8, fol. 29r-a; II, qu. 10, fol. 30r-b.
12. *Ibid.*, II, qu. 14, fol. 33r-b.
13. *Ibid.*, II, qus. 8, 9, 10, 13, fols. 29r-b, 30r-b–v-a, 31r-b–v-a.
14. *Ibid*, VIII, qu. 4, fol. 81v-b. MS Paris, BN 16401, fols. 149v–177v; "Utrum qualitas suscipiat magis et minus," BN 6559, fol. 121r.
15. M. Clagett, *The Science of Mechanics* (Madison, Wis., 1959; 2nd ed., 1961), pp. 536–537, lines 7, 8, 9.
16. *Abbreviationes libri physicorum Aristotelis*, VIII, not. 4, qu. IV (Venice or Pavia, *ca.* 1490), fols. L 4r-a–5r-a.

17. *Ibid.*, fol. L 5r-a.
18. *Quaestiones . . . physicorum*, VIII, qu. 9, fol. 85v-b.
19. G. Ritter, Studien zur Spätscholastik, II, *Via antiqua und via moderna . . .* (Heidelberg, 1922), p. 39 and *passim*.

BIBLIOGRAPHY

I. ORIGINAL WORKS. There are no modern eds. of Marsilius' writings, but only MSS and rare eds. of collections of questions and of commentaries on the physics of Aristotle and biological problems of generation and corruption. Among the former are "Abbreviatura physicorum sive quaestiones variorum abbreviatae," MS Vienna 5437, fols. 1r–410v; Erfurt O.78, *anno* 1346, fols. 41–132; Erfurt Q.314, *anno* 1394, fol. 106; Vienna VI, 5112, fols. 181r–283v, printed at Pavia *ca.* 1480; Venice or Pavia, *ca.* 1490; Venice, 1521—see A. C. Klebs, "Incunabula scientifica et medica," in *Osiris*, 4 (1938), 667; and *Quaestiones subtilissimae super octo libros physicorum IX* (different edition from Pavia and Lyons, 1518; repr. Venice, 1617), repr. under the name of Duns Scotus and inserted in Lyons 1639 among the works of Duns Scotus (Lyons, 1639). He also wrote works in the form of questions on the psycho-biological problems of Aristotle: "Quaestiones de parvorum naturalium libris," MS Erfurt F.334, *anno* 1421, fols. 1–61; and MS Novacella [near Bressanone], Convento dei Canonici Regolari, 440, fols. 1–88, 89–268; and "Quaestiones de generatione et corruptione": MS Florence, Riccardiana 745 (N. II 26), fols. 96–137v ("per manus Nycolay Montfort"); MS Florence, Riccardiana 746 (K. II 38), fol. 76, *anno* 1407; Milan, Ambrosiana G. 102 inf., fols. 1r-a–87v-a; Modena, Estense 687 (Alpha F 5, 20) (Kristeller, *Iter italicum*, I [London–Leiden, 1963], 372); Modena, Estense Fondo Campori 1374 (Gamma T 4, 18) (Vandini, 441); Padua, Biblioteca Universitaria MS 693 (Kristeller, *Iter . . .*, II [London–Leiden, 1967], 14); Venice, Marciana, 121a (2557) (G. Valentinelli, *Bibliotheca manuscripta ad S. Marci Venetiarum*, V, Venice, 1868, pp. 50–51), *anno* 1393; Marciana, 324 (4072) (G. Valentinelli, *Bibliotheca manuscripta ad S. Marci venetiarum*, VI, Venice, 1868, p. 218); Vienna 5494, fol. 209; Munich, Staatsbibliothek, 26929, *anno* 1407, fols. 88r-a–193r-b; Erfurt Q.311, *anno* 1414, fols. 1–74v; Oxford, Bodleian cm. 238, fol. 101; Vienna 4951, *anno* 1501, fols. 164r–223v—published at Padua, 1476 (?), 1480; Venice, 1493, 1504, 1505, 1518, 1520, 1567; Strasbourg, 1501, together with works by others; Paris, 1518.

He also wrote on the mutations of qualities: "Utrum qualitas suscipiat magis et minus," MS Paris, BN 16401, fols. 149v–177v; BN 6559, fol. 121r.

Marsilius' works on logic, such as commentaries on the logic of Aristotle in the nominalists' *via moderna* form are MS Vat. lat. 3072, "Tractatus de suppositionibus"; Pistoia, Archivio Capitolare del Duomo, MS 61 (Kristeller, *Iter*, II, p. 75); Rome, Vat. lat. 3072 (Kristeller, *Iter*, II, p. 316); and Turin, Biblioteca Nazionale G.III, 12 (Pasini, lat. 449), fols. 167r-a–171r-b; "Consequentiae," MS Rome, Vat. lat. 3065; "De obligationibus, insolubilia," Rome, Pal. lat. 995 (*Arist. lat.*, II [1955], 1190–1191, n. 1777), published in *Textus dialectices de suppositionibus, ampliationibus . . .* (Cracow, n.d.); commentaries on the *Parva logicalia* (Basel, 1487; Hagenow, 1495, 1503; Vienna, 1512, 1516; Turin, 1729); and *Expositio super analitica* (Venice, 1516, 1522).

Works on theological and moral arguments are *Quaestiones super quattuor libros Sententiarum* (Hagenow, 1497; Strasbourg, 1501); and commentaries on the ethics of Aristotle, MS Rome, Pal. lat. 1022 (Kristeller, *Iter*, II, 392).

II. SECONDARY LITERATURE. There are no specific monographs on Marsilius, only partial studies. See the following, listed chronologically: P. Duhem, *Études sur Léonard de Vinci*, III (Paris, 1913), 403–405; and *Le système du monde*, IV (Paris, 1916), 164–168; G. Ritter, "Marsilius von Inghen und die okkamistische Schule in Deutschland," in *Sitzungsberichte der Heidelberger Akademie der Wissenschaften*, phil. Kl. (1921), 4, 210; J. Fruytier, *Nieuw nederlandsch biografisch woordenboek*, VIII (Leiden, 1930), 903–904; A. Maier, *Die Vorläufer Galileis in 14 Jahrhundert* (Rome, 1949), p. 3 and *passim*; *Zwei Grundprobleme der scholastischen Naturphilosophie* (Rome, 1951), pp. 275 ff.; *An der Grenze von Scholastik . . .* (Rome, 1952), pp. 118 ff.; and *Metaphysische Hintergrunde der spätscholastischen Naturphilosophie* (Rome, 1955), pp. 40, 90, 133, 146, 222, 396; G. Federici Vescovini, "Problemi di fisica aristotelica . . .," in *Rivista di filosofia*, 51 (1960), 190–193, 209; cf. Blasii qu. de gener. II, 2. MS Vat. Chig. O.IV.41, f. 37 2b; A. Birkenmajer, *Études d'histoire des sciences et de la philosophie du moyen age*, I (Wrocław, 1970), 368, 612, 654; II (Wrocław, 1972), 181, 187, 192–194; and G. Federici Vescovini, *Le questioni "De anima" de Biagio Pela cani da Parma* (Florence, 1973), p. 35 and *passim*.

GRAZIELLA FEDERICI VESCOVINI

MARTENS, ADOLF (*b.* Backendorf bei Hagenow, Mecklenburg–Schwerin, Germany, 6 March 1850; *d.* Berlin, Germany, 24 July 1914), *materials testing, metallography.*

Martens was the son of Friedrich Martens, a tenant farmer. After attending the Realschule in Schwerin and gaining two years of practical experience, he studied mechanical engineering from 1868 to 1871 at the Königliche Gewerbeakademie in Berlin (later the Technische Hochschule of Berlin-Charlottenburg). At the end of his training in 1871, he entered the service of the Prussian State Railway, where he participated in the planning of the great bridges over the Vistula near Thorn and over the Memel near Tilsit. From 1875 to 1879 he was a member of the Commission for the Berlin-Nordhausen-Wetzlar Railway. In this position he had to supervise the preliminary work done by the companies supplying the iron superstructure of the bridges. He thus became involved, early in his career, with the techniques just then being developed for testing construction materials.

Martens, in this early period, was stimulated by a short book by Eduard Schott, *Die Kunstgiesserei in Eisen* (Brunswick, 1873), to begin metallographic studies for which he built his own microscope. His first publication, "Über die mikroskopische Untersuchung des Eisens" (1878), contained his observations on freshly fractured iron surfaces, as well as drawings of etched and polished surfaces. On this topic Martens wrote:

> A careful observer of all these results cannot but come to the conclusion that in pig iron the various combinations of iron are only mechanically mixed; during the process of cooling or crystallization they arrange themselves with most surprising regularity. So the microscopical investigation of iron has a very great chance of becoming one of the most useful methods of practical analysis.

Further works followed and brought Martens into close contact with contemporary metallographers, sometimes provoking lively debates.

In 1884, after a short time as an assistant at the newly founded Königliche Technische Hochschule of Berlin-Charlottenburg, he was appointed director of the associated Mechanisch-Technische Versuchsanstalt, which in 1903 became the Königliche Materialprüfungsamt of Berlin-Dahlem. The brilliant design and organization of this institute were essentially his work.

Metallography did not at first come within the range of the Mechanisch-Technische Versuchsanstalt, and Martens could continue his very successful metallographic studies only in his free time. He could not resume them on a larger scale until 1898, when the Mechanisch-Technische Versuchsanstalt established a metallographic laboratory. His co-worker Emil Heyn greatly developed the field and made the institute a first-rate metallographic laboratory.

Martens' works from this later period were concerned with all aspects of the testing of materials, and especially the development of new measuring methods and equipment. His *Handbuch der Materialienkunde* (1899) is a comprehensive work which earned him the high regard of his colleagues as well as many honors.

Martens was chosen vice-chairman of the International Society for Testing Materials (ISTM) at its founding in 1895; in 1897 he became chairman of the German Society.

Martens combined tireless research activity and unusual talents as a designer and organizer. He made a fundamental contribution to the knowledge of the properties of materials by presenting the results of his research in clear and exhaustive reports.

BIBLIOGRAPHY

I. ORIGINAL WORKS. Martens' works on metallography include "Über die mikroskopische Untersuchung des Eisens," in *Zeitschrift des Vereins deutscher Ingenieure*, **22** (1878), 11–18; "Zur Mikrostruktur des Spiegeleisens," *ibid.*, 480–488; "Über das mikroskopische Gefüge und die Rekristalisation des Roheisens, speziell des grauen Eisens," *ibid.*, **24** (1880), 398–406; "Mikroskop für die Untersuchung der Metalle," in *Stahl und Eisen*, **2** (1882), 423–425; "Untersuchungen über das Kleingefüge des schmiedbaren Eisens, besonders des Stahles," *ibid.*, **7** (1887), 235–242; "Die Mikroskopie der Metalle auf dem Ingenieurkongress zu Chicago 1893," *ibid.*, **14** (1894), 797–809; "Ferrit und Perlit," *ibid.*, **15** (1895), 537–539, a discussion between Martens and A. Sauveur; and "F. Osmonds Methode für die mikrographische Analyse des gekohlten Eisens," *ibid.*, **15** (1895), 954–957.

For articles on materials testing, see "Die Festigkeitseigenschaften des Magnesiums," in *Mitteilungen aus den K. technischen Versuchsanstalten zu Berlin*, **5** (1887), supp. 1; "Ergebnisse der Prüfung von Apparaten zur Untersuchung der Festigkeitseigenschaften von Papier," *ibid.*, supp. 3, pt. 2; "Untersuchungen über Festigkeitseigenschaften und Leitungsfähigkeit an deutschem und schwedischem Drahtmateriale," *ibid.*, supp. 2; "Festigkeitsuntersuchungen mit Zinkblechen der schlesischen AG für Bergbau und Zinkhüttenbetrieb zu Lipine, Oberschlesien," *ibid.*, **7** (1889), supp. 4; "Untersuchungen mit Eisenbahnmaterialien," *ibid.*, **8** (1890), supp. 2; and "Untersuchungen über den Einfluss der Wärme auf die Festigkeitseigenschaften des Eisens," *ibid.*, 159–214.

With H. Sollner, Martens wrote "Verhandlungen der in Wien im Jahre 1893 abgehaltenen Conferenz zur Vereinbarung einheitlicher Prüfungsmethoden für Bau- und Konstruktionsmaterialien," in *Mitteilungen aus dem Mechanisch-technischen Laboratorium der K. technischen Hochschule in München*, no. 23 (1895). Also see "Entspricht das zur Zeit übliche Prüfungsverfahren bei der Übernahme von Stahlschienen seinem Zweck?" in *Stahl und Eisen*, **20** (1900), 302–310; "Zugversuche mit eingekerbten Probekörpern," in *Zeitschrift des Vereins deutscher Ingenieure*, **45** (1901), 805–812; *Das Königliche Materialprüfungsamt der Technischen Hochschule Berlin auf dem Gelände der Domäne Dahlem beim Bahnhof Gross-Lichterfelde-West* (Berlin, 1904), written with M. Guth.

His later works include "Prüfung der Druckfestigkeit von Portlandzement," in *Verhandlungen des Vereins zur Beförderung des Gewerbefleisses*, **88** (1909), 179–186; "Über die Grundsätze für die Organisation des öffentlichen Materialprüfungswesens," in *Dinglers polytechnisches Journal*, **93** (1912), 557–559; and "Über die in den Jahren 1892 bis 1912 im Königl. Materialprüfungsamt ausgeführten Dauerbiegeversuche mit Flusseisen," in *Mitteilungen aus dem K. Materialprüfungsamt Gross-Lichterfelde*, **32** (1914), 51–85.

Martens' handbooks are *Handbuch der Materialienkunde für den Maschinenbau*, 2 vols. (Berlin, 1898–1912); and *Das Materialprüfungswesen unter besonderer Berücksichti-*

gung der am Kgl. Materialprüfungsamt zu Berlin-Lichterfelde üblichen Verfahren im Grundriss dargestellt (Stuttgart, 1912), written with F. W. Hinrichsen.

II. SECONDARY LITERATURE. Articles on Martens are "Adolf Martens," in *Metallographist*, **3** (1900), 178–181; "Adolf Martens †," in *Zeitschrift des Vereins deutscher Ingenieure*, **58** (1914), 1369–1370; and E. Heyn, "Adolf Martens †," in *Stahl und Eisen*, **34** (1914), 1393–1395.

FRANZ WEVER

MARTÍ FRANQUÉS (or **Martí d'Ardenya**), **ANTONIO DE** (*b*. Altafulla, Tarragona, Spain, 14 June 1750; *d*. Tarragona, 19 August 1832), *biology, geology, meteorology, chemistry.*

Martí Franqués belonged to a rich and noble Catalan family. He started his studies at the University of Cervera but left because of his disgust with the Scholastic atmosphere. He continued his education himself, first learning French, and later English, German, and Italian. Initially, as a member of the Sociedad de Amigos del País, he took an interest in promoting the development of the cotton-spinning, weaving, and chinaware industries in the region of Tarragona.

Martí Franqués later became interested in scientific matters, but he was a retiring person and almost never announced his discoveries. In 1785 he started analyses of air that concluded in establishing, on 12 May 1790, that the oxygen content of the atmosphere is between 21 and 22 percent. He devised an instrument to control the air pressure and temperature in his atmospheric analyses which was a forerunner of Walter Hempel's burette. In 1791 he became absorbed in the sexual reproduction of plants, and as a result of his experiments, he understood and defended Linnaeus against Spallanzani. In all these studies he demonstrated that he was aware of the latest developments of the leading scientists of that period, notably Priestley and Cavendish. He knew and admired the work of Lavoisier, but that did not prevent him from recognizing the priority of Cavendish in the synthesis of water.

The Peninsular War (1808–1814) curtailed Martí Franqués' experiments. The bombardment of Tarragona destroyed part of his laboratory, and he himself was taken prisoner by the French. After the war he continued his reproduction experiments, but they were much less important than the ones he had done previously.

Among his disciples and friends were the botanists Mariano Lagasca y Segura, Mariano de la Paz Graells, and the physicist Juan Agell.

BIBLIOGRAPHY

A notice by Torres Amat appeared in *Diario de Barcelona*, 25–26 May 1833. The best monograph is in Catalan by Antoni Quintana i Mari, "Antoni de Martí i Franqués (1750–1832)," in *Memòries de l'Acadèmia de Ciències i Arts de Barcelona*, **24** (1935), 1–309; the first 58 pages contain Martí's preserved scientific works. A critical analysis of them was made by E. Moles in his entrance speech for the Academia de Ciencias Exactas, Físicas y Naturales de Madrid (28 March 1934).

J. VERNET

MARTIANUS CAPELLA (*b*. Carthage; *fl*. Carthage, ca. A.D. 365–440), *transmission of knowledge.*

Martianus may have been a secondary school teacher or a rhetorician, and he appears to have pleaded cases as a *rhetor* or advocate. He was the author of *De nuptiis philologiae et Mercurii*, the most popular textbook in the Latin West during the early Middle Ages. Cast in the form of an allegory of a heavenly marriage, in which seven bridesmaids present a compendium of each of the liberal arts, this book became the foundation of the medieval curriculum of the trivium (books III–V) and quadrivium (VI–IX). The setting (I–II) became a model of heavenly journeys as late as Dante and contributed greatly to the popularity of the book. Although Martianus understood little more of the subject matter of the disciplines than what he presented in digest form, he was a key figure in the history of rhetoric, education, and science for a thousand years.

Owing to the disappearance in the early Middle Ages of Varro's book on the mathematical disciplines (*Disciplinae*, IV–VII), Martianus' quadrivium books, inspired by Varro's archetypal work, provide the best means of reconstructing the ancient Roman mathematical disciplines. Book VI, *De geometria*, proves to be not a book on geometry but a conspectus of *terra cognita*, reduced from the geographical books of Pliny the Elder's *Natural History* (III–VI) and the *Collectanea rerum memorabilium* of Solinus. Martianus closes with a ten-page digest of Euclidean geometry, drawn from some Latin primer in the Varronian tradition. This digest assumes importance as a rare sample of pre-Boethian Latin geometry. Book VII, *De arithmetica*, was the second most important treatise on arithmetic after Boethius' *De institutione arithmetica*. Martianus' ultimate sources were Nicomachus' *Introduction to Arithmetic* and Euclid's *Elements* VII–IX, but his immediate sources were Latin primers based upon these works. A. Dick cites the original passages in the apparatus of his edition. Martianus' arithmetic proper consists of classifications and definitions of the kinds of numbers (largely Nicomachean, with some Euclidean material) and Latin translations of the enunciations of thirty-six Euclidean arithmetical propositions. Euclid developed his proofs geometrically; Martianus used numerical illustrations.

Book VIII, *De astronomia*, is the best extant ancient Latin treatise on astronomy. Because of its systematic, proportionate, and comprehensive treatment, it is the only one that bears comparison with such popular Greek handbooks as Geminus' *Introduction to Phenomena*. Its excellence indicates that Greek traditions, transmitted to the Latin world by Varro, were fairly well preserved in digest form. Martianus deals with all the conventional topics: the celestial circles; northern and southern constellations; hours of daylight at the various latitudes; anomalies of the four seasons; and a discussion of the orbits of each of the planets, including the sun and moon. Martianus was the only Latin author to give a clear exposition of Heraclides' theory of the heliocentric motions of Venus and Mercury and was commended for this by Copernicus.

Book IX, *De harmonia*, largely drawn from Aristides Quintilianus' *Peri mousikes*, book I, is important for its Latin definitions of musical terms that have long puzzled medieval musicologists. Next to Boethius, Martianus was the most important ancient Latin authority on music.

BIBLIOGRAPHY

I. Original Works. The best ed. of *De nuptiis* is that of A. Dick (Leipzig, 1925). A new ed., to be published about 1976, is being prepared for the Teubner Library by J. A. Willis. A trans. of the complete work, with commentary, is W. H. Stahl, *Martianus Capella and the Seven Liberal Arts* (New York, 1971).

II. Secondary Literature. See W. H. Stahl, *The Quadrivium of Martianus Capella; a Study of Latin Traditions in the Mathematical Sciences from 50 B.C. to A.D. 1250* (New York, 1969); and *Roman Science; Origins, Development, and Influence to the Later Middle Ages* (Madison, Wis., 1962), which contains a chapter on Martianus and places him in the stream of Latin scientific writings. C. Leonardi's book-length census of Martianus' MSS describes 243 MSS and excerpts and discusses his influence in later ages: "I codici di Marziano Capella," in *Aevum*, **33** (1959), 443–489; **34** (1960), 1–99, 411–524.

W. H. STAHL

MARTIN, BENJAMIN (*b.* Worplesdon, Surrey, England, February 1704 [?]; *d.* London, England, 9 February 1782), *experimental philosophy, scientific instrumentation.*

Benjamin Martin was the son of John Martin, gentleman, of Broadstreet, near Worplesdon. Nothing is known of his education, but it seems probable that in science he was self-taught. In 1729 he married Mary Lover of Chichester, and at the time of his marriage was described as a merchant of Guildford. The couple had two children, a daughter, Maria, and a son, Joshua Lover Martin, who joined his father in the 1770's to form the firm of B. Martin and Son.

Soon after his marriage, Martin became a teacher, running his own boarding school at Chichester, where, in 1735, he published his first work, *The Philosophical Grammar;* it ran to eight editions. The second edition includes a description of a pocket microscope, suggesting that Martin was also engaged in inventing and possibly selling optical instruments. By 1743, he had become a traveling lecturer in experimental philosophy, for in that year he first published a textbook based on his course of lectures. Martin made a curiously inept attempt during this period to secure election to the Royal Society. In letters written in 1741 to Sir Hans Sloane and the duke of Richmond, he claimed that he found it an embarrassment when lecturing not to be a fellow, and therefore requested their support in acquiring the title. This approach found no favor at all, and Martin never achieved the desired fellowship.

By 1755 Martin had settled in London, for in January he launched a monthly journal, *The General Magazine of Arts and Sciences*, publication of which continued until 1765. Between September 1755 and May 1756, he set up in business at 171 Fleet Street. His shop soon became well-known for its extensive stock and for Martin's popular lecture-demonstrations, following in the tradition of the Hauksbees and Desaguliers. Martin also stimulated business by his constant publication of catalogues of the scientific instruments that he supplied and pamphlets on a wide range of scientific subjects.

Although Martin claimed to have invented and improved numerous instruments, he is more accurately to be described as a retailer than as an instrument-maker. Instruments bearing his name are to be found in many museums, and they cover a wide range of types. Among his inventions, the best known relate to the microscope. He is credited as the first to supply, in about 1740, a microscope fitted with a micrometer. To improve the image, he produced, from 1759, an objective with two lenses set one inch apart. It has been suggested that the screw thread on this type of objective has a linear descendant in the standard thread of the Royal Microscopical Society, which was established in 1858 and continues in use today.

Martin is remarkable as one of the great popularizers of science in the mid-eighteenth century. He became known internationally, and supplied Harvard College, Massachusetts, with a large proportion of the new instruments needed after the fire of 1764. Yet Martin's industry and popularity did not bring financial stability. He was declared a bankrupt in January 1782, and died, a few weeks after a suicide attempt, on 9 February.

BIBLIOGRAPHY

Benjamin Martin's publications are too numerous to cite here. P. J. Wallis lists more than sixty works in his biobibliography of British mathematical writers.

See also R. S. Clay and T. H. Court, *The History of the Microscope* (London, 1932), ch. 9; John R. Millburn, "Benjamin Martin and the Royal Society," in *Notes and Records of the Royal Society of London,* **28** (June 1973), 15–23; "Benjamin Martin and the Development of the Orrery," in *British Journal for the History of Science,* **6** (Dec. 1973), 378–399; G. L'E. Turner, "The Apparatus of Science," in *History of Science,* **9** (1970), 129–138; John Williams, "Some Account of the Martin Microscope, Purchased for the Society at the Sale of the Late Professor Quekett's Effects," in *Transactions of the Microscopical Society of London,* n.s. **10** (1862), 31–41; and "A Few Words More on Benjamin Martin," *ibid.,* n.s. **11** (1863), 1–4, which lists forty works by Martin.

G. L'E. TURNER

MARTIN, HENRY NEWELL (*b.* Newry, County Down, Ireland, 1 July 1848; *d.* Burley-in-Wharfedale, Yorkshire, England, 27 October 1896), *physiology.*

The son of a congregational minister and sometime schoolmaster, Martin was the oldest of twelve children. Tutored at home, he entered the Medical School of University College London at sixteen, while—as was customary—apprenticing himself to a local practitioner for clinical instruction.

The youthful Martin was particularly attracted by the teaching and example of Michael Foster, then physiology instructor at the Medical School; despite his long hours as apprentice physician, Martin soon mastered the subject sufficiently to win a place as Foster's demonstrator. When Foster was called to Cambridge as praelector in physiology at Trinity College, Martin followed, receiving a sholarship at Christ's College, where he was to place first in the natural science tripos. Martin also served as assistant to T. H. Huxley in the latter's innovative biology course at the Royal College of Science, South Kensington. Under Huxley's supervision, Martin performed the "chief labour" in writing *A Course of Practical Instruction in Elementary Biology* (1875). In the same year, Martin received the D.Sc. in physiology, the first ever granted at Cambridge. Still in his twenties, Martin was clearly one of England's most promising young physiologists.

At the same time, D. C. Gilman, president of the projected Johns Hopkins University in Baltimore, was hard at work in assembling a faculty equal to his hopes of establishing a truly research-oriented university in the United States. Huxley recommended Martin, who, after some negotiation, accepted the well-paid professorship. He was only twenty-eight.

Though Martin published only fifteen research papers in his abbreviated scholarly career, he did complete a series of significant investigations based on his success in surgically isolating a mammalian heart and perfusing it so as to create experimental situations in which he could evaluate the role of such variables as temperature, alcohol, and venous and arterial pressure in cardiac function. Martin was elected a fellow of the Royal Society on the basis of this work and in 1883 delivered the Society's Croonian Lecture on the influence of temperature variation upon heart beat.

Martin's institutional role was almost certainly more significant than his scientific work. When he arrived in Baltimore, only one other course in physiology was offered in the United States (by H. P. Bowditch at Harvard). Between 1876 and 1893 the Johns Hopkins University was to play a uniquely influential role in the establishment of a research-oriented scientific community in the United States. From his strategic position at the Hopkins, Martin was to exert a significant influence in this evolution, especially in the development of physiology. Although never a magnetic lecturer, Martin was a warm and successful graduate teacher and colleague; William T. Sedwick, William Councilman, Henry Sewall, George Sternberg, W. K. Brooks, and Martin's successor at Hopkins, William H. Howells, were among his students or sometime associates. When the American physiological society was organized in 1887, six of the twenty-four founding members were Martin's students. Not only did he create and sustain an atmosphere of scholarship in his own laboratory, but Martin also consistently advocated the need for basic science excellence in the Johns Hopkins projected medical school, which opened in 1893. Although of necessity he taught general biology and animal morphology, Martin thought consistently in disciplinary terms; he never lost sight of his identity as a physiologist, and he was deeply committed to establishing the independence of physiology from the needs and attitudes of clinical medicine.

Martin was not only active in the founding and early years of the American Physiological Society, but served on the editorial board of Foster's *Journal of Physiology*—even managing to wring a small subvention for it from the Johns Hopkins administration. In addition he edited and founded *Studies from the Biological Laboratory of the Johns Hopkins University*, five volumes of which appeared between 1877 and 1893.

Martin was also a defender of the university against the attacks of antivivisectionists and spokesmen of religious orthodoxy disturbed by the encroachments of evolutionary naturalism. A fortunate marriage to Hattie Pegram, the socially prominent widow of a Confederate officer, allowed him greater access to Baltimore society, and thus to serve more effectively as an advocate of the university. The young physiologist even offered a Saturday morning course in physiology for local teachers and normal school students. In the early 1890's Martin's health began to fail and in 1893 he resigned. With a small pension from the Hopkins trustees, he returned to England in an effort to restore his health. Despite attempts to continue working at Cambridge, Martin's health did not improve and he died in 1896.

BIBLIOGRAPHY

There is no full-scale biography of Martin. The Daniel Coit Gilman Papers at the Johns Hopkins University Library contain a good many Martin letters illuminating his years at Hopkins.

For briefer sketches of Martin's work, see C. S. Breathnach, "Henry Newell Martin (1848–1893). A Pioneer Physiologist," in *Medical History*, **13** (1969), 271–279; Henry Sewall, "Henry Newell Martin, Professor of Biology in Johns Hopkins University, 1876–1893," in *Bulletin of the Johns Hopkins Hospital*, **22** (1911), 327–333; Michael Foster, *Proceedings of the Royal Society*, **60** (1897), xx–xxiii; R. H. Chittenden, "Henry Newell Martin," in *Dictionary of American Biography*, XII, 337–338. See also the sketch by William Howells, Martin's immediate successor, in *The History of the American Physiological Society. Semi-Centennial, 1887–1937* (Baltimore, 1938), 15–18.

The best evaluation of Martin's role at Hopkins is to be found in Hugh Hawkins, *Pioneer: A History of the Johns Hopkins University. 1874–1889* (Ithaca, N.Y., 1960). Supplementary information may be found in Walter J. Meek, "The Beginnings of American Physiology," in *Annals of Medical History*, **10** (1928), 122–124; Gerald B. Webb and Desmond Powell, *Henry Sewall. Physiologist and Physician* (Baltimore, 1946). Martin's *Physiological Papers* were collected and published by the Johns Hopkins University Press as volume III of the *Memoirs From the Biological Laboratory of the Johns Hopkins University* (Baltimore, 1895). His text, *The Human Body* (New York, 1881), was used widely in the United States and went through several editions. With William Moale he wrote for classroom use a *Handbook of Vertebrate Dissection* (New York, 1881).

CHARLES E. ROSENBERG

MARTIN, RUDOLF (*b.* Zurich, Switzerland, 1 July 1864; *d.* Munich, Germany, 11 July 1925), *anthropology.*

Martin, one of Germany's most important anthropologists, was born to south German parents—his father came from Württemberg and his mother from Baden. For a short time his father worked in Zurich as a mechanical engineer, but he soon established his own machine works in Offenburg in Baden. Martin began his schooling in that city, passed the final secondary school examination there in 1884, and then enrolled in the law faculty of the Baden State University in Freiburg. After two semesters he changed his field to philosophy and left Freiburg in order to continue his studies at Leipzig. He was soon drawn back to the University of Freiburg by the presence of the zoologist Weismann. The latter had developed Darwin's ideas into a theory known as neo-Darwinism; and his lectures on the theory of evolution, the theory of natural selection, and the continuity of the germ plasm as the foundation of a theory of heredity made an indelible impression on the young Martin.

Weismann emphasized the exact formulation of problems and the scientifically demonstrable axioms of the new biological theories, and this clearly satisfied Martin more than the usual, more speculative theoretical lectures on philosophy. Martin was no doubt especially attracted by the possibilities of uniting scientific conceptions with philosophic views on the origin and destiny of man, possibilities that Weismann had presented to his students in important lectures at Freiburg beginning in 1880. Martin also attended the lectures and anatomic demonstrations of Wiedersheim and enthusiastically took part in the accompanying anatomic sections. With equal interest he followed the lectures of A. Riehl on critical philosophy and positivism, and Martin's preoccupation with Kant's ideas in anthropology may have led to his decision not to become a zoologist. His doctoral dissertation was "Kants philosophische Anschauungen in den Jahren 1762–1766," which he submitted, under the supervision of Riehl, to the philosophy faculty at Freiburg in 1887. These efforts in natural science and philosophy formed the basis of all his later work.

At the conclusion of his studies Martin visited, in 1887–1890, almost all the anthropological collections in Europe. He was especially impressed by the holdings of the École d'Anthropologie in Paris, where he twice worked as a volunteer assistant. He became acquainted with leading researchers such as Duval, P. Topinard, L.-P. Manouvrier, and the Demortillet brothers; it was they who persuaded him to return to France in order to work without the obligation to teach. It was in this period that Martin decided to devote himself to anthropology. In 1890–1891 he prepared his *Habilitationsschrift*, "Zur physischen Anthropologie der Feuerländer," which was based on an exact description and comparative anatomical evaluation of five Alakaluf tribesmen from Tierra del Fuego who had died in Zurich. With this essay he qualified as privatdocent in physical anthropology on the philosophy faculty at the University of Zurich.

When Georg Ruge was appointed director of Zurich's Institute of Anatomy in 1897, he immediately provided Martin with several rooms for anthropologic work. From this a separate anthropology institute was soon formed, and recognition for Martin was not long in coming. In 1899 Martin was named extraordinary professor of anthropology at Zurich and full professor in 1905. In 1897 he had made a major research expedition to Malaysia, where he took detailed anthropological measurements of a vast number of individuals of various tribes. He presented his results in 1905 in the monograph *Die Inlandstämme der malaiischen Halbinsel*. This classic work, which has not become obsolete, dealt with tribes existing at the most primitive level of culture then known. In his investigations of the Senoi and the Semang, Martin not only recorded accurately the anatomical and physiological characteristics of these peoples but also made fundamental observations regarding their dwellings, their history, and the entire complex of their social relationships. In addition he investigated their consanguinity with other primitive populations living in Malaysia. During this project he constructed new, more exact measuring instruments. In general, these instruments, considered the best available at the time, permitted him to obtain the first exact results that could both be employed in comparative studies and be effectively submitted to statistical procedures.

Martin was able to gather around himself in Zurich many gifted students; but his health, already weak at that time, forced him to confine himself to his research. Thus in 1911 he gave up his professorship at Zurich in order to retire to Versailles. There, assisted by his French colleagues and able to draw on the rich material in Paris, he began working on a textbook of anthropology conceived on a grand scale. It appeared in 1914, just before the start of World War I. Taken by surprise by the outbreak of war, Martin managed to flee to Germany from a seaside resort in southern France; however, all his scientific collections and personal assets were impounded. In 1917 he received an appointment as professor of anthropology at the University of Munich, where he remained for the rest of his life.

Martin's textbook, which is really a sort of handbook, makes it clear that he took into account all the tendencies within the field of anthropology and that he sharply distinguished it from certain other specialties. He thereby elevated this discipline from the status of an auxiliary science and endowed it with a thoroughly autonomous character. In his introduction to the nature and tasks of anthropology he states:

> Anthropology is the natural history of the hominids throughout their temporal and spatial distribution. Hence it is established (1) that anthropology is a science of groups, and that as a result human anatomy, physiology, etc. are excluded from its domain as sciences concerned with individuals; (2) that it deals with only the nature of the hominids; and (3) that it encompasses the entire realm of forms of this zoological group without any restriction. Anthropology therefore has the task of distinguishing all the extinct and recent forms occurring among the hominids, with respect to their corporal properties, of characterizing them, and of investigating their geographical distribution. . . .

In this program Martin placed special emphasis on the technique of anthropological investigation that he had developed. He wrote repeatedly concerning "instructions for body measurements" and "anthropometry."

Furthermore, to improve the teaching of anthropology Martin created first-rate wall charts that were well made and didactically effective. He was constantly preoccupied with adapting his textbook to current developments in the young science, but the second edition was only published posthumously (1928). Prepared by his anthropological co-worker and second wife, Stephanie Oppenheim, it appeared in three volumes. In 1956–1966 a successor to Martin's chair, Karl Saller, brought out a third edition, in four volumes.

In his later years, Martin turned to the anthropology of European peoples. In particular, prompted by the years of famine in Germany during and after World War I, he undertook important investigations into the influence of hunger on the development of schoolchildren. He also studied the effect of profession and sports on the physique of certain strata of the population. His subjects were students, especially the gymnasts who had gathered for the great German gymnastic festival held at Munich in 1923. In the meantime, however, his activity was severely restricted by heart disease; his death, which was the result of a heart attack, came as a surprise to those other than his close friends.

Martin was named Geheimer Regierungsrat and was an honorary or corresponding member of many scientific societies in Germany, Italy, England, Spain, Austria, France, Holland, and Russia. Only one year before his death he founded his own journal, the *Anthropologischer Anzeiger*. In it he published sensational studies on the reduced physical development of starving Munich schoolchildren in 1921–1923. His findings helped to bring about the introduction of remedial measures financed by American institutions, which were immediately effective.

Martin was extremely tolerant and objected to the use of malicious or polemical language against his scientific opponents. In his later years his favorite field of study was Indian philosophy and art. He was warmhearted to both students and friends. By his first wife he had three sons. During the final period of his life his second wife became his trusted co-worker; she also arranged his posthumous papers. As Martin observed, "We will never be completely finished with the investigation of life, and if occasionally we seek a provisional conclusion, we know very well that even the best we can give is no more than a step towards the better."

BIBLIOGRAPHY

I. ORIGINAL WORKS. A complete bibliography of Martin's works is in *Anthropologischer Anzeiger*, **3** (1926), 15–17. His most important works and papers are "Kants philosophische Anschauungen in den Jahren 1762–1766" (Ph.D. diss., University of Freiburg im Breisgau, 1887); "Zur physischen Anthropologie der Feuerländer," in *Archiv für Anthropologie*, **22** (1893), 155–217; "Altpatagonische Schädel," in *Vierteljahrsschrift der Naturforschenden Gesellschaft in Zürich*, **41** (1896), 496–537; "Die Ureinwohner der malayischen Halbinsel," in *Correspondenzblatt der Deutschen Gesellschaft für Anthropologie Ethnologie und Urgeschichte*, **30** (1899), 125–127; "Anthropologisches Instrumentarium," *ibid.*, 130–132; *Anthropologie als Wissenschaft und Lehrfach* (Jena, 1901); *Wandtafeln für den Unterricht in Anthropologie, Ethnologie und Geographie mit Verzeichnis und Beschreibung* (Zurich, 1902); "Über einige neue Instrumente und Hilfsmittel für den anthropologischen Unterricht," in *Korrespondenzblatt der Anthropologischen Gesellschaft*, **34** (1903), 127–132; and *Die Inlandstämme der malaiischen Halbinsel* ... (Jena, 1905). His textbook, *Lehrbuch der Anthropologie in systematischer Darstellung*, went through three eds. (Jena, 1914; 2nd ed., 1928; 3rd ed., Stuttgart, 1956–1966).

Martin's later works include "Über Domestikationsmerkmale beim Menschen," in *Naturwissenschaftliche Wochenschrift*, **30**, n.s. **14** (1915), 481–483; "Anthropologische Untersuchungen an Kriegsgefangenen," in *Umschau*, **19** (1915), 1017; "Anthropometrie," in *Münchener medizinische Wochenschrift*, **69** (1922), 383–389; *Körperverziehung* (Jena, 1922); "Anthropometrische und ärztliche Untersuchungen an Münchener Studierenden," in *Münchener medizinische Wochenschrift*, **71** (1924), 321–325, written with A. Alexander; "Die Körperbeschaffenheit der deutschen Turner," in *Monatsschrift für Turnen, Spiel und Sport*, **3** (1924), 53–61; "Körpermessungen und -wägungen an deutschen Schulkindern," in *Veröffentlichungen des K. Gesundheitsamtes*, separate supps. (pt. 1, 1922; pt. 2, 1923; pt. 3, 1924); "Die Körperentwicklung Münchener Volksschulkinder in den Jahren 1921, 1922 und 1923," in *Anthropologischer Anzeiger*, **1** (1924), 76–95; *Richtlinien für Körpermessungen und deren statistische Verarbeitung mit besonderer Berücksichtigung von Schülermessungen* (Munich, 1924); "Die Körperentwicklung Münchener Volksschulkinder im Jahre 1924," in *Anthropologischer Anzeiger*, **2** (1925), 59–78; and *Anthropometrie. Anleitung zu selbständigen anthropologischen Erhebungen und deren statistische Verarbeitung* (Berlin, 1925).

II. SECONDARY LITERATURE. See K. Saller, "Rudolf Martin†," in *Münchener medizinische Wochenschrift*, **72** (1925), 1343–1344; and E. Fischer, "Rudolf Martin†," in *Anatomischer Anzeiger*, **60** (1926), 443–448. Also see the article, "Rudolf Martin," in I. Fischer, ed., *Biographisches Lexikon der hervorragenden Ärzte der letzten fünfzig Jahre*, 2nd ed., II (Munich–Berlin, 1962), 998.

H. SCHADEWALDT

MARTÍNEZ, CRISÓSTOMO (*b.* Valencia, Spain, 1638; *d.* Flanders, 1694), *anatomy*.

Information about the early career of Martínez is almost nonexistent. He was associated with a circle of anatomists at the University of Valencia, where he began work on an anatomical atlas around 1680. In December 1686 he received a grant from Charles II which enabled him to advance his studies abroad. Martínez arrived in Paris on 19 July 1687 to continue work on his atlas, associating himself with Joseph-Guichard Duverney and other members of the recently founded Académie des Sciences. Accused of spying, he was obliged to flee France in 1690.

The anatomical work of Martínez survives in nineteen engravings and a few written descriptions. His macroscopic drawings, encompassing most of the human body, bespeak a functional interpretation of anatomy. His genius was most apparent, however, in microscopic studies of the structure of the human bone, work which placed him among the first generation of European microscopists, the only Spaniard so to qualify.

Both in his drawings and in his essay, "Generalidades acerca de los huesos" ("Generalities Concerning Bones"), Martínez sought to explain the processes of ossification from the embryo, through infantile bones without periosteum, to the mature bone structure. He studied the insertion of ligaments and muscles; the periosteum; the exterior pores of the bone; the structure of compact bone substance and of spongy bone tissue (this last was the subject of his best graphic work); and the function of bone marrow. His work rested on four concepts: the formation of fat from the blood (an iatrochemical notion accepted by most of his contemporaries); the presence of storage vesicles; the morphological and functional nature of the medulla; and the existence of adipose circulation. Martínez regarded the "adipose vessels" as his major discovery, and his work in this area reflected the great influence of Harvey among late seventeenth-century anatomists.

BIBLIOGRAPHY

I. ORIGINAL WORKS. The extant anatomical drawings and writings of Martínez are collected in José María López Piñero, ed., *El Atlas Anatómico de Crisóstomo Martínez* (Valencia, 1964). Of the nineteen drawings published by López Piñero, only three had been published before: no. XIX in *Nouvelles figures de proportions et d'anatomie du corps humain* (Paris, 1689; repr., Frankfurt–Leipzig, 1692); and nos. XVII and XIX in *Nouvelle esposition des deux grandes planches gravées et dessinées par Chrysostome Martinez, Espagnol, représentant des figures très singulières de proportions et d'anatomie*, with revisions of Martínez's text by J. B. Winslow (Paris, 1740; repr., 1780).

II. SECONDARY LITERATURE. Various aspects of Martínez' work are discussed in P. Dumaitre, "Un anatomiste espagnol à Paris au XVIIe siècle. Chrysostome Martinez et ses rarissimes planches d'anatomie," in *Médecine de France*, no. 154 (1964), 10–15; José M. López Piñero, "La repercusión en Francia de la obra anatómica de Crisóstomo Martínez," in *Cuadernos de Historia de la Medicina Española*, **6** (Salamanca, 1967), 87–100; and María Luz Terrada Ferrandis, *La anatomía microscópica en España (siglos XVII–XVIII)* (Salamanca, 1969).

THOMAS F. GLICK

MARTINI, FRANCESCO DI GIORGIO, also known as **Francesco di Siena** (*b.* Siena, Italy, 1439; *d.* Siena, November 1501), *architecture, sculpture, painting, technology.*

Little is known of Francesco's early life. He was apparently born to humble parents and trained as a painter, probably in Siena. He married twice, in 1467 and 1469. A document of the latter year shows that he, together with a certain Paolo d'Andrea, received a commission from the municipal authorities of Siena to improve the water supply system of that city. From this period of his career until his death it is possible to trace his activities with some facility; until 1477, when he entered the service of Federigo da Montefeltro, duke of Urbino, all records refer to Francesco as "dipintore," a painter.

In Urbino, Francesco participated not only in the decoration but also in the architectural design of the great ducal palace that Federigo was building. At a somewhat later date he became the duke's chief military engineer; he accompanied Federigo on his campaigns and was responsible for the design and maintenance of engines of war and artillery, as well as for the manufacture of gunpowder. He also built a large number of fortresses for the duke.

In 1479 Francesco went to southern Italy as artist and military engineer to Ferdinand I, king of Naples. He returned to Urbino in 1481, and remained there for some time after the death of Federigo in 1482. A number of documents suggest that he was concurrently in the employ of Sienese officials, however, and by 1485 he was again working primarily in Siena, as artist and city engineer. During this time he made frequent trips to other parts of Italy in the service of various rulers. In 1486 Francesco returned to Urbino; his skills had made him so famous that governments competed for his services.

Francesco went to Milan in 1490 at the request of Gian Galeazzo Sforza. He submitted a proposal for the completion of Milan's cathedral, which lacked its dome; his project was accepted for execution by local workmen. In the same year Francesco met Leonardo da Vinci (although they may have had some previous contact); in June the two men were at Pavia, inspecting the construction of the cathedral there. In 1490, too, Francesco may have been asked to submit a design for the façade of the cathedral of Florence.

Francesco was summoned to Naples by Alfonso, duke of Calabria (and king of Naples in 1494–1495), on three separate occasions in 1491, 1492, and 1495, respectively. On his last mission for Alfonso, Francesco used gunpowder to undermine and destroy the fortress of Castelnuovo, which was held by the forces of the invading French king, Charles VIII. Although earlier writers, among them Taccola, had discussed this technique, Francesco seems to have been the first to succeed with it. In 1499 Francesco returned to Urbino to advise on fortifications intended to stem the advance of Cesare Borgia's forces. He continued to be active as both an artist—he probably resumed painting in his later years—and an engineer until the time of his death.

Francesco's reputation lay in his work as a painter, sculptor, and architect, until the discovery that a number of important writings on technology, circulated anonymously, were in fact his. These treatises and notes mirror the full range of Francesco's concerns—among their subjects are civil and military engineering, surveying, hydraulic engineering, both offensive and defensive war machinery, mechanical technology (especially millworks, devices for raising water, and cranes), studies on proportion, and notes and relief drawings of Roman monuments (which he observed in the course of his travels). In all of these writings the influence of Vitruvius is clear. (Indeed, an autograph draft of Francesco's translation of Vitruvius' treatise is itself preserved in Florence.) Francesco's importance to the history of technology lies in these works, which were widely influential among his contemporaries and successors, although they were not printed under his name until the middle of the nineteenth century.

Although certain of Francesco's mechanical projects were borrowed from earlier authors (especially Taccola), they gain significance from the artistic and technological superiority of his rendering. His method of illustration was itself influential. One of his particular techniques, that of confining the machine illustrated within a frame, may be taken as an index to the extent of his authority in books on machinery in the sixteenth and seventeenth centuries. Many manuscript technical and military collectanea of this epoch also bear his mark, including those of Leonardo, whose inventory of books (*Codex Madrid II*) contains the entry "Francesco da Siena." Francesco's ideas appeared, without credit, in the later works of such composers of "Theaters of Machines" as Jacob de Strada, Vittorio Zonca, and Agostino Ramelli, as well as the somewhat later authors G. A. Böckler and Heinrich Zeising. The technology that Francesco represented even found its way, at quite an early date, to the Far East; the *Ch'i Ch'i T'u Shuo* ("Diagrams and Explanations of Wonderful Machines"), published in 1627 by the Jesuit missionary Johann Schreck and Wang Cheng, includes several devices that clearly derive from Francesco's work.

From such later books Francesco's ideas passed into the works of eighteenth-century writers, for example, Jacob Leupold and Stephan Switzer, and even into mechanical handbooks of the early nineteenth century. Some of the basic mechanisms described by J. A. Borgnis in his *Traité complet de mécanique appliquée* of 1818–1823, for example,

are still very similar to Francesco's prototypes. Even when the machines that Francesco described became obsolete, his renderings of them lingered as technological symbols, and as such they may be seen in the form of colophons of eighteenth- and nineteenth-century technical works.

Francesco's practical work as a military engineer was equally influential. Among his innovations was the system of fortification by bastions and curtains that replaced the medieval concept of the turreted castle. The final development of this phase of his work appeared in the great French fortresses designed by Vauban for Louis XIV.

BIBLIOGRAPHY

I. ORIGINAL WORKS. Francesco's writings are preserved in six MSS:

1. *Taccuino Vaticano*, Vatican Library, Rome, Urb. Lat. 1757, an autograph pocket encyclopedia, on vellum, with sketches of a great number of mechanical contrivances. The first entry is dated 1472; others are spread out over many years. Marginal notes in the hand of Leonardo da Vinci.

2. *British Museum Codex*, British Museum, London, 24.949, a series of drawings of machines, on vellum, dedicated to Federigo da Montefeltro, datable between 1474 and 1482. An excellent copy is Biblioteca Reale, Turin, Ser. Mil. 383.

3. *Codex Laurenziano Ashburnhamiano*, Laurentian Library, Florence, 361, datable *ca.* 1480, probably the first version of the *Treatise on Architecture*, with marginal illustrations.

4. *Codex Saluzziano*, Biblioteca Reale, Turin, 148, datable *ca.* 1485, a version of the immediately preceding, although lacking several chapters. Apparently a copy by a professional scribe, although the marginal illustrations may be in Francesco's own hand.

5. *Trattato d'architettura civile e militare*, Biblioteca Comunale, Siena, S.IV.4, datable *ca.* 1490, a copy on paper of a lost original.

6. *Codex Magliabechiano*, National Library, Florence, II.I.141, datable *ca.* 1492, an expanded and integrated version of the Siena manuscript above. Besides the beautifully illustrated text of the *Trattato*, it contains the autograph translation of Vitruvius and a collection of drawings of war machines and fortifications.

Editions of Francesco's work are Carlo Promis, ed., *Trattato di architettura civile e militare*, 2 vols. and atlas (Turin, 1841); and, more useful, Corrado Maltese, ed., *Trattati di architettura ingegniera e arte militare*, 2 vols. (Milan, 1967), which includes complete annotated transcriptions of the Turin, Siena, and Florence MSS, an index of variants and concordances, and reproductions of all illustrated pages.

II. SECONDARY LITERATURE. On Francesco and his work see Selwyn Brinton, *Francesco di Giorgio of Siena*, 2 vols.

(London, 1934–1935); P. Fontana, "I codici di Francesco di Giorgio Martini e di Mariano di Jacomo detto il Taccola," in *Actes du XIVᵉ Congrès International d'histoire de l'art* (Brussels, 1936), p. 102, which discusses the influence of Taccola on Francesco; G. Mancini, *Giorgio Vasari: Vite cinque annotate* (Florence, 1917); Roberto Papini, *Francesco di Giorgio architetto*, 3 vols. (Florence, 1946), a superb graphic presentation, but marred by polemics and unwarranted attributions; A. E. Popham and P. Pouncey, *Italian Drawings in the Department of Prints and Drawings in the British Museum: the XIVth and XVth Centuries* (London, 1950), which gives an accurate description of the British Museum codex; Ladislao Reti, "Francesco di Giorgio Martini's Treatise on Engineering and its Plagiarists," in *Technology and Culture*, **4**, no. 3 (1963), 287–298, on the transmission of Francesco's technological drawings; E. Rostagno and T. Lodi, *Indici e cataloghi VIII. I codici Ashburnhamiani della Biblioteca Mediceo-Laurenziana*, I (Rome, 1948), 468–474, a study of the early versions of the *Trattato;* Mario Salmi, *Disegni di Francesco di Giorgio nella Collezione Chigi Saracini* (Siena, 1947); Luigi Michelini Tocci, "Disegni e appunti autografi di Francesco di Giorgio in un codice del Taccola," in *Scritti di storia dell'arte in onore di Mario Salmi*, II (Rome, 1962), 202–212, which is concerned with Taccola's influence on Francesco; and Allen Stuart Weller, *Francesco di Giorgio 1439–1501* (Chicago, 1943), the best available biography of Francesco, with a bibliography complete up to 1942.

LADISLAO RETI

MARTINOVICS, IGNÁC (*b*. Pest, Hungary, 22 July 1755; *d*. Buda, Hungary, 20 May 1795), *chemistry*.

Martinovics, the son of an army officer, entered the Franciscan order and studied philosophy and theology at the universities of Pest and Vienna, but he soon displayed an interest in natural science and technology. He left the order and served as an army chaplain at various garrisons in the Hapsburg dominions. In Galicia, he became the secretary to Count Potocki and traveled with him through western Europe. In England and France, Martinovics became acquainted with the most distinguished scientists of the age and was exposed to the progressive ideas of the French Enlightenment. Thereafter chemistry and politics determined the course of his life.

After returning home, Martinovics accepted the chair of physics at the University of Lemberg (Lvov) in Galicia, where he remained from 1783 to 1791. At Lemberg he published his *Praelectiones physicae experimentalis* (1787), which showed that he still adhered to the phlogiston theory. He continued to oppose Lavoisier's theory of combustion and sought to refute it with experiments with fulminating gold.

He asserted that although combustion is indeed determined by a substance, that substance is not oxygen; the atmosphere plays no role in the explosion of fulminating gold, which therefore takes place without oxygen. Martinovics also carried out experiments on the solubility of gases in water; he ascertained that the solubility diminishes with decreasing pressure and increasing temperature. In 1791 he undertook distillation experiments on Galician petroleum and determined the combustibility and specific gravity of various fractions.

Martinovics also published many philosophical writings that reflected the atheistic and materialistic views of d'Holbach. Inspired by the French Revolution, he fought for political reform in the Hapsburg state. At first he hoped this could be accomplished legally. He entered the service of the reform-minded Emperor Leopold II and furnished him with information concerning the political intentions of the nobility and the Jesuits. Leopold's successor, Francis, frightened by the events of the French Revolution, changed his predecessor's policies and dismissed the reformers. Martinovics then joined in a plot to proclaim a republic. The plot was discovered, and Martinovics and four other conspirators were beheaded.

BIBLIOGRAPHY

A list of Martinovics' works is in Poggendorff, I, 65. On Martinovics, see V. Fraknoi, *Martinovics* (Budapest, 1921), in Hungarian; and Z. Szökefalvi-Nagy, "Ignatius Martinovics, 18th-century Chemist and Political Agitator," in *Journal of Chemical Education*, **41** (1964), 458.

FERENC SZABADVÁRY

MARTIUS, KARL FRIEDRICH PHILIPP VON (*b*. Erlangen, Germany, 17 April 1794; *d*. Munich, Germany, 13 December 1868), *botany, ethnology*.

The Martius family, many members of which had pursued learned professions, traced its lineage back to Galeottus Martius, who was a professor at Padua in 1450. Karl was the son of Ernst Wilhelm Martius, an apothecary and honorary professor of pharmacy at Erlangen University, and Regina Weinl, a noblewoman. Martius at an early age manifested a resolve to devote himself to science. He was also much interested in classical studies and composed many of his works in a very elegant Latin. In 1810 he was admitted to Erlangen University, where he studied medicine and received his M.D. with the dissertation *Plantarum horti academici Erlangensis* (Erlangen, 1814).

In 1814 Martius became an *élève* of the Royal Bavarian Academy at Munich and was appointed assistant to the conservator of the botanic garden, F. von Schrank. In this position he published his *Flora cryptogamica Erlangensis* (Nuremberg, 1817), which he had begun while at Erlangen. In 1816 he was admitted as a member of the Leopoldine Academy, of which he became director ephemeridum in 1858.

A man of superior talents, indefatigable energy, and excellent personal qualities, Martius attracted the attention of the older members of the Royal Academy. The king of Bavaria, Maximilian Joseph I, was a lover of botany and often selected Martius as his guide when visiting the botanic garden. His plans for sending scientific explorers to South America were realized in 1817, when an Austrian expedition was sent to Brazil. Martius and several other Bavarian scientists, including his companion, the zoologist Spix, went along. They left Trieste on 2 April 1817 and returned to Munich in December 1820. The Munich herbarium received 6,500 carefully preserved species of plants, which constituted a most valuable portion of its collection, and the botanic garden received many living plants and seeds from the expedition. This voyage laid the foundation of Martius' future success, and as a result of the expedition he was appointed a member of the Royal Bavarian Academy and assistant conservator of the botanic garden. In 1826, when King Ludwig I had transferred Landshut University to Munich, Martius was appointed professor of botany, and in 1832, when Schrank retired, he was named principal conservator of the botanic garden, institute, and collections. Among his students were A. Braun, H. von Mohl, K. Schimper, and O. Sendtner. In 1840 Martius became secretary of the physicomathematical section of the academy and was charged with all correspondence and commemorative addresses. The excellent style of these eulogies is comparable to that of the *éloges* of G. Cuvier. The decision of the government to erect the glass building of the Munich industrial exhibition within the area of the botanic garden deeply disappointed Martius, who had vainly remonstrated, and it caused him to resign his professorship and superintendence of the garden. After his retirement much of his time was taken up in editorial activities and scientific labors.

In 1823 Martius married Franciska Freiin von Stengel; they had four children.

BIBLIOGRAPHY

I. ORIGINAL WORKS. Martius wrote more than 150 books, monographs, and minor works, as well as several poems. His monograph, *Historia naturalis palmarum*, 3 vols. (Munich, 1823–1853), written in cooperation with H. von Mohl, A. Braun, and O. Sendtner, was highly appreciated. In 1840 he began his great work, the *Flora Brasiliensis*, 15 vols. (Munich, 1840–1906), assisted by many collaborators and financially supported by the Brazilian government. After his death this magnificent work was continued by several others such as A. Eichler and I. Urban. Together with Spix he wrote *Reise in Brasilien . . . in den Jahren 1817–1820*, 3 vols. (Munich, 1823–1831). The eulogies are contained in *Akademische Denkreden von C. F. Ph. von Martius* (Leipzig, 1866). Those of a later date are in *Sitzungsberichte der Bayerischen Akademie der Naturwissenschaften zu München* (Munich, 1868).

Martius also wrote about the potato disease, of which he had discovered the cause, in *Die Kartoffelepidemie* (Munich, 1842). One of his more important ethnological works is *Beiträge zur Ethnographie und Sprachenkunde Amerikas zumal Brasilien*, 2 vols. (Leipzig, 1867).

II. SECONDARY LITERATURE. For works about Martius, see A. W. Eichler, "C. F. Ph. v. Martius, Nekrolog," in *Flora*, **52** (1869), 3–13, 17–24; K. Goebel, *Zur Erinnerung an K. F. Ph. von Martius* (Munich, 1905); C. F. Meissner, *Denkschrift auf Carl Friedr. Phil. von Martius* (Munich, 1869); and the article by E. Wunschmann in vol. 20, *Allgemeine Deutsche Biographie*, 517–527.

A. P. M. SANDERS

MARTONNE, EMMANUEL-LOUIS-EUGÈNE DE

(*b.* Chabris, France, 1 April 1873; *d.* Sceaux, France, 24 July 1955), *geography*, *geomorphology*, *hydrography*.

The scion of a noble Breton family, Martonne was the son of Alfred de Martonne, an archivist, and the former Caroline Cadart. He entered the École Normale Supérieure in 1892 and three years later received a degree in history and geography. He subsequently attended the courses and worked in the laboratories of Richthofen at Berlin and of Penck and Hann at Vienna. Soon after his return to Paris he began fieldwork in Rumania and became proficient in the language.

In 1899 Martonne joined the geography department of the Faculty of Letters at the University of Rennes, where in the Faculty of Sciences he established a geographical laboratory equipped with maps, geological specimens, and simple surveying instruments. He wrote several articles on the peneplain and the coastal morphology of Brittany (1904–1906); but his main publications concerned mountain glaciation, particularly in the southern Carpathians.

In 1904 Martonne went on a long excursion to the American West and Mexico with William M. Davis, professor of geology at Harvard. He became devoted to Davis' methods of teaching, presentation and landform analysis; henceforth his interests leaned increasingly toward the physical branches of geography. In 1905 he joined the Faculty of Arts at the University of Lyons.

The turning point in Martonne's life came in 1909, when he succeeded Paul Vidal de la Blache, his father-in-law, as head of the department of geography in the Faculty of Letters at the Sorbonne. He held this post for thirty-five years, and from 1927 he combined it with the directorship of the Institut de Géographie. From the death of Vidal de la Blache in 1918 to his own retirement in 1944, Martonne was the recognized leader of the French school of geography. A leading international figure, he was responsible for organizing the meetings of the International Geographical Union from 1931 to 1938, serving as its president from 1949 to his death. The Académie des Sciences elected him a member in 1942; he also held honorary membership in a dozen foreign geographical societies and honorary doctorates from Cambridge and the University of Cluj (Rumania).

Martonne was the most important influence in the development of modern French geography into an autonomous science. As a scholar he was more interested in the patient accumulation of observed facts than in deductions, but, although cautious, he was fairly open-minded toward new concepts and techniques.

Martonne's approach to the natural sciences was essentially geographical, and he took a broad view of physical geography. After describing and mapping the distribution by area of a natural phenomenon, he usually tried to associate that distribution with some general law and so to seek causes for it. Thus he tended to place more importance on comparative spatial distribution than on genetic explanation and was more inclined to determine the causes of distribution than to elucidate the scientific properties of the phenomenon itself. Among his major contributions to geographical instruction in France were his insistence on practical laboratories and on a sound knowledge of cartography and surveying. To regional geography he contributed important general descriptions of Walachia (1902) and two volumes, on central Europe, to the *Géographie universelle* (1931–1932). His smaller regional syntheses on the Alps (1926) and the major geographical regions of France (1921) are masterly summaries.

In physical geography Martonne's chief contributions were to the study of mountain glaciation, peneplains, hydrography, and climatic geomorphology. His discussions of glacial erosion and the development of Alpine valleys show keen powers of observation and are his best works. He popularized the concept that steps and over-deepenings in the floors of glaciated valleys were associated with pre-existing breaks-of-slope caused by pre-glacial and Quaternary tectonic uplifts. His elaboration of the role of snow (nivation) in sculpturing mountain landforms was one of his more original themes.

Peneplains and other erosional flattenings always interested Martonne, and he preferred Davis' peneplanation theory to the eustatic ideas of Henri Baulig. Among the investigations he helped to initiate was an international study of terraces; the findings were edited by others for the International Geographical Union.

In hydrography Martonne published (1925–1928), with the collaboration of L. Aufrère, details of areas with endoreic (interior) drainage rather than exoreic drainage (flowing to the ocean). This survey and its world map showed that 27 percent (41 million square kilometers) of the continental land area did not drain to the oceans, whereas the previously accepted measurement had been 22 percent (33 million square kilometers). Martonne then proceeded to relate the enfeebled nature of certain drainage systems to an increase of aridity; he also propounded an index of aridity and the concept of areism, or absence of stream runoff, a condition that occurs on 17 percent of the continental land area. He traveled widely in the deserts of North Africa and South America, in an attempt to determine a more precise relationship between aridity and surface runoff, or drainage. His first index of aridity was $P/(T + 10)$, P being the annual precipitation in millimeters and T the mean annual temperature on the centigrade scale, 10 being added to avoid negative values. The resulting numerical scale of values was mapped as isograms, the lower values coinciding with areism and the higher with exoreism. In 1941 Martonne improved his aridity index by adopting a scale based on the arithmetical mean of the index of aridity for the year and for the driest month. But the scheme, useful for broad correlative purposes only, was soon supplanted by the evapotranspiration concept, which allowed water deficiency and surplus to be assessed more accurately.

Most of Martonne's ideas in climatic geomorphology had already been formulated by German geographers. His account of the geomorphological problems of Brazil (1940), however, contained original observations.

As a scientific geographer and educator Martonne will probably be remembered longest for his general summaries of physical geography. His chief regional exposition of systematic physical topics was *Géographie physique de la France* for *Géographie universelle* (1942). His main global exposition, *Traité de géo-*

graphie physique, first appeared as one volume in 1909 and achieved phenomenal success. It was entirely recast in three volumes in 1925–1927 and was kept up to date by careful pruning and enlargement. Its breadth of content, wide outlook, clarity of explanation, richness in diagrams—mostly by Martonne himself—and wise choice of typical rather than exotic examples earned it a well-deserved longevity.

BIBLIOGRAPHY

I. ORIGINAL WORKS. A complete list of Martonne's more than 200 publications is in the obituary by Jean Dresch, in *Bulletin de la Société géologique de France*, **6** (1956), 623–642; and in the archives of the Académie des Sciences, Institut de France, Paris. His articles were published mainly in *Comptes rendus . . . de l'Académie des sciences; Météorologie; Bulletin de la Société géologique de France;* and, above all, in *Annales de géographie*, of which he was a director from 1920 to 1940 and a chief director from 1940 to his death in 1955.

His major works are *La Valachie, essai de monographie géographique* (Paris, 1902), his dissertation for his doctorate in letters; *Recherches sur la distribution géographique de population en Valachie avec une étude critique sur les procédés de représentation de la répartition de la population* (Paris–Bucharest, 1903); "La période glaciaire dans les Karpates méridionales," in *Comptes rendus du Congrès international de géologie*, Vienne, 1903 (1904), 691–702; "La pénéplaine et les côtes bretonnes," in *Annales de géographie*, **15** (1906), 213–236, 299–328; *Recherches sur l'évolution morphologique des Alpes de Transylvanie (Karpates méridionales)* (Paris, 1907), his dissertation for his doctorate in natural sciences; "Sur l'inégale répartition de l'érosion glaciaire dans le lit des glaciers alpins," in *Comptes rendus . . . de l'Académie des sciences*, **149** (1909), 1413–1415; "L'érosion glaciaire et la formation des vallées alpines," in *Annales de géographie*, **19** (1910), 289–317; **20** (1911), 1–29; "L'évolution des vallées glaciaires alpines, en particulier dans les Alpes du Dauphiné," in *Bulletin de la Société géologique de France*, **12** (1912), 516–549; *Atlas photographique des formes du relief terrestre* (Paris, 1914), compiled with J. Brunhes and E. Chaix; and "Le climat facteur du relief," in *Scientia*, **13** (1913), 339–355.

Other works are "The Carpathians," in *Geographical Review*, **3** (1917), 417–437; "Essai de carte ethnographique des pays roumains," in *Annales de géographie*, **29** (1920), 181–198; "Le rôle morphologique de la neige en montagne," in *Géographie*, **34** (1920), 255–267; *Les régions géographiques de la France* (Paris, 1921); "Le massif du Bihar (Roumanie)," in *Annales de géographie*, **31** (1922), 313–340; "Extension du drainage océanique," in *Comptes rendus . . . de l'Académie des sciences*, **180** (1925), 939–942, written with L. Aufrère; "Aréisme et l'indice d'aridité," *ibid.*, **182** (1926), 1395–1398; "Une nouvelle fonction climatologique: L'indice d'aridité," in *Météorologie*, **68** (1926), 449–458; *Les Alpes. Géographie générale* (Paris,

1926); *L'extension des régions privées d'écoulement vers l'océan* (Paris, 1928), written with L. Aufrère; *Europe centrale*, 2 vols. (Paris, 1931–1932); "Les régions arides du nord argentin et chilien," in *Bulletin de l'Association de géographes français*, **79** (1934), 58–62; "Sur la formule de l'indice d'aridité," in *Comptes rendus . . . de l'Académie des sciences*, **200** (1935), 166–168, written with Mme R. Fayol; "Problèmes morphologiques du Brésil tropical Atlantique," in *Annales de géographie*, **49** (1940), 16–27, 106–129; "Carte morphologique de la France," in *Atlas de France* (Paris, 1941); "Nouvelle carte mondiale de l'indice d'aridité," in *Météorologie*, **17** (1941), 3–26, and *Annales de géographie*, **51** (1942), 241–250; *Géographie physique de la France* (Paris, 1942); "Géographie zonale. La zone tropicale," in *Annales de géographie*, **55** (1946), 1–18; and *Géographie aérienne* (Paris, 1949).

His major work was *Traité de géographie physique* (Paris, 1909; 2nd ed., 1913; 3rd ed., 1921). The 4th ed. appeared in 3 vols.: I, *Notions générales. Climat. Hydrographie* (Paris, 1925); II, *Le relief du sol* (Paris, 1925); III, *Biogéographie* (Paris, 1927), written with A. Chevalier and L. Cuénot. The latest eds., as of 1970, are I, 9th ed. (Paris, 1957); II, 10th ed. (Paris, 1958); and III, 7th ed. (Paris, 1955). Abridged eds. were issued at Paris from 1922 and at London, in English, from 1927.

II. SECONDARY LITERATURE. The chief assessments of Martonne's work and influence are André Cholley, in *Annales de géographie*, **65** (1956), 1–14; Donatien Cot, in *Comptes rendus . . . de l'Académie des sciences*, **241** (1955), 713–716; Jean Dresch, in *Bulletin de la Société géologique de France*, **6** (1956), 623–642, with bibliography; and André Meynier, in his *Histoire de la pensée géographique en France: 1872–1969* (Paris, 1969), *passim*.

ROBERT P. BECKINSALE

MARUM, MARTIN (MARTINUS) VAN (*b.* Delft, Netherlands, 20 March 1750; *d.* Haarlem, Netherlands, 26 December 1837), *natural philosophy, medicine, botany.*

Van Marum's father, Petrus, a construction engineer and surveyor, moved from Groningen to Delft to marry Cornelia van Oudheusden in 1744. Martin attended elementary school and grammar school at Delft; but when his father returned to Groningen in 1764, he matriculated at Groningen University. One of his teachers was Peter Camper, who greatly influenced his studies and stimulated his special interest in plant physiology, a subject hardly studied in the Netherlands in those days. On 7 August 1773, he obtained his Ph.D. for a dissertation on the circulation of plant juices. On 21 August 1773 he received his medical degree with a study of comparative animal-plant physiology. The first thesis was highly esteemed abroad. When van Marum was not appointed professor of botany, as he had been promised, he abandoned his physiological studies, although he could not refrain from experimenting in this field later on.

Van Marum subsequently studied electricity. In cooperation with Gerhard Kuyper he developed an electrical machine with shellac disks drawn through mercury. A description was published in 1776, and translations into German and French followed.

From 1776 to 1780 van Marum practiced medicine in Haarlem. He was at once elected a member of the Netherlands Society of Sciences, and was appointed a lecturer in philosophy and mathematics. In 1777 the Society appointed him director of their rapidly expanding cabinet of natural curiosities. He then lived on the museum's premises.

In 1781 van Marum married Joanna Bosch, heiress of a prosperous printer, and thus he acquired a piece of land, on which he started to cultivate plants in 1783. His new appointment as director of Teyler's Cabinet of Physical and Natural Curiosities and Library left him little time for working his own garden, but it brought him his greatest fame.

The organization of Teyler's Museum was left entirely to van Marum, and he soon obtained a large electrical machine made under his supervision by John Cuthbertson of Amsterdam. Its disks had a diameter of sixty-five inches, the largest possible at the time. Van Marum thought that results obtained with such enormous discharges were bound to bring order to the chaos of concepts about the mysterious "electrical matter." He described the experiments with this machine and great battery of Leyden jars in three volumes of *Verhandelingen uitgeven door Teyler's tweede Genootschap* (1785, 1787, 1795). These experiments were greatly admired and repeated all over Europe. From his experiments with the large machine van Marum concluded that Franklin was correct in his theory of a single electric fluid. For this support Franklin expressed his appreciation. Volta also greatly admired van Marum's work, and informed him in 1792 of his own experiments; van Marum later introduced the term "Voltaic pile." Working with C. H. Pfaff, van Marum conclusively proved static and galvanic electricity to be identical.

From 1782 van Marum regularly made trips abroad. In Paris in 1785 he met Lavoisier and saw his assistants at work. After his return home, he made his own experimental test and became convinced of the validity of Lavoisier's combustion theory. He contributed greatly to the acceptance of the "new chemistry" in the Netherlands by his *Schets der Leere van Lavoisier*, published as a supplement to the *Verhandelingen uitgeven door Teyler's tweede Genootschap* (1787). He applied himself especially to the simplification of the required instruments, thus making the experiments less costly and enabling many chemists to repeat them. His gasometer was also a very important instrument.

Van Marum, in cooperation with van Troostwijk, discovered carbon monoxide. He continued his experiments to decompose and synthesize water, as he had seen done in Paris, and he oxidized various metals and then decomposed the oxides. During his experiments he had smelled ozone, but he did not recognize it to be a form of oxygen. Van Marum was the first to observe condensation of liquid ammonia from the gas, but he failed to realize that other gases would condense under the proper conditions of temperature and pressure. For this experiment van Marum built his own convertible air pump and compressor. In 1798 the *Verhandelingen uitgeven door Teyler's tweede Genootschap* included the description of these chemical experiments.

In 1794 van Marum was appointed secretary of the Netherlands Society of Sciences. After the French occupation of the Netherlands in 1795 there was little opportunity for scientific research, and funds for acquiring new instruments steadily decreased. Van Marum then applied himself more to the study of paleontology and geology, collecting much material and information during his various travels. He had already been able to procure valuable items for Teyler's Museum. In 1784 he bought the fossil *Mosasaurus camperi*, which had been found on the St. Pietersberg hill in Limburg; it was then still called "the head of an unknown marine animal." G. Cuvier later concluded that it was a lizard's head, and thus a land animal, which it had already been assumed to be by Peter Camper's son, Adriaan.

When traveling in Switzerland in 1802, van Marum bought the *Homo diluvii testis et theoskopos*, so named by Scheuchzer (1726). Cuvier examined this fossil at Haarlem in 1811, and concluded that it was a salamander. Van Marum also rearranged the whole collection of minerals in Teyler's Museum according to the methods of Cuvier, at that time the greatest authority in paleontology, geology, and mineralogy. Van Marum always tried to procure the latest and the best scientific information.

In 1803 van Marum bought a country house with a large garden, in which he cultivated mainly South African plants, especially aloes. He contributed greatly to the publication of Prince Joseph of Salm-Dyck's descriptive catalog of aloes by supplying him with many new species and data. He also maintained correspondence with C. P. Thunberg, Banks, Jacquin, and Jacquin's son, Joseph Franz.

Van Marum was actively interested in many aspects of human welfare: the prevention of air pollution from carbon monoxide, the treatment of victims of drowning, the construction of a portable fire engine, ventilation in factories and aboard ships, improvements of Papin's digester to produce cheap food for the poor, lightning rods, especially for windmills, and steam baths for cholera patients. He also gave many public lectures on various subjects. In 1808 he and three colleagues were asked to draft a constitution for the Royal Institute of Sciences (the present Royal Netherlands Academy of Sciences). He also was a member of the committee for the organization of higher education (1814).

Although van Marum made no great scientific discoveries, he greatly influenced the dissemination of knowledge in those fields of science that made great progress during his lifetime.

BIBLIOGRAPHY

A complete bibliography by J. G. de Bruyn may be found in R. J. Forbes, ed., *Martinus van Marum, Life and Work*, I (Haarlem, 1969), 287–320. Van Marum's principal publications are numbers 1, 3, 10, 11, 35, and 40.

ALIDA M. MUNTENDAM

AL-MARWAZĪ. See Ḥabash al-Ḥāsib.

MARX, KARL HEINRICH (*b.* Trier, Germany, 5 May 1818; *d.* London, England, 14 March 1883), *philosophy*.

For a complete study of his life and works, see Supplement.

MASCAGNI, PAOLO (*b.* Pomarance, Volterra, Italy, 25 January 1755; *d.* Florence, Italy, 19 October 1815), *anatomy*.

Mascagni, whom Lalande included among the learned men of Siena, graduated at the age of twenty and, four years later was appointed professor. At that time the Academy of Sciences of Paris proposed to "determine and demonstrate the system of the lymphatic vessels." The theory of the lymphatic vessels had been all but forgotten in Italy; and although Frederik Ruysch had tried to reawaken interest in the subject in Holland, Albrecht Haller, by denying the existence of lymphatic vessels in certain parts of the body, had cast doubt on the entire lymphatic system.

By 1784 Mascagni was able to send the Academy the first part of a work on the lymphatic vessels illustrated with numerous plates. Although his work, *Vasorum lymphaticorum historia*, arrived late, he was awarded a special prize. The *Historia* paved the way for progress in anatomy, physiology, and clinical medicine, for 50 percent of the lymphatic vessels now known were discovered by Mascagni.

In studying the origin of the lymphatic vessels, Mascagni established that every vessel must in its course enter one or more lymph glands. He rearranged and completed the observations of others and overhauled their techniques. Mascagni also performed experiments, using the mercury injection method and so improving it that it surpassed all preceding techniques. In the light of his excellent results, the simplicity of the technique is truly surprising. The only instrument used was a tubular needle bent at a right angle; yet he observed, named, and described nearly all the lymph glands and vessels of the human body, checking earlier observations and carrying out new ones.

Mascagni examined the views of Boerhaave and his followers, who believed that the lymphatics arose from the tips of the arteries and were shaped like ramified conical vessels. These vessels formed canals that gradually became thinner; and these canals, by continuing into the veins, brought some sort of material to the blood and therefore were related to the lymphatic system. Mascagni demonstrated, however, that such arterial and venous lymphatics did not exist. After examining the work of Noguez, Hamberger, and Hoffmann and the results of his own researches, Mascagni concluded that the lymphatic system originates from all the cavities and surfaces of the body, both internal and external, and is related to the absorbing function. By means of colored injections he demonstrated the communication between the lymphs and the serous vessels.

Mascagni was appointed professor of anatomy at Pisa; he was also invited to hold professorships at Bologna and Padua, but accepted the vacant post at Florence. Indeed, the Tuscan government, desirous of securing his services, not only created one professorship covering anatomy, physiology, chemistry, and the teaching of art anatomy but also doubled the stipend. In appreciation of this generous offer, Mascagni began to prepare anatomical models for use by students of sculpture and painting. The various systems of the human body were to be represented on life-size figures, a grandiose concept that was carried out with the help of illustrations by Sienese artists. The huge cost of this colossal editorial venture obliged Mascagni to draw on his salary and even to mortgage the family estate. These generous efforts failed to yield the desired results, for he died before completing his lifework.

BIBLIOGRAPHY

Mascagni's first published writing was *Vasorum lymphaticorum historia* (Siena, 1784), the intro. to a work on lymphatic vessels. Of greater importance is *Vasorum lymphaticorum corporis humani historia et iconographia* (Siena, 1787). Mascagni also published commentaries on mineralogy, agriculture, chemistry, and physics.

His first posthumously published work was that on anatomy for use by students of sculpture and painting (Florence, 1816). There followed two introductions to the *Anatomia:* the Antonmarchi edition, prepared under the supervision of Antonmarchi, who was Napoleon's physician and Mascagni's pupil; and the edition prepared in Milan by Farnese. The latter is inferior because the redrawn plates are not as good as those in the Antonmarchi version. These editions were followed by the plates of the animal and vegetable organs illustrated in the intro. to the *Anatomia* (Florence, 1819).

Mascagni's monumental *Anatomia universa XLIV tabulis aeneis iuxta archetjpum hominis adulti accuratissime repraesentata* (Pisa, 1823) is so large that one of its designers—Antonio Serantoni, a designer, engraver, and modeler in wax—prepared a special personal ed. in color: *Anatomia universale descrittiva del Professor Paolo Mascagni* (Florence, 1833), reproduced with copper plates smaller than those in the Pisa ed. Mascagni's important works also include the many wax models preserved in Italian and foreign museums.

FEDERICO ALLODI

MASCART, ÉLEUTHÈRE ÉLIE NICOLAS (*b.* Quarouble, France, 20 February 1837; *d.* Paris, France, 26 August 1908), *physics.*

The son of a teacher, Mascart received his secondary education at the *collège* in Valenciennes, after which he became *maître répétiteur* at the *lycées* in Lille (1856–1857) and Douai (1857–1858). His thorough mathematical preparation at Douai enabled him in 1858 to enter the École Normale Supérieure in Paris. Three years later he became *agrégé-préparateur* at the École Normale, and in July 1864 he received his doctorate. Shortly thereafter he married a Mlle Briot.

After teaching physics at the *lycée* in Metz (1864–1866) and publishing his first book, *Éléments de mécanique* (Paris, 1866; 9th ed., 1910), his former professor of physics, Verdet, helped him secure a post in Paris at the Collège Chaptal. He soon transferred, first to the Lycée Napoléon and then to the Lycée de Versailles. In December 1868 he left

secondary education for good to become Régnault's assistant at the Collège de France. In May 1872, his scientific career having been interrupted by the Franco-Prussian War, he succeeded Régnault as professor of physics, a chair that he held for the rest of his life. In 1878 he was also chosen to be the first director of the Bureau Central Météorologique. In December 1884 he was elected to J. C. Jamin's place in the French Academy of Sciences; he served as permanent secretary and, in 1904, president.

Mascart's scientific career was marked not by great discoveries but by a steady stream of first-rate experimental and theoretical work in optics, electricity, magnetism, and meteorology. The first problem he attacked—the subject of his thesis—was a systematic and precise spectroscopic exploration (using photographic detection techniques) of the ultraviolet region of the solar spectrum, in which he greatly increased the number of lines of known wavelength. At the same time he accurately determined the relative wavelengths of the principal emission lines of ten selected metals and argued that all of his data agreed well with a modified version of Cauchy's dispersion formula. A more detailed extension of these experiments, which Fizeau termed the "most thorough and most satisfying" work since Fraunhofer's, won for Mascart the 1866 Prix Bordin.

During the course of this work and in the years immediately following it, Mascart made several individually significant observations, including the existence of triplets in the spectrum of magnesium. Undoubtedly the most valuable aspect of this period was the thorough preparation in experimental optics that it gave him. When the Academy in 1870 proposed for the Grand Prix des Sciences Mathématiques the experimental determination of the modifications that light experiences in its mode of propagation and its properties as a result of the movement of the source and observer, Mascart was ready to compete for it. Several years of painstaking researches followed, at the end of which Mascart found himself forced to the purely negative conclusion that refraction and diffraction experiments, independent of whether terrestrial sources or sunlight is used, are incapable of detecting the motion of the earth through the ether. Double refraction and other optical experiments yielded the same negative result. While contemporary interpretations of these experiments had to be modified later in the light of special relativity theory, the great importance of Mascart's work was recognized by the Academy when it awarded Mascart the Grand Prix in 1874.

Optical researches of various kinds—experiments in physiological optics, determinations of the indices of refraction and dispersive powers of numerous gases, studies on metallic reflection and color, theoretical work on the rainbow and on the formation of interference fringes under various conditions—continued to occupy much of Mascart's time both before and after 1874, especially until the publication of his well-known three-volume *Traité d'optique* (Paris, 1889–1893). Concurrently, however, his interests were extending into the fields of electricity and magnetism. He studied, for example, electrical machines (1873) and the efficiencies of various motors (1877–1878), the propagation of electricity in conductors (1878), the theory of induced currents (1880, 1883), the interaction of two electrified spheres (1884), diamagnetism (1886), means for determining the positions of the poles of a bar magnet (1887), and the propagation of electromagnetic waves (1893–1894). Perhaps Mascart's most important and precise work involved the determination of the electrochemical equivalent of silver (1884) and, with F. de Nerville and R. Benoit, the absolute value of the ohm (1884–1885). Once again he incorporated his researches into textbooks: first into his two-volume *Traité d'électricité statique* (Paris, 1876) and then into his two-volume *Leçons sur l'électricité et le magnétisme*, written with J. Joubert (Paris, 1882–1886; English trans. by E. Atkinson, *A Treatise on Electricity and Magnetism* [London, 1883–1888]; 2nd French ed., 1896–1897), which was the first French textbook that attempted to treat synthetically the work of Maxwell, Kelvin, and Helmholtz. Since it concentrated on applications as well as on theory, it became a standard work for engineers as well as for physicists.

Mascart's third major area of scientific activity was meteorology, which made greater demands on his time after he became director of the Bureau Central Météorologique (1878). In succeeding years he traveled widely as a member of an international committee charged with defining pressing meteorological questions and organizing international meteorological conferences. He also helped organize an international scientific polar expedition, as well as a French expedition to Cape Horn. The major goal of the latter was to map the magnetic field of the earth, a subject to which he repeatedly returned throughout the 1880's and 1890's and on which he published an extensive textbook, *Traité de magnétisme terrestre* (Paris, 1900). Concurrently, he carried out studies on atmospheric electricity (1878–1882), on the amount of carbonic acid in the air (1882), on the terrestrial variations of gravitational attraction (1882–1883) and its possible diurnal variation (1893), on the theory of cyclone formation (1887–1888), and on the mass of the atmosphere (1892).

Beginning in the late 1870's Mascart played an increasingly prominent role in national and international scientific organizations and events. Indeed, a substantial portion of his own researches stemmed directly from issues raised at the congresses he attended or presided over. Thus, for example, at the 1881 Exposition Internationale d'Électricité in Paris, it became clear that one of the most important tasks confronting physicists was to originate a universal and coherent system of electrical units. The agreement finally reached on the definitions of the volt and the ohm prompted Mascart to carry out his determinations of the electrochemical equivalent of silver and of the absolute value of the ohm (final agreement was reached in Chicago in 1893). At a number of later congresses of electricians and meteorologists, Mascart played leading organizational and official roles. As president of the general assembly of the Société Internationale des Électriciens held in Paris in May 1887, he was instrumental in creating the Laboratoire Central d'Électricité and the École Supérieure d'Électricité. He was repeatedly called upon to serve as a consultant to the French government on matters relating to national defense, public electrical and lighting facilities, and public instruction. Only in the last year of his life did he also consent to advise two private industries. His general prestige is reflected in his election in 1892 as a foreign member of the Royal Society and in his election in 1900 as vice-president of the Institution of Electrical Engineers, the first time this post was ever held by a non-British citizen.

Of medium height and of great physical stamina, Mascart was a leader who could readily get to the essence of arguments and quietly persuade others of a course of action in which he believed. An experimental physicist with a thorough command of mathematics, he could easily step outside of his laboratory and point the way to practical results in technology or policy making. He was a *grand officier* of the Légion d'Honneur, an honor—one of his many—that he valued very highly. He died after a serious operation, at the age of seventy-one.

BIBLIOGRAPHY

I. ORIGINAL WORKS. Mascart's most important papers are "Recherches sur le spectre solaire ultra-violet et sur la détermination des longueurs d'onde," in *Annales scientifiques de l'École normale supérieure*, **1** (1864), 219–262, his doctoral thesis, also published separately (Paris, 1864); "Recherches sur la détermination des longueurs d'onde," *ibid.*, **4** (1867), 7–37, the 1866 Prix Bordin memoir; "Sur les modifications qu'éprouve la lumière par suite du mouvement de la source lumineuse et du mouvement de l'observateur," *ibid.*, 2nd ser., **1** (1872), 157–214; **3** (1874), 363–420, the 1874 Grand Prix memoir; "Sur l'équivalent électrochimique de l'argent," in *Journal de physique théorique et appliquée*, 2nd ser., **3** (1884), 283–286; and "Détermination de l'ohm et de sa valeur en colonne mercurielle," in *Annales de chimie et de physique*, 4th ser., **6** (1885), 5–86, written with F. de Nerville and R. Benoit. An interesting review article of Mascart's is "The Age of Electricity," in *Report of the Board of Regents of the Smithsonian Institution* (1894), 153–172. His many textbooks—he was one of the most prolific textbook writers of all time—are cited above.

II. SECONDARY LITERATURE. See Paul Janet, "La vie et les oeuvres de E. Mascart," in *Revue générale des sciences pures et appliquées*, **20** (1909), 574–593; the obituary notices in *Nature*, **78** (1908), 446–448; and *Journal de physique théorique et appliquée*, 4th ser., **7** (1908), 745; and the portrait in Edward D. Adams, *Niagara Power*, I (Niagara Falls, N.Y., 1927), 191.

ROGER H. STUEWER

MASCHERONI, LORENZO (*b*. Castagneta, near Bergamo, Italy, 13 May 1750; *d*. Paris, France, 14 July 1800), *mathematics*.

Mascheroni was the son of Paolo Mascheroni dell'Olmo, a prosperous landowner, and Maria Ciribelli. He was ordained a priest at seventeen and at twenty was teaching rhetoric and then, from 1778, physics and mathematics at the seminary of Bergamo. His *Nuove ricerche su l'equilibrio delle vòlte* (1785) led to his appointment as professor of algebra and geometry at the University of Pavia in 1786. In 1789 and 1793 he was rector of the university and, from 1788 to 1791, was head of the Accademia degli Affidati. Mascheroni was a member of the Academy of Padua, of the Royal Academy of Mantua, and of the Società Italiana delle Scienze. In his *Adnotationes ad calculum integrale Euleri* (1790) he calculated Euler's constant, sometimes called the Euler-Mascheroni constant, to thirty-two decimal places; the figure was corrected from the twentieth decimal place by Johann von Soldner in 1809.

In 1797 Mascheroni was appointed deputy to the legislative body in Milan. Sent to Paris by a commission to study the new system of money and of weights and measures, he published his findings in 1798 but was prevented from returning home by the Austrian occupation of Milan in 1799. Also a poet, Mascheroni dedicated his *Geometria del compasso* (1797) to Napoleon in verse; his celebrated *Invito a Lesbia Cidonia* (1793) glorifies the athenaeum of Pavia. He died after a brief illness, apparently from the complications of a cold. The poet Monti mourned his death in the *Mascheroniana*.

Mascheroni's *Nuove ricerche* is a well-composed work on statics, and the *Adnotationes* shows a profound understanding of Euler's calculus. He is best known, however, for his *Geometria del compasso*, in which he shows that all plane construction problems that can be solved with ruler and compass can also be solved with compass alone. It is understood that the given and unknowns are points; in particular, a straight line is considered known if two points of it are known.

In the preface Mascheroni recounts the genesis of his work. He was moved initially by a desire to make an original contribution to elementary geometry. It occurred to him that ruler and compass could perhaps be separated, as water can be separated into two gases; but he was also assailed by doubts and fears often attendant upon research. He then chanced to reread an article on the way Graham and Bird had divided their great astronomical quadrant, and he realized that the division had been made by compass alone, although, to be sure, by trial and error. This encouraged him, and he continued his work with two purposes in mind: to give a theoretical solution to the problem of constructions with compass alone and to offer practical constructions that might be of help in making precision instruments. The second concern is shown in the brief solutions of many specific problems and in a chapter on approximate solutions.

The theoretical solution (see especially §191) depends on the solution of the following problems: (1) to bisect a given circular arc of given center; (2) to add and subtract given segments; (3) to find the fourth proportional to three given segments; (4) to find the intersection of two given lines; and (5) to find the intersection of a given line and given circle.

In 1906 August Adler applied the theory of inversion to the Mascheroni constructions. Since this theory places lines and circles on an equal footing, it sheds light on Mascheroni's problem; but the solution via inversion is not as elegant—and certainly not as simple or as brief—as Mascheroni's.

Mascheroni's theory is but a chapter in the long history of geometrical constructions by specified means. The limitation to ruler and compass occurs in book I of Euclid's *Elements*—at least the first three postulates have been called the postulates of construction; and there are even reasons to suppose that Euclid's so-called axiomatic procedure is really only an axiomatization of the Euclidean constructions.

Euclid, of course, had inherited a tradition of restricting construction to ruler and compass. Oenopides is credited by Proclus with the construction for dropping a perpendicular (*Elements* I.12) and with the method of transferring an angle (I.23). The tradition itself appears to be of religious origin (see Seidenberg, 1959, 1962).

About 980, the Arab mathematician Abu'l-Wafā' proposed using a ruler and a compass of fixed opening, and in the sixteenth century da Vinci, Dürer, Cardano, Tartaglia, and Ferrari were also concerned with this restriction. In 1672 Georg Mohr showed that all the construction problems of the first six books of the *Elements* can be done with compass alone. Lambert in 1774 discussed the problem "Given a parallelogram, construct, with ruler only, a parallel to a given line."

Poncelet, who mentions Mascheroni in this connection, showed in 1822 that in the presence of a given circle with given center, all the Euclidean constructions can be carried out with ruler alone. This has also been credited to Jacob Steiner, although he had heard of Poncelet's result, or "conjecture," as he called it. Poncelet and others also studied constructions with ruler alone; abstractly, his result is related to the axiomatic introduction of coordinates in the projective plane. Johannes Trolle Hjelmslev and others have studied the analogue of the Mascheroni constructions in non-Euclidean geometry.

The question has recently been posed whether the notion of two points being a unit apart could serve as the sole primitive notion in Euclidean plane geometry. An affirmative answer was given, based on a device of Peaucellier's for converting circular motion into rectilineal motion.

In 1928 Mohr's *Euclides danicus*, which had fallen into obscurity, was republished with a preface by Hjelmslev, according to whom Mascheroni's result had been known and systematically expounded 125 years earlier by Mohr. The justice of this judgment and the question of the independence of Mascheroni's work will now be examined.

The term "independent invention" is used in two different but often confused senses. Anthropologists use it in reference to the appearance of identical, or similar, complex phenomena in different cultures. A controversy rages, the opposing positions of which, perhaps stripped of necessary qualifications, can be put thus: According to the "independent inventionists," the appearance of identical social phenomena in different cultures (especially in New World and Old World cultures) is evidence for the view that the human mind works similarly under similar circumstances; for the "diffusionists," it is evidence of a historical connection, but not necessarily a direct one.

The historian, dealing with a single community,

uses the term in a different sense. When he says two inventions are independent, he means that each was made without direct reliance on the other. Simultaneous and independent solutions of outstanding problems that are widely published in the scholarly press are no more surprising than the simultaneous solutions by schoolboys of an assigned problem; and the simultaneous development in similar directions of a common fund of knowledge can also be expected. Even so, examples of independent identical innovations are rare and difficult to establish.

Although five centuries separate Abu'l-Wafā' and Leonardo, presumably no one will doubt that the Italians got the compass problem of a single opening from the Arabs (or, possibly, that both got it from a third source).

When the works of Mascheroni and Mohr are compared, it is apparent that the main ideas of their solutions of individual problems are in most cases quite different. In particular, this can be said for the bisection of a given segment. Moreover, the problem of bisection plays no role in Mascheroni's general solution, whereas it is central in Mohr's constructions. Still more significantly, the general problem is not formulated in Mohr's book. Thus, any suggestion of Mascheroni's direct reliance on Mohr would be quite inappropriate. Of course, the possibility cannot be excluded that Mascheroni, who explicitly denied knowledge that anyone had previously treated the matter, had heard of a partial formulation of the problem.

It appears that Hjelmslev's judgment is not entirely accurate. Mohr's book is quite remarkable and contains the basis for a simple proof of Mascheroni's result, but there is no evidence within the book itself that Mohr formulated the problem of constructions with compass alone in complete generality.

BIBLIOGRAPHY

I. Original Works. Mascheroni's mathematical works are *Nuove ricerche su l'equilibrio delle vòlte* (Bergamo, 1785); *Adnotationes ad calculum integrale Euleri* (Pavia, 1790); and *Geometria del compasso* (Pavia, 1797). A nonmathematical work is *Invito a Lesbia Cidonia* (Pavia, 1793).

II. Secondary Literature. Biographical details are presented in A. Fiamazzo, *Nuovo contributo alla biografia di L. Mascheroni*, 2 vols. (Bergamo, 1904); J. W. L. Glaisher, "History of Euler's Constant," in *Messenger of Mathematics*, **1** (1872), 25–30; G. Loria and C. Alasia, "Bibliographie de Mascheroni," in *Intermédiaire des mathématiciens*, **19** (1912), 92–94; and G. Natali, "Mascheroni," in *Enciclopedia italiana*, XXII (Rome, 1934), 496.

Adler's application of the theory of inversion to Mascheroni's constructions is presented in his *Theorie der geometrischen Konstruktionen* (Leipzig, 1906).

Support for the view that Euclid's so-called axiomatic procedure is merely an axiomatization of Euclidean constructions may be found in A. Seidenberg, "Peg and Cord in Ancient Greek Geometry," in *Scripta mathematica*, **24** (1959), 107–122; and "The Ritual Origin of Geometry," in *Archive for History of Exact Sciences*, **1** (1962), 488–527. Opposition to the above view is presented in T. L. Heath's ed. of Euclid's *Elements*, I, 124; and A. D. Steele, "Über die Rolle von Zirkel und Lineal in der griechischen Mathematik," in *Quellen und Studien zur Geschichte der Mathematik, Astronomie und Physik*, Abt. B, **3** (1936), 287–369. W. M. Kutta, "Zur Geschichte der Geometrie mit constanter Zirkelöffnung," in *Nova acta Academiae Caesarae Leopoldino Carolinae*, **71** (1898), 71–101, discusses the use of a ruler and a compass of fixed opening.

Georg Mohr's *Euclides danicus* was translated into German by J. Pál and provided with a foreword by J. Hjelmslev (Copenhagen, 1928). Lambert's work is referred to in R. C. Archibald, "Outline of the History of Mathematics," in *American Mathematical Monthly*, **56**, no. 1, supp. (1949), note 277, 98.

Poncelet's and Steiner's contributions can be found in Poncelet's *Traité des propriétés projectives des figures*, 2nd ed. (Paris, 1865), I, 181–184, 413–414; and in Steiner's *Geometrical Constructions With a Ruler*, translated by M. E. Stark and edited by R. C. Archibald (New York, 1950), p. 10.

Analogues of Mascheroni's work in non-Euclidean geometry are discussed in J. Hjelmslev, "Om et af den danske Matematiker Georg Mohr udgivet skrift *Euclides Danicus*," in *Matematisk tidsskrift*, B (1928), 1–7; and in articles by A. S. Smogorzhevsky, V. F. Rogachenko, and K. K. Mokrishchev that are reviewed in *Mathematical Reviews*, **14** (1953), 576, 1007; **15** (1954), 148; and **17** (1956), 885, 998.

The question of whether the notion of two points being a unit apart can be the sole primitive notion in Euclidean plane geometry is discussed in R. M. Robinson, "Binary Relations as Primitive Notions in Elementary Geometry," in Leon Henkin, Patrick Suppes, and Alfred Tarski, eds., *The Axiomatic Method With Special Reference to Geometry and Physics* (Amsterdam, 1959), 68–85.

A. SEIDENBERG

MASERES, FRANCIS (*b.* London, England, 15 December 1731; *d.* Reigate, Surrey, England, 19 May 1824), *mathematics*.

Maseres was the son of a physician who was descended from a family that had been forced to flee France by the revocation of the Edict of Nantes. At Clare College, Cambridge, he obtained his B.A. degree in 1752 with highest honors in both classics and mathematics. Upon receiving the M.A. and a fellowship from his college, he moved to the Temple and was later called to the bar. After spending a few years in the practice of law with little success, he was appointed attorney general for Quebec, in which post he served until 1769. His career in the new world was distinguished "by his loyalty during the American contest and his zeal for the interests of the province." Upon his return to England he was appointed cursitor baron of the Exchequer, an office which he held until his death at the age of ninety-three. During this period of his life he was generally known as Baron Maseres. In addition he was at different times deputy recorder of London and senior judge of the sheriff's court.

Three aspects of Maseres' career are noteworthy. The first is his interest in political matters, particularly in the affairs of Canada and the American colonies. Of a considerable number of essays along these lines from Maseres' pen, the following are typical: (1) "Considerations on the expediency of admitting Representatives from the American Colonies to the House of Commons" (1770); (2) "Account of Proceedings of British and other Protestants of the Province of Quebec to establish a House of Assembly" (anon.), (1775); (3) "The Canadian Freeholder, a Dialogue shewing the Sentiments of the Bulk of the Freeholders on the late Quebeck Act" (1776–1779); (4) "Select Tracts on Civil Wars in England, in the Reign of Charles I" (1815).

A second aspect of Maseres' long career is the peculiar nature of his mathematical contributions, reflecting his complete lack of creative ability together with naive individualism. For a proper perspective, one must recall that Maseres' works were written about a century and a half after Viète and Harriot had ushered in the period of "symbolic algebra." While Viète had rejected negative roots of equations, certain immediate precursors of Maseres, notably Cotes, De Moivre, Taylor, and Maclaurin, had gone far beyond this stage, as had his contemporaries on the Continent: Lambert, Lagrange, and Laplace. Despite these advances, some quirk in the young Maseres compelled him to reject that part of algebra which was not arithmetic, probably because he could not understand it, although by his own confession others might comprehend it. Unfortunately this prejudice against "negative and impossible quantities" affected much of his later work. Thus in one of his earliest publications, *Dissertation on the Use of the Negative Sign in Algebra* (1758), he writes as follows.

If any single quantity is marked either with the sign + or the sign − without affecting some other quantity ...

the mark will have no meaning or signification; thus if it be said that the square of −5, or the product of −5 into −5, is equal to +25, such an assertion must either signify no more than 5 times 5 is equal to 25 without any regard to the signs, or it must be mere nonsense or unintelligible jargon.

Curiously enough, in addition to Maseres, two other contemporary mathematicians opposed the generalized concept of positive and negative integers: William Frend, father-in-law of De Morgan, and Robert Simson. Maseres unfortunately influenced the teaching of algebra for several decades, as may be seen from textbooks of T. Manning (1796); N. Vilant (1798); and W. Ludlam (1809).

Perhaps the many publications with which he strove to bring mathematics to a much wider public were the most notable aspect of Maseres' legacy. Some were original works; others were reprints of the works of distinguished mathematicians. His original books are characterized by extreme prolixity, occasioned by his rejection of algebra, and the consequent proliferation of particular cases. For example, in the *Dissertation* alluded to above, which is virtually a treatise on elementary algebra, the discussion of basic rules and the solution of quadratic and cubic equations occupy three hundred quarto pages.

Of the reprints that Maseres made at his own expense, the most significant is the *Scriptores logarithmici* (1791–1807), six volumes devoted to the subject of logarithms, including the works of Kepler, Napier, Snellius, and others, interspersed with original tracts on related subjects. Other republications include the following: (1) *Scriptores optici* (1823), a reprint of the optical essays of James Gregory, Descartes, Schooten, Huygens, Halley, and Barrow; (2) Jakob I Bernoulli's tract on permutations and combinations; (3) Colson's translation of Agnesi's *Analytical Institutions*; (4) Hale's Latin treatise on fluxions (1800); and (5) several tracts on English history. Presumably a number of authors were indebted to Maseres for financial assistance of this sort. There can be little doubt of his sincerity and generosity, even if somewhat misplaced.

BIBLIOGRAPHY

I. ORIGINAL WORKS.

(1) *A Dissertation on the Use of the Negative Sign in Algebra: containing a demonstration of the rules usually given concerning it; and shewing how quadratic and cubic equations may be explained, without the consideration of negative roots. To which is added, as an appendix, Mr. Machin's quadrature of the circle* (London, 1758).

(2) *Elements of Plane Trigonometry ... with a disserta-*

tion on the nature and use of logarithms (London, 1760).

(3) *A proposal for establishing life-annuities in parishes for the benefit of the industrious poor* (London, 1772).

(4) *Principles of the Doctrine of Life Annuities explained in a familiar manner so as to be intelligible to persons not acquainted with the Doctrine of Chances, and accompanied with a variety of New Tables, accurately computed from observations* (London, 1783).

(5) *Scriptores Logarithmici, or a collection of several curious Tracts on the Nature and Construction of Logarithms, mentioned in Dr. Hutton's Historical Introduction to his New Edition of Sherwin's Mathematical Tables*, 6 vols. (London, 1791–1807).

(6) *The Doctrine of Permutations and Combinations, being an essential and fundamental part of the Doctrine of Chances; as it is delivered by Mr. James Bernoulli, in his excellent Treatise on the Doctrine of Chances, intitled, Ars Conjectandi, and by the celebrated Dr. John Wallis, of Oxford, in a tract intitled from the subject, and published at the end of his Treatise on Algebra; in the former of which tract is contained, a Demonstration of Sir Isaac Newton's famous Binomial Theorem, in the cases of integral powers, and of the reciprocals of integral powers. Together with some other useful mathematical tracts* (London, 1795).

(7) "An Appendix by F. Maseres," in William Frend, *The Principles of Algebra*, 2 vols. in 1 (London, 1796–1799), 211–456. Also "Observations on Mr. Raphson's method of resolving affected equations of all degrees by approximation," *ibid.*, vol. 2, 457–581.

(8) *Tracts on the Resolution of Affected Algebraick Equations by Dr. Halley's, Mr. Raphson's and Sir I. Newton's, Methods of Approximation* [*with those of W. Frend and J. Kersey*] (London, 1800).

(9) *Tracts on the Resolution of Cubick and Biquadratick Equations* (London, 1803).

II. SECONDARY LITERATURE.

(10) *The Penny Cyclopaedia of the Society for the Diffusion of Useful Knowledge*, **14** (London, 1837), 480–481.

(11) *The Gentlemen's Magazine* (June 1824); contains a list of Maseres' political writings.

(12) Moritz Cantor, *Vorlesungen über die Geschichte der Mathematik*, IV (Leipzig, 1913), 80, 86–87, 92, 149–151, 271, 302; references to some periodical articles published by Maseres.

WILLIAM L. SCHAAF

MĀSHĀ'ALLĀH (*fl.* Baghdad, 762–*ca.* 815), *astrology.*

The son of Athari (his father's name is sometimes written Abrī or Sāriya), Māshā'allāh was a Jew from Baṣra (sometimes wrongly written Miṣr [Egypt]). His name in Hebrew was Manasse (Mīshā, according to Ibn al-Qifṭī); in Persian, Yazdān Khwāst (British Museum, MS Add. 23,400). This last form is of particular interest, since Māshā'allāh was one of those early 'Abbāsid astrologers who introduced the Sassanian version of the predictive art to the Arabs; he was particularly indebted to the Pahlavī translation of Dorotheus of Sidon and to the *Zīk i Shahriyārān*, or *Royal Astronomical Tables*, issued under the patronage of Khusrau Anūshirwān in 556. He was also acquainted with some Greek material (perhaps through Arabic versions of Syriac texts) and would have acquired some knowledge of Indian science, both through the Pahlavī texts that he read and through such Indian scientists as the teacher of al-Fazārī and Kanaka, who visited the courts of al-Manṣūr and Hārūn al-Rashīd.

It is during al-Manṣūr's reign that Māshā'allāh's name first appears: he participated in the astrological deliberations that led to the decision to found Baghdad on 30 July 762 (*Journal of Near Eastern Studies*, **29** [1970], 104). Several of his works contain horoscopes that can be dated between 762 and 809 and were cast during his lifetime. Ibn al-Nadīm states that Māshā'allāh lived into the reign of al-Ma'mūn, which began in 813; but the absence of any information about his activities after 809 indicates that he probably did not live long after 813.

Māshā'allāh wrote on virtually every aspect of astrology, as the bibliography below demonstrates. His most interesting works for the historian of astronomy are his astrological history, from which we derive almost all that we know of Anūshirwān's *Royal Tables*. His brief and rather primitive *De scientia motus orbis* combines Peripatetic physics, Ptolemaic planetary theory, and astrology in such a way that, in conjunction with its use of the Syrian names of the months, one strongly suspects that it is based on the peculiar doctrines of Ḥarrān, to which al-Kindī and Abū Ma'shar were also attracted. In fact, Māshā'allāh's works are often echoed in Abū Ma'shar's; and in the list below references have been made to the corresponding items in the list of works given in the article on Abū Ma'shar in the *Dictionary of Scientific Biography* (I, 32–39).

The basis of this list of Māshā'allāh's works is that given by Ibn al-Nadīm in his *Fihrist* (G. Flügel, ed. [Leipzig 1871], 273–274); this was copied by Ibn al-Qifṭī in his *Ta'rīkh al-ḥukamā'* (J. Lippert, ed. [Leipzig, 1903], 327), although the published text stops at book V of item 9. This bibliography is supplemented from various sources, the most important of which are F. J. Carmody, *Arabic Astronomical and Astrological Sciences in Latin Translation* (Berkeley–Los Angeles, 1956), 23–38, and L. Thorndike, "The Latin Translations of Astrological Works by Messahala," in *Osiris*, **12** (1956), 49–72.

1. Ibn al-Nadīm (hereafter N) 1. *Kitāb al-mawālīd*

al-kabīr ("Great Book of Nativities"), in fourteen books. See Abū Ma'shar 4. This apparently exists in a Latin translation made by Hugo Sanctallensis and dedicated to Michael, bishop of Tarazona from 1119 to 1151; see C. H. Haskins, *Studies in the History of Mediaeval Science*, 2nd ed. (Cambridge, Mass., 1927), 76, and Carmody, item 13.

2. N 2. *Fī al-qirānāt wa 'l-adyān wa 'l-milal* ("On Conjunctions and Peoples and Religions"), in twenty-one chapters. See Abū Ma'shar 8. This work, written shortly before 813, survives in an epitome by Ibn Hibintā that is published in E. S. Kennedy and D. Pingree, *The Astrological History of Māshā'allāh* (Cambridge, Mass., 1971), 1–38. For a different interpretation of the astronomy upon which the casting of the horoscopes in this work is based, see J. J. Burckhardt and B. L. van der Waerden, "Das astronomische System der persischen Tafeln I," in *Centaurus*, **13** (1968), 1–28.

3. N 3. *Kitāb maṭraḥ al-shu'ā'* ("Book of the Projection of Ray[s]"). This lost work is referred to by Abū Ma'shar, as quoted by his pupil Abū Sa'īd Shādhān in his *Mudhākarāt* (*Catalogus codicum astrologorum Graecorum*, XI, pt. 1 [Brussels, 1932], 171–172); see also al-Bīrūnī, *Rasā'il* (Hyderabad–Deccan, 1948), pt. 3, 80.

4. N 4. *Kitāb al-ma'ānī* ("Book of Definitions"). Māshā'allāh refers to this nonextant work in 16, below (Kennedy and Pingree, *The Astrological History*, p. 130).

5. N 5. *Kitāb ṣana'at al-asṭurlāb wa 'l-'amal bihā* ("Book of the Construction of an Astrolabe and Its Use"). This survives only in a Latin translation (see Carmody, item 1). It was first published by G. Reisch, *Margarita philosophica nova* (Strasbourg, 1512; repr. Strasbourg, 1515; O. Finé, ed., Basel, 1535; repr. Basel, 1583; and trans. into Italian by G. P. Gallucci [Venice, 1599]). The third part of the treatise, on the use of the astrolabe, was edited by W. W. Skeat, *A Treatise on the Astrolabe; Addressed to His Son Lowys by Geoffrey Chaucer A.D. 1391* (London, 1872; repr. London, 1905), 88–104. The best edition now is by R. T. Gunther, *Early Science in Oxford*, V (Oxford, 1929), 195–231; for the catalog of stars see P. Kunitzsch, *Typen von Sternverzeichnissen in astronomischen Handschriften des zehnten bis vierzehnten Jahrhunderts* (Wiesbaden, 1966), 47–50. Not from Māshā'allāh's treatise are the fragment published by J. M. Millás Vallicrosa, *Las traducciones orientales en los manuscritos de la Biblioteca catedral de Toledo* (Madrid, 1942), 313–321 (see Kunitzsch, pp. 23–30), and the first table in Gunther (see Kunitzsch, pp. 51–58, who argues that this catalog is a product of the school of al-Majrīṭī).

6. N 6. *Kitāb dhāt al-ḥalaq* ("Book of the Armillary Sphere"). Nothing more is known of this treatise.

7. N 7. *Kitāb al-amṭār wa 'l-riyāḥ* ("Book of Rains and Winds"). See Abū Ma'shar 34. The Arabic text has been published by G. Levi della Vida, "Un opuscolo astrologico di Mâsâ'allâh," in *Rivista degli studi orientali,* **14** (1933–1934), 270–281. The Latin translation by Drogon [?] was edited by M. A. Šangin, *Catalogus codicum astrologorum Graecorum,* XII (Brussels, 1936), 210–216; see Carmody, item 15, and Thorndike, pp. 67–68.

8. N 8. *Kitāb al-sahmayn* ("Book of the Two Lots [of Fortune and of the Demon]"). See Abū Ma'shar 14.

9. N 9. *Kitāb al-ma'rūf bi 'l-sābi' wa 'l-'ishrīn* ("The Book Known as the Twenty-seventh"), in six books: I, "On the Beginnings of Works"; II, "On the Overthrow of the Government"; III, "On Interrogations"; IV, "On Aspects"; V, "On Occurrences"; VI, "On the *tasyīrāt* ('astrological cycles') of the Luminaries and What They Indicate." This work is probably the source of many excerpts from Māshā'allāh found in the Arabic compendiums of al-Ṣaymarī, al-Qaṣrānī, and others, as well as in the manuscript Laleli 2122 at the Süleymaniye Library in Istanbul. It may also be the source of the following translations:

a. *De cogitationibus (De interrogationibus).* Published by Bonetus Locatellus (Venice, 1493; repr. Venice, 1519) and by I. Heller (Nuremberg, 1549); Carmody, item 5 (who mentions a French translation of the Latin), and Thorndike, pp. 53–54 and 56–62. There is also a Hebrew translation of a work on interrogations (M. Steinschneider, *Die hebräischen Übersetzungen des Mittelalters und die Juden als Dolmetscher* [Berlin, 1893], 600–602), and a *Kitāb al-Masā'il* ("Book of Interrogations") was known to Ḥājjī Khalīfa *(Lexicon bibliographicum et encyclopaedicum,* G. Flügel, ed., VII [Leipzig, 1858], 386).

b. *De occultis,* which survives in two versions; see Carmody, items 9 and 10, and Thorndike, pp. 54–56.

c. *Liber iudiciorum;* see Carmody, item 14.

d. *De interpretationibus,* edited by I. Heller (Nuremberg, 1549). To it may also belong the *De testimoniis lune, De stationibus planetarum,* and *De electionibus horarum* (see Carmody, items 16, 17, and 18), if they are truly by Māshā'allāh.

10. N 10. *Kitāb al-ḥurūf* ("Book of Letters").

11. N 11. *Kitāb al-sulṭān* ("Book of Government").

12. N 12. *Kitāb al-safar* ("Book of Travel").

13. N 13. *Kitāb al-as'ār* ("Book of Prices"). This short treatise, which contains a horoscope dated 24 June 773 (Kennedy and Pingree, *The Astrological History,* p. 185), is extant in Bodleian MS Marsh 618 and Escorial MS Ar. 938. The *Liber super annona* or *De mercibus* may be the Latin version; see Carmody, item 11, and Thorndike, pp. 68–69.

14. N 14. *Kitāb al-mawālīd* ("Book of Nativities"). This work, based largely on Dorotheus of Sidon with some additions from a Byzantine source of the sixth century, and itself the basis of the main work of Māshā'allāh's pupil al-Khayyāṭ, survives only in Latin; see Carmody, item 12. It has been edited by Kennedy and Pingree, *The Astrological History,* pp. 145–174.

15. N 15. *Kitāb taḥwīl sinī al-mawālīd* ("Book of the Revolution[s] of the Years of Nativities"). See Abū Ma'shar 19. This work is lost, but many fragments of it can be recovered from the *Majmū' aqāwīl al-ḥukamā'* of al-Dāmaghānī.

16. N 16. *Kitāb al-duwal wa 'l-milal* ("Book of Dynasties and Religions"). This is probably identical with the *Fī qiyām al-khulafā' wa ma'rifat qiyām kull malik* ("On the Installation of the Caliphs and the Knowledge of the Installation of Every King"), which was written during the reign of Hārūn al-Rashīd and is translated in Kennedy and Pingree, *The Astrological History,* pp. 129–143.

17. N 17. *Kitāb al-ḥukm 'alā 'l-ijtimā'āt wa 'l-istiqbālāt* ("Book of Judgment[s] According to the Conjunctions and Oppositions [of the Sun and Moon]").

18. N 18. *Al-Kitāb al-murdī* ("The Pleasing Book").

19. N 19. *Kitāb al-ṣuwar wa 'l-ḥukm 'alāyhā* ("Book of Constellations and Judgment[s] According to Them"). See Abū Ma'shar 17 and 18. This may be the *Kitāb al-amthāl* ("Book of Images") in Ayasofya Library, Istanbul, MS 2672.

20. *De revolutionibus annorum mundi,* in forty-six chapters. This Latin translation of a lost Arabic original was published by Bonetus Locatellus (Venice, 1493, 1519) and by I. Heller (Nuremberg, 1549); see Carmody, item 2, and Thorndike, pp. 66–67.

21. *Epistola de rebus eclipsium* or *De ratione circuli et stellarum,* in twelve chapters. This Latin translation by John of Seville was published by Bonetus Locatellus (Venice, 1493, 1519), by I. Heller (Nuremberg, 1549), and by N. Pruckner, *Iulii Firmici Materni . . . Astronomicōn libri VIII* (Basel, 1533; repr. Basel, 1551), pt. 2, 115–118; see Carmody, item 7 (who mentions a French translation of the Latin), and Thorndike, pp. 62–66. A Hebrew translation made by Ibn Ezra in 1148 was commented on by Abraham Yagel at the end of the sixteenth century (see M. Steinschneider, *Die hebräischen Übersetzungen,* pp. 602–603). Abraham's Hebrew was translated into English by B. Goldstein, "The Book on Eclipses of Masha'allah," in *Physis* (Florence), **6** (1964), 205–213.

22. *Super significationibus planetarum in nativitate,*

in twenty-six chapters. This Latin translation by John of Seville [?] of a lost Arabic original based largely on Dorotheus of Sidon was published by I. Heller (Nuremberg, 1549); see Carmody, item 4.

23. *De septem planetis*, in nine chapters, is sometimes ascribed to Jirjis; see Carmody, item 6.

24. *De receptione*, in twelve chapters, is a Latin translation by John of Seville of a lost Arabic original that contained horoscopes dated between 13 February 791 and 30 November 794 (Kennedy and Pingree, *The Astrological History*, pp. 175–178; E. S. Kennedy, "A Horoscope of Messehalla in the Chaucer Equatorium Manuscript," in *Speculum*, **34** [1959], 629–630). It was published by Bonetus Locatellus (Venice, 1493, 1519) and by I. Heller (Nuremberg, 1549); see Carmody, item 3 (who mentions a French translation of the Latin), and Thorndike, pp. 50–53.

25. *De scientia motus orbis* or *De elementis et orbibus coelestibus*, in twenty-seven chapters. This important Latin translation by Gerard of Cremona of the lost Arabic original of this exposition of apparently Harranian doctrines was published by I. Stabius (Nuremberg, 1504) and by I. Heller (Nuremberg, 1549); see Carmody, item 8. There is an Irish adaptation edited by M. Power, *An Irish Astronomical Tract* (London, 1914).

26. *De electionibus*. This text, which quotes Dorotheus, is ascribed to Māshā'allāh and Ptolemy but is probably by neither. It was published by P. Liechtenstein (Venice, 1509) and by T. Rees (Paris, 1513).

27. *Mafātīḥ al-qaḍāʾ* ("The Keys of Judgments"). The Arabic original of this treatise is lost, but there is a manuscript of a Persian translation (see C. A. Storey, *Persian Literature*, II, pt. 1 [London, 1958], 38–39, who doubts the attribution to Māshā'allāh) and a Latin epitome of a *Septem claves* of Māshā'allāh, edited by M. A. Šangin, "Latinskaya parafraza iz utrachennogo sochinenia Mashallaha 'Semi Kluchey'" ("A Latin Paraphrase From Māshā'allāh's Lost Work 'The Keys of Judgment'"), in *Zapiski kollegii vostokovedov*, **5** (1930), 235–242.

28. *Aḥkām al-qirānāt wa 'l-mumāzajāt* ("Judgments of Conjunctions and Mixtures"). This lost work is mentioned by Ḥājjī Khalīfa, I, 175.

BIBLIOGRAPHY

Many further fragments of Māshā'allāh's voluminous writings can be found in Arabic texts (such as those by Abū Maʿshar, al-Hāshimī, and al-Bīrūnī) and in Greek (particularly in Vaticanus Graecus 1056; see *Catalogus codicum astrologorum Graecorum*, I [Brussels, 1898], 81–82, and Kennedy and Pingree, *The Astrological History*,

pp. 178–184). Until this material has been examined, it cannot be said that any complete survey of Māshā'allāh's work exists. Apart from the present attempt to fill the gap, the only previous survey—besides the works cited in the body of this article—is H. Suter, *Die Mathematiker und Astronomen der Araber und ihre Werke* (Leipzig, 1900), 5–6.

DAVID PINGREE

MASKELYNE, NEVIL (*b*. London, England, 6 October 1732; *d*. Greenwich, England, 9 February 1811), *astronomy*.

The last male heir of an ancient Wiltshire family that probably originated in Normandy, Maskelyne was educated at Westminster School, where he received a good grounding in the classics. During his vacations, he was tutored in writing and arithmetic. He enjoyed reading and was fascinated by optics and astronomy, through which he was led to the study of mathematics as the indispensable tool for the proper understanding of these related sciences. Having mastered in a few months the elements of geometry and algebra, he then applied this knowledge to other aspects of natural philosophy, particularly mechanics, pneumatics, and hydrostatics. He furthered these studies at Trinity College, Cambridge, graduating in 1754 as seventh wrangler. After being ordained in 1755, he accepted a curacy near London; there, rather than seeking a livelihood in the Anglican Church, he devoted many of his leisure hours to assisting the astronomer royal, James Bradley, in computing tables of refraction. He was elected a fellow of Trinity College, Cambridge, in 1758 and of the Royal Society the following year.

On Bradley's recommendation, Maskelyne was sent in 1761 by the British government to the island of St. Helena to observe the transit of Venus, from which the distance of the earth from the sun can be deduced. Unfortunately, clouds prevented his observing the time of emersion of this planet; and an error in his observations of the meridian zenith distance of the bright star Sirius—due to a fault in suspending his zenith sector—prevented him from testing the supposition that it exhibited a small but measurable parallax.

Maskelyne was more successful with observations made during the voyage for the purpose of investigating the reliability of the lunar distance method of determining longitude at sea. The lunar tables that he employed were those of Tobias Mayer, transmitted to London in 1755 to support his application for a large parliamentary bounty offered to "such person or persons as shall discover the longitude at sea." The instrument used for making the necessary angular measurements of lunar distances and celestial altitudes was a reflecting quadrant of the type invented by John Hadley in 1731 and already in widespread use among seamen. In his book *The British Mariners Guide* (London, 1763) he gave detailed instructions on how to use and rectify this instrument, and examples of how to apply the lunar tables in calculating the longitude.

A prime objective of Maskelyne's second voyage, to Bridgetown in Barbados in 1764, was to assess the accuracy of the rival chronometer method of longitude determination, championed by John Harrison, before a decision could be made on its claim for a parliamentary award; this necessitated Maskelyne's making astronomical observations to establish the longitude of Barbados. He was also ordered by the Board of Longitude to investigate the comparative accuracy of two additional means of longitude determination based upon observations of the satellites of Jupiter and on occultations of stars by the moon. He was further entrusted with the testing of a marine chair designed by a certain Mr. Christopher Irwin, which he found to be quite impracticable for assisting observations made at sea.

At a memorable meeting of the Board of Longitude (9 February 1765), at which the sums to be awarded to Harrison and Mayer were specified, Maskelyne, who had just been appointed astronomer royal, arranged for four naval officers to be in attendance to testify to the general utility of the lunar-distance method for finding longitude at sea to within 1° or 60 miles. He also presented a memorial in which he proposed that the practical application of the method could be facilitated by the preparation of a nautical ephemeris with auxiliary tables and explanations. These plans crystallized less than two years later with the publication of the *Nautical Almanac* for 1767. Maskelyne also assumed the responsibility of supervising the printing and publishing of Mayer's lunar theory (1767) and his solar and lunar tables (1770), and he prepared "Requisite Tables" (1767) for eliminating the effects of astronomical refraction and parallax from the observed lunar distances. He continued to superintend the ever-increasing work of the computers and comparers of the annual *Nautical Almanac* until his death more than forty years later.

This periodical is undoubtedly Maskelyne's greatest monument to astronomical science. It is still a useful navigational aid even though the lunar distance tables themselves became obsolete by the beginning of the twentieth century, mainly as a result of the exceptionally high degree of reliability of chronometers.

Among Maskelyne's onerous duties at the Royal Observatory was to assess the performances of a considerable number of chronometers submitted for an official trial by other pioneers of watchmaking—Thomas Mudge, John Arnold, Josiah Emery, and Thomas Earnshaw. The controversial results of these comparative tests, which stemmed from an ambiguity in defining "accuracy" and "error" in the case of chronometers, had the desirable effect of establishing a consistent system of rating and the introduction in 1823 of "trial-" or "test-numbers," which were modified by George Airy in 1840 to a system that is still used.

In a famous experiment of 1774 Maskelyne attempted to determine the earth's density from measurements of the deviation of a plumb line produced by the gravitational attraction of Mt. Schiehallion, in Scotland. By observing the slight difference in the zenith distances of certain stars at two observing stations on the north and south faces of the mountain, and making due allowance for the effect of their latitude difference by means of geodetic measurements, Maskelyne identified the residual displacement of 11.7" with the sum of the deviations in the direction of the vertical to the earth's surface on each side of this conveniently symmetrical mountain. This was the first convincing experimental demonstration of the universality of gravitation, in the sense that it operates not only between the bodies of the solar system but also between the elements of matter of which each body is composed. With the aid of his friend Charles Hutton and John Playfair, who estimated the density of the rocks and total mass of that mountain relative to the mass of the earth, Maskelyne concluded the mean density of the earth to be between 4.867 and 4.559 times that of water, a result that compares quite well with the presently accepted value of 5.52.

BIBLIOGRAPHY

No definitive biography of Maskelyne has been written, but accounts of his life and work are to be found in standard encyclopedic works such as *Encyclopaedia Britannica*, 8th ed. (1857), XIV, 334–336; and *Dictionary of National Biography*, rev. ed., XII, 1299–1301; from which references to other biographical sources may be obtained. Precise references to Maskelyne's contributions to the *Philosophical Transactions of the Royal Society* between 1760 and 1808 and to his other publications are in D. W. Dewhirst's new ed. of J. C. Houzeau and A. Lancaster, *General Bibliography of Astronomy to the Year 1880*, 2 vols. (London, 1964). No fewer than 168 batches of Maskelyne's papers are preserved in the records room of the Royal Greenwich Observatory. Photocopies of some other unpublished writings, still in the possession of one of his heirs, are in the MS department of the National Maritime Museum, London (Reference PGR/38/1). Other repositories of his correspondence include the libraries of the Royal Society of London, the British Museum, the Fitzwilliam Museum and university library in Cambridge, the Bodleian Library in Oxford, the university library in Göttingen, and the private archives of the earl of Bute at Rothesay, Scotland.

ERIC G. FORBES

MASON, CHARLES (b. Wherr, Gloucestershire, England, baptized 1 May 1728; d. Philadelphia, Pennsylvania, 25 October 1786), astronomy, geodesy.

Little is known of Mason's early life. He was one of at least four children of Charles Mason, and it is likely that he received his early education at Tetbury Grammar School. He may have received additional tuition from Robert Stratford, a schoolmaster and mathematician at Sapperton, a village near Wherr. At any rate, he seems to have acquired a considerable competence in plane and spherical trigonometry, practical and spherical astronomy, and geodesy. In 1756 he joined the staff of the Royal Observatory as assistant to the director, James Bradley. Mason held this post until 1760, and may be assumed to have aided Bradley in his extensive stellar, solar, planetary, and lunar astrometric work.

In 1761 Mason joined forces with an associate, Jeremiah Dixon, to observe the transit of Venus of 6 June. Their expedition was sponsored by the Royal Society as part of an international effort to establish the solar parallax (measure of the distance to the sun); they were to make observations at Bencoolen, Sumatra, but were delayed by an attack from a French frigate and actually observed the transit at the Cape of Good Hope. On their return voyage they stopped at St. Helena, where another party had observed the transit under the direction of Nevil Maskelyne, and assisted in gathering tidal and gravitational data.

In 1763 Mason and Dixon were named by Nathaniel Bliss, astronomer royal, to go to the American colonies to resolve the question of the common boundaries of Pennsylvania, Maryland, Delaware, and Virginia. (The Penn and Calvert families had disputed such boundaries for some eighty years, and it was perhaps at their request that Bliss made his recommendation.) Mason and Dixon arrived in Philadelphia on 15 November and immediately set about their task. The best-known lines of the demarcation are those that extend from east to west, mostly along the southern border of Pennsylvania, for a combined distance of 244.483 miles westward from the west shore of the Delaware River.

While in America Mason and Dixon also undertook a commission from the Royal Society to measure a degree of latitude. They chose the latitude of 39°11′56.5″ as the mid-point of their arc and determined the value of one degree on it as 68.7291 miles (according to the Clarke spheroid of 1866, the value is actually 68.9833 miles). Cavendish reviewed their result and concluded that the normal to the geoid had been vitiated by topographical and subsurface anomalies in mass distribution. Mason and Dixon also conducted studies of the variation of gravity with latitude before they left America for England on 11 September 1768.

Mason returned to England in time to take part in another Royal Society expedition to observe a transit of Venus. The transit occurred on 3 June 1769; Mason was in charge of the station at Cavan, County Donegal, Ireland. Despite cloud conditions, he was able to record the times of the first external contact and the first internal contact; he reported his results in a forty-three-page paper read to the Royal Society on 7 November 1770.

During this period the Royal Society also was concerned with the problem of measuring the mass and density of the earth. A procedure earlier outlined by Newton pointed out that the presence of a topographical protuberance would vitiate the direction of the vertical and therefore affect latitude observations. If a mountain of suitable shape, preferably hemispherical or conical, could be found, it would only be necessary to determine its mass by borings and topographical studies and then observe the latitude on each side of it along a meridian and finally determine the distance between the two stations by methods of plane or geodetic surveying. The mass and density of the earth would then follow from a simple trigonometrical relationship. In implementing this plan Mason, after studying the topography of northern England and Scotland, chose Mt. Schiehallion in Perthshire as most nearly answering Newton's specifications. Maskelyne then carried out the proposed research.

Mason also worked with the Commissioners of Longitude, particularly in connection with the Nautical Almanac of 1773, for which he prepared a catalog of the positions of 387 fixed stars from observations made by Bradley and precessed to the epoch of 1760. In 1778 he published "Lunar Tables in Longitude and Latitude According to the Newtonian Laws of Gravity"; he finished an improved set of these tables at Sapperton in 1780. Mason's work was cited in each annual edition of the *Nautical Almanac* for some thirty years; between 1770 and 1781 the commissioners paid him £1,317. Although there is little documentation of Mason's activities from 1781 until 1786, it is reasonable to suppose that he continued to work with the Royal Observatory and the Commissioners of Longitude.

In 1786 Mason returned to the United States, accompanied by his second wife and eight children. Although he held no particular commission, it may be surmised that he expected that considerable geodetic work would be necessary in establishing the boundaries of the states then being incorporated into the Union. During the Atlantic crossing he became ill, however; he never recovered and died in Philadelphia. He was interred in Christ Church cemetery, where Benjamin Franklin lies. He had been a member of the American Society (now the American Philosophical Society) since 1768. At his death Mason left all his manuscripts and scientific papers to John Ewing, provost of the University of Pennsylvania, who was himself a distinguished mathematician and astronomer.

BIBLIOGRAPHY

I. ORIGINAL WORKS. The whereabouts of Mason's MSS and papers is not known today. His publications include "Observations Made at the Cape of Good Hope," in *Philosophical Transactions of the Royal Society*, **52** (1762), 378–394, written with Jeremiah Dixon; and "Astronomical Observations Made at Cavan ...," *ibid.*, **60** (1770), 454–497.

II. SECONDARY LITERATURE. On Mason and his work see T. D. Cope, "The First Scientific Expedition of Charles Mason and Jeremiah Dixon," in *Pennsylvania History*, **12**, no. 1 (1945), 3–12; "Mason and Dixon—English Men of Science," in *Delaware Notes*, 22nd ser. (1949), 13–32; T. D. Cope and H. W. Robinson, "Charles Mason, Jeremiah Dixon and the Royal Society," in *Notes and Records. Royal Society of London*, **9** (1951), 55–58, 78; A. Hughlett Mason, "The Journal of Charles Mason and Jeremiah Dixon Transcribed From the Original in the U.S. National Archives ...," in *Memoirs of the American Philosophical Society*, **76** (1969), 25; and H. W. Robinson, "A Note on Charles Mason's Ancestry and His Family," in *Proceedings of the American Philosophical Society*, **93**, no. 2 (1949), 134–136.

A. HUGHLETT MASON

MASSA, NICCOLO (*b.* Venice, Italy, 1485; *d.* Venice, 1569), *medicine.*

Massa, a medical graduate of Padua, practiced medicine in Venice, where he was known chiefly as clinician and syphilologist. Owing to his belief that the physician ought to have a sound knowledge of anatomy, he undertook a program of dissection and investigation of the human body at least from 1526 to 1533, producing an unillustrated anatomical treatise entitled *Liber introductorius anatomiae* (Venice, 1536), which remained the best brief textbook of the subject for a generation.

The *Liber introductorius anatomiae* is arranged according to the medieval pattern of anatomy established by Mondino, that is, an approach to the subject derived from the necessity of dissecting the most perishable organs first. It is based partly on the work of earlier writers, especially Galen, and partly on its author's own dissections carried out in the convent of SS. John and Paul (fols. 26r, 56v) and the hospital of SS. Peter and Paul (fols. 10r, 26r) in Venice as well as others performed on the bodies of stillborn infants (fols. 7v, 43v).

Since Massa was over fifty years old when he composed his book, its text does not reflect to any large degree the alterations in favor of classical anatomical terminology that the humanists were introducing at the time. Nevertheless he was the first to employ the term *panniculus carnosus* (fol. 8r). Of his descriptions it may be said that he provided a relatively good account of the abdominal wall, noted the tendinous intersections of the rectus abdominis muscle (fol. 11v), and referred very briefly to the inguinal canal (fol. 13r). He described the intestinal canal with some accuracy (fols. 18v–23r), including an account of the appendix, which he thought tended to disappear with maturity (fols. 20v–21r). He mentioned the variation in size of the spleen in ailments involving that organ, declaring that he had observed it "very large and extending into the lower parts" (fol. 26v). He declared the liver to be divided usually into five lobes, although sometimes finding it undivided or divided into only two parts (fol. 27r), but asserted that the portal vein is always divided into five main branches (fol. 27r). In his description of the kidneys he proved by blowing through a reed that the cavity of the renal veins is not continuous with that of the sinus of the kidney (fol. 31v). This contribution was important, even though the fact had been alluded to earlier by Berengario da Carpi, since the kidneys were usually thought to be filters straining urine out of blood. Massa held that the right kidney is normally higher than the left, although he declared that he had twice seen the reverse (fol. 32r). He briefly noted the difference in the levels of origin of the spermatic vessels on the two sides (fol. 33r)—a fact known to Mondino—and made brief reference to the prostate (fol. 34r), the first reference to that organ. He denied the belief in the seven-celled uterus, declaring the uterus to contain only a single cavity (fol. 45r).

Massa gave credence to the existence of the *rete mirabile* in the human brain, but admitted that there was disagreement on this matter, and wrote "some dare to say that this *rete* is a figment of Galen . . . but I myself have often seen and demonstrated it . . . though sometimes I have found it to be very small" (fols. 89v–90r). Generally speaking, Massa's long description of the brain was traditional and unsatisfactory. On the other hand Massa was the first after Berengario da Carpi to refer to the malleus and incus, although his short statement refers to both ossicles under the word *malleolus* (fols. 93r–v). Thus he left to Vesalius the opportunity of providing better and more appropriate names.

Within its limits, and despite a considerable residue of Galenic anatomy, the *Liber introductorius anatomiae* contains shrewd observations often tempered by curious errors. For examples of the latter, it describes certain nonexistent cardiac valves (fol. 55v), and Massa asserted that he had sometimes found a third ventricle in the heart (fol. 56r). Despite its merits the book is distinctly pre-Vesalian. The reissue of the book in 1559 was unsuccessful.

BIBLIOGRAPHY

In addition to a few autobiographical notes in the *Liber introductorius anatomiae*, what further information there is on the life of Massa is in Luigi Nardo, "Dell'anatomia in Venezia," in *Ateneo Veneto*, fasc. 2–3 (1897), with additional notes by Cesare Musatti. The full title of Massa's anatomical treatise is *Liber introductorius anatomiae, sive dissectionis corporis humani, nunc primum ab ipso auctore in lucem aeditus, in quo quamplurima membra, operationes, & utilitates tam ab antiquis, quam a modernis praetermissa manifestantur. Venetiis in vico sancti Moysi, aput* [sic] *signum archangeli Raphaelis, in aedibus Francisci Bindoni, ac Maphei Pasini, socios* [sic], *accuratissimae* [sic] *impressum. Mense Novembri, MDXXXVI.* The reissue of 1559 was also published in Venice, *Ex officina Stellae Jordani Zilleti.*

C. D. O'MALLEY

MASSON, ANTOINE-PHILIBERT (*b.* Auxonne, France, 22 or 23 August 1806; *d.* Paris, France, 1 December 1860), *physics.*

Having completed a bachelor of arts program in Nancy, Antoine Masson subsequently received his bachelor of sciences degree from the École Normale Supérieure in Paris. In 1831, after a year of teaching

mathematics at Montpellier, he moved to Caen, where he taught physical sciences at the Collège Royal until 1839. Unaware of the discoveries of Joseph Henry or William Jenkins, Masson in 1834 observed independently the self-induction of a voltaic circuit. Three years later he described his investigation of this phenomenon and, utilizing a toothed wheel as an interrupter, demonstrated the tetanic effect of a series of rapidly repeated self-induced currents. Employing a similar toothed wheel to interrupt an independent primary circuit, Masson constructed some of the earliest induction coils. In 1841, together with Louis Breguet, he described a high-tension induction coil of the type Ruhmkorff subsequently perfected. In the interim, having in 1836 successfully defended a doctoral thesis elaborating Ampère's work in electrodynamics, Masson had returned to Paris and from 1841 taught physics at the Lycée Louis-le-Grand and at the École Centrale.

Masson's subsequent researches spanned the breadth of contemporary physics and continued unabated until his death in 1860. To clarify the relations among heat, light, and electricity, between 1844 and 1854 he conducted an intensive investigation of the spark produced by electrical discharges through various media. In conjunction with L. Courtépée and J.-C. Jamin, he also examined during these years the absorption of radiant heat and light by different substances, confirming the conclusions of Melloni. In addition, he investigated aspects of electrical telegraphy, acoustics, the elasticity of solid bodies, and the discharge of induction coils through partial vacuums, as well as related chemical and physical problems. He was a member of the Académie des Sciences, Arts, et Belles-Lettres of Caen, the Société Royale of Liège, and the Société Philomatique in Paris. He received the Légion d'Honneur and, although never elected, was nominated in 1851 and 1860 to the Académie des Sciences of Paris.

BIBLIOGRAPHY

I. ORIGINAL WORKS. Accounts of Masson's researches appeared almost annually between 1835 and 1858, for the most part in the *Annales de chimie et de physique* or the *Comptes rendus . . . de l'Académie des sciences*. Although Poggendorff, II, col. 75, lists most of these papers, see also Masson's own *Notice sur les travaux scientifiques de M. A. Masson* (Paris, 1851). Several of these papers were also reprinted separately. Other published works include *Théorie physique et mathématique des phénomènes électrodynamiques et du magnétisme* (Paris, 1838); *École centrale des arts et manufactures. Cours de physique générale* [1841–1842, 1843–1844], 2 vols. (Paris, n.d.); *Mémoire sur l'étin-*

celle électrique (Haarlem, 1854); and *Nouvelle théorie de la voix* (Paris, 1858).

II. SECONDARY LITERATURE. Although briefly mentioned in most of the standard secondary sources, the only extended discussion of Masson is Louis Jovignot, "Un grand savant bourguignon du XIXᵉ siècle: Antoine Masson," in *Revue d'histoire des sciences et de leurs applications*, **1** (1948), 337–350.

DAVID W. CORSON

MAST, SAMUEL OTTMAR (*b.* Ann Arbor, Michigan, 3 October 1871; *d.* Baltimore, Maryland, 3 February 1947), *botany*.

Mast attended elementary school in his home state and received a teaching certificate from the State Normal College in Ypsilanti, Michigan, in 1897. He received a B.Sc. from the University of Michigan in 1899, and in 1906 he obtained his Ph.D. in zoology from Harvard. After graduation from Michigan Mast started an uninterrupted teaching career, which lasted forty-three years. From 1899 to 1908 he was professor of biology and botany at Hope College, Holland, Michigan, and then associate professor of biology and professor of botany at Goucher College, Baltimore, Maryland, where he remained until 1911. He then joined the faculty of Johns Hopkins University and became the director of the zoological laboratory in 1938, when Jennings retired. Mast published his book *Light and the Behavior of Organisms* in 1911, and most of his later research was on the reactions of lower organisms to stimuli, especially light. His contractile-hydraulic theory of amoeboid movement, proposed in 1926, continues to be basic in the explanation of this phenomenon. His careful study of the metabolism of the colorless flagellate *Chilomonas paramecium* (1933), showing its ability to synthesize organic compounds in the dark, is also a classic in the field.

During his long working life, Mast published almost 200 papers and books. Besides being a member of many scientific societies, he was awarded the Cartwright Prize by Columbia University in 1909. The State Normal College at Ypsilanti awarded him an honorary M.Pd. in 1912, and the University of Michigan the Sc.D. in 1941, a year before he retired.

BIBLIOGRAPHY

I. ORIGINAL WORKS. Among Mast's important works are "Structure, Movement, Locomotion and Stimulation in *Amoeba*," in *Journal of Morphology*, **4** (1926), 347–425, written with D. M. Pace; and "Synthesis From Inorganic Compounds of Starch, Fats, Proteins and Protoplasm in the Colorless Animal *Chilomonas paramecium*," in *Protoplasma*, **20** (1933), 326–358.

II. SECONDARY LITERATURE. See D. H. Wenrich, "Some American Pioneers in Protozoology," in *Journal of Protozoology*, **3** (1956), 17; and the obituary notice by C. G. Wilber, "Samuel O. Mast (1871–1947)," in *Transactions of the American Microscopical Society*, **67** (1948), 82–83.

ENRIQUE BELTRÁN

MÄSTLIN, MICHAEL (*b.* Göppingen, Germany, 30 September 1550; *d.* Tübingen, Germany, 20 October 1631), *astronomy*.

Earthshine was correctly explained for the first time in print by Mästlin.[1] He matriculated at Tübingen University on 3 December 1568 and received the B.A. (30 March 1569) and M.A. (1 August 1571) before entering the theological course.[2] To his reprint of Erasmus Reinhold's *Prussian Tables*, Mästlin added a brief appendix in 1571, and his 1573 essay on the nova of 1572 was impressive enough to be incorporated in its entirety into the *Progymnasmata* of Tycho Brahe.[3] Lacking observational instruments, Mästlin stretched a thread through the nova and two pairs of previously known stars. He took the celestial longitude and latitude of these four fixed points directly from the star catalog of Copernicus, of whose *Revolutions* he had acquired a copy in 1570. (Mästlin's heavily annotated copy of the *Revolutions* is preserved at Schaffhausen, Switzerland.) The intersection of the arcs of the great circles passing through the two pairs of his reference stars gave Mästlin the position of the 1572 nova, and its nondisplacement from them convinced him that it was indeed a new star; thus, coming-into-being could occur in heaven as well as on earth, contrary to the traditional dogma.

Having served as the assistant to Philipp Apian (1531–1589), professor of mathematics at Tübingen, Mästlin replaced him when Apian went on leave in 1575. This arrangement was not renewed, however, for on 24 October 1576 Mästlin was appointed to a Lutheran pastorate in Backnang. In April 1577 he married Margaret Grüninger, who bore him three daughters and three sons.[4] Ludwig became a physician after enrolling at Tübingen on 26 February 1594 and obtaining the B.A. on 5 April 1598 and the M.A. on 13 February 1600.[5] In that year Michael, Jr., a painter, ran away from home and was later said to be hiding among the Jesuits.[6] Margaret married Tobias Olbert (M.A., Tübingen, 15 February 1598) on 7 December 1602; Anna Maria also married a Lutheran clergyman, Johann Wolfgang Mögling;

and Sabina married Burckhardt Rümelin, a Tübingen law student in 1606 and court attorney in 1624.[7]

Mästlin was designated professor of mathematics at Heidelberg University on 19 November 1580.[8] In discussing that year's comet he declared that the unsoundness of the Aristotelian cosmology had been revealed to him by three great celestial events occurring over a period of eight years: the 1572 nova and the comets of 1577 and 1580.

Having failed to detect any perceptible parallax in the comet of 1577, Mästlin concluded that it was not a sublunar but, rather, a supralunar body. Remarking that "according to Abū Ma'shar, who flourished about A.D. 844, a comet was seen above the sphere of Venus," he asked, "What would have been the physical cause of this [phenomenon], if we are to believe that comets have no place other than the region of the [four] elements?"[9] Rejecting the conventional classification of comets as meteorological phenomena, he located the comet of 1577 in the sphere of Venus.

Nevertheless, in his *Epitome of Astronomy*, an introductory textbook begun while he was still a student at Tübingen and so popular that it ran through seven editions between 1582 and 1624, Mästlin expounded the traditional view as easier for beginners to understand. He advised Protestant governments to reject the Gregorian calendar as a papal scheme to regain control over territories that had escaped from its grasp. All of his books and writings appeared on the Index of Pope Sixtus V in 1590.[10]

In a public address at Tübingen University on 22 September 1602, on the basis of his chronological researches Mästlin put Jesus' birth more than four years before the conventional date.[11] On 23 May 1584 he had replaced Apian, who had been dismissed for refusing to sign the oath of religious allegiance; he later bought Apian's library from the latter's widow.[12] Mästlin, a man of slight build, unlike the massive ancestor from whom his surname was derived,[13] was elected dean of the Tübingen Arts Faculty eight times between 1588 and 1629. He taught there for forty-seven years, until his death in 1631.

His first wife having died on 15 February 1588, on 28 January 1589 Mästlin married Margaret Burckhardt (19 March 1564–18 February 1622), who bore him nine children.[14] Sabina, the second Mästlin daughter to bear this name, was buried on 9 July 1596, before attaining the age of seven, and a third Sabina was born on 22 June 1599.[15] A second Margaret, christened on 16 December 1604, died on 31 August 1609.[16] Augustus, born on 13 January 1598, died on 16 February 1598.[17] Anna Dorothea married a Lutheran clergyman, Andrew Osiander (M.A.,

Tübingen, 1610), in 1614.[18] Gottfried, baptized on 12 October 1595, received his B.A. at Tübingen on 31 March 1612, his M.A. on 16 August 1615, and became a professor of languages there in 1627.[19] Matthew acquired his B.A. at Tübingen on 17 March 1619 and the M.A. on 20 February 1622. He married on 24 November 1622; taught school at Gerlingen; and worked as a caretaker in Knittlingen, where he was buried on 6 February 1661.[20]

In his 1578 discussion of the comet of 1577, Mästlin announced his "adoption of the cosmology of Copernicus, truly the foremost astronomer since Ptolemy." In 1632 Galileo attributed his acceptance of Copernicanism to two or three lectures, delivered shortly after he had completed his philosophy course, by a foreign professor whose identity (or very existence) is uncertain.[21] Hence in 1650 Gerhard Johann Voss (1577–1649) posthumously initiated the legend—which has been uncritically repeated by influential writers for centuries—that the foreigner responsible for Galileo's Copernicanism was Mästlin.[22] The latter, however, was really responsible for the Copernicanism of Johannes Kepler, who attended Mästlin's classroom lectures at Tübingen and heard him expound the superiority of the Copernican astronomy over the Ptolemaic.[23] The pupil-teacher relationship between Kepler and Mästlin ripened into a lifelong affectionate friendship, each sincerely acknowledging the other's valuable assistance. No finer example of the educational process at its best can be found in the entire history of science.

NOTES

1. The key passage was translated into English by Edward Rosen, *Kepler's Conversation*, 117–119, 157.
2. *Die Matrikeln der Universität Tübingen*, I (Stuttgart, 1906), 487.
3. Tycho Brahe, *Opera omnia*, III (Copenhagen, 1916), 58–62.
4. Karl Steiff, "Der Tübinger Professor . . .," 51–53.
5. *Matrikeln . . . Tübingen*, I, 708; Johannes Kepler, *Gesammelte Werke*, XIII, 211:119–121, 232:527–528.
6. Kepler, *op. cit.*, XIV, 157:73–82, 354:473–475.
7. *Diarium Martini Crusii*, III (Tübingen, 1958), 515:25–26; *Matrikeln . . . Tübingen*, I, 707; II, 7. Steiff, *op. cit.*, 53, erroneously assigned this Sabina to Mästlin's second marriage.
8. *Die Matrikel der Universität Heidelberg*, II (Heidelberg, 1886), 92.
9. Mästlin's statement about Abū Ma'shar, Islam's foremost astrologer, was undoubtedly based on Cardano's *Astronomical Aphorisms*, published as a supplement to *Hieronymi Cardani Libelli V* (Nuremberg, 1547), as cited by Willy Hartner, *Oriens-Occidens* (Hildesheim, 1968), 503.
10. Heinrich Reusch, ed., *Die Indices librorum prohibitorum des sechszehnten Jahrhunderts* (Tübingen, 1896; repr. Nieuwkoop, 1961), 504, 566.
11. Kepler, *op. cit.*, XVII, 56:100–103.
12. *Matrikeln . . . Tübingen*, I, 624; Siegmund Günther, *Peter und Philipp Apian* (Amsterdam, 1967, repr. of 1882 ed.),

107–109; Ernst Zinner, *Entstehung und Ausbreitung der Coppernicanischen Lehre*, 453.

13. Edward Rosen, *Kepler's Somnium*, 64–65; H. M. Decker, "Die Ahnen des Astronomen Mästlin," 103–104.
14. W. Bardili, "Ergänzungen zur 'Geistesmutter,'" 114.
15. *Diarium . . . Crusii*, I, 128:18–20; Kepler, *op. cit.*, XIII, 368:28; XIV, 43:5, 463:5.
16. K. E. von Marchtaler, "Ein Beitrag zur Familienforschung Mästlin," 179.
17. Kepler, *op. cit.*, XIII, 184:179–180, 209:12–14.
18. "1604" in Steiff, *op. cit.*, 53, is a misprint; *Matrikeln . . . Tübingen*, II, 41.
19. *Matrikeln . . . Tübingen*, II, 57.
20. *Ibid.*, 72; Marchtaler, *op. cit.*, 179–180.
21. Galileo Galilei, *Opere*, national ed., VII (Florence, 1897; repr. 1968), 154:5–10.
22. G. J. Voss, *De universae mathesios natura et constitutione liber, cui subjungitur chronologia mathematicorum* (Amsterdam, 1650), 192.
23. Kepler, *op. cit.*, I, 9:11–21.

BIBLIOGRAPHY

I. ORIGINAL WORKS. Writings published under Mästlin's name are *Ephemeris nova anni 1577* (Tübingen, 1576); *Observatio et demonstratio cometae aetherei, qui anno 1577 et 1578 . . . apparuit* (Tübingen, 1578); *Ephemerides novae ab anno . . . 1577 ad annum 1590* (Tübingen, 1580), preceded by Regiomontanus' brief *Commentary on the Ephemerides* and Mästlin's additions thereto, as well as a portrait of Mästlin, aged twenty-eight; *Consideratio et observatio cometae aetherei astronomica, qui anno 1580 . . . apparuit* (Heidelberg, 1581), with the same portrait as in the 1580 work; *De astronomiae principalibus et primis fundamentis disputatio* (Heidelberg, 1582), the respondent on 20 January 1582 being Jeremiah Jecklin or Jacobus of Ulm (M.A., Heidelberg, 24 July 1582)—the title is preceded by "Divino rectoris astrorum favente numine," a religious formula which has been listed as though it identified a separate publication; *De astronomiae hypothesibus sive de circulis sphaericis et orbibus theoricis disputatio* (Heidelberg, 1582), the respondent being Matthias Mener (M.A., Heidelberg, 19 Feb. 1583); *Epitome astronomiae* (Heidelberg, 1582; Tübingen, 1588, 1593, 1597, 1598, 1610, 1624); *Ausführlicher und gründtlicher Bericht von der . . . Jarrechnung* (Heidelberg, 1583), cited by Mästlin in a later calendar tract written in Latin as his "Dialexis germanica," which has sometimes been registered as though it were a separate publication, also repr., with additions, in *Nothwendige und gründtliche Bedenckhen von dem . . . Kalender* (Heidelberg, 1584); *Alterum examen novi pontificialis Gregoriani Kalendarii* (Tübingen, 1586); and *Defensio alterius sui examinis* (Tübingen, 1588).

He also wrote *Tres disputationes astronomicae et geographicae* (Tübingen, 1592): *De climatibus* (the respondent being Wolfgang Hohenfelder), *De diebus naturalibus et artificialibus* (the respondent being Ludwig Hohenfelder), *De zonis* (the respondent being George Achatius Enenckel) —each of these disputations has its own title page and separate pagination; *Disputatio de eclipsibus solis et lunae* (Tübingen, 1596), the respondent on 15 Jan. 1596 being Marcus Hohenfelder; *Geographische Landtafel, Stuttgart–*

Rome (Reutlingen, 1601); *Disputatio de multivariis motuum planetarum in coelo apparentibus irregularitatibus, seu regularibus inaequalitatibus, earumque causis astronomicis* (Tübingen, 1606), the respondent on 21–22 Feb. 1606 being Samuel Hafenreffer; *Chronologicae theses et tabulae*, Samuel Hafenreffer, ed. (Tübingen, 1641, 1646)—Hafenreffer's copy of the Mästlin MS had been approved by the author; *Synopsis chronologiae sacrae*, Johann Valentin Andreae, ed. (Lüneburg, 1642), recorded by Jacob Friderich Reimmann, *Versuch einer Einleitung in die historiam literariam*, III, pt. 2 (Halle, 1710), 369–370; and *Perpetuae dilucidationes tabularum Prutenicarum coelestium motuum* (Tübingen, 1652), listed in Jean Graesse, *Trésor de libres rares*, IV (Dresden, 1863), 333, and Poggendorff, II, 170.

Mästlin's writings published in works by other authors are "Observatio mathematica," appended to Nicodemus Frischlin, *Consideratio novae stellae, quae mense Novembri, anni . . . 1572 . . . apparuit* (Tübingen, 1573); "Demonstratio astronomica loci stellae novae," completed on 4 Mar. 1573, in Tycho Brahe, *Astronomiae instauratae progymnasmata* (Prague, 1602), pt. 3, ch. 8; "De dimensionibus orbium et sphaerarum coelestium," in Johannes Kepler, *Mysterium cosmographicum* (Tübingen, 1596), 161–181; autobiography, dated 23 Sept. 1609, in Hermann Staigmüller, "Württembergische Mathematiker," in *Württembergische Vierteljahrshefte für Landesgeschichte*, **12** (1903), 227–256, see 234–235; appendix to a proposed ed. of Copernicus written in 1621, in Christian Frisch, ed., *Joannis Kepleri astronomi opera omnia*, I (Frankfurt-Erlangen, 1858), 56–58; and "Observationes Moestlinianae," in Lucius Barrettus (Albert Curtius), *Historia coelestis* (Augsburg, 1666), esp. lxxv–lxxvi—according to the *Paralipomena* (at *sig.* Zzzzz2ʳ), these observations, written in Mästlin's own hand, were transferred by Wilhelm Schickard (the author of a [lost?] funeral oration for Mästlin) to a MS forming part of a collection bought for the Holy Roman Emperor Ferdinand III and preserved in the National Library, Vienna.

Original writings erroneously listed as printed, although still in MS, are "Apologia examinum suorum" (or "Examina, eorundemque apologia"), the title of a work projected by Mästlin in answer to Clavius' attack on *Ausführlicher und gründtlicher Bericht von der . . . Jarrechnung*, *Alterum examen novi pontificialis Gregoriani Kalendarii*, and *Defensio alterius sui examinis* was registered in the book fair catalog for 1593, which presence led bibliographers to list it as though it had been printed at Tübingen in 1593 (or 1597)—actually, Mästlin never finished writing this, which remains a torso in Vienna, National Library Codex 12411 (E. Zinner, *Entstehung und Ausbreitung . . .*, 435, no. 151); "Horologiorum solarium sciotericorum in superficiebus planis descriptionis et delineationis universalis informatio," which, although it has been listed as a book printed at Tübingen in 1590, is actually an unpublished MS written by the hand of Gottfried Mästlin, dated 20 July 1613, and preserved in the library of Erlangen University: *Katalog der Handschriften der Universitätsbibliothek Erlangen*, Hans Fischer, ed., II (Erlangen, 1936), 485, no. 838; and "De cometa anni 1618" (Tübingen, 1619) or "Astronomischer Discurs, von dem Cometen, so in Anno 1618 im November zu erscheinen angefangen und bis Februar dies 1619. Jars am Himmel gesehen worden" (Tübingen, 1619) is listed as printed in both Latin and German but the unpublished MS in German, ready for the printer, still lies in the Württembergische Landesbibliothek, Stuttgart, Codex math. Q. 15a–b.

Unpublished MSS, ready for the printer, are "Iudicium . . . de opere astronomico D. Frischlini," dated 18 Jan. 1586 (David Friderich Strauss, *Leben und Schriften des Dichters und Philologen Nicodemus Frischlin* [Frankfurt, 1856], 330); "Modus, ratio et fundamenta compositionis tabularum directionum Regiomontani et Reinholdi," Stuttgart Landesbibliothek, Codex math. Q. 15a–b; "Commentarius in 1. et 2. librum Euclidis cum demonstrationibus regularum algebraicarum," Vienna, National Library, Codex 12411 (E. Zinner, *Entstehung und Ausbreitung* . . ., 440, no. 260); "Emendatio sphalmatum typographicorum in Opere Palatino quodam geometrico et in Magno Canone Rhetici, nec non demonstratio, canonem tangentium et secantium in eodem Magno Canone Rhetici iuxta finem quadrantis minus exactum esse," Vienna, National Library (*Tabulae codicum manu scriptorum praeter graecos et orientales in Bibliotheca Palatina Vindobonensi asservatorum*, VI [Vienna, 1873], 253, no. 10913); and "Tractatus brevis de dimensione triangulorum rectilineorum et sphaericorum," written by the hand of Gottfried Mästlin, dated Oct. 1612, preserved at Erlangen—see *Katalog der Handschriften der Universitätsbibliothek Erlangen*, II, 485, no. 839.

Other unpublished MSS are listed in Vienna, National Library, Codex 12411; *Tabulae codicum . . . in Bibliotheca Palatina Vindobonensi; Katalog der Handschriften der Universitätsbibliothek Erlangen; Die historischen Handschriften der k. öffentlichen Bibliothek zu Stuttgart*, W. von Heyd, ed., I (Stuttgart, 1889), 257: Codex hist. fol. 603, Mästlin's correspondence with Johann Weidner; 283: Codex hist. fol. 657, biography of Mästlin by Johann Gottlieb Friedrich von Bohnenberger (1765–1831); Codex math. fol. 14b and Q. 15a–b; *Verzeichnis der Handschriften im deutschen Reich*, II, *Die Handschriften der Universitätsbibliothek Graz*, Anton Kern, ed., I (Leipzig, 1939), 82, no. 159 (15): a letter from Johann Reinhard Ziegler in Mainz to Paul Guldin in Rome, dated 5 Apr. 1611, regarding Mästlin's acquisition of a telescope; and *Kataloge der Herzog-August-Bibliothek Wolfenbüttel, Die Augusteischen Handschriften*, II (Frankfurt, 1966 [repr. of 1895 ed.]), 118–120, no. 2174: 15.3.Aug. fol.—also see Ernst Zinner, *Verzeichnis der astronomischen Handschriften des deutschen Kulturgebietes* (Munich, 1925), 217–219.

Published correspondence consists of Mästlin's letters to, from, and about Kepler, in Johannes Kepler, *Gesammelte Werke* (Munich, 1937–   ), part of which was trans. into German in *Johannes Kepler in seinen Briefen*, Max Caspar and Walther von Dyck, eds., 2 vols. (Munich–Berlin, 1930); and five letters to Mästlin from Simon Marius, in Ernst Zinner, "Zur Ehrenrettung des Simon Marius," in *Vierteljahrsschrift der Astronomischen Gesellschaft* (Leipzig), **77** (1942), 40–45.

Works edited by Mästlin are Erasmus Reinhold, *Prutenicae tabulae* (Tübingen, 1571), with an appendix, dated 1571, by Mästlin on p. 143; and George Joachim Rheticus, *Narratio prima*, in Johannes Kepler's *Mysterium cosmographicum* (Tübingen, 1596), 93–160, with Mästlin's preface, dated 1 Oct. 1596, at 86–90, and numerous notes by him in the margins.

A misattribution is *Problema astronomicum: Die Situs der Sternen, Planetarum oder Cometarum zu observiren ohne Instrumenta* (n.p., 1619). The Latin original of this trans. into German by Matthew Beger was misattributed to Mästlin by J. C. Houzeau and Albert Lancaster, *Bibliographie générale de l'astronomie*, I, pt. 1 (Brussels, 1887; repr. London, 1964), 603, where the work of Beger (miscalled Begern) is incorrectly listed as a translation of Mästlin's *Tres disputationes*. . . . Actually, Beger translated from Adriaan Metius' *Astronomiae universae institutiones* (Franeker, 1606–1608) an excerpt in which Metius discussed Mästlin's method of observing without the aid of any instruments.

II. SECONDARY LITERATURE. See Peter Aufgebauer, "Die Gregorianische Kalenderreform im Urteil zeitgenössischer Astronomen," in *Sterne*, **45** (1969), 118–121; Walter Bardili, "Ergänzungen zur 'Geistesmutter,' " in *Blätter für Württembergische Familienkunde*, **8** (1939–1941), 113–119; J. G. F. von Bohnenberger, "Michael Mästlin," in *Württembergische Vierteljahrshefte für Landesgeschichte*, **12** (1903), 244–247; Erhard Cellius, *Imagines professorum Tubingensium* (Tübingen, 1596), sig. I 4v, woodcut portrait of Mästlin, aged forty-five; Hans Martin Decker, "Die Ahnen des Astronomen Mästlin," in *Blätter für Württembergische Familienkunde*, **8** (1939–1941), 102–104; Siegmund Günther, *Beiträge zur Geschichte der neueren Mathematik* (Ansbach, 1881), 15–25; and "Mästlin," in *Allgemeine deutsche Biographie*, XX, 575–580, also repr. (Berlin, 1970), XLV, 669; C. Doris Hellman, *The Comet of 1577* (New York, 1941; repr. 1971), 137–159; Johannes Kepler, *Gesammelte Werke* (Munich, 1937–   ); and Viktor Kommerell, "Michael Mästlin," in *Schwäbische Lebensbilder*, IV (Stuttgart, 1948), 86–100.

Also see Paul Löffler, "Michael Mästlin zu seinem 300. Todestag," in *Tübinger Chronik-Amtsblatt für den Oberamtsbezirk Tübingen*, **87**, no. 245 (20 Oct. 1931), 4r; Kurt Erhard von Marchtaler, "Ein Beitrag zur Familienforschung Mästlin," in *Blätter für Württembergische Familienkunde*, **8** (1939–1941), 178–180; Edward Rosen, "Kepler and the Lutheran Attitude Toward Copernicanism," in *Vistas in Astronomy* (in press); *Kepler's Somnium* (Madison, Wis., 1967), xvi, repro. of an oil portrait of Mästlin painted in 1619; Karl Steiff, "Der Tübinger Professor der Mathematik und Astronomie Michael Mästlin," in *Literarische Beilage des Staats-Anzeiger für Württemberg* (30 Apr. 1892), 49–64, 126–128; Ernst Zinner, *Entstehung und Ausbreitung der Coppernicanischen Lehre* (Erlangen, 1943); and Edward Rosen, *Kepler's Conversation with Galileo's Sidereal Messenger* (New York–London, 1965).

EDWARD ROSEN

AL-MAS'ŪDĪ, ABU 'L-ḤASAN 'ALĪ IBN AL-ḤUSAYN IBN 'ALĪ (*b*. Baghdad; *d*. al-Fusṭāṭ [old Cairo], Egypt, September/October 956 or 957), *geography, history.*

While still relatively young, al-Mas'ūdī left Baghdad about 915, spending the rest of his life traveling until he settled in Egypt toward the end of his life. He journeyed extensively in Khurāsān, Sijistān (southern Afghanistan), Kirmān, Fārs, Qūmīs, Jurjān, Ṭabaristān, Jibāl (Media), Khūzistān, Iraq (southern half of Mesopotamia), and Jazīra (northern half of Mesopotamia) until 941; and in Syria, Yemen, Ḥaḍramawt, Shaḥr, and Egypt between 941 and 956. He also visited Sind, India, and East Africa and sailed on the Caspian Sea, the Mediterranean, the Red Sea, and the Arabian Sea. His claims to have visited Java, Indochina, or China do not seem to be correct, however, since there is no internal evidence to support them in his extant works. Nor did he visit Madagascar, Ceylon, or Tibet, as is believed by some scholars. Apart from his urge to see the wonders of the world (*al-'ajā'ib*), his travels were motivated by his conviction that true knowledge could be acquired only through personal experience and observation.

Al-Mas'ūdī was a prolific writer; nearly thirty-seven works can be enumerated from his extant writings and from other sources. He wrote on a great variety of subjects: history, geography, jurisprudence, theology, genealogy, and the art of government and administration. Only two of these works have survived completely: *Murūj al-dhahab wa ma'ādin al-jawhar*, completed in November/December 947 and revised in 956, and *Al-Tanbīh wa 'l-ishrāf*, completed a year before his death. His magnum opus, *Kitāb Akhbār al-zamān wa man abādahu 'l-ḥidthān*, a world history and geography in about thirty volumes (*funūn*), is lost except for its first volume, which is preserved in Vienna (there is another manuscript in Berlin; see C. Brockelmann, *Encyclopaedia of Islam*, 1st ed.). A number of manuscripts and printed works bearing different titles—*Mukhtaṣar al-'ajā'ib* (French translation by Carra de Vaux, *L'abrégé des merveilles* [Paris, 1898]); *Kitāb Akhbār al-zamān wa man abādahu 'l-ḥidthān* ('Abd Allāh al-Ṣāwī, ed. [Cairo, 1938]); *Kitāb al-Ausaṭ; Kitāb 'ajā'ib al-dunyā* (or *Kitāb al-'ajā'ib*)—are incorrectly ascribed to him. In fact, they seem to belong to the *'ajā'ib* literature produced in abundance in the medieval period. This consisted of collections of sailors' tales about the Indian Ocean and legends about ancient Egypt, among other subjects. Similarly, *Ithbāt al-waṣiyya li'l-Imām 'Alī ibn Abī Ṭālib* (al-Najaf, Iraq, 1955) does does not seem to be al-Mas'ūdī's work.

Al-Mas'ūdī was a Mu'tazilite thinker with Shī'a

leanings. Believing that knowledge accumulated and advanced with the passage of time, he disagreed with those scholars who uncritically accepted the "ancients" *(salaf)* as final authorities and who minimized the importance of the knowledge of the contemporary savants *(khalaf)*: "And often a latter-day writer, because of his great accumulation of experiences, and of his wariness of an uncritical imitation of his predecessors and of his caution against pitfalls, is better in his documentation and more thorough in his authorship. Again, since he discovers new things not known to former generations, the sciences steadily progress to unknown limits and ends" (*Tanbīh*, p. 76). Thus we find him openly challenging traditionalism *(taqlīd)*, which from the twelfth century exerted a deadly influence on the progress of scientific knowledge and learning and hence was the main cause of the decline of the Islamic society in the Middle Ages.

As a historian al-Mas'ūdī made important contributions to Arab historiography in the Middle Ages. He believed that to obtain a true and objective picture of the history of a nation, a historian ought to consult the primary sources available in that country and not depend upon secondary sources, which are likely to distort facts. He followed this principle in the case of the history of ancient Iran (*Tanbīh*, p. 105). For his history of the world he not only utilized a large number of Arabic historical works available to him but also incorporated into it the vast amount of rich material on different countries and kingdoms that he had collected during his travels. Besides dealing with the history of Islam in the traditional manner —from the time of the Prophet Muḥammad up to his own times—he surveyed the histories of important nations and races who lived before the rise of Islam in the seventh century and also covered, as far as possible, the contemporary history of the Byzantine Empire, some European nations, India, and China. His approach to history was, therefore, both scientific and objective. He was one of the first Muslim historians to set the trend of secularism in historiography, for he included in his works the histories of a large number of non-Islamic nations. In his enthusiasm to record everything at his disposal, however, he uncritically related legends and popular beliefs side by side with history.

Al-Mas'ūdī conceived of geography as an essential prerequisite of history, and hence a survey of world geography preceded his account of world history. He emphasized that geographical environment deeply influenced the character, temperament, and structure —as well as the color—of the animal and plant life found in a particular region. He was fully acquainted with ancient Greek, Indian, and Iranian geographical thought and concepts through Arabic translations of the literature and was equally well versed in contemporary Arabic geographical literature. His knowledge of geography covered almost all branches of the subject, and his system was based mainly on the Greeks. Thus, he belonged to the "secular" school of Arab geographers rather than to the Islamic Balkhī school, the followers of which took Mecca as the center of the world and made their geographical ideas conform to the concepts found in the Koran. Having had a wide experience of the οἰκουμένη and endowed with a critical mind, al-Mas'ūdī was able to challenge some of the concepts of the "theoreticians" and to rectify the confused knowledge of the Arab geographers of his time. For instance, he was not fully convinced of the Ptolemaic theory of the existence of a *terra incognita* in the southern hemisphere, according to which the Indian Ocean was believed to be surrounded by land on all sides except in the east, where it was joined with the Pacific by a sea passage. He says he was told by the sailors of the Indian Ocean *(al-bahr al-habashī)* that this sea had no limits toward the south *(Murūj,* I, 281–282; see S. M. Ahmad, "The Arabs and the Rounding of the Cape of Good Hope," in *Dr. Zakir Husain Presentation Volume* [New Delhi, 1968]).

Al-Mas'ūdī was not a philosopher, but he was deeply interested in Greek philosophy, as is evident from his writings. As a theologian he refuted the Greek materialist concept that the world is eternal *(qadīm)* and argued in favor of the Islamic belief that the world had come into existence in time *(hādith).* His style is simple and direct; but he made full use of Arabic poetry, which imparts a literary touch to his writings. There is little doubt that he was one of the most original thinkers of medieval Islam.

BIBLIOGRAPHY

I. ORIGINAL WORKS. Al-Mas'ūdī's extant works are *Murūj al-dhabab wa ma'ādin al-Jawhar, Les prairies d'or,* Arabic text and French trans. by C. Barbier de Meynard and Pavet de Courteille, 9 vols. (Paris, 1861–1877), also rev. ed. of the Arabic text by Charles Pellat, 3 vols. (Beirut, 1966–1970); and *Kitāb al-Tanbīh wa 'l-ishrāf,* M. J. de Goeje, ed., vol. VIII of Bibliotheca Geographorum Arabicorum (Leiden, 1893–1894), trans. into French by Carra de Vaux as *Le livre de l'avertissement et de la revision* (Paris, 1897).

II. SECONDARY LITERATURE. See S. Maqbul Ahmad, "Al-Mas'ūdī's Contributions to Medieval Arab Geography," in *Islamic Culture* (Hyderabad), **27**, no. 2 (Apr. 1953), 61–77, and **28**, no. 1 (Jan. 1954), 275–286; and "Travels of Abu 'l-Hasan 'Alī ibn al-Husayn al-Mas'ūdī," *ibid.,* **28**, no. 4 (Oct. 1954), 509–524; C. Brockelmann,

"Al-Mas'ūdī," in *Encyclopaedia of Islam,* 1st ed. (Leiden, 1936); I. I. Krachkovsky, *Istoria arabskoy geograficheskoy literatury* (Moscow–Leningrad, 1957), trans. into Arabic by Salāh al-Dīn 'Uthmān Hāshim as *Ta'rikh al-adab al-jughrāfī al-'Arabi* (Cairo, 1963), pt. 1, 177–186; *Al-Mas'ūdī Millenary Commemoration Volume,* S. Maqbul Ahmad and A. Rahman, eds. (Aligarh, 1960); and M. Reinaud, *Géographie d'Aboulféda,* I, *Introduction générale à la géographie des orientaux* (Paris, 1848).

On the *'ajā'ib* literature, see S. M. Ahmad, "The Aligarh Manuscript of al-Mas'ūdī's *'Ajāib al-Dunyā,*" in *Majalla-i 'Ulūm-i Islāmīya* (1960), 102–110; C. Brockelmann, *Geschichte der arabischen Literatur,* I (Leiden, 1943), 150–152 and supp. I (Leiden, 1937), 220–221; Carra de Vaux, in *Journal Asiatique,* 9th ser., **7**; Hājjī Khalīfa, *Kashf al-zunūn,* II (Istanbul, 1943), 1126; Qutbuddīn Collection, no. 36/1, Maulana Azad Library, Aligarh; M. Reinaud, *Géographie d'Aboulféda,* I, *Introduction générale à la géographie des orientaux* (Paris, 1848); and P. Voorhoeve, *Handlist of Arabic Manuscripts* (Leiden, 1957), 4.

S. MAQBUL AHMAD

MATHER, WILLIAM WILLIAMS (*b.* Brooklyn, Connecticut, 24 May 1804; *d.* Columbus, Ohio, 25 February 1859), *geology.*

Mather was a member of the New England Mather family, famous in the ministry, education, and literature. A boyhood interest in chemistry led him to mineralogy. In 1823 he entered West Point Military Academy and graduated in 1828. He remained in the army for eight years, partly on regular duty and partly as assistant professor of chemistry, mineralogy, and geology. In 1833 he published *Elements of Geology for the Use of Schools,* which went through at least five editions. He was on topographic duty in 1835 as assistant geologist to G. W. Featherstonhaugh in making a geological study of the country from Green Bay, Wisconsin, to the Coteau des Prairies, in southwestern Minnesota. He resigned from the army in 1836 and Governor Marcy of New York appointed him geologist in charge of the first geological district of the New York survey. He completed his final report in 1843. During this time he organized the first geological survey of Ohio (1837–1840); was professor of natural science at Ohio University (1842–1845), and vice-president and acting president in 1845; acting professor of chemistry, mineralogy, and geology at Marietta College in 1846. He returned to Ohio University as vice-president and professor of natural science in 1847. From 1850 he was active as secretary and agricultural chemist of the Ohio State Board of Agriculture, as well as consultant on mineral resources for railroads in Kentucky and Ohio. An expert on coal geology, he had large interests in the development of Ohio coal lands.

"Not possessing the genius which dazzles, [Mather] had the intellect which achieved valuable results by patient and conscientious industry" (*Popular Science Monthly*, **49** [1896], 555). His most important geological work is embodied in his massive final report on the New York survey, which is notable not only for its vast detail of the structure and classification of the strata but also for the breadth of its coverage. His sections on the red rocks of the Catskill Mountains and his descriptions of the Quaternary deposits of the lower Hudson River valley and Long Island are still useful, although he did not accept Agassiz's glacial theory. He was one of the first to recognize that the much disputed Taconic rocks are mainly metamorphosed early Paleozoic sediments and that the rocks of the Hudson highlands correspond in age and lithology to the ancient rocks of the Adirondacks.

BIBLIOGRAPHY

I. ORIGINAL WORKS. Mather's most important work is *Geology of New York. Part I, Comprising the Geology of the First Geological District* (Albany, 1843).

II. SECONDARY LITERATURE. See the unsigned "Sketch of Williams Mather," in *Popular Science Monthly*, **49** (1896), 550–555, with portrait; I. J. Austin, "William Williams Mather," in *New England Historic-Genealogical Society, Memorial Biographies*, **3** (1883), 339–355; C. H. Hitchcock, "Sketch of William Williams Mather," in *American Geologist*, **19** (1897), 1–15, with portrait and a list of his publications; and Charles Whittlesey, "Personnel of the First Geological Survey of Ohio," in *Magazine of Western History*, **2** (1885), 73–87.

JOHN W. WELLS

MATHEWS, GEORGE BALLARD (*b*. London, England, 23 February 1861; *d*. Liverpool, England, 19 March 1922), *mathematics*.

Born of a Herefordshire family, Mathews was educated at Ludlow Grammar School; at University College, London; and at St. John's College, Cambridge. In 1883 he headed the list in the Cambridge mathematical tripos. In 1884 he was elected a fellow of St. John's, but in the same year he was appointed to the chair of mathematics at the newly established University College of North Wales at Bangor. He resigned the Bangor chair in 1896 and returned to lecture at Cambridge. He gave up this appointment in 1911, when he was appointed to a special lectureship at Bangor. He was elected to the Royal Society in 1897.

Mathews was an accomplished classical scholar; and besides Latin and Greek he was proficient in Hebrew, Sanskrit, and Arabic. He also possessed great musical knowledge and skill. His versatility led a colleague at Bangor to assert that Mathews could equally well fill four or more chairs at the college.

In mathematics Mathews' main interest was in the classical theory of numbers, and most of his research papers deal with topics in this field. His book on the theory of numbers, of which only the first of two promised volumes appeared, discusses in detail the Gaussian theory of quadratic forms and its developments by Dirichlet, Eisenstein, and H. J. S. Smith; it also contains a chapter on prime numbers that is concerned largely with describing Riemann's memoir, at that time little known in England. Since the book was published in 1892, it was not possible to mention the proofs of the prime number theorem, first given by Hadamard and Vallée Poussin in 1896. In a related field, his 1907 tract on algebraic equations gave a clear exposition of the Galois theory in relation to the theory of groups.

A collaboration with Andrew Gray, then professor of physics at Bangor, produced a book on Bessel functions, the first substantial text on this subject in English. The theory is developed carefully and rigorously, but throughout the book stress is laid on applications to electricity, hydrodynamics, and diffraction; in this respect the book retained its value even after the publication in 1922 of Watson's standard treatise on the theory of these functions.

Mathews' book on projective geometry had two main aims: first, to develop the principles of projective geometry without any appeal to the concept of distance and on the basis of a simple but not minimal set of axioms; and second, to expound Staudt's theory of complex elements as defined by real involutions. Much material on the projective properties of conics and quadrics is included. The topics were relatively novel in English texts, although the first volume of Oswald Veblen and J. W. Young's *Projective Geometry* had just become available.

Mathews' research papers advanced the study of higher arithmetic, and his books were equally valuable, since they gave English readers access to fields of study not then adequately expounded for the English-speaking world.

BIBLIOGRAPHY

I. ORIGINAL WORKS. Mathews' books are *Theory of Numbers* (Cambridge, 1892); *A Treatise on Bessel Func-*

tions and Their Applications to Physics (London, 1895; 2nd ed., rev. by T. M. MacRobert), written with A. Gray; *Algebraic Equations*, Cambridge Mathematical Tracts, no. 6 (Cambridge, 1907; 3rd ed., rev. by W. E. H. Berwick); and *Projective Geometry* (London, 1914). The 2nd ed. of R. F. Scott's *Theory of Determinants* (London, 1904) was revised by Mathews.

Most of Mathews' research papers were published in *Proceedings of the London Mathematical Society* and *Messenger of Mathematics*.

II. SECONDARY LITERATURE. See the obituary notices by W. E. H. Berwick, in *Proceedings of the London Mathematical Society*, 2nd ser., **21** (1923), xlvi–l; and A. Gray, in *Mathematical Gazette*, **11** (1922), 133–136.

T. A. A. BROADBENT

MATHIEU, ÉMILE LÉONARD (*b.* Metz, France, 15 May 1835; *d.* Nancy, France, 19 October 1890), *mathematics, mathematical physics.*

Mathieu showed an early aptitude for Latin and Greek at school in Metz; but in his teens he discovered mathematics, and while a student at the École Polytechnique in Paris he passed all the courses in eighteen months. He took his *docteur ès sciences* in March 1859, with a thesis on transitive functions, but had to work as a private tutor until 1869, when he was appointed to a chair of mathematics at Besançon. He moved to Nancy in 1874, where he remained as professor until his death.

Although Mathieu showed great promise in his early years, he never received such normal signs of approbation as a Paris chair or election to the Académie des Sciences. From his late twenties his main efforts were devoted to the then unfashionable continuation of the great French tradition of mathematical physics, and he extended in sophistication the formation and solution of partial differential equations for a wide range of physical problems. Most of his papers in these fields received their definitive form in his projected *Traité de physique mathématique*, the eighth volume of which he had just begun at the time of his death. These volumes and a treatise on analytical dynamics can be taken as the basis for assessing his achievements in applied mathematics, for they contain considered versions, and often extensions, of the results that he had first published in his research papers. Mathieu's first major investigation (in the early 1860's) was an examination of the surfaces of vibration that arise as disturbances from Fresnel waves by considering the dispersive properties of light. His later interest in the polarization of light led him to rework a number of problems in view of certain disclosed weaknesses in Cauchy's analyses.

One of Mathieu's main interests was in potential theory, in which he introduced a new distinction between first and second potential. "First potential" was the standard idea, defined, for example, at a point for a body V by an expression of the form

$$\int_V \frac{1}{r} f(x, y, z)\, dv; \qquad (1)$$

but Mathieu also considered the "second potential"

$$\int_V r f(x, y, z)\, dv, \qquad (2)$$

the properties of which he found especially useful in solving the fourth-order partial differential equation

$$\nabla^2 \nabla^2 w = 0. \qquad (3)$$

His interest in (3) arose especially in problems of elasticity; and in relating and comparing his solutions with problems in heat diffusion (where he had investigated various special distributions in cylindrical bodies), he was led to generalized solutions for partial differential equations and to solutions for problems of the elasticity of three-dimensional bodies, especially those of anisotropic elasticity or subject to noninfinitesimal deformations. Mathieu applied these results to the especially difficult problem of the vibration of bells, and he also made general applications of his ideas of potential theory to the study of dielectrics and magnetic induction. In his treatment of electrodynamics he suggested that the traversal of a conductor by an electric current gave rise to a pair of neighboring layers of electricity, rather than just a single layer.

Mathieu introduced many new ideas in the study of capillarity, improving upon Poisson's results concerning the change of density in a fluid at its edges. His most notable achievement in this field was to analyze the capillary forces acting on an arbitrary body immersed in a liquid, but in general his results proved to be at variance with experimental findings.

In celestial mechanics Mathieu extended Poisson's results on the secular variation of the great axes of the orbits of planets and on the formulas for their perturbation; he also analyzed the motion of the axes of rotation of the earth and produced estimates of the variation in latitude of a point on the earth. Mathieu studied the three-body problem and applied his results to the calculation of the perturbations of Jupiter and Saturn. In analytical mechanics, he gave new demonstrations of the Hamiltonian systems of equations and of the principle of least action, as well as carrying out many analyses of compound motion, especially those that took into account the motion of the earth.

In all his work Mathieu built principally on solution methods introduced by Fourier and problems investigated by Poisson, Cauchy, and Lamé. The best-known of his achievements, directly linked with his name, are the "Mathieu functions," which arise in solving the two-dimensional wave equation for the motion of an elliptic membrane. After separation of the variables, both space variables satisfy an ordinary differential equation sometimes known as Mathieu's equation:

$$\frac{d^2u}{dz^2} + (a + 16b \cos 2z)u = 0, \qquad (4)$$

whose solutions are the Mathieu functions $ce_n(z, b)$, $se_n(z, b)$. These functions are usually expressed as trigonometric series in z, each of which takes an infinite power series coefficient in b; but many of their properties, including orthogonality, can be developed from (4) and from various implicit forms. Both equation (4) and the functions were an important source of problems for analysis from Mathieu's initial paper of 1868 until the second decade of the twentieth century. The functions themselves are a special case of the hypergeometric function, and Mathieu's contributions to pure mathematics included a paper on that function. He also wrote on elliptic functions and especially on various questions concerned with or involving higher algebra—the theory of substitutions and transitive functions (his earliest work, and based on extensions to the results of his thesis) and biquadratic residues. In fact, his earliest work was in pure mathematics; not until his thirties did applied mathematics assume a dominant role in his thought.

Mathieu's shy and retiring nature may have accounted to some extent for the lack of worldly success in his life and career; but among his colleagues he won only friendship and respect. Apart from a serious illness in his twenty-eighth year, which seems to have prevented him from taking over Lamé's lecture courses at the Sorbonne in 1866, he enjoyed good health until the illness that caused his death.

BIBLIOGRAPHY

I. Original Works. The 7 vols. of Mathieu's *Traité de physique mathématique* were published at Paris: *Cours de physique mathématique* (1874); *Théorie de la capillarité* (1883); *Théorie du potentiel et ses applications à l'électrostatique et au magnetisme*, 2 vols. (1885–1886), also trans. into German (1890); *Théorie de l'électrodynamique* (1888); and *Théorie de l'élasticité des corps solides*, 2 vols. (1890). The 3 vols. that were still projected at his death were to

have dealt with optics, the theory of gases, and acoustics. His other book was *Dynamique analytique* (Paris, 1878). His papers were published mostly in *Journal de physique*, *Journal für die reine und angewandte Mathematik*, and especially in *Journal des mathématiques pures et appliquées*. A comprehensive list of references can be found in Poggendorff, IV, 1972.

II. Secondary Literature. The two principal writings are P. Duhem, "Émile Mathieu, His Life and Works," in *Bulletin of the New York Mathematical Society*, **1** (1891–1892), 156–168, translated by A. Ziwet; and G. Floquet, "Émile Mathieu," in *Bulletin . . . de la Société des sciences de Nancy*, 2nd ser., **11** (1891), 1–34. A good treatment of Mathieu's equation and functions may be found in E. T. Whittaker and G. N. Watson, *A Course of Modern Analysis* (Cambridge, 1928), ch. 19.

I. Grattan-Guinness

MATHURĀNĀTHA ŚARMAN (*fl.* Bengal, India, 1609), *astronomy.*

Mathurānātha, who enjoyed the titles Vidyālaṅkāra ("Ornament of Wisdom") and Cakravartin ("Emperor"), composed the *Ravisiddhāntamañjarī* in 1609. This is an astronomical text in four chapters accompanied by extensive tables (see Supplement) based on the parameters of the *Saurapakṣa* with the admixture of some from the adjusted *Saurapakṣa*; the epoch is 29 March 1609. His is one of the primary sets of tables belonging to this school in Bengal. Another set of tables, the *Viśvahita*, is sometimes attributed to him, but its author is, rather, Rāghavānanda Śarman. Mathurānātha also wrote a *Praśnaratnāṅkura* and a *Pañcāṅgaratna*, but little is known of either.

BIBLIOGRAPHY

The *Ravisiddhāntamañjarī* was edited by Viśvambhara Jyotiṣārṇava as *Bibliotheca Indica*, no. 198 (Calcutta, 1911); the tables are analyzed by D. Pingree, *Sanskrit Astronomical Tables in England* (Madras, 1973), 128–134.

David Pingree

MATRUCHOT, LOUIS (*b.* Verrey-sous-Salmasse, near Dijon, France, 14 January 1863; *d.* Paris, France, 5 July 1921), *mycology.*

Matruchot was admitted to the École Normale Supérieure in 1885. After passing the *agrégation* he became assistant science librarian there in 1888. In 1901 he was named lecturer in botany at the Sorbonne, where he also held a professorship in mycology. He was a member of the Société Biologique and of the Société Mycologique; as president of the latter he presented an honorary membership to George Safford Torrey of Harvard. His doctoral thesis, on the Mucedinaceae, was published in 1892.

Matruchot applied Pasteur's techniques to the study of the effects of various culture media upon the polymorphism and reproduction of fungi. He was thereby able to demonstrate the facultative parasitism of *Melanosporum parasitica;* he also found three different forms of *Bulgaria sarcoides*—having solitary, coalescent, and sterile mycelia, respectively—and discovered the relationship between *Cladobotryum ternatum* and *Graphium penicilloides.* Having identified the perfect stage of *Gliocadium,* he was able to place it among the Perisporaceae; he identified *Cunninghamella africana* through the use of *Pitocephalus,* a parasite of the Mucoraceae family, as a biological indicator. Matruchot also showed symbiotic association between *Gliocephalis hyalina* and a bacterium and developed a cytological technique by which a Mortierella was inoculated with such pigmented organisms as *Bacillus violaceus* or fusaria; he was then able to demonstrate some constituents of the host in the extracted pigment.

Matruchot's research on fungi pathogenic to men and animals opened a new field of medical investigation. He showed that certain infections that had previously been treated as lymphatic tuberculosis or syphilis were in fact fungal in nature. He found the yeast stage of *Sporotrichum gougeroti* in an infected leg muscle; discovered the fungus that caused subcutaneous nodules in a forearm (naming it *Mastigocladium blochii*); described a *Trichophyton* that is pathogenic in horses and that resembles Gymnoascaceae in its conidia, although it mimics Ctenomyces in its perfect stage; and finally discovered *Microbacillus synovialis* to be the cause of a condition similar to acute arthritis.

Matruchot also obtained the conidial stage of *Cryptococcus farcimonosus* in a medium containing sugar, which he kept at 25° C., and he was first to make pure cultures of *Phytospora infestans,* the agent of potato blight, for which he was awarded the Prix Bordin in 1911. He developed new techniques for the cultivation of mushrooms and truffles, and was honored by the Academy of Agriculture for having discovered the cause of the pollution of the Étang des Suisses in the park of Versailles.

In addition to his work as a mycologist, Matruchot wrote outlines in chemistry and physics for the use of his students, and contributed to archaeological research in his native province, the Côte-d'Or. He died of appendicitis at the age of fifty-eight.

BIBLIOGRAPHY

I. ORIGINAL WORKS. A complete bibliography of Matruchot's scientific works is in Costantin (see below). His doctoral thesis was published as *Recherches sur le développement de quelques mucédinées* (Paris, 1892); and two course outlines, *Livret de chimie* (Paris, 1897) and *Livret de physique* (Paris, 1897). His papers include "Sur la culture de quelques champignons Ascomycètes," in *Bulletin de la Société mycologique de France,* **9** (1893), 246–249; "Sur la structure du protoplasma fondamental dans une espèce de *Mortierella,*" in *Comptes rendus hebdomadaires des séances de l'Académie des sciences,* **123** (1896), 1321; "*Gliocéphalis hyalina,*" in *Bulletin de la Société mycologique de France,* **15** (1899), 254–262; "Sur la culture pure du *Phytophora infestans,* de Bary, agent de la maladie de la pomme de terre," *ibid.,* **16** (1900), 209–210, written with Marin Molliard; "Une mucorinée purement conidienne, *Cunninghamella africana,* étude éthologique et morphologique," in *Revue mycologique,* **26** (1904), 83–85; "Sur un nouveau groupe de champignons pathogènes agents des Sporotrichoses," in *Comptes rendus hebdomadaires des séances de l'Académie des sciences,* **150** (1910), 543–545; "Études sur les mauvaises odeurs de la pièce d'eau des Suisses à Versailles: nature, origine, causes et remèdes," in *Comptes rendus de la Société biologique de France,* **75** (1913), 611, written with M. Desroche; "Un microbe nouveau, *Mycobacillus synoviale* causant chez l'homme une maladie évoluant comme le rhumatisme articulaire," in *Comptes rendus hebdomadaires des séances de l'Académie des sciences,* **164** (1917), 652–655; and "Sur la forme conidienne du champignon agent de la lymphangite épizoolique," in *Bulletin de la Société mycologique de France,* **38,** supp. (1921), 76–77, written with Brocq-Rousseau.

II. SECONDARY LITERATURE. M. J. Costantin's obituary notice of Matruchot is in *Bulletin de la Société mycologique de France,* **38** (1922), 127–139. See also Paul Portier, "Louis Matruchot," in *Comptes rendus de la Société biologique de France,* **85** (1921), 322–323.

DENISE MADELEINE PLOUX, S.N.J.M.

MATTEUCCI, CARLO (*b.* Forlì, Italy, 2 June 1811; *d.* Leghorn, Italy, 24 June 1868), *physiology, physics.*

The son of Vincenzo Matteucci, a physician, and Chiara Folfi, Matteucci attended the University of Bologna from 1825 to 1828, when he graduated with a degree in physics. At the age of sixteen he prepared his first published paper, on meteorology.

In October 1829 Matteucci went to Paris, at his father's expense, and spent eight months attending scientific lectures at the Sorbonne. He returned to Forlì in June 1830. He received his first academic appointment in 1840, when he was appointed professor of physics at the University of Pisa on the advice of

Alexander von Humboldt. In the meantime he carried out electrophysiological investigations, first at his father's home and later in a small laboratory in Ravenna. His reports, presented to the Académie des Sciences by Arago and Edmond Becquerel, made his "name known through the European Continent," as Faraday wrote when Matteucci was only twenty-two. In 1842, at Pisa, he made his most famous discovery, the induced twitch, and began publishing his works in English, with a series of memoirs sent to the Royal Society.

A liberal, Matteucci was involved in the great political upheaval of 1848, which spread through most of the Continent. He was sent by the new Tuscan government to the Frankfurt Parliament, with the aim of establishing contacts with the German liberals. He did not lose his chair of physics after the restoration; in fact, the grand duke of Tuscany gave him —a political adversary—the funds necessary to build the first large institute of physics. When Italy was united, Matteucci became a senator for life and in 1862, as minister of education, reorganized the Scuola Normale Superiore of Pisa as the first Italian institute for advanced studies.

Working on torpedoes, Matteucci found that the discharges of the electric organ of the fish were due to impulses arising in the fourth lobe of the medulla, which he called the electric lobe. Mechanical or galvanic stimulation of this lobe constantly produced the electric discharge, the sign of which was not reversed when the direction of the stimulating current was reversed. This discharge could also be produced reflexly by applying pressure to the fish's eyes or by stimulating its body. Both spontaneous and induced discharges occurred after ablation of the cerebral hemispheres, of the optic lobes, and the cerebellum; but they could not be observed after bilateral ablation of the electric lobe.

The existence of the phenomenon of animal electricity had already been definitely proved with Galvani's last experiment (1797), and it is now clear that the twitch he produced was due to the currents of injury of sciatic nerve fibers, a phenomenon made possible by the polarization of their intact membranes. It remained for Matteucci to prove in 1842 that a current could constantly be detected when the electrodes of the galvanometer were placed in contact with the intact surface and with the interior (wounded portion) of a muscle. That the wounded part was always negative with respect to the normal surface was later demonstrated by Emil du Bois-Reymond, who in 1843 confirmed Matteucci's observation.

Although in 1838 Matteucci had recognized that the frog's resting potential (the difference in potential between the interior and exterior of a muscle fiber at rest) was, paradoxically, abolished by strychnine tetanus, it remained for du Bois-Reymond to demonstrate in 1848 that during the muscle contraction there was a "negative variation" of the injury currents. Just a year before the first preliminary note by du Bois-Reymond (1843), however, Matteucci had presented to the Académie des Sciences his report on the "induced twitch." In an experimental demonstration he gave at Paris in the presence of Humboldt and of several members of the Academy, he showed that when the sciatic nerve of the galvanoscopic frog leg was placed upon the leg muscle of another frog, the contraction of the latter muscle "induced" the contraction of the galvanoscopic leg. Becquerel immediately repeated and confirmed this experiment and gave the correct interpretation: that the nerve of the galvanoscopic leg was stimulated by the action currents of the contracting muscle of the other frog. Matteucci accepted this interpretation but failed to see the relation between his discovery and the phenomenon of the negative variation. This was done for the first time in Johannes Müller's *Handbuch der Physiologie des Menschen* (1844) and in du Bois-Reymond's *Untersuchungen über thierische Electricität* (1848–1849).

Although Matteucci was scientifically active until the end of his life, his most important work in physiology was carried out between 1836 and 1844 on the neural mechanisms of the electric discharge of torpedoes, on the resting potential of the frog's muscle, and especially on the action currents, which he discovered. His reluctance to admit that an electric phenomenon could disappear as a consequence of an active physiological process (the "negative variation") led Matteucci in 1845 to reject his own galvanometric findings of 1838 and Becquerel's interpretation of the induced twitch. This was the major error in the life of an outstanding scientist, whose work greatly influenced nineteenth-century electrophysiology.

BIBLIOGRAPHY

A list of 269 papers written by Matteucci is in Royal Society *Catalogue of Scientific Papers*, IV, 285–293; VIII, 354–355. His major books are *Essai sur les phénomènes électriques des animaux* (Paris, 1840); and *Traité des phénomènes électro-physiologiques des animaux* (Paris, 1844).

On Matteucci and his work, see N. Bianchi, *Carlo Matteucci e l'Italia del suo tempo* (Turin, 1874), with a complete bibliography of his works; and G. Moruzzi, "L'opera elettrofisiologica di Carlo Matteucci," in *Physis*, 6 (1964), 101–140, with a partial listing of his works and bibliography of secondary literature.

GIUSEPPE MORUZZI

MATTHIESSEN, AUGUSTUS (*b.* London, England, 2 January 1831; *d.* London, 6 October 1870), *chemistry.*

As a young child Matthiessen suffered a seizure that left him handicapped with a permanent twitching of the right hand. As a result he was considered unfit physically for most careers and was sent to learn farming. During his three-year stay on a farm, he nevertheless developed an interest in chemistry. At this time agricultural chemistry was attracting wide attention as a result of the writings of Liebig. It therefore was natural for Matthiessen to choose the University of Giessen to continue his education in chemistry, and he took his Ph.D. there in 1853.

From 1853 to 1857 Matthiessen worked in Bunsen's laboratory at the University of Heidelberg. Under Bunsen's direction Matthiessen prepared significant quantities of lithium, strontium, magnesium, and calcium by electrolysis of their fused salts. He then carried out a study with Kirchhoff on the electrical conductivity of these metals and of sodium and potassium.

In 1857 Matthiessen left Heidelberg and returned to London. He worked for a few months in Hofmann's laboratory at the Royal College of Chemistry. Here he studied the steps in the action of nitrous acid on aniline. Soon he moved to a small laboratory in his home and worked there for four years. At this time he began one of his most important studies, on the chemistry of narcotine and related opium alkaloids. In 1861 Matthiessen was elected a fellow of the Royal Society. He held the lectureship in chemistry at St. Mary's Hospital Medical School from 1862 to 1868, and then became a lecturer at St. Bartholomew's Medical School, both schools of the University of London. During this time he pursued research on the electrical, physical, and chemical properties of metals and their alloys. From 1862 to 1865 he served on the British Association Committee on the Standards of Electrical Resistance. Augustus Matthiessen committed suicide on 6 October 1870.

BIBLIOGRAPHY

I. Original Works. A list of Matthiessen's publications can be found in the Royal Society's *Catalogue of Scientific Papers.* Among his important works are the following: "On the Electric Conducting Power of the Metals of the Alkalies and Alkaline Earths," in *Philosophical Magazine,* **13** (1857), 81–90; "On the Electric Conducting Power of Copper and its Alloys," in *Proceedings of the Royal Society,* **11** (1860–1862), 126–131; and a series of papers on the chemical constitution of the opium alkaloids.

II. Secondary Literature. Obituaries of Matthiessen appeared in: *Nature,* **2** (1870), 517–518; *Journal of the Chemical Society,* **24** (1871), 615–617; *American Journal of Science,* **101** (1871), 73–74; and *Proceedings of the Royal Society,* **18** (1870), 111. An account of the details of his suicide appeared in *The Times* (London), 8 October 1870, p. 5, col. 5.

Daniel P. Jones

MATTIOLI, PIETRO ANDREA GREGORIO (*b.* Siena, Italy, 12 March 1501; *d.* Trento, Italy, January/February 1577), *medicine, botany.*

Mattioli was the son of Francesco Mattioli, a physician, and Lucrezia Buoninsegni. After moving with his family to Venice, where his father practiced medicine, Mattioli was sent to Padua and began the study of Greek and Latin, rhetoric, astronomy, geometry, and philosophy. He soon developed an interest in medicine and natural history, his main concerns until he received a degree in medicine at the University of Padua in 1523.

After his father's death Mattioli returned with his mother to Siena, which was then experiencing civil unrest. He therefore left Siena and, wishing to improve his skill in surgery, moved to Perugia, where he studied under Gregorio Caravita. About 1520 he moved to Rome, where he attended the Santo Spirito Hospital and the San Giacomo Xenodochium for incurables, where he frequently dissected cadavers of syphilis victims. Mattioli also continued his interest in natural history and botany, making direct observations of herbs and plants. Following the sack of Rome in 1527, he moved to Trento.

In 1528, at Cles in Val di Non, Trentino–Alto Adige, Mattioli married a young woman named Elisabetta; in 1545 they had a son, Paolo (Pavolino), who died in childhood. During his stay in Trentino, where he began to practice medicine, Mattioli became an intimate friend, adviser, and physician to Cardinal Bernardo Clesio, bishop of Trento, who developed a great esteem for Mattioli. While in Trentino, Mattioli continued his observations of plants and wrote his first book.

After Cardinal Clesio's death in 1539, Mattioli moved to Gorizia, apparently at the request of the inhabitants of that city, to practice medicine. His medical and natural history interests had increased and had developed particularly in phytology, both through the study of books and through direct observations of plants; in 1544 he published *Di Pedacio Dioscoride anazarbeo libri cinque,* which, through revisions and expansions, made him famous. In 1554 Mattioli was called to Prague, where he served first at the court of Ferdinand I and then at that of Maximilian II.

After the death of his first wife in 1557, Mattioli married Girolama di Varmo, of a noble Friuli family; they had two sons, Ferdinando and Massimiliano. In 1570 he married his third wife, Susanna Cherubina, of Trentino, by whom he had three children—Pietro Andrea, Lucrezia, and Eufemia.

In 1570, after visiting Verona, Mattioli left Prague and returned to the Tirol. He died of the plague at Trento apparently in January or February 1577. Buried in the cathedral, he is commemorated by a monument bearing his effigy in bas-relief.

Endowed with a wide-ranging knowledge, Mattioli concerned himself with a great variety of subjects, most of them involving botany and materia medica.

De morbi gallici curandi ratione, dialogus (Bologna, 1530), written in 1528 during his stay in Trentino and reprinted several times, was Mattioli's first work. A traditional examination of the origins and treatment of syphilis, it deals with the modes of propagation and symptomatology, including buboes in the groin, which, according to some authors, Mattioli was the first to describe. The discussion centers on the efficacy of the potion obtained from guaiacum, or holy wood. In view of the large number of works dealing with holy wood, it is difficult to recognize any original contribution that Mattioli may have made.

Magno palazzo del cardinale di Trento (Venice, 1539), an elegant poem of some 450 octaves, is a description in verse of the cultured and humanistic environment of the palace of Cardinal Clesio.

Geografia di Claudio Ptolemeo Alessandrino (Venice, 1548), another nonmedical book, is an Italian translation of Ptolemy's *Geography* and one of the earliest Italian translations from Latin of classical scientific writing.

Apologia adversus Amathum Lusitanum cum censura in eiusdem enarrationes (Venice, 1558) is a short work mainly polemical in content.

Epistola de bulbocastaneo . . . (Prague, 1558) illuminates Mattioli's scientific personality through his new botanical methods and his contributions regarding the identification of plants mentioned by the ancients, their synonyms and proper names, and their spelling.

Epistolarum medicinalium libri quinque (Prague, 1561) contains the names of celebrated contemporary scientists, notably Konrad Gesner, Ulisse Aldrovandi, Francesco Calzolari, Giacomo Antonio Cortuso, and Gabriele Falloppio. It is a series of writings on various medical subjects, including alchemy, magnetism, pharmacology, and the causes and symptoms of diseases. Mattioli deals fully with plants in general

—identification, curative powers—and with medicinal plants in particular, listing properties and habitats, and outlining methods for collecting and preserving samples.

Commentarii a Dioscoride is the work with which Mattioli's name is chiefly linked. The first edition, *Di Pedacio Dioscoride anazarbeo libri cinque. Dell'historia, et materia medicinale tradotti in lingua volgare italiana da M. Pietro Andrea Mathiolo Sanese medico. Con amplissimi discorsi, et comenti, et doctissime annotationi, et censure del medesimo interprete* . . . (Venice, 1544), is an Italian version of Dioscorides' *De materia medica* ($\Pi\epsilon\rho\grave{\iota}$ $\H{\upsilon}\lambda\eta\varsigma$ $\iota\alpha\tau\rho\iota\kappa\^{\eta}\varsigma$). Mattioli's original purpose was relatively modest: it was to provide doctors and apothecaries with a practical treatise in Italian with a commentary that would enable them to identify the medicinal plants mentioned by Dioscorides. This first edition, without illustrations, probably had a limited circulation. The highly successful Venice edition of 1548, also in Italian and with a new commentary, was entirely rewritten and was reprinted in 1550 and 1552.

It was probably this success that induced Mattioli to publish his first Latin translation of Dioscorides' *Commentarii, in libros sex Pedacii Dioscoridis anazarbei, De medica materia. Adjectis quam plurimis plantarum et animalium imaginibus, eodem authore* (Venice, 1554), an edition of broader purpose than the previous ones. Unlike the Italian versions, this Latin edition —enriched by synonyms in various languages, provided with a special commentary, and accompanied by numerous illustrations valuable for the reader's identification of Dioscorides' simples—rendered the work accessible to scholars throughout Europe. From then Mattioli's name was linked with that of Dioscorides. Further editions and reprints of the *Commentarii* continued practically without interruption until the eighteenth century. There were versions also in German, French, and Bohemian.

A critical examination of the features and the sometimes complex vicissitudes of the *Commentarii* would constitute an interesting chapter in the history of bibliology. Fundamental to the work's success is its conception and execution as a practical scientific treatise. It was intended for daily use by physicians, herbalists, and others, who could find descriptions and notes on medicinal plants and herbs, Greek and Latin names and synonyms, and the equivalents in other languages. The work made it possible to identify and compare its plants and herbs with those mentioned by Dioscorides and also with those found in nature.

The *Commentarii* thus differed profoundly from translations by other authors, who generally insisted

179

on lexical and grammatical aspects rather than on medical and botanical aims. Mattioli supported his work with new information, partly derived from his direct observation of plants and herbs and partly obtained from other authors. Many of the illustrations were reproductions of his own drawings or elaborations of drawings made by other authors; the rest were derived from original drawings placed at his disposal by other scholars.

From the scientific point of view, Mattioli's work did not always win approval. Sachs, for example, asserted that Mattioli's study of the medicinal effects of plants took priority to the observation of their morphological characteristics. Certainly Mattioli's interest in botany was not primary but proceeded from his interest in therapy, and it was medicine that led him back to the observation of nature. Mattioli's commentary on Dioscorides' text was aimed largely at the practical purpose of medicinal phytognosis and acquired intrinsic value both through the wealth of its descriptive details of each plant and through its accurate drawings. Mattioli may therefore be considered a member of the Vesalian school of morphological observation.

BIBLIOGRAPHY

The following works, which were consulted in the writing of this article, are also of value as sources concerning Mattioli's writings, letters, MSS, and iconography, as well as the literature on him: Vincenzo Cappelletti, "Nota sulla medicina umbra del Rinascimento: Pietro Andrea Mattioli," in *Atti del IV Convegno di studi umbri* (Perugia, 1967), pp. 513–532; Jerry Stannard, "P. A. Mattioli: Sixteenth-Century Commentator on Dioscorides," in University of Kansas Libraries, *Bibliographical Contributions*, I (Lawrence, Kans., 1969), 59–81; Giovanni Battista de Toni, "Pierandrea Mattioli," in Aldo Mieli, ed., *Gli scienziati italiani dall'inizio del medio evo ai giorni nostri . . .*, I (Rome, 1921), 382–387; and *La vita di Pietro Andrea Mattioli*, collected from his works by Giuseppe Fabiani, edited with additions and notes by Luciano Banchi (Siena, 1872).

BRUNO ZANOBIO

MATUYAMA (MATSUYAMA), MOTONORI (*b.* Uyeda [now Usa], Japan, 25 October 1884; *d.* Yamaguchi, Japan, 27 January 1958), *physics, geophysics, geology.*

Matuyama was the son of a Zen abbot, Tengai Sumiye. In 1910 he was adopted by the Matsuyama family, whose daughter, Matsuye Matsuyama, he married. He altered the romanized spelling of his adoptive name in about 1926, in conformity with a then new convention of transliteration. Matuyama received his early education in the schools of Kiyosuye and Chōfu, then entered Hiroshima Normal College (now the University of Hiroshima), where he studied physics and mathematics, graduating in 1907. After a year of teaching at a junior high school in Tomioka, Matuyama entered the Imperial University in Kyoto to further his study of physics; he graduated in 1911, then took up postgraduate study of geophysics with Toshi Shida and astronomy with Shizō Shinjō. With Shida he began work on what became one of his chief fields of research, the determination of gravity by pendulum. Matuyama's first papers were written in collaboration with his teacher and constitute the third and sixth parts of Shida's "On the Elasticity of the Earth and the Earth's Crust" of 1912.

Matuyama was appointed lecturer at the Imperial University in 1913; three years later he was promoted to assistant professor of the Geophysical Institute. His doctoral dissertation, which he published in 1918, was entitled "Determination of the Second Derivatives of the Gravitational Potential on Jaluit Atoll," and contained the results of experiments performed with the Eötvös gravity-variometer to determine the depth of the atoll. Matuyama had spent a month on Jaluit with a collaborator, H. Kaneko, in February 1915; his paper was the first to suggest that the determination of microfeatures of the gravity field of the earth could reveal geological substructure. It became the basis for the development in Japan of the torsion-balance method of prospecting for underground minerals.

In 1919 Matuyama left Japan for the United States to study geophysics with T. C. Chamberlin at the University of Chicago. While there he conducted laboratory experiments on ice designed to illuminate the mechanics of glacial movement. His results were published in 1920 as "On Some Physical Properties of Ice." Chamberlin wrote an introductory note to the paper, in which Matuyama stated the conclusion:

> These facts seem to show that gliding planes parallel to the base of each crystal are not the controlling factor in the deformation of ice and probably are not even an important factor. But instead, adjustment along the contact surfaces of adjacent crystals and perhaps the development of planes of weakness in the constituent crystals parallel to their long axis seem more effective in the process of deformation.

Matuyama returned to Japan in December 1921; the following January he was appointed professor of theoretical geology at the Imperial University. He once again took up the determination of gravity by pendulum. As early as 1911, while he was still a postgraduate student, Matuyama had participated in the national gravity survey of the Imperial Japanese Geodetic Commission; from 1927 until 1932 he extended the survey to Korea and Manchuria. In October 1934 and October 1935 he made a survey of marine gravity, using the Vening-Meinesz pendulum apparatus mounted in a navy submarine, in the Japan Trench and the area surrounding it. During the same period he also determined the gravity of nine islands in the Caroline and Mariana groups and as part of his maritime survey of 1935 landed his equipment on Chichijima in the Bonin Islands to determine its gravity. He found the free-air anomalies in these ten islands to range between +214 and +357 milligal, a result consistent in magnitude with those established for other oceanic islands.

One aspect of Matuyama's research on gravity was dictated by the request put to the Japanese delegation by the International Union of Geodesy and Geophysics, probably at the meeting of 1936, to carry out a gravity survey in the water areas surrounding the Japan Trench. The sea bottom of the landward side of the deepest line of the trench is the site of strong earthquakes that produce tsunami waves on the Pacific coast of northeast Honshu. In examining the distribution of free-air anomalies over the trench, Matuyama discovered that in the region of the northeast Pacific coasts of Honshu and the Pacific coast of Hokkaido the axis of the negative minimum of anomalies does not occur just above the axis of the maximum depths of the trench, contrary to expectations, but rather shifts landward, while the two axes are almost coincident in the southern part of the trench along the east side of the Fuji volcanic range. (Matuyama's associate Naoiti Kumagai took up these results a few years later and discovered a clear correlation between the earthquakes that occur in this area and the isostatic anomalies of great magnitude that are also apparent there.)

Matuyama was further concerned with the study of distribution of various kinds of coral reefs in the South Seas. The peculiarity of this distribution had first interested him on his visit to Jaluit atoll in 1915; he noted that in the Mariana group such reefs are elevated above sea level, while in the Marshalls they exist as atolls, or have subsided completely. He theorized that the ocean floor in this area had tilted eastward, and recommended to the Japanese Association for the Advancement of Science that a research commission be appointed to study the tilt of the sea bed in this area. A committee was appointed in 1934, and research stations were established on Saipan and on Jaluit atoll; no reports of their observations were published, however.

The last of Matuyama's main areas of research was the remnant magnetization of rocks. The first specimen that he examined was a basalt block from Genbudō, Tazima, in western Japan; he then extended his investigation to thirty-six specimens of basalt, each taken from a different site in Japan, Korea, and Manchuria. He subjected each specimen to tests for remnant magnetization, using Gauss's analysis of the vertical component of the magnetic field of the earth originating within the earth. Matuyama published his results in a series of papers. The most important, published in 1929 and entitled "On the Direction of Magnetization of Basalt in Japan, Tyōsen [Korea] and Manchuria," offers his conclusion that "According to Mercanton the earth's magnetic field was probably in a greatly different or nearly opposite state in the Permo-Carboniferous and Tertiary Periods, as compared to the present. From my results it seems as if the earth's magnetic field in the present area has changed even reversing itself in comparatively short times in the Miocene and also Quaternary Epochs." This work was widely influential, and the term "Matuyama Epoch" was coined to indicate the paleomagnetic period—from about the late Pliocene to the middle Pleistocene—during which the direction of magnetic field of the earth is supposed to have been opposite to what it is at present.

Matuyama also wrote a series of early papers on seismology, a subject which he originally pursued with Shida, and a great number of miscellaneous papers and books addressed to laymen and students. He served the Imperial University as dean of the Faculty of Science from June 1936 until December 1937; he retired from teaching in 1944 and was made professor emeritus in 1946. In May 1949 Matuyama was appointed president of the University of Yamaguchi; the following year he was elected a fellow of the Japan Academy. He had a lifelong interest in the Noh drama, and organized Noh groups among his neighbors and colleagues in both Kyoto and Yamaguchi. He died following the onset of acute myelogenous leukemia.

BIBLIOGRAPHY

Matuyama's important papers include "Note on Hecker's Observation of Horizontal Pendulums" and "Change of Plumb Line Referred to the Axis of the Earth as Found From the Result of the International Latitude Observations," pts. 3 and 6, respectively, of Toshi Shida, "On the Elasticity of the Earth and the Earth's Crust," in *Memoirs of the College of Science and Engineering, Kyoto*

Imperial University, **4**, no. 1 (1912), both written with Shida; "Determination of the Second Derivatives of the Gravitational Potential on the Jaluit Atoll," in *Memoirs of the College of Science, Kyoto Imperial University*, **3** (1918), 17–68; "On Some Physical Properties of Ice," in *Journal of Geology*, **28** (1920), 607–631; "On the Gravitational Field at the Fushun Colliery, Manchuria," in *Japanese Journal of Astronomy and Geophysics*, **2** (1924), 91–102; "Probable Subterranean Intrusion of Magma to the North of Sakurajima Volcano," in *Proceedings of the Third Pan-Pacific Science Congress* (Tokyo, 1926), 782–783; "Torsion Balance Observation and its Value in Prospecting" [in Japanese], in *Tōyō-Gakugei-Zasshi*, **520** (1926), 476–494; "On the Subterranean Structure Around Sakurajima Volcano Considered From the State of Gravitational Fields," in *Japanese Journal of Astronomy and Geophysics*, **4** (1927), 121–138; "Gravity Measurements in Tyōsen and Manchuria," in *Proceedings of the Fourth Pacific Science Congress* (Djakarta, 1929), 745–747; "Study of the Underground Structure of Suwa Basin by Means of the Eötvös Gravity-Variometer," *ibid.*, 869–872; "On the Direction of Magnetization of Basalt in Japan, Tyōsen and Manchuria," *ibid.*, 567–569, and in *Proceedings of the Imperial Academy of Japan*, **5** (1929), 203–205; "Subterranean Structure of Takamati Oil Field Revealed by Gravitational Method," in *Japanese Journal of Astronomy and Geophysics*, **7** (1930), 47–81, written with H. Higasinaka; "Relative Measurements of Gravity in Japan, Tyōsen and Manchuria Since 1921," in *Travaux. Association internationale de géodésie*, Japan Report no. 2, **11** (1933), 1–6; "Measurements of Gravity Over Nippon Trench on Board H. I. M. Submarine Ro-57. Preliminary Report," in *Proceedings of the Imperial Academy of Japan*, **10** (1934), 625–628; "Distribution of Gravity Over the Nippon Trench and Related Areas," *ibid.*, **12** (1936), 93–95; and "Gravity Survey by the Japanese Geodetic Commission Since 1932," in *Travaux. Association internationale de géodésie*, Japan Report no. 2, **12** (1936), 1–8.

NAOITI KUMAGAI

MAUGUIN, CHARLES VICTOR (*b.* Provins, France, 19 September 1878; *d.* Paris, France, 25 April 1958), *crystallography, mineralogy.*

Mauguin was the son of a baker in Provins, a small city fifty miles southeast of Paris. He attended primary school in Provins and, from 1894 to 1897, the École Primaire of Melun, in order to become a teacher. He began his university career in Montereau, where he also taught at the elementary school, while preparing for the entrance examination for the École Normale of Saint-Cloud, which he attended from 1902 to 1904. At this school, established to train teachers for the *écoles normales primaires*, students received thorough instruction in mathematics, physics, chemistry, and

the natural sciences. A brilliant student, Mauguin attracted the attention of L. J. Simon, who suggested that he work in his organic chemistry laboratory at the École Normale Supérieure in Paris. In 1910 Mauguin defended his doctoral thesis, "Les amides bromées-sodées et leur rôle dans la transposition d'Hofmann."

At the Sorbonne, Mauguin took the mathematics courses of Émile Picard, Poincaré, and Goursat and attended the lectures given there in 1905 by Pierre Curie on symmetry in physical phenomena—his first contact with crystallography. He then attended the courses of Frédéric Wallerant, the professor of mineralogy and crystallography. The latter was interested in liquid crystals, which had been discovered a few years previously by the German physicist Otto Lehmann. These organic substances, in a well-defined temperature interval between the liquid and the solid phase, present a curious state of matter that is characterized by the great fluidity of liquids and optical properties similar to those of crystals.

Attracted by crystallography, in 1910 Mauguin became Wallerant's assistant in the mineralogy laboratory of the Sorbonne in order to study liquid crystals. His memoirs on this subject published from 1910 to 1914 are fundamental to an understanding of the liquid-crystal state. He was named lecturer in mineralogy at the Faculty of Sciences of Bordeaux in 1912 and professor of mineralogy at the Faculty of Sciences of Nancy in 1913. He was mobilized in the infantry upon the declaration of war and later worked in a chemistry laboratory. At the end of 1919 he returned to the Sorbonne as a lecturer and in 1933 succeeded Wallerant in the chair of mineralogy, which he occupied until his retirement in 1948. All of his researches were concerned essentially with the diffraction of X rays by crystals.

Mauguin's marriage in 1907 to Louise Gaudebert was childless. Mme Mauguin became blind in 1930; and from then on, they led a retiring life and died within a few months of one another. Until the end of his life, Mauguin preserved an intellectual and youthful enthusiasm for science; his whole life was devoted to studies of extremely varied questions. Long interested in mathematics, especially group theory and Laplace-Fourier transforms, he later turned his interest to theoretical physics and in his last years paid special attention to biological work dealing with the genesis of life. He was a remarkable teacher who could clarify the most difficult questions. His great pleasure, before his wife's illness, was to go on excursions in the mountains and woods to search for plants; he was an excellent botanist and was president of the Mycological Society of France. He was also laureate of the Institut de France in 1922 and in 1928. In 1937 he was elected a member of the Académie des Sciences.

Mauguin's first researches in organic chemistry dealt with the amides $RCONH_2$, in which he replaced the two hydrogen atoms with one atom of bromine and one of sodium; the liberation of NaBr furnished isocyanates $O \cdot CN \cdot R$. He thus established a close link between the amides and the ureides, which play a role of great importance in the chemistry of the living cell. Throughout his life Mauguin was interested in the biological aspect of chemistry.

In the temperature region that characterizes the liquid-crystal state, the liquid crystal appears in the form of a turbid liquid, almost opaque when in a thick layer. Some scientists explained this cloudiness by the presence of an insoluble impurity. Mauguin showed that the liquid is made up of birefringent elements in random orientation so that it loses its transparency. Azoxyanisole and azoxyphenetole, which in the turbid phase are extremely fluid, become homogeneous and perfectly transparent when a uniform orientation is imposed on the birefringent elements, either by the action of a magnetic field or by suitable surface actions.

Placed between the poles of an electromagnet, the liquid-crystal phase behaves, optically, like strongly birefringent uniaxial crystal with optical axis parallel to the magnetic field. Mauguin made a complete optical study of this phenomenon, measured the indices of refraction, and reproduced all the classic experiments of optical crystallography.

Similarly, when melted between two completely clean glass plates, azoxyanisole yields a transparent homogeneous phase and behaves like a uniaxial crystal with optical axis perpendicular to the surface. If azoxyanisole is melted on a freshly cleaved flake of muscovite, the optical axis is parallel to the cleavage plane (001) in a direction (100) 30° from the plane of symmetry (010); this fact, unexpected at the time (1912), was explained by Mauguin after X rays showed that the plane of symmetry of mica is a plane of glide symmetry. If the melting takes place between the two surfaces of a cleavage, the two optical axes in contact with the two flakes form an angle of 60°; the result is a helicoidal structure, of which Mauguin made a detailed theoretical and experimental study. These results, established with remarkable rigor and clarity, excited great interest and are still valuable.

Upon returning to the laboratory after World War I, Mauguin, impressed with the importance for crystallography of the discoveries of Laue and the Braggs, devoted himself completely to X-ray crystallographic studies. In 1923 he published the atomic structure of cinnabar, followed by those of calomel and graphite. He next undertook long crystal-chemical researches on the micas and the chlorites, among which the unity of crystallographic properties is in contrast with the variety of chemical compositions. Mauguin determined the chemical composition of a great number of micas; their density; and, by means of X rays, the absolute values of their cell dimensions. He was thus able to determine the number of atoms contained in the unit cell. He established that the crystal motif for all the micas always includes twelve oxygen and fluorine atoms, although the number of cations varies within large limits and can be fractional, proving that the simple motif is not always repeated identically in the crystal (*Bulletin de la Société française de minéralogie*, **51** [1928], 285–332). In the chlorites the crystal motif always has eighteen oxygen atoms.

Mauguin worked a great deal on group theory; his memoir of 1931 represented the 230 Schönflies-Federov groups by simple symbols, describing the symmetry elements precisely and expressing directly the symmetry operations determined by X-ray diffraction. These symbols, slightly modified following a collaborative effort with C. Hermann, are universally employed and have made Mauguin's name familiar to crystallographers.

BIBLIOGRAPHY

The papers by Mauguin referred to in the text are "Étude des micas au moyen des rayons x," in *Bulletin de la Société française de minéralogie*, **51** (1928), 285–332; "La maille cristalline des chlorites," *ibid.*, **53** (1930), 279–300; and "Sur le symbolisme des groupes de répétition ou de symétrie des assemblages cristallins," in *Zeitschrift für Krystallographie*, **79** (1931), 542–558.

On Mauguin and his work see P. P. Ewald, *Fifty Years of X-Ray Diffraction* (Utrecht, 1962), pp. 335–340; and J. Wyart, "Ch. Mauguin 1878–1958," in *Bulletin de la Société française de minéralogie et de cristallographie*, **81** (1958), 171–172.

JEAN WYART

MAUNDER, EDWARD WALTER (*b.* London, England, 12 April 1851; *d.* London, 21 March 1928), *astronomy.*

Maunder attended the school attached to University College, London, and took some additional courses at King's College there. He then worked briefly in a London bank before taking the first examination ever given by the British Civil Service Commission for the post of photographic and spectroscopic assistant in the Royal Observatory at Greenwich. By appointing Maunder to this new post in 1873, the observatory—which had been concerned since its founding with positional astronomy—made a formal commitment to astrophysical observations. Maunder worked at Greenwich for forty years, largely under the direction of W. H. M. Christie; the primary task assigned him was the photographic observation of the sun and the subsequent measurement of sunspots.

Of Maunder's first wife, who died in 1888, little is known. His second wife, whom he married in 1895, was Annie S. D. Russell, a competent and active astronomer. In 1889 she graduated from Girton College, Cambridge, as Senior Optime in the Mathematical Tripos, thus earning the highest mathematical honor then available to women. In 1891 she was appointed "lady computer" at Greenwich, charged with examining and measuring the sunspot photographs taken by Maunder. Thenceforth, she worked closely with Maunder.

When the Greenwich record of sunspots was begun on 17 April 1874, the periodicity, equatorial drift, and variation of rotation with latitude of sunspots had already been established. In addition to verifying these facts, Maunder's daily photographs—taken first on wet plates, later on dry—made possible a search for other regularities. To this end Maunder tabulated various sunspot features, such as number, area, changes, position, and motion. From these data he drew conclusions concerning the relation between rotation period and latitude of sunspots, the position of the solar axis of rotation, the correlation between solar rotation and terrestrial magnetic disturbances, the variation in time of the mean spotted area of the sun, and the latitudinal distribution of sunspot centers. With a spectroscope attached to the observatory's great equatorial, Maunder observed solar prominences, the radial motion of stars, and the spectra of planets, comets, novae, and nebulae. The results were undistinguished.

Maunder traveled outside England to observe six solar eclipses. As a member of the official British party, Maunder photographed the corona from Carriacou in the West Indies in 1886, and from Mauritius in 1901. In 1905 he went to Canada as a guest of the Canadian government. The other three expeditions, under the auspices of the British Astronomical Association, were organized for the most part by Maunder himself. In 1896 they went to Vadsö, Norway, in 1898 to India, and in 1900 to Algeria. In India, Maunder and his wife made separate observations: she, with instruments of her own devising, photographed a coronal streamer extending to six solar radii—the longest ever photographed.

After his election as fellow in 1875, Maunder took an active part in the affairs of the Royal Astronomical Society, serving as council member for many years and secretary from 1892 to 1897. Despite its many advantages, this society did not satisfy the needs of many British astronomers. Therefore, in 1890, largely through the efforts of Maunder and his brother Thomas Frid Maunder, the British Astronomical Association was founded. Its purposes were twofold: "To meet the wishes and needs of those who find the subscription of the R.A.S. too high or its papers too advanced, or who are, in the case of ladies, practically excluded from becoming Fellows" and "to afford a means of direction and organization in the work of observation to amateur astronomers." For the rest of his life Maunder supported this popular organization, serving as president in 1894–1896 and as director at various times of the Mars section, the solar section, and the colored star section. He edited the association's *Journal* for about ten years; during his presidency this job was undertaken by his wife. Previously, from 1881 to 1887, he had edited *Observatory*, the journal founded by Christie.

The literary output of Maunder and his wife was prodigious. The results of their astronomical observations were communicated primarily to the *Monthly Notices of the Royal Astronomical Society* and the *Journal of the British Astronomical Association*. For many years both *Nature* and *Knowledge* contained frequent articles by the Maunders on popular astronomy, astronomical researches, and the history of astronomy—notably astronomical records in the Bible.

BIBLIOGRAPHY

I. ORIGINAL WORKS. Maunder's books include *The Royal Observatory, Greenwich, A Glance at its History and Work* (London, 1902); *Astronomy Without a Telescope* (London, 1903), derived largely from articles in *Knowledge; Astronomy of the Bible: An Elementary Commentary on the Astronomical References of Holy Scripture* (London, 1908); *The Science of the Stars* (London–Edinburgh, 1912); *Are the Planets Inhabited?* (London–New York, 1913); *Sir William Huggins and Spectroscopic Astronomy* (London–Edinburgh, 1913); and the astronomical section of *The International Standard Bible Encyclopaedia* (Chicago, 1915). See also *The Heavens and Their Story* (London, 1910), written with his wife. Articles by the Maunders are listed in the Royal Society *Catalogue of Scientific Papers*, X, 749–750; XVII, 102; and the annual volumes of the *International Catalogue of Scientific Literature*.

II. SECONDARY LITERATURE. There are obituaries of Maunder by H. P. H. in *Journal of the British Astronomical Association*, **38** (1927–1928), 229–233 (see also 165–168);

and in *Monthly Notices of the Royal Astronomical Society*, **89** (1928–1929), 313–318. The obituary of A. S. D. R. Maunder, written by M. A. Evershed, appeared in the *Journal of the British Astronomical Association*, **57** (1946–1947), 238.

DEBORAH JEAN WARNER

MAUPAS, FRANÇOIS ÉMILE (*b.* Vaudry, Calvados, France, 2 July 1842; *d.* Algiers, Algeria, 18 October 1916), *zoology, biology.*

The son of Pierre-Augustin Maupas, deputy mayor of Vaudry, and of Marie Adèle Geffroy, Maupas attended the municipal secondary school and then entered the École des Chartes. In 1867 he became archivist of the Department of Cantal, where he developed an interest in natural science and, in particular, in free protozoans. He spent his vacations in Paris in order to work in the laboratories of the Muséum d'Histoire Naturelle and of the Sorbonne. In 1870 Maupas was appointed an archivist in Algiers and then curator of the Bibliothèque Nationale. In his leisure moments he pursued research in zoological microscopy at home with rudimentary instruments. Maupas never married, and he lived the life of an isolated researcher. On 27 June 1901 he was elected a corresponding member of the Academy of Sciences, and in 1903 he received an honorary doctorate from the University of Heidelberg.

Maupas's scientific work was devoted entirely to sexuality and reproduction among the protozoans, rotifers, nematodes, and oligochaetes, which he studied with the aid of extremely ingenious breeding and culture techniques. Among the ciliates he investigated cultures bearing on hundreds of generations. He carefully examined the phenomenon of conjugation, which he discovered, and demonstrated the overall unity of the process and of its secondary features. He likewise analyzed the transformations of the nucleus. Maupas at first believed that this phenomenon effected a rejuvenation of the offspring after a long period of multiplication that produced a fatal aging—a view contradicting Weismann's theories on the "immortality" of the infusorians. His observations were later confirmed by other protistologists—who showed, however, that senescence does not have the absolute and inevitable character that Maupas had attributed to it. He also demonstrated that there are two categories of females in the rotifers: those which are parthenogenetic, producing only females, and those which can also be fertilized. If the latter are not impregnated, they yield only males; if they are fertilized they will produce special eggs which undergo later development and always produce females.

Among the nematodes, Maupas studied free and parasitic species. Among the free forms (Rhabditida) he showed that the postembryonic development consisted of five stages, of which the fifth is the adult stage (Maupas's law); and he demonstrated that in the parasitic forms the third stage, which is part of the molt of the second, is the infesting form. He provided more precise data on the phenomenon of encystment and studied parthenogenesis and hermaphroditism with self-fertilization, as well as cross-fertilization. These investigations earned him the Grand Prize in physical sciences of the Institut de France (1901). With L. G. Seurat he made observations on the strongyles, parasitic nematodes which are agents of bronchopneumonia in sheep in Algeria, and specified the etiology of this disease. Some of Maupas's investigations of the nematodes were published posthumously (1919). He also worked on freshwater oligochaetes *(Nais, Dero, Pristina, Aelosoma),* of which he obtained cultures prolonged for several months.

A complete naturalist, Maupas also published geological and botanical observations. In addition, he translated important German scientific works. Maupas was virtually unique among biologists of the second half of the nineteenth century in his ability to produce fundamental zoological work, without scientific training and through work in isolation with incredibly simple means and no real laboratory or collaborators.

BIBLIOGRAPHY

I. ORIGINAL WORKS. Maupas's principal publications are "Contribution à l'étude morphologique et anatomique des infusoires ciliés," in *Archives de zoologie expérimentale et générale,* 2nd ser., **1** (1883), 427–664; "Recherches expérimentales sur la multiplication des infusoires ciliés," *ibid.,* **6** (1888), 165–277; "Sur la multiplication agame de quelques métazoaires inférieurs," in *Comptes rendus . . . de l'Académie des sciences,* **109** (1889), 270–272; "Le rajeunissement caryogamique chez les ciliés," in *Archives de zoologie expérimentale et générale,* 2nd ser., **7** (1889), 149–517; "Sur la fécondation de l'*Hydatina scuta,*" in *Comptes rendus . . . de l'Académie des sciences,* **111** (1890), 505–507; "Sur la multiplication et la fécondation de l'*Hydatina scuta,*" *ibid.,* 310–312; "Sur le déterminisme de la sexualité chez l'*Hydatina scuta,*" *ibid.,* **113** (1891), 388–390; "La mue et l'enkystement chez les nématodes," in *Archives de zoologie expérimentale,* 3rd ser., **7** (1900), 563–632; "Modes et formes de reproduction des nématodes," *ibid.,* **8** (1901), 463–624; "Sur le mécanisme de l'accouplement chez les nématodes," in *Comptes rendus . . . de la*

Société de biologie, **79** (1916), 614–618, written with L. G. Seurat; "Essais d'hybridation chez les nématodes," in *Bulletin biologique de la France et de la Belgique,* **52** (1919), 467–486; and "Expériences sur la reproduction asexuelle des oligochètes," *ibid.,* **53** (1919), 150–160.

Among Maupas's translations is H. Burmeister, *Histoire de la création* (Paris, 1870).

II. SECONDARY LITERATURE. See M. Caullery, *Inauguration de la plaque commémorative apposée sur la maison habitée par Émile Maupas à Alger, le mercredi 6 avril 1932* (Paris, 1932), with portrait; and E. Sergent, "Émile Maupas prince des protozoologistes," in *Archives de l'Institut Pasteur d'Algérie,* **33** (1955), 59–70.

JEAN THÉODORIDÈS

MAUPERTUIS, PIERRE LOUIS MOREAU DE (*b.* St.-Malo, France, 28 September 1698; *d.* Basel, Switzerland, 27 July 1759), *mathematics, biology, physics.*

It was said of Maupertuis, in the official eulogy by Samuel Formey, that "Madame Moreau idolized her son rather than loved him. She could not refuse him anything." It seems highly probable that the spoiled child inevitably developed some of those personality characteristics that later made him not only proud but intransigent and incapable of bearing criticism, traits that ultimately led to great unpleasantness in his life and, quite literally, to his undoing.

After private schooling Maupertuis went to Paris at the age of sixteen to study under Le Blond, but he found ordinary philosophical disciplines quite distasteful. In 1717 he began to study music; but he soon developed a strong interest in mathematics, which he pursued under the tutelage of Guisnée and, later, Nicole. Maupertuis was elected to the Academy of Sciences in 1723, at the age of twenty-five, and presented a dissertation, "Sur la forme des instruments de musique." This was soon followed by a mathematical memoir on maxima and minima, some biological observations on a species of salamander, and two mathematical works of much promise: "Sur la quadrature et rectification des figures formées par le roulement des polygones reguliers" and "Sur une nouvelle manière de développer les courbes."

In 1728 Maupertuis made a trip to London that was to exert a major influence upon his subsequent career. From a conceptual world of Cartesian vortices he was transported into the scientific milieu of Newtonian mechanics, and he was quickly converted to these views. From this time on, Maupertuis was the foremost proponent of the Newtonian movement in France and a convinced defender of Newton's ideas about the shape of the earth. After returning to France he visited Basel, where he was befriended by the Bernoullis.

While pursuing, in conjunction with Clairaut, further studies in mathematics—resulting in a steady flow of notable memoirs—Maupertuis was readying his first work on Newtonian principles, "Discours sur les différentes figures des astres" (1732). It brought him the attention of the Marquise du Châtelet and of Voltaire, both of whom he instructed in the new doctrines. His position as the leading Continental Newtonian was confirmed the following year by his "Sur la figure de la terre et sur les moyens que l'astronomie et la géographie fournissent pour la déterminer," which was accompanied by a complementary memoir by Clairaut.

Thus it came about that in 1735 France sent an expedition to Peru under the leadership of La Condamine and another to Lapland under the leadership of Maupertuis. Clairaut, Camus, and other scientists accompanied the latter. The mission of each expedition was to measure as accurately as possible the length of a degree along the meridian of longitude. If, indeed, the earth is flattened toward the poles, as Newton had predicted, the degree of longitude should be longer in far northern latitudes than near the equator. The voyage began on 2 May 1736 and lasted over a year. The local base for the expedition's fieldwork was Torneå, in northern Sweden—then, according to Maupertuis, a town of fifty or sixty houses and wooden cabins. On the return journey the ship was wrecked in the Baltic Sea, but without loss of life, instruments, or records.

Maupertuis reached Paris on 20 August 1737, only to meet with a rather chilly reception. Envy and jealousy were already at work; he had few Newtonian supporters in France except Voltaire; and La Condamine's expedition had not yet returned from Peru. At this time Maupertuis found respite at Saint-Malo and at Cirey, where Mme du Châtelet and Voltaire made him welcome. He stayed only briefly at Cirey, however, intending to revisit Basel. There he met Samuel König, a young student of Johann I Bernoulli. He persuaded König to accompany him back to Cirey, where König behaved so arrogantly that he angered Mme du Châtelet, who through this episode became temporarily estranged from Maupertuis.

The laborious analysis of the data on the length of the arc of a meridional degree at various latitudes took much time and created much controversy. The measurements made in France had to be corrected. In December 1739 Maupertuis announced to the Academy the value found for the distance along the meridian between Paris and Amiens. The expedition to Peru having returned after an arduous three years, the degree between Quito and Cuenca was added to the comparisons. Still later (1751) measurements made by Lacaille at the Cape of Good Hope permitted a fourth comparison.

In a final revision of the reports on the "Opérations pour déterminer la figure de la terre" (*Oeuvres*, IV, 335) Maupertuis summarized the corrected measurements for a degree of longitude as follows:

	Latitude	Toises
Peru	0°30'	56,768
Cape of Good Hope	33°18'	56,994
France	49°23'	57,199
Lapland	66°10'	57,395

In 1738 Voltaire recommended Maupertuis to Frederick the Great, who was eager to rehabilitate the academy of sciences at Berlin. Frederick commenced overtures to Maupertuis, who visited Berlin after publication of his new, anonymously printed *Éléments de géographie* and his reconciliation with Mme du Châtelet. In Berlin he met Francesco Algarotti and the family of M. de Borck, whose daughter he was later to marry. After the outbreak of the War of the Austrian Succession, Maupertuis joined Frederick in Silesia, only to be captured when his horse bolted into the enemy lines. For a time he was feared dead by his friends, but Maupertuis soon emerged safely in Vienna; ominously, he took offense at the jests of Voltaire regarding his military exploit.

Maupertuis was elected to the Académie Française in 1743. In 1744 he presented the memoir "Accord de différentes lois de la nature" and published "Dissertation sur le nègre blanc." The latter was the precursor of the *Vénus physique* of 1745, which was an enlarged and more fully analyzed argument against the then-dominant biological theory of the preformation of the embryo. Maupertuis argued convincingly that the embryo could not be preformed, either in the egg or in the animalcule (spermatozoon), since hereditary characteristics could be passed down equally through the male or the female parent. He rejected the vitalistic notion that some "essence" from one of the parents could affect the preformed fetus in the other parent, or that maternal impressions could mold the characteristics of the offspring. A strict mechanist, although a believer in the epigenetic view of the origin of the embryo, he looked for some corporeal contribution from each parent as a basis of heredity.

In the middle of 1745 Maupertuis finally accepted Frederick's invitation and took up residence in Berlin. In the same year he married Mlle de Borck; and on 3 March 1746 he was installed as president of the Academy. His first contribution was the brief paper "Les lois du mouvement et du repos," in which he set forth the famous principle of least action, which he regarded as his own most significant scientific contribution. It states simply that "in all the changes that take place in the universe, the sum of the products of each body multiplied by the distance it moves and by the speed with which it moves is the least possible" (*Oeuvres*, II, 328). That is, this quantity tends to a minimum. This principle was later clarified and expounded by Euler, developed by Hamilton and Lagrange, and incorporated in modern times into quantum mechanics and the biological principle of homeostasis. As Maupertuis himself said:

The laws of movement thus deduced [from this principle], being found to be precisely the same as those observed in nature, we can admire the application of it to all phenomena, in the movement of animals, in the vegetation of plants, in the revolution of the heavenly bodies: and the spectacle of the universe becomes so much the grander, so much the more beautiful, so much worthier of its Author. . . .

These laws, so beautiful and so simple, are perhaps the only ones which the Creator and Organizer of things has established in matter in order to effect all the phenomena of the visible world [*Oeuvres*, I, 44–45].

Maupertuis clearly was successful in attracting to Berlin scientific luminaries who greatly enhanced the luster of the new Academy. Euler, one of the greatest mathematicians of the day, was already there. La Mettrie came in 1748; Mérian and Meckel in 1750; and, in the same year, after the death of Mme du Châtelet, Voltaire arrived in Berlin. With others the brusque impatience of Maupertuis rendered his efforts less successful. On the whole, however, matters were going well when the celebrated "affaire König" erupted. Samuel König, a protégé of Maupertuis, after having been elected a member of the Academy, visited Berlin, was warmly received by Maupertuis, and shortly thereafter submitted a dissertation attacking the validity of the principle of least action and then—most strangely for a devoted adherent of Leibniz—ascribed the discredited law to the latter, citing a letter from Leibniz to Hermann. Maupertuis was incensed. He demanded that the letter be produced. König produced a copy but stated that the original was in the hands of a certain Swiss named Henzi, who had been decapitated at Bern following involvement in a conspiracy. After exhaustive search no trace of the letter was found in Henzi's belongings. Maupertuis then demanded that the Academy take action against König.

At the same time Maupertuis was embroiled in a controversy between Haller and La Mettrie. The latter had dedicated to Haller, much to Haller's dismay, his *L'homme machine* (1748). La Mettrie had, in response to Haller's rejection, responded with a diatribe. Haller demanded an apology; but inasmuch as La Mettrie died at just that time, Maupertuis tried —without success—to assuage Haller with a polite letter. The episode certainly contributed to the extraordinary bitterness and tension that Maupertuis experienced in 1751.

Nevertheless, at this very time Maupertuis was able to publish one of his most significant works, later called *Système de la nature*. A sequel to the *Vénus physique*, it was a theoretical speculation on the nature of biparental heredity that included, as evidence, an account of a study of polydactyly in the family of a Berlin barber-surgeon, Jacob Ruhe, and the first careful and explicit analysis of the transmission of a dominant hereditary trait in man. Not only did Maupertuis demonstrate that polydactyly is transmitted through either the male or the female parent, but he also made a complete record of all normal as well as abnormal members of the family. He furthermore calculated the mathematical probability that the trait would occur coincidentally in the three successive generations of the Ruhe family had it not been inherited.

On the basis of this study, Maupertuis founded a theory of the formation of the fetus and the nature of heredity that was at least a century ahead of its time. He postulated the existence of hereditary particles present in the semen of the male and female parents and corresponding to the parts of the fetus to be produced. They would come together by chemical attraction, each particle from the male parent joining a corresponding particle from the female parent. Chemical affinity would also account for the proper formation of adjacent parts, since particles representing adjacent parts would be more alike than those of remote parts. At certain times the maternal character would dominate; at others the paternal character. The theory was applied to explain the nature of hybrids between species and their well-known sterility; and it was extended to account for aberrations with extra structures as well as to those characterized by a missing part. The origin of new sorts of particles, as well as the presence of those representing ancestral types, was envisaged. Finally, Maupertuis thought it possible that new species might originate through the geographical isolation of such variations.

During 1752 the König affair reached a climax and a hearing was held, from which Maupertuis absented himself. The letter cited by König was held to be unauthentic and undeserving of credence, and König resigned from the Academy—only to issue a public appeal and defense. Voltaire had already run afoul of Maupertuis, and jealousy existed between them regarding their influence with the king. Maupertuis had shown scant enthusiasm for a proposed monumental dictionary of metaphysics, to be developed by the Academy as a counterpoise to the *Encyclopédie*, for Maupertuis considered the talents of the Berlin Academy insufficient to keep such a work from being superficial. In September 1752 Voltaire attacked Maupertuis, charging him not only with plagiarism and error but also with persecution of honest opponents and with tyranny over the Academy. In the *Diatribe du Docteur Akakia*, Voltaire poured invective on the ideas that Maupertuis had expressed in his *Lettre sur le progrès des sciences* (1752) and *Lettres* (1752)—in which, among other daring speculations regarding the future course of science, Maupertuis had included his most substantial account of the investigation of polydactyly in the Ruhe family and of his own breeding experiments with Iceland dogs. In *Micromégas* Voltaire made fun of the voyage to Lapland undertaken to measure the arc of the meridian and lampooned Maupertuis's amorous adventures in the North. His mockery made a great contrast with the grandiloquent words that he had once inscribed beneath a portrait of Maupertuis. In vain Frederick supported Maupertuis and tried to restore good feeling. Maupertuis was crushed, his health gave way, and he requested a leave to recuperate at Saint-Malo. Pursued by an unceasing volley of Voltaire's most savage satires, Maupertuis withdrew. He remained at Saint-Malo until the spring of 1754, when he returned to Berlin at Frederick's insistence. Here he delivered the eulogy of his friend Montesquieu, who died at Paris early in 1755. He departed again for France, a very sick man, in May 1756. Greatly distressed by the outbreak of the Seven Years' War, he decided to return home by way of Switzerland. He went to Toulouse, whence he set out again in May 1758. At Basel, too ill to proceed, he was received warmly by his old friend Johann Bernoulli. On 27 July 1759, before his wife could reach him, he died and was buried in Dornach.

Maupertuis was a man of singular aspect. He was very short. His body was always in motion; he had numerous tics. He was careless of his apparel. Perhaps he was always endeavoring to attract attention. Perhaps he shared the Napoleonic complex of little men. Certainly he was both highly original and possessed of qualities that attracted friends, especially among the ladies; the Marquise du Châtelet and many other Frenchwomen corresponded regularly with him. He could be gay as well as fiery and violent. Above all he was proud, both of his intelligence and of his accomplishments, and to attack either was to wound him deeply. Above all, he could not understand the character of König, whom he had sponsored and who then gratuitously attacked him, or of Voltaire, whose adulation and friendship so quickly turned to malice and vituperation.

A philosopher as well as a scientist, Maupertuis proved himself a powerful and original thinker in *Essai de cosmologie* (1750). According to A. O. Lovejoy, he anticipated Beccaria and Bentham and, along with Helvétius, represents "the headwaters of the important stream of utilitarian influence which became so broad and sweeping a current through the work of the Benthamites" (*Popular Science Monthly*, **65** [1904], 340). He rejected the favorite eighteenth-century argument in favor of God—the argument from design—and instead, like Hume, he formulated a view of adaptation based on the elimination of the unfit. He recognized that Newton's laws are insufficient to explain chemistry, and even more so life, and turned to Leibniz for ideas about the properties of consciousness. In the *Système de la Nature* we may, with Ernst Cassirer (*Philosophy of the Enlightenment*, p. 86), see an attempt to "reconcile the two great opponents of the philosophy of nature of the seventeenth century," Newton and Leibniz. Yet in it must also be recognized a highly original work based on his own investigations of heredity. In his effort to introduce a calculus of pleasure and pain, in order to evaluate the good life and to measure happiness, Maupertuis proposed that the amount of pleasure or pain is a product of intensity and duration. This formulation is strictly analogous to his principle of least action in the physical world and shows how he extended his philosophy of nature into a philosophy of life.

BIBLIOGRAPHY

The works of Maupertuis are collected in *Oeuvres*, 4 vols. (Lyons, 1756). For his life see Grandjean de Fouchy, "Éloge de Maupertuis," in L. Angliviel de la Beaumelle, *Vie de Maupertuis* (Paris, 1856); Damiron, *Mémoires sur Maupertuis* (Paris, 1858); and P. Brunet, *Maupertuis*, I. *Étude Biographique* (Paris, 1929).

See also B. Glass, "Maupertuis, Pioneer of Genetics and Evolution," in B. Glass, O. Temkin, and W. Straus, Jr., eds., *Forerunners of Darwin, 1745–1859* (Baltimore, 1959); and Ernst Cassirer, *The Philosophy of the Enlightenment* (Princeton, 1951).

BENTLEY GLASS

MAURER, JULIUS MAXIMILIAN (*b*. Freiburg im Breisgau, Germany, 14 July 1857; *d*. Zurich, Switzerland, 21 January 1938), *meteorology, astronomy*.

Maurer was born in Germany but passed his whole life in Switzerland, where his parents settled when he was one year old. He attended the Eidgenössische Technische Hochschule at Zurich and studied astronomy at the University of Zurich. In 1879 he became an assistant at the Eidgenössische Sternwarte in Zurich, and in 1882 he received his doctorate for a thesis on the extinction of starlight in the atmosphere. In 1881 he was appointed adjunct at the Schweizerische Meteorologische Zentralanstalt, which was at that time connected with the observatory; soon afterwards the two institutions were separated administratively. In 1905, Maurer became director of the Zentralanstalt; he retired in 1934. He was a member of many scientific societies, and he was also an honorary citizen of Zurich from 1900.

Maurer worked mainly on radiation problems. In his early years, he dealt with the astronomical aspects of radiation. Later he became interested in questions of radiation in meteorology. His papers on total solar radiation and on nighttime heat loss by radiation made these topics as clear as was possible at the end of the nineteenth century.

Some meteorological instruments were constructed by Maurer, including barographs and instruments recording solar radiation. His position as director of the Zentralanstalt stimulated him to climatological researches. In 1909, together with R. Billwiller, Jr., and C. Hess, he published *Das Klima der Schweiz*, which contained detailed critical discussions on the climate of Switzerland. Maurer continued work on these problems and published papers on glacial variations, freezing of lakes, and general climatological problems.

BIBLIOGRAPHY

Among Maurer's works are "Die theoretische Darstellung des Temperaturgangs in der Nacht und die Wärmestrahlung der Atmosphäre," in *Meteorologische Zeitschrift*, **4** (1887), 189; "Beobachtungen über die irdische Strahlenbrechung bei typischen Formen der Luftdruckverteilung," *ibid.*, **22** (1905), 49; and *Das Klima der Schweiz*, 2 vols. (Frauenfeld, 1909–1910), written with R. Billwiller, Jr., and C. Hess. Many of Maurer's papers on detailed questions of climatology in Switzerland appeared in *Meteorologische Zeitschrift*. There is no secondary literature on Maurer.

F. SCHMEIDLER

MAURO, FRA (*d*. Murano, near Venice, Italy, 20 October 1459 [?]), *geography*.

Fra Mauro, author of the last of the great medieval world maps, was a monk of the Camaldolese order and, in all probability, head of a cartographic workshop in the Camaldolese monastery of San Michele di Murano, in the lagoon of Venice. Of his life very little is known other than that he worked at San Michele from about 1443 until his death and that his fame as a mapmaker spread as far as Portugal. There are records of payments made by the king of Portugal to the monastery in the late 1450's, and a statement on the map reads: "I have copies of maps made by the Portuguese."

The world map now in the Biblioteca Nazionale Marciana in Venice is the sole surviving work that can be positively identified as Fra Mauro's. Drawn on vellum, the circular map is 1.96 meters in diameter, and its quadrangular frame measures 2.23 meters on each side. The mapmaker's colors are well preserved, and legends both on the map and in the corners outside its circular outline are fully legible. The map is oriented to the south on the top; a legend on the back states that it was completed on 26 August 1460, which would indicate that the last touches were added after Fra Mauro's death in the previous year.

Fra Mauro's map represents an encyclopedic storehouse of contemporary geographic and cosmographic information. It is limited to Europe, Asia, and part of Africa and shows Iceland and the Canary Islands to the west. It includes the first mention of "Zimpagu" (Japan) on any European map; it extends to the Urals in the north; and its southern limit is probably at the latitude of Madagascar. The mapmaker and his assistants used a variety of sources: medieval navigation charts of European origin; the accounts of travelers, especially Marco Polo and the fifteenth-century Venetian merchant and traveler Niccolò de' Conti; Arabic sailing directions and travel accounts; and, possibly, information obtained from Ethiopian delegates to the council of Florence (1438–1445).

Fra Mauro's work is a milestone in the history of geography and cartography for the wealth of its information, both correct and distorted; its wide range of cartographic and geographic data on remote parts of Asia and, to a lesser extent, of Africa; and its clearly transitional character, from the medieval to Renaissance worldview.

BIBLIOGRAPHY

The first detailed study of Fra Mauro's world map was Placido Zurla, *Il mappamondo di Fra Mauro camaldolese* (Venice, 1808). The authoritative reference, accompanied by a complete section-by-section color reproduction of the map and transcription of all legends, is Tullia Gasparrini Leporace, *Il mappamondo di Fra Mauro* (Rome, 1956), with introductory essay by Roberto Almagià.

GEORGE KISH

MAUROLICO, FRANCESCO (*b*. Messina, Italy, 16 September 1494; *d*. near Messina, 21 or 22 July 1575), *mathematics, astronomy, optics.*

Maurolico's name is variously transcribed as Maurolyco, Marulì, Marulli, and, in Latin, Maurolicus, Maurolycus, and Maurolycius. He was the son of Antonio Maurolico, master of the Messina mint, and his wife, Penuccia or Ranuccia. The family came from Greece, from which they had fled to Sicily to escape the Turks; Maurolico learned Greek, as well as astronomy, from his father. In 1521 he was ordained priest; he later became a Benedictine. Except for short sojourns in Rome and Naples, he lived his whole life in Sicily.

Maurolico's patrons included Giovanni de Vega, Charles V's viceroy of Sicily, who entrusted him with the mathematical education of one of his sons; and Giovanni Ventimiglia and his son, Simon, both marquises of Geraci and princes of Castelbuono and governors ("stradigò") of Messina. In 1550 Simon conferred upon Maurolico the abbey of Santa Maria del Parto (today also known as the Santuario di San Guglielmo), near Castelbuono. Maurolico also held a number of civil commissions in Messina; he served as head of the mint, he was in charge (with the architect Ferramolino) of maintaining the fortifications of the city on behalf of Charles V, and he was appointed to write a history of Sicily, which, as *Sicanicarum rerum compendium*, was published in Messina in 1562. Most important, he gave public lectures on mathematics at the University of Messina, where he was appointed professor in 1569.

Although Maurolico himself referred to a vast literary production (in his *Cosmographia* and *Opuscula*), only a few of his works were printed, although these are enough to show him as an outstanding scholar. In addition to writing his own books, Maurolico translated, commented upon, reconstructed, and edited works by a number of ancient authors. His first work in this vein, published in Messina in 1558, included treatises on the sphere by Theodosius of Bythinia "ex traditione Maurolyci"; by Menelaus of Alexandria "ex traditione eiusdem"; and by Maurolico himself. The book also contained a work by Autolycus of Pitane on the moving sphere, translations of the *De habitationibus* of Theodosius and the *Phaenomena* of Euclid, trigonometric tables, a mathematical compendium, and a work entitled "Maurolyci de sphaera sermo."

This early book is especially noteworthy for two reasons. First, the Neapolitan mathematician Giuseppe d'Auria furthered the dissemination of Maurolico's work by including his annotations in later editions of Autolycus' *Sphaera* and Theodosius' *De habitationibus* (Rome, 1588), as well as of Euclid's *Phaenomena* (Rome, 1591). Second, J. B. J. Delambre, in his *Histoire de l'astronomie du moyen âge*, stated that Maurolico had been the first to make use of the trigonometric function of the secant. Maurolico did give a table of numerical values for the secants of 0° to 45° (the "tabella benefica"), but Copernicus had certainly preceded him in its use.

Maurolico's two other major books on ancient mathematics—one on Apollonius' *Conics*, and the other a collection of the works of Archimedes—were published only after his death. In *Emendatio et restitutio conicorum Apollonii Pergaei* (Messina, 1654), Maurolico attempted to reconstruct books V and VI of the *Conics* from the brief references to them that Apollonius provided in his preface to the entire work. In Maurolico's time, only the first four books were known in the Greek original; he completed his restoration in 1547, and a similar reconstruction of book V was published by Vincenzo Viviani in 1659. (Although Maurolico's work is less famous than Viviani's, both Libri and Gino Loria cite it as an example of his genius.) Maurolico's collection of Archimedes' works, *Admirandi Archimedis Syracusani monumenta omnia mathematica quae extant . . . ex traditione doctissimi viri D. Francisci Maurolici* (Palermo, 1685), was based upon an earlier partial edition by Borelli (Messina, 1670–1672), which was almost completely lost.

Among the most important of Maurolico's extant books are *Cosmographia* (Venice, 1543), written in the form of three dialogues; *Opuscula mathematica* (Venice, 1575), a collection of eight treatises; *Photismi de lumine et umbra ad perspectivam et radiorum incidentiam facientes* (possibly Venice, 1575, and certainly Naples, 1611); and *Problemata mechanica . . . et ad magnetem et ad pixidem nauticam pertinentia* (Messina, 1613). In addition to these, a number of Maurolico's manuscripts held by the Bibliothèque Nationale, Paris, were published by Federico Napoli in 1876; these include a letter of 8 August 1556, in which Maurolico reported on his mathematical studies to his patron Giovanni de Vega; a brief treatise, previously thought to be lost, entitled "Demonstratio algebrae"; books I and II of a 1555 "Geometricarum quaestionum"; and a "Brevis demonstratio centri in parabola," dated 1565.

Of the mathematical works edited by Napoli, the "Demonstratio algebrae" is elementary in its concerns, dealing with simple second-degree problems and derivations from them. "Geometricarum quaestionum" is primarily devoted to trigonometry and solid geometry, but touches upon geodesy in offering a proposal for a new method for measuring the earth, a method previously discussed in the *Cosmographia* and later taken up by Jean Picard for measuring the meridian (1669–1671). In the "Brevis demonstratio centri in parabola," Maurolico chose to deal with a problem related to mechanics—which he also treated in his edition of Archimedes—the determination of the center of gravity of a segment of a paraboloid of revolution cut off by a plane perpendicular to its axis.

The greatest number of Maurolico's mathematical writings are gathered in the *Opuscula mathematica;* indeed, the second volume of that work, "Arithmeticorum libri duo," is wholly devoted to that subject and contains, among other things, some notable research on the theory of numbers. This includes, in particular, a treatment of polygonal numbers that is more complete than that of Diophantus, to which Maurolico added a number of simple and ingenious proofs. L. E. Dickson has remarked upon Maurolico's argument that every perfect number is hexagonal, and therefore triangular, while Baldassarre Boncompagni noted his proof of a peculiarity of the succession of odd numbers. That property had been enunciated by Nicomachus of Gerasa, Iamblichus, and Boethius, among others.

Among the topics related to mathematics in the *Opuscula* are chronology (the treatise "Computus ecclesiasticus") and gnomonics (in two treatises, both entitled "De lineis horariis," one of which also discusses conics). The work also contains writing on Euclid's *Elements* (for which see also the unpublished Bibliothèque Nationale, Paris, manuscript Fonds Latin 7463). Of particular interest, too, is a passage on a correlation between regular polyhedrons, which was commented upon by J. H. T. Müller, and later by Moritz Cantor. The balance of Maurolico's known mathematical work is contained in three manuscripts, mostly on geometrical problems, in the Biblioteca Nazionale Centrale Vittorio Emanuele in Rome; they have been described by Luigi De Marchi.

Maurolico's work in astronomy includes the first treatise collected in the *Opuscula*, "De sphaera liber unus," in which he criticized Copernicus. In another item of the collection, "De instrumentis astronomicis," Maurolico described the principal astronomical instruments and discussed their theory, use, and history—a subject similar to that treated in one of his first publications, the rare and little-known tract *Quadrati fabrica et eius usus* (Venice, 1546). In practical astronomy, Maurolico observed the nova that appeared in the constellation Cassiopeia in 1572. Until recently all that was known of this observation was contained in the short extracts from an unknown work by Maurolico that were published by Clavius in his *In Sphaeram Ioannis de Sacro Bosco commentarius* (Rome, 1581). In 1960, however, C. Doris Hellman published an apograph manuscript that she had found in the Biblioteca Nazionale of Naples. This manuscript contains a full account of Maurolico's observation; it is dated 6 November 1572, and is clear evidence that Maurolico's observation preceded by at least five days the more famous one made by Tycho Brahe.

Maurolico also did important work in optics; indeed, according to Libri, "it is in his research on optics, above all, that Maurolico showed the most sagacity" (*Histoire*, III, 116). The chief record of this research is *Photismi de lumine et umbra*, in which Maurolico discussed the rainbow, the theory of vision, the effects of lenses, the principal phenomena of dioptrics and catoptrics, radiant heat, photometry, and caustics. Maurolico's work on caustics was anticipated by that of Leonardo da Vinci (as was his research on centers of gravity), but Leonardo's work was not published until long after Maurolico's. Libri further characterized the *Photismi de lumine et umbra* as "full of curious facts and ingenious research" (*Histoire*, III, 118), and Sarton suggested that it might be the most remarkable optical treatise of the sixteenth century outside the tradition of Alhazen, or even the best optical book of the Renaissance (*Six Wings*, 84, 85).

Maurolico applied his broad scientific knowledge to a number of other fields. One treatise in the *Opuscula*, "Musicae traditiones," is devoted to music. The *Problemata mechanica* published in 1613 is concerned with mechanics and magnetism, as is, to some degree, the "Brevis demonstratio." His contributions to geodesy have already been discussed; he made an additional contribution to geography with a map of Sicily, drawn about 1541 at the request of Jacopo Gastaldo (who published it in 1575)—this map was also incorporated by Abraham Ortelius in his *Theatrum orbis terrarum*. Maurolico wrote on the fish of Sicily, in a letter to Pierre Gilles d'Albi, dated 1 March 1543 and published by Domenico Sestini in 1807, and on the eruption of Mt. Etna, in a letter to Cardinal Pietro Bembo, dated 4 May 1546 and published by Giuseppe Spezi in 1862. Finally, he enjoyed some contemporary fame as a meteorologist, based upon a weather prediction that he made for John of Austria upon the latter's departure from Messina prior to the Battle of Lepanto (1571).

BIBLIOGRAPHY

I. ORIGINAL WORKS. Almost all of Maurolico's writings have been mentioned in the text. For further information see Pietro Riccardi, *Biblioteca matematica italiana* (Modena, 1870–1928; repr. Milan, 1952), articles "Archimede," "Auria," "Maurolico"; and Federico Napoli, "Intorno alla vita ed ai lavori di Francesco Maurolico," pref. to "Scritti inediti di Francesco Maurolico," in *Bullettino di bibliografia e di storia delle scienze matematiche e fisiche*, **9** (1876), 1–121, on p. 5 of which is a list of codices of the Bibliothèque Nationale, Paris, containing autographs by Maurolico (Fonds Latin, nos. 6177, 7249, 7251, 7459, 7462–7468, 7471, 7472A, 7473). On this see also Federico Napoli, "Nota intorno ad alcuni manoscritti di Maurolico della Biblioteca Parigina," in *Rivista sicula di scienze, letteratura ed arti*, **8** (1872), 185–192.

See also Luigi De Marchi, "Di tre manoscritti del Maurolicio che si trovano nella Biblioteca Vittorio Emanuele di Roma," in Eneström's *Bibliotheca mathematica* (1885), cols. 141–144, 193–195. In the codices described by De Marchi (marked 32, 33, 34; formerly S. Pantaleo 115, 116, 117), there is a letter from Maurolico to Prince Barresi di Pietraperzia, dated 11 Sept. 1571, which was published by De Marchi in "Una lettera inedita di Francesco Maurolico a proposito della battaglia di Lepanto," in *Rendiconti dell'Istituto lombardo di scienze e lettere*, **16** (1883), 464–467; this letter, De Marchi observes, may be considered as Maurolico's scientific will.

Maurolico's letter to Cardinal Bembo of 4 May 1546 is in Giuseppe Spezi, *Lettere inedite del Card. Pietro Bembo e di altri scrittori del secolo XVI, tratte da codici Vaticani e Barberiniani* (Rome, 1862), pp. 79–84. A letter from Maurolico to Cardinal Antonio Amulio dated 1 Dec. 1568 is in Baldassarre Boncompagni, "Intorno ad una proprietà de' numeri dispari," in *Bullettino di bibliografia e di storia delle scienze matematiche e fisiche*, **8** (1875), 51–62, see pp. 55–56, where a MS on arithmetic by Maurolico is cited (Codex Vat. lat. no. 3131) and the dedicatory letter which precedes it is published.

The work on the nova of 1572 is in "Maurolyco's 'Lost' Essay on the New Star of 1572," transcribed, translated, and edited by C. Doris Hellman, in *Isis*, **51** (1960), 322–336; the MS, in the Biblioteca Nazionale of Naples (cod. I E 56, fols. 2r–10r), perhaps a copy of an autograph version, is entitled "Super nova stella: Que hoc anno iuxta Cassiopes apparere cepit considerationes."

The work on Sicilian fish is in Domenico Sestini, *Viaggi e opuscoli diversi* (Berlin, 1807), 285–302, with notes on pp. 303–313 and mention of the MS used on p. xiii; see also *Tractatus per epistolam Francisci Maurolici ad Petrum Gillium de piscibus siculis Codice manu auctoris exarato, Aloisius Facciolà messanensis nunc primum edidit* (Palermo, 1893). An English translation of the *Photismi* is *The Photismi de Lumine of Maurolycus. A Chapter in Late Medieval Optics*, Henry Crew, trans. (New York, 1940).

The rare pamphlet on the quadrant is in the personal library of Dr. Carlo Viganò, Brescia, Italy. Its full title is *Quadrati fabrica et eius usus, ut hoc solo instrumento,* caeteris praetermissis, uniusquisq. mathematicus, contentus esse possit, per Franciscum Maurolycum nuper edita. Illustriss. D. D. Ioanni Vigintimillio Ieraciensium Marchioni, D. (Venice, 1546). In colophons to various parts of the text Maurolico gives the dates 6 Apr. 1541, 18 Apr. 1541, and 11 Jan. 1542. The work consists of eleven numbered pages and one unnumbered page with a table of stars.

II. SECONDARY LITERATURE. Older biographies and bibliographies on Maurolico include Francesco della Foresta, Vita dell'abbate del Parto D. Francesco Maurolyco (Messina, 1613), written by the nephew and namesake of the subject; Antonino Mongitore, "Maurolico," in Biblioteca sicula, I (Palermo, 1707), 226–227; Domenico Scinà, Elogio di Francesco Maurolico (Palermo, 1808); and Girolamo Tiraboschi, "Maurolico," in Storia della letteratura italiana, VII (Milan, 1824), 728–734.

Two valuable monographs from the late nineteenth century are Giuseppe Rossi, Francesco Maurolico e il risorgimento filosofico e scientifico in Italia nel secolo XVI (Messina, 1888); and Giacomo Macrì, "Francesco Maurolico nella vita e negli scritti," in R. Accademia Peloritana, Commemorazione del IV centenario di Francesco Maurolico MDCCCXCIV (Messina, 1896), p. iii–iv, 1–198. The latter volume also contains "Ricordi inediti di Francesco Maurolico," illustrated by Giuseppe Arenaprimo di Montechiaro, p. 199–230, with three plates reproducing handwritten items by Maurolico.

Maurolico is discussed in the following standard histories of mathematics: J. E. Montucla, Histoire des mathématiques, 2 vols. (Paris, 1758), I, 563, 571–572, 695–698; Guglielmo Libri, Histoire des sciences mathématiques en Italie, 3 vols. (Paris, 1837–1841), III, 102–118; Moritz Cantor, Vorlesungen über Geschichte der Mathematik, 4 vols. (Leipzig, 1880–1908), II, 558–559, 575, passim; and David Eugene Smith, History of Mathematics, 2 vols. (Boston, 1924–1925), I, 301–302, and II, 622. See also Florian Cajori, A History of Mathematical Notations, 2 vols. (La Salle, Ill., 1928–1929), I, 349, 362, 402, and II, 150.

Maurolico's work on mathematicians of antiquity is discussed in Vincenzo Flauti, "Sull'Archimede e l'Apollonio di Maurolico. Osservazioni storico-critiche," in Memorie della Accademia delle scienze di Napoli, 2 (1855–1857), lxxxiv–xciv; and Gino Loria, Le scienze esatte nell'antica Grecia (Milan, 1914), 219, 354, 434, 435, 502, 510, 511, 513, 515. On Maurolico as editor of Autolycus, see the following works by Joseph Mogenet: "Pierre Forcadel traducteur de Autolycus," in Archives internationales d'histoire des sciences (1950), 114–128; and "Autolycus de Pitane: Histoire du texte, suivie de l'édition critique des traités De la sphère en mouvement et Des levers et couchers," in Université de Louvain, Recueil de travaux d'histoire et de philologie, 3rd ser., fasc. 37 (1950), 23, 26, 27, 30–36, 38–42, 48–50, 176.

Arithmetic is treated in Mariano Fontana, "Osservazioni storiche sopra l'aritmetica di Francesco Maurolico," in Memorie dell'Istituto nazionale italiano (Bologna), Fis.-mat. cl., 2, pt. 1 (1808), 275–296; Baldassarre Boncompagni, "Intorno ad una proprietà de' numeri dispari" (see

above); and Leonard Eugene Dickson, History of the Theory of Numbers (Washington, D.C., 1919; repr. New York, 1952, 1966), I, 9, 20, and II, 5, 6.

On the use of the principle of mathematical induction by Maurolico, anticipated by Euclid, see the following writings by Giovanni Vacca: "Maurolycus, the First Discoverer of the Principle of Mathematical Induction," in Bulletin of the American Mathematical Society, 16 (1909–1910), 70–73; "Sulla storia del principio d'induzione completa," in Loria's Bollettino di bibliografia e storia delle scienze matematiche, 12 (1910), 33–35; and "Sur le principe d'induction mathématique," in Revue de métaphysique et de morale, 19 (1911), 30–33. See also W. H. Bussey, "The Origin of Mathematical Induction," in American Mathematical Monthly, 24 (1917), 199–207; Léon Brunschvicg, Les étapes de la philosophie mathématique, 3rd ed. (Paris, 1929), 481–484; and Hans Freudenthal, "Zur Geschichte der vollständigen Induktion," in Archives internationales d'histoire des sciences (1953), 17–37.

Maurolico's geometry is treated in Michel Chasles, Aperçu historique sur l'origine et le développement des méthodes en géometrie, 2nd ed. (Paris, 1875), 120, 291, 293, 345, 496, 516; J. H. T. Müller, "Zur Geschichte des Dualismus in der Geometrie," in Grunert's Archiv der Mathematik und Physik, 34 (1860), 1–6; and Federico Amodeo, "Il trattato sulle coniche di Francesco Maurolico," in Eneström's Bibliotheca mathematica, 3rd ser., 9 (1908–1909), 123–138.

On centers of gravity, see Margaret E. Baron, The Origins of the Infinitesimal Calculus (Oxford, 1969), 90–94.

Astronomy is discussed in J. B. J. Delambre, Histoire de l'astronomie du moyen âge (Paris, 1819; repr. New York, 1965), 437–441; J. L. E. Dreyer, A History of Astronomy From Thales to Kepler (New York, 1953), 257, 295, 356–357, formerly entitled History of the Planetary Systems From Thales to Kepler (Cambridge, 1906); Lynn Thorndike, A History of Magic and Experimental Science, V (New York, 1941), 304, 360, 421, 426, and VI (New York, 1941), 27, 74, 179–180, 382; and Edward Rosen, "Maurolico's Attitude Toward Copernicus," in Proceedings of the American Philosophical Society, 101 (1957), 177–194.

On Maurolico's contributions to geodesy, see Pietro Riccardi, "Cenni sulla storia della geodesia in Italia dalle prime epoche fin oltre alla metà del secolo XIX," in Memorie della Accademia delle scienze di Bologna, 3rd ser., 10 (1879), 431–528, see 518–519; and "Sopra un antico metodo per determinare il semidiametro della terra," ibid., 4th ser., 7 (1887), 17–22; and Ottavio Zanotti-Bianco, "Sopra una vecchia e poco nota misura del semidiametro terrestre," in Atti della Accademia delle scienze di Torino, 19 (1883–1884), 791–794.

On optics, besides works by Libri, Crew, and Sarton already cited, see the following writings of Vasco Ronchi: Optics, the Science of Vision, trans. and rev. by Edward Rosen (New York, 1957), 39–40, 265; "L'optique au XVIe siècle," in La science au seizième siècle. Colloque international de Royaumont, 1–4 juillet 1957 (Paris, 1960), 47–65, and The Nature of Light, trans. by V. Barocas

(London, 1970), 78, 99ss., 223. See also A. C. Crombie, "The Mechanistic Hypothesis and the Scientific Study of Vision," in S. Bradbury and G. L'E. Turner, eds., *Historical Aspects of Microscopy* (Cambridge, 1967), 3–112 (see 43–46), and in *Proceedings of the Royal Microscopical Society*, 2, pt. 1 (1967).

On music, see Salvatore Pugliatti, "Le *Musicae traditiones* di Francesco Maurolico" in *Atti dell'Accademia peloritana*, **48** (1951–1967). On p. 336 is mentioned a MS, which contains three papers of Maurolico: "De divisione artium," "De quantitate," "De proportione." This MS was recently found by Monsignor Graziano Bellifemine in the Library and Museum of the Seminario Vescovile at Molfetta.

On Maurolico as a man of letters, historian, and philosopher, see G. Macrì, "Francesco Maurolico nella vita e negli scritti" (see above), pp. 48–62, 123–151; Valentino Labate, "Le fonti del *Sicanicarum rerum compendium* di Francesco Maurolico," in *Atti dell'Accademia peloritana*, **13** (1898–1899), 53–84; and L. Perroni-Grande, "F. Maurolico professore dell'Università messinese e dantista," in R. Accademia Peloritana, *CCCL anniversario della Università di Messina. Contributo storico* (Messina, 1900), 15–41, which includes the notarial act containing the nomination of Maurolico as professor at the University of Messina.

Other writings to be consulted are Luigi De Marchi, "Sull'ortografia del nome del matematico messinese Maurolicio," in Eneström's *Biblioteca mathematica* (1886), cols. 90–92; and several biobibliographical writings by Edward Rosen: "The Date of Maurolico's Death," in *Scripta mathematica*, **22** (1956), 285–286; "Maurolico Was an Abbot," in *Archives internationales d'histoire des sciences* (1956), 349–350; "De Morgan's Incorrect Description of Maurolico's Books," in *Papers of the Bibliographical Society of America*, **51** (1957), 111–118; "Was Maurolico's Essay on the Nova of 1572 Printed?," in *Isis*, **48** (1957), 171–175; "The Title of Maurolico's *Photismi*," in *American Journal of Physics*, **25** (1957), 226–228; and "The Editions of Maurolico's Mathematical Works," in *Scripta mathematica*, **24** (1959), 56–76.

ARNALDO MASOTTI

MAURY, ANTONIA CAETANA DE PAIVA PEREIRA (*b*. Cold Spring-on-Hudson, New York, 21 March 1866; *d*. Dobbs Ferry, New York, 8 January 1952), *astronomy*.

Antonia Maury was the daughter of Mytton and Virginia Draper Maury, a niece of Henry Draper, and granddaughter of John William Draper, a pioneer in the application of photography to astronomy. Her background was rich and varied, for her father was a naturalist and editor of a geographical magazine, as well as a professional minister. Although she worked chiefly as an astronomer, she was also an active ornithologist. Her sister, Carlotta Joaquina Maury (1874–1938), became a paleontologist specializing in Venezuelan and Brazilian stratigraphy.

Shortly after graduating from Vassar in 1887, Miss Maury became an assistant at the Harvard College Observatory, where during the next eight years she carried out her most perceptive and creative research. At that time the observatory director, Edward C. Pickering, was engaged in a program of stellar spectroscopy, and he had just found that the spectral lines of the star Mizar were double on one plate but single on others. Additional photographs established Mizar as the first spectroscopic binary, and Miss Maury was the first to determine its period, 104 days. In 1889 she herself discovered the second such star, Beta Aurigae, with a period of about four days.

In 1890 Williamina Fleming's *Draper Catalogue of Stellar Spectra* was published, with an initial classification of more than 10,000 stars. To Miss Maury was assigned a more detailed study of the brighter stars, made possible by placing three or four prisms in front of the eleven-inch Draper refractor (a telescope originally owned by her uncle, Henry Draper, and given to Harvard by his widow). Miss Maury soon concluded that the single spectral sequence of the *Draper Catalogue* was inadequate for representing all the observed peculiarities. In particular, for stars of the early spectral groups she assumed the existence of three collateral divisions (designated *a*, *b*, and *c*) characterized by the width and distinctness of their lines. In her system, *a* stars had normal lines, *b*, hazy lines, and *c*, sharp lines. Intermediate cases were designated *ab* or *ac*. Her catalogue, based on an examination of about 4,800 photographs, included her elaborate classification of 681 bright stars of the northern skies (*Annals of Harvard College Observatory*, **28**, pt. 1 [1896]).

Miss Maury's painstaking classifications enabled Ejnar Hertzsprung to verify his discovery of two distinct varieties of stars—dwarfs (divisions *a* and *b*) and giants (*c*). Unfortunately, Hertzsprung's interpretation was scarcely exploited at Harvard and in later work there, the *a*, *b*, *c* distinction was largely ignored in favor of the more elementary Draper system, as extended by Annie Jump Cannon. This led Hertzsprung to write to Pickering (22 July 1908):

> In my opinion the separation by Antonia C. Maury of the c- and ac-stars is the most important advancement in stellar classification since the trials by Vogel and Secchi .... To neglect the c-properties in classifying stellar spectra, I think, is nearly the same thing as if the zoologist, who has detected the deciding differences between a whale and a fish, would continue in classifying them together.

Miss Maury's temperament was little suited to the often tedious observatory routine, and as early as 1891 her connection with Harvard became an on-again off-again affair. After her paper on spectral classification was finally published, for several years she lectured on astronomy in various cities; between lectures she accepted private pupils and an occasional teaching position. In 1908 she returned to Harvard Observatory as a research associate, resuming her earlier studies of spectroscopic binaries. She spent many years investigating the complex spectrum of the binary Beta Lyrae, details of which were published in the *Annals of Harvard College Observatory*, **84**, no. 8 (1933). After retiring in 1935, at the age of sixty-nine, she served for several years as curator of the Draper Park Museum at Hastings-on-Hudson, New York, paying nearly annual visits to the Harvard Observatory to examine the current spectra of Beta Lyrae.

BIBLIOGRAPHY

Miss Maury's chief publications are noted in the text. A short obituary by Dorrit Hoffleit appears in *Sky and Telescope*, **11** (1952), 106. The best source is Bessie Zaban Jones and Lyle Gifford Boyd, *The Harvard College Observatory* (Cambridge, 1971), 395–400; see also Solon I. Bailey, *The History and Work of Harvard Observatory, 1839–1927* (New York, 1931).

OWEN GINGERICH

MAURY, MATTHEW FONTAINE (*b.* near Fredericksburg, Virginia, 14 January 1806; *d.* Lexington, Virginia, 1 February 1873), *physical geography, meteorology, oceanography.*

Maury was the seventh child of a small planter, Richard Maury, who was a descendant of a Huguenot family that had come to Virginia from Ireland about 1718, and the former Diana Minor, whose English and Dutch forebears had settled in Virginia by 1650. He grew up in Williamson County, Tennessee, where his family moved in 1810. On graduating from Harpeth Academy in 1825, he followed his deceased eldest brother into the U.S. Navy, where his career flourished until 1839, when a stagecoach accident left him too lame for further duty at sea. Maury nevertheless remained a naval officer, serving in Washington and writing vigorously in the causes of naval reform, Southern expansionism, and those branches of science that could be applied to seafaring. He resigned his commission in 1861 to join the Confederate Navy. In England for the Confederacy from 1862 until

May 1865, Maury next served Emperor Maximilian of Mexico until 1866, when he returned to England to write geography textbooks. Not until 1868 did he return to the United States, where he was professor of physics at Virginia Military Institute until his death. In 1834 Maury married Ann Herndon, a distant cousin; they had five daughters and three sons.

Maury's scientific career began with two articles and a textbook on navigation. These made him an obvious choice for the U.S. Navy exploring expedition, to which he was appointed astronomer in September 1837 by Thomas ap Catesby Jones, the expedition's first leader. Maury's role was brief; he joined Jones and the other officers in resigning in November following Jones's repeated disagreements with Secretary of the Navy Mahlon Dickerson. After a number of senior officers declined, command of the expedition went to Charles Wilkes, who as head of the Navy's Depot of Charts and Instruments had traveled to Europe to obtain the expedition's apparatus.

The depot, set up in 1830 to issue navigational supplies to the fleet, had become under Wilkes an astronomical observatory as well. His successor, James M. Gilliss, who had studied astronomy in Paris, carried the quest for a national observatory one step further when he convinced Congress in 1842 that the depot needed a new observatory building. Dispatched to Europe for ideas and instruments, Gilliss was succeeded at the depot by Maury, who was thus rewarded with an important shore billet for leading the fight to reorganize the Navy.

When the observatory building was completed in 1844, the Virginians had their revenge for Wilkes's takeover of the exploring expedition: Secretary of the Navy John Y. Mason chose Maury to head the new "National Observatory." Maury threw himself and his staff into the strenuous program of observations that his rival, Gilliss, had planned, and he began to publish the results. But Maury's poor qualifications for astronomy and his proprietary attitude toward the work done at the observatory created hostility toward him in the intense competition for scarce resources within the American scientific community. This hostility seems justified. Considering that Maury was in charge of one of the world's major observatories for almost seventeen years and that he had substantial funds at his disposal, his contributions to astronomy seem small. Between 1844 and 1861 he published fewer than twenty papers—all observational—and seven catalogs of observations.

Maury failed to accomplish more in astronomy because his main interest lay in improving the technology of navigation, for which the science of the earth was more relevant than the science of the heavens. Upon taking charge of the depot in 1842, he moved it out of Wilkes's house. The move revealed an accumulation of manuscript ships' logs. Maury's insight that the data on winds and currents in these logs could be brought together to chart the general circulation of atmosphere and ocean was the basis for his chief contribution to science.

Maury began to publish his *Wind and Current Charts*—beginning with the North Atlantic in 1847—and to issue them free to mariners in exchange for abstract logs of the winds and currents of their voyages. The result was a series of charts and (after 1850) accompanying sailing directions that presented a climatic picture of the surface winds and currents for all the oceans.

Maury's chief aim in issuing these charts was the promotion of maritime commerce. He was thus more a technologist than a scientist, interested in knowledge less for its own sake than as a means to practical achievement. Pressed by the growth of steam propulsion, the sailing fleets of the world were making great progress in improving their technology about 1850, and Maury was the leading developer of the "software" of sail. After 1849, when the rush to California's gold fields became the main stage for the conflict between sail and steam, he claimed that his charts shortened sailing passages considerably in the competition between the sailing route round Cape Horn and the steamer-railroad route across Panama.

Another commercial stimulation to Maury's scientific endeavors came from submarine telegraphy. U.S. Navy vessels sounded the North Atlantic under Maury's direction from 1849 to 1853; and from their results he prepared the first bathymetrical chart, using 1,000-fathom contours. By distributing the bottom samples collected on these cruises to J. W. Bailey at West Point and C. G. Ehrenberg at Berlin, Maury made possible their pioneering studies in marine micropaleontology.

Inspired by the example of Alexander von Humboldt, many men of science in the second quarter of the nineteenth century were devoting their efforts to collecting on a large scale the data of physical phenomena on earth. Maury's charts were important instances of this kind of empirical science. The need to standardize observations made at widely separated points required international cooperation, which led in turn to international scientific meetings. The spread of the telegraph made possible a synoptic meteorology; and in response to a tentative British proposal for American cooperation in weather observations on land, Maury organized a conference at Brussels in 1853, the first of a series of international meteoro-

logical meetings. Maury, the leader in systematizing observations at sea, hoped to extend his own efforts to land. But his plans for the conference to unify weather reporting for both land and ocean ran into opposition at home; at the insistence of the American and British governments, the Brussels conference dealt only with the sea. The final report, written largely by Maury, organized uniform weather reporting at sea. This system was extended to the land after his death.

Maury's scientific achievements were organizational and empirical; they earned him the praise of European leaders of science, including Humboldt. Maury's attempts to interpret his data, however, were largely without merit in the eyes of scientific colleagues. He expressed them in the pious language of natural theology at a time when most scientists had succeeded in purging their writings of all religious references. Beginning with an article on the Gulf Stream in 1844, Maury developed theories of the general circulation of atmosphere and ocean, first in articles and in *Explanation and Sailing Directions to Accompany the Wind and Current Charts* (1850 *et seq.*) and then in his best-known work, *Physical Geography of the Sea* (1855), a loosely organized compilation of Maury's earlier writings on meteorology and oceanography. Reprinted many times in America and England and translated into six European languages, it was received enthusiastically in general and religious journals, critically in scientific ones. Maury's response to his critics was either to ignore them or to defend vigorously his original ideas. Since he was unwilling to modify his theories in the light of criticism, Maury's importance to the history of ideas of wind and water motion lies in the stimulus he gave to others, especially William Ferrel, who were forced by the popularity of Maury's book to improve upon his unphysical interpretations.

Almost no one accepted Maury's idea—based on Faraday's demonstration that oxygen is paramagnetic—that fluctuations in the wind are due to the earth's magnetism. Maury's scheme of the general circulation of the atmosphere required that vertical air currents move across each other in the calm belts of the tropics and the equator, and that horizontal winds converge to low-pressure areas around the poles. The latter requirement was contrary to the evidence; the former, physically implausible. Maury ignored Ferrel's alternative scheme, despite its explicit challenge. Maury's ideas on ocean circulation were not much sounder. He offered a vigorous argument for "thermo-haline" forces; but unable, like most of his contemporaries, to accept multiple causes, he accompanied it with an equally vigorous argument against wind stress, based on his erroneous belief that a Gulf Stream driven by the wind would be flowing uphill. He believed (incorrectly) that variations in salinity were more important than variations in temperature in causing currents, and he was also the principal exponent of the idea that the sea around the North Pole is free of ice.

Maury's failure to revise his theories in the light of criticism and new evidence, and his aggressive promotion in Congress of his own brand of science, brought him increasingly into conflict with the leaders of the growing American scientific community. At first Maury was given the place that his position in Washington merited. He was one of the founders of the American Association for the Advancement of Science, which in 1849 formed one committee to urge more funds for Maury's charts and appointed Maury himself to several others. But in 1851, when a committee was formed to organize the land meteorology of North America, Maury was not appointed. His claim that he should organize observations on land as he had on the ocean was a threat to the network established by Joseph Henry at the Smithsonian Institution, and in the presidential address to the A.A.A.S. in that year Alexander Dallas Bache spoke of the dangers to American science "from a modified charlatanism, which makes merit in one subject an excuse for asking authority in others, or in all" (*Proceedings of the American Association for the Advancement of Science*, **6** [1852], xliv). Their opposition to Maury led to the restriction of the 1853 Brussels conference to marine meteorology. Maury continued to present papers to the annual meetings of the A.A.A.S. until his book appeared in 1855; but he ceased to be a member in 1859, after his continuing effort to take over land meteorology had again been thwarted by Henry and his allies. His hope had been to benefit agriculture as his maritime meteorology had benefited navigation.

Although his cherished theories never received the support that he believed they deserved, Maury was widely honored for his achievements, both in his lifetime and afterward. He was decorated by the sovereigns of Denmark, Portugal, and Russia; received honorary degrees from Columbian College (now George Washington University [1853]) and the universities of Cambridge (1868) and North Carolina (1852); and became a member of a number of scientific academies and societies.

BIBLIOGRAPHY

I. ORIGINAL WORKS. *The Physical Geography of the Sea* is available in a modern ed. (Cambridge, Mass., 1963).

Lists of Maury's other works are in Ralph M. Brown, "Bibliography of Commander Matthew Fontaine Maury," which is *Bulletin of the Virginia Polytechnic Institute*, **37**, no. 12 (1944); and in F. L. Williams, *Matthew Fontaine Maury* (see below), 693–710.

II. SECONDARY LITERATURE. The massive biography by Frances L. Williams, *Matthew Fontaine Maury. Scientist of the Sea* (New Brunswick, N.J., 1963), contains much more material than earlier ones, together with footnotes and a complete bibliography. Each of its three predecessors, however, is useful: Diana Corbin, *Life* (London, 1888), contains family reminiscences by Maury's daughter; Charles L. Lewis, *Maury* (Annapolis, 1927), an account of the efforts after Maury's death to keep his name alive; and John W. Wayland, *Pathfinder of the Seas* (Richmond, Va., 1930), a chronology and a number of photographs not in the other works. All four biographies take Maury's scientific achievement at his own valuation; only Williams provides the reader with the evidence for an independent judgment.

Maury's science is carefully evaluated in John Leighly's brilliant introduction to the 1963 repr. of *Physical Geography of the Sea* and his equally important "M. F. Maury in His Time," in Proceedings of the First International Congress of the History of Oceanography, *Bulletin de l'Institut océanographique de Monaco*, spec. no. 2 (1968), 147–159. Leighly's incisive treatments supersede all previous writings on Maury's work in meteorology and oceanography. For Maury's work in a broader scientific context, see Margaret Deacon, *Scientists and the Sea 1650–1900* (London, 1970), ch. 13; in the context of American science, A. Hunter Dupree, *Science in the Federal Government* (Cambridge, Mass., 1957).

HAROLD L. BURSTYN

MAWSON, SIR DOUGLAS (*b.* Bradford, Yorkshire, England, 5 May 1882; *d.* Adelaide, Australia, 14 October 1958), *geology.*

Douglas Mawson was the younger son of Robert Mawson and Margaret Ann Moore, both of long-established Yorkshire families. The family sailed to Australia in 1884, where the father eventually attained some success as a lumber merchant. The boys were educated at Rooty Hill country school and later at Fort Street Public School, Sydney. Mawson entered the University of Sydney in 1899, took a bachelor of engineering degree in 1901, and under the influence of T. W. E. David, professor of geology, decided to become a geologist. He received a bachelor of science degree in 1904, doctor of science in 1909 (South Australia), became a fellow of the Royal Society in 1923, and received a doctor of science degree from the University of Sydney in 1952. After joining the staff at the University of Adelaide in 1905 as lecturer on mineralogy and petrology, he became the first professor of geology in 1920 and remained there until his retirement in 1952.

Mawson was honorary curator of minerals at the South Australian Museum and chairman of the board of governors at the time of his death. He was also a foundation fellow of the Australian Academy of Science and an honorary member of the Geological Society of Australia. His scientific awards are too numerous to be listed here. He married Francisca Adriana ("Paquita") Deprat, daughter of a mining engineer, on 31 March 1914 and had two daughters, Patricia and Jessica.

Douglas Mawson was foremost an explorer-geologist. His first expedition to the New Hebrides in 1903 was followed by his participation in Sir Ernest Shackleton's 1907–1909 expedition to Antarctica, where Mawson ascended Mt. Erebus and mapped the position of the South Magnetic Pole, helping to man-haul sledges for some 1,300 miles. He then helped organize and commanded two Antarctic expeditions. In the first, the Australasian Antarctic Expedition (1911–1914), six parties worked in Queen Mary Land and Adélie Land. Mawson's two companions died—Ninnis falling to his death in a crevasse 315 miles from base, and Mertz dying more than a hundred miles from safety—and he struggled back alone for the last 115 miles, reaching the winter base over a month later. His epic is well told in *The Home of the Blizzard*. As commander of the British Australian New Zealand Antarctic Research Expedition (BANZARE) in 1929–1931, he traveled to subantarctic islands and to Kemp Land and Enderby Land as far west as 45°E.

Although not a first-rank scientific investigator, Mawson established an outstanding department at Adelaide and worked extensively on geological problems of South Australia, notably on the Precambrian Adelaide System. He insisted on the fusing of scientific and geographic exploration, and his highly successful pioneering expeditions inspired public and government support.

BIBLIOGRAPHY

I. Original Works. Mawson's writings include "The Geology of the New Hebrides," in *Proceedings of the Linnean Society of New South Wales*, **3** (1905), 400–485; "The Australasian Antarctic Expedition, 1911–1914," in *Geographical Journal*, **44** (1914), 257–286; *The Home of the Blizzard: Being the Story of the Australasian Antarctic Expedition 1911–1914*, 2 vols. (London, 1915); *The Winning of Australian Antarctica* (Sydney, 1963), the geographical report of the BANZARE 1929–1931 research expedition;

Macquarie Island: Its Geography and Geology, Australasian Antarctic Expedition 1911–1914, Scientific Reports, ser. A, vol. V (Sydney, 1943); and "The Adelaide Series As Developed Along the Western Margin of the Flinders Ranges," in *Transactions of the Royal Society of South Australia*, **71**, pt. 2 (1947), 259–280.

II. Secondary Literature. See Charles Francis Laseron, *South With Mawson* (London, 1947), reminiscences of the Australasian Antarctic expedition of 1911–1914; Paquita Mawson, *Mawson of the Antarctic* (London, 1961); and A. Grenfell Price, *Mawson's B.A.N.Z.A.R.E. Voyage 1929–1931, Based on the Mawson Papers* (Sydney, 1963).

J. B. Waterhouse

MAXIMOV. See **Maksimov.**

MAXWELL, JAMES CLERK (*b*. Edinburgh, Scotland, 13 June 1831; *d*. Cambridge, England, 5 November 1879), *physics.*

Maxwell was a descendant of the Clerks of Penicuik, a family prominent in Edinburgh from 1670 on, who had twice intermarried during the eighteenth century with the heiresses of the Maxwells of Middlebie, illegitimate offspring of the eighth Lord Maxwell. His father, John Clerk (Maxwell), younger brother of Sir George Clerk, M.P., inherited the Middlebie property and took the name Maxwell in consequence of some earlier legal manipulations which prevented the two family properties being held together. The estate, some 1,500 acres of farmland near Dalbeattie in Galloway (southwestern Scotland), descended to Maxwell; and much of his scientific writing was done there. Maxwell's mother was Frances Cay, daughter of R. Hodshon Cay, a member of a Northumbrian family residing in Edinburgh. She died when he was eight years old. On both parents' sides Maxwell inherited intellectual traditions connected with the law, as was common in cultivated Edinburgh families. John Clerk Maxwell had been trained as an advocate, but his chief interest was in practical, technical matters. He was a fellow of the Royal Society of Edinburgh and published one scientific paper, a proposal for an automatic-feed printing press. Maxwell's father was a Presbyterian and his mother an Episcopalian. Maxwell himself maintained a strong Christian faith, with a strain of mysticism which has affinities with the religious traditions of the Galloway region, where he grew up.

From 1841 Maxwell attended Edinburgh Academy, where he met his lifelong friend and biographer, the Platonic scholar Lewis Campbell, and P. G. Tait. He entered Edinburgh University in 1847 and came under the influence of the physicist and alpinist James David Forbes and the metaphysician Sir William Hamilton. In 1850 he went up to Cambridge (Peterhouse one term, then Trinity), where he studied under the great private tutor William Hopkins and was also influenced by G. G. Stokes and William Whewell. He graduated second wrangler and first Smith's prizeman (bracketed equal with E. J. Routh) in 1854. He became a fellow of Trinity in 1855. Maxwell held professorships at Marischal College, Aberdeen, and King's College, London, from 1856 to 1865, when he retired from regular academic life to write his celebrated *Treatise on Electricity and Magnetism* and to put into effect a long-cherished scheme for enlarging his house. During the four years 1866, 1867, 1869, and 1870, he also served as examiner or moderator in the Cambridge mathematical tripos, instituting some widely praised reforms in the substance and style of the examinations. In 1871 he was appointed first professor of experimental physics at Cambridge and planned and developed the Cavendish Laboratory. On 4 July 1858 he married Katherine Mary Dewar, daughter of the principal of Marischal College and seven years his senior. They had no children. He died in 1879 at the age of forty-eight from abdominal cancer.

Maxwell's place in the history of physics is fixed by his revolutionary investigations in electromagnetism and the kinetic theory of gases, along with substantial contributions in several other theoretical and experimental fields: (1) color vision, (2) the theory of Saturn's rings, (3) geometrical optics, (4) photoelasticity, (5) thermodynamics, (6) the theory of servomechanisms (governors), (7) viscoelasticity, (8) reciprocal diagrams in engineering structures, and (9) relaxation processes. He wrote four books and about one hundred papers. He was joint scientific editor with T. H. Huxley of the famous ninth edition of the *Encyclopaedia Britannica*, to which he contributed many articles. His grasp of both the history and the philosophy of science was exceptional, as may be seen from the interesting philosophical asides in his original papers and from his general writings. His *Unpublished Electrical Researches of the Hon. Henry Cavendish* (1879) is a classic of scientific editing, with a unique series of notes on investigations suggested by Cavendish's work.

It was Maxwell's habit to work on different subjects in sequence, sometimes with an interval of several years between successive papers in the same field. Six years elapsed between his first and second papers on electricity (1855, 1861), twelve years between his

second and third major papers on kinetic theory (1867, 1879). The account of his work must therefore be grouped by subject rather than in strict chronological order; a description of his juvenile papers and the studies on color vision and Saturn's rings is useful in illustrating his intellectual development up to 1859.

Juvenilia (1845–1854). Maxwell's first paper was published when he was fourteen years old. It followed the efforts of D. R. Hay, a well-known decorative artist in Edinburgh, to find a method of drawing a perfect oval similar to the string property of the ellipse. Maxwell discovered that when the string used for the ellipse is folded back on itself n times toward one focus and m times toward the other, a true oval is generated, one of the kind first studied by Descartes in connection with the refraction of light. Although Descartes had described ways of generating the curves, Maxwell's method was new. His father showed the results to J. D. Forbes, who secured publication in the *Proceedings of the Royal Society of Edinburgh*. Shortly afterward Maxwell wrote a remarkable manuscript, which is reproduced in facsimile by his biographers, on the geometrical and optical properties of ovals and related curves of higher order. It afforded a foretaste of two of his lifelong characteristics: thoroughness and a predilection for geometrical reasoning. Both qualities, traditional in Scottish education, were powerfully reinforced for Maxwell by his teacher at Edinburgh Academy, James Gloag, a man of "strenuous character and quaint originality" to whom "mathematics was a mental and moral discipline."[1]

Three of Maxwell's next four papers were on geometrical subjects. One, "On the Theory of Rolling Curves" (1848), analyzed the differential geometry of families of curves generated like the cycloid, by one figure rolling on another. Another (1853) was a brief investigation in geometrical optics, leading to the beautiful discovery of the "fish-eye" lens. The third was "Transformation of Surfaces by Bending," which extended work begun by Gauss. The only paper from this period with a strictly physical subject was "On the Equilibrium of Elastic Solids," written in 1850 shortly before Maxwell went up to Cambridge. In 1847 he had been taken by his uncle John Cay to visit the private laboratory of the experimental optician William Nicol, from whom he received a pair of polarizing prisms. With these he investigated the phenomenon of induced double refraction in strained glass, which had been discovered in 1826 by another famous Scottish experimenter, Sir David Brewster. Maxwell's studies led him to the papers of Cauchy and Stokes. He developed a simple axiomatic formulation of the general theory of elasticity, solved various problems, and offered a conjectural explanation of induced double refraction based on strain functions. The alternative interpretation based on stress functions had been given earlier by F. E. Neumann, but Maxwell's theory was independent and better. The usefulness of photoelastic techniques in studying stress distributions in engineering structures is well-known: retrospectively the paper is even more important as Maxwell's first encounter with continuum mechanics. Its significance for his researches on the electromagnetic field and (more surprisingly) gas theory will shortly appear.

Color Vision (1850–1870). Maxwell created the science of quantitative colorimetry. He proved that all colors may be matched by mixtures of three spectral stimuli, provided subtraction as well as addition of stimuli is allowed. He revived Thomas Young's three-receptor theory of color vision and demonstrated that color blindness is due to the ineffectiveness of one or more receptors. He also projected the first color photograph and made other noteworthy contributions to physiological optics.

Credit for reviving Young's theory of vision is usually given to Helmholtz. His claim cannot be sustained. The paper it is based on, published in 1852, contained useful work, but Helmholtz overlooked the essential step of putting negative quantities in the color equations and explicitly rejected the three-receptor hypothesis;[2] and although Grassmann in 1854 pointed out fallacies in his reasoning, there is no evidence that Helmholtz followed the argument through to a conclusion until after Maxwell's work appeared. Artists had indeed known centuries before Maxwell or Helmholtz that the three so-called primary pigments, red, yellow, and blue, yield any desired hue by mixture; but several things clouded interpretation of the phenomena and hindered acceptance of Young's idea. One was the weight of Newton's claim that the prismatic spectrum contains seven primary colors rather than three. Another was the cool reception given to Young's theory of light, which extended to his theory of vision. The course of speculation between Young and Maxwell has never been clearly charted. In Britain the three-receptor theory did nearly gain acceptance during the 1820's. It was favorably discussed by John Herschel and Dalton as well as by Young: Herschel in particular suggested that Dalton's red blindness might come from the absence of one of Young's three receptors.[3] A curious complication supervened, however. During the 1830's Brewster performed experiments with absorption filters by which he claimed to demonstrate the existence of three kinds of light, distributed in various proportions throughout the spectrum. Color according to him

was thus an objective property of light, not a physiological function of the human eye. Brewster's interpretations were founded on his stubborn belief in the corpuscular theory of light, but the experiments seemed good and were accepted even by Herschel until Helmholtz eventually traced the effects to imperfect focusing. During the same period from 1830 on, wide general progress was made in physiological optics throughout Europe, in which the names of Purkinje, Haidinger, Johannes Müller, and Wartmann are memorable. In Britain the first statistical survey of color deficiency was conducted by George Wilson of Edinburgh—the chemist, and biographer of Cavendish—who brought to the subject a nice touch of topical alarmism through his lurid warnings about the dangers inherent in nighttime railway signaling. It was in an appendix to Wilson's monograph *On Colour Blindness* (1855) that Maxwell's first account of his researches appeared.

Maxwell began experiments on color mixing in 1849 in Forbes's laboratory at Edinburgh. At that time Edinburgh was unusually rich in students of color: besides Forbes, Wilson, and Brewster, there were William Swan, a physician interested in the eye, and D. R. Hay, who, in addition to his work in the geometry of design, had written a book entitled *Nomenclature of Colours* (1839) and supplied Forbes and Maxwell with tinted papers and tiles for their investigations. The experiments consisted in observing hues generated by colored sectors on a rapidly spinning disk. Forbes first repeated a standard experiment in which a series of colors representing those of the spectrum combine to give gray. He then tried to produce gray from combinations of red, yellow, and blue but failed—"and the reason was found to be, that blue and yellow do not make green, but a pinkish tint, when neither prevails in the combination."[4] No addition of red to this could produce a neutral tint.

Using a top with adjustable sectors of tinted paper, Forbes and Maxwell went on to obtain quantitative color equations, employing red, blue, and *green* as primaries. Interestingly, Young, in one little-known passage, had made the same substitution.[5] The standard rules for mixing pigments were explained by Maxwell, and independently by Helmholtz, as a secondary process, with the pigments acting as filters to light reflected from the underlying surface.

In 1854, after his graduation from Cambridge, Maxwell was able to resume these researches, which Forbes had been compelled by a severe illness to abandon. He improved the top by adding a second set of adjustable sectors of smaller diameter than the first, to make accurate color comparisons, and obtained equations for several groups of observers which could be manipulated algebraically in a consistent manner. For color-deficient observers only two variables were needed. Maxwell then went on to prove that Newton's method of displaying colors on a circle with white at the center implicitly satisfies the three-receptor theory, since it is equivalent to representing each color datum by a point in a three-dimensional space. With the experimental results plotted on a triangle having red, blue, and green corners, after the method of Young and Forbes, there is a white point w inside and an ordered curve of spectral colors outside the triangle very similar to Newton's circle. Adapting terminology from D. R. Hay, Maxwell distinguished three new variables—hue (spectral color), tint (degree of saturation), shade (intensity of illumination)—corresponding to "angular position with respect to w, distance from w, and coefficient [of intensity]." There is an easy transformation from these variables and to the representation of colors as a sum of three primaries: hence "the relation between the two methods of reducing the elements to three becomes a matter of geometry."[6] All this is most modern. In later correspondence with Stokes (1862), Maxwell described manipulations of color coordinates to reduce data from different observers to a common white point. The advantages of this procedure were also pointed out by C. J. Monro in a letter to Maxwell, dated 3 March 1871, which was published in Campbell and Garnett's *Life of James Clerk Maxwell* (1882), although other workers in colorimetry entirely ignored the idea until Ives and Guild rediscovered it fifty years later.[7]

To go further, a new instrument less susceptible than the color top to conditions of illumination and properties of paper was called for. Accordingly Maxwell devised what he called his "colour-box," in which mixtures of spectral stimulants were directly compared with a matching white field. The original version, perfected in 1858, consisted of two wooden boxes, each about three feet long, joined at an angle, containing a pair of refracting prisms at the intersection. An eyepiece was placed at one end; at the other were three slits, adjustable in position and aperture, which could be set at positions corresponding to any three wavelengths A, B, C in the spectrum formed by projecting white light through the eyepiece. By the principle of reciprocity, white light entering the slits yielded mixtures of A, B, C at the eyepiece, with intensities determined by the widths of the slits. Light from the same source (a sheet illuminated by sunlight) entered another aperture and was reflected past the edge of the second prism to the eyepiece, where the observer saw, side by side, two fields which

he could match in hue and intensity. The spectrum locus determined by Maxwell's observer K (his wife) is shown in Figure 1, together with the results of König and Abney (1903, 1913) and the 1931 standard observer. The Maxwells come out of the comparison rather well. Maxwell designed two other "colourboxes" on the same general principle. The second was made portable by the use of folded optics on the principle afterward adapted to the spectroscope by Littrow. The third gave hues of exceptional spectral purity by adopting a "double monochromator" principle, illuminating the slits with the spectrum from a second train of prisms symmetrically disposed rather than with direct sunlight. With it Maxwell studied variations of color sensitivity across the retina, a subject he had become interested in through his observations of the "Maxwell spot."

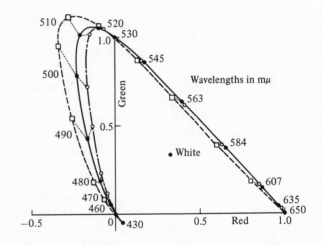

FIGURE 1. Spectrum loci determined by different experimenters.

——— ○   Maxwell 1860 (observer K)
- - - □   König, Abney 1903, 1913 (recalculated Weaver)
——— ●   C.I.E. standard observer 1931 (Wright, Guild)

Most people, when they look at an extended source of polarized light, intermittently perceive a curious pair of yellow structures resembling a figure eight, with purple wings at the waist. These are the "brushes" discovered by Haidinger in 1844. They may be seen especially clearly by looking at a blue surface through a Nicol prism. Maxwell studied them with the prisms he had received from Nicol; and at the British Association meeting of 1850 he proposed attributing them to a polarizing structure in the yellow spot on the retina, a hypothesis which brought him into an amusing confrontation with Brewster, who attributed them to the cornea.[8] Maxwell's explanation is now accepted. In 1855 he noticed, in the blue region of the spectrum formed by looking through a prism at a vertical slit, an elongated dark spot which moved up and down with the eye and possessed the same polarizing structure as Haidinger's brushes. This is the Maxwell spot. Later his wife discovered that she could not see the spot, there being almost no yellow pigment on her retinas. Noticing also a large discrepancy between her white point and his, Maxwell then found that his own color matches contained much less blue in the extrafoveal region and he proceeded to investigate variations of sensitivity across the retina for a large number of observers. He was able to exhibit the yellow spot—as he wrote to C. J. Monro in 1870—to "all who have it,—and all have it except Col. Strange, F. R. S., my late father-in-law and my wife,—whether they be Negroes, Jews, Parsees, Armenians, Russians, Italians, Germans, Frenchmen, Poles, etc."[9] Summaries of the work appeared in two brief papers and in a delightful correspondence with Monro, which also contains an interesting discussion on differences in color nomenclature between ancient and modern languages.

In 1861 Maxwell projected the first trichromatic color photograph at the Royal Institution before an audience which included Faraday. The subject was a tartan ribbon photographed through red, green, and blue filters by Thomas Sutton, a colleague at King's College, London, and then projected through the same filters. An odd fact which remained without explanation for many years was that the wet collodion plates used should not have given any red image, since that photographic process is completely insensitive to red. Yet contemporary descriptions make it clear that the colors were reproduced with some fidelity. In 1960 R. M. Evans and his colleagues at Kodak Research Laboratories, in a first-class piece of historical detective work, established that the red dyes in Maxwell's ribbon also reflected ultraviolet light in a region just coinciding with a pass band in the ferric thiocyanate solution used as a filter. The "red" image was really obtained with ultraviolet light! The hypothesis is confirmed by the fact that the original red plate preserved at Cambridge is slightly out of focus, although Sutton carefully refocused the camera for visible red light. A repetition of the experiment under modern conditions gave a "surprisingly colorful reproduction of the original scene."[10]

Saturn's Rings (1855–1859). In 1855 the topic of the fourth Adams prize at Cambridge was announced as an investigation of the motions and stability of the rings of Saturn. Some calculations on Saturn's rings, treated as solid bodies, had been given as early as 1787 by Laplace. He established that a uniform rigid ring would disintegrate unless (1) it is rotating at a speed where the centrifugal force balances the attraction of the planet and (2) the ratio ρ_r/ρ_s of its density to the density of Saturn exceeds a critical value 0.8, such that the attractions between inner and outer portions of the ring exceed the differences between centrifugal and gravitational forces at different radii. Also, the motions of a uniform ring are dynamically unstable: any displacement from equilibrium leads to an increased attraction in the direction of displacement, precipitating the ring against the planet. Laplace conjectured, however, that the motion is somehow stabilized by irregularities in the mass distribution; and in his dogmatic way asserted that the rings of Saturn are irregular solid bodies. That was where the theory still stood in 1855; meanwhile, a new dark ring and further divisions in the existing rings had been observed, along with some evidence for slow changes in the overall dimensions of the system during the 200 years since its discovery. The examiners, James Challis, Samuel Parkinson, and William Thomson (the future Lord Kelvin), called for explanations of each point and an investigation of dynamical stability on the hypothesis that the rings are: (1) solid, (2) fluid, (3) composed of "masses of matter not mutually coherent."[11] These were the questions on which Maxwell spent much time between 1855 and 1859 in the essay to which the prize was awarded.

Maxwell took up first the theory of the solid ring where Laplace had left it, and determined conditions for stability of a ring of arbitrary shape. Forming equations of motion in terms of the potential at the center of Saturn due to the ring, he obtained two restrictions on the first derivatives of the potential for uniform motion, and then, by a Taylor expansion, three more conditions on the second derivatives for stable motion. Maxwell next transformed these results into conditions on the first three coefficients of a Fourier series in the mass distribution. He was able to show that almost every conceivable ring was unstable except the curious special case of a uniform ring loaded at one point with a mass between 4.43 and 4.87 times the remaining mass. There the uneven distribution makes the total attraction act toward a point outside the ring in such a way that the instabilities affecting the moment of inertia are counteracted by a couple which alters the angular momentum. But such a ring would collapse under the uneven stress, and its lopsidedness would be plainly visible. The hypothesis of a solid ring is untenable.

In considering nonrigid rings Maxwell again utilized Fourier's theorem, but in a different way, examining the stability of various rings by expanding disturbances in their form into a series of waves. He took as a starting model, with which more complex structures could later be compared, a ring of solid satellites, equally spaced and all of equal mass. The motions may be resolved into four components: rotation about Saturn with constant angular velocity ω and small displacement ρ, σ, ζ in directions radial, tangential, and normal to the plane of the ring. Normal displacements of any satellite are manifestly stable, for the components of attraction to the other bodies always constitute a restoring force. Tangential disturbances might be expected to be unstable, since the attractions to neighboring satellites are in the direction of displacement; but Maxwell discovered that radial and tangential waves of a given order may be coupled together in a stable manner because the radial motions generate Coriolis forces through the rotation about the planet, which counterbalance the gravitational forces due to tangential motions. Detailed analysis revealed four kinds of waves, grouped in two pairs, all of which are stable if the mass of the central body is great enough. The motions are rather complicated; and Maxwell, "for the edification of sensible image worshippers,"[12] had a mechanical model constructed to illustrate them in a ring of thirty-six satellites. Waves of the first two kinds move in opposite directions with respect to a point on the rotating ring, with a velocity nearly equal to ω/n, where ω is the angular velocity of the ring and n the number of undulations. Thus if there are five undulations the wave velocity is 1/5 of the ring velocity. Each satellite describes an elliptical path about its mean position in a sense opposite to the rotation of the ring itself, the major axis of the ellipse being approximately twice the minor axis and lying near the tangential plane. If the number of satellites is μ, the highest-order waves, which are most likely to disrupt the ring, have $\mu/2$ undulations. The stability criterion is

$$S > 0.4352\mu^2 R, \qquad (1)$$

S and R being the masses of Saturn and the ring. Stability is determined by tangential forces; the parameter defining them must lie between 0 and $0.07\omega^2$.

For rings of finite breadth Maxwell's procedure was to examine simplified models which bracket the true situation. He began with rings whose inner and outer parts are so strongly bound together that they rotate uniformly. Such rings may be called semirigid. They are evidently subject to Laplace's criterion of cohesion $\rho_r/\rho_s > 0.8$ but, like a ring of satellites, are also subject to conditions of stability against tangential disturbances. Maxwell established that tangential forces disrupt a semirigid ring of particles unless

$\rho_r/\rho_s < 0.003$ and one of incompressible fluid unless $\rho_r/\rho_s < 0.024$. Since neither is compatible with Laplace's criterion, neither kind of semirigid ring is stable. Various arguments then disposed of other gaseous and liquid rings, leaving as the only stable structure concentric circles of small satellites, each moving at a speed appropriate to its distance from Saturn. Such rings cannot be treated independently: they attract one another. Maxwell presented a lengthy investigation of mutual perturbations between two rings. Usually they are stable; but at certain radii waves of different order may come into resonance and cause disruption, making particles fly off in all directions and collide with other rings. Maxwell estimated the rate of loss of energy and concluded that the whole system of rings would slowly spread out, as the observations indicated. He did not then study the general problem of motion among colliding bodies, but his unpublished manuscripts include one from 1863 applying the statistical methods that he later developed in the kinetic theory of gases to Saturn's rings.

In 1895 A. A. Belopolsky and C. Keeler independently confirmed the differential rotation of the rings by spectroscopic observations. Later the gaps between successive rings were attributed to resonances between orbital motions of the primary satellites of Saturn and local ring oscillations. More recently A. F. Cook and F. A. Franklin, using kinetic theory techniques, have shown that heat generated in collisions makes the rings expand in thickness unless it is removed by radiation, and have obtained closer restrictions on structure and density. Maxwell's density limit $\rho_r/\rho_s > 0.003$ has sometimes been interpreted as a limit on the actual rings; in reality it applies only to semirigid rings, where stability depends on tangential forces. With differential rotation the tangential waves are heavily damped and stability depends on radial motions. The true upper limit on ρ_r/ρ_s appears to be in the range 0.04 to 0.20. Spectroscopic evidence suggests the particles may be crystals of ice or carbon dioxide.[13]

The essay on Saturn's rings illustrates Maxwell's debt to Cambridge as sharply as the experiments on color vision reveal his debt to Edinburgh. It also established his scientific maturity. Success with a classical problem of such magnitude gave a mathematical self-assurance vitally important to his later work. Many letters testify to the concentrated effort involved, not the least interesting amongst them being one to a Cambridge friend, H. R. Droop: "I am very busy with Saturn on top of my regular work. He is all remodelled and recast, but I have more to do to him yet for I wish to redeem the character of mathematicians and make it intelligible."[14] To the graceful literary style and analytical clarity established there, two further broad qualities were added in Maxwell's work over the next two decades. The great papers of the 1860's continued at much the same level of analytical technique, with epoch-making advances in physical and philosophic insight. The books and articles of the 1870's display growing mastery of mathematical abstraction in the use of matrices, vectors and quaternions, Hamiltonian dynamics, special functions, and considerations of symmetry and topology. The contrasting ways in which these different phases of Maxwell's mature researches reflect his interaction with his contemporaries and his influence on the next scientific generation form a fascinating study which has not yet received due attention.

Electricity, Magnetism, and the Electromagnetic Theory of Light (1854–1879). Maxwell's electrical researches began a few weeks after his graduation from Cambridge in 1854, and ended just before his death twenty-five years later with a referee's report on a paper by G. F. FitzGerald. They fall into two broad cycles, with 1868 roughly the dividing point: the first a period of five major papers on the foundations of electromagnetic theory, the second a period of extension with the *Treatise on Electricity and Magnetism*, the *Elementary Treatise on Electricity*, and a dozen shorter papers on special problems. The position of the *Treatise* is peculiar. Most readers come to it expecting a systematic exposition of its author's ideas which makes further reference to earlier writings unnecessary. With many writers the expectation might be legitimate; with Maxwell it is a mistake. In a later conversation he remarked that the aim of the *Treatise* was not to expound his theory finally to the world but to educate himself by presenting a view of the stage he had reached.[15] This is a clue well worth pondering. The truth is that by 1868 Maxwell had already begun to think beyond his theory. He saw electricity not as just another branch of physics but as a subject of unique strategic importance, "as an aid to the interpretation of nature . . . and promoting the progress of science."[16] Wishing, therefore, to follow up questions with wider scientific ramifications, he gave the *Treatise* a loose-knit structure, organized on historical and experimental rather than deductive lines. Ideas are exhibited at different phases of growth in different places; different sections are developed independently, with gaps, inconsistencies, or even flat contradictions in argument. It is a studio rather than a finished work of art. The studio, being Maxwell's, is tidily arranged; and once one has grasped what is going on, it is wonderfully instructive to watch the artist at work; but anyone who finds himself there unawares is courting bewilderment, the more so if he overlooks Maxwell's advice to read the four parts of the *Treatise* in parallel rather than in sequence. It is, for example, disconcerting to be told on reaching section 585, halfway through volume II, that Maxwell is now about to "begin again from a new foundation without any assumption except those of the dynamical theory as stated in Chapter VII." Similar difficulties occur throughout. The next fifty years endorsed Maxwell's judgment about the special importance of electricity to physics as a whole. His premature death occurred just as his ideas were gaining adherents and he was starting an extensive revision of the *Treatise*. Not the least unfortunate consequence was that the definitive exposition of his theory which he intended was never written.

Seen in retrospect, the course of physics up to about 1820 is a triumph of the Newtonian scientific program. The "forces" of nature—heat, light, electricity, magnetism, chemical action—were being progressively reduced to instantaneous attractions and repulsions between the particles of a series of fluids. Magnetism and static electricity were already known to obey inverse-square laws similar to the law of gravitation. The first forty years of the nineteenth century saw a growing reaction against such a division of phenomena in favor of some kind of "correlation of forces." Oersted's discovery of electromagnetism in 1820 was at once the first vindication and the most powerful stimulus of the new tendency, yet at the same time it was oddly disturbing. The action he observed between an electric current and a magnet differed from known phenomena in two essential ways: it was developed by electricity in motion, and the magnet was neither attracted to nor repelled by—but set transversely to—the wire carrying the current. To such a strange phenomenon widely different reactions were possible. Faraday took it as a new irreducible fact by which his other ideas were to be shaped. André Marie Ampère and his followers sought to reconcile it with existing views about instantaneous action at a distance.

Shortly after Oersted's discovery Ampère discovered that a force also exists between two electric currents and put forward the brilliant hypothesis that all magnetism is electrical in origin. In 1826 he established a formula (not to be confused with the one attached to his name in textbooks) which reduced the known magnetic and electromagnetic phenomena to an inverse-square force along the line joining two current elements idl, $i'dl'$ separated by a distance r,

$$F_{ii'} = \frac{ii'\,dl\,dl'}{r^2}\,G, \qquad (2)$$

where G is a complex geometrical factor involving the angles between r, dl, and dl'. In 1845 F. E. Neumann derived the potential function corresponding to Ampère's force and extended the theory to electromagnetic induction. Another extension developed by Wilhelm Weber was to combine Ampère's law with the law of electrostatics to form a new theory, which also accounted for electromagnetic induction, treating the electric current as the flow of two equal and opposite groups of charged particles, subject to a force whose direction was always along the line joining two particles e, e', but whose magnitude depended on their relative velocity $\dot{r}$ and relative acceleration $\ddot{r}$ along that line,

$$F_{ee'} = \frac{ee'}{r^2}\left[1 - \frac{1}{c^2}(\dot{r}^2 - 2r\ddot{r})\right], \qquad (3)$$

c being a constant with dimensions of velocity. In 1856 Kohlrausch and Weber determined c experimentally by measuring the ratio of electrostatic to electrodynamic forces. Its value in the special units of Weber's theory was about two-thirds the velocity of light. Equations (2) and (3) and Neumann's potential theory provided the starting points for almost all the work done in Europe on electromagnetic theory until the 1870's.

The determining influences on Maxwell were Faraday and William Thomson. Faraday's great discoveries—electromagnetic induction, dielectric phenomena, the laws of electrochemistry, diamagnetism, magneto-optical rotation—all sprang from the search for correlations of forces. They formed, in Maxwell's words, "the nucleus of everything electric since 1830."[17] His contributions to theory lay in the progressive extension of ideas about lines of electric and magnetic force. His early discovery of electromagnetic rotations (the first electric motor) made him skeptical about attractive and repulsive forces, and his ideas rapidly advanced after 1831 with his success in describing electromagnetic induction by the motion of lines of magnetic force through the inductive circuit. In studying dielectric and electrolytic processes he imagined (wrongly) that their transmission in curved lines could not be reconciled with the hypothesis of direct action at a distance, attributing them instead to successive actions of contiguous portions of matter in the space between charged bodies. In his work on paramagnetism and diamagnetism he conceived the notion of magnetic conductivity (permeability); and finally, in the most brilliant of of his conceptual papers, written in 1852, when he was sixty, he extended the principle of contiguous action in a general qualitative description of magnetic and electromagnetic phenomena, based on the assumption that lines of magnetic force have the physical property of shortening themselves and repelling each other sideways. A quantitative formulation of the last hypothesis was given by Maxwell in 1861.

Thomson's contribution began in 1841, while he was an undergraduate at Cambridge. His first paper established a formal analogy between the equations of electrostatics and the equations for flow of heat. Consider a point source of heat P embedded in a homogeneous conducting medium. Since the surface area of a sphere is $4\pi r^2$, the heat flux ϕ through a small area dS at a distance r from P is proportional to $1/r^2$ in analogy with Coulomb's electrostatic law; thus by appropriate substitution a problem in electricity may be transposed into one in the theory of heat. Originally Thomson used the analogy as a source of analytical technique; but in 1845 he went on to examine and dispose of Faraday's widely accepted claim that dielectric action cannot be reconciled with Coulomb's law and, conversely, to supply the first exact mathematical description of lines of electric force. Later Thomson and Maxwell between them established a general similitude among static vector fields subject to the conditions of continuity and incompressibility, proving that identical equations describe (1) streamlines of frictionless incompressible fluids through porous media, (2) lines of flow of heat, (3) current electricity, and (4) lines of force in magnetostatics and electrostatics.

Since it was Thomson's peculiar genius to generate powerful disconnected insights rather than complete theories, much of his work is best described piecemeal along with Maxwell's; but certain of his ideas from the 1840's may first be mentioned, notably the method of electric images, a second formal analogy between magnetic forces and rotational strains in an elastic solid, and, most important, the many applications of energy principles to electricity which followed his involvement with thermodynamics. Amongst other things Thomson is responsible for the standard expressions $\frac{1}{2}Li^2$ and $\frac{1}{2}CV^2$ for energy in an inductance and in a condenser. He and (independently) Helmholtz also applied energy principles to give an extraordinarily simple derivation of Neumann's induction equation. It so happened that the discussion of energy principles had a curious two-sided impact on Weber's hypothesis. In 1846 Helmholtz presented an argument which seemed to show that the hypothesis was inconsistent with the principle of conservation of energy. His conclusion was widely accepted and formed one of the grounds on which Maxwell opposed the theory, but in 1869 Weber succeeded in rebutting it. By then, however, Maxwell had developed his theory, and the implication of the Thomson-Helmholtz argument had become clearer: that any theory which is consistent with energy principles automatically predicts induction. In retrospect, therefore, although Helmholtz was wrong in his first criticism, the agreement between Weber's theory and experiment was also less compelling than Weber and his friends had supposed.

Maxwell's first paper, "On Faraday's Line of Force" (1855–1856), was divided into two parts, with supplementary examples. Its origin may be traced in a long correspondence with Thomson, edited by Larmor in 1936.[18] Part 1 was an exposition of the analogy between lines of force and streamlines in an incompressible fluid. It contained one notable extension to Thomson's treatment of the subject and also an illuminating opening discourse on the philosophical significance of analogies between different branches of physics. This was a theme to which Maxwell returned more than once. His biographers print in full an essay entitled "Analogies in Nature," which he read a few months later (February 1856) to the famous Apostles Club at Cambridge; this puts the subject in a wider setting and deserves careful reading despite its involved and cryptic style. Here, as elsewhere, Maxwell's metaphysical speculation discloses the influence of Sir William Hamilton, specifically of Hamilton's Kantian view that all human knowledge is of relations rather than of things. The use Maxwell saw in the method of analogy was twofold. It cross-fertilized technique between different fields, and it served as a golden mean between analytic abstraction and the method of hypothesis. The essence of analogy (in contrast with identity) being partial resemblance, its limits must be recognized as clearly as its existence; yet analogies may help in guarding against too facile commitment to a hypothesis. The analogy of an electric current to two phenomena as different as conduction of heat and the motion of a fluid should, Maxwell later observed, prevent physicists from hastily assuming that "electricity is either a substance like water, or a state of agitation like heat."[19] The analogy is geometrical: "a similarity between relations, not a similarity between the things related."[20]

Maxwell improved the presentation of the hydrodynamic analogy chiefly by considering the resistive medium through which the fluid moves. When an incompressible fluid goes from one medium into another of different porosity, the flow is continuous but a pressure difference develops across the boundary. Also, when one medium is replaced by another of different porosity, equivalent effects may be obtained formally by introducing appropriate sources or sinks of fluid at the boundary. These results were an impor-

tant aid to calculation and helped in explaining several processes that occur in magnetic and dielectric materials. Another step was to consider a medium in which the porosity varies with direction. The necessary equations had been supplied by Stokes in a paper on the conduction of heat in crystals. They led to the remarkable conclusion that the vector **a** which defines the direction of fluid motion is not in general parallel to **α**, the direction of maximum pressure gradient. The two functions are linked by the equation

$$\mathbf{a} = \mathbf{K}\boldsymbol{\alpha}, \qquad (4)$$

where **K** is a tensor quantity describing the porosity. Applying the analogy to magnetism, Maxwell distinguished two vectors, the magnetic induction and the magnetic force, to which he later attached the symbols **B** and **H**. The parallel quantities in current electricity were the current density **I** and the electromotive intensity **E**. The distinction between **B** and **H** provided the key to a description of "magnecrystallic induction," a force observed in crystalline magnetic materials by Faraday. Maxwell later identified the two quantities with the two definitions of magnetic force that Thomson had found to be required in developing parallel magnetostatic and electromagnetic theories of magnetism. The question of the two magnetic vectors **B** and **H** has disturbed several generations of students of electromagnetism. Maxwell's discussion gives a far clearer starting point than anything to be found in the majority of modern textbooks on the subject.

This physical distinction based on the hydrodynamic analogy led Maxwell to make an important mathematical distinction between two classes of vector functions, which he then called "quantities" and "intensities," later "fluxes" and "forces." A flux **a** is a vector subject to the continuity equation and is integrated over a surface; a force **α** (in Maxwell's generalized sense of the term) is a vector usually, but not always, derivable from a single-valued potential function and is integrated along a line. The functions **B** and **I** are fluxes; **H** and **E** are forces.

The close parallel that exists between electric currents and magnetic lines of force, which had been seen qualitatively by Faraday, was the concluding theme of Part 1 of Maxwell's paper. Part 2 covered electromagnetism proper. In it Maxwell developed a new formal theory of electromagnetic processes. The starting point was an identity established by Ampère and Gauss between the magnetic effects of a closed electric current and those of a uniformly magnetized iron shell of the same perimeter. In analytic method the discussion followed Thomson's "Mathematical Theory of Magnetism" (1851), as well as making extensive use of a theorem first proved by Thomson in 1847, in a letter to Stokes, and first published by Stokes as an examination question in the Smith's prize paper taken by Maxwell in February 1854. This was the well-known equality (Stokes's theorem) between the integral of a vector function around a closed curve and the integral of its curl over the enclosed surface. The original analysis given by Maxwell was Cartesian, but since in 1870 he himself introduced the terms "curl," "divergence," and "gradient" to denote the relevant vector operations, the notation may legitimately be modernized. The relationship between the flux and force vectors **a** and α contained in equation (4) has already been discussed. Pursuing a line of analysis started by Thomson, Maxwell now proceeded to show that any flux vector **a** may be related to a second, distinct force vector α' through the equation

$$\mathbf{a} = \operatorname{curl} \alpha' + \operatorname{grad} \beta, \tag{5}$$

where β is a scalar function. Applying (4), (5) and other equations, Maxwell obtained a complete set of equations between the four vectors **E**, **I**, **B**, **H**, which describe electric currents and magnetic lines of force. He then went on to derive another vector function, for which he afterward used the symbol **A**, such that

$$\mathbf{B} = \operatorname{curl} \mathbf{A} + \operatorname{grad} \varphi, \tag{6}$$

where the second term on the right-hand side may, in the absence of free magnetic poles, be eliminated by appropriate change of variables. Maxwell proved that the electromotive force **E** developed during induction is $-\partial \mathbf{A}/\partial t$ and that the total energy of an electromagnetic system is $\int \mathbf{I} \cdot \mathbf{A} \, dV$. Thus the new function provided equations to represent ordinary magnetic action, electromagnetic induction, and the forces between closed currents. Maxwell called it the electrotonic function, following some speculations of Faraday's about a hypothetical state of stress in matter, the "electrotonic state." Later he identified it as a generalization of Neumann's electrodynamic potential and established other properties (to be discussed shortly).

The 1856 paper has been eclipsed by Maxwell's later work, but its originality and importance are greater than is usually thought. Besides interpreting Faraday's work and giving the electrotonic function, it contained the germ of a number of ideas which Maxwell was to revive or modify in 1868 and later: (1) an integral representation of the field equations (1868), (2) the treatment of electrical action as analogous to the motion of an incompressible fluid (1869, 1873), (3) the classification of vector functions

into forces and fluxes (1870), and (4) an interesting formal symmetry in the equations connecting **A**, **B**, **E**, and **H**, different from the symmetry commonly recognized in the completed field equations. The paper ended with solutions to a series of problems, including an application of the electrotonic function to calculate the action of a magnetic field on a spinning conducting sphere.

Maxwell's next paper, "On Physical Lines of Force" (1861–1862), began as an attempt to devise a medium occupying space which would account for the stresses associated by Faraday with lines of magnetic force. It ended with the stunning discovery that vibrations of the medium have properties identical with light. The original aim was one Maxwell had considered in 1856, and although he explicitly rejected any literal interpretation of the analogy between magnetic action and fluid motion, the meaning of the analogy can be extended by picturing a magnet as a kind of suction tube which draws in fluid ether at one end and expels it from the other. That idea had been suggested by Euler in 1761;[21] it leads to a most remarkable result first published by Thomson in 1870 but probably known to Maxwell earlier.[22] Geometrically the flow between two such tubes is identical with the lines of force between two magnets, but physically the actions are reciprocal: like ends of the tubes are *attracted* according to the inverse-square law; unlike ends are repelled. The difference is that in a fluid the Bernoulli forces create a pressure minimum where the streamlines are closest, while Faraday's hypothesis requires a pressure maximum.

The clue to to a medium having a right stress distribution came from an unexpected source. During the 1840's the engineer W. J. M. Rankine (who like Maxwell had been a student of Forbes's at Edinburgh) worked out a new theory of matter with applications to thermodynamics and the properties of gases, based on the hypothesis that molecules are small nuclei in an ethereal atmosphere, fixed in space but rotating at speeds proportional to temperature. In 1851 Thomson refereed one of Rankine's papers. He was then concerning himself with thermodynamics, but five years later it dawned on him that molecular rotation was just the thing to account for the magneto-optical effect.[23] Faraday had observed a slight rotation in the plane of polarization of light passing through a block of glass between the poles of a magnet. Using an analogy with a pendulum suspended from a spinning arm, Thomson concluded that the effect could be attributed to coupling between the ether vibrations and a spinning motion of the molecules of glass about the lines of force. Maxwell's theory of physical lines of force consisted in extending this hypothesis of rotation in the magnetic field from ordinary matter to an ether. The influence of Thomson and Rankine is established by direct reference and by Maxwell's use of Rankine's term "molecular vortices" in the titles of each of the four parts of the paper. The charm of the story is that barely twelve months had passed since Maxwell had given the death blow to Rankine's theory of gases through his own work on kinetic theory.

Consider an array of vortices embedded in incompressible fluid. Normally the pressure is identical in all directions, but rotation causes centrifugal forces which make each vortex contract longitudinally and exert radial pressure. This is exactly the stress distribution proposed by Faraday for physical lines of force. By making the angular velocity of each vortex proportional to the local magnetic intensity, Maxwell obtained formulas identical with the existing theories for forces between magnets, steady currents, and diamagnetic bodies. Next came the problem of electromagnetic induction. It required some understanding of the action of electric currents on the vortex medium. That tied in with another question: how could two adjacent vortices rotate freely in the same sense,

since their surfaces move in opposite directions? Figure 2, reproduced from Part 2 of the paper, illustrates Maxwell's highly tentative solution. Each vortex is separated from its neighbors by a layer of minute particles, identified with electricity, counter-rotating like the idle wheels of a gear train.

On this view electricity, instead of being a fluid confined to conductors, becomes an entity of a new kind, disseminated through space. In conductors it is free to move (though subject to resistance); in insulators (including the ultimate insulator, space) it remains fixed. The magnetic and inductive actions of currents are then visualized as follows. When a current flows in a wire A, it makes the adjacent vortices rotate; these in turn engage the next layer of particles and so on until an infinite series of vortex rings, which constitute lines of force, fills the surrounding space. For induction consider a second wire B with finite resistance, parallel to A. A steady current in A will not affect B; but any change in A will communicate an impulse through the intervening particles and vortices, causing a reverse current in B, which is then dissipated through resistance. This is induction. Quite unex-

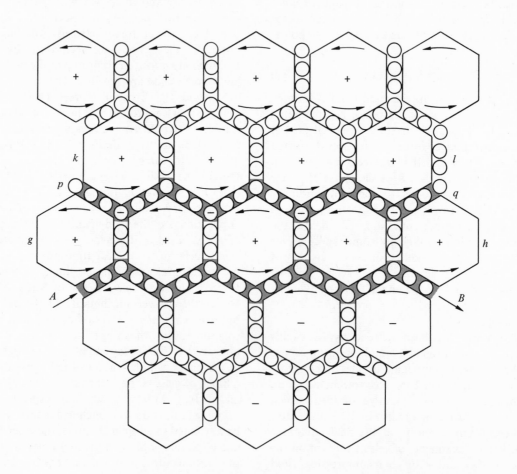

FIGURE 2. Model of molecular vortices and electric particles (1861).

pectedly the model also suggested a physical interpretation of the electrotonic function. In analyzing machinery several engineers, including Rankine, had found it useful to add to the motion of a mechanical part terms incorporating effects of connected gears and linkages, which they called the "reduced" inertia or momentum of the system. Maxwell discovered that the electrotonic function corresponds to the reduced momentum of the vortex system at each point. The equation for induced electromotive force $\mathbf{E} = \partial\mathbf{A}/\partial t$ is the generalized electrical equivalent of Newton's equation between force and rate of change of momentum.

There is good evidence internal and external to the paper that Maxwell meant originally to end here and did not begin Part 3 until Part 2 had been printed.[24] Meanwhile, he had been considering the relation between electric currents and the induction of charge through a dielectric. In 1854 he had remarked to Thomson that a literal treatment of the analogy between streamlines and lines of electric force would make induction nothing more than an extreme case of conduction.[25] Now, with the picture of electricity as disseminated in space, Maxwell hit upon a better description, based partly on Faraday's ideas, by making the vortex medium elastic. The forces between charged bodies could be attributed to potential energy stored in the medium by elastic distortion, as magnetic forces are attributed to stored rotational energy; and the difference between conduction and static electric induction is analogous to the difference between viscous and elastic processes in matter.

Two amazing consequences swiftly followed. First, since the electric particles surrounding a conductor are now capable of elastic displacement, a varying current is no longer entirely confined like water in a pipe: it penetrates to some extent into the space surrounding the wire. Here was the first glimmering of Maxwell's "displacement current." Second, any elastic substance with density ρ and shear modulus m can transmit transverse waves with velocity $v = \sqrt{m/\rho}$. Making some ad hoc assumptions about the elastic structure of the vortex medium, Maxwell derived while he was in Scotland formulas connecting ρ and m with electromagnetic quantities, which implied a numerical relationship between v and Weber's constant c. Returning to London for the academic year, Maxwell looked up the result of Kohlrausch and Weber's experiment to determine c, and after putting their data in a form suitable for insertion into his equation he found that for a medium having a magnetic permeability μ equal to unity v was almost equal to the velocity of light. With excitement manifested in italics he wrote: "we can scarcely avoid the inference that *light consists in the transverse undulations of the same medium which is the cause of electric and magnetic phenomena*."[26] Thus the great discovery was made; and Maxwell, following a calculation on the dielectric properties of birefringent crystals, returned in Part 4 to his starting point, the magneto-optical effect, and replaced Thomson's spinning pendulum analogy with a more detailed theory in better accord with experiment.

In 1861 the British Association formed a committee under Thomson's chairmanship to determine a set of internationally acceptable electrical standards following the work of Weber. At Thomson's urging, a new absolute system of units was adopted, similar to Weber's, but based on energy principles rather than on a hypothetical electrodynamic force law. The first experiment was on the standard of resistance, and in 1862 Maxwell was appointed to the committee to help with that task. His third paper, "On the Elementary Relations of Electrical Quantities," written in 1863 with the assistance of Fleeming Jenkin, supplied a vital step in his development, often overlooked through its having been, most unfortunately, omitted from the *Scientific Papers*.[27] Extending a procedure begun by Fourier in the theory of heat, Maxwell set forth definitions of electric and magnetic quantities related to measures M, L, T of mass, length, and time, to provide the first—and one may also think the most lucid—exposition of that dual system of electrical units commonly but incorrectly known as the Gaussian system.[28] The paper introduced the notation, which was to become standard, expressing dimensional relations as products of powers of M, L, T enclosed in brackets, with separate dimensionless multipliers. For every quantity the ratio of the two absolute definitions, based on forces between electric charges and forces between magnetic poles, proved to be some power of a constant c with dimensions $[LT^{-1}]$ and magnitude $\sqrt{2}$ times Weber's constant, or very nearly the velocity of light. The analysis disclosed five different classes of experiments from which c might be determined. One was a direct comparison of electrostatic and electromagnetic forces carried out by Maxwell and C. Hockin in 1868, and two others were started by Maxwell at Cambridge in the 1870's.[29] The results of many experiments over the next few years progressively converged with the measured velocity of light.

By 1863, then, Maxwell had found a link of a purely phenomenological kind between electromagnetic quantities and the velocity of light. His fourth paper, "A Dynamical Theory of the Electromagnetic Field," published in 1865, clinched matters. It provided a new theoretical framework for the subject, based on experiment and a few general dynamical principles, from which the propagation of electromagnetic waves through space followed without any special assumptions about molecular vortices or the forces between electric particles. This was the work of which Maxwell, in a rare moment of unveiled exuberance, wrote to his cousin Charles Cay, the mathematics master at Clifton College: "I have also a paper afloat, containing an electromagnetic theory of light, which, till I am convinced to the contrary, I hold to be great guns."[30]

Several factors, scientific and philosophical, settled the disposition of Maxwell's artillery. From the beginning he had stressed the provisional character of the vortex model, especially its peculiar gearing of particles and vortices. Rankine was a cautionary example. In an article on thermodynamics written in 1877 Maxwell illuminated his own thought by observing that the vortex theory of matter, which at first served Rankine well, later became an encumbrance, distracting his attention from the general considerations on which thermodynamic formulas properly rest.[31] Maxwell wished to avoid that trap. Yet he did not abandon all the ground gained in 1862. The idea of treating light and electromagnetism as processes in a common medium remained sound. Furthermore, the new theory was, as the title of the paper stated, a dynamical one: the medium remained subject to the general principles of dynamics. The novelty consisted in deducing wave propagation from equations related to electrical experiments instead of from a detailed mechanism; that was why the theory became known as the electromagnetic theory of light. Again Sir William Hamilton's influence is discernible. Maxwell's decision to replace the vortex model of electromagnetic and optical processes by an analysis of the relations between the two classes of phenomena is a concretization of Hamilton's doctrine of the relativity of knowledge: all human knowledge is of relations between objects rather than of objects in themselves.

More specifically the theory rested on three main principles. Maxwell retained the idea that electric and magnetic energy are disseminated, merely avoiding commitment to hypotheses about their mechanical forms in space. Here it is worth noticing that his formal expressions $\mathbf{B} \cdot \mathbf{H}/8\pi$ and $\mathbf{D} \cdot \mathbf{E}/8\pi$ for the two energy densities simply extend and interpret physically an integral transformation of Thomson's.[32] Next Maxwell revived various ideas about the geometry of lines of force from the 1856 paper. Third, and most important, he replaced the vortex hypothesis with a new macroscopic analogy between inductive circuits and coupled dynamical systems. The analogy

seems to have germinated in Maxwell's mind in 1863, while he was working out the theory of the British Association resistance experiment.[33] In part it goes back to Thomson, especially to Thomson's use of energy principles in the theory of the electric telegraph.[34] It may be illustrated in various ways, of which the model shown in Figure 3, which Maxwell had constructed in 1874, is the most convenient.[35] Two wheels, P and Q, are geared together through a

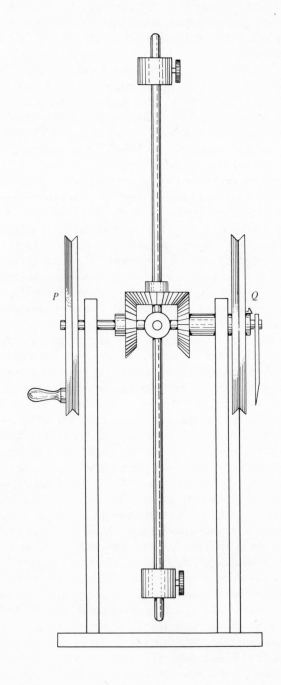

FIGURE 3. Dynamical analogy for two inductively coupled circuits (1865, 1874).

210

differential mechanism with adjustable flyweights. Rotations of P and Q represent currents in two circuits; the moments of inertia represent coefficients of induction; a frictional band attached to Q represents the resistance of the secondary circuit. Every feature of electromagnetic induction is seen here. So long as P rotates uniformly, Q remains stationary; but when P is started or stopped, a reverse impulse is transmitted to Q. This impulse is determined by the acceleration, the coefficient of coupling, and the inertia and resistance of Q, in exact analogy with an electrical system. Again the definitive quantity has the nature of momentum, determined in the mechanical model by the positions of the flyweights and in the electromagnetic analog by the geometry of the circuits. The total "electrokinetic momentum" **p** is $Li + \sum_j M_j i_j$, where L and i are the self-inductance and current in a particular circuit and the M_j's and i_j's are the mutual inductances and currents of neighboring circuits. Since **p** is the integral of the function **A** round the circuit, the analogy carries through at the macroscopic level Maxwell's identification of **A** with the "reduced momentum" of the field. Combined with conservation of energy, it also gives the mechanical actions between circuits. Helmholtz and Thomson had applied energy principles to deduce the law of induction from Ampère's force law; Maxwell inverted and generalized their argument to calculate forces from the induction formulas. Thus his first analytic treatment of the electrotonic function was metamorphosed into a complete dynamical theory of the field.

In the *Treatise* Maxwell extended the dynamical formalism by a more thoroughgoing application of Lagrange's equations than he had attempted in 1865. His doing so coincided with a general movement among British and European mathematicians about then toward wider use of the methods of analytical dynamics in physical problems. The course of that movement in Britain may be followed through Cayley's two British Association reports on advanced dynamics of 1857 and 1862, Routh's *Treatise on the Dynamics of a System of Rigid Bodies* (1860, 1868), and Thomson and Tait's *Treatise on Natural Philosophy* (first edition 1867). Maxwell helped Thomson and Tait with comments on many sections of their text. Then, with the freshness of outlook that makes his work so appealing, he turned the current fad to his own ends by applying it to electromagnetism. Using arguments extraordinarily modern in flavor about the symmetry and vector structure of the terms, he expressed the Lagrangian for an electromagnetic system in its most general form. Green and others had developed similar arguments in studying the dynamics of the luminiferous ether, but the use Maxwell made of Lagrangian techniques was new to the point of being almost a new approach to physical theory—though many years were to pass before other physicists fully exploited the ground he had broken. The beauty of the Lagrangian method is that it allows new terms to be incorporated in the theory automatically as they arise, with a minimum of physical hypothesis. One that Maxwell devoted a chapter of the *Treatise* to was the magneto-optical effect. By a powerful application of symmetry considerations he put Thomson's argument of 1856 on a rigorous basis and proved that any dynamical explanation of the rotation of the plane of polarized light must depend on local rotation in the magnetic field. In later terminology, the induction **B** is an axial vector, and the electrons in matter precess about the applied field: these are the elements of truth behind the molecular vortex hypothesis. Characteristically Maxwell did not limit his thinking to the general symmetry argument: he tested it by attempting to invent counterexamples. Elsewhere he wrote, "I have also tried a great many hypotheses [to explain the magneto-optical effect] besides those which I have published, and have been astonished at the way in which conditions likely to produce rotation are exactly neutralized by others not seen at first."[36] A further instance of the power of the Lagrangian methods, covered in the *Treatise*, is Maxwell's analysis of cross-terms linking electrical and mechanical phenomena. This he did partly at the suggestion of J. W. Strutt (Lord Rayleigh).[37] He identified three possible electromechanical effects, later detected by Barnett (1908), Einstein and de Haas (1916), and Tolman and Stewart (1916). The Barnett effect is a magnetic moment induced in a rapidly spinning iron bar. Maxwell himself had looked for the inverse phenomenon in 1861 during an experiment in search of the angular momentum of molecular vortices.[38]

In 1865, and again in the *Treatise*, Maxwell's next step after completing the dynamical analogy was to develop a group of eight equations describing the electromagnetic field. They are set out in the table with subsidiary equations according to the form adopted in the *Treatise*. The principle they embody is that electromagnetic processes are transmitted by the separate and independent action of each charge (or magnetized body) on the surrounding space rather than by direct action at a distance. Formulas for the forces between moving charged bodies may indeed be derived from Maxwell's equations, but the action is not along the line joining them and can be reconciled with dynamical principles only by taking into account the exchange of momentum with the field.[39] Maxwell remarked that the equations might be condensed, but "to eliminate a quantity which expresses a useful idea would be rather a loss than a gain in this stage of our enquiry."[40] He had in fact simplified the equations in his fifth major paper, the short but important "Note on the Electromagnetic Theory of Light" (1868), writing them in an integral form without the function **A**, based on four postulates derived from electrical experiments. This may be called the electrical formulation of the theory, in contrast with the original dynamical formulation. It was later independently developed by Heaviside and Hertz and passed into the textbooks. It has the advantage of compactness and analytical symmetry, but its scope is more restricted and to some extent it concealed from the next generation of physicists ideas familiar to Maxwell which proved important later on. Two points in the table deserve comment for the modern reader. Equations (B) and (C) appear slightly unfamiliar, because (B) contains terms defined for a particular laboratory frame of reference, while (C), the so-called Lorentz force formula, contains a term in grad Ω for the force on isolated magnetic poles, should such exist. Elsewhere in the *Treatise*[41] Maxwell began the investigation of moving frames of reference, a subject which in Einstein's hands was to revolutionize physics. The second point concerns the addition of the displacement current $\dot{\mathbf{D}}$ to the

General Equations of the Electromagnetic Field (1873)

A	Magnetic Induction	$\mathbf{B} = \mathrm{curl}\ \mathbf{A}$
B	Electromotive Force	$\mathbf{E} = \mathbf{v} \wedge \mathbf{B} - \dot{\mathbf{A}} - \mathrm{grad}\ \psi$
C	Mechanical Force	$\mathbf{F} = \mathbf{I} \wedge \mathbf{B} + e\mathbf{E} - m\ \mathrm{grad}\ \Omega$
D	Magnetization	$\mathbf{B} = \mathbf{H} + 4\pi\mathbf{J}$
E	Electric Currents	$4\pi\mathbf{I} = \mathrm{curl}\ \mathbf{H}$
F	Current of Conduction	$\mathbf{I}' = C\mathbf{E}$
G	Electric Displacement	$\mathbf{D} = (1/4\pi)\ \mathbf{KE}$
H	True Currents	$\mathbf{I} = \mathbf{I}' + \dot{\mathbf{D}}$
J	Induced Magnetization	$\mathbf{B} = \mu\mathbf{H}$
K	Electric Volume Density	$e = \mathrm{div}\ \mathbf{D}$
L	Magnetic Volume Density	$m = \mathrm{div}\ \mathbf{J}$

Note: Maxwell used **S** rather than **I** for electric current density.

current of conduction **I**'. In Maxwell's treatment (unlike later textbooks) the extra term appears almost without explanation, arising as it does from his analogy between the paired phenomena of conduction and static induction in electricity and viscous flow and elastic displacement in the theory of materials. More will be said below about the implications of Maxwell's view.

Maxwell gave three distinct proofs of the existence of electromagnetic waves in 1865, 1868, and 1873. The disturbance has dual form, consisting in waves of magnetic force and electric displacement with motions perpendicular to the propagation vector and to each other. An alternative view given in the *Treatise* is to represent it as a transverse wave of the function **A**. In either version the theory yields strictly transverse motion, automatically eliminating the longitudinal waves which had embarrassed previous theories of light.

Among later developments, the generation and detection of radio waves by Hertz in 1888 stands supreme; but there were others of nearly comparable interest. In the *Treatise* Maxwell established that light, on the electromagnetic theory, exerts a radiation pressure. Radiation pressure had been the subject of much speculation since the early eighteenth century; before Maxwell most people had assumed that its existence would be a crucial argument in favor of a corpuscular rather than a wave theory of light. When William Crookes discovered his radiometer effect in 1874, shortly after the publication of Maxwell's *Treatise*, some persons thought that he had observed radiation pressure, but the disturbance was much larger than the predicted value and in the wrong direction, and was caused, as will be explained below, by convection currents in the residual gas. Maxwell's formula was confirmed experimentally by Lebedev in 1900. The effect has implications in many branches of physics. It accounts for the repulsion of comets' tails by the sun; it is, as Boltzmann proved in 1884, critical to the theory of blackbody radiation; it may be used in deriving classically the time-dilation formula of special relativity; it fixes the mass-range of stars.

Another very fruitful new area of research started by Maxwell was on the connections between electrical and optical properties of bodies. He obtained expressions for the torque on a birefringent crystal suspended in an electric field, for the relation between refractive index and dielectric constant in transparent media, and for the relation between optical absorption and electrical conductivity in metals. In the long wavelength limit the refractive index may be expected on the simplest theory to be proportional to the square root of the dielectric constant. Measurements by Boltzmann, J. E. H. Gordon, J. Hopkinson, and others confirmed Maxwell's formula in gases and paraffin oils, but in some materials (most obviously, water) they revealed large discrepancies. These and like problems, including Maxwell's own observation of a discrepancy between the observed and predicted ratios of optical absorption to electrical conductivity in gold leaf, formed a basis for decades of research on electro-optical phenomena. Much of what was done during the 1880's and 1890's should be seen as the beginnings of modern research on solid-state physics, though a full interpretation waited on the development of the quantum theory of solids.

In classical optics Maxwell's theory worked a revolution that is now rarely perceived. A popular fiction among twentieth-century physicists is that mechanical theories of the ether were universally accepted and universally successful during the nineteenth century, until shaken by the null result of the Michelson-Morley experiment on the motion of the earth through the ether. This little piece of textbook folklore is wrong in both its positive and its negative assertions. More will be said below about the Michelson-Morley experiment, but long before that the classical ether theories were beset with grave difficulties on their own ground. The problem was to find a consistent dynamical foundation for the wave theory of light. During the 1820's Fresnel had given his well-known formulas for double refraction and for the reflection of polarized light; they were confirmed later with extraordinary experimental accuracy, but Fresnel's successors had immense trouble in reconciling them with each other on any mechanical theory of the ether. In 1862 Stokes summarized forty years of arduous research, during which a dozen different ethers had been tried and found wanting, by remarking that in his opinion the true dynamical theory of double refraction was yet to be found.[42] In 1865 Maxwell obtained Fresnel's wave surface for double refraction from the electromagnetic theory in the most straightforward way, completely avoiding the ad hoc supplementary conditions required in the mechanical theories. He did not then derive the reflection formulas, being uncertain about boundary conditions at high frequency;[43] but in 1874 H. A. Lorentz obtained them also very simply, using the static boundary condition Maxwell had given in 1856. An equivalent calculation, probably independent, appears in an undated manuscript of Maxwell's at Cambridge. The whole matter was investigated in two very powerful critical papers by Rayleigh (1881) and Gibbs (1888), and in the cycle of work begun by Thomson in his 1884 *Baltimore Lectures*. Rayleigh and Gibbs proved that Maxwell's were the only equations that give formulas for refraction, reflection, and scattering of light consistent with each other and with experiment.[44] Brief reference is appropriate here to James MacCullagh's semi-mechanical theory of 1845, in which the ether was assigned a property of rotational elasticity different from the elastic properties of any ordinary substance. After Stokes in 1862 had raised formidable objections against the stability of MacCullagh's medium, it was taken as disproved until FitzGerald and Larmor noticed a formal resemblance between MacCullagh's and Maxwell's equations. Since then the two theories have usually been considered homologous. In truth neither Stokes's objections to, nor Larmor's claims for, MacCullagh's theory can be sustained. A dynamically stable medium with rotational elasticity supplied by gyrostatic action was invented by Thomson in 1889.[45] On the other hand, whereas MacCullagh made kinetic energy essentially linear and elastic energy rotational, Maxwell identified magnetism with rotational kinetic energy and electrification with a linear elastic displacement. Very peculiar assumptions about the action of the ether on matter are necessary to carry MacCullagh's theory through at the molecular level; Maxwell's extends naturally and immediately to the ionic theory of matter. Even as an optical hypothesis, apart from its other virtues, the position of Maxwell's theory is unique.

Maxwell's statements about the luminiferous ether have an ambiguity which needs double care in view of the intellectual confusion of much twentieth-century comment on the subject. Selective quotation can make him sound as mechanistic as Thomson became in the 1880's or as Machian as Einstein was in the early 1900's. The *Treatise* concludes flatly that "there must be a medium or substance in which . . . energy exists after it leaves one body and before it reaches [an] other";[46] a later letter dismisses the ether as a "most conjectural scientific hypothesis."[47] Some remarks simply express the ultimate skepticism behind Maxwell's working faith in science. Others hinge on the view he inherited from Whewell that reality is ordered in a series of tiers, each more or less complete in itself, each built on the one below, and that the key to discovery lies in finding "appropriate ideas"[48] to describe the tier one is concerned with. By 1865 Maxwell was convinced that magnetic and electric energy are disseminated in space. As a "very probable hypothesis" he favored identifying the two forms of energy with "the motion and the strain of one and the same medium,"[49] but definite knowledge about one tier must be distinguished from reasonable speculation about the next. That was the philosophic point of the Lagrangian method. In Hamilton's terminology the best short statement of Maxwell's position is that we may believe in the existence of the ether without direct knowledge of its properties; we know only relations between the phenomena it accounts for. In a striking passage from the article on thermodynamics mentioned above, perhaps written after seeing the famous bells at Terling near Rayleigh's estate, Maxwell compared the situation to that of a group of bellringers confronted with ropes going to invisible machinery in the bell loft. Lagrange's equations supply the "appropriate idea" expressing neither more nor less than is known about the visible motions: whether more detailed information about the machinery can be gained later remains open. In Maxwell's, as in many later applications of Lagrange's method, the energies involve electrical, not mechanical, quantities. If the "very probable hypothesis" is followed out and one term is equated with ordinary kinetic energy, then, as Thomson found in 1855, a lower limit to the density ρ of a mechanical ether can be calculated from the known energy density of sunlight.[50] The flaw in Thomson's argument lies in assuming an energy density $\frac{1}{2}\rho v^2$; it is resolved in relativistic dynamics by the mass-energy relation; the rest mass of the photon is zero. Considerations of this kind indicate the subtlety of the scientific transformation wrought by relativity theory. It eliminated the arguments for an ether of fixed position and finite density, yet it preserved intact Maxwell's equations and his fundamental idea of disseminated electrical energy. More light is thrown on Maxwell's own opinions about the problem of relative and absolute motion and the connection between dynamics and other branches of physics by the delightful monograph *Matter and Motion*, published in 1876.

Maxwell's influence in suggesting the Michelson-Morley ether-drift experiment is widely acknowleged, but the story is a curiously tangled one. It originates in the problem of the aberration of starlight. During the course of a year the apparent positions of stars, as fixed by transit measurements, vary by ± 20.5 arc-seconds. This effect was discovered in 1728 by Bradley. He attributed it to the lateral motion of the telescope traveling at velocity v with the earth about the sun. On the corpuscular theory of light the motion causes a displacement of the image, while the particles travel from the objective to the focus, through an angular range v/c just equal to the observed displacement. An explanation of aberration on the wave theory of light is harder to come by. If the ether were a gas like the earth's atmosphere (as was first supposed), it would be carried along with the telescope and one scarcely would expect any displacement. Young in 1804 therefore proposed that the ether must pass between the atoms in the telescope wall "as freely perhaps as the wind passes through a grove of trees."[51] The idea had promise, but in working it out other phenomena needed to be considered, many of which further illustrate the difficulties of classical ethers. To explain Maxwell's involvement I depart from chronology and give the facts roughly in the order in which they presented themselves to him.

In 1859 Fizeau proved experimentally that the velocity of light in a moving column of water is greater downstream than upstream. A natural supposition is that the water drags the ether along with it. This contradicts Young's hypothesis in its most primitive form; however, the modified velocity was not $c + w$ but $c + w(1 - 1/\mu^2)$, where μ is the refractive index of water, and that tallied with a more sophisticated theory of aberration due to Fresnel. Fresnel held the conviction (not actually verified until 1871) that the aberration coefficient in a telescope full of water must remain unchanged, which on Young's theory it does not. He was able to satisfy that requirement by combining Young's hypothesis with the further assumption that refraction is due to condensation of the ether in ordinary matter, the ether-density in a medium of refractive index μ being μ^2 times its value in free space. With the excess ether carried along by matter one obtains the quoted formula, which is in consequence still known as the "Fresnel drag" term, though it stands on broader foundations, as Larmor afterwards proved. Indeed Fresnel's condensation hypothesis is logically inconsistent with another principle that became accepted in the 1820's, namely, that the ether, to convey transverse but not longitudinal waves, must be an incompressible solid. A dissatisfaction with Fresnel's "startling assumptions" made Stokes in 1846 propose a radically new theory of aberration, treating the ether as a viscoelastic substance, like pitch or glass. For the rapid vibrations of light the ether acts as a solid, but for the slow motions of the solar system it resembles a viscous liquid, a portion of which is dragged along with each planetary body. A plausible circuital condition on the motion gives a deflection v/c for a beam of light approaching the earth, identical with the displacement that occurs inside the telescope in the other theories.

Some time in 1862 or 1863 Maxwell read Fizeau's paper and thought out an experiment to detect the ether wind. Since refraction is caused by differences in the velocity of light in different media, one might expect the Fresnel drag to modify the refraction of a glass prism moving through the ether. Maxwell calculated that the additional deflection in a 60° prism moving at the earth's velocity would be 17 arc-seconds. He arranged a train of three prisms with a return mirror behind them in the manner of his portable "colour-box," and set up what would now be called an autocollimator to look for the deflection, using a telescope with an illuminated eyepiece in which the image of the crosshair was refocused on itself after passing to and fro through the prisms. The displacement from ether motion could be seen by mounting the apparatus on a turntable, where the effect would reverse on rotating through 180°, giving an overall deflection after the double passage of $2\frac{1}{2}$ arc-minutes: easily measurable. Maxwell could detect nothing, so in April 1864 he sent Stokes a paper for the Royal Society concluding that "the result of the experiment is decidedly negative to the hypothesis about the motion of the ether in the form stated here."[52]

Maxwell had blundered. Though he did not then know it, the French engineer Arago had done a crude version of the same experiment in 1810 (with errors too large for his result to have real significance), and Fresnel had based his theory on Arago's negative result. Stokes knew all this, having written an article on the subject in 1845; he replied, pointing out Maxwell's error, which had been to overlook the compensating change in density that occurs because the ether satisfies a continuity equation at the boundary.[53] Maxwell withdrew the paper. He did give a description of the experiment three years later, with a corrected interpretation, in a letter to the astronomer William Huggins, who included it in his pioneering paper of 1868 on the measurement of the radial velocities of stars from the Doppler shifts of their spectral lines.[54] There the matter rested until the last year of Maxwell's life. Then in his article "Ether" for the *Encyclopaedia Britannica* he again reviewed the problem of motion through the ether. The only possible earth-based experiment was to measure variations in the velocity of light on a double journey between two mirrors. Maxwell concluded that the time differences in different directions, being of the order v^2/c^2, would be too small to detect. He proposed another method from timing the eclipses of the moons of Jupiter, which he later described in more detail in a letter to the American astronomer D. P. Todd, published after his death in the Royal Society *Proceedings* and in *Nature*.[55] His statements there about the difficulties of the earth-based experiment served as a challenge to the young Albert Michelson, who at once invented his famous interferometer to do it.

The negative result of the experiment swung Michelson and everyone else behind Stokes's theory of aberration. In 1885, however, Lorentz discovered that Stokes's circuital condition on the motion of the ether is incompatible with having the ether stationary at the earth's surface. Lorentz advanced a new theory combining some of Stokes's ideas with some of Fresnel's; he also pointed out an oversight in Michelson's (and Maxwell's) analysis of the experiment, which halved the magnitude of the predicted effect, bringing it near the limits of the observations. Michelson and Morley then repeated the experiment

with many improvements. Their conclusive results were published in 1887. In 1889 FitzGerald wrote to the American journal *Science* explaining the negative result by his contraction hypothesis.[56] The same idea was advanced independently by Lorentz in 1893. Physics texts often refer to the FitzGerald-Lorentz contraction as an ad hoc assumption dreamed up to save appearances. It was not. The force between two electric charges is a function of their motion with respect to a common frame: Maxwell had shown it (incompletely and in another context) in the *Treatise*.[57] Hence, as FitzGerald stated, all one need assume to explain the negative result of the Michelson-Morley experiment is that intermolecular forces obey the same laws as electromagnetic forces. The real (and great) merit of the special theory of relativity was pedagogical. It arranged the old confusing material in a clear deductive pattern.

Reference may be made to some more technical contributions from Maxwell's later work. A short paper of 1868, written after seeing an experiment by W. R. Grove, gave the first theoretical treatment of resonant alternating current circuits.[58] Portions of the *Treatise* applied quaternion formulas discovered by Tait to the field equations, and paved the way for Heaviside's and Gibbs's developments of vector analysis. Maxwell put these and various related matters in a wider context in a paper of 1870, "On the Mathematical Classification of Physical Quantities." He coined the terms "curl," "convergence" (negative divergence), and "gradient" for the various products of the vector operator ∇ on scalar and vector quantities, with the less familiar but instructive term "concentration" for the operation ∇^2, which gives the excess of a scalar V at a point over its average through the surrounding region.[59] He extended also his previous treatment of force and flux vectors, introduced the important distinction between what are now (after W. Voigt) known as axial and polar vectors, and in other papers gave a useful physical treatment of the two classes of tensors later distinguished mathematically as covariant and contravariant.[60] Further analytical developments in the *Treatise* include applications of reciprocal theorems to electrostatics, a general treatment of Green's functions, topological methods in field and network theory, and the beautiful polar representation of spherical harmonic functions.[61] The *Treatise* also contains important contributions to experimental technique, such as the well-known "Maxwell bridge" circuit for determining the magnitude of an inductance.[62]

A consequence of the displacement hypothesis which Maxwell himself did not truly grasp until 1869 is that all electric currents, even in apparently open circuits, are in reality closed.[63] But with that a new interpretation of electric charge became necessary. This is a subject of great difficulty, one of the most controversial in all Maxwell's writings. Many critics from Heinrich Hertz on have come to feel that a consistent view of the nature of charge and electric current, compatible with Maxwell's statements, simply does not exist. I believe these authors to be mistaken, although I admit that Maxwell gave them grounds for complaint, both by his laziness over plus and minus signs and by the fact that in parts of his work where the interpretation of charge was not the central issue he slipped back into terminology—and even ideas— not really compatible with his underlying view. The question is all the harder because the problem it touches (the relation between particles and fields) has continued as a difficulty in physics down to the present day. A full critical discussion would take many pages. I shall content myself with a short dogmatic statement, cautioning the reader that other opinions are possible.

Before Maxwell, electricity had been represented as an independent fluid (or pair of fluids), the excess or deficiency of which constitutes a charge. But if currents are invariably closed, how can charge accumulate anywhere? Part, but only part, of the answer lies in the hypothesis, hinted at by Faraday and clearly stated by Maxwell in 1865, that electrostatic action is entirely a matter of dielectric polarization, with the conductor serving not as a receptacle for electric fluid but as a bounding surface for unbalanced polarization of the surrounding medium. The difference between the old and new interpretations of charge, illustrated in Figure 4(a) and (b), looks simple; but underneath are problems that Maxwell's followers found bafflingly obscure. One source of confusion was that the polarization in 4(b) differs from that in the theory of material dielectrics proposed earlier by Thomson and Mossotti[64] (Figure 4[c]), which made the effective charge Q at the boundary the sum of a real charge Q_0 on the conductor and an apparent charge $-Q'$ on the dielectric surface. In Maxwell's interpretation the polarization extends from material dielectrics to space itself; all charge is in a sense apparent charge, and the motion is in the opposite direction. All might have been well had Maxwell in the *Treatise* not discussed the difference between charge on a conductor and charge on a dielectric surface in language similar to Mossotti's and if he had adopted a less liberal approach to the distinction between plus and minus signs. As it was, with the

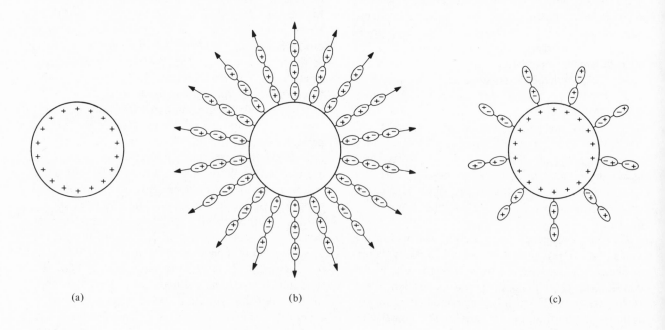

(a)

(b)

(c)

Conventional
electric fluid.

Maxwell-Faraday: all charge attributed to unbalanced dielectric polarization.

Thomson-Mossotti: real charge on conductor combined with apparent charge due to unbalanced polarization of a material dielectric.

FIGURE 4.   Representations of a charged conductor.

further novelty of totally closed currents, most people from Hertz on shook their heads in despair.

Yet the two analogies on which Maxwell based his ideas—those between the motion of electricity and an incompressible fluid and between static induction and displacement—are both sound. The escape lies in recognizing the radical difference in meaning of the two charges illustrated in 4(a) and 4(b). Maxwell's current is not the motion of charge, but the motion of a continuous *uncharged* quantity (not necessarily a substance); his charge is the measure of the displacement of that quantity relative to space. To the question puzzling Hertz—whether charge is the cause of polarization or polarization the cause of charge— the answer is "neither." For Maxwell electromotive force is the fundamental quantity. It causes polarization; polarization creates stresses in the field; charge is the measure of stress. All these ideas are traceable to Maxwell; but nowhere, it must be conceded, are they fairly set out. The representation of electricity as an uncharged fluid may seem incompatible with electron theory. Actually it is not; and one of the oddities in Maxwell's development is that the clue to reconciling the two ideas rests in the treatment of charges as sources and sinks of incompressible fluid given in his 1856 paper. That essentially was the principle of the ether-electron theory worked out by Larmor in 1899.

Few things illustrate better the subtlety of physical analogy than Maxwell's developing interpretations of the function **A**. His original discussion in 1856 was purely analytic. The dynamical theory led him to its representation as a property of electricity analogous to momentum, which reached fulfillment after his death in the expression $(m\mathbf{v} + e\mathbf{A}/c)$ for the canonical momentum of the electron, $m\mathbf{v}$ being the momentum of the free particle and $e\mathbf{A}/c$ the reduced momentum contributed by sources in the surrounding field. In 1871 he perceived another, entirely different analogy for **A**. Considered in relation to electrodynamic forces it resembles a potential, as may be seen by comparing the equation $F = \mathrm{grad}(\mathbf{i} \cdot \mathbf{A})$ for force on a conductor carrying a current with the equation $F = \mathrm{grad}(e\Phi)$ for force on a charged body. Maxwell introduced the terms "vector" and "scalar potential" for **A** and Φ and recognized, probably for the first time, that **A** was a generalization of F. E. Neumann's electrodynamic potential, though his formulation differed in spirit and substance from Neumann's, since it started from the field equations and incorporated displacement current. The formulas were later rearranged by FitzGerald, Liénard, and Wiechert as retarded potentials of the conduction currents, thus uncovering their common ground with

L. V. Lorenz's propagated action theory of electrodynamics. Both of Maxwell's analogies may be carried through in detail: that is, equations in **A** exist analogous to every equation in dynamics involving momentum and every equation in potential theory involving Φ. The resemblance of a single function to two quantities so different as momentum and potential depends on the peculiar relation between electromotive and electrodynamic forces: the electromotive force generated by induction is proportional to the velocity of the conductor times the electrodynamic force acting on it. The momentum analogy was little appreciated until 1959, when Y. Aharonov and D. J. Bohm pointed out some unexpected effects tied to the canonical momentum in quantum mechanics.[65]

Statistical and Molecular Physics (1859–1878). The problem of determining the motions of large numbers of colliding bodies came to Maxwell's attention while he was investigating Saturn's rings. He dismissed it then as hopelessly complicated; but in April 1859, as he was finishing his essay for publication, he chanced to read a new paper by Rudolf Clausius on the kinetic theory of gases, which convinced him otherwise and made him transfer his interest to gas theory.

The idea of attributing pressure in gases to the random impacts of molecules against the walls of the containing vessel had been suggested before. Prevailing opinion, however, still favored Newton's hypothesis of static repulsion between molecules or one of its variants, such as Rankine's vortex hypothesis. Maxwell had been taught the static theory of gases as a student at Edinburgh. Behind the victory of kinetic theory led by Clausius and Maxwell lay two distinct scientific advances: the doctrine of conservation of energy, and an accumulation of enough experimental information about gases to shape a worthwhile theory. Many of the new discoveries from 1780 on, such as Dalton's law of partial pressures, the law of equivalent volumes, and measurements on the failure of the ideal gas equation near liquefaction, came as by-products of chemical investigations. Two developments especially important to Maxwell were Thomas Graham's long series of experiments on diffusion, transpiration, and allied phenomena, also begun as chemical researches, and Stokes's analysis of gas viscosity, made in 1850 as part of a study on the damping of pendulums for gravitational measurements. Maxwell had used Stokes's data in treating the hypothesis of gaseous rings for Saturn. Viscosity naturally became one of his first subjects for calculation in kinetic theory; to his astonishment the predicted coefficient was independent of the pressure of the gas. The experiments of his wife and himself between 1863 and 1865, which confirmed this seeming paradox, fixed the success of the theory.

Clausius' work appeared in two papers of 1857 and 1858, each of which contained results important to Maxwell. The first gave a greatly improved derivation of the known formula connecting pressure and volume in a system of moving molecules:

$$pV = \tfrac{1}{3}nm\overline{v^2},\qquad(7)$$

where m is the mass of a molecule, $\overline{v^2}$ its mean square velocity, and n the total number of molecules, from which, knowing the density at a given pressure, Clausius deduced (as others had done earlier) that the average speed must be several hundred meters per second. Another matter, whose full significance only became apparent after Maxwell's work, was the exchange of energy between the translational and rotational motions of molecules. Clausius guessed that the average energies associated with the two types of motion would settle down to a constant ratio σ, and from thermodynamical reasoning he derived an equation relating σ to the ratio γ of the two specific heats of a gas.

Clausius' second paper was written to counter a criticism by the Dutch meteorologist C. H. D. Buys Ballot, who objected that gas molecules could never be going as fast as Clausius imagined, since the odor of a pungent gas takes minutes to permeate a room. Clausius replied that molecules of finite diameter must be repeatedly colliding and rebounding in new directions, and he deduced from statistical arguments that the probability W of a molecule's traveling a distance L without collision is

$$W = e^{-L/l},\qquad(8)$$

where l is a characteristic "mean free path." Assuming for convenience that all molecules have equal velocity, Clausius found

$$\frac{1}{l} = \frac{4}{3}\,\pi s^2 N,\qquad(9)$$

where s is their diameter and N their number density. He could not determine the quantities explicitly but guessed that l/s might be about 1,000, from which l had to be a very small distance. Since by equation (8) only a minute fraction of molecules travel more than a few mean free paths without collision, Buys Ballot's objection to kinetic theory was fallacious.

Although Clausius had based his investigation on the simplifying assumption that all molecules of any one kind have the same velocity, he recognized that the velocities would in reality spread over a range of values. The first five propositions of Maxwell's "Illustrations of the Dynamical Theory of Gases"

(1860) led to a statistical formula for the distribution of velocities in a gas at uniform pressure, as follows. Let the components of molecular velocity in three axes be x, y, z. Then the number dN of molecules whose velocities lie between x and $x + dx$, y and $y + dy$, z and $z + dz$ is $Nf(x) f(y) f(z)\, dx\, dy\, dz$. But since the axes are arbitrary, dN depends only on the molecular speed v, where $v^2 = x^2 + y^2 + z^2$ and the distribution must satisfy the functional relation

$$f(x) f(y) f(z) = \phi(x^2 + y^2 + z^2),\qquad(10)$$

the solution of which is an exponential. Applying the fact that N is finite, the resolved components of velocity in a given direction may be shown to have a distribution function identical in form with Laplace's bell-shaped "normal distribution" in the theory of errors:

$$dN_x = \frac{N}{\alpha\sqrt{\pi}}\, e^{-x^2/\alpha^2}\, dx,\qquad(11)$$

where α is a quantity with dimensions of velocity. The number of particles summed over all directions with speeds between v and $v + dv$ is

$$dN_v = \frac{4N}{\alpha^3\sqrt{\pi}}\, v^2 e^{-v^2/\alpha^2}\, dv.\qquad(12)$$

Related formulas give the distributions in systems of two or more kinds of molecules. From them with (11) and (12) Maxwell was able to determine mean values of various products and powers of the velocities used in calculating gas properties.

The derivation of equations (11) and (12) marks the beginning of a new epoch in physics. Statistical methods had long been used for analyzing observations, both in physics and in the social sciences, but Maxwell's idea of describing actual physical processes by a statistical function was an extraordinary novelty. Its origin and validity deserve careful study. Intuitively equation (12) is plausible enough, since dN_v approaches zero as v approaches zero and infinity and has a maximum at $v = \alpha$, consistent with the natural physical expectation that only a few molecules will have very high or very low speeds. Empirically it was verified years later in experiments with molecular beams. Yet the assumption that the three resolved components of velocity are distributed independently is one which, as Maxwell later conceded, "may appear precarious";[66] and the whole derivation conveys a strange impression of having nothing to do with molecules or their collisions. Its roots go back to Maxwell's Edinburgh days. His interest in probability theory was aroused in 1848 by Forbes, who reexamined a statistical argument for the existence of binary stars put forward in 1767 by the Reverend John Michell. Over the next few years he read thoroughly the statistical writings of Laplace and Boole and also another item of peculiar interest, a long essay by Sir John Herschel in the *Edinburgh Review* for June 1850 on Adolphe Quetelet's *Theory of Probability as Applied to the Moral and Social Sciences*. Herschel's review ranged over many issues, social and otherwise; and a contemporary letter to Lewis Campbell leaves no doubt that Maxwell had read it.[67] One passage embodied a popular derivation of the law of least squares applied to random distributions in two dimensions, based on the supposed independence of probabilities along different axes. The family resemblance to Maxwell's derivation of equation (11) is striking. Thus early reading on statistics, study of gaseous rings for Saturn, and ideas from Clausius about probability and free path all contributed to Maxwell's development of kinetic theory.

In his second paper, published in 1867, Maxwell offered a new derivation of the distribution law tied directly to molecular encounters. To maintain equilibrium the distribution function must satisfy the relation $f(v_1)f(v_2) = f(v_1')f(v_2')$ where v_1 and v_1' are velocities of molecule 1 and v_2 and v_2' of molecule 2 before and after encounter. Combination with the energy equation yielded formulas corresponding to (11) and (12). This established the equilibrium of the exponential distribution but not its uniqueness. From considerations of cyclic collision processes Maxwell sketched an argument that any velocity distribution would ultimately converge to the same form. The proof of the theorem in full mathematical rigor is still an open problem. Boltzmann gave an interesting extended version of Maxwell's argument in his *Lectures on Gas Theory* (1892). Earlier he had formulated another approach (the *H*-theorem), which bears on the subject and is even more important as part of the development that eventually transcended gas theory and led to the separate science of statistical mechanics. One further point that has been examined by various writers is the status of Maxwell's original derivation of the exponential law. Since the result is correct the hypotheses on which it was based must in some sense be justifiable. The best proof along Maxwell's first lines appears to be one given by M. Kac in 1939.[68]

Maxwell next applied the distribution function to evaluate coefficients of viscosity, diffusion, and heat conduction, as well as other properties of gases not studied by Clausius. He interpreted viscosity as the transfer of momentum between successive layers of molecules moving, like Saturn's rings, with different transverse velocities. The probability of a molecule's starting in a layer dz and ending in dz' is found from

Clausius' equation (8) in combination with the distribution function. Integration gives the total frictional drag and an equation for the viscosity coefficient,

$$\mu = \tfrac{1}{3}\rho \bar{l}\bar{v}, \qquad (13)$$

where ρ is the density, $\bar{l}$ the mean free path, and $\bar{v}$ the mean molecular speed. Since $\bar{l}$ is inversely proportional to ρ, the viscosity is independent of pressure. The physical explanation of this result, given by Maxwell in a letter to Stokes of 30 May 1859, is that although the number of molecules increases with pressure, the average distance over which each one carries momentum decreases with pressure.[69] It holds experimentally over a wide range, only breaking down when ρ is so high that $\bar{l}$ becomes comparable with the diameter of a molecule or so low that it is comparable with the dimensions of the apparatus. Maxwell was able to calculate a numerical value for the free path by substituting into (13) a value for μ/ρ from Stokes's data and a value for $\bar{v}$ from (7). The result was 5.6×10^{-6} cm. for air at atmospheric pressure and room temperature, which is within a factor of two of the current value. The calculations for diffusion and heat conduction proceeded along similar lines by determining the number of molecules and quantity of energy transferred in the gas. Applying the diffusion formulas to Graham's experiments, Maxwell made a second, independent estimate of the free path in air as 6.3×10^{-6} cm. The good agreement between the results greatly strengthened the plausibility of the theory. There were, however, errors of principle and of arithmetic in some of the calculations, which Clausius exposed—not without a certain scholarly relish—in a new paper of 1862. The chief mistake lay in continuing to use an isotropic distribution function in the presence of density and pressure gradients. Clausius offered a corrected theory; but since he persisted in assuming constant molecular velocity, it too was unsatisfactory. Maxwell wrote out his own revised theory in 1864; but having meanwhile become dissatisfied with the whole mean free path method, he withheld the details. The true value of Clausius' criticism was to show the need for a formulation of kinetic theory consistent with known macroscopic equations. Maxwell was to produce it in 1867.

One further important topic covered in the 1860 papers was the distribution of energy among different modes of motion of the molecules. Maxwell first established an equality, which had previously been somewhat sketchily derived by both Waterston and Clausius, between the average energies of translation of two sets of colliding particles with different molecular weights. He deduced that equal volumes of gas at fixed temperature and pressure contain the same number of molecules, accounting for the law of equivalent volumes in chemistry. Later, following out Clausius' thoughts on specific heat, he studied the distribution of energy between translational and rotational motions of rough spherical particles and found that there too the average energies are equal. These two statistical equalities, between the separate translational motions of different molecular species and between the rotational and translational motions of a single species, are examples of a deep general principle in statistical mechanics, the "equipartition principle." The second was an embarrassing surprise; for if molecules are point particles incapable of rotation, Clausius' formula makes the specific heat ratio 1.666, and if they are rough spheres it makes it 1.333. The experimental mean for several gases was 1.408. Maxwell was so upset that he stated that the discrepancy "overturned the whole hypothesis."[70] His further wrestlings with equipartition in the 1870's will be discussed below.

The measurements of gaseous viscosity at different pressures and temperatures made by Maxwell and his wife[71] in 1865 were their most useful contribution to experimental physics. The "Dynamical Theory of Gases," which followed, was Maxwell's greatest single paper. The experiment consisted in observing the decay of oscillations of a stack of disks torsionally suspended in a sealed chamber. Over the ranges studied, the viscosity μ was independent of pressure, as predicted, and very nearly a linear function of the absolute temperature T. But equation (12) implies that μ should vary as $T^{1/2}$. The hypothesis that gas molecules are freely colliding spheres is therefore too simple, and Maxwell accordingly developed a new theory treating them as point centers of force subject to an inverse nth power repulsion. In a theory of this kind the mean free path ceases to be a clear-cut concept: molecules do not travel in straight lines but in complicated orbits with deflections and distances varying with velocity and initial path. Yet some quantity descriptive of the heterogeneous structure of the gas is needed. Maxwell replaced the characteristic distance l by a characteristic time, the "modulus of time of relaxation" of stresses in the gas. A second need, exposed by Clausius' critical paper of 1862, was for a systematic procedure to connect molecular motions with the known macroscopic gas laws. On both points Maxwell's thinking was influenced by Stokes's work on the general equations of viscosity and elasticity.

Elasticity may be defined as a stress developed in a body in reaction to change of form. Both solids and fluids exhibit elasticity of volume; solids alone are elastic against change of shape. A fluid resists changes of shape through its viscosity, but the resistance is evanescent: motion generates stresses proportional to velocity rather than displacement. In 1845 Stokes wrote a powerful paper giving a new treatment of the equations of motion of a viscous fluid. He noticed while doing so that if the time derivatives in the equations are replaced by spatial derivatives, they become the equations of stress for an elastic solid. Poisson also had noticed this transformation, but Stokes went further and remarked that viscosity and elasticity seem to be physically related through time. Substances like pitch and glass react as solids to rapid disturbances and as viscous liquids to slow ones. Stokes utilized this idea in the theory of aberration already described; other physicists also followed it up, among them Forbes, who, as an alpinist, applied it to the motions of glaciers. Maxwell's early letters contain several references to Forbes's opinions.[72] His youthful work on elasticity made him acquainted with Stokes's paper, and in 1861, as explained above in the section on electricity, he applied the analogy of viscosity and elasticity in another way to the processes of conduction and static induction through dielectrics.

During the experiments on gases Maxwell's attention was again directed to viscoelastic phenomena through having to correct for losses in the torsion wire from which his apparatus was suspended. His 1867 paper proposed a new method of specifying viscosity in extension of Stokes's theory. In an ideal solid free from viscosity, a distortion or strain S of any kind creates a constant stress F equal to E times S, where E is the coefficient of elasticity for that particular kind of strain. In a viscous body F is not constant but tends to disappear. Maxwell conjectured that the rate of relaxation of stress is proportional to F, in which case the process may be described formally by the differential equation

$$\frac{dF}{dt} = E\frac{dS}{dt} - \frac{F}{\tau}, \tag{14}$$

which gives an exponential decay of stress governed by the relaxation time τ. Processes short compared with τ are elastic; processes of longer duration are viscous. The viscosity μ is equal to E_s times τ, where E_s is the instantaneous rigidity against shearing stresses. A given substance may depart from solidity either by having small rigidity or short relaxation time, or both. Maxwell seems to have arrived at (14) from a comparison with Thomson's telegraphy equations, inverting the analogy between electrical and mechanical systems that he had developed in 1865. A test that immediately occurred to him was to look for induced double refraction in a moving fluid, comparable to the double refraction in strained solids discovered by Brewster, which he himself had analyzed in his paper of 1850 on the equilibrium of elastic solids. After some difficulty Maxwell eventually demonstrated in 1873 that a solution of Canada balsam in water exhibits temporary double refraction with a relaxation time of order 10^{-2} seconds.[73] Maxwell's theory of stress relaxation formed the starting point of the science of rheology and affected indirectly every branch of physics, as may be seen from the widespread use of his term "relaxation time." Its immediate purpose lay in reaching a new formulation of the kinetic theory of gases.

Consider a group of molecules moving about in a box. Their impact on the walls exerts pressure. If the volume is changed from V to $V + dV$, the pressure will change by an amount $-p\, dV/V$. But in the theory of elasticity the differential stress due to an isotropic change of volume is $-E\, dV/V$, where E is the cubical elasticity. The elasticity of a gas is proportional to its pressure. Suppose now the pressure is reduced until the mean free path is much greater than the dimensions of the box; and let the walls be rough, so that the molecules rebound at random, and also flexible. Then in addition to the pressure there will be continued exchange of the transverse components of momentum from wall to wall, making the box, even though it is flexible, resist shearing stresses. In other words, a rarefied gas behaves like an elastic solid! Let this property be called quasi-solidity. Following the ideas expressed in equation (14), the viscosity of a gas at ordinary pressures may be conceived of as the relaxation of stresses by molecular encounters. Since elasticity varies as pressure, μ is proportional to $p\tau$ and the relaxation time of a gas at normal pressures is inversely proportional to its density. Although the concept of free path is elusive when there are forces between molecules, some link evidently exists between it and the relaxation time. Maxwell gave it in 1879 in a footnote to his last paper, added in response to a query by Thomson.[74] For a gas composed of rigid-elastic spheres, the product of τ with the mean speed $\bar{v}$ of the molecules is a characteristic distance λ, whose ratio to the mean free path $\bar{l}$ is $8/3\pi$. The free path is a special formulation of the relaxation concept applicable only to freely colliding particles of finite diameter.

To calculate the motions of a pair of molecules subject to an inverse nth power repulsion was a straightforward exercise in orbital dynamics. For the statistical specification of encounters, Maxwell wrote the number dN_1 of molecules of a particular type with molecular weight M, and velocities between ξ_1 and $\xi_1 + d\xi$, etc. as $f(\xi_1 \eta_1 \zeta_1)\, d\xi_1\, d\eta_1\, d\zeta_1$, as in the first paper, with a similar expression for molecules of another type with molecular weight M_2. The velocities of two such groups being defined, their relative velocity V_{12} is also a definite quantity; and the number of encounters between them occurring in time δt can be expressed in terms of orbit parameters. It is $V_{12}b\, db\, d\phi\, dN_1\, dN_2\, \delta t$, where b is the distance between parallel asymptotes before and after an encounter and ϕ is the angle determining the plane in which V_{12} and b lie. If Q is some quantity describing the motion of molecules in group 1, which may be any power or product of powers of the velocities or their components, and if Q' is its value after an encounter, the net rate of change in the quantity for the entire group is $(Q' - Q)$ times the number of encounters per second, or

$$\frac{\delta}{\delta t}(Q\, dN_1) = (Q' - Q)\, V_{12}b\, db\, d\phi\, dN_1\, dN_2. \quad (15)$$

Equation (13) is the fundamental equation of Maxwell's revised transfer theory, replacing the earlier equations based on Clausius' probability formula (8). With the explicit relation between V_{12} and b inserted from the orbit equation, the relative velocity enters the integral of (15) as a factor $V_{12}^{(n-5)/(n-1)}$, which means that although integration generally requires knowledge of the distribution function f_2 under nonequilibrium conditions, in the special case of molecules subject to an inverse fifth-power repulsion V_{12} drops out and the final result may be written immediately as $\bar{Q}N_2$, where $\bar{Q}$ is the mean value of the quantity and N_2 is the total number of molecules of type 2. The simplification may be understood, as Boltzmann later pointed out, by noticing that the number of deflections through a given angle is the product of two factors, one of which (the cross section for scattering) decreases with V_{12}, while the other (the number of collisions) increases with V_{12}.[75] When n is 5, the two factors are exactly balanced. Molecules subject to this law are now called Maxwellian. By a happy coincidence their viscosity is directly proportional to the absolute temperature, in agreement with Maxwell's experiment, although not with more precise measurements made later.

With this Maxwell was in a position to determine the scattering integrals and calculate physical properties of gases. Even with the simplification of inverse fifth-power forces the mathematical task remained formidable, and an impressive feature was the notation Maxwell developed to keep track of different problems. One general equation described transfer of quantities across a plane with different Q's giving the velocities, pressures, and heat fluxes in a gas. Next to be considered were variations of $\bar{Q}$ within a given element of volume. These might occur through the actions of encounters or external forces on molecules within the element or, alternatively, through the passage of molecules to or from the surrounding region. Denoting variations of the first kind by the symbol δ and variations of the second kind by ∂, Maxwell got his general equation of transfer:

$$\frac{\partial}{\partial t}\,\bar{Q}N + \left(\frac{du}{dx} + \frac{dv}{dy} + \frac{dw}{dz}\right) + \frac{d}{dx}\,(\bar{\xi Q}N)$$
$$+ \frac{d}{dy}\,(\bar{\eta Q}N) + \frac{d}{dz}\,(\bar{\zeta Q}N) = \frac{\delta}{\delta t}\,QN, \quad (16)$$

where u, v, w are components of the translational velocity of the gas; the differential symbol d gives total variations with respect to position and time; and subscripts are added to δ, to distinguish variations due to encounters with molecules of the same kind, molecules of a different kind, and the action of external forces. With Q equal to mass, (16) reduces to the ordinary equation of continuity in hydrodynamics. With Q equal to the momentum per unit volume, (16) in combination with the appropriate expression for

$$\frac{\delta}{\delta t}\,QN$$ derived from (15) reduces to an equation

of motion. From this, or rather from its generalization to mixtures of more than one kind of molecule, Maxwell derived Dalton's law of partial pressures, and formulas for diffusion applicable to Graham's experiments. With Q energy, (16) yields an equation giving the law of equivalent volumes and formulas for specific heats, thermal effects of diffusion, and coefficients of viscosity in simple and mixed gases. The viscosity equation replacing (12) for Maxwellian molecules is

$$\mu = 0.3416k \left(\frac{M}{K}\right)^{\frac{1}{2}} T, \quad (17)$$

where k is Boltzmann's constant, M is molecular weight, and K is the scaling constant for the forces.

The hardest area of investigation was heat conduction. That was where Maxwell had gone astray in 1860. In the exact theory effects of thermal gradients occur when Q in equation (16) is of the third order in ξ, η, ζ. Maxwell found an expression for the thermal conductivity of a gas in terms of its viscosity, density, and specific heat. The ratio of these quantities, which is known as the Prandtl number, "but which ought to be called the Maxwell number,"[76] is one of several dimensionless ratios used in applying similarity principles to the solution of problems in fluid dynamics. For a monatomic gas it is nearly a constant

over a wide range of temperatures and pressures. Another matter, in which Maxwell became interested through considering the stability of the earth's atmosphere, was the equilibrium of temperature in a vertical column of gas under gravity. The correct result was known from thermodynamics, but its derivation from gas theory gave Maxwell great trouble. It comes out right only if the ratio of the two statistical averages $\bar{\xi^4}/|\,\bar{\xi^2}\,|^2$ has the particular value 3 given by the exponential distribution law. The calculation thus supplied evidence in favor of the law. More light on the same subject came in Boltzmann's first paper on kinetic theory, written in 1868. Boltzmann investigated the distribution law by a method based on Maxwell's, but included the external forces directly in the energy equation to be combined with Maxwell's collision equation $f(v_1)\,f(v_2) = f(v_1')\,f(v_2')$. The distribution function assumed the form $e^{-E/kT}$, where E is the sum of the kinetic and potential energies of the molecule. In 1873 Maxwell gave a greatly simplified derivation of Boltzmann's result during a correspondence in *Nature* about the equilibrium of the atmosphere. He then confessed that his first calculation for the 1867 paper, which gave a temperature distribution that would have generated unending convection currents, nearly shattered his faith in kinetic theory.

Maxwell never attempted to solve the transfer equations for forces other than the inverse fifth power. In 1872 Boltzmann rearranged (16) into an integro-differential equation for f, from which the transport coefficients could in principle be calculated; but despite much effort he failed to reach any solution except for Maxwellian molecules. It was not until 1911–1917 that S. Chapman and D. Enskog developed general methods of determining the coefficients. One interesting result was Chapman's expression for viscosity of a gas made up of hard spheres, which had a form equivalent to (12) but with a numerical coefficient 50 percent higher than Maxwell's and 12 percent higher than that obtained from the mean free path method with corrections for statistical averaging and persistence of velocities derived by Tait and Jeans. So even for the hard-sphere gas the simple theory fails in quantitative accuracy.

For some years after 1867 Maxwell made only sporadic contributions to gas theory. In 1873 he gave a revised theory of diffusion for the hard-sphere gas, from which he developed estimates of the size of molecules, following the work of Loschmidt (1865), Johnstone Stoney (1868), and Thomson (1870). In 1875, following van der Waals, he applied calculations on intermolecular forces to the problem of continuity between the liquid and gaseous states of matter.

In 1876 he gave a new theory of capillarity, also based on considerations about intermolecular forces, which stimulated new research on surface phenomena. Of all the questions about molecules which Maxwell puzzled over during this period the most urgent concerned their structure. His uneasiness about the discrepancy between the measured and calculated specific heat ratios of gases has already been referred to. The uneasiness increased after 1868 when Boltzmann extended the equipartition theorem to every degree of freedom in a dynamical system composed of material particles; and it turned to alarm with the emergence of a new area of research: spectrum analysis. From 1858 onwards, following the experiments of Bunsen and Kirchhoff, several people, including Maxwell, worked out a qualitative explanation of the bright lines in chemical spectra, attributing them to resonant vibrations of molecules excited by their mutual collisions. The broad truth of the hypothesis seemed certain; but it led, as Maxwell immediately saw, to two questions, neither of which was answered until after his death. First, the identity of spectra implies that an atom in Sirius and an atom in Arcturus must be identical in all the details of their internal structure. There must be some universal dimensional constant determining vibration frequency: "each molecule . . . throughout the universe bears impressed on it the stamp of a metric system as distinctly as does the metre of the Archives of Paris, or the double royal cubit of the Temple of Karnac."[77] The royal cubit proved to be Planck's quantum of action discovered in 1900. The other question, also answered only by quantum theory, concerned the influence of molecular vibrations on the specific heat ratio. There were not three or six degrees of freedom, but dozens. There was no way of reconciling the specific heat and spectroscopic data with each other and the equipartition principle. The more Maxwell examined the problem the more baffled he became. In his last discussion, written in 1877, after summarizing and rejecting all the attempts from Boltzmann on to wriggle out of the difficulty, he concluded that nothing remained but to adopt that attitude of "thoroughly conscious ignorance that is the prelude to every real advance in knowledge."[78]

During his last two years Maxwell returned to molecular physics in earnest and produced two full-length papers, strikingly different in scope, each among the most powerful he ever wrote. The first, "On Boltzmann's Theorem on the Average Distribution of Energy in a System of Material Points," followed a line of thought started by Boltzmann, who in 1868 had offered a new conjectural derivation of the distribution law based on combinatorial theory.

A strange feature of the analysis was that it seemed to be free from restrictions on the time spent in encounters between molecules. Hence, as Maxwell was quick to point out,[79] both the distribution factor $e^{-E/kT}$ and the equipartition theorem should apply to solids and liquids as well as gases: a conclusion as fascinating and disturbing as equipartition itself.

Maxwell now gave his own investigation of the statistical problem, based partly on Boltzmann's ideas and partly on an extension of them contained in H. W. Watson's *Treatise on the Kinetic Theory of Gases*.[80] Following Watson, Maxwell used Hamilton's form of the dynamical equations, and adopted the device of representing the state of motion of a large number n of particles by the location of a single point in a "phase-space" of $2n$ dimensions, the coordinates of which are the positions and momenta of the particles. Boltzmann had applied similar methods in configuration space, but the Hamiltonian formalism has advantages in simplicity and elegance. Maxwell then postulated, as Boltzmann had done, that the system would in the course of time pass through every phase of motion consistent with the energy equation. This postulate obviously breaks down in special instances, of which Maxwell gave some examples, but he argued that it should hold approximately for large numbers of particles, where discontinuous jumps due to collisions make the particles jog off one smooth trajectory to another. The validity of this hypothesis, sometimes called the ergodic hypothesis, was afterwards much discussed, often with considerable misrepresentation of Maxwell's opinions. Maxwell next introduced a new formal device for handling the statistical averages. In place of the actual system of particles under study, many similar systems are conceived to exist simultaneously, with identical energies but different initial conditions. The statistical problem is then transformed into determining the number of systems in a given state at any instant, rather than the development in time of a single system. The method had in some degree been foreshadowed by Boltzmann in 1872. It was later very greatly extended by Gibbs, following whom it is known as the method of "ensemble averaging." Maxwell's main conclusion was that the validity of the distribution and equipartition laws in a system of material particles is not restricted to binary encounters. An important result of a more technical kind was an exact calculation of the microcanonical density of the gas, with an expression for its asymptotic form as the number n of degrees of freedom in the system goes to infinity, while the ratio E/n is held constant. According to C. Truesdell, although the hypotheses on which the theorem was based were rather special, "no better proof was given until the work of Darwin and Fowler."[76] Together with Boltzmann's articles this paper of Maxwell's marks the emergence of statistical mechanics as an independent science.

One feature of the paper "On Boltzmann's Theorem," eminently characteristic of Maxwell, is that the analysis, for all its abstraction, ends with a concrete suggestion for an experiment, based on considering the rotational degrees of freedom. Maxwell proved that the densities of the constituent components in a rotating mixture of gases would be the same as if each gas were present by itself. Hence gaseous mixtures could be separated by means of a centrifuge. The method also promised much more accurate diffusion data than was hitherto available. Maxwell's correspondence before his death discloses a plan to set up experiments at Cambridge.[81] Many years later it became a standard technique for separating gases commercially.

Maxwell's last major paper on any subject was "On Stresses in Rarefied Gases Arising From Inequalities of Temperature." Between 1873 and 1876 the scientific world had been stirred by William Crookes's experiments with the radiometer, the well-known device composed of a partially evacuated chamber containing a paddle wheel with vanes blackened on one side and silvered on the other, which spins rapidly when radiant heat impinges on it. At first many people, Maxwell included, were tempted to ascribe the motion to light pressure, but the forces were much greater than predicted from the electromagnetic theory, and in the wrong direction. The influence of the residual gas was soon established; and from 1874 on partial explanations were advanced by Osborne Reynolds, Johnstone Stoney, and others. The tenor of these explanations was that the blackened surfaces absorb radiation and, being hot, make the gas molecules rebound with higher average velocity than do the reflecting surfaces. That plausible but false notion is still perpetuated in many textbooks. A striking observation is that the stresses increase as the pressure is reduced. In 1875 Tait and James Dewar drew the significant conclusion that large stresses occur when the mean free path is comparable with the dimensions of the vanes. At higher pressures some equalizing process enters to reduce the effect.

Such was the state of affairs in 1877, when Maxwell and Reynolds independently renewed the attack. Maxwell was thoroughly familiar with the radiometer controversy, having acted as a referee for many of the original papers, as well as seeing and experimenting with radiometers himself. His work went forward in several stages, during which the comments of Thomson, who refereed his paper, and his own reaction as a referee for Reynolds' paper had important influences. He began by applying the exact transfer theory to the hypothesis that the stresses arise from the increased velocity of molecules rebounding from a heated surface, expanding the distribution function in the form

$$[1 + F(\xi, \eta, \zeta)] e^{-(\xi^2+\eta^2+\zeta^2)/kT}, \qquad (18)$$

where F is a sum of powers and products of ξ, η, ζ up to the third degree, and then calculating the effect of temperature gradients in the gas. This expansion later became the first step of Chapman's elaborate procedure for determining transport coefficients under any force law, but Maxwell kept to inverse fifth-power forces "for the sake of being able to effect the integrations."[82] The result was a stress proportional to d^2T/dn^2, the second derivative of temperature with respect to distance, correcting a formula given earlier by Stoney, where the stress was proportional to dT/dn. The stress increases when the pressure is lowered, reaching a maximum when the relaxation time τ becomes comparable with the time $d/\bar{v}$, in which a molecule traverses the dimension d of the body—that is, Tait and Dewar's conjecture in the language of the exact theory.

At this point Maxwell made an awkward discovery. Although the stresses are indeed large, when the flow of heat is uniform (as in the radiometer) they automatically distribute themselves in such a way that the forces on each element of gas are in equilibrium. The result is a very general consequence of the fact that the stresses depend on d^2T/dn^2; it is almost independent of the shape of the source; the straightforward explanation of the motions by normal stresses must, therefore, be rejected. Yet the radiometer moves. To escape the dilemma, Maxwell turned to tangential stresses at the edges of the vanes. Here the phenomenon known as "slip" proved all-important. When a viscous fluid moves past a solid body, it generates tangential stresses by sliding over the surface with a finite velocity v_s. According to experiments by Kundt and Warburg in 1875, v_s in gases is equal to SG/μ, where S is the stress and G is a coefficient expressed empirically by $G = 8/\rho$. Thus slip effects increase as the pressure is reduced; and as Maxwell pointed out in 1878,[83] convection currents due to tangential stresses should become dominant in the radiometer, completely destroying the simplicity of the original hypothesis.

The second phase of Maxwell's investigation followed a report by Thomson urging him to treat the gas–surface interaction, and his own report on Reynolds' paper. Reynolds also had decided that the effect must depend on tangential stresses, and he devised an experiment to study them under simplified conditions. When a temperature difference ΔT is set up across a porous plug between two vessels containing gas at pressure p, a pressure difference Δp develops between them proportional to $\Delta T/p$. Reynolds called this new effect "thermal transpiration." Maxwell gave a simple qualitative explanation in his report, and in an appendix added to his own paper in May 1879 he developed a semiempirical theory accounting for it and for the radiometer effect. The method was to assume that a fraction f of molecules striking any surface are temporarily absorbed and reemitted diffusely, while the remaining $(1 - f)$ are specularly reflected. Application of the transfer equations gave a formula for the velocity v_s of gas moving past an unequally heated surface, in which one term was the standard slip formula and two further terms predicted convection currents due to thermal gradients. The theory provided an explicit expression $\frac{2}{3}(2/f - 1)\bar{l}$ for the coefficient G, where $\bar{l}$ is the effective mean free path; from this, using Kundt and Warburg's data, Maxwell deduced that f is about 0.5 for air in contact with glass. Maxwell also obtained a formula for transpiration pressure, and showed that both radiometer and transpiration effects are in the correct direction and increase with reduction of pressure, in agreement with experiment.

Maxwell's paper created the science of rarefied gas dynamics. His formulas for stress and heat flux in the body of the gas were contributions of permanent value, while his investigation of surface effects started a vast body of research extending to the present day. Quantities similar to f later became known as "accommodation coefficients" and were applied to many kinds of gas–surface interaction. One other contribution of great beauty contained in notes added to the paper in May and June 1879 was an application of the methods of spherical harmonic analysis to gas theory. It exemplified the process which Maxwell elsewhere called the "cross-fertilization of the sciences."[84] He was engaged in revising the chapter on spherical harmonics for the second edition of the *Treatise on Electricity and Magnetism*, when he realized that the harmonic expansion used in potential theory could equally be applied to the expansion of the components ξ, η, ζ of molecular velocity. A standard theorem on products of surface and zonal harmonics, which is discussed in the *Treatise*, eliminates odd terms in the expansion of variations of F, greatly simplifying the calculations.[85] With this and other simplifications Maxwell carried the approximations to higher order and added an extra term to the equation of motion of a gas subject to variations in temperature.

It is a tribute to Maxwell's genius that on two occasions his papers on transfer theory stimulated fresh work long after the period at which science usually receives historical embalming. In 1910 Chapman read them, and "with the ignorant hardihood of youth,"[86] knowing nothing of the fruitless toil that had been spent on the equations during the interval, began his investigation that yielded solutions under any force law. In 1956 E. Ikenberry and C. Truesdell again returned to Maxwell. They obtained an exact representation formula for the collision integral of any spherical harmonic for inverse-fifth-power molecules, using which they explored various iterative techniques for solving the transfer equations. One technique, which they called "Maxwellian iteration" from its resemblance to Maxwell's procedure in the 1879 paper, yielded much more compact derivations than the Chapman-Enskog procedure; and with it Ikenberry and Truesdell carried solutions for pressure and energy flux in the gas one stage further than had previously been attempted. Truesdell also discovered an exact solution for steady rectilinear flow, by means of which he exposed certain shortcomings of the iterative methods. Speaking of the "magnificent genius of Maxwell" these authors concluded their appraisal by remarking that it passed over all developments in kinetic theory since 1879 and went back "for its source and inspiration to what Maxwell left us."[87]

Other Scientific Work. Maxwell's remaining work may be summarized more shortly, though not as being of small account. His early discovery of the perfect imaging properties of the "fish-eye" lens extended to a lifelong interest in the laws of optical instruments. In a medium whose refractive index varies as $\mu_0 a^2/(a^2 + r^2)$, where μ_0 and a are constants and r is the distance from the origin, all rays proceeding from any single point are focused exactly at another point. The calculation was "suggested by the contemplation of the structure of the crystalline lens in fish."[88] Real fishes' eyes of course only approximate roughly to Maxwell's medium. Not until R. K. Luneberg revived the subject in 1944 were other instances of perfect imaging devices found.[89] In 1853, shortly after discovering the "fish-eye," Maxwell came across the early eighteenth-century writings on geometrical optics by Roger Cotes and Archibald Smith, in which, as he said to his father, "I find many things far better than what is new."[90] He went on to formulate a new approach to the subject, combining the principle of perfect imaging with Cotes's neglected theorem on "apparent distance." Recent years have seen a revival of interest in Maxwell's method.[91] During the 1870's he returned to it and wrote three papers on the application of Hamilton's characteristic function to lens systems, which seems to have been about the earliest attempt to reduce Hamilton's general theory of ray optics to practice. Another striking paper was on cyclidal wave surfaces. It was illustrated with stereoscopic views of different classes of cyclide and contained a description of Maxwell's real-image stereoscope.

The most pleasing of the minor inventions was his adjustable "dynamical top" (1856), which carried a disk with four quadrants (red, blue, green, yellow) that formed gray when spinning axially, "but burst into brilliant colors when the axis is disturbed." He was led to search records at Greenwich for evidence of the earth's 10-month nutation predicted by Euler, which was detected in modified form by Chandler in 1891.

During his regular lectures at King's College, London, Maxwell was accustomed to present some of Rankine's work on the calculation of stresses in frameworks. In 1864 Rankine offered an important new theorem,[92] which Maxwell then developed into a geometrical discussion entitled "On Reciprocal Figures and Diagrams of Forces." The principle was an extension of the well-known triangle of forces in statics. Corresponding to any rectilinear figure, another figure may be drawn with lines parallel to the first, but arranged so that lines converging to a point in one figure form closed polygons in the other. The

lengths of lines in the polygon supply the ratios of forces needed to maintain the original point in equilibrium. Maxwell gave a method for developing complex figures systematically, and derived a series of general theorems on properties of reciprocal figures in two and three dimensions. He combined the method with energy principles and later, after refereeing a paper on elasticity by G. B. Airy, extended it to stresses in continuous media.[93] Figure 5 reproduces diagrams of a girder bridge and its reciprocal given by Maxwell in 1870. Reciprocal theorems and diagrams are useful in many fields of science besides elasticity. Maxwell investigated similar theorems (some of them already known) in electricity. His student Donald MacAlister, the physiologist, applied the method to bone structures. Another application from a later period is the use of reciprocal lattices to determine atomic configurations by X-ray crystallography.

In the British Association experiment on electrical resistance, Maxwell and his colleagues used a speed governor to ensure that the coil rotated uniformly. In principle it resembled James Watt's steam-engine governor: centrifugal force made weights attached to the driven shaft fly out and adjust a control valve.[94] Maxwell studied its behavior carefully; and four years later, in 1868, after reading a paper by William Siemens[95] on the practical limitations of governors, he gave an analytical treatment of the subject. He determined conditions for stability in various simple

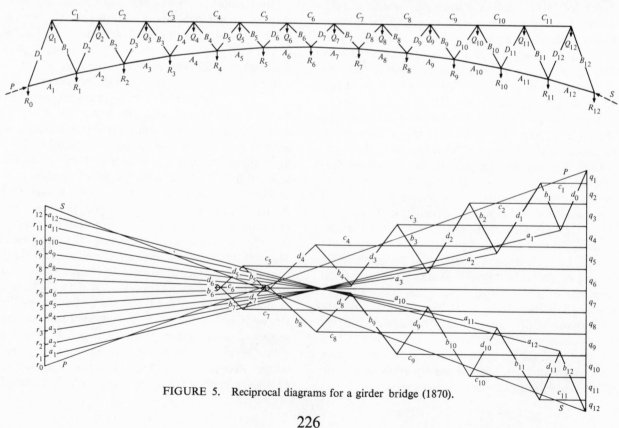

FIGURE 5.   Reciprocal diagrams for a girder bridge (1870).

cases, including one fifth-order system representing a combination of two devices invented by Thomson and Fleeming Jenkin, and investigated effects of natural damping and of variations in the driven load, as well as the onset of instabilities. Maxwell's paper "On Governors" is generally regarded as the foundation of control theory. Norbert Wiener coined the name "cybernetics" in its honor, from κυβερνητης, the Greek for "steersman," from which, via a Latin corruption, the word "governor" is etymologically descended.[96]

Maxwell's textbook *Theory of Heat* was published in 1870 and went through several editions with extensive revisions. Chiefly an exposition of standard results, it did contain one far-reaching innovation, the "Maxwell relations" between the thermodynamical variables, pressure, volume, entropy, and temperature, and their partial derivatives. In conceptual spirit they resemble Maxwell's field equations in electricity, by which they were obviously suggested; they are an ordered collection of relationships between fundamental quantities from which practically useful formulas follow. Several of the individual terms had previously been given by other writers. Maxwell's derivation was a deceptively simple geometrical argument based on the pressure-volume diagram. Applications of geometry to thermodynamics underwent an extraordinary development in 1873 through Gibbs's work on entropy-volume-temperature surfaces, of which Maxwell instantly became a powerful advocate. Maxwell's papers and correspondence contain much of related interest, including an independent development of the chemical potential and an admirable discussion of the classification of thermodynamic quantities in a little-known article, "On Gibbs' Thermodynamic Formulation for Coexistent Phases." In 1908 this paper was reprinted at the request of the energeticist W. Ostwald, with notes by Larmor.[97] One more important personage in the *Theory of Heat* was Maxwell's "sorting demon" (so named by Thomson), a member of a class of "very small BUT lively beings incapable of doing work but able to open and shut valves which move without friction and inertia"[98] and thereby defeat the second law of thermodynamics. The demon points to the statistical character of the law. His activities are related to the so-called "reversibility paradox" discussed first by Thomson in 1874—that is, the problem of reconciling the irreversible increase in entropy of the universe demanded by thermodynamics with the dynamical laws governing the motions of molecules, which are reversible with respect to time. A more formal view of the statistical basis of thermodynamics was supplied by Boltzmann in 1877 in the famous equation $S = k \overline{\log W}$, which relates entropy S to a quantity W expressing the molecular disorder of a system.

Much of Maxwell's last eight years was devoted to Cambridge and the Cavendish Laboratory. Many papers by Cambridge mathematicians of the period acknowledge suggestions by him. The design of the laboratory embodied many ingenious features: clear corridors and stairwells for experiments needing large horizontal and vertical distances, an iron-free room for magnetic measurements, built-in antivibration tables for sensitive instruments supported by piano wires from the roof brackets, and so on. The construction of the building and much of the equipment were paid for by the Duke of Devonshire, but after 1876 Maxwell had to spend substantial sums out of his own pocket to keep the laboratory going. A characteristic of the work done under his direction was an emphasis on measurements of extreme precision, in marked contrast to the "string-and-sealing-wax" tradition of research later built up by J. J. Thomson. Examples were D. MacAlister's test of the inverse-square law in electrostatics; G. Chrystal's test of the linear form of Ohm's law; J. H. Poynting's improved version (the first of many) of Cavendish's experiment to measure the gravitational constant; and R. T. Glazebrook's determination of the optical wave surface for birefringent crystals. In each instance the precision was several orders of magnitude higher than anything previously attempted. "You see," wrote Maxwell to Joule, "that the age of heroic experiments is not yet past."[99]

NOTES

1. C. G. Knott, *Life and Scientific Work of Peter Guthrie Tait* (Cambridge, 1911), 4, 5.
2. C. W. F. Everitt, in *Applied Optics*, 6 (1967), 644–645.
3. W. C. Henry, *Life of Dalton* (London, 1854), 25–27, letter of 20 May 1833; the letter was familiar to Maxwell through G. Wilson, *Researches on Colour Blindness* (Edinburgh, 1855), 60, in which his own work was first published. See also J. Herschel, "Treatise on Light," in *Encyclopaedia Metropolitana* (London, 1843), 403.
4. *Papers*, I, 146.
5. T. Young, *Lectures on Natural Philosophy*, I (London, 1807), 440; as was known to Maxwell, *Papers*, I, 150. The choice had also been suggested by C. E. Wünsch, *Versuche und Beobachtungen über die Farben des Lichtes* (Leipzig, 1792), of which an abstract is given in *Annales de chimie*, 64 (1807), 135. This rare reference is noted in one of Maxwell's memorandum books preserved at King's College, London.
6. *Papers*, I, 135.
7. J. Larmor, ed., *Memoir and Scientific Correspondence of Sir G. G. Stokes*, II (London, 1910), 22; *Life*, 376–379; W. D. Wright, *The Measurement of Colour* (London, 1944), 62 f.
8. *Life*, 489.
9. *Ibid.*, 347.
10. R. M. Evans, in *Journal of Photographic Science*, 9 (1961), 243; *Scientific American*, 205 (1961), 118.

11. *Papers*, I, 288. There is much of interest in the Challis-Thomson correspondence, Kelvin Papers, Cambridge University Library, file box 2.
12. *Life*, 295.
13. A. F. Cook and F. A. Franklin, in *Astronomical Journal*, **69** (1964), 173–200; **70** (1965), 704–720; **71** (1966), 10–19; also G. P. Kuiper, D. P. Cruikshank, and V. Fink, in *Bulletin of the American Astronomical Society*, **2** (1970), 235–236; and C. B. Pilcher, C. R. Chapman, L. A. Lebotsky, and H. H. Kieffer, *ibid.*, 239.
14. *Life*, 291.
15. Quoted by J. Larmor, in *Proceedings of the Royal Society*, **81** (1908), xix.
16. *Treatise*, preface, vi.
17. *Life*, 302.
18. *Proceedings of the Cambridge Philosophical Society. Mathematical and Physical Sciences*, **32** (1936), 695–750.
19. *Treatise*, I, sec. 72.
20. *Elementary Treatise*, sec. 64.
21. L. Euler, *Letters to a German Princess . . .*, H. Hunter, trans., II (London, 1795), 265–271; and known to Faraday, *Experimental Researches*, III, sec. 3263.
22. W. Thomson, *Papers on Electrostatics and Magnetism* (London, 1873), secs. 573 f., 733 f. See Maxwell's *Papers*, I, 453.
23. W. Thomson, in *Proceedings of the Royal Society*, **8** (1856), 150–158; repr. in *Baltimore Lectures* (London, 1890), app. F, 569–583.
24. J. Bromberg, Ph.D. thesis (Univ. of Wis., 1966); A. M. Bork, private communication.
25. *Proceedings of the Cambridge Philosophical Society*, **32** (1936), 704, letter of 13 Nov. 1854.
26. *Papers*, I, 500.
27. *Report of the British Association for the Advancement of Science*, 1st ser., **32** (1863), 130–163; repr. with interesting additions in F. Jenkin, *Reports of the Committee of Electrical Standards* (London, 1873), 59–96.
28. Gauss introduced only the definition of the magnetic pole; credit for the remaining parts of the system is shared by Weber, Thomson, and Maxwell.
29. I. B. Hopley, in *Annals of Science*, **15** (1959), 91–107.
30. *Life*, 342. Letter of 5 Jan. 1865.
31. *Papers*, II, 662–663.
32. W. Thomson, *Paper on Electrostatics and Magnetism* (London, 1873), 447–448n.
33. *Report of the British Association for the Advancement of Science*, 1st ser., **32** (1863), 163–176.
34. W. Thomson, *Mathematical and Physical Papers* (Cambridge, 1882–1911), II, 61–103.
35. *Treatise*, 3rd ed., II, 228. Other illustrations were given by Boltzmann and Rayleigh. The original MS of Maxwell's 1865 paper, preserved in the archives of the Royal Society, contains a curious canceled passage likening the action of two inductive circuits on the field to the action of two horses pulling on the swingletree of a carriage. This in essence is Rayleigh's analogy.
36. Comment on a paper by G. Forbes, in *Proceedings of the Royal Society of Edinburgh*, **9** (1878), 86.
37. *Treatise*, II, sec. 575; Rayleigh (4th Baron), *Life of Lord Rayleigh* (London, 1924), 48, letter from Maxwell to Rayleigh of 18 May 1870.
39. A subject on which much ink has been spilled; the clearest physical treatment is by L. Page and N. I. Adams, in *American Journal of Physics*, **13** (1945), 141.
40. *Treatise*, II, sec. 615.
41. *Ibid.*, secs. 600–601.
42. G. G. Stokes, *Mathematical and Physical Papers*, IV (Cambridge, 1904), 157–202.
43. J. Larmor, ed., *Memoir and Scientific Correspondence of Sir G. G. Stokes*, II (London, 1910), 25–26. Letter to Stokes of 15 October 1864.
44. Lord Rayleigh, *Scientific Papers*, I (Cambridge, 1900), 111–134, 518–536; J. Willard Gibbs, *Scientific Papers*, II (London, 1906), 223–246; see *Papers*, II, 772 f. for Maxwell's account.
45. Thomson, *Mathematical and Physical Papers*, III, 466, 468.
46. *Treatise*, II, sec. 866.
47. *Life*, 394, letter to Bishop Ellicott of 22 Nov. 1876.
48. W. Whewell, *Philosophy of the Inductive Sciences*, 2 vols. (London, 1840), *passim*. See *Life*, 215, letter to R. B. Litchfield of 6 June 1855.
49. *Papers*, I, 564.
50. Thomson, *Mathematical and Physical Papers*, II, 28; for Maxwell's comments, see *Papers*, II, 767–768.
51. T. Young, in *Philosophical Transactions of the Royal Society*, **94** (1804), 1.
52. Unpublished MS at Cambridge. "On an Experiment to Determine Whether the Motion of the Earth Influences the Refraction of Light."
53. The letter is lost but see Maxwell's reply dated 6 May 1864 in J. Larmor, ed., *Memoir and Scientific Correspondence of Sir G. G. Stokes*, II (London, 1910), 23–25. I am indebted to Dr. A. M. Bork for the connection, which is obscured by the first part of Larmor's footnote on p. 23.
54. W. Huggins, in *Philosophical Transactions of the Royal Society*, **158** (1868), 532.
55. *Nature*, **21** (1880), 314, 315. See Michelson's comments in *American Journal of Science*, **122** (1881), 120; also J. C. Adams to Maxwell (17 July 1879) on the feasibility of the astronomical test (Cambridge MSS).
56. Reprinted with the FitzGerald-Lorentz correspondence in S. G. Brush, *Isis*, **58** (1967), 230–232.
57. *Treatise*, II, sec. 769.
58. *Papers*, II, 121–124.
59. Cf. J. E. McDonald, in *American Journal of Physics*, **33** (1965), 706–711.
60. *Papers*, II, 329–331, 391–392.
61. In order of citation, secs. 86, 95–102, 19–21, 280–282 with app.; and 129.
62. Secs. 756–757 and app. to ch. 17.
63. The first statement is in a letter to Thomson of 5 June 1869, in *Proceedings of the Cambridge Philosophical Society*, **32** (1936), 738–739. See J. Bromberg, in *American Journal of Physics*, **36** (1968), 142–151.
64. Thomson, *Papers on Electrostatics and Magnetism*, 15–41, paper of 1845; F. O. Mossotti, in *Archives des sciences physiques et naturelles*, **6** (1847), 193.
65. Y. Aharonov and D. Bohm, in *Physical Review*, **115** (1959), 485–491; **123** (1961), 1511–1524.
66. *Papers*, II, 43.
67. *Life*, 142–143; C. C. Gillispie, *Scientific Change*, A. C. Crombie, ed. (London, 1963), 431 ff.; S. G. Brush, *Kinetic Theory*, I (Oxford, 1965), 30n.; Elizabeth Wolfe Garber, thesis (Case Institute, 1966), and in *Historical Studies in the Physical Sciences*, **2** (1970), 299; P. M. Heimann, in *Studies in History and Philosophy of Science*, **1** (1970), 189.
68. M. Kac, in *American Journal of Mathematics*, **61** (1939), 726–728. See also T. H. Gronwall, in *Acta mathematica*, **17** (1915), 1.
69. J. Larmor, ed., *Memoir and Scientific Correspondence of Sir G. G. Stokes*, II (London, 1910), 10.
70. *Report of the British Association for the Advancement of Science*, **28**, pt. 2 (1860), 16.
71. "My better $\frac{1}{2}$, who did all the real work of the kinetic theory is at present engaged in other researches. When she is done I will let you know her answer to your enquiry [about experimental data]." Postcard from Maxwell to Tait, 29 Dec. 1877, Cambridge MSS.
72. *Life*, 80.
73. *Papers*, II, 379–380.
74. *Papers*, II, 681. Royal Society Archives 1878, Maxwell 70, Thomson's report marked 123 in upper right-hand corner. See S. G. Brush and C. W. F. Everitt, in *Historical Studies in the Physical Sciences*, **1** (1969), 105–125.

75. See S. G. Brush, in *American Journal of Physics*, **24** (1962), 274n.
76. Letter from C. Truesdell to C. W. F. Everitt, 16 Dec. 1971.
77. *Papers*, II, 376.
78. *Nature*, **20** (1877), 242.
79. *Life*, 570; A. Schuster, *The Progress of Physics 1875–1878* (Cambridge, 1911), 29; also *History of Cavendish Laboratory* (London, 1910), 31.
80. See the two eds. of Watson's *Treatise on the Kinetic Theory of Gases* (Oxford, 1876; 2nd ed., 1893); and the commentaries on Maxwell's paper by Boltzmann, in *Philosophical Magazine*, **14** (1882), 299–312; by Rayleigh, *ibid.*, **33** (1892), 356–359, and *Scientific Papers*, III, 554; and by J. Larmor, *Mathematical and Physical Papers*, II (Cambridge, 1929), app. III, 743–748. Rayleigh incorrectly attributes one of Watson's results to Maxwell, as Watson, in the 2nd ed. of his book (pp. 22–23), succeeds in pointing out, without appearing to do so, with the beautiful oblique courtesy to be expected from the man who was, after all, the Rector of Berkswell.
81. *Life*, 570–571.
82. *Papers*, II, 692.
83. *Proceedings of the Royal Society*, **27** (1878), 304.
84. *Papers*, II, 742.
85. *Treatise*, I, sec. 135a.
86. Letter of 11 July 1961 from S. C. Chapman to S. G. Brush quoted in S. G. Brush, in *American Journal of Physics*, **24** (1962), 276n.
87. E. Ikenberry and C. Truesdell, in *Journal of Rational Mechanics and Analysis*, **5** (1956), 4–128.
88. *Papers*, I, 79.
89. R. K. Luneberg, *Lectures on Optical Design* (Providence, R.I., 1944), mimeographed notes.
90. *Life*, 221.
91. For example, C. G. Wynne, in *Proceedings of the Physical Society of London*, **65B** (1952), 429.
92. W. J. M. Rankine, *Miscellaneous Scientific Papers* (London, 1881), 564.
93. *Papers*, II, 161–207; Royal Society Archives 1869.
94. A photograph of the governor designed by Fleeming Jenkin is given by I. B. Hopley, in *Annals of Science*, **13** (1951), 268. See also Otto Mayr, in *Isis*, **62** (1971), 425–444; and *Notes and Records. Royal Society of London*, **26** (1971), 205–228.
95. C. W. Siemens, in *Philosophical Transactions of the Royal Society*, **156** (1866), 657–670.
96. Norbert Wiener, *Cybernetics, or Control and Communication in the Animal and the Machine* (Cambridge, Mass., 1948), 11–12.
97. *Philosophical Magazine*, **16** (1908), 818.
98. C. G. Knott, *Life and Scientific Work of Peter Guthrie Tait*, 214–215.
99. *History of the Cavendish Laboratory*, 31.

BIBLIOGRAPHY

I. ORIGINAL WORKS. Most of the technical papers were reprinted in *The Scientific Papers of J. Clerk Maxwell*, W. D. Niven, ed., 2 vols. (Cambridge, 1890; repr. New York, 1952), cited in the footnotes as *Papers*. About twenty papers and short articles were omitted from the collection; most may be found in *Nature, Electrician, Reports of the British Association, Proceedings of the London Mathematical Society, Proceedings of the Royal Society of Edinburgh,* and *Cambridge Reporter*. The abstracts of longer papers printed in the *Proceedings of the Royal Society* are also often of interest. Maxwell's books are *Theory of Heat* (London, 1870; 4th ed. greatly rev., 1875; 11th ed. rev. with notes by Lord Rayleigh, 1894); *Treatise on Electricity and Magnetism*, 2 vols. (Oxford, 1873); 2nd ed., W. D. Niven, ed. (1881); 3rd ed., J. J. Thomson, ed. (1891), cited as *Treatise*—revision of the 2nd ed. was cut short by Maxwell's death; the changes in the first eight chs. are extensive and significant; references here are to the 3rd ed.; *Matter and Motion* (London, 1877), 2nd ed., with appendixes by J. Larmor (1924); *Elementary Treatise on Electricity*, W. Garnett, ed. (Oxford, 1881; 2nd ed., rev., 1888), cited as *Elementary Treatise*; and *The Unpublished Electrical Writings of Hon. Henry Cavendish* (Cambridge, 1879), 2nd ed., with further notes by J. Larmor (1924), which contains an introductory essay and extensive notes by Maxwell.

II. SECONDARY LITERATURE. The standard biography is L. Campbell and W. Garnett, *The Life of James Clerk Maxwell* (London, 1882), cited as *Life;* 2nd ed., abridged but containing letters not given in 1st ed. (1884). Extensive correspondence appears in *Memoir and Scientific Correspondence of Sir George Gabriel Stokes*, J. Larmor, ed., 2 vols. (London, 1910); C. G. Knott, *Life and Scientific Work of Peter Guthrie Tait* (Cambridge, 1911); Silvanus P. Thomson, *Life of Lord Kelvin*, 2 vols. (London, 1912); J. Larmor, "The Origin of Clerk Maxwell's Electric Ideas as described in Familiar Letters to W. Thomson," in *Proceedings of the Cambridge Philosophical Society. Mathematical and Physical Sciences*, **32** (1936), 695–750, repr. as a separate vol. (Cambridge, 1937). Other letters or personal material will be found in standard biographies of W. C. and G. P. Bond, H. M. Butler, J. D. Forbes, J. G. Fraser, F. Galton, D. Gill, F. J. A. Hort, T. H. Huxley, Fleeming Jenkin, R. B. Litchfield, by Henrietta Litchfield (London, 1903), privately printed; a copy is in the library of the Working Men's College, London; C. S. Peirce, Lord Rayleigh, H. Sidgwick, W. Robertson Smith, Sir James FitzJames Stephen, and George Wilson, and in the collected papers of T. Andrews, Sir William Huggins, J. P. Joule, J. Larmor, and H. A. Rowland.

See also C. Popham Miles, *Early Death not Premature: Memoir of Francis L. Mackenzie* (Edinburgh, 1856), 216–218; W. Garnett, *Heroes of Science* (London, 1886); R. T. Glazebrook, *James Clerk Maxwell and Modern Physics* (London, 1896); F. W. Farrar, *Men I Have Known* (London, 1897); A. Schuster, *The Progress of Physics 1875–1908* (London, 1911); *Biographical Fragments* (London, 1932); and "The Maxwell Period," in *History of the Cavendish Laboratory 1871–1910* (London, 1910), no editor identified; *Aberdeen University Quarter-Centenary Volume* (Aberdeen, 1906); D. Gill, *History of the Royal Observatory, Cape of Good Hope* (London, 1913), xi–xiv, for Maxwell at Aberdeen; F. J. C. Hearnshaw, *History of King's College, London* (London, 1929; J. J. Thomson, ed., *James Clerk Maxwell 1831–1931* (Cambridge, 1931); J. G. Crowther, *British Scientists of the Nineteenth Century* (London, 1932); K. Pearson, "Old Tripos Days at Cambridge," in *Mathematical Gazette*, **20** (1936), 27; C. Domb, ed., *Clerk Maxwell and Modern Science* (London, 1963); and R. V. Jones, "James Clerk Maxwell at Aberdeen 1856–1860," in *Notes and Records. Royal Society of London*, **28** (1973), 57–81.

Useful general bibliographies are given by W. T. Scott, in *American Journal of Physics*, **31** (1963), 819–826, for the electromagnetic field concept; and by S. G. Brush in *Kinetic Theory* (Oxford, 1965, 1966, 1972) and in *American Journal of Physics*, **39** (1971), 631–640 for kinetic theory. For thermodynamics see Martin J. Klein in *American Scientist*, **58** (1970), 84–97. For the theory of governors see two articles by Otto Mayr in *Isis*, **62** (1971), 425–444; and *Notes and Records. Royal Society of London*, **26** (1971), 205–228; references to other early papers on governors are given in the later editions of E. J. Routh, *Treatise on the Dynamics of a System of Rigid Bodies*, II (6th ed., London, 1905), sec. 107.

For reciprocal diagrams see A. S. Niles, *Engineering*, **170** (1950), 194–198, and S. Timoshenko, *History of the Strength of Materials* (New York, 1953): both authors exaggerate the neglect of Maxwell's work by his contemporaries. *Studies in History and Philosophy of Science*, **1** (1970), 189–251 contains four articles on Maxwell with lengthy bibliographies.

The two principal collections of unpublished source materials are in the Archives of the Royal Society and in Cambridge University Library, Anderson Room, where the Stokes and Kelvin MSS should also be consulted. Materials elsewhere at Cambridge are in the Cavendish Laboratory, Peterhouse and Trinity College libraries, and the Cambridge Library. Other items are at Aberdeen University; St. Andrews University (Forbes MSS); Berlin, Staatsbibliothek der Stiftung Preussischer Kultur Besitz; Bodleian Library, Oxford (Mark Pattison MSS); Burndy Library, Norwalk, Conn.; Edinburgh University (Tait MSS); Glasgow University (Kelvin MSS); Göttingen, Niedersächsische Staats- und Universitätsbibliothek; Harvard University (Bond MSS); Imperial College, Lyon Playfair Library (Huxley MSS); Institute of Electrical Engineers (Heaviside MSS); Johns Hopkins University (Rowland MSS); Manchester Institute of Science and Technology (Joule MSS); Queen's University, Belfast (Andrews, J. Thomson MSS); Royal Institution (Faraday, Tyndall MSS); University of Rochester, Rush Rhees Library; U.S. Air Force Cambridge Center (Rayleigh MSS).

A large collection of watercolor paintings of Maxwell's childhood by Jemima Wedderburn (later Mrs. Hugh Blackburn) and others are now in the possession of Brigadier J. Wedderburn-Maxwell, D.S.O., M.C.

C. W. F. EVERITT

MAYER, ALFRED MARSHALL (*b.* Baltimore, Maryland, 13 November 1836; *d.* Hoboken, New Jersey, 13 July 1897), *physics*.

Mayer invented the method of floating tiny magnets in a magnetic field, used in the early twentieth century as a key to discovering or illustrating atomic structure. He studied classics at St. Mary's College in Baltimore but left at the age of sixteen to become a machinist. A self-educated analytical chemist, he published his first research paper at the age of nineteen; it brought him to the attention of Joseph Henry, who helped him to become assistant professor of physics and chemistry at the University of Maryland when he was only twenty and professor of physical science at Westminster College, Fulton, Missouri, in 1859. From 1863 to 1865 he studied in Paris, notably under Regnault, learning advanced physics, mathematics, and physiology. On his return to America, Mayer became professor of natural science at Pennsylvania College of Gettysburg (now Gettysburg College), and then, in 1867, professor of physics and astronomy at Lehigh University; in 1871 he organized the department of physics at the newly founded Stevens Institute of Technology, with which he was associated until his death.

Mayer's only academic degree was an honorary Ph.D. from Pennsylvania College of Gettysburg in 1866; he was a member of the National Academy of Sciences (1872), the American Philosophical Society, and the American Academy of Arts and Sciences.

Mayer conducted research in sound, heat, light, and gravity; devised a number of instruments for scientific measurement; and was the author of about one hundred publications, including fifty-four research articles and three scientific books. He was selected by the U.S. Nautical Almanac Office to direct the photographing of the solar eclipse of 7 August 1869; the results were considered remarkable for those early days of photography: a set of forty-two "perfect photographs," made at exposures of 0.002 second —five of them during the eighty-three seconds of total eclipse. His major scientific work was in acoustics; Mayer's Law gives a quantitative relation between pitch and the duration of residual auditory sensation. An avid sportsman, Mayer wrote widely about fishing and invented a rod with which, in 1884, he won first prize at the Amateur Minnow-Casting Tournament of the National Rod and Reel Association.

Mayer is most remembered (and cited) for his experiments in which magnetized needles were inserted into corks, which were then floated on water with their south poles upward, under the north pole of a powerful electromagnet. Under these conditions, certain definite stable configurations were observed "which suggested the manner in which atoms of molecules may be grouped in the formation of definite compounds" (Mayer and Woodward, p. 257) and which illustrated various properties of the constitution of matter. These experiments won high praise from Kelvin (*Nature*, **18** [1878], 13–14) and were later used by J. J. Thomson (*Electricity and Matter* [New Haven, 1904], pp. 114–117, 122; *The*

Corpuscular Theory of Matter [New York, 1907], p. 110) and others as a key to the way in which a characteristic number of electrons might be arranged within the atoms of each chemical element in relation to the periodic table. Mayer thus made a small but significant contribution to the theory of atomic structure.

BIBLIOGRAPHY

I. ORIGINAL WORKS. A full list of Mayer's scientific publications is given in Alfred G. Mayer and Robert S. Woodward, "Biographical Memoir of Alfred Marshall Mayer 1836–1897," in *Biographical Memoirs. National Academy of Sciences*, **8** (1916), 243–272. A list of his publications for the period 1871–1897 is given in his biography, in F. DeR. Furman, *Morton Memorial: A History of the Stevens Institute of Technology* (Hoboken, N.J., 1905), pp. 202–209.

Mayer's articles on the stable configurations of magnets floating freely in a magnetic field were published in *American Journal of Science*, 3rd ser., **15** (1878), 276–277, 477–478; **16** (1878), 247–256; and in *Scientific American*, supp. **5** (1878), 2045–2047, where these experiments are said "to illustrate the action of atomic forces and the molecular structure of matter . . ." (which includes allotropy, isomerism, and the kinetic theory of gases).

II. SECONDARY LITERATURE. Besides the two biographies mentioned above, see F. DeR. Furman's article on Mayer in the *Dictionary of American Biography*, XII. A biography based on personal recollections was published by W. LeConte Stevens in *Science*, n.s. **6** (1897), 261–269. Obituaries appeared in *Stevens Indicator*, **14** (1897), 367; *American Journal of Science*, 4th ser., **4** (1897), 161–164; and New York *Times* (14 July 1897), p. 5.

I. B. COHEN

MAYER, CHRISTIAN (*b.* Meseritsch, Moravia [now Mederizenhi, Czechoslovakia], 20 August 1719; *d.* Heidelberg, Germany, 17 April 1783), *astronomy*.

Claims that Mayer studied Greek, Latin, philosophy, theology, and mathematics at Brno, Vienna, Turnau, Rome, and Würzburg have not been confirmed. The first authenticated fact about his life is his entering the Jesuit novitiate at Mannheim on 13 September 1745, after he had left home because his father did not approve of his decision. He subsequently taught languages and then also mathematics in a Jesuit school at Aschaffenburg, spending his evenings making astronomical observations. In 1752 he was appointed professor of mathematics and physics at Heidelberg University, and in 1753 his first physical work was printed there. He also published a series of mathe-

matical and physical works at Heidelberg, but his main interest soon turned to astronomy.

In 1762 the elector palatine, Karl Theodor, who was very interested in the arts and sciences, constructed an astronomical observatory for Mayer at Schwetzingen, his summer residence. In 1772–1774 a second and larger observatory was erected at Mannheim, then the capital of the electoral Palatinate. This observatory was well equipped for the time, with instruments from the best British workshops. A great quadrant by Bird was installed in 1775 and other instruments were made by Dollond, Troughton, and Ramsden; but Mayer did not live to see the observatory acquire all the instruments he had requested. Appointed court astronomer, Mayer was relieved of his duties as a theologian (the Jesuit order was dissolved by Pope Clement XIV in 1773, which made such a step easier).

In the 1760's Mayer participated in the measurement of a degree of the meridian, inaugurated by Cassini de Thury, visiting Paris and also executing the measurement of a geodetic base in the plain of the Rhenish Palatinate. He observed the transits of Venus across the sun in 1761 and 1769, invited to Russia for the latter by Catherine II. He also drew up a map of the Russian empire for her.

In 1776 Mayer turned to a branch of astronomy not previously investigated: the observation of double stars of all classes. Mayer could not distinguish between truly binary stars and those that are nearly on a line of sight from the earth but distantly separated in space. He made uncritical observations of all such apparent pairs and compiled a catalog of those that were near enough to be doubles in his sense of the word. The work was superseded in 1782 by W. Herschel's catalog of double stars, but his pioneer work should not be forgotten.

Mayer became involved in a polemic with his colleagues, typical of the time and caused by his name for the double stars. In his lecture at the Mannheim Academy and in his first note published in a Mannheim newspaper in 1777, Mayer said he had discovered more than 100 satellites of fixed stars. This term was misunderstood and Mayer's colleagues inferred that he was claiming to have discovered planets of other fixed stars. Today we speak of a companion of a fixed star, such as the companion of Sirius. But the contemporary astronomers, especially Hell, argued against Mayer's observations—which marked the beginning of systematic observation and an important impetus to this new branch of astronomy.

Mayer's reputation was unharmed by the quarrels. He was widely known and published his observations in various foreign journals—including the United

States, an uncommon practice among European astronomers. He was a member of scientific academies and societies in London, Philadelphia, Mannheim, Munich, Bologna, and other cities.

BIBLIOGRAPHY

Mayer's writings include *Selecta physices experimentalis elementa mathematico-physica* (Heidelberg, 1753); *Disquisitio de momento virium mechanicarum* (Heidelberg, 1756); *Basis Palatina anno 1762 ad normam Academiae Regiae Parisinae scientiarum exactam bis dimensa . . .* (Mannheim, 1763); *Solis et lunae eclipseos observatio astronomica, facta Schwetzingae in specula nova electoralia* (Mannheim, 1764); "Observationes astronomicae," in *Philosophical Transactions of the Royal Society* (1764 and 1768); *Ad Augustissimam Russiarum omnium Imperatricem Catarinam II. Aliexiewnam expositio de transitu Veneris ante discum solis d. 23 Maji anno 1769* (St. Petersburg, 1769); *Nouvelle méthode pour lever . . . une carte générale exacte de toute la Russie . . .* (St. Petersburg, 1770); *Directio meridiani Palatini per speculam electorialem arcis aestivae Schwetzingensis ducti, observationibus et calculis definita* (Heidelberg, 1771); *Gründliche Vertheidigung neuer Beobachtungen von Fixstern Trabanten, welche zu Mannheim an der Sternwarte entdeckt worden sind* (Mannheim, 1778); *De novis in coelo sidereo phaenomenis, in miris stellarum fixarum comitibus Mannhemii detectis* (Mannheim, 1779); and "Observationes astronomicae," in *Transactions of the American Philosophical Society*, **2** (1786), 34–41.

On Mayer and his work, see J. L. Kluber, *Die Sternwarte zu Mannheim* (Mannheim, 1811), 58–59; and W. Meyer, "Geschichte der Doppelsterne," in *Vierteljahrsschrift d. naturforschenden Gesellschaft in Zurich* (1876), 695 ff.

H.-CHRIST. FREIESLEBEN

MAYER, CHRISTIAN GUSTAV ADOLPH (*b.* Leipzig, Germany, 15 February 1839; *d.* Gries bei Bozen, Austria [now Bolzano, Italy], 11 April 1908), *mathematics.*

The son of a wealthy Leipzig merchant family, Mayer studied mathematics and physics from 1857 to 1865 at Leipzig, Göttingen, Heidelberg, and chiefly at Königsberg under F. Neumann. In 1861 he received his doctorate from Heidelberg and qualified to lecture there in 1866. He became assistant professor in 1871 and full professor in 1890. In 1872 Mayer married Margerete Weigel. Poor health caused him to suspend his teaching activities early in 1908.

As a professor, Mayer enjoyed great respect from his colleagues and students. His activity as a researcher, which earned him membership in numerous learned societies, dealt essentially with the theory of differential equations, the calculus of variations, and theoretical mechanics. In his work, following Lagrange and Jacobi, he was capable of bringing out the inner relationship of these fields through emphasis on the principle of least action. Mayer achieved important individual results concerning the theory of integration of partial differential equations and the criteria for maxima and minima in variation problems. This work quickly brought him into close contact with the investigations on partial differential equations that Lie had under way at about the same time. Through subsequent works of Mayer, Lie's achievements became famous relatively quickly. Despite a great variety of methods and an outstanding mastery of calculation, Mayer was unable to develop the rigor necessary for the existence theorems of the calculus of variations; such rigor was displayed in exemplary fashion at approximately the same time by Weierstrass.

BIBLIOGRAPHY

Among Mayer's works are *Beiträge zur Theorie der Maxima und Minima einfacher Integrale* (Leipzig, 1866); *Geschichte des Prinzips der kleinsten Aktion* (Leipzig, 1877); and "Unbeschränkt integrable Systeme von linearen totalen Differentialgleichungen und die simultane Integration linearer partieller Differentialgleichungen," in *Mathematische Annalen*, **5** (1872), 448–470.

Also see the obituary notice by O. Holder, in *Berichte über die Verhandlungen der sächsischen Akademie der Wissenschaften zu Leipzig*, Math.-phys. Kl., **60** (1908), 353–373.

H. WUSSING

MAYER, JOHANN TOBIAS (*b.* Marbach, near Stuttgart, Germany, 17 February 1723; *d.* Göttingen, Germany, 20 February 1762), *cartography, astronomy.*

Mayer was the son of a cartwright, also named Johann Tobias Mayer, and his second wife, Maria Catherina Finken. In 1723 the father left his trade and went to work as the foreman of a well-digging crew in the nearby town of Esslingen, where his family joined him the following year. After his father's death in 1737 Mayer was taken into the local orphanage, while his mother found employment in St. Katharine's Hospital, where she remained until her death in 1737. It was probably through her occupation that Mayer found the opportunity to make architectural drawings of the hospital, as he did when he was barely fourteen years old. There is some evidence to indicate that he was encouraged in his draftmanship by Gottlieb David Kandler, a shoemaker who was subsequently responsible for the education of orphans in Esslingen.

Mayer's skill in architectural drawings also brought him to the attention of a certain Geiger, a non-commissioned officer in the Swabian district artillery, which was then garrisoned in Esslingen. Under Geiger's instruction, Mayer, in early 1739, prepared a book of plans and drawings of military fortifications. Later in the same year he drew a map of Esslingen and its surroundings (the oldest still extant), which was reproduced as a copper engraving by Gabriel Bodenehr of Augsburg in 1741.

Mayer's first book, written on the occasion of his eighteenth birthday, was published at about this same time. It was devoted to the application of analytic methods to the solution of geometrical problems, and in its preface Mayer acknowledged his debt to Christian von Wolff's *Anfangs-Gründe aller mathematischen Wissenschaften*, through which he had taught himself mathematics, a subject not included in the curriculum of the Esslingen Latin school, which he attended. The influence of Wolff's compendium is again apparent in the arrangement and content of Mayer's *Mathematischer Atlas* of 1745; the sixty plates of the latter work duplicate Wolff's choice of subjects—arithmetic, geometry, trigonometry, and analysis, as applied to mechanics, optics, astronomy, geography, chronology, gnomonics, pyrotechnics, and military and civil architecture. This atlas, published in Augsburg by the firm of Johann Andreas Pfeffel, for which Mayer worked during his brief stay there (from 1744 to 1746), provides a good index to the extent of his scientific and technical knowledge at that period. It was probably in Augsburg that he acquired much of his knowledge of French, Italian, and English. He also became acquainted with a local mechanic and optician, G. F. Brander.

Mayer left Augsburg to take up a post with the Homann Cartographic Bureau in Nuremberg. He spent five years there, which he devoted primarily to improving the state of cartography. To this end he collated geographical and astronomical data from the numerous printed and manuscript records to which the Homann office permitted him access. He also made personal observations of lunar occultations and other astronomical eclipse phenomena, using a nine-foot-focus telescope and a glass micrometer of his own design. Of more than thirty maps that he drew, the "mappa critica" of Germany is generally considered to be the most significant, since it established a new standard for the rigorous handling of geographical source materials and for the application of accurate astronomical methods in finding terrestrial latitude and longitude.

In order to facilitate the lunar eclipse method of longitude determination, Mayer in 1747 and 1748 made a large number of micrometric measurements of the angular diameter of the moon and of the times of its meridian transits. In his determinations of the selenographic coordinates of eighty-nine prominent lunar markings, he took account of the irregularity of the orbital and libratory motions of the moon and of the effect of its variable parallax. In addition his analysis correctly—although fortuitously—reduced twenty-seven conditional equations to three "normal" ones, a procedure that had never before been attempted, and one for which a theory had still to be developed.

Mayer was the editor of the *Kosmographische Nachrichten und Sammlungen auf das Jahr 1748*, which was published in Nuremberg in 1750, under the auspices of the newly established Cosmographical Society. The work contains Mayer's own description of his glass micrometer, his observations of the solar eclipse of 25 July 1748 and the occultations of a number of bright stars, his long treatise on the libration of the moon, and his argument as to why the moon cannot possess an atmosphere. The Cosmographical Society itself, founded by Johann Michael Franz, director of the Homann firm, was crucial in determining the nature, scope, and, to some degree, motivation of Mayer's subsequent scientific research. The aims of the mathematical class of the society, to which Mayer belonged, as set out by Franz in the preface to the *Homannisch-Haseschen Gesellschafts Atlas* (Nuremberg, 1747), define much of Mayer's later work.

In November 1750 Mayer was called to a professorship at the Georg-August Academy in Göttingen, a post that he took up after Easter of the following year. Shortly before he left Nuremberg he married Maria Victoria Gnüge; of their eight children, two, Johann Tobias and Georg Moritz, lived to maturity. Mayer's academic title, professor of economy, was purely nominal, since his actual duties were assigned, in his letter of appointment, as the teaching of practical (that is, applied) mathematics and research. His reputation as a cartographer and practical astronomer had preceded him, and was indeed the basis for his selection as professor.

Mayer's chief scientific concerns at this time were the investigation of astronomical refraction and lunar theory. In 1752 he drew up new lunar and solar tables, in which he attained an accuracy of $\pm 1'$, an achievement attributable to his skillful use of observational data, rather than to the originality of his theory or the superiority of his instruments. Mayer subsequently undertook an investigation of the celestial positions of the moon at conjunction and opposition; he compared the values that he obtained with those derivable from a systematic study of all lunar and solar eclipses reported since the invention of the astronomical telescope and the pendulum clock. His results led him to recognize that the discrepancies of up to $\pm 5'$ that he and his contemporaries had found were due largely to errors in the determination of star places and to the poor quality of their instruments.

Mayer's further astronomical researches consequently included the problem of the elimination of errors from a six-foot-radius mural quadrant made in 1755 by John Bird for installation in Mayer's newly completed observatory in Göttingen; the invention of a simple and accurate method for computing solar eclipses; the compilation of a catalogue of zodiacal stars; and the investigation of stellar proper motions. He wrote treatises on each of these topics that were published posthumously in Georg Christoph Lichtenberg's *Opera inedita Tobiae Mayeri* (Göttingen, 1775). This work also contains a treatise on the problem of accurately defining thermometric changes (an extension of Mayer's research on astronomical refraction) and another on a mathematical theory of color mixing (a topic that Mayer may have taken up in response to the need of the Homann firm, part of which had been transferred to Göttingen in 1755, to train unskilled workers in the accurate reproduction of maps). Appended to Lichtenberg's book, in accordance with one of Mayer's last wishes, is a copper engraving of Mayer's map of the moon; the original map and the forty detailed drawings from which it was constructed were also reproduced by photolithography more than a century later.

Others of Mayer's treatises, lecture notes, and correspondence have been neglected since their deposit, shortly after his death, in the Göttingen observatory archives, although abstracts of some of his lectures to the Göttingen Scientific Society were printed in the *Göttingische Anzeigen von gelehrten Sachen* between 1752 and 1762. His researches during these years included his efforts to improve the art of land measurement, for which purpose he invented a new goniometer and explored the application of the repeating principle of angle measurement, developed a new projective method for finding the areas of irregularly shaped fields, and transformed the common astrolabe into a precision instrument. He further applied the repeating principle to an instrument of his own invention, the repeating circle, which proved to be of use not only for the sea navigation for which it had been designed but also for making standard trigonometrical land surveys. (The instru-

ment used by Delambre and Méchain in their determination of the standard meter was a variant, designed by Borda, of the Mayer circle.)

Mayer also undertook to devise a method for finding geographical coordinates independently of astronomical observations. In so doing he arrived at a new theory of the magnet, based, like his lunar theory, on the principles of Newtonian mechanics. This theory represented a convincing demonstration of the validity of the inverse-square law of magnetic attraction and repulsion, and antedated Coulomb's well-known verification of that law by some twenty-five years. Mayer's manuscripts on this theory and on its application to the calculation of the variation and dip of a magnetic needle are among those that went virtually unnoticed after his death.

In 1763 Mayer's widow, acting upon another of his last requests, submitted to the British admiralty his *Theoria lunae juxta systema Newtonianum*, which contained the derivations of the equations upon which his lunar theory was based, and his *Tabulae motuum solis et lunae novae et correctae*, which were published in London in 1767 and 1770, respectively. The tables were edited by Maskelyne, and printed under his direct supervision; they were used to compute the lunar and solar ephemerides for the early editions of the *Nautical Almanac*. (They were superseded a decade later by tables employing essentially the same principles, but based upon the newer and more accurate observational data that were gradually being assembled at the Royal Observatory at Greenwich.) In 1765 the British parliament authorized Maria Mayer to receive an award of £3,000, in recognition of her husband's claim, lodged ten years before, for one of the prizes offered to "any Person or Persons as shall Discover the Longitude at Sea."

BIBLIOGRAPHY

A comprehensive list of Mayer's publications is given in Poggendorff, II, 91, the sole omission being his article "Versuch einer Erklärung des Erdbebens," in *Hannoverischen nützlichen Sammlungen* (1756), 290–296.

Mayer's scientific work is discussed by his official biographer, Siegmund Günther, in *Allgemeine deutsche Biographie*, XXI (1885), 109–116. His correspondence with Euler between 1751 and 1755, a valuable primary source of information about the former's contributions to the lunar theory, is in E. G. Forbes, ed., *The Euler-Mayer Correspondence (1751–1755)* (London, 1971).

The bulk of MS material relating to Mayer is preserved in Göttingen. The official classification of these papers is contained in the *Verzeichniss der Handschriften im Preussischen Staate I Hannover 3 Göttingen*, III (Berlin, 1894), 154–158. The title "Tobias Mayer's Nachlass, aufbewahrt in der K. Sternwarte" no longer applies, since the 70 items catalogued in this index were transferred to the Niedersächsische Staats- und Universitäts-Bibliothek, Göttingen, during the summer of 1965. In this same repository there is a booklet entitled "Briefe von und an J. Tobias Mayer," Cod. MS philos. 159. Cod. MS philos. 157 and Cod. MS Michaelis 320 are two other items worth consulting. *Personalakte Tobias Mayer* 4/Vb 18, and 4/Vf/1–4 are preserved in the Dekanate und Universität-Archiv, Göttingen. Some additional items of minor importance are also in the archives of the Göttingen Akademie der Wissenschaften.

The only significant MS collection outside Göttingen is "Betreffend der von Seiten des Prof. Tobias Mayer in Göttingen gelöste englische Preisfrage über die Bestimmung der Longitudo maris. 1754–1765," *Hannover Des.* 92 xxxiv no. II, 4, a', Staatsarchiv, Hannover. A few documents relating to the payment of the parliamentary award to Mayer's widow are in vol. I of the Board of Longitude papers at the Royal Greenwich Observatory (P.R.O. Ref. 529, pp. 143–155).

E. G. Forbes, ed., *The Unpublished Writings of Tobias Mayer*, 3 vols. (Göttingen, 1972), contains Mayer's writings on astronomy and geography, his lecture notes on artillery and mechanics, and his theory of the magnet and its application to terrestrial magnetism.

Mayer's role in the development of navigation and his dealings with the British Admiralty and Board of Longitude are discussed in E. G. Forbes, *The Birth of Scientific Navigation* (London, 1973).

                                            ERIC G. FORBES

MAYER, JULIUS ROBERT (*b*. Heilbronn, Württemberg [now Baden-Württemberg], Germany, 25 November 1814; *d*. Heilbronn, 20 March 1878), *physics, physiology.*

Robert Mayer was one of the early formulators of the principle of the conservation of energy. His father, Christian Jakob Mayer, maintained a prosperous apothecary shop in Heilbronn and married Katharina Elisabeth Heermann, daughter of a Heilbronn bookbinder. The couple had three sons, of whom Robert was the youngest; both the older brothers followed their father's profession.

Mayer attended the classical Gymnasium at Heilbronn until 1829, when he transferred to the evangelical theology seminary at Schöntal. Although he was a mediocre student, he passed the *Abitur* in 1832 and enrolled in the medical faculty at the University of Tübingen. In February 1837 he was arrested and expelled from the university for participation in a secret student society. The next year Mayer was allowed to take the doctorate of medicine, and in 1838 he also passed the state medical examinations with distinction. During the winter of 1839–1840 Mayer visited Paris and from February 1840 to February 1841 served as physician on a Dutch merchant ship on a voyage to the East Indies. While in Djakarta, Java, certain physiological observations convinced Mayer that motion and heat were interconvertible manifestations of a single, indestructible force in nature, and that this force was quantitatively conserved in any conversion. Mayer was inspired and occasionally obsessed by this insight. He elaborated his idea in various scientific papers which he published during the 1840's after his return to Germany.

Mayer settled in his native Heilbronn, where he took up a prosperous medical practice and held various civic posts. In 1842 he married Wilhelmine Regine Caroline Closs; the marriage produced seven children, five of whom died in infancy. Mayer maintained a conservative position during the Revolution of 1848, and this position led to his brief arrest by the insurgents and to a lasting estrangement from his brother Fritz. Depressed by these events and by his failure to obtain recognition for his scientific work, Mayer attempted suicide in May 1850. During the early 1850's he suffered recurrent fits of insanity, which necessitated several confinements in asylums at Göppingen, Kennenburg, and Winnenthal. Only after 1860 did Mayer gradually receive international recognition. He died in Heilbronn of tuberculosis in 1878.

Before his trip to Java, Mayer had shown much interest in science, but little creative ability. Flush with enthusiasm for his new idea about force, Mayer composed his "Ueber die quantitative und qualitative Bestimmung der Kräfte" immediately after his return to Heilbronn. In this paper Mayer groped toward a philosophical and mathematical expression of his new concept of force. Although he later altered the mathematical and the physical expressions of the ideas which he employed in this first paper, the philosophical and conceptual expressions remained virtually unchanged in his later work.

Mayer asserted that the task of science is to trace all phenomena back to their first causes. The laws of logic assure us that for every change there exists a first cause (*Ursache*), which is called a force (*Kraft*). In the world we observe "tension" or "difference" such as spatial separation or chemical difference existing between all matter. This tension is itself a force, and its effect is to prevent all bodies from quickly uniting themselves into a mathematical point. These tension-forces are indestructible, and their sum total in the universe is constant. Just as chemistry is the science of matter, so physics is the science of forces. Just as chemistry assumes that mass remains constant in every reaction, whatever qualitative changes the matter may undergo, so physics must also assume that forces are quantitatively conserved, no matter what conversions or qualitative changes of form they may undergo.

Although Mayer's mathematical-physical exposition of his ideas was highly original, it was also quite obscure and revealed his lack of acquaintance with the principles of mechanics. Mayer first considered a moving particle and argued that the measure of its "quantity of motion" is its mass times its speed. He then considered the special case of two particles, each having mass m and speed c and approaching each other on a straight line. The "quantitative determination" of the force of movement present is $2mc$. The "qualitative determination," however, is formally zero, since the motions are equal and opposite; this Mayer expressed by the symbolism $02mc$. Unless the particles are totally elastic, the "quantitative determination" of the force of motion present will be less after the collision than before the collision; for totally inelastic particles it will be zero after collision. The force present as motion is never lost, Mayer insisted; rather a part of it is "neutralized" in the collision and appears as heat. From this assertion Mayer generalized obscurely that all heat can be thought of as equal and opposite motions which neutralize each other, and that $02mc$ is somehow a universal mathematical expression for the force of heat. Finally Mayer showed how, in the more general case in which the colliding particles do not lie in a straight line, the parallelogram of forces may be employed to determine how much force of motion would be "neutralized" in the collision.

Upon completing "Ueber die . . . Bestimmung der Kräfte," Mayer submitted it to the *Annalen der Physik und Chemie* for publication. The editor Poggendorff ignored the paper and it was not printed. Although he was angry and disappointed, Mayer quickly became aware of the limitations of the treatise and immediately set himself to studying physics and mathematics. Between August 1841 and March 1842 Mayer discovered that mv^2, not mv, is the proper measure of the quantity of motion and that this form of force is identical to the *vis viva* of mechanics. He incorporated that discovery into his second paper, "Bemerkungen über die Kräfte der unbelebten Natur," which he had published in Liebig's *Annalen der Chemie* in May 1842.

In this second paper Mayer elaborated the conceptual basis of his theory, examining, he said, the precise meaning of the term "force." As in the previous paper, Mayer concluded that forces are first causes; hence the law *causa aequat effectum* assures us that force is quantitatively indestructible. Like matter, forces are objects which are able to assume different forms and which are indestructible. Forces differ from matter only because they are imponderable.

Elaborating an idea mentioned in his previous paper, Mayer asserted that the spatial separation of two bodies is itself a force. This force he called "fall-force" (*Fallkraft*). Where one object is the earth and the second object is near the earth's surface, the fall-force can be written md, m being the weight of the object and d its elevation. In actual fall, fall-force is converted into force of motion. Mayer expressed this conversion as $md = mc^2$, where c is the velocity attained by an object of weight m in falling the distance d to the earth's surface.

On the basis of this concept of fall-force, Mayer concluded that gravity is not a force at all but a "characteristic of matter." Gravity cannot be a force, Mayer argued, because it is not the sufficient cause of motion; in addition to gravity, spatial separation is prerequisite to fall. If gravity were a force, then it would be a force which constantly produces an effect without itself being consumed; this, however, would violate the principle of the conservation of force. Throughout all his later papers and letters Mayer clung staunchly to this position. He continually argued that the entity "force" in its Newtonian sense is illogically and misleadingly named and that hence a different term should be introduced for it. The word "force" should be reserved for the substantial, quantitative entity conserved in conversions. Even after physics later adopted the term "energy" to describe Mayer's concept of force, Mayer continued to feel that the idea of force as a conserved entity was conceptually prior to the Newtonian entity and that hence the traditional name "force" should have been reserved for his own concept of force.

After discussing the interconvertibility of fall-force and force of motion in his 1842 paper, Mayer noted that motion is often observed to disappear without producing an equivalent amount of other motion or fall-force. In these cases motion is converted into a different form of force, namely heat. Fall-force, motion, and heat are different manifestations of one indestructible force, and hence they maintain definite quantitative relationships among themselves. This means, Mayer concluded, that there must exist in nature a constant numerical value which expresses the mechanical equivalent of heat. He stated that this value is 365 kilogram-meters per kilocalorie; that is, the fall-force in a mass of one kilogram raised 365 meters is equal to the heat-force required to raise one kilogram of water one degree centigrade.

Although Mayer's 1842 paper merely stated the

mechanical equivalent of heat without giving its derivation, later papers also gave his method. Let x be the amount of heat in calories required to raise one cubic centimeter of air from $0°$ C. to $1°$ C. at constant volume. To raise the same cubic centimeter of air one degree centigrade at constant pressure will require a larger amount of heat, say $x + y$, since, in the volume expansion, work must be done against the force which maintains constant pressure. If this latter expansion is carried out under a mercury column, then the extra heat y will go into raising that mercury column. Hence if P is the weight of the mercury column and h is the distance that it is raised in the expansion, we can write $y = Ph$; the problem is to find y. From published data Mayer knew that 3.47×10^{-4} calories are required in order to raise one cubic centimeter of air one degree centigrade under a constant pressure of 1,033 gm./cm.^{2} (that is, 76 cm. of mercury); hence $x + y = 3.47 \times 10^{-4}$ calories. He also knew from data of Dulong that the ratio of the specific heats of air at constant volume and at constant pressure is 1/1.421; hence $x/(x + y) =$ 1/1.421. Knowing the value of $x + y$, Mayer then easily found $y = 1.03 \times 10^{-4}$ calories. Since the expansion was known to raise the mercury column 1/274 centimeters, Mayer then had for the equation $y = Ph$,

$$1.03 \times 10^{-4} \text{ cal.} = 1,033 \text{ gm.} \times 1/274 \text{ cm.}$$

The reduction of these figures yielded the equation 1 kilocalorie = 365 kilogram-meters.

Mayer's derivation of the mechanical equivalent of heat was as accurate as the value chosen for the ratio of specific heats would permit. Mayer's derivation rests upon the assumption that his cubic centimeter of air does no internal work during free expansion; that is, that all of the heat y goes to raise the mercury column. Although in 1842 Mayer already knew of an experimental result by Gay-Lussac which would substantiate this assumption, he did not invoke it publicly until three years later (1845).

The paper of 1842 set out Mayer's definitive view on the conservation of force and established his claim to priority; historically the paper also provides insight into the processes through which Mayer arrived at his theory. During the 1840's various European scientists and engineers were formulating ideas which were suggestive of the conservation of energy. Several different interests influenced these formulations. Among these interests was the growing concern with the efficiency of steam engines and with the many new conversion processes which were being discovered in electricity, magnetism, and chemistry. Mayer's early papers show little interest in these

problems but instead suggest that philosophical and conceptual considerations largely guided Mayer's theorizing. One of these considerations was his constant identification of force and cause; another was his intuitive understanding of force as a substantial, quantitative entity. The source of these ideas of Mayer's and their relationship to the larger context of German science and philosophy remain unsolved historical problems. Both concepts seem to have been unique to German science and to have led Mayer to interpret familiar phenomena in a radically new way. An example of this interpretation can be seen in the events which apparently led Mayer to his initial speculations about force conservation.

Like several other formulators of the conservation principle, Mayer was led to his theory through physiological, not physical, considerations. While letting the blood of European sailors who had recently arrived in Java in July 1840, Mayer had been impressed by the surprising redness of their venous blood. Mayer attributed this redness to the unaccustomed heat of the tropics. Since a lower rate of metabolic combustion would suffice to maintain the body heat, the body extracted less oxygen from the red arterial blood. This observation struck Mayer as a remarkable confirmation of the chemical theory of animal heat, and he quickly generalized that the oxidation of foodstuff is the only possible source of animal heat. Conceiving of the animal economy as a force-conversion process—the input and outgo of which must always balance—Mayer realized that chemical force which is latent in food is the only input and that this input could be expressed quantitatively as the heat obtained from the oxidation of the food. To this point Mayer's reasoning differed little from contemporary physiological theory, but once it was reached Mayer proceeded to a conceptual leap which was well beyond any facts at his disposal. He decided that not only the heat produced by the animal directly as body heat, but also that heat produced indirectly through friction resulting ultimately from the animal's muscular exertion must be balanced against this input of chemical force. Muscle force and also body heat must be derived from the chemical force latent in food. If the animal's intake and expenditure of force are to balance, then all these manifestations of force must be quantitatively conserved in all the force conversions which occur within the animal body. This inference, however fruitful, seemed to rest largely upon Mayer's preconceived notion of force and conversion rather than upon any empirical observations.

Immediately after his return from Java Mayer had planned a paper on physiology which would set out these ideas, but he purposely postponed the paper in order first to lay a proper physical basis for the theory. Having done so in the treatise of 1842, he published privately at Heilbronn in 1845 *Die organische Bewegung in ihrem Zusammenhang mit dem Stoffwechsel*, his most original and comprehensive paper. In this work Mayer again set out the physical basis of his theory, this time extending the ideal of force conservation to magnetic, electrical, and chemical forces. In *Die organische Bewegung* he described the basic force conversions of the organic world. Plants convert the sun's heat and light into latent chemical force; animals consume this chemical force as food; animals then convert that force to body heat and mechanical muscle force in their life processes.

Mayer intended *Die organische Bewegung* not only to establish the conservation of force as the basis of physiology, but also to refute views held by the organic chemist Liebig. In 1842 Liebig had published his influential and controversial book *Die Thierchemie oder die organische Chemie in ihrer Anwendung auf Physiologie und Pathologie*. In that work Liebig had come out as a champion of the chemical theory of animal heat, which Lavoisier and Laplace had first proposed in 1777. Reasoning much as Mayer had done, Liebig had concluded that animal heat produced from any source other than the oxidation of food was tantamount to the production of force from nothing. Hence he concluded that the oxidation of food is the sole source of animal heat. Liebig also believed that muscle force was derived ultimately from chemical force through an intermediary vital force localized in the protein substances of muscle tissue. Well aware of Liebig's acquaintance with his 1842 paper, Mayer regarded *Die organische Chemie* as possible plagiarism and as a definite threat to his priority. In his *Die organische Bewegung* Mayer joined Liebig in championing the chemical theory of animal heat, but he then proceeded to refute Liebig's other views wherever possible.

Mayer opened his attack on Liebig by criticizing Liebig's frequent recourse to vitalism. The vital force served various functions in Liebig's theory, the chief function being to prevent the living body from spontaneously beginning to putrefy, its tissues being constantly in the presence of oxygen and moisture. Mayer denied that putrefaction would occur in the tissues as spontaneously as Liebig had assumed. Mayer argued that if putrefaction did occur the putrefying parts would nevertheless be carried off in the blood as rapidly as they began to decay. Hence postulating a vital force was not merely unscientific, it was unnecessary.

Liebig had argued further that while starch and sugar are oxidized in the blood to produce heat, only the protein-bearing muscle tissue can undergo the chemical change necessary to produce mechanical muscle force. Hence those changes occur in the muscle, not in the blood; the muscle literally consumes itself in exertion. Against this argument Mayer employed his mechanical equivalent of heat to compute the amount of muscle tissue which must be consumed daily in order to support the exertions of a working animal. The high rate of assimilation necessary continuously to replace that loss, Mayer argued, made Liebig's theory improbable at best. He concluded that it seemed most reasonable to assume all oxidation to occur within the blood, whatever the form and locus of the force released. At the end of his 1845 paper Mayer finally reconciled the main observations of classical irritability theory with his own hypothesis and argued the dependence of the contractile force upon the blood supply.

Die organische Bewegung exercised little influence on German physiology, although Mayer's attack on Liebig's vital force found enthusiastic response, and the work received several favorable reviews. After 1845 Liebig's younger disciples quietly dropped his speculations about the vital force, much as Mayer had suggested. The issue of muscle decomposition remained controversial among physiologists, although by 1870 it was agreed that the oxidation of carbohydrates in addition to proteins contributed to the production of muscle energy. Mayer's writings had little direct influence on either of these developments.

Immediately after publishing his treatise on physiology, Mayer applied his theory of force conservation to a second critical problem which he had treated unsatisfactorily in 1841: the source of the heat of the sun. In 1846 he advanced an explanation of solar heat which he incorporated into a memoir submitted to the Paris Academy, "Sur la production de la lumière et de la chaleur du soleil," and into the expanded *Beiträge zur Dynamik des Himmels in populärer Darstellungen*, which was published privately at Heilbronn in 1848. After demonstrating in these papers the insufficiency of any chemical combustion to sustain the sun's enormous radiation, Mayer advanced what rapidly became known as the "meteoric hypothesis" of the sun's heat. Mayer speculated that matter, mostly in the form of meteors, daily enters the solar system in immense quantities and begins to orbit the sun. Friction with the luminiferous ether causes this matter gradually to spiral into the sun at inordinate velocities. Upon striking the sun this matter yields up its kinetic energy as light and heat. Mayer employed his mechanical equivalent of heat to show that each unit of mass striking the sun would yield four thousand to eight thousand times as much heat as would be produced by the combustion of an equivalent mass of carbon. Hence if the quantity of matter falling into the sun is assumed to be sufficiently large, this process can sustain the sun's total output of heat.

After 1850 the meteoric hypothesis received wide currency, largely on account of versions of the theory which were advanced independently of Mayer by Waterston and William Thomson. The explanation of solar heat that won general acceptance and that survived well into the twentieth century, however, was proposed by Helmholtz in a popular lecture of 1854, "Ueber die Wechselwirkung der Naturkräfte und die darauf bezüglichen Ermittlungen der Physik." According to Helmholtz the sun's heat is sustained by the gradual cooling and contraction of the sun's mass. As the sun's density increases the sun's matter yields its potential energy directly as heat. Although this was not a true meteoric hypothesis, Helmholtz' explanation of the sun's heat resembled Mayer's in many respects. Mayer's hypothesis may have influenced Helmholtz in the formulation of his own hypothesis, for by 1854 Helmholtz knew of Mayer's 1848 treatise and had discussed it in his 1854 lecture shortly before setting out his own views on the origin of solar energy.

Mayer's astronomical papers also revived another hypothesis which was to become important after 1850. In the *Dynamik des Himmels* of 1848 and in his 1851 memoir, "De l'influence des marées sur la rotation de la terre," Mayer showed that tidal friction deflects the major axis of the earth's tidal spheroid some thirty-five degrees from the earth-moon line. Hence the moon's gravitation exercises a constant retarding couple on the earth's rotation, a couple which gradually dissipates the earth's energy of rotation as heat.

Although minute, this quantity is perceptible. Citing Laplace, Mayer noted that on the basis of data from ancient eclipses, the length of the day, and hence the velocity of rotation of the earth, can be shown to have been constant to within .002 seconds over the last 2,500 years. This failure to observe the predicted retardation due to tidal friction indicated to Mayer the presence of a compensating phenomenon. He found this in geology. By 1848 many geologists believed that the earth had originally condensed as a molten mass and had since then been cooling at an undetermined rate. This theory faced a critical difficulty, for cooling should have produced a contraction of the earth, which in turn should have accelerated its rotation. No such acceleration could be observed, and Laplace had already used the apparent constancy

of the day to prove that no contraction greater than fifteen centimeters could have occurred within the last 2,500 years. At this juncture Mayer boldly hypothesized that tidal retardation of the earth's rotation is offset by the acceleration due to cooling and contraction. Mayer pointed out that this assumption rescued both hypotheses and reconciled both with the observed constancy of the day. The predicted retardation of .0625 seconds in 2,500 years, Mayer showed, would permit an offsetting contraction of the earth's radius by 4.5 meters.

The influence of Mayer's speculations is difficult to assess; the 1848 treatise was not widely read, while the memoirs to Paris had been reported upon but not printed. In 1858 Ferrel published a similar hypothesis, apparently independently of Mayer, and noted that tidal retardation and the earth's contraction might produce compensating changes in the earth's rotation. In 1865 Delaunay invoked tidal friction to explain a newly discovered inequality in the moon's motion and noted that the hypothesis of tidal friction had already been formulated in several printed works.

The *Dynamik des Himmels* marked the end of Mayer's creative career, for his numerous later articles were primarily popular or retrospective. At this point Mayer had received almost no recognition in important scientific circles, and to this disappointment was added the frustration of seeing other men independently advance ideas similar to his own. Liebig had anticipated many of Mayer's views in 1842, and in 1845 Karl Holtzmann computed a mechanical equivalent of heat without reference to Mayer. In 1847 Helmholtz set out a complete mathematical treatment of force conservation in his treatise *Ueber die Erhaltung der Kraft*. Mayer's main rival was Joule, and in 1848 Mayer became embroiled with him in a priority dispute carried out mainly through the Paris Academy. Although the dispute remained inconclusive, it later developed bitter nationalistic overtones when other scientists took up the quarrel.

After 1858 Mayer's fortunes improved. Helmholtz apparently read Mayer's early papers around 1852, and thereafter he argued Mayer's priority in his own widely read works. Clausius, too, regarded Mayer deferentially as the founder of the conservation principle and began to correspond with him in 1862. Through Clausius, Mayer was put in touch with Tyndall, who quickly became Mayer's English champion in the priority dispute with Joule, Thomson, and Tait. During the 1860's many of Mayer's early articles were translated into English, and in 1871 Mayer received the Royal Society's Copley Medal. In 1870 he was voted a corresponding member of the Paris Academy of Sciences and was awarded the Prix Poncelet.

Although the scientific world lionized Mayer before his death in 1878, in reality he exercised little influence on European science. In every field in which he worked his principal ideas were later formulated independently by others and were well established in science before his own contributions were recognized. In an age in which German science was rapidly becoming professionalized, Mayer remained a thorough dilettante. He conducted almost no experiments, and although he had an exact, numerical turn of mind, he neither fully understood mathematical analysis nor ever employed it in his papers. His scientific style, his status as an outsider to the scientific community, and his lack of institutional affiliation were all factors that limited Mayer's access to influential journals and publishers and hampered the acceptance of his ideas. Mayer was a conceptual thinker whose genius lay in the boldness of his hypotheses and in his ability to synthesize the work of others. Mayer actually possessed only one creative idea—his insight into the nature of force—but he tenaciously pursued that insight and lived to see it established in physics as the principle of the conservation of energy.

BIBLIOGRAPHY

Mayer's major scientific works were collected in Jacob J. Weyrauch, ed., *Die Mechanik der Wärme*, 3rd ed. (Stuttgart, 1893). Mayer's letters, short papers, and other documents related to his career were reprinted as Jacob J. Weyrauch, ed., *Kleinere Schriften und Briefe von Robert Mayer* (Stuttgart, 1893). In both works Weyrauch provides not only extensive nn. and commentary, but also a thorough biog. of Mayer. Other documents relating to Mayer's career and family background are included in the commemorative vol., Helmut Schmolz and Hubert Weckbach, eds., *J. Robert Mayer. Sein Leben und Werk in Dokumenten* (Weissenhorn, 1964).

Existing biographies of Mayer tend to whiggishness; one of the better ones is S. Friedländer, *Julius Robert Mayer* (Leipzig, 1905). On Mayer's place in the formulation of the principle of the conservation of energy and on the European context of his work, see Thomas S. Kuhn, "Energy Conservation as an Example of Simultaneous Discovery," in Marshall Clagett, ed., *Critical Problems in the History of Science* (Madison, Wis., 1959), 321–356. Mayer's concepts of force and causation are discussed by B. Hell in "Robert Mayer," in *Kantstudien*, **19** (1914), 222–248. Although he does not mention Mayer, Frederic L. Holmes discusses the milieu of German physiology in the 1840's in his intro. to Liebig's *Animal Chemistry*, facs. ed. (New York, 1964). On Mayer's role in astrophysical speculations see Agnes M. Clerke, *A Popular History of Astronomy During the Nineteenth Century*, 3rd ed. (London, 1893), esp. 332–334, 376–388.

R. STEVEN TURNER

MAYER-EYMAR, KARL (*b.* Marseilles, France, 29 June 1826; *d.* Zurich, Switzerland, 25 February 1907), *paleontology, stratigraphy.*

The son of a Swiss merchant, Mayer-Eymar received his early schooling in Rennes and St. Gall. He entered the University of Zurich in 1846, first studying medicine and then natural history and geology. After graduating, he worked in Paris from 1851 to 1854, principally at the Muséum d'Histoire Naturelle under d'Orbigny. In 1858 he was appointed assistant in the geology institute of the Zurich Polytechnische Hochschule. Shortly afterward, he became a *Privatdozent* and curator of the collections, and in 1875 he was named professor. He held these latter posts until his death and never married. His contemporaries described Mayer-Eymar as an original and sometimes picturesque character. Around 1865 he added the anagram Eymar to his patronymic to avert confusion with other persons of that name; thenceforth he wrote his name Mayer-Eymar.

Mayer-Eymar's chief field of interest was the biostratigraphy and paleontology of mollusks, mainly of the Tertiary and, to a lesser extent, of the Jurassic and the Cretaceous. A passionate and successful collector from his school days on, he investigated in particular the Tertiary terranes of many western European and Mediterranean countries and brought extensive collections back to Zurich. He published voluminous lists and descriptions of these materials and of others sent to him from abroad. Some of his accounts included new species and genera, but most of them were without illustrations. This omission lessened the usefulness of many of his publications.

Mayer-Eymar's stratigraphical works were of great importance and have been of some influence until the present day. In 1858 appeared his first major publication on the subdivision of the Tertiary, which he divided into stages according to lithological and faunal criteria named after typical localities in the Tertiary basins of western Europe. He introduced many new names for these stages, a number of which were never adopted or were in use for only a short time; others, however, are still employed, although with somewhat modified definitions (for instance, Bartonian, Tongrian, Aquitanian, Helvetian, Tortonian, Plaisancian). He published similar subdivisions on the Jurassic and Cretaceous. For the publication of his stratigraphic researches he employed mainly autographed synoptic tables, which he frequently republished in improved form.

His profound paleontological knowledge frequently enabled Mayer-Eymar to make definitive decisions concerning stratigraphical problems. In 1876, he clarified the much discussed question of whether the glaciers of the southern Alps were contemporaneous with the Pliocene sea in northern Italy. He demonstrated that the glacial deposits contained layers with Quaternary mollusks and therefore had to be more recent than the late Pliocene marine sediments of the Astian.

BIBLIOGRAPHY

I. ORIGINAL WORKS. Mayer-Eymar's writings include "Versuch einer neuen Klassifikation der Tertiär-Gebilde Europas," in *Verhandlungen der Schweizerischen naturforschenden Gesellschaft* (Trogen) (1858), 165–199; "Catalogue systématique et descriptif des mollusques tertiaires, qui se trouvent au Musée fédéral de Zurich," in *Vierteljahrsschrift der naturforschenden Gesellschaft in Zürich*, **11** (1866), 301–337; **12** (1867), 241–303; **13** (1868), 21–105, 163–200; **15** (1870), 31–82; "Systematisches Verzeichnis der Versteinerungen des Helvetian der Schweiz und Schwabens," in *Beiträge zur geologischen Karte der Schweiz*, **11** (1872), 475–511; "La vérité sur la mer glaciale au pied des Alpes," in *Bulletin de la Société géologique de France*, 3rd ser., **4** (1876), 199–222; the synoptic tables, published in Zurich in 1900: *Classification et terminologie des terrains tertiaires d'Europe, Classification et terminologie des terrains crétaciques d'Europe*, and *Classification et terminologie des terrains jurassiques d'Europe*, and many articles on fossil mollusks and stratigraphic problems in *Journal de conchyliologie*, **5–49** (1856–1902), and in *Vierteljahrsschrift der naturforschenden Gesellschaft in Zurich*, **6-49** (1861–1904).

II. SECONDARY LITERATURE. See G. F. Dollfus, "Nécrologie Ch. Mayer-Eymar," in *Journal de conchyliologie*, **56** (1908), 145–162; A. Heim and L. Rollier, "Dr. Karl Mayer-Eymar 1826–1907," in *Verhandlungen der Schweizerischen naturforschenden Gesellschaft* Vers. (Fribourg), **90** (1908), xl–xlix, with complete bibliography; and F. Sacco, "Carlo Mayer-Eymar. Cenni biografici," in *Bollettino della Società geologica italiana*, **26** (1907), 585–602, with a 127-title bibliography.

HEINZ TOBIEN

MAYO, HERBERT (*b.* London, England, 3 May 1796; *d.* Bad Weilbach, Germany, 15 May 1852), *neurology*.

Herbert was the third son of John Mayo; his father and his eldest brother, Thomas, were prominent physicians in London. He was a pupil of Charles Bell at the Windmill Street Anatomy School (1812–1815) and graduated M.D. at Leiden in 1818. He was admitted a member of the Royal College of Surgeons by examination in 1819 and elected among the first fellows in 1843. He practiced surgery and taught anatomy in London from 1819 to 1843, becoming senior surgeon to the Middlesex Hospital, where he founded the Medical School in 1836; he also wrote many successful textbooks.

Charles Bell had circulated privately in 1811 his *Idea of a New Anatomy of the Brain*, which showed that the anterior roots of the nerves alone have motor functions; ten years later, in 1821, Bell contributed to the *Philosophical Transactions* a paper "On the Nerves; Giving an Account of Some Experiments on Their Structure and Functions, Which Lead to a New Arrangement of the System." Bell here put forward the concept of the motor function of the anterior and the sensory function of the posterior roots, but as Claude Bernard later wrote, "drowned in philosophical considerations so obscure or diffuse that it is difficult to find places where his opinions are succinctly stated."

Mayo announced his independent discoveries of the physiology of the nerves in his *Anatomical and Physiological Commentaries*; the first part (August 1822) included a paper which described "Experiments to Determine the Influence of the Portio Dura of the Seventh and the Facial Branches of the Fifth Pair of Nerves"; part two (July 1823) opened with a paper "On the Cerebral Nerves With Reference to Sensation and Voluntary Motion," and it concluded with "Remarks Upon the Spinal Chord and the Nervous System Generally." Mayo attributed sensibility to the fifth nerve and motor power to the seventh nerve, and he showed that a circumscribed segment of the nervous system sufficed to produce muscular action. He wrote that "An influence may be propagated from the sentient nerves of a part to their correspondent nerves of motion through the intervention of that part alone of the nervous system to which they are mutually attached"; the term "reflex" was applied to this phenomenon by Marshall Hall in 1833. Neither Bell nor Mayo seems to have known at this time that François Magendie had achieved similar results in research which was reported in Paris (1821–1823). Bell protested his claim to priority against both Mayo and Magendie.

Mayo supplemented the fifteen plates in his *Commentaries* by an atlas of six larger plates (each plate was printed in an outline and a shaded version) entitled *A Series of Engravings Intended to Illustrate the Structure of the Brain and Spinal Chord* (1827).

The brief text is pure descriptive anatomy, except for a paragraph (p. iii) in which Mayo stated,

> The filaments of which the nerves consist have the office of conductors. We may therefore infer that the white threads which enter so largely into the composition of the spinal marrow, the medulla oblongata, and the brain, likewise serve as media for conveying impressions. The justice of this conclusion in the instance of the spinal marrow has been proved by experiments made on animals.

He added that his observations would prove useful for pathologists in explaining "interruption or impairment of functions."

Although he made no further original discoveries, Mayo retained his interest in neurology. In his *Outlines of Human Physiology* (3rd ed., 1833, p. 219) he gave "an extension of the original law respecting the place of origin of the nerves." He published a pamphlet on the *Powers of the Roots of the Nerves* in 1837 in reply to R. D. Grainger's *Observations on the Structure and Function of the Spinal Cord*; Mayo described this as a restatement of his views after conversations with Grainger. In an appendix he discussed recent demonstrations of hypnotism, "magnetic sleep," by Baron Dupotet and concluded that "persons susceptible of it may be thrown into a kind of trance by the influence of imagination excited through the senses." He also anticipated a possible value for anesthetizing a patient before "a surgical operation of little severity." In the main pamphlet Mayo also stated: "Nerves, it was discovered by the independent researches of Sir C. Bell, M. Magendie, and myself (each having contributed his separate share to the result) are of two kinds only, one *sentient*, the other *voluntary*." He did not discuss Bell's claims, but recorded (p. 8) the highest regard for Magendie's results and integrity, and he mentioned (p. 20) that "Dr Marshall Hall, who invented the term 'reflex action,' has followed out the idea with great diligence, showing fresh instances parallel to my own, which I reduced to one theory in 1823."

Mayo's final work on the subject was his monograph *The Nervous System* (1842). This was begun as a physiological introduction for a reissue of the 1827 *Engravings*, but in the event the illustrations were not reprinted. Mayo wrote that his new "survey of the nervous system and the reflections to which it gave rise did not elicit much that is new, yet display what has been discovered with new distinctness and force."

Mayo retired to Germany in 1843 for hydropathic treatment as a victim of "rheumatic gout," and while there he wrote on *The Cold Water Cure* and on *Mesmerism*. He died in Germany at the age of fifty-six, survived by his wife, a son, and two daughters.

BIBLIOGRAPHY

I. ORIGINAL WORKS. His writings on neurology are *Anatomical and Physiological Commentaries*, pt. 1 (August 1822), pt. 2 (July 1823); *A Series of Engravings Intended to Illustrate the Structure of the Brain and Spinal Chord in Man* (1827); *Powers of the Roots of the Nerves in Health and Disease, Likewise On Magnetic Sleep* (1837); and *The Nervous System and Its Functions* (1842).

Textbooks which Mayo wrote include *A Course of Dissections for Students* (1825); *Outlines of Human Physiology* (1827, 1829, 1833, 1837); *Observations on Injuries and Diseases of the Rectum* (1833; Washington, 1834); *Outlines of Human Pathology* (1836; Philadelphia, 1839; 1841), trans. into German (1838–1839); *The Philosophy of Living* (1837, 1838, 1851); *Management of the Organs of Digestion in Health and Disease* (1837, 1840); *A Treatise on Siphilis* (1840), trans. into German (1841); *The Cold Water Cure* (1845); and *Letters on the Truths in Popular Superstitions With an Account of Mesmerism* (Frankfurt, 1849), 2nd and 3rd eds. (Edinburgh, 1851).

II. SECONDARY LITERATURE. Biographical memoirs of Mayo are in the *Dictionary of National Biography*, XXXVII (1894); D'A. Power, ed., *Plarr's Lives of the Fellows of the Royal College of Surgeons* (1930); and John F. Fulton, *Selected Readings in the History of Physiology*, 2nd ed., Leonard G. Wilson, ed. (1966), 285–286.

WILLIAM LeFANU

MAYOW, JOHN (*b.* Bray, near Looe, England, December 1641; *d.* London, England, September 1679), *physiology, chemistry.*

Mayow was the second son of Phillip Mayowe, a member of the well-established, substantial, and multi-branched Mayow family of Cornwall. His grandfather Philip acquired the manor of Bray in 1564; he was one of the nine charter burgesses of East Looe when the town received its charter of incorporation from Queen Elizabeth in 1587. He appears on his altar tomb in alderman's robes with the epitaph "Phillipe Maiowe of East, Looe, Gentleman." John's father is referred to in the parish register that records John's baptism as "Mr. Phillip Mayowe, Gent."

Mayow matriculated at Wadham College, Oxford, on 2 July 1658 and was received as a commoner and admitted scholar on 23 September 1659. On 3 November 1660 he was elected to a fellowship at All Souls College, Oxford. He graduated bachelor of common law on 5 July 1670 and obtained the further privilege of studying medicine. After leaving Oxford in 1670 he entered medical practice, at least during the summer season at Bath. In the 1670's he seems to have spent considerable time during the fall and winter months in London. Robert Hooke records several meetings with Mayow in his *Diary* from 1674 through 1677. On Hooke's recommendation Mayow was elected fellow of the Royal Society on 30 November 1678.

Mayow is best known for his studies on the interrelated problems of atmospheric composition, aerial nitre, combustion, and respiration. He has occasionally been regarded, usually uncritically, as an unappreciated precursor of Lavoisier. In fact, Mayow's work was vigorously scrutinized—both in a friendly and in a hostile spirit—in his own time and again in the late eighteenth century after the discovery of oxygen. In the last several decades, the question of his originality and importance has been a subject of scholarly debate.

Mayow's first publication, a thin volume entitled *Tractatus duo*, was printed at Oxford in 1668. The two tracts, the first on respiration and the second on rickets, demonstrated his involvement in the scientific and medical issues and literature of his day. In "De respiratione," Mayow specifically cited the work of his English contemporaries Robert Boyle, Nathaniel Highmore, and Thomas Willis, and of the Italian Marcello Malpighi. He also took note of experiments on the inflation of the lungs "recently performed at the Royal Society" by Robert Hooke and Richard Lower, and textual nuances suggest that he may likewise have been familiar with such recent publications as Swammerdam's *Tractatus . . . de respiratione usuque pulmonum* (Leiden, 1667), reviewed in the *Philosophical Transactions* for October 1667. Mayow's second essay, "De rachitide," shows a familiarity with Francis Glisson's *De rachitide, sive morbo puerili . . .* (London, 1650), although Mayow departed sharply from Glisson by offering a highly abbreviated account of the symptomatology and therapeutics and a more iatromechanical version of the etiology of rickets.

The real interest and importance of the *Tractatus duo*, however, lies in the striking originality of Mayow's juxtaposition of contemporary physiological ideas in "De respiratione." Thus, after describing with some novelty the mechanics of thoracic dilatation and pulmonary inflation, Mayow argued that respiration serves principally to convey a supply of fine nitrous particles from the air to the blood. This "nitrous air" is necessary to life, for when it is missing from the mass of inspired air, respiration does not produce its usual good effect. The nitrous particles are needed to react with the "sulphureous" parts of the sanguinary stream, and this reaction causes a gentle and necessary

fermentation in the pulmonary vessels, the heart, and the arteries. Moreover, the nitrous air is also essential to the beating of the heart. Like other muscles, the heart contracts macroscopically because an "explosion" occurs microscopically within its fibres. The explosion, which inflates the muscles, results specifically from the violent interaction of the "nitro-saline" particles of the inspired air with the animal spirits fashioned from the "volatile salt" of the blood.

Mayow was here fusing in a very original way two recent Oxford physiological traditions. First, he adopted the "nitrous pabulum" theory originally advanced by Ralph Bathurst in Oxford lectures of 1654 and later remembered by Robert Hooke and improved in his *Micrographia* of 1665.[1] Second, Mayow endorsed Willis' essential ideas about the explosion mechanism for muscular contraction. But whereas Willis had attributed explosive inflation to the violent, gunpowder-like interaction of the "spirituous-saline" animal spirits with the "sulphureous" parts of the blood, Mayow contended that the blood and spirits could not possibly react explosively, for if they could they would already have done so before the spirits were distilled from the blood in the cortex of the brain. Mayow was thus able to avoid apparent contradiction and to account for the otherwise perplexing fact that death follows so suddenly upon the cessation of respiration. Failure to inspire fresh supplies of nitrous particles mixed with the larger bulk of air could now be understood to lead instantaneously to the stopping of heartbeat; and stoppage of heartbeat immediately curtails the distribution of animal spirits throughout the body. Since, Mayow asserted, the life of animals consists in the distribution of animal spirits, death quickly follows upon the cessation of respiration.

Thus, in 1668, Mayow wrote as a product of and a participant in the Oxford physiology to which he was thoroughly exposed as a student and fellow. His ideas were interesting, although his contemporaries considered them fundamentally unexceptional; they were well reviewed and apparently well received. The *Tractatus duo* was accorded the lead review in the November 1668 number of the *Philosophical Transactions* where Mayow's theories were clearly summarized in considerable detail with no suggestion of skepticism or hostility.

Between 1668 and 1674, perhaps encouraged by the initial reception of his views on respiration, Mayow attempted a clarification, expansion, and refining of his ideas, both on physiology and on chemistry. He may well have been influenced by the publication of several closely related books and essays: Richard Lower, *Tractatus de corde* (1669); Malachi Thruston,

De respirationis usus primario (1670); Thomas Willis, *De sanguinis accensione* (1670) and *De motu musculari* (1670); and Robert Boyle, *Tracts . . . Containing New Experiments, Touching the Relation Betwixt Flame and Air* (1672) and *Tracts . . . About Some Hidden Qualities of the Air* (1674). Meanwhile Hooke continued to report to the Royal Society about experiments on combustion, respiration, and the action of the air and of nitrous compounds. In 1674 Mayow referred directly to several of these efforts, and allusions suggest a familiarity with the rest. In any case, by 1674 Mayow, aware of contemporary developments, had expanded his *Tractatus duo* into *Tractatus quinque* by the addition of three new essays: "De sal-nitro et spiritu nitro-aereo"; "De respiratione foetus in utero et ovo"; and "De motu musculari et spiritibus animalibus."

In the first essay, by far the longest and most important, Mayow offered a chemical history of nitre and nitro-aerial spirit. His primary intention seems to have been to distinguish between these two distinct substances, which the vague vocabulary of his contemporaries (and his own) had previously confused. Nitre (saltpeter) is a triply complex salt. It consists of spirit of nitre (nitric acid) combined with a fixed salt of the earth; spirit of nitre is in turn derived from the "ethereal and igneous" nitro-aerial spirit of atmospheric air (oxygen?) in combination with the "Salino-metallic parts" of common "Terrestrial sulphur." It is the nitro-aerial spirit, harbored in turn in the spirit of nitre and in common nitre, that is the active and "igneous" substance in nitrous compounds. It is the chemical agent responsible for sustaining combustion and producing fermentation. Flame consists essentially in nitro-aerial spirit thrown to brisk motion by interacting with sulphureous particles, whereas fermentation is the general effervescence of nitro-aerial particles reacting with salino-sulphureous ones. Moreover, the caustic qualities of acids derive from the active and igneous nitro-aerial particles within them.

Having clarified the respective roles and chemical relations of the several nitrous substances, Mayow next explores a wide range of problems to which he makes the nitro-aerial spirit relevant. His exploration ranges from meteorological fantasies about thunder and lightning quite happily and deliberately modeled on Descartes's *Principia philosophiae*, through speculations on the role of nitro-aerial spirit in transmitting the pulse of light, to—most significantly—ingenious experimental investigations of the role of nitro-aerial spirit in combustion and respiration. In pursuit of this latter problem, Mayow dexterously employed a variety of experimental techniques that represented subtle though important improvements on contemporary practice, notably that of Boyle. For example, Mayow was able to transfer gases collected over water more neatly than did Boyle, who had to use two air pumps for this operation.[2] Mayow also experimented with animals and candles breathing or burning over water, using cupping glasses, water troughs, and bell jars. He always carefully adjusted water levels with a special siphon arrangement, and with this apparatus he was able to observe the breathing of an animal in a closed space. He was thus able to test his earlier assertion that there are nitrous particles diffused in a larger bulk of otherwise useless air, an assertion that Hooke had repeated, unverified, to the Royal Society early in the 1670's.[3] Mayow now observed the gradual rise of water into the space occupied by the breathing animal. The rise of water continued until there was a diminution of one-fourteenth of the original volume of air. Mayow explained this diminution as the result of the passing of nitro-aerial particles, which normally account for the elasticity of atmospheric air, from the air through the lungs and into the blood. There, finally, the nitro-aerial particles fermentatively interact with sulphureous particles, producing animal heat in the process and changing the blood from dark purple to light scarlet.

Mayow's two other essays in *Tractatus quinque*, "De respiratione foetus in utero et ovo" and "De motu musculari et spiritibus animalibus," primarily supplement and clarify physiological views that he had earlier expressed in *Tractatus duo*. In the first of these essays Mayow contended that embryos require nitro-aerial particles as surely as do respiring animals. The umbilical arteries convey the appropriate particles either from the maternal bloodstream or from the albuminous humor of the egg, whence they are temporarily collected from the nitro-aerial particles supplied by the heat of the incubating fowl. In the second essay Mayow somewhat revised his 1668 views on muscular contraction. Aware of Steno's recently published findings on the action of muscles, Mayow contended that muscles contract by "contortion" rather than by inflation. The active agent, however, is still nitro-aerial particles, which were now said to be the very substance of animal spirits; and these spirits produce the necessary effervescence when they come in contact with the salino-sulphureous particles of the blood in the muscular fibrils.

The immediate reception of *Tractatus quinque* was decidedly less favorable than that of *Tractatus duo*. Mayow's work again earned a lead review in the *Philosophical Transactions*, a lengthy one in the July 1674 number. Now, however, the detailed summary showed suggestions of sarcasm and disbelief. Detailed marginal notes called attention to works by Boyle and others, the impression being clearly and perhaps deliberately created that Mayow owed debts to his contemporaries that he did not fully acknowledge. The review was probably written by Henry Oldenburg, a friend of Boyle and secretary of the Royal Society. In a letter to Boyle of July 1674, Oldenburg commented that "some learned and knowing men speak very slightly of the *quinque Tractatus* of *J.M.* and a particular friend of yours and mine told me yesterday, that as far as he had read him, he would shew to any impartial and considering man more errors than one in every page."[4]

To a large extent personal loyalty and scientific partisanship lay behind Oldenburg's remark. At just this time Boyle and Hooke were conducting a polite but unmistakable debate about the nature of nitrous compounds and the role of the air in respiration and combustion. Close as Oldenburg was to Boyle, he was distant from Hooke, who several times accused Oldenburg of personal malice.[5] In striking contrast to the hostility that Hooke felt in Oldenburg, Mayow seemed eager to support Hooke's side of the debate and, indeed, to provide experimental substantiation for his long-standing but still disputed views on chemistry, combustion, and respiration. Moreover, the elaborate hypothetical excursions with which Mayow filled much of *Tractatus quinque,* and which doubtless ran counter to the skeptical mood of Boyle and Oldenburg, were consistent with Hooke's increasing enthusiasm for explicit Cartesian hypothesizing in the 1670's and 1680's.[6] It seems no accident that Hooke and Mayow were friendly after the publication of *Tractatus quinque,* and that Hooke proposed Mayow for membership in the Royal Society after Oldenburg's death in 1677.

Other reactions to Mayow's views were mixed. In one work Boyle seemed to flirt briefly with Mayow's ideas, but by and large he remained aloof.[7] Other contemporaries cited Mayow's theories and experiments, and some continued to do so for several decades. In the eighteenth century Mayow still had a following which included the chemist and physiologist Stephen Hales. The bitter critics who also appeared were usually, like Archibald Pitcairne, of iatromechanical persuasion. There were also judicious conciliators. Albrecht von Haller, for example, a magisterial figure in mid-eighteenth-century physiology, devoted significant attention to Mayow's views in his much studied *Elementa physiologiae.* Yet with the passage of time, Mayow's special originality faded, even in the minds of his supporters; and he became generally but vaguely identified with Boyle, Hooke,

Lower, and those other seventeenth-century virtuosi who speculated on the role of the air in respiration and combustion.

With the discovery of oxygen the ground shifted considerably. Lavoisier himself had a copy of Mayow's book in his library, and several of his ideas and experiments seem to show important traces of Mayow's techniques and perhaps even his theories.[8] Lavoisier's contemporary Fourcroy discussed Mayow explicitly and remarked that his experiments had been more ingenious than those of his much noted countrymen Boyle and Hales.[9] In England, no doubt due in part to the hunger for national priority, a small Mayow revival began. Participating with various degrees of enthusiasm were Thomas Thomson, Thomas Beddoes, and G. D. Yeats. Beddoes and Yeats published extracts and analyses of *Tractatus quinque,* Beddoes' being *Chemical Experiments and Opinions. Extracted From a Work Published in the Last Century* (1790) and Yeats's *Observations on the Claims of the Moderns, to Some Discoveries in Chemistry and Physiology* (1798). Among the claims made for Mayow were that in 1674 he already knew the true cause of increased weight in metallic calcination (fixation of nitro-aerial particles = oxygen) and clearly recognized that certain bases are made acid by the addition of nitro-aerial particles (= oxygen, the acidifying principle).[10]

Throughout the nineteenth century and into the early twentieth there was a steady flow of commentary on Mayow and his originality *vis-à-vis* both immediate contemporaries and late-eighteenth-century successors. Several editions of his works were also published. More recently, especially since the publication of T. S. Patterson's long and biting "John Mayow in Contemporary Setting" (1931), Mayow's originality and importance have been considerably debated. Patterson contended that Mayow had been elevated to scientific preeminence by confusion and poor scholarship. In fact, Mayow was a derivative thinker who owed his important ideas to Boyle, Hooke, and Lower, among others. If Mayow contributed anything of his own to the *Tractatus quinque,* it was a penchant for fanciful hypothesizing and a general confusion. Further, according to Patterson, the later resurrection of Mayow as a precursor of Lavoisier was based on misreading and special pleading; Mayow's ideas, closely studied, were fundamentally different from Lavoisier's. Not the least significant difference was that Mayow and Lavoisier wrote in completely different ways about the gaseous state.

A steadily growing body of scholarship has developed since Patterson's article appeared. Working from one perspective, Henry Guerlac and Allen Debus have attempted to trace the alchemical and meteorological roots of Mayow's theories on aerial nitre and the nitrous compounds, and have thus begun to situate his work in a more cogent contemporary context. Partington has taken up Mayow's cause by working from another angle. Both in separately published articles and in long chapters in *A History of Chemistry*, he has vigorously defended Mayow's special talents and insights against Patterson's assault. Other scholars have also contributed important information.

It seems probable that both pro- and anti-Mayow scholars will be vindicated to a certain extent. It is already clear that several of Mayow's ideas had a long history or at least prehistory and that he acquired many notions from the contemporary intellectual environment. It seems equally to be correct that Mayow gave common and contemporary views—especially those popular at Oxford and the Royal Society—unique twists and imaginative interpretations. He was also an ingenious and talented experimenter, whatever his passion for Cartesian hypotheses. With regard to his putative anticipation of Lavoisier, it is well established that Mayow covered many of the basic chemical and physiological phenomena that Lavoisier later interpreted with new theories and improved data. Nonetheless, as Patterson has argued, a certain unbridgeable conceptual gulf separated Mayow's seventeenth-century formulations from Lavoisier's in the eighteenth century, even when they used similar or approximately similar experimental apparatus and materials. But quantumlike theoretical discontinuities within a continuum of experimental and theoretical concern with certain problems are a commonplace in the history of science.

NOTES

1. Bathurst's lectures were published by T. Warton in *The Life and Literary Remains of Ralph Bathurst* (London, 1761). Hooke's discussion of the "dissolution" of combustible bodies by "a substance inherent, and mixt with the Air, that is like, if not the very same, with that which is fixt in *Salt-peter*" is found on pp. 103–105 of the *Micrographia*.
2. J. R. Partington, *A History of Chemistry*, II (London, 1961), 604.
3. Douglas McKie, "Fire and the Flamma Vitalis: Boyle, Hooke and Mayow," in E. Ashworth Underwood, ed., *Science, Medicine and History*, I (Oxford, 1953), 482.
4. Robert Boyle, *Works*, VI (London, 1772), 285.
5. Margaret 'Espinasse, *Robert Hooke* (Berkeley, 1962), 63–65.
6. Theodore M. Brown, "Introduction," *The Posthumous Works of Robert Hooke* (London, 1971), 4–7.
7. McKie, *op. cit.*, pp. 483–484.
8. Partington, *op. cit.*, II, 592, 595.
9. *Ibid.*, p. 595.
10. T. S. Patterson, "John Mayow in Contemporary Setting," in *Isis*, 15 (1931), 49.

BIBLIOGRAPHY

I. Original Works. Mayow's two major publications were both originally published at Oxford but enjoyed several seventeenth-century reissues and special editions. *Tractatus duo* has never been translated as such. *Tractatus quinque*, which includes modified versions of the two 1668 essays, has been translated several times: in a Dutch trans. by Steven Blankaart (Amsterdam, 1683); a German trans. by J. Koellner (Jena, 1799); and an English trans. by A. Crum Brown and L. Dobbin (Edinburgh, 1907). A partial German trans. was published by F. G. Donnan, in Ostwalds Klassiker der exacten Wissenschaften no. 125 (Leipzig, 1901); and a partial French trans. by L. Ledru and H. C. Gaubert was published at Paris in 1840.

Contemporary English reactions to Mayow, with references, have been cited above. A favorable contemporaneous review of *Tractatus quinque* was published in *Journal des sçavans* (3 Feb. 1676).

II. Secondary Literature. There is as yet no detailed, full-length study of Mayow, although it has recently been called for. A number of recent studies are, however, of considerable utility. Principal among them are Walter Böhm, "John Mayow und Descartes," in *Sudhoffs Archiv für Geschichte der Medizin und der Wissenschaften*, 46 (1962), 45–68; "John Mayow and His Contemporaries," in *Ambix*, 11 (1963), 105–120; and "John Mayow und die Geschichte des Verbrennungsexperiments," in *Centaurus*, 11 (1967), 241–258; Allen G. Debus, "The Paracelsian Aerial Niter," in *Isis*, 55 (1964), 43–61; Henry Guerlac, "John Mayow and the Aerial Nitre," in *Actes du septième congrès international d'histoire des sciences* (Jerusalem, 1953), 332–349; and "The Poets' Nitre: Studies in the Chemistry of John Mayow—II," in *Isis*, 45 (1954), 243–255; Diana Long Hall, *From Mayow to Haller: A History of Respiratory Physiology in the Early Eighteenth Century*, unpublished diss. (Yale, 1966); Douglas McKie, "Fire and the Flamma Vitalis: Boyle, Hooke and Mayow," in E. Ashworth Underwood, ed., *Science, Medicine and History*, I (Oxford, 1953), 469–488; J. R. Partington, "The Life and Work of John Mayow," in *Isis*, 47 (1956), 217–230, 405–417; "Some Early Appraisals of the Work of John Mayow," *ibid.*, 50 (1959), 211–226; and *A History of Chemistry*, II (London, 1961), *passim*, but esp. ch. 16; and T. S. Patterson, "John Mayow in Contemporary Setting," in *Isis*, 15 (1931), 47–96, 504–546.

Of considerable help also are John F. Fulton, *A Bibliography of Two Oxford Physiologists: Richard Lower (1631–1691) and John Mayow (1643–1679)* (Oxford, 1935); and Douglas McKie, "John Mayow, 1641–1679," in *Nature*, 148 (1941), 728; and "The Birth and Descent of John Mayow," in *Philosophical Magazine and Journal of Science*, 33 (1942), 51–60.

Additional studies that throw light on Mayow's contemporary context are Hansruedi Isler, *Thomas Willis 1621–1675* (New York, 1968); D. J. Lysaght, "Hooke's Theory of Combustion," in *Ambix*, 1 (1937), 93–108; Alfred Myer and Raymond Hierons, "On Thomas Willis' Concepts of Neurophysiology," in *Medical History*, 9

(1965), 1–15, 142–155; and H. D. Turner, "Robert Hooke and Theories of Combustion," in *Centaurus*, **4** (1955–1956), 297–310.

THEODORE M. BROWN

MAYR (MARIUS), SIMON (*b.* Gunzenhausen, Germany, 20 January 1573; *d.* Ansbach, Germany, 26 December 1624), *astronomy.*

Mayr was the first to mention in print the nebula in Andromeda, to publish tables of the mean periodic motions of the four satellites of Jupiter then known, to direct attention to the variation in their brightness, and to identify the brightest of the four, which are still called by the names he bestowed on them.[1]

After studying at Gunzenhausen and later at the Margrave's School in Heilbronn from 1589 to 1601, he was appointed mathematician of the margrave of Ansbach and was sent to Prague, with a recommendation dated 22 May 1601, to join the staff of Tycho Brahe, the mathematician of Emperor Rudolph II.[2] Arriving toward the end of May, Mayr learned how to use Tycho's observational instruments.[3] He remained less than four months, however, since on 25 September he passed through Znojmo in Moravia, and then Vienna, on his way south.[4]

Deciding to study medicine in Padua, Mayr was admitted to the Association of German Students of the Arts in the University of Padua on 18 December 1601.[5] On that occasion he donated six Venetian lire to the association and in each of the next four years he contributed ten lire. Because the association's proctor was unable to complete his term of office, Mayr replaced him on 5 March 1604. On 27 July Mayr was elected librarian or second counselor, to serve until 14 April 1605. On 1 July 1605 he announced that he had to return home.[6] During this journey he spent the night of 25 July near Donauwörth.[7] The association's official minutes for 24 July record that he had misinformed it about the German law students' attitude toward an impending election.[8] In 1606 Mayr married Felicitas Lauer, daughter of his publisher in Nuremberg. In October 1613 he met Johannes Kepler, Brahe's successor as imperial mathematician, at the Diet held in Regensburg.[9]

Shortly after his arrival in Padua, on 24 December 1601, Mayr had observed a solar eclipse; and on 10 October 1604 he noticed that year's nova while with a pupil who a few years later, on 4 May 1607, was convicted of plagiarizing a work by Galileo.[10] In his published denunciation of the plagiarist, Galileo refrained from mentioning Mayr by name, perhaps to avoid arousing the powerful Association of German Students, but referred to him as an "old adversary," poisonous reptile, and "enemy . . . of all mankind."[11] Sixteen years later, after Galileo had left Padua, in his *Assayer* of 1623 he condemned Mayr's *World of Jupiter* (Nuremberg, 1614, two editions) as itself an outright plagiarism. But Galileo spoiled his case by suggesting that Jupiter's satellites had never been seen by Mayr, whose tables of their mean motions preceded and surpassed Galileo's.[12]

NOTES

1. Pierre Humberd, "Le baptême des satellites de Jupiter," in *Revue des questions scientifiques*, **117** (1940), 171, 175.
2. J. Klug, "Simon Marius . . .," p. 397; E. Zinner, "Zur Ehrenrettung . . .," pp. 25., 66, 70; Johannes Kepler, *Gesammelte Werke*, XIV (Munich, 1946), 168, 170.
3. Zinner, *op. cit.*, pp. 49, 54, 66.
4. *Ibid.*, pp. 59, 60, 61, 70.
5. Antonio Favaro, *Galileo Galilei a Padova*, Contributi alla Storia dell'Università di Padova, V (Padua, 1968), 218, with Mayr's coat of arms on p. 219; repr. of Favaro's *Stemmi ed inscrizioni concernenti personaggi galileiani nella Università di Padova* (Padua, 1893).
6. *Atti della nazione germanica artista nello studio di Padova*, Antonio Favaro, ed., Monumenti Storici Pubblicati dalla R. Deputazione Veneta di Storia Patria, no. 19–20, 1st ser., Documenti, no. 13–14 (Venice, 1911–1912), II, 189, 195, 211, 214, 220, 225, 231, 236.
7. Zinner, *op. cit.*, pp. 60, 72.
8. *Atti*, II, 238, 239.
9. Zinner, *op. cit.*, pp. 63, 71.
10. *Ibid.*, pp. 48, 51; *Le opere di Galileo Galilei*, II (Florence, 1891; repr. 1968), 293, 560.
11. *Ibid.*, 519.
12. *Ibid.*, VI (1896), 215, 217.

BIBLIOGRAPHY

I. ORIGINAL WORKS. Mayr's writings were listed by Ernst Zinner, in "Zur Ehrenrettung des Simon Marius," in *Vierteljahrsschrift der Astronomischen Gesellschaft*, **77** (Leipzig, 1942), 27–32. Mayr's *Mundus Jovialis* was trans. into English by Arthur Octavius Prickard in *Observatory*, **39** (1916), 367–381, 403–412, 443–452, 498–503.

II. SECONDARY LITERATURE. The Dutch Academy of Sciences announced a contest for the best essay submitted by 1 Jan. 1900 on the question whether Galileo was justified in condemning Mayr as a plagiarist. The only entry was submitted by Josef Klug, who published a revised version as "Simon Marius aus Gunzenhausen und Galileo Galilei," in *Abhandlungen der Bayerischen Akademie der Wissenschaften*, Math.-phys. Kl., **22** (1906), 385–526. Klug's attack on Mayr stimulated one of the judges, J. A. C. Oudemans, together with Johannes Bosscha, to defend Mayr in "Galilée et Marius," in *Archives néerlandaises des sciences exactes et naturelles*, 2nd ser., **8** (1903), 115–189. After the publication of Klug's article, the reasons why its original version had been rejected were explained by Bosscha in "Simon Marius, réhabilitation d'un astronome calomnié," in *Archives* *néerlandaises* . . ., 2nd ser., **12** (1907), 258–307, 490–528; G. S. Braddy, "Simon Marius (1570–1624)," in *Journal of the British Astronomical Association,* **81** (1970), 64–65.

See also J. B. J. Delambre, *Histoire de l'astronomie moderne* (New York–London, 1969 [repr. of 1821 ed.]), I, 634, 693–703; Antonio Favaro, "Galileo Galilei e Simone Mayr," in *Bibliotheca mathematica*, 3rd ser., **2** (1901), 220–223; "Galileo and Marius," in *Observatory*, **27** (1904), 199–200; "A proposito di Simone Mayr," in *Atti e memorie dell'Accademia di scienze, lettere ed arti* (Padua), n.s. **34** (1917–1918), 17–19; and *Galileo Galilei e lo studio di Padova*, 2 vols., Contributi alla Storia dell'Università di Padova, nos. 3–4 (Padua, 1966 [repr. of 1883 ed.]), I, 184, 192, 234, 340–347; Siegmund Günther, "Mayr," in *Allgemeine deutsche Biographie*, XXI (Leipzig, 1885; repr. Berlin, 1970), 141–146; J. H. Johnson, "The Discovery of the First Four Satellites of Jupiter," in *Journal of the British Astronomical Association*, **41** (1930–1931), 164–171; William Thynne Lynn, "Simon Marius and the Satellites of Jupiter," in *Observatory*, **26** (1903), 254–256; "Galilée et Marius," *ibid.*, 389–390; "Galileo and Marius," *ibid.*, **27** (1904), 63–64, 200–201; and "Simon Mayr," *ibid.*, **32** (1909), 355–356; Julius Meyer, "Osiander und Marius," in *Jahresbericht des historischen Vereins für Mittelfranken*, **44** (1892), 59–71; Pietro Pagnini, "Galileo and Simon Mayer," trans. by W. P. Henderson, in *Journal of the British Astronomical Association*, **41** (1930–1931), 415–422; and Emil Wohlwill, *Galilei und sein Kampf für die Copernicanische Lehre* (Wiesbaden, 1969 [repr. of 1909–1926 ed.]), II, 343–426.

EDWARD ROSEN

AL-MĀZINĪ. See **Abū Ḥāmid.**

MAZURKIEWICZ, STEFAN (*b.* Warsaw, Poland, 25 September 1888; *d.* Grodžisk Mazowiecki, near Warsaw, 19 June 1945), *mathematics.*

Mazurkiewicz was, with Zygmunt Janiszewski and Wacław Sierpiński, a founder of the contemporary Polish mathematical school and, in 1920, of its journal *Fundamenta mathematicae*, which is devoted to set theory and to related fields, including topology and foundations of mathematics.

The son of a noted lawyer, Mazurkiewicz received his secondary education at the lyceum in Warsaw. He passed his baccalaureate in 1907, studied mathematics at the universities of Cracow, Lvov, Munich, and Göttingen, and was awarded a Ph.D. in 1913 by the University of Lvov for his thesis, done under Sierpiński, on curves filling the square ("O krzywych wypełniajacych kwadrat"). Named professor of mathematics in 1915 at the University of Warsaw, he held this chair until his death. He was several times elected dean of the Faculty of Mathematical and Natural Sciences and, in 1937, prorector of the University of Warsaw. He was a member of the Polish Academy of Sciences and Letters; of the Warsaw Society of Sciences and Letters, which elected him its secretary-general in 1935; of the Polish Mathematical Society, which elected him its president for the years 1933–1935; and member of the editorial boards of *Fundamenta mathematicae* and the *Monografie matematyczne* from their beginnings. His book on the theory of probability was written in Warsaw during the German occupation of Poland. The manuscript was destroyed in 1944 when the Germans burned and destroyed Warsaw before their retreat; it was partly rewritten by Mazurkiewicz and published in Polish eleven years after his death. Gravely ill, Mazurkiewicz shared the lot of the people of Warsaw. He died in the outskirts of the city during an operation for gastric ulcer.

Mazurkiewicz' scientific activity was in two principal areas: topology with its applications to the theory of functions, and the theory of probability. The topology seminar given by him and Janiszewski, beginning in 1916, was probably the world's first in this discipline. He exerted a great influence on the scientific work of his students and collaborators by the range of the ideas and problems in which he was interested, by the inventive spirit with which he treated them, and by the diversity of the methods that he applied to them.

As early as 1913 Mazurkiewicz gave to topology an ingenious characterization of the continuous images of the segment of the straight line, known today as locally connected continua. He based it on the notions of the oscillation of a continuum at a point and on that of relative distance; the latter concept, which he introduced, was shown to be valuable for other purposes. This characterization therefore differs from those established at about the same time by Hans Hahn and by Sierpiński, which were based on other ideas. It is also this characterization that is linked with the Mazurkiewicz-Moore theorem on the arcwise connectedness of continua.

Mazurkiewicz' theorems, according to which every continuous function that transforms a compact linear set into a plane set with interior points takes the same value in at least three distinct points (a theorem established independently by Hahn), while every compact plane set that is devoid of interior point is a binary continuous image, enabled him to define the notion of dimension of compact sets as follows: the dimension of such a set C is at most n when n is the smallest whole number for which there exists a continuous function transforming onto C a nondense compact linear set and taking the same value in at most $n + 1$ distinct points of this set. This definition preceded by more than seven years that of Karl Menger and Pavel Uryson, to which it is equivalent for compact sets.

In a series of later publications Mazurkiewicz contributed considerably to the development of topology by means of solutions to several fundamental problems posed by Sierpiński, Karl Menger, Paul Alexandroff, Pavel Uryson, and others, through which he singularly deepened our knowledge, especially of the topological structure of the Euclidean plane. In solving the problem published by Sierpiński (in *Fundamenta mathematicae*, **2** [1921], 286), he constructed on the plane a closed connected set which is the sum of a denumerable infinity of disjoint closed sets (1924) and which, in addition, has the property that all these summands except one are connected; at the same time he showed (independently of R. L. Moore) that on the plane the connectedness of all the summands in question is impossible, although, according to a result of Sierpiński's, it ought to be possible in space. Mazurkiewicz also solved, affirmatively, Alexandroff's problem (1935) on the existence of an indecomposable continuum (that is, one which is the sum of not fewer than $2^{\aleph_0}$ subcontinua different from itself) in every continuum of more than one dimension; that of Menger (1929) on the existence, for every positive integer n, of weakly n-dimensional sets; and that of Uryson (1927) on the existence, for every integer $n > 1$, of separable complete n-dimensional spaces devoid of connected subsets containing more than one point. He also showed (1929) that if R is a region in n-dimensional Euclidean space and E is a set of $n - 2$ dimensions, then the difference $R - E$ is always connected and is even a semicontinuum.

Mazurkiewicz also contributed important results concerning the topological structure of curves, in particular concerning that of indecomposable continua, as well as an ingenious demonstration, by use of the Baire category method, that the family of hereditarily indecomposable continua of the plane, and therefore that the continua of less paradoxical structure occur in it only exceptionally (1930).

By applying the same method to the problems of the theory of functions, Mazurkiewicz showed (1931) that the set of periodic continuous functions f, for which the integral $\int_0^1 t^{-1}f(x + t) + f(x - t) - 2f(x)dt$ diverges everywhere, is of the second Baire category in the space of all continuous real functions, and that the same is true with the set of continuous functions which are nowhere differentiable. In addition he provided

the quite remarkable result that the set of continuous functions transforming the segment of the straight line into plane sets which contains Sierpiński's universal plane curve (universality here designating the presence of homeomorphic images of every plane curve) is also of the second Baire category. Among Mazurkiewicz' other results on functions are those concerning functional spaces and the sets in those spaces that are called projective (1936, 1937), as well as those regarding the set of singular points of an analytic function and the classical theorems of Eugène Roché, Julius Pál, and Michael Fekete.

In the theory of probability, Mazurkiewicz formulated and demonstrated, in a work published in Polish (1922), the strong law of large numbers (independently of Francesco Cantelli); established several axiom systems of this theory (1933, 1934); and constructed a universal separable space of random variables by suitably enlarging that of the random variables of the game of heads or tails to a complete space (1935). These results and many others were included and developed in his book on the theory of probability.

BIBLIOGRAPHY

I. ORIGINAL WORKS. Among the 130 of Mazurkiewicz' mathematical publications listed in *Fundamenta mathematicae*, **34** (1947), 326–331, the most important are "Sur les points multiples des courbes qui remplissent une aire plane," in *Prace matematyczno-fizyczne*, **26** (1915), 113–120; "Teoria zbiorów G_δ" ("Theory of G_δ Sets"), in *Wektor*, **7** (1918), 1–57; "O pewnej nowej formie uogólnienia twierdzenia Bernoulli'ego" ("On a New Generalization of Bernoulli's Theorem"), in *Wiadomości aktuarjalne*, **1** (1922), 1–8; "Sur les continus homogènes," in *Fundamenta mathematicae*, **5** (1924), 137–146; "Sur les continus plans non bornés," *ibid.*, 188–205; "Sur les continus absolument indécomposables," *ibid.*, **16** (1930), 151–159; "Sur le théorème de Rouché," in *Comptes rendus de la Société des sciences et des lettres de Varsovie*, **28** (1936), 78, 79; and "Sur les transformations continues des courbes," in *Fundamenta mathematicae*, **31** (1938), 247–258. See also the posthumous works *Podstawy rachunku prawdopodobieństwa* ("Foundations of the Calculus of Probability"), J. Łoś, ed., *Monografie Matematyczne*, no. 32 (Warsaw, 1956); and *Travaux de topologie et ses applications* (Warsaw, 1969), with a complete bibliography of Mazurkiewicz' 141 scientific publications.

II. SECONDARY LITERATURE. See P. S. Alexandroff, "Sur quelques manifestations de la collaboration entre les écoles mathématiques polonaise et soviétique dans le domaine de topologie et théorie des ensembles," in *Roczniki Polskiego towarzystwa matematycznego*, 2nd ser., *Wiadomości matematyczne*, **6** (1963), 175–180, a lecture delivered at the Polish Mathematical Society, Warsaw, 18 May 1962; and

C. Kuratowski, "Stefan Mazurkiewicz et son oeuvre scientifique," in *Fundamenta mathematicae*, **34** (1947), 316–331, repr. in S. Mazurkiewicz, *Travaux de topologie et ses applications* (Warsaw, 1969), pp. 9–26.

B. KNASTER

MÉCHAIN, PIERRE-FRANÇOIS-ANDRÉ (*b.* Laon, Aisne, France, 16 August 1744; *d.* Castellón de la Plana, Spain, 20 September 1804), *geodesy, astronomy*.

Méchain was the son of Pierre-François Méchain, a master ceiling plasterer of modest means, and Marie-Marguerite Roze. Young Méchain's mathematical ability attracted the attention of various local notables, who advised sending him to the École des Ponts et Chaussées in Paris. Lack of financial resources interrupted his studies there and he accepted a tutorship for two young noblemen about thirty miles from Paris.

In some fashion Méchain came into communication with Lalande, who sent him the proofs of the new second edition of his *Astronomie*. Filled with enthusiasm, Méchain made such rapid progress in this study that in 1772 Lalande procured for him a position as hydrographer at the naval map archives (Depôt de la Marine) in Versailles. The archives were then a seat of political patronage and intrigue, and, caught in the political crosscurrents, Méchain twice lost his job; but each time he was reinstated because of his competence as a map-maker. The archives were soon transferred to Paris, and there he drew up the maps for the shoreline from Nieuwpoort in Flanders to Saint-Malo. In 1777 Méchain married Thérèse Marjou, whom he met while working in Versailles; they had a daughter and two sons.

Beginning in 1780 he determined the network of fundamental points for large military maps of Germany and northern Italy.

Meanwhile Méchain was also active as an astronomical observer, his early efforts being crowned in 1781 with the discovery of not one but two comets. He calculated the orbits for both, and in the following year he calculated orbits for the comets of 1532 and 1661, proving, contrary to general expectation, that they were not the same. This research won both the 1782 prize of the Académie Royale des Sciences and admission to its ranks. Encouraged by these successes, Méchain threw himself into observing with still greater zeal, and ultimately discovered nine more comets, including the remarkable short-period one now named after Encke. He calculated the orbits for all of these, as well as thirteen found by other observers. In addition he found many nebulae, which were incorporated by Charles Messier into his famous catalogue of clusters and nebulae. In 1785 he became editor of the French national almanac, *Connoissance des temps*, and he prepared the seven volumes for 1788 to 1794.

In 1787 a joint Anglo-French project undertook the triangulation between the Greenwich and Paris observatories. Méchain was chosen as one of the French commissioners, along with Legendre and J.-D. Cassini. Both countries engaged in a friendly rivalry to produce new and more accurate measuring instruments. In France, Borda developed the principle of the *cercle répétiteur*, or repeating transit, in which after the first set of readings, the circle was clamped with the telescope and moved back to the original line of sight. In this way the angles could be measured against different segments of the circle, thus averaging out graduation errors. The commissioners systematically tested Borda's device, with Méchain using the older equipment; the tests demonstrated the great superiority of this new circle.

In 1790 the National Assembly approved an Academy proposal to establish a decimal system of measures, and Méchain and Delambre were designated to carry out the fundamental geodetic measurements for a new unit of length. This unit, the meter, was intended to be one ten-millionth part of the distance from the terrestrial pole to the equator, and it was to be based on an extended survey from Dunkerque to Barcelona. Méchain was assigned the shorter but more difficult southern zone, the previously unsurveyed region across the Pyrenees.

The new repeating transit became the fundamental instrument of the survey, but not until June 1792 was the new equipment, including parabolic mirrors for reflecting signals, ready. By this time the Revolution was engulfing France and the monarchy was tottering; Méchain with his suspicious array of instruments was arrested at Essonnes just south of Paris as a potential counterrevolutionary. Only with much difficulty was he located and released two months later, so that he could continue his journey to Spain. In September and October he swiftly carried out the triangulation between Perpignan and Barcelona. During the winter of 1792–1793 he undertook the astronomical observations to establish the latitude of Barcelona, almost at the southernmost limit of the meridian. At the same time he investigated the possibility of extending the meridian $2\frac{1}{2}°$ southward to the Balearic Islands. Otherwise, only a few weeks of work remained to complete the network across the frontier.

His plans were abruptly interrupted at the beginning of spring in 1793 when, invited by a friend to inspect a new hydraulic pump in the outskirts of Barcelona, he was involved in an accident. While trying to start the machine, the friend and an assistant were caught in the mechanism. Méchain, rushing to aid them, was struck by a lever that knocked him violently against the wall, breaking some ribs and a collarbone. He was unconscious for three days and afterward was forced to remain completely immobile for two months. By June he still did not have the use of his right arm; but, undeterred, he used his left hand to make the solar observations at the summer solstice.

During Méchain's convalescence, open war had broken out between Spain and France, and he was denied a passport to return home. Profiting from his captivity, he determined the latitude of Montjouy, just south of Barcelona, and surveyed the triangle connecting these points. He then noticed a 3″ discrepancy in the latitude previously obtained for Barcelona. Anguished by his failure to find the cause, and blaming himself for the error, he kept the discrepancy a carefully guarded secret. In the remaining years of his life he became a driven and tormented man, whose behavior was mysterious and inexplicable to his colleagues. Delambre, who found out the secret only when he inherited the notes, intimated that Méchain simply put too much trust in the precision of the repeating transit.

Eventually Méchain obtained a passport for Italy, and he managed to reach Genoa in September 1794. Saddened by the guillotining of several of his colleagues and in poor health, he delayed his return to France, not embarking for Marseilles until the following year. After additional hesitation he journeyed to the vicinity of Perpignan and in September 1795 resumed the triangulation. Méchain slowly continued his work through 1796 and 1797. Meanwhile, after a fifteen-month suspension for political reasons, Delambre proceeded with measurements of the northern part of the network and in April 1798 he invited Méchain to join him in linking the sections. Méchain remained incommunicado, and Delambre finally sought him out in Carcassonne. Méchain expressed a stubborn desire, inexplicable to Delambre, to return to Spain for further latitude determinations. Faced with the choice of returning to Paris and the warm welcome of his colleagues, or remaining forever an expatriate, Méchain reluctantly came back to Paris. There he was less than cooperative in presenting his observations to the commissioners charged with setting up the decimal metric system.

In Paris he was made director of the observatory, considered a just and tranquil reward for an astronomer who had labored so faithfully without a real astronomical position. But to Méchain nothing was

right, and in a remarkable letter to Franz von Zach he aired his complaints publicly (*Monatliche Correspondenz*, 2 [1800], 290–302). Always he yearned to return to Spain; and eventually the Bureau of Longitudes approved the extension of the meridian to the Balearic Islands, a project that would render his imperfect latitude of Barcelona unnecessary. The Bureau, believing that Méchain's abilities were best employed as director of the observatory, appointed another astronomer to extend the meridian, but to their surprise Méchain insisted on doing it himself.

The expedition left Paris on 26 April 1803, but encountered unexpected delays in Spain. When the ship at last departed for the islands, an epidemic of yellow fever broke out on board. Méchain eventually reached Ibiza, but he discovered that his mainland station at Montsia could not be sighted from the island. Thus he was obliged to change the pattern of triangles and survey a greater distance southward in the mountains along the Spanish coast. Exhausted by the work and further weakened by fever and a poor diet, he collapsed and died on 20 September 1804. Several years later the extension of the meridian was completed by Biot and Arago.

BIBLIOGRAPHY

I. ORIGINAL WORKS. Méchain's bibliography is found in J. M. Quérard, *La France littéraire*, V (Paris, 1830), 10–11, which along with several biographical encyclopedias, gives his death erroneously as 1805. Méchain's most important work was edited in three volumes by J. B. Delambre, *Base du système métrique décimal, ou Mesure de l'arc du méridien compris entre les parallèles de Dunkerque et Barcelone, exécutée en 1792 et années suivantes, par MM. Méchain et Delambre* (Paris, 1806–1810).

Many of Méchain's MSS are preserved at the Paris observatory; they are catalogued as C6.6–7 and E2.1–21 in G. Bigourdan, "Inventaire des manuscrits," in *Annales de l'observatoire de Paris. Mémoires*, 21 (Paris, 1895), 1–60. See also his "La prolongation de la méridienne de Paris, de Barcelone aux Baléares, d'après les correspondances inédites de Méchain, de Biot et d'Arago," in *Bulletin astronomique*, 17 (Paris, 1900), 348–368, 390–400, 467–480.

II. SECONDARY LITERATURE. J. B. Delambre's florid "Notice," in *Mémoires de l'Institut des sciences, lettres et arts, sciences mathématiques et physiques*, 6 (Paris, 1806), 1–28, was written before he knew why Méchain desired so ardently to return to Spain; for the earlier biography he refers the reader to Franz von Zach, "Pierre-François-André Méchain," in *Monatliche Correspondenz*, 2 (Gotha, 1800), 96–120. More balanced accounts by Delambre are in *Histoire de l'astronomie au dix-huitième siècle* (Paris, 1827), 755–767, and in Michaud's *Biographie universelle ancienne et moderne*, XXVII (Paris, after 1815), 454–458.

See also Delambre's *Grandeur et figure de la terre*, G. Bigourdan, ed. (Paris, 1912).

An excellent modern account with new material is by Joseph Laissus, "Un astronome Français en Espagne: Pierre-François-André Méchain (1744–1804)," in *Comptes rendus 94ᵉ Congrès national des sociétés savantes, Pau, 1969, sciences*, **1** (Paris, 1970), 37–59.

OWEN GINGERICH

MECHNIKOV. See **Metchnikoff.**

MECKEL, JOHANN FRIEDRICH (*b.* Halle, Germany, 13 October 1781; *d.* Halle, 31 October 1833), *anatomy, embryology, comparative anatomy*.

Belonging to the third generation of an illustrious family of physicians, Meckel was one of the greatest anatomists of his time. His painstaking observations in comparative and pathological anatomy furnished a wealth of new knowledge, which Meckel attempted to organize along certain evolutionary schemes popular in his day.

Although influenced by the contemporary ideas of *Naturphilosophie*, Meckel rejected pure speculation and stressed instead the acquisition of empirical data from which certain useful conclusions could be derived. Among his most lasting and impressive contributions was the study of the abnormalities occurring during the embryological development. Hence, Meckel's teratology was the first comprehensive description of birth defects, a detailed and sober analysis of a topic which had hitherto been approached with a great deal of fantasy and moral bias.

Meckel's grandfather, Johann Friedrich the Elder (1714–1774), had been one of Haller's most brilliant disciples, an anatomist endowed with great powers of observation and notable skill in the preparation of anatomical specimens. In turn Meckel's father, Phillip Friedrich (1755–1803), was a famous surgeon and obstetrician in Halle, where he taught for twenty-six years.

Young Meckel spent his student years between 1798 and 1801 in Halle, then a bastion of academic freedom and objective scientific inquiry. Among his teachers were Kurt Sprengel, famous for his botanical and historical studies, and, above all, his mentor Johann C. Reil, who inspired Meckel's studies in cerebral anatomy and was the true leader of the local medical school.

After studying anatomy under the direction of his father—he apparently detested the discipline in the beginning—Meckel transferred in 1801 to the University of Göttingen. There he studied comparative anatomy with the famous physician and anthropologist Blumenbach. His subsequent doctoral dissertation, defended at Halle in 1802, dealt with the subject of cardiac malfunctions. Meckel expanded the topic and eventually published it as an article in Reil's journal, the *Archiv für die Physiologie*.

Following his graduation Meckel visited Würzburg, then a stronghold of Schelling's philosophy of nature, and Vienna, where he met Johann P. Frank. In 1803 Meckel temporarily interrupted his travels, returning to Halle at his father's death. Thereafter he went to Paris where he met and worked with Georges Cuvier, Étienne Geoffroy Saint-Hilaire, and Alexander von Humboldt. Together with Cuvier, Meckel systematically analyzed the immense anatomical collection located at the Jardin des Plantes. The available material, sent back from Napoleon's campaigns abroad, was described by Cuvier in his *Leçons d'anatomie comparée*. Meckel translated Cuvier's five-volume work into German, a task which he completed in 1810.

Meckel returned to his native Halle in 1806 under tragic circumstances. The Napoleonic forces had occupied the city and dissolved the local university. Napoleon used Meckel's own home as temporary headquarters, an intrusion which may have aided in preserving the valuable anatomical collection of the Meckel family.

When the newly organized University of Halle opened its doors in May 1808, Meckel was appointed professor of normal and pathological anatomy, surgery, and obstetrics. He was at Halle until his death and set a harsh working schedule for himself. He gradually withdrew from social activities and grew bitter in the face of the academic mediocrity surrounding him. Furthermore, Meckel was impatient with the bureaucratic fetters imposed by the Prussian government, which treated Halle as a secondary and provincial city compared to the capital, Berlin.

Meckel's scientific aim was to arrive at an understanding of the great variety of organic forms. Such knowledge would, he hoped, reveal the uniformity of nature and expose its general laws. Meckel sought fundamental types amid the multiplicity of organisms, and accepted the idea that each higher evolutionary product must have traversed all the lower stages of development before achieving its position.

Moreover, Meckel adopted an Aristotelian position by clearly distinguishing between matter and form, the latter being provided by the *Lebenskraft*. His morphological studies were, therefore, geared to discovering the fundamental laws regulating the formation of the various organic categories. Meckel was interested in malformations because structural aberrations were the result of normal actions attributable to the vital force, which he tried to understand.

Meckel achieved such insights through exhaustive observations rather than arm-chair philosophy— witness his three-volume *Handbuch der pathologischen Anatomie* (1812–1816) and six-volume *System der vergleichenden Anatomie* (1821–1831). Among Meckel's discoveries was the diverticulum—which now carries his name—in the distal small bowel, a vestige between the intestinal tract and the yolk sac.

In 1815 Meckel became the editor of Reil's journal, then known as *Deutsches Archiv für die Physiologie*, which listed among its distinguished collaborators Autenrieth, Blumenbach, Döllinger, Kielmeyer, Sprengel, and others. Meckel wrote a preface to the first volume stressing that only articles based on observations and experiments would be printed. He hoped that such an approach would gradually prevail in German science in order to obviate the ridicule incurred by speculation. But Meckel also decried mindless experimentation.

Meckel emphasized the need for work in comparative anatomy and embryology. An early article concerned the development of the central nervous system in mammals, a study followed by new observations related to the evolution of the gut, heart, and lungs. Interspersed with these careful monographs were numerous shorter articles. They covered subject matters as varied as the generation of earthworms, bleeding diatheses, development of human teeth, and the cerebral anatomy of birds.

From 1826 until his death, Meckel was the editor of the *Archiv für Anatomie und Physiologie*, a continuation of the previous publication. His last articles dealt to a considerable degree with malformations as well as with vascular and pulmonary development.

Meckel's adherence to a *Lebenskraft* or vital force and denial of mechanical factors in embryological development were strongly disputed by successors who viewed life in strict physicochemical terms. Although his interpretations rapidly became obsolete, Meckel's material remained an extremely valuable source for those interested in comparative anatomy and in congenital malformations.

BIBLIOGRAPHY

I. ORIGINAL WORKS. A complete bibliography of Meckel's works, prepared in a chronological order, is in Beneke (see below), pp. 155–159. Meckel's work on comparative anatomy is contained in his *Beyträge zur vergleichenden Anatomie*, 2 vols. (Leipzig, 1808–1812), and the more extensive publication, *System der vergleichenden Anatomie*, 6 vols. (Halle, 1821–1831). He also published a large number of articles which can be found in the *Deutsches Archiv für die Physiologie*, 1–8 (1815–1823) and the *Archiv für Anatomie und Physiologie*, 1–6 (1826–1832).

Among those works of Meckel available in English is the *Manual of General Anatomy*, translated from a French version by A. S. Doane (London, 1837), and the *Manual of Descriptive and Pathological Anatomy*, also from the French by the same English translator, 2 vols. (London, 1838).

II. SECONDARY LITERATURE. The only extensive biography of Meckel is Rudolf Beneke, *Johann Friedrich Meckel der Jüngere* (Halle, 1934). Shorter notices appeared in the *Medicinische Wochenschrift für Hamburg*, 1 (1833), as well as in August Hirsch's *Biographisches Lexikon*, 2nd ed., IV (Munich, 1932), 145–146. A recent article reviewing Meckel's interest in birth defects is Owen E. Clark, "The Contributions of J. F. Meckel, the Younger, to the Science of Teratology," in *Journal of the History of Medicine and Allied Sciences*, 24 (1969), 310–322. A short description of the genealogy of the Meckel family and the collection of their skulls is contained in H. Schierhorn and R. Schmidt, "Beitrag zur Genealogie und Kraniologie der Familie Meckel," in *Verhandlungen der anatomischen Gesellschaft Jena*, 63 (1969), 591–599. The conceptual background for the contemporary German interest in embryology is given by Owsei Temkin, "German Concepts of Ontogeny and History Around 1800," in *Bulletin of the History of Medicine*, 24 (1950), 227–246.

GUENTER B. RISSE

MEDICUS, FRIEDRICH CASIMIR (Medikus, Friedrich Kasimir) (*b.* Grumbach, Rhineland, Germany, 6 January 1736; *d.* Mannheim, Germany, 15 July 1808), *botany.*

Medicus was the most prolific, bitter, witty, and sarcastic of those contemporary opponents of Linnaeus who ignored or assailed his innovations. Apart from invective and references to Linnaeus' shortcomings, errors, and inconsistencies, Medicus' numerous works contain many firsthand botanical observations, particularly on *Leguminosae, Cruciferae, Malvaceae,* and *Rosaceae,* and are of both historical and nomenclatural importance.

After studying medicine at the universities of Tübingen, Strasbourg, and Heidelberg, in 1759 he became garrison doctor at Mannheim, in the Palatinate (Pfalz), then ruled by the Elector Carl Theodor. The latter founded in 1763 the Academia Theodoro-Palatina of Mannheim and in 1766 an associated botanic garden at Medicus' instigation. In 1766 Medicus spent five months on sick leave in Paris, becoming friendly with the botanists Duhamel du

Monceau, Bernard de Jussieu, and Adanson, all of whom favored the generic concepts and nomenclature of Tournefort rather than those of Linnaeus, his successor. Returning to Mannheim, Medicus abandoned medicine for botany and became director of the Mannheim botanic garden. In his many publications based on the study of living plants, he thereafter never lost an opportunity to criticize the works and character of Linnaeus. He angrily called attention to a basic practical weakness of Linnaeus' generic descriptions: being originally based on the study of one or two species, they often failed to cover adequately other species later added by Linnaeus to the genus by virtue of similarity in habit rather than technical details. He restored many Tournefortian genera and rejected many Linnaean generic names.

It is uncertain how widely his works, written mostly in German rather than Latin, were read at the time. He undoubtedly greatly influenced Conrad Moench at Marburg, whose relatively well-known *Methodus plantas horti botanici et agri Marburgensis* (1794–1802) brought the same Tournefortian concepts and names to more general notice, although their valid post-Linnaean publication dates from Miller's *Gardeners Dictionary Abridged* of 1754. Unfortunately, both the Mannheim academy and garden, to which Medicus had given so much attention, suffered almost irreparable damage when Mannheim was heavily bombarded in 1795 and 1799. The academy was closed, its books sold, and the garden did not long outlast the death of Medicus in 1808.

BIBLIOGRAPHY

I. ORIGINAL WORKS. Medicus was a prolific and combative writer. G. Pritzel, *Thesaurus litterature botanicae* (Leipzig, 1872), 211, lists 16 publications, of which the most notable are *Theodora speciosa* (Mannheim, 1786); "Versuch einer neuen Lehrart der Pflanzen," in *Vorlesungen der churpfälzischen physikalisch-ökonomischen Gesellschaft*, **2** (1787), 327–460; *Philosophische Botanik*, 2 vols. (Mannheim, 1789–1791); *Pflanzengattungen* (Mannheim, 1792); *Geschichte der Botanik unserer Zeiten* (Mannheim, 1793); and *Beyträge zur Pflanzen-Anatomie* (Leipzig, 1799–1801).

II. SECONDARY LITERATURE. See (listed in chronological order) A. Kistner, *Die Pflege der Naturwissenschaften in Mannheim zur Zeit Karl Theodors* (Mannheim, 1930); G. Schmid, "Linné im Urteil Johann Beckmanns, mit besonderer Bezeihung auf F. C. Medicus," in *Svenska linnésällskapets årsskrift*, **20** (1937), 47–70; W. T. Stearn, "Botanical gardens and botanical literature in the eighteenth century," in Rachel Hunt, *Catalogue of Botanical Books . . .*, II (Pittsburgh, 1961), xli–cxl; and "Early Marburg Botany," in Conrad Moench, *Methodus plantas*

horti . . ., Otto Koeltz, ed. (Koenigstein–Taunus, 1966), xi–xv; and F. A. Stafleu, *Linnaeus and the Linnaeans* (Utrecht, 1971), 260–265.

WILLIAM T. STEARN

MEDINA, PEDRO DE (*b*. Seville [?], Spain, 1493; *d*. Seville, 1576), *cosmography*, *navigation*.

Little is known about the life of Medina, who wrote both literary and navigational works during Spain's golden age. He was a cleric, and may have graduated from the University of Seville. It is certain that for part of his career he was librarian to the duke of Medina-Sidonia, for whom he composed a family chronicle that was published in 1561. His other philosophical and historical works date from the same period of his life.

Medina was also a teacher of mathematics and a founder of marine science. King Charles I gave him a warrant (dated Toledo, 20 December 1538) to draw charts and prepare pilot books and other devices necessary to navigation to the Indies. In 1549 he was named "cosmógrafo de honor." In addition to charts and sailing directions, Medina made astrolabes, quadrants, mariner's compasses, forestaffs, and other navigational instruments; it is possible that he himself performed some actual practical navigation.

Medina's first navigational book was the *Arte de navegar*, which is supposed to have inspired Bernardino Baldi's great didactic poem "Nautica." Medina's work contains two fundamental errors, however, in that he failed to recognize the exactness of the plane chart (Mercator's projection of the world was made in 1569) and posited the constancy of the magnetic declination (although his sailing directions do take account of the variation of the magnetic pole).

Medina further became active in the professional argument between cosmographers and pilots, maintaining that the existing instructions for the determination of altitude and use of the mariner's compass prepared by the Seville school of cosmographers contained a number of serious errors. His "Suma de Cosmografía" was never published; it is preserved in the Biblioteca Capitular Colombina in Seville, and contains material on astrology, philosophy, and navigation.

BIBLIOGRAPHY

I. ORIGINAL WORKS. Medina's literary works include *Libro de verdad* (Valladolid, 1545; repr. Málaga, 1620); *Libro de las grandezas y cosas memorables de España* (Seville, 1548 and 1549; repr. Alcalá de Henares, 1566);

and *Crónica breve de España* (Seville, 1548), which was commissioned by Queen Isabella I before her death in 1504.

His navigational writings comprise *El arte de navegar* (Seville–Valladolid, 1545; Seville, 1548), with trans. into German, French, English, and Italian; *Tabulae Hispaniae geographica* (Seville, 1560); "Suma de Cosmografia," an unpublished work of 1561 (MS in Biblioteca Capitular Colombina, Seville); and *Regimiento de navegación* (Seville, 1563).

II. SECONDARY LITERATURE. On Medina and his work, see *Diccionario Enciclopédico Hispano-Americano*, XII (Barcelona, 1893), 692-693. See also Angel Gonzalez Palencia, *La primera guia de la España Imperial* (Madrid, 1940); Rafael Pardo de Figueroa, *Pedro de Medina y su "Libro de las Grandezas"* (Madrid, 1927); *Regimiento de navegación de Pedro de Medina 1563* (Cadiz, 1867); Martin Fernandez de Navarrete, *Biblioteca marítima española* (Madrid, 1851); and *Dissertación sobre la historia de la naútica* (Madrid, 1846).

J. M. LÓPEZ DE AZCONA

MEEK, FIELDING BRADFORD (*b.* Madison, Indiana, 10 December 1817; *d.* Washington, D. C., 21 December 1876), *paleontology, geology*.

Meek was an exceptionally able paleontologist who made substantial pioneering contributions to knowledge of extinct faunas and stratigraphic geology. Little is known of his early life in Indiana and Kentucky, except that frail health and the early death of his father rendered his childhood and young adulthood difficult. As a youth he devoted most of his time to the study of natural history. He failed in business, partly because of his preoccupation with fossils, and supported himself as a portrait painter. His first work in geology was as an assistant to D. D. Owen in 1848 and 1849.

From 1852 until 1858 he served as an assistant to James Hall, paleontologist of New York, at Albany. During this interval he worked two summers for the Geological Survey of Missouri and spent the summer of 1853 exploring, with F. V. Hayden, the Badlands of South Dakota and surrounding areas. Accounts and letters indicate that throughout this time Hall tyrannized and exploited his modest and retiring assistant.

In 1857 Meek first recognized the occurrence of Permian fossils in North America. Unfortunately, he became involved in a bitter controversy concerning the priority of this discovery. He also felt, probably justifiably, that Hall was claiming credit for other significant age determinations that he had made.

In 1858 Meek left Albany and became the first full-time paleontologist associated with the Smithsonian Institution. Although he received no salary, Joseph Henry permitted him to live in the south tower of the Smithsonian building. Progressive deafness and continued poor health combined to limit his professional contacts.

Despite his physical handicaps, Meek completed a prodigious quantity of descriptions of invertebrate fossils and probably ranks only behind Hall and C. D. Walcott in sheer volume of published pages. Although many works were published jointly with his associate Hayden or with A. H. Worthen of the Illinois Geological Survey, it is likely that almost all of this work, including many plates of illustrations, was done entirely by Meek. Meek also published for the Ohio and California Geological Surveys.

Meek's principal contributions may be divided into three parts. The first, begun while he was still at Albany, included descriptions and interpretations of fossils collected by Hayden before the Civil War and laid the groundwork for stratigraphic and age interpretations of rocks of the Great Plains. The second part comprised his descriptions of the Paleozoic fossils of Illinois, especially those of Mississippian and Pennsylvanian age. His third great body of work relates to the U. S. Geological and Geographical Survey of the Territories, with which his name is closely associated, although he was never formally employed by it. He is particularly noted for investigations of freshwater faunas at the Mesozoic-Cenozoic boundary.

Meek described invertebrate fossils of almost every phylum from all geologic periods, from Cambrian to Tertiary and over a wide area. His descriptions and observations on fossils are still valid; and his geologic interpretations, based on these fossils, have contributed materially to a better understanding of the geology of about half of the United States.

BIBLIOGRAPHY

I. ORIGINAL WORKS. Meek's bibliography (see below) contains 106 titles, some of which were written with F. V. Hayden or A. H. Worthen. Following the conventional practice of the times, a number of these are merely preliminary accounts of fossil descriptions, but they are more than balanced by his massive contributions to the Geological Survey of Illinois and to the U.S. Geological and Geographical Survey.

II. SECONDARY LITERATURE. C. A. White, in *American Geologist*, **18** (1896), 337–350, gives a brief account of Meek's life based in part on a memorial of 1877. This work and a similar shorter version for *Biographical Memoirs. National Academy of Sciences* (1902), 77–91, include a bibliography of Meek's works. G. P. Merrill, *Contributions to the History of American Geology*, U.S.

National Museum Annual Report for 1904 (Washington, 1906), provides some additional material on his relations with Hall and priority in scientific discovery.

ELLIS L. YOCHELSON

MEGGERS, WILLIAM FREDERICK (*b*. Clintonville, Wisconsin, 13 July 1888; *d*. Washington, D. C., 19 November 1966), *physics*.

Meggers was reared on a farm near Clintonville, Wisconsin, to which his parents, John Meggers and the former Bertha Bork, had emigrated from Pomerania in 1872. A self-made man who placed a high value on education, he supported himself while attending Ripon College (1910), largely by playing a trombone in a dance orchestra, and earned his doctorate at Johns Hopkins University (1917).

Inspired by Bohr's classical work "On the Constitution of Atoms and Molecules," he chose spectroscopy as his lifework. After serving as assistant in the new spectroscopy section at the U.S. Bureau of Standards, he became chief of the section in 1919, a post he held until 1958.

His achievements provide a lasting contribution to our knowledge of atomic structure. He was an expert in observing, measuring, and interpreting optical spectra. From intricate spectra he deciphered the quantum structure of many atoms and ions: energy levels, terms, quantum numbers, and configurations. He worked on some fifty spectra of about thirty elements—a unique record. His generosity in sharing his splendid line lists with co-workers was outstanding.

Meggers' name will always be associated with standard wavelengths of light. For almost a decade he was president of the Commission of the International Astronomical Union, which was responsible for recommending international standards. The first such standards, dating from 1910, were interferometric measurements of lines observed with an iron arc as source.

He developed an electrodeless ^{198}Hg lamp, which he hoped would be accepted as the source for the primary standard of length, but it was not adopted. In 1958, however, he reported the first interferometric wavelength measurement, by using radiation emitted from an electrodeless thorium halide lamp. Some five hundred thorium wavelengths now supersede the early iron standards, with at least a tenfold increase in accuracy.

A pioneer in spectrochemistry, Meggers fully realized the value of utilizing laboratory spectra for identification and quantitative analysis of commercial substances. To this end he instituted an extensive program in which the spectra of seventy metallic elements were observed under standardized conditions, and the relative intensities of some 39,000 spectral lines were determined to provide requisite data for quantitative work.

He was an excellent photographer and was a member of the Bureau orchestra in the early days. He had valuable coin and stamp collections, which he left to the American Institute of Physics to establish a foundation for training students in science.

He served also on many important committees and received many high honors. It has been truly said that "all of these are trivial compared to the esteem and admiration of his colleagues" [P. D. Foote]. Meggers was content to spend hours at a comparator measuring wavelengths of spectral lines. From these patiently accumulated, reliable data he solved many intricate problems on atomic structure, which to him was an abundant reward for his years of painstaking effort.

His zest for knowledge took other turns. He invested heavily in many collections, ranging from buttons to light bulbs to phonographs, with the belief that they had educational value. They were housed in the "Meggers Museum of Science and Technology," located over his garage, and he and his friends spent pleasant evenings in this museum enjoying travelogues illustrated by the splendid color slides he accumulated on his extensive travels, or listening to favorite records played on the large "Regina" music box. On 13 July 1920 Meggers married Edith (Marie) Raddant; they had two sons and a daughter.

BIBLIOGRAPHY

A complete bibliography of Meggers' writings is included in Paul D. Foote's biographical memoir; see *Biographical Memoirs. National Academy of Sciences*, **41** (1970), 319–340. His most important writings include "Measurements on the Index of Refraction of Air for Wavelengths From 2218 Å to 9000 Å," in *Scientific Papers of the United States Bureau of Standards*, **14** (1918), 697–740, with C. G. Peters; "Solar and Terrestrial Absorption in the Sun's Spectrum From 6500 Å to 9000 Å," in *Publications of the Allegheny Observatory, University of Pittsburgh*, **6**, no. 3 (1919), 13–44; "Interference Measurements in the Spectra of Argon, Krypton, and Xenon," in *Scientific Papers of the National Bureau of Standards*, **17** (1921), 193–202; "Standard Solar Wavelengths (3592–7148 Å)," in *Journal of Research of the National Bureau of Standards*, **1** (1928), 297–317, with K. Burns and C. C. Kiess; "Infrared Arc Spectra Photographed with Xenocyanine," in *Journal of Research of the National Bureau of Standards*, **9** (1932), 309–326, with C. C. Kiess; "Term Analysis of the First Spectrum of Vanadium," in *Journal of Research of the National Bureau of Standards*, **17** (1936), 125–192, with H. N. Russell;

Index to the Literature on Spectrochemical Analysis 1920–1939, (Philadelphia, 1941), with B. F. Scribner; "Spectroscopy, Past, Present, and Future," in *Journal of the Optical Society of America,* **36** (1946), 431–448; "Dr. W. F. Meggers, Ives Medalist for 1947," in *Journal of the Optical Society of America,* **38,** no. 1 (1948), 1–6; "Zeeman Effect," in *Encyclopaedia Britannica,* XXIII; "Wavelengths From Thorium-Halide Lamps," in *Journal of Research of the National Bureau of Standards,* **61,** no. 2 (1958), 95–103, with Robert W. Stanley; "Table of Wavenumbers," in *National Bureau of Standards Monographs,* **3** (1960), with Charles DeWitt Coleman and William R. Bozman; "Tables of Spectral-Line Intensities," *ibid.,* **32** (1961), with Charles H. Corliss and Bourdon F. Scribner; "Spectra Inform Us About Atoms," in *Physics Teacher,* **2,** no. 7 (1964), 303–311; *Key to the Welch Periodic Chart of the Atoms* (Chicago, 1965); "More Wavelengths From Thorium Lamps," in *Journal of Research of the National Bureau of Standards,* **69A,** no. 2 (1965), 109–118, with Robert W. Stanley; "Mees Medal Ceremony," in *Journal of the Optical Society of America,* **55,** no. 4 (1965), 341–345; "Dr. William F. Meggers," in *Arcs and Sparks,* **12,** no. 1 (1967), 3–4; and "The Second Spectrum of Ytterbium (Yb II)," in *Journal of Research of the National Bureau of Standards,* **71A,** no. 6 (1967), 396–544, edited by Charlotte E. Moore.

CHARLOTTE E. MOORE

MEINESZ, F. A. VENING. See **Vening Meinesz, Felix A.**

MEINZER, OSCAR EDWARD (*b.* near Davis, Illinois, 28 November 1876; *d.* Washington, D. C., 14 June 1948), *ground-water hydrology.*

Meinzer was the son of William and Mary Julia Meinzer. He graduated *magna cum laude* from Beloit College, Wisconsin, in 1901. He was a graduate student in geology at the University of Chicago (1906–1907) and received the Ph.D., *magna cum laude,* in 1922. His career in the United States Geological Survey began as geologic aide in June 1906. He married Alice Breckenridge Crawford in October 1906. Meinzer became junior geologist on ground-water investigations (1907), acting chief (1912), and chief, ground-water division (1913), a post which he held until retirement on 30 November 1946. In that same year he received an honorary doctorate from Beloit College.

During his thirty-four years as the chief, ground-water division (now branch) of the United States Geological Survey, Meinzer became the main architect in development of the modern science of ground-water hydrology. He organized and trained a large number of scientists and engineers, many of whom became recognized international authorities in this vastly expanded field. When he began, the study of underground water was an insignificant and poorly appreciated art.

During his early years as chief, he initiated the development of the science of ground-water hydrology. He realized that in addition to locating and defining ground-water basins, as had been the earlier practice, the principles governing occurrence, movement, and discharge of ground water must be determined, and methods had to be devised and tested for determining the quantity and quality of available ground water. In order to standardize terms and describe principles, he prepared *Outline of Ground-Water Hydrology, With Definitions,* and *The Occurrence of Ground Water in the United States, With a Discussion of Principles.* Among his definitions he proposed the term "phreatophyte" taken from Greek roots meaning a "well plant," which like a water well taps the ground-water supply especially in arid regions in contrast to most plants which derive their water from soil moisture in humid regions. That term, together with many of his logical definitions, continues to be used. In his definitions he explained the significant difference between "porosity" and "effective porosity" and the relation of these terms to specific yield, which many hydrologists failed to recognize.

The need for more precise and comprehensive methods to determine the perennial yield of aquifers led him to devise a quantitative approach. In a report, *Outline of Methods for Estimating Ground-Water Supplies,* Meinzer described twenty-six approaches, eleven of which are applicable, though not exclusively, to aquifers and parts of aquifers under water table conditions. Five of the methods are applicable to aquifers in which water moves considerable distances from intake to discharge areas.

As part of the study of ground-water hydrology, Meinzer established a laboratory, where, along with other experiments and tests, he was able to prove that as long as the flow of water through granular material is laminar, the velocity is directly proportional to the hydraulic gradient—that is, the flow conforms to Darcy's law. For field investigations Meinzer proposed and encouraged development of geophysical methods and such instrumentation as automatic water-stage recorders on wells. He was in the vanguard of those pioneers who urged pumping tests and other analytical tests on wells to obtain quantitative information on the water-bearing properties of aquifers. Among these was the method of Gunter Thiem, which was tested in the field and described by L. K. Wenzel.

The quantitative methods described by Wenzel, and those developed by C. V. Theis, and later C. E. Jacobs and others under Meinzer's supervision, provided additional means for determining the perennial yield of aquifers.

Meinzer also emphasized the need for studying the chemical quality and geochemistry of water, as well as salt-water encroachment in aquifers. Among the research studies on geochemistry were investigations of natural softening of water and the source of some elements, such as fluoride. One of the early reports, prepared by John S. Brown under Meinzer's supervision, introduced to this country the Ghyben-Herzberg formula to estimate the extent of salt-water encroachment in aquifers in which fresh water is in dynamic equilibrium with sea water.

Meinzer recognized that aquifers are functional components of the hydrologic cycle and that ground-water investigations require special skills of the geologist, engineer, physicist, chemist, and others. He pioneered in the teaming of men of these disciplines, in particular geologists and engineers. Beginning about 1930, as the demand for ground-water investigations began to increase rapidly, Meinzer and his assistants trained and supervised dozens of geologists and engineers, many of whom, with that fundamental training, were able to develop more sophisticated tools and techniques.

BIBLIOGRAPHY

I. ORIGINAL WORKS. Meinzer was author or coauthor of more than 100 reports and papers dealing with ground water, as listed on pages 202–206 of a memorial to Oscar Edward Meinzer by A. Nelson Sayre, published in *Proceedings Volume (1948) of the Geological Society of America* (April 1949), 197–206. "The Occurrence of Ground Water in the United States, With a Discussion of Principles," was published in 1923 as *U.S. Geological Survey Water-Supply Paper 489*. The report served as his dissertation for his Ph.D. at the University of Chicago.

His "Outline of Ground-Water Hydrology, With Definitions" was also published in 1923 as *U.S. Geological Survey Water-Supply Paper 494*. His definition of the coefficient of hydraulic permeability as used in hydrologic work of the U.S. Geological Survey, defined and illustrated in his paper "Movements of Ground Water," in *Bulletin of the American Association of Petroleum Geologists*, **20**, no. 6 (1936), is an example of Meinzer's ability to express technical terms so clearly that they can be understood by the layman.

His report "Large Springs in the United States," published in 1927 as *U.S. Geological Survey Water-Supply Paper 557*, continues to serve as a model for later reports on large springs. Meinzer's *Water-Supply Paper 577*, "Plants as Indicators of Ground Water," was published

in the same year. *Water-Supply Paper 640*, prepared under Meinzer's direction and close supervision, is cited in the fourth edition of *Suggestions to Authors of the Reports of the United States Geological Survey* as a model for the preparation of ground-water reports.

"Outline of Methods for Estimating Ground-Water Supplies" was published as *U.S. Geological Survey Water-Supply Paper 638-C*, 99–144.

Meinzer's "Ground-Water in the United States, a Summary of Ground-Water Conditions and Resources, Utilization of Water from Wells and Springs, Methods of Scientific Investigation, and Literature Relating to the Subject" was published in 1939 as *U.S. Geological Survey Water-Supply Paper 836-D*, 157–232.

Meinzer was editor and coauthor with twenty-three associates of a book, *Hydrology*, published in the *Physics of the Earth Series*, vol. 9 (New York, 1942). The part of the book written by Meinzer, as with all of his reports, stands out as an example of his excellent, plain, terse, readable style of writing.

Three of his latest papers were (1) "Problems of the Perennial Yield of Artesian Aquifers," in *Economic Geology*, **40** (1945), 159–163; (2) "General Principles of Artificial Ground-Water Recharge," in *Economic Geology*, **41** (1946), 191–201; and (3) "Hydrology in Relation to Economic Geology," *ibid.*, 1–12. His last paper, *Suggestions as to Future Research in Ground-Water Hydrology*, serves as a guide for continuing research.

II. SECONDARY LITERATURE. A biography and a complete bibliography are given by Sayre, in *Proceedings Volume (1948) of the Geological Society of America*, pp. 197–206, cited above. A brief biography by Sayre is published in *Transactions, American Geophysical Union*, **29**, no. 4 (1948), 455–456. A longer discussion of Meinzer is given by O. M. Hackett, "The Father of Modern Ground-Water Hydrology," in *Ground Water*, **3**, no. 2 (April 1965). A brief biography is given in *American Men of Science*. Thirty-one of his U.S. Geological Survey Water-Supply Papers are listed in *Publications of the Geological Survey, U.S. Department of the Interior, 1879–1961*. *U.S. Geological Survey Water-Supply Paper 992* lists his reports up to 1946, and *Water-Supply Paper 1492* gives an annotated bibliography for his later reports. The following U.S. Geological Survey bulletins in *Bibliography of North American Geology* list most of his reports for years indicated: Bull. 746–747 for the period through 1918; Bull. 823, pts. 1 and 2 for years 1919–1928; Bull. 937, pts. 1 and 2 for years 1929–1939; and Bull. 1049, pts. 1 and 2, 1940–1949.

V. T. STRINGFIELD

MEISSNER, GEORG (*b.* Hannover, Germany, 19 November 1829; *d.* Göttingen, Germany, 30 March 1905), *anatomy, physiology.*

Meissner was the son of a senior law-court official, Adolf Meissner. As a student he displayed only average talents, his wish to study medicine becoming strong only during his last years at school. After passing the final examination, he left school in the spring of 1849. He began to study medicine at Göttingen in the summer term of 1849. There he had a fatherly friend and patron in Rudolph Wagner, who was professor of physiology, comparative anatomy, and zoology. While still a student Meissner took an active part in Wagner's investigations in anatomy and, especially, in microscopy. At Göttingen he became a lifelong friend of Theodor Billroth. The two were united by their great love for music and by their interest in microscopic anatomy. In the autumn of 1851 Meissner and Billroth accompanied Wagner on a research expedition to Trieste, in order to investigate the origins and endings of the nerves in the torpedo. Meissner provided the drawings, which were printed by Wagner in his *Icones physiologicae*. The expedition was also concerned with analyzing the electrical organ of the torpedo. At Trieste, Meissner became acquainted with Johannes Müller, whom he esteemed highly. It was also in 1851 that Meissner conducted intensive comparative microscopic investigations on the cells and fibers of the *nervus acusticus*. In 1852 he studied the tactile corpuscles of the skin which today bear his name. The results were first published under the names of Wagner and Meissner; but in Meissner's doctoral thesis the same results were again published, this time under his name alone, as *Beiträge zur Anatomie und Physiologie der Haut* (Leipzig, 1853), and a fierce controversy over priority ensued between Wagner and Meissner.

After finishing his studies in the spring of 1853, Meissner went to Berlin to attend the lectures of Johannes Müller and Lukas Schönlein. In April 1853 he left for Munich to attend the lectures of Siebold, Emil Harless, and Liebig. In August he there received a letter from Wagner, who claimed the discovery of the tactile cells for his own and demanded a public resolution of the matter. Meissner rejected this proposal politely but firmly, and bad feeling between teacher and pupil persisted until 1859.

In 1855, at the age of twenty-six, Meissner was appointed full professor of anatomy and physiology at the University of Basel. Two years later he accepted a professorship of physiology, zoology, and histology at the University of Freiburg im Breisgau. At Freiburg he married the daughter of the mineralogist and poet Franz Ritter von Kobell; they had two sons.

In 1859 Wagner and Meissner were reconciled. Wagner, who until then had held the joint chair of physiology, comparative anatomy, and zoology, turned over his duties in physiology to Meissner, who thus became the first occupant of the separate chair of physiology at Göttingen. He took office after Easter of 1860 and held the chair until 1901, when he retired because of asthma.

He also was not very sociable. His lectures on physiology, which were illustrated by many experiments, were always well prepared and vivid. Here his talent for drawing, especially for microscopic drawings, served him well.

The number of Meissner's publications is not great. Those composed between 1853 and 1858 dealt chiefly with problems of microscopy, especially as related to the skin (Meissner's tactile cells). In 1857 he described the submucosal nerve plexus of the intestinal wall, which is now called Meissner's plexus. After 1858 he wrote largely on physiological-chemical problems. He was mainly concerned with the nature and the decomposition of protein compounds in the digestive system. The results of his investigations, undertaken alone as well as with collaborators, were published in *Zeitschrift für rationelle Medizin*, edited by his friend Jakob Henle. In 1861 Meissner constructed a new electrometer, a mirror galvanometer. The ensuing electrophysiological investigations led him to propose a new theory concerning the generation of electric potentials through the deformation of biological tissues. This suggestion provoked a devastating critique in 1867 by Emil du Bois-Reymond, the Nestor of electrophysiology. Meissner's experiments on protein also failed to meet with recognition. He was so offended that after 1869 he published nothing more under his own name. His collaborators included Carl Büttner, Friedrich Jolly, Heinrich Boruttau, Otto Weiss, and Karl Flügge. The bacteriologist Robert Koch was among his pupils.

BIBLIOGRAPHY

I. ORIGINAL WORKS. Meissner's memoirs are listed in the Royal Society *Catalogue of Scientific Papers*, IV, 326–327; and VIII, 375. His writings include *Über das Vorhandensein bisher unbekannter eigentümlicher Tastkörperchen (Corpuscula tactus) in den Gefühlswärzchen der menschlichen Haut und über die Endausbreitung sensitiver Nerven* (Göttingen, 1852), written with R. Wagner; *Beiträge zur Anatomie und Physiologie der Haut* (Leipzig, 1853); "Über die Nerven der Darmwand," in *Zeitschrift für rationelle Medizin*, n.s. **8** (1857), 364–366; "Über die Verdauung der Eiweisskörper," *ibid.*, 3rd ser. **7** (1859), 1–26; **8** (1859), 280–303; **10** (1860), 1–32; **12** (1861), 46–67, written with C. Büttner; **14** (1862), 78–96, 303–319, written with L. Thiry; "Zur Kenntnis des elektrischen Verhaltens des Muskels," *ibid.*, **12** (1861), 344–353; "Über das Entstehen der Bernsteinsäure im tierischen Stoffwechsel," *ibid.*, **24** (1865), 97–112, written with F. Jolly; and *Untersuchungen über das Entstehen der Hippursäure* *im tierischen Organismus* (Hannover, 1866), written with C. K. Shepard.

II. SECONDARY LITERATURE. See Heinrich Boruttau, "Zum Andenken an Georg Meissner," in *Pflügers Archiv für die gesamte Physiologie* . . ., **110** (1905), 351–399, with portrait and bibliography; Otto Damsch, "Georg Meissner†," in *Deutsche medizinische Wochenschrift*, **31** (1905), 758–759; Gottfried Müller, *Georg Meissner, sein Leben und seine Werke* (Düsseldorf, 1935), especially for letters to Wagner; Gernot Rath, "Georg Meissners Tagebuch seiner Triestreise (1851)," in *Sudhoffs Archiv für Geschichte der Medizin und der Naturwissenschaften*, **38** (1954), 129–164; and Otto Weiss, "Georg Meissner," in *Münchener medizinische Wochenschrift*, **52** (1905), 1206–1207.

See also Walter von Brunn, ed., *Jugendbriefe Theodor Billroths an Georg Meissner* (Leipzig, 1941).

K. E. ROTHSCHUH

MEITNER, LISE (*b.* Vienna, Austria, 7 November 1878; *d.* Cambridge, England, 27 October 1968), *physics.*

Meitner was the third of eight children of Hedwig Skovran and Philipp Meitner, a lawyer. Although both parents were of Jewish background (and the father was a freethinker), all the children were baptized and Meitner was raised as a Protestant. Her interest in physics apparently began very early, but her parents encouraged her to study for the state examination in French, so that she could support herself as a teacher should the need arise. Meitner passed the examination, then studied privately for the test that permitted her to enter the University of Vienna in 1901. At the university she met with some rudeness from her fellows (a female student then being something of a freak) but was inspired by her teachers, particularly Boltzmann. She was the second woman to receive a doctorate in science from the university; her dissertation, in 1905, was on heat conduction in non-homogeneous materials.

After graduation Meitner remained in Vienna for a time, during which she was introduced to the new subject of radioactivity by Stephan Meyer. Although she then had no notion of making the study of radioactivity her life's work, she did design and perform one of the first experiments to demonstrate that alpha rays are slightly deflected in passing through matter. But she was also interested in theoretical physics; she requested and obtained her father's (very modest) financial support to go to Berlin to study with Planck—for a year or two, as she thought.

Meitner enrolled for Planck's lectures, but had some difficulty finding a place to do experimental work until she met Otto Hahn, who was looking for a physicist to help him in his work on the chemistry of radioactivity. Hahn himself was working at the Chemical Institute, under Emil Fischer, who did not allow women in his laboratory (although two years later, after women's education had been regularized in Berlin, he welcomed Meitner). Hahn and Meitner equipped a carpenter's workshop for radiation measurement and set to work. Hahn, the chemist, was primarily interested in the discovery of new elements and the examination of their properties, while Meitner was more concerned with disentangling their radiations. They were pioneers, and a great deal of their first work was based on false assumptions—such as H. W. Schmidt's idea that beta rays of defined energy follow an exponential absorption law—so that most of their early papers are of largely historical interest.

In 1912 Meitner joined the Kaiser-Wilhelm Institut für Chemie, newly opened in Berlin-Dahlem. World War I interrupted her work; Hahn was called to military service, and Meitner volunteered as a roentgenographic nurse with the Austrian army. On her leaves she went back to Berlin to measure radioactive substances; Hahn's leaves sometimes coincided with hers, so that they could occasionally continue their collaboration. Since in the study of radioactive substances measurements made at fairly long intervals may be desirable to allow some activities to build up and others decay, Hahn and Meitner were able to make a virtue of necessity. By this time they were searching for the still unknown precursor of actinium; they reported their success at the end of the war, naming the new element protactinium.

In 1918 Meitner was appointed head of the physics department of the Kaiser-Wilhelm Institut. She also maintained her rather tenuous connection with the University of Berlin—from 1912 to 1915 she had been Planck's assistant, and after the war she became a docent. Her inaugural lecture was given in 1922; it concerned cosmic physics (reported in the press as "cosmetic physics"). Meitner was appointed extraordinary professor in 1926; she never gave any courses, although she did contribute to the weekly physics colloquia, in which her colleagues included Planck, Einstein, Nernst, Gustav Hertz, and Schroedinger.

Meitner continued her work toward clarifying the relationships between beta and gamma rays. It had by then become clear that while some radioactive substances emitted an electron from the nucleus, others did not. The electrons that these latter substances, the alpha emitters, released must therefore come from the outer shell (as was presumably the case for some of those issued by the true electron emitters), and must therefore be regarded as secondary. There remained the determination of which of the many electron lines then identified were primary electrons from the nucleus. Ellis, at Cambridge, thought that none of them were, but rather that the primary electrons constituted the continuous spectrum that Chadwick had discovered as early as 1914. Meitner disagreed, in the belief that Chadwick's method was inadequate for the discrimination of such a spectrum. Chadwick had counted electrons deflected by a fixed angle in a variable magnetic field; Meitner had always put her faith in photographing electrons. In 1922 she published the measurements that she had made using Danysz' method of focusing the electrons by deflection through 180°. This technique emphasized the narrow electron lines, while the continuous spectrum appeared to be very faint, and Meitner attributed the latter to secondary effects.

Meitner's skepticism was, moreover, a product of her belief that, like alpha particles, primary electrons must form a group of well-defined energy. Her conviction was in the spirit of the quantum theory, which was then being applied to nuclei (largely by Gamow).

If the primary electrons display a continuous spectrum it must be, she thought, because they lose varying amounts of energy in the form of X rays on passing through the strong electric field that surrounds the nucleus, or perhaps in collisions with atomic electrons. The primary energy would then correspond to the highest energy found in the continuous spectrum. In 1927, however, Ellis and Wooster measured the heat generated by electron-emitting nuclei and thus found that each electron gives to its surrounding material an energy equal to the mean energy of the continuous spectrum, not its top energy as Meitner's view demanded. With Wilhelm Orthmann, Meitner immediately set out to check Ellis and Wooster's result; she reported good agreement with their data in the paper that she and Orthmann published jointly in 1929.

The growing evidence for the continuous distribution of energy of primary electrons emitted in beta decay led Pauli to write to Meitner and Geiger a letter in which he proposed the existence of a new neutral particle—later called the neutrino—that should be emitted together with the electron and would at random share the energy available to it. Pauli had to assume that this particle was too elusive to be detected by means then available, and, indeed, effects due to free neutrinos were not actually found until 1956.

Although Meitner's belief in the simplicity of nature had led her astray in regard to the distribution of energy of primary electrons, she was correct in her theory that electron lines were generated from the outer electron shell. She measured the electron lines of actinium to demonstrate that they were produced

from the shells of the newly formed—rather than the decaying—nucleus. She thus showed that gamma rays follow upon radioactive transformation, rather than acting as the triggering mechanism for it (as Ellis had suggested). She further observed and correctly interpreted those radiationless transitions in which an electron, on dropping into a vacancy in an inner shell, ejects another electron from the atom, a phenomenon usually named for Auger, who independently described it about two years later in a different context.

Although Meitner never invented a laboratory instrument or technique of her own, she rapidly adopted any new methods developed by others that seemed to her to be useful in her work. For example, she encouraged her student Gerhard Schmidt to make use of Millikan's droplet technique to study the ionization density of alpha particles, and introduced C. T. R. Wilson's cloud chamber—which had been neglected since its invention in 1911—into her Berlin laboratory and applied it in innovative researches (as, for instance, the study of slow electrons, for which she employed the device at greatly lowered pressure). Among her own investigations, she was one of the first (with Phillip, in a paper dated March 1933) to observe and report on positrons formed from gamma rays.

Meitner had accurately measured the attenuation of hard gamma rays in their passage through matter even earlier, when she realized the potential of the new Geiger-Mueller counter for measuring the attenuation of well-collinated, narrow beams of gamma rays. The main purpose of that measurement was to test the Klein-Nishina formula for the Compton effect, and she found good agreement for light elements, up to magnesium. She discovered, however, that attenuation increased with atomic number; she suspected an effect of nuclear structure, perhaps a resonance, and therefore searched for the scattering of gamma rays with unchanged wavelength. (In 1933 it was discovered that the excess attenuation was due to the formation of electron-positron pairs, rather than to scattering.)

In the early 1930's nuclear physics advanced dramatically: the neutron was discovered in 1932, the positron in 1933, and artificial radioactivity in 1934. Meitner and her colleagues published a number of short papers in the light of these rapid developments. In 1934 Meitner resumed work with Hahn to follow up results obtained by Fermi, who had bombarded uranium with neutrons and had found several radioactive products which he thought must be due to a transuranic element since neutron bombardment had invariably led to the formation of a heavier, usually beta-radioactive, isotope of the bombarded element (except for the lightest elements, where a nucleus of lower atomic number might result from the ejection of a charged particle such as a proton or a helium nucleus).

In his investigation of this phenomenon, Hahn discovered several decay products for uranium, some of which might be presumed to be transuranic, with atomic numbers greater than 92. He and Meitner set out to isolate such elements by precipitating an irradiated and acidified uranium salt solution with hydrogen sulfide in order to eliminate all elements between polonium (84) and uranium (92); they assumed that the remaining precipitate must contain only transuranic elements. To be sure, Ida Noddack had suggested that the formation of transuranic elements could not be regarded as proven until it could be established that such elements were not, in fact, identical with any elements between hydrogen and uranium, but her paper was little read and uninfluential. Meitner and Hahn were thus considerably surprised when Irene Curie and Savitch reported irradiating uranium to find a product with penetrating beta rays and a half-life of three-and-one-half hours. Curie further noted that this substance behaved chemically somewhat like thorium. (Hahn and Meitner, using sulfide precipitation, would have missed that.) By implication, then, a uranium nucleus upon being hit by a neutron might emit an alpha particle—a helium nucleus—which seemed unlikely. Later Curie changed her view and pointed to the similarity of her three-and-one-half-hour substance with lanthanum, foreshadowing, but not formulating, the concept of nuclear fission.

Meitner set one of her students, Gottfried von Droste, to look for such alpha particles, but he failed to find them. By studying substances not precipitated as sulfide, Hahn and Strassmann found yet more products, with actinium-like properties and, startlingly, three others with the properties of radium, four places below uranium on the atomic scale.

These results puzzled Meitner, who was unable to reconcile them with nuclear theory. It was at this point, however, that she was forced to interrupt her researches and leave Germany, where the Nazi racial laws had made it increasingly difficult for her to work. Although the Kaiser-Wilhelm Institut was to some degree autonomous, Nazi policies were being enforced even there, and Meitner's situation became critical when the occupation of Austria robbed her of the protection of her foreign nationality. She had never concealed her Jewish origin; her Austrian passport was invalid, and her dismissal from the institute certain. The Dutch physicist Peter Debye communicated (through Scherrer in Zürich) with Dirk Coster at the University of Groningen, and Coster arranged that Meitner be allowed to enter Holland, despite her lack of papers. No one except Hahn knew that she was leaving Germany for good.

Meitner remained in Holland for only a short time, then went to Denmark, where she was the guest of Niels Bohr and his wife. Although Copenhagen offered her good facilities for research, and although there were a number of younger nuclear physicists working there (including her nephew, O. R. Frisch), Meitner soon chose to accept an invitation from Manne Siegbahn to work in the new Nobel Institute in Stockholm, where a cyclotron was being constructed. Meitner was sixty years old when she went to Sweden; she nonetheless acquired a good command of the language, built up a small research group, and eventually published a number of short papers, most of them on the properties of new radioactive species formed with the cyclotron.

Meitner made her most famous contribution to science shortly after she arrived in Stockholm, however. Worried by Hahn's statement that neutron bombardment of uranium leads to isotopes of radium, she had written to Hahn to ask for irrefutable data concerning the properties of these substances. Her request led Hahn and Strassmann to undertake a series of tests designed to demonstrate that these products were chemically identical to radium, as their earlier investigations had suggested. Hahn wrote to inform her that in these tests, he and Strassmann had found that, like radium, these substances could be precipitated with barium but, surprisingly, were then inseparable from it. They therefore reluctantly concluded that the decay products were isotopes of barium, rather than radium. The evidence for transuranic elements was thus placed in doubt, since sulfide precipitation did not eliminate elements lighter than polonium.

Meitner discussed this news with Frisch. It soon became clear that Bohr's droplet model of the nucleus must provide the clue to understanding how barium nuclei could be formed from uranium nuclei, which are almost twice as heavy. Frisch suggested that the division into two smaller nuclei was made possible through the mutual repulsion of the many protons of the uranium nucleus, making it behave like a droplet in which the surface tension has been greatly reduced by its electric charge. Meitner estimated the difference between the mass of the uranium nucleus (plus the extra neutron with which it had been bombarded) and the slightly smaller total mass of the two fragment nuclei; from this she worked out (by Einstein's mass-energy equivalence) the large amount of energy that was bound to be released. The two mutually repulsed fragments would, indeed, be driven apart with an energy that agreed with her value, so it all fitted.

Meitner and Frisch reported these findings in a joint

paper that described this "nuclear fission" (composed over the telephone, since she was in Stockholm and he had returned to Copenhagen). A few months later they jointly demonstrated experimentally that radioactive fission fragments could be collected on a water surface close to a uranium layer undergoing neutron irradiation. They further showed that the sulfide precipitated from the material so obtained had a decay curve of the same shape as the precipitate derived directly from the irradiated uranium. They concluded that no observable amounts of transuranic elements were produced, capable of affecting their counters.

Meitner had, however, previously demonstrated that one of the products of slow-neutron irradiation of uranium was a uranium isotope of twenty-four minutes half-life; by measuring the resonance cross section she concluded that it was U-239, formed by the capture of a neutron in U-238. Although she realized that its observed beta decay must lead to the formation of a transuranic element, she was not able to observe the very soft radiation of that daughter substance. (Macmillan later found this substance, neptunium; the next generation, plutonium, was the explosive of the first atomic bomb.) Meitner was invited to join the team at work on the development of the nuclear-fission bomb; she refused, and hoped until the very end that the project would prove impossible. Except for a brief note on the asymmetry of fission fragments, she did no more work in nuclear fission.

In 1946 Meitner spent half a year in Washington, D. C., as a visiting professor at Catholic University. In 1947 she retired from the Nobel Institute and went to work in the small laboratory that the Swedish Atomic Energy Commission had established for her at the Royal Institute of Technology. She later moved to the laboratory of the Royal Academy for Engineering Sciences, where an experimental nuclear reactor was being built. In 1960, having spent twenty-two years in Sweden, Meitner retired to Cambridge (England). She continued to travel, lecture, and attend concerts (her love of music was lifelong), but she gradually gave up these activities as her strength ebbed. She died a few days before her ninetieth birthday.

BIBLIOGRAPHY

Meitner's earlier writings include "Über die Zerstreuung der α-Strahlen," in *Berichte der Deutschen physikalischen Gesellschaft,* **8** (1907), 489; "Eine neue Methode zur Herstellung radioaktiver Zerfallsprodukte; Thorium D, ein kurzlebiges Produkt des Thoriums," in *Verhandlungen der Deutschen physikalischen Gesellschaft,* **11** (1909), 55, written with O. Hahn; "Vorträge aus dem Gebiet der Radioaktivität," in *Physikalische Zeitschrift,* **12** (1911), 147; "Magnetische Spektren der β-Strahlen des Radiums,"

ibid., 1099, written with O. von Baeyer and O. Hahn; "Die Muttersubstanz des Actiniums, ein neues radioaktives Element von langer Lebensdauer," *ibid.,* **19** (1918), 208, written with O. Hahn; "Über die verschiedenen Arten des radioaktiven Zerfalls und die Möglichkeit ihrer Deutung aus der Kernstruktur," in *Zeitschrift für Physik,* **4** (1921), 146; "Die γ-Strahlung der Actiniumreihe und der Nachweis, dass die γ-Strahlen erst nach erfolgtem Atomzerfall emittiert werden," *ibid.,* **34** (1925), 807; "Einige Bemerkungen zur Isotopie der Elemente," in *Naturwissenschaften,* **14** (1926), 719; "Experimentelle Bestimmung der Reichweite homogener β-Strahlen," *ibid.,* 1199; "Über eine absolute Bestimmung der Energie der primären β-Strahlen von Radium E," in *Zeitschrift für Physik,* **60** (1930), 143, written with W. Orthmann; and "Über das Absorptionsgesetz für kurzwellige γ-Strahlung," *ibid.,* **67** (1931), 147, written with H. H. Hupfeld.

Later works are "Die Anregung positiver Elektronen durch γ-Strahlen von Th C″," in *Naturwissenschaften,* **21** (1933), 468, written with K. Philipp; *Kernphysikalische Vorträge am Physikalischen Institut der Eidgenössischen technischen Hochschule* (Berlin, 1936); "Über die Umwandlungsreihen des Urans, die durch Neutronenbestrahlung erzeugt werden," in *Zeitschrift für Physik,* **106** (1937), 249, written with O. Hahn and F. Strassmann; "Künstliche Umwandlungsprozesse bei Bestrahlung des Thoriums mit Neutronen; Auftreten isomerer Reihen durch Abspaltung von α-Strahlen," *ibid.,* **109** (1938), 538, written with O. Hahn and F. Strassmann; "Trans-Urane als künstliche radioaktive Umwandlungsprodukte des Urans," in *Scientia* (Jan. 1938), written with O. Hahn; "Disintegration of Uranium by Neutrons; a New Type of Nuclear Reaction," in *Nature,* **143** (1939), 239, written with O. R. Frisch; "Resonance Energy of the Th Capture Process," in *Physical Review,* **60** (1941), 58; "Spaltung und Schalenmodell des Atomkernes," in *Arkiv för fysik,* **4** (1950), 383—see *Nature,* **165** (1950), 561; "Die Anwendung des Rückstosses bei Atomkernprozessen," in *Zeitschrift für Physik,* **133** (1952), 141; "Einige Erinnerungen an das Kaiser-Wilhelm-Institut für Chemie in Berlin-Dahlem," in *Naturwissenschaften,* **41** (1954), 97; and "Looking Back," in *Bulletin of the Atomic Scientists* (Nov. 1964), 2.

A biography with extensive bibliography is by O. R. Frisch, in *Biographical Memoirs of Fellows of the Royal Society,* **16** (Nov. 1970), 405–420.

O. R. FRISCH

MELA, POMPONIUS. See **Pomponius Mela.**

MELLANBY, EDWARD (*b.* West Hartlepool, Durham, England, 8 April 1884; *d.* Mill Hill, London, England, 30 January 1955), *pharmacology.*

For a complete study of his life and work see Supplement.

MELLO, FRANCISCO DE (*b.* Lisbon, Portugal, 1490; *d.* Évora, Portugal, 27 April 1536), *mathematics.*

The son of a nobleman, Manuel de Mello, and Beatriz de Silva, Mello was a protégé of the Portuguese king Manuel I, who sent him to Paris to study. Mello graduated in theology and mathematics; his teacher was Pierre Brissot, who gave him a thorough grounding in the works of Euclid and Archimedes. On his return to Portugal, Mello was appointed tutor to the king's children. He may have served in an official capacity in navigating the Atlantic in order to determine the boundaries of the Spanish and Portuguese territories as defined by the Holy See. He was also to some degree involved in Portuguese politics, and shortly before his death was rewarded with the bishopric of Goa (it is not known whether he actually accepted this post, although it is certain that he never went there).

Mello enjoyed considerable fame as a scientist; as such, Gil Vicente dedicated to him some verses in the introduction to the *Auto da feira.* He was also firmly within the humanistic tradition of his time; his friends included Nicolás Clenard, Juan Luis Vives, and his fellow mathematician Gaspar de Lax. Many of his own works were destroyed by the fire that followed the Lisbon earthquake of 1755. Among his mathematical writings are "De videndi ratione atque oculorum forma," a commentary on Euclid's *Optica*; "De incidentibus in humidis," a commentary on Archimedes' hydrostatics; and an "Elements of Geometry," which would seem to be derived from Jābir ibn Aflaḥ. His nonscientific writings included translations from Latin authors and funerary poems.

Mello should not be confused with the great historian Francisco Manuel de Mello (1611–1667), who also wrote on mathematics.

BIBLIOGRAPHY

On Mello and his work see M. Bataillon, "Erasme et la cour de Portugal," in *Études sur le Portugal au temps de l'humanisme* (Coimbra, 1952), 49–100; Diego Barbosa Machado, *Bibliotheca Lusitana* (Lisbon, 1747), 197–198; Felipe Picatoste y Rodríguez, *Apuntes para una biblioteca científica española del siglo XVI* (Madrid, 1891), 167; Antonio Ribeiro dos Santos, *Memoria da vida e escritos de Don Francisco de Mello*, Memórias de literatura portuguesa publicadas pela Academia Real das sciencias de Lisboa, VII (Lisbon, 1806), 237–249; and Inocencio Francisco da Silva, *Diccionario bibliografico portugues*, III (Lisbon, 1859), 8–10.

JUAN VERNET

MELLONI, MACEDONIO (*b.* Parma, Italy, 11 April 1798; *d.* Portici, Italy, 11 August 1854), *physics.*

Melloni spent his early professional life as a professor of physics at the University of Parma between 1824 and 1831. Political difficulties arising out of the 1830 rebellions forced him to flee to Paris, where he lived without a position until 1839. He returned to Italy to become director of a conservatory of physics in Naples, where, until 1848, he also directed the meteorological observatory on Vesuvius.

As a physicist Melloni was concerned mainly with the properties of radiant heat, or calorific radiation as it was then called. Since 1820 it had been thought, after a suggestion by Ampère, that the rays of light and those of heat are different manifestations of the same process. According to Young and Fresnel light is a transverse disturbance or wave propagated through a ubiquitous medium called the "luminiferous ether." Rays of heat were thought to be modifications of these waves, not very, if at all, different from the rays of light. There were, however, difficulties with this view which centered about the propagation of heat and light through matter. If, it was thought, heat rays and light rays are the same things, then there should be little difference in the ways they are transmitted through matter. Thus an optically transparent body should transmit the heat it intercepts in the same manner it transmits the light that impinges upon it. The problem was that in many instances the effects of radiant heat on matter are very unlike those of light.

Early in his career Melloni became convinced that, while radiant heat is a wave in ether as is light, it is not the same kind of a disturbance as a ray of light. His first experiments were designed to pinpoint the differences between these two kinds of propagation. In 1832, for example, Melloni attempted to show that, contrary to general belief, radiant heat and light are not transmitted in the same amounts through a given transparent body. In his experiment he demonstrated that the quantity of heat a body transmits is not related in any degree to its transparency, that is, to the amount of light which it can transmit. In fact the only relationship he could find was between the body's permeability to heat and its index of refraction (1). This strengthened him in his belief that heat rays and light are both ethereal vibrations but not the same kind of vibration.

Between 1833 and 1840 Melloni continued in his attempts to find the differences between heat and light. His experimental accounts, if read singly, often seem to be showing that heat and light are the same, not that they differ. But Melloni expected to find many similarities—since both are ethereal vibrations. What he sought were the differences in their effects. He showed in 1833 that the same body has different effects on heat and light; radiant heat, for example, is unaffected by the same polarization arrangement that extinguishes light (3). By 1835 Melloni was certain ". . . that light and radiant heat are effects directly produced by two different causes" (4). These causes are both molecular vibrations that set the ether in motion, but the molecules move differently when producing the vibrations of heat than they do when producing those of light. As he continued in his investigations he found that the rays of heat can actually be polarized, but in a way bearing no relation to the effects of the same polarization apparatus on light—further evidence, he thought, of the different origins of these two kinds of ethereal motions (2).

Between 1834 and 1840 Melloni began to concentrate on the behavior of bodies transmitting heat radiation. He was by then certain that heat and light are distinct modes of the same process, ethereal propagation, and he looked for those details of the transfer of heat that distinguished it from that of light. His theoretical distinction between the two kinds of waves aided him because he was always looking for differences and not similarities. For example, it was held that the amount of light that is transmitted by a body depends somehow upon the state of its surface, upon its degree of smoothness or lack of irregularities. Melloni, because he distinguished between heat and light, did not believe that this would be strictly true for heat. In 1839 he tried to show that, if a smooth-surfaced body transmits heat more readily than one with a rough surface, it is not because of some special surface regularity, as it is with light, but because the polishing necessary to make the surface smooth had so altered its elasticity that the rate at which it could transmit the vibrations of heat was also changed (6, 7). The importance of Melloni's work for later generations lies in the detailed investigations he made into the behavior of heat and the new knowledge about it that resulted.

BIBLIOGRAPHY

Melloni's writings include (1) "Expériences relatives à la transmission du calorique rayonnant par divers liquides," in *Bibliothèque universelle des sciences et arts . . .*, **49** (1832), 337–340, written with P. Prevost; (2) "Mémoire sur la transmission libre de la chaleur rayonnante par différens corps solides et liquides," in *Annales de chimie*, **53** (1833), 5–73; (3) "Nouvelles recherches sur la transmission immédiate de la chaleur rayonnante par différens corps solides et liquides," *ibid.*, **55** (1833), 337–397; (4) "Note sur la réflexion de la chaleur rayonnante," *ibid.*, **60** (1835), 402–426; (5) "Mémoire sur la polarisation de la chaleur," *ibid.*, **61** (1836), 375–410; (6) "De la prétendue influence que les aspérités et le poli des surfaces exercent sur le pouvoir émissif des corps," *ibid.*, **70** (1839), 435–444; and (7) "Sur la constance de l'absorption . . .," *ibid.*, **75** (1840), 337–388.

JED Z. BUCHWALD

MELTZER, SAMUEL JAMES (*b.* Ponevyezh, Russia [now Panevezhis, Lithuanian S.S.R.], 22 March 1851; *d.* New York, N.Y., 7 November 1920), *physiology*, *pharmacology*.

Meltzer was the son of Simon Meltzer, a teacher, and Taube Kowars. The family were orthodox Jews and Samuel's early education was obtained at a rabbinical seminary, but he decided against a religious vocation. After his marriage he studied at the Realgymnasium in Königsberg. He also attempted unsuccessfully to operate a soap-manufacturing business. In 1876 Meltzer entered the University of Berlin, where he studied philosophy and medicine. Under the direction of the physiologist Hugo Kronecker, he pursued experimental studies on the mechanism of swallowing. He received his medical degree in 1882.

Meltzer soon immigrated to the United States, settling in New York City, where he practiced medicine. In order to continue research he made arrangements to have access to laboratory facilities, particularly William Henry Welch's laboratory at Bellevue Hospital. In 1904 he joined the staff of the recently created Rockefeller Institute for Medical Research; he was head of the department of physiology and pharmacology until his retirement in 1919.

Meltzer's intimate acquaintance with both medical practice and research allowed him to serve as a liaison between practitioners and scientific investigators. He played an important role in the founding and early development of several scientific or medical societies, including the Society for Experimental Biology and Medicine—familiarly called the Meltzer Verein for many years. His strong belief in the cosmopolitanism of science led him to organize the Fraternitas Medicorum, an international medical brotherhood, during World War I, and thousands of American medical men joined the organization before its activities were suspended when the United States entered the conflict.

Meltzer also made contributions to pharmacology, pathology, and clinical medicine, as well as to physiology, his major field of interest. He was too inclined to speculate about his experimental results and to seek the general principles that govern physiological phenomena. In his 1882 medical dissertation on the swallowing reflex, he first outlined the theory of inhibition, which influenced much of his subsequent work. During the course of his studies on the act of swallowing, he noted that reflex stimulation of inspiratory muscles is accompanied by reflex inhibition of expiratory muscles, and vice versa. He postulated that this reciprocal arrangement must exist for other antagonistic muscles in the body for the purpose of efficient motor action. In 1893 Charles Sherrington, apparently unaware of Meltzer's work, showed that the contraction of an extensor in the limb is accompanied by a relaxation of its opposing flexor, and vice versa (specifically predicted by Meltzer). Sherrington called this relationship reciprocal innervation.

Meltzer developed the idea of combined action of opposing processes into a general theory. He believed that every excitation or stimulation of a tissue was accompanied by a corresponding inhibitory impulse. Physiological phenomena are a result of the compromise between these two fundamental, antagonistic life forces—excitation and inhibition. Although his dualistic conception of life processes did not gain wide acceptance, it was an important stimulus to his own experimental work.

One of Meltzer's most important experimental studies dealt with the pharmacological effect of magnesium salts. These compounds were shown to produce a state of unconsciousness and muscle relaxation in animals which was readily reversed by the injection of calcium chloride. This work added magnesium to the elements known to play a part in the activity of the cell, and Meltzer believed he had found the element in the body that is especially concerned with inhibition.

Another important series of researches dealt with artificial respiration. Meltzer and John Auer developed the technique of intratracheal insufflation, whereby the lungs are kept inflated by blowing a stream of air through a tube inserted into the trachea. By including an anesthetic vapor in the air stream, anesthetization could be produced at the same time as artificial respiration. The technique was valuable in thoracic surgery as a simple means of keeping the lungs inflated after the chest had been opened.

Meltzer's other significant contributions included the hypothesis that bronchial asthma is a phenomenon of anaphylaxis, the introduction of the engineering term "factors of safety" to describe the reserve powers of organisms, and researches with his daughter Clara on the effects of adrenaline on the blood vessels and on the muscles of the iris.

BIBLIOGRAPHY

I. ORIGINAL WORKS. For a bibliography of Meltzer's publications, see William Howell, "Biographical Memoir, Samuel James Meltzer, 1851–1920," in *Memoirs of the National Academy of Sciences*, Scientific Memoir Series, **21** (1926), 15–23. Meltzer discussed his theory of inhibition in detail in "Inhibition," in *New York Medical Journal*, **69** (1899), 661–666, 699–703, 739–743. The enduring influence of this theory on his work is illustrated in one of his last papers, "The Dualistic Conception of the Processes of Animal Life," in *Transactions of the Association of American Physicians*, **35** (1920), 247–257. His main experimental work on magnesium salts is described in a series of four papers written with John Auer under the general title "Physiological and Pharmacological Studies of Magnesium Salts," in *American Journal of Physiology*, **14-17** (1905–1906). For a description of the technique of intratracheal insufflation, see "The Method of Respiration by Intratracheal Insufflation: Its Scientific Principle and Its Practical Availability in Medicine and Surgery," in *Medical Record*, **77** (1910), 477–483, which is followed by several articles by other authors on the surgical use of this technique. Other important papers include "Bronchial Asthma as a Phenomenon of Anaphylaxis," in *Journal of the American Medical Association*, **55** (1910), 1021–1024; and "The Factors of Safety in Animal Structure and Animal Economy," in *Science*, **25** (1907), 481–498.

II. SECONDARY LITERATURE. The best biography is the memoir by William Howell cited above. See also Howell's memoir in *Science*, n.s. **53** (1921), 99–106; and R. H. Chittenden's article in the *Dictionary of American Biography*, XII (1933), 519–520. George Corner, *A History of The Rockefeller Institute, 1901–1953, Origins and Growth* (New York, 1964), discusses Meltzer and his work—see esp. pp. 117–120. A special supp. to vol. **18** (1921) of *Proceedings of the Society for Experimental Biology and Medicine*, entitled "Memorial Number for Samuel James Meltzer, Founder and First President of the Society for Experimental Biology and Medicine," contains several biographical sketches by colleagues.

JOHN PARASCANDOLA

MELVILL, THOMAS (*b.* Glasgow [?], Scotland, 1726; *d.* Geneva, Switzerland, December 1753), *astronomy, physics.*

Thomas Melvill noted the yellow spectrum of sodium and considered a means of testing a suggested relation between the velocity of light and its color.

Melvill's origins are obscure, but at a relatively late age, in 1748 and 1749, he studied divinity at the University of Glasgow, where he acquired a taste for experimental philosophy from Alexander Wilson. Together they used kites to investigate the change in atmospheric temperature with altitude. Melvill studied Newton's *Opticks* closely. In a paper "Observations on Light and Colours," given to the Medical Society of Edinburgh on 3 January and 7 February 1752, he wrote of his use of a prism for examining color in flames (*Edinburgh Physical and Literary Essays*, II [Edinburgh, 1752], 35). The property of common salt, whereby it turns a flame yellow, was probably well recognized, but Melvill was seemingly the first to treat the coloration in any way quantitatively. He studied the spectrum of burning alcohol into which he introduced in turn sal ammoniac, potash, alum, niter, and sea salt, noting the persistence of the yellow component of the spectrum, and he remarked that this yellow color was of a definite degree of refrangibility. His work appears to have had little influence, and the origins of spectrum analysis are not usually traced back before W. H. Wollaston's discovery of dark solar lines (1802).

As an explanation of the different refrangibilities of light of different colors, in terms of the corpuscular theory, Melvill suggested that the several colored rays were projected with various velocities from the luminous body—the violet with the least. A letter to Bradley, written from Geneva, dated 2 February 1753, and read to the Royal Society on 8 March 1753, pointed out an interesting consequence regarding aberration. Depending on velocity, the aberration would be different for different colors, and the satellites of Jupiter would gradually change color in one way (white to violet) on entering the planet's shadow, and another way (red to white) on leaving the shadow. This effect was not observed, and the suggestion was soon forgotten. Its originality is in some doubt, since Courtivron's *Traité d'optique*, published in 1752 and readily available to Melvill in Geneva, contained not only the fundamental hypothesis but its consequences for the appearance of Jupiter.

Melvill developed the idea further in a letter of 2 June 1753, and suggested that Bradley's observations of aberration revealed the ratio of the velocities of light, not in space and air, but in space and in the humors of the eye. He believed that it would be necessary to reject what he called "Sir Isaac Newton's whole doctrine of refraction by an accelerating or retarding power," if the consequences of his new hypothesis were not confirmed. Dying at the age of twenty-seven, he scarcely lived long enough to be disappointed at the neglect of his letter, which contains essentially the same idea as that adopted by Alexander Wilson's son, Patrick, who long afterwards discussed the consequences for an observer with a water-filled telescope. Conclusions drawn by Wilson and Robison (*Philosophical Transactions of the Royal Society*, **74** [1784], 35) were put to the test by Arago and communicated to the Institut de France in 1810 (*Comptes-rendus hebdomadaires des séances de l'Académie des sciences*, **8** [1839], 326, and **36** [1853], 38).

At the close of his second letter to Bradley, Melvill

stated that he had designed and had made in Geneva a timepiece with a conical pendulum, the virtues of which he extolled. His early death deprived physics of a gifted and ingenious experimenter.

BIBLIOGRAPHY

I. Original Works. Melvill published only the papers cited above. The letter of 2 June 1753 was unpublished until it was printed by S. P. Rigaud in *Miscellaneous Works and Correspondence of the Rev. James Bradley* (Oxford, 1832), 483–487. The letter is now at Oxford, Bodleian Library, MS Bradley 44, f. 112.

II. Secondary Literature. On Melvill and his work see Brewster's *Edinburgh Journal of Science, Technology and Photographic Art*, **10** (1829), 5; A. M. Clerke, *History of Astronomy During the Nineteenth Century*, 3rd ed. (London, 1893), 165; and E. T. Whittaker, *History of the Theories of Aether and Electricity*, 2nd ed., I (Edinburgh, 1951), 99, 367.

J. D. North

MENABREA, LUIGI FEDERICO (*b.* Chambéry, Savoy, 4 September 1809; *d.* St. Cassin [near Chambéry], France, 24 May 1896), *structural and military engineering, mathematics.*

Menabrea is known to scientists as one of the most important men in the development of energy methods in the theory of elasticity and structures, and to others as a distinguished general and statesman, each group being generally little aware of Menabrea's accomplishments in the other fields. Indeed, it is remarkable that he was able to make significant contributions in both types of activities.

Menabrea first studied engineering and then mathematics at the University of Turin. Upon graduation he entered the army corps of engineers. When Charles Albert acceded to the throne in 1831, Cavour resigned his army commission, and Menabrea replaced Cavour at the Alpine fortress of Bardo. Menabrea soon left to become professor of mechanics and construction at the Military Academy of the Kingdom of Sardinia at Turin and at the University of Turin. To this early period belongs his exposition and extension of Babbage's invention of a mechanical calculator to be published in 1842.

His political career started at this time. Between the years 1848 and 1859 King Charles Albert entrusted Menabrea with diplomatic missions to Modena and Parma. Menabrea then entered Parliament (where he championed proposals for Alpine tunneling) and was attached successively to the ministries of war and foreign affairs. At the same time he attained the rank of major general and was commander in chief of the army engineers in the Lombard campaigns of 1859. He directed siege and fortification works and also the artifical flooding of the plains between the Dora Baltea and the Sesia rivers to obstruct the Austrian advance.

During this time (1857–1858) Menabrea's early scientific papers were published, in which he gave the first precise formulation of the methods of structural analysis based on the "virtual work principle" earlier examined by A. Dorna. He studied an elastic truss in these papers and enunciated his "principle of elasticity," calling it also "principle of least work." He stated that when an elastic system attains equilibrium under external forces, the work done by the tensions and compressions in the internal members of the system is a minimum.

Menabrea's political and military advance continued. In 1860 he became lieutenant-general, conducted sieges at Ancona, Capua, and Gaeta, was appointed senator, and was granted the title of count. He was minister of the navy under Ricasoli from June 1861 to May 1862 and from January to April 1863 and minister of public works from December 1862 to September 1864 (under Farini and Minghetti). He was named Italian plenipotentiary for the peace negotiations with Austria in 1866. In October 1867 he succeeded Rattazzi as premier, holding simultaneously the portfolio of foreign minister, and remained in these posts in three cabinets until December 1869. During this turbulent period he was faced with the difficult situation created by Garibaldi's invasion of the Papal States. Menabrea issued the famous proclamation of 27 October 1868, in which he disavowed Garibaldi, against whom he instituted judicial proceedings. He protested against the pope's temporal power, insisted on the Italian prerogative of interference in Rome, and contended against infringement of Italian rights in repeated negotiations with Napoleon III and the pope.

In 1868 Menabrea published a new demonstration of his principle of least work, which, although superior to the preceding one, still failed to note the independence of the variations of the internal forces and of the elongations of the members of the structure. This oversight was criticized by Sabbia, Genocchi, and Castigliano, giving rise to a controversy lasting until 1875, which is described in the article on Castigliano. In 1870 Menabrea published jointly with the French mathematician J. L. F. Bertrand (1822–1900) a note that advanced the first valid proof of his principle.

In order to deprive Menabrea of influence as aide-de-camp to King Victor Emmanuel II, and to get him out of the country, Giovanni Lanza, his successor as premier, appointed him ambassador to London, and

in 1882 to Paris. In 1875 he was made marquis of Valdora; he retired from public life in 1892.

Menabrea's place in the history of Italy is assured; his role in the introduction of concepts of work and energy into analytical mechanics and engineering has been overshadowed by the greater fame of Castigliano. In the United States, for example, Menabrea is hardly mentioned, although in Continental and particularly Italian textbooks the correct distinction between Menabrea's and Castigliano's theorems is generally made. Menabrea's methods placed these concepts for the first time very clearly before the engineering profession and thus started the essential work of education which was completed by Castigliano.

BIBLIOGRAPHY

I. ORIGINAL WORKS. Menabrea's principal scientific works consist of seven papers, as follows: "Notions sur la machine analytique de Charles Babbage," in *Bibliothèque Universelle de Genève*, n.s. **41** (1842), 352–376; "Principio generale per determinare le tensioni e le pressioni in un sistema elastico," a seminar presented to the Reale Accademia delle Scienze di Torino in 1857, which was then printed as "Nouveau principe sur la distribution des tensions dans les systèmes élastiques," in *Comptes rendus hebdomadaires des séances de l'Académie des sciences*, **46** (1858), 1056. Then followed "Étude de Statique Physique —Principe général pour déterminer les pressions et les tensions dans un système élastique," in *Memorie della Reale Accademia delle scienze di Torino*, 2nd ser., **25** (1868), 141. An abstract of Bertrand's letter to General Menabrea was published jointly by Menabrea and Bertrand in *Atti della Reale Accademia delle scienze*, **5** (1 May 1870), 702.

The last two contributions are the reply to criticism in "Un'ultima lettera sulle peripezie della serie di Lagrange in risposta al Prof. Angelo Genocchi per L. F. Menabrea, A. D. B. Boncompagni," in *Bullettino di bibliografia e di storia delle scienze matematiche e fisiche*, **6** (October 1873), 435, and the memoir which raised the dispute with Castigliano, i.e., "Sulla determinazione delle tensioni e delle pressioni ne sistemi elastici," in *Atti della Reale Accademia dei Lincei*, 2nd ser., **2** (1875), 201.

II. SECONDARY LITERATURE. The reader is referred to the article on Alberto Castigliano for a listing of pertinent works, and to Menabrea's autobiography, covering the years up to 1871, published as *Memorie*, L. Briguglio and L. Bulferetti, eds. (Florence, 1971).

BRUNO A. BOLEY

MENAECHMUS (*fl.* Athens and Cyzicus, middle of fourth century B.C.), *mathematics.*

In the summary of the history of Greek geometry given by Proclus, derived at this point from Eudemus, it is stated that "Amyclas of Heraclea, one of the friends of Plato, and Menaechmus, a pupil of Eudoxus and associate of Plato, and his brother Dinostratus made the whole of geometry still more perfect."[1] There is no reason to doubt that this Menaechmus is to be identified with the Manaechmus who is described in the *Suda Lexicon* as "a Platonic philosopher of Alopeconnesus, or according to some of Proconnesus, who wrote works of philosophy and three books on Plato's *Republic*."[2] Alopeconnesus was in the Thracian Chersonese, and Proconnesus (the Island of Marmara) was in the Propontis (the Sea of Marmara), no great distance from it; and both were near Cyzicus (Kapidaği Yarimadasi, Turkey), where Eudoxus took up his abode and where Helicon, another pupil, was born.[3] This dating of Menaechmus, about the middle of the fourth century B.C., accords with an agreeable anecdote reproduced by Stobaeus from the grammarian Serenus; when Alexander the Great requested Menaechmus to teach him geometry by an easy method, Menaechmus replied: "O king, for traveling through the country there are private roads and royal roads, but in geometry there is one road for all."[4] A similar story is told of Euclid and Ptolemy I;[5] but it would be natural to transfer it to the more famous geometer, and the attribution to Menaechmus is to be preferred. If true, it would suggest that Menaechmus was the mathematical tutor of Alexander. He could have been introduced to Alexander by Aristotle, who had close relations with the mathematicians of Cyzicus.[6] A phrase used by Proclus in two places—οἱ περὶ Μέναιχμον μαθηματικοί—implies that Menaechmus had a school;[7] and Allman has argued cogently that this was the mathematical school of Cyzicus, of which Eudoxus and Helicon (probably) were heads before him and Polemarchus and Callippus after him.[8]

According to Proclus, Menaechmus differentiated between two senses in which the word στοιχεῖον, "element," is used.[9] In one sense it means any proposition leading to another proposition, as Euclid I.1 is an element in the proof of I.2, or I.4 is in that of I.5; and in this sense propositions may be said to be elements of each other if they can be established reciprocally—for example, the relation between the sum of the interior angles of a rectilineal figure and the sum of the exterior angles. In the second sense an element is a simple constituent of a composite entity, and in this sense not every proposition is an element but only those having a primordial relation to the conclusion, as the postulates have to the theorems. As Proclus notes, this is the sense in which "element" is used by Euclid, and Menaechmus may have helped to fix this terminology.

In another passage Proclus shows that many so-called conversions of propositions are false and are not properly called conversions, that is, not every converse of a proposition is true.[10] As an example he notes that every hexagonal number is triangular but not every triangular number is hexagonal, and he adds that these matters have not escaped the notice of the mathematicians in the circle of Menaechmus and Amphinomus.

In yet another passage Proclus discusses the division of propositions into problems and theorems.[11] While the followers of Speusippus and Amphinomus held that all propositions were theorems, the school of Menaechmus maintained that they were all problems but that there were two types of problems: at one time the aim is to find the thing sought, at another to see what some definite thing is, or to what kind it belongs, or what change it has undergone, or what relation it has to something else. Proclus considers that both schools were right; it might be argued with equal justice that both were wrong and that the distinction between theorem and problem is valid.

It is clear from these references that Menaechmus gave much attention to the philosophy and technology of mathematics. He must also have applied himself to mathematical astronomy, for Theon of Smyrna records that Menaechmus and Callippus introduced the system of "deferent" and "counteracting" spheres into the explanation of the movements of the heavenly bodies (οἱ τὰς μὲν φερούσας, τὰς δὲ ἀνελιττούσας εἰσηγήσαντο).[12] The terms mean that one of the spheres bears the heavenly body; the other corrects its motion so as to account for the apparent irregularities of their paths. Eudoxus was the first to devise a mathematical model to explain the motions of the sun and planets, and he did so by a highly ingenious system of concentric spheres, the common center being the center of the earth. The sun, moon, and planets were each regarded as fixed on the equator of a moving sphere; the poles of that sphere were themselves borne round on a larger concentric sphere moving about two different poles with a different speed; and so on. For the sun and moon Eudoxus postulated three spheres; for the planets, four. The modifications in this system made by Callippus are known in some detail. For example, he added one sphere for each planet except Jupiter and Saturn and two spheres for the sun and the moon—five in all. Nothing more is known of Menaechmus' contribution than what Theon relates, but he would appear to have been working on the same lines as Callippus. T. H. Martin conjectured that Menaechmus made his contribution in his commentary on Plato's *Republic* when dealing with the passage on the distaff of the Fates.[13]

It is not, however, on these achievements but on the discovery of the conic sections that the fame of Menaechmus chiefly rests. Democritus had speculated on plane sections of a cone parallel to the base and very near to each other,[14] and other geometers must have cut the cone (and cylinder) by sections not parallel to the base; but Menaechmus is the first who is known to have identified the resulting sections as curves with definite properties.

The discovery was a by-product of the search for a method of duplicating the cube. Hippocrates had shown that this could be reduced to the problem of finding two mean proportionals between two lines, and Menaechmus showed that the two means could be obtained by the intersection of a parabola and a hyperbola. His solution is given in a collection of such solutions preserved by Eutocius in his commentary on Archimedes' *On the Sphere and the Cylinder*.[15] Another of the solutions, by Eratosthenes, is introduced by a letter purporting to be from Eratosthenes to Ptolemy Euergetes.[16] The letter is spurious, but it quotes a genuine epigram by Eratosthenes written on a votive pillar to which was attached a device for effecting the solution mechanically. The epigram included the lines:[17]

> Try not to do the difficult task of the cylinders of Archytas, or to cut the cones in the triads of Menaechmus or to draw such a pattern of lines as is described by the god-fearing Eudoxus.

Proclus, in a passage derived from Geminus, also attributes the discovery of the conic sections to Menaechmus and cites a line from the verses of Eratosthenes in the form Μὴ δὲ Μεναιχμίους κωνοτομεῖν τριάδας.[18] He notes again in his commentary on Plato's *Timaeus* that Menaechmus solved the problem of finding two means by "conic lines" but says that he prefers to transcribe Archytas' solution.[19]

Eratosthenes' epigram implies not only that Menaechmus was aware of the conic sections but that he was aware of all three types and saw them as sections of a cone—that is, not as plane curves that he later identified with sections of a cone. The proof itself shows also that he knew the properties of the asymptotes of a hyperbola,[20] at least of a rectangular hyperbola, which is astonishing when it is remembered that Apollonius does not introduce the asymptotes until his second book, after the properties of the diameter and ordinates have been proved. There are no signs of any knowledge of the conic sections before Menaechmus, but with him it suddenly blossomed forth into full flower.[21]

The proof as we have it cannot reproduce the words of Menaechmus himself and no doubt has been recast by Eutocius in his own language, or by someone earlier.[22] It uses the terms παραβολή and ὑπερβολή, although these words were first coined by Apollonius; and we have the evidence of Geminus, as transmitted by Eutocius, that "the ancients" (οἱ παλαιοί) used the names "section of a right-angled cone" for the parabola, "section of an obtuse-angled cone" for the hyperbola, and "section of an acute-angled cone" for the ellipse.[23] This is undeniable evidence that at the time of "the ancients" the three curves were conceived as sections of three types of cone. But how ancient were "the ancients"? Pappus gives a similar account to that of Geminus but says these names were given by Aristaeus;[24] and there is some reason to believe that the name used by Menaechmus for the ellipse was θυρεός, because its oval shape resembled a shield.[25] The question of name is not so important as the question behind it: whether Menaechmus discovered his curves as sections of cones or whether he investigated them as plane curves, which were only later (by Aristaeus?) identified with the curves obtained by plane sections of a cone. It will be necessary to return to this question later.

The term ἀσύμπτωτοι, employed by Eutocius, would also not have been used by Menaechmus, who probably used the expression αἱ ἔγγιστα εὐθεῖαι τῆς τοῦ ἀμβλυγωνίου κώνου τομῆς, or simply αἱ ἔγγιστα, which is found in Archimedes, who also employed the old names for the sections. Other terms that Menaechmus would not have used are ἄξων, "axis," and ὀρθία πλευρά, or *latus rectum*.

By way of introduction to Menaechmus' proof it may be pointed out that if x, y are two mean proportionals between a, b, so that

$$a : x = x : y = y : b,$$

then

$$x^2 = ay$$

and

$$xy = ab.$$

These are easily recognized today as the equations of a parabola referred to a diameter and a tangent at its extremity as axes and the equation of a hyperbola referred to its asymptotes as axes; the means may therefore be obtained as the intercepts on the axes of a point of intersection of a parabola and hyperbola, but Menaechmus had to discover *ab initio* that there were such curves and to ascertain their properties.

He proceeded by way of analysis and synthesis.

Suppose the problem solved. Let a, b be the given straight lines and x, y the mean proportionals—where the letters both indicate the lines and are a measure of

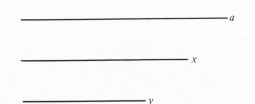

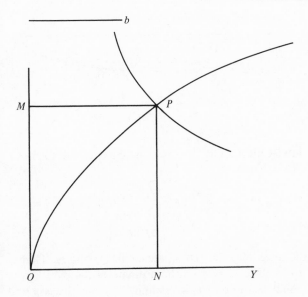

FIGURE 1

and let the perpendiculars PM, PN be drawn. Then by the property of the parabola

$$PN^2 = a \cdot ON,$$

that is,

$$a : PN = PN : ON,$$

and by the property of the hyperbola

$$ab = PN \cdot PM$$
$$= PN \cdot ON.$$

Therefore

$$a : PN = ON : b,$$

and

$$a : PN = PN : ON = ON : b.$$

Let a straight line x be drawn equal to PN and a straight line y equal to ON. Then a, x, y, b are in continuous proportion.

This solution is followed in the manuscripts of Eutocius by another solution introduced with the word Ἄλλως, "Otherwise," in which the two means are obtained by the intersection of two parabolas.

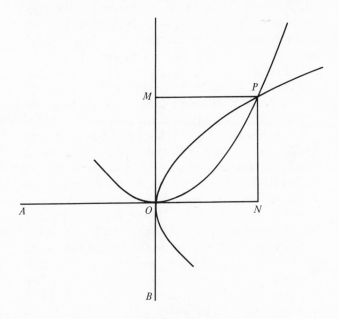

FIGURE 2

In the figure, AO, BO are the two given straight lines, the two parabolas through O intersect at P, and it is easily shown that

$$BO : ON = ON : OM = OM : OA,$$

or

$$a : x = x : y = y : b.$$

their length—so that $a : x = x : y = y : b$. On a straight line OY given in position and terminating at O, let $ON = y$ be cut off, and let there be drawn perpendicular to it at N the straight line $PN = x$. Because $a : x = x : y$, it follows that $ay = x^2$ or $a \cdot ON = x^2$, that is, $a \cdot ON = PN^2$, so that P lies on a parabola through O. Let the parallels PM, OM be drawn. Since xy is given, being equal to ab, $PM \cdot PN$ is also given; and therefore P lies on a hyperbola in the asymptotes OM, ON. P is therefore determined as the intersection of the parabola and hyperbola.

In the synthesis the straight lines a, b are given, and OY is given in position with O as an end point. Through O let there be drawn a parabola having OY as its axis and *latus rectum a*. Then the squares on the ordinates drawn at right angles to OY are equal to the rectangle contained by the *latus rectum* and the abscissa. Let OP be the parabola, let OM be drawn perpendicular to OY, and in the asymptotes OM, OY let there be drawn a hyperbola such that the rectangle contained by the straight lines drawn parallel to OM, ON is equal to the rectangle contained by a, b (that is, $PM \cdot PN = ab$). Let it cut the parabola at P,

271

The proof is established by analysis and synthesis as in the first proof, and it corresponds to the equations

$$x^2 = ay$$
$$y^2 = bx.$$

It has hitherto been assumed by all writers on the subject that this second proof is also by Menaechmus, but G. J. Toomer has discovered as proposition 10 of the Arabic text of Diocles' *On Burning Mirrors* a solution of the problem of two mean proportionals by the intersection of two parabolas with axes at right angles to each other, and with *latera recta* equal to the two extremes, which looks remarkably like the second solution;[26] and it is followed as proposition 11 by another solution which is identical in its mathematical content with that attributed to Diocles by Eutocius. Toomer believes that the second solution should therefore be attributed to Diocles, not to Menaechmus. A final judgment must await publication of his edition of Diocles, but it may at once be noted that there are differences as well as resemblances. In particular, in the Arabic text Diocles starts from the focus-directrix property of the parabola—of which Menaechmus shows no awareness—and in order to get his means deduces from it the property that the ordinate at any point is a mean proportional between the abscissa and the *latus rectum*. It could be that Diocles found his solution independently, or he may have made a conscious adaptation of Menaechmus' solution in order to start from the focus-directrix property.

C. A. Bretschneider first showed how Menaechmus could have investigated the curves, and his suggestion has been generally followed.[27] In a semicircle the perpendicular from any point on the circumference to the diameter is a mean proportional between the segments of the diameter. This property would have been familiar before Menaechmus, and Bretschneider thinks it probable that he would have sought some similar property for the conic sections. We know from Geminus, as transmitted by Eutocius, that "the ancients" generated the conic sections by a plane section at right angles to one side (generator) of the cone, getting different curves according to whether the cone was right-angled, obtuse-angled, or acute-angled.[28] If *ABC* is a right-angled cone and *DEF* is a plane section at right angles at *D* to the generator *AC*, the resulting curve where the plane intersects the cone is a parabola. Let *J* be any point in *DE*, and through *J* let there be drawn a plane parallel to the base of the cone. It will cut the cone in a circle. Let it meet the parabola at *K*. The planes *DEF* and *HKG* are both perpendicular to the plane *BAC*, and their line of

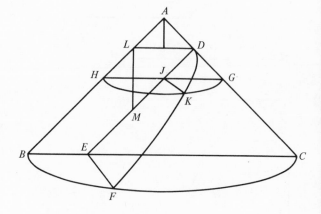

FIGURE 3

intersection *JK* is thus perpendicular to the diameter *HG*. Therefore,

$$JK^2 = HJ \cdot JG$$
$$= LD \cdot JG$$
$$= DJ \cdot DM,$$

because *JDG* and *DLM* are similar triangles. That is to say, the square on the ordinate of the parabola is equal to the rectangle contained by the abscissa and a given straight line *(latus rectum)*, which is the fundamental property of the curve. Bretschneider demonstrates in similar manner the corresponding properties for the ellipse and hyperbola.

Despite Eratosthenes' epigram, the clear statement of Geminus, and the evidence of the early names, it has been doubted whether Menaechmus first obtained the curves as sections of a cone. Charles Taylor suggests that they were discovered as plane loci in investigations of the problem of doubling the cube.[29] In support he argues that Menaechmus used a machine for drawing conics, that in his solutions he uses only the parabola and hyperbola, and that the ellipse—the most obvious of the sections of a cone—is treated last by Apollonius; but he agrees that the conception of a conic as a plane locus was immediately lost. If it be the case that such names as "section of a right-angled cone" were introduced by Aristaeus after the time of Menaechmus, this raises a slight presumption that Menaechmus did not obtain the curves as sections of a cone; but it can hardly outweigh the evidence of Eratosthenes and Geminus.[30]

Allman believes that Menaechmus was led to his discovery by a study of Archytas' solution of the problem of doubling the cube. "In the solution of Archytas the same conceptions are made use of and the same course of reasoning is pursued, which, in the hands of his successor and contemporary Menaechmus, led to the discovery of the three conic sections."[31] This is more than likely. The brilliant solution of Archytas must have made a tremendous splash in the mathematical pool of ancient Greece.

If it be granted that Menaechmus knew how to obtain a hyperbola by a section of an obtuse-angled cone perpendicular to a generator, how did he obtain the rectangular hyperbola required for his proof? H. G. Zeuthen showed how this could be done.[32] In Figure 4, TKC is a plane section through the axis

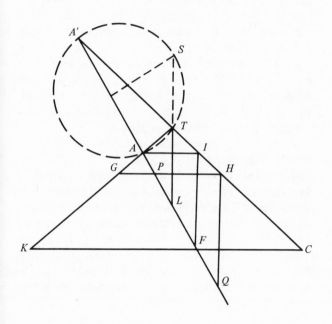

FIGURE 4

of an obtuse-angled cone, AP is a perpendicular to the generator TK, and a plane section through A parallel to the base meets TC at I. If P is the foot of an ordinate to the hyperbola with value y, then

$$y^2 = GP \cdot PH$$
$$= AP \cdot PQ$$
$$= AP \cdot \frac{AF}{A'A} \cdot A'P$$
$$= \frac{2AL}{A'A} \cdot x \cdot x',$$

where $AP = x$ and $A'P = x'$.

The hyperbola will be rectangular if $A'A = 2AL$. The problem is therefore as follows: Given a straight line $A'A$, and AL along $A'A$ produced equal to

$A'A/2$ to find a cone such that L is on its axis and the section through AL perpendicular to the generator through A is a rectangular hyperbola with $A'A$ as transverse axis. That is to say, the problem is to find a point T on the straight line through A perpendicular to $A'A$ such that TL bisects the angle that is the supplement of $A'TA$. Suppose that T has been found. The circle circumscribing the triangle $A'AT$ will meet LT produced in some point S; and because the angle $A'AT$ is right, $A'T$ is its diameter. Therefore $A'SL$ is right and S lies on the circle having $A'L$ as its diameter. But

$$\angle AA'S = \text{supplement of } \angle ATS$$
$$= \angle ATL$$
$$= \angle LTC$$
$$= \angle A'TS,$$

whence it follows that the segments AS, $A'S$ are equal and S lies on the perpendicular to the midpoint of $A'A$. Therefore S is determined as the intersection of the perpendicular to the midpoint of $A'A$ with the circle drawn on $A'L$ as diameter; and if SL is drawn, T, the vertex of the cone, is obtained as the intersection of SL with the perpendicular to $A'A$ at A.

Some writers, such as Allman, have doubted whether Menaechmus could have been aware of the asymptotes of a hyperbola;[33] but unless it is held that Eutocius rewrote Menaechmus' proof so completely that it really ceased to be Menaechmus, the evidence is compelling. It is easy to see (again following

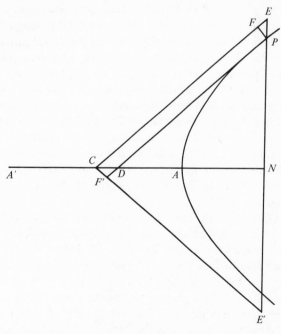

FIGURE 5

Zeuthen) how in the case of a rectangular hyperbola Menaechmus could have deduced the asymptote property from the axial property without difficulty.[34]

Let AA' be the transverse axis of a rectangular hyperbola, and CE, CE' its asymptotes meeting at right angles at C. Let P be any point on the curve and N the foot of the perpendicular to AA' (the principal ordinate). Let PF, PF' be drawn perpendicular to the asymptotes. Then

$$CA^2 = CN^2 - PN^2, \text{ by the axial property}$$
$$= CN \cdot NE - PN \cdot ND$$
$$= 2(\triangle CNE - \triangle PND)$$
$$= 2 \text{ quadrilateral } CDPE$$
$$= 2 \text{ rectangle } CF'PF, \text{ since } \triangle PEF = \triangle CDF',$$
$$= 2PF \cdot PF'.$$

$\therefore PF \cdot PF' = \frac{1}{2}CA^2$, which is the asymptote property.

Alternatively,

$$CA^2 = CN^2 - PN^2$$
$$= EN^2 - PN^2$$
$$= (EN - PN)(EN + PN)$$
$$= (EN - PN)(PN + NE')$$
$$= EP \cdot PE'$$
$$= \sqrt{2}PF \cdot \sqrt{2}PF', \text{ because } \angle PEF \text{ is } 45°.$$

$\therefore PF \cdot PF' = \frac{1}{2}CA^2.$

The letter of the pseudo-Eratosthenes to Ptolemy Euergetes says that certain Delians, having been commanded by an oracle to double one of their altars, sent a mission to the geometers with Plato in the Academy. Archytas solved the problem by means of half-cylinders, and Eudoxus by means of the so-called curved lines. Although they were able to solve the problem theoretically, none of them except Menaechmus was able to apply his solution in practice—and Menaechmus only to a small extent and with difficulty.[35] According to Plutarch, Plato censured Eudoxus, Archytas, Menaechmus, and their circle for trying to reduce the doubling of the cube to mechanical devices, for in this way geometry was made to slip back from the incorporeal world to the things of sense.[36]

Despite this emphatic evidence, Bretschneider considers it doubtful whether Menaechmus had an instrument for drawing his curves.[37] He notes that it is possible to find a series of points on each curve but agrees that this is a troublesome method of obtaining a curve without some mechanical device. Allman develops this hint and believes that by the familiar Pythagorean process of the "application" (παραβολή) of areas, which later gave its name to the parabola,

Menaechmus could have found as many points as he pleased—"with the greatest facility"—on the parabola $y^2 = px$; that, having solved the Delian problem by the intersection of two parabolas, he later found it easier to employ one parabola and the hyperbola $xy = a^2$, "the construction of which by points is even easier than that of the parabola"; and that this was the way by which in practice he drew the curves.[38] He also implies that this was what the pseudo-Eratosthenes and Plutarch had in mind. The evidence, however, seems inescapable that Menaechmus attempted to find some mechanical device for tracing the curves. Bretschneider's objection that no trace of any such instrument has survived is not substantial. Centuries later, Isidorus of Miletus is said to have invented a compass, διαβήτης, for drawing the parabola in Menaechmus' first solution.[39] Every schoolchild knows, of course, how to draw the conic sections with a ruler, string, and pins;[40] but this easy method was not open to Menaechmus, since it depends upon the focus-directrix property.

There is a possible solution to this dilemma, so simple that apparently it has not hitherto been propounded, although Heath came near to doing so. In Eutocius' collection of solutions to the problem of doubling the cube is a mechanical solution attributed to Plato.[41] It is now universally agreed that it cannot be by Plato because of his censure of mechanical solutions, which fits in with his whole philosophy. M. Cantor, however, thought it possible that he worked it out in a spirit of contempt, just to show how

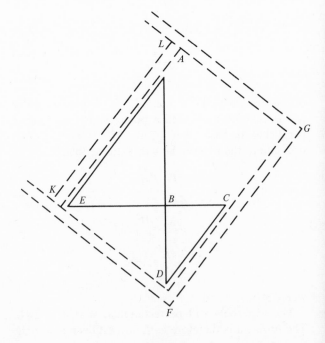

FIGURE 6

274

easy such things were in comparison with the real business of the philosopher.[42] The lines between which it is desired to find two means are placed at right angles, as *AB*, *BC*. The dotted figure *FGLK* is an instrument in which a ruler *KL* moves in slots in the two vertical sides so as to be always parallel to the base *FG*. The instrument is moved so that *FG* is made to pass through *C*, and *F* lies on *AB* produced. The ruler is then moved so that *KL* passes through *A*. If *K* does not then lie on *CB* produced, the instrument is manipulated until the four following conditions are all fulfilled: *FG* passes through *C*; *F* lies on *AB* produced; *KL* passes through *A*; *K* lies on *CB* produced. The conditions can be satisfied with difficulty—δυσχερῶς, as the pseudo-Eratosthenes says —and when it is done,

$$AB : BE = BE : BD = BD : BC,$$

so that *EB*, *BD* are the required means.

The arrangement of the extremes and the means in Figure 6 is exactly the same as in the second solution attributed to Menaechmus. "Hence," says Heath, "it seems probable that someone who had Menaechmus' second solution before him worked to show how the same representation of the four straight lines could be got by a mechanical construction as an alternative to the use of conics."[43] But why not Menaechmus himself? If he was the author, it would be easy for the tradition to refer it to his master, Plato. This cannot be proved or disproved, but it would be the simplest explanation of all the facts.

NOTES

1. Proclus, *In primum Euclidis*, G. Friedlein, ed. (Leipzig, 1873; repr. Hildesheim, 1967), 67.8–12. An English trans. is Glenn R. Morrow, *Proclus: A Commentary on the First Book of Euclid's Elements* (Princeton, 1970), 55–56. For Dinostratus see *Dictionary of Scientific Biography*, IV, 103–105.
2. *Suda Lexicon*, A. Adler, ed., *M.* No. 140, I, pt. 3 (Leipzig, 1933), 317–318. It is entirely in character that the *Suda* not only misspells Menaechmus' name but omits his most important achievement. The *Suda* is followed by Eudocia, *Violarium*, No. 665, H. Flach, ed. (Leipzig, 1880), p. 494.3–5.
3. Also Athenaeus of Cyzicus, if that is the correct interpretation of the name in Proclus, *op. cit.*, 67.16, as seems probable, but it could possibly be understood as Cyzicinus of Athens.
4. Stobaeus, *Anthologium*, C. Wachsmuth, ed., II (Leipzig, 1884), 228.30–33.
5. Proclus, *op. cit.*, 68.13–17.
6. G. J. Allman, *Greek Geometry From Thales to Euclid* (Dublin–London, 1889), 154, n. 2, 179 and n. 42.
7. *Op. cit.*, 78.9, 254.4.
8. *Op. cit.*, 171–172.
9. *Op. cit.*, 72.23–73.14. This passage is subjected to an elaborate analysis by Malcolm Brown in "A Pre-Aristotelian Mathematician on Deductive Order," in *Philosophy and Humanism: Essays in Honor of Paul Oskar Kristeller* (New York, in press). Brown sees Menaechmus as the champion of the relativity of mathematical principles and Aristotle as the champion of their absolute character.
10. *Ibid.*, 253.16–254.5.
11. *Ibid.*, 77.6–79.2.
12. *Liber de astronomia*, T. H. Martin, ed. (Paris, 1849; repr. Groningen, 1971), 330.19–332.3; *Expositio rerum mathematicarum ad legendum Platonem utilium*, E. Hiller, ed. (Leipzig, 1878), 201.22–202.2.
13. *Liber de astronomia*, "Dissertatio," 59–60; *Republic*, X, 616–617.
14. Plutarch, *De communibus notitiis contra Stoicos* 39.3, 1079E, M. Pohlenz and R. Westman, eds., in *Plutarchi Moralia*, VI, fasc. 2 (Leipzig, 1959), 72.3–11. Plutarch writes on the authority of Chrysippus.
15. *Commentarii in libros De sphaera et cylindro*, in *Archimedis opera omnia*, J. L. Heiberg, ed., 2nd ed., III (Leipzig, 1915; repr. Stuttgart, 1972), 54.26–106.24.
16. For Eratosthenes there is now available P. M. Fraser, *Eratosthenes of Cyrene* (London, 1971), which was the 1970 "Lecture on a Master Mind" of the British Academy.
17. Eutocius, *op. cit.*, 96.16–19; διζήση is the conjecture of Ulrich von Wilamowitz-Moellendorff for the solecism διζηαι of the MS.
18. *Op. cit.*, 111.20–23.
19. *In Platonis Timaeum ad* 32A, B, E. Diehl, ed. (Leipzig, 1914), pp. 33.29–34.4. The promise to transcribe Archytas is not redeemed in this work.
20. Allman, *op. cit.*, is skeptical on this point. "Menaechmus may have discovered the asymptotes; but, in my judgement, we are not justified in making this assertion, on account of the fact, which is undoubted, that the solutions of Menaechmus have not come down to us in his own words" (p. 170). "There is no evidence, however, for the inference that Menaechmus ... knew of the existence of the asymptotes of the hyperbola, and its equation in relation to them" (p. 177).
21. The first historian of Greek mathematics, J. E. Montucla, was deeply impressed by this fact. Writing of the proof by means of the parabola and hyperbola between asymptotes he notes, "Cette dernière montre même qu'on avoit fait à cette époque quelque chose de plus que les premiers pas dans cette théorie" (*Histoire des mathématiques*, I [Paris, 1758], 178). And again, "On ne peut y méconnoître une théorie déjà assez sçavante de ces courbes" (p. 183).
22. This appears to have been first recognized by N. T. Reimer, *Historia problematis de cubi duplicatione* (Göttingen, 1798), 68, n.
23. *Commentaria in Conica*, in *Apollonii Pergaei quae ... exstant ...*, J. L. Heiberg, ed., II (Leipzig, 1893), 168.17–170.27.
24. *Collectio*, F. Hultsch, ed., II (Berlin, 1877), VII.30–31, pp. 672.20–24, 674.16–19; Hultsch attributes the second passage to an interpolator.
25. In the following passages of Greek authors θυρεός and ἔλλειψις are used interchangeably: Eutocius, *Commentaria in Conica*, Heiberg, ed., II, 176.6; Proclus, *In primum Euclidis*, Friedlein, ed., 103.6, 9, 10, 111.6 (citing Geminus), 126.19, 20–21, 22. The name appears also to have been familiar to Euclid, for in the preface to the *Phaenomena*, in *Euclidis opera omnia*, J. L. Heiberg and H. Menge, eds., VIII (Leipzig, 1916), 6.5–7, he says: "If a cone or cylinder be cut by a plane not parallel to the base, the section is a section of an acute-angled cone which is like a shield (θυρεός)." From such passages Heiberg concluded that θυρεός was the term used for the ellipse by Menaechmus ("Nogle Bidrag til de graeske Mathematikeres Terminologi," in *Philologisk-historiske Samfunds Mindeskrift*, XXVI [Copenhagen, 1879], 7; *Litterärgeschichtliche Studien über Euklid* [Leipzig, 1882], 88). The primary meaning of θυρεός is "stone put against a door" (to keep it shut)—so H. G. Liddell and R. Scott, *A Greek-English Lexicon*, new ed.,

H. Stuart Jones (Oxford, 1940)—whence it comes to mean "oblong shield" (shaped like a door).

26. Dublin, Chester Beatty Library, Chester Beatty MS Arabic no. 5255, fols. 1–26.

27. *Die Geometrie und die Geometer vor Euklides* (Leipzig, 1870), 157–158.

28. *Commentaria in conica*, Heiberg, ed., II, 168.17–170.18.

29. *Introduction to the Ancient and Modern Geometry of Conics* (Cambridge, 1881), xxxi, xxxiii, xliii.

30. There is a similar uncertainty about the term "solid loci" (στερεοὶ τόποι). According to Pappus (*Collectio*, VII.30, Hultsch, ed., II, 672.21), Aristaeus wrote five books of *Solid loci* connected with (or continuous with) the *Conics*. This implies that "solid loci" were conics; and the name suggests that when it was given, the curves were regarded as sections of a solid, in contrast with "plane loci" such as straight lines and "linear loci," which were higher curves. But there can be no certainty that the name is older than Aristaeus. T. L. Heath, *A History of Greek Mathematics*, II (Oxford, 1921), 117–118, gives an alternative explanation, deriving plane, solid, and linear loci from plane, solid, and linear problems; but he concedes that it would be natural to speak of the conic sections as solid loci, "especially as they were in fact produced from sections of a solid figure, the cone."

31. *Op. cit.*, 115. In detail he writes:

In each investigation two planes are perpendicular to an underlying plane; and the intersection of the two planes is a common ordinate to two curves lying one in each plane. In one of the intersecting planes the curve is in each case a semi-circle, and the common ordinate is, therefore, a mean proportional between the segments of its diameter. So far the investigation is the same for all. Now, from the consideration of the figure in the underlying plane—which is different in each case—it follows that:—in the first case—the solution of Archytas—the ordinate in the second intersecting plane is a mean proportional between the segments of its base, whence it is inferred that the extremity of the ordinate in this plane also lies on a semi-circle; in the second case—the section of the right-angled cone—the ordinate is a mean proportional between a given straight line and the abscissa; and, lastly, in the third case—the section of an acute-angled cone—the ordinate is proportional to the geometric mean between the segments of the base [p. 169].

32. *Die Lehre von den Kegelschnitten im Altertum*, R. von Fischer-Benzon, ed. (Copenhagen, 1886), repr. with foreword and index by J. E. Hofmann (Hildesheim, 1966), 464–465. T. L. Heath, who followed Zeuthen's method in *Apollonius of Perga* (Cambridge, 1896), xxvi–xxviii, gives a different method in *A History of Greek Mathematics*, II, 113–114, for determining *T*. He shows that *T* is on the circle which is the locus of all points such that their distances from *A′*, *A* are in the ratio 3:1, and *T* is determined as the intersection of the perpendicular to *A′A* at *A* with this circle.

33. See n. 20.

34. *Op. cit.*, 463–464.

35. Eutocius, *Commentarii in libros De sphaera et cylindro*, in *Archimedis opera omnia*, J. L. Heiberg, ed., III, 88.23–90.11. There are similar accounts of the Delian mission in other authors. Plutarch, *De genio Socratis*, 7, 579A–D, P. H. De Lacy and B. Einarson, eds., Loeb Classical Library (London–Cambridge, Mass., 1959), 396.17–398.22, says that Plato referred the Delians to Eudoxus of Cnidus and Helicon of Cyzicus; John Philoponus, *Commentary on the Posterior Analytics of Aristotle*, 1.vii, 75b12, M. Wallies, ed., *Commentaria in Aristotelem Graeca*, XIII, pt. 3 (Berlin, 1909), p. 102.7–18, is in general agreement but omits the references to the geometers. Theon of Smyrna, *Expositio*, E. Hiller, ed., 2.3–12, quoting a lost work of Eratosthenes entitled *Platonicus*, says the god gave this oracle to the Delians, not because he wanted his altar doubled but because he wished to reproach the Greeks for their neglect of mathematics and contempt for geometry. Plutarch also in another work, *De E apud Delphos*, c. 6, 386E, F. C. Babbitt, ed., Loeb Classical Library, Plutarch's *Moralia*, V (London–Cambridge, Mass., 1936), p. 210.6–11 agrees that the god was trying to get the Greeks to pursue geometry rather than to have his altar doubled.

36. Plutarch, *Quaestiones conviviales*, viii.2.1, 718E–F, E. L. Minar, W. C. Helmbold, and F. H. Sandbach, eds., Loeb Classical Library, *Plutarch's Moralia*, IX, trans. as *Table Talk* (London–Cambridge, Mass., 1961), pp. 120.20–122.7. The same censure of Eudoxus and Archytas is repeated in Plutarch, "Vita Marcelli," xiv.5–6, *Plutarch's Lives*, B. Perrin, ed., V, Loeb Classical Library (London–Cambridge, Mass., 1917; repr. 1961), pp. 470.17–472.6, but here there is no mention of Menaechmus.

37. *Op. cit.*, 162.

38. *Op. cit.*, 176–177.

39. [Eutocius], *Commentarii in libros De sphaera et cylindro*, in *Archimedis opera omnia*, Heiberg, ed., III, 84.7–11. The words are bracketed by Heiberg and are no doubt an interpolation made by one of the pupils of Isidorus, who revised Eudocius' text.

40. Charles Smith, *Geometrical Conics* (London, 1894), 32, 84, 125.

41. Eutocius, *Commentarii in libros De sphaera et cylindro*, in *Archimedis opera omnia*, Heiberg, ed., III, 56.13–58.14.

42. *Vorlesungen über Geschichte der Mathematik*, 3rd ed., I (Leipzig, 1907), 234.

43. T. L. Heath, *A History of Greek Mathematics*, I (Oxford, 1921), 256.

BIBLIOGRAPHY

Menaechmus is known to have written a commentary on Plato's *Republic* in three books and other philosophical works, and he must have written at least one work in which he described his discovery of the conic sections. (Whether he wrote a separate book on the subject has been doubted, since Pappus, *Collectio*, F. Hultsch, ed., II [Berlin, 1877], VII 30, p. 672, does not mention any treatise on conics before those of Euclid and Aristaeus.) None of his works has survived. The fragments relating to his life and work are collected in Max C. P. Schmidt, "Die Fragmente des Mathematikers Menaechmus," in *Philologus*, **42** (1884), 77–81. Malcolm Brown (see below) believes that a passage in Proclus, *op. cit.*, 72.23–73.9, may be a quotation from Menaechmus.

The most complete account of Menaechmus is still that of G. J. Allman, *Greek Geometry From Thales to Euclid* (Dublin–London, 1889), 153–179, reproducing an article which appeared in *Hermathena*, no. 12 (July 1886), 105–130. Other accounts to which reference may profitably be made are C. A. Bretschneider, *Die Geometrie und die Geometer vor Eukleides* (Leipzig, 1870), 155–163; H. G. Zeuthen, *Keglesnitslaeren i Oldtiden* (Copenhagen, 1885), German trans. *Die Lehre von den Kegelschnitten im Altertum*, R. von Fischer-Benzon, ed. (Copenhagen, 1886), repr. with foreword and index by J. E. Hofmann (Hildesheim, 1966), 457–467; T. L. Heath, *Apollonius of Perga* (Cambridge, 1896), xvii–xxx; and *A History of Greek Mathematics* (Oxford, 1921), I, 251–255, II, 110–116; J. L. Coolidge, *A History of the Conic Sections and Quadric*

Surfaces (Oxford, 1945), 1–5; Malcolm Brown, "A Pre-Aristotelian Mathematician on Deductive Order," in *Philosophy and Humanism: Essays in Honor of Paul Oskar Kristeller* (New York, in press).

IVOR BULMER-THOMAS

MENDEL, JOHANN GREGOR (*b.* Heinzendorf, Austria [now Hynčice, Czechoslovakia], 22 July 1822; *d.* Brno, Austria [now Czechoslovakia], 6 January 1884), *genetics, meteorology.*

At the February and March 1865 meetings of the Natural Sciences Society of Brno, J. G. Mendel first presented an account of his eight years of experimental work on artificial plant hybridization. His paper was published in the Society's *Verhandlungen* in 1866 but went unnoticed. In 1900, within a two-month period, there appeared three preliminary reports by Hugo de Vries, Carl Correns, and Erich von Tschermak, who, working independently in Amsterdam, Tübingen, and Vienna respectively, attained the same results almost simultaneously. Each of them stated that just before completing his work, he learned that he had been preceded, by several decades, by a virtually unknown monk. Mendel's experimental work, designed after long contemplation of the problem, painstakingly executed on an extensive scale, intelligently analyzed and interpreted, and presented straightforwardly and clearly, yielded results of such general and far-reaching significance that his paper became the basis of the science of genetics.

Mendel's father, Anton, was a peasant. He served in the army during the Napoleonic Wars and later was able to turn his experience acquired in other regions to the improvement of his farm. Mendel's mother was the daughter of a village gardener, and other of his ancestors were professional gardeners in service at the local manor. Heinzendorf was on the border between the Czech- and German-speaking areas; the Mendel family spoke German, but about one-fourth of their ancestors were of Czech extraction. Mendel himself later lived on excellent terms with both. After the death of two infant girls, a daughter, Veronica, was born to the couple (1820), followed by Johann (1822), and another daughter, Theresia (1829). In the primary school the enlightened Reverend Schreiber, vicar of the neighboring village, taught the children natural science in addition to elementary subjects, and encouraged the cultivation of fruit trees both at the school and by the parishioners. Mendel also helped his father in grafting fruit trees in their orchard.

Since Mendel showed exceptional abilities, his parents, on the advice of the vicar and the village schoolmaster, sent the boy in 1833 to the Piarist secondary school in nearby Leipnik (Lipník), and a year later to the Gymnasium in Troppau (Opava), where he spent six years. He left with a certificate *primae classis cum eminentia*, the designation referring to his industriousness, knowledge, and ability. In 1838 Mendel's father suffered serious injuries during his statutory labor, and had to retire and turn over his farm to his son-in-law. Mendel had to earn his living by private tutoring. The physical and mental strain affected his health so much that in his fifth year at the Gymnasium he had to interrupt his studies for several months. He recovered, completed his secondary studies, and in 1840 enrolled in the philosophy course, as preparation for higher studies, at the University of Olmütz (Olomouc). His efforts to find private pupils were in vain, however, because he had no references. This new distress and frustration brought on further illness, this time for a longer period, so that Mendel had to spend a year with his parents to recover. But he refused to give up his studies and become a farmer. His younger sister, Theresia, offered him a part of her dowry to help him return to Olmütz and complete the two-year philosophy course. He accepted and thus became acquainted with the elements of philosophy, physics, and mathematics, including—in a course given by J. Fux—the principles of combinatorial operations, which he later employed with great success in his research. His physics professor, F. Franz, in 1843 recommended the admission of this "young man of very solid character, almost the best in his own branch," to the Augustinian monastery in Brno, where Franz himself had stayed for nearly twenty years.

Mendel entered the monastery on 9 October 1843 with the name Gregor. He did so out of necessity and without feeling in himself a vocation for holy orders. But he soon realized that now he was free of all financial worries and that he had found the best possible conditions for pursuing his studies. The monastery was a center of learning and scientific endeavor, and many of its members were teachers at the Gymnasium or at the Philosophical Institute. The monastery was supported mainly by the income from its estates. F. C. Napp (1792–1867), who was the abbot from 1824, devoted much energy to the improvement of agriculture; he was a member of the Central Board of the Moravian Agricultural Society and later its president. He wanted one of his monks to teach natural sciences and agriculture at the Philosophical Institute, and he established the tradition of experimenting with plants in the monastery garden. When Mendel entered the order, Matthew Klácel, a teacher of philosophy (1808–1882), was directing the experimental garden and investigating variation, heredity, and evolution in plants. He enjoyed a high reputation among the Brno botanists, and drew upon his experience in natural history to formulate ideas on the Hegelian philosophy of gradual development that ultimately led to his dismissal and emigration to America. Klácel guided Mendel in his first studies in science and later put him in charge of the experimental garden.

During his theological studies (1844–1848) Mendel, in accordance with the abbot's interests, also attended courses at the Philosophical Institute in agriculture, pomology, and viticulture given by F. Diebl (1770–1859), who, in his textbook of plant production, *Abhandlungen aus der Landwirtschaftskunde für Landwirthe . . .* (2 vols., Brno, 1835), had described artificial pollination as the main method of plant improvement. In these lectures Mendel also learned of the methods of sheep breeding introduced by F. Geisslern (1751–1824). Diebl was, with Napp, among the main organizers of the Congress of German Agriculturists at Brno in 1840, where hybridization as a method of fruit-tree breeding was discussed.

After he finished his theological studies, Mendel was appointed chaplain to the parish served by the monastery, his duty being to see to the spiritual welfare of the patients in the neighboring hospital. But Mendel was extremely sensitive, and could not bear to witness suffering; he was overcome by fear and shyness and again became very depressed, almost to the point of illness. The sympathetic abbot relieved him of this duty and sent him as a substitute teacher to the grammar school at Znojmo in southern Moravia.

Mendel enjoyed teaching and so impressed both his pupils and his colleagues that at the end of his first year the headmaster recommended him for the university examination for teachers of natural sciences, which would allow him a regular appointment. Mendel passed well in physics and meteorology, but failed in geology and zoology. Since the failure seemed to be due largely to Mendel's lack of a university education, Andreas Baumgartner, the professor of physics, advised Napp to send Mendel to the University of Vienna.

At the university Mendel attended lectures on experimental physics by Doppler and on the construction and use of physical apparatus by Andreas von Ettinghausen (1796–1878), who had earlier published a book on combinatorial analysis, *Die combinatorische Analysis* (Vienna, 1826). It is clear that some of the methods described there later influenced Mendel's derivation of series in the hybrid progeny. Mendel also attended lectures on paleontology, botany, zoology, and chemistry, and was especially influenced by the professor of plant physiology, Franz Unger, who also gave a practical course on

organizing botanical experiments. In his research Unger turned from the investigation of forms of fossil plants, to the influence of soil upon plants, to the causes of variation. He was known for his views on evolution, and in his lectures emphasized that sexual generation was the basis of the origin of the great variety in cultured plants. He sought to explain the evolution of new plant forms by the combination of the simplest elements in the cell, surmising their existence but unable to prove it. In Vienna, Mendel also thoroughly studied Gaertner's *Versuche und Beobachtungen über die Bastardzeugung im Pflanzenreich* (Stuttgart, 1849), in which nearly 10,000 separate experiments with 700 plant species yielding hybrids were described. In his copy, preserved in the Mendelianum, Mendel marked pages where pea hybrids are mentioned and also made notes on pairs of *Pisum* characteristics, some of which later appeared in his experimental program.

During his studies Mendel became a member of the Zoologisch-botanischer Verein in Vienna and published his first two short communications in its *Verhandlungen* (1853, 1854). They concerned damage to plant cultures by some insects.

After his return to Brno, Mendel was appointed substitute teacher of physics and natural history at the Brno Technical School. His superior was A. Zawadski (1798–1868), previously professor of physics and applied mathematics and dean of the Philosophical Faculty at the University of Lvov. He had come to Brno in 1854, after being dismissed for alleged responsibility for student uprisings in 1848. Zawadski was a man of wide scientific interests, ranging from botany, zoology, and paleontology to evolution. On his nomination Mendel became a member of the natural science section of the Agricultural Society in Brno.

As a teacher Mendel was highly appreciated both by students and colleagues. His task was not easy, for the classes were large, some with over 100 students. After his first year his headmaster reported that Mendel was a good experimentalist and, with rather scanty equipment, was able to give excellent demonstrations in both physics and natural history.

After his return from Vienna, Mendel also began experimenting with peas. The most arduous aspect was artificial pollination. He began the work in 1856, when he was also preparing for his second university examination for teachers of natural science, which took place in May 1856. Once again the instability of his psychological constitution betrayed him. He broke down during the written examination, withdrew from the other parts, and returned to Brno. There he became so seriously ill that his father and uncle came all the way from Silesia to see him. It was their only visit to him in Brno. Indirect evidence suggests that his indisposition derived from the stress of his studies and preoccupation with his research problems, compounded by the memory of his experience with the previous examination. After this failure he attempted no further degrees, and remained a substitute teacher until 1868, when he gave up teaching.

In 1868 Mendel was elected abbot of the monastery, which involved many official duties. He also became a member of the Central Board of the Agricultural Society and was entrusted with distribution of subsidies for promoting farming; from 1870 he was frequently elected to its executive committee. He took an active part in the organization of the first statistical service for agriculture. Later he also reported on scientific literature and cooperated with the editorial board of the society's journal, *Mittheilungen der K. K. Mährisch-schlesischen Gesellschaft zur Beförderung des Ackerbaues, der Natur- und Landeskunde.* Near the end of his life he was considered for the society's presidency, but he refused to accept this honor because of his poor health. From 1863 Mendel was also a member of the Brno Horticultural Society and after 1870 he belonged to the Society of Apiculturists, and influenced the development of both these fields.

Mendel soon became known for his liberal views, which he demonstrated by public support for the nominees of the Liberal Party in the general election of 1871. When the victorious Liberal government issued a law requiring a large contribution by the monastery to the religious fund, Mendel refused to pay the new taxes. After 1875 he was thus involved in a lengthy conflict with the authorities, which led to the sequestration of monastery land. In a last attempt to regain Mendel's support for the Liberal party, he was offered a place on the board of directors of the Moravian Mortgage Bank in 1876, and was even proposed for the office of its governor in 1881. Mendel persisted in his opposition, however, convinced that he was fighting for the rights of the monastery. The tension eventually had a deleterious effect on Mendel's health; he died of chronic inflammation of the kidneys with edema, uremia, and cardiac hypertrophy. At his funeral nobody was aware that an outstanding scientist was being buried, even though Mendel's experiments on *Pisum* were remembered by the fruit growers of Brno and in the obituary notices of local newspapers.

Work. *Meteorological Studies.* Mendel began his meteorological studies in 1856 and was soon recognized as the only authority on this subject in Moravia. In his first meteorological paper, published in 1863, he summarized graphically the results of observations at Brno, using the statistical principle to compare the data for a given year with average conditions of the previous fifteen years. Between 1863 and 1869, the paper was followed by five similar communications concerned with the whole of Moravia. Later Mendel published three meteorological reports describing exceptional storm phenomena. He also devoted much time to the observation of sunspots, assuming that they had some relation to the weather. In 1877, with his support, weather forecasts for farmers in Moravia were issued, the first in central Europe.

As always, there was a practical aspect to Mendel's pursuits and interests, but the primary motivation was scientific. The best example is his paper on the tornado that he observed at Brno in 1870. He began with a careful description and followed it with a new interpretation, which was that the observed phenomena were vortices engendered by encounters between conflicting air currents. This interpretation was overlooked, as were his hybridization experiments, even by those who advanced similar explanations many years later. These studies, although remote from his main work and far less important, have much in common methodologically with his studies of hybridization. They grew out of his habit of scrupulously collecting and recording data, thinking in quantitative terms, and subjecting observational data to statistical treatment.

Plant Hybridization. Mendel's principal work was the outcome of ten years of tedious experiments in plant growing and crossing; seed gathering and careful labeling; and observing, sorting, and counting almost 30,000 plants. It is hardly conceivable that it could have been accomplished without a precise plan and a preconceived idea of the results to be expected. There is evidence that Mendel began with an inductive hypothesis carefully framed so as to be testable in his experimental program.

From his previous experience Mendel was familiar with methods for improvement of cultivated plants. Both his teachers, Diebel and Unger, had pointed to hybridization as the source for this improvement. But hybridization was an empirical procedure, and Unger therefore stressed the necessity of studying the nature of variability. He suggested that it might be possible to find an explanation in the combination of hypothetical elements within the cells. Mendel's approach was the common one of reducing the problem to an elementary level and formulating a hypothesis that could be proved or disproved by experiments.

Between 1856 and 1863 Mendel cultivated and tested at least 28,000 plants, carefully analyzing seven pairs of seed and plant characteristics. This was his main experimental program. His original idea was that heredity is particulate, contrary to the model of "blending inheritance" generally accepted at that time. In the pea plants hereditary particles to be investigated are in pairs. Mendel called them "elements" and attributed them to the respective parents. From one parent plant comes an element determining, for instance, round seed shape; from the other parent, an element governing the development of the angular shape. In the first generation all hybrids are alike, exhibiting one of the parental characteristics (round seed shape) in unchanged form. Mendel called such a characteristic "dominant"; the other (angular shape), which remains latent and appears in the next generation, he called "recessive." The "elements" determining each paired character pass in the germ cells of the hybrids, without influencing each other, so that one of each pair of "elements" passes in every pollen (sperm) and in every egg (ovule) cell. In fertilization, the element marked by Mendel A, denoting dominant round seed shape, and the element a, denoting the recessive angular shape, meet at random, the resulting combination of "elements" being

$$\tfrac{1}{4}AA + \tfrac{1}{4}Aa + \tfrac{1}{4}aA + \tfrac{1}{4}aa.$$

In hybrid progeny both parental forms appear again; and Mendel's explanation of this segregation of parental traits was called, after 1900, Mendel's law (or principle) of segregation.

In his simplest experiments with crossing pea plants that differed in only one trait pair, Mendel cultivated nearly 14,000 plants and explained the progeny of the hybrid in terms of the series $A + 2\,Aa + a$. At the same time he conformed to the view of K. F. von Gaertner and J. G. Koelreuter that hybrids have a tendency to revert to the parental forms. Mendel then called his explanation of hybrid progeny "the law of development thus found," which he tested further in a case "when several different traits are united in the hybrid through fertilization." Hereditary elements belonging to different pairs of traits, for example A and a for the round and angular seed shapes and B and b for the yellow and green seed colors, recombine the individual series $A + 2\,Aa + a$ and $B + 2\,Bb + b$, resulting in terms of a combination series:

$$AB + Ab + aB + ab + 2\,ABb + 2\,aBb$$
$$+ 2\,AaB + 2\,Aab + AaBb.$$

In his paper Mendel also illustrated a recombination of three trait pairs, showing every expected combination of characteristics and relevant elements in actual counts of offspring. He also observed that 128 constant associations of seven alternative and mutually exclusive characteristics were actually obtained—that being the expansion of 2^7, and the maximum number theoretically possible. His conclusion was that the "behavior of each of different traits in a hybrid association is independent of all other differences in the two parental plants," which principle was later called Mendel's law of independent assortment.

The generalization of Mendel's explanation was that "if n denotes the number of characteristic differences in two parental plants, then 3^n is the number of terms in the combination series, 4^n the number of individuals that belong to the series, and 2^n the number of combinations that remain constant."

In his second lecture to the Natural Sciences Society of Brno (March 1865) Mendel presented his hypothesis explaining "the development of hybrids in separate generations," and furnished both a theoretical and experimental proof of his assumption by crossing hybrids with constant dominant and constant recessive forms. His explanation was "that hybrids form germinal and pollen cells that in their composition correspond in equal numbers to all the constant forms resulting from the combination of traits united through fertilization."

At this meeting Mendel also described briefly his experiments with other plant species, the object of which was to determine "whether the law of development discovered for *Pisum* is also valid for hybrids of other plants." He predicted that "through this approach we can learn to understand the extraordinary diversity in the coloration of our ornamental flowers." In his concluding remarks he compared the observations made on *Pisum* with the results obtained by Koelreuter and Gaertner, especially those on hybrid characteristics. Mendel could not agree with the assumption that in some cases hybrid offspring remain "exactly like the hybrid and propagate unchanged," as Gaertner believed.

Mendel also touched on the experimental transformation of one species into another by artificial fertilization. In a simple experiment with *Pisum* he exhibited transformation from the viewpoint of his theory, explaining why some transformations took longer than others. He noted that Koelreuter's transformation experiments proceeded "in a manner similar to that in *Pisum*," and that in this way "the entire process of transformation would have a rather simple explanation." In this connection Mendel opposed Gaertner's view "that a species has fixed limits beyond which it cannot change," and he thus asserted his conviction that his theory favored the assumption of continuous evolution.

In the opening paragraph of his paper Mendel stated

that his experiments were initiated by "artificial fertilization undertaken on ornamental plants to obtain new color variants," and he emphasized the significance of such investigations in establishing "the evolutionary history of organic forms." Subsequently he often mentioned that "law of development" but without using the terms "inheritance" or "hereditary." By the "law of development" he certainly meant the law governing the evolution of cultured plants. He also assumed that his theory was valid in generality because "no basic difference could exist in important matters, since unity in the plan of development of organic life is beyond doubt."

In comparison with his predecessors, Mendel was original in his approach, in his method, and in his interpretation of experimental results. He reduced the hitherto extremely complex problem of crossing and heredity to an elementary level appropriate to exact analysis. He left nothing to chance. The choice of *Pisum* as his main experimental material resulted both from his study of the literature and from numerous preliminary experiments. He very carefully selected varieties whose purity had been assured by several years of cultivation under strictly controlled conditions. The hybridized varieties differed in only a few characteristics, and those that did not allow a clear distinction were discarded. Limiting the characteristics to a small number enabled Mendel to distinguish all possible combinations. His introduction of simple symbols that permitted comparing the experimental results definitively with the theory was very important. Altogether new was his use of large populations of experimental plants, which allowed him to express his experimental results in numbers and subject them to mathematical treatment. By the statistical analysis of large numbers Mendel succeeded in extracting "laws" from seemingly random phenomena. This method, quite common today, was then entirely novel. Mendel, inspired by physical sciences, was the first to apply it to the solution of a basic biological problem and to explain the significance of a numerical ratio. His great powers of abstraction enabled him to synthesize the raw experimental data and to reveal the basic principles operating in nature.

Mendel's manuscript, as read at the 1865 meetings, was published without change in the Natural Sciences Society's *Verhandlungen* in 1866. The other members, however, could hardly have grasped either the main idea or the great significance of his discoveries. The *Verhandlungen* was distributed to 134 scientific institutions in various countries, including those in New York, Chicago, and Washington. Mendel commissioned forty reprints, two of which have been found in Brno and five others elsewhere; one was sent to

Naegeli and another to Anton Kerner, two contemporary authorities on hybridization.

Further Research. The main results of Mendel's experiments and their interpretation, which constituted his whole theory, were reported in "Versuche über Pflanzenhybriden" (1866). This memoir was his magnum opus, one of the most important papers in the history of biology, and the foundation of genetic studies. Mendel had confidence in his experimental work and its rational interpretation; but he did observe "that the results I obtained were not easily compatible with our contemporary scientific knowledge and that under [such] circumstances publication of one such isolated experiment was doubly dangerous, dangerous for the experimenter and for the cause he represented. Thus I made every effort to verify the results obtained with *Pisum*." He was aware that there would be difficulty in "finding plants suitable for another extended series of experiments and that under unfavorable circumstances years might elapse without my obtaining the desired information." Nevertheless he tried very hard to confirm, as far as possible, the general validity of the experiments, first with other genera of plants (some experiments extending to four to six generations) and then with animals. After 1866, however, he published only a single short paper on *Hieracium* hybrids (1869). But the great efforts he devoted to this goal are evident from his letters written from 1866 to 1873 to Naegeli. They amount to scientific reports containing many details of his work, of the problems he encountered, and of the results he obtained. The discussion is extremely sober, objective, and scientific—a patient reaction to Naegeli's "mistrustful caution" regarding his experiments. The letters also convey Mendel's personality: his sincere endeavor to reach the truth, his truly scientific spirit, his modesty in the calm defense of his viewpoint. This correspondence remained unknown until 1905, when it was published by Naegeli's pupil, Carl Correns.

Mendel's experiments demonstrated that hybrids of *Matthiola*, *Zea*, and *Mirabilis* (like those of *Phaseolus* reported in the first paper) "behave exactly like those of *Pisum*." There still remained the question "whether variable hybrids of other plant species show complete agreement in their behavior with hybrids of *Pisum*." In the relevant contemporary literature it was reported that some hybrids (such as Aa) remain constant (A), which contradicted the generalization of Mendel's results. The genus *Hieracium* (hawkweed) seemed to Mendel most suitable for solving this question.

Mendel's *Hieracium* research project was also connected with some taxonomical questions, since the transitional forms of a highly polymorphic genus like *Hieracium* were very difficult to classify. The results of his four years' work, reported at the meeting of the Natural Sciences Society in Brno on 9 June 1869 and published in the society's *Verhandlungen* in 1870, were disappointing. He had to admit that in his *Hieracium* experiments "the exactly opposite phenomenon seems to be exhibited" as compared with *Pisum*. Subsequently, however, he carefully added that the whole matter "is still an open question, which may well be raised but not as yet answered." These experiments were extremely laborious and delicate because of the minuteness of the flowers and their particular structure; Mendel succeeded in obtaining only six hybrids, and only one to three specimens of each. Another obstacle was to be explained only in 1903: that *Hieracium* reproduces partly by apogamy, so that in many instances offspring are not formed by cross-pollination and are all alike, as though derived from cuttings.

Mendel discussed these experiments and the problems involved in more detail in his letters to Naegeli. The small number of *Hieracium* hybrids he obtained did not allow any definite conclusion, and it is surprising that eventually he found the theoretical explanation even in this case. Notes in Mendel's handwriting brought to light only recently in the Mendelianum indicate that he insisted on his idea of variable hybrids and, assuming polygene action, he tried to explain that in *Salix*, as in *Hieracium*, a multifactor crossing takes place and that the segregation of their hybrids follows the same principle as in *Pisum*. According to this assumption, the reported constancy exhibited by the extremely variable *Hieracium* hybrids would be only apparent.

Mendel centered his efforts on proving that a certain system operates in nature and that its laws could be formulated. It required a great capacity for abstraction and simplification of the extremely complex set of observed phenomena. He had to focus his attention on the main issues; otherwise he would have become lost in the complexities of nature, as had all his predecessors who found many isolated phenomena but did not synthesize them into a coherent system. Many potentially interesting observations had to be left out of consideration in the first phase. Thus, it has been often overlooked that besides the main findings, Mendel noted several phenomena attributed, after 1900, to other scientists: the intermediate forms of heredity, the additive action of his "elements," like that of genes, and complete linkage. He also described, in principle, the frequencies of "elements" in the population. Later, as his extant fragmentary notes show, he imagined the existence of the interaction of the "elements" and of an action like

that later called polygenic. He also suggested that egg cells and pollen cells contain different hereditary units for the development of sex.

After 1871 Mendel conducted hybridization experiments on bees, hoping to prove his theory in the animal kingdom. He kept about fifty bee varieties, which he attempted to cross in order to obtain "a new synthetic race." He was not successful, however, because of the complex problem of the controlled mating of queen bees. In these experiments he also proved the hybrid effect on fertility of bees.

Mendel must have been greatly disappointed that there was no recognition of his scientific work and that even Naegeli missed its essential feature and did not grasp the historical significance of his theory. Naegeli's attention was focused on other problems, and Mendel's findings did not fit into his manner of thinking. Thus he raised objections—in fact not relevant—to Mendel's experiments and rejected his rational conclusions. Mendel was not understood in his time. Only in the following decades did the discoveries of the material basis of what was later called Mendelian—behavior of the nucleus in cell division, constancy in each species of the number of chromosomes, the longitudinal splitting of chromosomes, the reduction division during the maturation of germ cells, and the restitution of the number of chromosomes in fertilization—prepare the way for understanding the cytological basis of Mendelian inheritance and for its general acceptance.

The absence of response and recognition was one of the reasons that Mendel stopped publishing the results of his later experiments and observations. He did, nonetheless, take satisfaction and pleasure in the application of his theory in the breeding of new varieties of fruit trees and in propagating the idea of hybridization among local gardeners and horticulturists.

Mendel and Darwin. After Mendel's rediscovery in 1900, Mendelism was often opposed to the Darwinian theory of natural selection, and unfortunately so, for the apparent opposition was based on misunderstanding. In fact, the modern theory of descent and heredity has two foundations, one laid by Darwin and the other by Mendel, and both indispensable. It was in 1926, however, that Chetwerikov attempted a synthesis of Darwinian and Mendelian theories, a move completed in 1930–1932 by R. A. Fisher, Sewall Wright, and J. B. S. Haldane. The importance of Mendel for the theory of evolution rests in his demonstration of the mechanism that is the primary source of variability in plant and animal populations, on which natural selection subsequently operates.

When he wrote his paper, Mendel was already acquainted with Darwin's *On the Origin of Species*.

A copy of its German translation with Mendel's marginalia, preserved in the Mendelianum in Brno, shows Mendel's deep interest in this work. Similar marginalia are in the Brno copies of other Darwin books. Mendel's notes show his readiness to accept the theory of natural selection. He rejected the Darwinian provisional hypothesis of pangenesis, however, as contradicting in principle his own interpretation of the formation and development of hybrids. Like Darwin, Mendel was convinced that "it is impossible to draw a sharp line between species and variations."

On the other hand, Darwin, looking for the causes of variations, seems never to have realized that the clue to this problem was in the hybridization experiments. He never learned about Mendel's work, although almost the only book in which it was cited, S. O. Focke's *Pflanzenmischlinge* . . . (1881), is known to have passed through his hands.

Mendel was a lonely, unrecognized genius. Yet the rediscovery of his work brought to a close an era of speculation on heredity, which then became a subject of scientific analysis. He opened a new path to the study of heredity and revealed a new mechanism operating in the process of evolution. Every generation of biologists has found something new in his fundamental experiments. The science of genetics, which had both its origins and a powerful impetus in Mendel's work, has advanced with prodigious speed, linking many branches of biology (cytology in particular) with mathematics, physics, and chemistry. This development has led to a deeper understanding of man and nature with far-reaching theoretical implications and practical consequences.

BIBLIOGRAPHY

I. ORIGINAL WORKS. Mendel published thirteen papers, two of which were on plant-damaging insects, nine on meteorology, and two—the most important—on plant hybrids. Most of them, including seven on meteorology and the two on plant hybrids, were published in *Verhandlungen des Naturforschenden Vereins in Brünn*, **1** (1863) to **9** (1871). A list of them was published by J. Křiženecký in *Gregor Johann Mendel 1822–1884. Texte und Quellen zu seinem Wirken und Leben* (Leipzig, 1965), along with the text of the 1865 paper, revised according to the original MS. Another critical ed. of the 1865 paper was edited, with the text of the 1869 paper on *Hieracium* hybrids, an introduction, and commentaries, by F. Weiling as *Ostwalds Klassiker der Exakten Wissenschaften*, n.s. VI (Brunswick, 1970). There are numerous trans. in many languages of Mendel's magnum opus, "Versuche über Pflanzenhybriden." Most are listed in M. Jakubíček and J. Kubíček, *Bibliographia Mendeliana* (Brno, 1965); and M. Jakubíček, *Bibliographia Mendeliana. Supplementum*

1965–1969 (Brno, 1970). Trans. into English have been published several times since C. T. Druery's trans. was modified and corrected by W. Bateson in *Mendel's Principles of Heredity. A Defence* (Cambridge, 1902); this was republished by J. H. Bennett as *Experiments in Plant Hybridization—Gregor Mendel* (Edinburgh, 1965). A new English trans. was edited by C. Stern and E. R. Sherwood, *The Origins of Genetics. A Mendel Source Book* (San Francisco–London, 1966), which includes the paper on *Hieracium* hybrids and ten of Mendel's letters to Naegeli. The letters were first published by Carl Correns, "Gregor Mendel's Briefe an Carl Nägeli 1866–1873," in *Abhandlungen der Königlichen sächsischen Gesellschaft der Wissenschaften*, Math.-phys. Kl., **29** (1905), 189–265, and their English trans. in *Genetics*, **35** (1950), 1–29.

Besides the thirteen full-length papers by Mendel, over twenty minor publications, mostly book reviews from 1870–1882 signed with the initial "M" or "m," have been identified.

II. SECONDARY LITERATURE. The first—and still the best—detailed biography is H. Iltis, *Gregor Johann Mendel. Leben, Werk und Wirkung* (Berlin, 1924), translated into English as *Life of Mendel* (New York, 1932; 2nd ed., 1966). Additional information was published by O. Richter, *Johann Gregor Mendel wie er wirklich war* (Brno, 1943). Literature on Mendel's work and his importance in the history of biology is extremely plentiful. Over 800 titles are listed in Jakubíček and Kubíček's *Bibliographia Mendeliana* and in its supp. (see above). The most important recent literature includes "Commemoration of the Publication of Gregor Mendel's Pioneer Experiments in Genetics," in *Proceedings of the American Philosophical Society*, **109**, no. 4 (1965), 189–248; F. A. E. Crew, *The Foundations of Genetics* (Oxford, 1966); L. C. Dunn, *Genetics in the 20th Century. Essays on the Progress of Genetics During Its First 50 Years* (New York, 1951); and *A Short History of Genetics* (New York, 1965); R. A. Fisher, "Has Mendel's Work Been Rediscovered?" in *Annals of Science*, **1** (1936), 115–137; A. E. Gaissinovich, *Zarozhdenie genetiky* (Moscow, 1967); J. Křiženecký, ed., *Fundamenta genetica* (Brno, 1965); M. Sosna, ed., *G. Mendel Memorial Symposium (Brno, 1965)* (Prague, 1966); R. C. Olby, *Origins of Mendelism* (London, 1966); H. Stubbe, *Kurze Geschichte der Genetik bis zur Wiederentdeckung der Vererbungsregeln Gregor Mendels* (Jena, 1963); and A. H. Sturtevant, *A History of Genetics* (New York, 1965).

Over 700 original documents relating to Mendel have been preserved in the Mendelianum, established in 1964 by the Moravian Museum in the former Augustinian monastery at Brno. Since 1966 it has published annually the series *Folia Mendeliana;* no. 6 (1971) contains important papers, including an elucidation of the problem of the triple rediscovery of Mendel's work, presented at the international Gregor Mendel Colloquium, held at Brno, 29 June–3 July 1970. The rediscovery of Mendel's work is further discussed in V. Orel, *The Secret of Mendel's Discovery* (Tokyo, 1973), in Japanese.

V. KRUTA
V. OREL

MENDEL, LAFAYETTE BENEDICT (*b.* Delhi, New York, 5 February 1872; *d.* New Haven, Connecticut, 9 December 1935), *physiological chemistry*.

Lafayette Benedict Mendel was the elder of two sons of Benedict Mendel, a merchant in Delhi, New York, and Pauline Ullman. Both parents migrated to the United States from Germany. Mendel prepared for Yale College in the local schools and in 1887, at the age of fifteen, obtained a New York State scholarship by competitive examination. At Yale he studied mainly the classics, economics, and the humanities, but on graduation in 1891 was awarded a fellowship that enabled him to enter the graduate course in physiological chemistry under Russell H. Chittenden of the Sheffield Scientific School.

Although poorly prepared in chemistry and physics and without experience in laboratory work, Mendel completed the requirements for the Ph.D. in two years with a thesis on the proteolysis of the crystalline hempseed protein edestin. This investigation was of no lasting significance, but the work aroused his interest in protein chemistry, and especially in the properties of the proteins of plant seeds. This was to have great influence upon his later career.

Mendel joined the teaching staff of the Sheffield Laboratory of Physiological Chemistry in the fall of 1893. He took a year's leave of absence in 1895 and went to Germany, where he studied physiology at Breslau with R. Heidenhain and chemistry at Freiburg im Breisgau with E. Baumann. He quickly established his position in Heidenhain's laboratory by demonstrating the preparation of crystalline edestin from hempseed, something that the professor had never seen before.

In 1897 Mendel was appointed assistant professor and in 1903 full professor of physiological chemistry in the Sheffield Scientific School. In 1921 he was made Sterling professor of physiological chemistry at Yale University, one of the first of these distinguished appointments, with membership in the faculties of the graduate and medical schools. Mendel was a most effective teacher. His lectures were clear and forceful, scholarly and stimulating. In his seminars, where weekly discussions of current advances in biochemistry were held, he taught his students to teach, always insisting on dignity in presentation, good English style, and accuracy of statement, qualities that he illustrated in his own discussions of the matter at hand. He communicated his own enthusiasm to his students and took a close personal interest in all of them, winning their confidence and respect and caring for their interests long after they had left Yale for positions elsewhere.

Mendel's early scientific work illustrates the influence of his teachers: from Chittenden the interest in proteins, from Heidenhain that in experimental physiology, and from Baumann the biochemistry of such compounds as creatine, choline, taurine, the purines, and especially the iodine-containing substances of the thyroid gland. With the collaboration of colleagues on the faculty and of a steadily increasing number of graduate students, papers were published on such subjects as the nitrogen metabolism of the cat, the formation of uric acid, the paths of excretion of a number of inorganic ions, the metabolism of iodine, of allantoin, of kynurenic acid, and of several pyrimidines and purines. His interest in nutrition was aroused early. The first paper on the subject was published in 1898 and dealt with the nutritive value of various edible fungi. As early as 1906 he began his studies of growth, one or another aspect of which was dealt with in about seventy subsequent papers.

Mendel is remembered chiefly as coauthor, with Thomas B. Osborne of the Connecticut Agricultural Experiment Station in New Haven, of more than one hundred papers on the subject of nutrition. This collaboration began in 1905 with a study of the proteins of the castor bean, especially the highly toxic albumin ricin. Osborne, with his assistant Isaac F. Harris, prepared the proteins, and Mendel did the physiological tests. Their most active preparation of ricin was fatal to rabbits at a dose of two one-thousandths of a milligram per kilogram, and they thoroughly established the protein nature of this extraordinary poison, then a matter of debate.

The collaboration with Osborne on the nutritive effect of proteins began in 1909. Osborne had become an internationally known authority on the preparation and properties of the proteins of plant seeds and upon their analysis by the then current methods. The question had arisen whether substances of such widely varied amino acid composition were equally effective for the protein nutrition of animals, a matter upon which divergent opinions were held, and he invited Mendel to join him in an investigation of the subject. Together they devised improved experimental methods for feeding white rats, including accurate measurements of food intake, and adopted the general principle that in a successful experiment the food must maintain the weight of the rat for a substantial fraction of its life span. Rats had been used previously for studies of nutrition by a number of European investigators, such as V. Henriques in Copenhagen and W. Falta in Basel. They had also been used in this country by Henry H. Donaldson of the Wistar Institute in Philadelphia and by E. V. McCollum of the University of Wisconsin.

Aided by annual grants from the Carnegie Institution of Washington, they soon established that the diet must contain adequate amounts of lysine and tryptophan, supplied either as such or combined in the protein of the diet. This was the first convincing proof that certain amino acids are essential components of the diet and cannot be synthesized by the animal organism. Despite every care nutritive failure ultimately supervened. A preparation obtained by evaporating milk serum to dryness, the so-called protein-free milk, greatly postponed such failures when included in the food; but, even so, sudden and dramatic losses of weight and ultimately death occurred. The animals could be saved by furnishing a diet which contained dried whole milk, but not by one containing dried skim milk. This difference led to an examination of the effect of supplying butter for a part of the lard in the food. The result was a demonstration that butter contains an organic substance, obviously present only in trace amounts, which is essential in the nutrition of the rat. This finding was the discovery of vitamin A. Unfortunately for Osborne and Mendel, McCollum at the University of Wisconsin had made a similar observation and had submitted his results for publication a few weeks before Osborne and Mendel's paper was received. McCollum is thus regarded in the history of biochemistry as the discoverer of vitamin A.

Nevertheless, the independent and almost simultaneous publication of so important a conclusion from two laboratories greatly strengthened the position of both groups of investigators, and the doctrine that an adequate diet must supply trace amounts of hitherto unrecognized organic substances was at once widely accepted. It led within a few years to a complete revolution in the science of nutrition. The "protein-free milk" was recognized to contain a second such essential, which was soon designated water-soluble vitamin B, and Osborne and Mendel for some ten years devoted much study to the distribution of these essential substances in natural food products and to the elucidation of the complexities of the water-soluble vitamins.

Once they had established that diets of purified food materials could be compounded upon which rats would grow well and live indefinitely, Osborne and Mendel carried out many studies of growth. From the beginning of the period of collaboration with Osborne, Mendel's bibliography contains 289 titles. Of these, 24 percent contain the word "growth." Perhaps the most striking result was the demonstration that the growth of a young animal could be indefinitely suppressed and then resumed by manipulation of the diet with respect to the supply of lysine. Growth could occur at any age.

Notwithstanding the time and effort expended upon the collaboration with Osborne, Mendel also directed the activities of many graduate students. Especial attention was given to the chemistry and metabolism of fats and to the regulation of blood volume by the supply of salts. He was frequently invited to give lectures and also served as a consultant not only to his medical colleagues but also to the food industry. Withal, he was a professor who is remembered by his students with deep affection and respect. Always approachable and kindly, ever ready with suggestions for the solution of practical problems or with helpful reference to the literature of his subject, of which he was a complete master, his influence upon science at Yale and especially upon the medical applications of nutrition was great. Largely through his own efforts nutrition was transformed during his lifetime from empiricism to a clearly recognized branch of biochemistry founded upon scientific principles. When it is realized that the modern poultry and meat industries rely entirely upon the proper supply to the animals of vitamins and of proteins of correct and adequate amino acid composition, the benefit to practical agriculture of Mendel's work is almost incalculable.

BIBLIOGRAPHY

I. Original Works. Mendel's bibliography in Russell H. Chittenden's memoir, *Biographical Memoirs of the National Academy of Sciences*, XVIII (1937), lists titles of 326 papers, nearly all being records of scientific research published between 1894 and 1935. It is incomplete since Mendel, who prepared it, did not include numerous editorials in the *Journal of the American Medical Association* and many book reviews and similar less important writings. Of these papers 111 were written in collaboration with Thomas B. Osborne of the Connecticut Agricultural Experiment Station and record joint experiments made between 1910 and 1928 in Osborne's laboratory with financial support by the Carnegie Institution of Washington and the Connecticut Station. Most of them were published in the *Journal of Biological Chemistry*. After Osborne's retirement in 1928 and death in 1929, the work at the station was continued until Mendel's death in 1935, some fifteen papers being published with several junior collaborators. During this same period Mendel published ninety-seven papers in collaboration with graduate students or colleagues on the Yale faculty, and forty-one, mainly reviews of various aspects of nutrition, of which he was sole author. Mendel gave lectures subsequently published before the Harvey Society of New York in 1906 and 1914 and also gave the Herter Lectures at University and Bellevue Hospital Medical College in New York in 1914. In 1923 he gave the Hitchcock Lectures at the University of California and in 1930 was Cutler Lecturer at the Harvard Medical School.

Publications in book form include *Feeding Experiments with Isolated Food-substances*, 2 pts., Carnegie Institution of Washington Publication No. 156 (1911); *Changes in the Food Supply and Their Relation to Nutrition* (New Haven, 1916); and *Nutrition the Chemistry of Life* (New Haven, 1923).

II. Secondary Literature. In addition to the memoir by Chittenden mentioned above, there is a tribute by A. H. Smith, in *Journal of Nutrition*, **60** (1956), 3.

H. B. Vickery

MENDELEEV, DMITRY IVANOVICH (*b.* Tobolsk, Siberia [now Tyumen Oblast, R.S.F.S.R.], Russia, 8 February 1834; *d.* St. Petersburg [now Leningrad], Russia, 2 February 1907), *chemistry*.

Mendeleev was the fourteenth and last child of Ivan Pavlovich Mendeleev, a teacher of Russian literature, and Maria Dmitrievna Kornileva, who came of an old merchant family (she herself owned a glass factory near Tobolsk). His mother, who died when he was fifteen, played a large part in Mendeleev's early education and was strongly influential in shaping the views that he held throughout his life. Mendeleev entered the Tobolsk Gymnasium when he was seven, and graduated from it in 1849; while there he learned to dislike ancient languages and theology and to enjoy history, mathematics, and physics. In Tobolsk Mendeleev, who lived with his family near the glass-works, also acquired an interest in industrial affairs and, through the group of Decembrists exiled there, a love of liberty.

Shortly before her death, Mendeleev's mother took him to St. Petersburg, where in 1850 he enrolled in the faculty of physics and mathematics of the Main Pedagogical Institute, a progressive institution in which the revolutionary democrat Nikolai Dobrolyubov was a fellow student. Among his teachers were the chemist A. A. Voskresensky, who gave his pupils a taste for chemical experiment (and of whose lectures Mendeleev wrote down detailed descriptions that are preserved in the Mendeleev Museum in Leningrad); the zoologist Brandt, who interested Mendeleev in the classification of animals (his notes on this subject are also preserved); the geologist and mineralogist Kutorga, who immediately assigned him the chemical analysis of orthosilicate and pyroxene, and thus introduced him to research techniques; and the pedagogue Vyshnegradsky, who influenced his ideas on education. Mendeleev graduated from the Institute in 1855 with a brilliant record, but his hot temper led him into a quarrel with an important official of the Ministry of Education, and his first teaching assignment was therefore to the Simferopol Gymnasium, which was closed because of the Crimean War.

After two months in the Crimea, where he was unable to work, Mendeleev went to Odessa as a teacher in the lyceum, and there took up the continuation of his early scientific work. He had already begun to investigate the relationships between the crystal forms and chemical composition of substances. On graduating from the Institute, he had written a dissertation entitled "Izomorfizm v svyazi s drugimi otno sheniami formy k sostavu" ("Isomorphism in Connection With Other Relations of Form to Composition"). It was published in *Gorny zhurnal* ("Mining Journal") in 1856. The writing of this work in itself led Mendeleev still further into the comparative study of the chemical properties of substances; his master's dissertation, prepared while he was in Odessa, was entitled "Udelnye obemy" ("Specific Volumes") and was a direct extension of the earlier articles, in which he had raised the question of whether the chemical and crystallographic properties of substances have any relation to their specific volumes.

During this same period, Mendeleev, in order to support himself, also wrote articles for *Novosti estestvenykh nauk* ("News of Natural Sciences") and reviews for *Zhurnal ministerstva narodnogo prosveshchenia* ("Journal of the Ministry of Public Education"). At a slightly later date he wrote an article on gas fuel and the Bessemer process for *Promyshlenny listik* ("Industrial Notes"). From this time, the application of science to industry and economics was a pronounced and recurrent preoccupation in his work.

In September 1856 Mendeleev defended a master's thesis at the University of St. Petersburg, expressing his adherence to the chemical ideas of Gerhardt, to which he remained loyal throughout his life. Among other topics, he made known his agreement with unitary and type theories and his opposition to Berzelius' electrolytic theory of the formation of chemical compounds. Mendeleev adhered to Gerhardt's ideas all his life, and in consequence later years found him resisting Arrhenius' electrolytic theory, rejecting the concept of the ion as an electrically charged molecular fragment, and refusing to recognize the reality of the electron. He was opposed in general to linking chemistry with electricity and preferred associating it with physics as the science of mass. His predilection found its most brilliant vindication in the correlation he achieved between the chemical properties and the atomic weights of elements. Nor was he a chemical mechanist in the methodological sense then fashionable in certain quarters. Chemistry in his view was an independent science, albeit a physical one.

In October 1856 Mendeleev defended a thesis *pro venia legendi* to obtain the status of privatdocent in the university. His subject was the structure of silicon compounds. In January 1857 he began to give lectures in chemistry and to conduct research at the university's laboratories. In 1859–1860 Mendeleev worked at the University of Heidelberg, where he first collaborated with Bunsen, and then established his own laboratory. He studied capillary phenomena and the deviations of gases and vapors from the laws of perfect gases. In 1860, he discovered the phenomenon of critical temperature—the temperature at which a gas or vapor may be liquefied by the application of pressure alone—which he called the "absolute temperature of boiling." He was thereby led to consider once again the relationship between the physical and chemical properties of particles and their mass. He was convinced that the force of chemical affinity was identical to the force of cohesion; he looked upon his work, then, as falling within the realm of physical chemistry, the ground upon which chemistry, physics, and mathematics met.

Mendeleev took part in the first International Chemical Congress, held at Karlsruhe in 1860. The idea of the congress had been Kekulé's; its purpose was the standardization of such basic concepts of chemistry as atomic, molecular, and equivalent weights, since the prevailing use of a variety of atomic and other weights had considerably impeded the development of the discipline. At the congress Mendeleev met a number of prominent chemists, including Dumas, Wurtz, Zinin, and Cannizzaro, whose championship of Gerhardt's notions impressed him deeply. His account of the congress, in a letter to his teacher Voskresensky, was published in the St. Petersburg *Vedomosti* ("Record") in the same year.

In February 1861, on his return to St. Petersburg, Mendeleev published *Opyt teorii predelov organicheskikh soedineny* ("Attempt at a Theory of Limits of Organic Compounds"), in which he stated that the percentage of such elements as oxygen, hydrogen, and nitrogen could not exceed a certain maximum value when combined with carbon—a theory that brought him into direct opposition to the structural theories of organic chemistry. On this theory he based his text *Organicheskaya khimia* ("Organic Chemistry"), which was published in the same year (a second edition was brought out in 1863) and which won the Demidov Prize.

From January 1864 to December 1866 Mendeleev was professor of chemistry at the St. Petersburg Technological Institute and a docent on the staff of

the university. In addition, he carried out scientific assignments for three or f each year, wrote books, edited tra participated in the compilation of a clopedia, for which he wrote articles on the pr of chemicals and technical chemistry, including production of alcohol and alcoholometry. In 1865 he defended a thesis for the doctorate in chemistry, "O soedinenii spirta s vodoyu" ("On the Compounds of Alcohol With Water"). In it he first developed the characteristic view that solutions are chemical compounds and that dissolving one substance in another is not to be distinguished from other forms of chemical combination. In this thesis, he also adhered to the principles of chemical atomism.

At this same time Mendeleev, stimulated by the stormy social conditions that followed on the abolition of serfdom in Russia, became more strongly attracted to the practical problems facing the national economy. He began to study petroleum, traveling to Baku for that purpose in 1863; he attended the great industrial expositions held in Moscow in 1865 and in Paris in 1867; he purchased the estate of Boblovo, near Klin, in 1865 to demonstrate how agriculture could be put on a rational scientific basis; and he joined the Free Economic Society, where he lectured on such subjects as experimental agriculture, cooperative cheesemaking, and experiments with fertilizers. In 1862 he also married Feozva Nikitichna Leshchevaya; they had a son and a daughter.

It is appropriate here to consider how Mendeleev's work was situated in the context of the major scientific advances of the earlier nineteenth century. He had learned of the cell theory in the lectures on botany given at the Pedagogical Institute. Out of a belief in the unity of forces of nature had developed the law of the conservation of energy, which was fundamental to the study of chemical transformations in their relation to physical properties. The Darwinian theory of evolution had come to dominate the study of living nature, and considering the way in which the periodic law in its turn followed out of these fundamental discoveries, William Crookes could later refer to Mendeleev's theory as "inorganic Darwinism."

Mendeleev was also active in the growth of Russian chemical organizations during the 1860's. He participated in drawing up the bylaws of the Russian Chemical Society, which was founded in 1868, and he systematically presented the results of his researches at its meetings. The journal of the society was also important to the growth of the discipline within Russia, and Mendeleev chose to publish many of his findings in it. He further communicated his work to the chemical section of the Russian congresses for natural the first was held in December 1867.

A turning point in Mendeleev's career occurred in October 1867, when he was appointed to the chair of chemistry at the University of St. Petersburg. In preparing for his lectures he found nothing which he could recommend to his students as a text, so he set out to write his own. He derived his basic plan for his book from Gerhardt's theory of types, whereby elements were grouped by valence in relation to hydrogen. The typical elements hydrogen (1), oxygen (2), nitrogen (3), and carbon (4) were listed first, followed, in the same order, by the halogens (1) and the alkali metals (1).

Mendeleev entitled his book *Osnovy khimii* ("Principles of Chemistry"); he finished the first part of it, ending with the halogens, at the end of 1868. During the first two months of 1869 he wrote the first two chapters—on alkali metals and specific heat—of the second part. In spite of their common univalency, he organized the halogens and alkali metals so as to point up their contrary chemical relationships. It then remained to organize them according to another, more basic quantitative variable (or system of ordering), namely, their atomic weight. It may be noted that all Mendeleev's early work—his studies of the chemical properties of substances, his work on specific weights and their relationships to atomic and molecular weights, his investigations of the limits of compounds, and his study of atomic weights and their correlation with elements—had fitted him to undertake such a task, which was to culminate in the grand synthesis of the periodic law.

On 1 March 1869 Mendeleev was making preparations to leave St. Petersburg for a trip to Tver (now Kalinin) and then to other provincial towns. The Free Economic Society had given him a commission to investigate the methods in use for making cheeses in artels. It was on the very day of his departure that he realized the answer to the question of what group of elements should be placed next after the alkali metals in his *Osnovy khimii*. The principle of atomicity required treating copper and silver as a transitional group, since they gave compounds of both the $CuCl_2$ and AgCl types; it therefore seemed logical to place them next to the alkali metals, which they most closely resemble in chemical properties. In seeking a quantitative basis to justify such a transition, Mendeleev had the crucial idea of arranging the several groups of elements in the order of atomic weights, a sequence which gave him the following tabulation:

		Ca = 40	Sr = 87.6	Ba = 137
Li = 7	Na = 23	K = 39	Rb = 85.4	Cs = 133
		F = 19	Cl = 35.5	Br = 80	Te = 127

Clearly there was a regular progression in the differences between the atomic weights of the elements in the vertical columns (the future periods), and this arrangement made it possible to place other elements of intermediate atomic weight in the gaps in the table. In working out the final stages of his discovery, Mendeleev used the method of "chemical solitaire," writing out the names or symbols of the elements, together with their atomic weights and other properties, on cards. The procedure was an adaptation of the game of patience, which he liked to play for relaxation.

Mendeleev's work toward the *Osnovy khimii* thus led him to the periodic law, which he formulated in March 1869: "Elements placed according to the value of their atomic weights present a clear periodicity of properties." The work of the Karlsruhe congress had contributed to its discovery; clearly, it would have been impossible to find any relationship between the elements using the old atomic weights—Ca = 20, Sr = 43.8, and Ba = 63.5, for example. The necessity to establish correct atomic weights was indeed what first led Mendeleev to investigate the connections among the elements; from this investigation he proceeded inductively to the periodic law, upon which he was then able to construct a system of elements. He used deduction, however, to predict consequences from his still incomplete discovery, moving from the general to the particular to test the validity of the law. For example, immediately following his discovery of the periodic law, Mendeleev proposed changing the generally accepted weight for beryllium—14—to 9.4, ascribing to its oxide (after I. Avdeev) the formula BeO (by analogy with magnesia, MgO) and not Be_2O_3 (by analogy with alumina, Al_2O_3). He thus correctly determined the place of beryllium in his system of elements. He also predicted three undiscovered elements in the future groups III and IV of his system, which he called eka-aluminum, ekasilicon, and ekazirconium.

Mendeleev's first report of his discovery was "Opyt sistemy elementov, osnovannoy na ikh atomnom vese i khimicheskom skhodstve" ("Attempt at a System of Elements Based on Their Atomic Weight and Chemical Affinity"); he presented it in more detail in "Sootnoshenie svoystv s atomnym vesom elementov" ("Relation of the Properties to the Atomic Weights of the Elements"), which was read to the Russian Chemical Society in March 1869 by N. A. Menshutkin (since Mendeleev himself was away visiting cheesemaking cooperatives). In preparing the latter report, Mendeleev developed several variant tables of elements, including one in which even- and odd-valenced elements were placed in two separate columns. He discovered gaps at three points—between hydrogen and lithium, between fluorine and sodium, and between chlorine and potassium—and predicted that these lacunae would be filled by then-unknown elements having atomic weights of approximately 2, 20, and 36—that is, by helium, neon, and argon.

At first Mendeleev could subsume under the periodic law only isomorphism and atomic weight; in each of these early papers, too, he presented only the quantitative argument for the analytical expression of the law in the form of the increase of atomic weights. The first paper in particular contained many ambiguities and imprecisions; lead, for example, was placed in the same group as calcium and barium, while thallium occupied the same group as sodium and potassium, and uranium was grouped with boron and aluminum. Having been occupied with studies leading up to the law for fifteen years—since 1854—Mendeleev then formulated it in a single day. He spent the next three years in further perfecting it, and continued to be concerned with its finer points until 1907.

In the work that immediately followed his statement of the law, Mendeleev returned to his earlier investigation of specific volumes, studying the physical function of the rule that showed that uranium should be ascribed a doubled atomic weight. Many elements, including tellurium and lead, had therefore to be assigned new places on the table. Mendeleev presented this new result to the Second Congress of Russian Natural Scientists in August 1869, in a report entitled "Ob atomnom vese prostykh tel" ("On the Atomic Weight of Simple Bodies"). He then proceeded to use the same argument to determine chemical functions; having recognized the importance of the simplicity of oxides as compound types, he proceeded to clarify the seven fundamental groups that extend from the alkali metal oxides of form R_2O to the halogen oxides of form R_2O_7. Mendeleev communicated this finding to the October meeting of the Russian Chemical Society in the memoir "O kolichestve kisloroda v solyanykh okislakh i ob atomnosti elementov" ("On the Quantity of Oxygen in Salt Oxides and on the Valence of Elements"). By 1870, he had taken into account the presence of compounds of the type RO_4 for osmium and ruthenium, and had therefore introduced an eighth group into his classification.

Mendeleev himself summarized the studies that had brought him to the periodic law in a later edition of Osnovy khimii, in which he commented on "four aspects of matter," representing the measurable properties of elements and their compounds: "(a) isomorphism, or the similarity of crystal forms and their ability to form isomorphic mixtures; (b) the relation of specific volumes of similar compounds or elements; (c) the composition of their compound salts; and (d) the relations of the atomic weights of elements." He concluded that these "four aspects" are important because "when a certain property is measured, it ceases to have an arbitrary and subjective character and gives objectivity to the equation."

Since the periodic law was dependent upon the quantitative relation between atomic weight, as an independent variable, and its physical and chemical properties, Mendeleev in 1870 took up the problem of developing an entire "natural system of elements." He employed deduction to reach the boldest and most far-reaching logical consequences of the law that he had discovered, so that he might, by verification of these consequences, confirm the law itself.

Mendeleev simultaneously described various groups of elements for inclusion in the Osnovy khimii and made them the subject of extended laboratory research. He examined molybdenum, tungsten, titanium, uranium, and the rare metals, and in November 1870 he wrote two articles. In the first, "O meste tseria v sisteme elementov" ("On the Place of Cerium in the System of Elements"), he introduced a theoretically corrected value for the atomic weight of cerium—138, instead of the previously accepted 92—and determined its new place within his system. In the second article, "Estestvennaya sistema elementov i primenenie ee k ukazaniyu svoystv neotkrytykh elementov" ("The Natural System of Elements and Its Application to Indicate the Properties of Undiscovered Elements"), Mendeleev predicted that because of the volatility of its salts, eka-aluminum would be discovered by spectroscopic means.

The Osnovy khimii was finished in February 1871. Among the important ideas that the work embodied was Mendeleev's notion of the complexity of the chemical elements and their formation from "ultimates." He stated that the bivalence (II) of magnesium and calcium could be explained as a result of the close blending of monovalent (I) sodium and potassium with monovalent (I) hydrogen:

$$Na_{23}^{I} + H_1^{I} = Mg_{24}^{II}; \qquad K_{39}^{I} + H_1^{I} = Ca_{40}^{II},$$

a formulation that may be seen as a confused premonition of the later rule of displacement.

In March 1871, two years after his discovery of the law, Mendeleev first named it "periodic." That summer he published in Justus Liebigs Annalen der Chemie his article "Die periodische Gesetzmässigkeit der chemischen Elemente," which he later characterized as "the best summary of my views and ideas on the periodicity of the elements and the original after which so much was written later about this system. This was the main reason for my scientific fame, because much was confirmed—much later." In the fall of that year Mendeleev turned to conducting research on rare earth metals to determine their place among the elements of group IV. One of his goals was to find the ekasilicon (later called germanium) that he had predicted. He also conducted research on hydrates and complex compounds, especially those of ammonia, and gave public lectures in which he combined chemical topics with philosophical ones.

The reception of the periodic law caused Mendeleev considerable mental anguish. In the sharp and prolonged battle that was soon joined, the law at first had few advocates, even among Russian chemists. Its opponents, who were especially vocal in Germany and England, included those chemists who thought in exclusively empirical terms and who were unable to acknowledge the validity of theoretical thinking; Bunsen, Zinin, Lars Nilson, and Carl Petersen were prominent among them. Petersen not only doubted the generality of the periodic law but also defended the contradictory view of the trivalence of beryllium. In Germany, Rammelsberg also took issue with a particular point, attempting in 1872 to refute Mendeleev's proposed correction for the atomic weights of cerium and its close neighbors. Mendeleev answered this charge the following year in an article entitled "O primenimosti periodicheskogo zakona k tseritovym metallam" ("On the Application of the Periodic Law to Cerite Metals"), in which he demonstrated that the facts introduced by Rammelsberg "strengthen, not refute, my proposed changes in the atomic weight of cerium."

A number of other chemists specializing in the system of the elements either attacked Mendeleev's law or disputed his priority. Lothar Meyer, for example, proposed in 1870 a representation for the atomic volumes of the elements in the form of a broken zigzag line. Blomstrand and E. H. von Blomhauer developed a spiral system, also in 1870. Mendeleev answered these and other claims to the periodic law— and also claims against it—in the article "K voprosu o sisteme elementov" ("Toward the Question of a System of Elements"), published in March 1871. Basically, however, he had no patience with disputes over priority, and although by taste an internationalist in science, he engaged in such disputes only when others denigrated Russian achievements.

The years 1871 to 1874 saw the acceptance by a number of chemists of Mendeleev's corrected atomic weights for several elements. Bunsen consented to Mendeleev's value for indium; Rammelsberg and

Roscoe, to that for uranium; Cleve, to that for the rare earth metals (which for yttrium confirmed the values found earlier by Marc Delafontaine, Bunsen, and J. F. Bahr); and Chidenius and Delafontaine, to that for thorium. Nevertheless, the majority of scientists did not accept Mendeleev's discovery for some time; the first textbook on organic chemistry to be based on the law was published in St. Petersburg by Richter only in 1874. Wurtz's *Théorie atomique* further helped to propagate Mendeleev's ideas. At about the same time, Brauner spoke in favor of Mendeleev's corrected weight for chlorine and set out to determine the density of the vapors of beryllium chloride, as Nilson and Petersen had also done— Brauner's determination of the weight of beryllium was a major confirmation of the generality of Mendeleev's law.

The discovery of the three elements predicted by Mendeleev was, however, of decisive importance in the acceptance of his law. In 1875 Lecoq de Boisbaudran, knowing nothing of Mendeleev's work, discovered by spectroscopic methods a new metal, which he named gallium. Both in the nature of its discovery and in a number of its properties gallium coincided with Mendeleev's prediction for eka-aluminum, but its specific weight at first seemed to be less than predicted. Hearing of the discovery, Mendeleev sent to France "Zametka po povodu otkrytia gallia" ("Note on the Occasion of the Discovery of Gallium"), in which he insisted that gallium was in fact his eka-aluminum. Although Lecoq de Boisbaudran objected to this interpretation, he made a second determination of the specific weight of gallium and confirmed that such was indeed the case. From that moment the periodic law was no longer a mere hypothesis, and the scientific world was astounded to note that Mendeleev, the theorist, had seen the properties of a new element more clearly than the chemist who had empirically discovered it. From this time, too, Mendeleev's work came to be more widely known; in 1877 Crookes placed in the *Quarterly Journal of Science* an abstract, entitled "The Chemistry of the Future," of Mendeleev's summarizing article of 1871, while in 1879 a French translation of the full article, with a new introduction, was published by G. G. Quesneville in the *Moniteur scientifique*.

The discovery of gallium was incorporated into the third edition of *Osnovy khimii* in 1877. The fourth edition, of 1881–1882, mentioned the discovery of scandium—the ekaboron predicted by Mendeleev—by Nilson, in 1879. Winkler discovered germanium in 1886; its properties matched precisely those of Mendeleev's ekasilicon, and the discovery of germanium figured in the fifth edition of Mendeleev's book in 1889. This edition also contained, within a single frame, reproductions of portraits of Lecoq de Boisbaudran, Nilson, Winkler, and Brauner. The composite bore the caption "Reinforcers of the Periodic Law."

The periodic law might now be considered proven, and Mendeleev presented a summary of the research leading to it in his Faraday lecture, "The Periodic Law of the Chemical Elements," which he delivered at the invitation of the Chemical Society of London on the occasion of the twentieth anniversary of his discovery. He spoke of the scientists who preceded him in his work as well as those who later contributed to the development of the law, and dealt with both the history and what might be called the prehistory of it. During the same visit to London Mendeleev was also invited to lecture before the Royal Institution of Great Britain. In this speech, "An Attempt at the Application to Chemistry of One of Newton's Principles," he sought to oppose the concept of chemical structure to the hypothesis that the mutual influence of atoms within the molecule is in concord with Newton's third law of motion. In both these lectures (which he published in 1889 as *Dva Londonskikh chtenia* ["Two London Lectures"]), Mendeleev did not confine himself to chemistry, but went on to draw philosophical generalities that embraced the whole of the natural sciences.

Even while he was working toward the periodic law and its proofs, Mendeleev was also concerned with the problem of the liquefaction of gases. As early as 1870 he discussed the necessity of intensive cooling in the process, while in December 1871 he suddenly turned to purely physical research on permanent gases and their compressibility. In initiating this investigation, he hoped to find the hypothetical "universal ether," which he believed to be an extraordinarily thin gas that must, in his system, occupy the place above hydrogen. Although his primary goal was unreachable, in the course of his studies Mendeleev discovered a number of deviations of gases from the Boyle-Mariotte law, and gave a more precise equation for the state of real gases. His work then assumed a more practical slant, and he turned to aeronautical research; giving a general form to his experiments on the temperature of the upper layers of the atmosphere (1875) in the report "Ob opytakh nad uprugostyu gazov" ("On Experiments on the Elasticity of Gases"), published in 1881. In 1887 Mendeleev made a solo balloon ascension from Klin, for the purpose of observing a solar eclipse.

After 1884, Mendeleev concerned himself with the expansion of liquids and in particular with the specific weights of aqueous solutions of various substances. He was able to conclude that in such solutions discontinuous relationships exist between the solvent and the solute, attesting to the existence of determinate chemical relationships—a necessary condition, according to chemical atomic theory. Mendeleev thus arrived at a chemical theory of solutions, which he opposed to the theory of electrolytic dissociation of dilute aqueous solutions set forth by Arrhenius. Mendeleev stated his theory both in his *Issledovanie vodnykh rastvorov po udelnomu vesu* ("Research on Aqueous Solutions According to Their Specific Weight") of 1887 and in the fifth edition of *Osnovy khimii*.

From the last years of the 1870's Mendeleev was also concerned with the production of petroleum. In 1876 he visited the United States; in the resultant book, *Neftyanaya promyshlennost v Severo-amerikanskom shtate Pensilvanii i na Kavkaze* ("Petroleum Production in the North American State of Pennsylvania and in the Caucasus"), he advanced a theory of the inorganic origin of petroleum. Mendeleev traveled to Baku, too, to study oilfields. He did further research on the uses of petroleum, including its medical applications; in 1878 he employed petroleum as a self-treatment for pleurisy. In 1880–1881, Mendeleev wrote a series of reports of the results of his Caucasian journeys, and thus became engaged in a dispute with Nobel over the proper location of petroleum refineries. In 1883, with *Po voprosy o nefti* ("On a Question of Petroleum"), he entered into a discussion with Markovnikov; in the same year and the one following he wrote a series of works on the refining of both Baku and American oil. In an article of 1889 he denied recurrent rumors of the exhaustion of the Baku fields.

By the end of the 1880's Mendeleev had added an investigation of the coal industry to his practical concerns; he visited the Donets Basin to study mining and wrote *Budushchaya sila, pokoyushchayasya na beregakh Dontsa* ("Future Power Lying on the Banks of the Donets"; 1888). None of his efforts toward the development of domestic industry was successful, however; the czarist government chose to dismiss his remarkable ideas and projects as "professorial dreams."

The decades of the 1870's and 1880's marked a major transitional period in Mendeleev's life. The law that he had discovered was developed and confirmed, and he had turned to more commercial matters in the interest of the national economy; he had also left his family and entered into a second marriage, in 1882, with a young artist, Anna Ivanova Popova, by whom he had two sons and two daughters. He became increasingly concerned with philosophical matters, of which he wrote, "Much in me was changing; at that time I read much on religion, on sects, and philosophy, economic articles." His writings on philosophical themes included the articles "Ob ediniyse" ("On Unity"; 1870), "Pered kartinoyu A. I. Kuindzhi" ("Before a Picture of A. I. Kuindzhi"; 1880), "O edinstve veshchestva" ("On the Unity of Matter"; 1886), and, most importantly, the book *Materialy dlya suzhdenia o spiritizma* ("Material for an Opinion on Spiritism"; 1876), which embodied the results of the work of a special commission of the Physical Society of St. Petersburg. Of the last, Mendeleev later wrote, "I tried to fight against superstition . . . it took professors to act against the authority of professors. The result was right, spiritism was rejected."

The same period also saw a change in Mendeleev's academic status. In 1876 he was elected a corresponding member of the St. Petersburg Academy of Sciences; in 1880 he was defeated in an election for extraordinary membership by the reactionary majority of members of the physics and mathematics section, who had come to fear his democratic tendencies. In the course of the protests that followed this event, Butlerov published an article entitled "Russkaya ili tolko Imperatorskaya Akademia Nauk v S.-Peterburge" ("The Russian or Only an Imperial Academy of Sciences in St. Petersburg") and some twenty other scientific institutions elected Mendeleev an honorary member. In 1890 disorders broke out among the students at the University of St. Petersburg and Mendeleev undertook to deliver a student petition to the ministry of education. He was given a rude and insulting answer, tantamount to a demand for his personal resignation; he thus left the university, where he had taught for more than thirty years. On 3 April 1890 Mendeleev gave his last lecture to the students of the general chemistry course.

His teaching career at an end, Mendeleev decided to publish a newspaper in support of the protectionist policies that his investigations of petroleum and coal production had convinced him were the "sole means of saving Russia." Before he could begin this project, however, he received a commission from the naval ministry to conduct large-scale laboratory research on the production of smokeless powder—a secret project that took high priority. From 1890 to 1892, he also participated in a study of the tariff structure, at the invitation of the ministry of finance; this resulted in his *Tolkovy tarif* ("Comprehensive Tariff"), which was published in 1891–1892. The government was appreciative of his services, and Mendeleev rose rapidly in the bureaucracy, being appointed privy councillor in 1891.

From 1892 on, Mendeleev was concerned in the regulation of the system of weights and measures in Russia, a task that he discharged "with enthusiasm, since here the purely scientific was closely interwoven with the practical." In 1893 he was named director of the newly created Central Board of Weights and Measures, a post that he held until his death, and in connection with which he frequently traveled abroad. In the 1890's Mendeleev was also actively involved in problems of shipbuilding and the development of shipping routes. He participated in the design of the icebreaker *Ermak* (launched in 1899) and wrote on the progress of research in the northern Arctic Ocean (1901). He simultaneously studied the development of heavy industry in Russia, traveled to the Urals and to Siberia to observe the production of iron, began to publish a series entitled Biblioteka Promyshlennykh Znany ("Library of Industrial Knowledge")—for which he also compiled a curriculum—and wrote, in addition to several related books and articles, *Uchenie o promyshlennosti* ("Theory of Industry"; 1901), which contained a number of ideas that he later developed in his *Zavetnye mysli* ("Private Thoughts"; 1903–1905).

Nor was Mendeleev unconcerned with theoretical chemistry during these years. A sixth edition of *Osnovy khimii* was published in 1895; in it he expressed some skepticism about the discoveries (in 1894 and 1895, respectively) of the first inert gases, argon and helium. After Ramsay's 1898 discovery of their three analogues (which Ramsay had himself predicted), and after the determination of the place of the whole group as a zero valence group within the periodic system (1900), Mendeleev reconsidered his position and not only accepted the new elements but also grouped Ramsay among the "reinforcers of the periodic law."

Mendeleev denied the discovery of the electron, however, and in particular the explanation of radioactivity as the disintegration of atoms and the transformation of elements, thinking that these discoveries destroyed the very foundations of the periodic law. He disputed the transmutation of elements in his article "Zoloto iz serebra" ("Gold From Silver") of 1898; while in *Popytka khimicheskogo ponimania mirovogo efira* ("An Attempt at a Chemical Conception of the Universal Ether") of 1902, he introduced the erroneous notion that the universal ether is similar in nature to a very light inert gas and that it takes part in radioactive processes. In 1902 he visited the Paris laboratories of the Curies and Becquerel to study radioactivity further. He dealt with these questions in the seventh and eighth editions (1903 and 1906) of his textbook.

The fifth and later editions of the *Osnovy khimii*

were translated into the western European languages. In addition, from 1892 Mendeleev took an active part in the preparation of the great Brockhaus encyclopedia, which provided another vehicle for the dissemination of his ideas in western Europe. He introduced a section on chemistry and the production of chemicals and wrote the articles on matter, the periodic regularity of the chemical elements, and technology, among a number of other topics. His work as a whole amounted to more than 400 books and articles, as well as a large number of manuscripts, which are preserved in the D. I. Mendeleev Museum-Archive, Leningrad State University.

In 1894 Mendeleev was awarded the doctorate by both Oxford and Cambridge; his seventieth birthday was widely observed in 1904, as was the fiftieth anniversary of his scientific career the following year. In 1905 he attended the commemorative session of the Royal Society of London, and was awarded the Copley Medal; he was also a member of many Russian and foreign scientific societies. He held several czarist orders and the French government made him a member of the Legion of Honor. Following his death from heart failure, students followed his funeral to the Volkov Cemetery in St. Petersburg. They carried the periodic table of the elements high above the procession as the fitting emblem of Mendeleev's career.

BIBLIOGRAPHY

I. ORIGINAL WORKS. Mendeleev's works were published in Russian during his lifetime in the form of monographs and magazine and encyclopedia articles, many of which were translated into English, French, and German. For Mendeleev's own annotated bibliography of his works (1899) see *Sochinenia*, XXV, 686–776. After his death *Osnovy khimii* was reprinted many times, collections of his work appeared in the series Klassiki Nauki ("Classics of Science"), his archival material was published, and his complete works were published as *Sochinenia* ("Works"), 25 vols. (Leningrad, 1934–1952); a supp. vol. contains a detailed index.

Osnovy khimii ("Principles of Chemistry"), Mendeleev's main work, went through eight eds. during his lifetime: 1868–1871; 1872–1873; 1877; 1881–1882; 1889; 1895; 1903; 1906. The 1st ed., in 4 pts., was published in two vols. Starting with the 5th ed. the book was no longer divided into parts. In the 8th ed. all notes were placed at the end of the book as special appendixes. The periodic law is the focus of the work; beginning with the 3rd ed. (after the discovery of gallium in 1875) it is more prominent because it had been verified experimentally. Mendeleev rewrote each ed., including all new scientific data—particularly confirmations of the periodic law—and reanalyzing difficulties that had arisen to hinder its confirmation (inert

gases, radioactivity, radioactive and rare-earth elements). He also expanded the sections on the chemical industry and on philosophy and methodology. To update the posthumous 9th (1928) and 10th (1931) eds. a section by G. V. Wulff *et al.* was added on new trends in the construction of chemical principles. This new section was omitted from the 11th to 13th eds. (1932–1947).

The first English trans., *The Principles of Chemistry* (London, 1891), was made from the 5th ed. The 2nd (London, 1897) and 3rd (London, 1905; repr. New York, 1969) eds. were based on the 6th and 7th Russian eds., respectively. A German version, *Grundlagen der Chemie* (St. Petersburg, 1890), was based on the 5th ed. and a French trans., *Principes de chimie* (Paris, 1895), on the 6th ed.

Several articles from *Periodichesky zakon* ("Periodic Law"), B. M. Kedrov, ed., in the series Klassiki Nauki (Moscow, 1958), were published in other languages. Those in English are "The Periodic Law of the Chemical Elements" (written in 1871), in *Chemical News and Journal of Physical (Industrial) Science*, **40**, nos. 1042–1048 (1879); **41**, nos. 1049–1060 (1880), reviewed by W. Crookes, "The Chemistry of the Future," in *Quarterly Journal of Science*, no. 55 (July 1877), also published separately, George Kamensky, trans., as *An Attempt Towards a Chemical Conception of the Ether* (London, 1904); "An Attempt to Apply to Chemistry One of the Principles of Newton's Natural Philosophy," in *Chemical News*, **60**, no. 1545 (1889), 1–4; no. 1546, pp. 15–17; no. 1547, pp. 30–32, also published separately under the same title (London, 1889); and "The Periodic Law of the Chemical Elements (Faraday Lecture)," in *Journal of the Chemical Society*, **55** (1889), 634–656, repr. in *Faraday Lectures 1869–1928* (London, 1928). See also "The Relations Between the Properties and Atomic Weights of the Elements," in Henry M. Leicester and Herbert S. Klickstein, eds., *A Source Book in Chemistry 1400–1900* (New York, 1952), 438–444.

French translations include "Remarques à propos de la découverte du gallium," in *Comptes rendus . . . de l'Académie des sciences*, **81** (1875), 969–972; "La loi périodique des éléments chimiques (Faraday Lecture)," in *Moniteur scientifique*, 3rd ser., **9** (1879), 691 ff.; "La loi périodique des éléments chimiques," *ibid.*, 4th ser., **3**, pt. 2, no. 572 (1889), 899–904; and "Comment j'ai trouvé le système périodique des éléments," in *Revue générale de chimie pure et appliquée*, **1** (1899), 210 ff., 510 ff.—here, repr. under another title, is "Periodicheskaya zakonnost khimicheskikh elementov" ("Periodic Law of Chemical Elements"), from Brockhaus and Efron's *Entsiklopedichesky slovar* ("Encyclopedic Dictionary").

For German translations, see "Zur Frage über das System der chemischen Elemente," in *Berichte der Deutschen chemischen Gesellschaft*, **4** (1871), 348–352; "Die periodische Gesetzmässigkeit der chemischen Elemente," in *Justus Liebigs Annalen der Chemie*, supp. **8**, no. 2 (1871), 133–229, repr. in Ostwald's Klassiker, no. 68 (Leipzig, 1913), pp. 41–118; "Ueber die Stellung des Ceriums im System der Elemente," in *Bulletin de l'Académie des sciences de St. Petersbourg*, **16** (1871), 45–50; "Ueber die Anwendbarkeit des periodischen Gesetzes bei die Ceritmetallen," in *Justus Liebigs Annalen der Chemie*, **168**, no. 1 (1873), 45–63; "Zur Geschichte des periodischen Gesetzes," in *Berichte der Deutschen chemischen Gesellschaft*, **8** (1875), 1796–1804; and "Das natürliche System der chemischen Elemente," in Ostwald's Klassiker, no. 68 (Leipzig, 1913), pp. 20–40.

Publications from Mendeleev's scientific archives include *Novye materialy po istorii otkrytia periodicheskogo zakona* ("New Material on the History of the Discovery of the Periodic Law"), B. M. Kedrov, ed. (Moscow, 1950); *Nauchny arkhiv* ("Scientific Archive"), I, *Periodichesky zakon* ("The Periodic Law"), compiled and edited by B. M. Kedrov (Moscow, 1953), which includes theoretical material from 1869–1871. Notes on experiments related to the periodic law during this period will appear in vol. II, *Eksperimentalnye raboty* ("Experimental Works"). Material preceding the periodic law and directed toward it will be in vol. III, *Podgotovlenie otkrytia* ("Preparation for the Discovery"), and that which followed the discovery will be in vol. IV, *Razrabotka otkrytia* ("Development of the Discovery"); *Rastvory* ("Solutions"), K. P. Mishchenko, ed., in the series Klassiki Nauki (Leningrad, 1959); *Nauchny arkhiv. Osvoenie kraynego Severa* ("Scientific Archive. The Conquest of the Far North"), I, *Vysokie shiroty Severnogo Ledovitogo okeana* ("High Latitudes of the Northern Arctic Ocean"), A. I. Dubravin, ed. (Moscow–Leningrad, 1960); *Nauchny arkhiv. Rastvory* ("Scientific Archive. Solutions"), compiled by R. B. Dobrotin (Moscow–Leningrad, 1960); and *Izbrannye lektsii po khimii* ("Selected Lectures in Chemistry"), compiled by A. A. Makarenya *et al.* (Moscow, 1968), Mendeleev's chemistry lectures from 1864, 1870–1871, and 1889–1890.

For autobiographical source material, see *D. I. Mendeleev. Literaturnoe nasledstvo*, I, *Zametki i materialy D. I. Mendeleeva biograficheskogo kharaktera* (Leningrad, 1938), a collection of biographical notes and material; *Arkhiv D. I. Mendeleeva*, I, *Avtobiograficheskie materialy. Sbornik dokumentov* (Leningrad, 1951), with Mendeleev's bibliography of his works, pp. 39–130, as well as diary notes, chronology, a catalog of Mendeleev's personal library, and a list of the contents of his scientific archives; and M. D. Mendeleeva, ed., *Nauchnoe nasledstvo* ("Scientific Heritage"), Natural Science Ser., II (Moscow–Leningrad, 1951): see pp. 111–256 for Mendeleev's diaries for 1861–1862, and pp. 257–294 for his letters concerning his work on smokeless powder, P. M. Lukyanov, ed.

II. SECONDARY LITERATURE. Biographical works on Mendeleev include N. A. Figurovsky, *Dmitry Ivanovich Mendeleev* (Moscow, 1961); B. Kedrov and T. Chentsova, *Brauner—spodvizhnik Mendeleeva* (Moscow, 1960), written by Mendeleev's associate, with their correspondence and material on their elaboration of the periodic law; A. A. Makarenya *et al.*, eds., *D. I. Mendeleev v vospominaniakh sovremennikov* ("Mendeleev Recalled by His Contemporaries"; Moscow, 1969), with recollections of his friends, students, acquaintances, and relatives; A. I. Mendeleeva, *Mendeleev v zhizni* ("Mendeleev in Life"; Moscow, 1928), written by Mendeleev's second wife; M. N. Mladentsev and V. E. Tishchenko, *Mendeleev, ego zhizn i deyatelnost*

("Mendeleev, His Life and Work"), I (Moscow–Leningrad, 1938)—Tishchenko was Mendeleev's laboratory assistant and the biography goes as far as 1861; O. N. Pisarzhevsky, *Dmitry Ivanovich Mendeleev* (Moscow, 1959); and *Semeynaya khronika* ("Family Chronicle"; St. Petersburg, 1908), letters from his relatives and recollections by his niece, N. Y. Gubkinaya.

On the history of the discovery and development of the periodic law, see L. A. Chugaev, *Periodicheskaya sistema khimicheskikh elementov* ("The Periodic System of the Chemical Elements"; St. Petersburg, 1913); K. Danzer, *Dmitri I. Mendelejew und Lothar Meyer. Die Schöpfer des Periodensystems der chemischen Elemente* (Leipzig, 1971); B. M. Kedrov, *Razvitie ponyatia elementa ot Mendeleeva do nashikh dney* ("The Development of the Concept of the Element From Mendeleev to Our Times"; Moscow–Leningrad, 1948), pp. 24–71, 220–239; *Evolyutsia ponyatia elementa v khimii* ("The Evolution of the Concept of the Element in Chemistry"; Moscow, 1956), pp. 137–161, 188–294; *Den odnogo velikogo otkrytia* ("The Day of One Great Discovery"; Moscow, 1958), also translated into French as "Le 1er mars 1869; jour de la découverte de la loi périodique par D. I. Mendeléev," in *Cahiers d'histoire mondiale*, VI, 3, 644–656, gives the history of the discovery of the periodic law on 1 Mar. 1869 and includes many archival documents; *Filosofsky analiz pervykh trudov D. I. Mendeleeva o periodicheskom zakone (1869–1871)* ("A Philosophical Analysis of the First Works of D. I. Mendeleev on the Periodic Law [1869–1871]"; Moscow, 1959), a continuation of the preceding work; *Tri aspekta atomistiki* ("Three Aspects of Atomic Theory"), III, *Zakon Mendeleeva. Logiko-istorichesky aspekt* ("Mendeleev's Law. Logical-Historical Aspect"; Moscow, 1969); *Mikroanatomia velikogo otkrytia. K 100-letiyu zakona Mendeleeva* ("Microanatomy of the Great Discovery. For the 100th Anniversary of Mendeleev's Discovery"; Moscow, 1970); B. M. Kedrov and D. N. Trifonov, *Zakon periodichnosti i khimicheskie elementy. Otkrytia i khronologia* ("The Law of Periodicity and the Chemical Elements. Discoveries and Chronology"; Moscow, 1969); Paul Kolodkine, *Dmitri Mendeleiv et la loi périodique* (Paris, 1963); V. A. Krotikov, "The Mendeleev Archives and Museum of the Leningrad University," in *Journal of Chemical Education*, **37** (1960), 625–628; V. Y. Kurbatov, *Zakon D. I. Mendeleeva* ("D. I. Mendeleev's Law"; Leningrad, 1925); Henry M. Leicester, "Dmitrii Ivanovich Mendeleev," in Eduard Farber, ed., *Great Chemists* (New York, 1961), 719–732; A. A. Makarenya, *D. I. Mendeleev o radioaktivnosti i slozhnosti elementov* ("D. I. Mendeleev on Radioactivity and the Complexity of the Elements"), 2nd ed. (Moscow, 1965); and *D. I. Mendeleev i fiziko-khimicheskie nauki* ("D. I. Mendeleev and the Physicochemical Sciences"; Moscow, 1972), an attempt at a scientific biography; F. A. Paneth, "Radioactivity and the Completion of the Periodic System," in *Nature*, **149** (23 May 1942), 565–568; *Periodichesky zakon D. I. Mendeleeva i ego filosofskoe znachenie* ("Periodic Law of D. I. Mendeleev and Its Philosophical Significance"; Moscow, 1947), a collection of articles by A. N. Bakh, A. F. Joffe, A. E. Fersmann,

A. V. Rakovsky, B. M. Kedrov, G. S. Vasetsky, and B. N. Vyropaev; *Periodichesky zakon i stroenie atoma* ("The Periodic Law and Atomic Structure"; Moscow, 1971), a collection of articles; O. N. Pisarzhevsky, *Dmitrii Ivanovich Mendeleev. His Life and Work* (Moscow, 1959); Daniel Posin, *Mendeleyev, the Story of a Great Scientist* (New York, 1948); E. Rabinowitsch and E. Thilo, *Periodisches System. Geschichte und Theorie* (Stuttgart, 1930), trans. into Russian as *Periodicheskaya sistema elementov. Istoria i teoria* (Moscow–Leningrad, 1933), pt. 1, esp. ch. 5; N. N. Semenov, ed., *Sto let periodicheskogo zakona khimicheskikh elementov* ("A Hundred Years of the Periodic Law of the Chemical Elements") (Moscow, 1969); *75 let periodicheskogo zakona D. I. Mendeleeva i Russkogo khimicheskogo obshchestva* ("Seventy-five Years of Mendeleev's Periodic Law and the Russian Chemical Society"; Moscow–Leningrad, 1947), a collection of articles with a bibliography on pp. 261–265; T. E. Thorpe, *Essays in Historical Chemistry* (London, 1911), 483–499; W. A. Tilden, *Famous Chemists* (London, 1921), 241–258; D. N. Trifonov, *O kolichestvennoy interpretatsii periodichnosti* ("On the Quantitative Interpretation of Periodicity"; Moscow, 1971), pp. 16–31; *Voprosy estestvoznania i tekhniki* ("Questions of Natural Science and Technology"), no. 4 (29) (Moscow, 1969), a collection commemorating the centenary of the periodic law; Alexander Vucinich, "Mendeleev's Views on Science and Society," in *Isis*, **58** (1967), 342–351; and *Science in Russian Culture* (Stanford, Calif., 1970), 147–165; and *Yubileynomu Mendeleevskomu sezdu v oznamenovanie 100-letney godovshchiny so dnya rozhdenia D. I. Mendeleeva. Varianty periodicheskoy sistemy* ("Mendeleev Anniversary Congress in Recognition of the Centenary of D. I. Mendeleev's Birth. Variants of the Periodic System"), collected by M. A. Blokh (Leningrad, 1934).

On other aspects of Mendeleev's life and work, see V. P. Barzakovsky and R. B. Dobrotin, *Trudy D. I. Mendeleeva v oblasti khimii silikatov i stekloobraznogo sostoyania* ("Mendeleev's Works on the Chemistry of Silicates and Glass-Making"; Moscow, 1960); T. S. Kudryavtseva and M. E. Shekhter, *Mendeleev i ugolnaya promyshlennost Rossii* ("Mendeleev and the Russian Coal Industry"; Moscow, 1952); A. A. Makarenya and I. N. Filimonova, *D. I. Mendeleev i Peterburgsky universitet* ("Mendeleev and St. Petersburg University"; Leningrad, 1969); V. E. Parkhomenko, *D. I. Mendeleev i russkoe neftyanoe delo* ("Mendeleev and the Russian Petroleum Industry"; Moscow, 1957); S. I. Volfkovich *et al.*, eds., *D. I. Mendeleev. Raboty po selskomu khozyaystvu i lesovodstvu* ("Mendeleev. Works on Agriculture and Forestry; Moscow, 1954); and G. A. Zabrodsky, *Mirovozzrenie D. I. Mendeleeva* ("Mendeleev's World View"; Moscow, 1957), issued to commemorate the fiftieth anniversary of his death.

B. M. Kedrov

MENEGHETTI, EGIDIO (*b.* Verona, Italy, 14 November 1892; *d.* Padua, Italy, 4 March 1961), *experimental pharmacology.*

Meneghetti was the son of Umberto Meneghetti and Clorinda Stegagno; both his father and grandfather were physicians. He attended school in Verona, then entered the University of Padua, where from 1913 to 1914 he worked under Luigi Sabbatani, director of the Institute of Pharmacology. He graduated *cum laude* in 1916. Meneghetti was named chief of the pharmacology laboratory in 1919; in 1922 he became teacher of experimental pharmacology. In 1926 he left Padua to take up a similar post at Camerino. Two years later he accepted an appointment at the University of Palermo, then, in 1932, returned to Padua as professor of pharmacology. He was chosen rector of the university in 1945 after the Liberation, and in 1951 founded the Centro di Studio per la Chemoterapia there.

Meneghetti's first important scientific work, in 1921, concerned the relationship of the hemolytic and fixative actions of metals to their place in the table of atomic weights. He used the techniques of quantitative biophysics to demonstrate that such actions increase in intensity as the ionic tension of the metallic solution decreases. He was also concerned with technology; in 1925 he improved the apparatus by which artifical circulation could be maintained in the isolated heart of a frog. By 1928, however, he had formulated the basis for his subsequent researches; in his inaugural lecture at the University of Palermo, given on 5 March of that year, Meneghetti stated that experimental biochemistry and cell physiology must constitute the basis of modern pharmacology.

The greatest part of Meneghetti's pharmacological contributions concern the occasionally overlapping fields of colloids and toxicology. His first work on colloids was his article *Über die pharmakologischen Wirkung des kolloidalen Arsensulfids*, published in 1921. He developed this line of inquiry in a series of works, written between 1924 and 1934, on the trivalent and pentavalent compounds of antimony and in articles (in 1930 and 1937) on the salts of silver, gold, and copper. He demonstrated that substances that are of limited solubility in water may be introduced into the circulatory system (or injected locally) in the colloidal state.

In a series of researches conducted between 1924 and 1926 Meneghetti showed a specific effect of colloidal sulfur of antimony when it is injected into a vein. He was able to demonstrate that it lodged in the histiocytes of the bone marrow, thereby disrupting erythropoiesis, as is evidenced by the appearance of immature erythrocytes in the blood. (Two conditions are necessary to the observation of this erythroneocytosis—the granules of the colloidal preparation must be extremely fine, and the injection must be made slowly; otherwise the substance is exhibited more strongly in the macrophagic reticuloendothelial cells of the lungs and liver.) Meneghetti's proof that erythroblasts can be produced in the blood by the fixation of a toxic substance in the reticuloendothelial cells of the bone marrow was a major contribution toward the understanding of the pathogenesis of blood diseases (see his very important work *Emopatia primitiva da solfuro di antimonio colloidale* [1926]).

Meneghetti devoted ten works to toxicology between 1928 and 1936. In them he examined the efficacy of the therapeutic use of sodium thiosulfate and tetrathionate to counter mercury, lead, and cyanide poisoning. In 1936 he also conducted research on the thiazinic dyes, including methylene blue and toluidin blue, two highly dispersed electropositive colloids, and on the action, similar to that of digitalis, of alkaloid substances derived from *Erythrophloeum* (work which was developed in 1939 by Meneghetti's student Renato Santi). In the same year, too, he returned to the study of the reticuloendothelial system to demonstrate the presence of histiocytes in the pulmonary alveoli. In his article "Il polmone come sede di azione e come via di assorbimento di farmaci," Meneghetti posited a relationship between the activity of these alveolar cells and the absorption of drugs into the lung, a new route for the chemotherapeutic treatment of infectious diseases. He further took up the question of the special conditions that might macrophagically fix such electropositive colloids as the cupric oxide in the lung: in particular he noted the relation of blood coagulability to cell permeability, and therefore to granulopexis.

Meneghetti conducted a long series of investigations of the factors that can modify the relation between the degree of dispersion of colloids and the intensity of their action. In 1939 he drew upon his results to state that such highly stable colloids as the electropositive ones have a rapid and intense action that recommends them for pharmacological use. He thus completed some of his earlier researches; a decade before, he had pronounced the colloidal state to be the "pharmacological" one. In later work (1943 and 1954) he went on to investigate the relationship between the molecular structure and pharmacological action of the sulfa drugs and antibiotics.

Meneghetti wrote more than a hundred scientific works. He was also concerned with the history of medicine and with social problems—his book *Biologia rivoluzionaria* was published posthumously in 1962. He was a humanist and a patriot; he was decorated four times for valor in World War I, and in World War II, in which he lost both his wife and his daughter in an air raid, he showed equal courage as a member of the Resistance.

BIBLIOGRAPHY

I. ORIGINAL WORKS. Among Meneghetti's earliest publications is a brief *Curriculum vitae* (Padua, 1925). His inaugural lecture at the University of Palermo is "Chimismo, forma, funzione e fenomeni colloidali," in *Biochimica e terapia sperimentale*, **15** (1928), 77–98. His *Elementi di Farmacologia* (Padua, 1934) went through many eds. and revisions; the 9th ed. was entitled *Farmacologia*, 2 vols. (Padua, 1958). Meneghetti wrote more than 100 articles on his research, including reports on the toxicology of arsenic, erythrocytes, antimony, sulfur, and the histiocytic system. For a complete bibliography, see Renato Santi, "Commemorazione . . ." (below).

Meneghetti published two reports on his chemotherapy study center, "Centro di Studio per la Chemoterapia. Attività svolta nel quinquennio 1951–1955," in *Ricerca scientifica*, **26** (1956), 72–99; and "Centro di Studio . . . 1956–1960," *ibid.*, **30** (1960), 2228–2240. He also contributed many articles to *Enciclopedia medica italiana* (Rome, 1952). Two works were published posthumously, *Biologia rivoluzionaria* (Padua, 1962); and *Poesie e prose* (Vicenza, 1963), with a preface by E. Opocher and D. Valeri, which is a collection of works showing his civil and social concerns.

II. SECONDARY LITERATURE. See M. Aloisi, "Ricordo di Egidio Meneghetti nell'anniversario della sua morte," in *Atti dell'Accademia nazionale dei Lincei. Rendiconti*, fasc. 2 (1962), 78–83; A. Cestari, "In memoria di Egidio Meneghetti," in *Ricerca scientifica*, 2nd ser., **1**, pt. 1 (1961), 123–128; M. Messini, "Egidio Meneghetti a un anno dalla morte," in *Clinica terapeutica*, **22** (1962), 461–465; and R. Santi, "Egidio Meneghetti," in *Archivio italiano di scienze farmacologiche*, 3rd ser., **11** (1961), 183–186; and "Commemorazione di Egidio Meneghetti," in *Annuario dell'Università di Padova* (Padua, 1963), which contains a complete bibliography of Meneghetti's writings.

PIETRO FRANCESCHINI

MENELAUS OF ALEXANDRIA (*fl.* Alexandria and Rome, A.D. 100), *geometry, trigonometry, astronomy.*

Ptolemy records that Menelaus made two astronomical observations at Rome in the first year of the reign of Trajan, that is, A.D. 98.[1] This dating accords with Plutarch's choice of him as a character in a dialogue supposed to have taken place at or near Rome some time after A.D. 75.[2] He is called "Menelaus of Alexandria" by Pappus and Proclus.[3] Nothing more is known of his life.

The first of the observations that Ptolemy records was the occultation of the star Spica by the moon at the tenth hour in the night (that is, 4 A.M. in seasonal hours or 5 A.M. in standard hours) of the fifteenth-sixteenth of the Egyptian month Mechir and its emergence at the eleventh hour.[4] In the second observation Menelaus noticed that at the eleventh hour in the night of 18–19 Mechir the southern horn of the moon appeared to fall in line with the middle and southern stars in the brow of Scorpio, while its center fell to the east of this straight line and was as distant from the star in the middle of Scorpio as the middle star was from the southern, and the northern star of the brow was occulted.[5] Both these observations took place in year 845 of the era of Nabonassar (reigned 747–734 B.C.). By comparing the position of the stars as observed by Timocharis in year 454 of the era of Nabonassar, Ptolemy (and presumably Menelaus before him) concluded that the stars had advanced to the east by 3°55′ in 391 years, from which he confirmed the discovery originally made by Hipparchus that the equinox was moving westward at the rate of 1° a century. (The true figure is 1° in about seventy-two years.) It was by comparing the position of Spica in his day with that recorded by Timocharis that Hipparchus had been led to postulate the precession of the equinoxes.

A list of works attributed to Menelaus is given in the register of mathematicians in the *Fihrist* ("Index") of Ibn al-Nadīm (second half of tenth century). His entry reads:[6]

> He lived before Ptolemy, since the latter makes mention of him. He composed: *The Book on Spherical Propositions. On the Knowledge of the Weights and Distribution of Different Bodies*, composed at the commission of Domitian.[7] Three books on the *Elements of Geometry*, edited by Thābit ibn Qurra. The *Book on the Triangle*. Some of these have been translated into Arabic.

From references by the Arabic writers al-Battānī (*d.* 929), al-Ṣūfī (*d.* 986), and Ḥajjī-Khalīfa it has been deduced that Menelaus composed a catalog of the fixed stars, but there is some uncertainty whether the observations that he undoubtedly made were part of a full catalog.[8]

According to Pappus, Menelaus wrote a treatise on the settings of the signs of the zodiac.[9] Hipparchus had shown "by numbers" that the signs of the zodiac take unequal times to rise, but he had not dealt with their settings. Menelaus appears to have remedied the omission.[10] The work has not survived, nor did Pappus redeem his promise to examine it later, not at least in any surviving writings.

The problem can be solved rigorously only by the use of trigonometry,[11] and it is on his contributions to trigonometry that the fame of Menelaus chiefly rests. Theon of Alexandria noted that Hipparchus had treated chords in a circle in twelve books and Menelaus in six.[12] Almost certainly this means that Menelaus,

like Hipparchus before him, compiled a table of sines similar to that found in Ptolemy. For the Greeks, if *AB* is a chord of a circle, sin *AB* is half the chord subtended by double of the arc *AB* and a table of chords is, in effect, a table of sines. Menelaus' work has not survived.

Menelaus' major contribution to the rising science of trigonometry was contained in his *Sphaerica*, in three books. It is this work which entitles him to be regarded as the founder of spherical trigonometry and the first to have disengaged trigonometry from spherics and astronomy and to have made it a separate science. The work has not survived in Greek; but it was translated into Arabic, probably through a lost Syriac rendering, and from Arabic into Latin and Hebrew. There have been three printed Latin versions; and although it is debatable how much of them is due to Menelaus and how much to their editors, a modern study in German by A. A. Björnbo and a critical edition of the Arabic text with German translation by Max Krause make the content of Menelaus' work tolerably clear.[13]

Book I opens with the definition "A spherical triangle is the space included by arcs of great circles on the surface of a sphere," subject to the limitation that "these arcs are always less than a semicircle." This is the earliest known mention of a spherical triangle. Since the Arabic tradition makes Menelaus address a prince with the words, "O prince, I have discovered a splendid form of demonstrative reasoning," it would appear that he was claiming originality. This is, indeed, implied in a reference by Pappus, who, after describing how a spherical triangle is drawn, says, "Menelaus in his *Sphaerica* calls such a figure a *tripleuron* [τρίπλευρον]."[14] Euclid (in *Elements* I, defs. 19, 20) had used τρίπλευρον for plane rectilinear figures having three sides—that is, triangles —but in the body of his work, beginning with proposition 1, he regularly employed the term τρίγωνον, "triangle." Menelaus' deliberate choice of *tripleuron* for a spherical triangle shows a consciousness of innovation.

In book I Menelaus appears to make it his aim to prove for a spherical triangle propositions analogous to those of Euclid for a plane triangle in *Elements* I. In proposition 11 it is proved that the three angles of a spherical triangle are together greater than two right angles. Menelaus did not always use Euclid's form of proof even where it can be adapted to the sphere, and he avoided the use of indirect proofs by *reductio ad absurdum*. Sometimes his treatment, as of the "ambiguous case" in the congruence of triangles (prop. 13), is more complete than Euclid's.

Book I is an exercise in spherics in the old sense of

that term—the geometry of the surface of the sphere—and book II consists only of generalizations or extensions of Theodosius' *Sphaerica* needed in astronomy; the proofs, however, are quite different from those of Theodosius. It is in book III that spherical trigonometry is developed. It opens (prop. 1) with the proposition long since known as "Menelaus' theorem." This is best known from the proof in Ptolemy's *Syntaxis mathematica*, along with preliminary lemmas, but it is not there attributed by name to Menelaus.[15] According to the Arabic of Mansūr ibn 'Irāq as contained in a Leiden manuscript, the proof runs:[16]

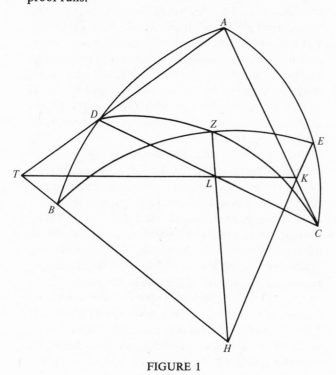

FIGURE 1

Between two arcs of great circles *ADB* and *AEC* let two other arcs of great circles intersect in *Z*. All four arcs are less than a semicircle. It is required to prove

$$\frac{\sin CE}{\sin EA} = \frac{\sin CZ}{\sin ZD} \cdot \frac{\sin DB}{\sin BA}.$$

Let *H* be the center of the circle and let *HZ*, *HB*, *HE* be drawn. *AD* and *BH* lie in a plane and, if they are not parallel, let *AD* meet *BH* in the direction of *D* at *T*. Draw the straight lines *AKC*, *DLC*, meeting *HE* in *K* and *HZ* in *L*, respectively. Because the arc *EZB* is in one plane and the triangle *ACD* is in another plane, the points *K*, *L*, *T* lie on the straight line which is the line of their intersection. (More clearly, because *HB*, *HZ*, *HE*, which are in one plane, respectively intersect the straight lines *AD*, *DC*, *CA*, which are also in one

plane, in the points *T*, *L*, *K*, these three points of intersection must lie on the straight line in which the two planes intersect.) Therefore, by what has become known as Menelaus' theorem in plane geometry (which is proved by Ptolemy, although not here),

$$\frac{CK}{KA} = \frac{CL}{LD} \cdot \frac{DT}{TA}.$$

But, as Ptolemy also shows,

$$\frac{CK}{KA} = \frac{\sin CE}{\sin EA}, \quad \frac{CL}{LD} = \frac{\sin CZ}{\sin ZD}, \quad \frac{DT}{TA} = \frac{\sin DB}{\sin BA},$$

and the conclusion follows.

Menelaus proceeds to prove the theorem for the cases where *AD* meets *HB* in the direction of *A* and where *AD* is parallel to *HB*. He also proves that

$$\frac{\sin CA}{\sin AE} = \frac{\sin CD}{\sin DZ} \cdot \frac{\sin ZB}{\sin BE}.$$

Björnbo observed that Menelaus proved the theorem in its most general and most concise form; Ptolemy proved only what he needed, and Theon loaded his pages with superfluous cases. But A. Rome challenged this view.[17] He considered that Ptolemy really covered all cases, that the completeness of Menelaus' treatment may have been due to subsequent amplification, and that Theon's prolixity was justified by the fact that he was lecturing to beginners.

In Ptolemy's *Syntaxis*, Menelaus' theorem is fundamental. For Menelaus himself it led to several interesting propositions, of which the most important is book III, proposition 5; it is important not so much in itself as in what it assumes. The proposition

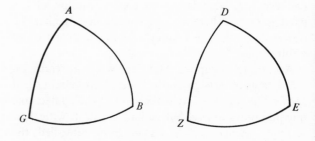

FIGURE 2

is that if in two spherical triangles *ABG*, *DEZ*, the angles *A*, *D* are both right, and the arcs *AG*, *DZ* are each less than a quarter of the circumference,

$$\frac{\sin(BG + GA)}{\sin(BG - GA)} = \frac{\sin(EZ + ZD)}{\sin(EZ - ZD)},$$

from which may be deduced the modern formula

$$\frac{\sin(a + b)}{\sin(a - b)} = \frac{1 + \cos C}{1 - \cos C},$$

or

$$\tan b = \tan a \cos C.$$

In the proof Menelaus casually assumes (to use modern lettering) that if four great circles drawn through any point O on a sphere are intersected in

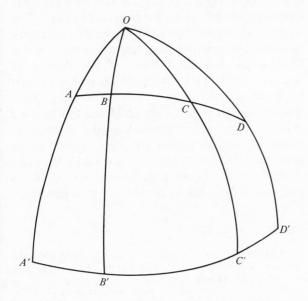

FIGURE 3

A, B, C, D and A', B', C', D' by two other great circles (transversals), then

$$\frac{\sin AD}{\sin DC} \cdot \frac{\sin BC}{\sin AB} = \frac{\sin A'D'}{\sin D'C'} \cdot \frac{\sin B'C'}{\sin A'B'}.$$

This is the anharmonic property, the property that the cross ratio or double ratio of the range (A, D : B, C) is unaltered by projection on to another great circle. There is, of course, a corresponding property for four concurrent lines in a plane cut by a transversal.

It is possible that Menelaus did not prove this property and the preliminary lemmas needed for book III, proposition 1, because he had done so in another work; but the balance of probability is that they were well known in his time and had been discovered by some earlier mathematician. The fact that Menelaus' theorem is proved, not as a proposition about a spherical triangle, but as a proposition about four arcs of great circles, suggests that this also was taken over from someone else. It would not be the

first time that credit has been given to the publicist of a discovery rather than to the discoverer. If this is so, it is tempting to think that both Menelaus' theorem and the anharmonic property go back to Hipparchus. This conjecture is reinforced by the fact that the corresponding plane theorems were included by Pappus as lemmas to Euclid's *Porisms* and therefore presumably were assumed by Euclid as known.[18]

When Ptolemy in the former of his two references to Menelaus called him "Menelaus the geometer,"[19] he may have had his trigonometrical work in mind, but Menelaus also contributed to geometry in the narrower sense. According to the *Fihrist*, he composed an *Elements of Geometry* which was edited by Thābit ibn Qurra (*d.* 901) and a *Book on the Triangle*. None of the former has survived, even in Arabic, and only a small part of the latter in Arabic;[20] but it was probably in one of these works that Menelaus gave the elegant alternative proof of Euclid, book I, proposition 25, which is preserved by Proclus.[21]

Euclid's enunciation is as follows: "If two triangles have the two sides equal to two sides respectively, but have [one] base greater than the base [of the other], they will also have [one of] the angle[s] contained by the equal straight lines greater [than the other]." He proved the theorem by *reductio ad absurdum*. Menelaus' proof was direct and is perhaps further evidence of his distaste for indirect proofs already manifested in the *Sphaerica*. Let the two triangles be ABC, DEF, with $AB = DE$, $AC = DF$, and $BC > EF$. From BC cut off BG equal to EF. At B make the angle GBH on the side of BC remote from A equal to angle DEF. Draw BH equal to DE. Join HG and produce HG to meet AC at K. Then the triangles BGH, DEF are congruent and $HG = DF = AC$. Now HK is greater than HG or AC, and therefore greater than AK. Thus angle KAH is greater than angle KHA. And since $AB = BH$, angle BAH = angle BHA. Therefore, by addition, angle BAC is greater than angle BHG, that is, greater than angle EDF.

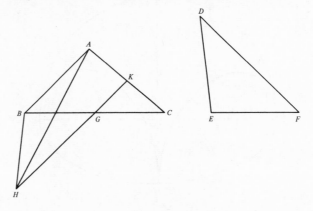

FIGURE 4

MENELAUS OF ALEXANDRIA

MENELAUS OF ALEXANDRIA

The *Liber trium fratrum de geometria*, written by Muḥammad, Aḥmad, and al-Ḥasan, the three sons of Mūsā ibn Shākir (Banū Mūsā) in the first half of the ninth century,[22] states that Menelaus' *Elements of Geometry* contained a solution of the problem of doubling the cube, which turns out to be Archytas' solution.

This bears on a statement by Pappus that Menelaus invented a curve which he called "the paradoxical curve" (γραμμὴ παράδοξος).[23] Pappus, writing of the so-called "surface loci," says that many even more complicated curves having very remarkable properties were discovered by Demetrius of Alexandria in his *Notes on Curves* and by Philo of Tyana as a result of weaving together plektoids[24] and other surfaces of all kinds. Several of the curves, he continues, were considered by more recent writers to be worthy of a longer treatment, in particular the curve called "paradoxical" by Menelaus.

If Menelaus really did reproduce Archytas' solution, which relies on the intersection of a tore and a cylinder, this lends support to a conjecture by Paul Tannery that the curve was none other than Viviani's curve of double curvature.[25] In 1692 Viviani set the learned men of Europe the problem "how to construct in a hemispherical cupola four equal windows such that when these areas are taken away, the remaining part of the curved surface shall be exactly capable of being geometrically squared." His own solution was to take through *O*, the center of the sphere, a diameter *BC* and to erect at *O* a perpendicular *OA* to the plane *BDCO*. In the plane *BACO* semicircles are described on the radii *BO*, *CO*, and on each a right half-cylinder is described. Each half-cylinder will, of course, touch the sphere internally; and the two half-cylinders will cut out of the hemispherical surface the openings *BDE*, *CDF*, with corresponding openings on the other side. The curve in which the half-cylinders

intersect the hemisphere is classified as a curve of the fourth order and first species, and it is a particular case of the *hippopede* used by Eudoxus to describe the motion of a planet. The portion left on the hemispherical surface is equal to the square on the diameter of the hemisphere, and Tannery conjectures that the property of this area being squarable was considered at that time, when the squaring of the circle was much in the air, to be a paradox. It is an attractive conjecture but incapable of proof on present evidence.

According to several Arabic sources[26] Menelaus wrote a book on mechanics, the title of which was something like *On the Nature of Mixed Bodies*.[27] This is presumably to be identified with the unnamed work by Menelaus on which al-Khāzinī draws in his *Kitāb mīzān al-ḥikma* ("Book of the Balance of Wisdom," 1121/1122). The fourth chapter of the first book quotes theorems by Menelaus respecting weight and lightness; the first chapter of the fourth book describes Archimedes' balance on the evidence of Menelaus; and the second and third chapters of the same book describe the balance devised by Menelaus himself and his use of it to analyze alloys, with a summary of the values he found for specific gravities.[28]

NOTES

1. *Syntaxis mathematica*, VII, 3, in *Claudii Ptolemaei opera quae exstant omnia*, J. L. Heiberg, ed., I, pt. 2 (Leipzig, 1903), pp. 30.18–19, 33.3–4.
2. Plutarch, *De facie quae in orbe lunae apparet*, 17, 930A, H. Cherniss and William C. Helmbold, eds., in *Moralia*, Loeb Classical Library, XII (London–Cambridge, Mass., 1957), 106.7–15. Lucius is the speaker and says, "In your presence, my dear Menelaus, I am ashamed to confute a mathematical proposition, the foundation, as it were, on which rests the subject of catoptrics. Yet it must be said that the proposition, 'All reflection occurs at equal angles,' is neither self-evident nor an admitted fact." Menelaus is not allowed by Plutarch to speak for himself, and it would be rash to assume from this reference that he made any contribution to optics. Cherniss thinks that "the conversation was meant to have taken place in or about Rome some time—and perhaps quite a long time—after A.D. 75" (p. 12).
3. Pappus, *Collectio*, VI.110, F. Hultsch, ed., II (Berlin, 1877), p. 102.1; Proclus, *In primum Euclidis*, G. Friedlein, ed. (Leipzig, 1873; repr. Hildesheim, 1967), 345.14; English trans., G. R. Morrow (Princeton, 1970).
4. Ptolemy, *op. cit.*, 30.18–32.3.
5. *Ibid.*, 33.3–34.8.
6. Heinrich Suter, "Das Mathematiker Verzeichniss im Fihrist des Ibn Abî Ja'kûb an-Nadim (Muhammad Ibn Ishāk)," in *Abhandlungen zur Geschichte der Mathematik*, no. 6 (Leipzig, 1892), 19.
7. This is unlikely to be correct and is probably an embroidering of the reference to Trajan in Ptolemy.
8. A. A. Björnbo, "Hat Menelaos einen Fixsternkatalog verfasst?" in *Bibliotheca mathematica*, 3rd ser., **2** (1901), 196–212.
9. Pappus, *op. cit.*, VI.110, vol. II, 600.25–602.1.
10. This at least is what the text of Pappus as we have it implies, but there is some reason to doubt whether the text can be correct. See Hultsch's note at the point.

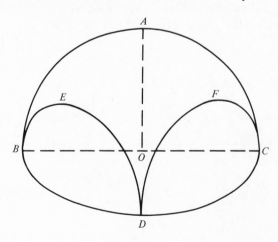

FIGURE 5

11. The inequality of the times was already known to Euclid, *Phaenomena*, *Euclidis opera omnia*, J. L. Heiberg and H. Menge, eds., VIII (Leipzig, 1916), props. 9, 12, 13, pp. 44, 62, 78; and Hypsicles (q.v.) attempted to calculate the times by an arithmetical progression. When Hipparchus is said to have solved the problem "by numbers," it presumably means that he was the first to have given a correct solution by trigonometrical methods.

12. *Commentary on the Syntaxis mathematica of Ptolemy*, A. Rome, ed., in the series Studi e Testi, LXXII (Vatican City, 1936), I.10, p. 451.4–5. For further discussion see A. Rome, "Premiers essais de trigonométrie rectiligne chez les Grecs," in *L'antiquité classique*, **2**, fasc. 1 (1933), 177–192; and a brief earlier note by the same author with the same title in *Annales de la Société scientifique de Bruxelles*, ser. A, **52**, pt. 1 (1932), 271–274.

13. The trans. and eds. are summarized by George Sarton, *Introduction to the History of Science*, I (Baltimore, 1927; repr. 1968), 253–254; and are more fully examined by A. A. Björnbo, *Studien über Menelaos' Sphärik* (Leipzig, 1902), 10–22, and Max Krause, *Die Sphärik von Menelaos aus Alexandrien* (Berlin, 1936), 1–116. See also the bibliography at the end of this article.

14. Pappus, *op. cit.*, VI.1, p. 476.16–17. This is part of the evidence for the genuineness of the definitions even though they do not appear in Gerard's Latin trans.

15. Ptolemy, *Syntaxis mathematica*, I.13, J. L. Heiberg, ed., I, pt. 1 (Leipzig, 1898), pp. 68.14–76.9. See also the commentary of Theon of Alexandria with the valuable notes of A. Rome, ed., *Commentaires de Pappus et de Théon d'Alexandrie sur l'Almageste*, II, *Théon d'Alexandrie*, which is Studi e Testi, LXXII (Vatican City, 1936), 535–570.

16. A. A. Björnbo, *Studien*, 88–92. Menelaus omits a general enunciation (πρότασις) and goes straight to the particular enunciation (ἔκθεσις). Björnbo (p. 92) regards this as partial evidence that the proposition was taken from some other work; but Rome, "Les explications de Théon d'Alexandrie sur le théorème de Ménélas," in *Annales de la Société scientifique de Bruxelles*, ser. A, **53**, pt. 1 (1933), 45, justly says that the length and complexity of a general enunciation, as given by Theon writing for his pupils, is a sufficient reason for the omission.

17. Björnbo, *Studien*, 92. A. Rome, "Les explications de Théon d'Alexandrie sur le théorème de Ménélas" (see n. 16), 39–50; and *Commentaires de Pappus et de Théon d'Alexandrie sur l'Almageste*, II, 554, n. 1 ("L'on est tenté de conclure que le complément de preuve établissant le théorème de Ménélas pour tous les cas, a été inventé à une date située entre Théon et les auteurs arabes qui nous font connaître les Sphériques.")

18. Pappus, *op. cit.*, VII.3–19, props. 129, 136, 137, 140, 142, 145, Hultsch ed., vol. II, pp. 870.3–872.22, 880.13–882.16, 882.17–884.9, 886.23–888.8, 890.3–892.2, 894.14–28. M. Chasles, "Aperçu historique sur l'origine et le développement des méthodes en géométrie," in *Mémoires couronnés par l'Académie royale des sciences et des belles-lettres de Bruxelles*, **2** (1837), 33, 39; and *Les trois livres de Porismes d'Euclide* (Paris, 1860), 11, 75–77, was the first to recognize the anharmonic property in the lemmas of Pappus and to see that "les propositions d'Euclide étaient de celles auxquelles conduisent naturellement les développements et les applications de la notion du rapport anharmonique, devenu fondamentale dans la géométrie moderne." Actually, in prop. 129 Pappus does not use four concurrent lines cut by two transversals but three concurrent lines cut by two transversals issuing from the same point. (The generality is not affected.) Props. 136 and 142 are the converse; prop. 137 is a particular case and prop. 140 its converse; prop. 145 is another case of prop. 129.

19. Ptolemy, *op. cit.*, 30.18.

20. M. Steinschneider, *Die arabischen Uebersetzungen aus dem Griechischen*, 2. Abschnitt, Mathematik §111–112, in *Zeit-schrift der Deutschen morgenländischen Gesellschaft*, **50** (1896), 199.

21. Proclus, *op. cit.*, 345.9–346.13.

22. M. Curtze first edited Gerard of Cremona's trans. in *Nova acta Academiae Caesareae Leopoldino Carolinae germanicae naturae curiosorum*, **49** (1885), 105–167. This is now superseded by the later and better ed. of M. Clagett, *Archimedes in the Middle Ages*, I (Madison, Wis., 1964), 223–367, see particularly 334–341, 365–366.

23. Pappus, *op. cit.*, IV.36, vol. I, p. 270.17–26.

24. A plektoid (πλεκτοειδὴς ἐπιφάνεια) is a twisted surface; the only other example of the word, also in Pappus, suggests that it may mean a conoid.

25. Paul Tannery, "Pour l'histoire des lignes et surfaces courbes dans l'antiquité," in *Bulletin des sciences mathématiques*, 2nd ser., **7** (1883), 289–291, repr. in his *Mémoires scientifiques*, II (Toulouse–Paris, 1912), 16–18. On Viviani's curve see *Acta eruditorum* (Leipzig, 1692), "Aenigma geometricum de miro opificio testudinis quadrabilis hemispherica a D. Pio Lisci Posillo geometra propositum die 4 April. A. 1692," pp. 274–275, also pp. 275–279, 370–371; Moritz Cantor, *Vorlesungen über Geschichte der Mathematik*, III (Leipzig, 1898), 205.

26. Among them the *Fihrist*, see n. 7.

27. In *Codex Escurialensis* 905 the title is given as *Liber de quantitate et distinctione corporum mixtorum* and in *Codex Escurialensis* 955 as *De corporum mistorum quantitate et pondere;* but J. G. Wenrich, *De auctorum graecorum versionibus et commentariis Syriacis, Arabicis, Persicisque* (Leipzig, 1842), 211, gives *De cognitione quantitatis discretae corporum permixtorum.*

28. N. Khanikoff, "Analysis and Extracts of the Book of the Balance of Wisdom," in *Journal of the American Oriental Society*, **6** (1859), 1–128, especially pp. 34, 85. Unfortunately Khanikoff does not translate the passage referring to Menelaus, but the whole Arabic text has since been published—*Kitāb mīzān al-ḥikma* (Hyderabad, 1940). For further information see *Dictionary of Scientific Biography*, VII.

BIBLIOGRAPHY

I. ORIGINAL WORKS. Menelaus wrote a work on spherics (the geometry of the surface of a sphere) in three books (the third treating spherical trigonometry); a work on chords in the circle, which would have included what is now called a table of sines; an elements of geometry, probably in three books; a book on the triangle, which may or may not have been a publication separate from the last-mentioned one; possibly a work on transcendental curves, including one called "paradoxical" that he discovered himself; a work on hydrostatics, dealing probably with the specific gravities of mixtures; a treatise on the setting of the signs of the zodiac; and a series of astronomical observations which may or may not have amounted to a catalog of the fixed stars.

None of these has survived in Greek, but after earlier efforts the *Sphaerica* was translated into Arabic by Isḥāq ibn Ḥunayn (*d.* 910/911), or possibly by his father, Ḥunayn ibn Isḥāq (*d.* 877), and the translation was revised by several eds., notably by Manṣūr ibn 'Irāq (1007/1008), whose redaction survives in the University library at Leiden as *Codex Leidensis* 930, and by Nasir al Dīn al-Ṭūsī (1265), whose work exists in many manuscripts. From Arabic the work was translated into Latin by Gerard of Cremona (*d.* 1187), and his trans. survives to varying extents in some

17 MSS; in many of them the author is called Mileus. The work was rendered into Hebrew by Jacob ben Māḥir ibn Tibbon (*ca.* 1273). The first printed ed. was a Latin version by Maurolico (Messina, 1558) from the Arabic; based on a poor MS, it is replete with interpolations. Nor was the Latin version of Mersenne (Paris, 1644) much better. Halley produced a Latin version which was published posthumously (Oxford, 1758) with a preface by G. Costard. Halley made some use of Arabic MSS, but in the main he has given a free rendering of the Hebrew version, with some mathematical treatment of his own. It held the field until Axel Anthon Björnbo produced his "Studien über Menelaos' Sphärik. Beiträge zur Geschichte der Sphärik und Trigonometrie der Griechen," in *Abhandlungen zur Geschichte der Mathematischen Wissenschaften*, **40** (1902), 1–154. After the introductory matter this amounts to a free German rendering of the *Sphaerica* based mainly on Halley's ed. and *Codex Leidensis* 930. It was the best work on Menelaus that existed for many years, but as a doctoral thesis, the work of a young man who had to rely on secondhand information, it had many deficiencies. The need for a satisfactory ed. of the Arabic text with a German trans. and notes on the history of the text was finally met when Max Krause, basing his work on the same Leiden MS, published "Die Sphärik von Menelaos aus Alexandrien in der Verbesserung von Abū Naṣr Manṣūr b. ʿAlī b. ʿIrāq mit Untersuchungen zur Geschichte des Textes bei den islamischen Mathematikern," in *Abhandlungen der Gesellschaft der Wissenschaften zu Göttingen*, Phil.-Hist. Klasse, 3rd ser., no. 17 (1936).

None of Menelaus' other works survives even in trans. except for a small part of his *Book on the Triangle* (if this is different from his *Elements of Geometry*). For notes on the Arabic translations, see M. Steinschneider, "Die arabischen Uebersetzungen aus dem Griechischen, 2. Abschnitt, Mathematik 111–112," in *Zeitschrift der Deutschen Morgenländischen Gesellschaft*, **50** (1896), 196–199.

It is possible that the proof of Menelaus' theorem given by Ptolemy, *Syntaxis mathematica*, in *Claudii Ptolemaei opera quae exstant omnia*, J. L. Heiberg, ed., I, pt. 1 (Leipzig, 1898), 74.9–76.9, reproduces, at least to some extent, the language of Menelaus; but in the absence of direct attribution there can be no certainty.

II. SECONDARY LITERATURE. The various references to Menelaus by Plutarch, Pappus, Proclus, and Arabic authors are given in the notes above. The chief modern literature is A. A. Björnbo, "Studien über Menelaos' Sphärik," mentioned above; and his "Hat Menelaos einen Fixsternkatalog verfasst?" in *Bibliotheca mathematica*, 3rd ser., **2** (1901), 196–212; Thomas Heath, *A History of Greek Mathematics*, II (Oxford, 1921), 260–273; A. Rome, "Premiers essais de trigonométrie rectiligne chez les Grecs," in *Annales de la Société scientifique de Bruxelles*, ser. A, **52**, pt. 2 (1932), 271–274; an expanded version with the same title is in *L'antiquité classique*, II, fasc. 1 (Louvain, 1933), 177–192; "Les explications de Théon d'Alexandrie sur le théorème de Ménélas," in *Annales de la Société scientifique de Bruxelles*, ser. A, **53**, pt. 1 (1933), 39–50; and *Commentaires de Pappus et de Théon d'Alexan-*

drie sur l'*Almageste*, II, *Théon d'Alexandrie*, Studi e Testi, LXXII (Vatican City, 1936), 535–570; and Max Krause, *Die Sphärik von Menelaos aus Alexandrien* (mentioned above).

IVOR BULMER-THOMAS

MENGHINI, VINCENZO ANTONIO (*b.* Budrio, Italy, 15 February 1704; *d.* Bologna, Italy, 27 January 1759), *medicine, chemistry.*

Menghini was the son of Domenico Menghini and Bartolomea Benelli. He graduated from the University of Bologna in philosophy and medicine on 18 June 1726. Ten years later he lectured there on logic. In the following year he lectured on theoretical medicine, and then, from 1738 until his death, he taught practical medicine at the same university. He was a member of the Academy of Sciences of the Bologna Institute, of which he was also president in 1748.

Menghini developed Galeazzi's research on the presence of iron in the blood, identifying the red corpuscles as the chief site of iron within the organism. He experimentally reduced an organ to ashes, then used a magnetized knife to extract iron particles from it. Since he suspected that the iron particles might be contained in the blood within the organ so treated (especially if it were muscle) he carefully washed out the blood before incinerating it, and found that the number of iron particles did perceptibly decrease. Having thus demonstrated that the iron in an organism is located primarily in the blood, Menghini continued his investigation in an effort to determine which of the three components of the blood—as described by Malpighi in *De polypo cordis*—actually contained the iron. He used Malpighi's method of repeatedly washing coagulum to separate the blood into its three parts, then examined each, thus determining that while iron was absent from both the serum and the bleached coagulum, it was abundant in the red corpuscles that remained in the washing liquid.

BIBLIOGRAPHY

I. ORIGINAL WORKS. Menghini's writings include "De ferrearum particularum sede in sanguine," in *De Bononiensi scientiarum et artium instituto atque academia commentarii*, II, pt. 2 (1746), 244–266; and "De ferrearum particularum progressu in sanguinem," *ibid.*, pt. 3 (1747), 475–488.

II. SECONDARY LITERATURE. On Menghini and his work see L. Belloni, "La scoperta del ferro nell'organismo," in *Atti dell'Accademia medica lombarda*, **20** (1965), 1809–1815; "Dal polipo del cuore (Malpighi 1666) al ferro dei globuli rossi," in *Simposi clinici*, **3** (1966), xvii–xxiv; A. Brighetti, "Il Menghini e la scoperta del ferro nel sangue," in *Atti del XXIII Congresso Nazionale di storia della medicina, Modena, 1967* (Rome, n.d.), 63–80; "Una lettera inedita di Vincenzo Menghini ad Ercole Lelli," in *Scritti in onore di Adalberto Pazzini* (Rome, 1968), 212–218; and "Una importante memoria inedita del Menghini sul ferro nel sangue," in *La clinica*, **28** (1968), 46–56; M. Medici, "Elogio di Vincenzo Menghini," in *Memorie dell'Accademia delle scienze dell'Istituto di Bologna. Memorie*, **9** (1858), 455–479; and V. Busacchi, "Vincenzo Menghini e la scoperta del ferro nel sangue," in *Bullettino delle scienze mediche*, **130** (1958), 202–205.

LUIGI BELLONI

MENGOLI, PIETRO (*b.* Bologna, Italy, 1625; *d.* Bologna, 1686), *mathematics.*

Mengoli's name appears in the register of the University of Bologna for the years between 1648 and 1686. He studied with Cavalieri, whom he succeeded in the chair of mathematics, and also took a degree in philosophy in 1650 and another in both civil and canon law in 1653. He was in addition ordained to the priesthood and from 1660 until his death served the parish of Santa Maria Maddalena, also in Bologna.

Mengoli's mathematics were superficially conservative. He did not subscribe to the innovations of Torricelli, and his own discoveries were set out in an abstruse Latin that made his works laborious to read. His books were nevertheless widely distributed in the seventeenth century, and were known to Collins, Wallis, and Leibniz; they were then almost forgotten, so that Mengoli's work has been studied again only recently. His significance to the history of science lies in the transitional position of his mathematics, midway between Cavalieri's method of indivisibles and Newton's fluxions and Leibniz' differentials.

In *Novae quadraturae arithmeticae* (Bologna, 1650), Mengoli took up Cataldi's work on infinite algorithms. As Eneström (1912) and Vacca (1915) have pointed out, he was the first to sum infinite series that were not geometric progressions and to demonstrate the existence of a series which, although its general term tends to zero, has a sum that can be greater than any number. In particular, he showed the divergence of the harmonic series

$$\sum_{n=1}^{\infty} \frac{1}{n} = 1 + \frac{1}{2} + \frac{1}{3} + \frac{1}{4} + \cdots,$$

preceding Jakob Bernoulli's demonstration of it by nearly forty years (it was known to Oresme in the fourteenth century). From this, Mengoli made the

general deduction that any series formed from the reciprocals of the terms of an arithmetic progression must diverge.

Mengoli also considered the series of the reciprocals of the triangular numbers

$$\frac{1}{3} + \frac{1}{6} + \frac{1}{10} + \cdots \frac{1}{\frac{n(n+1)}{2}} + \cdots,$$

and said that the sum is 1, because the sum of the first n terms is $n/(n+2)$, which (for suitably large n) differs from 1 by less than any given quantity. He then demonstrated the convergence of the series of the reciprocals of the numbers $n(n+r)$ to the result that

$$\sum_n \frac{1}{n(n+r)} = \frac{1}{n}\left(1 + \frac{1}{2} + \frac{1}{3} + \cdots + \frac{1}{r}\right),$$

and summed the reciprocals of the solid numbers,

$$\sum \frac{1}{n(n+1)(n+2)} = \frac{1}{4}.$$

In the *Geometriae speciosae elementa* (1659), Mengoli set out a logical arrangement of the concepts of limit and definite integral that anticipated the work of nineteenth-century mathematicians. In establishing a rigorous theory of limits, he considered a variable quantity as a ratio of magnitudes and hence needed to consider only positive limits. He then made the following definitions: a variable quantity that can be greater than any assignable number is called "quasi-infinite"; a variable quantity that can be smaller than any positive number is "quasi-nil"; and a variable quantity that can be both smaller than any number larger than a given positive number a and greater than any number smaller than a is "quasi-a."

Using these precise concepts of the infinite, the infinitesimal, and the limit, and working from simple inequalities valid between numerical ratios, he demonstrated (as Agostini recognized by translating his obscure exposition into modern symbols and terminology) the properties of the limit of the sum and the product, and showed that the properties of proportions are conserved also at the limit. The proofs obtain when such limits are neither 0 nor ∞; for this case Mengoli set out the properties of the infinitesimal calculus and the calculus of infinites some thirty years before Newton published them in his *Principia*.

Mengoli's predecessors (among them Archimedes, Kepler, Valerio, and Cavalieri) had assumed as intuitively evident that a plane figure has an area. By contrast, he proved the existence of the area by dividing an interval of the continuous figure $f(x)$ into n

parts and considering, alongside the figure to be squared (which he called the "form"), the figures formed by parallelograms constructed on each segment of the interval and having the areas (in modern notation):

$$s_n = \sum_{i=1}^{n} l_i(x_{i+1} - x_i), \quad \text{(inscribed figure)}$$

$$S_n = \sum_{i=1}^{n} L_i(x_{i+1} - x_i), \quad \text{(circumscribed figure)}$$

$$\left.\begin{array}{l} \sigma_n = \sum_{i=1}^{n} f(x_i)(x_{i+1} - x_i), \text{ or} \\[2mm] \sigma'_n = \sum_{i=1}^{n} f(x_{i+1})(x_{i+1} - x_i), \end{array}\right\} \text{(adscribed figure)}$$

where l_i and L_i denote, respectively, the minimum and maximum of $f(x)$ on the interval (x_i, x_{i+1}). Drawing upon the theory of limits that had worked so well in the study of series, Mengoli demonstrated that the sequences of the s_n and S_n tend to the same limit to which the sequences of the σ_n and σ'_n, compressed between them, also tend. Hence, since the figure to be squared is always compressed between the s_n and the S_n, it follows that this common limit is the area of the figure itself.

Mengoli also used this method to integrate the binomial differentials $Z^s(a - x)^r \, dx$ with whole and positive exponents. (He had, preceding Wallis, already integrated these some time before by the method of indivisibles.) Before publishing his results, however, he wished to give a rigorous basis to the method of indivisibles or to develop in its stead another method that would be immune to criticism. He therefore set out a purely arithmetic theory of logarithms; having given a definition of the logarithmic ratio similar to Euclid's definition of ratio between magnitudes, he then extended Euclid's book V to encompass his own logarithmic ratio. Mengoli also did significant work in logarithmic series (thirteen years before N. Mercator published his *Logarithmotecnia*).

In a short work of 1672, entitled *Circolo*, Mengoli calculated the integrals of the form

$$\int_0^1 x^{\frac{m}{2}}(1 - x)^{\frac{n}{2}} \, dx,$$

finding for $n/2$ the same infinite product that had already been given by Wallis. Mengoli published other, minor mathematical writings; in addition he was interested in astronomy, and wrote a short vernacular book on music, published in 1670.

BIBLIOGRAPHY

I. ORIGINAL WORKS. Mengoli's writings include *Novae quadraturae arithmeticae* (Bologna, 1650); *Geometriae speciosae elementa* (Bologna, 1659); *Speculazioni di musica* (Bologna, 1670); and *Circolo* (Bologna, 1672).

II. SECONDARY LITERATURE. On Mengoli and his work, see A. Agostini, "La teoria dei limiti in Pietro Mengoli," in *Periodico di matematiche*, 4th ser., **5** (1925), 18–30; "Il concetto di integrale definito in Pietro Mengoli," *ibid.*, 137–146; and "Pietro Mengoli," in *Enciclopedia italiana*, XXII (Milan, 1934), 585; E. Bortolotti, *La storia della matematica nella università di Bologna* (Bologna, 1947), 98–101, 137–138; G. Eneström, "Zur Geschichte der unendlichen Reihen in die Mitte des siebzehnten Jahrhunderte," in *Bibliotheca mathematica* (1912), 135–148; and G. Vacca, "Sulle scoperte di Pietro Mengoli," in *Atti dell'Accademia nazionale dei Lincei. Rendiconti* (Dec. 1915), 512.

A. NATUCCI

MENSHUTKIN, NIKOLAY ALEKSANDROVICH

(*b.* St. Petersburg, Russia, 24 October 1842; *d.* St. Petersburg, 5 February 1907), *chemistry*.

Menshutkin graduated from St. Petersburg University in 1862, having studied under A. A. Voskresensky and N. N. Sokolov. In 1866 he defended his master's thesis, "O vodorode fosforistoy kisloty, ne sposobnom k metallicheskomu zameshcheniyu pri obyknovennykh usloviyakh dlya kislot" ("On the Hydrogen of Phosphorous Acid, Which Is Not Replaceable by Metal Under the Usual Conditions for Acids"). After the defense of his doctoral dissertation, "Sintez i svoystva ureidov" ("The Synthesis and Properties of the Ureides"), in 1869, Menshutkin was appointed professor at St. Petersburg. From 1902 he was professor at the Petersburg Polytechnic Institute. His basic research involved the rate of chemical transformation of organic compounds in relation to the composition and structure of the reacting substances. This work appeared in the early stages of physical chemistry and played an important role in the development of chemical kinetics.

Menshutkin began his research in 1877 with the study of the reversibility of complex ester formation from alcohols and organic acids. He first showed that the reactivity of monovalent, bivalent, and multivalent alcohols depends on the structure of this carbon chain. He found that in the formation of esters the secondary alcohols react less rapidly than the primary ones. The kinetic method of determining the isomers of alcohols, which Menshutkin developed, was used to determine the structure of newly synthesized alcohols.

Studying the esterification of monobasic and polybasic organic acids, and oxy acids (1882), Menshutkin explained the influence of the molecular weights of alcohols and acids, and of temperature, on the formation of their complex esters.

After van't Hoff introduced the concept of the reaction-rate constant and gave examples of its application to the solution of structural questions (1884), Menshutkin compared the structures of alcohols and acids with the constants of the corresponding rates of reaction. The results confirmed his earlier conclusions. From 1887, Menshutkin investigated the influence of solvents on the rate of reaction. Defining the rate of reaction of triethylamine with ethyl iodide,

$$N(C_2H_5)_3 + C_2H_5I \rightarrow N(C_2H_5)_4I$$

in twenty-three different solvents, he found (1890) that this reaction in benzyl alcohol was 742 times faster than in hexane. Menshutkin's discovery of the influence of the medium on the rate of reaction was one of the most important achievements in the field of chemical kinetics.

Explaining the quantitative relation between the reactivity of organic compounds and their structure, Menshutkin found that any branching of the chain leads to a decrease in the value of the constant of velocity; substitution in the ortho position causes a decrease in velocity, but in meta- and para-positions it causes an increase in velocity. The accumulation of methyl groups in the α position decreases the velocity of esterification of aliphatic acids and alcohols.

In Menshutkin's study of the kinetics of esterification reactions he discovered that the reaction proceeds more readily with straight-chain than with cyclic compounds. For his work in chemical kinetics the Petersburg Academy of Sciences awarded Menshutkin the Lomonosov Prize in 1904.

Menshutkin was an outstanding teacher. He wrote a textbook, *Analiticheskaya khimia* ("Analytic Chemistry," 1871; 16th ed., 1931), which was translated into German and English and for several decades served as a reference book. In 1883 and 1884 he published the most detailed course of organic chemistry in Russian at that time (4th ed., 1901). He also wrote the first original work on the history of chemistry in the Russian language.

Menshutkin was one of the founders and leaders of the Russian Physical-Chemical Society, and from 1869 to 1900 he was editor of its journal. On his initiative and under his leadership were established the chemical laboratory of St. Petersburg University (1894) and the Petersburg Polytechnic Institute (1902).

BIBLIOGRAPHY

I. ORIGINAL WORKS. Menshutkin's works, apart from his textbook *Analiticheskaya khimia*, include "Issledovanie obrazovania uksusnykh efirov pervichnykh spirtov" ("Research on the Formation of Acetic Esters of Primary Alcohols"), in *Zhurnal Russkago fisiko-khimicheskago obshchestva*, **9** (1877), 318–319; "Rukovodstvo k opredeleniyu izomerii spirtov i kislot pri pomoshchi eterifikatsionnykh dannykh" ("A Guide to the Determination of Isomers of Alcohols and Acids With the Aid of Esterification Data"), *ibid.*, **13** (1881), 572; "O metode opredelenia khimicheskogo znachenia sostavlyayushchikh organicheskikh soedineny" ("On the Method of Determining the Chemical Significance of the Components of Organic Compounds"), *ibid.*, 67; "Issledovania raspadenia uksusnogo tretichnogo amida pri nagrevanii" ("Research on the Decomposition of Acetic Tertiary Amide During Heating"), *ibid.*, **14** (1882), 292–300; and "Issledovanie obrazovania amidov kislot" ("Research on the Formation of Amides of Acids"), *ibid.*, **16** (1884), 191–206.

See also *Lektsii organicheskoy khimii* ("Lectures in Organic Chemistry"), 2 vols. (St. Petersburg, 1883–1884); *Ocherk razvitia khimicheskikh vozzreny* ("A Sketch of the Development of Chemical Views"; St. Petersburg, 1888); "O vlianii khimicheski nedeyatelnoy zhidkoy sredy na skorost soedinenia trietilamina s iodgidrinami" ("On the Influence of Chemically Inactive Liquid Mediums on the Speed of Compound Formation of Triethylamine With Iodohydrins"), in *Zhurnal Russkago fisiko-khimicheskago obshchestva*, **22** (1890), 393–409; "Vlianie chisla tsepey na skorost obrazovania aminov" ("Influence of the Number of Chains on the Rate of Formation of Amines"), *ibid.*, **27** (1895), 96–118, 137–157; "O vlianii khimicheski nedeyatelnykh rastvoriteley na izmenenie raspredelenia skorostey reaktsii v ryadakh izomernykh aromaticheskikh soedineny" ("On the Influence of Chemically Inactive Solvents on the Change in the Determination of the Rate of Reaction in a Series of Isomeric Aromatic Compounds"), *ibid.*, **32** (1900), 46–60; and "Vlianie katalizatorov na obrazovanie anilidov i amidov" ("The Influence of Catalysts on the Formation of Anilides and Amides"), *ibid.*, **35** (1903), 343.

II. SECONDARY LITERATURE. See B. N. Menshutkin, *Zhizn i deyatelnost N. A. Menshutkina* ("Life and Work of N. A. Menshutkin"; St. Petersburg, 1908); and P. I. Staroselsky and Y. I. Soloviev, *Nikolay Aleksandrovich Menshutkin. Zhizn i deyatelnost* (". . . Life and Work"; Moscow, 1968).

Y. I. SOLOVIEV

MENURET DE CHAMBAUD, JEAN JACQUES

(*b*. Montélimar, France, 1733; *d*. Paris, France, 15 December 1815), *physiology, medicine.*

Having completed preliminary philosophical studies, presumably in Montélimar, Menuret received his medical degree from Montpellier and journeyed to

Paris to seek his fortune. His activity in the capital is evidenced by several notable contributions to the final series of volumes (1765) of the Diderot-d'Alembert *Encyclopédie*. Medical practice appears to have been his principal occupation; Menuret held minor appointments in the royal household (physician to the staff of the royal stables and consulting physician to the Comtesse d'Artois, wife of the future Charles X). Active in military service during the revolutionary wars (he joined General C. F. Dumouriez in his disgrace and flight from France), Menuret passed his final years in providing medical care for the poor of his section of Paris.

Menuret applied considerable learning and subtlety to consideration of the principal phenomena of life and to the methods deemed suitable for the study of vital activities. In his views he echoed those expressed by Théophile de Bordeu and others of similar conviction, and thus expounded further the central tenets of Montpellier vitalism. Observation assumed methodological preeminence; experimentation was virtually rejected. Observation respects the autonomy, the naturalness of the object or process under scrutiny; experiment "dismembers and combines and thereby produces phenomena quite different from those which nature presents."[1] This approach confirmed the faith upon which the Montpellier physiologists acted—the uniqueness of vital structure and processes necessarily excludes the possibility of an easy or even legitimate application of the methods or substance of other sciences to matters physiological.

Menuret regarded mechanistic explanation and its associated manipulative, experimental method as the principal enemy. One must begin with the characteristic manifestations of life (motion and sensory impressions), recognize in their ceaseless interaction the very essence of life, and then concede that these processes, while grounded in the physical constitution of the body (Menuret speaks of *molécules organiques*), will be no better understood even if translated into the language of contemporary physics or chemistry.

Such views were fully in accord with Menuret's central preoccupation, which was man and his relation to the medical art. Menuret was a physician with broad clinical experience; he was also a physician who claimed to regard practice as being far more important than theory. In medicine observation must absolutely displace experiment; the nature of man and the art demand no less.[2] For this reason the prospective physician required more the clinical experience won through apprenticeship or in the hospital and less a rigorous introduction to the sciences ancillary to medicine. "No profession," Menuret remarked of medicine, "demands more imperiously the harmonious cooperation of *science* and *virtue*."[3] The physician's virtue referred not to scientific learning but to the recognized and willingly accepted responsibility of the physician to the healing art and to its primary concern, the patient.

Montpellier medicine was noted for its clinical emphasis. It venerated Hippocrates and Sydenham, condemned (but often yielded to) speculative excesses, and sought, as part of its ambition to embrace all that affected the ailing patient, to determine with comprehensiveness and precision the factors which dictated the well-being or afflictions of man. Among these factors were climate and the general physical and social conditions under which men lived. Menuret devoted considerable attention to these matters. His medical surveys of Montélimar and Hamburg are worthy examples of medicogeographical interest; that of Paris is an invaluable guide to conditions influencing health and disease in the French capital during the closing years of the *ancien régime*.

NOTES

1. "Observation," in *Encyclopédie*, XI (1765), 313 (cited in Roger, *Sciences de la vie*, 632).
2. *Ibid.*, 315.
3. *Essai . . . de former des bons médecins*, 4.

BIBLIOGRAPHY

I. Original Works. Menuret contributed some forty articles (signed either "M" or by his name: see Roger, *Sciences de la vie*, p. 631) to the Diderot-d'Alembert *Encyclopédie*. Among these "Oeconomie animale" and "Observation" are of general interest; Albert Von Haller replied, under the same heading and in the *Supplément* to the *Encyclopédie*, to Menuret's views on the animal economy. Other works by Menuret include *Nouveau traité du pouls* (Amsterdam, 1767); *Avis aux mères sur la petite vérole et la rougeole* (Lyons, 1770); *Essai sur l'action de l'air dans les maladies contagieuses* (Paris, 1781); *Essai sur l'histoire médico-topographique de Paris* (Paris, 1786; 2nd ed., rev. and enl., 1804); *Essai sur les moyens de former des bons médecins* (Paris, 1791; 2nd ed., 1814); and *Discours sur la réunion de l'utile à l'agréable, même en médecine* (Paris, 1809). Menuret also published reflections on the utilization of fallow lands and the implications for health of the salt tax *(gabelle)*. He prepared two obituary notices: G. F. Venel (1777) and P. Chappon (1810).

II. Secondary Literature. Henri Zeiller provides the unique but, regrettably, muddled catalog of medical contributors to the *Encyclopédie: Les collaborateurs médicaux de l'Encyclopédie de Diderot et d'Alembert* (Paris, 1934); Zeiller wrongly reassigns the signature "M" from Menuret to the Dijon practitioner Hugues Maret. Biographical notices concerning Menuret are brief and provide few details; see F. L. Chaumeton, "Notice sur Jean Jacques Menuret de Chambaud," in *Journal universel des sciences médicales*, **1** (1816), 384–390; M. de Cubières–Palmézeaux, "Lettre sur Jean Jacques Menuret de Chambaud," in *Journal général de médecine*, **54** (1816), 415–429.

Reference to Menuret has virtually disappeared from modern historical literature. Exceptions are the invaluable accounts by Jacques Roger, *Les sciences de la vie dans la pensée française du XVIIIe siècle* (Paris, 1963), 631–634, and "Méthodes et modèles dans la préhistoire du vitalisme française," in *Actes du XIIe Congrès international d'histoire des sciences* (Paris, 1971), IIIB, 101–108. A roster of Menuret's contributions to the *Encyclopédie* is given in R. N. Schwab and W. E. Rex, "Inventory of Diderot's Encyclopédie," in *Studies on Voltaire and the Eighteenth Century*, **93** (1972), 216–217. For the context of Menuret's theoretical work see Frédéric Bérard, *Doctrine médicale de l'école médicale de Montpellier, et comparaison de ses principes avec ceux d'autres écoles d'Europe* (Montpellier, 1819), 3–77, and François Granel, "Théophile de Bordeu (1722–1776)," in *Pages médico-historiques montpelliéraines* (Montpellier, 1964), 87–97.

WILLIAM COLEMAN

MÉRAY, HUGUES CHARLES ROBERT (*b.* Chalon-sur-Saône, France, 12 November 1835; *d.* Dijon, France, 2 February 1911), *mathematics.*

Méray entered the École Normale Supérieure in 1854. After teaching at the lycée of St. Quentin from 1857 to 1859 he retired for seven years to a small village near Chalon-sur-Saône. In 1866 he became a lecturer at the University of Lyons and, in 1867, professor at the University of Dijon, where he spent the remainder of his career.

In his time he was a respected but not a leading mathematician. Méray is remembered for having anticipated, clearly and with only minor differences of style, Cantor's theory of irrational numbers, one of the main steps in the arithmetization of analysis.

Méray first expounded his theory in an article entitled "Remarques sur la nature des quantités définies par la condition de servir de limites à des variables données" (1869). His precise formulation in the framework of the terminology of the time and the place is of considerable historical interest.

I shall now reserve the name number or quantity to the integers and fractions; I shall call *progressive variable* any quantity v which takes its several values successively in unlimited numbers.

Let v_n be the value of v of rank n: if as n increases to infinity there exists a number V such that beginning with a suitable value of n, $V - v_n$ remains smaller than any quantity as small as might be supposed, one says that V is the limit of v and one sees immediately that

$v_{n+p} - v_n$ has zero for limit whatever the simultaneous laws of variation imposed on n and p.

If there is no such number it is no longer legitimate, analytically speaking, to claim that v has a limit; but if, in this case, the difference $v_{n+p} - v_n$ still converges to zero then the nature of v shows an extraordinary similarity with that of the variables which really possess limits. We need a special term in order to express the remarkable differentiation with which we are concerned: I shall say that the progressive variable is *convergent*, whether or not a numerical limit can be assigned to it.

The existence of a limit to a convergent variable permits greater ease in stating certain of its properties which do not depend on this particular question [i.e., whether or not there exists a numerical limit] and which frequently can be formulated directly only with much greater difficulty. One sees therefore that it is advantageous, in cases where there is no limit, to retain the same abbreviated language which is used properly when a limit exists, and in order to express the convergence of the variable one may say simply that *it possesses a fictitious limit*.

Here is a first example of the usefulness of this convention: if, when m and n both increase to infinity, the difference $u_m - v_n$ between two convergent variables tends to zero for a certain mutual dependence between the subscripts, then one proves easily that it remains infinitely small also for any other law [i.e., law of dependence between m and n]: I shall then say that the variables u and v are *equivalent*, and one sees immediately that two variables which are equivalent to a third variable are equivalent to each other [*loc. cit.* p. 284, in translation].

In this paper Méray also discussed the question of how to assign values to a given function for irrational values of the argument or arguments, and he suggested that this problem could always be solved by a passage to the limit. In this connection, as well as elsewhere in his writings, he did in fact assume a somewhat constructive point of view of the notion of a function, taking it for granted that a function can always be obtained constructively either by rational operations or by limiting processes.

The paper marked the first appearance in print of an "arithmetical" theory of irrational numbers. Some years earlier Weierstrass had, in his lectures, introduced the real numbers as sums of sequences or, more precisely, indexed sets, of rational numbers; but he had not published his theory and there is no trace of any influence of Weierstrass' thinking on Méray's. Dedekind also seems to have developed his theory of irrationals at an earlier date, but he did not publish it until after the appearance of Cantor's relevant paper in 1872. In that year Méray's *Nouveau précis d'analyse infinitésimale* was published in Paris. In the first chapter the author sketches again his theory of irrationals and remarks that however peculiar it might appear to be, compared with the classical traditions, he considers it more in agreement with the nature of the problem than the physical examples required in other approaches.

The *Nouveau précis* had as its principal aim the development of a theory of functions of complex variables based on the notion of a power series. Thus here again, Méray followed unconsciously in the footsteps of Weierstrass; consciously, he was developing the subject in the spirit of Lagrange but felt—rightly—that he could firmly establish what Lagrange had only conjectured. The book is in fact written with far greater attention to rigor than was customary in Méray's time.

Little regard was paid to Méray's main achievement until long after it was first produced, partly because of the obscurity of the journal in which it was published. But even in his review (1873) of the *Nouveau précis,* H. Laurent pays no attention to the theory, while gently chiding the author for using too narrow a notion of a function and for being too rigorous in a supposed textbook. At that time there was not in France—as there was in Germany—a sufficient appreciation of the kind of problem considered by Méray, and not until much later was it realized that he had produced a theory of a kind that had added luster to the names of some of the greatest mathematicians of the period.

Although Méray's theory of irrationals stands out above the remainder of his work, his development of it may be regarded as more than an accident. For elsewhere he also showed the same critical spirit, the same regard to detail, and the same independence of thought that led him to his greatest discovery.

BIBLIOGRAPHY

I. ORIGINAL WORKS. Méray's theory was published as "Remarques sur la nature des quantités définies par la condition de servir de limites à des variables données," in *Revue des sociétés savantes des départements*, Section sciences mathématiques, physiques et naturelles, 4th ser., **10** (1869), 280–289. Among his many treatises and textbooks are *Nouveaux éléments de géométrie* (Paris, 1874); *Exposition nouvelle de la théorie des formes linéaires et des déterminants* (Paris, 1884); and *Sur la convergence des développements des intégrales ordinaires d'un système d'équations différentielles totales ou partielles*, 2 vols. (Paris, 1890), written with Charles Riquier.

II. SECONDARY LITERATURE. Laurent's review of the *Nouveau précis* was published in *Bulletin des sciences mathématiques*, **4** (1873), 24–28. See also the biography of Méray in *La grande encyclopédie* XXIII (Paris, 1886), 692; and J. Molk, "Nombres irrationels et la notion de limite," in *Encyclopédie des sciences mathématiques pures et appliquées*, French ed., I (Paris, 1904), 133–160, after the German article by A. Pringsheim.

ABRAHAM ROBINSON

MERCATI, MICHELE (*b*. San Miniato, Italy, 13 April 1541; *d*. Rome, Italy, 25 June 1593), *medicine, natural sciences.*

Mercati was the elder son of Pietro Mercati, a doctor, and Alfonsina Fiaminga. He received his early education from his father and later enrolled at the University of Pisa, where he studied under Cesalpino. Possibly as a result of the specialized knowledge he received from Cesalpino, Mercati was called by Pope Pius V to direct the Vatican botanical garden, a post he retained under Gregory XIII and Sixtus V. He was very active in botany and contributed greatly to the development of the simples section of the botanical garden. He was early famous for his scientific achievements; when he was only twenty-seven, the future Grand Duke Ferdinand I of Tuscany honored him by elevating his family into the ranks of the Florentine aristocracy, while the same privilege was bestowed on him the following year by the Roman Senate. Pope Gregory XIII named him a member of the "pontifical family," and Mercati showed his gratitude by caring for the pope during his final illness. For Gregory XIII, Mercati wrote *Istruzione sopra la peste* (Rome, 1576), with the addition "Tre altre istruzioni sopra i veleni occultamente ministrati, podagra e paralisi"—which is, however, of limited scientific value. Pope Sixtus V held Mercati in great esteem and created him apostolic protonotary. He also sent him to Poland with Cardinal Aldobrandini (later Clement VIII) on a mission to King Sigismund III. It was during that journey that Mercati began writing from memory a book on the obelisks of Rome; it was published at Rome in 1589 under the title *Degli obelischi di Roma*. Clement VIII made Mercati chief physician and knight of the Order of Santo Spirito in Sassia.

Mercati suffered from bladder and kidney stones and gout. In 1582 he recovered from an attack of renal colic; he had another four years later. On the advice of his friend Filippo Neri he retired to the Oratorian monastery at Santa Maria in Vallicella, where he could receive better care. Again he recovered; but following a third attack in 1593 he died, at the age of fifty-two. He was treated by Filippo Neri and by his teacher Cesalpino, whom he had called to Rome years previously and for whom he had procured appointments as papal physician and professor at the

University of Rome. An autopsy on Mercati, possibly carried out by Cesalpino himself, showed the existence of two stones in the ureters, about sixty in the kidneys, and thirty-six in the gallbladder. Mercati was buried in the church of Santa Maria in Vallicella, in the tomb of the Mediobarba family. He had been a friend and correspondent not only of Filippo Neri and of famous cardinals, but also of persons renowned in the arts and sciences, including Marsilio Cognati, Pier Angelo Bargeo, Latino Latini, Girolamo Mercuriale, Aldrovandi, and Melchior Wieland (better known as Guilandinus). A portrait of Mercati engraved by Benoit Fariat (after Tintoretto) is the frontispiece of his *Metallotheca*.

As a naturalist Mercati's greatest interest lay in collecting minerals and fossils; this collection later formed the basis of the work that has made him famous: *Metallotheca. Opus posthumum, auctoritate et munificentia Clementis undecimi pontificis maximi e tenebris in lucem eductum; opera autem et studio Joannis Mariae Lancisii archiatri pontificii illustratum* (Rome, 1717).

Mercati was a good mineralogist and one of the founders of paleontology. He understood the true origin of stone implements, which in his day were considered to be the product of lightning. In his book he described, besides the Vatican collection of minerals, some stones of animal origin and the bladder stones that had been found by Lancisi during the autopsy of Pope Innocent XI.

Mercati's book is illustrated by beautiful copper engravings which, with the manuscript of the work, were rediscovered by Carlo Roberto Dati in the eighteenth century.

BIBLIOGRAPHY

In addition to Mercati's writings mentioned above, on Mercati and his work see P. Capparoni, "Michele Mercati (1541–1593)," in *Profili bio-bibliografici di medici e naturalisti celebri italiani dal secolo XV al secolo XVIII* (Rome, 1932), pp. 48–50; E. Gurlt, *Geschichte der Chirurgie und ihrer Ausübung*, II (repr. Hildesheim, 1964), 482–483; W. Haberling and J. L. Pagel, "Mercati, Michele," in *Lexicon der hervorragen den Ärzte aller Zeiten und Völker*, W. Haberling, F. Hübotter, and H. Vierordt, eds., 2nd ed., IV (Berlin–Vienna, 1932), 169–170; and G. Montalenti, *Storia delle scienze*, N. Abbagnano, ed., III, pt. 1 (Turin, 1962), 353.

LORIS PREMUDA

MERCATOR, GERARDUS (or **Gerhard Kremer**) (*b*. Rupelmonde, Flanders, 5 March 1512; *d*. Duisburg, Germany, 2 December 1594), *geography*.

Mercator's family name was Kremer, but he latinized it on entering the University of Louvain in 1530. Philosophy and theology were his principal subjects at Louvain, and he retained a concern with these matters throughout his life. Soon after his graduation he became concerned with mathematics and astronomy, studied these subjects informally under the guidance of Gemma Frisius, and acquired considerable skills as an engraver. His first known work was a globe, made in 1536; the following year he published his first map—of Palestine. Mercator was a man of many talents, well versed in mathematics, astronomy, geography, and theology, and was also a great artist whose contributions to calligraphy and engraving influenced several generations of artisans. His lasting fame rests on his contributions to mapmaking: he was undoubtedly the most influential of cartographers.

Mercator's maps cover a variety of subjects. During his sojourn at Louvain (1530–1552), besides his map of Palestine, he made maps of the world, globes, and scientific instruments and also established a reputation as a surveyor. Accused of heresy in 1544, and imprisoned for several months, he was released for lack of evidence, and in 1552 moved to Duisburg, where he became cosmographer to the duke of Cleves. His years at Duisburg were most fruitful: he published the first modern maps of Europe and of Britain, prepared an excellent edition of Ptolemy, and in 1569 published a world map on a new projection that still bears his name.

The 1569 world map of Mercator was designed for seamen. In order to lay out his course easily, the navigator needed a map where a line of constant bearing would cross all meridians at the same angle. Mercator designed a cylindrical projection, tangent at the equator; on it meridians and parallels are straight lines, intersecting at right angles, and distortion gradually increases toward the poles. Such a map shows loxodromes as straight lines, and for small areas it conforms to shapes, but tends to distort large areas, especially at high latitudes. Nonetheless, the Mercator projection, as modified at the end of the sixteenth century by Wright and Molyneux, remains the most important tool of the navigator.

Mercator's second great contribution to geography and cartography was the collection of maps he designed, engraved, and published during the last years of his life. It consisted of detailed and remarkably accurate maps of western and southern Europe. In 1595, the year after Mercator's death, his son, Rumold, published the entire collection under the title "Atlas— or Cosmographic Meditations on the Structure of the World," the first time the word "atlas" was used to designate a collection of maps.

BIBLIOGRAPHY

The most detailed and authoritative biography of Mercator is the work of H. Averdunk and J. Müller-Reinhard, *Gerhard Mercator und die Geographen unter seinen Nachkommen*, which is *Petermanns Mitteilungen, Ergänzungsheft*, no. 182 (1914). His correspondence was published by M. Van Durme, *Correspondance Mercatorienne* (Anvers, 1959). Among the many studies dealing with Mercator's life and works, a special publication, on the occasion of the 450th anniversary of his birth, is "Gerhard Mercator— 1512–1594: zum 450. Geburtstag," in *Duisburger Forschungen*, **6** (1962).

GEORGE KISH

MERCATOR, NICOLAUS (Kauffman, Niklaus) (*b.* Eutin [?], Schleswig-Holstein, Denmark [now Germany], *ca.* 1619; *d.* Paris, France, 14 January [?] 1687), *mathematics, astronomy.*

His father was probably the Martin Kauffman who taught school at Oldenburg in Holstein from 1623 and died there in 1638. Doubtless educated in boyhood at his father's school, Nicolaus graduated from the University of Rostock and was appointed to the Faculty of Philosophy in 1642. At Copenhagen University in 1648 he superintended a "Disputatio physica de spiritibus et innato calido" and over the next five years produced several short textbooks on elementary astronomy and spherical trigonometry; one of his title pages at this time describes him as "mathematician and writer on travels to the Indies."

His tract on calendar improvement (1653) caught Cromwell's eye in England and, whether invited or not, he subsequently left Denmark for London. There he resided for almost thirty years and came universally to be known by his latinized name, an "anglicization" which he himself soon adopted. Unable to find a position in a university, Mercator earned a living as a mathematical tutor, but soon he made the acquaintance of Oughtred, Pell, Collins, and other practitioners. In November 1666, on the strength of his newly invented marine chronometer, he was elected a fellow of the Royal Society; earlier, in Oldenburg's *Philosophical Transactions of the Royal Society*, he had wagered the profits (seemingly nonexistent) from his invention against anyone who could match his expertise in the theory of Gerard Mercator's map. Through his Latin version (1669) of Kinckhuysen's Dutch *Algebra*, commissioned by Collins at Seth Ward's suggestion, he came into contact with Newton, and the two men later exchanged letters on lunar theory. Aubrey portrays Mercator at this time as "of little stature, perfect; black haire, . . . darke eie,

but of great vivacity of spirit . . . of a soft temper . . . (*amat Venerem aliquantum*): of a prodigious invention, and will be acquainted (familiarly) with nobody." In September 1676 Hooke unsuccessfully proposed Mercator as Mathematical Master at Christ's Hospital. In 1683 he accepted Colbert's commission to plan the waterworks at Versailles, but died soon afterward, having fallen out with his patron.

Mercator's early scientific work is known only through the university textbooks which he wrote in the early 1650's; if not markedly original, they show his firm grasp of essentials. His *Trigonometria sphaericorum logarithmica* (1651) gives neat logarithmic solutions of the standard cases of right and oblique triangles and tabulates the logarithms of sine, cosine, tangent, and cotangent functions (his "Logarithmus," "Antilogarithmus," "Hapsologarithmus," and "Anthapsologarithmus") at $1'$ intervals. His *Cosmographia* (1651) and *Astronomia* (1651) deal respectively with the physical geography of the earth and the elements of spherical astronomy. In his *Rationes mathematicae* (1653) he insists on drawing a basic distinction between rational and irrational numbers: the difference in music is that between harmony and dissonance; in astronomy that between a Keplerian "harmonice mundi" and the observable solar, lunar, and planetary motions. In the tract *De emendatione annua* (1653[?]) he urges the reform of the 365-day year into months of (in sequence) 29, 29, 30, 30, 31, 31, 32, 31, 31, 31, 30, and 30 days.

Mercator's first published book in England, *Hypothesis astronomica nova* (1664), in effect combines Kepler's hypothesis (that planets travel in elliptical orbits round the sun, with the sun at one focus) with his vicarious hypothesis (in which the equant circle is centered in the line of apsides at a distance from the sun roughly 5/8 times the doubled eccentricity): Mercator sets this ratio exactly equal to the "divine section" $(\sqrt{5} - 1)/2$, with an error even in the case of Mars of less than $2'$. (Here a mystical streak in his personality gleams through, for he compares his hypothesis to a knock-kneed man standing with arms outstretched, a "living image of Eternity and the Trinity." He later expounded similar insights in an unpublished manuscript on *Astrologia rationalis*.) Subsequently, in 1670, he showed his skill in theoretical astronomy by demolishing G. D. Cassini's 1669 method for determining the lines of apsides of a planetary orbit, given three solar sightings. He showed that it reduced to the Boulliau-Ward hypothesis of mean motion round an upper-focus equant and pointed out its observational inaccuracy. (His enunciation of the "true" Keplerian hypothesis, that time in orbit is proportional to the focal sector swept out by the planet's radius vector, may well have been the source of Newton's knowledge of this basic law.) The two books of his *Institutiones astronomicae* (1676) offered the student an excellent grounding in contemporary theory, and Newton used them to fill gaps in his rather shaky knowledge of planetary and lunar theory. Some slight hint of the practical scientist is afforded by the barometric measurements made during the previous half year, which Mercator registered at the Royal Society in July 1667. No working drawings are extant of the Huygenian pendulum watch—which he designed in 1666—or of its marine mounting (by gimbal suspension), but an example "of a foote diameter" was made.

Mercator is remembered above all as a mathematician. In 1666 he claimed to be able to prove the identity of "the Logarithmical Tangent-line beginning at 45 deg." with the "true Meridian-line of the Sea-Charte" (Mercator map). This declaration is not authenticated but not necessarily empty. It is difficult to determine how far his researches into finite differences—which were restricted to the advancing-differences formula—were independent of Harriot's unpublished manuscripts on the topic, to which Mercator perhaps had access. In his best-known work, *Logarithmotechnia* (1668), he constructed logarithms from first principles (if $a^b = c$, then $b = \log_a c$), making ingenious use of the inequality

$$\left(\frac{a + px}{a - px}\right) < \left(\frac{a + x}{a - x}\right)^p, \qquad p = 1/2, 1/3, \cdots,$$

while in supplement (a late addition to the manuscript submitted in 1667) he used the St. Vincent-Sarasa hyperbola-area model to establish, independently of Hudde and Newton, the series expansion

$$\text{lognat}(1 + x) = \int_0^x 1/(1 + x) \cdot dx$$
$$= x - \tfrac{1}{2}x^2 + \tfrac{1}{3}x^3 \cdots.$$

The circulation by Collins of the "De analysi," composed hurriedly by Newton as a riposte, seems to have effectively blocked Mercator's plans to publish a complementary *Cyclomathia* with allied expansions (on Newtonian lines) of circle integrals. The "Introductio brevis" which he added in 1678 to Martyn's second edition of the anonymous *Euclidis elementa geometrica* commendably sought to simplify the Euclidean definitions for the beginner by introducing motion proofs: a circle is generated as the ripple on the surface of a stagnant pool when a stone is dropped at its center, a line as the instantaneous meet of two such congruent wave fronts. His

Hypothesis astronomica nova contains the first publication of the polar equation of an ellipse referred to a focus.

BIBLIOGRAPHY

I. ORIGINAL WORKS. The trio of textbooks put out by Mercator at Danzig in 1651 appeared under the titles *Cosmographia, sive descriptio coeli et terrae in circulos . . .; Trigonometria sphaericorum logarithmica, . . . cum canone triangulorum emendatissimo . . .;* and *Astronomia sphaerica decem problematis omnis ex fundamento tradita.* They were reissued shortly afterward at Leipzig . . . *Conformatae ad exactissimas docendi leges pro tironibus, . . . privatis hactenus experimentis comprobatae.* At Copenhagen Mercator published in 1653 his study on mathematical rationality, *Rationes mathematicae subductae,* and also his propagandist tract on calendar improvement, *De emendatione annua diatribae duae. . . .*

During the next ten years he apparently wrote nothing for the press, but at length produced his *Hypothesis astronomica nova, et consensus ejus cum observationibus* (London, 1664). His wager regarding the logarithmic nature of the Mercator map was announced in "Certain Problems Touching Some Points of Navigation," in *Philosophical Transactions of the Royal Society,* **1**, no. 13 (4 June 1666), 215–218. In 1668 appeared his major work, *Logarithmotechnia: sive methodus construendi logarithmos nova, accurata, & facilis; scripto antehàc communicata, anno sc. 1667 nonis Augusti: cui nunc accedit vera quadratura hyperbolae, & inventio summae logarithmorum* (London, 1668), later reprinted in F. Maseres, *Scriptores logarithmici,* I (London, 1791), 169–196; to Wallis' "account" of it in *Philosophical Transactions of the Royal Society,* **3**, no. 38 (17 Aug. 1668), 753–759, Mercator added "Some further Illustration," *ibid.,* 759–764. For a page-by-page analysis of the bk. see J. E. Hofmann, "Nicolaus Mercators *Logarithmotechnia* (1668)," in *Deutsche Mathematik,* **3** (1938), 446–466. His "Some Considerations . . . Concerning the Geometrick and direct Method of Signior Cassini for finding the Apogees, Excentricities and Anomalies of the Planets; as that was printed in the *Journal des sçavans* of Septemb. 2. 1669" appeared in *Philosophical Transactions of the Royal Society,* **5**, no. 57 (25 Mar. 1670), 1168–1175.

His astronomical compendium, *Institutionum astronomicarum libri duo, de motu astrorum communi & proprio, secundum hypotheses veterum & recentiorum praecipuas . . .* came out at London in 1676 (reissued Padua, 1685): Newton's lightly annotated copy is now at Trinity College, Cambridge, NQ.10.152. In an app. to the compendium Mercator reprinted his earlier *Hypothesis nova* (the preface excluded). His "Introductio brevis, qua magnitudinum ortus ex genuinis principiis, & ortarum affectiones ex ipsa genesi derivantur" was adjoined in 1678 to John Martyn's repr. of the "Jesuit's Euclid," in *Euclidis elementa geometrica, novo ordine ac methodo fere, demonstrata* (London, 1666).

None of Mercator's correspondence with his contemporaries seems to have survived, although that with

Newton (1675–1676) on lunar vibration is digested in the *Institutiones astronomicae,* 286–287; compare the remark added by Newton to the third bk. of the third ed. of his *Principia,* Propositio XVII (London, 1726), 412. The MS (Bodleian, Oxford, Savile G.20⁴) of Mercator's Latin rendering of Kinckhuysen's *Algebra ofte Stelkonst* (Haarlem, 1661) is reproduced in *The Mathematical Papers of Isaac Newton,* II (Cambridge, 1968), 295–364, followed by Newton's "Observations" upon it, *ibid.,* 364–446.

Thomas Birch in his biography in *A General Dictionary Historical and Critical,* VII (London, 1738), 537–539 [= J. G. de Chaufepié, *Nouveau Dictionnaire historique et critique,* III (Amsterdam, 1753), 79], records the existence in Shirburn Castle of "a manuscript containing Theorems relating to the Resolution of Equations, the Method of Differences, and the Construction of Tables; and another, intitled, *Problema arithmeticum ad doctrinam de differentialium progressionibus pertinens*"; these are now in private possession. Birch also lists (*ibid.,* 539) the section titles of Mercator's unpublished "Astrologia rationalis, argumentis solidis explorata" (now Shirburn 180.F.34). Details of his chronometer are given by Birch in his *History of the Royal Society,* II (London, 1756), 110–114, 187, and in Oldenburg's letter to Leibniz of 18 December 1670 (C. I. Gerhardt, *Die Briefwechsel von G. W. Leibniz,* I [Berlin, 1899], 48). References to the lost treatise on circle quadrature, *Cyclomathia,* occur in John Collins' contemporary correspondence with James Gregory (see the *Gregory Memorial Volume* [London, 1939], 56, 60, 153).

II. Secondary Literature. J. E. Hofmann's *Nicolaus Mercator (Kauffman), sein Leben und Wirken, vorzugsweise als Mathematiker* (in *Akademie der Wissenschaften und der Literatur in Mainz [Abh. der Math.-Nat. Kl.],* no. 3 [1950]) is the best recent survey of Mercator's life and mathematical achievement. On his personality and habits see John Aubrey, *Letters . . . and Lives of Eminent Men,* II (London, 1813), 450–451, 473, or *Brief Lives* (London, 1949), 135, 142, 153–154. J.-B. Delambre gives a partially erroneous estimate of Mercator's equant hypothesis of planetary motion in his *Histoire de l'astronomie moderne,* II (Paris, 1821), 539–546; see also Curtis Wilson, "Kepler's Derivation of the Elliptical Path," in *Isis,* **59** (1968), 5–25, esp. 23.

D. T. Whiteside

MERICA, PAUL DYER (*b.* Warsaw, Indiana, 17 March 1889; *d.* Tarrytown, New York, 20 October 1957), *metallurgy.*

After receiving his A.B. from the University of Wisconsin in 1908, Merica taught physics in Wisconsin and "Western Subjects" in Hangchow, China, for two years before going to the University of Berlin, from which he obtained his Ph.D. in 1914. From 1914 to 1919 he was a physical metallurgist at the U.S. National Bureau of Standards, where he was involved with R. G. Waltenberg and H. Scott in research on the new alloy Duralumin, the properties of which

depended on precipitation hardening—the only method of hardening metals and alloys that was not known in or before classical times.

Merica was the first to show that such hardening resulted from a change of solubility with temperature (almost unsuspected in solids at the time), and he postulated that hardening required a critical dispersion of submicroscopic particles of $CuAl_2$ within the matrix crystals.

This theory inspired many studies of hardening in other alloy systems, especially when it was combined with the slip-interference theory of hardening advanced by Jeffries and R. S. Archer in 1921. X-ray diffraction later showed that the greatest hardness occurred before there were detectable particles of compound, and in 1932 Merica advanced his theory of "knots," that is, clusters with high concentration of solute atoms forming without breaking coherence with the parent lattice. The idea soon received quite independent experimental proof in the X-ray studies of Guinier and Preston. From 1919 until his death, Merica was with the International Nickel Company (director of research, 1919–1949; president, 1949–1952). He developed several precipitation-hardening alloys of nickel, nickel-bearing cast irons, and sheet alloys for corrosion-resistant and high temperature applications.

BIBLIOGRAPHY

I. Original Works. Merica's most influential papers are "Heat Treatment and Constitution of Duralumin," in *Scientific Papers of the United States Bureau of Standards,* **347** (1919), with R. G. Waltenberg and H. Scott; repr. in *Transactions of the American Institute of Mining and Metallurgical Engineers,* **64** (1920), 41–79; and "The Age-Hardening of Metals," *ibid.,* **99** (1932), 13–54.

II. Secondary Literature. For a complete list of Merica's publications and further biographical information, see Z. Jeffries, "Paul Dyer Merica," in *Biographical Memoirs. National Academy of Sciences,* **33** (1959), 226–239.

For a review of the history of precipitation-hardening, see H. Y. Hunsicker and H. C. Stumpf, "History of Precipitation Hardening," in C. S. Smith, ed., *The Sorby Centennial Symposium on the History of Metallurgy* (New York, 1965), 271–311.

Cyril Stanley Smith

MERRETT, CHRISTOPHER (*b.* Winchcomb, England, 16 February 1614; *d.* London, England, 19 August 1695), *natural history, glassmaking.*

Merrett, who like his father and younger son was baptized Christopher, was educated at Oxford, where he obtained the M.B. in 1636 and the M.D. in 1643. He had married Ann Jenour of Kempsford by the time he commenced practice in London about 1640. Admitted as a fellow of the College of Physicians in 1651, he became the first keeper of their new library and museum given by William Harvey and compiled its first printed catalog (1660). The founding of the Royal Society (1660), of which he was an original member, provided an outlet for Merrett's varied interests.

In 1662, at the suggestion of Robert Boyle and the instigation of the Royal Society, Merrett translated Antonio Neri's *L'arte vetraria* (1612), a pioneer work. By adding his own extensive observations on the construction of glassmaking furnaces, the types of glass being manufactured in England, and the raw materials used, Merrett gave considerable impetus to glassmaking in England and other European countries.

William How's *Phytologia* (1650) was still in demand when it went out of print. At the publisher's request Merrett wrote *Pinax rerum naturalium Britannicarum* (1666) to replace it. Since he was no fieldworker but a sedentary and inexpert naturalist, he enlisted all the help possible and revealed a wide knowledge of the relevant literature by giving more precise references than his predecessors had. By his own admission the list was imperfect ("inchoatus"). Although the large botanical section, with over 1,400 species and synonyms from Gerard and John Parkinson, was soon superseded, the section on mammals and birds is important as the first attempt to construct a British fauna. The name *Merrettia* was given to a group of unicellular algae by S. F. Gray.

When the College of Physicians was destroyed by fire in 1666, Merrett saved and looked after 150 books; but the College argued that since they now had no library, they had no need of a keeper. The last years of Merrett's life were clouded by the consequent dispute, which cost him his fellowship (1681), allegedly for nonattendance. His only medical publications were those that contributed to the war of mutual denigration between the physicians and the apothecaries.

BIBLIOGRAPHY

I. ORIGINAL WORKS. Merrett's main work is *Pinax rerum naturalium Britannicarum* (London, 1666; another ed., 1667). He translated A. Neri, *L'arte vetraria* as *The Art of Glass, . . . With Some Observations on the Author, . . .* (London, 1662); it also appeared in Latin (London, 1668), in German (Amsterdam, 1679; Frankfurt, 1689), and in French (Paris, 1752).

II. SECONDARY LITERATURE. See C. E. Raven, "William How and Christopher Merrett," in his *English Naturalists From Neckham to Ray* (Cambridge, 1947), 298–338; and W. E. S. Turner, "A Notable British Seventeenth Century Contribution to the Literature of Glass-Making," in *Glass Technology*, **6** (1962), 201–213.

LEONARD M. PAYNE

MERRIAM, CLINTON HART (*b.* New York, N. Y., 5 December 1855; *d.* Berkeley, California, 19 March 1942), *biology.*

Merriam was raised in Locust Grove, New York, on a farm bought by an ancestor in 1800; his father, Clinton L. Merriam, had retired there early from a brokerage firm. The boy's mother, Caroline Hart Merriam, and father both encouraged his interest in collecting birds. Through Spencer F. Baird, to whom his father introduced him, the boy was appointed, when only sixteen, to collect bird skins and eggs on Hayden's geological and geographical survey of the territories.

Merriam studied for three years at Yale, then received an M.D. from the College of Physicians and Surgeons in 1879. For six years he practiced medicine in Locust Grove, then accepted the new post of ornithologist in the entomological division of the U.S. Department of Agriculture. In 1905 this unit became the Bureau of Biological Survey, which Merriam continued to direct until 1910, when a trust fund established by Mrs. E. H. Harriman provided him with independent research money through the Smithsonian Institution.

Although most widely known for his definition of life zones of faunal distribution, Merriam also did significant groundwork in mammalian studies. Many of the 600 species he proposed have proved invalid, for Merriam was indeed a "splitter"; but he established the significance of cranial characters in mammalian classification, and he perfected preservation techniques. Under his direction the Biological Survey accumulated a vast collection of mammals, on which Merriam published extensively, from shrews to grizzly bears. Under the sponsorship of the Harriman fund, he devoted his later years to gathering data on the Indians of California.

An early conservationist, Merriam was the most active founder of the American Ornithologists' Union and a founder of the Washington Academy of Sciences, the American Society of Mammalogists, and the National Geographic Society. He served on the American-British fur-seal commission in 1891, and he was the scientific director and editor of all reports of the Harriman Alaska Expedition of 1899.

BIBLIOGRAPHY

I. ORIGINAL WORKS. Merriam's report on life zones was "Results of a Biological Survey of the San Francisco Mountain Region and Desert of the Little Colorado, Arizona," in *North American Fauna*, **3** (1890), 119–136. He was especially proud of his "Monographic Revision of the Pocket Gophers Family Geomyidae (Exclusive of the Species of *Thomomys*)," in *North American Fauna*, **8** (1895), 1–258. His publications, totaling nearly 500 titles, are included in Osgood (see below).

II. SECONDARY LITERATURE. Wilfred H. Osgood presented a thorough account of Merriam's life in "Biographical Memoir of Clinton Hart Merriam," in *Biographical Memoirs. National Academy of Sciences*, **24** (1944), 1–57, which includes a bibliography. A. L. Kroeber, "C. Hart Merriam as Anthropologist," in C. Hart Merriam, *Studies of California Indians* (Berkeley, 1955), vii–xiv, covers Merriam's work on California Indians; and Peter Matthiesen, *Wildlife in America* (New York, 1959), touches on Merriam as a biologist and conservationist.

ELIZABETH NOBLE SHOR

MERRIAM, JOHN CAMPBELL (*b*. Hopkinton, Iowa, 20 October 1869; *d*. Oakland, California, 30 October 1945), *paleontology*.

Merriam was the son of Charles and Margaret Merriam. He took a B.S. degree at Lenox College, Iowa, then in 1887 moved with his family to Berkeley, California, where he attended the University of California, studing botany under E. L. Green and geology with Joseph Le Conte. In 1893 he took his doctorate in vertebrate paleontology at Munich. The following year he became an instructor at the University of California and in 1912 chairman of the new department of paleontology. In 1896 he married Ada Gertrude Little, who bore him three sons. She died in 1940, and in 1941 he married Margaret Webb.

Merriam helped pioneer the study of paleontology on the West Coast. The early explorations were followed by a period of stagnation, broken in the early 1890's by workers from both Stanford and the University of California. Between 1896 and 1908 Merriam published papers on Tertiary molluscan faunas, Tertiary echinoids, and the Triassic Ichthyosauria. In 1901 he published an important work on the John Day Basin in Oregon, and after 1905 he published many descriptions of the Tertiary mammalian faunas of the Rancho La Brea tar pits in Los Angeles.

In 1917 Merriam began two additional activities that led him away from research in paleontology: he helped found and became president of the pioneer conservation organization, the Save-the-Redwoods League, and he was elected chairman of the Committee

on Scientific Research of the California State Council of Defense. The latter post led him to Washington, D.C., to aid in the war effort, and eventually to his becoming president (1920–1938) of the Carnegie Institution of Washington. During these two decades he was very active in the National Academy of Sciences and was a leader in science administration and conservation. Conservative in his social beliefs, he was considered more serious than jovial by his colleagues.

BIBLIOGRAPHY

I. ORIGINAL WORKS. Merriam's writings are collected in *Published Papers and Addresses of John Campbell Merriam*, 4 vols. (Washington, D.C., 1938); vol. IV contains his nonscientific writings. His MSS are in the Manuscript Division, Library of Congress and the Bancroft Library, Univ. of California, Berkeley.

II. SECONDARY LITERATURE. A biographical sketch and extensive bibliography of Merriam's work, by Chester Stock, appear in *Biographical Memoirs. National Academy of Sciences*, **26** (1951), 208–232; see also Chester Stock, "Memorial to John Campbell Merriam," in *Proceedings. Geological Society of America* for 1946 (1947), 182–197; and Ralph W. Chaney, "John Campbell Merriam," in *Yearbook. American Philosophical Society* for 1945 (1946), 381–387. A sketch of his scientific and philosophical thought appears in Chester Stock, "John Campbell Merriam as Scientist and Philosopher," in Carnegie Institution of Washington, *Cooperation in Research* (Washington, D.C., 1938), 765–778.

CARROLL PURSELL

MERRILL, GEORGE PERKINS (*b*. Auburn, Maine, 31 May 1854; *d*. Auburn, 15 August 1929), *geology*, *meteoritics*.

Merrill was a descendant of Nathaniel Merrill, who had settled in the Massachusetts Bay Colony in the 1630's. His father, Lucius Merrill, was a carpenter and cabinetmaker. His mother, Anne Elizabeth Jones, was the daughter of the Reverend Elijah Jones of Minot, Maine, whose scholarship had a profound influence upon the intellectual life of his grandson. One of seven children, Merrill began to earn his own living at an early age, finding employment as a farmhand and in shoe factories. He was twenty-two years old when he entered the Maine State College of Agriculture and the Mechanic Arts (now the University of Maine), where he majored in chemistry and graduated with a B.Sc. degree in 1879. He then became a laboratory assistant, working on the chemistry of foods, at Wesleyan University, Middletown,

Connecticut. There he became acquainted with G. Brown Goode, formerly curator of Wesleyan's museum collections and at that time in charge of the U.S. National Museum in the Smithsonian Institution and director of the survey of fisheries for the tenth census. Goode appointed Merrill to the census staff in 1880 and to the Museum staff in 1881 as aid to George W. Hawes, who had just become curator of the geological collections. After Hawes's death in 1882, Merrill was put in charge of petrology and physical geology; and in 1897 he became head curator of the department of geology in the U.S. National Museum, a position that he held until his death. He also served as part-time professor of geology and mineralogy at Columbian College (renamed George Washington University in 1904) from 1893 to 1915.

Merrill was married in 1883 to Sarah Farington, of Portland, Maine. She died in 1894, leaving one son and three daughters. He was married again in 1900 to Katherine L. Vancey of Virginia, by whom he had one daughter. He was of sturdy build, alert and active, accustomed to long hours in office and laboratory; an avid reader, he was fond of poetry and music. Austere and reserved on first acquaintance, to his many friends Merrill displayed a warm and generous heart. He was a member of the National Academy of Sciences; the American Philosophical Society; the Geological Society of America, of which he was vice-president in 1920; the Washington, the Maryland, and the Philadelphia academies of science; and the Geological Society of Washington, of which he was president in 1906–1907; and a corresponding member of the American Institute of Architects.

Merrill made scientific contributions in at least five distinct areas. As a museum administrator he built up the department of geology in the U.S. National Museum and made it one of the world's greatest and best-organized geological collections. Introduced by Hawes to the new petrologic technique of microscopic study of thin sections of rocks, he applied that procedure to the large collection of building stones assembled in connection with the tenth census and enlarged in succeeding years. This not only led to the publication of his most widely read book, *Stones for Building and Decoration*, but also established such a reputation for him that he was influential in the selection of stones for many governmental buildings, most notably the Lincoln Memorial. These studies naturally turned Merrill's attention to the processes of rock weathering. Here his early training in chemistry proved valuable and his *Treatise on Rocks, Rock Weathering, and Soils* was immediately hailed by European as well as American geologists, and led to his recognition in agricultural circles as the out-

standing authority of his time on soils and their origin.

A fourth area in which Merrill's scientific contributions were especially notable involved the study of meteorites. He was one of the first to "regard the meteorites as world matter"; and in 1906 he correctly identified Coon Butte, near Canyon Diablo, Arizona (now known as Meteor Crater), as an impact crater. Last among his areas of accomplishment was that of the history of geological science; his three works on this subject (1906, 1920, 1924) are indispensable source material.

Among Merrill's many honors were an honorary Ph.D. from what is now the University of Maine, in 1889, the Sc.D. from George Washington University in 1917, and the J. L. Smith gold medal of the National Academy of Sciences in 1922.

BIBLIOGRAPHY

I. ORIGINAL WORKS. Merrill's writings include "On the Collection of Maine Building Stones in the United States National Museum," in *Proceedings of the United States National Museum*, **6** (1883), 165–183; "Report on the Building Stones of the United States and Statistics of the Quarry Industry for 1880," in *Tenth Census United States*, X (Washington, D.C., 1884), bound as part of vol. X, but with separate pagination; "The Collection of Building and Ornamental Stones in the United States National Museum," in *Report of the Board of Regents of the Smithsonian Institution* for 1886 (Washington, D.C., 1889), pt. 2, 277–648; *Stones for Building and Decoration* (New York, 1891; 2nd ed., 1897; 3rd ed., 1903); "Disintegration of the Granitic Rocks of the District of Columbia," in *Bulletin of the Geological Society of America*, **6** (1895), 321–332; "The Principles of Rock Weathering," in *Journal of Geology*, **4** (1896), 704–724, 850–871; and *A Treatise on Rocks, Rock Weathering, and Soils* (New York, 1897; new ed., 1906).

Later works are *The Non-metallic Minerals, Their Occurrence and Uses* (New York, 1904); "Contributions to the History of American Geology," in *Report of the United States National Museum* for 1904 (1906), 189–733; "The Meteor Crater of Canyon Diablo, Arizona," in *Smithsonian Miscellaneous Collections*, **50** (1908), 461–498; "The Composition of Stony Meteorites, Compared With That of Terrestrial Igneous Rocks and Considered With Reference to Their Efficacy in World Making," in *American Journal of Science*, 4th ser., **27** (1909), 469–474; "Handbook and Descriptive Catalogue of the Meteorite Collections in the United States National Museum," *Bulletin. United States National Museum*, no. 94 (1916); "Contributions to a History of American State Geological and Natural History Surveys," *ibid.*, no. 100 (1920); "On Chondrules and Chondritic Structure in Meteorites," in *Proceedings of the National Academy of Sciences* . . ., **6** (1920), 449–472; *The First One Hundred Years of American Geology* (New Haven, Conn., 1924); "The Present Condition of

Knowledge on the Composition of Meteorites," in *Proceedings of the American Philosophical Society*, **65** (1926), 119–130; and "Composition and Structure of Meteorites," *Bulletin. United States National Museum*, no. 149 (1930).

II. SECONDARY LITERATURE. Biographies of Merrill are Waldemar Lindgren, in *Biographical Memoirs. National Academy of Sciences*, **17** (1935), 31–53, which includes a bibliography of 196 titles; and Charles Schuchert, in *Bulletin of the Geological Society of America*, **42** (1931), 95–122, with a bibliography of 196 titles.

KIRTLEY F. MATHER

MERSENNE, MARIN (*b*. Oizé, Maine, France, 8 September 1588; *d*. Paris, France, 1 September 1648), *natural philosophy, acoustics, music, mechanics, optics, scientific communication.*

> The sciences have sworn among themselves an inviolable partnership; it is almost impossible to separate them, for they would rather suffer than be torn apart; and if anyone persists in doing so, he gets for his trouble only imperfect and confused fragments. Yet they do not arrive all together, but they hold each other by the hand so that they follow one another in a natural order which it is dangerous to change, because they refuse to enter in any other way where they are called. . . .[1]

Mersenne's most general contribution to European culture was this vision of the developing community of the sciences. It could be achieved only by the cultivation of the particular:

> Philosophy would long ago have reached a high level if our predecessors and fathers had put this into practice; and we would not waste time on the primary difficulties, which appear now as severe as in the first centuries which noticed them. We would have the experience of assured phenomena, which would serve as principles for a solid reasoning; truth would not be so deeply sunken; nature would have taken off most of her envelopes; one would see the marvels she contains in all her individuals. . . .[1]

These complaints had long been heard, yet "most men are glad to find work done, but few want to apply themselves to it, and many think that this search is useless or ridiculous."[1] He offered his scientific study of music as a particular reparation of a general fault.

Born into a family of laborers, Mersenne entered the new Jesuit *collège* at La Flèche in 1604 and remained there until 1609. After two years of theology at the Sorbonne, in 1611 he joined the Order of Minims and in 1619 returned to Paris to the Minim Convent de l'Annonciade near Place Royale, now

Place des Vosges. There he remained, except for brief journeys, until his death in 1648.[2] The Minims recognized that Mersenne could best serve their interests through an apostolate of the intellect. He made his entry upon the European intellectual scene in his earliest publications, with a discussion of ancient and modern science in support of a characteristic theological argument. He aimed to use the certifiable successes of natural science as a demonstration of truth against contemporary errors dangerous to religion and the morals of youth. In his vast and diffuse *Quaestiones in Genesim* (1623) he defended orthodox theology against "atheists, magicians, deists and suchlike,"[3] especially Francesco Giorgio, Telesio, Bruno, Francesco Patrizzi, Campanella, and above all his contemporary Robert Fludd, by attacking atomism and the whole range of Hermetic, Cabalist, and "naturalist" doctrines of occult powers and harmonies and of the Creation. In the same volume he included a special refutation of Giorgio,[4] and he continued his attack on this group in *L'impiété des déistes, athées, et libertins de ce temps* (1624). This attack on magic and the occult in defense of the rationality of nature attracted the attention of Pierre Gassendi, whom he met in 1624 and who became his closest friend.[5]

Mersenne's next work, the *Synopsis mathematica* (1626), was a collection of classical and recent texts on mathematics and mechanics. After that came *La vérité des sciences, contre les sceptiques ou Pyrrhoniens*, a long defense of the possibility of true human knowledge against the Pyrrhonic skepticism developed especially by Montaigne. Thus religion and morality had some rational basis. Yet while he stood with Aristotle in arguing that nature was both rational and knowable, he denied that theologians had to be tied to Aristotle.[6] Against the qualitative, verbal Aristotelian physics he came to argue that nature was rational, its actions limited by quantitative laws, because it was a mechanism.[7]

From about 1623 Mersenne began to make the careful selection of *savants* who met at his convent in Paris or corresponded with him from all over Europe and as far afield as Tunisia, Syria, and Constantinople. His regular visitors or correspondents came to include Peiresc, Gassendi, Descartes,[8] the Roman musicologist Giovanni Battista Doni, Roberval, Beeckman, J. B. van Helmont, Fermat, Hobbes, and the Pascals. It was in Mersenne's quarters that in 1647 the young Blaise Pascal first met Descartes.[9] Mersenne's role as secretary of the republic of scientific letters, with a strong point of view of his own, became institutionalized in the Academia Parisiensis, which he organized in 1635.[10] His monument as an architect of the European scientific community is the rich edition of his *Correspondance* published in Paris in the present century.

Mersenne developed his mature natural philosophy in relation to two fundamental questions. The first was the validity in physics of the axiomatic theory of truly scientific demonstration described in Aristotle's *Posterior Analytics* and exemplified in contemporary discussions especially by Euclid's geometry. Mersenne entered in the wake of the sixteenth-century debate on skepticism. The second question was the acceptability of a strictly mechanistic conception of nature. Opinions about these two questions decided what was believed to be discoverable in nature and what any particular inquiry had discovered. Opinions about the second also decided how to deal with the relationship of perceiver to world perceived, and so with the information communicated, especially through vision and hearing.

Mersenne's approach to these problems represents a persistent style in science. He took up his characteristic position on the first in the course of the debate over the new astronomy. He treated the decree of 1616 against Copernicus with Northern independence and moved in his early writings from rejection of the hypothesis of the earth's motions because sufficient evidence was lacking,[11] to preference for it as the most plausible. Copernicus' hypothesis, he said, had been neither refuted nor demonstrated: "I have never liked the attitude of people who want to look for, or feign, or imagine reasons or demonstrations where there are none; it is better to confess our ignorance than abuse the world."[12] But Mersenne reacted strongly against theologically sensitive extensions of the new cosmology, especially the doctrines of a plurality of worlds and of the infinity of the universe.[13] He took particular exception to Giordano Bruno: "one of the wickedest men whom the earth has ever supported . . . who seems to have invented a new manner of philosophizing only in order to make underhand attacks on the Christian religion."[14] He maintained that ecclesiastics had the right to condemn opinions likely to scandalize their flocks and merely advised moderation in censorship, because in the end "the true philosophy never conflicts with the belief of the Church."[15]

Through the Christian philosopher defending true knowledge against the skeptic in *La vérité des sciences*, and in later essays, Mersenne defined the kind of rational knowledge he held to be available. He found in Francis Bacon a program for real scientific knowledge, but he reproached him for failing to keep abreast of the "progress of the sciences" and for proposing the impossible goal of penetrating "the nature of things."[16] Only God knew the essences of things.

God's inscrutable omnipotence, which denied men independent rational knowledge of his reasons, and the logical impossibility of demonstrating causes uniquely determined by effects reduced the order of nature for men simply to an order of contingent fact. Mersenne concluded that the only knowledge of the physical world available to men was that of the quantitative externals of effects, and that the only hope of science was to explore these externals by means of experiment and the most probable hypotheses. But this was true knowledge, able to guide men's actions, even though theology and logic showed it to be less than that claimed to be possible by Aristotle.[17]

In 1629, after some earlier approaches, Mersenne wrote to Galileo, offering his services in publishing "the new system of the motion of the earth which you have perfected, but which you cannot publish because of the prohibition of the Inquisition."[18] Galileo did not reply to this generous offer—nor, indeed, to any of Mersenne's later letters to him. But Mersenne was not put off. He had come to see in Galileo's work a supreme illustration of the rationality of nature governed by mechanical laws and, so far as these laws went, of the true program for natural science.[19] In 1633 he published his first critique of Galileo's *Dialogo* (1632) in his *Traité des mouvemens et de la cheute des corps pesans et de la proportion de leurs différentes vitesses, dans lequel l'on verra plusieurs expériences très exactes.*[20] His first response to hearing of Galileo's condemnation in that year was to agree with the need for the Church to preserve Scripture from error;[21] yet he came forward at once with a French version (with additions of his own) of Galileo's unpublished early treatise on mechanics under the title *Les méchaniques de Galilée* (1634), and with a summary account of the first two days of the *Dialogo* and of the trial in *Les questions théologiques, physiques, morales, et mathématiques* (1634).

Mersenne's mature natural philosophy appeared in *Les questions* and three other works in the same year: *Questions inouyës, Questions harmoniques,* and *Les préludes de l'harmonie universelle.*[22] He made it plain that Galileo had not been condemned for heresy; and although he wrote later that he would not be prepared to risk schism for the new astronomy,[23] in 1634 he planned to write a defense of Galileo.[24] He gave this up. Mersenne disagreed with Galileo's claim to "necessary demonstrations" on the general ground that no physical science had "the force of perfect demonstration;"[25] and like most of his contemporaries he was unconvinced by the dynamical arguments so far produced by Galileo or anyone else. Yet while he saw the question of the earth's motion as undecided, he encouraged the search for fresh quantitative evidence which alone would make it possible "to distinguish the way nature acts in these movements, and to make a decision about it."[26]

Mersenne's conclusion that an inescapable "ignorance of true causes"[27] was imposed by the human situation gave him a scientific style interestingly different from that of Galileo and of Descartes. They aimed at certainty in physical science; Mersenne, disbelieving in the possibility of certainty, aimed at precision. Galileo's lack of precision in his first published mention of his experiments on acceleration down an inclined plane in the *Dialogo* led Mersenne to doubt whether he had really performed them. His own carefully repeated experiments, using a seconds pendulum to measure time, confirmed the "duplicate proportion" between distance and time deduced by Galileo but gave values nearly twice as great for the actual distances fallen. He commented that "one should not rely too much only on reasoning."[28] On many occasions Mersenne's too close attention to the untidy facts of observation may have deprived him of theoretical insight; but his insistence on the careful specification of experimental procedures, repetition of experiments, publication of the numerical results of actual measurements as distinct from those calculated from theory, and recognition of approximations marked a notable step in the organization of experimental science in the seventeenth century. Amid many words and some credulity, the works of his maturity, especially on acoustics and optics, contain models of "expériences bien reglées et bien faites"[29] and of rational appreciation of the limits of measurement and of discovery.

While strict demonstration was beyond natural science, Mersenne maintained that the imitation of God's works in nature by means of technological artifacts gave experimental natural philosophy an opening into possible explanations of phenomena. In this way he linked his experimental method with the second fundamental question for his natural philosophy—the conception of nature as a mechanism—and with the method of the hypothetical model. Characteristically it was through theological issues that he developed the central idea that living things were automatons. He used it as a weapon in his campaign for the uniqueness of human reason and of its power to grasp true knowledge and moral responsibility, against the false doctrines both of "les naturalistes,"[30] who asserted human participation in a world soul, and of the skeptics, who threw doubt on human superiority over the animals. After his visit to Beeckman, Descartes, and J. B. van Helmont in the Netherlands in 1630,[31] Mersenne came to hold that, on the analogy of sound, light was a form of purely

corporeal propagation. Although he remained unconvinced by the evidence for any of the current theories of light and sound and changed his views several times, his restriction of the choice to physical motions gave him (like Descartes) a method of asking how these motions affected a sentient being.[32] He disposed finally of the arguments against the uniqueness of man by declaring animals to be simply automatons, explicitly first in *Les préludes de l'harmonie universelle* (1634):

> ... for the animals, which we resemble and which would be our equals if we did not have reason, do not reflect upon the actions or the passions of their external or internal senses, and do not know what is color, odor or sound, or if there is any difference between these objects, to which they are moved rather than moving themselves there. This comes about by the force of the impression that the different objects make on their organs and on their senses, for they cannot discern if it is more appropriate to go and drink or eat or do something else, and they do not eat or drink or do anything else except when the presence of objects, or the animal imagination [*l'imagination brutalle*], necessitates them and transports them to their objects, without their knowing what they do, whether good or bad; which would happen to us just as to them if we were destitute of reason, for they have no enlightenment except what they must have to take their nourishment and to serve us for the uses to which God has destined them.[33]

So one could say of the animals that they knew nothing of the world impinging upon them, "that they do not so much act as be put into action, and that objects make an impression on their senses such that it is necessary for them to follow it just as it is necessary for the wheels of a clock to follow the weights and the spring that pulls them."[34] Yet Mersenne did not say, like Descartes, that animals were machines identical in kind with the artificial machines made by men. He wrote that the movements of the heart would be understood without mystery if one could discover its mechanism,[35] but men could imitate God's productions in nature only externally and quantitatively. The essence remained hidden. Nevertheless, men's artificial imitations could become testable hypotheses or models for explaining natural phenomena.[36] The quantitative relations within natural phenomena represented the rational and stable *harmonie universelle* that God had chosen to exhibit, both within the structure of his physical creation and in the information about it that men were in a position to discover and communicate.

Mersenne selected for his own particular field of positive inquiry, and for the elimination of magic and the irrational, the mode of operation of vision and of heard sound, and of the languages of men and animals. His first original contributions to acoustics (on vibrating strings), as well as analyses of ancient and modern musical theory and optics, appeared in *Quaestiones in Genesim* (1623). In the same year he announced in his *Observationes*[37] on Francesco Giorgio's plans for a systematic science of sound, "le grand oeuvre de la musique,"[38] which henceforth became his chief intellectual preoccupation. The first sketches appeared in the *Traité de l'harmonie universelle* (1627),[39] *Questions harmoniques* (1634), and *Les préludes de l'harmonie universelle* (1634). Meanwhile, by 1629 Mersenne had planned and soon afterward began writing simultaneously two sets of treatises, in French and in Latin, which together form his great systematic work and were published as the two parts of *Harmonie universelle, contenant la théorie et la pratique de la musique* (1636, 1637), and the eight books of *Harmonicorum libri* with *Harmonicorum instrumentorum libri IV* (1636).[40] Before the final sections of *Harmonie universelle* were in print, he read in Paris, in the winter of 1636–1637, a manuscript of the first day of Galileo's *Discorsi* (1638) containing an account of conclusions about acoustics and the pendulum similar to his own.[41] Mersenne's next work on these subjects was his French summary and critical discussion of Galileo's book in *Les nouvelles pensées de Galilée* (1639). Later he published the results of further acoustical researches in three related works, *Cogitata physico-mathematica* (1644), *Universae geometriae mixtaeque mathematicae synopsis* (1644), and *Novarum observationum physico-mathematicarum tomus III* (1647). The last contains a summary of his contributions to the science of sound.

Parallel discussions of light and vision, beginning in *Quaestiones in Genesim* and Mersenne's correspondence from this time, run especially through *Harmonie universelle* and *Harmonicorum libri*, the *Cogitata*, and *Universae geometriae synopsis*. The inclusion in the optical section of *Universae geometriae synopsis* of unpublished work by Walter Warner, and of a version of Hobbes's treatise on optics with its mechanistic psychology, reflects Mersenne's close English connections at this time. His final contributions to optics, including experimental studies of visual acuity and binocular vision and a critical discussion of current hypotheses on the nature of light, appeared posthumously in *L'optique et la catoptrique* (1651).

Mersenne's scientific analysis of sound and of its effects on the ear and the soul began with the fundamental demonstration that pitch is proportional to frequency and hence that the musical intervals (octave, fifth, fourth, and so on) are ratios of frequencies of vibrations, whatever instrument produces them.

The essential propositions were established by G. B. Benedetti (*ca.* 1563), Galileo's father, Vincenzio Galilei (1589–1590), Beeckman (1614–1615), and, finally, Mersenne (1623–1634). Mersenne gave an experimental proof by counting the slow vibrations of very long strings against time measured by pulse beats or a seconds pendulum. He then used the laws he had completed (now bearing his name), relating frequency to the length, tension, and specific gravity of strings, to calculate frequencies too rapid to count. Similar relations were established for wind and percussion instruments. The demonstration of these propositions made it possible to offer quantitative physical explanations of consonance, dissonance, and resonance.[42]

An allied outstanding discovery apparently made first by Mersenne was the law that the frequency of a pendulum is inversely proportional to the square root of the length. His first statement of this was printed by 30 June 1634, about a year before Galileo's was written.[43] Exploring further acoustical quantities, Mersenne pioneered the scientific study of the upper and lower limits of audible frequencies, of harmonics, and of the measurement of the speed of sound, which he showed to be independent of pitch and loudness. He established that the intensity of sound, like that of light, is inversely proportional to the distance from its source.[44] Mersenne's discussions, after his visit to Italy in 1644, of the Italian and later French experiments with a Torricellian vacuum helped to make a live issue of this whole subject and its bearing on the true medium of sound and on the existence of atmospheric pressure.[45] Besides these contributions to science, collaboration with Doni on an ambitious plan for a comprehensive historical work on the theory and practice of ancient and modern music[46] yielded a rich collection of descriptions and illustrations of instruments, making *Harmonie universelle* and its Latin counterpart essential sources for musicology.

In keeping with his empirical philosophy, Mersenne looked for purely rational explanations of the motions and dispositions of the soul brought about by music. He aimed to put an end to all ideas of magical and occult powers of words and sounds.[47] At the same time he offered a rational analysis of language, arguing that if it was language that chiefly distinguished men from animals, this was a fundamental distinction, for language meant conscious understanding of meaning. The speech and jargon of animals was a kind of communication, but not language, for they mindlessly emitted and responded to messages simply as automatons.[48] Mersenne soon rejected any idea that there were natural names revealing the natures of things and firmly proposed a purely rational theory of language that made words simply conventional physical signs. Because all men possessed reason, they had developed languages in which spoken or written words signified meanings. But just as the effects of music varied with temperament, race, period, and culture, so different groups of men had come to express their common understanding of meaning in a variety of languages diversified by their different historical experiences, environments, needs, temperaments, and customs.[49] In this analysis of common elements Mersenne saw a means of inventing a perfect universal language that could convey information without error. Basing his linguistic experiments on a calculus of permutations and combinations, he proposed a system that would convey the only knowledge of things available to men, that of their quantitative externals. Such a language of quantities "could be called natural and universal"[50] and would be a perfect means of philosophical communication.

Descartes's famous comment that this perfect language could be achieved only in an earthly paradise[51] was true in a way perhaps not intended, for "le bon Père Mersenne" seems to have lived mentally in just such a paradise. "A man of simple, innocent, pure heart, without guile," Gassendi wrote three days after his friend had died in his arms. "A man than whom none was more painstaking, inquiring, experienced. A man whom all the arts and sciences to whose advance he tirelessly devoted himself, by investigating or by deliberating or by stimulating others, will justly mourn."[52] With almost his last breath Mersenne asked for an autopsy to discover the cause of his death. *Maxime de Minimis*.[53] He illustrates the creativeness of gifts of personality distinct from those of sheer originality in the scientific movement.

NOTES

1. Mersenne, *Les préludes de l'harmonie universelle* (Paris, 1634), 135–139.
2. Lenoble, *Mersenne*, 15 ff.
3. Mersenne, *Quaestiones celeberrime in Genesim, cum accurata textus explicatione. In hoc volumine athei, et deistae impugnantur, et expurgantur, et Vulgata editio ab haereticorum calumniis vindicatur. Graecorum et Hebraeorum musica instauratur. . . . Opus theologis, philosophis, medicis, iuriconsultis, mathematicis, musicis vero, et catoptricis praesertim utile . . .* (Paris, 1623), preface.
4. Mersenne, *Observationes et emendationes ad Francisci Georgii Veneti problemata* (Paris, 1623).
5. Mersenne, *Correspondance*, I, 190–193; Lenoble, *Mersenne*, xviii, 28.
6. *Quaestiones in Genesim*, preface.
7. Mersenne, *Les méchaniques de Galilée* (1634), "Épistre dédicatoire," ch. 1.
8. It seems likely that he met Descartes in either 1623 or 1625, before or after the latter's journey to Italy: see *Correspon-*

dance, I, 149; and Lenoble, *Mersenne*, 1, 17, 31, 314–316, for the improbability of their friendship at La Flèche as boys separated by seven and a half years in age, and other misconceptions of their relationship promulgated by Descartes's biographer Adrien Baillet.
9. A. Baillet, *La vie de Monsieur Des-Cartes*, II (1691), 327–328; Jacqueline Pascal's letter of 25 Sept. 1647, in Blaise Pascal, *Oeuvres*, L. Brunschvicg, P. Boutroux, and F. Gazier, eds., II (Paris, 1908), 39–48. Pascal in his "Histoire de la roulette" gave Mersenne the credit for being the first to consider, about 1615, the curve produced by "le roulement des roues": *Oeuvres*, VIII (1914), 195; cf. Mersenne, *Correspondance*, I, 13, 183–184, and II, 598–599.
10. *Correspondance*, I, xliii–xliv, V, 209–211, 371; Lenoble, *Mersenne*, 1, 35–36, 48, 233–234, 586–594. Mersenne had for more than a decade been a member of the Cabinet des Frères Dupuy; for this and the various proposals he made beginning in 1623 for national and international cooperation through academies of theology in which scientific and other experts assisted, of science and mathematics, and of music, see the *Correspondance*, I, 45, 106–107, 129, 136–137, 169–172, V, 301–302; *Quaestiones in Genesim*, preface, dedication, and cols. 1510–1511, 1683–1687; *La vérité des sciences*, 206–224, 751–752, 913–914; *Traité de l'harmonie universelle*, 50, 255–256.
11. *Quaestiones in Genesim*, preface and cols. 841–850, 879–920. He gave considerable attention to Kepler, whom he supported against Fludd: cf. cols. 1016, 1556–1562; *Correspondance*, I, 131–132, 147–148; Lenoble, *Mersenne*, 224–225, 367–370, 394–413.
12. *L'impiété des déistes*, II, 200–201; cf. 198.
13. *Quaestiones in Genesim*, cols. 57, 85, 892–893, 903–904, 1081–1096, 1164; cf. *Correspondance*, I, 130–135.
14. *L'impiété*, I, 230–231; cf. II, 326–342, 363–364, 475.
15. *La vérité*, 111; cf. *L'impiété*, II, 479, 494–495.
16. *La vérité*, 109, 212–213; cf. 913–914.
17. *Ibid.*, 13–15, 226; *Les questions théologiques* (1634), "Épistre" and pp. 9–11, 16–19, 116–117, 123–124, 178–183, 229; *Questions inouyës* (1634), 69–78, 130–131, 153–154; see notes 25–27.
18. *Correspondance*, II, 175.
19. Cf. note 7.
20. *Correspondance*, III, 437–439, 561–568, 630–633.
21. Letter of 8 Feb. 1634, *ibid.*, IV, 37–38.
22. *Ibid.*, IV, 76–78, 156–157; cf. III, 570–572.
23. Mersenne to Martinus Ruarus, 1 Apr. 1644, in Ruarus' *Epistolarum selectarum centuria* (Paris, 1677), 269; Lenoble, *Mersenne*, 413.
24. *Correspondance*, IV, 226, 232, 267–268, 406–407, 411–412, V, 106, 127, 214; note 22. Cf. Descartes's letters to Mersenne during 1633–1635 on Galileo: *ibid.*, III, 557–560; IV, 26–29, 50–52, 97–99, 297–300; V, 127.
25. *Les questions théologiques*, 116–117; cf. 18–19, 43–44, 164.
26. *Harmonie universelle* (1636), "Traitez de la nature des sons et des mouvemens," I, prop. xxxiii, p. 76; cf. II, props. xix, xxi, pp. 149–150, 154–155. The same attitude appears in the *Cogitata physico-mathematica* (1644), "Hydraulica," 251, 260, and "Ballistica," 81–82; in the *Universae geometriae synopsis* (1644), "Cosmographia," preface, 258; and in Roberval's dedication to his "Aristarchus," printed in Mersenne's *Novarum observationum tomus III* (1647).
27. *Les questions théologiques*, 18–19; cf. *Harmonie universelle*, "Première preface générale"; see notes 20, 29.
28. *Harmonie universelle*, "Traitez . . . des sons," II, prop. vii, coroll. 1, p. 112; cf. prop. i, pp. 85–88, and prop vii, pp. 108–112; and for his seconds pendulum, prop. xv, pp. 135–137, prop. xxii, coroll. 9, p. 220; *Correspondance*, IV, 409–411; A. Koyré, "An Experiment in Measurement." These criticisms may have provoked Galileo to describe his experiment in more detail in the *Discorsi* (1638); Mersenne again repeated the experiment and wrote in *Les nouvelles pensées de Galilée* (1639) that, with a ball

heavy enough not to be significantly affected by air resistance, he found "les mesmes proportions" (pp. 188–189).

29. *Harmonie universelle*, "Traitez . . . des sons," III, prop. v, p. 167; cf. *Novarum observationum . . . tomus III*, 113, on reason guiding the senses.

30. *Les préludes*, 118; cf. *Quaestiones in Genesim*, cols. 130, 937–948, 1262–1272; *L'impiété*, II, 360–378, 390–391, 401–437; *La vérité*, 15–20, 25–36, 179–189; *Les questions théologiques*, 229–232.

31. See for this visit, *Correspondance*, II, 486, 506–507, 522–525.

32. See for discussions about light and sound, *ibid.*, I, 329–330, 333–335, II, 107–108, 116–124, 248–249, 282–283, 293–296, 353, 456–459, 467–477, 669–670, III, 35–42, 48–49; *Quaestiones in Genesim*, cols. 742, 1561, 1892; *La vérité*, 69–72; *Traité de l'harmonie universelle*, preface and p. 7; *Les questions théologiques*, 67–69, 105–106, and 164 of the expurgated ed. (Lenoble, *Mersenne*, xx, 399–401, 518; *Correspondance*, IV, 74–76, 203–206, 267–271); *Harmonie universelle*, "Traitez de la nature des sons," I, props. i–ii, viii–x, xxv, xxxii, pp. 1–6, 14–19, 44–48, 73–74; *Harmonicorum libri*, I, props. ii–vi, pp. 1–3; *Cogitata physico-mathematica*, "Harmonia," 261–271, "Ballistica," preface and pp. 74–82 (on Hobbes, etc.); *Universae geometriae . . . synopsis*, "Praefatio utilis in synopsim mathematicam," sec. x, and pp. 471 bis–487, 548, 567–571 (by Hobbes); *L'optique et la catoptrique* (1651), 1–3, 49–54, 77–92; Lenoble, *Mersenne*, 107–108, 317–318, 370–371, 414–418, 421–424, 478–486; note 44.

33. *Les préludes*, 156–159. Their correspondence and Mersenne's publications leave uncertain what Mersenne knew at this time of the earlier ideas developed by Descartes in the *Regulae*, left unfinished in 1629, and *Le monde* and *L'homme*, begun in the same year.

34. *Harmonie universelle* (1637), "Traitez de la voix," I, prop. lii, p. 79; cf. note 47.

35. *Les questions théologiques*, 76–81; cf. 183. Mersenne sent a copy of William Harvey's *De motu cordis* (1628) together with a set of Fludd's works to Gassendi in Dec. 1628 and discussed the circulation of the blood with Descartes: *Correspondance*, II, 181–182, 189, 268; III, 346, 349–350; VIII, 296.

36. *La vérité*, preface; *Harmonie universelle*, "Traitez de la voix," II, prop. xxii, pp. 159–160, "Nouvelles observations physiques et mathématiques," I, coroll. 5, pp. 7–8.

37. Cols. 439–440; see note 4.

38. *La vérité*, 567; cf. preface and 370–371, 579, 981.

39. "Sommaire"; cf. *Correspondance*, I, 195–196, 204.

40. Mersenne created a major bibliographical problem by writing these treatises simultaneously with numerous revisions and repetitions, and by having the different sections printed separately: scarcely any two of the extant copies have the same contents in the same order; cf. Lenoble, *Mersenne*, xxi–xxvi; see note 41.

41. Galileo Galilei, *Opere*, A. Favaro, ed., XVI (Florence, 1905), 524, XVII (1907), 63–64, 80–81; Mersenne, *Correspondance*, VI, 83–84, 241–243, cf. 216, 237; *Harmonie universelle* (1637), "Seconde observation"; cf. *Les nouvelles pensées de Galilée* (1639), preface and 66–67, 72, 92, 96–99, 104–105, 109–110; cf. *Correspondance*, VII, 107–109, 317–320; see note 42.

42. *Quaestiones in Genesim*, cols. 1556–1562, 1699, 1710; *La vérité*, 370–371, 567, 614–620; *Traité de l'harmonie universelle*, 147–148, 447; *Harmonicorum libri*, I, prop. ii, II, props. vi–viii, xvii–xxi, xxxiii–xxxv, IV, prop. xxvii; *Harmonie universelle*: "Traité des instrumens," I, props. v, xii, xvi, III, props. vii, xvii; "Traitez . . . des sons," I, props. i, vii, xiii, III, props. i, v, vi, xv; "Traitez de la voix," I, prop. lii; "Traitez des consonances," I, props. vi, x, xii, xvii, xviii, xix, xxii, II, prop. x. Mersenne wrote from Paris on 20 Mar. 1634 to Peiresc in Aix-en-Provence that after more than ten years of work he had finished his "grand oeuvre de l'*Harmonie universelle*," of which he sent "le premier cayer" (*Correspondance*, IV, 81–82). The earliest section in which he gave an extensive analysis of the physical quantities determining the notes and intervals produced by vibrating strings, bells, and pipes, and used this to explain resonance, consonance, and dissonance seems to have been the "Traitez des consonances," I, "Des consonances." This was in print by 2 Feb. 1635 (Mersenne to Doni, *Correspondance*, V, 40–41). Internal references and the *Correspondance*, IV–V, indicate that he was writing at the same time, during 1634, the "Traité des instrumens" (I–III) and the *Harmonicorum libri* (I–IV); see Crombie, *Galileo and Mersenne* (forthcoming).

43. Mersenne published this law first in one of his original additions to *Les méchaniques de Galilée*, 7th addition, p. 77. The "privilège du roy" gives 30 June 1634 as the date on which the printing was completed: cf. Mersenne, *Correspondance*, IV, 76–77, 207–212, and the new ed. of *Les méchaniques* by Rochot (1966). The work was bound with Mersenne's *Les questions théologiques* and presumably sent with that to Doni by way of Peiresc in 1634 (Mersenne to Peiresc, 28 July 1634; Doni to Mersenne, 8 Nov. 1634; *Correspondance*, IV, 267, 384–385, appendix III, 444–455). Élie Diodati sent a copy of *Les méchaniques* from Paris to Galileo on 10 Apr. 1635 (*ibid.*, V, 132; cf. VI, 242). For Mersenne's use of this pendulum law, and his possible derivation of it from the law of falling bodies, see also *Harmonicorum libri*, II, props. xxvi–xxix; *Harmonie universelle*, "Traitez des instrumens," I, props. xix–xx; "Traitez . . . des sons," III, "Du mouvement," props. xxi, xxiii. Galileo's correspondence with Fulgenzio Micanzio in Venice between 19 Nov. 1634 and 7 Apr. 1635 (*Opere*, XVI, 163, 177, 193, 200–201, 203, 208–210, 214, 217–233, 236–237, 239–244, 254) indicates that he had not written the last part of the first day of the *Discorsi* (in which he discussed the pendulum and acoustics) by the latter date. His letter of 9 June 1635 to Diodati, saying that he had sent a copy to Giovanni Pieroni, and subsequent correspondence (*Opere*, XVI, 272–274, 300–304, 359–361) establishes this as the latest date of composition. This copy survives in Biblioteca Nazionale Centrale, Florence, MS Banco Raro 31; cf. note 40.

44. For these subjects see, respectively, *Harmonie universelle*, "Traitez des instrumens," I, prop. xix, III, prop. xvii, "Traitez . . . des sons," III, prop. vi, "Traitez de la voix," I, prop. lii; *Harmonicorum libri*, II, props. xviii, xxxiii; *Harmonie universelle*, "Traitez des instrumens," IV, prop. ix, VI, prop. xlii, VII, prop. xviii, "Nouvelles observations," IV; *Harmonicorum instrumentorum libri IV*, I, prop. xxxiii, III, prop. xxvii; cf. *Quaestiones in Genesim*, col. 1560; *Harmonie universelle*, "Traitez . . . des sons," I, props. vii, viii, xiii, xvii, xxi, III, prop. xxii, "De l'utilité de l'harmonie," prop. ix; *Novarum observationum . . . tomus III*, "Reflectiones physico-mathematicae," ch. 20; *Harmonie universelle*, "Traitez . . . des sons," I, props. xii, xv, cf. props. iii, iv (coroll. 30), and III, prop. xxi, coroll. 4; *Harmonicorum libri*, II, prop. xxxix.

45. *Novarum observationum . . . tomus III*, "Praefatio ad lectorem," "Praefatio secunda," and pp. 84–96, 216–218; cf. de Waard, *L'expérience barométrique*, 117–131; Lenoble, *Mersenne*, xxx, 431–436; Middleton, *The History of the Barometer*, 33–54.

46. Cf. *Correspondance*, III, 395, 512–513, IV, 80, 345, 368, VII, 393–394; G. B. Doni, *Annotazioni sopra il compendio de' generi, e de' modi della musica* (Rome, 1640), 277–280.

47. *Quaestiones in Genesim*, cols. 1619–1624; *La vérité*, 16–17, 32, 69–72; *Les préludes*, 212, 219–222; *Questions harmoniques*, 91–99; *Harmonie universelle*, "Préface générale au lecteur," "Traitez . . . des sons," I, props. i–ii, "Traitez de la voix," I, "Traitez des consonances," I, prop. xxxiii; *Harmonicorum libri*, I, prop. ii; Lenoble, *Mersenne*, 522–531.

48. *Harmonie universelle*, "Traitez de la voix," I, prop. xxxix, pp. 49–52; cf. props. vii–xii, xxxviii; cf. note 33.
49. *Quaestiones in Genesim*, cols. 23–24, 470–471, 702–704, 1197–1202, 1217, 1383–1398, 1692; MS continuation, Bibliothèque Nationale, Paris, MS lat. 17, 262, pp. 511, 536 (Lenoble, *Mersenne*, xiii–xiv, 514–517); *L'impiété*, 167; *La vérité*, 67–76, 544–580; *Traité de l'harmonie universelle*, "Sommaire," item 9; *Questions inouÿes*, 95–101, 120–122; *Harmonie universelle*, "Préface générale au lecteur" and "Traitez de la voix," preface, I, II, props. vii–xii; *Harmonicorum libri*, VII; Mersenne's discussions from 1621 to 1640 with Guillaume Bredeau, Descartes, Jean Beaugrand, Peiresc, Gassendi, Comenius, and others are in *Correspondance*, I, 61–63, 102–103; II, 323–329, 374–375; III, 254–262; IV, 329; V, 136–140; VI, 4–6; VII, 447–448; X, 264–274; Lenoble, *Mersenne*, 96–109, 514–521.
50. *Les questions théologiques*, quest. xxxiv, "Peut-on inventer une nouvelle science des sons, qui se nomme psophologie?" p. 158 (expurgated ed.); *Harmonie universelle*, "Traitez . . . des sons," I, prop. xxiv (language played on a lute), "Traitez de la voix," I, props. xii, xlvii–l (artificial rational languages), "De l'utilité de l'harmonie," prop. ix (symbolic language, acoustical telegraph). Cf. his proposals for methods of imitating human speech with instruments and for teaching deaf-mutes to speak and communicate: *Harmonie universelle*, "Traitez de la voix," I, props. x–xi, li, "Traitez des instrumens," II, prop. ix; cf. *Correspondance*, III, 354, 358–359, 375, 378, IV, 258–259, 262–263, 280, 289, 294 (1633–1634). On instruments for imitating human speech see "Traitez des instrumens," VI, props. xxxi–xxxii, xxxvi, VII, prop. xxx; *Correspondance*, III, 2–9, 538–553, 578–597, V, 269–272, 293–294, 299–300, 410–415, 478–482 (1631–1635).
51. Descartes to Mersenne, 20 Nov. 1629, in Mersenne, *Correspondance*, II, 323–329; cf. 374–375, IV, 329, 332, V, 134–140, VI, 4, 6.
52. Gassendi to Louis de Valois, 4 Sept. 1648, *Opera*, VI (Lyons, 1658), 291; Lenoble, *Mersenne*, 596, cf. 58; cf. Coste, *Vie*, 13, 99–101; Mersenne, *Correspondance*, I, xxx.
53. Constantijn Huygens, in a poem cited by Thuillier, *Diarium . . .*, II, 104; cf. Lenoble, *Mersenne*, 597, who also quotes a poem by Hobbes on Mersenne.

BIBLIOGRAPHY

I. ORIGINAL WORKS. A list of Mersenne's published and unpublished writings is in R. Lenoble, *Mersenne ou la naissance du mécanisme* (Paris, 1943), "Bibliographie," which also contains a list of publications on Mersenne from the seventeenth century. His main books are named in the text; all were published at Paris. There is a recent edition of *Les méchaniques de Galilée* by B. Rochot (Paris, 1966); and Mersenne's own copy of *Harmonie universelle*, with his annotations made during 1637–1648, has been reprinted in facsimile by the Centre National de la Recherche Scientifique (Paris, 1965). Above all there is Mersenne's *Correspondance*, C. de Waard, R. Pintard, and B. Rochot, eds. (Paris, 1932–   ), which includes information about his publications and MSS.

II. SECONDARY LITERATURE. The first biography was the valuable study written immediately after Mersenne's death by a fellow Minim, Hilarion de Coste, *La vie du R. P. Marin Mersenne, théologien, philosophe et mathématicien, de l'Ordre des Pères Minim* (Paris, 1649). A second main source for his life is René Thuillier, *Diarium patrum, fratrum et sororum Ordinis Minimorum Provinciae Franciae*

sive Parisiensis qui religiose obierunt ab anno 1506 ad annum 1700 (Paris, 1709). The critical problems are discussed in the *Correspondance*, I (1932), xix–lv; in this his career, publications, and relations with his contemporaries can be followed in detail from 1617.

The major study of Mersenne's life and thought is Lenoble's *Mersenne*. A valuable monograph is H. Ludwig, *Marin Mersenne und seine Musiklehre* (Halle–Berlin, 1935). For particular aspects there are C. de Waard, *L'expérience barométrique* (Thouars, 1936), and W. E. K. Middleton, *The History of the Barometer* (Baltimore, 1964), on the Torricellian vacuum; Mario M. Rossi, *Alle fonti del deismo e del materialismo moderni* (Florence, 1942), on his relation to deism; A. Koyré, "An Experiment in Measurement," in *Proceedings of the American Philosophical Society*, **97** (1953), 222–237, repr. in his *Metaphysics and Measurement* (London, 1968), on his critique of Galileo's experiments on acceleration; R. H. Popkin, *The History of Scepticism From Erasmus to Descartes* (Assen, Netherlands, 1964), on his relation to contemporary skepticism; F. A. Yates, *Giordano Bruno and the Hermetic Tradition* (London, 1964), on his relation to Hermeticism; A. C. Crombie, "Mathematics, Music and Medical Science," in *Actes du XIIᵉ Congrès international d'histoire des sciences: Paris 1968* (Paris, 1971), 295–310, on his science of sound; and W. L. Hine, "Mersenne and Copernicanism," in *Isis*, **64** (1973), 18–32. A further substantial discussion of his natural philosophy, with special reference to vision, heard sound and language, is included in A. C. Crombie, with the collaboration of A. Carugo, *Galileo and Mersenne: Science, Nature and the Senses in the Sixteenth and Early Seventeenth Centuries*, 2 vols. (forthcoming).

A. C. CROMBIE

MÉRY, JEAN (*b.* Vatan, France, 6 January 1645; *d.* Paris, France, 3 November 1722), *anatomy, surgery, pathology.*

Intent on following in his father's profession, Méry traveled to Paris at the age of eighteen to study surgery at the Hôtel-Dieu, then the best place to learn surgical practice. In addition to his regular studies, Méry undertook clandestine dissections whenever fresh human material became available to him. After completing his preparations he set up a private surgical practice, becoming well known, particularly in lithotomy. Much of his career was centered at the Hôtel-Dieu, where he was surgeon from 1681 and chief surgeon from 1700. He was appointed a senior surgeon at Les Invalides, Paris, in 1683. In 1684 Méry was elected to the Academy of Sciences. He also had connections with the French court. In 1681 he was appointed surgeon to the queen and later was sent by the court on at least two medical missions. Méry traveled to England in 1692 for the court, but the purpose of this trip is unknown.

Méry tended to be taciturn, has been described as argumentative, and often saw his family only at meals. He did a thorough job at the Hôtel-Dieu, both in his hospital practice and in training young surgeons. The balance of his time was divided between the Academy and his anatomical research.

Most of Méry's researches were comparative-anatomical and pathological. The pathological researches were mostly descriptive in character and covered a wide range of situations, although most of them were concerned with human developmental malformations. Of greater interest are his researches in comparative anatomy, including his physiological investigations. In the latter his methods were comparative and were based on preserved and dried anatomical specimens. Because of the limited preservation techniques available, this approach could be deceptive.

After his election to the Academy in 1684, Méry became closely associated with the comparative-anatomical work led by Claude Perrault and J.-G. Duverney. As a member of this group, Méry made contributions to their joint publications, in which each man's specific contributions usually cannot be determined. Méry worked closely with Duverney until about 1693, when their differing interpretations of mammalian fetal circulation estranged them. The coolness that resulted was apparent to Martin Lister, when he visited Paris in 1698. Méry probably did more to retard than to aid the understanding of this problem. Méry claimed that the blood flowed from the left to the right through the foramen ovale in the interatrial septum. This view was prevalent enough that Haller took time to refute it. Méry initially formulated his theory from a false analogy between a tortoise heart and a fetal mammalian heart. Ultimately he based his theory of fetal circulation on a comparison of the cross sections of the pulmonary artery and the aorta, concluding that not all of the blood passing through the pulmonary artery and returning to the heart by the pulmonary vein could pass into the aorta. Instead, he thought, a portion of that blood passed through the foramen ovale from the left to the right side of the heart.

Méry erred in assuming that the cross section of an artery is the only factor determining the amount of blood that can flow through it. He compounded this error by his method of measuring the relative cross sections of the arteries. He may have used fresh preparations for his measurements on cows and sheep. For those on human beings, he probably used preserved specimens, dried ones as a rule. The results were inconsistent at best. For example, Martin Lister described a fetal heart that he saw in Méry's collection

which had no valve for the foramen ovale, and which was open in both directions and had a diameter nearly equal to that of the aorta. For two decades numerous arguments were presented on both sides of the controversy between Méry's views and the traditional views dating back to Harvey and Lower. Méry held his views against all opposition to the end.

In other areas of anatomy Méry demonstrated that he was a capable and careful worker, making a number of valuable contributions to the anatomy of a wide range of animals. He described the urethral glands named after Cowper some years before Cowper's description, and he preceded Winslow in a description of the eustachian valve, although he misinterpreted its function as part of his concept of the mammalian fetal circulation.

BIBLIOGRAPHY

I. ORIGINAL WORKS. For a list of Méry's anatomical studies in *Mémoires de l'Académie royale des sciences*, see either the 1734 index volumes or J. D. Reuss, *Repertorium commentationum ... a societatibus litterariis editorum*, 16 vols. (Gottingen, 1801–1820). Much of the controversy on fetal circulation is contained in *Nouveau système de la circulation du sang par le trou ovale dans le foetus humain; avec les réponses aux objections de Messieurs Duverney, Tauvri, Verheyen, Silvestre & Buissiere contre cette hypothèse* (Paris, 1700), as well as scattered papers. He made unidentified contributions which were incorporated in *Mémoires pour servir à l'histoire naturelle des animaux* (Paris, 1732–1734).

II. SECONDARY LITERATURE. Principal biographical sources are the article in *Biographie universelle ancienne et moderne*, XXVIII (Paris); Bernard Le Bouyer de Fontenelle, "Éloge," in *Oeuvres de M. de Fontenelle*, VI (Amsterdam, 1754); and Martin Lister, *A Journey to Paris in the Year 1698* (London, 1699), *passim*. There are numerous references to Méry throughout the appropriate years of the *Histoire de l'Académie royale des sciences*. For Méry's theory of fetal circulation see Kenneth J. Franklin, "Jean Méry (1645–1722) and His Ideas on the Foetal Blood Flow," in *Annals of Science*, **5** (1945), 203–338; and for some of his other anatomical work see F. J. Cole, *A History of Comparative Anatomy from Aristotle to the Eighteenth Century* (London, 1944).

WESLEY C. WILLIAMS

MESHCHERSKY, IVAN VSEVOLODOVICH (*b.* Arkhangelsk, Russia, 10 August 1859; *d.* Leningrad, U.S.S.R., 7 January 1935), *mechanics, mathematics.*

Meshchersky was born into a family of modest means, but succeeded in obtaining a good education. He was enrolled in the Arkhangelsk Gymnasium in

1871, and graduated from it with a gold medal after seven years. He entered St. Petersburg University in 1878, and undertook the study of mathematics, attending the lectures of Chebyshev, A. N. Korkin, and A. Possé; he simultaneously studied mechanics. He graduated in 1882 but remained at the university to begin his own academic career. He passed the examinations for the master's degree in applied mathematics in 1889 and became a *Privatdozent* the following year.

In 1891 Meshchersky was appointed to the chair of mechanics at the St. Petersburg Women's College, a post that he retained until 1919, when the college was incorporated into the university. In 1897 he defended a dissertation entitled *Dinamika tochki peremennoy massy* ("The Dynamics of a Point of Variable Mass") before the Physics and Mathematics Faculty of St. Petersburg University and was awarded a doctorate in applied mathematics. In 1902 Meshchersky was invited to head the department of applied mathematics at the newly founded St. Petersburg Polytechnic Institute (now the Leningrad M. I. Kalin Polytechnic Institute), for which he had helped to develop a curriculum.

Meshchersky taught at St. Petersburg University for twenty-five years and at the Polytechnic Institute for thirty-three. He was a conscientious and innovative pedagogue. Among other things, he was concerned with drafting a scientific-methodological guide to the teaching of mathematics and mechanics; his *Prepodavanie mekhaniki i mekhanicheskie kollektsii v nekotorykh vysshikh uchebnykh zavedeniakh Italii, Frantsii, Shveytsarii i Germanii* ("The Teaching of Mechanics and Mechanics Collections in Certain Institutions of Higher Education in Italy, France, Switzerland, and Germany"; 1895) contributed significantly toward raising the standards of the teaching of mechanics in Russia. Meshchersky's own course in theoretical mechanics became famous, while his textbook on that subject, *Sbornik zadach po teoreticheskoy mekhanike* ("A Collection of Problems in Theoretical Mechanics"), published in 1914, went through twenty-four editions and became a standard work.

Meshchersky's purely scientific work was devoted to the motion of bodies of variable mass. He reported the results of his first investigations of the problem at a meeting of the St. Petersburg Mathematical Society held on 27 January 1893, then made it the subject of the doctoral dissertation that he presented four years later. He began the thesis *Dinamika tochki peremennoy massy* with a discussion of the many instances in which the mass of a moving body changes, citing as examples the increase of the mass

of the earth occasioned by meteorites falling on it; the increase of the mass of an iceberg with freezing and its decrease with thawing; the increase of the mass of the sun through its gathering of cosmic dust and its decrease with radiation; the decrease of the mass of a rocket as its fuel is consumed; the decrease of the mass of a balloon as its ballast is discarded; and the increase of the mass of a captive balloon as it draws its tether with it in rising.

Having defined the problem, Meshchersky considered it physically. He established that if the mass of a point changes during motion, then Newton's second law of motion must be replaced by an equation of the motion of a point of variable mass wherein $m \frac{d\bar{v}}{dt} = \bar{F} + \bar{R}$ ($\bar{F}$ and $\bar{R}$ being the given and the reactive forces, respectively), where $\bar{F}$ and $\bar{R} = \frac{dm}{dt} \bar{U}_r$.

This natural generalization of the equation of motion of classical mechanics is now called Meshchersky's equation. In his second important work, "Uravnenia dvizhenia tochki peremennoy massy v obshchem sluchae" ("Equations of the Motion of a Point of Variable Mass in the General Case," 1904), Meshchersky gave his theory a definitive and elegant expression, establishing the general equation of motion of a point of which the mass is changing by the simultaneous incorporation and elimination of particles.

In developing the theoretical foundations of the dynamics of a point of variable mass, Meshchersky opened a new area of theoretical mechanics. He also examined a number of specific problems, including the ascending motion of a rocket and the vertical motion of a balloon. His exceptionally thorough general investigation of the motion of a point of variable mass under the influence of a central force led to a new celestial mechanics; he was further concerned with the motions of comets. He was, moreover, the first to formulate, from given external forces and given trajectories, the so-called inverse problems in determining the law for the change of mass.

Meshchersky published a number of papers on general mechanics. In "Differentsialnye svyazi v sluchae odnoy materialnoy tochki" ("Differential Ties in the Case of One Material Point"; 1887), he examined the motion of a point subjected to a nonholonomic tie, which is neither ideal nor linear. In "O teoreme Puassona pri sushchestvovanii uslovnykh uravneny" ("On Poisson's Theorem on the Existence of Conditional Arbitrary Equations"; 1890), he took up the integration of dynamical equations, while in "Sur un problème de Jacobi" (1894), he gave a generalization of Jacobi's results. A paper of 1919, "Gidrodinamicheskaya analogia prokatki" ("A Hydrodynamic Analogue of Rolling"), is of particular interest because it contains Meshchersky's ingenious attempt to elucidate the equations of motion rolling bodies in terms of those for a viscous fluid.

Meshchersky's work on the motion of bodies of variable mass remains his most important contribution to science. His pioneering studies formed the basis for much of the rocket technology and dynamics that was developed rapidly following World War II.

BIBLIOGRAPHY

I. ORIGINAL WORKS. Meshchersky's writings include "Davlenie na klin v potoke neogranichennoy shiriny dvukh izmereny" ("The Pressure on a Wedge in a Two-Dimensional Stream of Unbounded Width"), in *Zhurnal Russkago fiziko-khimicheskago obshchestva pri Imperatorskago St.-Peterburskago universitete*, **18** (1886); "Differentsialnye svyazi v sluchae odnoy materialnoy tochki" ("Differential Bonds in the Case of One Material Point"), in *Soobshchenie Kharkovskogo matematicheskogo obshchestva* (1887), 68–79; *Prepodavanie mekhaniki i mekhanicheskie kollektsii v nekotorykh vysshikh uchebnykh zavedeniakh Italii, Frantsii, Shveytsarii i Germanii* ("The Teaching of Mechanics and Mechanics Collections in Certain Institutions of Higher Education in Italy, France, Switzerland, and Germany"; St. Petersburg, 1895); *Dinamika tochki peremennoy massy* ("The Dynamics of a Point of Variable Mass"; St. Petersburg, 1897); and *O vrashchenii tyazhelogo tverdogo tela s razvertyvayushcheysya tyazheloy nityu okolo gorizontalnoy osi* ("On the Rotation of a Heavy Solid Body Having an Unwinding Heavy Thread About Its Horizontal Axis"; St. Petersburg, 1899).

Later writings include "Über die Integration der Bewegungsgleichungen im Probleme zweier Körper von veränderlicher Masse," in *Astronomische Nachrichten*, **159**, no. 3807 (1902); "Uravnenia dvizhenia tochki peremennoy massy v obshchem sluchae" ("Equations of the Motion of a Point of Variable Mass in the General Case"), in *Izvestiya S-Peterburgskago politekhnicheskago instituta Imperatora Petra Velikago*, **1** (1904); *Sbornik zadach po teoreticheskoy mekhanike* ("Collection of Problems in Theoretical Mechanics"; St. Petersburg, 1914); "Zadachi iz dinamiki peremennoy massy" ("Problems From the Dynamics of a Variable Mass"), in *Izvestiya S-Peterburgskago politekhnicheskago instituta Imperatora Petra Velikago*, **27** (1918); and "Gidrodinamicheskaya analogia prokatki" ("A Hydrodynamic Analogue of Rolling"), *ibid.*, **28** (1919).

II. SECONDARY LITERATURE. See Y. L. Geronimus, "Ivan Vsevolodovich Meshchersky (1859–1935)," in *Ocherki o rabotakh korifeev russkoy mekhaniki* ("Essays on the Works of the Leading Figures of Russian Mechanics"; Moscow, 1952); A. T. Grigorian, "Ivan Vsevolodovich Meshchersky (k 100-letiyu so dnya rozhdenia)" ("Ivan Vsevolodovich Meshchersky [on the Centenary of His Birth]"), in *Voprosy istorii estestvoznaniya i tekhniki* (1959), no. 7; and "Mekhanika tel peremennoy massy I. V. Meshcherskogo" ("I. V. Meshchersky's Mechanics of Bodies of Variable Mass"), in *Evolyutsia mekhaniki v Rossii* ("The Evolution of Mechanics in Russia"; Moscow, 1967); A. A. Kosmodemyansky, "Ivan Vsevolodovich Meshchersky (1859–1935)," in *Lyudi russkoy nauki* ("People of Russian Science"; Moscow, 1961), 216–222; and E. L. Nikolai, "Prof. I. V. Meshchersky [Nekrolog]," in *Prikladnaya matematika i mekhanika*, **3**, no. 1 (1936).

A. T. GRIGORIAN

MESMER, FRANZ ANTON (*b.* Iznang, Germany, 23 May 1734; *d.* Meersburg, Germany, 5 March 1815), *medicine, origins of hypnosis.*

Mesmer was born and raised in the Swabian village of Iznang near the Lake of Constance. His father was a forester employed by the archbishop of Constance; his mother, the daughter of a locksmith; and his family, large (Franz Anton was the third of nine children), Catholic, and not particularly prosperous. By the time he began to propound his theory of animal magnetism or mesmerism, Mesmer had risen through the educational systems of Bavaria and Austria and had advanced to a position of some prominence in Viennese society through his marriage to a wealthy widow, Maria Anna von Posch, on 16 January 1768. Mesmerism therefore may have been the product of an ambitious *arriviste* but not of a mountebank. The man and the "ism" represent a period when medicine was attempting to assimilate advances in the physical and biological sciences and when scientists often indulged in cosmological speculations that read like science fiction today but passed as respectable varieties of Newtonianism in the eighteenth century.

After preliminary studies in a local monastic school, Mesmer spent four years at the Jesuit University of Dillingen (Bavaria), presumably as a scholarship student preparing for the priesthood. He then attended the University of Ingolstadt for a brief period and in 1759 entered the University of Vienna as a law student. Having changed to medicine and completed the standard course of studies, he received his doctorate in 1766. A year later he began practice as a member of the faculty of medicine in what was one of Europe's most advanced medical centers; for the Vienna school was then in its prime, owing to the patronage of Maria Theresa and the leadership of Gerhard van Swieten and Jan Ingenhousz.

Mesmer later traced his theory of animal magnetism to his doctoral thesis, *Dissertatio physico-medica de planetarum influxu.* At the time of its defense, however, the thesis did not strike the Viennese authorities as a revolutionary new theory of medicine. On the contrary, it showed a common tendency to speculate about invisible fluids, which derived both from Cartesianism and from the later queries in Newton's *Opticks* as well as from Newton's remarks about the "most subtle spirit which pervades and lies hid in all gross bodies" in the last paragraph of his *Principia.* The immediate source of Mesmer's fluid was Richard Mead's *De imperio solis ac lunae in corpora humana et morbis inde oriundis* (London, 1704), a work upon which Mesmer's thesis drew heavily. Mead had argued that gravity produced "tides" in the atmosphere as well as in water and that the planets could therefore affect the fluidal balance of the human body. Mesmer associated this "animal gravitation" with health: physical soundness resulted from the "harmony" between the organs of the body and the planets—a proposition, he emphasized, that had nothing to do with the fictions of astrology.

The proposition took on new life for Mesmer when he began treating his own patients. Inspired by the experiments of Maximilian Hell, a court astronomer and Jesuit priest, who used magnets in the treatment of disease, Mesmer applied magnets to his patients' bodies and produced remarkable results, especially in the case of a young woman suffering from hysteria. Unlike Hell, Mesmer did not attribute his cures to any power in the magnets themselves. Instead, he argued that the body was analogous to a magnet and that the fluid ebbed and flowed according to the laws of magnetic attraction. Having moved from "animal gravitation" to "animal magnetism," he announced his new theory in *Sendschreiben an einen auswärtigen Arzt . . .* (Vienna, 1775).

By this time Mesmer had moved into a comfortable town house in Vienna, which he used as a clinic. His marriage brought him enough wealth to pursue his experiments at his leisure and enough leisure to indulge his passion for music. Mesmer knew Gluck, seems to have been acquainted with Haydn, and saw a great deal of the Mozarts. The first production of a Mozart opera, *Bastien und Bastienne,* took place in Mesmer's garden, and Mozart later made room for mesmerism in a scene in *Così fan tutte.* In general, the ten years between Mesmer's marriage in 1768 and his departure from Vienna in 1778 seem to have been a time of prosperity and some prominence. He built up a repertoire of techniques and cures; he gave lectures and demonstrations; and he traveled through Hungary, Switzerland, and Bavaria, where he was made a member of the Bavarian Academy of Sciences at Munich in 1775. Mesmer also developed a taste for

publicity. He staged and announced his cures in a manner that offended some of Vienna's most influential doctors. Offense developed into open hostility in 1777 during a dispute over Mesmer's treatment of Maria-Theresa von Paradies, a celebrated blind pianist who was eventually removed from Mesmer's care by her parents. In these circumstances Mesmer decided to leave Vienna and perhaps also to leave his wife, who did not accompany him through the later episodes of his career.

The next and most spectacular episode began with Mesmer's arrival in Paris in February 1778. He set up a clinic in the Place Vendôme and the nearby village of Créteil and then began an elaborate campaign to win recognition of his "discovery" from France's leading scientific bodies. Helped by some influential converts and an ever-increasing throng of patients, who testified that they had been cured of everything from paralysis to what the French then called "vapeurs," Mesmer seized the public's imagination and alienated the Faculty of Medicine of the University of Paris, the Royal Society of Medicine, and the Academy of Sciences. The defenders of orthodox medicine took offense at what the public found most appealing about mesmerism—not its theory but its extravagant practices. Instead of bleeding and applying purgatives, the mesmerists ran their fingers over their patients' bodies, searching out "poles" through which they infused mesmeric fluid. By the 1780's Mesmer had given up the use of magnets; but he had perfected other devices, notably his famous "tub," a mesmeric version of the Leyden jar, which stored fluid and dispensed it through iron bars that patients applied to their sick areas. Mesmer transmitted his invisible fluid through all sorts of media—ropes, trees, "chains" of patients holding hands—and he usually sent it coursing through the air by gestures with his hands. He reasoned that his own body acted as an animal type of magnet, reinforcing the fluid in the bodies of his patients. Disease resulted from an "obstacle" to the flow of the fluid. Mesmerizing broke through the obstacle by producing a "crisis," often signaled by convulsions, and then restoring "harmony," a state in which the body responded to the salubrious flow of fluid through all of nature.

Mesmerism presented itself to the French as a "natural" medicine at a time when the cult of nature and the popular enthusiasm for science had reached a peak. Mesmer did not produce any proof of his theory or any rigorous description of experiments that could be repeated and verified by others; but like contemporary chemists and physicists, he seemed able to put his invisible fluid to work. Scores of Parisians fell into "crises" at the touch of Mesmer's hand and recovered with a new sense of being at harmony with the world. The mesmerists published hundreds of carefully documented and even notarized case histories. And they produced an enormous barrage of propaganda—at least 200 books and pamphlets, more than were written on any other single subject during the decade before the opening phase of the Revolution in 1787.

Thus mesmerism became a *cause célèbre*, a movement, which eventually even eclipsed Mesmer himself. He limited his part in the polemics to two pamphlets, written by or for him: *Mémoire sur la découverte du magnétisme animal* (1779) and *Précis historique des faits relatifs au magnétisme animal* (1781). The first contained twenty-seven rather vague propositions, which is as close as Mesmer came to systematizing his ideas. He left the system-building to his disciples, notably Nicolas Bergasse, who produced many of the articles and letters issued in Mesmer's name as well as his own mesmeric treatise, *Considérations sur le magnétisme animal* (1784). The disciples also formed a sort of Masonic secret society, the Société de l'Harmonie Universelle, which developed affiliates in most of France's major cities. The spread of the new medicine alarmed not only the old doctors but also the government. A royal commission composed of distinguished doctors and academicians, including Bailly, Lavoisier, and Franklin, reported in 1784 that, far from being able to cure disease, Mesmer's fluid did not exist. The report badly damaged the movement, which later dissolved into schisms and heresies. Mesmer finally left his followers to their quarrels and, after a period of traveling through England, Austria, Germany, and Italy, settled in Switzerland, where he spent most of the last thirty years of his life in relative seclusion.

Considered as a movement, mesmerism suggests some of the varieties of pre-Romanticism and popular science in the late eighteenth century. It did not spend itself as an intellectual force for almost a hundred years, as the mesmerist passages in the works of Hoffmann, Hugo, and Poe testify. But as a scientific theory mesmerism offered only a thin and unoriginal assortment of ideas. Although Mesmer's own writings contained little sustained theorizing, they provided enough for his enemies to detect all manner of occultist and vitalistic influences and to align him with William Maxwell, the Scottish physician, author of *De Medicina Magnetica* (1769), Robert Fludd, J. B. van Helmont, and Paracelsus—when they did not categorize him with Cagliostro. This version of his intellectual ancestry seems convincing enough, if one adds Newton and Mead to the list. But nothing proves that Mesmer was a charlatan. He seems to have

believed sincerely in his theory, although he also showed a fierce determination to convert it into cash: he charged ten louis a month for the use of his "tubs"; and he made a fortune from the Société de l'Harmonie Universelle, which, in return, claimed exclusive proprietorship of his deepest "secrets."

In terms of the development of medicine, the techniques of mesmerizing proved more influential than its theory. By concentrating on the "rapport" of patient and doctor, Mesmer seems to have dealt effectively with nervous disorders. He certainly had, to put it mildly, a forceful bedside manner; and in 1784 his followers, led by the Chastenet de Puységur brothers, extended mesmeric "rapport" into something new: mesmerically induced hypnosis. Later groups of hypnotists, particularly in the mesmerist sects of Lyons and Strasbourg, abandoned the hypothesis of a cosmic fluid. In the nineteenth century hypnosis, shorn of Mesmer's cosmology and perfected by James Braid and J. M. Charcot, became an accepted medical practice. And finally, through Charcot's impact on Freud, mesmerism exerted some influence on the development of psychoanalysis, another unorthodox product of the Viennese school.

BIBLIOGRAPHY

I. ORIGINAL WORKS. Mesmer's own works contain only a sketchy version of his system. The most important are *Dissertatio physico-medica de planetarum influxu* (Vienna, 1766); *Schreiben über die Magnetkur* (n.p., 1766); *Mémoire sur la découverte du magnétisme animal* (Geneva, 1779); *Précis historique des faits relatifs au magnétisme animal* (London, 1781); and *Mesmerismus oder System der Wechselwirkungen, Theorie und Anwendung des thierischen Magnetismus als die allgemeine Heilkunde zur Erhaltung des Menschen*, K. C. Wolfart, ed. (Berlin, 1814). There are some unpublished letters by Mesmer and his followers in the Bibliothèque Nationale, fonds français, 1690.

II. SECONDARY LITERATURE. For a thorough but incomplete bibliography of early works on Mesmer and mesmerism, see Alexis Dureau, *Notes bibliographiques pour servir à l'histoire du magnétisme animal* (Paris, 1869). Most of the important source material is contained in the fourteen enormous volumes of the mesmerist collection in the Bibliothèque Nationale, 4° Tb 62.1.

Biographies of Mesmer tend to treat him as a forgotten pioneer of hypnosis and Freudianism: Margaret Goldsmith, *Franz Anton Mesmer: The History of an Idea* (London, 1934); E. V. M. Louis, *Les origines de la doctrine du magnétisme animal: Mesmer et la Société de l'harmonie* (Paris, 1898); Rudolf Tischner, *Franz Anton Mesmer, Leben, Werk und Wirkungen* (Munich, 1928); Jean Vinchon, *Mesmer et son secret* (Paris, 1936); and Stefan Zweig, *Mental Healers: Franz Anton Mesmer, Mary Baker Eddy, Sigmund Freud* (London, 1933).

For a more scholarly treatment of aspects of Mesmer's life and thought, see R. Lenoir, "Le mesmérisme et le système du monde," in *Revue d'histoire de la philosophie*, **1** (1927), 192–219, 294–321; Bernhard Milt, *Franz Anton Mesmer und Seine Beziehungen zur Schweiz: Magie und Heilkunde zu Lavaters Zeit* (Zurich, 1953); and Frank Pattie, "Mesmer's Medical Dissertation and Its Debt to Mead's *De Imperio Solis ac Lunae*," in *Journal of the History of Medicine and Allied Sciences*, **11** (1956), 275–287.

Works concentrating on mesmerism as a movement rather than as a philosophy are Robert Darnton, *Mesmerism and the End of the Enlightenment in France* (Cambridge, Mass., 1968); and Louis Figuier, *Histoire du merveilleux dans les temps modernes*, 2nd ed., III (Paris, 1860).

ROBERT DARNTON

MESNIL, FÉLIX (*b*. Ormonville-la-Petite, Manche, France, 12 December 1868; *d*. Paris, France, 15 February 1938), *zoology, general biology, tropical medicine*.

Mesnil, whose family had been farmers in Normandy for several generations, attended the school in his village. One of his uncles, a physician in the navy, recognized Mesnil's exceptional ability and arranged for him to enter the lycée in Cherbourg and then the Lycée Saint-Louis in Paris. At the age of eighteen he was accepted by both the École Polytechnique and the École Normale Supérieure; he chose the latter because of the interest in natural history he had developed during his boyhood. He passed the *agrégation* in the natural sciences in 1891 and obtained his doctorate in 1895 with a work on the resistance of lower vertebrates to microbial invasions. After passing the *agrégation* he spent several months at universities in central Europe. Upon returning, he entered the Institut Pasteur and remained there throughout his career. While serving as assistant and secretary to Pasteur, he began to work in Metchnikoff's laboratory, where he acquired experimental technique. Mesnil became *agrégé préparateur* in 1892, laboratory director in 1898, and professor in 1910.

Mesnil's work was varied, much of it oriented toward general biology; important memoirs dealt with systematic, ecological, and ethological zoology. For more than thirty years, during summer vacations Mesnil had the opportunity to study—first alone and then, beginning in 1914, with his brother-in-law Caullery—the fauna of St. Martin Cove, near the Cap de la Hague, and of the neighboring coasts. This research resulted in the description of many new genera and species of annelids, crustaceans, enteropneusts, turbellarians, Orthonectida, and protozoans. A great number of investigations were devoted to the annelid polychaetes—to their morphology, in order to establish their phylogenetic relationships; to their sexual maturity (epitokous forms); and to their asexual reproduction (schizogenesis, regeneration). Mesnil, who was interested in parasitism, discovered that condition in the Monstrillidae. With Caullery, he described *Xenocoeloma brumpti*, a parasite of *Polycirrus arenivorus*; the two scientists furnished a precise analysis of its morphology, of the penetration of the larva into the annelid, and of its complex development. They also studied isopod parasites of sea acorns and spheromes; *Fecampia* (turbellarian rhabdocoeles that are internal parasites of crustaceans); and the Orthonectida and their life cycle.

Alone or with Caullery and A. Laveran (the latter discovered the hematozoon of malaria), Mesnil examined the parasitic protozoans: gregarines, coccidia, Myxosporidia, Microsporidia, infusoria, and flagellates. From 1900 to 1916 Mesnil was concerned especially with the trypanosomes and trypanosomiases: chemotherapy, determination of the species, experimental constitution of heritable strains, infectious power and virulence, reactions of the organism, and the resistance of certain strains to medicines and serums. He was also interested in natural and acquired immunity. He and Laveran devised the test that bears their names for detecting the specific identity of the trypanosomes.

Mesnil reported on many works in microbiology and general biology for various French journals. With G. Bertrand, A. Besredka, Amédée Borrel, C. Delezenne, and A. C. Marie he founded the *Bulletin de l'Institut Pasteur* and he was also its editor. In 1907 he participated in founding the Société de Pathologie Exotique, of which he was secretary-general (1908–1920), then vice-president and president (1924–1927).

Mesnil belonged to the Académie des Sciences (1921), the Académie de Médecine, and (as founding member) the Académie des Sciences Coloniales. He was a commander of the Légion d'Honneur. In 1920 he received the Mary Kingsley Medal of the Liverpool School of Tropical Medicine, and in 1926 C. M. Wenyon dedicated his *Textbook of Protistology* to Mesnil. Among Mesnil's students were E. Roubaud, E. Chalton, A. Lwof, and S. Volkonsky.

Mesnil's learning was prodigious and his memory legendary. Kind and easily approachable, he gave advice and support to everyone. The archives of the Académie des Sciences contain his portrait and autograph manuscripts.

BIBLIOGRAPHY

I. ORIGINAL WORKS. A complete bibliography is in *Titres et travaux scientifiques (1893–1920)* (Laval, 1921). Mesnil's major book was *Trypanosomes et trypanosomiases* (Paris, 1904; 2nd ed., enl., 1912), written with Laveran.

His early articles include "Sur la résistance des vertébrés inférieurs aux infections microbiennes artificielles," his doctoral diss., published in *Annales de l'Institut Pasteur*, **9** (1895), 301–351; "Études de morphologie externe chez les annélides. I. Les spionidiens des côtes de la Manche," in *Bulletin scientifique de la France et de la Belgique*, **29** (1896), 110–268; ". . . II. Remarques complémentaires sur les spionidiens. La nouvelle famille des disomidiens. La place des aonides" and ". . . III. Formes intermédiaires entre les maldaniens et les arénicoliens," *ibid.*, **30** (1897), 83–101 and 144–168; ". . . IV. La famille nouvelle des levinséniens. Révision des ariciens. Affinités des deux familles. Les apistobranchiens," *ibid.*, **31** (1898), 126–149, written with Caullery.

Between 1900 and 1910 he wrote "Recherches sur l'*Hemioniscus balani* épicaride parasite des balanes," in *Bulletin scientifique de la France et de la Belgique*, **34** (1901), 316–362, written with Caullery; "Recherches sur les orthonectides," in *Archives d'anatomie microscopique*, **4** (1901), 381–470, written with Caullery; "Les trypanosomes des poissons," in *Archiv für Protistenkunde*, **1** (1902), 475–498, written with Laveran; "Recherches sur les *Fecampia*, turbellariés rhabdocèles parasites internes des crustacés," in *Annales de la Faculté des sciences de Marseille*, **13** (1903), 131–167, written with Caullery; "Contribution à l'étude des entéropneustes," in *Zoologische Jahrbuch Abteilung für Anatomie*, **20** (1904), 227–256, written with Caullery; "Recherches sur les haplosporidies," in *Archives de zoologie expérimentale et générale*, 4th ser., **4** (1905), 101–181, written with Caullery; and "Sur les propriétés préventives du sérum des animaux trypanosomiés. Races résistantes à ces sérums," in *Annales de l'Institut Pasteur*, **23** (1909), 129–154, written with E. Brimont.

After 1910 he published "Sur deux monstrilides parasites d'annélides," in *Bulletin scientifique de la France et de la Belgique*, **48** (1914), 15–29, written with Caullery; "Notes biologiques sur les mares à *Lithothamnion* de la Hague," in *Bulletin de la Société zoologique de France*, **40** (1915), 160–161, 176–178, 198–200, written with Caullery; "*Xenocoeloma brumpti*, copépode parasite de *Polycirrus arenivorus*," in *Bulletin biologique de la France et de la Belgique*, **53** (1919), 161–233, written with Caullery; and "*Ancyroniscus bonnieri*, épicaride parasite d'un sphéromide (*Dynamene bidentulata*)," *ibid.*, **44** (1920), 1–36, written with Caullery.

II. SECONDARY LITERATURE. Obituaries include M. Caullery, in *Presse médicale*, no. 21 (12 Mar. 1938), 401–402; and in *Bulletin biologique de la France et de la Belgique*, **77** (1938); and G. Ramon, in *Bulletin de l'Académie de médecine*, **119** (1938), 241–247. Unsigned obituaries are in *Bulletin de la Société de pathologie exotique*, **31** (1938), 173–177; *Bulletin de l'Institut Pasteur*, **36** (1938), 177–179; *Annales de l'Institut Pasteur*, **60** (1938), 221–226; and *Archives de l'Institut Pasteur*, **16** (1938), 1–2.

ANDRÉE TÉTRY

MESSAHALA. See **Māshāllāh.**

MESSIER, CHARLES (*b.* Badonviller, Lorraine, France, 26 June 1730; *d.* Paris, France, 11 or 12 April 1817), *astronomy.*

Messier was the tenth of twelve children; his father died when the boy was eleven years old. In October 1751 he arrived in Paris, where (according to J. B. Delambre, virtually the sole biographical source) he had only a neat, legible hand and some practice in drawing to recommend him. The astronomer Joseph-Nicolas Delisle hired him to record observations and to copy maps of Peking and of the great wall of China. In 1755 Delisle, by trading his large collection of books and maps to the French government, received for himself an annuity and for Messier an appointment as clerk with a salary of 500 francs plus room and board at the observatory in the Hôtel de Cluny. There Messier undertook the series of observations that gradually secured his fame.

In 1759 the comet predicted by Halley reached perihelion, and in anticipation of the return Delisle set Messier on a systematic search for the object. Unfortunately the perturbations from Jupiter were underestimated and Messier surveyed too restricted an area. Finally he recovered the comet on 21 January 1759, but Delisle demanded strict secrecy. Unknown to French astronomers, Halley's comet had already been observed in Saxony; and only after this news reached Paris did Delisle reveal Messier's discovery. The incorrigible Delisle followed the same procedure with a comet that Messier discovered on 21 January 1760.

Soon thereafter Delisle, who was in his seventies, retired and left Messier to carry out comet searches. For the next fifteen years Messier claimed a virtual monopoly on comet discoveries. According to Lalande, Messier observed a total of forty-one comets, claiming twenty-one as his own (*Bibliographie astronomique* [Paris, 1803], 796). By stricter modern standards twelve or thirteen initial discoveries from Comet 1759 III to Comet 1798 I, and three additional independent ones, can be attributed to him. J.-F. La Harpe records that Messier's having to tend his wife on her deathbed cost him the discovery of yet another comet, which was identified instead by a certain Montagne of Limoges. When friends consoled him for the loss he had suffered, he wept for the comet and barely remembered to sigh, "Ah, cette pauvre femme."

As a result of these discoveries Messier became a member of the Royal Society of London in 1764 and of the academies at Berlin and St. Petersburg, and his title was changed from clerk to *astronome*. The French savants were reluctant to admit a mere observer to their academy, but finally in 1770, two years after Delisle's death, he gained entry. Ultimately he also became a member of several academies in Sweden, of the Netherlands Society of Sciences, and of the Institute of Bologna; and in 1806 he received the cross of the Legion of Honor.

Immediately after his election to the Academy, Messier began publication of a long series of memoirs, invariably devoted to observations and often accompanied by elegant maps of his own design. His first memoir, "Catalogue des nébuleuses et des amas d'étoiles, que l'on découvre parmi les étoiles fixes" (*Mémoires de mathématiques et physique de l'Académie des sciences* for 1771 [1774], 435–461), remains his most enduring contribution. In it he describes forty-five of what are today the most celebrated nebulae and clusters, including M1, the Crab Nebula; M13, the globular star cluster in Hercules; and M31, the Andromeda Galaxy.

In 1780 Messier added twenty-three new objects, publishing a list of sixty-eight objects in the *Connoissance des temps* for 1783. A year later he again augmented his list, to a total of 103, for the *Connoissance des temps* for 1784; many of the new nebulae were first found by his colleague P. F. A. Méchain. The two supplements revealed for the first time the remarkable abundance of faint nebulae in the constellations Virgo and Coma Berenices, now recognized as the Virgo cluster of galaxies.

At various times Messier used over a dozen telescopes for his observations, but none larger than his favorite 7.5-inch Gregorian. His contemporary Jean-Sylvain Bailly carried out some experimental comparisons showing that the inefficient speculum metal surfaces of the reflector gave it a light-gathering power equivalent to a 3.5-inch refractor. Messier also undertook observations with one of the new Dollond achromatic refractors, which had an aperture of 3.5 inches and a magnification of 120. These small telescopes stand in marked contrast to the giant reflectors constructed by William Herschel during Messier's lifetime. Herschel quickly outstripped Messier's brief list, finding literally thousands of faint nebulae. Looking back on his work, Messier wrote in the *Connaissance des temps* for 1800/1801:

> What caused me to undertake the catalog was the nebula I discovered above the southern horn of Taurus on September 12, 1758, while observing the comet of that year. . . . This nebula had such a resemblance to a comet, in its form and brightness, that I endeavored to find others, so that astronomers would not confuse these same nebulae with comets just beginning to shine. I

observed further with the proper refractors for the search of comets, and this is the purpose I had in forming the catalog. After me, the celebrated Herschel published a catalog of 2,000 that he had observed. This unveiling of the sky, made with instruments of great aperture, does not help in a perusal of the sky for faint comets. Thus my object is different from his, as I only need nebulae visible in a telescope of two feet [length].

Besides the comets and nebulae Messier observed eclipses, occultations, sunspots, the new planet Uranus, and the transits of Mercury and Venus. In 1767 he sailed aboard the *Aurore* for nearly four months, testing instruments for longitude determinations at the request of the Academy. A man of single-minded purpose, he pressed his observational abilities to the utmost but, unskilled in mathematics, left the calculations to others.

On 6 November 1781 a severe accident interrupted Messier's observing for an entire year. Walking in a park with his friend Bochart de Saron, a presiding judge of the Parlement of Paris, Messier entered what he assumed to be a grotto. Instead it was an icehouse; and he fell nearly twenty-five feet onto the ice, breaking an arm, thigh, wrist, and two ribs. Although he was attended by the leading Academy surgeons, Messier sustained a permanent limp.

In 1802, when Messier was seventy-two, Herschel visited Paris and wrote in his diary:

> A few days ago I saw Mr. Messier at his lodgings. He complained of having suffered much from his accident of falling into an ice cellar. He is still very assiduous in observing, and regretted that he had not interest enough to get the windows mended in a kind of tower where his instruments are; but keeps up his spirits. He appeared to be a very sensible man in conversation. Merit is not always rewarded as it ought to be.

As Harlow Shapley wrote in *Star Clusters* (New York, 1930), ". . . the systematic listing by Messier in 1784 marked an epoch in the recording of observations. . . . He is remembered for his catalogue; forgotten as the applause-seeking discoverer of comets."

BIBLIOGRAPHY

I. ORIGINAL WORKS. Messier's bibliography is found in J. M. Quérard, *La France littéraire*, V (Paris, 1830), 90–91. Messier published detailed accounts of his lifetime of observations, with incidental biographical material, in *Connaissance des tems* for 1798–1799, 1799–1800, 1800–1801, 1807–1808, 1809, and 1810. His catalog of nebulae and clusters, cited in the text, found its final form in *Connoissance des temps* for 1784 (Paris, 1781), 227–269. For an English trans. of this paper, see Kenneth Glyn

Jones, "The Search for the Nebulae—VIII," in *Journal of the British Astronomical Association*, **79** (1969), 357–370.

II. SECONDARY LITERATURE. The principal sources are J. B. Delambre's "Notice," in *Histoire de l'Académie royale des sciences de l'Institut de France* for 1817 (1819), 83–92; and his somewhat rewritten biography in *Histoire de l'astronomie au dix-huitième siècle* (Paris, 1827), 767–774; see also J.-F. La Harpe, *Correspondance littéraire*, 6 vols. in 5 (Paris, 1801–1807), I, 97–98.

Recent material includes Owen Gingerich, "Messier and His Catalogue," in *Sky and Telescope*, **12** (1953), 255–258, 288–291; and Kenneth Glyn Jones, *Messier's Nebulae and Star Clusters* (London, 1968), 376–410. See also C. Flammarion, "Nébuleuse et amas d'étoiles de Messier," in *Bulletin de la Société astronomique de France*, **31** (1917), 385–400.

OWEN GINGERICH

MESYATSEV, IVAN ILLARIONOVICH (*b.* 1885; *d.* Moscow, U.S.S.R., 7 May 1940), *earth science, oceanography.*

In 1908 Mesyatsev entered the natural sciences section of the department of physics and mathematics of Moscow University. During his student years he displayed great ability in teaching and research; and in 1912, after he graduated from the university, he remained in the department of invertebrate zoology to prepare for a professorship.

Although Mesyatsev's first works were in embryology, histology, and protozoology, his scientific interests later became more involved with marine ichthyology and its application to the fishing industry. In 1920 he headed a pioneering group of Soviet zoologists who worked on a plan to set up the first special scientific oceanographic institute in the country, the Plavmornin.

Established in 1921, Plavmornin was oriented to research on the country's northern seas, especially the Barents Sea. Mesyatsev was placed in charge of all its expeditionary activity, and in 1928 was appointed its director. He organized the construction of the institute's special scientific ship, the *Perseus*, and its systematic research expeditions on the Barents Sea. He himself participated in many of these trips. Mesyatsev succeeded, through careful study of the biology and environment of fish in that sea, in establishing its rich potential for the fishing industry.

Mesyatsev was director of the State Oceanographic Institute from 1929 and manager of the oceanography laboratory of the All-Union Scientific-Research Institute of Ocean Fishing Economy and Oceanography from 1933.

In 1934, as president of the Government Commission for the Determination of Fish Resources of the Caspian Sea, Mesyatsev developed a special method for measuring the supply of fish, which was later used by other specialists in the Sea of Azov. In 1937–1939 Mesyatsev came to conclusions, important for the fishing industry, about the behavior of schools of fish and introduced into ichthyology a clear definition of schooling.

Despite his great load of scientific and administrative work, Mesyatsev found time for teaching as professor of zoology at Moscow University.

BIBLIOGRAPHY

I. ORIGINAL WORKS. Mesyatsev's most important works are "K embriologii mollyuskov" ("Toward an Embryology of Mollusks"), in *Dnevnik zoologicheskogo otdelenia Obshchestva lyubiteley estestvoznania, antropologii i ethografii*, n.s., **1**, no. 4 (1913); *Plavychy morskoy nauchny institut i ego eksepditsia 1921 god. Otchet nachalnika polyarnoy eksepditsii* ("The Floating Ocean Scientific Institute and Its Expedition of 1921: An Account by the Chief of the Polar Expedition"; Moscow, 1922); *Materialy k zoogeografii russkikh severnykh morey* ("Material for a Zoogeography of the Russian Northern Oceans"; Moscow, 1923); "Stroenie kosyakov rybnykh stad" ("The Structure of Schools of Fish"), in *Izvestia Akademii nauk SSSR, seria biologicheskaya*, no. 3 (1937); "O strukture kosyakov treski" ("On the Structure of Schools of Cod"), in *Trudy VNIRO*, IV (Moscow, 1939).

II. SECONDARY LITERATURE. See the foreword to *Trudy VNIRO*, LX (Moscow, 1966); "Kratkaya biografia I. I. Mesyatsev" ("A Short Biography of I. I. Mesyatsev"), in *Bolshaya sovetskaya entsiklopedia* ("Great Soviet Encyclopedia"), 2nd ed., XXVII (1954), 209; and A. D. Starostin, "Zhizn i nauchnaya deyatelnost I. I. Mesyatseva" ("Life and Scientific Career of I. I. Mesyatsev"), in *Trudy VNIRO*, LX (Moscow, 1966), 11–18.

A. F. PLAKHOTNIK

METCHNIKOFF, ELIE (*b.* Ivanovka, Kharkov Province, Russia, 16 May 1845; *d.* Paris, France, 15 July 1916), *embryology, comparative anatomy, pathology, bacteriology, immunology.*

Elie was the youngest of the five children of Ilia Ivanovitch Metchnikoff and Emilia Nevahovna, the daughter of the Jewish writer Leo Nevahovna. His mother played an important role in the boy's education and encouraged his scientific career. A tutor to the family stimulated Elie to become interested in the wonders of natural history at an early age. In 1856 he enrolled in the Kharkov Lycée, where he made a splendid academic record, his main passion being biology. At this time he read Buckle's *History of*

Civilization in England, and throughout his life strongly adhered to one of Buckle's main tenets, that through science would come man's advancement.

Elie's mother dissuaded him from the study of medicine because she believed that he was too sensitive for such a career. He did win her approval to study physiology and zoology, to which he increasingly devoted his life. The seventeen-year-old student was especially interested in the subject of protoplasm and decided to go to Würzburg to study with Koelliker. The German term did not begin in September. Disappointed, lonely, and bewildered in the strange city, Metchnikoff hurried back home, content to study for two years at the university in Kharkov. In 1864 he studied the sea fauna on the North Sea island of Heligoland, a naturalist's paradise. Here the botanist Ferdinand Cohn gave Metchnikoff friendly guidance and advised him to continue his work with Rudolf Leuckart at Giessen. Metchnikoff made his first real scientific discovery in Leuckart's laboratory when he found an interesting example of alternation of generations (sexual and asexual) in nematodes. In Giessen, Metchnikoff also read Fritz Müller's *Für Darwin.* The German enthusiasm for the theory of evolution greatly influenced him. He worked feverishly and began to suffer from severe eyestrain. This malady prevented him for a time from using his chief research tool, the microscope.

In 1865 Metchnikoff went to Naples, where he began a systematic study of the development of germ layers in invertebrate embryos, a subject less well understood at the time than the similar development in vertebrate embryos. Metchnikoff devoted many years to studying the comparative development of the embryonic layers of lower animals. Like many zoologists of the immediate post-*Origin of Species* period, Metchnikoff's constant aim was to show that in their development the lower animals follow a plan similar to that of the higher animals. He thus attempted to establish a definite link between the two divisions and to add to the theory of evolution. In Naples he befriended another young Russian zoologist, Aleksandr Kovalevsky, with whom he collaborated on several embryological studies.

Because cholera was epidemic in Naples in the autumn of 1865, Metchnikoff decided to continue his studies in Germany. He went to Göttingen, where he briefly worked with W. M. Keferstein and then with Henle. In the following summer he went to Munich to study with Siebold. After again doing research together in Naples, Kovalevsky and Metchnikoff returned to Russia in 1867 to obtain their doctoral degrees in St. Petersburg. For their work on the development of germ layers in invertebrate embryos,

they shared the prestigious Karl Ernst von Baer prize, presented by the discoverer of the human ovum. Metchnikoff also received a faculty position at the new University of Odessa. At age twenty-two the instructor was younger than some of his pupils. He soon was embroiled in a controversy with a senior colleague over attendance at a scientific meeting. The conflict was resolved, but Metchnikoff thought the atmosphere at the university in St. Petersburg would be more conducive to work and teaching and when he was offered a job there in 1868 he gladly accepted. The move proved a disappointment, for the working conditions were, if anything, worse than in Odessa. Metchnikoff was barely able to make ends meet, and he led a lonely existence.

He did meet Ludmilla Federovna, who on one occasion nursed him during an illness. They were married in 1869. Trouble was already on the horizon. The bride was disabled by severe "bronchitis," and she had to be carried to the church in a chair. For the next five years Metchnikoff devoted himself to caring for his wife, who subsequently died of the tuberculous disease already present on her wedding day. To enable him to take Ludmilla to a warmer climate, he did translations besides his teaching and researches. His eyesight again weakened, and he became extremely distraught. In the winter of 1873 he hurried to Madeira to see Ludmilla, who by now was extremely sick. She died in April 1873, and Metchnikoff collapsed. He did not attend the funeral and on his way back to Russia attempted suicide. He swallowed a large dose of morphine, which caused him to vomit, thereby sparing his life.

After this period of tragedy and exhaustion, Metchnikoff slowly returned to his scientific work, but his eyesight was not sufficiently restored to allow microscopic work. Instead he planned an anthropological trip to the Kalmuk steppes, where he observed the natives and carried out comparative physical measurements. He concluded that the development of Mongol natives was arrested in comparison with that of the Caucasian race, although relative bodily proportions were the same. He ascribed the growth lag of the Kalmuks to a state of slight but chronic intoxication, which was the effect of the habitual drinking of fermented milk.

The trip helped Metchnikoff to recover from the hardships of the previous five years and restored his eyesight. He again returned to his job in Odessa, to which he had been recalled in 1872. Metchnikoff was already well established in the scientific world by this time. He had published twenty-five papers, most of which dealt with the development and characteristics of invertebrates, and Odessa afforded him ample material for collecting sea fauna. Moreover, he was a successful and popular lecturer. In 1875 he married Olga Belokopitova, a young student who lived with her large family in the apartment directly over Metchnikoff's. It was a happy marriage, and his wife was a devoted companion and co-worker for the remainder of his life.

Political pressures, student unrest, and Olga's severe bout of typhoid fever in 1880 led Metchnikoff to a second suicide attempt. He injected himself with the spirochete of relapsing fever. A long illness resulted, but he recovered with a renewed zest for life. Cardiac disturbances, from which he suffered in his last years, seem to have begun with his bout of relapsing fever, but the eyestrain, a great cause of worry and inconvenience in earlier years, never did return.

In 1880 the Metchnikoffs spent the summer on Mme Metchnikoff's family farm. A beetle infestation was destroying the grainfields, and Metchnikoff studied the insects and found that some had died from a fungus infection. He conceived the idea of starting an epidemic among the beetles. After experimenting with the idea in the laboratory, he had some success in its implementation in the fields. This study was the starting point for his interest in the infectious diseases. A remarkably similar chain of events occurred in the career of Pasteur, who would in future years play a significant role in Metchnikoff's life.

By 1882 the unrest in Russia, and at the University of Odessa in particular, was so great that the non-political Metchnikoff wished to leave for the quiet atmosphere of Messina, where he could better devote himself to science. In Messina he made his greatest scientific discovery, the role of phagocytes in the defense of the animal body; but the related strands of this concept of the cellular mechanism of immunity had begun to take shape somewhat earlier.

While working in Giessen in 1865, Metchnikoff had studied and observed intracellular digestion in roundworm (*Fabricia*). He compared this type of digestion to that found in some protozoans and saw in the similarity one more proof of a genetic connection between a lower and somewhat higher animal form. A dozen years later he published another paper that dealt with the digestive process and in 1880 "Über die intracelluläre Verdauung bei Coelenteraten." Here he showed that endodermal and mesodermal cells take up carmine granules suspended in water. He did not discover the exact mode of uptake of dye by the cell.

This phenomenon was not an original discovery by Metchnikoff. In 1862 Ernst Haeckel had described in his monograph on *Radiolaria* white blood cells ingesting dye particles. Several other investigators reported similar results, but it was Metchnikoff who made the proper interpretation and who realized the significance of the link between phagocytic digestion and the body's defense.

In Messina in 1882 Metchnikoff observed that the mobile cells in a transparent starfish larva surrounded intruding foreign bodies, a phenomenon similar to the inflammatory response in animals with a vascular system. These mobile cells were derived not from the endoderm, the layer that gives rise to the digestive system, but from the mesoderm. Metchnikoff reasoned correctly that these mesodermal cells might serve in the defense of the animal against intruders and that this observation had very wide implications. He devoted the next twenty-five years to the development and popularization of his theory. As he later explained, "Thus it was in Messina that the great event of my scientific life took place. A zoologist until then, I suddenly became a pathologist."

Both Kleinenberg and Virchow, who were in Messina that summer of 1882, encouraged Metchnikoff. Carl Claus in Vienna urged Metchnikoff to publish his findings, and in 1883 the first of many papers appeared in which Metchnikoff explored the newly developing field of immunology. In Claus's *Arbeiten*, Metchnikoff first used the term phagocyte, derived from the Greek, instead of *Fresszellen* (eating cells). Metchnikoff had been studying the evolution of the alimentary tract. One question that had arisen was whether the lower metazoa retained the power of using mesodermal and also endodermal cells for digestion. He observed that in starfish larvae the wandering or mobile cells of mesodermal origin were active in the metamorphosis of the larva. These cells resorbed the parts of the larva that were no longer used. By simple experiment Metchnikoff showed that it was but a short step from resorption of useless parts to a similar role when a foreign particle was introduced into the organism.

In the next years Metchnikoff showed that the mobile cells (the white blood corpuscles) of the higher animals and man also developed from the mesodermal layer of the embryo and were responsible for ridding the body of foreign invaders, especially bacteria. Although Virchow supported him and published Metchnikoff's papers in his *Archiv für pathologische Anatomie und Physiologie und für klinische Medizin*, the phagocyte theory ran counter to many commonly held theories of the time.

For instance, Julius Cohnheim, a pupil of Virchow's, had shown that the pus cells of the inflammatory process were derivatives of the bloodstream, and not of the surrounding connective tissue, as Virchow had claimed. Cohnheim further maintained that without blood vessels to bring the white blood cells, there could be no inflammation. Metchnikoff claimed that the action of mobile cells in clearing an organism of foreign material or no-longer-useful parts was a form of inflammation. According to Metchnikoff, furthermore, one could observe this action in starfish larva altogether lacking a vascular system.

A serious objection to this new theory of bodily defense was the currently held idea that the white blood cells took up invading particles or bacteria and spread them throughout the body. These phagocytes of Metchnikoff were then far from salutary and were believed to be helpful to the invader rather than to the host. There was also the usual resistance to major innovations in thought or approach.

Metchnikoff had been in a number of scientific and personal fights in his early career, and it was natural that he now became a staunch defender of his new theory. He devised new experiments and new arguments and warded off one attack after another upon his brainchild. Much of his voluminous writing in the years 1883 to 1910 was dedicated to elaboration or modification of the role of phagocytes in inflammation and immunity; but he always held tenaciously to the underlying idea of the central role of the phagocytes.

By 1886 Metchnikoff was well known as a biologist and also as a microbiologist and pathologist, and was invited back to Odessa, where he had taught from 1873 to 1882. The city had established a bacteriological institute similar to the Pasteur Institute of Paris. In Odessa there was to be a combination of basic research and the production of antirabies vaccine.

Metchnikoff headed the Institute in 1886 and part of 1887, but found that the internal strife among the members and his inability to carry out immunizations himself, because he was not a physician, combined to make life and work there unpleasant. He and his wife traveled to various centers in Europe in search of a congenial place to settle. It was Pasteur in Paris who made them most welcome and who gave Metchnikoff a laboratory in which to work. In 1888 the Metchnikoffs moved to Paris, where Elie worked for the last twenty-eight years of his life. This was an honorary position because Metchnikoff had sufficient income from his parents-in-law's estate to live without salary.

Metchnikoff quickly became a revered member of the small circle of the Institute, where friendships and working relationships were close. He began to attract students to his laboratory and set most of them to work answering the various objections to the theory of phagocytosis, elucidating ways in which the white blood cells were attracted to and ingested bacteria, or determining how, in general, the mechanism of immunity worked. Among his many talented students

was Bordet, who in 1919 received the Nobel Prize for his work on complement fixation.

Metchnikoff also gave public lectures, for he believed the popularization of science to be important. In 1891 he delivered a series of talks on inflammation. In these talks Metchnikoff dealt with the history of the various theories of inflammation and their investigation, and chiefly with the role of phagocytes in the animal kingdom. The lectures were well-attended and Pasteur himself came. The series was published as *Leçons sur la pathologie comparée de l'inflammation* in 1892 and in English translation in the following year.

Metchnikoff felt that the decade 1895–1905 was the happiest period of his life. He and his wife lived outside of Paris in Sèvres, and he came to the Institute each morning by train. He continued his research in immunity and also into the problem of fever and the mechanisms of infection. While attending the International Medical Congress in Paris in 1900, he realized that there should be a summary of his and his antagonists' different theories. He began to write a large and comprehensive book, *L'immunité dans les maladies infectieuses* (1901). This book was a magnificent review of the entire field of both comparative and human immunology. The work was also, of course, a defense of the theory of phagocytosis, which the humoral theory of immunity seriously challenged. The work of the German bacteriologists, especially Emil Behring, Paul Ehrlich, and Robert Koch, which led to discovery of many new bacteria, toxins, and antitoxins, strengthened the beliefs of those who held to a noncellular theory of immunity. Even before the English edition of *Immunity in Infectious Diseases* was issued in 1905, two British investigators, A. E. Wright and S. R. Douglas, put forth their theory of opsonins, which postulated that something in the fluid portions of the blood helped the white blood cells to digest bacteria. Hence a compromise was beginning to take shape. In 1908 Metchnikoff and Ehrlich shared the Nobel Prize for their researches illuminating the understanding of immunity.

After the *Immunity* was finished, Metchnikoff turned his attention to the problems of aging and the idea of death. With his friend and co-worker Émile Roux, he began to study syphilis, one disease that was known to be implicated in cardiovascular pathology. In 1903 Metchnikoff and Roux discovered that syphilis was transmissible to monkeys, thereby destroying the old theory that the disease was exclusively human and inaccessible to experiment. They also showed the importance and efficacy of early treatment of the primary lesion with mercurial ointment.

In a series of books and lectures between 1903 and 1910 Metchnikoff developed his thoughts on the prolongation of life. He stressed proper hygienic and dietary rules. His idea of orthobiosis, or right living, included careful attention to the flora of the intestinal canal. He believed that intestinal putrefaction was harmful and that the introduction of lactic-acid bacilli, as in yogurt, accounted for the longevity of the Bulgars. He introduced sour milk into his own diet and thought that his health improved. Although his name became associated with a commercial yogurt preparation, he had not endorsed it and realized no profit from it.

In his *Nature of Man* Metchnikoff argued that when diseases have been suppressed and life has been hygienically regulated, death would come only with extreme old age. Death would then be natural, accepted gratefully, and robbed of its terrors.

The outbreak of World War I in 1914 was a profound shock to Metchnikoff. Not only was there an interruption of the work of the Pasteur Institute, but Metchnikoff was forced to acknowledge that science had not yet brought man to that stage of civilization which he had envisioned. When he became ill and weaker in the summer of 1916, he faced death placidly, according to the tenets of his own philosophy. He was moved from his country house to the rooms at the Pasteur Institute that had been occupied by Pasteur. There he died of cardiac failure on 15 July 1916.

BIBLIOGRAPHY

I. ORIGINAL WORKS. A complete list of Metchnikoff's arts. and bks. is available in the Zeiss trans. of Olga Metchnikoff's biog. (see below). A less complete list may be found in the English trans. and in the Dover repr. of the *Lectures on Inflammation*. "Metchnikoff" is the preferred spelling. The name appears that way on the French original eds. of his work. American catalogs usually list it under "Mechnikov."

The major bks. by Metchnikoff that have been translated into English are included here. The French original and the German translations often predated the English by one to four years: *Lectures on the Comparative Pathology of Inflammation*, delivered at the Pasteur Institute in 1891, trans. by F. A. and E. H. Starling (London, 1893), repr. with a new intro. by Arthur M. Silverstein (New York, 1968); *The Nature of Man; Studies in Optimistic Philosophy*, trans. by P. C. Mitchell (New York, 1903); *Immunity in Infectious Diseases*, trans. by F. G. Binnie (Cambridge, 1905), repr. with a new intro. by Gert H. Brieger (New York, 1968); *The New Hygiene. Three Lectures on the Prevention of Infectious Diseases* (London, 1906); *The Prolongation of Life: Optimistic Studies*, trans. by P. C. Mitchell (New York, 1908); and *The Founders of Modern Medicine; Pasteur, Koch, Lister*, trans. by D. Berger (New York, 1939), which was originally published in 1933.

II. SECONDARY LITERATURE. The most important source for details of Metchnikoff's life and work is the memoir written by his wife, Olga Metchnikoff, *Life of Elie Metchnikoff 1845–1916*, trans. by E. Ray Lankester (Boston, 1921). Heinz Zeiss translated the original French into a German ed., *Elias Metschnikow, Leben und Werk* (Jena, 1932), in which he included many additional letters, excellent nn., and the most complete bibliog. of Metchnikoff's writings that I have seen. A. Besredka, a devoted student and co-worker, wrote *Histoire d'une idée, l'oeuvre de E. Metchnikoff* (Paris, 1921). Pierre Lépine, *Elie Metchnikoff et l'immunologie* (Vichy, 1966), is helpful for personal details and for its many photographs.

Useful arts. include Alice G. Elftman, "Metchnikoff as a Zoologist," in *Victor Robinson Memorial Volume* (New York, 1948), 49–60; R. B. Vaughn, "The Romantic Rationalist, a Study of Elie Metchnikoff," in *Medical History*, **10** (1965), 201–215; and Denise Wrotnowska, "Elie Metchnikoff quelques documents inédits conservés au Musée Pasteur," in *Archives internationales d'histoire des sciences*, **21** (1968), 115–136.

GERT H. BRIEGER

METIUS, ADRIAEN (*b.* Alkmaar, Netherlands, 3 December 1571; *d.* Franeker, Frisia [now Netherlands], 1635), *mathematics, instrument making*; **[METIUS], ADRIAEN ANTHONISZ** (*b.* Alkmaar [?], Netherlands, *ca.* 1543; *d.* Alkmaar [?], 20 November 1620), *military engineering, cartography*; **METIUS, JACOB** (*b.* Alkmaar, Netherlands; *d.* Alkmaar, June 1628), *mathematics, instrument making*.

The father, Adriaen Anthonisz, was a cartographer and military engineer for the States of Holland, and between 1582 and 1601 he was burgomaster of Alkmaar several times. In an unpublished pamphlet *Tegens de quadrature des circkels van Mr. Simon van Eycke* (1584), he gave, according to his son Adriaen (1625), the value of 355/113 for what we now denote by π, stating that it differs from the true value by less than 1/100,000. He obtained it by averaging numerators and denominators of the values 377/120 and 333/106. (This value had already been obtained by Tsu Chung-chih in the fifth century.) Anthonisz built fortifications in the war against Spain, drew charts of cities and military works, and wrote on sundials and astronomical problems. In the receipt for his burial the name Metius, adopted by some of his sons, is mentioned. The origin of the name is uncertain: some derive it from Metz, others from the family name Schelven (*schelf = rick =* Latin *meta*), it may also simply be related to *metiri* (to measure). Anthonisz and his wife Suida Dircksd. had one daughter and six sons, of whom two, Adriaen and Jacob, became widely known.

The second son, Adriaen, educated at the Latin school in Alkmaar, entered the recently founded University of Franeker in Frisia in 1589, and in 1594 continued his studies at the University of Leiden. Among his teachers in Leiden were the mathematicians Rudolf Snellius and Van Ceulen. Like his townsman Blaeu, Adriaen worked under Tycho Brahe at his observatory on the island of Hven; he then went to Rostock and Jena, where in 1595 he gave his first lectures. He returned to the Netherlands where he assisted his father in his military engineering until, in 1598, he was appointed professor extraordinarius at Franeker; in the same year he published his first book, *Doctrina spherica*.

Adriaen became professor ordinarius of mathematics, surveying, navigation, military engineering, and astronomy at Franeker in 1600, a position he held until his death. He bought mathematical and astronomical instruments, observed sunspots, and showed familiarity with the telescope, of which his brother Jacob was a coinventor. He especially appreciated its use for measuring instruments. In his *Geometria practica* (Franeker, 1625) he described a triangulation of part of Frisia, made shortly after Rudolf Snellius' son Willebrord had published his triangulation of the west Netherlands in *Eratosthenes batavus* (1617). Adriaen was a popular and efficient teacher who stressed the training of Frisian surveyors. His lectures were well attended by an international audience including, in 1629, Descartes. In 1625 Adriaen received an honorary doctorate in medicine from Franeker. He was married twice, first to Jetske Andreae, and then to Cecelia Vertest. He left no children. His motto was "Simpliciter et sine strepitu."

Adriaen's books cover all fields that he taught, and although they show little originality, they were widely used in his time. He followed Tycho Brahe's theory of the solar system, but also showed respect for the Copernican system. While not accepting astrology, he did believe in alchemy, and spent money in the search for the transmutation of metals.

His brother Jacob was as shy as Adriaen was sociable. He became an instrument maker in Alkmaar, specializing in the grinding of lenses. He made several inventions but rarely showed them to others, even to his brother. He was one of the claimants to the invention of the telescope, and is mentioned as such by Descartes in his *Dioptrique* (1637). Jacob was indeed one of the first to bring a concave and a convex lens together in a tube, thus constructing a telescope. In 1608 he applied for a patent on such an instrument but unfortunately a similar request had been made a few weeks earlier by H. Lippershey of Middelburg. This disappointment may have intensified Jacob's shyness. Adriaen, in several of his books after 1614, refers to his brother's "perspicilla" (telescope). He expresses the hope that he would allow others to share in his discoveries, but Jacob remained secretive. Before his death he destroyed his instruments so that, as a contemporary said, "the perfection of his art has died and been buried with him."

BIBLIOGRAPHY

I. ORIGINAL WORKS. A satisfactory bibliography of Adriaen Metius' works does not exist. Boeles lists seventeen titles, de Waard eighteen, and Bierens De Haan thirty-three, but some are reprints, trans., or collections. Boeles also lists a map of Frisia and a celestial globe from J. Janssonius' cartographic workshop (1648). Some titles are *Institutiones astronomiae et geographicae*, found together with *Geographische Onderwysinghe, waer in ghehandeld wordt die Beschryvinghe ende Afmetinghe des Aertsche Globe* (Franeker, 1614; Amsterdam, 1621); *Arithmetica et geometrica nova* (Franeker, 1625); *Arithmeticae libri II et geometriae libri VI. Hic adiungitur trigonometriae planorum methodus succincta* (Leiden, 1626); *Geometria practica* (Franeker, 1625), which states that "Parens P. M. illustrium D. D. Ordinum Confoederatarum Belgiae Provinciarum Geometra" found $\pi = 355/113$ (pp. 88–89; "P. M." is clearly "pia memoria"—Anthonisz died in 1620—and not P. Metius, as has occasionally been claimed to justify the term "ratio of Metius"); *Maet-constigh Lineael . . . alsmede de Sterckten-Bouwinghe ofte Fortificatie* (Franeker, 1626), which is a trans. of part of *Arithmeticae libri II . . .*, in which is described an early form of a calculating mechanism; *Eeuwighe Handt-calendrier* (Amsterdam, 1627; Rotterdam, 1628); *Tafelen van de Declinatie des Sons* (Franeker, 1627); *Astronomische ende Geographische Onderwysinghe* (Amsterdam, 1632); *Manuale arithmeticae et geometriae practica* (Franeker, 1633; 1646); *Opera omnia astronomia* (Amsterdam, 1632–1633), which contains the *canon sinuum, tangentium et secantium ad radium* 10,000,000.

II. SECONDARY LITERATURE. On the father and sons see C. de Waard, "Anthonisz" and "Metius," in *Nieuw Nederlandsch Biographisch Woordenboek*, I (Leiden, 1911), 155–158, 1325–1329 (in Dutch). In "Anthonisz," he gives an account of Anthonisz' MSS and published material. On Anthonisz' value of π see D. Bierens De Haan, "Adriaan Metius," in *Bouwstoffen voor de geschiedenis der wis- en natuurkundige wetenschappen in de Nederlanden*, XII, repr. from *Verslagen en Mededeelingen K. Akademie van Wetenschappen Amsterdam, Afdeling Natuurkunde*, 2nd ser., **12** (1878), 1–35. The same author's *Bibliographie neerlandaise historique et scientifique sur les sciences mathématiques et physiques* (Rome, 1883; Nieuwkoop, 1960) lists thirty-three works of Adriaen; this is a reprint of articles in *Bullettino di bibliografia e di storia delle scienze matematiche*, **14**

(1881), and **15** (1882), esp. 258–259. Also see his "Notice sur quelques quadrateurs du cercle dans les Pays-Bas," *ibid.*, **7** (1874), 99–104; and "Notice sur un pamphlet mathématique hollandais," *ibid.*, **11** (1878), 383–452. On Adriaen also see W. B. S. Boeles, *Frieslands Hoogeschool*, II (Leeuwarden, 1879), 70–75; and H. K. Schippers, "Fuotprinten fan in mannich Fryske stjerrekundigen," in *Beaken*, **24** (1962), 77–104 (in Frisian). On Jacob, see C. de Waard, *De uitvinding der verrekijkers* (The Hague, 1906).

D. J. STRUIK

METON (*fl.* Athens, second half of fifth century B.C.), *astronomy.*

Meton was the son of Pausanias, an Athenian from the deme (local subdivision of Attica) Leuconoe. He is dated by his observation of the summer solstice on 27 June 432 B.C.[1] He was still active nearly eighteen years later, for the story is told of a ruse whereby he avoided military service either for himself or for his son (the more probable version) on the Athenian expedition to Sicily that set out in 415, by pretending to be mad and setting fire to his house.[2] Furthermore, he is introduced as a character in Aristophanes' comedy *The Birds*, produced early in 414, and mentioned in Phrynichus' *Monotropos*, produced at the same festival as *The Birds*.[3] That is all we know about his life.

No written work by Meton survives; and we have to reconstruct what he did, and its purpose, from a few scattered references in ancient literature. Any such reconstruction involves some guesswork, and there is considerable disagreement on this subject among modern scholars. The following account seems to me to represent the evidence best.

Meton was famous in antiquity for his introduction of a nineteen-year lunisolar calendaric cycle, in ancient times usually called ἐννεακαιδεκετηρίς ("nineteen-year period") and sometimes the "great year" or "year of Meton," in modern times often called the "Metonic cycle." In Meton's time all Greek civil calendars, including the Athenian, were lunisolar. That is, the months were theoretically (although often not in practice) true lunar months, with the new moon occurring on the first of the month. Since the mean synodic month is slightly longer than 29.5 days, calendar months were normally either 30 days long ("full" months) or 29 days long ("hollow" months). The years, on the other hand, were supposed to be solar. Now twelve true lunar months make up only about 354 days. Therefore it was necessary to intercalate a thirteenth month in some years in order to keep the calendar roughly in step with the seasons

(the year at Athens, as in most Greek states, began near the summer solstice). All the extant primary evidence (in the form of dated inscriptions and coins) from Athens and elsewhere suggests that at no period was a fixed rule for intercalation of a thirteenth month adopted by any Greek state. Instead, each intercalation was determined by the decision of a magistrate (probably the eponymous archon at Athens) or an official body.

In constructing his nineteen-year cycle Meton used the fact (known before his time) that nineteen solar years correspond very well, on the average, to 235 true synodic months. This means that during one nineteen-year period a thirteenth month has to be intercalated seven times. Meton must have prescribed rules for the places of those seven intercalations. In addition, we are told that his cycle contained precisely 6,940 days.[4] This means that 110 of the 235 months in the cycle were hollow and the other 125 full. Thus Meton must also have prescribed rules for the sequence of full and hollow months throughout the cycle. Since it is probable that he derived the equation of nineteen years with 235 months from Babylonian practice (see below), it might seem plausible to assume that, like the Babylonians, he intercalated in the third, sixth, eighth, eleventh, fourteenth, seventeenth, and nineteenth years of his cycle. There is no evidence whatever for his having adopted this or any other scheme, however, and all modern attempts to reconstruct his intercalation system are futile. The same is true for reconstructions of his sequence of full and hollow months (in this case we cannot even refer to Babylonian practice, since their nineteen-year cycle did not contain a fixed number of days: instead, the length of each month was determined by observation of the new crescent). The only other information we have on the Metonic cycle is that it used the month names of the Athenian civil calendar[5] and that the first Metonic cycle began on 27 June 432 B.C., in the archonship of Apseudes at Athens—which was, according to Meton, the day of the summer solstice and the thirteenth day of Skirophorion (the twelfth month) in his calendar.

The evidence for the last statement needs examination. The chief authority is Diodorus, who says: "In the archonship of Apseudes at Athens . . . Meton the son of Pausanias, who has a reputation in astronomy, set out the so-called nineteen-year period, taking the beginning from the thirteenth of Skirophorion at Athens . . ." (XII, 36). One might assume that Meton would start his cycle from the beginning of the first month—Hekatombaion 1—and it would be possible to interpret Diodorus as meaning that the first day of Meton's cycle (his Hekatombaion 1) coincided with

Skirophorion 13 of the Athenian civil calendar of that year. That this is not so is shown by a fragment of an inscription found at Miletus, probably part of a calendar, which reads: "from the summer solstice in the archonship of Apseudes on Skirophorion 13, which was Phamenoth 21 according to the Egyptians, until the [solstice] in the archonship of Polykleitos on Skirophorion 14, or Pauni 1 according to the Egyptians."[6]

The equations with the Egyptian calendar plus the archon years enable us to determine these dates as 27 June 432 B.C. and 26 June 109 B.C., respectively. They are exactly seventeen nineteen-year periods apart; and one can deduce, first, that the second date is not an observed solstice but one computed from the first by means of a fixed calendrical scheme and, second, that the Skirophorion dates must have been taken not from the Athenian civil calendar but from an artificial astronomical calendar. The first is the starting date of Meton's first cycle. The second must be the date in the current Callippic cycle, for the interval corresponds to 323 years of $365\frac{1}{4}$ days.[7] The transition from Metonic to Callippic reckoning may also explain the shift of one day (from 13 to 14 Skirophorion) of the date of the solstice after an integer number of nineteen-year cycles. It may seem strange that Meton began his cycle elsewhere than at the beginning of a year (in contrast, when Callippus introduced his "improved" cycle, he began it at a solstice that coincided roughly with a new moon and thus was able to begin the year there too). But one can begin a cycle at an arbitrary point within it, and we know that Meton himself had observed the solstice of 432. No doubt he wished to begin at a point well-established astronomically.

Enormous confusion has arisen over the Metonic cycle because many scholars since Scaliger have assumed that Meton's purpose was to reform the Athenian civil calendar and that he succeeded (at least in part). Not only is there no evidence for the latter belief, but the former too is not supported by our texts. Instead, we may state confidently that his purpose in publishing the "nineteen-year cycle" was to provide a fixed calendrical scheme for recording astronomical data. Thus, if one was told that event A occurred on day 6 of the month Metageitnion in the second year of the cycle and event B on day 21 of the month Anthesterion of the fourth year, it was possible to determine the exact interval between the two—this was, in general, not possible between dates in the Athenian or any other Greek civil calendar. We can see from references in Ptolemy's *Almagest* that the cycle, as reformed by Callippus, was used for astronomical dating as late as Hipparchus (128 B.C.).

Ptolemy preferred to use the Egyptian calendar, with a fixed year length of 365 days, for the same purpose.

It is likely that what Meton published was in fact an astronomical calendar for nineteen years. If this assumption is correct, the calendar listed for each year the dates of the solstices and equinoxes, of the morning and evening risings and settings of certain prominent stars and constellations (that is, their first and last appearances just before dawn and just after sunset), and weather predictions associated with the various astronomical phenomena. All of this, except the equinoxes, was traditional Greek "astronomy,"[8] but Meton's observations of the intervals between phenomena may have been more accurate than his predecessors'. There exist a number of astronomical calendars of the type described, both in manuscript and (fragmentarily) on stone,[9] but all cover just one year. In these the months are either "zodiacal" (the time taken by the sun to traverse one sign of the zodiac), Egyptian, or Julian.[10] All three types are impossible or unlikely for Meton's time; and it is preferable to assume that he used synodic months and hence, necessarily, a nineteen-year calendar.[11] It is certain, at least, that Meton did publish an astronomical calendar. It is one of the authorities listed by Ptolemy,[12] and it is referred to by others.

Meton's chief claim to fame, apart from his cycle, is that he is the first Greek of whom we can say with certainty that he undertook serious astronomical observations. His solstice observations are the earliest that Ptolemy thought worth attention, even if inaccurate. (The only recorded observation is more than a day too early.) We are told that Meton erected an instrument for observing solstices (a ἡλιοτρόπιον) on the hill of the Pnyx in Athens.[13] The form of this instrument is entirely conjectural; but any upright gnomon would serve the purpose, provided one could observe its longest and shortest midday shadow.

It is commonly supposed that Meton also observed equinoxes, since he assumed unequal lengths for the seasons. One source quotes figures for the lengths of the seasons, beginning with the summer solstice, of ninety, ninety, and ninety-two days (and hence, by inference, ninety-three for the fourth).[14] But these figures (which are very inaccurate) can equally well be explained by a crude schematic distribution of the times spent by the sun in each of the twelve zodiacal signs into intervals of thirty and thirty-one days.[15] This would imply that the equinoxes were not observed. The first Greek of whom we can say with certainty that he determined the lengths of the seasons by observation, and drew the conclusion that the sun has an anomalistic motion, is Callippus (*ca.* 330 B.C.).

The question of Babylonian influence on Meton is

relevant. A standard nineteen-year intercalation cycle was in regular use in the civil calendar of Babylonia from 367 B.C. and seems to have been known there, although not uniformly used, from the early fifth century. We are informed by an early source that Meton derived his nineteen-year cycle from a certain Phaeinos who was a resident alien at Athens.[16] It is possible that Phaeinos was an Asian Greek who acted as transmitter of Babylonian astronomical knowledge. A further connection of Meton with Babylonian astronomy is that he put the equinoxes and solstices at 8° of their respective zodiacal signs.[17] This is characteristic of "System B" in Babylonian astronomical texts.

Meton is also called a "geometer" in some ancient sources. In Aristophanes' *The Birds* he comes on stage equipped with the geometer's traditional rule and compasses and proceeds to "square the circle" in an absurd manner. It would be hazardous to draw any inference about the real Meton's mathematical interests from this burlesque. Similarly, we cannot conclude that he engaged in town planning or hydrography from the representations of him in contemporary comedies drawing plans for Cloudcuckooland or drilling wells. He remains an obscure figure; but he and his associate Euctemon were probably of importance in giving an initial impetus to astronomical observation, however crude, in Greece. His cycle, although later superseded by other reference systems, provided the first adequate framework for recording astronomical data.

NOTES

1. Reported by Ptolemy, *Almagest*, III, 1.
2. Differing versions in Plutarch, "Nicias," 13.5; Plutarch, "Alcibiades," 17.4–5; Aelian, *Varia Historia*, 10.7.
3. Aristophanes, *Birds*, 992–1020, with the scholion on 997.
4. Ptolemy, *Almagest*, III, 1; Geminus, VIII, 51; Censorinus, 18.8.
5. The best evidence for this is that Callippus used them in his cycle, which was a slight modification of Meton's. See, for instance, Ptolemy, *Almagest*, VII, 3 (Heiberg, ed., II, 28).
6. *Sitzungsberichte der K. Preussischen Akademie der Wissenschaften zu Berlin* (1904), no. 1, 96.
7. The Callippic cycle differed from the Metonic in assuming a year length of 365¼ days. Hence to 76 years it assigned 27,759 days, a day less than the corresponding 4 Metonic cycles (Geminus, VIII, 59–60). Otherwise the Callippic cycle of 76 years was, presumably, identical to 4 consecutive Metonic cycles. The first Callippic cycle began at the summer solstice (probably 28 June) 330 B.C.
8. Found, for example, in Hesiod's *Works and Days*, which is some 300 years earlier.
9. Such a calendar, when inscribed on permanent material, was often provided with a hole at each entry to receive a peg to mark the current date. Hence it was called παράπηγμα ("that which has a peg beside it").
10. Examples of the first are Geminus' calendar (Geminus,

Elementa astronomiae, Manitius, ed., 210–232) and the Miletus parapegma (*Sitzungsberichte der K. Preussischen Akademie der Wissenschaften zu Berlin* [1904], no. 1, 102–111); of the second, Ptolemy's *Phaseis* (*Calendaria Graeca*, Wachsmuth, ed., 211–274); and of the third, the calendar of Clodius Tuscus (*Sitzungsberichte der Heidelberger Akademie der Wissenschaften*, Phil.-hist. Kl. [1914], no. 3).
11. A nineteen-year calendar is suggested by the scholion on Aratus, 753 (Maass, ed., *Commentariorum in Aratum reliquiae*, 478), and by Diodorus, XII, 36.3.
12. *Phaseis*, in *Calendaria Graeca*, Wachsmuth, ed., 275.
13. Philochorus, fr. 122, Jacoby, ed.
14. *Eudoxi Ars astronomica*, Blass, ed., 25. The figures quoted are attributed to Euctemon, but the two are so often coupled in the context of astronomical observations (as by Ptolemy in the passages referred to in notes 1 and 10) that it is plausible to associate Meton with these season lengths too. This is confirmed by Simplicius, *In De caelo*, Heiberg, ed., 497.
15. See Albert Rehm, "Das Parapegma des Euktemon" ("Griechische Kalender," F. Boll, ed., III), in *Sitzungsberichte der Heidelberger Akademie der Wissenschaften*, Phil.-hist. Kl. (1913), no. 3, 9.
16. Theophrastus, *De signis*, 4.
17. Columella, *De re rustica*, IX, 14.12.

BIBLIOGRAPHY

The principal ancient passages concerning Meton are Ptolemy, *Almagest*, III, 1 (*Claudii Ptolemaei Opera quae exstant omnia*, I, *Syntaxis mathematica*, J. L. Heiberg, ed., pt. 1 [Leipzig, 1898], 205–207); Diodorus, *Bibliotheca historica*, XII, 36 (F. Vogel, ed. [Leipzig, 1890], II, 395); Geminus, *Elementa astronomiae*, VIII, 50–56 (K. Manitius, ed. [Leipzig, 1898], 120–122); Censorinus, *De die natali*, 18.8 (Otto Jahn, ed. [Berlin, 1845], 54); Aristophanes, *The Birds*, ll. 992–1020, with the scholion on l. 997 (printed as fr. 122 of Philochorus by F. Jacoby, *Die Fragmente der Griechischen Historiker*, III B [Leiden, 1950], 135); Theophrastus, *De signis*, 4 (*Theophrasti Opera*, F. Wimmer, ed. [Leipzig, 1862], III, 116); the scholion on Aratus, 752–753, in *Commentariorum in Aratum reliquiae*, E. Maass, ed. (Berlin, 1898), 478; Ptolemy, *Phaseis*, 93D, in *Calendaria Graeca*, C. Wachsmuth, ed. (with Ioannes Lydus, *Liber de Ostentis*) (Leipzig, 1897), 275 (see also index, 360, under Μέτων); Columella, *De re rustica*, IX, 14.12 (*ibid.*, 303); *Eudoxi Ars astronomica*, F. Blass, ed. (Kiel, 1887), 25; Simplicius, *In Aristotelis De caelo commentaria*, J. L. Heiberg, ed. (*Commentaria in Aristotelem Graeca*, VII) (Berlin, 1894), 497; Plutarch, "Life of Nicias," 13.5, and "Life of Alcibiades," 17.4–5 (*Plutarch's Lives*, B. Perrin, ed. [Cambridge, Mass., 1916], III, 254–256, and IV, 44–46); and Aelian, *Varia Historia*, 10.7 and 13.12 (R. Hercher, ed. [Leipzig, 1866], 109, 149).

There is no satisfactory modern account of Meton. Most are vitiated by the belief that the "Metonic cycle" is somehow reflected in the Athenian civil calendar. For a refutation of this belief and a history of scholarly discussion of the question, see W. Kendrick Pritchett, "The Choiseul Marble," in *University of California Publications. Classical Studies*, **5** (1970), 39–97. The fragments of the Miletus parapegma(ta) were published by H. Diels and

A. Rehm, "Parapegmenfragmente aus Milet," in *Sitzungsberichte der K. Preussischen Akademie der Wissenschaften zu Berlin* (1904), no. 1, 92–111; and by A. Rehm, "Weiteres zu den milesischen Parapegmen," *ibid.*, 752–759. For references to other partially preserved ancient parapegmata, see A. Rehm, "Parapegma," in Pauly-Wissowa, *Realencyclopädie der classischen Altertumswissenschaft*, 1st ser., XVIII, pt. 2, cols. 1299–1302; for eds. of the Italian ones, with excellent photographs, see *Inscriptiones Italiae*, XIII, pt. 2, A. Degrassi, ed. (Rome, 1963), 299–313.

Many of the ancient astronomical calendars preserved in MS were collected by C. Wachsmuth in his *Calendaria Graeca* (see above). See also the series "Griechische Kalender," F. Boll, ed., in *Sitzungsberichte der Heidelberger Akademie der Wissenschaften*, Phil.-hist. Kl. (1910), no. 16, (1911), no. 1, (1913), no. 3, (1914), no. 3 and (1920), no. 15. On the nineteen-year cycle in Babylonia, see R. A. Parker and W. H. Dubberstein, *Babylonian Chronology 625 B.C.–A.D. 75*, Brown University Studies, XIX (Providence, 1956), esp. 1–6. On System B in Babylonian astronomy see O. Neugebauer, *Astronomical Cuneiform Texts*, I (London, 1955), 69–85 (for the vernal point in Aries 8° see 72). A well-informed conjecture about the site of Meton's instrument for observing solstices on the Pnyx at Athens was advanced by K. Kouroniotes and Homer A. Thompson, "The Pnyx in Athens," in *Hesperia*, **1** (1932), 207–211.

G. J. Toomer

METTENIUS, GEORG HEINRICH (*b*. Frankfurt am Main, Germany, 24 November 1823; *d*. Leipzig, Germany, 19 August 1866), *botany*.

Mettenius was the son of a Frankfurt merchant. He studied medicine at Heidelberg from 1841 to 1845, defending a doctoral dissertation, *De Salvinia*, in 1845. After periods of further study in Heligoland, Berlin, Vienna, and Fiume, he became a *Privatdozent* at Heidelberg. He moved to Freiburg im Breisgau as professor extraordinarius in 1851. In 1852, following the death of Gustav Kunze, he became professor of botany and director of the botanic garden at Leipzig. Kunze had assembled a rich collection of living plants and herbarium specimens of ferns. This abundant material led Mettenius to concentrate his attention thereafter on pteridological studies.

In June 1859 Mettenius married Cecile Braun, second daughter of the Berlin botanist Alexander Braun; her sister married the Königsberg botanist Robert Caspary on the same day. Mettenius' life, according to Caspary, was the most regular possible:

> At five o'clock he began the work of the day and finished it punctually at ten in the evening. His whole mind was turned towards the study of plants and especially of ferns. . . . Mettenius generally took the whole

management of the garden upon himself, being out by six o'clock in the morning and directing the operations of each of the labourers.

By such incessant toil, he accomplished much in his relatively short life. An athletic man of great bodily strength, he was in splendid health when he contracted cholera during the epidemic of 1866, and died suddenly at the age of forty-two. His years of intensive study of ferns were leading to comprehensive monographs on the species of individual genera. He had already published, in the *Abhandlungen der Senckenbergischen Naturforschenden Gesellschaft*, on *Polypodium* in 1856; *Plagiogyra*, *Phegopteris*, and *Aspidium* in 1858; and *Cheilanthes* and *Asplenium* in 1859. These writings revised existing classifications, and, together with his *Filices Lechlerianae Chilenses et Peruanae* (1856–1859), *Filices horti botanici Lipsiensis* (1856), and *Ueber die Hymenophyllaceae* (1864), place him among the leading pteridologists of the nineteenth century.

Like J. W. Hooker, Mettenius preferred a few large genera divided into sections instead of a multitude of smaller genera as proposed by his older contemporaries C. B. Presl, John Smith, and Fée (see *Webbia*, **17** [1962], 207–222). His work remains important for its detailed and precise descriptions of species.

BIBLIOGRAPHY

I. Original Works. Some of Mettenius' pteridological publications were issued both as parts of the *Abhandlungen herausgegeben von der Senckenbergischen Naturforschenden Gesellschaft*, 2–3 (Frankfurt am Main, 1856–1860), and as separates; for their precise dates of publication, see W. T. Stearn, "Pteridological Publications of G. H. Mettinius," in *Journal of the Society for the Bibliography of Natural History*, **4** (1967), 287–289.

II. Secondary Literature. The main source of biographical information is in the obituary by his brother-in-law, Robert Caspary, in *Gardeners' Chronicle* (1866), 1018; repr. in *Journal of Botany*, **4** (1866), 388–391, with a list of publications. Various references occur in the biography of his father-in-law by Cecile Braun Mettenius, *Alexander Braun's Leben nach seinem handschriftlichen Nachlass dargestellt* (Berlin, 1882).

William T. Stearn

METZGER, HÉLÈNE (*b*. Chatou, near Paris, France, 26 August 1889; *d*. on the way to Auschwitz, Poland, after February 1944), *chemistry, history of science, philosophy*.

The daughter of Paul Bruhl and Jenny Adler, and the niece of Lucien Lévy-Bruhl, Hélène Metzger earned the *brevet supérieur* at a time when girls did not go to lycée to prepare for the *baccalauréat* and rarely attended university. She studied mineralogy with Frédéric Wallerant in his laboratory at the Sorbonne and in May 1912 received a *diplôme d'études supérieures* in physics under him for her memoir "Étude cristallographique du chlorate de lithium."

On 13 May 1913 she married Paul Metzger, a professor of history and geography at Lyons. In September 1914 he was reported missing in one of the first battles of World War I. A widow at twenty-five, she henceforth devoted herself entirely to research, commencing with her work on crystallography. Animated by a wide-ranging curiosity and an eminently philosophic cast of mind, she became interested in a historical approach to science.

Hélène Metzger's abilities as historian of science were evident as early as 1918 in her doctoral thesis, *La genèse de la science des cristaux*, which she defended in Paris. In this work she showed how crystallography slowly became differentiated from mineralogy, physics, and chemistry, until at the end of the eighteenth century it had developed into an independent science. Convinced that scientific revolutions are the visible effect of a previous underlying current, she took chemistry as an example and conceived a vast plan that was to lead her research from the beginning of the seventeenth century to Lavoisier. The general title was *Les doctrines chimiques en France, du début du XVIIᵉ à la fin du XVIIIᵉ siècle*. The first part appeared in 1923, and in 1924 it won for its author the Prix Binoux of the Académie des Sciences. Nicolas Lemery was the central character, but importance was accorded to authors little known until then.

Newton, Stahl, Boerhaave et la doctrine chimique, published in 1930, may be considered the second installment of the projected work. Sections of what would have been the third part can be found in lectures delivered in 1932–1933 at the Institut d'Histoire des Sciences of the University of Paris; they were published in 1935 under the title *La philosophie de la matière chez Lavoisier*.

A synthetic view of the history of chemistry, as Hélène Metzger conceived of it, can be found in the little volume *La chimie*, written in 1926 (published in 1930) for the series Histoire du Monde, edited by Eugène Cavaignac.

Drawn to philosophical reflection and preoccupied by epistemological problems, Hélène Metzger submitted an essay to a contest held by the Académie des Sciences Morales et Politiques that won the Prix Bordin in philosophy in 1925 and was published in 1926 under the title *Les concepts scientifiques*. This study deals with both psychology and logic and takes examples from the history of science to show how concepts arise and become transformed and how they can be classified.

A disciple of both Émile Meyerson and Lucien Lévy-Bruhl, Hélène Metzger was not satisfied with a strictly positivist position. She followed Meyerson in seeking out the philosophical bases of science, and Lévy-Bruhl in extending her investigations to the nonrational aspects of thought, which are as prevalent in the civilized as in the primitive mind. It was the activity of the entire human intellect that she wanted to uncover by following the scientists in their groping; she was as interested in "false" ideas as in those currently considered "true." For her, religious, metaphysical, and scientific ideas formed a unified whole in a given historical period, and she believed that one group could not properly be studied by artificially separating it from others. If that viewpoint is widely accepted today, it is partly because she helped to establish it.

The best example of Hélène Metzger's approach is the thesis she presented to the fifth section of the École Pratique des Hautes Études in 1938, published as *Attraction universelle et religion naturelle chez quelques commentateurs anglais de Newton*. Encouraged by Léon Brunschvicg, she wished to pursue this synthetic study of the development of scientific and philosophical thought by a thorough examination of the work of Condillac in relation to that of Lavoisier and the chemists of the end of the eighteenth century. Unfortunately, this project was never carried out; after the beginning of the German occupation of Paris, she moved to Lyons to work, at the Bureau d'Études Israélites, on a study of Jewish monotheism. Her conclusions appeared in 1947 in *Revue philosophique*; the preamble was published in 1954 in a volume prepared by her brother, Adrien Bruhl: *La science, l'appel de la religion et la volonté humaine*. Hélène Metzger was arrested in the Rue Vaubécour in Lyons in February 1944, deported to Drancy, and then sent to Auschwitz; it has proved impossible to establish the circumstances and the date of her death.

During the interwar years Hélène Metzger's works—which included many articles in *Isis*, *Archeion*, and *Scientia* and her contributions to the *Vocabulaire historique* (prepared by the Centre International de Synthèse), which appeared in *Revue de synthèse* and *Revue d'histoire des sciences et de leurs applications*—had a considerable impact on the history of science and on epistemology. Her personal influence among historians of science was still more decisive. She participated in the first four international congresses of the history of science and was a charter member of the Comité International d'Histoire des Sciences (converted into the Académie Internationale d'Histoire des Sciences in 1929). She served as its administrator-treasurer from 5 June 1931 until her arrest. She organized the Academy's library in the Rue Colbert in Paris, and her philosophical concerns are clearly reflected in its holdings.

In 1939 Hélène Metzger was placed in charge of the history of science library of the Centre International de Synthèse. An ardent participant in all the meetings of its history of science section—as is attested by the issues of *Archeion*—and secretary of the Groupe Français d'Historiens des Sciences, she enlivened the discussions with her subtle and often ironic remarks, which were always pertinent and erudite, if somewhat disconcerting in their impulsiveness. Cordial to young scholars and to French and foreign colleagues, she was an inceptive influence for many studies. Aldo Mieli, Pierre Brunet, Federigo Enriques, Alexandre Koyré, George Sarton, Paul Mouy, and Robert Lenoble all derived inspiration for their work from their contact with Hélène Metzger.

BIBLIOGRAPHY

I. Original Works. Metzger's books are *La genèse de la science des cristaux* (Paris, 1918; repr. 1970); *Les doctrines chimiques en France, du début du XVIIe à la fin du XVIIIe siècle* (Paris, 1923; repr. 1970); *Les concepts scientifiques* (Paris, 1926); *La civilisation européenne*, pt. 4, *La chimie* (Paris, 1930); *Newton, Stahl, Boerhaave et la doctrine chimique* (Paris, 1930); *La philosophie de la matière chez Lavoisier* (Paris, 1935); *Attraction universelle et religion naturelle chez quelques commentateurs anglais de Newton* (Paris, 1938); and *La science, l'appel de la religion et la volonté humaine* (Paris, 1954).

Her principal articles are "L'évolution du règne métallique d'après les alchimistes du XVIIe siècle," in *Isis*, **4** (1922), 464–483; "La philosophie de la matière chez Stahl et ses disciples," *ibid.*, **8** (1925), 427–464; "Newton et l'évolution de la théorie chimique," in *Archeion*, **9** (1928), 243–256, 433–461, and **10** (1929; incorrectly numbered **11**), 13–25—the three parts were also brought together in a booklet (Rome, n.d.); "La philosophie de Lucien Lévy-Bruhl et l'histoire des sciences," in *Archeion*, **12** (1930), 15–24; "Eugène Chevreul historien de la chimie," *ibid.*, **14** (1932), 6–11; "Introduction à l'étude du rôle de Lavoisier dans l'histoire des sciences," *ibid.*, 31–50; "L'historien des sciences doit-il se faire le contemporain des savants dont il parle?" *ibid.*, **15** (1933), 34–44; "Tribunal de l'histoire et théorie de la connaissance scientifique," *ibid.*, **17** (1935), 1–18; "La signification de l'histoire de la pensée scientifique," in *Scientia*, **57** (June 1935), 449–453; "L'*a priori* dans la doctrine scientifique et l'histoire des sciences," in *Archeion*, **18** (1936), 29–79; "La méthode philosophique dans l'histoire des sciences," *ibid.*, **19** (1937), 204–216; "Alchimie. Communication pour servir au Vocabulaire historique," in *Revue de synthèse*, **16**, no. 1 (Apr. 1938), 43–53; and "Atomisme. Communication pour servir au Vocabulaire historique," in *Revue d'histoire des sciences et de leurs applications*, **1**, no. 1 (July 1947), 51–62.

II. Secondary Literature. See Marie Boas, in *Archives internationales d'histoire des sciences*, **12** (1959), 432–435; Pierre Brunet, in *Revue d'histoire des sciences et de leurs applications*, **1**, no. 1 (July 1947), 68–70; and Suzanne Delorme, in *Archives internationales d'histoire des sciences*, **1** (1948), 326–327.

Suzanne Delorme

MEUSNIER DE LA PLACE, JEAN-BAPTISTE-MARIE-CHARLES (*b.* Tours, France, 19 June 1754; *d.* Mainz, Germany, 17 June 1793), *mathematics, physics, engineering.*

Meusnier was the son of Jean-Baptiste Meusnier and Anne le Normand Delaplace. The family was for generations engaged in law and administration; the father was a counsel attached to a court (*présidial*) at Tours. He tutored his son, and only during his last years at Tours did Meusnier go to school.

From 1771 to 1773 Meusnier was privately tutored at Paris for entrance into the military academy at Mézières, where he studied in 1774–1775 and graduated as second lieutenant in the Engineering Corps. His mathematics teacher was Gaspard Monge, under whom Meusnier did his only published mathematical work, on the theory of surfaces.

His paper, read at the Paris Academy of Sciences in 1776, supposedly led d'Alembert to state: "Meusnier commence comme je finis." It also led to Meusnier's election, at twenty-one, as a corresponding member of the Academy. He was placed in charge of continuing the descriptions of machines approved by the Academy, and in February 1777 he presented to the Academy the seventh volume of the *Recueil des machines approuvées par l'Académie*. During 1777, now a first lieutenant, he was sent to Verdun to study mining and sapping. From 1779 to 1788 he worked as a military engineer on the harborworks of Cherbourg, where he displayed great ingenuity and perseverance, despite red tape and intrigues, in the building of the breakwater and the fortification of Île Pelée. To provide drinking water for this island he spent much time on experiments on the desalinization of seawater. In March 1783 Meusnier, sent into debt by his work, presented his machine to the Academy.

During 1783 the first balloon ascensions took place. Meusnier, on leaves of absence from Cherbourg, began to study the theory of this new field, aerostation. In December 1783 he read before the Academy his "Mémoire sur l'équilibre des machines aéro-statiques." The next month he was elected a full member of the Academy and was immediately appointed to a committee on aerostation, other members of which were Lavoisier, Berthollet, and Condorcet. The results of his work on this committee were presented in November 1784 in "Précis des travaux faits à l'Académie des sciences pour la perfection des machines aérostatiques," with a theory and detailed construction plans for dirigible balloons. It led to no practical results at the time.

During this period Meusnier began a collaboration with Lavoisier on the synthesis and analysis of water; Meusnier was especially interested in the production of hydrogen in quantity from water. On 21 April 1784 they presented to the Academy a continuation of the paper presented in June 1783 by Lavoisier and Laplace on the synthesis of water from oxygen and hydrogen: "Mémoire où l'on prouve par la décom-position de l'eau que ce fluide n'est point une substance simple . . . ." It was also a heavy blow against the phlogiston theory, which Berthollet and others soon abandoned in favor of Lavoisier's "théorie française." Meusnier also collaborated with Lavoisier on the improvement of oil lamps for city street illumination. Their ideas were contemporary with those of Aimé Argand and perhaps inspired the construction of his lamp.

In May 1787 Meusnier became a captain; in July 1788, he was promoted to *aide-maréchal général des logis au corps de l'État Major* and major.

From then on his career was with the army, and in July 1789 he became a lieutenant colonel. With his friends Monge and Berthollet he joined the Jacobins in 1790. With many other academicians he was appointed to the Bureau de Consultation Pour les Arts et Métiers to study inventions useful to the state. Meusnier invented a machine for engraving assignats that greatly reduced the possibility of producing counterfeit notes. In February 1792 he was appointed colonel, then *adjutant général colonel*, and in September 1792 field marshal. Sent in February 1793 to the armies of the Rhine commanded by Custine, he participated in the defense of the fortress of Kassel during the siege of Mainz by the Prussians. He was wounded on 5 June and died twelve days later. His remains were brought to Paris (Goethe witnessed the procession leaving Mainz; see his *Kampagne in Frankreich*), and were later transferred to Tours, where in 1888 a bust was erected on a pedestal containing his ashes.

The "Mémoire sur la courbure des surfaces," read in 1776 and published in 1785, was written after Monge had shown him Euler's paper on this subject

(*Mémoires de l'Académie des Sciences* [Berlin, 1760]). In the "Mémoire" Meusnier derived "Meusnier's theorem" on the curvature, at a point of a surface, of plane sections with a common tangent and also found, as special solutions of Lagrange's differential equation of the minimal surfaces (1760), the catenoid and the right helicoid. His results can be found in any book on differential geometry. In the "Mémoire" on aerostation (1783) Meusnier presented a theory of the equilibrium of a balloon, the dynamics of ascension, and the rules for maneuvering a balloon. To maintain appropriate altitude even with the disposal of ballast he proposed a balloon filled with hydrogen containing a smaller balloon filled with air (known as *ballonet d'air*); he also suggested a model with air in the larger balloon and hydrogen in the smaller. In the "Précis" of 1784, the result of a great many test experiments, Meusnier gave a detailed plan for the construction of a dirigible balloon in the form of an elongated ellipsoid with another balloon inside. For propulsion he suggested revolving air screws worked by a crew. He described two possibilities: a small dirigible 130 feet long carrying six men and one 260 feet long (130 feet minor axis) with a crew of thirty and food for sixty days, able to fly around the earth. In his formula for the stability of the balloon,

$$n = \left(\frac{P + E}{P}\right) \times \frac{3}{2}\left(\frac{l^2 - h^2}{h^2}\right) \times \frac{(h - x)^2}{3h - 2x},$$

n is the distance from the metacenter to the center of the balloon, P the weight of the objects collected at the center of the gondola, E the weight of the balloon as concentrated at the center, l and h the major and minor axes of the balloon, and x the height of the hydrogen when the balloon is on earth, the hydrogen rising above the air in the balloon.

The principle of the revolving screw had also occurred to David Bushnell of Connecticut in the construction of his submarine (1776–1777). Meusnier knew of Bushnell's invention.

After Cavendish had shown nonquantitatively in 1781 that the combination of oxygen and hydrogen yields water, Lavoisier and Laplace in 1783 presented to the Academy an account of their work on the synthesis of water; Monge had also performed this experiment. Meusnier suggested more exact measure-ments to Lavoisier and constructed precision instruments for this purpose. Their "Mémoire" of April 1784 showed how they had decomposed water into its components; the hydrogen was obtained as a gas and the oxygen in the form of an iron oxide. For many this famous experiment carried convincing evidence against the phlogiston theory.

BIBLIOGRAPHY

I. Original Works. "Mémoire sur la courbure des surfaces" appeared in *Mémoires de mathématique et de physique présentés par divers sçavans*, **10** (1785), pt. 2, 477–510. The "Mémoire" and the "Précis" on aerostation were published, with other material, by G. Darboux in *Mémoires de l'Académie des sciences*, 2nd ser., **51** (1910), 1–128. This includes the "Atlas de dessins relatifs à un projet de machine aérostatique" of 1784, presented in a photographic reproduction to the Academy in 1886 by General Perrier. The "Mémoire où l'on prouve par la décomposition de l'eau . . .," written with Lavoisier, is in *Mémoires de l'Académie royale des sciences pour 1781* (1784), 269–283. See also "Description d'un appareil propre à manoeuvrer différentes espèces d'air dans les expériences qui exigent des volumes considérables," *ibid., 1782* (1785), 466; "Sur les moyens d'opérer l'entière combustion de l'huile et d'augmenter la lumière des lampes," *ibid., 1784* (1787), 390–398. There is MS material in the Archives of the Académie des Sciences, the Institut de France, the Archives Historiques de la Guerre, and the Bibliothèque du Génie, all in Paris. Details are given by J. Laissus (see below).

II. Secondary Literature. "Notice sur le général Meusnier," in *Revue rétrospective*, 2nd ser., **4** (1835), 77–99, contains biographical notes on Meusnier by Monge and others, the originals of which have not been found. Partly based on these is Darboux's "Notice historique sur le général Meusnier," in his *Éloges académiques et discours* (Paris, 1912), 218–262, also in *Mémoires de l'Académie des Sciences*, 2nd ser., **51** (see above). In it are many particulars on Meusnier's work in Cherbourg and in the army of the Revolution. See also L. Louvet, in *Nouvelle biographie générale*, XXXV (1865), cols. 264–267. Bibliographical details based on independent research in the printed and MS materials are in J. Laissus, "Le général Meusnier de la Place, membre de l'Académie royale des sciences," in *Comptes rendus du 93ᵉ Congrès national des sociétés savantes, Tours, 1968*, Section des Sciences, II (Paris, 1971), 75–101. Meusnier's work on decomposition of water can be studied in books on Lavoisier. His works on aerostation have been analyzed by F. Letonné, "Le général Meusnier et ses idées sur la navigation aérienne," in *Revue du génie militaire*, **2** (1888), 247–258; and by Voyer, "Les lois de Meusnier," *ibid.*, **23** (1902), 421–430; "Le ballonet de Meusnier," *ibid.*, 521–532; and "Le général Meusnier et les ballons dirigeables," *ibid.*, **24** (1902), 135–156—German trans. in *Illustrierte aeronautische Mitteilungen*, **9** (1905), 137–144, 353–361, 373–387. The third of these papers gives a proof of Meusnier's stability formula. See also G. Béthuys, *Les aérostations militaires* (Paris, 1894), 137–146. On the Argand lamp see S. T. McCoy, *French Inventions of the Eighteenth Century* (Lexington, Ky., 1952), 52–56.

On the papers relating to the collaboration between Lavoisier and Meusnier, see also D. I. Duveen and H. S. Klickstein, *Bibliography of the Works of Antoine Laurent Lavoisier 1743–1794* (London, 1954), index, p. 462.

On Bushnell see D. J. Struik, *Yankee Science in the Making* (New York, 1962), 83, 453.

D. J. Struik

MEYEN, FRANZ JULIUS FERDINAND (*b*. Tilsit, Prussia [now Sovetsk, U.S.S.R.], 28 June 1804; *d*. Berlin, Germany, 2 September 1840), *botany*.

Meyen's father, who was president of the commercial court in Tilsit, died in 1811. Meyen attended the Gymnasium in Tilsit until 1819, when he had to begin an apprenticeship to an apothecary in Memel, Prussia. In 1821 his brother in Berlin offered him the chance to continue his schooling so that he could enter a university. From 1823 to 1826 Meyen studied medicine at the Friedrich Wilhelms Institut, where military physicians were trained. At the same time, however, he also attended the zoology lectures of H. Lichtenstein and K. A. Rudolphi and the botany lectures of Johann Horkel, K. H. Schultz, and H. F. Link at the University of Berlin. He received his medical degree in October 1826 with a dissertation entitled "De primis vitae phaenomenis in fluidis formativis et de circulatione sanguinis in parenchymate." Until 1830 he was a military physician in Berlin, Cologne, Bonn, and Potsdam. In this period he published three monographs and eleven journal articles.

In 1830, through the influence of Alexander von Humboldt, Meyen obtained the post of doctor on the royal cargo ship *Prinzess Louise*. His assignment, during a world cruise lasting nearly two years, was to collect natural history specimens and make scientific observations. He made long excursions in the western part of South America, climbing the Andes in Chile and Peru up to the snow line. Later in the voyage he spent some time in the Sandwich Islands (Hawaii), the Philippines, and China. Wherever he went, he collected plants, and in China took an interest in Chinese gardening.

Upon returning to Prussia, Meyen began to prepare his material; he published a general account of the voyage in 1834–1835. The scientific presentation of the collections appeared in the *Nova Acta Leopoldina* (XVI, XVII, and XIX [1832–1834, 1835, 1843]). At first Meyen published only the articles on zoology and ethnography; of the plants he described only the lichens (with J. von Flotow).

In August 1834 Meyen was named extraordinary professor in the Philosophy Faculty of the University of Berlin. He received this appointment—which followed his being granted an honorary doctorate by the University of Bonn—on the basis of the description of his voyage and of his earlier works. He then continued his study of phytotomy and plant physiology. Meyen's most important scientific publication was *Phytotomie*. Written when he was twenty-five, it presented the new field of microscopic plant anatomy. The book appeared at the beginning of about ten years of intensive microscopic investigations of plants and animals. At the end of this period the Schleiden-Schwann cell theory had fully emerged. Meyen's *Phytotomie* did not in every respect represent progress, but its comprehensive summary of the subject provided a strong impetus to further research. In response to the much-discussed question of the type and number of the elementary plant organs, Meyen described the cells, spiral tubes, and sap vessels. For the various forms of cellular tissue he introduced new designations—mesenchyma and pleurenchyma—to be added to those already used by Link—parenchyma and prosenchyma.

Before Meyen's research, only the structure of the cellular reticulum was considered important, but he investigated the contents of the cell as well. Most notably, he described in detail the movements that could be observed within it. As early as 1827 he published a paper entitled "Über die eigentümliche Säftebewegung in den Zellen der Pflanzen." This movement had first been observed in 1774 by Bonaventura Corti in the cells of *Chara*. For this reason Meyen's cognomen as a member of the Imperial Leopoldine-Caroline Academy of Science was Corti. In *Phytotomie* he also treated movements of fluids throughout the plant. He viewed the lactiferous tubes as circulatory organs and "as the highest thing that the plant produces." The fluid circulating within them corresponded, he thought, to the blood of animals.

In 1837 there appeared the first volume of Meyen's other major work: *Neues System der Pflanzen-Physiologie*. Meyen expressed the wish that the book be considered a continuation and improvement of his *Phytotomie*. This first volume is in fact a reworking of *Phytotomie*; once again the content of plant cells is examined and described more fully than in the writings of other contemporary students of microscopic plant anatomy. The amalgamation of physiological and morphological problems, more evident here than in *Phytotomie*, corresponded to the conception of the relationship between anatomy and physiology held in zoology since the beginning of the nineteenth century. In the preface to the *Neues System* Meyen stated that the time had arrived "when one could attempt to study plant physiology in just the same way as animal physiology."

For his essay "Ueber die neusten Fortschritte der Anatomie und Physiologie der Gewächse" Meyen received, among other honors, the prize offered by the Teyler Society of Haarlem for the best paper on that subject. For his "Ueber die Secretions-Organe der Pflanzen" he was awarded the prize of the Royal Society of Science of Göttingen. Both these awards were presented in 1836.

Meyen's importance for botany lies much less in discovery than in the intensive and wide-ranging study of microscopic anatomy in connection with physiology. The breadth of his interests can be seen from the fact that he published the "Jahresberichte über die Resultate der Arbeiten im Felde der physiologischen Botanik" for the years 1834–1839 for A. F. A. Wiegmann's *Archiv für Naturgeschichte*. He also wrote a work on plant geography and one on plant pathology.

BIBLIOGRAPHY

Meyen's most important works are *Phytotomie* (Berlin, 1830); *Ueber die Bewegung der Säfte in den Pflanzen. Ein Schreiben an die Königliche Akademie der Wissenschaften zu Paris* (Berlin, 1834); and *Neues System der Pflanzen-Physiologie*, 3 vols. (Berlin, 1837–1839).

A biography with a complete bibliography is J. T. C. Ratzeburg, "Meyen's Lebenslauf," in *Nova acta Academiae Caesareae Leopoldina Carolinae germanicae naturae curiosorum*, **19** (1843), xiii–xxxii.

HANS QUERNER

MEYER, CHRISTIAN ERICH HERMANN VON (*b.* Frankfurt, Germany, 3 September 1801; *d.* Frankfurt, 2 April 1869), *paleontology.*

Meyer came from on old Frankfurt family; his father was a lawyer and later mayor of Frankfurt. Meyer was born with clubfeet, which handicapped his movement. He was educated in Frankfurt, then he worked for a year in a glasswork and for three years as an apprentice in a banking house. From 1822 to 1827 he studied finance and natural science, especially geology and mineralogy, at Heidelberg, Munich, and Berlin, where he met Hegel and Humboldt. On returning to Frankfurt he devoted all his time and energy to paleontology, publishing numerous works in rapid succession, visiting museums and collections, and attending professional congresses. He soon became a known and respected paleontologist, who received material for study and publication from all of Germany and neighboring countries.

In 1837, Meyer entered the financial administration of the Bundestag—the parliament of the German Confederation, which was then under Austrian leadership; in 1863 he became its director of finances. Consequently, from 1837 he could carry out his paleontological studies only during his spare time. Nevertheless, in 1860 he rejected an appointment as professor at the University of Göttingen in order to maintain his scientific independence. Meyer never married. He was sociable, had charming manners, and was respected and loved by his fellow citizens for his sincerity and civic service.

The main subject of Meyer's scientific studies was the fossil vertebrates. His chief work in this field is the four-volume *Fauna der Vorwelt*, which contains 132 plates of outstanding drawings done by Meyer himself. In these books Meyer described vertebrates—chiefly from Germany—of the Miocene, Jurassic, Triassic, Permian, and Carboniferous. He also wrote articles for journals; 103 of his paleontological writings were published in *Palaeontographica*, which he founded in 1846 with Wilhelm Dunker.

Meyer considered all classes of vertebrates—fishes, amphibians, reptiles, birds, and mammals—and was, in fact, one of the most distinguished vertebrate paleontologists of his time in Europe. He also published studies on the crustaceans, the crinoids, the Asterozoans, and the cephalopods. His descriptions are characterized by great accuracy, by clarity of expression, and by first-rate drawings. Meyer produced no original theories, no ingenious hypotheses; yet he did not lose sight of the broader connections among his detailed studies. He repeatedly criticized Cuvier's law of correlation and, as early as 1832, wrote a survey of the vertebrates then known, their stratigraphic distribution, emergence, and evolution.

BIBLIOGRAPHY

I. ORIGINAL WORKS. Meyer's books include *Palaeologica, zur Geschichte der Erde und ihrer Geschöpfe* (Frankfurt, 1832); *Die fossilen Zähne und Knochen und ihre Ablagerung in der Gegend von Georgensgmünd in Bayern* (Frankfurt, 1834); *Beiträge zur Paläontologie Württemberg's, enthaltend die fossilen Wirbelthierreste aus den Triasgebilden mit besonderer Rücksicht auf die Labyrinthodonten des Keupers* (Stuttgart, 1844), written with T. Plieninger; *Zur Fauna der Vorwelt: Erste Abtheilung. Fossile Säugetiere, Vögel und Reptilien aus dem Molasse-Mergel von Oeningen* (Frankfurt, 1845); *Zweite Abtheilung. Die Saurier des Muschelkalks mit Rücksicht auf die Saurier aus Buntem Sandstein und Keuper* (Frankfurt, 1847–1855); *Dritte Abtheilung. Saurier aus dem Kupferschiefer der Zechsteinformation* (Frankfurt, 1856); and *Vierte Abtheilung. Reptilien aus dem lithographischen Schiefer in Deutschland und Frankreich* (Frankfurt, 1860).

Among his articles are "Reptilien aus der Steinkohlenformation in Deutschland," in *Palaeontographica*, 6 (1856–1858), 59–219; "Reptilien aus dem Stubensandstein des obern Keupers," *ibid.*, 7 (1861), 253–346; and "Studien über das Genus Mastodon," *ibid.*, 17 (1867–1870), 1–72.

II. SECONDARY LITERATURE. On Meyer or his work, see T. H. Huxley, "The Life of Hermann Christian Erich von Meyer. The Anniversary Address of the President," in *Quarterly Journal of the Geological Society of London*, 26 (1870), xxxiv–xxxvi; F. von Kobell, "Nekrolog auf Hermann v. Meyer," in *Sitzungsberichte der Bayerischen Akademie der Wissenschaften zu München*, 1 (1871), 403–407; M. Pfannenstiel, "Unbekannte Briefe von Sir Charles Lyell an Hermann von Meyer," in *Bulletin of the Geological Institution of the University of Uppsala*, 40 (1961), 1–15; J. J. Rein, "Dr. Christian Erich Hermann von Meyer. Eine biographische Skizze," in *Bericht der Senckenbergischen naturforschenden Gesellschaft in Frankfurt a. M.* (1868–1869), report of the anniversary of 30 May 1869, pp. 13–17; W. Struve, "H. von Meyer und die Senckenbergische Paläontologie," in "Zur Geschichte der paläozoologisch-geologischen Abteilung des Natur-Museums und Forschungs-Instituts Senckenberg," in *Senckenbergiana lethaea*, 48 (1967), 64–75; and C. A. Zittel, *Denkschrift auf Christ. Erich Hermann von Meyer* (Munich, 1870), with complete bibliography.

HEINZ TOBIEN

MEYER, JOHANN FRIEDRICH (*b.* Osnabrück, Hannover [now German Federal Republic], 24 October 1705; *d.* Osnabrück, 2 November 1765), *chemistry*.

Meyer is best known for having been wrong. Just a few years after Joseph Black explained that the difference between the mild and the caustic alkalies lies in the presence or absence of "fixed air" (1756), Meyer published his *Chymische Versuche zur näheren Erkenntniss des ungelöschten Kalchs* (1764). In this work he argued that causticity in alkalies arose from a substance that entered the mild alkalies from the fire. He called this substance *acidum pingue* and characterized it as a combination of a previously unknown acid substance with the matter of fire or light. It was, Meyer said, responsible for "sharp" properties and thus was found in acids, caustic alkalies, and fire. It was not to be confused with phlogiston, which turned calxes into metals; *acidum pingue* calcined metals, causing the famous—or notorious—weight gain. Meyer's peculiar theory of the *acidum pingue* combined features from the Paracelsian sulfur of metals and Lemery's "matter of fire." The theory avoided one set of errors by attributing the "augmented calx" to a gain of matter, but it incurred others by claiming causticity to be a result of an accession of *acidum pingue*.

Meyer's father, who died in 1714, was a physician; his mother, the daughter of an apothecary. Meyer was intended for the clergy but, he said, "Providence made me a pharmacist." He went at age fifteen into his grandmother's apothecary shop, where he served six years as an apprentice. After working as a journeyman in Leipzig, Nordhausen (where he studied mining and metallurgy), Frankfurt am Main, Trier, and Halle, he returned to Osnabrück and in 1737 inherited his grandmother's shop. The following year he married a clergyman's daughter, who died in 1759; they had no children.

Meyer's work was highly respected on the Continent in the 1760's and early 1770's; and his theory of causticity was accepted by a number of chemists, including Baumé, Pörner, and Wiegleb. Black took special care to answer point by point this challenge to his own findings. Lavoisier and Guyton de Morveau avowed at different times that Meyer's writings had considerable merit. But with the explication over the next fifteen years of the role of oxygen in combustion and acidification, and with the recognition that Black's work had inaugurated this great train of discoveries in pneumatic chemistry, Meyer's claim to a place among the builders of eighteenth-century chemistry suffered a blow from which it has never recovered.

BIBLIOGRAPHY

I. ORIGINAL WORKS. *Chymische Versuche zur näheren Erkenntniss des ungelöschten Kalchs* . . . (Hannover–Leipzig, 1764; 2nd ed., 1770) was translated into French by F. F. Dreux (Paris, 1765). *Alchymistische Briefe* . . . (Hannover, 1767) is available in a French trans. by Dreux (Paris, 1767). Johann Christian Wiegleb, *Kleine chymische Abhandlungen von dem grossen Nutzen der Erkenntniss des Acidi pinguis bey der Erklärung vieler chymischen Erscheinungen* (Langensalza, 1767), draws freely and expands upon Meyer's *Versuche*, and contains a short autobiographical sketch by Meyer (on which the present article is based), edited by E. G. Baldinger.

II. SECONDARY LITERATURE. See Henry Guerlac, *Lavoisier: The Crucial Year* (Ithaca, N.Y., 1961), 48–49, and the literature cited there; and J. R. Partington, *A History of Chemistry*, III (London, 1962), 145–146, 152–153, 388–389, 519–520.

STUART PIERSON

MEYER, JULIUS LOTHAR (*b.* Varel, Oldenburg, Germany, 19 August 1830; *d.* Tübingen, Germany, 11 April 1895), *chemistry*.

(Julius) Lothar Meyer was the fourth of seven children of Heinrich Friedrich August Jacob Meyer, a prominent physician in Varel. His mother, the former Anna Sophie Wilhelmine Biermann, was the daughter of another physician of that town. Both Lothar and his brother, Oskar Emil, later a physicist, began their studies with the intention of entering medicine. Brought up as a Lutheran, Meyer first attended a private school, then the newly founded Bürgerschule in Varel, supplementing this education with private instruction in Latin and Greek. Delicate in his early years, he suffered such severe headaches at age fourteen that his father advised complete discontinuance of academic studies and placed him as an assistant to the chief gardener at the summer palace of the grand duke of Oldenburg, at Rastede. After a year his health was sufficiently restored for him to enter the Gymnasium at Oldenburg, from which he graduated in 1851. In the summer of that year Meyer began to study medicine at the University of Zurich, and in 1853 he moved to Würzburg, where Virchow was lecturing on pathology. He received the M.D. the following year. Encouraged by Carl Ludwig, his former physiology professor at Zurich, Meyer turned from medicine to physiological chemistry and went to Heidelberg to study under Bunsen. The latter's work on gas analysis particularly attracted him, and in 1856 Meyer completed his investigation *Ueber die Gase des Blutes*, which was accepted by the Würzburg Faculty of Medicine as his doctoral dissertation. F. Beilstein, H. H. Landolt, H. E. Roscoe, A. von Baeyer, and F. A. Kekulé were in Heidelberg at the same time. Lectures by Kirchhoff moved Meyer further toward physical chemistry.

At the suggestion of his brother, Meyer moved to Königsberg in the fall of 1856, to attend Franz Neumann's lectures on mathematical physics. He also pursued there his earlier physiological interests by studying the effect of carbon monoxide on the blood. When he moved to Breslau in 1858, this investigation was accepted by the Philosophy Faculty as his dissertation for the Ph.D. In February 1859 Meyer established himself as *Privatdozent* in physics and chemistry at Breslau with a critical historical work, "Über die chemischen Lehren von Berthollet und Berzelius." That same spring he took over the direction of the chemical laboratory in the physiological institute and lectured on organic, inorganic, physiological, and biological chemistry. During his stay at Breslau the first edition of his *Die modernen Theorien der Chemie und ihre Bedeutung für die chemische Statik* appeared (1864). It went through five editions and was translated into English, French, and Russian.

Meyer had attended the 1860 Karlsruhe Congress, where he heard Cannizzaro and read his paper on the use of Avogadro's hypothesis and the law of Dulong and Petit in establishing atomic weights and formulas. Meyer edited Cannizzaro's paper for Ostwald's

Klassiker der Exacten Wissenschaften and describes in that work how "the scales fell from my eyes and my doubts disappeared and were replaced by a feeling of quiet certainty." Meyer's *Moderne Theorien* was a direct outcome of that experience. In a brief obituary in 1895 the book was described as "not especially well received at first, but as years passed it exerted a more and more powerful influence on the thoughts of chemists. From a flimsy pamphlet it grew to a stately volume, and it has generally been recognized as the best presentation of the fundamental principles of chemistry until the physicochemical movement began."[1]

Meyer was called to the School of Forestry at Neustadt-Eberswalde in 1866 for his first independent position. The same year he married Johanna Volkmann; they had four children. In 1868 Meyer succeeded C. Weltzien as professor of chemistry and director of the chemical laboratories at the Karlsruhe Polytechnic Institute. His final move, in 1876, was to Tübingen, where he taught until his death.

Two major events occurred in the early years of Meyer's stay at Karlsruhe. Mendeleev's 1869 paper on the periodic table led him to submit his own matured ideas for publication in December of that year. The paper was published in March 1870. In the summer of 1870 the Franco-Prussian War broke out; and Meyer made use of his medical abilities, helping to organize an emergency hospital in the buildings of the Polytechnic.

Meyer's Tübingen years at last offered an opportunity for intensive pursuit of his major interests. In excellent health until his sudden death, he guided the work of over sixty doctoral candidates; and with his associate Karl Seubert he published a careful analysis of the best atomic weight determinations available until then. In 1890 Meyer published *Grundzüge der theoretischen Chemie*, a less technical account of the theoretical foundations of chemistry than the later editions of his *Moderne Theorien* had become.

Outside his work in chemistry, Meyer read Greek and Latin classics and retained his love for gardening, learned in his youth. He was concerned with higher education and gave a number of lectures—later published—on that subject. For the year 1894–1895 he was elected rector of Tübingen University.

Meyer received the Davy Medal of the Royal Society jointly with Mendeleev in 1882. In 1883 he became a foreign honorary member of the Chemical Society (London) and in 1888 and 1891 corresponding member of the Prussian and St. Petersburg Academies of Sciences, respectively. He was given a title of nobility by decree of the Württemberg crown in 1892.

Meyer's earliest research dealt with physiological aspects of the uptake of gases by the blood. Building on previous studies by G. Magnus, he was able to demonstrate in 1856 that oxygen absorption by blood in the lungs occurs independently of pressure. This suggested to him that some possibly loose chemical linkage occurred. When he turned his attention to carbon monoxide poisoning, Meyer demonstrated a similar chemical linkage between that gas and a constituent of the blood. Further, he found that the amounts of oxygen and carbon monoxide taken up by the blood were in a simple molecular ratio, the carbon monoxide being able to expel volume for volume the oxygen already in the blood. This suggested to him that the same constituent of blood reacted with both gases. His preliminary searches for this constituent were unsuccessful. Hemoglobin was discovered by Hoppe-Seyler in 1864.[2]

Although these physiological studies were of considerable importance, Meyer's greatest achievement is no doubt tied to his work on the periodic classification of the elements. Meyer and Mendeleev both received their major stimulus for these considerations at the 1860 Karlsruhe Congress through Cannizzaro's paper on atomic weights. By 1862, Meyer had completed the manuscript of *Moderne Theorien*, including a table of twenty-eight elements in order of increasing atomic weight. Meyer felt that by the early 1860's considerable unity had finally been achieved regarding the fundamental principles of chemistry; and it was the purpose of his book to present these theoretical foundations.

Meyer saw J. W. Döbereiner and M. von Pettenkofer as his direct precursors and later edited their key papers. In 1816–1817, and more fully in 1829, Döbereiner had drawn attention to the fact that similar chemical elements often occurred in groups of three and that the arithmetic mean of the atomic weights of the lightest and heaviest elements often corresponded closely to the atomic weight of the third member of the group. His "triads" included calcium, strontium, and barium; lithium, sodium, and potassium; chlorine, bromine, and iodine; sulfur, selenium, and tellurium. Such a quantitative relationship suggested to some the likelihood that atoms were not the ultimate building blocks of nature—that they were composite, with the differences in weight of successive members of triads representing weights of more fundamental units.

Pettenkofer, pursuing Döbereiner's ideas, pointed to the parallelism between regular increases in equivalent weights of similar elements and increases in molecular weights of successive members of homologous series in organic chemistry.[3] Thus $CH_3 = 15$, $C_2H_5 = 29$, $C_3H_7 = 43$, $C_4H_9 = 57$,

$C_5H_{11} = 71$. The common increment (of 14) in these weights suggested that organic radicals may well hold the clue to the nature of the internal structure of inorganic atoms. Similar ideas were independently developed by Dumas, who spoke about them to the British Association for the Advancement of Science in 1851 but did not publish them until 1857.[4] Further attempts at systematizing the elements known to Meyer were made by J. H. Gladstone (1853), J. P. Cooke (1854), W. Odling (1857), and E. Lenssen (1857).

No progress beyond the arithmetic comparisons of weights of similar elements was likely as long as no clear distinction was made between equivalent and atomic weights, and no path to the values of the latter was generally accepted. That clarification was achieved by Cannizzaro at Karlsruhe in 1860, and almost immediately further relations between the elements became apparent. In 1862 A. E. Béguyer de Chancourtois plotted atomic weights of elements on a "telluric screw," on which similar elements would fall directly below each other. J. A. R. Newlands, beginning in 1863, organized the elements by their atomic weights, as computed by Cannizzaro's methods, into ten families (later reduced to eight). In an early table blanks were left for undiscovered elements; but these later disappeared in the eight-family version of 1865, which Newlands claimed as illustrating a "law of octaves."

Near the end of the first edition of Meyer's *Moderne Theorien*, the author points to the evidences for the composite nature of atoms, emphasizing the parallelism between series of related elements and organic compounds. He then appends a tabulation (see Figure 1) of twenty-eight elements, arranged according to increasing atomic weight, in six families that have valences of 4, 3, 2, 1, 1, and 2, respectively. Thus the integral stepwise change in valence as atomic weight increases was in print by 1864. A relation between families, and hence between dissimilar yet neighboring elements, was clearly established. Meyer remained interested also in constant increments within families and left a space for an as yet undiscovered element between silicon and tin, clearly indicating its probable atomic weight to be $28.5 + 44.55$, or 73.1. His next publication on the subject appeared after Mendeleev's historic 1869 paper, which Meyer had seen only in its abbreviated German form.[5]

Meyer's independent establishment of the central principles underlying the periodic table of the elements was demonstrated in 1893, when Adolf Remelé, his successor at Neustadt-Eberswalde, showed him a handwritten draft periodic table (Figure 2) designed by Meyer for the second edition of *Moderne Theorien* and given to Remelé in July 1868. Its notation "§91" makes clear its intended use for the second edition. It differs from the 1864 table mainly by the addition of twenty-four elements and nine families. These were the B-subgroups, the characteristics of which Meyer later claimed to have discovered independently. Hydrogen, boron, and indium are not in the table, and aluminum appears in both column 3

	4 werthig	3 werthig	2 werthig	1 werthig	1 werthig	2 werthig
	—	—	—	—	Li = 7.03	(Be = 9.3?)
Differenz =	—	—	—	—	16.02	(14.7)
	C = 12.0	N = 14.04	O = 16.00	Fl = 19.0	Na = 23.05	Mg = 24.0
Differenz =	16.5	16.96	16.07	16.46	16.08	16.0
	Si = 28.5	P = 31.0	S = 32.07	Cl = 35.46	K = 39.13	Ca = 40.0
Differenz =	$\frac{89.1}{2} = 44.55$	44.0	46.7	44.51	46.3	47.6
	—	As = 75.0	Se = 78.8	Br = 79.97	Rb = 85.4	Sr = 87.6
Differenz =	$\frac{89.1}{2} = 44.55$	45.6	49.5	46.8	47.6	49.5
	Sn = 117.6	Sb = 120.6	Te = 128.3	I = 126.8	Cs = 133.0	Ba = 137.1
Differenz =	89.4 = 2 × 44.7	87.4 = 2 × 43.7	—	—	(71 = 2 × 35.5)	—
	Pb = 207.0	Bi = 208.0	—	—	(Tl = 204?)	—

FIGURE 1.   Meyer's periodic table of 1864.

MEYER

1	2	3	4	5	6	7	8	9	10	11	12	13	14	15
s 91														
											Li = 7.03	Be = 9.3		
											16.02	14.7		
							C = 12.00	N = 14.04	O = 16.00	Fl = 19.0	Na = 23.05	Mg = 24.0		
							16.5	16.96	16.07	16.46	16.08	16.0		
		Al = 27.3	Al = 27.3				Si = 28.5	P = 31.0	S = 32.07	Cl = 35.46	K = 39.13	Ca = 40.0	Ti = 48	Mo = 92
		$\frac{28.7}{2} = 14.3$					$\frac{89.1}{2} = 44.55$	44.0	46.7	44.51	46.3	47.6	42	45
Cr = 52.6	Mn = 55.1	Fe = 56.0	Co = 58.7	Ni = 58.7	Cu = 63.5	Zn = 65.0	–	As = 75.0	Se = 78.8	Br = 79.97	Rb = 85.4	Sr = 87.6	Zr = 90	Vd = 137
	49.2	48.3	47.3		44.4	46.9	$\frac{89.1}{2} = 44.55$	45.6	49.5	46.8	47.6	49.5	47.6	47
	Ru = 104.3	Rh = 104.3	Pd = 106.0		Ag = 107.94	Cd = 111.9	Sn = 117.6	Sb = 120.6	Te = 128.3	I = 126.8	Cs = 133.0	Ba = 137.1	Ta = 137.6	W = 184
	92.8 = 2 x 46.4	92.8 = 2 x 46.4	93 = 2 x 46.5		88.8 = 2 x 44.4	88.3 = 2 x 44.15	89.4 = 2 x 44.7	87.4 = 2 x 43.7			71 = 2 x 35.5			
	Pt = 197.1	Ir = 197.1	Os = 199.0		Au = 196.7	Hg = 200.2	Pb = 207.0	Bi = 208.0			?Tl = 204?			

FIGURE 2. Meyer's 1868 table, published in 1895.

and column 4. Boron, indium, and aluminum properly belong in a family between columns 7 and 8. Meyer placed lead (Pb) correctly in column 8, while Mendeleev put it with calcium, strontium, and barium. Remelé's disclosure was published by Seubert after Meyer's death.[6]

In Meyer's classic paper of 1870, he adopted Mendeleev's use of a vertical form for the periodic table, publishing a table (Figure 3) in which the relation of the A- and B-subgroups of the chemical families is for the first time clearly indicated.[7] He also attached his graphical representation of the variation of atomic volume of the solid elements (volume divided by atomic weight) when plotted against atomic weight (Figure 4), for which he is most generally known. Both Meyer and Mendeleev emphasized that there is a periodic variation, a succession of maxima and minima, in several physical and chemical properties when they are examined as functions of atomic weight. Meyer began this paper with the assertion that

it is most improbable that the chemical elements are absolutely undecomposable and referred to the ideas of Prout, Pettenkofer, and Dumas. As for the gaps in the table, he suggested that they would be filled through careful redeterminations of the atomic weights of known elements or through the discovery of new ones.

The significance of atomic weights in the demonstration of chemical periodicity, and the suspicion that some atomic weights were not accurate, led Meyer and Seubert to examine critically and to recalculate all atomic weights then considered important. Their study was published in 1883. All atomic weights were referred to the standard of unity for the atomic weight of hydrogen, a standard Meyer championed. Wilhelm Ostwald, on the other hand, strongly urged the adoption of $O = 16.000$ as standard, a view accepted in 1898 by a special committee of the German Chemical Society consisting of Landolt, Ostwald, and Seubert. In 1903 the newly created International

I	II	III	IV	V	VI	VII	VIII	IX
	B = 11.0	Al = 27.3		--		?In = 113.4		Tl = 202.7
			--	--			--	
	C = 11.97	Si = 28		--		Sn = 117.8		Pb = 206.4
			Ti = 48		Zr = 89.7		--	
	N = 14.01	P = 30.9		As = 74.9		Sb = 122.1		Bi = 207.5
			V = 51.2		Nb = 93.7		Ta = 182.2	
	O = 15.96	S = 31.98		Sc = 78		Te = 128?		--
			Cr = 52.4		Mo = 95.6		W = 183.5	
--	F = 19.1	Cl = 35.38		Br = 79.75		I = 126.5		--
			Mn = 54.8		Ru = 103.5		Os = 198.6?	
			Fe = 55.9		Rh = 104.1		Ir = 196.7	
			Co = Ni = 58.6		Pd = 106.2		Pt = 196.7	
Li = 7.01	Na = 22.99	K = 39.04		Rb = 85.2		Cs = 132.7		--
			Cu = 63.3		Ag = 107.66		Au = 196.2	
?Be = 9.3	Mg = 23.9	Ca = 39.9		Sr = 87.0		Ba = 136.8		--
			Zn = 64.9		Cd = 111.6		Hg = 199.8	

Difference from I to II and from II to III about = 16.
Difference from III to V, Iv to VI, V to VII fluctuating around 46.
Difference from VI to VIII, from VII to IX = 88 to 92.

FIGURE 3.　Meyer's 1870 table showing subgroups A (columns V, VII, IX) and B (IV, VI, VIII).

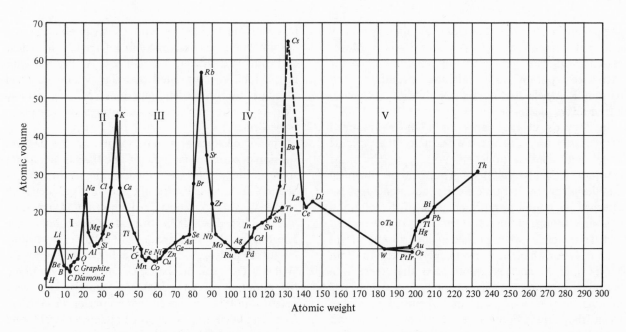

FIGURE 4.   Meyer's 1870 graph of atomic volume plotted against atomic weight. (A redraft of Bailey's version which appeared in *Philosophical Magazine*, 5th ser., **13** [1882], 31.)

Commission on Atomic Weights decided to publish parallel tables based on H = 1 and O = 16, a practice followed for many years. The arguments for the oxygen standard were that the O:H ratio was for many years in doubt and that far more elements formed stable compounds with oxygen than with hydrogen.

In organic structural theory Meyer became involved in discussions of the structure of benzene. In 1865 Kekulé had proposed ring formula I; but this predicted two substances $C_6H_4X_2$, each having the two substituents, X, on adjacent carbons (II and III). Only one

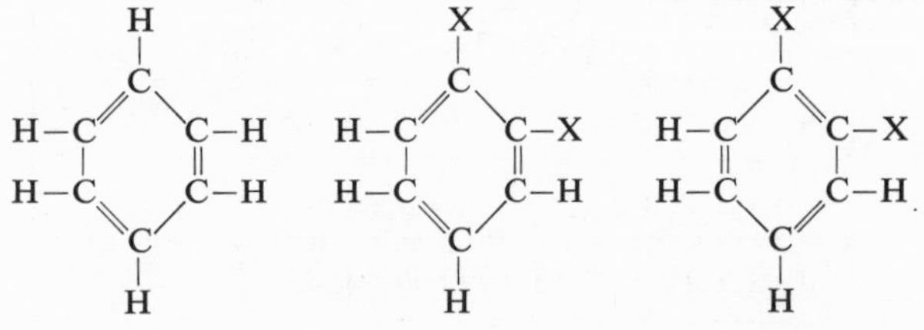

FIGURE 5

was ever found, and in 1872 Kekulé proposed a complex atomic oscillation mechanism in order to make all carbon atoms equivalent.[8] In the same year, in the second edition of *Moderne Theorien*, Meyer proposed a much simpler solution. He suggested that each carbon used only three of its four affinities, leaving one valence unsatisfied. His formula was the

first of a series of "centric" formulas proposed by a number of chemists. The unused valences point to the center of the ring.

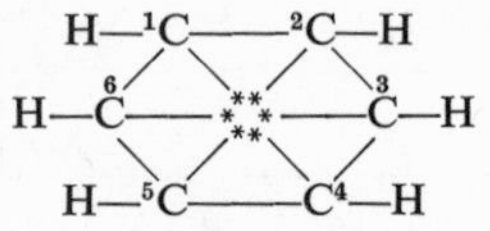

FIGURE 6

Meyer studied a number of benzene substitution reactions, particularly the nitration of benzene and its derivatives. He examined the effects of time, temperature, solvent, and concentration of reagents, feeling that chemists must go beyond a mere interest in the nature and quantity of products and must subject chemical reactions themselves to quantitative study. He examined reagents that facilitated chlorination and oxidation, the so-called chlorine and oxygen carriers, thus laying some of the groundwork for Ostwald's extensive revision of the concept of catalysis (1894). Meyer's studies of the effects of reagent concentration on chemical reactions served to confirm the law of mass action enunciated by C. M. Guldberg and P. Waage. In the fourth edition of *Moderne Theorien* (1883), he included a major new section, constituting more than a third of the book, entitled "Dynamik der Atome."

Meyer and his students investigated a number of physical properties, such as the boiling points, of structurally related organic compounds, seeking relations between these properties and molecular structure. His wide-ranging interests and mechanical skill led Meyer to devise or improve many pieces of apparatus, often adopted by other chemists. He pleaded with chemists to systematize inorganic chemistry on the basis of the periodic table, in order to approach the organization of subject matter achieved in organic chemistry.

NOTES

1. I. R., "Lothar Meyer," in *Journal of the American Chemical Society*, **17** (1895), 471–472.
2. F. Hoppe-Seyler, "Ueber die optischen und chemischen Eigenschaften des Blutfarbstoffs," in *Virchows Archiv für pathologische Anatomie und Physiologie und für klinische Medizin*, **29** (1864), 233–235.
3. M. Pettenkofer, "Ueber die regelmässigen Abstände der Aequivalentzahlen der sogenannten einfachen Radicalen," in *Münchener Gelehrten Anzeigen*, **30** (1850), 261–272; repr. with new intro. by the author in *Annalen der Chemie*, **105** (1858), 187–202.
4. J. B. A. Dumas, "Mémoire sur les équivalents des corps simples," in *Comptes rendus . . . de l'Académie des sciences*, **45** (1857), 709–731; **46** (1858), 951–953; **47** (1858), 1026–1034.
5. D. Mendeleev, "Sootnoshenie svoistv s atomnym vesom elementov" ("The Correlation Between the Properties and the Atomic Weights of the Elements"), in *Zhurnal Russkago fiziko-khimicheskago obshchestva pri Imperatorskago St-Peterburgskago universitete*, **1** (1869), 60–77; *Zeitschrift für Chemie*, **12** (1869), 405–406.
6. K. Seubert, "Zur Geschichte des periodischen Systems," in *Zeitschrift für anorganische . . . Chemie*, **9** (1895), 334–338.
7. L. Meyer, "Die Natur der chemischen Elemente als Function ihrer Atomgewichte," in *Justus Liebigs Annalen der Chemie*, supp. **7** (1870), 354–364.
8. F. A. Kekulé, "Ueber einige Condensationsproducte des Aldehyds," in *Annalen der Chemie*, **162** (1872), 77–124.

BIBLIOGRAPHY

I. ORIGINAL WORKS. Meyer's publications and those of students under his direction are listed in the extensive obituaries by K. Seubert, in *Berichte der Deutschen chemischen Gesellschaft*, **28R** (1895), 1109–1146; and P. P. Bedson, in *Journal of the Chemical Society*, **69** (1896), 1402–1439, repr. in *Memorial Lectures Delivered Before the Chemical Society, 1893–1900* (London, 1901). Bedson's bibliography is copied from Seubert's. Unfortunately the listing of doctoral publications is given under the year of the dissertation and not the year of publication of the journal article. The volume of each journal article is, however, given. The bibliography includes, in addition to Meyer's technical articles, a number of his obituaries and more general lectures and papers, particularly on education and the nature of the university.

Meyer's major work is *Die modernen Theorien der Chemie und ihre Bedeutung für die chemische Statik* (Breslau, 1864, 1872, 1876, 1883, 1884). The 1st ed. was translated into Russian as *Novieishie teorii khimii ikh znacherie dlya khimicheskoy statiki* (St. Petersburg, 1866). The 5th ed. was translated into English by P. Phillips Bedson and W.

Carleton Williams, *Modern Theories of Chemistry* (London, 1888), and French by A. Bloch and J. Meunier, *Les théories modernes de la chimie et leur application à la mécanique chimique*, 2 vols. (Paris, 1887–1889). His less technical account of the same subject appeared as *Grundzüge der theoretischen Chemie* (Leipzig, 1890; 2nd ed., 1893); there is an English trans. by P. Phillips Bedson and W. C. Williams, *Outlines of Theoretical Chemistry* (London, 1892).

Lothar Meyer and Karl Seubert published *Die Atomgewichte der Elemente aus den Originalzahlen neu berechnet* (Leipzig, 1883).

Meyer edited two works in Ostwald's Klassiker der Exacten Wissenschaften: no. 30, *Abriss eines Lehrganges der theoretischen Chemie, vorgetragen von Prof. S. Cannizzaro* (Leipzig, 1891); and no. 66, *Die Anfänge des natürlichen Systemes der chemischen Elemente. Abhandlungen von J. W. Döbereiner und Max Pettenkofer* (Leipzig, 1895), which contains a historical survey by Meyer of the further development of the doctrine of the triads of the elements. Meyer's major contributions on the periodic law (1864, 1870) were published with those of Mendeleev in Ostwald's Klassiker, no. 68, edited with commentary by Karl Seubert: *Das natürliche System der chemischen Elemente, Abhandlungen von L. Meyer und D. Mendeleeff* (Leipzig, 1895).

The paper that established Meyer as codiscoverer of the periodic law is "Die Natur der chemischen Elemente als Function ihrer Atomgewichte," in *Justus Liebigs Annalen der Chemie*, supp. **7** (1870), 354–364.

II. SECONDARY LITERATURE. In addition to the major obituaries by Seubert and Bedson (see above), there is P. Walden, "Meyer, Mendelejeff, Ramsay, und das periodische System der Elemente," in G. Bugge, ed., *Das Buch der grossen Chemiker*, II (Berlin, 1930), 229–287, with further bibliographic sources on p. 508. Brief biographical sketches were written by J. H. Long, in *Journal of the American Chemical Society*, **17** (1895), 664–666; and R. Winderlich, in *Journal of Chemical Education*, **27** (1950), 365–368.

Meyer's work and its context are discussed in some detail in P. Venable, *The Development of the Periodic Law* (Easton, Pa., 1896), 96–108; and in Ida Freund, *The Study of Chemical Composition* (Cambridge, 1904; repr. New York, 1968), esp. ch. 16.

The question of Mendeleev's priority in enunciating the periodic law was discussed under the title "Zur Geschichte der periodischen Atomistik" by L. Meyer, in *Berichte der Deutschen chemischen Gesellschaft*, **13** (1880), 259–265, 2043–2044; by D. Mendeleev, *ibid.*, 1796–1804; and K. Seubert, in *Zeitschrift für anorganische . . . Chemie*, **9** (1895), 334–338. See also J. W. van Spronsen, "The Priority Conflict Between Mendeleev and Meyer," in *Journal of Chemical Education*, **46** (1969), 136–139; J. W. van Spronsen, *The Periodic System of Chemical Elements: A History of the First Hundred Years* (Amsterdam–London–New York, 1969), 124–132; and H. Cassebaum and G. B. Kauffman, "The Periodic System of the Chemical Elements: The Search for Its Discoverer," in *Isis*, **62** (1971), 314–327.

OTTO THEODOR BENFEY

MEYER, KURT HEINRICH (*b*. Dorpat, Russia, 29 September 1883; *d*. Menton, France, 14 April 1952), *organic chemistry*.

Meyer's father, Hans Horst Meyer, was a pharmacologist who also taught at the German-speaking University of Dorpat. Meyer was educated mainly in Germany and studied chemistry at the universities of Marburg, Freiburg, and Leipzig; among his teachers were Hantzsch and Ostwald. After receiving the doctorate in 1907, he traveled for a year to America, to Rutherford's department of physics at Manchester, and to Ramsay's department of chemistry at London; he then settled in Munich, where the school of organic chemistry was led by Adolf von Baeyer. There Meyer carried out the studies on keto-enol tautomerism that first made his reputation, including the determination by a simple titration of the amount of enol in samples of ethyl acetoacetate. He also discovered some new coupling reactions of diazonium salts and worked on a possible industrial synthesis of formamide from carbon monoxide and ammonia and, with F. Bergius, on the large-scale hydrolysis of chlorobenzene to phenol.

Meyer spent three years on war service as an artillery officer but was recalled in 1917 to work with Haber on chemical warfare. When peace came, he returned to Munich, where organic chemistry was under Willstätter's direction, and returned to his previous interests. Notably, with H. Hopff he isolated the pure enol form of ethyl acetoacetate by "aseptic distillation," avoiding the presence of any impurities that might catalyze the conversion to the keto form.

In 1921 Meyer left academic life to become director of the headquarters laboratories of the firm of Badische Anilin- und Sodafabrik (BASF) at Ludwigshafen. He organized a large and active research group whose interests, although wide, were concerned mainly with dyeing and dyestuffs. His own interests became increasingly centered on the chemistry of natural high polymers, a study to which he recruited the young physical chemist Herman Francis Mark. Their results, published in 1930, were a landmark in the development of the subject. In a lucid survey of naturally occurring organic polymers (cellulose, starch, proteins, rubber) the authors, although giving due weight to the then fashionable theory of "small building blocks," found themselves more in sympathy with the concept of true macromolecules, which was being vigorously promoted by Staudinger.

Especially after the incorporation of BASF into the huge I. G. Farbenindustrie complex in 1926, Meyer found that his research work was increasingly hindered by the cares of administration. The political situation in Germany also caused him justifiable anxiety, and in 1932 he left the country to take the chair of inorganic and organic chemistry at the University of Geneva. Although he had to accustom himself to lecturing in French, a language with which he was unfamiliar, he was a successful teacher and again built up a fine research school. With his collaborators (notably A. J. A. van der Wyk) Meyer continued his studies of cellulose and chitin, the permeability of synthetic membranes, and the thermodynamics of large molecules in solution; and developed a theory of muscle contraction by analogy with the contraction of rubber. Investigation of the structure of amylopectin, the branched-chain constituent of starch, led to extensive work on the crystallization, characterization, and specificity of enzymes, a subject that occupied his last years. Meyer died suddenly while on holiday.

BIBLIOGRAPHY

I. ORIGINAL WORKS. Meyer's main work is *Der Aufbau der hochpolymeren organischen Naturstoffe* (Leipzig, 1930), written with H. F. Mark. The 2nd ed. (Leipzig, 1940) was in 2 vols., one by Meyer, dealing with the chemical aspects of the subject, and the other by Mark, concerned with physics. Meyer's volume was trans. into English by L. E. R. Picken and published as *Natural and Synthetic High Polymers* (New York, 1942; 2nd ed., 1950). Meyer wrote many scientific papers, usually with collaborators. A complete list of works is in Poggendorff, V, 843–844, VI, 1717, and VIIa, 3, 283–285.

II. SECONDARY LITERATURE. There is a memorial article by R. Jeanloz in *Advances in Carbohydrate Chemistry*, **11** (1956), xiii–xviii, with portrait. The more important obituary notices include H. Mark, in *Angewandte Chemie*, **64** (1952), 521–523; L. E. R. Picken, in *Nature*, **169** (1952), 820; and A. J. A. van der Wyk, in *Helvetica chimica acta*, **35** (1952), 1418–1422.

W. V. FARRAR

MEYER, VICTOR (*b*. Berlin, Germany, 8 September 1848; *d*. Heidelberg, Germany, 8 August 1897), *chemistry*.

Victor Meyer was the second son of Jacques and Bertha Meyer. The elder Meyer, a prosperous Jewish merchant in calico printing and dyeing, wanted his sons to become chemists, but Victor's foremost desire was to be an actor. Hoping that his interests would change, the family persuaded him to attend some lectures at Heidelberg, where his brother Richard was a student. He then enrolled at Berlin and transferred to Heidelberg in 1865. He was suddenly converted to chemistry on encountering the renowned Bunsen. His dramatic gifts were to be employed as a striking and effective teacher.

At Heidelberg, Meyer studied under Bunsen, Erlenmeyer, Kopp, Kirchhoff, and Helmholtz. He headed the lists in all his courses and progressed so rapidly that he was awarded the Ph.D., *summa cum laude*, at the age of eighteen.

Bunsen was so impressed with Meyer that he immediately selected him to be his assistant. Meyer worked with Bunsen for one year, performing analyses of the mineral waters of Baden for the government. Bunsen then recommended him to Baeyer, whose laboratory at the Gewerbeakademie in Berlin was one of the most famous in Europe. Meyer spent three years with Baeyer (1868–1871), beginning his publications in organic chemistry during this period. His first professorship was at the Stuttgart Polytechnic in 1871. At the age of twenty-four he became a full professor and director of the chemical laboratories at the Eidgenössische Technische Hochschule at Zurich. Meyer celebrated this appointment with his engagement to Hedwig Davidson. They were married in 1873 and had five daughters.

Meyer had rejected offers from several institutions during his thirteen years in Zurich, when in 1885 the University of Göttingen asked him to take charge of the construction of its new chemical laboratories. No sooner were the laboratories completed in 1888 than Meyer received the offer of Bunsen's chair at Heidelberg. He felt obliged to remain at Göttingen and declined the offer. It was only Bunsen himself, intervening with the Prussian ministry for the release of Meyer from Göttingen, who enabled Meyer to become his successor at Heidelberg, a position Meyer held until his death in 1897.

An extremely attractive personality, Meyer was also a brilliant lecturer and attracted many students from both Europe and North America. He was a member of the academies of Berlin, Uppsala, and Göttingen, and president of the German Chemical Society.

Meyer's health declined during the 1880's. He suffered several breakdowns and was so frequently ill that he resorted to drugs in order to sleep. He became conscious that his long suffering was affecting his thinking and suddenly in the summer of 1897, suffering from continuous neuralgic pains, his nervous system shattered, he ended his life by taking prussic acid.

There is an unusually large number of important contributions in the more than 300 papers that Meyer published. His first significant paper appeared in 1870, when he described a new method for introducing the carboxyl group into an aromatic substance by heating the potassium salts of aromatic sulfonic acids with sodium formate. This method has been used ever since by organic chemists for the synthesis of aromatic acids. Meyer's primary purpose in this paper was to ascertain the constitution of benzene derivatives. The determination of the ring position of substituents in isomeric aromatic compounds was an unsettled problem, and Meyer established that salicylic acid and other compounds which had been assigned to the *meta* series were *ortho* derivatives. In a paper one year later Meyer listed many disubstituted benzoic acids in columns according to whether they were *ortho*, *meta*, or *para* compounds.

Meyer first attracted wide attention in 1872 with his work on the nitroparaffins. Aromatic nitro compounds were well known and easily prepared from aromatic hydrocarbons, but aliphatic nitro compounds existed only in scattered examples, obtained mostly by accident. Meyer proposed the existence of two series of isomeric organic nitrogen compounds: the nitrite and nitro compounds. During his year at Stuttgart, he discovered a general method for the preparation of nitroparaffins and made the subject his main research problem for his first four years at Zurich. Meyer found that alkyl iodides combined with silver nitrite to form true nitro compounds, the nitrogen atom being bound directly to a carbon atom, whereas the isomeric nitrites were esters. He explored this area so thoroughly that at the time of his death almost all that was known about nitro compounds was due to Meyer and his students.

Meyer disclosed the existence of two new classes of organic nitrogen substances from the surprising reactions of nitrous acid with the primary and secondary nitroparaffins. Primary nitro compounds formed acidic products which dissolved in alkali to form red salts. Secondary nitro compounds formed blue nonacidic products which did not dissolve in alkali. Meyer named these products "nitrolic acids" and "pseudonitroles" respectively. Since tertiary nitroparaffins did not react with nitrous acid, these color reactions served as a test to differentiate between primary, secondary, and tertiary radicals. Meyer and his students established the structural formulas for the nitrolic acids and pseudonitroles.

Meyer then explored a variety of organic nitrogen compounds and discovered several new types. His most important compound was his preparation of the first oximes by means of the reaction between hydroxylamine and an aldehyde or ketone. He proved that this was a general reaction with the carbonyl group, and he established the structure of oximes.

Victor Meyer's name is most closely associated with his vapor density method. Devised in three stages from 1876, the method was a product of his researches in organic chemistry, since it was necessary for him to determine the molecular formulas of the substances with which he was working. There were several methods available for determining the density of the vapors of liquids or solids, each having particular advantages and disadvantages. Meyer wanted a method that (1) utilized small amounts of a substance (he was working with new substances usually obtainable only in small quantities) and that (2) could be used at high temperatures (his substances often possessed high boiling points).

In 1876 he measured for the first time the vapor density of diphenyl, anthracene, anthraquinone, triphenylamine, p-dibromobenzene, and p-diphenyl-benzene by volatilizing them at the temperature of boiling sulfur. The following year, in order to make his method more flexible, he used the vapors of a variety of liquids, depending on the temperature required, instead of sulfur. Finally, in 1878 he presented his third and best-known modification. The vapor of a weighed substance displaced an equal volume of air, which in turn was measured by means of a burette. This method is more commonly used than any other, and Meyer's apparatus is found in most chemical laboratories.

These vapor density studies led to his endless series of pyrochemical researches, which he investigated until his last days at Heidelberg. Meyer hoped to get vapor density estimations at ever higher temperatures. He employed molten lead baths and platinum, platinum-iridium, and porcelain bulbs, which enabled him to study vapors at temperatures up to 3000° C. Very little was known about the molecular constitution of vapors at high temperatures. Meyer's method made possible the determination of the molecular state of many elements and inorganic substances. In 1879 he showed that the halogens dissociated at high temperatures. His pyrochemical investigations included vapor density determinations, the effect of temperature on the dissociation of substances, and the study of the ignition temperatures of explosive gas mixtures. In 1885 he published *Pyrochemische Untersuchungen*, a monograph on the subject.

A new area for investigation came about through a lecture demonstration that failed. In 1882 Meyer gave a series of lectures on benzene and its derivatives. His lectures were brilliant as usual, and the experiments performed before the class were well prepared. At one of these lectures Meyer wanted to show the students Baeyer's indophenine test for benzene, in which the addition of isatin and sulfuric acid to benzene produces the deep blue indophenine. The results were negative. Sandmeyer, Meyer's assistant, reminded him afterward that the benzene sample that had been used was not commercial benzene from coal tar but synthetic benzene prepared by the decarboxylation of benzoic acid.

Meyer's investigation of the indophenine reaction began the same day. He found that the purest samples of benzene from coal tar invariably gave the blue color reaction, but the color could be eliminated by first extracting the benzene with sulfuric acid. The sulfonated product on distillation gave Meyer an active "benzene," which again showed the indophenine reaction. Meyer proposed several hypotheses, one of which was that coal-tar benzene was a mixture of two substances with similar properties and that only one of these substances combined with isatin. In 1883 he isolated this substance and named it "thiophene" because it contains sulfur and is similar to phenyl compounds. He then rapidly developed the subject and was able in five years to publish a 300-page monograph, *Die Thiophengruppe* (1888), which contains a list of 106 papers by Meyer and his students. His main interest was in demonstrating the similarity between the chemistry of thiophene compounds and the chemistry of benzene. By 1885 he proved that thiophene has a ring structure and suggested that pyrrole and furan were analogous ring compounds.

Meyer contributed many papers on the negative nature of radicals, a topic which had interested him ever since he detected the acidic properties of the nitroparaffins. He could replace hydrogen in a nitroparaffin by an alkali metal and thereby form a salt. He explained that the acidic character is due to the influence of the nitro group on the hydrogen atoms bound to the same carbon atom. He noted that acidity can be induced in an inert hydrocarbon by the introduction of certain substituents, such as nitro, cyano, or phenyl radicals. In 1887 Meyer defined those groups which possessed acid-inducing properties as "negative," later termed "electrophilic" by Ingold in the context of the electronic theory of valence.

Continuing research on the oximes led Meyer into the realm of stereochemistry and the spatial effects of radicals. Meyer and his students noted that benzil forms more than one dioxime. In 1888 he and Karl von Auwers explained that the isomerism is due to lack of free rotation about the carbon-carbon single bond, an explanation at variance with van't Hoff's assumption of free rotation about such bonds. In so doing, they proposed the term "stereochemistry" in place of van't Hoff's "chemistry in space" as a more suitable name for phenomena involving spatial effects. Their explanation never appealed to chemists, and Hantzsch and Werner in 1890 presented an explanation based on the stereochemistry of nitrogen. This explanation proved to be more satisfactory, although

Meyer was critical to the end of his life of their spatial formulas.

Meyer's interest in spatial aspects of organic reactions continued during the 1890's, and in 1894 he identified the inhibiting effect known as "steric hindrance." Benzoic acid and most of its substitution products readily formed esters with alcohol at room temperature, but Meyer observed that trisubstituted benzoic acids do not form esters unless the carboxyl group is extended well beyond the ring by the interposition of a chain of carbon atoms. Further study showed that *meta* and *para* derivatives of benzoic acid esterify almost completely while their isomeric *diortho* compounds yield little or no ester. Meyer explained this as a spatial effect, the *ortho* substituent exerting a blocking action, which suppresses the esterification.

Concurrently with his stereochemical researches, Meyer published many papers exploring new types of aromatic iodine compounds. He revealed that iodine can exist in higher oxidation states in aromatic compounds. He first prepared an "iodoso" compound in 1892 by the oxidation of *o*-iodobenzoic acid; further oxidation produced an "iodoxy" compound. What was remarkable to him was his discovery in 1894 of a class of free organic bases, the "iodonium" compounds. He obtained the first member of this class by the interaction of iodoso- and iodoxyhydrocarbons. Iodosobenzene and iodoxybenzene yielded diphenyliodonium hydroxide:

$$C_6H_5-IO + C_6H_5-IO_2 + AgOH$$
$$\rightarrow (C_6H_5)_2I-OH + AgIO_3$$

Iodonium hydroxides are strong bases resembling the quaternary ammonium and ternary sulfonium bases.

Victor Meyer's concern for excellence in teaching found expression in a project with which he was occupied at the time of his death. With Paul Jacobson, his assistant at Heidelberg, he wrote a comprehensive treatise on organic chemistry, the *Lehrbuch der organischen Chemie*. This two-volume work, the second volume of which was incomplete when he died, remains the best extended treatment of the subject. The book was meant to be fresh and comprehensive. It included the most recent developments in theory, the authors being the first to use stereochemistry as a background for the subject. Written in an attractive style, it remains a rich source of information about both the principles of organic chemistry and of the chemistry of the classes of organic compounds and their individual members.

BIBLIOGRAPHY

I. ORIGINAL WORKS. Meyer wrote three major chemical treatises: *Pyrochemische Untersuchungen* (Brunswick, 1885), written with Carl Langer; *Die Thiophengruppe* (Brunswick, 1888); and *Lehrbuch der organischen Chemie*, 2 vols. (Leipzig, 1893–1903), written with Paul Jacobson.

Among his important papers are "Untersuchungen über die Constitution der zweifach-substituirten Benzole," in *Justus Liebigs Annalen der Chemie*, **156** (1870), 265–301, and **159** (1871), 1–27; "Über die Nitroverbindungen der Fettreihe," in *Berichte der Deutschen chemischen Gesellschaft*, **5** (1872), 399–406, 514–518, written with O. Stüber; "Über die Nitroverbindungen der Fettreihe," in *Justus Liebigs Annalen der Chemie*, **171** (1874), 1–56, and **175** (1875), 88–140; "Über die Pseudonitrole, die Isomeren der Nitrolsäuren," *ibid.*, **180** (1876), 133–155, written with J. Locher; "Zur Dampfdichtebestimmung," in *Berichte der Deutschen chemischen Gesellschaft*, **11** (1878), 1867–1870; "Über das Verhalten des Chlors bei höher Temperatur," *ibid.*, **12** (1879), 1426–1431, written with Carl Meyer; "Über stickstoffhaltige Acetonderivate," *ibid.*, **15** (1882), 1164–1167, written with Alois Janny; "Untersuchungen über die Strukturformel des Thiophens," *ibid.*, **18** (1885), 3005–3012, written with L. Gattermann and A. Kaiser; "Untersuchungen über die zweite van't Hoffsche Hypothese," *ibid.*, **21** (1888), 784–817, and "Über die isomeren Oxime unsymmetrischer Ketone und die Configuration der Hydroxylamins," *ibid.*, **23** (1890), 2403–2409, written with Karl Auwers; "Über Jodosobenzoësäure," *ibid.*, **25** (1892), 2632–2635, written with Wilhelm Wachter; "Über ein seltsames Gesetz bei der Esterbildung aromatischer Säuren," *ibid.*, **27** (1894), 510–512; "Das Gesetz der Esterbildung aromatischer Säuren," *ibid.*, 1580–1592, and "Weiteres über die Esterbildung aromatischer Säuren," *ibid.*, 3146–3156, written with J. Sudborough.

II. SECONDARY LITERATURE. The principal source on the life and work of Victor Meyer was composed by his brother Richard Meyer: *Victor Meyer. Leben und Wirken eines deutschen Chemikers und Naturforschers 1848–1897* (Leipzig, 1917).

Other important studies are Heinrich Biltz, in *Zeitschrift für anorganische Chemie*, **16** (1898), 1–14; Margaret Davis Cameron, "Victor Meyer and the Thiophene Compounds," in *Journal of Chemical Education*, **26** (1949), 521–524; Friedrich Challenger, "Victor Meyer's and Paul Jacobson's 'Lehrbuch der organischen Chemie': the Authors and Their Work," in *Journal of the Royal Institute of Chemistry*, **82** (1958), 164–169; Benjamin Harrow, *Eminent Chemists of Our Time*, 2nd ed. (New York, 1927), 177–195, 407–422; F. Henrich, in G. Bugge, ed., *Das Buch der grossen Chemiker*, II (Berlin, 1930), 374–390; B. Horowitz, in *Journal of the Franklin Institute*, **182** (1916), 363–394; Paul Jacobson, in *Allgemeine Deutsche Biographie*, LV (Leipzig, 1910), 833–841; and C. Liebermann, in *Berichte der Deutschen chemischen Gesellschaft*, **30** (1897), 2157–2168.

See also G. Lunge, in *Vierteljahrsschrift der Naturforschenden Gesellschaft in Zürich*, **42** (1897), 347–361; J. McCrae, "Recollections of Heidelberg and Victor Meyer: 1893–1895," in *Journal of the Royal Institute of Chemistry*, **82** (1958), 77–82; Richard Meyer, in *Berichte der Deutschen chemischen Gesellschaft*, **41** (1909), 4505–

4718; Gustav Schmidt, "The Discovery of the Nitroparaffins by Victor Meyer," in *Journal of Chemical Education*, **27** (1950), 557–559; J. Sudborough, "Victor Meyer," in *Proceedings of the Chemical Society* (1959), 137–141; and Edward Thorpe, *Essays in Historical Chemistry*, 3rd ed. (London, 1911), 422–482, which originally appeared as the "Victor Meyer Memorial Lecture," in *Journal of the Chemical Society*, **77** (1900), 169–206.

ALBERT B. COSTA

MEYER, WILHELM FRANZ (*b.* Magdeburg, Germany, 2 September 1856; *d.* Königsberg, Germany [now Kaliningrad, U.S.S.R.], 11 June 1934), *mathematics.*

Meyer studied in Leipzig and Munich, where he received his doctorate in 1878. He studied further in Berlin, where at that time Weierstrass, Kummer, and Kronecker were active. In 1880 he qualified for lecturing at the University of Tübingen, and in 1888 he became full professor at the Bergakademie of Clausthal–Zellerfeld. From October 1897 until October 1924, when he retired, he taught at the University of Königsberg.

Meyer was a many-sided and very knowledgeable mathematician, whose list of writings includes 136 titles. His principal field of interest, however, was geometry, especially algebraic geometry and the related projective invariant theory. His *Habilitationsschrift*, which was published in 1883 as *Apolarität und rationale Kurven*, shows this direction of his research. In this work he extended the apolarity theory, created by Reye, to a multidimensional projective geometry based on the theory of rational curves. At the time such considerations were not completely obvious.

Other of Meyer's works from this period deal with algebraic curves and their production, and with related algebraic questions. He early showed himself to be one of the leading experts on invariant theory. In 1892 he composed for the Deutsche Mathematiker-vereinigung a long report on this subject, which was translated into French, Italian, and Polish. In this work he presented the development of invariant theory from its beginning in the middle of the nineteenth century to the end of the century and the appearance of the decisive finiteness theorems of Gordan and Hilbert. Meyer also made many individual contributions to invariant theory. This area of research went somewhat out of fashion during his lifetime, however, chiefly as a result of Hilbert's work.

Meyer was one of the founders of the *Encyklopädie der mathematischen Wissenschaften*. He, H. Weber, and F. Klein were responsible for planning this project.

The *Encyklopädie*, which was conceived on a large scale, was supported from 1895 by a syndicate of German academies. From the turn of the century until the 1930's some twenty volumes appeared; they treated all fields of mathematics and their applications. Meyer wrote the articles on potential theory (with H. Burkhardt), invariant theory, the new geometry of the triangle (with G. Berkhan), third-order surfaces, and surfaces of the fourth and higher orders.

The editing of such a vast work required great effort and presupposed considerable knowledge. In this regard Meyer benefited from his extensive familiarity with the literature, gained in large measure through the 2,000 reviews that he wrote for *Fortschritte der Mathematik*; his knowledge of foreign languages was also very useful to him. Of special note are the articles on third- and fourth-degree surfaces, which he composed at an advanced age. At that period, around 1930, Meyer was the only German mathematician who still possessed a comprehensive view of the abundant material, produced mainly in the nineteenth century, on special algebraic curves and surfaces. Meyer conducted investigations in geometry of the triangle, handled in the spirit of Klein's Erlangen program, and gave lectures discussing the essential aspects of mathematical research in the spirit of the time and emphasizing the importance of simple algebraic identities, the symmetries of group theory, and transformation principles as a source of geometric theorems.

Meyer was an excellent teacher who had many students. Most East Prussian mathematics teachers at the beginning of the twentieth century were trained by him.

BIBLIOGRAPHY

An extensive listing of Meyer's writings can be found in Poggendorff, IV, 1001–1002; V, 841; and VI, 1714. They include *Apolarität und rationale Kurven, eine systematische Voruntersuchung zu einer allgemeinen Theorie der linearen Räume* (Tübingen, 1883); "Bericht über den gegenwärtigen Stand der Invariantentheorie," in *Jahresberichte der Deutschen Mathematiker-vereinigung*, **1** (1892), 79–292; and the following articles in *Encyklopädie der mathematischen Wissenschaften:* "Invariantentheorie," I, pt. 1, 320–403; "Potentialtheorie," II-A, pt.7-b, 464–503, written with H. Burkhardt; "Neuere Dreiecksgeometrie," III, pt.1-b, 1173–1276, written with G. Berkhan; "Flächen 3. Ordnung," III-C, pt. 10-a, 1437–1532; and "Flächen 4. und höherer Ordnung," III-C, 1533–1779.

An article on Meyer is B. Arndt, "W. F. Meyer zum Gedächtnis," in *Jahresberichte der Deutschen Mathematiker-vereinigung*, **45** (1935), 99–113.

W. BURAU

MEYERHOF, OTTO (*b.* Hannover, Germany, 12 April 1884; *d.* Philadelphia, Pennsylvania, 6 October 1951), *biochemistry.*

The son of Felix Meyerhof, merchant, and Bettina May, Meyerhof received the M.D. from the University of Heidelberg in 1909. While at the medical clinic of Ludolf von Krehl, he came under the influence of Otto Warburg, who turned Meyerhof's interest from psychology and philosophy to cellular physiology. He worked at the Institute of Physiology at the University of Kiel from 1913 to 1924 and then at the Kaiser Wilhelm Institute for Biology in Berlin–Dahlem until 1929, when he became head of the department of physiology at the Kaiser Wilhelm Institute for Medical Research in Heidelberg. Like other scientists of Jewish extraction, Meyerhof left Germany (in 1938) after the Nazi rise to power; he joined the Institute of Physico-chemical Biology in Paris but was forced to flee in 1940, when the Germans invaded France. He came to the United States late in 1940 and was research professor of physiological chemistry at the School of Medicine of the University of Pennsylvania until his death.

Meyerhof's work on the chemical processes in muscle laid the basis for the elucidation of the chemical pathway in the intracellular breakdown of glucose to provide energy for biological processes. In 1919 he demonstrated that during muscle contraction in the absence of oxygen, muscle glycogen is converted to lactic acid. In the presence of oxygen, about one-fifth of the lactic acid is oxidized to carbon dioxide and water; and the energy yielded by this oxidation is used to regenerate glycogen from the remaining lactic acid. This discovery provided a chemical basis for the interpretation of the heat changes during muscle contraction and subsequent recovery, studied by A. V. Hill in 1913–1914. Hill and Meyerhof shared the 1922 Nobel Prize in physiology or medicine, awarded in 1923.

Meyerhof's choice of muscle as the experimental material was prompted by his philosophical commitment to the idea that the dynamics of biological processes can be described in the language of chemistry and physics. From his early article "Zur Energetik der Zellvorgänge" (1913) to his last writings, this affirmation of the antivitalist position is evident; outside his scientific work he retained an attachment to the transcendental idealism of Kant and J. F. Fries.

In 1925 Meyerhof succeeded in extracting from muscle the group of enzymes responsible for the conversion of glycogen to lactic acid. This preparation of a cell-free glycolytic system was a counterpart of the earlier successful extraction from yeast of the enzyme system (zymase) that converts glucose to alcohol and carbon dioxide during fermentation (Buchner, 1897). In 1917–1918 Meyerhof had shown the presence in animal tissues of the "cozymase" of yeast fermentation, discovered by Harden and W. J. Young in 1906. After 1925 the study of the chemical pathway in the breakdown of glucose by muscle and by yeast was found to be very similar, and this pathway was shown to be operative in many other biological systems. The development pioneered by Meyerhof thus provided striking evidence of the unity of biochemical processes amid the manifold diversity of the forms of life.

The discovery of phosphocreatine (in 1926) and of adenosine triphosphate (in 1929) as constituents of mammalian muscle was followed by Einar Lundsgaard's demonstration in 1930 that muscle contraction depends more directly on the enzymic cleavage of these two substances than on the production of lactic acid. These advances provided essential links in Meyerhof's later analysis of the energy relations between chemical change and the physical events in muscle contraction, and his studies led to the recognition of the central role in muscle contraction (and in other energy-requiring processes of biological systems) of adenosine triphosphate, the resynthesis of which in muscle is driven by the breakdown of phosphocreatine and the production of lactic acid. His measurements of the heat released in the hydrolysis of adenosine triphosphate and related compounds, although subsequently refined, permitted the first quantitative estimates to be made of the efficiency of muscle operating as a chemical machine.

Meyerhof's influence on the development of biochemistry was profound and continued past the middle of the twentieth century through the work of his former students; noteworthy among them were Fritz Lipmann and Severo Ochoa, both Nobel laureates.

BIBLIOGRAPHY

I. ORIGINAL WORKS. Meyerhof's books include *Chemical Dynamics of Life Phenomena* (Philadelphia, 1925); *Die chemischen Vorgänge im Muskel und ihr Zusammenhang mit Arbeitsleistung und Wärmebildung* (Berlin, 1930); and *Chimie de la contraction musculaire* (Paris, 1933). He published some 400 scientific articles; a list of his publications is given in *Biographical Memoirs. National Academy of Sciences*, **34** (1960), 164–182.

II. SECONDARY LITERATURE. See D. Nachmansohn, S. Ochoa, and F. A. Lipmann, in *Science*, **115** (1952), 365–369; and C. L. Gemmill, *Medical College of Virginia Quarterly*, **2** (1966), 141–142.

JOSEPH S. FRUTON

MEYERSON, ÉMILE (*b.* Lyublin, Russia [now Lublin, Poland], 1859; *d.* Paris, France, 1933), *philosophy.*

For a complete study of his life and work, see Supplement.

MICHAEL, ARTHUR (*b.* Buffalo, New York, 7 August 1853; *d.* Orlando, Florida, 8 February 1942), *chemistry.*

Michael studied chemistry under Hofmann at Berlin (1871, 1875–1878), under Bunsen at Heidelberg (1872–1874), and under Wurtz at Paris (1879). He was professor of chemistry at Tufts College (1881–1889, 1894–1907) and Harvard University (1912–1936). A severe critic of mechanical interpretations of chemical phenomena, he introduced thermodynamic conceptions into organic chemical theory.

Michael's earliest studies included the discovery of several synthetic reactions. He was the first to synthesize a natural glucoside (helicin, 1879), and the method that he introduced became the standard synthetic route to this class of organic substances. His best-known synthetic method is the direct addition of the sodium derivatives of malonic, acetoacetic, or cyanoacetic esters to α, β-unsaturated esters, ketones, nitriles, amides, and sulfones (the Michael reaction, 1887). There had been no general method available for the conversion of unsaturated compounds into saturated compounds of a higher carbon series until Michael described his method of additive condensation in his article "Über die Addition von Natriumacetessig- und Natriummalonsäureäthern zu den Aethern ungesättigter Säuren."

Michael's primary concern was organic theory. From 1888 he developed a novel theory of organic reactions based on the thermodynamic concepts of free energy and entropy. He maintained that organic structural theory was too qualitative, pictorial, and mechanical; and he hoped to overcome these deficiencies with energetic conceptions. Michael made the second law of thermodynamics the fundamental principle governing organic reactions. He related the course of reactions to energy conversions, including addition and substitution reactions, molecular rearrangements, tautomerism, and stereochemistry within his theory. He concentrated much of his research on the theoretical aspects of addition to the double bond and the behavior of active methylene compounds.

In his role as critic of accepted views, Michael refused to accept Wislicenus' assumption that addition to unsaturated compounds always proceeded in the *cis* manner and that elimination reactions occurred more easily with *cis* isomers than with *trans* isomers. By carefully planned experiments he proved that *trans* additions and eliminations did occur and that all of the then accepted configurations of geometric isomers were erroneous (1895–1918).

Michael was a critic of all purely mechanical interpretations of organic reactions, such as steric hindrance and the strain hypothesis. He attempted over many years to show experimentally that these conceptions were extremely limited and inadequate as explanations of chemical phenomena and that they needed to be modified by considerations of chemical affinity and energy.

BIBLIOGRAPHY

I. ORIGINAL WORKS. Important papers by Michael include "On the Synthesis of Helicin and Phenolglucoside," in *American Chemical Journal*, **1** (1879), 305–312: "Über die Addition von Natriumacetessig- und Natriummalonsäureäthern zu den Aethern ungesättigter Säuren," in *Journal für praktische Chemie*, **35** (1887), 349–356; **43** (1891), 390–395; **45** (1892), 55–63; and **49** (1894), 20–25; "Untersuchungen über Alloisomerie," *ibid.*, **52** (1895), 289–325; "Über die Gesetze der Alloisomerie und Anwendung derselben zur Classificirung ungesättigter organischer Verbindungen," *ibid.*, 344–372; "Über einige Gesetze und deren Anwendung in der organischen Chemie," *ibid.*, **60** (1899), 286–384, 409–486; "Valenzhypothesen und der Verlauf chemischer Vorgänge," *ibid.*, **68** (1903), 487–520; "Stereoisomerism and the Law of Entropy," in *American Chemical Journal*, **39** (1908), 1–16; "Outline of a Theory of Organic Chemistry Founded on the Law of Entropy," in *Journal of the American Chemical Society*, **32** (1910), 990–1007; and "The Configurations of Organic Compounds and Their Relation to Chemical and Physical Properties," *ibid.*, **40** (1918), 704–723, 1674–1707.

II. SECONDARY LITERATURE. Brief accounts of Michael's life and work are Louis F. Fieser, Edward W. Forbes, and Arthur B. Lamb, in *Harvard University Gazette* (22 May 1943), 246–248; *Dictionary of American Biography*, supp. 3 (New York, 1973), 520–521; *National Cyclopaedia of American Biography*, XV (New York, 1916), 172; and W. T. Read, in *Industrial and Engineering Chemistry*, **22** (1930), 1137–1138. His thermodynamic conceptions are discussed by Ferdinand Henrich, in *Theories of Organic Chemistry*, T. B. Johnson and D. A. Hahn, trans. (New York, 1922), 569–584, and Albert B. Costa, "Arthur Michael (1853–1942): The Meeting of Thermodynamics and Organic Chemistry," in *Journal of Chemical Education*, **48** (1971), 243–246.

ALBERT B. COSTA

MICHAEL PSELLUS. See **Psellus, Michael.**

MICHAEL SCOT (*b.* before 1200; *d. ca.* 1235), *astrology, popularization of science, translation of scientific and philosophical works from the Arabic.*

Almost all information about Michael's life and work is uncertain; his posthumous fame as a wise or wicked magician bred legends and was increased by them. Although imaginative scholars have established undocumented traditions, no satisfactory analysis—linguistic, stylistic, or doctrinal—of writings ascribed to him has been carried out. It is thus impossible to determine the accuracy of many attributions.

Life. Michael's place of birth and details of his family are unknown. His appointment to an Irish archbishopric suggests that "Scot" meant, as it often did, "Irish"; his refusal on the ground of ignorance of the vernacular does not support this suggestion but does not exclude it. He was given benefices in England and Scotland with no explicit residence requirements; there is no sign that he lived in either place at any time. Nowhere in his geographical and meteorological works does he show any special interest in those countries or knowledge of them, and nothing points to English being his mother tongue. The ten Anglo-Saxon names of months that he mentioned are found in Bede; there might just be a nostalgic element in his words referring to the "Anglici" as beginning the year on Christmas night and flocking to their main churches on the first day of every month with offerings while the bells ring festively. Otherwise his examples, topical anecdotes, and descriptions give a more prominent position to several other countries than to Britain.

The date of Michael's birth can be guessed with a vague approximation by considering that he produced a translation about 1217 and that by early 1236 he was dead. The insistent recommendations for benefices in the mid-1220's suggest that he was then still young with a precocious interest in learning. It may well be that he was not born before 1195. In 1217, or not long after, Michael was in Toledo and had perhaps acquired some knowledge of Arabic. It was there that, with the help of Abuteus (or Andreas) Levita, a Jew later converted to Christianity, he translated a work of al-Biṭrūjī and—with or without help—some Aristotle from the Arabic. He may also have learned some Hebrew. In 1220 or 1221 he was staying in Bologna in the house of the widow of one Albertus Gallus; while there he had the opportunity to examine and describe in detail a tumor of the womb. By 1224 Michael was a priest and was addressed as "magister" by Pope Honorius III, who obtained for him benefices in Britain and appointed him to be archbishop of Cashel, Ireland; for the latter see he was also recommended by the pope to King Henry III. He renounced

the appointment as archbishop and was given further benefices by Stephen Langton, archbishop of Canterbury, at the instance of Honorius III and of Gregory IX (1225 and 1227). Nothing is known of Michael's university studies: his references to Paris and to some teaching he had done may indicate that he had been there, as either a student or teacher or both. In 1228 Leonardo Fibonacci of Pisa sent a revised copy of the *Liber abaci*, which Michael had solicited. The date 1231 occurs in one manuscript of a poetical prophecy on the future of many towns in northern Italy, requested by Bolognese dignitaries and ascribed to Michael in the later part of the century by the Parma chronicler Salimbene and by many manuscripts. It is probably to this prophecy that the poet Henry of Avranches referred when writing around the beginning of 1236 to Emperor Frederick II; Henry noted that Michael, who had predicted the fate of others, had himself succumbed to fate.

In his writings Michael presented himself as a highly regarded scientific companion and consultant to Frederick II, the most faithful among astrologers. It is as "astrologer to the emperor" that he is often referred to by Salimbene and other writers. No state or other documents survive to confirm or disprove the truth of this title; nor is it clear whether it would imply a regular attachment to the court. No doubt Frederick would have welcomed Michael's contribution to his scientific knowledge. Michael's dedications to him probably represent more than pleas or thanks for moral and social support; his skill in astrological forecasts may have been very welcome to an intelligent ruler who was not above putting some trust in this kind of "science" and to a shrewd politician for whom favorable prophecies had an undeniable propaganda value. Before the middle of 1232 Michael had dedicated to Frederick II his translation of Ibn Sīnā's treatise on animals. This is the only definite date concerning his relationship with the emperor. The dedications, introductions, and contents of his astrological works—taken together with Henry of Avranches's remarks—suggest that the relationship had been neither trivial nor brief in the last years before Michael's death. But it is reasonable to assume that Michael was not depending on Frederick II when, from 1224 to 1227, he relied on the papal curia's support for an income from British benefices or, perhaps, when he was dedicating to Stephen of Provins a translation of Aristotle's *De caelo* with commentary of Ibn Rushd (Averroës); in 1231 Stephen was in a key position to decide on the introduction and study of approved texts of Aristotle in the University of Paris.

There is not much evidence for assessing Michael's standing with his learned contemporaries, apart from

Frederick's interest, Leonardo Fibonacci's complimentary words, and the formal praises contained in the papal recommendations. The two first philosopher-scientists to express views on him after his death, Albertus Magnus and Roger Bacon, were scathing about his scientific knowledge and honesty, although Bacon recognized his merit in having introduced some Aristotle and Ibn Rushd into the Latin West in the early 1230's. What fame, praise, and blame he was accorded later were the result of his reputed magic powers, and the variety of scientific and astrological information presented in his treatises—especially, perhaps, the systematic section on the generation of human beings (book I of his *Physionomia*), which gained great popularity in the late fifteenth and the sixteenth centuries.

It may be that Roger Bacon hit on the one activity for which Michael deserves a place in the history of serious philosophical and scientific speculation. It was through his efforts that some of Ibn Rushd's commentaries on Aristotle came into circulation in Latin and led the way to a penetrating analysis of fundamental problems, such as those of the eternity of the world and the immortality of the soul; they also provided models of methodical interpretation of Aristotle's texts on sound, objective bases. It may also be that Bacon was right when he minimized Michael's linguistic achievements. There is no clear evidence of what his share was in producing the translations ascribed wholly or partly to him. The collaboration in this work by other interpreters, such as Abuteus, may have been much greater than just occasional help. The only research—and that very limited—made on Michael's method of translating suggests considerable inaccuracy, systematic changes in style between one work and another, and occasional recourse to existing Latin translations for increased ease and reliability.

Works. *Translations.* Al-Biṭrūjī's *In astrologia* (as given in a manuscript) or *De sphaera* (both these titles correspond to the Arabic *Fi 'l-hay'at*) or *De motibus celorum circularibus* (the title given by Roger Bacon) is preserved completely or incompletely in eleven manuscripts, all of the fourteenth or fifteenth century. The translation was made with the collaboration of Abuteus and was finished in Toledo on 18 August, probably in 1217 (other, less likely, years are 1207 and 1221). Michael took over long passages of Ptolemy, included by al-Biṭrūjī in his work, from Gerard of Cremona's translation of the *Almagest*. The *In astrologia* made accessible in Latin some recent Spanish-Arabic learning (the original Arabic text was finished about 1190). In it an attempt was made with the use of new mathematical methods to revive Aristotle's cosmology of concentric spheres as against

Ptolemy's system of epicycles and eccentrics. The translation had a certain success, as use of it by Roger Bacon, Grosseteste, Pseudo-Grosseteste, and Albertus Magnus in the thirteenth century testifies, and as the several manuscripts of the next centuries confirm.

Aristotle's *De animalibus* (*Historia animalium*, *De partibus animalium*, *De generatione animalium*), a literal translation made at Toledo, possibly before 1220, of the ninth-century Arabic version by Ibn al-Bitriq, is preserved in more than sixty manuscripts of the thirteenth and early fourteenth centuries. It exerted a considerable influence, mainly through Albertus Magnus' exposition and elaboration. It may have been used by Frederick II, but was soon superseded by William of Moerbeke's translation from the Greek (*ca.* 1260) and later—at the time of printing—by Theodore of Gaza's version (*ca.* 1475). It has been suggested, on the basis of two short references by Michael and an attribution in a manuscript, that he produced a complete translation of the *Nicomachean Ethics* from the Greek, of which book I (*Ethica nova*) was widely circulated and other sections or fragments still survive.

Ibn Sīnā's *De animalibus* or *Abbreviatio de animalibus* was the relevant part of the philosophical encyclopedia *Shifa*. The translation was dedicated to Frederick II, who used it in the preparation of his *De arte venandi*; it is preserved in thirty or more manuscripts of the thirteenth and early fourteenth centuries, some of which derive from the 1232 copy of the volume presented to the emperor.

Of Ibn Rushd's commentaries on and expositions of Aristotle's works, only the first one listed here was certainly edited by Michael, the second quite probably, the others with a smaller degree of probability. *Great Commentary on the De caelo*, with Aristotle's full text; a preface addressed to Stephen of Provins, mentioning the translation of al-Biṭrūjī's *In astrologia*, was written after 1217. Thirty or forty manuscripts still exist; and the work was often quoted by the Latin commentators and philosophers from the thirteenth to the sixteenth centuries. *Great Commentary on the De anima*, with the full text, is preserved in more than fifty manuscripts, three or four of which give Michael as the translator. This version was also translated into Hebrew in the fifteenth century. *Great Commentary on the Physics* is available with full text. At least the prologue, and possibly the whole work, was translated by Theodore of Antioch; only a few manuscripts of the more than fifty extant suggest Michael as the author of the translation. Suggestions of Michael's authorship of the following have no documentary support: *Great Commentary on Metaphysics* with the full text, I.1–4, II–X, XII, extant in fifty manuscripts (in another sixty there is only Aristotle's text, under the name of *Metaphysica nova*, by which title it is quoted in the commentary on Sacrobosco's *Sphaera* ascribed to Michael), *Expositions* (*Middle Commentaries*) *of Meteorologica* IV (twenty manuscripts), *De generatione et corruptione* (forty manuscripts), and the *Epitome of Parva naturalia* (fifty manuscripts).

Original Writings. A trilogy, consisting of the *Liber introductorius, Liber particularis*, and *Physionomia* (*De secretis nature*, including a section *De urinis*), is presented by Michael as a unit in a general foreword addressed to Frederick II after the middle of 1228; but the unity does not go further than that of a collection of independent treatises, each of which seems also to lack a definite unity of its own, even though each has an introduction. It appears that Michael collected those of his writings that he thought might interest the emperor, whatever their state of elaboration, and started preparing a volume to be presented to him. This work seems never to have been completed, since the epilogue mentioned in the foreword is nowhere to be found and the manuscript tradition—all later than about 1270—is too varied in form and content to suggest its dependence on a properly edited text.

The *Liber introductorius* is preserved in four manuscripts, each of them differing in many respects from the others and some of them containing later interpolations. It is divided into four sections and is said to have been written at Frederick's request. It is meant to be a compendium of astrological, scientific, and general lore extracted from the works of many authors and enlarged with some personal observation. It is directed to beginners and written in a simple style. The main matters dealt with are astronomy, partly mixed with and partly distinguishable from what may be more properly called astrology, including a systematic treatment of the individual heavenly bodies, their spheres, and their movements; general geography and meteorology (the five main zones of the earth, the climes of the northern temperate zone, the seven regions of the air—that is, dew, snow, hail, rain, honey, laudanum, manna); the tides, including a "new" theory based on the mixture of cold influx from the moon and hot influx from the sun; and some descriptive geography, unsystematic and poorly informed. Other matters discussed at some length concern medicine (advice on food, on how to cure mental states with the help of enchantresses and divines); music; the calendar; important numbers (especially the number seven); and some theology. Altogether there is little more than a collection of secondhand, blindly accepted, information; occa-

sionally there is an assessment of the views of other authorities (for instance, on the distance of the heavens from earth) or an exposition of contradictory doctrines that suggest a critical approach to a problem, indications that scientific inquiry must be applied to research on the terrestrial paradise, hell, and purgatory, some incidental information on things seen, habits of and differences between people of different races, reports of simple experiments made by him and the emperor, and some of his predictions. His sources range from the Bible and Ptolemy to al-Farghânî, Abū Ma'shar, and the *Toledan Tables*. From what has been published so far it is not clear whether Aristotle and Ibn Rushd have been put directly to use, and if so, to what extent.

The *Liber particularis*, a shorter book, is intended to supplement with a fuller and more advanced treatment some of the things expounded for "novices" in the *Liber introductorius*. All that this second book includes is to be "new" but necessary for a better acquaintance with the grand science: "He who has assimilated both books will have qualified for the title of new astrologer." According to Haskins, these additions concern mainly the reckoning of time; sun, moon, and stars; winds and tides; and various meteorological questions. Compared with the *Liber introductorius*, it is based more extensively on an Italian background and on Latin authors like Isidore of Seville, and on Aristotle's meteorological theories. The last part of the *Liber particularis* is the most interesting, for it contains a large number of questions purporting to have been put to Michael by Frederick II, together with his answers. Frederick had heard enough about the sun, moon, fixed stars, elements, world soul, pagan and Christian peoples, creatures moving on earth, plants, and metals; he now wanted to hear about the more inaccessible things leading to spiritual enjoyment and wisdom: paradise, purgatory, and hell; what supports the earth, the abyss, the heavens; the relationships and relative distances between the heavens; where God dwells and what angels and saints do in front of Him; where fresh and salt waters come from; how volcanic eruptions and sulfur springs come about. The answers are less interesting than the questions, and provide little more than known facts or pseudo facts, apart from some information on specific volcanic phenomena in Italy and some attempts to explain them; one chapter, alchemical in character, deals with metals and would seem not to belong among the answers to Frederick's questions.

The third part of the trilogy is preserved in three or four manuscripts. The title *Physionomia* fits little more than half of it; *De secretis nature*, in its vagueness, is more appropriate. The contents of this part are at least threefold. Most of what appears as book I in the printed editions contains a detailed treatise on generation of human beings, with anatomical and physiological descriptions, information on the best time for conception, on sexual behavior, and on the state of the fetus during each of the nine months after conception. The rest of book I deals with differences between genera and species of animals. Books II and III contain the *Physionomia* proper (apart from some chapters on dreams and auguries from sneezes). In these, a systematic survey of the different parts of the body, in connection with the basic or other qualities affecting them, is meant to show how souls are intrinsically dependent for their natures on the bodies that they inhabit: "animae sequuntur corpus." Book III is particularly concerned with showing that such parts of the body as hair, forehead, eyes, nails, and heels, if properly studied, can inform one of the virtues and vices of men and women. A section not included in the printed editions of the *Physionomia,* but published by itself, contains the short treatise *De urinis.*

A *Commentary on Sacrobosco's Sphaera* is ascribed to Michael Scot in the two old printed editions and—with some doubts—in the recent one, but it is anonymous in the two manuscripts containing some parts of it. Thorndike suggested that its twenty-eight "lectiones" somehow reflect a course of lectures. Whether authentic or not, this work is an important document belonging most probably to Michael's time. The following authors and works are the only ones mentioned or quoted, and none of them was unknown in Latin before Michael's death: Aristotle (*Physica, De caelo, Metaphysica* [*Prima philosophia*]*, De generatione et corruptione, Meteorologica, De anima, De sensu, Analytica posteriora*), pseudo-Aristotle (*De plantis, De proprietatibus elementorum*), Plato, al-Farghānī, Euclid, Boethius, Ibn Sīnā, Ibn Rushd (*De substantia orbis, Commentary on Metaphysics*), Theodosius of Bythinia (*Spherica*), and Mercurius (*De vita Deorum*); the method followed in the work is also consistent with the habits of that time.

The *Questiones Nicolai peripatetici* contains a few discussions on physical, chemical, and physiological topics, similar to those of the trilogy. They were ascribed to Michael by Albertus Magnus, who condemned them as rubbish, and are preserved, without the author's name, in several manuscripts. Six fragments from a *Divisio philosophie,* quoted as coming from a work by Michael in Vincent of Beauvais's *Speculum doctrinale,* contain a definition of philosophy, the basic classification into theoretical and practical sciences, and some account of two of the former sciences: mathematics and metaphysics. One

of the sources of these fragments is Dominicus Gundissalinus; others are found in Arabic texts.

The *Ars alchemie,* preserved in three manuscripts (two of them containing additional material, perhaps spurious), was designed to reveal the "secret of philosophers." In it metals are assimilated to planets, both classes being studied in their special natures; the transformation of Venus into the sun, of mercury into silver, and of lead into gold, and the nature of salts are the other main topics discussed in this treatise. The *Lumen luminum* may be one of the forms, perhaps the basic one, in which the *Dedalus grecus*—a work translated from the Arabic—has been preserved. It contains an alchemical and descriptive study of salts. A *Geomantia,* ascribed to Michael in one manuscript, has never been studied. Together with a short text, of *Experimenta necromantica,* which appears under his name in another manuscript, it completes what is known of Scot's or pseudo-Scot's more fanciful writings on the margins of science and magic. The few lines of the *Description of a Tumor* and two *Recipes* ascribed to him are all we have of his medical texts; and the *Vaticinium* (the prophecy in verse of 1231, mentioned above) is the only "prophetic" text, apart from the few passages of this kind in the *Liber introductorius.*

A *Theorica planetarum,* the *Ten Categories in Theology,* and the *Mensa philosophica* (the last printed under Michael's name and constituting a handbook of dietetics and of characterization of people, with many references to Latin authors known only after Michael's death) are probably to be ascribed, respectively, to Gerard of Cremona, John Scot Eriugena or one of his followers (being perhaps extracts from the *De divisione naturae*), and an anonymous author of the sixteenth century.

BIBLIOGRAPHY

I. ORIGINAL WORKS. The fifteenth-century eds. of the translations of Ibn Rushd are listed in *Gesamtkatalog der Wiegendrucke* under "Aristoteles." Other translations are al-Biṭrūjī, *In astrologia* (*De motibus celorum*), critical text by F. J. Carmody (Berkeley–Los Angeles, 1952); Aristotle, *De animalibus,* bk. X only in Gunnar Rudberg, *Zum sogenannten zehnten Buche der aristotelischen Tiergeschichte,* which is Skrifter Utgivna af Humanistika Vetenskapssampfundet i Uppsala, XIII, pt. 6 (Uppsala–Leipzig, 1911), 109–120, cf. 64–70; Ibn Sīnā, *Abbreviatio de animalibus* (Venice, ca. 1500, 1508); and Ibn Rushd, *Great Commentaries on De caelo, De anima, Physica,* and *Metaphysica,* expositions of *Meteorologica* and *De generatione et corruptione,* and *Epitome of Parva naturalia,* several eds. between 1472 and 1575, also critical eds. of *Great Commentary on De anima* and *Epitome of Parva naturalia* in Corpus

Commentariorum Averrois in Aristotelem, VI, pt. 1 (1953), and VII (1949), by F. S. Crawford and A. L. Shields, respectively. What remains of the Greco-Latin translation of the *Nicomachean Ethics* tentatively ascribed to Michael is available in a critical ed. by R. A. Gauthier in *Aristoteles Latinus*, XXVI, pts. 1–3, fasc. 2 (Leiden–Brussels, 1972), 63–165.

Michael's own works are *Liber introductorius*, unpub. except for a few passages (see Haskins and Thorndike, below); *Liber particularis*, unpub. except for an important section containing Frederick II's questions and Scot's answers in Haskins, *Studies in the History of Mediaeval Science*, pp. 292–298, and a few quotations, in Haskins, *op. cit.*, and Thorndike, *Michael Scot; Physionomia* or *De secretis naturae*, about 20 eds. in the fifteenth century and 20 in the sixteenth (the earliest, Bologna, 1477), all without *De urinis*—which is pub. in A. H. Querfeld, *Michael Scottus und seine Schrift De secretis naturae* (Leipzig, 1919) —as well as sixteenth- and seventeenth-century eds. (without *De urinis*) in Spanish, Italian, and French; *Commentary on Sacrobosco's Sphaera* (Bologna, 1495; Venice, 1531), new ed. by Lynn Thorndike in *The Sphere of Sacrobosco and Its Commentators* (Chicago, 1949), pp. 248–342; *Questiones Nicolai peripatetici*, unpub. except for some quotations and an English summary in Thorndike, *Michael Scot*, pp. 127–131; *Ars alchimie*, or *Magisterium*, available in complete ed. by S. H. Thomson in *Osiris*, 5 (1938), 523–559, and partially, from MSS not used by Thomson, in Haskins, "The Alchemy . . .," in *Isis*, 10 (1928), 350–356, and *Studies in Mediaeval Culture*, pp. 148–159.

Also available are *Lumen luminum* (and/or *Dedalus grecus*, perhaps trans. from the Arabic), edited by W. J. Brown in *An Enquire . . .*, pp. 240–265; The *Experimenta necromantica, ibid.*, pp. 231–234; *Division of Philosophy*, extant fragments pub. in Ludwig Baur, "Dominicus Gundissalinus, De divisione philosophie," in *Beiträge zur Geschichte der Philosophie des Mittelalters*, 4, nos. 2–3 (1903), 365–368; *Vaticinium*, or *Futura praesagia*, critical ed. by O. Holder-Egger in "Italienische Prophetieen des 13. Jahrhunderts, II," in *Neues Archiv der Gesellschaft für ältere deutsche Geschichtskunde*, 30 (1905), 321–386, see 349–377, also in *Cronica Fratris Salimbene*, Monumenta Germaniae Historica: Scriptores, XXXII (1905–1913), pp. 361–362; some recipes, in "Notes on Medical Texts," in *Janus*, 48 (1959), 148; *Description of a Tumor*, in M. R. James, *Catalogue of Manuscripts in . . . Gonville and Caius College*, I (Cambridge, 1907), 112, and facs. from MS in *Edinburgh Medical Journal* (1920), 56; and *Mensa philosophica*, several eds. in the sixteenth and seventeenth centuries, such as Leipzig, 1603.

The main MSS of most works and references to printed lists of MSS are in Lynn Thorndike and Pearl Kibre, *A Catalog of Incipits of Mediaeval Scientific Works in Latin*, rev. ed. (Cambridge, Mass., 1963), see index, col. 1864. For the MSS of translations of Aristotle and Ibn Rushd, and of the *Questiones Nicolai peripatetici*, see G. Lacombe, L. Minio-Paluello *et al.*, *Aristoteles latinus*, codices I–II with suppl., suppl. alt. (Rome–Cambridge–Bruges, 1939–

1961). For those of Ibn Sīnā, see M. T. d'Alverny, "Avicenna latinus," in *Archives d'histoire littéraire et doctrinale du moyen-âge*, 1961 (1962)–1970 (1971). For texts of which there are critical eds., see the relevant introductions or appendixes. For the rest, see Haskins, Thorndike, and Thomson (below).

II. SECONDARY LITERATURE. The most precise study of Michael's life and some of his works is still C. H. Haskins, *Studies in the History of Mediaeval Science*, 2nd ed. (Cambridge, Mass., 1927; repr. ch. 12). A more ample account of his life and of more of his works is Lynn Thorndike, *Michael Scot* (London, 1965). There is still much of value in J. W. Brown, *An Enquire Into the Life and Legend of Michael Scot* (Edinburgh, 1897); and in Lynn Thorndike, *A History of Magic and Experimental Science*, II (London, 1923), 307–337. See also John Ferguson, "A Short Biography and Bibliography of Michael Scot," in *Records of the Glasgow Bibliographical Society*, 9 (1931), 75–100; and George Sarton, *Introduction to the History of Science*, II, pt. 2 (Baltimore, 1931), 579–582.

For special aspects of Michael's life or works, see the introductions to the critical eds. and C. H. Haskins, *Studies in Mediaeval Culture* (Oxford, 1929), pp. 148–159 (on *Liber particularis*, Alchemy, Abuteus/Andreas of Palencia); "Two Roman Formularies in Philadelphia," in *Miscellanea Ehrle*, 4 (*Studi e testi*, 40) (1924), 275–286, on Michael's appointment as an archbishop and on Stephen of Provins; Petrus Pressutti, *Regesta Honorii Papae III*, II (Rome, 1895), 194, 227, 254, 334, on the appointments to the benefices; H. A. Wolfson, "Revised Plan of a Corpus Commentariorum Averrois in Aristotelem," in *Speculum*, 38 (1963), 88–104, on attribution of translations of Ibn Rushd to Michael; G. Rudberg, "Die Tiergeschichte des Michael Scotus und ihre mittelbare Quelle," in *Eranos*, 9 (1909), 92–128, on the relationship between the Greek original and Michael's trans. from the Arabic; and J. D. Comrie, "Michael Scot, a 13th Century Scientist and Physician," in *Edinburgh Medical Journal*, n.s. 25 (1920), 50–60.

On the *Physionomia*, its eds., contents, and sources, see A. H. Querfeld, *Michael Scottus und seine Schrift De secretis naturae* (Leipzig, 1919); C. Klebs, "Incunabula scientifica et medica," in *Osiris*, 4 (1938), 297–299; and R. Foerster, *De translatione latina physiognomonicorum quae feruntur Aristotelis* (Kiel, 1884), p. 22; and *De Aristotelis quae feruntur secretis secretorum commentarium* (Kiel, 1888), p. 29.

LORENZO MINIO-PALUELLO

MICHAUX, ANDRÉ (*b.* Satory, near Versailles, France, 7 March 1746; *d.* Madagascar [now Malagasy Republic], 13 November 1802), *botany.*

Michaux compiled the first flora for eastern America, mainly from his own specimens. He introduced many American plants into French horticulture and disseminated the camellia, silk tree, and tea olive in the Carolinas.

Michaux was the eldest son of the manager of the 500-acre royal farm at Satory. His father died when the boy was seventeen, and after four years at a boarding school Michaux became manager of the farm. At twenty-three he married Cécile Claye, daughter of a wealthy Beauce farmer. She died following the birth of their son, François André, and Michaux then began to concentrate on botany and horticulture.

He first studied under Le Monnier at Montreuil, near Versailles. Michaux pursued his botanical studies with Bernard de Jussieu at the Trianon (1777) and then at the Jardin des Plantes. He returned from a visit to England with seeds for Le Monnier and the influential Louis, duc de Noailles of Perpignan. In 1780 he botanized with Lamarck and André Thouin in the Auvergne and the Pyrenees, and he then spent three years traveling through Persia.

Although he wished to explore Tibet, the French government commissioned him to visit North America, particularly to investigate potential sources of ship timbers. With his son and a journeyman gardener, Pierre Paul Saunier, he embarked for New York on 1 September 1785. After two years of collecting and cultivating at Hackensack, New Jersey, Michaux sent 5,000 trees and twelve parcels of seed to France. In September 1787 he set out for Charleston, South Carolina, where he established a second garden. The reputed quinine substitute *Pinckneya* (Rubiaceae) especially interested him. William Bartram's discoveries early attracted Michaux's attention, and he botanized along the St. Johns River and its savannahs in Spanish Florida. Mark Catesby's *Natural History* prompted him to visit the Bahamas.

The last trip for which Michaux received support from the pre-Revolutionary French government was a difficult journey into the mountains of North Carolina. In 1792 Michaux made his longest trip—eight months—to Hudson Bay via the Saguenay River and Lake Mistassini. Then followed a three-month trip to Kentucky. Sponsored by the French revolutionary minister to the United States, Edmond Charles Genet, it was a political as well as botanical journey. In 1794 he returned to the coniferous forests of the southern Appalachians and then journeyed to the Illinois prairies. Thus ended ten years of exploration in America.

His personal funds exhausted, Michaux sailed for France from Charleston on 13 August 1796. He was shipwrecked off the Netherlands coast, and his specimens were only tediously salvaged. Arriving in France, he found the Republic unwilling to indemnify his private expenses or to support future explorations in America. He then set about writing on the American oaks, but before the engravings were completed, he accepted a position with Nicolas Baudin's government expedition to Australia. He stipulated that he be permitted to disembark at Mauritius for exploration and to establish a garden there. He then sailed for Madagascar to found a garden at Tamatave. Before he was able to explore the interior, he contracted a fever and died. Three different death dates have been published although Deleuze offers none; most, though weak, evidence supports that of 13 November 1802.

Michaux's success no doubt encouraged the French naturalists Louis Bosc and Palisot de Beauvois to visit America. His *Histoire des chênes de l'Amérique*, illustrated with twenty plates, mostly by Redouté, inspired an interest in forestry that was furthered by his son.

BIBLIOGRAPHY

I. ORIGINAL WORKS. Michaux's writings are *Histoire des chênes de l'Amérique* (Paris, 1801); "Mémoire sur les dattiers, avec des observations sur quelques moyens utiles aux progrès de l'agriculture dans les colonies occidentales," in *Journal de physique, de chemie, d'histoire naturelle et des arts*, **52** (1801), 325–335; and *Flora boreali-americana* (Paris, 1803; repr. with extensive introduction by J. Ewan, New York, 1973); none of them was seen in print by Michaux. G. A. Pritzel and others attributed the *Flora* to L. C. M. Richard, who assisted Michaux's son François in bringing out the work, but there is no peremptory reason for doubting its authorship. The type specimens of the *Flora* are preserved in a separate herbarium at the Muséum d'Histoire Naturelle, Paris.

II. SECONDARY LITERATURE. The primary source is J. P. F. Deleuze, "Notice historique sur André Michaux," in *Annales du Muséum national d'histoire naturelle*, **3** (1804), 191–227. Additional references will be found in *Dictionary of American Biography*, VI, 591–592; and Frans A. Stafleu, *Taxonomic Literature* (Utrecht, 1967), 309–310. Useful papers not mentioned by Stafleu are W. J. Robbins and Mary C. Howson, "André Michaux's New Jersey Garden and Pierre Paul Saunier, Journeyman Gardener," in *Proceedings of the American Philosophical Society*, **102** (1958), 351–370; and C. V. Morton, "Fern Herbarium of André Michaux," in *American Fern Journal*, **57** (1967), 166–182.

JOSEPH EWAN

MICHEL-LÉVY, AUGUSTE (*b.* Paris, France, 7 August 1844; *d.* Paris, 27 September 1911), *geology, mineralogy.*

The greater part of Michel-Lévy's scientific work was accomplished in collaboration with Ferdinand Fouqué. Jointly they introduced into France the study of rocks by microscopical petrography and artificially synthesized many igneous rocks in order to determine the conditions necessary for the production of their mineral constituents. In addition Michel-Lévy, working with feldspars, founded the method of statistical research on the constituents of rocks. He was the first to demonstrate the importance of birefringence in petrographic studies, and he determined this optical constant for a large number of minerals. In the field Michel-Lévy devoted twenty years to the study of the eastern part of the Massif Central, of the Morvan Massif, and of the western Alps.

Michel-Lévy's father was a noted military hygienist and president of the Académie de Médecine. Independently wealthy, Michel-Lévy was raised in an intellectual atmosphere devoted to both science and literature. As a result he won numerous prizes in the general *concours* from 1859 to 1861 and entered the École Polytechnique in 1862. He ranked first there and at the École des Mines, from which he graduated in 1867. Michel-Lévy entered the service of the Carte Géologique in 1870 and was its director from 1887 until his death. In 1879 he was appointed engineer of mines of the first class; he became chief engineer of this division in 1883; and he attained the highest rank, inspector general, in 1907. He was elected to the Académie des Sciences in 1896. In addition Michel-Lévy was a member of the administrative council of the Conservatoire National des Arts et Métiers, of the national council of hygiene of France, and of the council of public hygiene for the department of the Seine.

Together with Fouqué and Alfred Lacroix, Michel-Lévy pioneered the science of microscopical petrography in France. His two-volume work, *Minéralogie micrographique: Roches éruptives françaises* (1879), written with Fouqué, demonstrated the results of this method to French scientists. In it they also employed a new classificatory system for volcanic rocks, using as criteria mineralogical composition, structure, and chemical composition. In 1880, with Lacroix, Michel-Lévy published *Tableaux des minéraux des roches*; and in 1889 they produced *Les minéraux des roches*, which described the optical and chemical methods of studying minerals in thin sections and the microscopical features of rock-forming minerals. Michel-Lévy's *Étude sur la détermination des feldspaths dans les plaques minces* (1894) was a significant contribution to the microscopic study of feldspars in thin sections.

From 1878 to 1882 Michel-Lévy and Fouqué worked to synthesize igneous rocks artificially, believing that if they could determine the peculiar conditions surrounding the rocks' genesis, they might arrive at important geological conclusions. Despite the meager equipment of the laboratory at the Collège de France in which they carried out their experiments, they produced rocks having the mineralogical composition and structure identical with most of the volcanic rocks found in nature. They published jointly twenty-two articles and a book, *Synthèse des minéraux et des roches* (1882), which incorporated the results of their work. Their most important conclusions were that the degree of crystallinity depended largely upon the rate of cooling and that rocks of distinctly different mineralogical compositions would be formed from the same magma, depending upon the conditions of crystallization. Their failure to reproduce the trachytes and rhyolites demonstrated that in order to obtain the characteristic elements of these rocks, the presence of mineralizers was necessary to lessen the viscosity of the magma and to allow crystallization.

The principal result of Michel-Lévy's fieldwork in geology was in distinguishing the two successive phases of folding and dislocation of the Massif Central toward the end of the late Paleozoic. His analysis of the dislocations superimposed on the eastern portion of the Massif Central caused him to trace them to the east and to search for their influence on the tectonic movements and volcanic phenomena of the Tertiary. In conjunction with this research he mapped Clermont-Ferrand, studied the lavas of the neighboring regions, and explored and mapped portions of the western Alps.

BIBLIOGRAPHY

Michel-Lévy's chief publications treating the application of optical methods to the study of minerals in thin sections are *Minéralogie micrographique: Roches éruptives françaises* 2 vols. (Paris, 1879), written with F. Fouqué; *Tableaux des minéraux des roches* (Paris, 1880), written with A. Lacroix; *Les minéraux des roches* (Paris, 1889), written with A. Lacroix; and *Étude sur la détermination des feldspaths dans les plaques minces* (Paris, 1894). In petrography he collaborated with F. Fouqué in *Synthèse des minéraux et des roches* (Paris, 1882) and also published *Structures et classifications des roches éruptives* (Paris, 1889). In addition he published either alone or jointly some 150 articles on geological or mineralogical subjects, and he contributed 10 maps to the Carte Géologique.

A biography is Alfred Lacroix, *Notice historique sur Auguste Michel-Lévy* (Paris, 1914), which includes a complete bibliography.

JOHN G. BURKE

MICHELI, PIER ANTONIO (b. Florence, Italy, 11 December 1679; d. Florence, 1 January 1737), botany.

Micheli was the son of Pier Francesco Micheli, a laborer, and Maria Salvucci. The boy had only the most elementary schooling (Haller, in 1772, described him as "illiteratus et pauper"). He was, however, interested in plants from childhood, and his native talent won him the respect of, and eventually a prominent position among, the botanists of his time. He obtained the patronage of both the Grand Duke Cosimo III de' Medici and his successor Gian Gastone de' Medici; the generosity of these two men permitted him to devote himself completely to his studies. Micheli was nonetheless hampered by the lack of an academic degree and never held a post worthy of his talents. He was obliged to content himself with modest positions in the botanical gardens of Pisa and Florence, although he enjoyed considerable contemporary fame among both Italian and foreign botanists and conducted an extensive correspondence with them. He was further influential in founding, with a group of friends, the Società Botanica Fiorentina in 1716 and in the tutelage of a student of great ability, Giovanni Targioni-Tozzetti.

Micheli was a lifelong and tireless collector of plants. His travels for this purpose took him to the provinces of Venetia, Emilia-Romagna, Lazio, Abruzzi e Molise, the Marches, Campania, and Puglia; he was also extremely active in his native Tuscany. In 1708 and 1709 he made collecting expeditions to the Tirol, Austria, Bohemia, Thuringia, and Prussia. He was occasionally accompanied on these trips by Targioni-Tozzetti, who wrote of his skills as a collector:

> He was perspicacious and possessed a talent made expressly for natural history, and particularly for botany; his eye was so keen that as soon as he reached a meadow or other place full of grasses, he could immediately distinguish the rarest or most worthy of observation. He was also gifted with an acute critical capacity . . ., so that he could tell in an instant why other illustrious botanists had been in error, confusing one species with another, or multiplying them [Notizie della vita e delle opere di P. A. Micheli (Florence, 1858), 330].

In the seventeenth and eighteenth centuries the concept of species was crucial to the great botanical task of classification. Micheli's views on species were in large part derived from those of Joseph de Tournefort, but even more than Tournefort, Micheli realized the need for great caution in the problem of definition. Micheli's attitude was, in fact, quite close to that of Linnaeus, who expressed his admiration for

him. His concern is evident in the first part of his Nova plantarum genera of 1729. In this work Micheli considered some 1,900 species, of which nearly 1,400 were new. The greater number of these new species were thallophytes—fungi, lichens, liverworts, and mosses—which Micheli classified for the first time. Using two primitive microscopes, he was able to observe, again for the first time, such notable anatomical details as the antheridia and the archegones of mosses and the spores of fungi. He thus discovered, too, the generative function and the anatomy of the mycelium; for this discovery, among others, he may properly be considered the founder of mycology.

The Nova plantarum genera remained unfinished at the time of Micheli's death, and a considerable amount of the data that he had gathered—particularly material relating to algae, which attracted him as much as did fungi—was therefore never incorporated into it.

In addition to his botanical studies, Micheli was also concerned with zoology, paleontology, and geology. In 1710, while he was botanizing in Campania, he noticed the similarity of the rocks on the islands of Ischia and Procida to those of Vesuvius, and realized that the islands were, in fact, extinct volcanoes. In 1722, recalling this earlier observation, Micheli concluded that the hill of Radicofani in Tuscany and a number of outcroppings in nearby Lazio might also be extinct volcanoes; in 1734 he reached the same conclusion about Monte Amiata, also in Tuscany. His intuition proved to be correct; Micheli's suggestion represented the first recognition of an extinct volcano far from regions still active volcanically.

BIBLIOGRAPHY

I. ORIGINAL WORKS. Micheli's major work was Nova plantarum genera . . . (Florence, 1729). Some of his reports of his journey in 1708–1709 were published posthumously in G. Targioni-Tozzetti, Relazioni di alcuni viaggi fatti in diverse parti della Toscana . . . (Florence, 1768–1779), IX (1776), 338; X (1777), 134, 159, 177. Several unpublished manuscripts are in the library of the Istituto di Botanica of the University of Florence.

II. SECONDARY LITERATURE. G. Targioni-Tozzetti, Notizie della vita e delle opere di P. A. Micheli (Florence, 1858), with copious historical notes and extracts from Micheli's correspondence, edited by Antonio and Adolfo Targioni-Tozzetti, is an excellent source on the life of Micheli and his relations with contemporary scientists. See also G. Negri, "P. A. Micheli (1679–1737)," in Nuovo giornale botanico italiano, n.s. 45 (1938), lxxxi–cvii; and "P. A. Micheli botanico," in Atti della Società Colombaria fiorentina, meeting of 27 Dec. 1937, 47–67, and with an extensive bibliography on Micheli; and F. Rodolico, "P. A. Micheli e le prime ricerche sui vulcani spenti," in *Atti dell' Accademia toscana di scienze e lettere "La Colombaria,"* **27** (1962–1963), 353–360.

FRANCESCO RODOLICO

MICHELINI, FAMIANO (*b.* Rome, Italy, 31 August 1604; *d.* Florence, Italy, 20 January 1665), *hydraulics, medicine.*

In 1619, when he was only fifteen, Michelini entered the Piarists as a lay brother, under the name of Francesco di San Giuseppe. In 1621 the congregation was raised to the status of a religious order with the task of running free schools open to all, so that poor boys from their earliest years could be given both religious and secular education. The program of the order included a number of interesting teaching principles: religious instruction was not to take priority over other subjects; not only literature but also mathematics was to be taught; and all teachers had received a thorough training.

Michelini was therefore sent to continue his education in Genoa, where he studied mathematics with Somasco Antonio Santini. In 1629 he went to Florence, where the first schools of the order were to be opened, and took a letter (still extant) of introduction and recommendation to Galileo (from Giovanni Battista Baliani). One can follow his activities and movements until September 1641 through Galileo's manuscripts, which contain several letters from Michelini; and he is frequently mentioned in other letters of the time, especially those of Benedetto Castelli, to whom Michelini was introduced by Galileo when he went to Rome in 1634. In April 1634 Castelli wrote to Galileo, who had already been obliged to retire to Arcetri: "I am amazed by his [Michelini's] knowledge, surprised by the subtlety of his mind, delighted by the sincere love that he bears for you, and fascinated by his goodness."

In 1635 Michelini was called to teach mathematics at the Florentine court, and a little later he was asked to give instruction to the brothers of Ferdinand II de' Medici, Gian Carlo and Leopoldo—to whom he also gave lectures in physics and astronomy, which apparently were attended by the grand duke. In November 1636 Michelini was ordained a priest, and in 1648 he obtained the chair of mathematics at Pisa—vacant after the death of Vincenzo Renieri—because negotiations with Ismael Boulliau and William Oughtred had failed. In his inaugural lecture, now lost, Michelini declared that all knowledge is derived from the exact sciences. Following this principle, he applied the experimental method even to medicine, in which he was much interested although he was not a doctor; he is generally credited with paving the way for Redi's experiments and Borelli's theories. Among other things he recommended the use in many illnesses of abundant quantities of orange and lemon juice, and advised people to control their weight. But being generally misunderstood, he was made the object of much derision.

In 1655 Michelini left the chair at Pisa and sought the appointment of Borelli, then at Messina, to replace him. In 1657, already in poor health and afflicted by gout, he received permission to leave his religious order and, remaining a simple priest under his old name, went to Sicily as a pro-vicar to the new bishop of Patti. The latter soon died, however, and Michelini had to return to Florence, in even worse health and with no financial resources. He had the good fortune, though, to attract the patronage of Prince Leopold de' Medici, through whom, at the end of 1664, he was able to publish his book *Della direzione de' fiumi*. A few weeks after its publication he became seriously ill and died within a few days.

In the following years books and papers by Michelini appeared in the possession of Vincenzo Santini—certainly not through inheritance, as was once believed—and in 1671 Santini copied from one of the books the marginal notes written by the young Galileo on Archimedes' *De sphaera et cylindro,* comments that otherwise would have been lost.

Michelini was always reluctant to publish, and he left unpublished a number of "Discourses on Health," now lost, which however were known at least to Redi, his direct follower in the field. As for the book he published just before his death, Michelini's contemporary fame as an expert in hydraulics obviously did not depend on it. The relevant authorities had, many years before, sought his advice on important problems concerning water, such as the course of the Chiana River, the threat of silting in the Lagoon of Venice, and the control of the Arno for the protection of Pisa against floods. But now one can judge him only from his book, which has been much criticized because it includes several serious mistakes—for instance, the belief that stagnant water exerts pressure only on the bottom of its bed and not on the sides, even though Pascal's basic principle of hydrostatics had been known for sixteen years. But since Michelini was dealing exclusively with running water, this error does not invalidate the rest of the work, which contains many good suggestions. One of them was that it should be possible to protect and repair riverbeds with boxes—or, rather, bulkheads—full of stones. Unlike Torricelli, he recognized the theory that one of the factors determining the velocity of current is the gradient of the riverbed. Most significantly, he attributed to the viscosity of water the fact that the current is faster in the middle of a stream than near the banks. This idea was not accepted by his contemporaries.

For these and for other reasons, Michelini was referred to as his partial source by Domenico Guglielmini when, in his fundamental treatise *Della natura de' fiumi* (1697), he dealt with the control of riverbeds. This resulted in a reprint of Michelini's book (Bologna, 1700) and its inclusion in all the editions of the *Raccolta d'autori che trattano dell'acque*, beginning with the Florence edition of 1723.

BIBLIOGRAPHY

I. ORIGINAL WORKS. Michelini's surviving works are *Trattato della direzione de' Fiumi* (Florence, 1664; 2nd ed., Bologna, 1700); and "Risposta alla scrittura del Sig. Torricelli," in *Raccolta d'autori che trattano del moto dell'acque*, 2nd ed. (Florence, 1768), 121. His letters to Galileo are in Galileo, *Opere*, National Ed. (Florence, 1890–1909), XVI, 76, 139–140; XVII, 234–235, 316–317, 321–322, 399–400, 407, 411–412; XVIII, 35–36, 39–40, 128.

II. SECONDARY LITERATURE. See the following, listed chronologically: G. Targioni-Tozzetti, *Notizie degli aggrandimenti della scienze fisiche accaduti in Toscana nel corso di anni 60 del secolo XVII* (Florence, 1780; repr. Bologna, 1967), I, 188–204, 365; P. Riccardi, *Biblioteca matematica italiana*, II (Modena, 1870), 156–157; and A. Neri, "Il Padre Staderone," in *Rivista europea*, n.s. **23** (1881), 756–764; and G. Giovannozzi, *Scolopi galileiani*, which is *Pubblicazioni dell'Osservatorio Ximeniano dei PP. Scolopi*, no. 124 (Florence, 1917); and "Un capitolo inedito della storia del metodo sperimentale in Italia di R. Caverni," in *Atti della Pontificia Accademia Romana dei Nuovi Lincei*, **71** (1918), 171–189.

GIORGIO TABARRONI

MICHELL, JOHN (*b.* Nottinghamshire [?], England, 1724[?]; *d.* Thornhill, near Leeds, England, 21 April 1793), *astronomy.*

Michell earned a permanent place in the history of stellar astronomy for two signal accomplishments: he was the first to make a realistic estimate of the distance to the stars, and he discovered the existence of physical double stars. He was educated at Cambridge. After graduating from Queens' College with the M.A. (1752) and the B.D. (1761), he held the Woodwardian chair of geology at Cambridge (1762–1764). In 1767 he was appointed rector of St. Michael's Church in Thornhill, near Leeds—a post he held for the rest of his life. He is buried at Thornhill, where the parish register describes him as aged sixty-eight (hence the surmise that he was born in 1724).

Michell's published scientific work, which earned him election to the Royal Society in 1760, covered many subjects, including the cause of earthquakes (1760), observations of the comet of January 1760, a method for measuring degrees of longitude "upon parallels of the Equator" (1766), and an independent discovery with Coulomb of the torsion balance (1784). His greatest accomplishments were two investigations published in the *Philosophical Transactions of the Royal Society*: "An Inquiry Into the Probable Parallax and Magnitude of the Fixed Stars From the Quantity of Light Which They Afford Us, and the Particular Circumstances of Their Situation" (1767) and "On the Means of Discovering the Distance, Magnitude, etc. of the Fixed Stars" (1784).

In the first of these papers, Michell pointed out that the frequency of the angular separation of close pairs of stars known at that time deviated grossly from what one could expect for chance projection of stars uniformly distributed in space—there appeared to be an excessive number of close pairs—and, according to Michell: ". . . The natural conclusion from hence is, that it is highly probable, and next to a certainty in general, that such double stars as appear to consist of two or more stars placed very near together, do really consist of stars placed nearly together, and under the influence of some general law . . . to whatever cause this may be owing, whether to their mutual gravitation, or to some other law or appointment of the Creator." The directness of Michell's language perhaps leaves something to be desired; but the unimpeachable logic of his arguments gave a convincing theoretical proof of the existence of physical binary stars in the sky long before Herschel (1803) provided a compelling observational proof.

Michell's second great achievement was a realistic estimate of the distance to the stars, and he made it more than half a century before the first parallax of any fixed star had been measured. His argument was very neat and can be regarded as the precursor of the "photometric" parallaxes of the twentieth century. Michell noticed that Saturn at opposition appears in the sky as bright as the star Vega and exhibits an apparent disk about twenty seconds in diameter, one which from the sun would be seen as seventeen seconds across. Therefore Saturn's illuminated hemisphere clearly intercepts $(17/3600)^2(\pi/720)^2$ of the light sent out by the sun.

Now—and this is essential—if the sun and Vega were of equal intrinsic brightness, and Vega's apparent brightness is equal to that of Saturn, it follows (from the inverse-square law of the attenuation of brightness, already established by Bouguer) that Vega must be $(3600/17)(720/\pi)$, or 48,500, times as far from the sun as Saturn is. Moreover, since Saturn is known to be 9.5 times as far from the sun as the earth is, it follows that the distance to Vega should amount to $9.5 \times 48,500$, or some 460,000 astronomical units.

Although this value represents only about a quarter of the actual distance of Vega, first measured trigonometrically by F. G. W. Struve in 1837 (the underestimate resulting from Vega's being intrinsically much brighter than the sun), Michell's value was the first realistic estimate of the distance to any star.

Michell was apparently a man of wide interests, including music. Tradition has it that William Herschel was a frequent guest at Thornhill during his years as a young musician in Yorkshire, and he is even said to have received his introduction to mirror grinding from Michell. There is, however, no real evidence that Herschel turned to astronomical observation before his move to Bath some years later; and the story of his apprenticeship with Michell may, therefore, be apocryphal.

BIBLIOGRAPHY

I. ORIGINAL WORKS. Michell's papers appeared mainly in the *Philosophical Transactions of the Royal Society* and include "Conjectures Concerning the Cause and Observations Upon the Phenomena of Earthquakes," **51**, pt. 2 (1760), 566–634, also published separately (London, 1760); "Observations on the Same Comet [January 1760]," *ibid.*, 466–467; "A Recommendation of Hadley's Quadrant for Surveying," *ibid.*, **55** (1765), 70–78, also published separately (London, 1765); "Proposal of a Method for Measuring Degrees of Longitude Upon Parallels of the Equator," **56** (1766), 119–125, also published separately (London, 1767); "An Inquiry Into the Probable Parallax and Magnitude of the Fixed Stars From the Quantity of Light Which They Afford Us," *ibid.*, **57** (1767), 234–264, also published separately (London, 1768); and "On the Means of Discovering the Distance, Magnitude, etc. of the Fixed Stars," *ibid.*, **74** (1784), 35–57.

Michell was also author of *A Treatise of Artificial Magnets* (Cambridge, 1750; 2nd ed., 1751), translated into French as *Traité sur les aimans artificiels* (Paris, 1752); and *De arte medendi apud priscos musices* (London, 1766; 1783).

II. SECONDARY LITERATURE. See Archibald Geikie, *Memoir of John Michell* (Cambridge, 1918); and *Dictionary of National Biography*, XIII, 333–334.

ZDENĔK KOPAL

MICHELSON, ALBERT ABRAHAM (*b.* Strelno, Prussia [now Poland], 19 December 1852; *d.* Pasadena, California, 9 May 1931), *physics, optics, metrology.*

Precision measurement in experimental physics was Michelson's lifelong passion. In 1907 he became the first American citizen to win a Nobel Prize in one of the sciences, being so honored "for his precision optical instruments and the spectroscopic and metrological investigations conducted therewith." Michelson measured the speed of light in 1878 as his first venture into scientific research, and he repeatedly returned to the experimental determination of this fundamental constant over the next half century. Never fully satisfied with the precision of former measurements, he developed and took advantage of more advanced techniques and tools to increase the accuracy of his observations. He died, after several strokes, during an elaborate test of the velocity of light in a true partial vacuum over a mile-long course at Irvine, California; but the value later published by his colleagues ($299,774 \pm 11$ km./sec.) was probably less precise than Michelson's own optical determination over a twenty-two-mile course between mountains in southern California during 1924–1926 ($299,796 \pm 4$ km./sec.).

Born to parents of modest means in disputed territory between Prussia and Poland, Michelson at the age of four emigrated with his parents, Samuel and Rosalie Michelson, to San Francisco via New York and Panama. The elder Michelson became a merchant to gold-rush miners in California and later in Virginia City, Nevada, while his son was sent after the sixth grade to board first with relatives in San Francisco and then with Theodore Bradley, the headmaster of Boys' High School there. Bradley seems to have aroused young Michelson's interest in science and to have recognized and rewarded his talents in the laboratory. At Bradley's suggestion Michelson competed for a state appointment to the U.S. Naval Academy; but when three boys tied for first place in the scholastic examination and another was appointed, young Michelson decided to take his case, with a letter of recommendation from his congressman, to the White House. In 1869 he traveled to Washington, saw President Grant, and gained his appointment to Annapolis.

Graduating with the class of 1873, Michelson went to sea for several cruises before being reassigned to the academy as instructor in physical sciences. On 10 April 1877 Michelson married Margaret Heminway from a prosperous New York family; this marriage lasted twenty years and produced two sons and a daughter.

While teaching physics in 1878, Michelson became interested in improving upon Foucault's method for measuring the speed of light terrestrially. In July 1878, with a $2,000 gift from his father-in-law, Michelson was able to improve the revolving-mirror apparatus and to perfect his experiment—the fourth terrestrial measurement of the speed of light. He was preceded by Fizeau, Foucault, and Cornu. Simon Newcomb, superintendent of the Nautical Almanac Office, became interested in his work. In consequence, his first scientific notices and papers were published in 1878–1879, and he began to collaborate with Newcomb on a government-sponsored project to refine further the determination of the velocity of light. He obtained a leave of absence to do postgraduate study in Europe during 1880–1882. He studied with Helmholtz in Berlin, with Quincke in Heidelberg, and with Cornu, Mascart, and Lippman in Paris.

In the winter of 1880–1881, while working in Helmholtz' laboratory, Michelson thought of a means to try a second-order measurement of Maxwell's suggestion for testing the relative motion of the earth against the ubiquitous, if hypothetical, luminiferous ether. Drawing on the credit that Alexander Graham Bell maintained in his account with the Berlin instrument makers Schmidt and Haensch, Michelson designed an apparatus called an interferential refractometer, which he then used to test for relative motion, or an "aether-wind," by comparing the speed of two pencils of light split from a single beam and caused to traverse paths at right angles to each other upon a base that could be rotated between observations. At different azimuths it was expected that the recombined pencils forming interference fringes would shift past a fiducial mark and thereby give data from which could be calculated the "absolute motion" of the earth, with respect to the ether or the "fixed" stars, as it hurtles through space. This first ether-drift experiment was tried in Berlin, then at the Astrophysicalisches Observatorium at Potsdam, with disappointingly null results. The instrument itself was amazingly sensitive and versatile; but errors in experimental design, pointed out by A. Potier and later by H. A. Lorentz, together with the null results themselves and the theoretical difficulties with regard to what was meant by "absolute velocity," later led Michelson to consider the experiment a failure. The hypotheses of A. J. Fresnel concerning a universal stationary ether and of G. G. Stokes concerning astronomical aberration were thus called into question.

The undulatory theory of light as generally accepted in the 1880's simply assumed a luminiferous medium. This "aether" must pervade intermolecular spaces, of both transparent and opaque materials, as well as interstellar space. Hence, it should be at rest or stationary in the universe and therefore provide a reference frame against which to measure the earth's velocity. Michelson boldly denied the validity of this hypothesis of a *stationary* ether, but he always maintained the need for some kind of ether to explain the phenomena of the propagation of light. Ad hoc hypotheses soon seemed necessary to explain why no relative etherwind or relative motion appeared to be detectable in Michelson's interferometer at the surface of the earth. This curious puzzle piqued the interest of Lorentz, W. Thomson (later Lord Kelvin), and FitzGerald, among others.

In 1881 Michelson resigned from active duty, and the next year he joined the faculty of the new Case School of Applied Science in Cleveland, Ohio. There he set up improved apparatus, helping to check Simon Newcomb's velocity-of-light measurements and testing various colored lights for indexes of refraction in various media. In 1885 Michelson began a collaborative project with Edward W. Morley of Western Reserve, a senior experimentalist (and primarily a chemist) with an elaborate laboratory. Their first effort, undertaken at the suggestion of W. Thomson, and of Rayleigh and Gibbs, was to verify the Fizeau experiment, reported in 1859, that supposedly had confirmed Fresnel's drag coefficient by comparing the apparent velocities of light moving with and against a current of water. This "ether-drag" experiment worked out well and corroborated the suppositions of Fresnel, Maxwell, Stokes, and Rayleigh concerning astronomical aberration and an all-pervasive immaterial luminiferous medium.

Michelson and Morley next redesigned the 1881 ether-drift experiment to increase the path length almost tenfold and to reduce friction of rotation by floating a sandstone slab on a mercury bearing. During five days in July 1887 Michelson and Morley performed their test for the relative motion of the earth in orbit against a stationary ether. Their results were null and so discouraging that they abandoned any effort to continue with the tests they intended in the following autumn, winter, and spring. The sensitivity they had achieved with this new interferometer, about one-fourth part in one billion, was its own reward, however; and both innovators began to think of other uses for such instruments. Although the experimenters quickly forgot their disappointment, theorists, and notably FitzGerald, Larmor, Lorentz, and Poincaré, made much of their failure to find fringe shifts and to corroborate Fresnel and Stokes's wave theory of light.

Michelson accepted an offer in 1889 to move to the new Clark University at Worcester, Massachusetts. Concurrently he began to carry out a monumental metrological project that he and Morley had envisioned to determine experimentally the length of the international meter bar at Sèvres in terms of wavelengths of cadmium light. Adapting his refractometer as a comparator for lengths that could be reduced through spectroscopy and interferometric techniques to nonmaterial standards of length, Michelson found in 1892–1893 that the Paris meter bar was equal to 1,553,163.5 wavelengths of the red cadmium line. So elegant were the success and precision of this project that Michelson became internationally famous.

In 1893 Michelson moved to the new University of Chicago to head its department of physics. There he began to develop his interests in astrophysical spectroscopy. Diffraction gratings, a new harmonic analyzer, and the echelon spectroscope, as well as a large-scale vertical interferometer, were designed by and built for Michelson around the turn of the century. He was clearly recognized as one of the foremost experimental physicists of the nation and was invited to give the Lowell lectures at Harvard in 1899, later published as *Light Waves and Their Uses* (Chicago, 1903). Also in 1899, Michelson remarried, having been divorced, and took as his second wife Edna Stanton, who bore him three daughters.

When Einstein's three famous papers of 1905 appeared, one of which inaugurated the special theory of relativity by dispensing with the idea of an ether and by elevating the velocity of light into an absolute constant, Michelson was much too busy with prior commitments and with receiving honors to pay much heed.

The relation between Michelson's experimental work and Einstein's theories of relativity is complex and historically indirect. But the influence of his ether-drift tests on Lorentz, FitzGerald, Poincaré, W. Thomson, Lodge, Larmor, and other theoreticians around 1900 is less problematic and quite direct. Although scholars continue to debate the role of his classic ether-drift experiment, Michelson himself in his last years still spoke of "the beloved old ether (which is now abandoned, though I personally still cling a little to it)." He advised in 1927 in his last book that relativity theory be accorded a "generous acceptance," although he remained personally skeptical.

From 1901 to 1903 he had served as president of the American Physical Society, and in 1907 he received the Copley Medal from the Royal Society (London) in addition to the Nobel Prize. In all, during his half-century as an active scientist he was elected to honorary membership in more than twenty-five societies, was awarded eleven honorary degrees, and received seventeen medals. In 1910–1911 he served as president of the American Association for the Advancement of Science, and from 1923 to 1927 he presided over the National Academy of Sciences.

During World War I, Michelson returned to the navy as a sixty-five-year-old reserve officer. He helped perfect an optical range finder and demonstrated tolerances for imperfections in striated optical glasses. After the war the Eddington eclipse expedition of 1919 made Einstein and relativity theory almost synonymous with esoteric modern science. Although legend has much inflated the role of the Michelson-Morley experiment in supposedly providing the basis for Einstein's first work on the principle of relativity applied to electrodynamics, Michelson's corroborations of the speed of light as a virtual constant did in fact prove significant equally for the special and for the general theories of relativity.

Early in the 1920's Michelson began to spend more time in California at Mt. Wilson, in Pasadena, and at the California Institute of Technology. Besides teaching, his main work for almost a decade had been to perfect ruling engines for the production of better diffraction gratings. But administrative duties at the University of Chicago also weighed heavily upon him. In southern California, he could work and play in several well-equipped laboratories and also indulge his interest in tennis, billiards, chess, and watercolor painting. Tests for the rigidity of the earth (or earth-tide experiments) were followed by work with H. G. Gale toward an elaborate test near Chicago for the effect of the earth's rotation on the velocity of light. Other studies of the application of interference methods to astronomical problems led to the construction in 1920 of the celebrated stellar interferometer on the Hooker 100-inch telescope that measured the amazing angular diameter of α Orionis (Betelgeuse), which was found to have a disk subtending 0.047″ arc, or approximately 240 million miles in diameter. Still other tests and a geodetic survey under Michelson's supervision in southern California prepared the way for a measurement of the velocity of light between mountain peaks. The Mt. Wilson to the San Jacinto Mountains measurement (eighty-two miles) was scuttled because of smog in 1925; the Mt. Wilson to Mt. San Antonio measurement (twenty-two miles) was completed in 1926, and the value remains one of the best optical determinations ever made.

Meanwhile, George Ellery Hale, director of the Mt. Wilson Observatory, had invited to southern California Michelson's friend and successor at Case, Dayton C. Miller, who had worked with Morley on other ether-drift tests in 1900–1906 and had achieved eminence in acoustics. Miller was supposed to perfect the original Michelson-Morley experiment for all seasons and at a 6,000-foot altitude. After many vicissitudes he did so in 1925–1926 and, to the consternation or delight of a divided profession, Miller announced in his retiring address as president of the American Physical Society that he had finally found the absolute velocity of the solar system: about 200 km./sec. toward the head of the constellation Draco! This challenge spurred Michelson to take up ether-drift tests once again. In conjunction with F. G. Pease and F. Pearson, several very elaborate interferometers were built and operated briefly from 1926 through 1928 but to little avail. Neither Michelson nor his team—nor any other experimentalists later in the 1920's—were able to corroborate Miller's slight but positive results; and so Einstein stood verified largely on the authority of Michelson's reiterated word.

Michelson's second book, *Studies in Optics*, was published in 1927, the year before the Optical Society of America dedicated its annual meeting to him on the fiftieth anniversary of his scientific career. Michelson had used "Light Waves as Measuring Rods for Sounding the Infinite and the Infinitesimal," as the title of one of his last papers. When he died in 1931, he was hardly less a believer in the wave theory of light and its concomitant ether. Although he supported Einstein with few reservations, he was secure in the knowledge that he had indeed sounded the nature of light and found its field both infinite and infinitesimal.

BIBLIOGRAPHY

I. ORIGINAL WORKS. Michelson's books are *Light Waves and Their Uses* (Chicago, 1903); and *Studies in Optics* (Chicago, 1927). Translations and 78 articles are listed in Harvey B. Lemon, "Albert Abraham Michelson: The Man and the Man of Science," in *American Physics Teacher*, **4** (Feb. 1936), 1–11.

MS and memorabilia material are widely scattered, but the best collection is held by the Michelson Laboratory, Naval Weapons Center, China Lake, California. See D. Theodore McAllister, "Collecting Archives for the History of Science," in *American Archivist*, **32** (Oct. 1969), 327–332; and *Albert Abraham Michelson: The Man Who Taught a World to Measure*, Publication of the Michelson Museum, no. 3 (China Lake, Calif., 1970). See also holdings of the Bohr Library, American Institute of Physics, Center for History and Philosophy of Physics, 335 East 45th Street, New York, N.Y. 10017.

II. SECONDARY LITERATURE. See Bernard Jaffe, *Michelson and the Speed of Light*, Science Study series (Garden City, N.Y., 1960); Dorothy Michelson Livingston, "Michelson in the Navy; the Navy in Michelson," in *Proceedings of the United States Naval Institute*, **95**, no. 6 (June 1969), 72–79, a collection of papers and memorabilia that forms the basis for a biography of her father, *The Master of Light* (New York, 1973); Robert A. Millikan, "Albert A. Michelson," in *Biographical Memoirs. National Academy of Sciences*, **19**, no. 4 (1938), 120–147; "Proceedings of the Michelson Meeting of the Optical Society of America," in *Journal of the Optical Society of America*, **18**, no. 3 (Mar. 1929), 143–286; Robert S. Shankland, "Albert A. Michelson at Case," in *American Journal of Physics*, **17** (Nov. 1949), 487–490; and Loyd S. Swenson, Jr., *The Ethereal Aether: A History of the Michelson-Morley-Miller Aether-Drift Experiments 1880–1930* (Austin, Tex., 1972); Gerald Holton, "Einstein, Michelson, and the 'Crucial Experiment,' " in *Isis*, **60**, no. 202 (Summer 1969), 133–197; Jean M. Bennett, *et al.*, "Albert Michelson, Dean of American Optics–Life, Contributions to Science, and Influence on Modern-Day Physics," together with Robert S. Shankland, "Michelson's Role in the Development of Relativity," in *Applied Optics*, **12**, no. 10 (Oct. 1973), 2287 and 2253; Loyd S. Swenson, Jr., "The Michelson-Morley-Miller Experiments Before and After 1905," in *Journal for the History of Astronomy*, **1**, no. 1 (1970), 56–78.

LOYD S. SWENSON, JR.

MICHURIN, IVAN VLADIMIROVICH (*b*. Dolgoye, Russia [now Michurovka, U.S.S.R.], 28 October 1855; *d*. Michurinsk, U.S.S.R., 7 June 1935), *plant breeding*.

For a complete study of his life and work, see Supplement.

MIDDENDORF, ALEKSANDR FEDOROVICH (*b*. St. Petersburg, Russia, 6 August 1815; *d*. Khellenurme [now Estonian S.S.R.], 16 January 1894), *biogeography*.

Middendorf graduated from the Third Petersburg Gymnasium, of which his father was director, and, in 1837, from Dorpat University with an M.D. For two years he studied zoology, botany, and geognosy at universities in Germany and Austria. In 1839 and 1840 he taught zoology at Kiev University. During the summer of 1839, he traveled to the Kola Peninsula with Karl Ernst von Baer.

In 1844 Middendorf completed a two-year journey to northern and eastern Siberia commissioned by the St. Petersburg Academy of Sciences. In 1845 he was elected to membership in the Academy, and in 1852 he became its permanent secretary. A sharp decline in his health obliged Middendorf in 1865 to relinquish his post as academician, but he was retained as an honorary academician. Middendorf subsequently resided at his estate, Khellenurme, where he completed a multivolume account of his Siberian journey and also journeyed to the Baraba Steppe in Western Siberia, and to the Fergana Valley in Central Asia.

Middendorf gave a brilliant geographical description and an ecological and geographical analysis of the fauna of Siberia, in which he examined in detail the concept of species, the causes of changes of species, the adaptation of animals to their environment, and laws of the geographical distribution of animals, including the distribution of boreal species in a zone surrounding the pole. No less valuable is his description of the geographical distribution and ecological peculiarities of Siberia's vegetation.

Two tasks had been assigned to the expedition to Siberia: to study the quality and quantity of organic life and to verify the presence and distribution of the permafrost discovered in many Siberian locations, especially in Yakutsk.

Middendorf twice crossed the Taymyr Peninsula and in Yakutsk revealed the mysterious phenomenon of permafrost and laid the scientific bases of the study of frozen soil. He calculated the geothermal gradient in the Fedor Shergin well and, on the basis of this calculation, determined the depth of the frozen layer under Yakutsk to be 204 meters (10 meters less than the current value). In the third stage of the expedition Middendorf crossed the Dzhugdzhur Range and investigated the flora and fauna of the Okhotsk Sea coastal areas and of the Shantar Islands.

Middendorf's Siberian journey led to the establishment of the Russian Geographical Society.

BIBLIOGRAPHY

I. ORIGINAL WORKS. Middendorf's main work, published originally in German, was Reise in den aussersten Norden und Osten Sibiriens während der Jahre 1843 und 1844, 4 vols. (St. Petersburg, 1848–1875), dealing with the climatology, geognosy, botany, zoology, ethnography, and the flora and fauna of the region; the Russian ed. was Puteshestvie na sever i vostok Sibiri, 2 pts. (St. Petersburg, 1860–1878).

His other writings include "Medved bury" ("The Brown Bear"), in Y. Simashko, Russkaya fauna ili opisanie i izobrazhenie zhivotnykh, vodyashchikhsya v Imperii Rossyskoy ("Russian Fauna or a Description and Depiction of the Animals Found in the Russian Empire"), 2 pts. (St. Petersburg, 1850–1851), 187–295; "O sibirskikh mamontakh" ("On Siberian Mammoths"), in Vestnik estestvennykh nauk, nos. 26–27 (1860), 843–868, with additions by N. Lyaskovsky; "Golfstrim na vostoke ot Nordkapa" ("The Gulfstream East of North Cape"), in Zapiski Imperatorskoi akademii nauk, 19, no. 1 (1871), 73–101; "Baraba," ibid., 19, supp. (1871); and Ocherki Ferganskoy doliny ("Essays on the Fergana Valley"; St. Petersburg, 1882), with app. by F. Schmidt.

II. SECONDARY LITERATURE. There are biographies of Middendorf by K. Kirt (Tartu, 1963); N. I. Leonov (Moscow, 1967); and S. P. Naumov (Moscow, 1959), 323–331.

G. NAUMOV

MIDGLEY, THOMAS, JR. (b. Beaver Falls, Pennsylvania, 18 May 1889; d. Worthington, Ohio, 2 November 1944), chemistry.

Midgley was the son of Thomas Midgley, a successful inventor, and Hattie Lena Emerson. Following graduation from Betts Academy, he entered Cornell University where he took the course in mechanical engineering; he graduated in 1911. His subsequent work, however, lay in industrial chemistry, to which he brought a mastery of scientific fundamentals and a talent for ingenious experimentation.

In 1916, shortly after he had joined Charles F. Kettering's Dayton Engineering Laboratories, Midgley was assigned the problem of reducing internal-combustion knock. Gaseous detonation, or knock, was obstructing the development of Kettering's Delco engine; the phenomenon was only imperfectly understood, and was initially attributed to the ignition of the battery employed in Kettering's self-starting device for automobiles. From 1917 until 1921, Midgley used a variety of experimental techniques directed toward finding a chemical antiknock agent.

Midgley and Kettering assumed that knock was an inverse function of volatility. They first tried iodine as a fuel additive, supposing that a red dye might cause low-volatility fuel to absorb radiant heat and citing the example of the red-backed trailing arbutus that blooms under snow. They found that knocking did decrease greatly, although further tests demonstrated that the red color was inconsequential. They had nonetheless shown that a chemical antiknock agent does exist; since iodine proved impractical as a fuel additive, Midgley undertook to test at least one compound of each chemical element in an attempt to find something better. After months of research he established that aniline and its homologues—as well as other nitrogenous compounds—are effective chemical agents, but that they also give off an unbearable smell.

Midgley then began to make use of Robert E. Wilson's arrangement of the periodic table, which was based on Langmuir's theory of atomic structure and chemical valence. He employed a bouncing-pin indicator to measure knock quantitatively, then correlated these measurements with the table to establish trends; he thus discovered the antiknock properties of lead and, on 9 December 1921, singled out the remarkable effectiveness of tetraethyl lead. Added to gasoline, tetraethyl lead improved the engine compression ratio, thereby economizing fuel. The substance was put into large-scale production after a number of difficulties had been overcome, including a moratorium placed upon its use to allow a U. S. surgeon general's committee to investigate any possible danger of widespread lead poisoning. Midgley was then appointed general manager of the Ethyl Gasoline Corporation.

In 1930 Kettering, who was in charge of research at General Motors, asked Midgley to find a nontoxic, nonflammable, and cheap refrigerant for use in household appliances. Again drawing upon the periodic table, Midgley discovered dichlorodifluoromethane within three days, a compound that possessed all the desired qualities. He was less successful in his investigations of natural and synthetic rubber, however. These constitute the most purely scientific of his works.

Midgley received the four principal American medals for achievement in chemistry: the Nichols Medal (1922), the Perkin Medal (1937), the Priestley Medal (1941), and the Willard Gibbs Medal (1942). He was president of the American Chemical Society; in his presidential address to that body, delivered only a few months before he died, he suggested that scientists older than forty should remove themselves from positions requiring a high order of creativity, since he thought that most of the great discoveries and inventions had been made by workers between the ages of twenty-five and forty-five.

BIBLIOGRAPHY

I. ORIGINAL WORKS. Two articles indicative of Midgley's formal and informal communications are, respectively, "The Chemical Control of Gaseous Detonation With Particular Reference to the Internal-Combustion Engine," in *Journal of Industrial and Engineering Chemistry*, **14** (1922), 894–898, written with T. A. Boyd; and "From the Periodic Table to Production," *ibid.*, **29** (1937), 241–244.

II. SECONDARY LITERATURE. Biographical essays on Midgley include one by his mentor, professional associate, and friend, Charles F. Kettering: "Biographical Memoir of Thomas Midgley, Jr.," in *Biographical Memoirs. National Academy of Sciences*, **24** (1947), 361–380, which includes a list of 57 articles by Midgley but does not list his patents. An extremely useful essay is by Midgley's close research associate, T. A. Boyd: "Thomas Midgley, Jr.," in *Journal of the American Chemical Society*, **75** (1953), 2791–2795, also with a list of articles. Williams Haynes, the historian of the American chemical industry, has written an essay on Midgley in *Great Chemists*, Eduard Farber, ed. (New York, 1961), 1589–1597. On Midgley's work, especially the history of tetraethyl lead, see T. A. Boyd, "Pathfinding in Fuels and Engines," in *S.A.E. Quarterly Transactions*, **4** (1950), 182–185; and *Professional Amateur: The Biography of Charles Franklin Kettering* (New York, 1957); and Williams Haynes, *American Chemical Industry*, IV (New York, 1948).

THOMAS PARKE HUGHES

MIE, GUSTAV (*b.* Rostock, Germany, 29 September 1868; *d.* Freiburg im Breisgau, German Federal Republic, 13 February 1957), *physics*.

Mie, the son of a pastor, spent his childhood and went to high school in Rostock. He studied mathematics and the physical sciences at the University of Heidelberg, completing his doctorate in 1891 with a dissertation on a mathematical problem in partial differential equations. He then went to Dresden as a teacher of mathematics and physical sciences in a private school but did not stay there long. He accepted an assistantship in the Physics Institute of the Technische Hochschule in Karlsruhe. Mie's interests had turned from mathematics to physics, and in Karlsruhe, where Heinrich Hertz had done his famous experiments on electrical oscillations, Mie reassembled Hertz's apparatus and repeated the experiments. On completing his *Habilitation*, Mie became a *Privatdozent* at Karlsruhe in 1897.

Mie married in the spring of 1901. He was appointed extraordinary professor of experimental physics at the University of Greifswald in 1902 and was made an ordinary professor and director of its Physics Institute in 1905. He remained at Greifswald for fifteen years, a happy and scientifically productive period. From Greifswald, Mie moved to the University of Halle in 1917 as professor of experimental physics and stayed there until 1924. Mie then became the director of the Institute of Physics of the University of Freiburg im Breisgau, where he remained until his retirement in 1935.

In 1908 Mie published the rigorous electrodynamic calculation of light diffraction from spherical dielectric and conducting particles. This, together with the explanation of color effects, led to the discovery of the asymmetry in the intensity distribution and the precise determination of the optical constants of suspended particles. Called the Mie effect, it has had increasing importance in the determination of molecular clusters in solutions and the investigation of interstellar matter.

Before 1914, encouraged by Russian researches in the field, Mie solved the problem of the anomalous dispersion of water by using his quenched-spark oscillator as emitter and thermal elements connected with a spherically coated galvanometer as receiver. These experiments led to the determination of an invariant dielectric constant for water. They also brought understanding of the free rotation of polar groups in molecules and the frictional dispersion of dipole molecules in highly viscous solutions.

The other main direction of Mie's experimental work was a series of X-ray analyses of the crystal structure of organic compounds, especially anthracene and naphthalene, which he began at Halle soon after the work of the Braggs. Mie continued these studies in collaboration with Staudinger at Freiburg, and the investigation of different polyoxymethylenes (as the model substances for cellulose) led to the verification of the molecular lattice.

Mie's greatest personal involvement was in his effort to understand the fundamental and general principles of physical phenomena, and to state them suitably. At Greifswald, during 1912–1913, he made the first attempt to construct a complete theory of matter in the twentieth century. In an imaginative extension of Maxwell's theory in the framework of special relativity, the elementary particles known at that time (electrons and protons) appear in Mie's work as offspring of a universal electromagnetic field. His goal was to overcome the traditional opposition between "field" and "matter," thereby seeking to obtain a "unity of the physical world-view." In particular, he wanted to explain "the existence of an indivisible electron and to relate the phenomenon of gravitation to the existence of matter."

Three assumptions formed the basis of Mie's theory:

1. Electric and magnetic fields exist both inside and outside the electrons.

2. The principle of special relativity is valid throughout.

3. "The hitherto known states of the ether, namely the electric field, the magnetic field, the electric charge, and the charge current are entirely sufficient to describe all phenomena in the material world."

From these three assumptions, Mie was led to a generalization of the equations for the ether. This extension of the Maxwell-Lorentz theory was determined on the basis of the validity of the principle of conservation of energy and the existence of a localizable energy. Mie did not realize how many unnecessary assumptions were built into his derivation. His theory ran into serious difficulties, some of which stem from the fact that no one has succeeded in deriving solutions for static electrons in which the charge is "quantized."

Mie was the first to recognize the necessity of "quantizing" the field variables of the electromagnetic field, long before Heisenberg and Pauli developed the first fundamentals of a rational quantum field theory. This insight aroused the admiration of David Hilbert, who was inspired by the "deep ideas and original concepts on which Mie had built his electrodynamics." This theory, together with Einstein's ideas on gravitation and relativity, led Hilbert to develop an axiomatic theory of the foundations of physics, from which he derived the field equations of gravitation (together with their auxiliary conditions as given by the Bianchi identities) and the equations of the electromagnetic field.

Although Mie did not discover the appropriate "world function" that could account for the existence, asymmetry, and stability of the proton and the electron, his investigations later inspired the work of Max Born and Leopold Infeld on "nonlinear electrodynamics," which corresponded entirely with Mie's program. Mie's theory of matter would probably be regarded as his greatest contribution to physics.

The originality of Mie's ideas lay in his treatment of electromagnetic phenomena. His *Textbook on Electricity and Magnetism*, with the subtitle *An Experimental Physics of World-Ether*, was constructed on the fundamental distinction between the "quantities of intensity" and "quantities of magnitude." The "quantities of magnitude" are the length of a path or the duration of an event, the inertial mass of a body, and the electric charge. The "intensive" quantities are, for instance, "force" in mechanics, and the electric and magnetic field strengths E and B in the expression for Lorentz' ponderomotive force.

BIBLIOGRAPHY

I. ORIGINAL WORKS. Mie's articles include "Grundlagen einer Theorie der Materie," in *Annalen der Physik*, **37** (1912), 511–534; **39** (1912), 1–40; and **40** (1913), 1–66; and the autobiographical sketch "Aus meinem Leben," in *Zeitwende*, **19** (1948), 733–743.

Among his books are *Textbook of Electricity and Magnetism* (1910; 2nd ed., 1941; 3rd ed., 1948); *Die Grundlage der Quantentheorie* (Freiburg im Breisgau, 1926); *Elektrodynamik*, XI, pt. 1 of the series Handbuch der Experimentalphysik, W. Wien and F. Harms, eds. (Leipzig, 1932); *Molecules, Atoms and Ether; Die Einsteinsche Gravitationstheorie; Die Denkweise der Physik; Naturwissenschaft und Theologie;* and *Die Grundlagen der Mechanik* (1950).

II. SECONDARY LITERATURE. Articles on Mie are H. Hönl, "Intensitäts- und Quantitätsgrössen," in *Physikalische Blätter*, **24** (1968), 498–502, commemorating the centenary of Mie's birth; and W. Kast, "Gustav Mie," *ibid.*, **13** (1957), 129–131.

Max Born's review article on the Born-Infeld nonlinear electrodynamics, in *Annales de l'Institut Henri Poincaré*, **7** (1937), 155, gives an explicit discussion of the relation of this work to Mie's. For Mie's work on the field theory of matter see J. Mehra, "Einstein, Hilbert, and the Theory of Gravitation," in *The Physicist's Conception of Nature* (Dordrecht, 1973).

JAGDISH MEHRA

MIELI, ALDO (*b.* Leghorn, Italy, 4 December 1879; *d.* Florida, Argentina, 16 February 1950), *chemistry, history of science.*

Mieli graduated in chemistry from the University of Pisa, then went to Leipzig to attend Ostwald's lectures on physical chemistry. He next studied mathematics with Ulisse Dini and chemistry with Stanislas Cannizzaro and Emanuele Paternò. He was Paternò's assistant at the University of Rome from 1905 to 1912. He became a docent at that university in 1908; in the same year he also published two articles on chemistry. Mieli's interests at this time were not confined to chemistry, however. During the same period he wrote a number of articles of general cultural interest, as well as works on the philosophy of science and the relationships between science and art.

From 1912 on, Mieli began to devote himself to the history of science. He was one of the first to consider this study as an autonomous discipline, and his position was consolidated when he became the Italian bibliographic editor for *Isis*, which had just been founded. He also collaborated in editing the journal *Scientia* and edited the *Rivista di storia delle scienze mediche e naturali*, in whose pages he initiated a campaign to have the history of science taught in the universities. In 1913–1914, with E. Trollo, he began the series *Classici della Scienza e della Filosofia*, which was inspired by Ostwald's collection. In 1919 the publisher Nardecchia suggested that he take over the bibliographical work *Gli scienziati italiani*; while only one full volume (and part of another) appeared, it included studies by A. Boffito, A. Corsini, A. Favaro, G. Loria, and Mieli himself. The journal *Archivio di storia della scienza* was founded in the same year; Mieli became its editor in 1921 (after 1925, the journal was called *Archeion*).

At this time, too, Mieli invested his own money in founding the Leonardo da Vinci publishing house. Among its first publications were the *Universitas scriptorum* and the *Rivista di studi sessuali e di eugenetica* (Mieli was secretary of the Italian Society for Sexual Studies, and editor of its journal until 1928). The most notable of Mieli's own works that were published by his house are *Pagine di storia della chimica* (1922) and *Manuale di storia della scienza: Antichità* (1925).

In 1928 political considerations forced Mieli to leave Italy. He went to Paris, where he became director of the section for the history of science of the Centre International de Synthèse, to which he gave his large history of science library. He also continued to edit *Archeion* and, at a meeting of the International Congress of the Historical Sciences held in Oslo, proposed the formation of an International Committee for the History of Sciences. The members of the committee included Abel Rey, Sarton, Sigerist, Charles Singer, Sudhoff, and Lynn Thorndike; Mieli

served as secretary of the group and organized the First International Congress of the History of Science, held in Paris in May 1929. During this congress, the committee transformed itself into the International Academy for the History of Science, and *Archeion*, under Mieli's editorship, became its official journal.

In 1939, on the eve of World War II, Mieli again exiled himself. He went to Argentina, where from 1940 until 1943 he taught the history of science at the Universidad Nacional del Litoral in Santa Fé. He created an Institute for the History and Philosophy of Science, continued to edit *Archeion*, and published a summary of his lectures. In 1943, however, the political situation in Argentina, and especially the intervention of the government into university affairs, forced Mieli to leave Santa Fé, and he retired to Florida, near Buenos Aires, sadly spent in both health and finances. To recoup the latter, he began to write his *Panorama general de historia de la ciencia*. Of the eight volumes that he planned, two were published before his death; he saw only the proofs of volumes III, IV and V. (The work was finished by Desiderio Papp and José Babini; it was eventually published in twelve volumes.) Mieli was gravely ill for the last three years of his life. He gave up the editorship of *Archeion*, which became the *Archives internationales d'histoire des sciences*. In the first issue of the newly renamed journal Mieli wrote, "Je puis mourir tranquille en sachant qu'une partie, au moins, des multiples efforts que j'ai amplement déployés pendant ma vie, pour la réalisation de maints idéaux, va continuer à exercer son action bienfaisante."

BIBLIOGRAPHY

I. ORIGINAL WORKS. Mieli contributed significantly to the journals *Archeion*, *Archives internationales d'histoire des sciences*, *Archivio di storia della scienza*, *Gazzetta chimica italiana*, *Isis*, *Miniera italiana*, *Rendiconti della R. Accademia dei Lincei*, *Rendiconti della Società chimica italiana*, *Rivista di biologia*, *Rivista di filosofia*, *Rivista di storia critica delle scienze mediche e naturali*, and *Scientia* (Bologna).

His separate publications include *Influenza che esercita un sale in varie concentrazioni sulla velocità di decolorazione di soluzioni acquose di sostanze organiche sotto l'influenza della luce* (Rome, 1906), written with G. Bargellini; *Catalogo ragionato per una biblioteca di cultura generale. Storia delle scienze* (Milan, 1914); *Programma del corso di storia della chimica tenuto nella Università di Roma durante l'anno scolastico 1913–1914* (Chiusi, 1914); *La scienza greca: I prearistotelici. I. La scuola ionica, la scuola pitagorica, la scuola eleata, Herakleitos* (Florence, 1915); *Programma del corso di storia della chimica tenuto nell'Università di Roma durante l'anno scolastico 1914–1915* (Florence, 1915); *La storia della scienza in Italia* (Florence, 1916; Rome, 1926); *Per una cattedra di storia della scienza* (Florence, 1916); *Il libro dell'amore* (Florence, 1916), which he considered his spiritual testament; *Lavoisier* (Genoa, 1916; 2nd ed., Rome, 1926); *Lavori e scritti di Aldo Mieli. I. (1906–1916)* (Florence, 1917); *Pagine di storia della chimica* (Rome, 1922); *Manuale di storia della scienza: Antichità, storia, antologia, bibliografia* (Rome, 1925), trans. into French as *Histoire des sciences. Antiquité* (Paris, 1935); *Un viaggio in Germania. Impressioni ed appunti di uno storico della scienza* (Rome, 1927); *La science arabe et son rôle dans l'évolution scientifique mondiale* (Leiden, 1938), with additional material by H.-P.-J. Renaud, Max Mayerhof, and Julius Ruska; *El desarollo histórico de la historia de la ciencia y la función actual de los institutos de historia de la ciencia* (Santa Fé, 1939); *Sumario de un curso de historia de la ciencia en ciento veinte números* (Santa Fé, 1943); *Lavoisier y la formación de la teoría química moderna* (Buenos Aires, 1944); *Volta y el desarollo de la electricidad hasta el descubrimiento de la pila y de la corriente eléctrica* (Buenos Aires, 1945); *Panorama general de historia de la ciencia. I. El mundo antiguo: Griegos y Romanos. II. La época medieval, mundo islamico y occidente cristiano* (Buenos Aires, 1945); and *La teoría atómica química moderna desde sus orígenes con J. B. Richter, John Dalton y Gay-Lussac, hasta su definitivo desarollo con Stanislao Cannizzaro, el sistema periódico de los elementos y el número atómico* (Buenos Aires, 1947).

II. Secondary Literature. On Mieli and his work see Andrea Corsini, "Aldo Mieli," in *Rivista di storia delle scienze mediche e naturali*, **41**, no. 1 (1950), 111–113; and P. Sergescu, "Aldo Mieli," in *Actes du VIᵉ Congrès International d'histoire des sciences* (Amsterdam, 1951), 79–95.

Maria Luisa Righini Bonelli

MIERS, HENRY ALEXANDER (*b.* Rio de Janeiro, Brazil, 25 May 1858; *d.* London, England, 10 December 1942), *mineralogy.*

Miers was the third son of Francis Charles Miers, a civil engineer, and Susan Fry Miers. He won scholarships at Eton and Oxford, where he studied classics and science, and gained second-class honors in mathematics upon graduation in 1881. He was small in stature, and the handsome appearance and trim build that he retained for most of his life made him look younger than his years. His manner was that of a pleasant diplomat who endeavored to get things done by friendly negotiation, without controversy. Tempering this quality was an adventurous streak, which was nearly his undoing in an early balloon attempt and led him to travel extensively, to the Klondike, to South Africa, and to Russia.

Although he had no formal training directly related to crystallography, Miers prepared within a year for an opening as assistant at the British Museum by short stays with N. Story-Maskelyne at Oxford, W. J. Lewis at Cambridge, and Paul von Groth at Strasbourg. His work at the Museum, under Lazarus Fletcher, was largely concerned with descriptions of crystal forms. He first detected the merohedrism in cooperite and other minerals, thus helping to complete the recognition of the classes of naturally occurring crystal symmetry. He described a number of sulfosalt minerals in detail, and the complex morphology of these crystals led to his interest in crystal growth. Miers constructed an ingenious inverted goniometer for measuring crystal faces while they were growing in solution. This led to direct observation of the ubiquitous but variable presence of slightly divergent (vicinal) faces during crystal growth. He realized the role of growth in the matching of a low reticular density on such faces with the lower density of matter in the solution, but the real underlying reason did not become apparent for another fifty years.

After his appointment as Wayneflete professor of mineralogy at Oxford in 1895, Miers refined his apparatus so that it could also measure the concentration of solution at the growing crystal surface through the index of refraction as determined by total reflection. This ingenious approach enabled him and a group of students to observe directly the conditions of various styles of crystallization, from slow, regular growth of large crystals at low supersaturations to the shower of microscopic crystals at a critical high degree of supersaturation, which were correlative with Ostwald's metastable and labile conditions, respectively.

Miers began his teaching in 1886, when H. E. Armstrong asked him to give a course in crystallography at the recently opened City and Guilds of London Institute (later part of Imperial College). His most famous student was William J. Pope, later professor of chemistry at Manchester and then at Cambridge. William Barlow is said to have learned his crystallography from Miers, apparently without formally registering as a student. Students at Oxford who later gained prominence in the field were Thomas V. Barker and Harold Hartley. Miers completed his textbook on mineralogy in 1902; it went through a second edition in 1929 and was translated into French. It drew heavily on Dana's *Mineralogy* and, for its time, contained excellent discussions of, for example, crystal optics as treated by Lazarus Fletcher.[1] The description of internal structures of crystals, which was then only a theory, was relegated to an appendix, although Miers had certainly followed closely developments in the field.[2]

In 1908 Miers was appointed principal of the University of London, the first of a long series of administrative and committee posts that occupied most of his time and energy for the remainder of his life. Although his next appointment, as vice-chancellor of the University of Manchester (1915), also created a special chair of crystallography, he did not publish further scientific work. That his teaching there was influential is amply shown by one student, H. E. Buckley, who later became head of the crystallography department at Manchester and who included much from Miers in his book *Crystal Growth*.[3] Published in 1951, just as F. C. Frank's revolutionary theory of crystal growth by dislocations had appeared, it was the most important inspiration and source of information on earlier work for the new school of crystal growth in the 1950's.[4]

Miers was elected to the Royal Society in 1896 and knighted in 1912. He received half a dozen honorary degrees, the Wollaston Medal of the Geological Society of London, and numerous other honors.

NOTES

1. J. D. Dana, *System of Mineralogy*, 6th ed. by E. S. Dana (New York, 1892); E. S. Dana, *Textbook of Mineralogy* (New York, 1877). On crystal optics see Miers, *Mineralogy*, pp. 118–165; and Lazarus Fletcher, *The Optical Indicatrix and the Transmission of Light in Crystals* (London, 1892).
2. *Mineralogy*, pp. 283–287; Miers, "Some Recent Advances in the Theory of Crystal Structures," in *Nature*, **39** (1889), 277–283; "Homogeneity of Structure the Source of Crystal Symmetry," *ibid.*, **51** (1894), 79–142; "The Arrangement of Molecules in a Crystal," in *Science Progress*, **1** (1894), 483–500; "The Arrangement of the Atoms in a Crystal," *ibid.*, **3** (1895), 129–142; William Barlow, H. A. Miers, and G. F. Smith, "Report of Committee on the Structure of Crystals. Part I. Report on the Development of the Geometrical Theories of Crystal Structure," in *Report of the British Association for the Advancement of Science* (1901), 297–337.
3. H. E. Buckley, *Crystal Growth* (New York, 1951).
4. F. C. Frank, *Discussions of the Faraday Society*, **5** (1948), 48–54.

BIBLIOGRAPHY

I. Original Works. A complete bibliography is provided by L. J. Spencer in *Mineralogical Magazine*, **27** (1944), 23–28, including works on descriptive mineralogy and crystallography and on the growth of crystals; Miers's extensive reports on museums, libraries, and education; and the known MSS. In addition to his textbook, *Mineralogy, an Introduction to the Scientific Study of Minerals* (London, 1902; 2nd ed., revised by H. L. Bowman, 1929), the most important publications are perhaps "Contributions to the Study of Pyrargyrite and Proustite," in *Mineralogical Magazine*, **8** (1888), 27–102; "Xanthoconite and Ritteringite, With Remarks on the Red Silvers," *ibid.*, **10** (1893), 185–216; "An Enquiry Into the Variation of Angles Observed in Crystals; Especially of Potassium-Alum and

Ammonium-Alum," in *Philosophical Transactions of the Royal Society*, **202A** (1903), 459–523; and "The Refractive Indices of Crystallising Solutions With Especial Reference to the Passage From the Metastable to the Labile Condition," in *Journal of the Chemical Society*, **89** (1906), 413–454, written with F. Isaac.

II. Secondary Literature. A number of memorials were published, the most important being those of L. J. Spencer, in *Mineralogical Magazine*, **27** (1944), 17–23, with photograph; H. T. Tizard, in *Dictionary of National Biography, 1941–1950* (London, 1959), 588–590; and Sir Thomas Holland, in *Obituary Notices of Fellows of the Royal Society of London*, **12** (1943).

William T. Holser

MIESCHER, JOHANN FRIEDRICH II (*b.* Basel, Switzerland, 13 August 1844; *d.* Davos, Switzerland, 26 August 1895), *physiology, physiological chemistry*.

Shortly after his birth Miescher (who was known as Fritz because his father bore the same names) was taken with his family to the Bernese Emmental, where his father had just been appointed professor of pathological anatomy at the University of Bern. When local canton politics caused the elder Miescher's resignation in 1850, the family returned to Basel, where Miescher excelled at the Gymnasium and in the musical circle to which his father and his uncle, Wilhelm His, Sr., belonged, together with the famous chemist C. F. Schönbein.

Apart from a semester spent at Göttingen Miescher remained in Basel, where he qualified in 1868. He then did research on the composition of pus cells, working in Hoppe-Seyler's laboratory at Tübingen (from 1868 to 1869). From there he went to Carl Ludwig's physiological institute in Leipzig (from 1869 to 1870), and finally returned to Basel for the *Habilitation*. In 1871 he was appointed to the chair of physiology at the University of Basel, which had been vacated by his uncle. There he worked to isolate nuclein from the sperm heads of Rhine salmon and to solve the mystery of the fasting-reproductive stage of the male. His resources were meager, and working conditions poor. When the effects of tuberculosis necessitated treatment in a sanatorium, Miescher used the opportunity to study the effects of altitude on the constitution of the blood and observed the increase in the blood count of erythrocytes with increasing altitude. In 1885 the university built an institute for him, the Vesalianum, where he was joined by Bunge.

Miescher was an unimpressive teacher and an often obscure writer. His subtle mind demanded caution and qualifications; his indecision over the rival claims of physical and of chemical reductionism, coupled with his distrust of cytology, prevented him from unifying that subject with chemistry, as he had sought to do. Miescher nonetheless had an eye for a good problem and for appropriate research material; he was observant and painstaking, and if he sought to achieve more than the best techniques of his day could allow, he established a method for physiological chemistry that his successors eagerly exploited.

Miescher's first and most important discovery was a new class of compounds rich in organic phosphorus and forming the major constituent of cell nuclei. He rightly concluded that these "nucleins," as he called them, were as important a center of metabolic activity as the proteins. The product he obtained from the pepsin digestion of pus cells in 1869 was nucleohistone; five years later he isolated a purer form of nuclein from salmon spermatozoa and demonstrated the saltlike union between its two major constituents, an acid fraction ("pure nuclein," or DNA) and a basic fraction (which he called "protamine" and regarded as an alkaloid, rather than a protein). He left to others the task of establishing the detailed chemical constitution of these compounds, and his own knowledge of them was limited to their solubility characteristics, elementary components, and reactions with histochemical tests.

Instead Miescher preferred investigating the formation of large amounts of nuclein by the male salmon during the fasting period. He concluded that this activity is achieved only at the expense of the trunk muscles of the fish, and suggested that these muscles are progressively decomposed or "liquidated" because of reduced oxygen supply. He further attempted to trace these changes at the chemical level, thereby providing a remarkable early example of the "dynamic biochemistry" that F. G. Hopkins later advocated. (Miescher's effort was, however, unfortunate in that it encouraged others in persistent attempts to show that nucleic acids are derived from proteins; these researches in turn fostered a false view of nucleic acids as compounds formed between proteins and phosphoric acid.)

In histochemistry Miescher established a clear chemical distinction between the nucleus and cytoplasm, based on the presence of nuclein in the nucleus, a distinction that supporters of the chemical theory of staining gladly embraced. Miescher's own parallel studies of the staining reactions of the spermatozoa were in conflict with the results achieved by Walther Flemming and P. Schweigger-Seidel, however, and thus lent credence to those who, like Albert Fischer, sought to discredit the chemical theory of staining altogether.

Miescher's interpretation of fertilization vacillated between the extreme physicalist reductionism of his uncle and the chemical theory that his own work suggested. He was never able to accept the notion that the structures revealed by cytological staining are themselves carried by the sperm into the egg to contribute to the structure of the embryo. Miescher saw this morphological theory, as Hertwig called it, as flying in the face of the reductionist program to which he was committed.

Miescher died of tuberculosis before he had completed his last paper on nuclein. A full account of his studies on this was compiled and published by Ostwald Schmiedeberg.

BIBLIOGRAPHY

I. ORIGINAL WORKS. All of Miescher's papers and a selection of his letters will be found in *Die histochemischen und physiologischen Arbeiten von Friedrich Miescher. Gesammelt und herausgegeben von seinen Freunden* (Leipzig, 1897). His paper on the isolation of nuclein from pus is "Ueber die chemische Zusammensetzung der Eiterzellen," in F. Hoppe-Seyler's *Medisch-chemische Untersuchungen,* IV (Berlin, 1871), 441–460. His first publication on salmon nuclein is "Die Spermatozoen einiger Wirbelthiere. Ein Beitrag zur Histochemie," in *Verhandlungen der Naturforschenden Gesellschaft in Basel,* **6** (1874), 138–208; his last and posthumous paper was "Physiologisch-chemische Untersuchungen über die Lachsmilch von F. Miescher, nach den hinterlassenen Aufzeichnungen und Versuchsprotokollen des Autors und herausgegeben von O. Schmiedeberg," in *Archiv für experimentelle Pathologie und Pharmakologie,* **37** (1896), 100–155.

II. SECONDARY LITERATURE. The clearest account of Miescher's work on the chemistry of the nucleus is by A. Mirsky, "The Discovery of DNA," in *Scientific American,* **218** (1967), 78–88. Biographical information is in M. de Meuron-Landot, "Friedrich Miescher, l'homme qui a découvert les acides nucléiques," in *Histoire de la médecine,* **15** (1965), 2–25. Earlier studies include the following: K. Spiro, *Zur Erinnerung an Schönbein, Miescher und Bunge* (Basel, 1922), originally published in *Basler Nachrichten,* 12 and 19 Feb. 1922; J. P. Greenstein, "Friedrich Miescher, 1844–1895. Founder of Nuclear Chemistry," in *Scientific Monthly,* **57** (1943), 523–532. The best obituary notice is A. Jaquet, "Professor Friedrich Miescher Nachruf," in *Verhandlungen der Naturforschenden Gesellschaft in Basel,* **11** (1897), 399–417. Further information is contained in F. Suter *et al., Friedrich Miescher, 1844–1895. Vorträge gehalten anlässlich der Feier zum hunderte Geburtstag von Professor Friedrich Miescher in der Aula der Universität Basel am 15 Juni 1944* (Basel, 1944); and in *Helvetica physiologica et pharmacologica acta,* supp. 2 (1944).

ROBERT OLBY

MILHAUD, GASTON (*b*. Nîmes, France, 10 August 1858; *d*. Paris, France, 1 October 1918), *mathematics, philosophy of science.*

Milhaud, a village near Nîmes, once belonged to the bishop of Nîmes and thus was able to shelter a Marrano community. Gaston Milhaud's ancestors came from this locality. He was the third of the famous trio with the same Christian name who brought fame to Nîmes during the nineteenth century; the other two were the historian Gaston Boissier and the mathematician Gaston Darboux, whose student he was at the École Normale Supérieure.

In 1878 Milhaud qualified for both the École Normale Supérieure and the École Polytechnique; he chose the former. *Agrégé* in mathematics in 1881, he then taught mathematics at Le Havre for ten years. His meeting with Pierre Janet and the fruitful collaboration that followed during this period induced a shift in his interests. He translated du Bois-Reymond's *Théorie générale des fonctions*; wrote a number of articles for such journals as *Revue scientifique, Revue des études grecques,* and *Revue philosophique de la France et de l'étranger*; and was henceforth concerned with the philosophy of mathematics.

Appointed professor of mathematics at Montpellier in 1891, Milhaud gave a series of lectures on the origins of Greek science (published in 1893). In 1894, at Paris, he defended a Ph.D. dissertation on the conditions and limits of logical certainty. This remarkable work was decisive for his career. He was appointed to the chair of philosophy at the Faculty of Letters of Montpellier in 1895 and rapidly became, through his lectures and publications, a respected authority in a field that was then quite new. He also arranged meetings between investigators in various disciplines. In 1909 a chair was created for Milhaud at the Sorbonne in the history of philosophy in relation to science. Despite the decline in his health, which had always been delicate, he continued to be active and held this chair with distinction until his death.

It has been observed that the end of the nineteenth century witnessed two complementary movements in response to the crisis in the foundations of science: that of philosophers becoming scientists and that of scientists becoming philosophers. Milhaud is one of the best representatives of the latter trend. He modestly presented himself as a teacher who wished to do useful work in the history of science, which he conceived of as "inseparable from a critical examination of fundamental notions and inseparable from philosophical views that, underneath the precise data that are constantly accumulating, attempt to appear and to evaluate the progressive and continuous work being accomplished" (quoted in Pierre Janet, "Notice," p. 57).

Acutely aware of the effort required to amass and criticize data, Milhaud declared that he was not learned in this respect. Nevertheless, his many works on Greek science show that he accepted the burdens of scholarship; and his study of the arguments of Zeno of Elea is important and still worth consulting. He was also responsible for renewing knowledge of Descartes as a scientist, and his writings on this subject remain a reliable source. It was Milhaud's second son, Gérard, who with Charles Adam produced an improved edition of Descartes's correspondence.

Milhaud oriented the study of the history of science more toward philosophy. Certain of his views, although representative of his time, are now outmoded, notably those of continuous progress and the analysis of the conditions, role, and scope of demonstration in mathematics and physics. But his writings on logical contradiction, the limits of the affirmations that it appears to permit, and the critique of scientifically inspired deterministic metaphysical systems are still of interest and justify the considerable influence he has exerted. Milhaud also illustrated his contention that "science progresses in proportion to the disinterestedness with which it is pursued." Émile Boutroux said in proposing Milhaud's election to the Académie des Sciences Morales et Politiques in 1918: "By the soundness and originality of his findings in both the theoretical and the historical domains regarding a question of paramount importance, that of the relation between certainty and truth, this conscientious, modest, and penetrating investigator has performed a lasting service to science and to philosophy" (Pierre Janet, "Notice," p. 58).

BIBLIOGRAPHY

I. ORIGINAL WORKS. Milhaud's books include *Leçons sur les origines de la science grecque* (Paris, 1893); *Essai sur les conditions et les limites de la certitude logique* (Paris, 1894; 4th ed., 1924); *Le rationnel* (Paris, 1898); *Les philosophes géomètres de la Grèce: Platon et ses prédécesseurs* (Paris, 1900; 2nd ed., 1934); *Le positivisme et le progrès de l'esprit (Études critiques sur Auguste Comte)* (Paris, 1902); *Études sur la pensée scientifique chez les Grecs et chez les modernes* (Paris, 1906); *Nouvelles études sur l'histoire de la pensée scientifique* (Paris, 1911); *Descartes savant* (Paris, 1921); *Études sur Cournot* (Paris, 1927); and *La philosophie de Charles Renouvier* (Paris, 1927).

Among Milhaud's many articles, the following appeared in *Revue de métaphysique et de morale:* "Le concept du nombre chez les Pythagoriciens" (1893), 140–156; "Réponse à Brochard" (1893), 400–404, concerning Zeno of Elea; "L'idée d'ordre chez Auguste Comte" (1901), 385–406; "Le hasard chez Aristote et chez Cournot" (1902), 667–681; and *"La science et l'hypothèse* par H. Poincaré"

(1903), 773–781. See also "Science et religion chez Cournot," in *Bulletin de la Société française de philosophie* (Apr. 1911), 83–104.

II. SECONDARY LITERATURE. See André Bridoux, "Souvenirs concernant Gaston Milhaud," in *Bulletin de la Société française de philosophie*, **55**, no. 2 (1960), 109–112; Edmond Goblot, "Gaston Milhaud (1858–1918)," in *Isis*, **3** (1921), 391–395; Pierre Janet, "Notice sur Gaston Milhaud," in *Annuaire des anciens élèves de l'École normale supérieure* (1919), pp. 56–60; André Nadal, "Gaston Milhaud (1858–1918)," in *Revue d'histoire des sciences . . .* (Paris), **12**, no. 2 (1959), 97–110; Dominique Parodi, *La philosophie contemporaine en France* (Paris, 1919), pp. 211–216; and René Poirier, *Philosophes et savants français du XXe siècle*, II, *La philosophie de la science* (Paris, 1926), 55–80; and "Meyerson, Milhaud et le problème de l'épistémologie," in *Bulletin de la Société française de philosophie*, **55**, no. 2 (1960), 65–94.

PIERRE COSTABEL

MILL, JOHN STUART (*b.* London, England, 20 May 1806; *d.* Avignon, France, 8 May 1873), *philosophy, economics.*

Mill was the son of James Mill, a London Scot who had risen from humble origins to become a prominent intellectual, a collaborator of Jeremy Bentham, and a leading exponent of utilitarianism. Mill's childhood was a singular one. He was educated at home by his father, learning both Greek and Latin before he was nine years old. All religion was excluded from his upbringing. James Mill, an even more rigid adherent than Bentham to the rationalism of the Enlightenment, was determined to educate his son to be another philosopher in the same mold. At sixteen the younger Mill started to earn his living as a clerk in the East India Office, where his father was a senior official. At seventeen he published his first article, in the *Westminster Review*, and in the same year he made his debut as a radical reformer, spending a day or two in the police cells for distributing pamphlets recommending contraception as a solution to the population problem.

In his posthumously published *Autobiography*, Mill recalls that at the age of twenty he went through a period of acute depression, from which he was delivered by reading the poetry of Wordsworth. Through Wordsworth he met a romanticism that challenged the whole rationalistic ethos in which he had been so carefully bred. After this experience, wrote Mill, "I did not lose sight of . . . that part of the truth I had learned before . . . but I thought that it had consequences which required to be corrected, by joining other kinds of cultivation with it" (*Autobiog-*

raphy, p. 34). Mill's aim thenceforth became to produce a philosophy that combined the virtues of rationalism with those of romanticism; but the contradictions between them proved to be too fundamental for even the ablest mind to reconcile, and Mill's philosophy is marred by a certain incoherence that even his most fervent admirers cannot deny.

Mill's most important work in pure philosophy was his *System of Logic*, which he began at the age of twenty-four and completed thirteen years later. Soon after he had started work on it, Mill met a beautiful, intelligent, and imperious young woman named Harriet Taylor. He fell in love with her, and she with him; but she was already the wife of a wholesale druggist and the mother of two children. In the nineteen years before the druggist's death enabled them to marry, Mill and Harriet Taylor were constantly in each other's company—"Seelenfreunden" ("soul friends"), as they put it, but not lovers. Victorian society's frowns (and his own sense of guilt) drove Mill to lead a lonely life, and Mrs. Taylor's hold over his thinking was immense. She was not a Wordsworthian but a rationalist of the left—and, paradoxically, she reinforced the influence of James Mill's training rather than that of romanticism.

Mill's marriage to Harriet Taylor took place in 1851; but seven years later she died at Avignon, and Mill bought a house there to live near her tomb. But by this time Mill's books had made him famous, and in 1865 he was persuaded by the controversial and progressive Viscount Amberley to stand for election to Parliament in Westminster. Mill was elected, and he sat until 1868 as an independent Liberal M.P. He died at the age of sixty-six, having just become the agnostic's equivalent of a godfather to Amberley's son, Bertrand Russell.

Mill's central endeavor as a philosopher was to provide science with a better claim to truth than that afforded by the skeptical philosophers of the seventeenth and eighteenth centuries. Locke had written: "As to a *perfect* science of natural bodies (not to mention spiritual beings) we are, I think, so far from being capable of any such thing that I conclude it lost labour to look after it." Mill disagreed. Indeed, he wrote his *Logic* precisely to formulate "a *perfect* science of natural bodies"—or, in other words, a demonstrative theory of induction—by which he hoped to reduce the conditions of scientific proof "to strict rules and scientific tests, such as the syllogism is for ratiocination."

Mill called himself a "philosopher of experience"; he believed that all knowledge of the universe is derived from sensory observation, and he opposed those who claimed that some knowledge of synthetic truth is either innate or acquired by rational insight.

He was what has come to be known as an empiricist, although that word did not then have the commonly accepted usage it has today and Mill rejected it. But he tried to give what we should call empiricism a form that would satisfy the nineteenth century's demand for certainty.

Mill's *Logic* seeks to diminish the value of knowledge achieved deductively—that is, by deriving particulars from universals—and to vindicate the importance of knowledge derived inductively, by the accumulation of evidence from particulars. Our "universal" knowledge, Mill argued, comes from particulars. We begin with particulars and end with particulars, and it is the method of science that enables us to formulate the "universals" or "generalities" that the mind knows.

In book II of his *Logic*, Mill claimed that even mathematics is, in a way, inductive. In the manner of Kant he said that mathematical propositions are synthetic propositions about the world of measurable things, but he denied the Kantian view that the mind imposes categories on experience. He argued instead that mathematical propositions are experimental truths of a highly general kind. Mill did not even admit that they are necessarily true, except in the sense that it is psychologically impossible for us to doubt them. His mathematical theory has not had much support from theorists of later generations. He is generally considered to have failed to solve logical problems by proposing psychological answers, and the reform of deductive logic that was begun by Boole and completed by Mill's "godson" Russell has suggested that Mill was mistaken about what could be done with inductive logic.

Book III of Mill's *Logic* has been more influential. Here Mill explained what he means by induction. He said it depends on the "assumption" that nature is uniform and that its future course will be like that of the past. Elementary induction is based on the enumeration of like instances: "All the crows we have seen are black, therefore all crows are black." Mill next distinguished between uniformity of "togetherness" and uniformity of sequence. In the first class he put properties that exist at the same time and can be measured or counted so as to give our knowledge a formal order. The second class, uniformities of sequence, he called "causal"; and here, instead of mere enumerations, he believed we can establish laws. These laws are discovered with the aid of Mill's famous "eliminative methods of induction."

These methods are (1) the canon of agreement, which asserts that if those instances in which a phenomenon occurs have only one feature in common, then that feature contains the cause of the phenom-enon; (2) the canon of difference, which asserts that if those instances in which the phenomenon occurs differ from instances in which it does not occur in only one feature, then that one feature contains the cause of the phenomenon; (3) the canon of residues (a variant of the canon of difference), which asserts that if we take away from a phenomenon all the effects we know to be caused by certain antecedents, then the remainder is the effect of the remaining antecedents; (4) the canon of concomitant variations, which asserts that when one phenomenon varies only when another varies, there is either a causal relation between them or they are both causally related to a third factor.

Although Mill's "eliminative methods of induction" have figured prominently in subsequent controversies about scientific method, their value has been criticized on several grounds. First, they cannot be used to vindicate the assumptions on which they are grounded: the uniformity of nature and the ubiquity of causality. Second, no method of elimination can yield demonstrably certain conclusions about the candidates that remain, although it may well yield high probabilities. Third, science is not primarily interested in the kind of "common sense" causal relations that Mill's methods can be used to discover. Fourth, science is not properly understood as an inductive enterprise; it does not proceed by the observation of regularities in nature but by the use of conjecture and "experimental refutation."

Some of these objections to Mill's inductivism can be met by a more sophisticated reformulation of his thesis, but the consensus among twentieth-century specialists in scientific method is that the more skeptical approach of Mill's predecessors, including perhaps Kant as well as Locke and Hume, comes closer both to the realities of scientific discovery and to the exigencies of logic.

In 1848, shortly after the publication of his *Logic*, Mill brought out another of his most influential books, *The Principles of Political Economy*. This is a curious mixture of orthodox economic theories and arresting, original ideas. Some of the new ideas are expressed in the language of classical economics, so that the shock of them is softened. Mill maintained that "the economic man" is a fiction, a way of registering the tendency of men to pursue wealth. He suggested that economic principles should be tested by their stability in a particular era and by their ability to promote transition to another era.

In his review of political economy as a static science, Mill did little but repeat the principles laid down by Adam Smith and others about production and exchange, the dependence of wealth on production and of profit on the cost of labor, the token nature of money, the need to balance imports with exports, and so forth. It was when he turned from the static to the dynamic side of the subject, to economics as related to social progress, that Mill propelled economic thought into new channels.

He remained true to Malthus on the subject of the population problem. There was no remedy for poverty, he thought, unless excessive numbers could be reduced, although, unlike Malthus, Mill favored contraception as well as "moral restraint." But Mill differed from his predecessors in his understanding of the concept of property and on the distribution of wealth. Property rights were conventional; and although private property was a useful institution, the only basis of a sound entitlement was a man's own labor. There was no natural right to inheritance or to the ownership of land. In the first edition of his *Political Economy*, Mill criticized the socialist theories put forward by Louis Blanc and others as unrealistic, but in later editions he withdrew these strictures and wrote sympathetically of socialism. It is probable that he made these changes under pressure from Harriet Taylor, a convert to socialism.

The intrusion of socialist sentiments into a book that was substantially based on the principles of classical economics has seemed to some readers to be yet another mark of Mill's inconsistency. A similar criticism might be addressed to his writings on politics and ethics. In ethics Mill affirmed his adherence to his father's utilitarianism, the doctrine that the rightness of an act is to be measured by the extent to which it promotes pleasure. But Mill rejected his father's belief that pleasure has only quantitative differences. Ever since he had read Wordsworth, Mill had believed in the superiority of the "pleasures of the mind" over the brutish pleasures of the uncultivated: "Better Socrates dissatisfied than a pig satisfied." But Mill was never able to produce any utilitarian or empirical reason to justify this preference.

The same ardent belief in the values of culture influenced Mill's political theorizing. He was an eloquent champion of freedom; but although he sometimes defined freedom as the absence of constraint, he went on to speak of it as "self-perfection" and said that men should be free in order to improve themselves. Although Mill came out (as his father had done) in favor of democratic government, he proposed that democratic institutions should be carefully designed to prevent government by the majority: he wanted a form of government by a cultured elite that would rest upon the assent of a progressively more educated populace. Like many another intellectual of the Victorian period, Mill made something of a religion of the culture of the sensi-

bilities, notwithstanding his general belief, as an empiricist, that all real knowledge is scientific knowledge.

BIBLIOGRAPHY

I. ORIGINAL WORKS. A bibliography is N. MacMinn, J. R. Hainds, and J. M. McCrimmon, *The Bibliography of Published Works . . .* (Evanston, Ill., 1945). A more up-to-date bibliography is being published in serial form in the *Mill News Letter* (Toronto, 1965–   ).

Publication is in progress on the 13-vol. *Collected Works of John Stuart Mill* (Toronto, 1963–   ). Among his earlier writings are *A System of Logic*, 2 vols. (London, 1843); *Essays on Some Unsettled Questions of Political Economy* (London, 1844); *Principles of Political Economy*, 2 vols. (London, 1848); *On Liberty* (London, 1859), also repr. with *Representative Government* and an intro. by R. B. MacCallum (Oxford, 1946); *Thoughts on Parliamentary Reform* (London, 1859); *Dissertations and Discussions*, 2 vols. (London, 1859), articles repr. from periodicals, chiefly *Edinburgh Review* and *Westminster Review; Considerations on Representative Government* (London, 1861); *Utilitarianism* (London, 1863), also edited by J. Plamenatz (Oxford, 1949); *Auguste Comte and Positivism* (London, 1865); *An Examination of Sir William Hamilton's Philosophy* (London, 1865); *Inaugural Address to the University of St. Andrews* (London, 1867); *England and Ireland* (London, 1869); and *The Subjection of Women* (London, 1869), also edited with an intro. by S. Coit (London, 1906).

Works published later are *Autobiography*, Helen Taylor, ed. (London, 1873), repr., with an appendix of unpublished papers, and an intro. by H. J. Laski (London, 1924); *Three Essays on Religion* (London, 1874); *Chapters on Socialism*, W. D. F. Bliss, ed. (New York, 1891); *Early Essays*, J. W. M. Gibbs, ed. (London, 1897); *On Education*, F. A. Cavanagh, ed. (London, 1931), printed with writings on the same subject by James Mill; *The Spirit of the Age*, edited, with an intro., by F. A. von Hayek (Chicago, 1942), articles contributed to *Examiner* in 1831; *Four Dialogues of Plato*, edited, with an intro., by R. Borchardt (London, 1946); *On Bentham and Coleridge*, edited, with an intro., by F. R. Leavis (London, 1950), repr. from *Dissertations and Discussions; An Early Draft of John Stuart Mill's Autobiography*, J. Stillinger, ed. (Urbana, Ill., 1961); *Mill's Essays on Politics and Culture*, G. Himmelfarb, ed. (New York, 1962); *Mill's Essays on Literature and Society*, J. B. Schneewind, ed. (New York–London, 1965); and *Mill's Ethical Writings*, J. B. Schneewind, ed. (New York–London, 1965).

II. SECONDARY LITERATURE. Biographical studies are A. Bain, *John Stuart Mill* (London, 1882), a study of Mill and his philosophy, with personal recollections by a close friend of his later years; W. D. Christie, *J. S. Mill and Mr. Abraham Cowley, Q.C.* (London, 1873); G. J. Holyoak, *John Stuart Mill as the Working Class Knew Him* (London, 1873), a short personal memoir; and M. St. J. Packe, *The*

Life of John Stuart Mill (London, 1954), the standard biography.

Critical and expository studies include R. P. Anschutz, *The Philosophy of J. S. Mill* (Oxford, 1953), and K. Britton, *John Stuart Mill* (London, 1953), both written from the point of view of modern analytic philosophy; Britton stresses the lasting value of Mill's achievement and is less sharply critical of Mill's shortcomings than is the Anschutz work; M. Cowling, *Mill and Liberalism* (Cambridge, 1963), a brisk conservative criticism of Mill; R. Jackson, *Examination of the Deductive Logic of J. S. Mill* (Oxford, 1941); O. A. Kubitz, *The Development of John Stuart Mill's System of Logic* (Urbana, Ill., 1932); E. Nagel, ed., *Mill's Philosophy of Scientific Method* (New York, 1950)—this and the works of Jackson and Kubitz are up-to-date books concerned with Mill as a logician; E. Neff, *Carlyle and Mill* (New York, 1926), an instructive comparison of rival philosophies; B. Russell, *John Stuart Mill* (London, 1955); J. B. Schneewind, ed., *Mill: A Collection of Critical Essays* (New York, 1968), short studies of Mill's thought from a philosophical perspective; and C. L. Street, *Individualism and Individuality in the Philosophy of John Stuart Mill* (Milwaukee, Wis., 1926), a study of Mill's ethical and political theory.

MAURICE CRANSTON

MILLER, DAYTON CLARENCE (*b.* Strongsville, Ohio, 13 March 1866; *d.* Cleveland, Ohio, 22 February 1941), *physics*.

Miller was the son of Charles Webster Dewey Miller and the former Vienna Pomeroy. In 1886 he was graduated from Baldwin-Wallace College and in 1890 was awarded a doctorate in science from Princeton University, having studied under the astrophysicist Charles A. Young. Miller then joined the faculty of the Case School of Applied Science in Cleveland as an instructor of mathematics. He transferred to the physics department in 1893, the year he married Edith Easton. He remained at Case as professor of physics until his death.

Miller was an effective teacher, a captivating public lecturer, and a respected research scientist. In 1914 he was elected to the American Academy of Arts and Sciences, in 1919 to the American Philosophical Society, and in 1921 to the National Academy of Sciences. From 1918 until his death he held various offices in the American Physical Society, including the presidency for the 1925–1926 term. From 1927 to 1930 he was chairman of the National Research Council's Division of Physical Sciences, and from 1913 to 1933 he was president of the Acoustical Society of America.

Miller's work in acoustics grew out of a love for music that dated from childhood. His mother had been the church organist, his father had sung in the choir, and Miller himself was an accomplished flutist. Keenly interested in the physics of musical tones, he invented what he called the phonodeik in 1908, a mechanical device that recorded sound patterns photographically. During World War I he used the apparatus to analyze the nature of gun wave-forms for the National Research Council, which was developing improved techniques to locate enemy artillery by sonic means. After the war Miller became an expert in architectural acoustics, consulting on the interior design of a number of college chapels as well as Severance Hall, the home of the Cleveland Orchestra.

As a research physicist Miller was best known for his elaborate repetitions of the experiment that Albert A. Michelson and Edward W. Morley had performed with an interferometer in 1887 to detect the stationary luminiferous ether postulated by Maxwell. Miller did the experiment in collaboration with Morley between 1902 and 1904. Repeating it by himself on Mt. Wilson, California, between 1921 and 1926, he found a positive effect corresponding to an apparent relative motion of the earth and the ether of some ten kilometers per second in the plane of the interferometer. Though this velocity was about 70 percent less than expected, Miller fastened on his result as a refutation of Einstein's theory of relativity, which he was unwilling to accept on principle to the end of his life.

When Miller presented his data in 1925, he provoked considerable interest among physicists and was awarded a $1,000 annual prize by the American Association for the Advancement of Science. Antirelativists hailed his findings; relativists believed that they probably rested on experimental error. In the 1950's a group of physicists subjected Miller's Mt. Wilson data to statistical analysis. They found that only part of his positive readings could be attributed to random fluctuations. The rest seemed to result from an appreciable systematic effect whose magnitude varied with the conditions of observation. The cause of this effect appeared to be the large temperature changes which undoubtedly occurred in the poorly insulated shack that housed Miller's apparatus atop Mt. Wilson.

BIBLIOGRAPHY

I. ORIGINAL WORKS. Miller's personal papers and research notebooks are at Case Western Reserve University but are as yet unavailable to scholars. Miller's "The Ether Drift Experiment and the Determination of the Absolute Motion of the Earth," in *Reviews of Modern Physics*, **5** (July 1933), 203–242, is a comprehensive résumé of all Miller's repetitions of the Michelson-Morley experiment.

II. SECONDARY LITERATURE. Complete bibliographies of Miller's writings and introductions to his career are Harvey Fletcher, "Dayton Clarence Miller," in *Biographical Memoirs. National Academy of Sciences*, **23** (1945), 61–74; and Robert S. Shankland, "Dayton Clarence Miller: Physics Across Fifty Years," in *American Journal of Physics*, **9** (Oct. 1941), 273–283. Miller's ether-drift data is assessed in Shankland, *et al.*, "New Analysis of the Interferometer Observations of Dayton C. Miller," in *Reviews of Modern Physics*, **27** (Apr. 1955), 167–178; and his research is set in context in Loyd S. Swenson, Jr., *The Ethereal Aether: A History of the Michelson-Morley-Miller Aether-Drift Experiments, 1880–1930* (Austin, 1972).

DANIEL J. KEVLES

MILLER, GEORGE ABRAM (*b.* Lynnville, Pennsylvania, 31 July 1863; *d.* Urbana, Illinois, 10 February 1951), *mathematics*.

The description of Miller's rise to prominence in the world of mathematics is one of those Horatio Alger stories with which American intellectual history of the late nineteenth century is studded. He was the son of Nathan and Mary Sittler Miller and a descendant of one Christian Miller who had emigrated from Switzerland around 1720. Unable to continue his education without self-support, he began to teach school at the age of seventeen. He studied at Franklin and Marshall Academy in Lancaster during 1882–1883, then enrolled at Muhlenberg College, where he received the baccalaureate with honorable mention in 1887, the master of arts in 1890, and an honorary doctor of letters in 1936. Miller served as principal of the schools in Greeley, Kansas, during the year 1887–1888 and as professor of mathematics at Eureka College (Illinois) from 1888 to 1893. Cumberland University in Lebanon, Tennessee, granted him a doctorate in 1892; it was then possible to do course work by correspondence, and examinations in advanced courses were an acceptable substitute for thesis requirements. Miller was offering the same courses toward a doctorate to his students at Eureka. He spent the summers of 1889 and 1890 at the Johns Hopkins University and the University of Michigan but probably did not come under Frank Nelson Cole's influence until 1893, when he became an instructor at Michigan for three years and lived in Cole's home during the first two years of that period. It was Cole who inspired him to pursue the research in group theory that was to engage his talents for the rest of his life. Cole, incidentally, had been a pupil of Felix Klein, who had made groups basic in his "Erlanger Programm."

Miller spent the years 1895–1897 in Europe, attending the lectures of Sophus Lie at Leipzig and Camille Jordan in Paris. He soon was publishing papers independent of their specializations, although Lie had become instrumental in Miller's study of commutators and commutator subgroups and Jordan's interest in questions of primitivity and imprimitivity was reflected in Miller's investigations of those problems throughout his career.

Upon Miller's return to the United States, his European experience and mathematical productivity gained him an assistant professorship at Cornell (1897–1901). This was followed by an associate professorship at Stanford University (1901–1906), and in 1906 an appointment at the University of Illinois, an affiliation that lasted for the rest of his life—first as associate professor, then as professor, and finally as professor emeritus. His retirement in 1931 was from classroom responsibilities only, for he continued his research and writing in his office at the university. The university undertook, as "a fitting memorial of his contributions to mathematical scholarship and to the renown of the University," the collection and reprinting of Miller's studies in the theory of finite groups as well as other studies. It is said that of the more than 800 titles that appeared in some twenty periodicals over forty years approximately 400 made direct scientific contributions to that theory. Other papers were written in the hope that teachers of elementary and secondary mathematics might be inspired to study advanced mathematics. Miller himself aided in the preparation of these memorial volumes.

This was not the only legacy that Miller left to the University of Illinois. To the great surprise of the colleagues who knew him well, the university found itself after his death the beneficiary of a bequest valued at just under one million dollars, the accumulation of judicious investments. His wife, the former Cassandra Boggs of Urbana, had predeceased him in 1949 and there were no children.

Miller's interest in the history of mathematics was second only to that in the theory of finite groups. His articles on the history of his own subject were of particular significance and value. He became a severe critic of historical methodology in mathematics and was zealous in rooting out error in conjecture or assumed fact. His letters in the David Eugene Smith collection at Columbia University offer ample evidence of this missionary fervor. His "History of Elementary Mathematics" remained unpublished, although there was originally the intention to include it in a volume of the *Collected Papers*.

Miller was elected to the National Academy of Sciences in 1921 and was a fellow of the American

Academy of Arts and Sciences. In 1900, for his work in group theory, the Academy of Sciences of Cracow awarded him a prize that had not been given for fourteen years. This is said to have been the Academy's first award to an American for work in pure mathematics. He was a member of the London Mathematical Society, the Société Mathématique de France, and the Deutsche Mathematiker-Vereinigung, an honorary life member of the Indian Mathematical Society, and a corresponding member of the Real Sociedad Matemática Española. He was an active member and served in various high offices of the American Mathematical Society and the Mathematical Association of America, serving also as an editor of the latter's *American Mathematical Monthly* (1909–1915).

BIBLIOGRAPHY

I. ORIGINAL WORKS. Miller's writings were brought together in *The Collected Works of George Abram Miller*, 5 vols. (Urbana, Ill., 1935–1959). Two of his books are *Determinants* (1892) and *Historical Introduction to Mathematical Literature* (New York, 1916). A more detailed bibliography is in Poggendorff, IV, 1013; V, 855–857; and VI, 1737–1738. *Theory and Application of Finite Groups* (New York, 1916; repr. 1961) was written in collaboration with H. F. Blichfeldt and L. E. Dickson.

II. SECONDARY LITERATURE. See H. R. Brahana, "George Abram Miller (1863–1951)," in *Biographical Memoirs. National Academy of Sciences*, 30 (1957), 257–312, with a complete bibliography of Miller's writings (1892–1947) on 277–312. E. T. Bell makes occasional reference to Miller's work in "Fifty Years of Algebra in America, 1888–1938," in *American Mathematical Society Semicentennial Publications*, II, as does Florian Cajori in his *History of Mathematics*. See also J. W. A. Young, *Monographs on Topics of Modern Mathematics Relevant to the Elementary Field* (New York, 1911, 1915, 1927; repr. 1955); *American Men of Science* (New York, 1906), 219–220; and *National Cyclopedia of American Biography*, XVI (New York, 1918), 388.

CAROLYN EISELE

MILLER, HUGH (*b.* Cromarty, Scotland, 10 October 1802; *d.* Portobello, Scotland, 24 December 1856), *geology*.

Miller was the elder son of Hugh Miller by his second wife, Harriet. His father, the master of a fishing sloop, was drowned when Miller was five. At school the boy was unruly and independent; and instead of following the conventional education that was open to one of his intelligence and social position, he apprenticed himself to a stonemason at the age of seventeen and thereafter used his leisure to educate himself in natural history and literature. His geological studies arose directly from his work as a mason and from his interest in the history, scenery, and folklore of the Highlands. Miller discovered that the Old Red Sandstone was not (as was commonly believed) virtually devoid of fossils but contained in certain strata an abundant fauna of spectacular bony fish that constituted one of the earliest vertebrate faunas then known. His *Scenes and Legends of the North of Scotland* (1835) brought him recognition as a descriptive writer of striking power; in addition its chapter "The Antiquary of the World," describing geology as "the most poetical of all the sciences," led to correspondence with Roderick Murchison and thus to contact with the scientific community at large.

In 1834, after some twelve years as a journeyman mason, Miller exchanged an outdoor life for that of an accountant in a Cromarty bank; and in 1837 he married Lydia Fraser, an author of children's books. In 1839 he entered the patronage controversy in the Church of Scotland by publishing a powerful open letter to Lord Brougham; his abilities were immediately recognized by the "nonintrusion" party, and he was invited to Edinburgh to edit their newspaper, *The Witness*. Miller's leading articles (from 1840) made him at once one of the most prominent and influential figures in public life in Scotland. His eloquent style, passionate commitment, and independent position were deployed with great effectiveness in the protracted struggle for the right of Scottish people to control the appointment of ministers in the national church. When at the Disruption (1843) the Free Kirk seceded on this issue, Miller used his influence to try to prevent the new body from retreating into a "sectarian" position and to keep alive the ideal of a truly national but non-Erastian church. As an integral part of this ideal, he pleaded for public education to be undenominational and fully grounded in modern science: he believed that this would defend Christian faith not only against the "infidelity" of materialism but also against the "Puseyite" anti-intellectualism of the Oxford Movement and the literalistic obscurantism of the scriptural "antigeologists."

Soon after Miller's arrival in Edinburgh, the meeting there of the British Association for the Advancement of Science gave him an opportunity to meet many of the leading British scientists and also Louis Agassiz, then the greatest authority on fossil fish. His subsequent articles in *The Witness* on his own research and its implications were amplified into his first scientific book, *The Old Red Sandstone* (1841). Like all his books this was not a conventional scientific monograph but a series of discursive essays, leading the ordinary reader from a starting point in everyday experience, through the details of the anatomy of the most ancient fossil fish and the reconstruction of their environment, toward the broader implications that geology held for the place of man in nature and his relation to God. Miller was no naïve literalist (he had, for example, a most vivid sense of the vast antiquity of the earth), but he did believe that the fossil record confirmed in broad outline the cosmic drama depicted symbolically in the Bible. More particularly, his strong sense of man as a moral being, ultimately responsible to God, led him to attack vehemently any attempt to diminish that responsibility by blurring the distinction between man and the lower animals. Hence Lamarck's "theory of progression" by transmutation was abhorrent to him, and its revival in Robert Chambers' anonymous *Vestiges of Creation* (1844) disturbed him particularly because he saw its "infidel" tendencies spreading to the artisan classes.

Miller's reply to Chambers was delayed by a breakdown of health brought on by overwork and by silicosis contracted during his years as a mason; and in 1845 he left Scotland for the first time, subsequently publishing his *First Impressions of England* (1846) with perceptive comments on the new industrial society as well as frequent digressions on geology. On his return to Scotland he wrote *Foot-Prints of the Creator* (1847) in answer to the *Vestiges*. It was explicitly an attack on the metaphysical and theological implications of Chambers' work, but Miller used his own scientific research to focus his attack on one of the weakest points in the "development hypothesis." The fish of the Old Red Sandstone (and the few that had been found in still earlier strata) were not, he argued, the rudimentary quasi-embryonic forms that Chambers' theory required; on the contrary, these "Ganoids"— earliest vertebrates then known—"enter large in their stature and high in their organisation." The geological history of the fish suggested that they had been created already perfect, clearly distinct from other animals, and that a better case could be made out for their subsequent "degradation" than for their "progress," since the earliest representatives were in some ways the most complex. Miller's interpretation could be extended to the rest of the fossil record; and he thus derived (like Agassiz) a picture of overall "progress" achieved by distinct creative steps, each initiating a new and higher form of organization, culminating in man.

More accurately, however, Miller saw the final culmination of this vast history in an eschatological future kingdom of Christ. This Christological focus to Miller's interpretation of science distinguishes his

work sharply from that of most of his contemporaries, who were concerned to "reconcile" geology with religion. Miller was not interested in defending natural theology except as a prelude to existential commitment to God as revealed in Christ: dissociated from distinctively Christian beliefs, "a belief in the existence of a God is," he asserted, "of as little *ethical* value as a belief in the existence of the great sea-serpent." But by stating his opposition to evolutionary theory in terms of a characteristically stark antithesis—"the *law* of development *versus* the *miracle* of creation"—he placed his theology and his science in a vulnerable position during a period in which scientific plausibility was seen increasingly in terms of a metaphysical "principle of uniformity" that excluded the category of miracle altogether.

Miller published an attractive account of his life up to 1840 in *My Schools and Schoolmasters* (1854), which romanticizes his early life and exaggerates his humble origins. In the last years of his life he suffered increasingly from mental illness, and he finally committed suicide at his home near Edinburgh while seeing his last collection of essays, *The Testimony of the Rocks* (1857), through the press.

Miller's strictly original scientific work was of limited scope; his studies of early fossil fish did little more than amplify and correct some details of Murchison's stratigraphy and Agassiz's paleontology. His importance for nineteenth-century science lies, rather, in his use of outstanding literary abilities to broaden the taste for science in general and for geology in particular, and to encourage a humane concern for the fundamental significance of such studies: in the words of his biographer Mackenzie, "probably no single man since has so powerfully moved the common mind of Scotland, or dealt with it on more familiar and decisive terms."

BIBLIOGRAPHY

I. ORIGINAL WORKS. Miller's principal publications are *Scenes and Legends of the North of Scotland or the Traditional History of Cromarty* (Edinburgh, 1835); *The Old Red Sandstone: Or New Walks in an Old Field* (Edinburgh, 1841); *First Impressions of England and Its People* (London, 1846); *Foot-Prints of the Creator: Or, the Asterolepis of Stromness* (Edinburgh, 1847); *My Schools and Schoolmasters; Or, the Story of My Education* (Edinburgh, 1854); and *The Testimony of the Rocks; Or, Geology in Its Bearings on the Two Theologies, Natural and Revealed* (Edinburgh, 1857). Some of his correspondence is published in Peter Bayne, ed., *The Life and Letters of Hugh Miller*, 2 vols. (London, 1871).

II. SECONDARY LITERATURE. A short biography is W. Keith Leask, *Hugh Miller* (Edinburgh, 1896). W. M.

Mackenzie, *Hugh Miller. A Critical Study* (London, 1905) is penetrating although somewhat unsympathetic; Mackenzie's *Selections From the Writings of Hugh Miller* (Paisley, 1908) contains a well-chosen and balanced sample of Miller's work.

M. J. S. RUDWICK

MILLER, PHILIP (*b.* Bromley, Greenwich, or Deptford, London, England, 1691; *d.* Chelsea, London, 18 December 1771), *botany, horticulture.*

Miller, the most important horticultural writer of the eighteenth century, was curator of the Chelsea Physic Garden from 1722 to 1770. During this period, and largely through his skill as a grower and propagator and his extensive correspondence, the Chelsea botanic garden belonging to the Society of Apothecaries of London became famous throughout Europe and the North American colonies for its wealth of plants, which was continuously enriched by new introductions, notably from the West Indies, Mexico, eastern North America, and Europe. These plants Miller recorded in successive editions of his *Gardeners Dictionary* from 1731 to 1768. As Richard Pulteney stated in 1790, "He added to the theory and practice of gardening, that of the structure and characters of plants, and was early and practically versed in the methods of Ray and Tournefort." He derived his concept of genus and his generic names from the *Institutiones rei herbariae* (1700) of Tournefort, who recognized genera of first rank based on floral and fruiting characters and genera of second rank based on vegetative characters, whereas Linnaeus, Tournefort's successor and Miller's contemporary, in his *Species plantarum* (1753) recognized only first-rank genera and united Tournefort's second-rank genera with them— thus including, for example, *Abies* and *Larix* in *Pinus*. Miller accepted Linnaeus' classification and nomenclature reluctantly and never wholeheartedly. Thus in 1754, by continuing to use, in the fourth abridged edition of his *Gardeners Dictionary*, the Tournefortian names he had always used but which Linnaeus had suppressed in 1753, Miller brought these names back into post-Linnaean botanical literature and so became an inadvertent innovator; he is now cited as the authority for some eighty generic names, among them *Abies* and *Larix*, really derived from his predecessors. In the eighth edition (16 April 1768) of his *Gardeners Dictionary*, Miller at last adopted Linnaean binomial nomenclature for species; he also published some 400 specific names for plants imperfectly known or unknown to Linnaeus, or otherwise classified by him. These works of 1754 and 1768 earned Miller his lasting place in systematic botany.

Miller's father, a gardener of Scots origin, gave him a good schooling, and Miller early set up in business in the London area as a florist, grower of ornamental shrubs, and planter and designer of gardens. Thus he came to the notice of Sir Hans Sloane, who had bought the manor of Chelsea in 1712 and had become the ground landlord of the Chelsea site which the Society of Apothecaries had leased since 1673 for their physic garden, or *hortus medicus*. In 1722 Sloane transferred it in perpetuity to the Society of Apothecaries for use as a botanic garden. A condition in the deed of conveyance was that every year the Apothecaries should give the Royal Society fifty good herbarium specimens of distinct plants grown that year in the garden "and no one offered twice until the compleat number of two thousand plants have been delivered." This necessitated the continual introduction of new plants. On Sloane's recommendation, Miller was appointed head gardener in 1722. The Chelsea botanic garden then became possibly the most richly stocked of any garden of the mid-eighteenth century, and Miller recorded his firsthand experience in his publications. In 1724 he published his two-volume octavo *Gardeners and Florists Dictionary*, replaced in 1731 by the one-volume folio *Gardeners Dictionary*, of which eight editions appeared in his lifetime. They provide not only cultural but also descriptive botanical information, including the characters of each genus and diagnoses of the species. From them there arose after Miller's death a series of encyclopedic works on cultivated plants culminating in the Royal Horticultural Society's *Dictionary of Gardening* (1951).

Miller remained in charge of the Chelsea Physic Garden until 1770, when most reluctantly he retired with a pension. The mainspring of his life gone, he died the year after.

BIBLIOGRAPHY

Miller's main work is his *Gardeners Dictionary* (London, 1731; 2nd ed., 1733; 3rd ed., 1737–1739; 4th ed., 1743; 5th ed., 1747 [apparently no copy extant]; 6th ed., 1752; 7th ed., 1756–1759; 8th ed., 1768); the 8th is the most important ed., for it contains the binomial specific names attributed to Miller. The concise ed. "abridged" from the 1731 ed. was first published in 1733–1740; 2nd ed., 1741; 3rd ed., 1748; 4th ed., 1754; 5th ed., 1763; 6th ed., 1771— of these only the 4th ed. (1754) in 3 vols. is nomenclaturally important; it has been reprinted in facsimile (Lehre, German Federal Republic, 1969), with an introduction by W. T. Stearn (see below).

The main biographical sources are R. Pulteney, *Historical and Biographical Sketches of the Progress of Botany in England*, II (London, 1790), 241–242; J. Rogers, *The Vegetable Cultivator* (London, 1839), pp. 335–343, reprinted by W. T. Stearn in 1969 (see below); and C. Wall and H. C. Cameron, *A History of the Worshipful Society of Apothecaries of London* (London, 1963). Some further information is given in W. T. Stearn, "The Abridgement of Miller's Gardeners Dictionary," prefixed to the Historiae Naturalis Classica facs. of the 4th ed. (1754) of *Gardeners Dictionary Abridged* (Lehre, 1969); Hazel Le Rougetel, "Gardener Extraordinary: Philip Miller of Chelsea, 1691–1771," in *Journal of the Royal Horticultural Society*, **96** (1971), 556–563; and W. T. Stearn, "Philip Miller and the Plants from the Chelsea Physic Garden Presented to the Royal Society of London, 1723–1796," in *Botanical Society of Edinburgh Transactions*, **41** (1972), 293–307, in which is printed the deed of conveyance of the Chelsea Physic Garden.

WILLIAM T. STEARN

MILLER, WILLIAM ALLEN (*b.* Ipswich, England, 17 December 1817; *d.* Liverpool, England, 30 September 1870), *chemistry, spectroscopy, astronomy.*

A writer of widely used textbooks on chemistry, Miller pioneered the use of spectroscopic analysis in chemistry and the application to it of photography. With Huggins he subsequently extended his studies to planetary and stellar spectra, making comparisons with terrestrial sources, and was one of the first to produce reliable information as to the chemical constitution of the stars.

Miller was the son of Frances (née Bowyer) and William Miller, who after being secretary to the Birmingham General Hospital became a brewer in the Borough, London. After a year at Merchant Taylors' School, Northwood, Middlesex, Miller was sent to a Quaker school at Ackworth, Yorkshire. There he was taught by William Allen, after whom he had been named and who introduced him to chemistry and astronomy.

In 1832 Miller was apprenticed to his uncle, Bowyer Vaux, a surgeon at the Birmingham General Hospital; he left in 1837 to read medicine at King's College, London. In 1839 Miller received the Warneford Prize in theology and in 1840 was made demonstrator of chemistry after having spent some months in Liebig's laboratory at Giessen. He took his M.B. and M.D. in 1841–1842 and in 1841 became assistant lecturer under J. F. Daniell, whom he succeeded as professor of chemistry in 1845. He was made a fellow of the Royal Society in the latter year.

Miller's lecture notes formed the basis of his well-known textbooks of inorganic and organic chemistry, which went into many editions. His first important and original paper, "Additional Researches on the Electrolysis of Secondary Compounds," was written jointly with Daniell (*Philosophical Transactions of the Royal Society*, **134** [1844], 1–19; *Philosophical Magazine*, **25** [1844], 175–188). It was well known that the passage of a current through an electrolyte yielded decomposition products at the electrodes and also resulted in changes of concentration of the solution at different points in relation to the cathodes. Faraday had investigated the subject in 1835, but it was left to Daniell and Miller to propose an explanation in terms of a discrepancy between the mobilities of cation and anion, movement of the latter often being much the greater. Their hypothesis was more fully exploited by Hittorf (from 1853) and later by F. W. Kohlrausch (from 1876), whose theory of ionic movement is substantially that taught at an elementary level today.

During the 1840's it was slowly becoming appreciated that the spectra of flames were far from simple; Miller was perhaps the first to publish drawings of flame and absorption spectra, which he observed in a makeshift laboratory under the King's College lecture theater. He presented his findings to the Cambridge meeting of the British Association for the Advancement of Science in 1845, and they were printed in *Philosophical Magazine* (**27** [1845], 81–91). He drew the spectra of calcium, copper, and barium chlorides, boric acid, and strontium nitrate, each having bright lines and bands, and the common yellow D-line of sodium. The ubiquity of the D-line, and the newly found complexity in spectral structure, led some chemists almost to despair of ever laying down rigid rules of chemical spectrum analysis.

In 1861, before the Manchester meeting of the British Association, and 1862, before the Pharmaceutical Society of Great Britain, Miller gave another address with far-reaching consequences for spectroscopy. Rather than use a fluorescent screen for the study of the ultraviolet spectra of metals, he photographed them. This made it possible to record accurately the extraordinary complexity of the spectra. He was now able to find similarities between the characteristic spectra of certain metals, such as the cadmium, zinc, and magnesium group. His photographic plates were wet collodion, and his prisms were quartz. In all, he published spectra of twenty-five metals (*Philosophical Transactions of the Royal Society*, **152** [1862], 861–887).

In 1862 Miller joined forces with William Huggins, his neighbor at Tulse Hill, London, and together they arranged a telescope to give the spectra of celestial objects side by side with a comparison spectrum from a laboratory source. In Italy, Pietro Secchi was making a very extensive survey and in due course classified the spectra of more than 4,000 stars. Miller and Huggins, however, aimed at a smaller survey but one made with much greater precision. In March 1863, Miller was able to show a fine spectrophotograph of Sirius to an audience at the Royal Institution. He and Huggins paid especial attention to the spectra of the moon, Jupiter, and Mars. In 1867 they were jointly awarded the gold medal of the Royal Astronomical Society for their work (for a report of which see *Proceedings of the Royal Society*, **12** [1862–1863], 444–445; *Philosophical Transactions of the Royal Society*, **154** [1864], 413–436). Other examples of their work on fixed stars can be found in *Monthly Notices of the Royal Astronomical Society* (**26** [1866], 215–218) and *Proceedings of the Royal Society* (**15** [1867], 146–149). Their general conclusion was that although stars differ considerably one from another, they all have much chemically in common with the sun.

Miller was a deeply religious man and was indefatigable in applying his scientific talents to social ends, whether advising on the chemistry of the Metropolitan water supply, on the uniformity of weights and measures, on the establishment of regular meteorological observations (under the Board of Trade), or on the affairs of the Royal Mint, where he was Assayer. He worked hard for the Royal Society, of which he was treasurer for nine years, and helped to found the Chemical Society, of which he was twice president. He married Eliza Forrest in 1842. She died a year before him, and two daughters and a son survived them both.

BIBLIOGRAPHY

I. Original Works. For papers in addition to those mentioned in the text, see the Royal Society's *Catalogue of Scientific Papers*, IV (1870), 390, and VIII (1879), 406–407. Miller's longer works include *On the Importance of Chemistry to Medicine* (London, 1845); *Report ... in Reference to the Composition of the Lambeth Stone Ware and Aylesford Pottery Pipes* (London, 1855); *Elements of Chemistry Theoretical and Practical*, 3 vols. (London, 1855; 6th ed., 1877–1878); *Practical Hints to the Medical Student* (London, 1867); and *Introduction to the Study of Inorganic Chemistry* (London, 1871).

II. Secondary Literature. For further details of Miller's public life, see Agnes Clerke's notice on him in the *Dictionary of National Biography*, XIII, 429–430 and the first three obituaries listed there. See especially *Proceedings of the Royal Society*, **19** (1871), xix–xxvi. In most histories of spectroscopy Miller is given only slight attention. For the background to his work, see W. McGucken, *Nineteenth-Century Spectroscopy* (Baltimore, 1969).

J. D. North

MILLER, WILLIAM HALLOWES (*b*. Llandovery, Carmarthenshire, Wales, 6 April 1801; *d*. Cambridge, England, 20 May 1880), *crystallography, mineralogy*.

His father, Captain Francis Miller, who served in the American war, had a long military ancestry. By his first wife Captain Miller had three sons, all of whom entered the army, and two daughters. After losing his estate near Boston, Massachusetts, he retired to Wales to the small estate of Velindre near Llandovery and in 1800 married Ann Davies, the daughter of a Welsh vicar. William was the only child of this second marriage; his mother died a few days after his birth, but his father lived to the age of eighty-six, dying in 1820.

William was educated privately until he entered St. John's College, Cambridge, where he graduated B.A. as fifth wrangler in mathematics in 1826. In 1829 he became a fellow of St. John's and in 1831 published his first book—written in his characteristically lucid but terse style—*The Elements of Hydrostatics and Hydrodynamics*, which survived as a standard, though difficult, textbook into the fifties. Another mathematical textbook, *An Elementary Treatise on the Differential Calculus*, appeared in 1833 and passed through several editions. By then Miller had, in 1832, succeeded William Whewell as professor of mineralogy. He was elected F.R.S. in 1838. In 1841 came a curious diversion: the statutes of St. John's College required all fellows to proceed in time to holy orders except for four who should be doctors of medicine, and in order to retain his fellowship, Miller prepared himself for and took the M.D. He was obliged to vacate his fellowship on his marriage (5 November 1844) to Harriet Susan Minty, the daughter of R. V. Minty, a retired civil servant. They had two sons and four daughters. In 1875 he became a fellow of St. John's again under new statutes. In 1876 he suffered a stroke, which effectively brought his scientific life to a close four years before his death.

Miller's significant contribution to crystallography was made in *A Treatise on Crystallography* published in 1839 (translated into French by H. de Senarmont [1842], and into German with two new chapters by J. Grailich [1856], and again into German in abbreviated form by P. Joerres [1864]). Miller started with the fundamental assertion that crystallographic reference axes should be parallel to possible crystal edges; his system of indexing, a derivative from Whewell (*Philosophical Transactions of the Royal Society*, 1825), was based on a parametral plane (111) making intercepts a, b, c on such reference axes and was such that indices (hkl) were assigned to a plane making intercepts on the reference axes in the ratio $a/h : b/k : c/l$, where h, k, l are integers. The established German school of C. F. Naumann and C. S. Weiss had, to use the same nomenclature, assigned indices (*hkl*) to a plane making intercepts in the ratio *ah* : *bk* : *cl* on reference axes not restricted to parallelism with possible crystal edges. The algebraic advantages of "Millerian indices" were immediately apparent; the crystallographic superiority of Miller's reciprocal indices over Weiss's direct indices did not become apparent until Bravais's development of Haüy's rudimentary lattice concept in 1848, and not fully appreciated until Bragg's interpretation of the diffraction of X rays by crystals in 1912. But Miller's notation had quickly found favor with his contemporaries on grounds of convenience and had already served to codify an immense corpus of morphological observations in a thoroughly well-understood manner.

In the *Treatise* Miller had little to say about symmetry, but he explored crystal geometry to the full. The zone law of Weiss was simplified by the new notation, and zone symbols were defined in familiar form; the equations to the normal and the cos θ formula were developed; and the rational sine ratio, which was to be further developed in *A Tract on Crystallography* (1863), made its first appearance here. For the representation of three-dimensional angular relationships Miller followed F. E. Neumann in using spherical projection, but the stereographic projection, which subsequently acquired greater currency, and the gnomonic projection were discussed in the final chapter.

The new edition (1852) of William Phillips' *Elementary Introduction to Mineralogy* by H. J. Brooke and W. H. Miller was an entirely new book largely written, as Brooke states in the preface, by Miller, and it represents his principal contribution to mineralogy. It incorporated a vast amount of accurate goniometric data provided by Miller himself; it followed the *Treatise* in using spherical projection; and it made a tentative start in the use of polarized light for the characterization of transparent minerals. The *Introduction*, like the *Treatise*, soon eclipsed its contemporaries; it inspired Des Cloizeaux to produce his more elaborate *Manuel de minéralogie* (Paris, 1862–1893), and determined the form of all subsequent texts on descriptive mineralogy.

In 1843 Miller branched out into a new field on appointment to the parliamentary committee concerned with the preparation of new standards of length and weight consequent on the destruction of the old standards in the burning of the Houses of Parliament in 1834. His exceptionally accurate work was responsible for the construction of the new standard of weight (*Philosophical Transactions of the Royal Society*, 1856). In 1870 he was appointed to the Commission Internationale du Mètre.

Many honors fell to Miller in his lifetime. He was president of the Cambridge Philosophical Society (1857–1859) and foreign secretary of the Royal Society (1856–1873), being awarded a Royal Medal in 1870.

The exceptional breadth of Miller's scientific knowledge was recognized by his contemporaries. He was generous and hospitable to a point, yet remarkably spartan in his way of life. His ingenuity in constructing surprisingly accurate apparatus from simple, often homely, materials was notable. While no great traveler, he obviously enjoyed his trips to Paris for meetings of the Meter Commission, and he regularly holidayed in the Italian Tirol, where he simply enjoyed the scenery while his wife sketched it.

BIBLIOGRAPHY

I. Original Works. Miller's works include *The Elements of Hydrostatics and Hydrodynamics* (Cambridge, 1831); *An Elementary Treatise on the Differential Calculus* (Cambridge, 1833); *A Table of Mineralogical Species* (Cambridge, 1833); *A Treatise on Crystallography* (Cambridge, 1839); and William Phillips, *An Elementary Introduction to Mineralogy*, new ed. by H. J. Brooke and W. H. Miller (London, 1852).

II. Secondary Literature. On Miller or his work see N. Storey Maskelyne, *Nature*, **22** (1880), 247–249; T. G. Bonney, *Proceedings of the Royal Society*, **31** (1881), ii–vii; and J. P. Cooke, *Proceedings of the American Academy of Arts and Sciences*, **16** (1881), 460–468. Memorial of William Hallowes Miller by his wife (privately printed, Cambridge, 1881[?]).

Duncan McKie

MILLER, WILLIAM LASH (*b.* Galt, Canada, 10 September 1866; *d.* Toronto, Canada, 1 September 1940), *chemistry.*

During the last decade of the nineteenth century and the early part of the twentieth century Miller played a leading role in the development of chemistry in Canada. In accordance with the tradition of the time, classical studies formed a significant part of his undergraduate training at the University of Toronto, although this was leavened with courses in mathematics, physics, chemistry, biology, mineralogy, and geology. After receiving his B.A. degree in natural philosophy in 1887, Miller went to Germany. After spending some time in Berlin and Göttingen he proceeded to Munich, where he took his Ph.D. under Baeyer in 1890. He then moved to Leipzig to work in Ostwald's laboratory. This was a turning point in Miller's life, and he continued to spend his summers with Ostwald after he had become a member of the staff of the department of chemistry at Toronto and had received his second Ph.D. at Leipzig in 1892. It was at Leipzig that he first became acquainted with the elegance and applicability to chemistry of the thermodynamic approach of Josiah Willard Gibbs.

In a series of papers published largely in the *Transactions of the Connecticut Academy of Arts and Sciences* (1873–1883), Gibbs had laid the foundation for chemical thermodynamics; but it was left to Ostwald and Miller to translate Gibbs's highly theoretical treatment into laboratory terms. Most of Miller's academic life was devoted to this activity. In one of his first scientific papers (1892), he showed that the electromotive force of an electrochemical cell having a metallic electrode of mercury, lead, or tin was independent, at the melting point, of whether the metal was in the liquid or the solid state, and hence the factor determining the electromotive force at constant temperature and pressure must therefore be the chemical potential, or Gibbs free energy.

Miller was particularly adroit in applying and extending Gibbs's theories to polycomponent systems. When one of his students found that the addition of salt to an aqueous solution of alcohol raised the partial pressure of alcohol, an effect opposite to that predicted by then-current theories, he was able to show that this was a logical consequence of thermodynamic reasoning and proved it in the paper "On The Second Differential Coefficients of Gibbs Function ζ" (1897). His appreciation of the importance of having quantitative values for these second differential coefficients dominated his approach to both teaching and research. It also led, in later years, to some controversy between the Miller school of thermodynamics and that of G. N. Lewis at Berkeley. In retrospect, this controversy was seen to relate to a choice of formalism rather than logic. Lewis chose to use two quantities, the standard state and the activity coefficient, which are related to the first derivative of the Gibbs free energy; Miller used the second differential coefficient of the Gibbs free energy. Whereas Miller's choice was mathematically more elegant, and possibly a better method for the beginning student, the Lewis approach was more practical insofar as getting accurate data for real systems is concerned. Miller realized this difference, and saw to it that his students were exposed to the two approaches.

During his long career at Toronto, Miller had a record of outstanding research in several areas of physical chemistry: chemical equilibriums, rates of reaction, electrochemistry, transference numbers, overvoltage, high-current electric arcs, and diffusion. In his later years he was attracted by problems of a biochemical nature, particularly by growth factors for simple cells like the yeasts.

In 1894, when Miller was promoted to lecturer in chemistry, he introduced research as a regular part of the fourth year of the undergraduate honors program, a step that has been followed in many other disciplines and institutions. He was made associate professor in 1900 and professor in 1908. When World War I broke out, the head of Miller's department took leave to enter active military service and Miller became *de facto* head. He remained in that capacity until his retirement in 1937.

Miller's leadership in research was paralleled by his active role in many professional societies and academies in Canada, Great Britain, and the United States. As early as 1910 he was chairman of the Canadian Section of the Society of Chemical Industry. He was one of the chief organizers of the Canadian Institute of Chemistry (its president in 1926) and of the Canadian Chemical Association. All three societies were eventually amalgamated to form the present Chemical Institute of Canada. In 1926 Miller was the first Canadian to be made an honorary member of the American Chemical Society and served for many years as an associate editor of its *Journal*. He was active in the establishment of, and as an associate editor of, *Journal of Physical Chemistry*. His distinction as a scientist and his leadership in his profession were recognized when he was made a commander of the Order of the British Empire.

BIBLIOGRAPHY

I. Original Works. Miller's works include "Über die Umwandlung Chemischer Energie in Elektrische," in *Zeitschrift für physikalische Chemie*, **10** (1892), 459–466; "On the Second Differential Coefficients of Gibbs Function ζ. The Vapour Tensions, Freezing and Boiling Points of Ternary Mixtures," in *Journal of Physical Chemistry*, **1** (1896–1897), 633–642; "The Theory of the Direct Method of Determining Transport Numbers," in *Zeitschrift für physikalische Chemie*, **69** (1910), 436–441; "Mathematical Theory of the Changes in Concentration at the Electrode Brought About by Diffusion and by Chemical Reactions," in *Journal of Physical Chemistry*, **14** (1910), 816–885, written with T. R. Rosebrugh; "The Influence of Diffusion on Electromotive Force Produced in Solutions by Centrifugal Action," in *Transactions of the Electrochemical Society*, **21** (1912), 209–217; "Toxicity and Chemical Potential," in *Journal of Physical Chemistry*, **24** (1920), 562–569; "The Method of Willard Gibbs in Chemical Thermodynamics," in *Chemical Reviews,* **1** (1924–1925), 293–344; "Numerical Evaluation of Infinite Series and Integrals Which Arise in Certain Problems of Linear Heat Flow, Electrochemical Diffusion, etc.," in *Journal of Physical Chemistry*, **35** (1931), 2785–2884, written with A. R. Gordon.

II. Secondary Literature. See C. J. S. Warrington and R. V. V. Nicholls, *A History of Chemistry in Canada* (New

York, 1949), and the obituaries by Frank B. Kenrick, in *Proceedings of the Royal Society of Canada*, 3rd ser., **35** (1941), 131–134, and by Wilder D. Bancroft, in *Journal of the American Chemical Society*, **63** (1941), 1–2.

DONALD J. LE ROY

MILLIKAN, ROBERT ANDREWS (*b*. Morrison, Illinois, 22 March 1868; *d*. Pasadena, California, 19 December 1953), *physics*.

Millikan was the son of Silas Franklin Millikan, a Congregational preacher, and Mary Jane Andrews, a graduate of Oberlin who had been dean of women at a small college in Michigan. Raised in Maquoketa, Iowa, where his family moved in 1875, young Millikan enjoyed a storybook Midwestern American boyhood, fishing, farming, fooling, and learning next to nothing about science. In 1886 he enrolled in the preparatory department of Oberlin College and, in 1887, in the classical course of the college itself. Mainly because he did quite well in Greek, at the end of his sophomore year he was asked to teach an introductory physics class. Glad to have the job, Millikan plunged into the subject, liked it, and soon decided to make it his career.

Millikan graduated from Oberlin in 1891 and continued to teach physics to the preparatory students while successfully pursuing a course of self-instruction in Silvanus P. Thomson's *Dynamic Electric Machinery*. Awarded an M.A. for this achievement, in 1893 Millikan entered Columbia University on a fellowship as the sole graduate student in physics. He was impressed by the lectures of Michael I. Pupin, who emphasized the importance of mathematical techniques, and by the experimental deftness of Michelson, under whom he studied at the University of Chicago in the summer of 1894. Receiving his Ph.D. in 1895, Millikan went to Europe for postgraduate study, financed by a loan from Pupin. He heard Poincaré lecture at Paris, took a course from Planck at Berlin, and did research with Nernst at Göttingen. In 1896, the excitement of the discovery of X rays still fresh in his mind, Millikan joined the faculty of the University of Chicago as an assistant in physics.

There he soon met Greta Irvin Blanchard, the daughter of a successful manufacturer from Oak Park, Illinois. By the time the young couple was married in 1902, Millikan was pouring a large fraction of his considerable energies into the development of the physics curriculum, especially the introductory courses. In conjunction with this work, he wrote or coauthored a variety of textbooks and laboratory manuals which, like his *First Course in Physics* (1906), written with

Henry Gale, quickly became standards and sold steadily through the years. In 1907, largely because of his outstanding pedagogical achievements, Millikan was promoted to an associate professorship.

But Millikan was acutely aware that at the University of Chicago the major rewards went to those who contributed to the advancement of knowledge. Although he had consistently done research, even his most recent investigation, on the photoelectric effect, had failed to yield significant results. Unaware of Einstein's explanation of the effect, Millikan used a spark source of ultraviolet light to determine conclusively whether the photocurrent from various metals varied with temperature; as he found, it did not. Eager to earn a reputation in research, about 1908 he decided to shelve the writing of textbooks and concentrate on his work in the laboratory.

By 1909 Millikan was deeply involved in an attempt to measure the electronic charge. No one had yet obtained a reliable value for this fundamental constant, and some antiatomistic Continental physicists were insisting that it was not the constant of a unique particle but a statistical average of diverse electrical energies. Millikan launched his investigation with a technique developed by the British-born physicist H. A. Wilson; it consisted essentially of measuring, first, the rate at which a charged cloud of water vapor fell under the influence of gravity and then the modified rate under the counterforce of an electric field. Using Stokes's law of fall to determine the mass of the cloud, one could in principle compute the ionic charge. Millikan quickly recognized the numerous uncertainties in this technique, including the fact that evaporation at the surface of the cloud confused the measure of its rate of fall. Hoping to correct for this effect, he decided to study the evaporation history of the cloud while a strong electric field held it in a stationary position.

But when Millikan switched on the powerful field, the cloud disappeared; in its place were a few charged water drops moving slowly in response to the imposed electrical force. He quickly realized that it would be a good deal more accurate to determine the electronic charge by working with a single drop than with the swarm of particles in a cloud. Finding that he could make measurements on water drops for up to forty-five seconds before they evaporated, Millikan arrived at a value for *e* in 1909 which he considered accurate to within 2 percent. More important, he observed that the charge on any given water drop was always an integral multiple of an irreducible value. This result provided the most persuasive evidence yet that electrons were fundamental particles of identical charge and mass.

Late in 1909 Millikan greatly improved the drop method by substituting oil for water. Because of the relatively low volatility of this liquid, he could measure the rise and fall of the drops for up to four and a half hours. Spraying the chamber with radium radiation, he could change the charge on a single drop at will. His overall results decisively confirmed the integral-multiple values of the total charge. As for the determination of e itself, Millikan found that Stokes's law was inadequate for his experimental circumstances because the size of the drops was comparable with the mean free path of the air. Using the so-called Stokes-Cunningham version of the law, which took this condition into account, by late 1910 he had computed a charge for e of 4.891×10^{-10} e.s.u. Realizing that the accuracy of this figure was no better than that of the key constants involved in the computation, Millikan painstakingly reevaluated the coefficient of viscosity of air and the mean-free-path term in the Stokes-Cunningham law. In 1913 he published the value for the electronic charge, $4.774 \pm .009 \times 10^{-10}$ e.s.u., which would serve the world of science for a generation.

Off and on all the while, Millikan had continued his exploration of the photoelectric effect; about 1912, now aware of Einstein's interpretation of it, he began an intensive experimental study of the phenomenon, with the aim of testing the formula relating the frequency of the incident light to the retarding potential which cut off the photocurrent. No experimentalist had yet succeeded in proving or disproving the validity of the equation. Millikan took great care to avoid the mistakes that he and other physicists had previously made. Since a spark source of ultraviolet light induced spurious voltages in the apparatus, he used a high-pressure mercury-quartz lamp arranged to suppress stray light, especially on the short wavelength side. To extend the range of test well into the visible region, he made targets of alkali metals which were photosensitive up to 6,000 Å. Where others had adulterated their results by using photosensitive materials as the reference for the cutoff voltage, Millikan employed a Faraday cage of well-oxidized copper netting which was not photosensitive in the range of his incident radiation. Finally, he sought to reduce the inaccuracies introduced when the photocurrent near the cutoff point was too low to measure with precision. Having noticed that this current was highest when the metal was fresh, he fashioned his targets into thick cylinders and rigged up an electromagnetically operated knife to shave off the ends of the blocks.

By 1915, as the result of these meticulous investigations, Millikan had confirmed the validity of Einstein's equation in every detail. He not only demonstrated the linear relationship between the cutoff potential and the frequency of the incident light but also showed that the intercept of the graphed data on the voltage axis equaled the contact electromotive force, or work potential, of the target metal, a quantity which he had measured independently, to within 0.5 percent. In addition Millikan proved that the slope of the line equaled the ratio of Planck's constant to the electronic charge, and his work provided the best measure of h then available. Despite the conclusiveness of these results, Millikan did not believe that he had confirmed Einstein's theory of light quanta but only his equation for the photoeffect. In the face of all the evidence for the wave nature of light, he was convinced, as were most other physicists of the day, that the equation had to be based on a false, albeit evidently quite fruitful, hypothesis.

By 1916, when Millikan completed his major work on the photoeffect, he had already assumed more than a mere professor's role in the world of science. In 1913 he became a consultant to the research department of Western Electric, primarily to advise the company on vacuum tube problems. In 1914 he was elected to the American Philosophical Society and the American Academy of Arts and Sciences, in 1915 to the National Academy of Sciences, and in 1916 to the presidency of the American Physical Society, an office which he held for two years. Millikan also served as an associate editor of *Physical Review* from 1903 to 1916; and he was made an editor of *Proceedings of the National Academy of Sciences . . .*, which was started in the year of his election.

Early in 1917, after the United States broke diplomatic relations with Germany, Millikan went to Washington as a vice-chairman and director of research for the National Research Council, the organization which the National Academy of Sciences had recently created to help mobilize science for defense. Commissioned a lieutenant colonel in the Army Signal Corps, he served in his military capacity as the director of the Signal Corps Division of Science and Research and, in his National Research Council identity, as a member of the U.S. Navy's Special Board on Antisubmarine Devices. After a brief postwar period back at Chicago, in 1921 Millikan accepted appointment as chairman of the executive council and director of the Norman Bridge Laboratory at the newly renamed California Institute of Technology in Pasadena. In effect the president of the school, he was an able fund raiser and its enthusiastic spokesman; and under his leadership it quickly developed into one of the most distinguished scientific centers in the world.

Managing all the while to supervise many doctoral and postdoctoral fellows, Millikan maintained an active research career throughout the interwar years. One of the important subjects he investigated was the ability of electric fields on the order of a few hundred thousand volts per centimeter to draw electrons out of cold metals. By 1926, working in collaboration with Carl F. Eyring, a Caltech graduate student, Millikan had completed a thorough study of the phenomenon, using tungsten wires threaded along the axis of a hollow cylinder in high vacuum. The two men found that the field current, to use the term they introduced, depended only on the field gradient, not on the potential difference, between the wire and the walls of the cylinder. More important, within wide limitations the current was also entirely independent of temperature. Pointing out that these results violated Owen W. Richardson's theory of thermionic emission, Millikan and Eyring speculated that at relatively low temperatures some metallic electrons must not obey the law of equipartition. But in 1928 Oppenheimer, R. H. Fowler, and their co-workers showed independently that cold emission was a quantum mechanical result of the leakage of electrons through a potential barrier. In 1929 Charles C. Lauritsen, who was completing his doctoral research under Millikan, derived an empirical formula from their data which related the field current to the field gradient; and this equation was ultimately found to be experimentally indistinguishable from the quantum mechanical expression.

During the 1920's Millikan also did significant research in the "hot spark" spectra. As he knew, a high potential difference would maintain a spark source of ultraviolet radiation across two electrodes in a vacuum. The relative ease with which such radiation was absorbed had made its study difficult. In 1915 Millikan proposed that one could get around the problem of absorption by enclosing the path between the spark and a photographic plate entirely in a vacuum. To maximize the intensity of the spectrum, he had a grating ruled that would throw most of the light into the first order. Shortly after the war, with the apparatus now working reliably, Millikan and Ira S. Bowen, another Caltech graduate student, embarked upon a thorough study of the ultraviolet spectra of the lighter elements up to copper. By 1924 they had found and identified some 1,000 new lines. They had also extended the observable spectrum down to 136.6 Å and had helped to close the last gap between the optical and the X-ray frequencies.

In the course of this work, Millikan and Bowen found that the strongest lines were produced by atoms which had been stripped of their valence electrons.

Since the spectra of such hydrogen-like atoms ought to contain multiplets, they began, about the end of 1923, to study the fine spectra in the ultraviolet. By early 1924 they had found that the $2s$, $2p_1$, and $2p_2$ terms of the ultraviolet doublets corresponded precisely to the L_I, L_{II}, and L_{III} levels associated with the X-ray spectra of the heavier elements. Moreover, exactly the same relationship existed between the M and N X-ray levels and the higher ultraviolet multiplet terms. Millikan and Bowen concluded that the X-ray doublet laws based on Sommerfeld's relativistic orbital analysis could account for the doublets in the whole field of optics.

Yet, as they also pointed out in 1924, independently of Alfred Landé, this conclusion raised a serious difficulty for the theory of spectra. On the one hand, Sommerfeld's relativistic analysis of the X-ray doublets assigned a different azimuthal quantum number to the L_{II} and L_{III} terms. On the other hand, Bohr's spectral scheme accounted for the optical doublets by assuming different orientations for the same orbit; by definition, the p_1 and p_2 terms of the optical doublets possessed the same azimuthal quantum number. Since the results of Millikan and Bowen identified the L_{II} and L_{III} terms with the p_1 and p_2 levels, it seemed that one had to give up either Sommerfeld's relativistic explanation or the Bohr scheme of spectra. Millikan and Bowen could find no way out of the dilemma; but their forceful statement of it in 1924, coupled with Landé's, contributed to the ultimate resolution of the difficulty through G. E. Uhlenbeck and S. A. Goudsmit's postulation of electron spin in 1925.

In the 1920's Millikan also began an increasingly intensive program of research into the penetrating radiation which in mid-decade he would name "cosmic rays." In 1912 the Austrian-born physicist Victor Hess had found that atmospheric ionization increased with altitude up to 12,000 feet. But although Hess had argued that some kind of radiation was coming from the heavens, most physicists still attributed the phenomenon to some terrestrial cause, such as electrical discharges from thunderstorms or radioactivity. Millikan's initial experiments in the field, done with an unmanned sounding balloon in 1922 to a height of fifteen kilometers and with lead-shielded electroscopes atop Pike's Peak in 1923, failed to decide in favor of either interpretation. In the summer of 1925 Millikan proposed to settle the question by measuring the variation of ionization with depth in Muir Lake and Lake Arrowhead in the mountains of California. Snow-fed and separated by many miles, as well as 6,675 feet of atmosphere, each was likely to be free of both local radioactive disturbances and whatever atmospheric peculiarities might affect the ionization in the other.

Millikan's electroscopic measurements showed that the intensity of ionization at any given depth in Lake Arrowhead was the same as the intensity six feet lower in Muir Lake. Since the layer of atmosphere between the surfaces of the two lakes had precisely the absorptive power of six feet of water, the results decisively confirmed that the radiation was coming from the cosmos. Moreover, since the intensity of the ionization showed no diurnal variation, the radiation was uniformly distributed over all directions in space. And, finally, since Millikan detected ionization as far below the top of the atmosphere as the combined air and water equivalent of six feet of lead, it was evident that cosmic rays were a good deal more energetic than even the hardest known gamma rays.

To penetrate six feet of lead, charged particles would have to possess stores of energy then considered impossibly large; accordingly, Millikan assumed that cosmic rays must consist of photons. In 1926 he tested this assumption experimentally with what he considered confirmatory results. If cosmic rays were charged particles, their trajectories would be affected by the earth's magnetic field, so that more of them would strike the earth at higher than at lower latitudes. But Millikan could detect virtually no difference in cosmic ray flux at Lake Titicaca in South America from that at Muir Lake. And, although he ran his electroscope while sailing back from Mollendo, Peru, to Los Angeles, he found no variation of intensity with latitude at sea level.

Employing the photonic interpretation of cosmic rays, Millikan developed a theory of their origin in 1928. Combining the data from the balloon flight of 1922 with that of his terrestrial surveys, he graphed a curve of ionization versus depth which covered the range from sea level up to virtually the top of the atmosphere. Because no single coefficient of absorption could account for the curve, he inferred that cosmic rays were spread across a spectrum of energies. Going further, he argued that the experimental curve could be constructed from three different curves, each representing a different coefficient of absorption. According to this analysis, cosmic ray energies were not generally distributed but were clustered in three distinct bands.

To account for these bands, Millikan introduced what he called the "atom-building hypothesis." Using Dirac's formula for absorption through Compton scattering, Millikan computed the energy of the three bands from their absorption coefficients and found them equal to 26, 110, and 220 MEV. These figures equaled the mass defects of hydrogen, oxygen,

and silicon, which were known to be three of the most abundant elements of the universe. Millikan concluded that the photons striking the earth must be produced when four atoms of hydrogen somehow fused to form helium, sixteen to form oxygen, and twenty-eight to form silicon. In his summary of the argument, cosmic rays were the "birth cries" of atoms, a phrase which quickly achieved a good deal of notoriety among both the scientific and the lay publics.

Although in the late 1920's most physicists agreed with Millikan that cosmic rays were photons, few accepted his atom-building hypothesis. He had no proof of the uniqueness of his three absorption coefficients and could not convincingly explain away the kinetic difficulties involved in the spontaneous union of sixteen hydrogen atoms into oxygen, let alone twenty-eight into silicon. Moreover, some of his own experimental evidence cast doubt on the validity of using the Dirac formula to compute cosmic ray energies. Then, at the beginning of the 1930's, Millikan's assumption that the primary radiation consisted of photons was refuted by the work of other experimentalists, especially by Arthur Compton's conclusive detection of a latitude effect in 1932.

Millikan hotly contested Compton's findings. He had repeated his search for a latitude effect in the late 1920's, and in late 1932 he did so once more, again without success. But Millikan was the victim of experimental circumstance. In the longitudinal region of California, the dip in cosmic ray intensity began quite suddenly in the neighborhood of Los Angeles and quickly reached its maximum fall of some 7 percent less than two days' sail south of the city. In Millikan's initial search for the latitude effect—the voyage from Mollendo, Peru, to Los Angeles—his estimated error had been 6 percent. In most of his later searches, he went to the north of Pasadena, where the rise in intensity was too small to detect easily. In 1932 he sent H. Victor Neher, a young collaborator at Caltech, on a voyage to the south; but Neher did not get his electroscope working before he had passed the region of the dip.

By 1933, with Neher having now found a latitude effect, Millikan had admitted that some percentage of cosmic radiation must consist of charged particles. By 1935 he had also rejected the atom-building hypothesis, mainly because it was now clear that the bulk of cosmic radiation possessed energies much higher than the mass defects of the abundant elements. All the same, despite a vast array of contrary evidence and the overwhelming body of professional opinion, Millikan clung tenaciously to the assumption that some fraction of the primary cosmic radiation could be photons. In the late 1930's and early 1940's he searched for evidence in support of this view, measuring cosmic ray intensities around the world at sea level, in airplanes at high altitudes, and with unmanned sounding balloons up to the top of the atmosphere. On the basis of this data, he also developed a theory that cosmic ray photons originated in the spontaneous annihilation of atoms in interstellar space. No more convincing than its predecessor, this hypothesis became completely untenable, as Millikan himself admitted a few years before his death, after the detection of the π-meson in 1947 made it clear that the primary cosmic radiation consisted almost entirely of protons.

But however wrongheaded Millikan had been, his cosmic ray research yielded a valuable fund of experimental data. Moreover, in 1934, independently of Jacob Clay, he detected the variation of the latitude effect with longitude because of the dissymmetry of the earth's magnetic field. In a roundabout way even the atom-building hypothesis strikingly benefited the progress of science. In the late 1920's, troubled by the discrepancy between his experimental data and the predictions of both the Dirac absorption formula and its successor, the Klein-Nishina formula, Millikan recognized that he needed a measure of cosmic ray energies that was not based on absorption coefficients. To obtain a direct determination, he put Carl Anderson, a young research fellow at Caltech, to work with a cloud chamber set in a powerful magnetic field. In 1931 Anderson's studies of the trajectories of charged particles showed conclusively that the absorption of cosmic rays resulted from nuclear encounters as well as from Compton scattering. They also led to his detection of the positron in 1932.

Between the wars Millikan played a prominent role in the affairs of his profession. The president of the American Association for the Advancement of Science in 1929 and the holder of various offices in the National Academy of Sciences and the National Research Council, he was especially active as a member of the NRC fellowship board and as foreign secretary of the Academy. From 1922 to 1932 Millikan served as the American representative to the Committee on Intellectual Cooperation of the League of Nations. Throughout the interwar period he participated in the International Research Council; its successor, the International Council of Scientific Unions; and the affiliate of both, the International Union of Pure and Applied Physics. In 1933 Millikan was appointed by President Franklin D. Roosevelt to the Science Advisory Board, a joint venture of the Academy and the federal government to find ways to use science for economic recovery.

Millikan was an able popularizer and lecturer, and

after he won the Nobel Prize in 1923 he became perhaps the most famous American scientist of his day. An outspoken religious modernist, he was a leading exponent of the reconcilability of science and religion in the 1920's, the decade of the Scopes trial. Politically, Millikan was a conservative Republican. During the 1930's he vigorously opposed the New Deal, repeatedly denounced governmental intervention in the economy, and argued that the promotion of science, because it led to new industries and new jobs, was a much sounder way to achieve economic recovery. Always an internationalist, Millikan believed firmly in collective security. In the late 1930's, unlike many conservative Republicans at the time, including his good friend Herbert Hoover, he helped propagandize in favor of aid to the Allies; by early 1941 he was encouraging the conversion of Caltech from academic to military purposes.

During the war Millikan turned over an increasing fraction of his administrative responsibilities at Caltech to the younger staff members who were running the various defense projects. In 1946 he retired from his professorship and the chairmanship of the executive council. He remained active as a public lecturer and spoke frequently on the subject of science and religion. He was cool to the creation of the National Science Foundation and spoke often against federal aid to education. By the time of his death, Millikan had been awarded numerous medals, even more honorary degrees, and membership in twenty-one foreign scientific societies, including the Royal Society of London and the Institut de France.

BIBLIOGRAPHY

I. Original Works. A complete bibliography of Millikan's published work, which includes close to 300 scientific papers, is in Lee A. DuBridge and Paul S. Epstein, "Robert Andrews Millikan," in *Biographical Memoirs. National Academy of Sciences*, **33** (1959), 241–282. In *The Autobiography of Robert A. Millikan* (New York, 1950) Millikan provided valuable accounts of his childhood and education, work on the electronic charge and the photoeffect, and involvement in the mobilization of science during World War I; curiously, he devoted little space to his research in hot spark spectra or cosmic rays, and his account of the development of the California Institute of Technology must be used with special care. Millikan left a voluminous body of correspondence, which is now in the Caltech archives. Dating in the main from 1921, the collection contains substantial materials on the National Academy of Sciences–National Research Council and the administration of the California Institute of Technology, as well as a sizable amount of family and scientific letters. Another important batch of Millikan's letters is in the papers of

George Ellery Hale in the Caltech archives, which were also published in a microfilm edition (Pasadena, 1968) under the editorship of Daniel J. Kevles. The locations of other letters to and from Millikan are given in Thomas S. Kuhn, *et al.*, *Sources for the History of Quantum Mechanics* (Philadelphia, 1967), 68.

II. SECONDARY LITERATURE. Paul S. Epstein wrote an excellent résumé of Millikan's scientific work in "Robert A. Millikan as Physicist and Teacher," in *Reviews of Modern Physics*, **20** (Jan. 1948), 10–25, a volume published in honor of Millikan's eightieth birthday. A condensed version of Epstein's essay occupies part of the memoir written with DuBridge (see above), which is on the whole a useful introduction to Millikan's life. Millikan the famous scientist is treated in Daniel J. Kevles, "Millikan: Spokesman for Science in the Twenties," in *Engineering and Science*, **32** (Apr. 1969), 17–22.

DANIEL J. KEVLES

MILLINGTON, THOMAS (*b.* Newbury, Berkshire, England, 1628; *d.* London, England, 5 January 1704), *medicine.*

The son of Thomas Millington, Esquire, of Newbury, Millington was educated at Westminster School during the headmastership of Richard Busby. From Westminster he was elected a scholar to Trinity College, Cambridge, on 31 May 1645 and matriculated the following Easter. At Cambridge he was under the tutorship of James Duport and graduated B.A. in 1649. Shortly afterward he moved to Oxford, where he became fellow of All Souls and proceeded M.A. on 30 May 1651 (incorporated Cambridge 1657), B.D. on 8 July 1659, and M.D. on 9 July 1659. Why Millington moved is unclear, but Carter states that he was invited.[1] Possibly, in view of his close connections with the groups engaged in natural philosophy at Wadham, All Souls, and elsewhere, his interest in these activities was the cause.[2] He was particularly involved in the research on the brain conducted by the Willis-Wren-Lower circle.[3]

Candidate of the Royal College of Physicians on 30 September 1659, Millington became a fellow on 2 April 1672, although he still seems to have been living at Oxford. Appointed Sedleian professor of natural philosophy as successor to Willis in 1675, he gave his inaugural lecture on 12 April 1676; according to Wood it was "much commended."[4] Shortly afterward, however, he seems to have moved to London, although he retained his post at Oxford until his death, discharging his duties by deputy. (Among these deputies was John Keill, in 1700.) Physician in ordinary to William and Mary, as he was also to Queen Anne, Millington was knighted in March 1680.

Censor of the Royal College of Physicians in 1678, 1680, 1681, and 1684; Harveian orator in 1679; and treasurer from 1686 to 1689, he was consiliarius in 1691 and 1695, and served as president from 1696 until his death. Millington was licensed to marry Hannah King, widow of Henry King, on 23 February 1680; they had a son, Thomas (who seems to have gained notoriety as a beau), and a daughter, Anne.[5] In 1680 Bishop John Fell put forward Millington's name to William Sancroft, archbishop of Canterbury, for the vacant chair of medicine at Oxford.[6]

Millington's claim upon the attention of posterity is threefold: as a physician, as a man of wide-ranging intellectual activities, and as the reputed discoverer of sexuality in plants. This last claim rests entirely on a remark by Nehemiah Grew (to whom the discovery would otherwise be credited) in a discourse upon the anatomy of flowers read to the Royal Society on 9 November 1676. While discussing the role of the attire (stamens) in flowers, he said, "In Discorse hereof with our Learned *Savilian* [sic] Professor Sir *Thomas Millington*, he told me he conceived, That the Attire doth serve in the *Male*, for the *Generation* of the *Seed*. I immediately reply'd, That I was of the Opinion; and gave him some reasons for it, and answered some *Objections*, which might oppose them."[7] The emphasis here seems to be on the immediacy of Grew's reply and the reasons he provided in support of Millington's idea. This suggests that Grew had been considering the problem for some time, while for Millington it was still little more than an undeveloped insight. In the lack of any other evidence that Millington had been working on this particular subject, there seems no reason to ascribe priority to him over Grew in the enunciation and explanation of this phenomenon.

Millington impressed his contemporaries as a learned man, as indeed he still does, despite the scarcity of materials relating to him. Thanks partly to his learning and partly to a notably amiable disposition, he was much respected as a physician, being praised in Samuel Garth's "The Dispensary" under the name of Machaon and also by Sydenham. He had a highly fashionable practice—amassing, says Carter, a fortune of £60,000.[8] Millington was called to the deathbed of Charles II and was one of the physicians to perform the dissection of William III's body. As an officer and as president of the Royal College of Physicians, he was active and zealous during a somewhat disturbed period of the College's history but was unable to restore it from its moribund state. He was, however, instrumental in liquidating the College's £7,000 debt to the executors of Sir John Cutler in 1701, providing £2,000 himself. Linnaeus named the genus *Millingtonia* among the Bignoniaceae after him.

NOTES

1. Edmund Carter, *History of Cambridge* (London, 1753), 329.
2. Anthony Wood, *Life and Times*, A. Clarke, ed., I (Oxford, 1891), 201.
3. Thomas Willis, *Cerebri anatomici* (Oxford, 1664), dedicatory epistle.
4. *Op. cit.*, II, 343.
5. William Musgrave, ed., *Obituaries Prior to 1800 (as far as Relates to England, Scotland and Ireland)*, which is *Harleian Society*, XLVII (London, 1900), 201–202. Bodleian Library MS Rawlinson D 1160, fol. 34a.
6. Bodleian MS Tanner 36*, fol. 51.
7. Nehemiah Grew, *The Anatomy of Plants With an Idea of a Philosophical History of Plants* (London, 1682), bk. IV, ch. 5, 171.
8. *Op. cit.*, p. 350.

BIBLIOGRAPHY

I. ORIGINAL WORKS. Millington's only published work, prepared jointly with Sir Richard Blackmore and Sir Edward Hannes, was *The Report of the Physicians and Surgeons, Commanded to Assist at the Dissecting the Body of His Late Majesty at Kensington, March the Tenth MDCCII. From the Original Delivered to the Right Honourable the Privy Council* (London, 1702). Bodleian MS Rawlinson D 1041, "Sententiae collectae a Tho. Millington Cantabrigiensi anno 1648," and British Museum, Sloane MS 3565, "Celebriorum distinctionum synopsis Thomas Millington April 7 1646," are undergraduate notebooks. Sloane 2148, "De morbis in specie eorumque remedius: Tum logice tum empirice," is more a recipe book than a treatise.

II. SECONDARY LITERATURE. In addition to the references given in the notes, further discussions of Millington and the Royal College of Physicians can be found in W. Munk, *The Roll of the Royal College of Physicians of London* (London, 1878), 363–365; and Sir George Clark, *A History of the Royal College of Physicians*, 2 vols. (London, 1964–1966), I, 323, 358, 370; II, 469, 472, 474–475, 483, 487. For most purposes, the entry in *Dictionary of National Biography*, XIII, 442, is perfectly adequate.

A. J. TURNER

MILLON, AUGUSTE-NICOLAS-EUGÈNE (*b.* Châlons-sur-Marne, France, 24 April 1812; *d.* St.-Seine-l'Abbaye, France, 22 October 1867), *chemistry, agronomy, pharmacy.*

After completing his secondary education in Châlons-sur-Marne and working as a teaching assistant at the Collège Rollin in Paris, Millon decided on a medical career in the army. In 1832 he was admitted as a student to the Val-de-Grâce military teaching hospital in Paris, and two years later he qualified for active duty as a surgeon. He served successively in Bitche, Lyons, Algeria, and Metz; in 1836 he received the M.D. from the Paris Faculty of Medicine.

Millon's long interest in chemistry prompted him, however, to take up military pharmacy rather than surgery and medicine. A brief appointment as *préparateur* and tutor at the Val-de-Grâce was followed by a tour of duty at several military installations, and finally by a professorship of chemistry at the Val-de-Grâce in 1841. During the next six years Millon established himself as an outstanding chemist and teacher. Probably because of his unorthodox views, he was abruptly transferred in 1847 as professor to the military teaching hospital in Lille, which not only separated him from his students and friends but also seriously disrupted his scientific work. From 1850 until his retirement in 1865, he served as the top-ranking pharmacist for the French army in Algeria.

The years from 1837 to 1847, scientifically the most important period of Millon's life, were devoted largely to basic chemistry. His circle of friends and occasional collaborators included Pelouze, J. Reiset, F. Hoefer, Regnault, Louis Laveran, and F.-J.-J. Nicklès. Particularly noteworthy at this time were his studies of the nitrides of bromine, iodine, and cyanogen; of oxides of chlorine and iodine; of reactions of nitric acid on metals and of mercury salts with ammonia; and the investigation with J. Reiset of the nature of catalytic reactions. It was also during this decade that Millon discovered iodine dioxide, chlorites, ethyl nitrate, and the production of potassium iodate. In 1845 he launched the *Annuaire de chimie* with Reiset (in collaboration with Hoefer and Nicklès), seven volumes of which appeared before it was discontinued in 1851. Millon's lectures at the Val-de-Grâce formed the basis for his two-volume treatise, *Éléments de chimie organique* (Paris, 1845–1848).

After 1847 the direction and emphasis of Millon's scientific work changed, becoming more applied and diffuse. He devoted considerable time to studying wheat, especially its classification, constituents, conservation, and processing. Millon showed in 1848 that urea could be quantitatively analyzed by decomposing it with nitrous acid and determining the amount of carbon dioxide released. In 1849 he published his discovery of a sensitive reagent for detecting proteins made by dissolving mercury in concentrated nitric acid and diluting with water, which proved effective in the presence of tyrosine. Among the varied projects he pursued in Algeria were the extraction of perfumes from Algerian flowers, the chemistry of nitrification, the raising and commerce of leeches, quality control of milk, the study of alcoholic fermentation, and the analysis of mineral water.

BIBLIOGRAPHY

1. ORIGINAL WORKS. Most of Millon's work was published in entirety or as extracts in the *Comptes rendus . . . de l'Académie des sciences*, often appearing at the same time in the *Annales de chimie et de physique*. For a chronological list of Millon's published and unpublished material, see J. Reiset *et al.*, *E. Millon, sa vie, ses travaux de chimie et ses études économiques et agricoles sur l'Algérie* (Paris, 1870), 321–327. A bibliography of Millon's articles is in the Royal Society's *Catalogue of Scientific Papers*, IV (London, 1870), 393–395; VIII (London, 1879), 407–408.

II. SECONDARY LITERATURE. See A. Balland, *Les travaux de Millon sur les blés* (Paris, 1905); H.-P. Faure, *E. Millon, notice biographique, lue à la Société d'agriculture, commerce, sciences et arts du département de la Marne, dans la séance publique du 26 août 1868* (Châlons-sur-Marne, 1868); J. R. Partington, *A History of Chemistry*, IV (London–New York, 1964), 57, 84, 90, 342, 364, 427–429, 603; and J. Reiset *et al.*, *E. Millon . . .* (see above).

The centenary of Millon's death was the occasion for three articles: Jean Delga, "La carrière militaire d'Eugène Millon," in *Revue d'histoire de la pharmacie*, **19** (1968), 69–72; Pierre Malangeau, "L'oeuvre scientifique d'Eugène Millon," *ibid.*, 73–82; and André Quevauviller, "À propos du centenaire de la mort de Millon," *ibid.*, 83–86.

ALEX BERMAN

MILLS, WILLIAM HOBSON (*b.* London, England, 6 July 1873; *d.* Cambridge, England, 22 February 1959), *organic chemistry.*

Although Mills was born in London, his father, William Henry Mills, an architect, and his mother, Emily Wiles Quincey Hobson, came from Lincolnshire and returned there in the autumn of 1873; thus he always regarded himself as a Lincolnshire man. He was educated first at Spalding Grammar School and then at Uppingham School, where an accident in the snow caused the severing of an Achilles tendon and limited his outdoor activities, although in his mature years he could walk and cycle with considerable vigor. He entered Jesus College, Cambridge, in October 1892 and in due course obtained a first class in the natural sciences tripos, part I, in 1896 and in part II (chemistry) in 1897.

Mills then began research in the Cambridge University Chemical Laboratory under T. H. Easterfield (later Sir Thomas Easterfield); when the latter accepted the professorship of chemistry at Wellington, New Zealand, in 1899, Mills continued the work alone and was elected to a fellowship (tenable for six years) at Jesus College in 1899.

In October 1899 Mills went to Tübingen to work under Hans von Pechmann for two years, during which period he met N. V. Sidgwick of Oxford University; the two chemists, so similar in their interests, became friends for life. In 1902 Mills was appointed head of the chemical department of Northern Polytechnic Institute in London. In 1912 he returned to Cambridge, having been appointed to the demonstratorship to the Jacksonian professorship of natural philosophy and to a fellowship and lectureship at Jesus College. In 1919 he was appointed university lecturer, and in 1931 the university recognized the high quality of his work by creating a personal readership in stereochemistry, which he held until his retirement in 1938.

The major part of Mills's scientific work was devoted to stereochemistry and the cyanine dyes. Only brief mention of some of the highlights in each of these divisions will be made.

Stereochemistry. Certain types of oximes were known to exist in two or more isomeric forms, for which an explanation had been suggested by Hantzsch and Werner. This explanation was not accepted by many chemists, and Mills sought decisive experimental evidence for its accuracy. After investigating several compounds, Mills and B. C. Saunders (*Journal of the Chemical Society* [1931], 537) prepared the *o*-carboxyphenylhydrazone of β-methyl-trimethylene-dithiolcarbonate, which they resolved into optically active forms. Optical activity could arise in this compound only if the Hantzsch-Werner theory were correct.

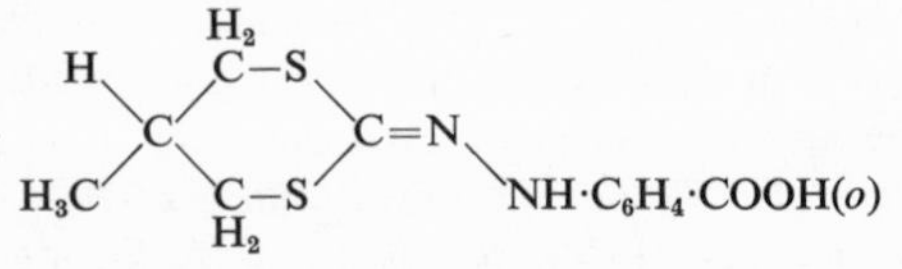

FIGURE 1. *o*-Carboxyphenylhydrazone of β-methyl-trimethylene-dithiolcarbonate.

It had been recognized that a spirocyclic compound consisting of two carbon rings linked together by a common carbon atom might show optical activity if the rings possessed appropriate substituents to ensure molecular dissymmetry. Mills and C. R. Nodder (*ibid.*, **119** [1921], 2094) synthesized and resolved into optically active forms the first such compound, the ketodilactone of benzophenone-2,4,2′,4′-tetracarboxylic acid.

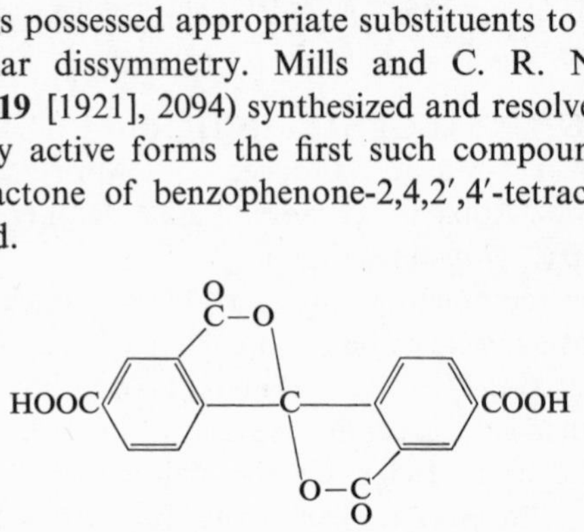

FIGURE 2. Ketodilactone of benzophenone-2,4,2′,4′-tetracarboxylic acid.

It had also long been recognized that a suitably substituted allene compound (3) would be dissym-

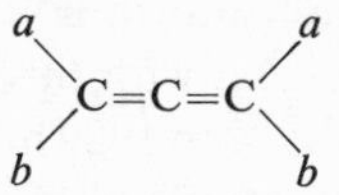

FIGURE 3. Example of an unsymmetrically substituted allene.

metric; but the synthesis of such a compound, bearing acidic or basic groups for resolution, had defied synthesis. P. Maitland and Mills, after about six years of persistent work, synthesized $\alpha\gamma$-biphenyl-$\alpha\gamma$-di-α-naphthylallyl alcohol, which by a stereospecific dehy-

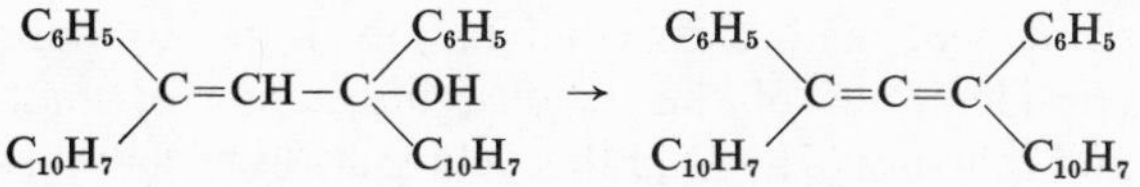

FIGURE 4. $\alpha\gamma$-Biphenyl-$\alpha\gamma$-di-α-naphthylallyl alcohol.

FIGURE 5. $\alpha\gamma$-Biphenyl-$\alpha\gamma$-di-α-naphthyl allene.

dration using dextro and levo camphorsulfonic acid, was converted into the optically active forms of $\alpha\gamma$-biphenyl-$\alpha\gamma$-di-α-naphthyl allene (5).

By extensions of these general methods, Mills and E. H. Warren (*ibid.*, **127** [1925], 2507) showed that the nitrogen atom of a quaternary ammonium salt had the tetrahedral configuration and was not situated in the center of a square-based pyramid. Furthermore, Mills and T. H. H. Quibell (*ibid.* [1935], 839) produced stereochemical evidence that the four-coordinated platinum atom had the planar, as distinct from the tetrahedral, configuration.

The fact that a biphenyl molecule, having suitable substituents in the 2,2'6,6'-positions, could show optical activity at first puzzled chemists. Mills was the first to point out in a simple diagram (*Chemistry and Industry*, **45** [1926], 884) that the size of these substituents could obstruct the free rotation of the two phenyl groups about their common axis, C_6H_5—C_6H_5, and such molecules could thus show optical activity. He became greatly interested in this subject of "restricted rotation" and later applied it to suitably substituted derivatives of naphthalene, quinoline, and benzene (with K. A. C. Elliott, *et al.*, in *Journal of the Chemical Society* [1928], 1291; [1932], 2209; [1939], 460).

Cyanine Dyes. In 1914 photographic plates and films were normally prepared with a silver bromide–silver iodide emulsion, which was sensitive only in the ultraviolet, violet, and blue regions. In 1905, however,

a German firm had synthesized a "photographic sensitizer" which, when incorporated into the emulsion, extended the sensitivity well into the red region. When in 1914–1915 the Western Front became essentially two parallel bands of heavily entrenched positions, it became imperative to detect as early as possible each day any work on these positions which the enemy had carried out during the previous night. The photographic reconnaissance of the British Royal Flying Corps (later the Royal Air Force) was under a great disadvantage, for their silver bromide–silver iodide plates were at their least sensitive in the red light of the early morning. The British authorities sent an urgent request to W. J. Pope, the head of the Cambridge University chemical department, to investigate the structure and the synthesis of Pinacyanol, which the Germans were using.

Pope enlisted the help of Mills and other workers, notably F. M. Hamer. This small team showed that Pinacyanol had the structure shown in Figure 6 and

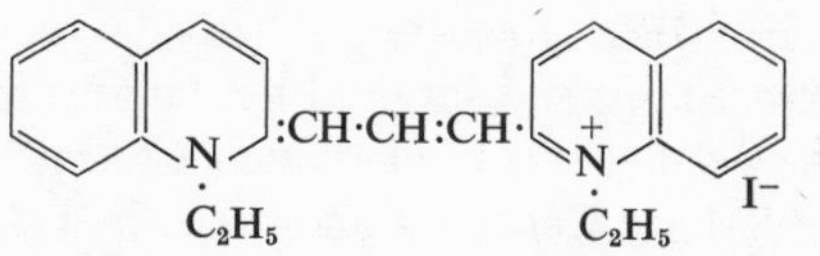

FIGURE 6. Pinacyanol (systematic name: 1,1'-Diethyl-2,2'-carbocyanine iodide).

developed a rapid synthesis of this compound and of other novel sensitizers such as the isocyanines. After the war Pope and Mills stated: "Throughout the war practically all the sensitizing dyestuffs used by the Allies in the manufacture of panchromatic plates were produced in this (i.e. the *Cambridge*) Laboratory" (*Photographic Journal*, **60** [1920], 183, 253). Mills and his co-workers subsequently continued the investigations of the various new types of sensitizers.

Mills was elected a fellow of the Royal Society in 1923 and received its Davy Medal in 1935. He was president of the Chemical Society for the years 1942–1943 and 1943–1944; his presidential addresses, entitled "The Stereochemistry of Labile Compounds" and "Old and New Views on Some Chemical Problems," respectively form the last of his chemical publications.

Retirement allowed Mills to devote himself to the study of natural history, in particular to the many subspecies of British bramble. His collection of *Rubi* is housed in the botany department of Cambridge University and is composed of about 2,200 specimens mounted in sheets and arranged in systematic order: he had specimens of 320 of the 389 "microspecies" of *Rubus fructicosus*.

BIBLIOGRAPHY

In addition to the works cited in the text see F. G. Mann's much fuller account of Mills and his work (with a photograph and a bibliography containing 73 entries) in *Biographical Memoirs of Fellows of the Royal Society*, **6** (Nov. 1960), 201.

FREDERICK G. MANN

MILNE, EDWARD ARTHUR (*b.* Hull, England, 14 February 1896; *d.* Dublin, Ireland, 21 September 1950), *astrophysics, cosmology.*

Milne was one of the foremost pioneers of theoretical astrophysics and modern cosmology, and his name was often linked with those of Eddington and Jeans, although, unlike them, he wrote no books on astronomy for the general public. He was the eldest of three brothers who all entered on scientific careers. His father, Sydney Arthur Milne, was headmaster of a Church of England school at Hessle, near Hull, in Yorkshire. His mother, born Edith Cockcroft, lived to an advanced age and survived her famous son.

Milne went to school at Hymers College, Hull, and entered Trinity College, Cambridge, in 1914 with an open scholarship in mathematics and natural science, having gained a record number of marks in the examination. The first World War had already begun when Milne went to Cambridge, but his defective eyesight prevented him from undertaking active military duties. Early in 1916 he accepted the invitation of the biophysicist A. V. Hill to join the Anti-Aircraft Experimental Section (as it was later called) of the Munitions Inventions Department. The work was largely concerned with ballistics and sound ranging and involved many problems relating to the atmosphere of the earth. This was the beginning of Milne's deep interest in atmospheric theory. For his war services he was awarded the M.B.E.

In 1919 Milne returned to Cambridge and soon afterward was elected a fellow of Trinity College. In 1920 H. F. Newall appointed him assistant director of the solar physics observatory. In 1924 he succeeded Sydney Chapman as Beyer professor of applied mathematics at the University of Manchester, a post which he held until January 1929, when he became first Rouse Ball professor of mathematics at Oxford and fellow of Wadham College. He held both these posts for the rest of his life but was granted leave of absence during the Second World War, from 1939 to 1944, in order to work at the Ordnance Board, at Chislehurst in Kent. There he dealt with a wide variety of problems, including ballistics, rockets, sound ranging, and the optimum distribution of guns.

Important though his researches were to military science, it is by his original contributions to astrophysics and cosmology that Milne's reputation must be judged. These fall into three clearly defined parts, which can be associated with three consecutive stages in his career. From 1920 to 1929 his researches centered on problems of radiative equilibrium and the theory of stellar atmospheres. From 1929 to 1932 he was mainly concerned with the theory of stellar structure, and from 1932 onward with relativity and cosmology.

Milne's interest in stellar atmospheres was first aroused by H. F. Newall, who sensed his special fitness for the task of tackling theoretical problems associated with the outermost layers of stars, particularly those that concern the transfer of radiation through an atmosphere and those relating to the ionization of the material. These problems have to be combined, and this combination leads to subtle considerations of the detailed interaction of matter and radiation. It was in this field that Milne first made his name in astronomical circles, and it was primarily through his work that by the end of the 1920's astrophysicists were provided with the theoretical techniques appropriate for the study of stellar atmospheres.

The idealized problem of radiative transfer through a scattering atmosphere without absorption was first studied by A. Schuster in a fundamental paper in 1905, and the theory of radiative equilibrium in an absorbing atmosphere was examined by K. Schwarzschild in 1906. Milne combined and extended these pioneer investigations. He soon realized that the concept of radiative equilibrium implies the constancy of the net flux of radiation through the atmosphere. He obtained an integral equation for this net flux and used it to derive a useful approximation for the dependence of temperature on optical depth. This work was not only of great scientific importance but also yielded a result of mathematical interest, an integral equation now known as Milne's equation.

In his Smith's Prize essay of 1922 (*Philosophical Transactions of the Royal Society*, **223A** [1922], 201–255), Milne extended his theory to the law of darkening of a stellar disk toward the limb and its relation to the distribution of energy in the star's continuous spectrum, assuming radiative equilibrium with a "gray" coefficient of absorption (that is, independent of wavelength). He demonstrated how closely this prediction was obeyed by the sun. Milne was the first to investigate the inverse problem of obtaining the temperature distribution from the observed darkening toward the limb. He also showed how both this and the observed continuous spectrum could be used to infer the dependence of opacity on frequency. (Milne's method was later used to show that the sun's opacity is in fact due to the negative hydrogen ion.) An admirable account of his theory and of related investigations was given by Milne in his "Thermodynamics of the Stars," published as a part of the *Handbuch der Astrophysik* (1930). It was a milestone in the history of the subject and was the starting point for more elaborate investigations by E. Hopf, S. Chandrasekhar, and others.

In 1923 Milne began a fruitful collaboration with R. H. Fowler on the intensities and widths of absorption lines in stellar spectra. This work was based on M. N. Saha's theory of high-temperature ionization. By modifying Saha's technique, Milne and Fowler developed a theory of the maximum intensity, instead of the marginal appearance, of any given absorption line in the spectral sequence. They deduced that the pressures of the levels in stellar atmospheres at which absorption lines are formed are of the order of 10^{-4} atmosphere, a value considerably lower than had previously been assumed. They were also able to determine a reliable temperature scale for the sequence of stellar spectra, one of the greatest advances in modern astrophysics. Although much of the work was Fowler's, the original key idea was Milne's.

Another problem to which Milne made a classic contribution was that of the escape of molecules from stellar and planetary atmospheres. In particular he investigated the equilibrium of the calcium chromosphere under the balance of gravitational forces and radiation pressure. He discovered that, for varying radiation from below, this equilibrium is unstable, so that in certain circumstances atoms can ultimately be ejected from the sun with velocities of the order of 1,000 kilometers a second.

Milne's numerous papers on stellar atmospheres led to his election as a fellow of the Royal Society in 1926, at the age of thirty, and culminated in his Bakerian lecture of 1929, "The Structure and Opacity of a Stellar Atmosphere." It was for his researches in this field that he was awarded the gold medal of the Royal Astronomical Society in 1935.

The second phase of Milne's research career in astrophysics began with his move to Oxford in 1929. During the following three years he devoted his main energies to elaborating a theory of stellar structure based on a constructive mathematical criticism of the pioneer researches of Sir Arthur Eddington. Although much of Milne's criticism of Eddington's work has not been generally accepted, his methods led to important developments, notably T. G. Cowling's fundamental study of the stability of gaseous stars and Chandrasekhar's standard theory of white dwarf stars. In particular Milne seems to have been the first to

suggest an association between the nova phenomenon and the collapse of a star from one configuration to another as a result of decreasing luminosity.

In May 1932 Milne turned his attention to the problem of the expansion of the universe. It occurred to him that this phenomenon might not be essentially different from the inevitable dispersion of a gas cloud liberated in empty space. Whatever its ultimate value, this simple idea fired his imagination and led him to develop an entirely new approach to theoretical cosmology. He abandoned the mathematically recondite method of general relativity and worked as far as possible in terms of special relativity and Euclidean space. He regarded Hubble's empirical law of simple proportionality of the distances and recessional speeds of the galaxies as immediately explicable in terms of uniform motion. This meant that the common ratio of the respective distances and speeds of the galaxies provided a direct measure of the age of the universe, that is, of the time that has elapsed since the initial pointlike singularity when the universe was "created." According to the scale of extragalactic distances determined by Hubble, this age was only some 2,000 million years, which is less than the ages now assigned to the sun and earth. According to the latest data bearing on Hubble's law, based on revised estimates of extragalactic distances, the age of the universe, if it is of Milne's type, would be nearer 10,000 million years, which is about twice the age now assigned to the sun and comparable with that currently assigned to the galaxy.

Milne's world model is not in accord with general relativity, according to which a homogeneous isotropic world model that expands uniformly must be devoid of matter. Milne was not dismayed at this discrepancy, but instead made his kinematic approach to cosmology the basis of a new deductive system of theoretical physics, which came to be called kinematic relativity. He introduced the useful term "cosmological principle" to signify that observers associated with galaxies in his model and in many others, including those based on general relativity, would see similar "world pictures."

Milne went on to derive from his model many properties analogous to the laws of dynamics, gravitation, and electromagnetic theory. These developments of his theory were not generally accepted, and it is now thought that the most important effect of his work was that it led to fresh attempts to analyze the concepts of time and space-time. In particular A. G. Walker proved, as a generalization of Milne's work, that the general metric of "orthodox" relativistic cosmology could be derived without appeal to general relativity, and G. J. Whitrow showed that special relativity can be based on determinations of distance in terms of time measurement by what is now called the radar technique. Milne himself was led to the conclusion that there may be different uniform scales of time operating in nature and that some of the fundamental constants of physics may vary with the cosmic epoch. He also showed, partly in collaboration with W. H. McCrea, that there exist useful Newtonian analogues of the expanding world models of relativistic cosmology and so was the founder of modern "Newtonian" cosmology.

Milne's philosophical outlook was best expressed in his inaugural lecture at Oxford in 1929, in which he claimed that the primary aim of mathematical physics is to build up a system of theory rather than to seek the solution of particular problems.

Small in stature, Milne had outstanding qualities of mind and was a continual fount of inspiration to others as well as to himself. Although as a young man he was stricken with epidemic encephalitis ("sleepy sickness"), he made a remarkable recovery. For about twenty years after he recovered from the initial attack in 1923 he remained a man who radiated energy and vitality. Nevertheless, he did not escape the usual long-delayed aftereffects of encephalitis; and in the last five years of his life he suffered from rigidity of muscles and tremor of the left arm. Milne had the humility and simplicity of character that often goes with scientific genius, and he bore personal misfortunes with courage, dignity, and religious conviction. Both his wives predeceased him in tragic circumstances, and he was left to bring up three young daughters and a son. In his later years his heart became affected, and he died suddenly in Dublin, where he had gone to attend a scientific meeting.

BIBLIOGRAPHY

I. ORIGINAL WORKS. "Thermodynamics of the Stars" and "Theory of Pulsating Stars" are in *Handbuch der Astrophysik*, III (Berlin, 1930), pt. 1, 65–255, and pt. 2, 804–821, respectively. Two of his books are *Relativity, Gravitation and World-Structure* (Oxford, 1935); and *Kinematic Relativity* (Oxford, 1948).

Milne contributed many original papers to scientific journals, notably *Monthly Notices of the Royal Astronomical Society*, *Philosophical Transactions of the Royal Society*, *Proceedings of the Royal Society* (sec. A), *Philosophical Magazine*, and *Zeitschrift für Astrophysik*. A complete list will be found at the end of the obituary notice by McCrea (see below).

Milne also wrote a valuable and highly individual textbook, *Vectorial Mechanics* (London, 1948), and left two other books in MS which were published posthumously: *Modern Cosmology and the Christian Idea of God the Creator* (Oxford, 1952) and *Life of James Hopwood Jeans* (Cambridge, 1952).

II. SECONDARY LITERATURE. Biographical notices are W. H. McCrea, in *Obituary Notices of Fellows of the Royal Society of London*, **7** (1951), 421–443; and in *Monthly Notices of the Royal Astronomical Society*, **111** (1951), III, 160–170. The latter is followed by a short notice, pp. 170–172, by H. H. Plaskett. There is a short biographical notice by G. J. Whitrow in *Nature*, **166** (1950), 715–716. McCrea also wrote the article on Milne in the *Dictionary of National Biography, 1941–1950*, pp. 594–595.

G. J. WHITROW

MILNE, JOHN (*b*. Liverpool, England, 30 December 1850; *d*. Shide, Isle of Wight, England, 31 July 1913), *seismology*.

The son of John Milne and Emma Twycross, Milne was educated at Liverpool and King's College, London, and later studied geology and mineralogy at the Royal School of Mines. He was an ardent and adventurous traveler, starting, as a schoolboy and without parental leave, with a dangerous exploration of the Vatnajökull in Iceland. After early experience as a mining engineer in Great Britain and Germany he spent two years investigating the mineral resources of Newfoundland and Labrador, and later wrote geological notes on his observations in Egypt, Arabia, and Siberia. He visited Funk Island, off the coast of Newfoundland, where he made a large collection of skeletons of the great auk. In 1874 he served as geologist in an expedition that sought to fix the site of Mt. Sinai.

In 1875 Milne was appointed professor of geology and mining at the Imperial College of Engineering, Tokyo. The journey to Japan took eleven months, part of it crossing Mongolia by camel in subzero weather. In Japan he turned to the study of earthquakes, the field in which he became world famous. He married Tone Noritsune, daughter of Horikawa Noritsune, the high priest of Hakodate. Milne retired from Japan in 1895 and went with his wife to Shide, on the Isle of Wight, where he continued in active seismological work until his death after a short illness in 1913. Throughout his work at Shide he was assisted by the British Association for the Advancement of Science, which had established a seismological committee and appointed Milne its secretary. The work was a labor of love in which he had the devoted services of a Japanese assistant, Shinobu Hirota; many of the expenses were defrayed by Milne himself. He became a fellow of the Royal Society in 1887 and was awarded the Lyell Medal of the Geological Society of London in 1894 and a Royal Medal in 1908. The emperor of Japan conferred upon him the Order of the Rising Sun.

Milne was the most noted of a group of British scientists in Japan who pioneered modern seismology. An earthquake at Yokohama on 22 February 1880 led them, on Milne's initiative, to form with their Japanese colleagues the Seismological Society of Japan, the first organization devoted exclusively to the study of earthquakes and volcanoes. Its work was crucial at a time when seismology was developing from a qualitative science, resting largely on geological observations and concerned with such matters as cataloging earthquake effects, into a science in which precise physical measurements are brought to bear. By 1892 Milne, in association with his colleagues J. A. Ewing and T. Gray, had developed a seismograph for recording horizontal components of the ground motion. It was reliable, compact, and simple enough to be installed on a worldwide basis and to provide a global coverage of ground movements due to large earthquakes. From that date the science of seismology as a branch of geophysics advanced apace, and seismological data began to be applied to unraveling the internal structure of the earth.

Milne's researches touched on nearly all aspects of seismology. From his Tokyo records he deduced that in large earthquakes the ground accelerations can be comparable with the vertical acceleration of gravity. He showed that earthquake accelerations are in general greater—and therefore more dangerous—on soft ground than on hard rock. He initiated experiments to study properties of earthquake waves by generating artificial shocks by explosives and other means and by examining records of the ensuing ground motions. In this way he obtained records showing groups of waves corresponding to the P and S (primary and secondary) waves of modern seismology. He devised methods of locating distant earthquake sources from his records and evolved early travel-time curves of earthquake waves in terms of the distances from the source. He compiled important earthquake catalogs, including one covering the seismic history of Japan from 295 B.C. and another on destructive world earthquakes. (It is estimated that he examined about one hundred thousand documents in the course of this work.)

Starting in 1881, Milne produced the seismological *General Reports* of the British Association for the Advancement of Science. Subsequently, on the Isle of Wight, he produced the "Shide circulars," which summarized the data gathered by a worldwide network of seismological stations set up by Milne and using his instruments. The Shide circulars were the forerunners of the *International Seismological Summary*, which, after Milne's death, became the basic source of instrument-gathered data on earthquakes.

With its recent successor, the *Bulletin of the International Seismological Center*, it has long been centrally important in world research on earthquakes.

Milne's success was due to the combination of scientific brilliance and adaptability with a genial disposition and capacity to interest others in his enthusiasms. He was modest, notably hospitable, gifted with a sense of humor, and generous to others in his scientific and pecuniary help.

BIBLIOGRAPHY

I. ORIGINAL WORKS. Milne was a prolific writer who contributed nearly 2,000 pages (about two-thirds of the entire content) of the *Transactions* and *Journal* of the Seismological Society of Japan during his editorship (1880–1895). He also published papers in the *Proceedings of the Royal Society*, *Geological Magazine*, and *Bulletin of the Seismological Society of America*. He wrote *Earthquakes and Other Earth Movements* (London, 1886); two eds. of a supp. volume, *Seismology*, appeared in 1898 and 1908. Among his noted publications are the Shide circulars and *A Catalogue of Destructive Earthquakes, A.D. 7 to A.D. 1899* (London, 1912), published by the British Association.

II. SECONDARY LITERATURE. A list of Milne's publications is given by H. Woodward, in *Geological Magazine*, **9** (Aug. 1912), 337–346. For details of Milne's life, see J.W.J., "Prof. John Milne, F.R.S.," in *Nature*, **91** (Aug. 1913), 587–588; J.P., "John Milne, 1850–1913," in *Proceedings of the Royal Society*, **84A** (Mar. 1914), xxii–xxv; **91** (Aug. 1913), 587–588; and C. Davison, *The Founders of Seismology* (Cambridge, 1927), ch. 10. Milne's *Earthquakes and Other Earth Movements* was revised by A. W. Lee (Philadelphia, 1939). For an account of Milne's work at Shide, see Mrs. Lou Henry Hoover, "John Milne, Seismologist," in *Bulletin of the Seismological Society of America*, **2**, no. 1 (Mar. 1912), 2–7.

K. E. BULLEN

MILNE-EDWARDS, HENRI (*b.* Bruges, Belgium, 23 October 1800; *d.* Paris, France, 29 July 1885), *zoology.*

The son of William Edwards, an English planter and militia colonel in Jamaica, and Elisabeth Vaux, Milne-Edwards was born in Bruges, where his parents had retired. (Milne, which he added to his father's name, was the married name of his godmother and half-sister by a previous marriage of his father.) When Belgium became independent, he chose French citizenship. After medical studies in Paris he acquired a solid background in zoology and in 1832 accepted a post as professor of hygiene and natural history at the École Centrale des Arts et Manufactures. Despite his delicate health, in addition to his teaching he undertook a vast program of research on the invertebrates. His success in this field earned him the Academy of Sciences' prize in experimental physiology in 1828 and his election to the zoology section of the Academy in 1838. Three years later he was appointed to the chair of entomology of the Museum of Natural History, where he had long had a laboratory. At the time the holder of this chair was responsible for the crustaceans, the myriapods, and the arachnids as well as the insects. Twenty years later the chair of mammalogy became vacant on the death of Isidore Geoffroy Saint-Hilaire, and Milne-Edwards was transferred to it at his own request. In the meantime he had been named professor, and then dean, of the Faculty of Sciences. He was a member of most of the scientific societies of his time and a commander of the Legion of Honor.

In contrast with the tendencies of his contemporaries, Milne-Edwards had been attracted since his youth to the study of the invertebrates, especially those inhabiting the coastal regions. With his friends from the Museum and later with his students, he organized scientific excursions along the shores of the English Channel. Not content with collecting and classifying the animals, he insisted on examining them in their habitat and observed their behavior, their movements, their localization according to the level of the tides, and their modes of obtaining food and of reproducing. Milne-Edwards recorded a wealth of observations in which physiological data were joined with data from comparative morphology. This method, essentially that of ecology, appeared to afford a novel approach to the marine invertebrates, although it was inspired by one that Georges Cuvier had applied to other groups. It led Milne-Edwards to brilliant discoveries and started the creation of maritime laboratories in France and abroad.

Milne-Edwards' first investigations were primarily concerned with crustaceans. He published a series of memoirs on most of their systems, including circulation, respiration, nerve, and muscle. He began this work with his friend Jean Audouin, who preceded him in the chair of entomology at the Museum, and who accompanied him on his expeditions to the Chausey Isles; he then continued it alone.

These anatomicophysiological investigations served as the basis for the comprehensive three-volume synthesis to which Milne-Edwards dedicated many years—the classic *Histoire naturelle des crustacés* (1834–1840). In this work he developed some highly original ideas. He reported that the Crustacea are made up of some twenty homologous metameric segments, the "zoonites," which are variously fashioned according to the functions they fulfill and the mode of life (free, fixed, or parasitic) of the species. The variety of possible natural combinations, within the limits of a basic framework, is thus virtually infinite. Among Milne-Edwards' other works are *Histoire naturelle des coralliaires* (1858–1860), *Monographie des polypes des terrains paléozoïques*, and the two-volume *Recherches pour servir à l'histoire des mammifères* (1868–1874).

As an adjunct to his teaching duties at the Faculty of Sciences Milne-Edwards gathered his lectures into a fourteen-volume publication, *Leçons sur la physiologie et l'anatomie comparée de l'homme et des animaux*, the composition of which was spread over more than twenty years (1857–1881). At the same time he provided a valuable development of his ideas on animal organization in *Introduction à la zoologie générale, ou considérations sur les tendances de la nature dans la constitution du règne animal* (1858). In this book Milne-Edwards set forth his principal discoveries. These concern the variations that obtain between animal groups, variations which in the final analysis display a great fundamental principle, the law of the division of labor within organisms. Milne-Edwards suspected the existence of this law with his first studies of crustaceans, and he verified it subsequently among the other groups. In the lower animals the same tissue can adapt to different functions. He observed this phenomenon, for example, in the coelenterates, where a single fragment was seen to be capable of regenerating the entire animal. But in animals of higher zoological order, this ability tends to disappear and is progressively replaced by a specialization of the tissues. Systems, or groups of related organs, become individualized in order to carry out precise and exclusive functions: a digestive system, a respiratory system, a reproductive system, and so on.

Within each system each organ has a well-defined role. Therefore the digestive system is divided into a digestive tube and the attached glands; and the digestive tube itself consists of a first region into which food is introduced, a second in which the nutriments undergo the action of the digestive juices, and a third where substances that are useful to the organism are absorbed and where waste products are eliminated. One could reconsider each of these regions and ascertain further subdivisions within them, varying according to diet and other factors. Such specializations, which become more and more precise, determine the rank of an organism in the animal series. It is in large part through the discovery, analysis, and application of these fundamental principles that

Milne-Edwards was for years the leader of the French naturalists and that his work remained famous long after his death.

BIBLIOGRAPHY

I. ORIGINAL WORKS. In addition to those described above, Milne-Edwards' works include *Manuel de matière médicale* (Paris, 1825), written with Vavasseur; *Manuel d'anatomie chirurgicale* (Paris, 1826); *Anatomie des crustacés* (Paris, 1832); *Recherches pour servir à l'histoire naturelle du littoral de la France* (Paris, 1832); *Éléments de zoologie* (Paris, 1834); *Discours sur les progrès des sciences dans les départements* (Paris, 1861); and *Rapport sur les progrès récents des sciences zoologiques en France* (Paris, 1867).

II. SECONDARY LITERATURE. See M. Berthelot, *Notice historique sur Henri Milne-Edwards, membre de l'Académie des sciences* (Paris, 1891); *Médaille d'honneur offerte à M. H. Milne Edwards. Allocutions de MM. de Quatrefages, Blanchard et J. B. Dumas* (Paris, 1881); and G. Pennetier, *Discours sur l'évolution des connaissances en histoire naturelle*, IV, *XVIIIᵉ–XIXᵉ siècles—zoologie* (Rouen, 1920), 497–501.

JEAN ANTHONY

MINDING, ERNST FERDINAND ADOLF (or **Ferdinand Gotlibovich**) (*b*. Kalisz, Poland, 23 January 1806; *d*. Dorpat, Russia [now Tartu, Estonian S.S.R.], 13 May 1885), *mathematics*.

Minding was a son of the town lawyer in Kalisz. After graduation in 1824 from the Gymnasium at Hirschberg (now Jelenia Góra, Poland), where the family had moved in 1807, Minding studied philology, philosophy, and physics at the universities of Halle and Berlin. In mathematics he was a self-taught amateur. After graduating from Berlin University in 1827, Minding taught mathematics in Gymnasiums for several years. In 1829 he received at Halle the doctorate in philosophy for his thesis on approximating the values of double integrals; from 1831 to 1843 he lectured on mathematics at Berlin University and from 1834 also at the Berlin Bauschule. At the university he lectured in 1831 and 1834 on the history of mathematics and gave a general introduction to the foundations and goals of the mathematical sciences. During these years he published thirty works, including several textbooks. Despite intensive pedagogical and scientific activity, Minding's position at Berlin was unsatisfactory; and he eagerly accepted an invitation to the University of Dorpat, where in 1842 the chair of mathematics of the Faculty of Philosophy was divided between one of pure mathematics, which was occupied by K. E. Senff, and one of applied mathematics, which was vacant. From 1843 to 1883 Minding was at the University of Dorpat as a full professor, giving both general and special courses in algebra, analysis, geometry, theory of probability, mechanics, and physics. In 1850 the Faculty of Philosophy was divided into that of physicomathematics and that of history-philology, and in 1851 Minding was elected to a four-year term as dean of the former division. In 1864 Minding and his family became Russian citizens. (In 1838 he had married Augusta Regler, and they had several children.) In the same year he was elected a corresponding member, and in 1879 an honorary member, of the St. Petersburg Academy of Sciences.

Minding's most important discoveries were in the differential geometry of surfaces; in these works he brilliantly continued the researches of Gauss, which had been published in 1828. In his first paper (1830), which dealt with the isoperimetric problem of determining on a given surface the shortest closed curve surrounding a given area (on the plane it is the circumference of a circle), he introduced the concept of geodesic curvature. It was independently discovered in 1848 by O. Bonnet, and it was he who named it geodesic curvature. Minding soon proved, as did Bonnet after him, the invariance of the geodesic curvature under bending of the surface. Neither of them knew that the same results had been presented in an earlier, unpublished paper of Gauss's (1825).

Minding's studies on the bending or the applicability of surfaces were especially remarkable. He first examined the bending of a particular class of surfaces (1838); incidentally, in the case of surfaces of revolution, he studied an example of the "applicability on a principal basis," which later became a preferred research topic for his disciple K. M. Peterson and for Peterson's followers in Moscow. He then proceeded to the general problem of determining the conditions for applicability of surfaces. Gauss had discovered (1828) that if one surface can be isometrically applied to another (so that the bending does not alter the lengths of curves), then the total curvature will be the same at all corresponding points.

In his article "Wie sich entscheiden lässt, ob zwei gegebene krumme Flächen auf einander abwickelbar sind oder nicht . . ." (1839), Minding stated the following sufficient condition for applicability: Two given surfaces of equal constant total curvature are applicable to one another isometrically, and this can be done in infinitely many different ways. He also investigated the corresponding problem for surfaces with a variable total curvature. Today "Minding's theorem" is found in all textbooks of differential geometry. Minding's papers, as well as Gauss's work of 1828, were great influences on the development of this branch of mathematics. In the article "Beiträge zur Theorie der kürzesten Linien auf krummen Flächen," which was published in Crelle's *Journal für die reine und angewandte Mathematik* (1840), Minding pointed out that when the trigonometric functions are replaced by corresponding hyperbolic ones, the trigonometric formulas in spherical trigonometry for the geodesic triangles on the surfaces with constant positive curvature are converted into the hyperbolic formulas for the surfaces with negative curvature. In 1837, Lobachevski showed (in an article that also appeared in Crelle's *Journal*) that the same relation exists between the trigonometric formulas for the sphere and the formulas in his "imaginary" (hyperbolic) geometry. The confrontation of these results might have led to the conclusion that two-dimensional hyperbolic geometry can be (partly) interpreted as the geometry of geodesics on a surface of constant negative curvature; but it was not until 1868 that Beltrami established this connection.

Starting from Euler's ideas, Minding proposed the method of solving the differential equation $M(x, y) \, dx + N(x, y) \, dy = 0$, where M and N are polynomials of some degree, based on determining the integrating factor by means of particular integrals of the equation. Minding's method, expounded in the paper "Beiträge zur Integration der Differentialgleichungen erster Ordnung zwischen zwei Veränderlichen," for which he received in 1861 the Demidov Prize of the St. Petersburg Academy of Sciences, was developed further by A. N. Korkin and others. Darboux (1878) worked independently, followed by E. Picard and others, in the same direction. Minding also published works on algebra (the elimination problem), the theory of continued fractions, the theory of algebraic functions, and analytic mechanics.

BIBLIOGRAPHY

I. Original Works. Minding's writings include "Ueber die Curven kürzesten Perimeters auf krummen Flächen," in *Journal für die reine und angewandte Mathematik*, **5** (1830), 297–304; "Bemerkung über die Abwickelung krummer Linien von Flächen," *ibid.*, **6** (1830), 159–161; "De valore integralium duplicum quam proxime inveniendo" (his doctoral diss., in the archives of the University of Halle), pub. with minor modifications as "Ueber die Berechnung des Näherungswertes doppelter Integrale," *ibid.*, 91–95; *Anfangsgründe der höheren Arithmetik* (Berlin, 1832); *Handbuch der Differential- und Integralrechnung nebst Anwendung auf die Geometrie* (Berlin, 1836); *Handbuch der Differential- und Integralrechnung und ihrer Anwendungen auf Geometrie und Mechanik. Zweiter Teil, enthaltend die Mechanik* (Berlin, 1838); "Ueber die Biegung gewisser Flächen," in *Journal für die reine und angewandte Mathematik*, **18** (1838), 297–302; "Wie sich entscheiden lässt, ob zwei gegebene krumme Flächen auf einander abwickelbar sind oder nicht; nebst Bemerkungen über die Flächen von unveränderlichem Krümmungsmasse," *ibid.*, **19** (1839), 370–387; "Beiträge zur Theorie der kürzesten Linien auf krummen Flächen," *ibid.*, **20** (1840), 323–327; and "Beiträge zur Integration der Differentialgleichungen erster Ordnung zwischen zwei Veränderlichen," in *Mémoires de l'Académie des sciences de St. Petersbourg*, 7th ser., **5**, no. 1 (1863), 1–95, also pub. separately in Russian trans. (St. Petersburg, 1862).

II. Secondary Literature. See R. I. Galchenkova *et al., Ferdinand Minding. 1806–1885* (Leningrad, 1970), which includes a complete list of Minding's works, pp. 205–210 (nos. 1–72), and extensive secondary literature, pp. 210–220 (nos. 73–289); A. Kneser, "Übersicht der wissenschaftlichen Arbeiten Ferdinand Minding's nebst biographischen Notizien," in *Zeitschrift für Mathematik und Physik*, Hist.-lit. Abt., **45** (1900), 113–128; I. Z. Shtokalo, ed., *Istoria otechestvennoy matematiki*, II (Kiev, 1967); A. Voss, "Abbildung und Abwickelung zweier Flächen auf einender abwickelbarer Flächen," in *Encyklopädie der mathematischen Wissenschaften*, III, pt. 6a (Leipzig, 1903), 355–440; and A. P. Youschkevitch, *Istoria matematiki v Rossii do 1917 g.* (Moscow, 1968).

A. Youschkevitch

MINEUR, HENRI (*b*. Lille, France, 7 March 1899; *d*. Paris, France, 7 May 1954), *astronomy, astrophysics, mathematics.*

Although he was first on the admissions list of the École Normale Supérieure in 1917, Mineur enlisted in the army and did not enter the school until after the end of World War I. After passing the *agrégation* in mathematics in 1921, he taught at the French *lycée* in Düsseldorf while pursuing the mathematical research he had begun in 1920. He received his doctorate in science in 1924 for his work on functional equations, in which he established an addition theorem for Fuchsian functions.

Mineur had been interested in astronomy from his youth, and in 1925 he left his teaching post to become astronomer at the Paris observatory. He made important contributions to several fields related to mathematical astronomy: celestial mechanics, analytic mechanics, statistics, and numerical calculus. His treatise on the method of least squares has become a classic.

It was in stellar astronomy, however, that Mineur's work was most sustained and fruitful. In particular, he detected the variation in the speed of near stars according to the distance from the galactic plane and the retrograde rotation of the system of globular clusters. He also corrected the coordinates of the galactic center and studied interstellar absorption. As early as 1944 he showed that an important correction had to be made in the zero of the period-luminosity relation of the Cepheids; this change led to a doubling of the scale of distances in the universe. All these results have been confirmed by recent investigations.

Mineur was a brilliant and unusual person who became thoroughly involved in many areas. Between 1940 and 1944 he was a member of the Resistance. He was a founder of the Centre National de la Recherche Scientifique and of the observatory of Saint-Michel in Haute-Provence. At his initiative the Institute d'Astrophysique was created at Paris in 1936; he was its director until his death, which occurred after five years of a serious heart and liver ailment. Mineur twice won prizes of the Académie des Sciences.

BIBLIOGRAPHY

I. Original Works. In kinematics and stellar dynamics Mineur's principal writings are "Rotation de la galaxie," in *Bulletin astronomique*, **5** (1925), 505–543; "Étude de mouvements propres moyens d'étoiles," *ibid.*, **6** (1930), 281–304; "Recherches sur les vitesses radiales résiduelles . . .," *ibid.*, **7** (1931), 321–352, written with his wife; *Éléments de statistique . . . stellaire*, Actualités Scientifiques et Industrielles, no. 116 (Paris, 1934); *Photographie stellaire . . .*, *ibid.*, no. 141 (Paris, 1934); *Dénombrement d'étoiles . . .*, *ibid.*, no. 225 (Paris, 1935); "Recherches sur la distribution de la matière absorbante . . .," in *Annales d'astrophysique*, **1** (1938), 97–128; "Sur la rotation galactique . . .," *ibid.*, 269–281; "Équilibre des nuages galactiques . . .," *ibid.*, **2** (1939), 1–244; "Zéro de la relation période-luminosité . . .," *ibid.*, **7** (1944), 160–186; and "Recherches théoriques sur les accélérations stellaires," *ibid.*, **13** (1950), 219–242. Some of these investigations are summarized in *L'espace interstellaire* (Paris, 1947).

In celestial and analytical mechanics, see especially "La mécanique des masses variables . . .," in *Annales scientifiques de l'École normale supérieure*, 3rd ser., **50** (1933), 1–69; "Étude théorique du mouvement séculaire de l'axe terrestre," in *Bulletin astronomique*, **13** (1947), 197–252; "Quelques propriétés . . . équations de la mécanique," *ibid.*, **13** (1948), 309–328; and "Recherche . . . dans le groupe canonique linéaire," *ibid.*, **15** (1950), 107–141.

In statistics and numerical calculus, see *Technique de la méthode des moindres carrés* (Paris, 1938); "Nouvelle méthode de lissage . . . période d'un phénomène," in *Annales d'astrophysique*, **6** (1943), 137–158; "Sur la meilleure représentation d'une variable aléatoire . . .," *ibid.*, **7** (1944), 17–30; and *Techniques de calcul numérique* (Paris, 1952).

His works in analysis include his doctoral dissertation, "Théorie analytique des groupes continus finis," in *Journal de mathématiques pures et appliquées*, 9th ser., **4** (1925),

23–108; and "Calcul différentiel absolu," in *Bulletin des sciences mathématiques*, 2nd ser., **52** (1928), 63–76.

II. Secondary Literature. See D. Barbier, "Henri Mineur," in *Annales d'astrophysique*, **17** (1954), 239–242; and J. Dufay, "Henri Mineur," in *Astronomie*, **70** (1956), 235–238.

Jacques R. Lévy

MINKOWSKI, HERMANN (*b.* Alexotas, Russia [now Lithuanian S.S.R.], 22 June 1864; *d.* Göttingen, Germany, 12 January 1909), *mathematics*.

Minkowski was born of German parents who returned to Germany and settled in Königsberg [now Kaliningrad, R.S.F.S.R.] when the boy was eight years old. His older brother Oskar became a famous pathologist. Except for three semesters at the University of Berlin, he received his higher education at Königsberg, where he became a lifelong friend of both Hilbert, who was a fellow student, and the slightly older Hurwitz, who was beginning his professorial career. In 1881 the Paris Academy of Sciences had announced a competition for the Grand Prix des Sciences Mathématiques to be awarded in 1883, the subject being the number of representations of an integer as a sum of five squares of integers; Eisenstein had given formulas for that number but without proof. The Academy was unaware that in 1867 H. J. Smith had published an outline of such a proof, and Smith now sent a detailed memoir developing his methods. Without knowledge of Smith's paper, the eighteen-year-old Minkowski, in a masterly manuscript of 140 pages, reconstructed the entire theory of quadratic forms in n variables with integral coefficients from Eisenstein's sparse indications. He gave an even better formulation than Smith's because he used a more natural and more general definition of the genus of a form. The Academy, unable to decide between two equally excellent, and substantially equivalent, works, awarded the Grand Prix to both Smith and Minkowski.

Minkowski received his doctorate in 1885 at Königsberg; he taught at Bonn until 1894, then returned to Königsberg for two years. In 1896 he went to Zurich, where he was Hurwitz' colleague until 1902; Hilbert then obtained the creation of a new professorship for him at Göttingen, where Minkowski taught until his death.

From his Grand Prix paper to his last work Minkowski never ceased to return to the arithmetic of quadratic forms in n variables ("n-ary forms"). Ever since Gauss's pioneering work on binary quadratic forms at the beginning of the nineteenth century, the generalization of his results to n-ary forms had been the goal of many mathematicians, including Eisenstein, Hermite, Smith, Jordan, and Poincaré. Minkowski's most important contributions to the theory were (1) for quadratic forms with rational coefficients, a characterization of equivalence of such forms under a linear transformation with rational coefficients, through a system of three invariants of the form and (2) in a paper of 1905, the completion of the theory of reduction for positive definite n-ary quadratic forms with real coefficients, begun by Hermite. The latter had defined a process yielding in each equivalence class (for transformations with integral coefficients) a finite set of "reduced" forms; but it was still possible for this set to consist in more than one form. Minkowski presented a new process of "reduction" giving a unique reduced form in each class. In the space of n-ary quadratic forms (of dimension $n(n + 1)/2$), the "fundamental domain" of all reduced forms proves to be a polyhedron; Minkowski made a detailed investigation of the relation of this domain to its neighbors and computed its volume, which enabled him to obtain asymptotic formulas for the number of equivalence classes of a given determinant, when the value of that determinant tends to infinity.

This 1905 paper was greatly influenced by the geometric outlook that Minkowski had developed fifteen years earlier—the "geometry of numbers," as he called it, his most original achievement. He was led to it by the theory of ternary quadratic forms. Following brief indications given by Gauss, Dirichlet had developed a geometrical method of reduction of positive definite ternary forms; Minkowski's brilliant idea was to use the concept of volume in conjunction with this geometric method, thus obtaining far better estimates than had been possible before. To make matters simpler, consider a binary positive definite quadratic form $F(x, y) = ax^2 + 2bxy + cy^2$. To say that F takes a value m when $x = p, y = q$ are integers, means, geometrically, that the ellipse E_m of equation $F(x, y) = m$ passes through the point (p, q). To find the minimum M of all such values m, obtained for p, q not both 0, Minkowski observed that for small α, certainly the ellipse E_α will not contain any such points; if one considers the ellipse $\frac{1}{2}E_\alpha$ and translates it by sending its center to every point (p, q) with integral coordinates, one obtains an infinite pattern of ellipses which do not touch each other. When α increases and reaches the value M, some of the corresponding ellipses will touch each other but no two will overlap. Now, if $A = ac - b^2$ is the area of the ellipse E_1, the ellipse $\frac{1}{2}E_M$ has area $AM^2/4$, $AM^2/4$ and the total area of the nonoverlapping ellipses which are translations of $\frac{1}{2}E_M$ and which have centers

at the points (p, q) with $|p| \leqslant n$ and $|q| \leqslant n$ is $(2n + 1)^2(AM^2/4)$. It is easy to see, however, that there is a constant $c > 0$ independent of n, such that all these ellipses are contained in a square of center 0 and of side $2n + 1 + c$, so that

$$(2n + 1)^2(AM^2/4) \leqslant (2n + 1 + c)^2;$$

letting n grow to infinity gives the inequality

$$\frac{AM^2}{4} \leqslant 1 \quad \text{or} \quad M \leqslant \frac{2}{\sqrt{A}}.$$

Not only can this argument be at once extended to spaces of arbitrary finite dimension, but Minkowski had a second highly original idea: He observed that in the preceding geometric argument, ellipses could be replaced by arbitrary convex symmetric curves (and, in higher-dimensional spaces, by symmetric convex bodies). By varying the nature of these convex bodies with extreme ingenuity (polyhedrons, cylinders), he immediately obtained far-reaching discoveries in many domains of number theory. For instance, by associating to an algebraic integer x in a field of algebraic numbers K of degree n over the rationals, the point in n dimensions having as coordinates the rational integers which are the coefficients of x with respect to a fixed basis, Minkowski gave lower bounds for the discriminant of K, which in particular proved that when $n > 1$, the discriminant may never be equal to 1 and that there are only a finite number of fields of discriminants bounded by a given number.

Minkowski's geometric methods also enabled him to reach a far better understanding of the theory of continued fractions and to generalize it into an algorithm which, at least theoretically, gives a criterion for a number to be algebraic. It was similar in principle to Lagrange's well-known criterion that quadratic irrationals are characterized by periodic continued fractions; but Minkowski also showed that, for his criterion, periodicity occurs in only a small number of cases, which he characterized completely. Finally, if, for instance, one considers (as above, but in three dimensions) an ellipsoid $F(x, y, z) = 1$ in relation to the lattice L of points with integral coordinates, the largest possible number M will be obtained when the translated ellipsoids are "packed together" as closely as possible. If one makes a linear transformation of the space transforming the ellipsoid in a sphere, L is transformed into another lattice consisting of linear combinations with integral coefficients of three vectors. The problem of finding the largest M, then, is equivalent to the "closest packing of spheres" in space, when the centers are at the vertices of a

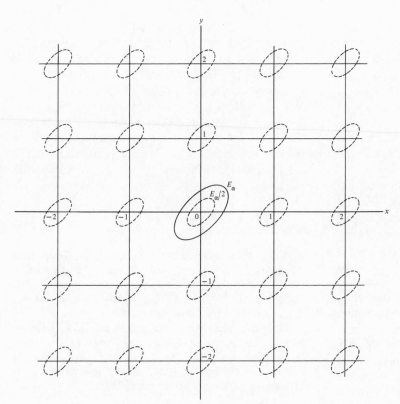

FIGURE 1

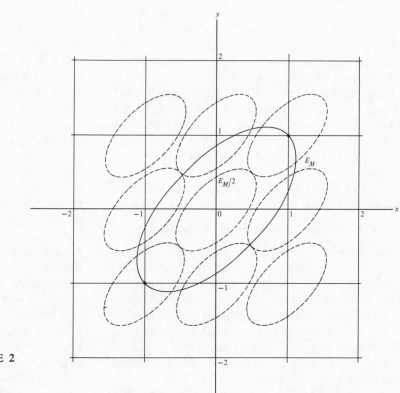

FIGURE 2

413

lattice L'; one has to find the lattice L' that gives this closest packing. Minkowski began the study of that difficult problem (which extends to any n-dimensional space) and of corresponding problems when spheres are replaced by some other type of convex set (particularly polyhedrons); they have been the subject of fruitful research ever since.

The intensive use of the concept of convexity in his "geometry of numbers" led Minkowski to investigate systematically the geometrical properties of convex sets in n-dimensional space, a subject that had barely been considered before. He was the first to understand the importance of the notion of hyperplane of support (both geometrically and analytically), and he proved the existence of such hyperplanes at each point of the boundary of a convex body. Long before the modern conception of a metric space was invented, Minkowski realized that a symmetric convex body in an n-dimensional space defines a new notion of "distance" on that space and, hence, a corresponding "geometry." His ideas thus paved the way for the founders of the theory of normed spaces in the 1920's and became the basis for modern functional analysis.

The evaluation of volumes of convex bodies led Minkowski to the very original concept of "mixed volume" of several convex bodies: when K_1, K_2, K_3 are three convex bodies in ordinary space and t_1, t_2, t_3 are three real numbers $\geqslant 0$, the points $t_1 x_1 + t_2 x_2 + t_3 x_3$, when x_j varies in K_j for $j = 1, 2, 3$, fill a new convex body, written $t_1 K_1 + t_2 K_2 + t_3 K_3$. When the volume of this new convex body is computed, it is seen to be a homogeneous polynomial in t_1, t_2, t_3 and the mixed volume $V(K_1, K_2, K_3)$ is the coefficient of $t_1 t_2 t_3$ in that polynomial. Minkowski discovered remarkable relations between these new quantities and more classical notions: if K_1 is a sphere of radius 1, then $V(K_1, K, K)$ is one third of the area of the convex surface bounding K; and $V(K_1, K_1, K)$ is one third of the mean value of the mean curvature of that surface. He also proved the inequality between mixed volumes

$$V(K_1, K_2, K_3)^2 \geqslant V(K_1, K_1, K_3)\, V(K_2, K_2, K_3),$$

from which he derived a new and simple proof of the isoperimetric property of the sphere. As a beautiful application of his concepts of hyperplane of support and of mixed volumes, Minkowski showed that a convex polyhedron having a given number m of faces is determined entirely by the areas and directions of the faces, a theorem that he generalized to convex surfaces by a passage to the limit. He also determined all convex bodies having constant width.

Minkowski was always interested in mathematical physics but did not work in that field until the last years of his life, when he participated in the movement of ideas that led to the theory of relativity. He was the first to conceive that the relativity principle formulated by Lorentz and Einstein led to the abandonment of the concept of space and time as separate entities and to their replacement by a four-dimensional "space-time," of which he gave a precise definition and initiated the mathematical study; it became the frame of all later developments of the theory and led Einstein to his bolder conception of generalized relativity.

BIBLIOGRAPHY

Minkowski's writings were collected in *Gesammelte Abhandlungen*, D. Hilbert, ed., 2 vols. (Leipzig–Berlin, 1911). Among his books are *Geometrie der Zahlen* (Leipzig, 1896; 2nd ed., 1910); and *Diophantische Approximationen* (Leipzig, 1907; repr. New York, 1957).

On Minkowski's work, see Harris Hancock, *Development of the Minkowski Geometry of Numbers* (New York, 1939); and Frederick W. Lanchester, *Relativity. An Elementary Explanation of the Space-Time Relations As Established by Minkowski* (London, 1935).

J. Dieudonné

MINNAERT, MARCEL GILLES JOZEF (*b.* Bruges, Belgium, 12 February 1893; *d.* Utrecht, Netherlands, 26 October 1970), *astronomy.*

Minnaert, one of the pioneers of solar research in the first half of the twentieth century, was professor at the University of Utrecht and director of its observatory from 1937 to 1963. His parents were teachers at normal schools and many of his other relatives were involved in teaching, which background undoubtedly determined his later interest in science and education. He studied biology at the University of Ghent and in 1914 defended—with the highest distinction—his doctoral thesis, "Contributions à la photobiologie quantitative."

At that time the University of Ghent, although situated in the heart of the Dutch-speaking part of Belgium, used French as the language of instruction, as did the other universities and most of the secondary schools in Flemish Belgium. Minnaert, who gradually realized that the linguistic problem was also a social problem related to the underdeveloped status of Flanders, joined associations of Flemish students and intellectuals who sought political equality and, later, relative independence (federalism) for both parts of Belgium. They also wished to convert the University of Ghent to the Dutch language. During the German occupation of Belgium in World War I, the latter goal was attained.

The urgent need for teachers at the new Flemish university induced Minnaert to go to Leiden in 1915–1916 to study physics. After his return to Ghent he was named associate professor of physics and remained in that post until 1918. At the end of the war those who had cooperated in the linguistic reform of the University of Ghent were accused of collaboration with the Germans, and many received long prison sentences. In order to escape that fate Minnaert moved to Utrecht, to which place he was attracted by the technique of objective photometry, then being developed at its physics laboratory by W. H. Julius, Ornstein, and Moll. He readily understood the importance of the technique because of his previous experience in photobiology, in which specialty the lack of quantitative measures was deeply felt. The director, W. H. Julius, had just set up a solar spectrograph—at that time the third in the world—intending to apply spectrophotometric techniques to the solar spectrum. Minnaert became interested in this work, and after Julius' death in 1924 he assumed the main responsibility for solar research at Utrecht. In 1925 he defended—cum laude—another thesis, this time in physics:"Onregelmatige straalkromming"("Irregular Refraction of Light").

At that time the basic requirements were available for quantitative research in solar physics: Bohr's atomic model, Saha's ionization law, the developments of quantum theory, and the new technique of quantitative spectrophotometry made possible the quantitative interpretation of the solar spectrum. Minnaert developed the concepts "equivalent width" and "curve of growth"; the theory of weak lines was carried further; and the intensity measurements of sunspots made possible the physical interpretation of these phenomena. This work, performed in the physics laboratory at Utrecht, culminated in 1940 in *Photometric Atlas of the Solar Spectrum* (in collaboration with Houtgast and Mulders), which is still a standard reference.

In 1937 Minnaert was named director of the University of Utrecht observatory, which he transformed into an astrophysical institute devoted mainly to the investigation of solar and stellar spectra. Yet his interests were wider than the sun: he studied comets and gaseous nebulae and was involved in lunar photometry; and during the last few years of his life he was a member of a working group of the International Astronomical Union concerned with naming the newly discovered formations on the hemisphere of the moon that is not visible from the earth. In 1970, two months before his death, Minnaert was elected president of the Commission for the Moon of the International Astronomical Union. His broad interest in science and nature led him to write these books: *De Natuurkunde van het vrije veld* ("Physics of the Open Field"), translated into many languages; *Dichters over Sterren* ("Poets on Stars"); and *De sterrekunde en de mensheid* ("Astronomy and Mankind").

In 1928 Minnaert married Maria Boergonje Coelingh, who defended her thesis in physics in 1938; they had two sons. Philosophically Minnaert defended determinism; politically he had strong left-wing sympathies but was too committed to science to link himself to any political party. Yet his political ideas were sufficiently known to the Germans for him to be imprisoned in 1942–1944.

Minnaert spoke ten languages fluently and could read in even more. Even so he was an enthusiastic defender of Esperanto—attracted by the simplicity and regularity of this artificial language which, he felt, could be of great importance for both scientific and social communication. He loved music and painting and cultivated both actively. Above all, Minnaert had a strong interest in humanity and its problems. He was admired and loved by his friends, students and co-workers, and respected by those who did not agree with his social or political ideas. In the last few years of his life he was very active in an international group purchasing books for the University of Hanoi, North Vietnam.

Minnaert was a member of the Royal Netherlands Academy of Arts and Sciences, of the Royal Belgian Academy of Science, Letters and Fine Arts, of the Kungl. Vetenskapsamhället of Uppsala, and of the Instituto de Coimbra; and associate of the Royal Astronomical Society of London. In 1947 he received the gold medal of the Royal Astronomical Society and in 1951 that of the Astronomical Society of the Pacific (Bruce Medal). He held honorary doctorates from the universities of Heidelberg, Moscow, and Nice.

BIBLIOGRAPHY

Minnaert's main publications were his diss., *Onregelmatige straalkromming* (Utrecht, 1925); *De Natuurkunde van de Zon* (The Hague, 1936); *De betekenis der zonnephysica voor de astrophysica* (Utrecht, 1937); *De Natuurkunde van het vrije veld* (Zutphen, 1937); *Photometric Atlas of the Solar Spectrum* (Amsterdam, 1940), with G. F. Mulders and J. Houtgast; *De sterrekunde en de mensheid* (The Hague, 1946); *Dichters over Sterren* (Arnhem, 1949); and *Practical Works in Elementary Astronomy* (Dordrecht, 1969). He was the author of many papers, of which a review is given in M. Minnaert, "Forty Years of Solar Spectroscopy," in C. de Jager, ed., *The Solar Spectrum*, the proceedings of a symposium held at the occasion of the seventieth anniversary of the birth of M. G. J. Minnaert (Dordrecht, 1965).

Minnaert also prepared the articles on Hoek, Kaiser, Hortensius, W. Julius, Pannekoek, and Stevin for this *Dictionary*.

C. DE JAGER

MINOT, CHARLES SEDGWICK (*b*. Roxbury, Massachusetts, 23 December 1852; *d*. Milton, Massachusetts, 19 November 1914), *anatomy, embryology*.

Minot was the second of three sons of William Minot and Katharine Sedgwick. A paternal ancestor was Jonathan Edwards; and on both sides, there were several distinguished lawyers and public figures. Growing up on his wealthy father's country estate, he early became interested in natural history and at the age of seventeen published articles on insect and bird life. He graduated from the Massachusetts Institute of Technology in 1872 and then entered the graduate school of Harvard College, where he worked under Henry P. Bowditch, spending a summer with Louis Agassiz at Penikese, Massachusetts. In 1873 he went to Leipzig to work with Karl Ludwig and Rudolf Leuckart. He was also at Paris for a few months with Louis-Antoine Ranvier and at Würzburg.

After his return to America in 1876, Minot completed in 1878 the requirements for his Harvard doctorate in science. After two years of private biological research, in 1880 he joined the Harvard faculty, at first in the dental school and, after 1883, in the department of histology and embryology of the school of medicine. There he began what became an outstanding collection of vertebrate embryos. To facilitate the work of sectioning them, he invented in 1886 the automatic rotary microtome, ever since in worldwide use. In 1892 Minot published his chief work, *Human Embryology*, a masterly summation of an unwieldy literature and a highly original presentation of the major problems of that branch of science. Among his many research accomplishments were an account of the microscopic structure of the human placenta and a description of the blood channels in the liver since known by his term "sinusoids."

Minot's wide-ranging intellect led him into very broad fields of thought. For a few years he was active in the American Society for Psychical Research, from which he withdrew when finally convinced of its unscientific outlook. Deep reflection about the nature of life, its origin, course, and termination guided his protracted studies of the growth of animals and the progressive changes in cell structure from birth to death.

Minot exerted wide influence on American biology of his time in his books, numerous papers in scientific journals, and lectures, all presented with clarity and stylistic elegance. Reserved in professional manner and sometimes sharply critical of other workers in matters of scientific judgment, he was a genial participant in the professional societies of natural history, anatomy, and physiology. He was one of a small group of biologists and medical scientists who broadened the study and teaching of anatomy in the United States to include not only gross morphology but also embryology, histology, and physical anthropology, and transformed the American Association of Anatomists from a small society with limited interests to its present breadth and strength.

Minot was elected to the National Academy of Sciences in 1897 and served as president of the American Society of Naturalists, the American Association of Anatomists, and the American Association for the Advancement of Science. His eminence in human and comparative embryology was recognized by honorary degrees from Yale, Toronto, St. Andrews, and Oxford universities and by a visiting professorship at Berlin.

BIBLIOGRAPHY

I. ORIGINAL WORKS. Minot's primary publications are *Human Embryology* (New York, 1892); "A Bibliography of Vertebrate Embryology," in *Memoirs of the Boston Society of Natural History*, **4**, no. 11 (1893), 487–614; *Laboratory Textbook of Embryology* (Philadelphia, 1903); and *The Problem of Life, Growth, and Death* (New York, 1908), in addition to about 180 scientific papers and lectures.

II. SECONDARY LITERATURE. On Minot and his work, see (listed chronologically) Henry H. Donaldson, "Charles Sedgwick Minot," in *Science*, n.s. **40** (1914), 926–927, a character study; Charles W. Eliot, "Charles Sedgwick Minot," *ibid.*, **41** (1915), 701–704; Frederic T. Lewis, "Charles Sedgwick Minot," in *Anatomical Record*, **10** (1915–1916), 133–164, with portrait and bibliography; Edward S. Morse, "Charles Sedgwick Minot, 1852–1914," in *Biographical Memoirs. National Academy of Sciences*, **14** (1920), 263–285, with portrait and complete bibliography.

GEORGE W. CORNER

MINOT, GEORGE RICHARDS (*b*. Boston, Massachusetts, 2 December 1885; *d*. Brookline, Massachusetts, 25 February 1950), *medicine*.

Minot was the eldest son of James Jackson Minot, a physician, and Elizabeth Whitney, from whom he inherited the inquisitiveness and industry of cultured forebears successful in Boston's business and professional life. In 1915 Minot married Marian Linzee

Weld of Milton, Massachusetts. He was an amateur naturalist, cultivator of irises, and summer sailor of the coast of Maine.

Minot received the A.B. from Harvard College in 1908 and the M.D. from Harvard Medical School in 1912. He was professor of medicine at Harvard University and director of the Harvard Medical Unit at the Boston City Hospital from 1928 to 1948. His outstanding contribution to medical science was the discovery in 1926, with William P. Murphy, of the successful treatment of pernicious anemia by liver feeding, for which they shared the 1934 Nobel Prize in physiology or medicine, with George H. Whipple of Rochester, N. Y.

While in the private practice of medicine in Boston with an appointment as associate in medicine at the Massachusetts General Hospital (1918–1923), Minot had become convinced of the inadequacy of the diets of many patients with pernicious anemia. Consequently, he was prepared to make a thorough trial of the effects of liver feeding when reported by Whipple as especially potent in preventing an experimental anemia due to chronic, periodic blood removal in dogs. In Minot's patients a prompt increase in the number of reticulocytes (young red blood cells) objectified the repeated association observed between daily liver feeding, clinical improvement, and progressive lessening of their hitherto fatally progressive anemia. This observation led shortly to the development of therapeutic liver extracts and to research by others eventually identifying their active principle as vitamin B_{12} in 1948.

Minot's work and that of numerous pupils during the decade after 1926 initiated a new era in clinical hematology by replacing the largely morphologic studies of the blood and of the blood-forming and blood-destroying organs with dynamic measurements of their functions. Today the use of radioisotopic labeling of the formed elements of the blood, together with biochemical and biophysical analyses, are extending this revolution in depth. Among the many significant contributions of Minot and his associates were early work on blood transfusion, blood coagulation, and blood platelets, and classical studies of the hematological effects of irradiation in chronic leukemias and lymphoid tumors. Later came successful treatment of hypochromic anemia with sufficient iron; and demonstration that hemophilia is due to lack of a globulin substance present in normal plasma.

BIBLIOGRAPHY

Minot's principal writings include "The Development of Liver Therapy in Pernicious Anaemia: A Nobel Lecture," in *Lancet* (1935), **1**, 361–364.

On Minot and his work, see W. B. Castle, "The Contributions of George Richards Minot to Experimental Medicine," in *New England Journal of Medicine*, **247** (1952), 585–592; and F. M. Rackemann, *The Inquisitive Physician: The Life and Times of George Richards Minot, A.B., M.D., D.Sc.* (Cambridge, Mass., 1956).

W. B. CASTLE

MIQUEL, FRIEDRICH ANTON WILHELM (*b.* Neuenhaus, Germany, 24 October 1811; *d.* Utrecht, Netherlands, 23 January 1871), *botany*.

Miquel was the son of a country physician. His university studies and subsequent academic career took place in the Netherlands. Trained as a physician at the University of Groningen, Miquel specialized in botany and was director of the Rotterdam botanic garden (1835–1846), professor of botany at Amsterdam (1846–1859) and at Utrecht (1859–1871), and director of the Rijksherbarium at Leiden (1862–1871). His numerous (296 items in his bibliography) botanical publications deal mainly with the floras of the former Netherlands East Indies, Surinam, and Japan, and with the Cycadaceae, Moraceae, and Piperaceae. He collaborated with C. F. P. von Martius on the *Flora brasiliensis*; was the first to publish a comprehensive flora of the Netherlands East Indies; and played an important background role in the development of the East Indian quinine industry. Miquel was also the founder of the University of Utrecht herbarium.

BIBLIOGRAPHY

I. ORIGINAL WORKS. Miquel's main writings are *Commentarii phytographici, quibus varia rei herbariae capita illustrantur* (Leiden, 1839); *Monographia Cycadearum* (Utrecht, 1842); *Sertum exoticum contenant des figures et descriptions de plantes nouvelles ou peu connues* (Rotterdam, 1843); *Systema Piperacearum* (Rotterdam, 1843); "Symbolae ad floram surinamensem," a series of 12 articles in *Linnaea*, **18–22** (1844–1849); "Illustrationes Piperacearum," *Nova acta Academiae Caesareae Leopoldino Carolinae germanicae naturae curiosorum*, **21**, supp. 1 (1846); *Stirpes surinamenses selectae* (Leiden, 1850); *Plantae junghuhnianae. Enumeratio plantarum, quas in insulis Java et Sumatra detexit Fr. Junghuhn* (Leiden, 1851[–1857]); *Flora van Nederlandsch Indië*, 3 vols. (Amsterdam–Leipzig, 1855–1859); and *Annales Musei botanici Lugduno Batavi*, 4 vols. (Amsterdam, 1863–1869).

II. SECONDARY LITERATURE. See F. A. Stafleu, "F. A. W. Miquel, Netherlands Botanist," in *Wentia*, **16** (1966), 1–95, a biography with complete bibliography and secondary references to published and unpublished sources; and *Taxonomic Literature* (Utrecht, 1967), pp. 315–324, for further bibliographical details.

FRANS A. STAFLEU

MIRBEL, CHARLES FRANÇOIS BRISSEAU DE (*b.* Paris, France, 27 March 1776; *d.* Paris, 12 September 1854), *botany.*

The son of a jurist, Mirbel began his studies in Paris at a private boarding school run by the Congregation of the Picpus; the Revolution forced him to interrupt his education and to seek refuge with his parents at Versailles. When he was conscripted during the Terror, he hid in Toulouse, waiting for conditions to become more settled. Through the aid of a friend Mirbel returned to Paris, where, in the office of Lazare Carnot, then member of the Committee of Public Safety, he did work in topography and military history.

In 1796, through his position as secretary to General Henri Clarke, Mirbel learned of a proscription list that included the name of a friend's relative. He warned the man immediately so that he could escape. Clarke ordered Mirbel's arrest, but he fled to the Pyrenees, profiting from his enforced exile by studying physics, mineralogy, and botany. His first research, carried out in collaboration with Louis Ramond de Carbonnières, professor of natural history at the École Centrale of Tarbes, dealt with the geological configuration of the Pyrenees.

In 1798, after two years of exile—and in order to escape military conscription to serve in the Egyptian campaign—Mirbel returned to Paris and obtained a post in the Museum of Natural History.

The following year Mirbel presented a memoir on ferns to the Academy of Sciences, and in 1801 and 1802 he submitted a series of articles on the structure of plants and on the seed and embryo. Thus he inaugurated the study of microscopical plant anatomy in France. He showed that the characteristics of the seed and of the embryo are identical for all plants of the same natural family, thereby laying the foundations of embryogenic classifications, which are still used.

In 1802 Mirbel married a young woman who was related through her mother to the Dandolo family of Venice. His wife's influence helped him to obtain the post of head gardener at Malmaison, the country palace of Napoleon and Josephine. On 9 May 1806 Mirbel presented to the Academy remarks on a system of comparative plant anatomy based on the organization of the flower and a memoir on plant fluids. At the end of 1806, seeking the financial security he had always lacked, Mirbel entered the service of Louis Bonaparte, king of Holland. On 17 March 1807 he was named a correspondent of the Academy of Sciences.

Mirbel's new duties afforded him sufficient time to pursue his research on plant organography and physiology. He was elected a member of the botany section of the Academy of Sciences on 31 October 1808. He was appointed supplementary professor of botany at the Faculty of Sciences in Paris, then the center of a renaissance in scientific education; Desfontaines, Gay-Lussac, and Poisson were teaching there. Mirbel's work benefited greatly from his association with the Faculty. Between 1809 and 1815, in a series of notes and memoirs and in his lectures, he challenged orthodox opinion by asserting the independence of plant cells in the different tissues. His *Éléments de botanique* (1815), which revealed his talents as a draftsman, contributed to the acceptance of his ideas.

In 1816, after Napoleon's abdication, Mirbel accepted the posts of secretary-general of the Ministry of the Interior and *maître des requêtes* of the Council of State, using his positions to obtain passage of measures that would advance science. He resigned on 20 February 1820 when, following a cabinet reorganization, his friend Élie Decazes, who had helped him to secure those posts, was named ambassador to England. Mirbel joined Decazes in England, where he met several English scientists.

On his return to France, Mirbel, whose wife had died, married Lezinka Rue, curator of Louis XVIII's art collection. He was appointed professor-administrator of the Jardin des Plantes in 1829, replacing Bosc, who had died. Mirbel's research activity was at its height from 1825 to 1846. Using the microscope he followed the first stages of the formation of the tissues and studied the origin, development, and organization of the phloem and wood. In his papers on the development of the ovule, on the structure of *Marchantia*, on the formation of the embryo, on the disposition of the tissues in the stems and roots of the monocotyledons, and on the cambium the rigor of the draftmanship strengthened the presentation of the material.

Between 1843 and 1845 Mirbel demonstrated that the cambium contains ternary substances and various nitrogenous materials, which include the most active parts of the plant, those that secrete cellulose and produce all the organic and mineral substances. In this pioneering work, therefore, living protoplasm was differentiated from the cell wall. The formation of the cuticle and the lignification of the vessels were described by means of simple chemical reactions in which Mirbel anticipated plant cytochemistry. Through the study of vascularization in date trees and other monocotyledons, he demonstrated that the plant is formed of two parts that begin at the collar: one descends into the soil, and the other rises above the substratum.

Mirbel was continuing his investigations when his second wife died of cholera in 1849. Exhausted and bereaved, Mirbel gradually lost his memory. He spent his last years in peaceful retirement, cared for by his daughter. He died in 1854, at the age of seventy-eight.

BIBLIOGRAPHY

I. ORIGINAL WORKS. A list of 67 papers written or coauthored by Mirbel is in Royal Society *Catalogue of Scientific Papers*, IV, 405–407. His principal works include *Traité d'anatomie et de physiologie végétales*, 2 vols. (Paris, 1802); *Histoire naturelle générale et particulière des plantes*, 18 vols. (Paris, 1802–1806), to which he contributed; *Éléments de physiologie végétale et de botanique*, 3 vols. (Paris, 1815); and *Physique végétale, ou Traité élémentaire de botanique* (Paris, 1832).

II. SECONDARY LITERATURE. See Élie Margollé, *Vie et travaux de M. de Mirbel d'après sa correspondance et des documents inédits* (St. Germain, 1863); and M. Payen's biography of Mirbel, in Michaud, *Biographie universelle*, new ed., XXVIII, 382–387; based largely on his *Éloge historique de M. de Mirbel* (Paris, 1858).

A. NOUGARÈDE

MISES, RICHARD VON (*b.* Lemberg, Austria [now Lvov, U.S.S.R.], 19 April 1883; *d.* Boston, Massachusetts, 14 July 1953), *mathematics, mechanics, probability.*

Von Mises was the second son of Arthur Edler von Mises, a technical expert with the Austrian state railways, and Adele von Landau. His elder brother, Ludwig, became a prominent economist; the younger brother died in infancy. After earning his doctorate in Vienna in 1907, Richard taught at universities in Europe and Turkey and then, from 1939, in the United States. In 1944 he became Gordon McKay professor of aerodynamics and applied mathematics at Harvard. During his European period, he married Hilda Pollaczek-Geiringer, one of his pupils. Proud to call himself an applied mathematician, he was the founder and editor, from 1921 to 1933, of the well-known *Zeitschrift für angewandte Mathematik und Mechanik*. He was a scholar with wide interests, who wrote perceptively on the philosophy of science from a positivist point of view, and who was also an authority on the poet Rilke.

Von Mises' early preoccupation with fluid mechanics led him into aerodynamics and aeronautics, subjects that in the years immediately before 1914 had received a major fillip from the success of heavier-than-air flying machines. He himself learned to fly and in the summer of 1913 gave what is believed to be the first university course on the mechanics of powered flight. After the outbreak of World War I he helped develop an Austrian air arm, and in 1915 the team he led produced a giant 600-horsepower military plane with an original wing profile of his own design (wing theory was perhaps his specialty).

In 1916 he published a booklet on flight, under the auspices of the Luftfahrarsenal in Vienna. It went into many enlarged editions and is the basis of *Theory of Flight*, published with collaborators in English toward the end of World War II. Other, allied topics to which he contributed were elasticity, plasticity, and turbulence. He also worked in various branches of pure mathematics, particularly numerical analysis.

Von Mises' concern with the border areas of mathematics and the experimental sciences was reflected in his giving much thought to probability and statistics. In 1919 he published two papers that, although little noticed at the time, inaugurated a new look at probability that was destined to become famous. The background to this contribution was the slow buildup, during the nineteenth century, of a frequency theory of probability, in contrast to the received classical theory of Laplace. The fathers of the frequency theory, Poisson in France and Ellis in England, had identified the probability of a given event in specified circumstances with the proportion of such events in a set of exactly similar circumstances, or trials. The weakness of this position is the necessary finiteness of the set, and there is no obvious way of extending the idea to those very large or infinite sets that in practice must be sampled for probabilistic information. The Cambridge logician John Venn improved the theory in 1866 by equating probability with the relative frequency of the event "in the long run," thereby introducing a mathematical limit and the infinite set. Nevertheless, even this reformation failed to make the theory compelling enough to tempt mathematicians to put it into rigorous terms; and Keynes in his *Treatise on Probability* (1921) expressed his inability to assess the frequency theory adequately because it had never been unambiguously formulated. This was the deficiency that Von Mises attempted to correct.

What Von Mises did was to splice two familiar notions, that of the Venn limit and that of a random sequence of events. Let us consider the matter in terms of a binary trial, the outcome of which is either a "success" or otherwise. Given an endless sequence of such trials, in the sense of Bernoulli binomial sampling, what can we say about it probabilistically? A meaningful answer, said Von Mises, is possible only if we postulate (1) the mathematical existence of a limiting value to the fraction successes/trials, and (2) the invariance of this limit for all possible infinite subsequences formed by any rule of place selection of trials that is independent of their outcomes. Then the limit can be called the probability of a success in the particular system. It then follows that the probability of a single event is formally meaningless; random sampling is a *sine qua non*; and the sequence (otherwise collective or sample space) must be clearly defined before any discussion of probability—in this strictly operational sense—can be undertaken.

The intuitive appeal of Von Mises' limiting-frequency theory is strong, and its spirit has influenced all modern statisticians. Remarkably, however, the mathematics of the theory, even after sophistication by leading probabilists, has never been rendered widely acceptable, and some authorities today do not mention Von Mises. In advanced work, the measure-theoretic approach initiated by Kolmogorov in 1933 is most favored. On the practical side, his statistical writings suffered from a foible: he denied the importance of small-sample theory. Von Mises' *Probability, Statistics, and Truth*, published in German in 1928 and in English in 1939, is not a pedagogic text but a semipopular account, very subjective in tone, good on the historic side, and in general notably stimulating.

BIBLIOGRAPHY

I. ORIGINAL WORKS. The core of Von Mises' work is to be found in the following six books: *Probability, Statistics and Truth* (New York, 1939; 2nd ed., 1957); *Theory of Flight* (New York, 1945); *Positivism, a Study in Human Understanding* (Cambridge, Mass., 1951); *Mathematical Theory of Compressible Fluid Flow* (New York, 1958), completed by Hilda Geiringer and G. S. S. Ludford; *Selected Papers of Richard von Mises*, Philipp P. Frank *et al.*, eds. (Providence, R.I., 1963); and *Mathematical Theory of Probability and Statistics* (New York, 1964), edited and complemented by Hilda Geiringer. His first papers on probability are "Fundamentalsätze der Wahrscheinlich-keitsrechnung," in *Mathematische Zeitschrift*, **4** (1919), 1–97; and "Grundlagen der Wahrscheinlichkeitsrech-nung," *ibid.*, **5** (1919), 52–99. A good bibliography of 143 works is in Garrett Birkhoff, Gustav Kuerti, and Gabor Szego, eds., *Studies in Mathematics and Mechanics Presented to Richard von Mises* (New York, 1954), which contains a portrait.

II. SECONDARY LITERATURE. The opening chapters of *Mathematical Theory of Probability and Statistics* (see above) contain a survey by Hilda Geiringer of other workers' developments of Von Mises' controversial theory, as well as a synopsis of Kolmogorov's rival theory and its relation to that of Von Mises. A critical essay review of this book by D. V. Lindley is in *Annals of Mathematical Statistics*, **37** (1966), 747–754. W. Kneale, *Probability and Induction* (London, 1949), marshals some logical arguments against limiting-frequency theories. On the other hand, H. Reichenbach, *The Theory of Probability* (Berkeley, 1949); Rudolf Carnap, *Logical Foundations of Probability* (Chicago, 1950); and Karl Popper, *The Logic of Scientific Discovery* (New York, 1958), are all, in different ways and with various emphases, derivative and sympathetic.

NORMAN T. GRIDGEMAN

MITCHELL, ELISHA (*b.* Washington, Connecticut, 19 August 1793; *d.* on Mount Mitchell, North Carolina, 27 June 1857), *natural history.*

Elisha Mitchell was the eldest son of Abner Mitchell, a farmer with substantial property, and Phoebe Eliot, a direct descendant of John Eliot, the "apostle to the Indians," who translated the Bible into Algonkian. A precocious child, he learned to read at an early age and possessed a nearly photographic memory. He attended school in Litchfield County, Connecticut, where he showed an interest in scholarship of all kinds, especially in natural science. Mitchell graduated from Yale in 1813 and in 1819 married Maria Sybil North, the educated daughter of a physician, by whom he had three sons (two of whom died in infancy) and four daughters. All his children received an excellent education, much of it imparted at home by their parents.

In 1816 Mitchell became a tutor at Yale, and in 1817 he was appointed professor of mathematics and natural philosophy at the University of North Carolina, in Chapel Hill. In the same year he received a license to preach and was ordained a minister of the Presbyterian church in 1821. In 1825 he transferred to the chair of chemistry, geology, and mineralogy at the university, a post that he held until his death. He received the honorary degree of doctor of divinity from the University of Alabama in 1838.

Mitchell accepted the scriptural account of the creation, and yet his *Elements of Geology*, a work published when he had been a minister for over twenty years, contained a sentence that showed him to be ahead of most of his contemporaries in accepting the principle of uniformitarianism: "A knowledge of the present will assist in explaining the past" (p. 64).

Mitchell was endowed not only with culture and learning but with humor, and he employed all these gifts in doing work in various fields. He earned respect as an authority on botany, geography, and geology, particularly of North Carolina. In his many cross-country trips on horseback and on foot, he not only took abundant scientific notes but made numerous friends. In 1842 he published the first geologic map of North Carolina and was the first to explain the origin of its gold deposits. He also wrote on meteorology and was a pioneer in applied soil science and in conservation.

Mitchell's lectures were all the more effective for being enlivened with humor. He was state geologist in 1826 and, during two brief periods, was acting president of the University of North Carolina. In addition he served as justice of the peace and town commissioner for Chapel Hill, preached on Sundays in the university chapel and the village church, prepared student manuals on natural history, botany, chemistry, geology, mineralogy, and certain religious topics, and contributed several scientific papers to the *American Journal of Science*.

Mitchell's richly varied career came to a tragic end in his sixty-fourth year. In 1839 he determined the altitude of the North Carolina peak now called Mount Mitchell, the highest mountain in the eastern United States. On a return to the summit in 1857 to verify his measurements and to attempt to settle a priority dispute, he lost his life in a fall from a cliff into a pool, in which he drowned. He is buried at the top of the mountain.

BIBLIOGRAPHY

I. ORIGINAL WORKS. Mitchell's writings include *Agricultural Speculations*, North Carolina Board of Agriculture (Raleigh, N.C., 1825), 49–58; *Report on the Geology of North Carolina*, pt. 3 (Raleigh, 1827), 1–27; "On the Character and Origin of the Low Country of North Carolina," in *American Journal of Science*, **13** (1828), 336–347; "On the Geology of the Gold Region of North Carolina," ibid., **16** (1829), 1–19, **17** (1829), 400; "On the Effect of Quantity of Matter in Modifying the Force of Chemical Attraction," *ibid.*, **16** (1829), 234–242; "On a Substitute for Welther's Tube of Safety, with Notices on other Subjects," *ibid.*, **17** (1830), 345–350; "On the Proximate Causes of Certain Winds and Storms," *ibid.*, **19** (1831), 248–292; "Analysis of the Protogaea of Leibnitz," *ibid.*, **20** (1831), 56–64; "On Storms and Meteorological Observations," *ibid.*, **20** (1831), 361–369; "Notice of the Height of Mountains in North Carolina," *ibid.*, **35** (1839), 377–380; *Elements of Geology With an Outline of the Geology of North Carolina* (n.p., 1842), with map; and *Diary of a Geological Tour*, James Sprunt Historical Monograph, no. 6 (Chapel Hill, N.C., 1905), with introduction and notes by K. P. Battle.

II. SECONDARY LITERATURE. See K. P. Battle, *History of the University of North Carolina*, I (Raleigh, N.C., 1907), II (1912); H. S. Chamberlain, "Life Story of Elisha Mitchell, D.D., 1793–1857, Professor in the University of North Carolina From 1818 Until His Death in 1857," unpublished MS, University of North Carolina Library, Chapel Hill (1951); F. B. Dexter, *Biographic Sketches of the Graduates of Yale College*, VI (New York, 1912), 586–589; G. P. Merrill, *Contributions to the History of American Geology*, U.S. National Museum Annual Report for 1904 (Washington, 1906), 285–286, 706; and *The First One Hundred Years of American Geology* (New York, 1964), 114–116; and Charles Phillips, "A Sketch of Elisha Mitchell," in *Journal of the Elisha Mitchell Scientific Society*, **1** (1883–1884), 9–18, with portrait on frontispiece.

ELLEN J. MOORE

MITCHELL, MARIA (*b.* Nantucket, Massachusetts, 1 August 1818; *d.* Lynn, Massachusetts, 28 June 1889), *astronomy.*

Maria Mitchell, the first woman astronomer in America, was the third of ten children of William and Lydia Coleman Mitchell. She was educated chiefly by her father, a man of wide culture. As a small child she helped him with the observations that he made for the purpose of checking the chronometers of whaling ships, while in 1831, during an annular eclipse of the sun, she assisted him in timing the contacts that he used to determine the longitude of Nantucket.

When she was eighteen, Maria Mitchell became librarian of the Nantucket Atheneum, a post that she held for twenty-four years. At the same time she conducted astronomical observations, sweeping the skies on clear evenings. It was thus that, on 1 October 1847, she discovered a new telescopic comet, for which discovery she was awarded a gold medal by the king of Denmark and became world famous.

From 1849 until 1868 Maria Mitchell was employed by the U.S. Nautical Almanac Office to compute the ephemerides of the planet Venus. She resigned her post there reluctantly when her academic duties at Vassar Female College, of which she had been a faculty member since its founding in 1865, demanded her full attention. At Vassar she was both professor of astronomy and director of the college observatory, positions that she fulfilled with great distinction until her death.

Maria Mitchell was the first woman to be elected to the American Academy of Arts and Sciences; she also belonged to the American Philosophical Society and to the American Association for the Advancement of Women (of which she was president in 1870 and subsequently chairman of its Committee on Women's Work in Science). Of the many memorials established in her honor after her death, the Nantucket Maria Mitchell Association (founded in 1902, with headquarters at her birthplace that incorporate an observatory, a science library, and a natural science museum) is of particular interest.

BIBLIOGRAPHY

Maria Mitchell's published scientific papers were short and few. Apart from the notes listed in Poggendorff, she wrote a few less technical articles for *Atlantic Monthly*, *Hours at Home*, and *Century*.

On Maria Mitchell and her work, see Phoebe Mitchell Kendall, *Maria Mitchell. Life, Letters, and Journals* (Boston, 1896); Helen Wright, *Sweeper in the Sky* (New York, 1950), and "Mitchell, Maria," in *Notable American Women*, II (Cambridge, Mass., 1971), 554–556; and *Annual Reports. Nantucket Maria Mitchell Association*.

DORRIT HOFFLEIT

MITCHELL, SILAS WEIR (*b.* Philadelphia, Pennsylvania, 15 February 1829; *d.* Philadelphia, 4 January 1914), *medicine, neurology.*

Mitchell's father, John Kearsley Mitchell, was professor of medicine at Jefferson Medical College, where the younger Mitchell graduated in 1850. He then spent a year in Europe attending the lectures of Claude Bernard and the microscopist Charles Philippe Robin. In 1851 he joined his father's Philadelphia medical practice, a practice that S. W. Mitchell continued until his own death in 1914.

Between 1852 and 1863 Mitchell published more than thirty papers on a variety of topics ranging from the toxic effects of rattlesnake venom to the crystalline forms of uric acid. The physiological bent of these early papers reflected his Paris experience; and though Mitchell always maintained an interest in toxicology, pharmacology, and physiology, his later writings were generally more clinically oriented. The nature of his clinical work was deeply affected by his medical experiences in the Civil War. He treated many patients with nerve injuries, post-traumatic epilepsy, and other neurological conditions at the Turner's Lane Hospital, the 400-bed army neurological hospital in Philadelphia where Mitchell was assigned.

In collaboration with William Keen, Jr., and George Morehouse, he published in 1864 the important study *Gunshot Wounds and Other Injuries of Nerves*. Mitchell later extended this treatise into a definitive monograph, *Injuries of Nerves and Their Consequences* (1872). By this time he was widely recognized as the outstanding American neurologist. His additional contributions to clinical neurology included papers on posthemiplegic chorea,[1] causalgia and traumatic neuralgia,[2] the effects of weather on painful amputation stumps,[3] various forms of headache,[4] and a rare condition he called erythromelalgia.[5] Mitchell also investigated the physiology of the cerebellum[6] and the cutaneous distribution of nerves,[7] described the cremasteric reflex,[8] and (with Morris J. Lewis) gave an early account of the phenomenon of sensory reinforcement of the deep tendon reflexes.[9]

Mitchell published two general neurological works, *Lectures on Diseases of the Nervous System—Especially in Women* (1881) and *Clinical Lessons on Nervous Diseases* (1897). His preeminence as a neurologist brought him many patients with functional and neurotic complaints. He was especially interested in hysteria, and a large portion of the two general treatises is devoted to the description and treatment of hysteria and related disorders. Mitchell popularized the "rest cure" in the management of many kinds of nervous diseases, both functional and organic.[10] His concern with therapeutics also resulted in a number of papers on the pharmacology of the bromides, lithium, and chloral hydrate.

In addition, Mitchell wrote novels, short stories, and poetry; indeed, in his later years his fame as a man of letters equaled his reputation as a physician. His home on Walnut Street was a longtime center of Philadelphia's intellectual life. Mitchell's intimates included William Osler, William Henry Welch, and John Shaw Billings.

NOTES

1. "Post-Paralytic Chorea," in *American Journal of the Medical Sciences*, **61** (1874), 342–352.
2. "Clinical Lecture on Certain Painful Affections of the Feet," in *Philadelphia Medical Times*, **3** (1872), 81–82, 113–115.
3. "The Relations of Pain to Weather," in *American Journal of the Medical Sciences*, **73** (1877), 305–329.
4. "Headaches, From Heat Stroke, From Fevers, After Meningitis, From Over Use of the Brain, From Eye Strain," in *Medical and Surgical Reporter*, **31** (1874), 67–70.
5. "On a Rare Vaso-motor Neurosis of the Extremities, and on the Maladies With Which It May Be Confounded," in *American Journal of the Medical Sciences*, **76** (1878), 17–36.
6. "Researches on the Physiology of the Cerebellum," *ibid.*, **57** (1869), 320–338.
7. "The Supply of Nerves to the Skin," in *Philadelphia Medical Times*, **4** (1874), 401–403.
8. "The Cremaster-Reflex," in *Journal of Nervous and Mental Diseases*, **6** (1879), 577–586.
9. "Physiological Studies of the Knee-jerk, and of the Reactions of Muscles Under Mechanical and Other Excitants," in *Medical News*, **48** (1886), 169–173, 198–203.
10. "Rest in Nervous Disease: Its Use and Abuse," in *A Series of American Clinical Lectures*, E. C. Seguin, ed., I (New York, 1875), 83–102; also in the semipopular book by Mitchell, *Fat and Blood* (Philadelphia, 1877).

BIBLIOGRAPHY

I. ORIGINAL WORKS. Mitchell wrote more than 170 medical and scientific papers. To the books and articles mentioned in the text and notes should be added the following: *Wear and Tear* (Philadelphia, 1871); *Nurse and Patient*

(Philadelphia, 1877); and *Doctor and Patient* (Philadelphia, 1888), all popular works.

Mitchell's lifelong interest in the physiological effects of snake venom led to a number of papers, including "Researches Upon the Venoms of Poisonous Snakes," in *Smithsonian Contributions to Knowledge*, **26** (1886), 1–186, written with Edward Reichert.

A complete bibliography of Mitchell's medical, scientific, and literary works may be found in Richard D. Walter, *S. Weir Mitchell, M.D., Neurologist: A Medical Biography* (Springfield, Ill., 1970), 207–222.

II. SECONDARY LITERATURE. Anna Robeson Burr, *Weir Mitchell—His Life and Letters* (New York, 1929), is an important source of letters and includes an autobiographical fragment. Ernest Earnest, *S. Weir Mitchell—Novelist and Physician* (Philadelphia, 1950), emphasizes his literary achievements. Mitchell's scientific and medical work is extensively considered in the volume by Richard Walter (see above). This book also contains a full bibliography of additional secondary literature.

WILLIAM F. BYNUM

MITSCHERLICH, EILHARD (*b.* Neuende, Oldenburg, Germany, 7 January 1794; *d.* Berlin, Germany, 28 February 1863), *chemistry, mineralogy.*

Mitscherlich was the son of a minister, also named Eilhard Mitscherlich, and Laura Meier. He received his early education at Jever, in the school directed by the historian F. C. Schlosser, who encouraged him to apply himself to the liberal arts. In 1811 Mitscherlich entered the University of Heidelberg, where he studied Oriental languages; he continued this pursuit at the University of Paris, which he entered in 1813. He learned Persian with particular enthusiasm and hoped to be a member of the legation that Napoleon intended to send there. When Napoleon's fall ended that prospect, Mitscherlich returned to Germany, where in 1817 he enrolled in the University of Göttingen to read science and medicine—a choice dictated by his determination to reach the Orient, as a ship's doctor if not as a diplomat.

Simultaneously with his medical studies, Mitscherlich completed the research on ancient Persian texts for which he was awarded the doctorate. At the same time, his interest increasingly turned toward chemistry, which was taught at Göttingen by F. Strohmeyer, who, in addition to his lectures, gave his students the opportunity to carry out certain laboratory experiments.

In 1818 Mitscherlich went to Berlin to work in the laboratory of the botanist Heinrich Link. There he began to study crystallography. He observed that the crystals of potassium phosphate and potassium arsenate appeared to be nearly identical in form and, his curiosity spurred, asked Gustav Rose to instruct him in exact crystallographic methods so that he could make precise measurements. He then applied spherical trigonometry to the data that he obtained, and was thereby able to confirm his first impression. He reported this finding in an article entitled "Ueber die Krystallisation der Saltze, in denen das Metall der Basis mit zwei Proportionen Sauerstoff verbunden ist," published in the *Abhandlungen der Preussischen Akademie der Wissenschaften* for 1818–1819 and translated into French for publication in the *Annales de chimie* in the following year.

In this important article Mitscherlich discussed the crystals of the sulfates of various metals. He demonstrated that these sulfates—as well as the double sulfates of potassium and ammonium—crystallize in like forms, provided that they bind the same quantity of water of crystallization. Thus, for sulfates of copper and manganese, he found the ratio between the oxygen of the oxide and that of the water of crystallization to be 1:5; while for zinc, nickel, and magnesium, the ratio is 1:7. He further stated his hope "that through crystallographic examination the composition of bodies will be determined with the same certainty and exactness as through chemical analysis."

Mitscherlich met Berzelius in 1819, when the latter was passing through Berlin. Berzelius had heard of Mitscherlich's work and recognized the significance of his findings. When the Prussian Ministry of Education offered Berzelius the chair of chemistry at the University of Berlin, left vacant on the death of Klaproth, Berzelius suggested appointing Mitscherlich in his stead. Mitscherlich was thought to be too young to fill the post, however, and a compromise was arranged whereby he would be sent to work with Berzelius in Stockholm for two years, in order to enlarge his knowledge of chemistry. In the course of this fruitful partnership Mitscherlich worked in Berzelius' laboratory, visited and studied the mines and metallurgical works at Falun, and acquired further experience in chemical analysis and inorganic chemistry. Most important, he continued his work on isomorphism.

In his second article on his crystallographic researches, "Om Förhållandet einellan Chemiska Sammansättningen och Krystallformen hos Arseniksyrade och Phosphorsyrade Salter" ("On the Relation Between the Chemical Composition and the Crystal Form of Salts of Arsenic and Phosphoric Acids"), published in *Kungliga Svenska vetenskapsakademiens handlingar* in 1822, Mitscherlich reported on new observations that he had made with Berzelius. Among his findings were that

... each arsenate has its corresponding phosphate, composed according to the same proportions, combined with the same amount of water and having nearly equal solubilities in water and acids; in fact the two series of salts differ in no respect except that the radical of the acid in one series is arsenic, while in the other it is phosphorus. ... Certain elements have the property of producing the same crystal form when in combination with an equal number of atoms of one or more common elements, and the elements, from this point of view, can be arranged in certain groups. For convenience I have called the elements belonging to the same group ... *isomorphous.*

He then stated his conclusion that

... an equal number of atoms, combined in the same way produce the same crystal forms and the crystal form does not depend on the nature of the atoms, but only on their number and mode of combination.

Mitscherlich further noted that the hydrate crystals of $NaO^2 + 2 PO^5$ (written today as $NaH_2PO_4 \cdot H_2O$) and $NaO^2 + 2 AsO^5$ ($NaH_2AsO_4 \cdot H_2O$) ordinarily exist in two different forms; but since the phosphate crystal also exists in another form identical to the usual form of the arsenate crystal, the criterion for isomorphism is met. He was thus the first to recognize the phenomenon now called dimorphism. In his next paper, "Ueber die Körper, welche in zwei verschiedene Formen krystallisieren," published in *Abhandlungen der Preussischen Akademie der Wissenschaften* for 1822–1823, he investigated this phenomenon in greater detail and presented a number of examples, including the rhombic and monoclinic forms of sulfur. (He thus refuted Haüy's crystallographic axiom, whereby crystal angles, particularly the angles of cleavage, are characteristic of a given substance.)

The statement of the law of isomorphism, made early in his career, marks Mitscherlich's most important contribution to chemistry—indeed, Berzelius considered Mitscherlich's discovery to be the most significant since that of chemical proportions. Berzelius himself found Mitscherlich's work to be of great use; he was at this time concerned with the determination of the atomic weights of the elements and the law of isomorphism provided him with a valuable tool. Since the relative atomic weight of an element could be determined only through a knowledge of how many atoms are contained in the molecule, Berzelius' task was simplified by the application of Mitscherlich's law—once he had established the atomic composition of one of the isomorphic compounds, those of the others could be assumed to correspond to it. He was thus able to check the atomic weights that he had set out in his *Lärbok i kemien*

of 1814 and presented corrected values for twenty-one elements in the second edition, which was published in 1826.

Mitscherlich refined his work on isomorphism from time to time throughout his scientific life. When it became clear that his original formulation of the law was too broad, he modified it (in 1832) to state more precisely that only certain elements can substitute for each other in crystal form. During the following years, too, Mitscherlich established the isomorphism that exists between a number of specific compounds, including sulfates, metallic selenates, potassium chromate and potassium manganate, and potassium perchlorate and potassium permanganate. All of his later work was conducted in Berlin, where he returned in 1822 to take up the post of assistant professor of chemistry at the university. He became full professor three years later. He was also a member of the Berlin Academy of Sciences and director of its laboratory, located in the observatory. He made extensive use of this installation for teaching as well as for research, since the university offered no facilities for practical instruction in chemistry.

Besides his sojourn in Sweden, Mitscherlich made other trips abroad to work with foreign scientists. In 1823–1824 he was in Paris, where he collaborated with Fresnel in investigating the alteration of the double refraction of crystals as a function of temperature; he also met Thenard and Gay-Lussac. In 1824 he visited Humphry Davy, Faraday, Wollaston, and Dalton in England, where he inspected a number of factories. Back in Berlin, he worked in a number of areas of both organic and inorganic chemistry, in addition to his studies of isomorphism.

In inorganic chemistry Mitscherlich investigated the higher compounds of manganese, including the mixture of manganate and permanganate that Glauber, in the seventeenth century, had called the "chameleon mineral." Mitscherlich offered an explanation for the transformations of this substance, establishing that its red and green salts are the derivatives of two different (manganic and permanganic) acids; he determined their chemical composition in 1830. Aschoff produced the anhydride of permanganic acid in Mitscherlich's laboratory, and Mitscherlich himself was the first to obtain iodine azide and selenic acid.

During the same period Mitscherlich was also concerned with vapor-density determinations. He modified Dumas's apparatus by employing a metal bath for measuring higher temperatures; he was thus able to determine the vapor densities of bromine, sulfur phosphorus, arsenic, mercury, sulfur trioxide, phosphorus pentachloride, calomel, and arsenic oxide.

His results were highly accurate in most instances. He further measured the pressure of water vapor over Glauber's salt, in response to a suggestion of Berzelius, who had hoped—erroneously—that a numerical indication of the affinity of water for various substances might be determined from the differences between the pressure of water vapor over those substances.

In organic chemistry, Mitscherlich in 1834 obtained benzene by the dry distillation of the calcium salt of benzoic acid. He found the product of the distillation to be identical with the "bicarburet of hydrogen" that Faraday had isolated from compressed oil-gas five years earlier. From his observation that benzoic acid might be a compound of benzene and carbon dioxide, Mitscherlich concluded that all organic acids must consist of hydrocarbons plus carbonic acid—a misconception that was long perpetuated. By vapor-density measurements, he reached the formula C_3H_3 (the present C_6H_6) for the composition of benzene, a quantity that corresponds in volume to one atom of hydrogen.

Mitscherlich went on to conduct experiments on various benzene derivatives. He obtained nitrobenzene from the reaction of benzene with fuming nitric acid (ordinary nitric acid does not react with benzene) and benzenesulfonic acid from the reaction of benzene with fuming sulfuric acid. He also obtained azobenzene, trichlorobenzene, hexachlorobenzene, and their corresponding bromine derivatives.

In 1834 Mitscherlich also showed that a mixture of ether and water distills out of a mixture of alcohol and diluted sulfuric acid; he suggested that in this case the sulfuric acid acts as a dehydrating agent. From this observation he developed his contact theory, whereby certain chemical reactions can take place only in the presence of certain other substances. Mitscherlich's theory was a direct predecessor of Berzelius' catalyst theory, which was, in fact, a refinement of it.

Mitscherlich further sought to explain fermentation by this theory, the "contact" in this process being yeast, which is necessary for the conversion of sugar into alcohol. He observed that if a test tube filled with yeast is dipped into a sugar solution, no fermentation occurs, whereas if the sugar is introduced directly into the tube that contains the yeast—or is brought into contact with it—fermentation does take place. Since it is not necessary that a contact agent be a chemical substance in Mitscherlich's theory, he was able to accept Cagniard de La Tour's assertion (of 1842) that yeast is a microorganism; indeed, Mitscherlich was the first chemist to do so.

In his experiments on fermentation Mitscherlich further discovered that yeast does not act directly on cane sugar; instead, an invert sugar, a kind of levorotatory "modified cane sugar" identical to the sugar formed by the action of acids on cane sugar, is formed first. He also established that 0.001 percent acid is sufficient to invert sugar solutions. He gave impetus to the sugar industry both by developing the first practical polarization apparatus and by devising a method to control polarization through polarimetric analysis.

Mitscherlich worked to improve the methods and accuracy of both organic and inorganic analytical chemistry. In 1855 he developed a toxicological detection index for white phosphorus, by which the substance to be tested was distilled with steam and the presence of phosphorus determined by luminescence in the condenser of the distilling apparatus. He was also the first to employ a mixture of potassium carbonate and sodium carbonate to produce fusion. For analyzing organic compounds, Mitscherlich constructed a combustion apparatus that differed from those of Berzelius and Liebig in that the combustion tube was heated by a spirit lamp, rather than by burning charcoal. The oxygen produced by the potassium chlorate was used to regenerate cupric oxide. Liebig, who was never on very good terms with Mitscherlich, pronounced the apparatus to be of little value.

Mitscherlich's early interest in geology and mineralogy continued throughout his life. He was particularly concerned with the production of artificial minerals through the fusion of silica with various metallic oxides, and achieved some valuable results in such experiments. In his last years he made a number of journeys to the most important European volcanoes to gather data toward a general theory of volcanoes, the subject of his last, posthumously published, articles. (It must be noted, however, that his work in volcanology produced little of significant value.)

Mitscherlich was perhaps most successful as a writer of textbooks. His *Lehrbuch der Chemie* was first published in 1829; by 1847 it had had four new editions in German, as well as two editions in French and one in English. The work contained Mitscherlich's lectures on all aspects of pure and applied chemistry, as well as a considerable amount of material on physics, all illustrated with a number of beautiful woodcuts. The lectures themselves are characterized by their exemplary clarity and ingenious experiments; the book was highly praised by Mitscherlich's contemporaries, including Berzelius and Liebig. As a teacher, Mitscherlich was aware that his students needed practical instruction; although his efforts to this end were in fact little more than perfunctory, he did take them on visits to factories.

Mitscherlich married and had five children, of whom the youngest, Alexander, also became a chemist. It was he, rather than his father, who discovered the Mitscherlich process for extracting cellulose from wood through boiling with calcium bisulfite, upon which discovery the German cellulose industry was based.

BIBLIOGRAPHY

I. Original Works. A more complete list of Mitscherlich's writings can be found in Poggendorff, II, cols. 160–162. His major book is *Lehrbuch der Chemie*, 2 vols. (1829; 4th ed., 1847), also trans. into French (1835) and into English by S. L. Hammick as *Practical Experimental Chemistry Adapted to Arts and Manufactures* (1838). Many of his shorter writings were brought together as *Gesammelte Schriften von Eilhard Mitscherlich. Lebensbild, Briefwechsel und Abhandlungen* (1896).

II. Secondary Literature. See G. Bugge, "Mitscherlich," in *Das Buch der Grossen Chemiker*, I (Berlin, 1929); F. Heinrich, "Zur Erinnerung an Eilhard Mitscherlich," in *Chemische Zeitung*, 37 (1913), 1369, 1398; H. Kopp, *Geschichte der Chemie*, I (Brunswick, 1843), 414; and *Die Entwicklung der Chemie in der neueren Zeit* (Munich, 1873), p. 417; A. Mitscherlich, in *E. Mitscherlichs Gesammelte Schriften* (Berlin, 1896); J. R. Partington, *A History of Chemistry*, IV (London, 1964); W. Prandtl, *Deutsche Chemiker* (Weinheim, 1956); G. Rose, "Eilhard Mitscherlich," in *Zeitschrift der Deutschen geologischen Gesellschaft*, 16 (1864), 21; and Williamson, "Eilhard Mitscherlich," in *Journal of the Chemical Society*, 17 (1864), 440.

F. Szabadváry

MITTAG-LEFFLER, MAGNUS GUSTAF (GÖSTA)

(*b.* Stockholm, Sweden, 16 March 1846; *d.* Stockholm, 7 July 1927), *mathematics.*

Mittag-Leffler was the eldest son of John Olaf Leffler and Gustava Wilhelmina Mittag. His father was a school principal and from 1867 to 1870 a deputy in the lower house of the Swedish parliament. The atmosphere at home was intellectually stimulating, and Mittag-Leffler's aptitude for mathematics was recognized and encouraged at an early age.

Mittag-Leffler entered the University of Uppsala in 1865 and obtained the doctorate in 1872. He remained at the university as a lecturer for a year, but in 1873 left on a traveling scholarship for Paris, Göttingen, and Berlin. On the advice of Hermite, whom he met in Paris, he went to study under Weierstrass in Berlin. Weierstrass exerted a decisive influence on his subsequent development.

In 1877 Mittag-Leffler wrote his *Habilitationsschrift* on the theory of elliptic function and, in consequence, was appointed professor of mathematics at the University of Helsinki. In 1881 he left Helsinki for Stockholm, where he became professor of mathematics at the newly established Högskola (later the University of Stockholm). He twice served as rector. Among his colleagues there were Sonya Kovalewsky and E. Phragmén. Mittag-Leffler was an excellent lecturer. Among his students were I. O. Bendixson, Helge von Koch, and E. I. Fredholm.

Mittag-Leffler was not among the mathematical giants of his time, but he did contribute several methods and results that have found a lasting place in the mathematical literature. His most important contributions clearly reflect Weierstrass' influence. Thus, where Weierstrass had given formulas for the representation of entire functions and of elliptic functions, Mittag-Leffler set himself the task of finding a representation for an arbitrary meromorphic function $f(z)$ which would display its behavior at its poles. The answer is of classical simplicity. Let $\{z_n\}$ be the set of poles of $f(z)$ so that $\{z_n\}$ is either finite or is infinite and possesses a limit point at infinity. In the former case the answer is trivial since $f(z)$ differs from an entire function only by the sum of its principal parts, $\sum h_n(z - z_n)$. In the latter case, this sum is infinite and may diverge. Convergence is reestablished by adding to the individual terms of the sums certain suitable polynomials.

A generalization of this result, also due to Mittag-Leffler, is concerned with the case where the set $\{z_n\}$ while still consisting of isolated points may have limit points also in the finite plane. Another field that was pioneered by Mittag-Leffler is that of the representation of an analytic function $f(z)$ beyond the circle of convergence of its power series round a given point. Taking this point, without loss of generality, as the origin, one defines the (principal) Mittag-Leffler star of the function with respect to the origin as the union of the straight segments extending from the origin to the first singularity of the function in that direction (or to infinity). Mittag-Leffler developed analytic expressions that represent $f(z)$ in the entire Mittag-Leffler star. The later evolutions of this subject led to its being subsumed under the heading of the theory of summability, where certain infinite matrices are now known as Mittag-Leffler matrices.

Mittag-Leffler was a prolific writer, and the list of his publications includes 119 items. But his importance as a research worker is overshadowed by his prominence as an organizer in many spheres of scientific activity. He was the founder and, for many years, the chief editor of the highly influential *Acta mathe-*

matica, to which he attracted important contributions by men such as E. Borel, G. Cantor, J. Hadamard, D. Hilbert, J. Jensen, V. Volterra, H. Weber, and above all H. Poincaré.

Mittag-Leffler's relationship with Cantor is of particular interest. Mittag-Leffler himself said of his work on meromorphic functions and of its generalizations that it had been his endeavor to subsume Weierstrass' and Cantor's approaches to analysis under a single point of view. And Cantor regarded Mittag-Leffler as one of his most influential friends and supporters in a hostile world.

Mittag-Leffler was very conscious of the importance of maintaining a record of the contemporary history of mathematics for posterity, and the pages of *Acta mathematica* contains reprints of many exchanges of letters between notable mathematicians of the period. He wrote a moving account of the relationship between Weierstrass and Sonya Kovalewsky.

He was one of the organizers of the first and of subsequent international congresses of mathematicians and was the recipient of many honors, including doctorates from the universities of Bologna, Oxford, Cambridge, Christiania (Oslo), Aberdeen, and St. Andrews.

Mittag-Leffler was married to Signe af Lindfors in 1882.

BIBLIOGRAPHY

Articles by Mittag-Leffler include "Sur la représentation analytique des fonctions monogènes uniformes d'une variable indépendante," in *Acta mathematica*, **4** (1884), 1–79, and "Weierstrass et Sonja Kowalewsky," *ibid.*, **39** (1923), 133–198. A complete bibliography is in N. E. G. Nörlund, "G. Mittag-Leffler," *ibid.*, **50** (1927), I-XXIII. See also A. Schoenflies, "Die Krisis in Cantor's mathematischem Schaffen," *ibid.*, 1–23, with "Zusätzliche Bemerkungen," by Mittag-Leffler, *ibid.*, 25–26; and E. Hille, "In Retrospect," 1962 Yale Mathematical Colloquium (mimeographed).

ABRAHAM ROBINSON

MITTASCH, ALWIN (*b.* Grossdehsa, Germany, 27 December 1869; *d.* Heidelberg, Germany, 4 June 1953), *physical chemistry.*

Mittasch was a leading authority on contact catalysis. As head of catalytic research for the Badische Anilin- und Soda-Fabrik (BASF) he guided the research that led to inexpensive, durable compound catalysts for the Haber-Bosch synthetic ammonia process, the Ostwald process for oxidation of ammonia to nitric acid, the water gas reaction, and various

hydrogenations in the gas phase. His career and private life were singularly untroubled, touched only marginally by the military and political upheavals through which he lived.

The fourth of the six children of a village schoolmaster, Mittasch grew up happily in Wendish Saxony. For lack of money the boy was sent to a teacher-training school instead of a university. At nineteen Mittasch began teaching in a rural grade school. Three years later, in 1892, he secured an appointment to a city school in Leipzig. Here he soon attended public lectures at the university, being particularly drawn to those of Ostwald on energy relations in chemical systems. He resolved to become a middle school science teacher, but as his undergraduate studies progressed, and with Ostwald's encouragement, he determined to become a physical chemist. After seven years of university studies (in addition to full-time teaching), Mittasch advanced to doctoral candidacy. His thesis under Max Bodenstein, on the kinetics and catalytic aspects of nickel carbonyl formation and decomposition, led directly to a career in catalytic chemistry.

After short interludes as Ostwald's assistant and then as analyst in a lead and zinc fabricating company, he was hired by the BASF in 1904. Here Mittasch assisted Carl Bosch in seeking an industrial process for fixing nitrogen via cyanides or nitrides. This work was abandoned in 1909 in favor of the commercially more promising Haber ammonia synthesis directly from nitrogen and hydrogen. However, the experience that he had just gained helped Mittasch in seeking a cheaper catalyst than Haber's osmium. Assuming that in the Haber process the metal catalyst briefly forms a nitride intermediate and remembering that nitride formation occurs best in the presence of certain stable oxides, Mittasch directed an exhaustive search that led not only to an optimal, cheap catalyst of iron, aluminum, and potassium oxides, but also to much knowledge about catalyst poisons and activators. His discovery of the utility of compounded catalysts formed the basis of a massive research program he directed at the BASF for the next two decades. Besides the catalysts for important industrial processes his research yielded much data on high pressure and temperature reactions in the gaseous phase. He became particularly impressed by the manner in which the selection of a specific catalytic mixture can favor the yield of a desired compound while inhibiting the formation of other possible products.

After his retirement in 1934, he made this last observation the basis of an elaborate philosophy of causality, about which he wrote two books and several articles. Much better received by critics than these often abstruse writings were his scholarly and extensive publications on the history of catalysis.

BIBLIOGRAPHY

I. ORIGINAL WORKS. Mittasch wrote some twenty-one books, which include *Von Davy und Döbereiner bis Deacon, ein Halbes Jahrhundert grenzfläschenkatalyse* (Berlin, 1932), with Erich Theis; *Julius Robert Mayer's Kausalbegriff* (Berlin, 1940); *Geschichte der Amoniaksynthese* (Weinheim, 1951); *Wilhelm Ostwalds Auflösungstheorie* (Heidelberg, 1951); and *Friedrich Nietzsche als Naturphilosoph* (Stuttgart, 1952).

Mittasch's numerous patents and technical articles and much else that he published can be located through the *Chemisches Zentralblatt* and *Chemical Abstracts*. His published speeches, books, book reviews, and articles of a historical, philosophical, and broader scientific nature are listed in an "Autobibliography" on pp. 747–759 of his book *Von der Chemie zur Philosophie* (Ulm, 1948); a supplement covering 1948–1953 is provided at the close of the obituary written by Karl Holdermann, "Alwin Mittasch in Memoriam," in *Chemische Berichte*, **90** (1957), LIV The archive of the BASF reports that it holds some of Mittasch's correspondence and other papers of minor historical significance. There is also an unpublished autobiography, *Chronik meines Lebens*, the location of which is unknown.

II. SECONDARY LITERATURE. Several obituaries and tributes are listed in the bibliography by Karl Holdermann. There are others at the BASF archives. In addition there is a chapter on "Alwin Mittasch," by Alfred von Nagel, in *Ludwigshafener Chemiker*, I (Dusseldorf, 1958), 137–170.

See also Eduard Farber, "From Chemistry to Philosophy: The Way of Alwin Mittasch (1869–1953)," in *Chymia*, **11** (1966), 157–178.

JOHN J. BEER

MIVART, ST. GEORGE JACKSON (*b.* London, England, 30 November 1827; *d.* London, 1 April 1900), *biology, natural history*.

Mivart was born of well-to-do parents who were members of the rising nonprofessional middle class. His father's associations in natural history encouraged him to develop his own interests in that field, which he did through reading and collecting. An expected enrollment at either Oxford or Cambridge was prevented by his conversion at seventeen to Roman Catholicism. He prepared instead for a career in law and was admitted to the bar in 1851.

Mivart's primary interests in natural history persisted, and he came to know many of the naturalists of his day, particularly Owen and Huxley. The latter demonstrated to Mivart the excitement of natural history as a discipline in its own right. It was undoubtedly through Huxley's influence that Mivart worked in the 1860's and 1870's on his series of papers on Primate comparative anatomy. Huxley viewed the development of a precise body of knowledge about the Primates as significant to the elaboration and documentation of Darwinian evolution. The prosimians themselves had not been systematically studied as a group; and Mivart's work, which culminated in "On *Lepilemur* and *Cheirogaleus* and the Zoological Rank of the Lemuroidea" (1873), was a major contribution to an understanding of this enigmatic Primate group and their systematic relationship to the rest of the order.

Meanwhile Mivart attained a modest reputation in comparative anatomy; he published a series of descriptive studies, lectured to lay audiences, and from 1862 to 1884 taught anatomy at St. Mary's Hospital Medical School in London. Mivart had been a member of the Royal Institution since 1849, and he was elected fellow of the Zoological Society in 1858, of the Linnean Society in 1862, and of the Royal Society in 1869.

Although he was initially an adherent of the new biology for which Huxley was the most articulate spokesman, and for which Darwinism was the most influential method, Mivart regarded the tendency to universalize and to reify organic evolution as a threat both to the truths of his own Catholicism and to his more restricted definition of the canons of science. The conflict led to the publication of *On the Genesis of Species* (1871) and *Man and Apes* (1873); in both works Mivart criticized Darwinism as insufficient to explain anomalies in the data of observation or to answer the more general questions which dealt with the initiation of specific forms which must precede the action of natural selection. Such attacks on Darwinism—which were coupled with what were defined as insulting personal allusions—precipitated a formal break with Huxley and the Darwinians and through them Mivart's removal from the main current of natural science, so that after 1873, although he continued to publish, his work appeared more and more dated.

Mivart's attempts to reconcile his Catholicism with his science were equally destructive to his position as a prominent Catholic layman. In a series of articles and books which began with *Contemporary Evolution* (1873–1876), he sought to inject a modernist spirit born of the new science into the still conservative theology, structure, and practice of the Catholic Church. His arguments were attacked with increasing bitterness and finally rejected. Six weeks before his death he was excommunicated. Mivart stands as an important symbol and victim of the deep conflicts in science and in the intellectual milieu of the nineteenth century.

BIBLIOGRAPHY

For descriptions of Mivart's life and works see Jacob W. Gruber, *A Conscience in Conflict: The Life of St. George Mivart* (New York, 1960), and Peter Vorzimmer, *Charles Darwin: The Years of Controversy* (Philadelphia, 1970).

JACOB W. GRUBER

MÖBIUS, AUGUST FERDINAND (*b*. Schulpforta, near Naumburg, Germany, 17 November 1790; *d*. Leipzig, Germany, 26 September 1868), *mathematics, astronomy.*

Möbius was the only child of Johann Heinrich Möbius, a dancing teacher in Schulpforta until his death in 1793, and the former Johanne Catharine Christiane Keil, a descendant of Luther. His father's unmarried brother succeeded him as dancing teacher and as provider for the family until his own death in 1804. Möbius was taught at home until his thirteenth year, by which time he had already shown an interest in mathematics. He pursued formal education from 1803 to 1809 in Schulpforta, where he studied mathematics under Johann Gottlieb Schmidt. In 1809 he entered Leipzig University with the intention of studying law, but his early love for mathematics soon came to dominance. Consequently he studied mathematics under Moritz von Prasse, physics with Ludwig Wilhelm Gilbert, and astronomy with Mollweide, whose assistant he became.

Having been selected for a traveling fellowship, he left Leipzig in May 1813, a few months before the Battle of Leipzig, and went to Göttingen, where he spent two semesters studying theoretical astronomy with Gauss. He then proceeded to Halle for studies in mathematics with Johann Friedrich Pfaff. When in 1814 Prasse died, Mollweide succeeded him as mathematics professor, thereby opening up the position in astronomy at Leipzig. The position was given to Möbius, who received his doctorate from Leipzig in 1814 and qualified for instruction in early 1815 with his *De peculiaribus quibusdam aequationum trigonometricarum affectionibus*. In the same year he published his doctoral thesis entitled *De computandis occultationibus fixarum per planetas*. In spring 1816 he became extraordinary professor of astronomy at Leipzig and also observer at the observatory. In preparation for these duties he visited a number of the leading German observatories and eventually made recommendations for the refurbishing and reconstruction of the observatory at Leipzig; these were carried out by 1821. Other instruments were added later, including a six-foot Fraunhofer refractor.

In 1820 Möbius' mother, who had come to live with him, died. Shortly thereafter he married Dorothea Christiane Johanna Rothe, whose subsequent blindness did not prevent her from raising a daughter, Emilie, and two sons, Theodor and Paul Heinrich, both of whom became distinguished literary scholars. The former is best known for his research on Scandinavian and Icelandic literature; the latter is sometimes confused with Paul Julius Möbius the neurologist, who was Möbius' grandson.

Although Möbius was offered attractive positions as an astronomer at Greifswald in 1816 and as a mathematician at Dorpat in 1819, he refused them both to remain at Leipzig. In 1829 he became a corresponding member of the Berlin Academy of Sciences, but it was not until 1844, after he had been invited to succeed J. F. Fries at Jena, that Leipzig promoted him to ordinary professor of astronomy and higher mechanics. The slowness of his promotion and his modest salary have been attributed to his quiet and reserved manner, while his refusal to leave Leipzig stemmed from his love for his native Saxony and the quality of Leipzig University. In 1848 Möbius became director of the observatory, and d'Arrest became the observer and eventually his son-in-law. Möbius rarely traveled, and in general his life centered around his study, the observatory, and his family. His writings were fully developed and original; he was not widely read in the mathematical literature of his day and consequently found at times that others had previously discovered ideas presented in his writings. Also his investigations were frequently aimed not so much at finding new results, but rather at developing more effective and simpler means for treating existing areas. In 1868, not long after having celebrated his fiftieth year of teaching at Leipzig, Möbius died; his wife's death had come nine years earlier.

Möbius' scientific contributions may be divided into two areas—astronomy and mathematics. Like his contemporaries Gauss and W. R. Hamilton, Möbius was employed as an astronomer but made his most important contributions to mathematics.

His early publications were in astronomy; two short papers on Juno and Pallas were followed by the separate publication in 1815 of his doctoral dissertation on occultation phenomena (see above) and in 1816 by his *De minima variatione azimuthi stellarum circulos parallelos uniformiter describentium com-*

mentatio. By 1823 his observational activities had borne fruit to the extent that he published his only work of that sort, his *Beobachtungen auf der Königlichen Universitäts-Sternwarte zu Leipzig.* He published a few observational papers in later decades and in the 1830's made measurements on terrestrial magnetism. He also published two popular treatises on the path of Halley's comet (1835) and on the fundamental laws of astronomy (1836), the latter having gone through many editions. His greatest contribution to astronomy was his *Die Elemente der Mechanik des Himmels* (1843), wherein he gave a thorough mathematical treatment of celestial mechanics without the use of higher mathematics. Although astronomical amateurs could therefore read the book, it nevertheless contained results important to professionals. Moreover he introduced (for the first time, he thought) the use of vectorial addition and subtraction to represent velocities and forces and effectively showed the computational usefulness of that very ancient mathematical device, the epicycle.

When Mollweide died in 1825, Möbius hoped to follow his example by exchanging his own position in astronomy for that in mathematics, but in 1826 M. W. Drobisch was selected. In the following year Möbius published his greatest work, which later became a mathematical classic. Möbius' *Der barycentrische Calcul: Ein neues Hülfsmittel zur analytischen Behandlung der Geometrie* (1827) was not only his most important mathematical publication, but also the source of much of his later work. He had come upon the fundamental ideas for his barycentric calculus in 1818 and by 1821 decided that they merited book-length treatment. In an appendix to his 1823 astronomical treatise, he had given a first discussion of his new method. As he stated in the foreword to his 1827 treatise, the concept of the centroid had been recognized by Archimedes as a useful tool for geometrical investigations.

Möbius proceeded from the well-known law of mechanics, that a combination of weights positioned at various points can be replaced by a single weight of magnitude equal to the sum of the individual weights and positioned at the center of gravity of the combination. Thus Möbius constructed a mathematical system, the fundamental entities of which were points, to each of which a weight or numerical coefficient was assigned. The position of any point could be expressed in this system by varying the numerical coefficients of any four or more noncoplaner points. Thus Möbius used an equation such as $aA + bB + cC \equiv D$, where a, b, c are numerical coefficients (positive or negative), and A, B, C, D are points, to express the fact that if A, B, C are not collinear, then D must lie in the plane of A, B, C. Möbius went on in his treatise to apply this method with noteworthy success to many important geometrical problems. Since barycentric coordinates are a form of homogeneous coordinates, their creator is recognized with Feuerbach and Plücker, whose publications were independent and nearly simultaneous, as a discoverer of homogeneous coordinates.

Moreover Möbius developed important results in projective and affine geometry and also was among the first fully to appreciate the principle of duality and to give a thorough treatment of the cross ratio. He was the first mathematician to make use of a system wherein geometrical entities, such as lines, plane figures, and solids, were consistently treated as spatially oriented and to which a positive or negative sign could be affixed. Moreover he presented in this work the construction now known as the Möbius net. Finally at one point in the treatise he commented that two equal and similar solid figures, which are however mirror images of each other, could be made to coincide, if one were "able to let one system make a half revolution in a space of four dimensions. But since such a space cannot be conceived, this coincidence is impossible in this case" (*Werke*, I, 172).

Nearly all of Möbius' subsequent mathematical publications appeared in Crelle's *Journal für die reine und angewandte Mathematik* and from 1846 in either the *Abhandlungen* . . . or the *Berichte der Königlichen Sächsischen Gesellschaft der Wissenschaften zu Leipzig.* Some of these merit special attention. An 1828 paper discussed two tetrahedrons which mutually circumscribe and inscribe each other; such tetrahedrons are now known as Möbius tetrahedrons. Two dioptrical papers appeared in 1830 wherein Möbius used continued fractions to develop his results; another optical paper appeared in 1855 based on the concept of collineation. The Möbius function in number theory was presented in an 1832 paper, but most of his energies during the 1830's went into a series of papers on statics, which culminated in his 1837 two-volume *Lehrbuch der Statik*, wherein he treated the subject, following Poinsot, through combining individual forces with couples of forces and introduced the concept of a null system.

It is frequently stated that in 1840 Möbius posed for the first time the four-color conjecture, that is, that four colors are sufficient for the unambiguous construction of any map, no matter how complex, on a plane surface. This attribution is, however, incorrect; its source lies in the correct statement that in 1840 Möbius presented a lecture in which he posed the problem of how a kingdom might be divided into five regions in such a way that every region would border on each of the four other regions. In 1846 Möbius published a treatment of spherical trigonometry based on his barycentric calculus and in 1852 a paper on lines of the third order. His 1855 "Theorie der Kreisverwandschaft in rein geometrischer Darstellung" is the culmination of a number of studies on circular transformations, which are now frequently called Möbius transformations.

Möbius had been visited in 1844 by a high school teacher, Hermann Grassmann, whose now famous *Ausdehnungslehre* of 1844 contained among other things results similar to Möbius' point system of analysis. Grassmann requested Möbius to review the book, but Möbius failed to appreciate it, as did many others. When Grassmann in 1846 won the prize in a mathematical contest, which he had entered at Möbius' suggestion, Möbius did agree to write a commentary on the prize-winning essay. This 1847 work was the only significant published analysis of Grassmann's ideas until the late 1860's, when their significance was realized. Möbius was stimulated in the early 1860's to write his own treatise, "Ueber geometrische Addition und Multiplication," but this was not published until nineteen years after his death.

Möbius is now most frequently remembered for his discovery of the one-sided surface called the Möbius strip, which is formed by taking a rectangular strip of paper and connecting its ends after giving it a half twist (*Werke*, II, 484–485). The Paris Academy had offered a prize for research on the geometrical theory of polyhedrons, and in 1858 Möbius began to prepare an essay on this subject. The results of his essay were for the most part given in two important papers: his "Theorie der elementaren Verwandtschaft" of 1863 and his "Ueber die Bestimmung des Inhaltes eines Polyëders" of 1865. The latter contains his discovery of the "Möbius strip" and proof that there are polyhedrons to which no volume can be assigned. Curt Reinhardt has shown from an examination of Möbius' notebooks that he discovered this surface around September 1858 (*Werke*, II, 517–521); this date is significant, since it is now known that Johann Benedict Listing discovered the same surface in July 1858 and published his discovery in 1861. Listing and Möbius, who worked independently of each other, should thus share the credit for this discovery.

BIBLIOGRAPHY

I. ORIGINAL WORKS. Möbius' main publications, including his three long books, are collected in R. Baltzer, F. Klein, and W. Scheibner, eds., *Gesammelte Werke*, 4 vols. (Leipzig, 1885–1887). The second and fourth volumes contain previously unpublished writings, and the fourth contains a useful discussion of Möbius' manuscripts by C. Reinhardt.

II. SECONDARY LITERATURE. The best discussion of Möbius' life and astronomical activities is contained in C. Bruhns, *Die Astronomen auf der Pleissenburg* (Leipzig, 1879). The best treatment of his mathematical work is by R. Baltzer in Möbius, *Werke*, I, v–xx. See also H. Gretschel, "August Ferdinand Möbius," in *Archiv der Mathematik und Physik*, **49**, *Literarischer Bericht*, CLXXXXV (1869), 1–9; and M. Cantor, "Möbius," in *Allgemeine deutsche Biographie*, XX (1885), 38–43. A useful discussion of his barycentric calculus is R. E. Allardice, "The Barycentric Calculus of Möbius," in *Proceedings of the Edinburgh Mathematical Society*, **10** (1892), 2–21, and selections from his treatise on this subject are given in English in D. E. Smith, ed., *A Source Book in Mathematics*, II (New York, 1959), 525–526, 670–676. K. O. May in his "The Origin of the Four-Color Conjecture," in *Mathematics Teacher*, **60** (1967), 516–519, clarifies Möbius' relationship to this conjecture, and M. Crowe, in *A History of Vector Analysis* (Notre Dame, Ind., 1967), treats Möbius' relationship to vectorial analysis and to Grassmann. See also E. Kötter, "Die Entwickelung der synthetischen Geometrie," in *Jahresbericht der Deutschen Mathematikervereinigung*, **5**, pt. 2 (1901), 1–486.

MICHAEL J. CROWE

MÖBIUS, KARL AUGUST (*b.* Eilenburg, Germany, 7 February 1825; *d.* Berlin, Germany, 26 April 1908), *zoology.*

The son of Gottlob Möbius, a wheelwright, and the former Sophie Kaps, Möbius was trained as an elementary school teacher at the private training college in Eilenburg, and from 1844 to 1849 he taught at Seesen, in the Harz Mountains. His strong interest in science led him, despite difficulties, to Berlin, where he had to pass the *Reifeprüfung* (certificate examination) to enter the university. He studied natural science until 1853 under Johannes Müller, C. G. Ehrenberg, Eilhard Mitscherlich, E. H. Beyrich, and the zoologist A. A. H. Lichtenstein; for a time he was the latter's assistant. Inspired by Humboldt's writings, Möbius hoped to join scientific expeditions to the tropics. Since it appeared that the first opportunity would arise in Hamburg, he took a position there in 1853 as a teacher of natural science at the Johanneum grammar school. In 1855 he married Helene Meyer, sister of the zoologist and philosopher Jürgen-Bona Meyer. He soon joined the administration of the Hamburg Museum of Natural History and in 1863 was a cofounder of the Hamburg zoo. Möbius was responsible for the construction of Germany's first public aquarium.

From 1860 Möbius carried out regular investigations of the fauna of the Kieler Bucht; the first volume of his *Fauna der Kieler Bucht* appeared in 1865. In the introduction to this work he set forth a program and methodology for modern ecology. The topography and variations in depth, the plant and animal life of the Kieler Bucht were characterized. The concept of "life community" ("Lebensgemeinschaft" or "Biocönose") was introduced, although Möbius did not define it more precisely until 1877. Through his scientific connections, Möbius was appointed to the chair of zoology at the University of Kiel in 1868. The following year, on a commission from the Prussian government, he traveled along the coasts of France and England to investigate the possibility of promoting mussel and oyster breeding on the German coasts. During the succeeding years he took part in further marine biological research expeditions to the North Sea and Baltic Sea. In 1874 Möbius' wish to visit the tropics was fulfilled; he joined an expedition to Mauritius and the Seychelles, during which he studied chiefly marine fauna and coral reefs. His *Die Auster und die Austernwirtschaft* (1877) contains a clear definition of the concept of "Biocönose."

In 1881 a zoology institute built according to Möbius' plans was opened at Kiel. Its museum was for decades considered a model for such establishments. Möbius left Kiel in 1887 to become director of the new natural history museum in Berlin. He considered his chief task there to be the creation of a large and impressive collection. In 1901 he presided over the International Congress of Zoology at Berlin.

Möbius' scientific work was extensive and very broad in scope. The major portion was devoted to marine biology, including applied research on invertebrates and fishery biology. He also studied the formation of pearls and investigated the biology and anatomy of the whale. Of special scientific importance are his studies on the Foraminifera and the related discovery that the *Eozoon canadense*, which had been considered a living creature, is actually a mineral aggregate. Also of value are Möbius' works on species and the theory of evolution, on animal geography and nomenclature, on animal psychology, on the administration of museums, and on ornithology.

BIBLIOGRAPHY

A complete bibliography is included in Friedrich Dahl, "Karl August Möbius. Ein kurzes Lebensbild, nach authentischen Quellen entworfen," in *Zoologische Jahrbücher*, supp. no. 8 (1905), 1–22, with four potraits. See also obituaries by R. von Hanstein, in *Naturwissenschaft-liche Rundschau*, **23** (1908), 361–373; H. Conwentz, in *Schriften der Naturforschenden Gesellschaft in Danzig*, n.s. **12** (1909), xviii–xx; and C. Matzdorff, in *Monatshefte für den Naturwissenschaftlichen Unterricht*, **2** (1909), 433–448; and L. Gebhardt, *Die Ornithologen Mitteleuropas* (Giessen, 1964).

HANS QUERNER

MOCIÑO, JOSÉ MARIANO (*b.* Temascaltepec, Mexico, 24 [?] September 1757; *d.* Barcelona, Spain, 19 May 1820), *botany.*

In botanical literature Mociño is the generally accepted spelling. The owner of the name always signed it Moziño. On the title page of *Noticias de Nutka* it is written Moziño Suarez de Figueroa. His mother's name was Manuela Losada, and the name under which his degree of bachelor of medicine was conferred was José Mariano Moziño Suares Losada. Nineteenth-century authors wrote the name Mocinno, Moçino, Mozino, or Mozinno.

Mociño studied for a career in theology, philosophy, and history, then about 1784 turned to the natural sciences. After medical training at the University of Mexico, he became committed to botany, and in March 1790 he joined the Royal Botanical Expedition to New Spain, which under the direction of Martín Sessé had been exploring in Mexico since 1787. He continued as a member of the expedition until its effective termination in 1804, traveling to western Mexico (1790–1791), to the coast of California and Nutka Island (1792–1793), the Atlantic slope of Mexico (1793–1794), and Central America (1795–1799).

When the period of exploration came to an end (1803), Mociño and Sessé went to Spain to complete their work and to get support for a new *Flora Mexicana*, to be based on their collections and the approximately 1,400 paintings made by the expedition's artists, Athanasio Echeverría and Vicente de la Cerda. The Napoleonic government then in power in Spain did not support the *Flora*; Sessé died in 1808; Mociño assumed responsibility for the manuscripts and paintings, and when he was forced to leave Madrid with the retreating French (1812), he carried a part of the material with him to Montpellier, where he worked with the botanist Augustin-Pyramus de Candolle. Most of the manuscripts of the *Flora Mexicana* were lost before they came into Candolle's hands, but most of the paintings were saved and some of them formed the bases for almost three hundred new species of plants described by Candolle. Mociño returned to Spain, probably in 1820, and died the same year.

The *Plantae Novae Hispaniae* (1887–1891) and the *Flora Mexicana* (1891–1897), two posthumous volumes, together comprise almost the sum of the original publication which resulted from the Royal Botanical Expedition. The names of Sessé and Mociño are commonly linked (and in that order) in any mention of the botanical work of the expedition, but their contributions seem to have been quite different. Both were competent and active botanists as shown by their existing analyses and descriptions of plants according to the Linnaean method. Sessé was the more competent administrator, with numerous responsibilities and an enormous amount of paper work, and he seems to have delegated much of the purely botanical work to Mociño. The latter was charged, for example, with the preparation of *Plantae Novae Hispaniae*—the entire manuscript is in his handwriting—which he completed in a little over a year after joining the group. The archives at the Instituto Botánico in Madrid contain various inventories of paintings and specimens summarizing the botanical activities of the expedition; which inventories are also for the most part in Mociño's hand. The herbarium of Sessé and Mociño, which is also at Madrid, contains much internal evidence that Mociño began and attempted to carry on some final organization of the specimens leading to publication of a flora of New Spain. That Mociño was a scholar—neither merely a collector nor a menial assistant—is attested by the opinions of his contemporaries and by his surviving reports on his expeditions to Nutka and to the Volcán de Tuxtla in Veracruz. He had some facility with languages; he wrote Latin well, and when in Nutka he soon learned the language of the aborigines well enough to serve as the interpreter for the Spanish party.

The surviving remains of the abortive Botanical Expedition include more than 10,000 herbarium specimens, some 1,300 paintings, and a mass of sorted and unsorted manuscript material. Through Mociño's efforts the paintings came to play a part in the development of nineteenth-century botany, and twentieth-century interpretation of the collections and other documents, including the paintings, has been made possible largely through the manuscripts that Mociño compiled systematically while he was in Mexico.

BIBLIOGRAPHY

I. ORIGINAL WORKS. Two vols., attributed to Sessé and Mociño jointly, were published in Mexico between 1887 and 1897. These appeared first in pts., as supps. to the periodical *La Naturaleza*. *Plantae Novae Hispaniae* (1887–1891), 1–184, I–XIII, was based on a MS written by

Mociño, completed at Guadalajara, Jalisco, forwarded from there to the Viceroy, the Conde de Revilla-Gigedo, in July 1791, and now in the archives of the Instituto Botánico "A. J. Cavanilles," Madrid. It is a complete flora, including the species of flowering plants studied by the Botanical Expedition up to about the beginning of 1791. A 2nd ed. was published in bk. form in 1893.

Flora Mexicana (1891–1897, pp. I–XI [intro.], 1–263, and I–XV [index]) was based on a very heterogeneous sers. of nn. on individual plant species from many parts of Spanish America. These nn. comprised a part, but by no means all, of those prepared by the members of the Botanical Expedition. The nn. were found in no particular order in the archives in Madrid; they were organized by the editor into the Linnaean classes and published without careful study or collation. A 2nd ed. was published in bk. form in 1894, before the later pts. of the 1st ed. appeared in *La Naturaleza*.

Mociño's own writings are listed by Rickett (v. inf.). The most important are the *Noticias de Nutka*, first published in *Gazeta de Guatemala* (1803–1804), then in bk. form by Alberto M. Carreño, ed. (Mexico, 1913), I–CIX, 1–117. This account of Nutka includes descriptions of the island itself and its inhabitants, comments on the then prevailing political situation, and a vocabulary of about five hundred words. Included in the 1913 vol. is Mociño's report on his ascent of the Mexican volcano of Tuxtla "Descripción del Volcán de Tuxtla," in *Noticias de Nutka* (Mexico, 1913), 103–117.

Original letters, memoranda, and other documents relative to the Botanical Expedition to New Spain and the Royal Botanical Garden in Mexico, are to be found in the Mexican National Archives, the *Archivo General de la Nación*, in the section *Historia*, vols. 460–466, 527. A few documents apparently of similar origin are in the William L. Clements Library, University of Michigan, Ann Arbor. The richest source of MS material in Spain is the archive of the Instituto Botánico "A. J. Cavanilles," Madrid; here are most of the existing MSS having to do with strictly botanical matters, for example, the MS of *Plantae Novae Hispaniae*, various botanical descriptions, fragments of unpublished floras including a *Flora guatemalensis* by Mociño, inventories of paintings and collections from the different excursions which were carried out in Mexico. Descriptions or copies of most of these inventories have been published by Arias Divito or in the papers cited by him. Arias Divito also lists (p. 307) the other major sources of MS material in Madrid and Seville.

II. SECONDARY LITERATURE. An extensively documented account of Sessé, Mociño, and their co-workers, based primarily on materials in the *Archivo General de la Nación*, Mexico, is H. W. Rickett, "The Royal Botanical Expedition to New Spain," in *Chronica botanica*, **11** (1947), 1–86. Juan Carlos Arias Divito, *Las expediciones científicas españolas durante el siglo XVIII* (Madrid, 1968), is based primarily on Spanish archival sources; it includes copies of many previously unpublished inventories of plants, animals, and paintings, and a considerable bibliog. that supplements the references cited by Rickett. Additional information, especially relative to the members of the Malaspina Expedition who were in Mexico at the same time as the Royal Botanical Expedition, may be found in Iris Higbie Wilson, "Scientific Aspects of Spanish Exploration in New Spain During the Late Eighteenth Century," (Ph.D. diss., Univ. of Southern California, 1962).

The original account of the intercourse between Mociño and Candolle and the story of the copying of some 1,200 paintings by 120 artists in ten days is told in *Mémoires et souvenirs de Augustin-Pyramus de Candolle* (Geneva, 1862), 219–221, 288–290.

ROGERS MCVAUGH

MOENCH, CONRAD (*b.* Kassel, Germany, 20 August 1744; *d.* Marburg, Germany, 6 January 1805), *botany.*

Moench, the son of a pharmacist, worked for six and a half years in pharmacies in Hannover, Bern, and Strasbourg before returning to take charge of his family's pharmacy, the Apotheke zum Einhorn, in Kassel. He had studied pharmacy, botany, chemistry, and mineralogy; in 1781 he became professor of botany at the Collegium Medicum Carolinianum attached to the court of the landgrave of Hesse-Kassel at Kassel. In 1785 the college and its professors were transferred to Marburg and incorporated into the Philipps-Universität, which had been founded there in 1527.

Moench initiated a new period in the teaching of botany at Marburg. Under his supervision, a site for a botanic garden was prepared in 1786; the following year it was planted with material brought from the Kassel botanic garden. Strongly influenced by the Mannheim botanist C. F. Medicus, a bitter opponent of Linnaeus, Moench likewise frequently rejected Linnaean classification, generic concepts, and nomenclature, restoring the names and genera of Tournefort wherever possible, and often subdividing Linnaean genera. His rebellion against the dominant Linnaean taxonomy of the period found expression in the *Methodus plantas horti botanici et agri Marburgensis a staminum situ describendi*, published at Marburg in 1794. The *Methodus* deals with 674 species, including both those cultivated in the Marburg botanic garden and those growing wild in the Marburg district. In it Moench used names at variance with those of most floristic works of the time. A *Supplementum ad Methodum plantas* of 1802 added 634 more flowering plants.

Moench's works remain nomenclaturally important because, although they include many generic names that have never been adopted elsewhere, they also comprise a number of generally accepted ones, among them *Bergenia, Cedronella, Froelichia, Kniphofia,*

Myosoton, Olearia, and *Sorghum.* Moench also provided various binomial specific names needed to avoid tautonyms—*Fagopyrum esculentum* and *Omphalodes verna,* for example—although most of his new names are now considered technically illegitimate. In dealing with the *Leguminosae,* Moench, a follower of Medicus, overlooked an important paper published by the latter in 1787 and thus renamed plants already named by him.

BIBLIOGRAPHY

I. ORIGINAL WORKS. Moench's most important works, *Methodus plantas horti botanici et agri Marburgensis a staminum situ describendi* (Marburg, 1794) and *Supplementum ad Methodum plantas* (Marburg, 1802), are repr. in facsimile with an intro. by W. T. Stearn, *Early Marburg Botany* (Königstein, 1966).

II. SECONDARY LITERATURE. On Moench and his work, see F. Grundlach, *Catalogus professorum academiae Marburgensis* (Marburg, 1927); C. Rommel, *Memoriam Conradi Moench* (Marburg, 1805); R. Schmitz, "Naturwissenschaft an der Universität Marburg," in *Sitzungsberichte der Gesellschaft zu Beförderung der gesamten Naturwissenschaften zu Marburg,* **83–84** (1963), 1–33, with portrait; and W. T. Stearn, *Early Marburg Botany* (cited above), for the nomenclature and concepts of Medicus and Moench in opposition to those of Linnaeus, as well as for their nomenclatural conflict with each other.

WILLIAM T. STEARN

MOERBEKE, WILLIAM OF, also known as **Guillelmus de Moerbeka** (*b.* Moerbeke, Belgium [?], *ca.* 1220–1235; *d.* before 26 October 1286), *philosophy, geometry, biology.*

Moerbeke, a Dominican, was one of the most productive and eminent translators from Greek into Latin of philosophical and scientific works written between the fourth century B.C. and the sixth century A.D. A spectacular widening and increase of the Greek sources for study and speculation in the second half of the thirteenth century and later times were due to Moerbeke's insatiable desire to pass on to Latin-reading students the yet undiscovered or rediscovered treasures of Greek civilization, his extensive linguistic knowledge, his indefatigable search for first-class works, and his philosophical vision.

There is little evidence concerning Moerbeke's life apart from some names of places and dates at which he produced a particular translation: they are enough, however, to suggest reasons why he did not have much time to write original works. He was at Nicaea, Asia Minor, in the spring of 1260, and in Thebes—where Dominicans had been present at least since 1253—in December of that same year. He was at

Viterbo, then a papal residence, in November 1267, May 1268, and June 1271. From 1272, at the latest, until April 1278 Moerbeke held the office of chaplain and penitentiary to the pope: in this capacity he visited the courts of Savoy and France pleading for help with the Ninth Crusade (March 1272), absolved an Augustinian prior from excommunication (1272, from Orvieto, seat of the papal curia), and authorized Albertus Magnus to absolve two abbeys in Cologne from censures (November 1274). In the same period (May–July 1274) he took part in the Second Council of Lyons, which was meant to bring about the reunion with the Greek Church; there, with Greek dignitaries, he sang the Creed in Greek in a pontifical mass. In October 1277 he was active at Viterbo. From April 1278 until his death he was archbishop of Corinth.

The three or four contemporaries with whom it is definitely known that Moerbeke had some contact were all scientists. The Silesian Witelo, who was in Viterbo toward the end of 1268, dedicated his *Perspectiva* to Moerbeke. In the introduction Witelo sheds some light on Moerbeke's philosophical doctrines and explains that they were never put in writing because Moerbeke was kept too busy by his ecclesiastical and pastoral duties and by his work as a translator. Henry Bate of Malines, a distinguished astronomer, was asked by Moerbeke, whom he met at Lyons in 1274, to write a treatise on the astrolabe; Henry immediately obliged and dedicated his *Magistralis compositio astrolabii* to his compatriot (October 1274). The physician Rosellus of Arezzo, who may have attended Pope Gregory X at his death-bed in Arezzo (1276), is the addressee of Moerbeke's dedication of his version of Galen's *De alimentis* (Viterbo, October 1277). Finally, some evidence seems to suggest that Moerbeke met the mathematician and astronomer Campanus of Novara at the papal curia.

Moerbeke may well have been in touch with Aquinas at or near Rome before 1269 or between 1271 and 1274, but there is no reliable direct evidence of any personal relationship. It is a commonplace, repeated *ad nauseam* by almost all historians and scholars concerned with either Aquinas or Moerbeke, that the latter was prompted by the former to undertake his work as a translator, especially as a translator of Aristotle. This is most probably nothing more than a legend originating in hagiography, when "evidence" was offered by William of Tocco, a confrère of Aquinas, for the latter's canonization, about forty years after his death. What remains true is that Aquinas, like other philosophers of his time, used some—by no means all—of Moerbeke's translations soon after they were made.

Works. Only one original work by Moerbeke is preserved, under the title *Geomantia* ("Divination From Earth"). It was dedicated to his nephew Arnulphus and seems to have been quite popular: several manuscripts in Latin and one manuscript of a French translation made in 1347 by Walter of Brittany are still extant, but the treatise does not seem to have been studied by modern scholars. The authenticity of the attribution has been doubted on the ground that a "faithful follower of Aquinas" could not have written a treatise on matters condemned by the master, but the premise is unfounded. There is no reason to believe that the *Geomantia* is a translation from the Greek or Arabic. Witelo's evidence strongly supports the evidence for the attribution found in the manuscripts. Addressing himself to Moerbeke in the introduction to his *Perspectiva*, he says:

> As an assiduous investigator of the whole of reality, you saw that the intelligible being which proceeds from the first principles is connected in a causal way with individual beings; and when you were inquiring into the individual causes of these individual beings, it occurred to you that there is something wonderful in the way in which the influence of divine power flows into things of the lower world passing through the powers of the higher world . . .; you saw that what is acted upon varies not only in accordance with the variety of the acting powers, but also in accordance with the variety of the modes of action; consequently you decided to dedicate yourself to the "occult" inquiry of this state of affairs.

Preliminary studies of the *Geomantia* have shown a vocabulary consistent with Moerbeke's translations; explicit mentions of the causal chain from God through the heavens to events on earth, of the occult nature of at least some part of geomancy, as indicated by Witelo; and attribution to "Frater Guillelmus de Moerbeka domini pape penitentiarius." MCCCLXXXVII in some manuscripts should be MCCLXXVI because of Moerbeke's death date, Witelo's statements, and the description "penitentiarius" and not "archiepiscopus Corinthiensis."

We do not know whether Moerbeke wrote any other original works; but we still possess many, if not all, of the translations which he made from the Greek. He undertook this activity, he says, "in spite of the hard work and tediousness which it involves, in order to provide Latin scholars with new material for study" and "in order that my efforts should add to the light to which Latins have access." His knowledge of the Greek language, perhaps scanty when he first embarked on translations, improved greatly in the course of the more than twenty years which he devoted partly to them. In this field Moerbeke was a very exacting scholar and philologist, comparable only, in the thirteenth century, with Robert Grosseteste. The unfavorable criticism brought against his versions— even against his latest and best—does not take into account two facts: first, that Greek scholarship among Latins in the thirteenth century was not the product of a long tradition and well-organized schools but the hard-won possession of isolated individuals; and second, that a very sound philosophy of language, accompanied by the need for detailed, literal interpretation of authoritative texts—biblical, legal, scientific, philosophical—required that translations should be strictly faithful, word by word, to the original. Within these limits Moerbeke was often excellent, although, like all translators, he made mistakes. He was meticulous in his quest for exactitude; he would search the Latin vocabulary with a sound critical sense and great knowledge, in order to find words which could convey to the intelligent reader the meaning of the Greek terms. If his search failed to produce the necessary results, he would form new Latin words by compounding two terms, or adding prefixes and suffixes on the Greek pattern, or even combining Greek and Latin elements: a typical example would be his rendering of αὐτοκίνητον by "automobile." In extreme cases he would resort to that great source of enrichment of a language, the transliteration, with slight adaptations, of foreign—in his case Greek—words. A test of Moerbeke's care in trying to pass on as much as possible of Aristotle's "light" can be found in his revisions, based on Greek manuscripts, of translations produced by such scholars as Boethius and James of Venice: in most cases where he introduced a change, a misinterpretation was put right, a serious mistake corrected, or a more appropriate shade of meaning introduced if his predecessor had missed a finer point. His scientific attitude toward language is also revealed by his attempt to reproduce the exact Greek sounds (mainly those of Byzantine Greek) in his transliteration of names or of newly introduced technical terms, for instance, by using "kh" for the Greek Χ.

Moerbeke applied his interest and gifts as a translator to four aims: (a) completing and improving the Latins' knowledge of Aristotle's works in all their encyclopedic extent; (b) making available to Latin readers some of the most valuable and comprehensive elaborations of Aristotle's treatises on logic, philosophy of nature, and psychology which had been written between about A.D. 200 and 550; (c) propagating the doctrines of Proclus, the greatest systematizer of Neoplatonic philosophy, on which Moerbeke's own philosophy so much depended; (d) introducing into the Latin West a more exact and extensive knowledge

of Archimedes' achievements in mathematics and physics. He also contributed in a smaller measure to the knowledge of Greek medical literature and of works by Ptolemy, Hero, Alexander of Aphrodisias, and Plato.

Evidence for Moerbeke's authorship of the versions ascribed to him varies in strength. In a number of instances—all concerning works by Aristotle—he only revised, more or less thoroughly, versions made by earlier scholars. In the following survey two asterisks indicate the titles of translations for which the evidence of authorship is direct (the translator's name accompanying the text itself); a single asterisk indicates the titles of versions for which evidence is elicited from a linguistic analysis. Dates and places where the translations were made are given only in the relatively few instances for which the evidence is found at the end of the translation itself. Within square brackets is a short indication of the best existing edition, whenever this has been ascertained, or of one old edition (original or a reprint). Some additional information on editions will be found in the bibliography.

The translations or revisions so far identified and ascribed with some degree of probability to Moerbeke are the following:

I. Plato (see Proclus).

II. Aristotle.

(1) Works never before translated into Latin:
 **Politica, *one version of bks. I–II.11 [P. Michaud-Quantin, Bruges, 1961] and **one complete [F. Susemihl, Leipzig, 1872; bks. I–III.8, with Aquinas' commentary, H. F. Dondaine and L. Bataillon, Rome, 1972].
 *Poetica, 1278 [L. Minio-Paluello, Brussels, 1968].
 **Metaphysica, bk. XI [Venice, 1562, and with Aquinas' commentary].
 *De motu animalium [L. Torraca, Naples, 1958].
 *De progressu animalium [unpublished].

(2) Works never before translated into Latin from the Greek:
 *Historia animalium [bk. I, G. Rudberg, Uppsala, 1908; bk. X.6, Rudberg, Uppsala, 1911; bks. II–IX unpublished].
 **De partibus animalium, Thebes, 1260 [unpublished].
 *De generatione animalium, two recensions [H. J. Drossaart Lulofs, Bruges, 1966].
 **Meteorologica, bks. I–III [with Aquinas].
 *De caelo, bks. III–IV [with Aquinas].

(3) Works of which Latin translations from the Greek already existed and which were translated anew by Moerbeke:

Categoriae, 1266 [L. Minio-Paluello, Bruges, 1961; also (first half) A. Pattin, Louvain, 1971].
De interpretatione, 1268 [G. Verbeke and L. Minio-Paluello, Bruges, 1965].
**Meteorologica*, bk. IV [with Aquinas' commentary].
De caelo, bks. I–II [with Aquinas' commentary].
**Rhetorica*, *first recension [unpublished]; **second recension [L. Spengel, Leipzig, 1867].

(4) Works translated from the Greek by other scholars and revised by Moerbeke:

Analytica posteriora, translated by James of Venice [L. Minio-Paluello and B. G. Dod, Bruges, 1968].
De sophisticis elenchis, translated by Boethius [B. G. Dod and L. Minio-Paluello, in press].
Physica, translated by James of Venice [with Aquinas' commentary].
De generatione et corruptione, translated by an unknown scholar [with Aquinas].
De anima, translated by James of Venice [with Aquinas].
Parva naturalia, translated by various scholars:
De sensu and *De memoria* [with Aquinas];
De somno et vigilia [H. J. Drossaart Lulofs, n.p., 1943]; *De insomniis et De divinatione* [H. J. Drossaart Lulofs, Leiden, 1947]; *De longitudine*, *De iuventute*, *De morte*, *De respiratione* [Venice, 1496].
De coloribus, incomplete, translated by an unknown scholar [E. Franceschini, Louvain, 1955].
**Metaphysica*, bks. I–X and XII–XIV [Venice, 1562] and I–X, XII [with Aquinas].
Ethica Nicomachea, translated by Robert Grosseteste [R.-A. Gauthier, Leiden–Brussels, 1973].

III. Commentators on Aristotle.

(1) Alexander of Aphrodisias:

**In meteorologica*, Nicaea, 1260 [A. J. Smet, Louvain, 1968]; *In De sensu* [C. Thurot, Paris, 1875].

(2) Themistius:

In De anima, Viterbo, 1267 [G. Verbeke, Louvain, 1957].

(3) Ammonius:

In De interpretatione, 1268 [G. Verbeke, Louvain, 1961].

(4) Philoponus:

In De anima, bks. I.3 and **III.4–9, 1268 [G. Verbeke, Louvain, 1966].

(5) Simplicius:

In categorias, 1266 [Venice, 1516; also (first half) A. Pattin, Louvain, 1971]; **In De caelo*, Viterbo, 1271 [Venice, 1540].

IV. Proclus.

**Elementatio theologica*, Viterbo, 1268 [C. Vansteenkiste, 1951].
**De decem dubitationibus*, **De providentia et fato*, **De malorum subsistentia*, Corinth, 1280 [H. Boese, Berlin, 1960].
In Platonis Parmenidis priorem partem commentarium, including Plato's *Parmenides* as far as 142A (shortly before 1286; authenticated by Henry Bate) [extensive sections edited by V. Cousin, Paris, 1820; last section, lost in Greek, and Plato's text edited by R. Klibansky and L. Labowsky, London, 1953].
In Platonis Timaeum commentarium, extracts, containing also a few passages from Plato's *Timaeus* [G. Verbeke, Louvain, 1953].

V. Alexander of Aphrodisias (see also above, under Commentators on Aristotle).

De fato ad imperatores and *De fato*, which is *De anima*, bk. II (authorship authenticated by the surviving Greek manuscript owned by Moerbeke and carrying his autograph title of possession) [P. Thillet, Paris, 1963].

VI. Archimedes.

De quam pluribus theorematibus, which is *De lineis spiralibus*, 1269 [J. L. Heiberg, Leipzig, 1890].
De centris gravium, which is *De planis aeque repentibus*, 1269 [N. Tartaglia, Venice, 1543].
Quadratura parabolae, 1269 [L. Gauricus, Venice, 1503].
Dimensio circuli, 1269 [L. Gauricus, Venice, 1503; partly, J. L. Heiberg, Leipzig, 1890].
De sphaera et cylindro, 1269 [introduction to bks. I and II, J. L. Heiberg, Copenhagen, 1887, and Leiden, 1890, respectively].
De conoidalibus et sphaeroidalibus, 1269 [unpublished].
De insidentibus aquae, 1269 [bk. I, N. Tartaglia, Venice, 1543; both books, Curtius Troianus, Venice, 1565; collations by J. L. Heiberg, Leipzig, 1890; several sections edited by Heiberg, Leipzig, 1913].

VII. Commentator on Archimedes and Eutocius.

On the De sphaera et cylindro, 1269 [a small section edited by J. L. Heiberg, Leipzig, 1890]; *On the De centris gravium*, 1269 [unpublished].

VIII. Hero of Alexandria.

Catoptrica, which is Pseudo-Ptolemy, *De speculis*, 1269 [W. (G.) Schmidt, Leipzig, 1901].

IX. Ptolemy.

De Analemmate, 1269 [J. L. Heiberg, Leipzig, 1907].

X. Galen.

**De alimentis*, Viterbo, 1277 [Venice, 1490].

XI. Pseudo-Hippocrates.

**De prognosticationibus aegritudinum secundum motum lunae*, which is (?) *Astronomia* [Padua, 1483].

Some Latin translations attributed at different times to Moerbeke have been proved or can be proved not to be by him. Among them are the Pseudo-Aristotelian *Rhetorica ad Alexandrum* (by Anaximenes of Lampsacus) and *Oeconomica* and Hero of Alexandria's [?] *Pneumatica* or *De aquarum conductibus*.

Influence. Moerbeke's influence can be assessed from different points of view.

1. The popularity of many of his Aristotelian translations is evidenced by the surviving manuscripts of the thirteenth to the fifteenth centuries; printed editions of the fifteenth, sixteenth, and later centuries; and versions or adaptations into French, English, Greek, and Spanish made in the fourteenth, sixteenth, nineteenth, and twentieth centuries. From about 100 to nearly 300 manuscripts and up to a dozen printed editions exist of works which had never before been translated into Greek, or older translations of which had been superseded or revised. This means that these works became accessible—and to a large extent comprehensible—to most Latin-reading students of philosophy, and that the philosophical language adopted by Moerbeke (and in some cases his interpretations) has influenced philosophical culture since the thirteenth century.

2. The introduction into the Western Latin world—and the consequent extensive study in universities and ecclesiastical and monastic schools, or the less extensive but still very influential study by specialists—of works of Aristotle, Proclus, and Archimedes which had been practically lost sight of for several centuries. An extreme example is provided by Aristotle's *Politica*, which had never been the object of more than exceptional study—and that only among Greeks before the fifth and in the eleventh century—and was almost discovered for the world at large, and introduced as one of the basic classics of political thought, by Moerbeke through his translation. Again, it was through Moerbeke's translations that some of Proclus' works were taken up by eminent philosophers and became essential ingredients of philosophical outlooks which affected the background and contents of some of the great schools of thought of the later Middle Ages, Renaissance, and more recent times. This is particularly true for the *Elementatio theologica*, in which Moerbeke discovered the original text of those propositions which formed the nucleus of the *De causis*, possibly the most influential carrier of Neoplatonic doctrines, transmitted via the Arabic to the Latin schools of the late twelfth and following centuries; it is also true of Proclus' *In Platonis Parmenidis . . . commentarium* and *De providentia et fato*. A similar influence was exerted by the translations of Themistius' and Philoponus' commentaries on the *De anima*, of Simplicius' on the *Categoriae* and *De caelo*, and of Ammonius' on the *De interpretatione*. The importance of Moerbeke's translations of Archimedes has been sketched in a masterly way by M. Clagett in his article on Archimedes in vol. I of this Dictionary.

3. A better knowledge of the actual Greek texts of several works came about through Moerbeke's versions. In a few cases they are the only evidence for lost Greek texts (the whole of Hero's *Catoptrica* and Pseudo-Hippocrates' *De prognosticationibus secundum motum lunae*; an important section of Proclus' *Commentary on the Parmenides*; and some sections of Proclus' smaller treatises and of Archimedes' *De insidentibus aquae*). Apart from two instances, Moerbeke used for his translations manuscripts now lost or not yet identified; on many points some of them provide us with better evidence of the Greek originals than the known Greek manuscripts: this is especially the case for Aristotle's *Politica*. For every single work Moerbeke's translations add to our knowledge of the tradition and history of the Greek texts.

BIBLIOGRAPHY

I. ORIGINAL WORKS. Abundant bibliographical information can be found in G. Lacombe, L. Minio-Paluello *et al.*, *Aristoteles Latinus*, *Codices: Pars prior* (Rome, 1939; Bruges, 1957), 21–38; *Pars posterior et supplementa* (Cambridge, 1955), 773–782, 1277; and *Supplementa altera* (Bruges, 1961), 7–17. See also M. Grabmann, *Guglielmo di Moerbeke O.P., il traduttore delle opere di Aristotele*, vol. II of *I papi del duecento e l'Aristotelismo*, Miscellanea Historiae Pontificiae, XI (no. 20) (Rome, 1946), *passim*; and in the relevant sections of *Bulletin thomiste* and *Bulletin de théologie ancienne et médiévale*.

The existing MSS of translations from Aristotle and his commentators are listed and described in the 3 vols. cited above of *Aristoteles Latinus, Codices*; those of Archimedes in V. Rose, *Deutsche Literaturzeitung* (1884), 210–213, and J. L. Heiberg, "Neue Studien zu Archimedes," in *Abhandlungen zur Geschichte der Mathematik*, **5** (1890), 1–84; for Pseudo-Hippocrates, see H. Diels, "Die Handschriften der antiken Aerzte I," in *Abhandlungen der Preussischen Akademie der Wissenschaften* (1905). Most scholarly eds. contain additional information on the MSS. No survey was made of the printed eds. of Latin versions of Aristotle, accompanied or not accompanied by commentaries by Ibn Rushd, Aquinas, or others. The *Gesamtkatalog der Wiegendrucke* contains, under "Aristoteles" and the names of commentators, short descriptions of most eds. printed, or thought to have been printed, before 1501 but does not give sufficient identifications of the authors of the translations. The oldest eds. of some of Moerbeke's Aristotelian translations are found in fifteenth- and sixteenth-century printed texts. The eds. of Aristotelian writings mentioned in the text and carrying dates later than 1960 are contained in the series Aristoteles Latinus (part of the Corpus Philosophorum Medii Aevi); those of Aristotelian commentaries cited in the text dated 1957 and later are part of the Corpus Latinum Commentariorum in Aristotelem Graecorum; and most of those mentioned as being "with Aquinas" are found in the modern critical ed. of Aquinas' works, the Leonine ed. (Rome, 1882–　). A critical ed. of all the translations from Archimedes and Eutocius based on Moerbeke's autograph is in vol. II of M. Clagett, *Archimedes in the Middle Ages*. The MSS of the *Geomantia* known to date are listed in L. Thorndike and P. Kibre, *A Catalog of Incipits of Mediaeval Scientific Writings in Latin* (1963).

II. SECONDARY LITERATURE. By far the most exhaustive study of Moerbeke's life and the best collection of evidence, information on the works which he translated and on the opinions expressed on them through the centuries, and references to modern scholarly studies is Grabmann's *Guglielmo di Moerbeke, il traduttore . . .* (cited above). This work suffers, however, from the wartime circumstances in which the material was being assembled and from the fact that it was left to be edited and translated into "Germitalian" by rather incompetent hands; the misprints affecting essential data are far too numerous. Its extreme bias in favor of Aquinas' and the popes' share in providing Moerbeke with the initiatives which were in fact his own is all-pervasive and misleading. Among the older works mention should be made of the article on Moerbeke in I. Quétif and I. Échard, *Scriptores ordinis praedicatorum*, I (Paris, 1791), 388–391. The best modern, concise, and critical survey listing Moerbeke's translations and their more important eds. is in P. Thillet's version of Alexander of Aphrodisias' *De fato* (cited in text); unfortunately, he ascribes to Moerbeke more recent Latin translations of Archimedes and Eutocius. For Moerbeke's early stay in Greece, see O. van der Vat, *Die Anfänge der Franziskaner Mission . . . im nahen Orient . . .* (Werl, 1934); B. Altaner's two long articles on the missionaries' linguistic knowledge in the Middle East, in *Zeitschrift für Kirchengeschichte*, **53** (1934) and **55** (1936); V. Laurent, "Le Pape Alexandre IV et l'empire de Nicée," in *Échos d'Orient*, **38** (1935), 26–55; K. M. Setton, "The Byzantine Background to the Italian Renaissance," in *Proceedings of the American Philosophical Society*, **100** (1956), esp. 31–35.

On Witelo and Bate, see C. Baeumker, *Witelo, ein Philosoph . . .*, III, pt. 2 of *Beiträge zur Philosophie des Mittelalters* (Münster, 1908); G. Wallerand, "Henri Bate de Malines et Thomas d'Aquin," in *Revue néoscolastique de philosophie*, **36** (1934), 387–410, and his ed. of the first part of Bate's *Speculum*, *Les philosophes belges*, XI, pt. 1 (Louvain, 1931). On the question of Aquinas' influence on Moerbeke, the best critical assessment is in R.-A. Gauthier's intro. to *Sententia libri ethicorum*, I, which is vol. XLVIII of *S. Thomae de Aquino opera omnia* (Rome, 1969), 232*–235*, 264*–265*. A page from Moerbeke's holograph of his Archimedes is reproduced in B. Kattenbach *et al.*, *Exempla scripturarum*, II (Rome, 1929), pl. 20; and his autograph inscription of property of the Greek MS of Alexander's *De fato* is reproduced in L. Labowsky, "William of Moerbeke's Manuscript of Alexander of Aphrodisias," in *Mediaeval and Renaissance Studies*, n.s. **5** (1961), 155–162.

Studies on Moerbeke's works and on their influence have been directed mainly to aspects of his method as a translator, particularly to his vocabulary, often for the purpose of ascertaining or suggesting his authorship or of distinguishing his version from those by other scholars. Apart from the extensive "indices verborum" which accompany most modern eds. of his texts (esp. the vols. in Aristoteles Latinus and Corpus Latinum Commentariorum Graecorum and the eds. by Drossaart Lulofs and Thillet cited in text as well as the forthcoming vol. II of Clagett's *Archimedes*) and linguistic analyses in some of the introductions (again by Clagett, Lulofs, Thillet, Verbeke, Vansteenkiste, and Rudberg), there are many special inquiries: F. H. Fobes, "Mediaeval Versions of Aristotle's *Meteorology*," in *Classical Philology*, **10** (1915), 297–314; F. Pelster, "Die griechisch-lateinischen Metaphysikuebersetzungen des Mittelalters," in *Beiträge zur Geschichte der Philosophie des Mittelalters*, supp. **2** (1923), 89–118; L. Minio-Paluello, "Guglielmo di Moerbeke traduttore della 'Poetica' d'Aristotele, 1278," in *Rivista di filosofia neoscolastica*, **39** (1947), 1–17; "Henri Aristippe, Guillaume de Moerbeke et les traductions latines médiévales des *Météorologiques* et du *De generatione et corruptione*," in *Revue philosophique de Louvain*, **45** (1947), 206–235; D. J. Allan, "Mediaeval Versions of Aristotle *De caelo* and the *Commentary* of Simplicius," in *Mediaeval and Renaissance Studies*, **2** (1950), 82–120.

Various points and aspects of Moerbeke's influence, the dates of his translations in relation to the dates of works in which use was made of them, and commentaries based on his versions have been the object of scholarly study in many books and articles devoted to wider issues. To those already mentioned one may add D. A. Callus, "Les sources de Saint Thomas," in *Aristote et Saint-Thomas d'Aquin: Journées d'études* (Louvain–Paris, 1957), 93–174;

A. Dondaine, reviews in *Bulletin Thomiste* (1924 ff.); R. A. Gauthier's intro. to Thomas Aquinas, *Contra gentiles, livre premier* (Paris, 1961); B. Geyer, "Die Uebersetzungen der aristotelischen Metaphysik bei Albertus Magnus und Thomas . . .," in *Philosophisches Jahrbuch*, **30** (1917), 392–415; J. Isaac, *Le Peri Hermeneias en Occident de Boèce à Saint Thomas* (Paris, 1953); R. Klibansky, "Ein Proklosfund und seine Bedeutung," in *Sitzungsberichte der Heidelberger Akademie der Wissenschaften*, Phil.-hist. Kl., **5** (1928–1929); and "Plato's *Parmenides* in the Middle Ages and the Renaissance," in *Mediaeval and Renaissance Studies*, **1** (1943), 281–330; H. Lohr, "Mediaeval Latin Aristotle Commentaries," in *Traditio*, **23** (1967 ff.); A. Mansion, "Le commentaire de Saint Thomas sur le *De sensu et sensato* d'Aristote," in *Mélanges Mandonnet* (Paris, 1930), 83–102; C. Martin, "The Commentaries on the *Politics* of Aristotle in the Late Thirteenth and Early Fourteenth Centuries" (D. Phil. thesis, Oxford University, 1949; copy at the Bodleian Library, Oxford); and B. Schneider, *Die mittelalterlichen greichisch-lateinischen Uebersetzungen der Aristotelischen Rhetorik* (Berlin, 1971).

The study of the Greek tradition through Moerbeke's texts has been carried out extensively both in the process of editing the Greek texts—see, for instance, Heiberg's ed. of Archimedes and Eutocius (Leipzig, 1910–1915) and W. L. Newman's ed. of Aristotle's *Politica* (Oxford, 1887) —and as part of the Aristoteles Latinus (every vol. contains the results of this study). Many separate studies were devoted to problems in this field, including E. Lobel, "The Medieval Latin Poetics," in *Proceedings of the British Academy*, **17** (1931), 309–334, and the work of B. Schneider cited above.

Lorenzo Minio-Paluello

MOFFETT (MOUFET, MUFFET), THOMAS (*b.* London, England, 1553; *d.* Bulbridge, Wiltshire, England, 5 June 1604), *medicine, entomology.*

Moffett was the second son of a London haberdasher, Thomas Moffett, and Alice Ashley. He was educated at the Merchant Taylors' School and at Cambridge, where he studied medicine under John Caius, with Thomas Penny as a fellow student. After graduating in 1573 he read medicine in Basel, where he received the M.D. in 1578 and published several of his medical theses. He accepted the Paracelsian system of treating disease with drugs and advocated it on his return to England. In 1579 he visited Italy and Spain; he there studied the silkworm, which he later described in his entomology. A poem on the silkworm by "T.M." is usually attributed to him. In 1580 Moffett married his first wife, Jane Wheeler, who died in 1600, and traveled again in Germany before returning to Cambridge in 1582. On a visit to Denmark in 1582 he met Severinus, to whom he dedicated his book *De jure et praestantia chemicorum medicamentorum dialogus apologeticus*, published in Frankfurt in 1584 and widely read on the Continent.

Settling in England, Moffett practiced as a physician in Ipswich for a time, then established himself in London. He became a fellow of the College of Physicians in 1588. His professional attendance on the nobility brought him to the court of Elizabeth I, but the Earl of Pembroke persuaded him to move to Wiltshire, and secured for him a seat as Member of Parliament for Wilton in 1597, which he held until his death in 1604. His second wife, the widow Catherine Brown, survived him with their daughter.

Moffett is remembered today mainly for two works, both published posthumously. The *Theatrum insectorum* which bears his name has a complex history. When Konrad Gesner died in 1565 he left an unfinished book on entomology: this was eventually sold to his friend Thomas Penny, who had already done some work of his own on Gesner's collection of insects. Penny also acquired the notes on insects made by Edward Wotton of Oxford, and made some progress in amalgamating the information before his death in 1589. The work was then rescued from Penny's heir by his Cambridge friend Moffett, who added a number of descriptions and drawings from his own observations in England and on the Continent— including a number of "lesser living creatures," spiders, crustacea, and worms. Moffett prepared a manuscript with a fine title page engraved by William Rogers, with portraits of Moffett himself, Gesner, Wotton, and Penny. The title page was dated 1589; by 1590 Moffett was negotiating for publication in The Hague. That fell through, however, and he was unable to find a printer in England, probably because there was little demand in England for a book on natural history. After Moffett's death his apothecary Darnell sold the manuscript to Sir Theodore Mayerne, who, after having found a printer only with great difficulty, eventually published it in 1634. Since illustrations for the mass market had to be done cheaply, the book appeared with woodcuts and without the original title page. It was translated into English and issued as part of Edward Topsell's *History of Four-Footed Beasts and Serpents* in 1658.

The *Theatrum insectorum* itself is a systematic treatise dealing with the habits, habitat, breeding, and economic importance of insects, beginning with bees, which are accorded the most detailed treatment. The observations and illustrations, although usually thought inferior to those published by Aldrovandi in 1602, are of considerable interest. Moffett usually described the larval and adult forms separately, and was aware that "There are so many kindes of Butterflies as there are of the Cankerwormes." He further discussed the emergence of either normal butterflies or "ordinaries Flyes" (now known to be parasitic wasps) from similar pupae and described both the depredations wrought by locusts in Europe and their use as food. He also recorded observations of the movement of the tongue of the chameleon in feeding.

Moffett's other work was *Health's Improvement*, which was edited by Christopher Bennet and published in 1655. Designed for the layman to a greater degree than were the medical works published in Frankfurt and Nuremberg, the book is concerned mainly with food and diet, but includes descriptions of animals and fishes used for food, and is of particular interest for two chapters of observations about wild birds. While few of these observations were original, together they constitute the first printed list of British birds. Moffett was one of the first to recognize migration in birds and referred to woodcock and snipe "when they have rested themselves after their long flight from beyond the Seas, and are fat"; he also mentioned crane breeding in the fens, a practice that ceased shortly after Moffett's own time. In his *Panzoologia* (1661), Robert Lovell used Moffett's descriptions of both birds and insects extensively.

BIBLIOGRAPHY

I. Original Works. Of Moffett's two scientific works, the manuscript of *Theatrum insectorum* is in the British Museum, Sloane MS 4014. It was first published as *Insectorum, sive minimorum animalium* (London, 1634); the English trans. by John Rowland was issued as the third vol. of Edward Topsell, *The History of Four-Footed Beasts and Serpents. Whereunto is now added The Theater of Insects; or, lesser Living Creatures: as Bees, Flies, Caterpillars, to Spiders, Worms &c. by T. Muffet* (London, 1658); facs. repr. has a new intro. by Willy Ley (London, 1967). For *Health's Improvement: or, Rules Comprizing and Discovering the Nature, Method and Manner of Preparing all Sorts of Foods Used in this Nation* (London, 1655), a second ed. was "corrected and enlarged by Christopher Bennet . . . to which is now prefix'd, a short view of the author's life and writings by Mr. Oldys, and an introduction by R. James" (London, 1746). Other of Moffett's works are listed in the *Athenae Cantabrigiensis* (below).

II. Secondary Literature. The first biography of Moffett is by W. Oldys in the 1746 edition of *Health's Improvement*, pp. vii–xxxii, and includes the text of his will. There is an early evaluation of Moffett's medical ability by John Aikin in *Biographical Memoirs of Medicine in Great Britain* (London, 1780), 168–175. The article by Sidney Lee in *Dictionary of National Biography* includes a comprehensive survey of the manuscript sources for Moffett's life, and gives a short bibliography of early sources. C. H. Cooper and T. Cooper, *Athenae Cantabri-giensis, II, 1568–1609* (Cambridge, 1861), 400–402, 554, is a good account of Moffett's life with the most comprehensive bibliography of his works and sources of biographical material, mainly nineteenth century. The chapter on Moffett in C. E. Raven, *English Naturalists from Neckham to Ray* (Cambridge, 1947), ch. 10, 172–191, is critical of Moffett's originality and accuracy, and collates his information with that given by other naturalists.

The history of the *Theatrum insectorum* is in M. Burr, "Unpublished for Over Three Hundred Years: the Original Title-Page for the First Book on Natural History Printed in England," in *Field*, 27 August (1938), 495; H. M. Fraser, "Moufet's Theatrum Insectorum," in *Gesnerus*, **3** (1946), 131; and B. Milt, "Some Explanatory Notes to Mr. H. M. Fraser's Article about Moufet's Theatrum Insectorum," *ibid.*, 132–134. The text of Moffett's notes on ornithology is included in W. H. Mullens, *Thomas Muffett*, Hastings and St. Leonards Natural History Society, Occasional Publication no. 5 (1911).

Diana M. Simpkins

MOHL, HUGO VON (*b.* Stuttgart, Germany, 8 April 1805; *d.* Tübingen, Germany, 1 April 1872), *biology.*

Born into a respected bourgeois family, Mohl had three brothers who gained reputations in scholarship, economics, and politics; his brother Jules, a naturalized Frenchman, was professor of Persian at the Collège de France from 1847 to 1876 (on the Mohl brothers see Vapereau [1870]). Mohl had a classical education; but from an early age he demonstrated a predilection for science, especially for botany and optics, thus early revealing his vocation: it was in the field of microscopic botany that he made his most remarkable contributions. He studied medicine at Tübingen and in 1827 presented a work on the structure and movement of the climbing plants, a problem which concerned botanists throughout the nineteenth century. Mohl's doctoral thesis (1828) was devoted to the constitution of the pores of plants. In 1832 he was appointed professor of physiology at Bern and in 1835 professor of botany at Tübingen, a chair he occupied until his death.

Mohl's scientific work deals with extremely diverse areas of botany. Among them he devoted himself to the technical problems of the microscope that he himself was able to construct and recorded his findings in a manual on microscopy (1846).

After a century Mohl remains famous for his works on the microscopic anatomy of plants and for his contributions to knowledge of the plant cell. The publication which gives the best picture of his way of working and thinking is the comprehensive memoir "Die vegetabilische Zelle" (1853), in Wagner's *Handwörterbuch der Physiologie*, a classic reference work of the period. In this study Mohl sketched a veritable panorama of botany, taking as a base the cell, which he viewed as an "elementary organ." He summarized his own work, claiming priority in certain cases, and subjected the publications of his predecessors and contemporaries to a critical examination. He recalled that he was the first to demonstrate the fusion of aligned cells in the formation of ducts and to observe intracellular movements. He examined the structure of the cell and its derivatives, its generation by division or free formation, and its physiology as an organ of nutrition, of reproduction, and of movement. For Mohl the cell is composed of the membrane, the primordial utricle, the protoplasm, the nucleus, and the cellular fluid. He arrived at this conception after meticulous studies, which were the first efforts in cytochemistry. An impartial examination makes it appear that Mohl did not go beyond the discoveries of Raspail, which he did not know of and nowhere cites (cf. Klein [1936]).

The history of biology credits Mohl with the invention of the term "protoplasm" (independently of Purkyně, who had already used it in a different sense). A careful reading of the texts reveals that Mohl saw in this substance a preliminary material in cellular generation. This position is all the more surprising because he was one of the first to describe the generation of cells in plants by division starting from preexisting cells. The notion of protoplasm was integrated into the knowledge of the period; but it is a derivative sense of this word, defined by Max Schultze in 1861, which has survived in contemporary biology (cf. Robin [1872] and Klein [1936]). Mohl always limited himself to descriptions of concrete facts and carefully avoided drawing general conclusions from them; moreover, he did not write a synthetic exposition clearly summarizing his stand on the cell theory, which was then in full development.

Mohl had a happy childhood and adolescence, and a university career and personal life without difficulties. He remained unmarried and never attempted to surround himself with a circle of pupils. He was known as a meticulous worker, very clever with his hands, who brought a great number of precise details to bear on very circumscribed problems. He was one of the founders of the *Botanische Zeitung* (1843), one of the most famous periodicals of modern botany. He was also one of the promoters of the creation of the Faculty of Sciences at Tübingen, the first of its kind in Germany. From the time of his inauguration (1863) he proclaimed his hostility toward speculative thought and, in particular, to German *Naturphilosophie*, which was then in its dying stages (cf. Bünning [1963]).

Mohl's great ability was recognized very early in his life. He was awarded many decorations and honorific titles, a fact to which he drew attention. Among numerous academies and learned societies, he was a corresponding member of the Institut de France at a very early age (1838). The Order of the Crown of Württemberg, bestowed in 1843, conferred upon him a title of nobility. He died in his sleep on Easter day 1872. The laudatory obituary of De Bary (1872) and the biography of Sachs (1875) have perpetuated his memory in contemporary biology.

BIBLIOGRAPHY

I. ORIGINAL WORKS. Among Mohl's writings are *Mikrographie, oder Anleitung zur Kenntniss und zum Gebrauche des Mikroskops* (Tübingen, 1846); "Sur le mouvement du suc à l'intérieur des cellules," in *Annales des sciences naturelles*. Botanique, 3rd ser., **6** (1846), 84–96; "Saftbewegung im Inneren der Zellen," in *Botanische Zeitung*, **4** (1846), 73–78; 89–94; and "Die vegetabilische Zelle," in Rudolph Wagner, *Handwörterbuch der Physiologie*, IV (Brunswick, 1853), 167–309.

II. SECONDARY LITERATURE. See A. de Bary, "Hugo von Mohl," in *Botanische Zeitung*, **30** (1872), 561–579, with complete bibliography; E. Bünning, "Hugo von Mohl (1805–1872)," in H. Freund and A. Berg, *Geschichte der Mikroskopie*, I (Frankfurt, 1963), 273–280, with portrait; M. Klein, *Histoire des origines de la théorie cellulaire* (Paris, 1936), 60; C. Robin, *Anatomie et physiologie cellulaires* (Paris, 1873), 7, 249; J. Sachs, *Geschichte der Botanik vom 16. Jahrhundert bis 1860* (Munich, 1875), 315–335; and G. Vapereau, *Dictionnaire universel des contemporains*, 4th ed. (Paris, 1870), 1285–1286.

MARC KLEIN

MOHN, HENRIK (*b.* Bergen, Norway, 15 May 1835; *d.* Christiania [now Oslo], Norway, 12 September 1916), *meteorology, oceanography.*

Mohn became interested in science during his first year at the University of Christiania, where in 1858 he received his master's degree in mineralogy. Soon afterward he wrote a prize essay on the position of cometary orbits and became assistant professor of astronomy. In 1866 he was appointed director of the new Norwegian Meteorological Institute, which under his guidance grew into an important organization with 450 stations all over the country. From 1866 to 1913 he occupied the first chair of meteorology at the University of Christiania.

Mohn's many endeavors in practical meteorology resulted in a very wide range of publications. A series of annual bulletins and other reports and climatic tables for Norway were written or edited by him. Particular works dealt with thunderstorms, fog signals, and other subjects. He also perfected the hypsometer for measuring altitude by the boiling point of water.

With G. O. Sars, Mohn planned the Norwegian North Atlantic expeditions, participating in the three voyages that occupied the summers of 1876, 1877, and 1878. He edited the general report and wrote the sections on meteorology and oceanography. He also edited the meteorological data from Nansen's *Fram* expedition through the Northwest Passage of 1893–1896, from the Arctic expedition of 1898–1902, and from Amundsen's South Pole expedition of 1912–1913. Beginning in 1870, Mohn became very active in international organizations. At his death he was recognized as the grand old man of European meteorology.

Mohn was not only a brilliant empiricist, but also deeply interested in theory. His studies, with C. M. Guldberg, on the motions of the atmosphere (1876–1880) utilized the Coriolis law and also took into account friction between the atmosphere and the earth. The Mohn-Guldberg equations meant a breakthrough for dynamical meteorology and gave the first (although incomplete) theoretical foundation of the work begun by Buys Ballot, William Ferrel, and others. The new ideas were propagated in a book which, from a small and rather popular Norwegian version, developed into a comprehensive manual of meteorology that was translated into several languages.

BIBLIOGRAPHY

I. ORIGINAL WORKS. Mohn's writings include *Om Kometbaners indbyrdes Beliggenhed* (Christiania, 1861), trans. into French as *Mémoire sur la situation réciproque des comètes* (Christiania, 1861); *Norsk meteorologisk Aarbog* (Christiania, 1867 ff.); *Det Norske Meteorologiske Instituts Storm Atlas, Atlas des tempêtes* (Christiania, 1870); "Om Vind og Vejr," in *Folkevennen*, (1872), ; *Grundzüge der Meteorologie* (Berlin, 1875, 1879, 1883), trans. into Finnish (Helsinki, 1880) and into French (Paris, 1884); *Études sur les mouvements de l'atmosphère*, 2 vols. (Christiania, 1876–1880), written with C. M. Guldberg; *Den Norske Nordhavs-Expedition 1876–1878. The Norwegian North Atlantic Expedition. General Report* (Christiania, 1880); "Studien über Nebelsignale," in *Annalen der Hydrographie und maritime Meteorologie* (1882, 1893, 1895); *Den Norske Nordhavs-Expedition 1876–1878. . . . Meteorology* (Christiania, 1883); *Nordhavets Dybder, Temperatur og Strømninger* (Christiania, 1887); *Tordenbygernes Hyppighed i Norge 1867–83* (Christiania, 1887); *Les orages dans la peninsule scandinave* (Uppsala, 1888), written with H. H. Hildebrandsson; *Om Taage-*

signaler (Christiania, 1897); "Das Hypsometer als Luftdruckmesser und seine Anwendung zur Bestimmung der Schwerekorrektion," in *Skrifter . . . det Norske videnskapsakademi i Oslo*, Math.-naturvis. Kl. (1899); and "Neue Studien über das Hypsometer," in *Meteorologische Zeitschrift* (1908).

II. SECONDARY LITERATURE. See V. Bjerknes, *Meteorologien in Norge* (Christiania, 1917); the unsigned *Christian Joachim Mohn, hans forfaedres liv og efterkommere* (Oslo, 1928), 318 ff.; and T. Hesselberg, "Mohn, Henrik," in *Norsk Biografisk Leksikon*, IX (Oslo, 1939), 290 ff.

OLAF PEDERSEN

MOHOROVIČIĆ, ANDRIJA (*b.* Volosko, Istria, Croatia, 23 January 1857; *d.* Zagreb, Yugoslavia, 18 December 1936), *meteorology, seismology.*

Mohorovičić's father was a shipwright; his mother died shortly after his birth. A brilliant pupil at the grammar school in Rijeka, he entered the University of Prague in 1875, graduating in mathematics and physics. One of his teachers at Prague was Ernst Mach. There followed a period as a secondary school teacher, and in 1882 he was appointed to the Royal Nautical School in Bakar (Buccari), near Rijeka, where he taught, among other things, meteorology and oceanography. His interests turned strongly toward meteorology and in 1887 he founded the Meteorological Station of Bakar. In 1891 he was appointed professor at the Main Technical School in Zagreb, where in 1892 he became director of the meteorological observatory. In 1897 he received his doctorate from the University of Zagreb, becoming an unsalaried lecturer there the same year and reader in 1910.

Most meteorological centers in Croatia had been set up under control from Budapest. Mohorovičić campaigned actively to remove this control and in 1900 he succeeded in having the Zagreb observatory established as meteorological center for all Croatia and Slavonia, completely independent of Budapest, as the Royal Regional Center for Meteorology and Geodynamics. Soon after the turn of the century, seismology became his dominant interest and the field in which he became famous. He retired in 1921 when the reorganized Royal Regional Center was renamed the Geophysical Institute. Although troubled by weak eyesight since 1916, he continued in active seismological research until 1926.

Mohorovičić's fame rests nearly entirely on the results of his very thorough investigation of the destructive earthquake of 8 October 1909, which occurred about thirty miles south of Zagreb, in the Kulpa valley of Croatia. Previously the velocities of P

and *S* (primary and secondary) seismic waves had been treated as varying continuously with the depth, apart from minor discontinuities connected with geographic features such as sedimentary deposits, mountain ranges, and ocean floors. In his study of records of the Kulpa valley earthquake, however, Mohorovičić detected the presence of two distinct pairs of *P* and *S* phases recorded by seismographs at distances between 125 and 450 miles from the epicenter of the earthquake. His careful analysis showed that one of the pairs was associated with markedly slower speeds of wave travel. Mohorovičić correctly interpreted the observations as showing that the focus of the earthquake was inside a distinct outer layer of the earth; that the slower *P* and *S* waves had traveled directly to observing stations through this layer; and that the paths of the faster waves had been mostly below the layer, having been refracted when passing down from the focus through the separating boundary and later refracted upward through this boundary to the surface. He calculated the thickness of the layer as 30–35 miles. The work of other seismologists later confirmed this discovery, though reducing his estimate of the layer thickness, and showed that the layer was worldwide.

This outer layer of the earth is now conventionally called the crust, and the region between the crust and the central core (at a depth of 1,800 miles) is known as the mantle (originally the shell). The boundary separating the crust and the mantle is now called the Mohorovičić discontinuity (sometimes the *M* discontinuity). Its depth below the earth's surface is now known to be about 20 miles in continental shield areas, somewhat greater under large mountain ranges, but only 3–6 miles below ocean floors. Across the Mohorovičić discontinuity, the seismic *P* velocity changes fairly rapidly from about 4 to 5 miles per second and the *S* velocity from about $2\frac{1}{2}$ to 3 miles per second. The Mohorovičić discontinuity was the second major boundary to be discovered below the earth's surface by seismological means; in 1906 R. D. Oldham had established the existence of the central core. The depth of the boundary separating mantle and core was accurately determined by Beno Gutenberg in 1914.

One outcome of Mohorovičić's work on the 1909 earthquake was a classification of earthquakes for investigative purposes into near and distant earthquakes. Near earthquakes are well recorded within about 600 miles of the epicenter and within this range show low-velocity phases of the type that Mohorovičić had found. In distant earthquakes the dominant interest is on records taken beyond this distance.

The name of Mohorovičić caught the public fancy in 1957 when the International Association of Seismology and Physics of the Earth's Interior sponsored a proposal, the Mohole project, to drill through the earth's crust to just below the Mohorovičić discontinuity. In the hands of journalists the discontinuity soon came to be referred to as the Moho.

As a meteorologist Mohorovičić was noted for his great organizational ability, his insistence on high standards of precision wherever he had responsibilities, and his success in circumventing bureaucracy. His research papers dealt with such subjects as cloud movements, the variation of atmospheric temperature with height, rainfall in Zagreb, and a tornado. Mohorovičić was also noted for his deep appreciation of what was needed to produce an up-to-date seismological observatory. In 1901, soon after the Royal Regional Center had been set up, a strong earthquake was felt in Zagreb, as a consequence of which he and a colleague were able to secure for the center a reliable seismograph constructed by the noted Italian seismologist G. Agamennone. With the addition of further equipment, including a Wiechert seismograph and equipment for ensuring precise timing, the center had become by 1908 one of the leading seismological observatories in central Europe. The thoroughness of this preparation was a major factor in the success of his study of the 1909 Kulpa valley earthquake.

Mohorovičić contributed research papers on a variety of other topics in seismology. He evolved a method of determining earthquake epicenters and constructed curves giving the travel times of seismic waves over distances of up to 10,000 miles from the source. He also carried out macroseismic studies—the investigation of the salient features of an earthquake from reports of observations of surface effects (geological effects, effects on buildings, bridges, among others) taken over a wide area surrounding the epicenter, and he investigated the subject of constructing earthquake-proof buildings. His ideas on improving the construction of seismographs were unrealized due to insufficient financial support.

Mohorovičić was most punctilious, tenacious, and meticulous in all his scientific work, and was known for always talking to the point. He was keen and enthusiastic in his undertakings and intolerant of slipshod work. Even after his eyesight began to fail, he worked far into the night reading specialized papers on seismology. An extremely good-humored man, he was idolized by his colleagues. His success was partly due to his unusual linguistic ability. At the age of fifteen, he spoke Croatian, Italian, English, and French, and later spoke German, Czech, Latin, and classical Greek as well. His son Stjepan is also a distinguished seismologist. Mohorovičić was elected to the Yugoslav Academy of Sciences in 1898 and was secretary of the mathematics and science section from 1918 to 1922.

BIBLIOGRAPHY

I. ORIGINAL WORKS. Mohorovičić's best-known publication is "Das Beben vom 8.X.1909," in *Jahrbuch des meteorologischen Observatoriums in Zagreb* for 1909, pt. 4, par. 1 (1910), 1–67. The essential content of this paper was published in French by E. Rothé, "Sur la propagation des ondes sismiques au voisinage de l'épicentre. Préliminaires continues et trajets à réfraction," in *Publications du Bureau central séismologique international*, ser. A, Travaux scientifiques, fasc. **1** (1924), 17–59. Mohorovičić published a total of 21 papers on meteorology and seismology from 1888 to 1926, mostly in journals published in Zagreb; a full list is held by the University of Zagreb.

II. SECONDARY LITERATURE. The proceedings of a symposium held in Zagreb in March 1968 in honor of Mohorovičić include an article by his student and collaborator Josip Mokrović, "Andrija Mohorovičić—sein Leben und Wirken."

K. E. BULLEN

MOHR, CARL FRIEDRICH (*b*. Koblenz, then France [now Germany], 4 November 1806; *d*. Bonn, Germany, 28 September 1879), *analytical chemistry, physical chemistry, agricultural chemistry, geology.*

Mohr's father, Karl, was an apothecary and city councillor. After completing secondary school, Mohr attended the University of Bonn, where he studied botany, chemistry, and mineralogy. After gaining practical experience with his father, he attended the chemistry lectures of Leopold Gmelin at Heidelberg and those of Heinrich Rose in analytical chemistry at Berlin. He then obtained his degree in pharmacy and took over his father's business. Besides attending to the business, he was interested in various areas of science. In 1833 he married Jacobine Derichs; they had three sons and two daughters.

In 1837 Mohr published an essay, "Ansichten über die Natur der Wärme," in which he wrote: "Apart from the known chemical elements, there exists in nature only one agent, and that is force; it can show itself in appropriate relationships as motion, chemical affinity, cohesion, electricity, light, heat or magnetism. And out of each of these kinds of phenomena all the others can be produced" (*Zeitschrift für Physik, Mathematik und verwandte Wissenschaften*, **5** [1837], 419). On the basis of this statement, he later claimed priority regarding the law of the conservation of energy. In 1847 Mohr

wrote a commentary on the Prussian pharmacopoeia and *Lehrbuch der pharmazeutischen Technik*. In this period he also carried out titrimetric experiments, the results of which are in *Lehrbuch der chemisch-analytischen Titriermethode* (1855). In the meantime Mohr had established a vinegar factory with his son-in-law and purchased an estate at Metternich, to which he moved after selling his apothecary's shop. He now concerned himself with fermentation and the cultivation of grapes, and wrote popular books on these subjects. He also experimented with artificial fertilizers, following the ideas of his close friend Liebig. In 1863 his factory failed, and Mohr found himself and his family in financial difficulties. Through Liebig's help he qualified as a *Privatdozent* at the University of Berlin, at the age of fifty-nine. A short time later he moved to Bonn and was *Dozent* at the university there. He soon turned to new areas of research and studied geology, on which science he developed original but wholly incorrect opinions.

Mohr's attention next turned to thermodynamics. He recalled his statement on force and had it reprinted in a book. His commentary on it is chracteristic: "This passage was written by me thirty-three years ago and contains, as I now see, the main features of the mechanical theory of heat." Mohr published several works in this field; but because he lacked the necessary mathematical knowledge, his works were failures.

Mohr had a passionate, critical, and combative nature and was therefore unpopular with his colleagues. He was active in many areas, yet much of his activity was marked by dilettantism. He was a skillful author and wrote many books.

Mohr's most lasting contribution was in titration. His *Lehrbuch . . . Titriermethode* was the first successful compendium in this new field of analytical chemistry; It went through eight new editions between 1856 and 1913 and was translated into several languages. Mohr invented many new titration procedures and examined and often improved most of the older ones. Many methods and designs of apparatus bear his name: the Mohr test for iron and chloride determination, the Mohr pinchcock burette, the Mohr balance for the determination of specific gravity, and Mohr's salt (ferrous ammonium sulfate) are evidence of his skill in the laboratory. The cooling device generally called the Liebig reflux and the useful cork borer were also invented by Mohr.

BIBLIOGRAPHY

I. ORIGINAL WORKS. Mohr's writings include *Commentar zur preussischen Pharmacopöe*, 2 vols. (Brunswick,

1847; 2nd ed., 1853); *Lehrbuch der pharmazeutischen Technik* (Brunswick, 1847; 2nd ed., 1853), also trans. into English as *Practical Pharmacy* (London, 1848) and as *Practice of Pharmacy* (Philadelphia, 1849); *Taschenbuch der chemischen Receptirkunst* (Hamburg, 1854); *Lehrbuch der chemisch-analytischen Titriermethode* (Brunswick, 1855; 6th and 7th eds., with A. Classen, 1880 and 1896; 8th ed., with H. Beckurts, 1912), trans. into French as *Traité d'analyse chimique par la méthode des liqueurs titrées* (Paris, 1888); *Der Weinstock und der Wein* (Koblenz, 1864); *Geschichte der Erde* (Bonn, 1866); *Mechanische Theorie der chemischen Affinität und die neuere Chemie* (Brunswick, 1868); and *Allgemeine Theorie der Bewegung und der Kraft als Grundlage der Physik und Chemie* (Brunswick, 1874). Many of his articles appeared in Poggendorff's *Annalen der Physik* and *Justus Liebigs Annalen der Chemie*.

II. SECONDARY LITERATURE. See E. E. Aynsley and W. A. Campbell, "Karl Friedrich Mohr's Contributions to Chemical Apparatus," in *School Science Review* (1959), 312; R. Hasenclever, "Erinnerungen an Friedrich Mohr," in *Berichte der Deutschen chemischen Gesellschaft*, **33** (1900), 3827; G. Kahlbaum, *Justus von Liebig und Friedrich Mohr in ihren Briefen* (Leipzig, 1904); Ralph E. Oesper, "Karl Friedrich Mohr," in *Journal of Chemical Education*, **4** (1927), 1357; J. R. Partington, *History of Chemistry*, IV (London, 1964), 317–318; J. M. Scott, "Karl Friedrich Mohr, Father of Volumetric Analysis," in *Chymia*, **3** (1950), 191; and F. Szabadváry, *History of Analytical Chemistry* (Oxford–New York, 1966), pp. 241–250, also available in German, *Geschichte der analytischen Chemie* (Brunswick, 1966), pp. 245–257.

F. SZABADVÁRY

MOHR, CHRISTIAN OTTO (*b.* Wesselburen, Holstein, 8 October 1835; *d.* Dresden, Germany, 2 October 1918), *civil engineering.*

A descendent of Holstein landowners, Mohr studied engineering at the Polytechnic Institute of Hannover, which he entered in 1851. As an engineer for the state railroads of Hannover and Oldenburg, he not only built some notable bridges but also began to publish original research papers. He published continuously into his eighties. In 1867 Mohr became professor of mechanics and civil engineering at the Technische Hochschule in Stuttgart and, from 1873, at Dresden, where he remained after his retirement in 1900. Commensurate with his steadily growing fame, he received the usual honors in generous measure. Many of his students, including Föppl, described Mohr as their most remarkable teacher. He was of imposing height, proud and taciturn; his ideals in lecturing as well as in writing were simplicity, clarity, and conciseness.

With the exception of one textbook, Mohr published only original research papers. In his first publication

(1860), on the theory of continuous beams, he presented the three-moments equation (derived earlier by Clapeyron and Bertot) for the first time in general form by adding terms to account for vertical variations of the supports. In 1868, recognizing that the differential equation of the elastic line has the same form as that of the funicular curve, he developed the method of influence lines, which makes it possible to determine the deflections of a loaded beam, even of varying cross section, without requiring the integration of its differential equation. In 1874 he independently rediscovered a method of determining the stresses in statically indeterminate frameworks that had been published, somewhat obscurely, by Maxwell ten years earlier. "Mohr's stress circle," his most widely known contribution, was described in a paper of 1882. Following a suggestion (1866) of Karl Culmann he devised a simple graphic representation of the stresses at one point. Mohr's theory of failure, based upon the concept of the stress circle, has been widely accepted in engineering practice.

BIBLIOGRAPHY

I. ORIGINAL WORKS. Apart from the textbook *Technische Mechanik* (Stuttgart, 1877), Mohr wrote only research papers, which were collected as *Abhandlungen aus dem Gebiete der technischen Mechanik* (Berlin, 1906).

II. SECONDARY LITERATURE. Biographical information on Mohr can be found in three articles by W. Gehler: "Christian Otto Mohr," in *Festschrift Otto Mohr zum 80. Geburtstag* (Berlin, 1916), v–vii; "Otto Mohr," in *Zentralblatt der Bauverwaltung*, **38** (1918), 425; and "Otto Mohr," in *Zeitschrift des Vereins deutscher Ingenieure*, **62** (1918), 114. See also Poggendorff, V, 868; VI, 1761. Mohr's technical work is discussed extensively in Stephen P. Timoshenko, *History of Strength of Materials* (New York, 1953), *passim*.

OTTO MAYR

MOHR, GEORG (*b.* Copenhagen, Denmark, 1 April 1640; *d.* Kieslingswalde, near Görlitz, Germany, 26 January 1697), *mathematics.*

Mohr was the son of David Mohrendal (or Mohrenthal), a hospital inspector and tradesman. His parents taught him reading, writing, and basic arithmetic, but his love for mathematics could not be satisfied in Denmark, and in 1662 he went to Holland, where Huygens was teaching, and later to England and France. He returned to Denmark, but about 1687 he went again to Holland, this time because of a difference with King Christian V. Wishing to be scientifically independent, he remained aloof from official positions; but Tschirnhausen finally persuaded him to come to Kieslingswalde to participate in his mathematical projects. Mohr went there in 1695, accompanied by his wife, whom he had married in 1687, and by his three-year-old son. Only one of his works, the *Euclides danicus* (1672), a valuable short work, is known today; but his son claimed that he wrote three books on mathematics and philosophy that were well received by scholars.

Mohr is often mentioned in the intellectual correspondence of the day. He corresponded with Leibniz, with Pieter van Gent, and with Ameldonck Bloeck, a member of Spinoza's circle. In 1675 Oldenburg sent Leibniz a work of Mohr's on the root extraction of $A + \sqrt{B}$. Leibniz, in a letter of 1676 to Oldenburg in which he refers to "Georgius Mohr Danus, in geometria et analysi versatissimus," mentions that he learned from Mohr that Collins had the expansions for $\sin x$ and $\arcsin x$. Unfortunately, little else of Mohr's scientific activity is known.

In 1928 Mohr's *Euclides danicus*, which had fallen into obscurity, was republished with a preface by J. Hjelmslev. Hjelmslev recognized that in 1672 Mohr had been dealing with a problem made famous 125 years later by Mascheroni, namely, that of making constructions with compass alone.

The book has two parts: the first consists of the constructions of the first six books of Euclid; the second, of various constructions. The problem of finding the intersection of two lines, which is of some theoretical importance, is solved incidentally in the second part in connection with the construction of a circle through two given points and tangent to a given line.

Hjelmslev made the acute observation that a minor variant of Mohr's constructions enables one to add and subtract segments on the sphere and in the hyperbolic plane.

The obscurity that befell Mohr and his book can be attributed, in some degree, to the presentation of the material. In the body of the book, Mohr does not state the issue until the very last paragraph, although the lines are referred to as "imagined" *(gedachte)*. In the dedication to Christian V, he does say that he believes he has done something new, and on the title page the issue is explicitly stated. Still, it would be easy for an inattentive reader to misjudge the value of the book.

According to Hjelmslev, Mascheroni's result—that all ruler and compass constructions can be done by compass alone—was already known and systematically expounded by Mohr. (The justice of this judgment and the question of the independence of Mascheroni's work are examined in the article on Mascheroni.)

The laconic Mohr tells us nothing about the genesis of his ideas. A guess is that the fundamental problem stems from a similar problem, that of the compass of a single opening, which was posed in the contests of the great Renaissance mathematicians. This conjecture might be supported by a historical study of the problems in the second part of the book: νεύσεις (inclinations) problems; maxima-minima problems; the problem of Pothenot, solved in 1617 by Snellius in his *Eratosthenes batavus;* and problems in perspective.

BIBLIOGRAPHY

Mohr's *Euclides danicus* (Amsterdam, 1672) was translated into German by J. Pál, with a foreword by J. Hjelmslev (Copenhagen, 1928).

Hjelmslev has written two articles on Mohr: "Om et af den danske matematiker Georg Mohr udgivet skrift *Euclides Danicus*," in *Matematisk Tidsskrift*, B (1928), 1–7; and "Beiträge zur Lebenabschreibung von Georg Mohr (1640–1697)," in *Kongelige Danske Videnskabernes Selskabs Skrifter, Math.-fysiske Meddelelser*, **11** (1931), 3–23.

A. SEIDENBERG

MOHS, FRIEDRICH (*b*. Gernrode, Anhalt-Bernburg, Germany, 29 January 1773; *d*. Agordo, Tirol, Italy, 29 September 1839), *mineralogy, geology*.

One of Abraham Werner's outstanding students, Mohs made his primary scientific contribution in systematic mineralogy. He also proposed the scale of hardness for minerals, which is named for him and which is still in use.

Mohs displayed a marked interest in science at an early age and received a private education before entering the University of Halle in 1797. In 1798 he matriculated at the mining academy at Freiberg, where in addition to physics and mathematics he studied mineralogy under Werner. In 1802 Mohs was invited to Great Britain by his fellow students George Mitchell and Robert Jameson to participate in the planning of a mining academy at Dublin. Although the proposed academy was never established, the journey enabled Mohs to study the geology and mineralogy of Ireland and Scotland and to make lasting friends among Scottish geologists.

On Mitchell's recommendation, Mohs in 1802 was commissioned by J. F. von der Null, a Viennese banker, to prepare a systematic description of his important mineral collection. In 1804 Mohs published a two-volume description of this collection and two other works, *Beschreibung des Gruben gebäudes*

Himmelfürst ohnweit Freiberg and *Über die oryktognostische Klassifikation, nebst Versuch eines auf blosse äussere Kennzeichen gegründeten Mineralsystems*, in which he first expressed his misgivings with Werner's approach to mineralogy. In 1810, while on one of his frequent mining and mineralogical explorations, he encountered Werner at Carlsbad. Failing to convince Werner of the inadequacy of his mineralogical method, Mohs determined to establish systematic mineralogy on a completely new basis.

In 1811 Archduke Johann established the Johanneum in Graz, and Mohs was appointed curator of the mineral collection and charged with adding to it the minerals and rocks of Styria. Mohs enlisted the young scholar Wilhelm Haidinger to help in this work, and Haidinger remained with Mohs until 1822. In 1812 Mohs became professor of mineralogy at the Johanneum and in the same year revealed the basis of his new classificatory system in his *Versuch einer Elementar-Methode zur naturhistorischen Bestimmung und Erkennung der Fossilien*, in which he first proposed his hardness scale for minerals. Miners and mineralogists had long been accustomed to scratch a mineral to aid in determining the species. In an attempt to make this method more certain, Mohs proposed a scale of increasing hardness from one to ten as follows: talc, 1; gypsum, 2; calcite, 3; fluorite, 4; apatite, 5; feldspar, 6; quartz, 7; topaz, 8; corundum, 9; and diamond, 10. Intermediate degrees of hardness were subsequently added to the Mohs scale. Mineralogists did not commonly employ the scale until the 1820's, after the publication of the English translation of Mohs's *Die Charaktere der Klassen, Ordnungen, Geschlecter, und Arten der naturhistorischen Mineral-Systems*, in which the scale was prominently featured.

Mohs remained at Graz until 1817. During this period he worked at perfecting his method of mineral classification, giving particular attention to the possible arrangements of minerals in crystal systems based on external symmetry. In 1817 he again traveled extensively in Great Britain, impressing Scottish mineralogists in particular with his novel ideas. Following Werner's death in 1817 Mohs was called to Freiberg as professor of mineralogy, and he assumed this post in the autumn of 1818.

In 1822 and 1824 Mohs published his two-volume *Grund-Riss der Mineralogie*, the first volume of which was largely devoted to the explanation of his ideas concerning crystallography and the second to a systematic description of minerals. Mohs postulated four crystal systems based on external symmetry: rhombohedral (hexagonal), pyramidal (tetragonal), prismatic (orthorhombic), and tessular (cubic). These divisions were similar to those proposed in 1816–1817

by Christian Samuel Weiss, who had approached the problem in much the same manner. Mohs, however, did not refer to Weiss's prior publication, and Weiss publicly accused him of plagiarism. Mohs defended himself in a letter to the *Edinburgh Philosophical Journal* (**8** [1823], 275–290), explaining that his dissatisfaction with Haüy's crystallographic concepts had led him to develop his own ideas.

Mohs, however, had surpassed Weiss in his analysis. In the first volume of *Grund-Riss* (pp. 56 ff.) he mentioned the possible existence of symmetry systems in which the crystallographic axes were not mutually perpendicular; and in the second volume (pp. vi–viii) he affirmed their existence. These new systems, the monoclinic and the triclinic, were described by K. F. Naumann in 1824 and were fully developed by Mohs in 1832. *Grund-Riss*, substantially amended and revised, was translated into English by Wilhelm Haidinger as *Treatise on Mineralogy* (1825). Mohs's classificatory system, based primarily on crystal form, hardness, and specific gravity, was not received favorably by most mineralogists.

In 1826 Mohs resigned his professorship at Freiberg to accept a position in Vienna, first to reorganize the imperial collection, which he augmented by the acquisition of the von der Null collection, and then as professor of mineralogy at the university in 1828. In 1835 he resigned to become imperial counselor of the exchequer in charge of mining and monetary affairs. This position required him to travel frequently to all parts of the Austro-Hungarian empire. He died while on a journey to inspect the volcanic areas of southern Italy.

BIBLIOGRAPHY

I. ORIGINAL WORKS. Mohs's chief works are *Beschreibung des Gruben gebäudes Himmelfürst ohnweit Freiberg* (Vienna, 1804); *Des Herrn J. F. von der Null Mineralien-Kabinet*, 2 vols. (Vienna, 1804); *Über die oryktognostische Klassifikation, nebst Versuch eines auf blosse äussere Kennzeichen gegründeten Mineralsystems* (Vienna, 1804); *Versuch einer Elementar-Methode zur naturhistorischen Bestimmung und Erkennung der Fossilien* (Vienna, 1812); *Die Charaktere der Klassen, Ordnungen, Geschlecter, und Arten der naturhistorischen Mineral-Systems* (Dresden, 1820), translated as *The Characters of the Classes, Orders, Genera, and Species, or the Characteristics of the Natural-History System of Mineralogy* (Edinburgh, 1820); *Grund-Riss der Mineralogie*, 2 vols. (Dresden, 1822–1824), translated, revised, and expanded by Wilhelm Haidinger as *Treatise on Mineralogy, or the Natural History of the Mineral Kingdom*, 3 vols. (Edinburgh, 1825); *Leichtfässliche Anfangsgründe der Naturgeschichte des Mineralreiches*, 2 vols. (Vienna, 1832–1839), vol. II completed by F. X. M.

Zippe; *Anleitung zum Schürfen* (Vienna, 1838); and the posthumous *Die ersten Begriffe der Mineralogie und Geognosie für engehende Bergbeamte*, 2 vols. (Vienna, 1842).

II. SECONDARY WORKS. The principal biographical source for Mohs, which includes an autobiography to 1830, is Wilhelm Fuchs, G. Haltmeyer, and F. Leydolt, eds., *Friedrich Mohs und sein Wirken in wissenschaftlicher Hinsicht: ein biographischer Versuch entworfen und zur Enthüllingsfeier seines Monumentes im st. st. Johanneums-Garten zu Grätz* (Vienna, 1843). Other sources are *Festschrift zur hundertjährigen Jubiläum der Bergakademie zu Freiberg* (Dresden, 1866), 24–28; Franz von Kobell, *Geschichte der Mineralogie* (Munich, 1864), 216–222; Paul Groth, *Entwicklungsgeschichte der mineralogischen Wissenschaften* (Berlin, 1926), 249–250; and *Allgemeine deutsche Biographie*, XXII (Leipzig, 1885), 76–79.

JOHN G. BURKE

MOISEEV, NIKOLAY DMITRIEVICH (*b.* Perm, Russia, 16 December 1902; *d.* Moscow, U.S.S.R., 6 December 1955), *celestial mechanics, astronomy, mathematics.*

After graduating from the Perm Gymnasium in 1919, Moiseev entered the Faculty of Physics and Mathematics of Perm State University, where he also worked as a laboratory assistant. In 1922 he transferred to Moscow University, from which he graduated in 1923, having specialized in astronomy. In 1922 he became a junior scientific co-worker at the State Astrophysics Institute (since 1931 part of the P. K. Sternberg Astronomical Institute). After completing his graduate work there, in 1929 Moiseev defended his dissertation "O nekotorykh osnovnykh voprosakh teorii proiskhozhdenia komet, meteorov i kosmicheskoy pyli" ("On Certain Basic Questions of the Theory of the Origin of Comets, Meteors, and Cosmic Dust"). From 1929 to 1947 he taught mathematics at the N. E. Zhukovsky Military Air Academy. In 1935 he was awarded the degree of doctor of physics and mathematical sciences and the title of professor. He was director of the department of celestial mechanics at the University of Moscow from 1938 to 1955 and was head of the P. K. Sternberg Astronomical Institute from 1939 to 1943.

The recognized leader of the Moscow school of celestial mechanics, Moiseev published more than 120 works on the mechanical theory of cometary forms; the cosmogony of comets, meteors, and cosmic dust; theoretical gravimetry, including an original method (the "nonregularized earth") used in the theory of determining the forms of geoids from gravimetric observations; and dynamic cosmogony. To the study of the general characteristics of the trajectories of celestial bodies he applied qualitative methods based on the use of differential equations of movement and certain known integrals. He introduced qualitative regional characteristics of the trajectory, such as its contacts with certain given curves and surfaces and its longitudinal and transversal stability.

Moiseev applied qualitative methods to problems of certain specific celestial bodies, and his investigations of the characteristics of stability of orbital motion found many applications in problems of airplane and missile dynamics. His 1949 monograph *Ocherki razvitia teorii ustoychivosti* ("Essays of the Development of the Theory of Stability") presented a historical analysis of the subject from antiquity to the twentieth century.

From 1940 to 1955 Moiseev published the results of his investigations on secular and periodic perturbations and the motions of celestial bodies. He developed concepts of the internal and external environments and twofold averaging. Moiseev established his own, interpolational-average scheme to supplement those of Gauss and Delaunay. Approximate empirical integrals of motion, deduced from observations of celestial bodies, were used for averaging the force function. This method allows the integration of the averaged differential equations of motion and the computation of the ephemerides of perturbation of motion.

Moiseev's chief contributions to mathematics were his two new methods of solving systems of linear differential equations: the method of determinant integrals and the interational method.

BIBLIOGRAPHY

I. ORIGINAL WORKS. Moiseev's early writings are "O vychislenii kometotsentricheskikh koordinat chastitsy kometnogo khvosta" ("On the Computation of the Comet-centered Coordinates of the Particles of the Comet Tail"), in *Russkii astronomicheskii zhurnal*, **1**, pt. 2 (1924), 79–86; "O khvoste komety 1901 I" ("On the Tail of the Comet of 1901 I"), *ibid.*, **2**, pt. 1 (1925), 73–84; "O vychislenii effektivnoy sily i momenta izverzhenia chastitsy kometnogo khvosta" ("On the Computation of the Effective Force and Moment of Ejection of the Particles of a Comet Tail"), *ibid.*, **2**, pt. 2 (1925), 54–60; and "O stroenii sinkhronnykh konoidov" ("On the Structure of Synchronic Conoids"), *ibid.*, **4**, pt. 3 (1927), 184–190.

Subsequent works are "Über einige Grundfragen der Theorie des Ursprungs der Kometen, Meteoren und des kosmischen Staubes (Kosmogonische Studien)" in *Trudy Gosudarstvennogo astrofizicheskogo instituta*, **5**, no. 1 (1930), 1–87; *Trudy Gosudarstvennogo astronomicheskogo instituta im P. K. Sternberga*, **5**, no. 2 (1933), 1–63; *Astronomicheskii Zhurnal*, **9**, nos. 1–2 (1932), 30–52; and *Trudy*

Gosudarstvennogo astronomicheskogo instituta im P. K. Sternberga, **6**, no. 1 (1935), 5–28, 50–58; "Intorno alla legge di resistenza al moto dei corpi in un mezzo pulviscolare," in *Atti dell'Accademia nazionale dei Lincei. Rendiconti*, **15** (1932), 135–139, 377–381, 443–447; "Sulle curve definite da un sistema di equazioni differenziali di secondo ordine," *ibid.*, Ser. 6a, **20** (1934), 178–182, 256–265, 321–327; "O nekotorykh obshchikh metodakh kachestvennogo izuchenia form dvizhenia v problemakh nebesnoy mekhaniki" ("On Certain General Methods of Qualitative Study of the Forms of Motion in Problems of Celestial Mechanics"), in *Trudy Gosudarstvennogo astronomicheskogo instituta im P. K. Sternberga*, **7**, pt. 1 (1936), 5–127; **9**, pt. 2 (1939), 5–45, 47–81, 165–166; **14**, pt. 1 (1940), 7–68; **15**, pt. 1 (1945), 7–26; and "O nekotorykh svoystvakh traektory v ogranichennoy probleme trekh tel" ("On Certain Properties of Trajectories in a Limited Three-Body Problem"), *ibid.*, **7**, pt. 1 (1936), 129–225; **9**, pt. 1 (1936), 44–71; **9**, pt. 2 (1939), 82–114, 116–131, 167–170; **15**, pt. 1 (1945), 27–74.

Also published in the 1930's were "Über die Relativkrummung der zwei benachbarten Trajektorien. Zum Frage über die Stabilität nach Jacobi," in *Astronomicheskii Zhurnal*, **13**, no. 1 (1936), 78–83; "Su alcune proposizioni di morfologia dei movimenti nei problemi dinamichi analoghi a quello del tre corpi," in *Revista de ciencias* (Lima), **39** (1937), 45–50; "Über Stabilität Wahrscheinlichkeitsstrehnung," in *Mathematische Zeitschrift*, **42**, no. 4 (1937), 513–537; "O postroenii oblastey sploshnoy ustoychivosti i neustoychivosti v smysle Lyapunova" ("On the Construction of Areas of Continuous Stability and Instability in Lyapunov's Sense"), in *Doklady Akademii nauk SSSR*, **20**, no. 6 (1938), 419–422; and "O fazovykh oblastyakh sploshnoy ustoychivosti i neustoychivosti" ("On Phase Areas of Continuous Stability and Instability"), *ibid.*, 423–425.

Moiseev's later works are "O nekotorykh osnovnykh uproshchennykh skhemakh nebesnoy mekhaniki, poluchaemykh pri pomoshchi osredenenia raznykh variantov problemy trekh tel" ("On Certain Basic Simplified Schemes of Celestial Mechanics Obtained With the Aid of Averaging Different Variants of the Problem of Three Bodies"), in *Trudy Gosudarstvennogo astronomicheskogo instituta im Sternberga*, **15**, pt. 1 (1945), 75–117; **20** (1951), 147–176; **21** (1952), 3–18; **24** (1954), 3–16; and in *Vestnik Moskovskogo gosudarstvennogo universiteta*, no. 2 (1950), 29–37; "A. M. Lyapunov i ego trudy po teorii ustoychivosti" ("A. M. Lyapunov and His Works on the Theory of Stability"), in *Uchenya zapiski Moskovskogo gosudarstvennogo universiteta*, no. 91 (1947), 129–147; "Kosmogonia" ("Cosmogony"), in the collection of papers, *Astronomia v SSSR za 30 let* ("Astronomy in the U.S.S.R. for Thirty Years"; Moscow–Leningrad, 1948), 184–191; *Ocherki razvitia teorii ustoychivosti* ("Essays of the Development of the Theory of Stability"; Moscow–Leningrad, 1949); and "Obshchii ocherk razvitia mekhaniki vo Rossii i v SSSR" ("A General Sketch of the Development of Mechanics in Russia and in the U.S.S.R."), in the collection of papers, *Mekhanika v SSSR za 30 let*

("Mechanics in the U.S.S.R. for Thirty Years"; Moscow–Leningrad, 1950), 11–57.

The following were published posthumously: "Ob ortointerpolyatsionnom osrednennom variante ogranichennoy zadachi trekh tochek" ("On the Orthointerpolational Averaging Variant of the Limited Problem of Three Points"), in *Trudy Gosudarstvennogo astronomicheskogo instituta im P. K. Sternberga*, **28** (1960), 9–24; and *Ocherk razvitia mekhaniki* ("Essay of the Development of Mechanics"; Moscow, 1961).

II. SECONDARY LITERATURE. On Moiseev and his work, see (listed in chronological order) the obituary in *Astronomicheskii tsirkulyar Akademii nauk SSSR*, no. 166 (1956), 24–25; and the biographies in *Trudy Gosudarstvennogo astronomicheskogo instituta im P. K. Shternberga*, **28** (1960), 5–9, with a list of 15 of Moiseev's works; *Ocherk razvitia mekhaniki* (cited above), 4–11, with bibliography of 21 works; and E. N. Rakcheev, in *Vestnik Moskovskogo gosudarstvennogo universiteta*, Seria matematika, mekhanika, no. 4 (1961), 71–77, published on the fifth anniversary of his death, with bibliography of 49 works. See also M. S. Yarov-Yarovoy, "Raboty v oblasti nebesnoy mekhaniki v MGU za 50 let (1917–1967 gg.)" ("Works in the Area of Celestial Mechanics at Moscow State University for Fifty Years"), in *Trudy Gosudarstvennogo astronomicheskogo instituta im P. K. Sternberga*, **41** (1968), 86–103.

P. G. KULIKOVSKY

MOISSAN, FERDINAND-FRÉDÉRIC-HENRI (*b.* Paris, France, 28 September 1852; *d.* Paris, 20 February 1907), *chemistry.*

Born into a family of modest means, Moissan lived in Paris until 1864, when his parents moved to Meaux. He attended the municipal college there but did not complete his studies; instead he returned to Paris to work for two years as a pharmacy apprentice. In 1872 he went to work in the laboratory of Edmond Frémy at the Muséum d'Histoire Naturelle but shortly after transferred to Pierre-Paul Dehérain's laboratory, also at the Muséum, where he began research in plant physiology under Dehérain's direction. Conscious of his need for more formal academic training, Moissan studied in Paris, earned the *baccalauréat* (1874) and the *licence* (1877), qualified as first-class pharmacist at the École Supérieure de Pharmacie (1879), and received the *docteur ès sciences physiques* from the Faculté des Sciences (1880).

Impressed with Moissan's ability, Dehérain collaborated with his young protégé in a study of plant respiration which was published in 1874. By this time Moissan had definitely decided on inorganic chemistry as his main interest. His early investigation of the oxides of iron and related metals, and particularly the compounds of chromium, attracted the attention of

Henri Sainte-Claire Deville and H. J. Debray, who encouraged him. This work formed the basis of Moissan's doctoral thesis of 1880 and preoccupied him to a large extent during the next three years. For some time he directed a private analytical laboratory and also served as *maître de conférences* and *chef des travaux pratiques* at the École Supérieure de Pharmacie (1879–1883). A happy marriage with Léonie Lugan of Meaux in 1882 and the financial and moral support of his father-in-law enabled Moissan to pursue his scientific objectives with a minimum of distraction. That same year he also competed successfully for an *agrégation* at the École Supérieure de Pharmacie.

In 1884 Moissan began his remarkable research on the compounds of fluorine, which was to lead him to the isolation of this element. Previous attempts by others to obtain fluorine had not been successful because of the toxicity of fluorine compounds and the difficulty in designing suitable apparatus. Efforts by Davy, Gay-Lussac, and Thenard had not only been fruitless but injurious to their health. George J. and Thomas Knox of Ireland were seriously affected; and for the Belgian chemist Paulin Louyet and the French chemist Jérôme Nicklès these investigations proved fatal. Frémy was equally unsuccessful in preparing fluorine, as was George Gore of England. Although Moissan's initial experiments to isolate fluorine, including the electrolytic decomposition of phosphorus trifluoride and arsenic trifluoride, had also failed and proved injurious to his health, he persisted and on 26 June 1886 finally succeeded. This difficult feat was accomplished by using an electrolyte of dry potassium acid fluoride dissolved in anhydrous hydrofluoric acid. For the reaction Moissan employed a platinum U-tube containing two platinum-iridium electrodes, closed by fluorite caps and cooled by methyl chloride. At the anode an electric current yielded a gas which by its strong reaction with silicon was shown to be fluorine. Moissan's continuing investigation of the chemistry of fluorine subsequently resulted in the discovery of a number of fluorides such as carbon tetrafluoride, ethyl fluoride, methyl and isobutyl fluorides (with M. Meslans), and sulfuryl fluoride (with P. Lebeau). In collaboration with James Dewar he both liquefied (1897, 1903) and solidified fluorine (1903).

Meanwhile, Moissan had turned his attention to the production of artificial diamonds and in the process constructed his famous electric furnace, which, although simple in design, proved to be a technological tool of the first order. The original model, which he subsequently improved, was demonstrated to the Academy of Sciences in December 1892. It consisted of two blocks of lime, one laid on the other, with a hollow space in the center for a crucible, and a longitudinal groove for two carbon electrodes which produced a high-temperature electric arc. In one experiment Moissan heated iron and carbonized sugar in his electric furnace, causing the carbon to dissolve in the molten iron. He then subjected the mixture to rapid cooling in cold water, causing the iron to solidify with enormous pressure, producing carbon particles of microscopic size that appeared to have the physical characteristics of diamond. Moissan and his contemporaries believed that diamonds had finally been synthesized by this method, a conclusion that has been rejected in recent years. Nevertheless, Moissan's electric furnace provided great impetus to the development of high-temperature chemistry. With this apparatus he prepared and studied refractory oxides, silicides, borides, and carbides; he succeeded in volatilizing many metals; and, by reducing metallic oxides with carbon, he obtained such metals as manganese, chromium, uranium, tungsten, vanadium, molybdenum, titanium, and zirconium. The electrochemical and metallurgical applications to industry of Moissan's work became immediately apparent, for example in the large-scale production of acetylene from calcium carbide.

Academic recognition came to Moissan in December 1886 with his appointment to a professorship in toxicology at the École Supérieure de Pharmacie. In 1899 he became professor of inorganic chemistry at this same institution and in 1900 he succeeded Troost in the chair of inorganic chemistry at the Faculty of Sciences. Moissan received the Nobel Prize for chemistry in 1906 and was elected to membership in numerous learned societies both in France and abroad. Through the originality of his research and the effectiveness of his teaching, Moissan attracted an increasing number of students and exerted a remarkable influence on the progress of inorganic chemistry.

BIBLIOGRAPHY

I. ORIGINAL WORKS. Moissan was a prolific writer and his papers and monographs (written either by himself or in collaboration with others) number more than three hundred—including such major works as *Le four électrique* (Paris, 1897), *Le fluor et ses composés* (Paris, 1900), and the five-volume collaborative work which he edited, *Traité de chimie minérale* (Paris, 1904–1906).

Comprehensive listings of Moissan's publications were compiled by Alexander Gutbier, *Zur Erinnerung an Moissan* (Erlangen, 1908), 268–285; and Paul Lebeau, "Notice sur la vie et les travaux de Henri Moissan," in *Bulletin. Société chimique de France*, 4th ser., **3** (1908), xxv–xxxviii.

II. SECONDARY LITERATURE. For accounts of Moissan's life and work, see *Centenaire de l'École supérieure de phar-*

macie de l'Université de Paris, 1803–1903 (Paris, 1904), 249–257; Alexander Gutbier, *Zur Erinnerung an Moissan* (Erlangen, 1908); Benjamin Harrow, *Eminent Chemists of Our Time*, 2nd ed. (New York, 1927), 135–154, 374–388; A. J. Ihde, *The Development of Modern Chemistry* (New York, 1964), 367–369; Paul Lebeau, "Notice sur la vie et les travaux de Henri Moissan," in *Bulletin. Société chimique de France*, 4th ser., **3** (1908), i–xxxviii; J. R. Partington, *A History of Chemistry*, IV (London–New York, 1964), 911–914; Sir William Ramsay, "Moissan Memorial Lecture," in *Journal of the Chemical Society*, **101** (1912), 477–488; and Alfred Stock, "Henri Moissan," in *Berichte der Deutschen chemischen Gesellschaft*, **40** (1907), 5099–5130.

Evidence disputing Moissan's claim to the production of diamonds has been presented by F. P. Bundy, *et al.*, "Man-Made Diamonds," in *Nature*, **176** (9 July 1955), 51–55.

For a discussion of the background and discovery of fluorine, see Louis Domange, "Les débuts de la chimie du fluor," in *Proceedings of the Chemical Society* (June/July 1959), 172–176; and M. E. Weeks, *Discovery of the Elements*, 6th ed. (Easton, Pa., 1956), 755–770.

ALEX BERMAN

MOIVRE, ABRAHAM DE (*b*. Vitry-le-François, France, 26 May 1667; *d*. London, England, 27 November 1754), *probability*.

De Moivre was one of the many gifted Protestants who emigrated from France to England following the revocation of the Edict of Nantes in 1685. His formal education was French, but his contributions were made within the Royal Society of London. His father, a provincial surgeon of modest means, assured him of a competent but undistinguished classical education. It began at the tolerant Catholic village school and continued at the Protestant Academy at Sedan. After the latter was suppressed for its profession of faith, De Moivre had to study at Saumur. It is said that he read mathematics on the side, almost in secret, and that Christiaan Huygens' work on the mathematics of games of chance, *De ratiociniis in ludo aleae* (Leiden, 1657), formed part of this clandestine study. He received no thorough instruction in mathematics until he went to Paris in 1684 to read the later books of Euclid and other texts under the supervision of Jacques Ozanam.

His Protestant biographers say that De Moivre, like so many of his coreligionists, was imprisoned during the religious tumult of 1685 and not released until 1688. Other, nearly contemporary sources report him in England by 1686. There he took up his lifelong, unprofitable occupation as a tutor in mathematics. On arrival in London, De Moivre knew many of the classic texts, but a chance encounter with

Newton's *Principia* showed him how much he had to learn. He mastered the book quickly; later he told how he cut out the huge pages and read them while walking from pupil to pupil. Edmond Halley, then assistant secretary of the Royal Society, was sufficiently impressed to take him up after meeting him in 1692; it was he who communicated De Moivre's first paper, on Newton's doctrine of fluxions, to the Royal Society in 1695 and saw to his election by 1697. (In 1735 De Moivre was elected fellow of the Berlin Academy of Sciences, but not until 1754 did the Paris Academy follow suit.)

Once Halley had made him known, De Moivre's talents became esteemed. He was able to dedicate his first book, *The Doctrine of Chances*, to Newton; and the aging Newton would, it is said, turn students away with "Go to Mr. De Moivre; he knows these things better than I do." He was admired in the verse of Alexander Pope ("Essay on Man" II, 104) and was appointed to the grand commission of 1710, by means of which the Royal Society sought to settle the Leibniz-Newton dispute over the origin of the calculus. Yet throughout his life De Moivre had to eke out a living as tutor, author, and expert on practical applications of probability in gambling and annuities. Despite his powerful friends he found little patronage. He canvassed support in England and even begged Johann I Bernoulli to get Leibniz to intercede on his behalf for a chair of mathematics at Cambridge, but to no avail. He was left complaining of the waste of his time spent walking between the homes of his pupils. At the age of eighty-seven De Moivre succumbed to lethargy. He was sleeping twenty hours a day, and it became a joke that he slept a quarter of an hour more every day and would die when he slept the whole day through.

De Moivre's masterpiece is *The Doctrine of Chances*. A Latin version appeared as "De mensura sortis" in *Philosophical Transactions of the Royal Society* (1711). Successively expanded versions under the English title were published in 1718, 1738, and 1756. The only systematic treatises on probability printed before 1711 were Huygens' *De ratiociniis in ludo aleae* and Pierre Rémond de Montmort's *Essay d'analyse sur les jeux de hazard* (Paris, 1708). Problems which had been posed in these two books prompted De Moivre's earliest work and, incidentally, caused a feud between Montmort and De Moivre on the subject of originality and priority.

The most memorable of De Moivre's discoveries emerged only slowly. This is his approximation to the binomial probability distribution, which, as the normal or Gaussian distribution, became the most fruitful single instrument of discovery used in probability theory and statistics for the next two centuries. In De Moivre's own time his discovery enormously clarified the concept of probability. At least since the fifteenth century there had been substantial work on games of chance that recognized the existence of stable frequencies in nature. But in the classic work of Huygens and even in that of Montmort, the reader was usually given, in the context of a game or lottery, a set of events of equal probability—a set of what were often called "chances"—and he was asked to derive further probabilities or expectations from this fundamental set. No one had a clear mathematical formulation of how "chances" and stable frequencies are related. Jakob I Bernoulli provided a first answer in part IV of his *Ars conjectandi* (Basel, 1713), where he proved what is now called the weak law of large numbers; De Moivre's approximation to the binomial distribution was conceived as an attempt to improve on Bernoulli.

In some experiment, let the ratio of favorable to unfavorable "chances" be *p*. In *n* repeated trials of the experiment, let *m* be the number of successes. Consider any interval around *p*, bounded by two limits. Bernoulli proved that the probability that *m/n* should lie between these limits increases with increasing *n* and approaches 1 as *n* grows without bound. But although he could establish the fact of convergence, Bernoulli could not tell at what rate the probability converges. He did obtain some idea of this rate by computing numerical examples for particular values of *n* and *p*, but he was unable to state the principles that underlie his discovery. That was left for De Moivre.

De Moivre's solution was published as a Latin pamphlet dated 13 November 1733. Introducing his translation of, and comments on, this work at the end of the last edition of *The Doctrine of Chances*, he took "the liberty to say, that this is the hardest Problem that can be proposed on the Subject of Chance" (p. 242). In this problem the probability of getting exactly *m* successes in *n* trials is expressed by the *m*th term in the expansion of $(a + b)^n$—that is, $\binom{n}{m} a^m b^{n-m}$, where *a* is the given ratio of chances and $b = 1 - a$. Hence the probability of obtaining a proportion of successes lying between the two limits is a problem in "approximating the Sum of the Terms of the Binomial $(a + b)^n$ expanded into a Series" (p. 243).

Working first with the binomial expansion of $(1 + 1)^n$, De Moivre obtained what is now recognized as *n*! approximated by Stirling's formula—that is, $cn^{n+\frac{1}{2}}e^{-n}$. He knew the constant *c* only as the limiting sum of an infinite series: "I desisted in proceeding farther till my worthy and learned Friend Mr. James Stirling, who had applied after me to that inquiry," discovered that $c = \sqrt{2\pi}$ (p. 244). Hence what is now called Stirling's formula is at least as much the work of De Moivre as of Stirling.

With his approximation of *n*! De Moivre was able, for example, to sum the terms of the binomial from any point up to the central term. This summation is equivalent to the modern normal approximation and is, indeed, the first occurrence of the normal probability integral. He even appears to have perceived, although he did not name, the parameter now called the standard deviation *σ*. It was left for Laplace and Gauss to construct the equation of the normal curve in its form

$$\int \frac{1}{\sigma \sqrt{2\pi}} e^{-\frac{1}{2}\left(\frac{x-\mu}{\sigma}\right)^2} dx;$$

but De Moivre obtained, in a series of examples, expressions that are logically equivalent to this. He understood the rate of the convergence that Bernoulli had discovered and saw that the "error" —that is, the likely difference of the observed frequency from the true ratio of "chances"—decreases in inverse proportion to the square of the number of trials.

De Moivre's approximation is a theorem in probability theory: given the initial law about the distribution of chances, he could approximate the probability that observed frequencies should lie within any two assigned limits. Unlike some later workers, he did not imagine that his result would solve the converse statistical problem—namely, given the observed frequencies, to approximate the probability that the initial law about the ratio of chances lies within any two limits. But he did think his theorem bore on statistics. After summarizing his theorem, he reasoned:

> *Conversely*, if from numberless Observations we find the Ratio of the Events to converge to a determinate quantity, as to the Ratio of P to Q; then we conclude that this Ratio expresses the determinate Law according to which the Event is to happen. For let that Law be expressed not by the ratio P : Q, but by some other, as R : S; then would the Ratio of the Events converge to this last, and not to the former: which contradicts our *Hypothesis* [p. 251].

Nowhere in *The Doctrine of Chances* is this converse reasoning put to any serious mathematical use, yet its conceptual value is great. For De Moivre, it seemed to resolve the philosophical paradox of finding regularities within events postulated to be random. As he expressed it in the third edition, "altho' Chance produces Irregularities, still the Odds will be infinitely great, that in process of Time, those Irregularities will bear no proportion to the recurrency of that Order which naturally results from ORIGINAL DESIGN" (p. 251).

All the mathematical problems treated by De Moivre before setting out his approximation to the binomial distribution are closely related to earlier work by Huygens and Montmort. They include the first intimation of another approximation to the binomial distribution, now usually named for Poisson. In the normal approximation, the given ratio of chances is constant at p; and as n increases, so does np. In the Poisson approximation, np is constant, so that as n grows, p tends to zero. It is useful in studying the probabilities of rather infrequent events. Although De Moivre worked out a particular case of the Poisson approximation, he does not appear to have guessed its subsequent uses in probability theory.

Also included in *The Doctrine of Chances* are great advances in problems concerning the duration of play; a clearer formulation of combinatorial problems about chances; the use of difference equations and their solutions using recurring series; and, as illustrated by the work on the normal approximation, the use of generating functions, which, by the time of Laplace, came to play a fundamental role in probability mathematics.

Although no statistics are found in *The Doctrine of Chances*, De Moivre did have a great interest in the analysis of mortality statistics and the foundation of the theory of annuities. Perhaps this originated from his friendship with Halley, who in 1693 had written on annuities for the Royal Society, partly in protest at the inane life annuities still being sold by the British government, in which the age of the annuitant was not considered relevant. Halley had very meager mortality data from which to work; but his article, together with the earlier "political arithmetic" of John Graunt and William Petty, prompted the keeping of more accurate and more relevant records. By 1724, when De Moivre published the first edition of *Annuities on Lives*, he could base his computations on many more facts. Even so, he found it convenient to base most of his computations on Halley's data, derived from only five years of observation in the city of Breslau; he claimed that other results confirmed the substantial accuracy of those data. In his tables De Moivre found it convenient to suppose that the death rate is uniform after the age of twelve. He did not pretend that the rate is absolutely uniform, as a matter of objective fact, but argued for uniformity partly because of its mathematical simplicity and partly because the mortality

records were still so erratically collected that precise curve fitting was unwarranted.

De Moivre's contribution to annuities lies not in his evaluation of the demographic facts then known but in his derivation of formulas for annuities based on a postulated law of mortality and constant rates of interest on money. Here one finds the treatment of joint annuities on several lives, the inheritance of annuities, problems about the fair division of the costs of a tontine, and other contracts in which both age and interest on capital are relevant. This mathematics became a standard part of all subsequent commercial applications in England. Yet the authorship of this work was a matter of controversy. De Moivre's first edition appeared in 1725; in 1742 Thomas Simpson published *The Doctrine of Annuities and Reversions Deduced From General and Evident Principles*. De Moivre republished in the next year, bitter at what, with some justice, he claimed to be the plagiarization of his work. Since the sale of his books was a real part of his small income, money must have played as great a part as pride in this dispute.

Throughout his life De Moivre published occasional papers on other branches of mathematics. Most of them offered solutions to fairly ephemeral problems in Newton's calculus; in his youth some of this work led him into yet another imbroglio about authorship, involving some minor figures from Scotland, especially George Cheyne. In these lesser works, however, there is one trigonometric equation the discovery of which is sufficiently undisputed that it is still often called De Moivre's theorem:

$$(\cos \varphi + i \sin \varphi)^n = \cos n\varphi + i \sin n\varphi.$$

This result was first stated in 1722 but had been anticipated by a related formula in 1707. It entails or suggests a great many valuable identities and thus became one of the most useful steps in the early development of complex number theory.

BIBLIOGRAPHY

I. ORIGINAL WORKS. De Moivre's two books are *The Doctrine of Chances* (London, 1718; 2nd ed., 1738; 3rd ed., 1756; photo. repr. of 2nd ed., London, 1967; photo. repr. of 3rd ed., together with the biography by Helen M. Walker, New York, 1967); and *A Treatise of Annuities on Lives* (London, 1725), repr. in the 3rd ed. of *The Doctrine of Chances*. Mathematical papers are in *Philosophical Transactions of the Royal Society* between 1695 and 1744 (nos. 216, 230, 240, 265, 278, 309, 329, 341, 345, 352, 360, 373, 374, 451, 473). "De mensura sortis" is no. 329; the trigonometric equation called De Moivre's formula is in 373 and is anticipated in 309. *Approximatio ad summam terminorum binomii* $(a + b)^n$ *in seriem expansi* is reprinted by R. C. Archibald, "A Rare Pamphlet of De Moivre and Some of His Discoveries," in *Isis*, **8** (1926), 671–684. Correspondence with Johann I Bernoulli is published in K. Wollenshläger, "Der mathematische Briefwechsel zwischen Johann I Bernoulli und Abraham de Moivre," in *Verhandlungen der Naturforschenden Gesellschaft in Basel*, **43** (1933), 151–317. I. Schneider (below) lists all known publications and correspondence of De Moivre.

II. SECONDARY LITERATURE. Ivo Schneider, "Der Mathematiker Abraham de Moivre," in *Archive for History of Exact Sciences*, **5** (1968–1969), 177–317, is the definitive study of De Moivre's life and work. For other biography, see Helen M. Walker, "Abraham de Moivre," in *Scripta mathematica*, **2** (1934), 316–333, reprinted in 1967 (see above), and Mathew Maty, *Mémoire sur la vie et sur les écrits de Mr. Abraham de Moivre* (The Hague, 1760).

For other surveys of the work on probability, see Isaac Todhunter, *A History of Probability From the Time of Pascal to That of Laplace* (London, 1865; photo. repr. New York, 1949), 135–193; and F. N. David, *Gods, Games and Gambling* (London, 1962), 161–180, 254–267.

IAN HACKING

MOLDENHAWER, JOHANN JACOB PAUL (*b.* Hamburg, Germany, 11 February 1766; *d.* Kiel, Germany, 22 August 1827), *plant anatomy.*

Moldenhawer was one of the principal founders of plant anatomy. His chief work, published in 1812, reflects substantially the extensive knowledge acquired in this field during the period 1800–1830. During these years, which were characterized by a wealth of polemical tracts on the structure of the basic plant organs, he went his own way in his research and in his studies.

Moldenhawer was the son of the theologian and preacher Johann Heinrich Daniel Moldenhawer and his third wife. He studied theology, following the example of his elder brother, Daniel Gotthilf, a distinguished scholar of Greek and oriental languages and of dogmatics. Moldenhawer lived with his brother both as a student in Kiel until 1783 and in Copenhagen, where he was a candidate in theology. It is not known when he turned to the study of science, a change concurrent with his interest in literature, but it was probably in the mid-1780's. He was especially attracted to botany. Evidence of Moldenhawer's interest in these two areas is provided by his first publication, *Tentamen in historiam plantarum Theophrasti* (Hamburg, 1791), a philological study of Peripatetic botany based on ancient sources. On 13 April 1792 Moldenhawer was appointed extraordinary professor of botany and fruit-tree culture at the Faculty of Philosophy of the University of Kiel. He also lectured regularly on classical Greek literature, especially Pindar. He was able to do this because of his philological training while a theology student.

The scene of Moldenhawer's most important work was the fruit-tree nursery in Düsternbrook, near Kiel, which was associated with his professorship and which was run by Moldenhawer with great conscientiousness. He botanized only occasionally and directed work at the nursery toward applied botany, especially phytotomy, his major interest. Through use of the nursery, its library, and its five microscopes, Moldenhawer was able to produce his *Beiträge zur Anatomie der Pflanzen* (Kiel, 1812). This lifework, prepared over eighteen years of unremitting research, is notable for its critical insights and methodical observations.

The *Beiträge* contains important findings concerning plant anatomy that were made possible by a preparation method of Moldenhawer's own devising. He allowed the cells and vessels, which he recognized as structural elements, to macerate by decaying in water, then separated out the parts to be examined. His success was attributable to his use of the monocotyledonous corn plant as a subject of investigation and demonstration because of its simple structure and quick growth. The illustrations surpassed all earlier representations of plant anatomy. They included the first accurate depictions of the structure of the disputed fissured openings of the epidermis. By completely isolating the cells and vessels in his preparations Moldenhawer demonstrated that the cell wall is closed on all sides. This discovery clarified a long-contested question, since the membrane was seen to be doubled between two closely packed cellular spaces in intact tissue. Moldenhawer's later reputation was diminished primarily because he assumed, incorrectly, that cells and vessels were held together by a fibrous network. This assumption, all the more misleading because of his mistaken nomenclature, was in accord with Grew's hypothesis. On the other hand, Moldenhawer devised the concept of the vascular tissue *(Gefässbündel)*, opposing it to that of the parenchyma. Herein lay his greatest achievement; with this radical new histological orientation he created the foundation of the theory of secondary thickening of woody stems, thereby separating himself most strikingly from the ideas of his predecessors (Grew, Malpighi) and contemporaries (Mirbel). Unfortunately, he never carried out his intention, expressed in 1812, of publishing a detailed work on the structure and development of the spiral vessels, one of his favorite objects of study.

In 1795 Moldenhawer married Catherina Dorothea Gädechens. They had one daughter, Pauline Mathilde, born in 1803. The family lived in Brunswick and later in Düsternbrook. Widely known and honored as a botanist, Moldenhawer was awarded the Danebrog Order in 1813 and was named king's counsel in 1824. He received a further honor in 1821, when H. A. Schrader named a legume genus *Moldenhawera*. Through a bequest of his daughter (1845) the botanical gardens of the University of Kiel received Moldenhawer's herbarium, which encompassed 120 files of plants arranged according to the systems of Forskål, Förster, and Linnaeus.

BIBLIOGRAPHY

Moldenhawer's two major works are mentioned in the text. See the obituary in *Neuer Nekrolog der Deutschen*, V, pt. 2 (Ilmenau, 1829); and the article in *Allgemeine deutsche Biographie,* XXII (Leipzig, 1885). For the report on his daughter's bequest to the University of Kiel, see *Botanische Zeitung*, **3** (1845), 262; and Prahl (cited below), II, 38.

For works about Moldenhawer see J. H. Barnhart, *The New York Botanical Garden. Biographical Notes Upon Botanists* (Mschr.), II (Boston, 1965); C. Harms, *Lebenbeschreibung* (Kiel, 1851); E. Hofmann, "Philologie," in *Geschichte der Philosophischen Fakultät*, pt. 2, K. Jordan and E. Hofmann, eds., *Geschichte der Christian-Albrechts-Universität Kiel 1665–1965*, V (Neumünster, 1969); P. Knuth, *Geschichte der Botanik in Schleswig-Holstein* (Kiel–Leipzig, 1890–1892); M. Möbius, *Geschichte der Botanik* (Jena, 1937); and F. Overbeck, "Botanik," in *Geschichte der Mathematik, der Naturwissenschaften und der Landwirtschaftswissenschaften*, K. Jordan, ed., *Geschichte der Christian-Albrechts-Universität Kiel 1665–1965*, VI (Neumünster, 1968). See also P. Prahl, ed., *Kritische Flora der Provinz Schleswig-Holstein, des angrenzenden Gebiets der Hansastädte Hamburg und Lübeck und des Fürstentums Lübeck*, 2 vols. (Kiel, 1888–1890); H. Röhrich, "Memoria horti medici Academiae Kiliensis III," in *Schleswig-Holsteinisches Ärzteblatt*, **18** (1965), 376–382; J. Sachs, "Geschichte der Botanik vom 16. Jahrhundert bis 1860," in *Geschichte der Wissenschaften in Deutschland*, XV (Munich, 1875); F. Volbehr and R. Weyl, in R. Bülck and H. J. Newiger, eds., *Professoren und Dozenten der Christian-Albrechts-Universität zu Kiel 1665–1954*, 4th ed. (Kiel, 1956); and O. F. Wiegand, *Bibliographie zur Geschichte der Christian-Albrechts-Universität Kiel* (Kiel, 1964).

JÖRN HENNING WOLF

MOLESCHOTT, JACOB (*b.* 's Hertogenbosch, Netherlands, 9 August 1822; *d.* Rome, Italy, 20 May 1893), *medicine, physiology.*

Moleschott's father, Johannes Franciscus Gabriel Moleschott, was a physician; his mother was the former Elisabeth Antonia van der Monde. He attended the Gymnasium at Cleves, Germany, then studied medicine at Heidelberg (1842–1845) under Tiedemann, Naegele, and Henle, while also pursuing his interest in the philosophy of Ludwig Feuerbach, Karl Vogt, and Hegel. On 22 January 1845 he received his medical degree with the thesis *De Malpighianis pulmonum vesiculis*. It had been written under the direction of Jakob Henle, who had instructed him in the use of the microscope. Moleschott then settled in Utrecht as a general practitioner. He was a pupil of G. J. Mulder from 1845 to 1847; in Mulder's laboratory he met the physiologists F. C. Donders (who did not share his enthusiasm for materialistic monism) and I. van Deen. With them he conducted an extensive scientific and private correspondence, much of which has been preserved.

While still a student Moleschott entered a prize competition sponsored by the Teyler's Society in Haarlem and received an award. His growing interest in physiology led him to publish, with Donders and van Deen, the first Dutch journal (in German) for anatomy and physiology: *Holländische Beiträge zu den anatomischen und physiologischen Wissenschaften* (1846–1848). In 1848 Moleschott violently opposed the appointment of H. J. Halbertsma as professor of anatomy and physiology at Leiden because his friend van Deen had been passed over. Moleschott was made *Privatdozent* in physiology and anthropology at Heidelberg in 1847 and resigned in 1854 after having been sharply reprimanded by the rector and senate because they felt that he was misleading the students. (Among other things, he had spoken out in favor of cremation.) He was appointed professor of physiology at Zurich in 1856, giving an oration, "Licht und Leben," based upon his own observations. In the following year he started publication of the journal *Untersuchungen zur Naturlehre des Menschen und der Thiere*, which he edited and which was continued until 1894 under G. Colasanti and S. Fubini.

While in Zurich, Moleschott was especially concerned with research on the cardiac nervous system, the respiratory system, the smooth muscles, and embryology, the last being closely connected with his teaching. At the urging of Cavour he was appointed professor of experimental physiology and physiological chemistry at Turin in 1861. He became professor at the "Sapienza" in Rome in 1879 and later a senator. (For many years he had studied the Italian language and literature; he became an Italian citizen.)

Moleschott's special interests were in the metabolism of plants and animals, and in the effect of light on it in nutrition. His most important work, *Kreislauf des Lebens* (1852), concerned the structure and function of the brain and contained arguments against Liebig's *Chemische Briefe* and strong statements favoring Moleschott's own materialistic view of life. The work was highly praised by Humboldt and was translated into French, Italian, and Russian.

It cannot be said that Moleschott possessed great creativity; but he did have a strong love for science, especially experimental physiology. He died of erysipelas at the age of seventy. His library was donated to the University of Turin.

BIBLIOGRAPHY

I. Original Works. Moleschott's writings include *Kritische Betrachtung von Liebig's Theorie der Ernährung der Pflanzen, im Jahre 1844 gekrönte Preisschrift* (Haarlem, 1845); *De Malpighianis pulmonum vesiculis dissertatio* (Heidelberg, 1845); *Holländische Beiträge zu den anatomischen und physiologischen Wissenschaften* (Dusseldorf-Utrecht, 1846–1848), written with F. C. Donders and I. van Deen; *Lehre der Nahrungsmittel* (Erlangen, 1850; 2nd ed., 1858); *Physiologie der Nahrungsmittel* (Darmstadt, 1850; 2nd ed., Giessen, 1859); *Physiologie des Stoffwechsels in Pflanzen und Thieren* (Erlangen, 1851); *Der Kreislauf des Lebens* (Mainz, 1852; 5th ed., 2 vols., Mainz–Giessen, 1877, 1887), also trans. into French (Paris, 1866); *Untersuchungen zur Naturlehre des Menschen und der Thiere*, 15 vols. (Frankfurt–Giessen, 1857–1892), of which the last contains a list of his works; and *Für meine Freunde. Lebenserinnerungen* (Giessen, 1894; 2nd ed., 1901).

With G. E. V. Schneevoogt, Moleschott translated Carl Rokitansky's *Handboek der bijzondere ziektekundige ontleedkunde*, 2 vols. (Haarlem, 1849).

II. Secondary Literature. See A. Cantani and W. Haberling, in *Biographisches Lexicon hervorragender Aerzte*, IV (Berlin–Vienna, 1932), 232; I. van Esso, "Jacob Moleschott," in *Nederlands tijdschrift voor geneeskunde*, **93** (1949), 1; A. A. Guye, "Jacob Moleschott," *ibid.*, **28** (1892), 325; R. E. de Haan, *Jacob Moleschott* (Haarlem, 1883); M. A. van Herwerden, "Eine Freundschaft von drei Physiologen," in *Gids*, **7** (1914), 448, also in *Janus*, **20** (1915), 174–201, 409–436; and the article in *Nieuw nederlandsch biografisch woordenboek*, III (Leiden, 1914), 874; C. A. Pekelharing, "Jakob Moleschott," in *Nederlands tijdschrift voor geneeskunde*, **29** (1893), 1741; and B. J. Stokvis, "Jacob Moleschott," in *Gids*, **5** (1892), 339.

See also *In memoria di Jacopo Moleschott* (Rome, 1894), which includes a bibliography of his works.

A. M. Geist-Hofman

MOLIÈRES, JOSEPH PRIVAT DE. See **Privat de Molières, Joseph.**

MOLIN, FEDOR EDUARDOVICH (*b.* Riga, Russia, 10 September 1861; *d.* Tomsk, U.S.S.R., 25 December 1941), *mathematics.*

Molin graduated from the same Gymnasium in Riga at which his father was a teacher. He then entered the Faculty of Physics and Mathematics at Dorpat University (now Tartu University), from which he graduated in 1883 with the rank of candidate and remained in the department of astronomy to prepare for a teaching career. In the same year he was sent to Leipzig University, where he attended the lectures of Felix Klein and Carl Neumann. Under the guidance of Klein he wrote his master's thesis ("Über die lineare Transformation der elliptischen Functionen"), which he defended in 1885 at Dorpat, where he then became *Dozent.*

During this period Molin became acquainted with the works of Sophus Lie and began to study hypercomplex systems. His most profound results in this field were presented in his doctoral dissertation, which he defended in 1892. Despite his outstanding work, Molin was unable to obtain a professorship at Dorpat and in 1900 moved to Tomsk, in west-central Siberia, where he found himself cut off from centers of scientific activity. He occupied the chair of mathematics at Tomsk Technological Institute and from 1918 was professor at Tomsk University. In 1934 he received the title Honored Worker of Science.

Molin obtained fundamental results in the theory of algebras and the theory of representation of groups. In his doctoral dissertation, which concerned the structure of an arbitrary algebra of finite rank over a field of complex numbers C, he showed that a simple algebra over C is isomorphic to a complete ring of matrices. He also introduced the concept of a radical (the term was introduced by Frobenius) and showed that the structure of an arbitrary algebra is reduced essentially into the case where factor algebra by a radical decomposes into a direct sum of simple algebras. Cartan later obtained the same results, which he introduced into the case of an algebra over a field of real numbers. In 1907 Wedderburn extended Molin's and Cartan's results into the case of an algebra over an arbitrary field.

Studying the theory of representation of groups, Molin explicitly introduced a group ring and showed that it is a semisimple algebra broken into the direct sum of S simple algebras, where S is the order of the center. This proved the decomposability of the regular representation into irreducible parts. Molin showed that every irreducible representation of the group is contained in the regular representation. He also demonstrated that representations of groups up to equivalence are determined by their traces. At the same time analogous results were obtained in a different way by Frobenius, who later became acquainted with Molin's research and valued it highly.

BIBLIOGRAPHY

I. ORIGINAL WORKS. Molin's writings include "Über die lineare Transformation der elliptischen Functionen" (Dorpat, 1885), his master's thesis; "Über Systeme höherer complexer Zahlen," in *Mathematische Annalen*, **41** (1893), 83–156, his doctoral dissertation; "Eine Bemerkung über endlichen linearen Substitutionsgruppen," in *Sitzungsberichte der Naturforscher-Gesellschaft bei der Universität Jurjew*, no. 11 (1896–1898), 259–276; "Über die Anzahl der Variabelen einer irreductibelen Substitutionsgruppen," *ibid.*, 277–288; and "Über die Invarianten der linearen Substitutionsgruppen," in *Sitzungsberichte der Preussischen Akademie der Wissenschaften zu Berlin*, **52** (1897), 1152–1156.

II. SECONDARY LITERATURE. See N. Bourbaki, *Éléments d'histoire des mathématiques* (Paris, 1969), 152, 154; and N. F. Kanunov, *O rabotakh F. E. Molina po teorii predstavlenia grupp* ("On the Works of F. E. Molin on the Theory of the Representation of Groups"), no. 17 in the series Istoriko-Matematicheskie Issledovania ("Historical–Mathematical Research"), G. F. Rybkin and A. P. Youschkevitch, eds. (Moscow, 1966), 57–88.

J. G. BASHMAKOVA

MOLINA, JUAN IGNACIO (*b.* Guaraculen, Talca, Chile, 24 June 1740; *d.* Bologna, Italy, 12 September 1829), *natural history*.

Molina received his early education at Talca; when he was sixteen, he entered the Jesuit college at Concepción, where he studied languages and the natural sciences. He entered the Jesuit order and was made librarian of the college, but in 1768 he had to leave Chile because of the expulsion of the Jesuits from the Spanish dominions. Molina received holy orders upon arrival at Imola, Italy; and in 1774 he was appointed professor of natural sciences at the Institute of Bologna, where he wrote most of his works. Some of his lectures maintained the analogy of the matter of living organisms and of minerals and the idea of the evolution of human beings, and he was censured by his superiors. Molina, who remains the classic author on the natural history of Chile, incorporated the observations of A. F. Frézier and Feuillée in the 1776 revised edition of his *Compendio*.

BIBLIOGRAPHY

I. ORIGINAL WORKS. Molina first published *Compendio della storia geografica, naturale, e civile del regno del Chile* (Bologna, 1776) anonymously; it was greatly improved in its 2nd ed., *Saggio sulla storia naturale del Chile* (Bologna, 1782). *Storia civile* (Bologna, 1786) was trans. into German, Spanish, French, and English. Molina's pupils published his 14 major essays on natural history under the title *Memorie di storia naturale lette in Bologna nelle adunaza dell'Istituto*, 2 vols. (Bologna, 1821).

II. SECONDARY LITERATURE. See Rodolfo Jaramillo Barriga, *El abate Juan Ignacio Molina, primer evolucionista y precursor de Teilhard de Chardin* (Santiago de Chile, 1963); Enrique Laval, "La medicina en el abate Molina," in *Anales chilenos de historia de la medicina* (1965); and Miguel Rojas Mix, in *Anales de la Universidad de Chile* (1965).

FRANCISCO GUERRA

MOLL, FRIEDRICH RUDOLF HEINRICH CARL (*b.* Culm, Germany, 31 January 1882; *d.* Berlin, Germany, 8 May 1951), *naval engineering, wood technology*.

After working on the docks and as a shipwright, Moll studied shipbuilding at the Technische Hochschule in Berlin-Charlottenburg from 1902 to 1907. Following his graduation he worked as an engine operator on English trawlers, then, in 1909, received a doctorate in engineering for a work on the possible causes of disappearance of long-missing trawlers.

From 1907 Moll was chiefly concerned with the preservation of wood. He obtained contracts to construct plants for impregnating telephone poles with mercuric chloride and studied this process (kyanizing) from a scientific, as well as technical, point of view. He published a large number of papers on both the biological and chemical aspects of preserving wood. From 1911 Moll privately built wood treatment works in a number of countries and his operations acquired an international reputation.

In 1920 Moll was awarded the doctor of philosophy degree by the University of Berlin for a study of the toxic effects of salts on fungi. Without giving up his profession of wood technologist, he qualified as a university lecturer and was *Privatdozent* at the Technische Hochschule in Berlin-Charlottenburg from 1922 until 1936, lecturing on the preservation of wood. He was thus led to prepare a comprehensive course of lectures on wood technology. Moll was a member of several national and international wood preservation societies and his authoritative papers appeared in many technical journals.

All of Moll's publications endorse the kyanization process that he had helped to develop. Although he rejected in principle the use of arsenic as a preservative agent, he fully recognized that other, more sophisticated agents—including the bifluorides—must be the future means of preserving wood. After World War II Moll did work in Berlin on a number of topics, including the geographic distribution of the Teredinidae in Africa. He also worked closely with American wood experts on developing techniques for protection against shipworms.

BIBLIOGRAPHY

I. ORIGINAL WORKS. Moll's writings include *Über die Ursachen des Unterganges der verschollenen Fisch-dampfer* (Berlin, 1909); "Schutz des Bauholzes in den Tropen gegen die Zerstörung durch die Termiten," in *Tropenpflanzer*, **18** (1915), 591–605; "Untersuchungen über Gesetzmässigkeiten in der Holzkonservierung. Die Giftwirkung anorganischer Verbindungen (Salze) auf Pilze," in *Zentralblatt für Bakteriologie, Parasitenkunde, Infektionskrankheiten und Hygiene*, **51** (1920), 257–279; *Das Schiff in der bildenden Kunst* (Bonn, 1929); *Der Schiffbauer in der bildenden Kunst* (Berlin, 1930); *Künstliche Holztrocknung* (Berlin, 1930); "Teredinidae of the British Museum," in *Proceedings of the Malacological Society of London*, **19** (1931), 201–218; *Der Schutz des Bauholzes und die Schädlingsbekämpfung mit chemischen Mitteln* (Karlsruhe, 1939); *Die Terediniden im königlichen Museum für Naturkunde zu Brüssel* (Brussels, 1940); "Übersicht über die Terediniden des Museums für Naturkunde Berlin," in *Sitzungsberichte der Gesellschaft naturforschender Freunde zu Berlin 1940* (1941), 152–219; *Zeitgemässe Verwendung von Holz in Bauwesen* (Berlin, 1942); and *Geographical Distribution of the Teredinidae of Africa* (London, 1949).

II. SECONDARY LITERATURE. Obituaries include that by Max Seidel, in *Norddeutsche Holzwirtschaft*, **5** (1951), 148–149; and those in *Chemiker Zeitung*, **75** (1951), 313–314; and *Holz-Zentralblatt*, **77** (1951), 794.

KURT MAUEL

MOLL, GERARD (*b.* Amsterdam, Netherlands, 18 January 1785; *d.* Amsterdam, 17 January 1838), *astronomy, physics.*

Moll had an enthusiastic interest in many of the physical sciences of his day. His contributions ranged from observing a transit of Mercury to determining the speed of sound.

Moll's father, a well-to-do businessman, was also named Gerard; his mother was the former Anna Diersen. Although destined for a commercial career, Moll met and talked to sea captains while serving his apprenticeship in Amsterdam, and became intrigued with the art of celestial navigation—to such an extent that he decided to change to astronomy as his life's work.

Moll studied at the University of Amsterdam, receiving his Ph.D. in 1809, and then continued his studies for some months in Paris. Returning to Holland in 1812, he was appointed director of the observatory in Utrecht. When that university was reorganized in 1815, Moll became professor of physics as well, and continued in both these positions until his death.

With little financial support and a crumbling observatory building, Moll contributed to astronomy rather more by personal contacts with scientists in other countries—especially in Great Britain—than by observing the heavens. His main astronomical accomplishment seems to have been his observation of the transit of Mercury of 5 May 1832.

In physics Moll made several contributions. With Albert van Beek he measured the speed of sound; an artillery battalion was placed at the experimenters' disposal, cannon were fired simultaneously—at night—from hills about nine miles apart, and the interval between light flash and sound was recorded at either end and then averaged. The value obtained was 332.05 m./sec. (the currently accepted value is 331.45).

Moll also extended the pioneering observations of H. C. Oersted, published in 1820, on the magnetic field that surrounds a wire carrying an electric current. He also investigated the lifting capacities of the electromagnets based on this phenomenon.

In recognition of his services on a commission dealing with weights and measures, the Kingdom of the Netherlands in 1815 appointed Moll *chevalier* of the Order of the Belgian Lion. In 1835 the University of Edinburgh gave him an honorary LL.D., and in 1836 the University of Dublin followed suit. Moll was buried beside his mother in Amerongen, some fifteen miles east of Utrecht.

BIBLIOGRAPHY

I. ORIGINAL WORKS. The experimental work referred to above is described in "An Account of Experiments on the Velocity of Sound, Made in Holland," in *Philosophical Transactions of the Royal Society*, **114** (1824), 425–456, written with A. van Beek; *Electro-magnetische Proeven* (Amsterdam, 1830); "Ueber die Bildung künstlicher Magnete mittelst der Voltaschen Kette," in *Annalen der Physik und Chemie*, 2nd ser., **29** (1833), 468–479; and "On the Transit of Mercury of May 5, 1832," in *Memoirs of the Royal Astronomical Society*, **6** (1833), 111–117.

A list of fifty articles by Moll appears in the Royal Society *Catalogue of Scientific Papers*, IV, 433–434. There is some duplication of subject matter, as Moll's work tended to appear simultaneously in at least two countries.

II. SECONDARY LITERATURE. An unsigned obituary of Moll appeared in *Annual Register* for 1838 (London, 1839), app., p. 198. A more extensive notice, by A. Quetelet, in *Annuaire de l'Académie des sciences, des lettres, et des beaux-arts de Belgique*, **5** (1839), 63–79, refers to other sources of biographical information in Dutch and Latin.

Note: The so-called Moll's thermopile was invented by Willem Jan Henri Moll in 1913.

SALLY H. DIEKE

MÖLLER, DIDRIK MAGNUS AXEL (*b.* Sjörup, Sweden, 16 February 1830; *d.* Lund, Sweden, 26 October 1896), *astronomy*.

Möller studied at the University of Lund, where in 1853 he became a docent, in 1855 associate professor, and in 1863 full professor. He was also director of the observatory, which he founded, until his resignation in 1895.

Möller's predecessor, John Mortimer Agardh, had sought to establish an observatory at Lund, but his efforts bore fruit only after his death. The government granted money for an observatory in 1863, and during the following years Möller devoted much of his time to its completion. The main building, still in use, was dedicated in 1867. Among the instruments Möller ordered were a refractor with a nine-inch objective and a thirteen-foot focal length, installed in 1867, and a meridian circle with a six-inch aperture and a seven-foot focal length, mounted in 1874. He intended these two instruments to be used simultaneously. Differential measurements of moving objects (comets and planets) and stars were made with the refractor, and accurate positions of the stars were determined with the meridian circle. Positions of about 11,000 stars in the declination zone $+35°$ to $+40°$ were measured with the meridian circle, and observations of planets, comets, and double stars were made with the refractor. The recently modernized meridian circle is still in use.

Möller's most important contributions to astronomy concern the motion of the comet discovered in 1843 by the French astronomer H. Faye and that of the asteroid Pandora. His interest in Faye's comet was aroused by J. F. Encke, who, on the basis of Newton's law, had computed the orbit of a comet of very short period (3.3 years) first seen in 1786 (later called Encke's comet) and found that the comet showed a retardation in relation to the computed positions. His explanation was that in interplanetary space there is a low-density medium which slows the motion of the comet. Möller started to test Encke's hypothesis by using Faye's comet, which has a period of 7.5 years.

He first concluded that the observations of this comet indeed indicated a retardation in comparison with theory. But through new, laborious, and careful calculations he was able to show that full agreement between theory and observations was obtained on the basis of Newton's theory: when the comet was observed in 1865, 1873, and 1880, the agreement was perfect. Encke's hypothesis could be rejected. For this brilliant work Möller was awarded the gold medal of the Royal Astronomical Society in 1881.

In several papers Möller studied the motion of the asteroid Pandora. He first calculated the special perturbations and later, according to Hansen's method, the general perturbations, including certain second-order perturbations depending on the masses of Jupiter and Saturn. In this case too Möller, through his skillful and accurate calculations, reached extremely good agreement with the observations. Besides his theoretical work Möller performed extensive series of observations of planets and comets.

Möller was an exceptionally able person, and was frequently called on for special commissions by the university and other agencies. He served as rector of the university in 1874–1875 and 1891–1895.

BIBLIOGRAPHY

Möller contributed many articles on Faye's comet and Planet 55 Pandora to *Astronomische Nachrichten* and *Vierteljahrsschrift der Astronomischen Gesellschaft*. Poggendorff, III, 924, gives a list of these and other publications.

In addition see Erik Holmberg, "Lundensisk astronomi under ett sekel," in *Cassiopeia* (1949), 21–27; Anders Lindstedt, "Didrik Magnus Axel Möller," in *Minnesteckning, Kungliga Svenska Vetenskapakademiens lefnadsteckningar*, **4** (1899–1912), no. 79; and Carl Schalén, Nils Hansson, and Arvid Leide, "Astronomiska Observatoriet vid Lunds Universitet," in *Lunds Universitets historia*, **4** (1968), 52–72.

C. SCHALÉN

MOLLIARD, MARIN (*b.* Châtillon-Colligny, Loiret, France, 8 June 1866; *d.* Paris, France, 24 July 1944), *plant physiology*.

For fifty years after his graduation from the École Normale Supérieure in 1894, Molliard taught and worked at the Faculty of Sciences of the Sorbonne; he was its dean for six years and had the first chair of plant physiology in France created for him. Deeply imbued with Lamarck's ideas, he devoted all his writings to the influence of the environment on plants. He stated:

The most general idea which emerges from my studies is that plants, even the most differentiated, are extremely plastic, much more so than has been admitted until now, that their structure is closely dependent on their chemistry, the latter being influenced by external conditions; it is therefore an experimental confirmation that my researches contribute to Lamarck's theory, insofar as its essential features are concerned [*Oeuvres scientifiques*, p. 6].

Molliard began by investigating the morphological transformations that certain parasites produce in plants and that lead to the formation of galls; his last works were concerned with the conditions of tuberization in the potato *(Solanum tuberosum)*. In order to carry out precise studies, he controlled all the nutrients. He also eliminated all possible parasites by cultivating his plants, particularly radishes, in an aseptic environment from germination to fructification.

Molliard systematically investigated the mineral nourishment of the mold *Sterigmatocystis nigra*. Normally it lives on sucrose, which it transforms into carbon dioxide and water by respiration; only a very small amount of organic acids appears in the medium. If too little nitrogen is furnished, a large quantity of citric acid is produced in the medium. If too little phosphorus is supplied, the medium abounds in both citric acid and oxalic acid. If potassium is lacking, only oxalic acid is abundant. If all of the mineral elements are reduced, gluconic acid appears. Hence, well before Hans Krebs discovered the acid cycle named for him, Molliard drew attention to the importance of organic acids in intermediate metabolism.

Molliard's studies on the radish are famous. Cultivated aseptically, provided with light but in an atmosphere without any carbon dioxide—and consequently without the assimilation of chlorophyll—the plant absorbs glucides through its roots. If the supply of glucides is abundant, the form of the radish is altered; the glucides no longer accumulate in the tissues as sucrose or monosaccharides but as starch. The reserves, instead of remaining in the root, move into the stem, which swells and acquires the characteristics and appearance of a subterranean stem. The organic nutrition totally transforms the physiology of the plant and thus modifies its microscopic appearance and morphology.

Through multiple experiments of the same kind Molliard showed that it is possible, by varying only the nutrition, to transform ordinary leaves into cotyledons. In addition, certain leaves can be changed into thorns and certain thorns into leaves. He also showed that parasitic plants like the dodder *(Cuscuta)*, which ordinarily feeds on clover and alfalfa to which it attaches itself by its suckers, are able, if they receive suitable nutrition, to live independently without suckers but with abundant chlorophyll.

Molliard was the leading authority on plant physiology in France. He spent the whole of his professional life in the same laboratory, on the second floor of the old Sorbonne building. From 1894 to 1940 all plant physiologists in France were more or less his direct pupils. His writings consist primarily of short notes to the Academy of Sciences, of which he was a very influential member.

BIBLIOGRAPHY

Molliard's most important book is *Nutrition de la plante*, 4 vols. (Paris, 1923). Among his many papers are the series with the general title "Recherches physiologiques sur les galles," in *Revue générale de botanique*, **25** (1913), 225–252, 285–307, 341–370; most appear in *Oeuvres scientifiques* (Paris, 1936), which consists of works republished or abridged under the supervision of a group of his students and friends. See also the obituary by Charles Maurain in *Comptes rendus hebdomadaires des séances de l'Académie des sciences*, **219** (1944), 144–147.

JULES CARLES

MOLLIER, RICHARD (*b*. Trieste, 30 November 1863; *d*. Dresden, Germany, 13 March 1935), *thermodynamics.*

Mollier was the eldest son of German parents. His father, Eduard Mollier, a Rhinelander, was a naval engineer at, and later director of, a Trieste machine factory; his mother (née von Dyck) was a native of Munich. After graduating *summa cum laude* (1882) from the local German Gymnasium, Mollier studied mathematics and physics at the universities of Graz and Munich. He soon transferred to the Technische Hochschule of Munich, where Moritz Schröter and Carl von Linde became his most influential teachers. He graduated in 1888 and, after a brief engineering practice at his father's factory in Trieste, became Schröter's assistant in 1890. His first scientific investigations were his *Habilitation* thesis on thermal diagrams in the theory of machines (1892) and his doctoral dissertation at the University of Munich on the entropy of vapors (1895). In 1896 Felix Klein, who was conducting a wide-ranging campaign to reunite science and technology, called Mollier to the University of Göttingen to introduce "technical physics" into the curriculum. Mollier's stay was brief. Feeling isolated in a purely scientific atmosphere, he was delighted to answer an invitation in 1897 to succeed Gustav Zeuner at the Technische Hochschule of Dresden. In this post, as professor of the theory of machines and director of the machine laboratory, Mollier spent his working life. He subsequently received international recognition for his contributions to thermodynamics, as well as the concomitant honors.

Mollier was unassuming and kindly, if somewhat retiring, and he took his teaching duties seriously. His lectures, prepared by a unique method, were much praised. Using no notes, he would compose and memorize them, so that clarity of organization and simplicity of style were combined with spontaneity. Several of his pupils became notable contributors to thermodynamics, including F. Bošnjaković, F. Merkel, Wilhelm Nusselt, and Rudolf Plank—as well as his own sister Hilde Mollier, who later married the electronics pioneer H. G. Barkhausen.

Although his engineering colleagues considered Mollier a pure theoretician—instead of experimenting himself, he based his findings upon the empirical data of others—his role was actually that of a mediator between the theoretical work of Clausius and J. W. Gibbs (whose work he knew through Ostwald's 1892 German translation) and the realm of practical engineering. From the beginning his interest centered on the properties of thermodynamic media and their effective presentation in the form of charts and diagrams. It was here that he made his crucial contribution. Engineers had traditionally visualized thermodynamic processes in terms of the pressure-volume (P-V) diagram with which they were familiar from practical experience with the steam engine indicator. This diagram, however, obscured the significance of the second law of thermodynamics. In 1873 Gibbs had suggested an alternative in the temperature-entropy (T-S) diagram where Carnot processes stand out as simple rectangles, and the degree of approximation of actual thermodynamic processes to ideal ones can be easily judged. It was at this point that Mollier introduced the concept of *enthalpy,* a property of state that was then little known (1902). This property had been defined in 1875 by Gibbs, under the name "heat function for constant pressure," as the sum of internal energy and of the product of pressure and volume (the term "enthalpy" was coined later by Kamerlingh Onnes). Like Clausius' entropy, enthalpy is an abstract property that cannot be measured directly. Its great advantage is that it describes energy changes in thermodynamic systems without requiring a distinction between heat and work. Employing this new property of state, in 1904 Mollier devised an enthalpy-entropy (H-S) diagram, which

retained most of the advantages of the T-S diagram, while acquiring some additional ones. While vertical lines signified, as before, reversible processes, horizontal lines in it described processes of constant energy; the diagram thus demonstrated in strikingly simple fashion the essence of both the first and the second law of thermodynamics. Quantities of work, which in the P-V and the T-S diagrams had appeared as an area, as well as discharge velocities through adiabatic nozzles, were represented here simply as vertical distances. Although the H-S diagram quickly became a principal tool of power and refrigeration engineers, to Mollier it was merely an element in a broad reorganization of thermodynamic practice. He also developed a new system of thermodynamic computation in which enthalpy played an important role, and as a basis for such calculations he published charts and diagrams of the properties of steam and of various refrigerants (his steam tables, first published in 1906, quickly went through seven editions). Besides the H-S diagram he proposed a number of other enthalpy diagrams, which have all become known, upon recommendation of the U.S. Bureau of Standards in 1923, as Mollier diagrams.

Mollier also contributed to other areas of thermodynamics. In 1897 he published an important study on heat transfer, before turning this subject over to his pupil Wilhelm Nusselt, who soon made fundamental contributions to it. His presentation of the first mathematical analysis of the process of combustion (1921) has proven of lasting utility.

BIBLIOGRAPHY

I. Original Works. Except for the chapter "Wärme," in Akademischer Verein Hütte, *Hütte: Des Ingenieurs Taschenbuch,* 18th ed. (Berlin, 1902), and *Neue Tabellen und Diagramme für Wasserdampf* (Berlin, 1906; 7th ed., 1932), Mollier's publications were confined to journals. His most important research papers are "Über die kalorischen Eigenschaften der Kohlensäure und anderer technisch wichtiger Dämpfe," in *Zeitschrift für die gesamte Kälteindustrie,* **2** (1895), 66–70, 85–91; "Über die kalorischen Eigenschaften der Kohlensäure ausserhalb des Sättigungsgebietes," *ibid.,* **3** (1896), 65–69, 90–92; "Über den Wärmedurchgang und die darauf bezüglichen Versuchsergebnisse," in *Zeitschrift des Vereins deutscher Ingenieure,* **41** (1897), 153–162, 197–202; "Über die Beurteilung der Dampfmaschinen," *ibid.,* **42** (1898), 685–689; "Dampftafel für schweflige Säure," in *Zeitschrift für die gesamte Kälteindustrie,* **10** (1903), 125–127; "Neue Diagramme zur technischen Wärmelehre," in *Zeitschrift des Vereins deutscher Ingenieure,* **48** (1904), 271–275; "Gleichungen und Diagramme zu den Vorgängen im Gasgenerator," *ibid.,* **51** (1907), 532–536; "Die physikalischen

Grundlagen der Kältetechnik," in *Zeitschrift für die gesamte Kälteindustrie*, **16** (1909), 186–190; "Die technische Darstellung der Zustandsgleichungen," in *Physikalische Zeitschrift*, **21** (1920), 457–463; "Die Gleichungen des Verbrennungsvorganges," in *Zeitschrift des Vereins deutscher Ingenieure*, **65** (1921), 1095–1096; "Ein neues Diagramm für Gasluftgemische," *ibid.*, **67** (1923), 869–872; and "Das i/x-Diagramm für Dampfluftgemische," *ibid.*, **73** (1929), 1009–1013.

II. SECONDARY LITERATURE. The following are particularly useful for biographical data: N. Elsner, "Richard Mollier als Mensch und Wissenschaftler," in *Wissenschaftliche Zeitschrift der Technischen Universität Dresden*, **13** (1964), 1101–1103; Heinz Jungnickel, "Kältetechnik— Stand und Entwicklung," *ibid.*, 1105–1106; Walter Pauer, "Erinnerungen an Richard Mollier," *ibid.*, 1103–1104; and Rudolf Plank, "Richard Mollier zum 70. Geburtstag," in *Zeitschrift für die gesamte Kälteindustrie*, **40** (1933), 165–167; and "Richard Mollier," in *Kältetechnik*, **15** (1963), 342–344. Poggendorff, VI, 1766; and VIIa, pt. 3, 342; gives a number of further references.

OTTO MAYR

MOLLWEIDE, KARL BRANDAN (*b.* Wolfenbüttel, Germany, 3 February 1774; *d.* Leipzig, Germany, 10 March 1825), *astronomy, mathematics*.

Mollweide graduated from the University of Halle, then became a teacher of mathematics in the Pädagogium of the Franckesche Stiftung there. In 1811 he was appointed to a position at Leipzig University, where he worked in the astronomical observatory that had been established in the old castle of Pleissenburg; the post carried with it the title of professor, and the following year he was made full professor of astronomy. In 1814 Mollweide was appointed to the chair of mathematics, one of the old and privileged university posts that carried with it the right to become dean or rector; he was twice dean during his eleven-year tenure at Leipzig.

Mollweide's two professorships left him little time to make astronomical observations—during term he usually gave four courses that met for fourteen to sixteen hours weekly. In his astronomy courses he emphasized the fixing of stellar positions, although he also treated the other branches of the subject; his mathematical courses comprised arithmetic, algebra, analysis, stereometry, trigonometry, analytical geometry, conics, and the theory of probability. He nevertheless was able to publish a number of scientific works; some of them represented his own researches, others were editions of standard authors and logarithmic tables.

Certain trigonometrical formulas and a conformal map projection are named for Mollweide. He is also known for his youthful dispute with Goethe over the latter's *Farbenlehre*, in which he defended the Newtonian theory of colors that Goethe was never able to accept.

BIBLIOGRAPHY

A more complete list of Mollweide's writings is in Poggendorff, II, cols. 180–181. They include "Beweis dass die Bonne'sche Entwerfungsart die Länder ihrem Flächeninhalt auf der Kugel gemäss darstellt," in *Monatliche Correspondenz zur Beförderung der Erd- und Himmelskunde*, **13** (1806); "Analytische Theorie der stereographische Projektion," *ibid.*, **14** (1806); "Einige Projektionsarten der sphäroidischen Erde," *ibid.*, **16** (1807); *Prüfung der Farbenlehre des Herrn von Göthe und Verteidigung des Newtonschen Systems gegen dieselbe* (Halle, 1810); *Darstellungen der optischen Irrtümer in Herrn von Göthes Farbenlehre* (Halle, 1811); *Commentatio mathematico-philologica* (Leipzig, 1813); *Kurzgefasste Beschreibung der künstliche Erd- und Himmelskugel . . .* (Leipzig, 1818); *Multiplex et continuus seriorum transformatio exemplo quodem illustratur* (Leipzig, 1820); and *Formula valorem praesentem pensionum annuarum comptandi recognitio et disputatio* (Leipzig, 1823).

A short biography of Mollweide by Siegmund Günther is in *Allgemeine deutsche Biographie*, XXII (Leipzig, 1885), 151–154.

H.-CHRIST. FREIESLEBEN

MOLYNEUX, SAMUEL (*b.* Chester, England, 18 July 1689; *d.* Kew, England, 13 April 1728), *astronomy, optics*.

Samuel Molyneux was the only son of William Molyneux to survive infancy. His mother died in 1691 and he was raised by his father, who zealously undertook his education on Lockean principles. His father died in 1698, leaving him to the care of his uncle, Thomas Molyneux. He entered Trinity College, Dublin, when he was sixteen, and there formed a friendship with George Berkeley, who dedicated his *Miscellanea Mathematica* to him in 1707. Molyneux received the B.A. in 1708, and the M.A. in 1710. In 1717 he married Lady Elizabeth Capel, who inherited a large sum of money and a residence outside London, Kew House, in 1721. Molyneux was thus able to devote himself to the study of astronomy and optics. He was elected fellow of the Royal Society in 1712.

Molyneux's most important astronomical investigations were undertaken in collaboration with his close friend James Bradley. In 1725 the two scientists decided to examine for themselves the validity of Robert Hooke's supposed detection of a large parallax for γ Draconis. To this end they ordered a large zenith sector with a radius of twenty-four feet from George Graham, the distinguished London instrument maker. The sector was set up on 26 November 1725 at Molyneux's residence, passing through holes in the ceilings and roof. Observations of γ Draconis on 3, 5, 11, and 12 December 1725 did not, however, reveal any change in the apparent position of the star.

Bradley observed the star again on 17 December "chiefly through curiosity," and to his great surprise found that it had moved southward, in the opposite direction to that which would arise from the projected parallax. Observations performed throughout the next twelve months revealed that the star exhibited an annual circular movement. Anxious to ascertain the laws of this phenomenon and to discover its physical cause, Bradley had Graham construct a more versatile sector than Molyneux's—one having a larger angular range. Molyneux helped set up this instrument at Bradley's aunt's residence at Wanstead on 19 August 1727. By 29 December 1727, Bradley had completed the observations necessary for his discovery of the aberration of light. The two scientists further worked together from 1723 to 1725 to improve methods of constructing reflecting telescopes; their efforts here did much to help bring reflecting telescopes into more general use.

In addition to his scientific activities, Molyneux pursued an active and noteworthy career in politics. He was a member of the English parliaments of 1715, 1726, and 1727, and a member of the Irish parliament of 1727. On 29 July 1727 he was appointed a lord of the admiralty, in which office he devised several schemes for the improvement of the navy. It was probably because of the pressure of public business arising from this appointment that he was unable to continue his astronomical observations after helping Bradley to set up his sector. Kew House was demolished in 1804 and a sundial, erected by William IV in 1834, now commemorates the observations made there.

BIBLIOGRAPHY

I. Original Works. Molyneux's writings include "A Relation of the Strange Effects of Thunder and Lightning, which Happened at Mrs. Close's House at New-Forge, in the County of Down in Ireland, on the 9th of August, 1707," in *Philosophical Transactions of the Royal Society*, **26** (1708), 36–40; "Sectio Oculorum Duorum Cataractâ Affectorum," *ibid.*, **33** (1724), 149–150; "The Method of Grinding and Polishing Glasses for Telescopes, Extracted from Mr. Huygens and Other Authors," in Robert Smith, *A Compleat System of Optics* (Cambridge, 1738), 281–301; "The Method of Casting, Grinding and Polishing Metals for Reflecting Telescopes, Begun by the Honourable

Samuel Molyneux Esquire, and Continued by John Hadley Esquire, Vice-President of the Royal Society," *ibid.*, 301–312; "Sir Isaac Newton's Reflecting Telescope Made and Described by the Honourable Samuel Molyneux Esquire, and Presented by Him to His Majesty John V. King of Portugal: with Other Kinds of Mechanisms for This and for Mr. Gregory's Reflecting Telescope," *ibid.*, 363–368; "A Description of an Instrument Set up at Kew, in Surrey, for Investigating the Annual Parallax of the Fixed Stars, with an Account of the Observations Made Therewith," in James Bradley, *Miscellaneous Works and Correspondence of the Rev. James Bradley*, S. P. Rigaud, ed. (Oxford, 1832), 93–115; and "Observations Made at Kew," *ibid.*, 116–193, which includes observations by James Bradley after 22 April 1726.

II. Secondary Literature. An excellent account of Molyneux's education can be gleaned from the extensive exchange of letters between William and Thomas Molyneux and John Locke in *The Works of John Locke*, IX (London, 1823), 289–472. See also the article on Molyneux by Agnes M. Clerke in *Dictionary of National Biography*.

Howard Plotkin

MOLYNEUX, WILLIAM (*b.* Dublin, Ireland, 17 April 1656; *d.* Dublin, 11 October 1698), *astronomy, physics*.

Molyneux was the son of Samuel and Margaret Dowdall Molyneux. He was born at his father's house in New Row near Ormond-Gate. The father was of an old family and, although trained in law, took up a military career during the turbulent 1640's. He was proficient in mathematics and as master gunner of Ireland, performed numerous gunnery experiments.

A delicate child, Molyneux was educated at a Dublin grammar school and entered Trinity College, Dublin, on 10 April 1671, under the tutelage of William Palliser (later archbishop of Cashel). After taking his bachelor of arts degree in 1675 he was sent by his father to prepare for the legal profession at the Middle Temple. He had little zeal for the law and, expecting an independent income, preferred to follow his own interests in natural philosophy. In 1678 he returned to Dublin to marry Lucy Domvile, daughter of the attorney general Sir William Domvile. Her ill health and subsequent blindness imposed a tragic family burden until her death on 9 May 1691.

After a vain attempt to secure a cure for his wife's ills, Molyneux returned to his studies in natural philosophy. While at Trinity he had already turned from Aristotelianism and began the study of Descartes, Gassendi, Bacon, and Digby. He also studied the *Philosophical Transactions of the Royal Society*. In April 1680 Molyneux published his first work, a translation of Descartes's *Six Metaphysical Meditations*, for which he wrote a brief introduction and a short sketch of Descartes's life. This book, published in London, appears to be among the first English translations of Descartes. In the summer of 1682 he undertook to publish some queries concerning a description of Ireland in connection with Moses Pitt's *English Atlas*, an abortive attempt that left Molyneux with vast heaps of uncorrelated materials.

In October 1683 Molyneux formed a Dublin scientific society in an attempt to emulate the Royal Society of London. He brought together at a coffee-house on Cock Hill about a dozen men to discourse on philosophy and mathematics. They were soon invited by Robert Huntington, provost of Trinity College, to meet at his home, where in January 1684 they adopted the name Dublin Philosophical Society and elected Molyneux their first secretary. Despite his initial pessimism, the society flourished, many scientific papers were read, and correspondence was initiated with the Royal Society and with the Oxford Philosophical Society. The Dublin group was dispersed under the government of Tyrconnell in 1687, but resumed its activities for a brief period in 1693.

During this time Molyneux began a lengthy correspondence with John Flamsteed, astronomer royal, and strengthened his connections with the Royal Society, of which he was elected a fellow in 1685. The most important of his numerous articles published in the *Philosophical Transactions* include papers on the hygroscope, optics, and astronomy. In the short work *Sciothericum telescopium* (1686), he described a telescopic sundial constructed for him in London by Richard Whitehead.

Fearing for their lives under Tyrconnell's rule, Molyneux and his family left Ireland in January 1689 to settle in Chester, England. There Molyneux wrote his best-known scientific work, the *Dioptrica nova*, the first treatise on optics published in English. Printed at London in 1692, it was intended as a complete and clear treatise of current optical knowledge independent of any hypothesis concerning the nature of light. Appended to it was Halley's famous theorem for finding the foci of lenses. A popular text, it was reprinted in 1709 and provided a scientific base for Berkeley's *Essay Towards a New Theory of Vision*. The book was widely distributed, and Molyneux personally sent copies to Newton, Halley, Locke, Hooke, Boyle, Flamsteed, and Huygens. Its publication ended his friendship with Flamsteed, who, according to Molyneux, took umbrage at the lack of prominence accorded his work.

In the dedicatory epistle, Molyneux lavishly praised Locke's *Essay Concerning Human Understanding*;

Locke's letter thanking him initiated a lengthy correspondence that was ended only by Molyneux's death in 1698. It was during the course of this exchange that Molyneux first posed the famous problem known by his name: Would a blind man, suddenly granted his vision, be able to distinguish by sight alone between a sphere and a cube that he had touched when sightless? Both Molyneux and Locke, as well as Berkeley, decided in the negative.

Through the influence of the duke of Ormonde, in 1684 Molyneux shared the post of surveyor general with William Robinson, but he was removed from the position by Tyrconnell in 1688. In 1691 the family returned from Chester to Dublin, where his wife died. Their son, Samuel, later became a noted astronomer. In 1692 Molyneux was chosen to represent the University of Dublin in Parliament and served for a short time. His services pleased the government and the university, and he was nominated a commissioner of forfeited estates in Ireland (a post he declined) and was awarded an honorary doctorate of laws in 1693.

Molyneux is best remembered for *The Case of Ireland's Being Bound by Acts of Parliament in England Stated* (1698), in which he argued for Ireland's autonomy and against the English Parliament's right to legislate for it. He died of a lifelong affliction, kidney stones, and was interred in St. Audoen's Church, Dublin, in the tomb of his grandfather, Sir William Usher.

BIBLIOGRAPHY

I. ORIGINAL WORKS. Molyneux's major published works are his translation of Descartes's *Six Metaphysical Meditations* (London, 1680); *Sciothericum telescopium* (Dublin, 1686); *Dioptrica nova* (London, 1692; 2nd ed., 1709); and *The Case of Ireland's Being Bound by Acts of Parliament in England Stated* (Dublin, 1698). His published articles appeared mainly in the *Philosophical Transactions of the Royal Society*, **14–19** (1684–1697).

The main repositories of his MSS are the Civic Centre Archives, Southampton, which possesses the bulk of his correspondence with Flamsteed and his translations of Galileo and Torricelli on mechanics, now being edited for publication by R. Kargon; and Trinity College, Dublin. The British Museum has Molyneux's own copy of the *Dioptrica nova* with MS notes; letters of Molyneux to Hans Sloane on Newton's *Principia*, a 2nd ed. of which Molyneux offered to underwrite (Sloane MS 4036); and the minute and register book of the Dublin Philosophical Society (Add. MS 4811).

Much of the society's correspondence with the Oxford Philosophical Society is in R. T. Gunther, *Early Science in Oxford*, IV (Oxford, 1925), 129–208; and its correspondence with the Royal Society, in T. Birch, *History of the*

Royal Society, IV (London, 1757), *passim. Dublin University Magazine*, **18** (1841), 305–327, 470–490, 604–619, 744–764, contains four articles with long extracts from Molyneux's correspondence with his brother Thomas. Molyneux's correspondence with John Locke, first published in *Some Familiar Letters Between Mr. Locke and Several of His Friends* (London, 1708), is reprinted in *The Works of John Locke*, 11th ed., IX (London, 1812).

II. SECONDARY LITERATURE. The major biographical source is still Molyneux's autobiographical sketch (1694) in Capel Molyneux, *An Account of the Family and Descendants of Sir Thomas Molyneux, Kt.* (Evesham, 1820). *Biographia Britannica* (London, 1760) has a lengthy account, as does Pierre Bayle, *A General Dictionary Historical and Critical*, J. P. Bernard, T. Birch, and J. Lockman, eds., 10 vols. (London, 1734–1741), which also contains part of the Molyneux-Flamsteed correspondence. There is a short MS biography, probably by Birch, in the British Museum, Add. MS 4223. See also Robert Dunlop's article in *Dictionary of National Biography*.

More recent works are Colin Turbayne, "Berkeley and Molyneux on Retinal Images," in *Journal of the History of Ideas*, **16** (1955); I. Ehrenpreis, *Swift: The Man, His Works and the Age*, I (Cambridge, Mass., 1962), 43–88; K. T. Hoppen, "The Royal Society and Ireland: William Molyneux, F.R.S.," in *Notes and Records. Royal Society of London*, **18** (1963), 125–135; and *The Common Scientist in the Seventeenth Century* (Charlottesville, Va., 1970), 90–190, which contains a good account of Molyneux's work and an excellent bibliography.

ROBERT H. KARGON

MONARDES, NICOLÁS BAUTISTA (*b.* Seville, Spain, *ca.* 1493; *d.* Seville, 10 October 1588), *medicine, natural history.*

Monardes was the son of Nicoloso de Monardis, an Italian bookseller, and Ana de Alfaro, daughter of a physician. He received a bachelor's degree in arts in 1530 and in medicine in 1533, both from the University of Alcalá de Henares, and the doctorate in medicine at Seville in 1547. In 1537 he married Catalina Morales, daughter of García Perez Morales, professor of medicine at Seville. They had seven children, some of whom went to America; their father, however, had to learn about American drugs at Seville's docks. Monardes had a good medical practice as well as considerable investments and businesses, which included the importation of drugs and the slave trade, the latter involving him in bankruptcy. After the death of his wife in 1577 Monardes took holy orders; he died eleven years later of a cerebral hemorrhage.

Monardes was the best-known and most widely read Spanish physician in Europe in the sixteenth century: his books were translated into Latin, English, Italian, French, German, and Dutch; and through his writings the American materia medica began to be known. He also published works on pharmacology, toxicology, medicine, therapeutics, phlebotomy, iron, and snow. He was an expert botanist; and because of his careful descriptions of drugs and the tests he carried out in animals to ascertain their medicinal properties, he is considered one of the founders of pharmacognosy and experimental pharmacology.

BIBLIOGRAPHY

I. ORIGINAL WORKS. The earliest book by Monardes, a survey of materia medica prior to the introduction of American drugs, was *Pharmacodilosis* (Seville, 1536). The study on venesection, *De secanda vena in pleuritii* (Seville, 1539), was reprinted at Antwerp in 1551, 1564, and 1943. The booklet on the medicinal properties of the rose, *De rosa et partibus eius* (Seville, *ca.* 1540), was also reprinted in *Archaeion* (Santa Fé, Argentina, 1941–1942). Monardes' fame grew after the publication of his first book on American drugs, *Dos libros. El uno que trata de todas las cosas que traen de nuestras Indias Occidentales* . . . (Seville, 1565; repr. 1569). The *Segunda parte del libro de todas las cosas* . . . (Seville, 1571) contains the description of tobacco, among other drugs. He also published a book on snow, *Libro que trata de la nieve* (Seville, 1571). Some of these works were translated and published abroad. A book containing all of Monardes' printed works on the American drugs plus those on the bezoar, viper's-grass, iron, and snow, *Primera, y segunda y tercera partes de la historia medicinal de las cosas que se traen de nuestras Indias Occidentales que se sirven en medicina* . . . (Seville, 1574), was soon translated into Italian, English, Latin, and French, and reprinted in Spanish (1580); up to 50 eds. of his works have been recorded. Monardes also edited Jean d'Avignon's *Sevillana medicina* (Seville, 1545; repr. 1885).

II. SECONDARY LITERATURE. There are several biographies on Monardes. Joaquín Olmedilla y Puig, *Estudio histórico de* . . . *Monardes* (Madrid, 1897); and Carlos Pereyra, *Monardes y el exotismo médico en el siglo XVI* (Madrid, 1936), were superseded by the data found in Seville's archives by Francisco Rodríguez Marín and presented in *La verdadera biografía del doctor Nicolás Monardes* (Madrid, 1925). Corrected biographical information, a study of Monardes' pharmacological work, and a bibliographical survey are in Francisco Guerra, *Nicolás Bautista Monardes, su vida y su obra* (Mexico City, 1961).

FRANCISCO GUERRA

MOND, LUDWIG (*b.* Kassel, Germany, 7 March 1839; *d.* London, England, 11 December 1909), *industrial chemistry.*

Mond is remembered for three contributions to the chemical industry: the establishment of the ammonia soda process in England; the development of an efficient power gas plant; and the discovery of nickel carbonyl, which led to a new process for extracting nickel from its ores.

Born into a wealthy and cultured Jewish family, Mond began his chemical education in 1855 under Kolbe at Marburg; from 1856 to 1859 he worked with Bunsen at Heidelberg. The next eight years were spent in acquiring experience in chemical manufacturing, especially of soda, ammonia, and acetic acid, in Germany, England, and Holland. In 1867 he settled in Widnes, one of the centers of the Leblanc soda trade in England.

Many unsuccessful attempts had been made to develop a simpler alternative to the Leblanc process by treating salt solutions with ammonia and carbon dioxide. By 1865 Ernest Solvay in Belgium had brought the process to some measure of efficiency, and a meeting between Mond and Solvay led to Mond's acquisition in 1872 of a license to use the process in England. Seven years of unceasing effort (during which time he often slept at the plant) enabled Mond to solve the chemical engineering problems posed by the handling of large volumes of liquids and gases, and by 1880 the success of the venture was assured. The corporation of Brunner and Mond (1881) was the first real threat to the survival of the Leblanc soda trade.

The search for a cheap source of ammonia for his soda works led Mond to examine ways of obtaining ammonia from coal. He devised in 1889 a system that burned coal in gas producers using a mixture of air and steam. In addition to ammonia the system yielded a cheap gas suitable for most industrial heating purposes. To promote its local use, the South Staffordshire Mond Gas Company was formed, and to develop the process overseas Mond founded the Power Gas Corporation.

From 1884 Mond and his assistant Carl Langer were concerned with recovering chlorine from waste ammonium chloride by distilling over heated metal oxides. Nickel valves in the plant became corroded, although this did not happen in the laboratory apparatus. Carbon monoxide in the kiln gases used to sweep ammonia out of the plant proved to be the reason. Experiments showed that nickel combined with carbon monoxide under gentle heat to form nickel carbonyl $Ni(CO)_4$, which on thermal decomposition yielded pure nickel. Mond's last industrial enterprise was the creation in 1900 of the Mond Nickel Company to link mines in Canada with extraction works in Wales.

Mond believed that the study of pure science is the best preparation for a career in industry. He used his great wealth wisely; particularly notable gifts were the Davy-Faraday Laboratory at the Royal Institution and financial support to the Royal Society for the *Catalogue of Scientific Papers*. He also bequeathed his collection of Italian paintings to his adopted country.

BIBLIOGRAPHY

I. ORIGINAL WORKS. Seventeen papers are listed in the Royal Society *Catalogue of Scientific Papers*, XVII, 318. The developments outlined in the text were all described by Mond in their historical setting. For ammonia-soda see "On the Origin of the Ammonia-soda Process," in *Journal of the Society of Chemical Industry*, **4** (1885), 527–529; on power gas, "The Commercial Production of Ammonium Salts," *ibid.*, **8** (1889), 505–510; on nickel carbonyl and nickel extraction, "On Nickel Carbon Oxide and Its Application in Arts and Manufactures," in *Report of the British Association for the Advancement of Science* (1891), 602–607; and "The History of the Process of Nickel Extraction," in *Journal of the Society of Chemical Industry*, **14** (1895), 945–946. There is also a valuable historical survey of chlorine manufacture in *Report of the British Association for the Advancement of Science* (1896), 734–745.

II. SECONDARY LITERATURE. The most useful obituary is in *Journal of the Chemical Society*, **113** (1918), 318–334. Not well known but very valuable is F. G. Donnan's published lecture to the (Royal) Institute of Chemistry, *Ludwig Mond F.R.S., 1839–1909* (London, 1939). More general is J. M. Cohen, *Life of Ludwig Mond* (London, 1956).

W. A. CAMPBELL

MONDEVILLE. See **Henry of Mondeville.**

MONDINO DE' LUZZI (also **Liucci** or **Liuzzi**) (*b.* Bologna, Italy, *ca.* 1275; *d.* Bologna, 1326), *anatomy.*

The name Mondino was probably an endearing form of Raimondo. The Luzzi family was prominent in Florence, but Mondino's father, Nerino Frazoli de' Luzzi, and his uncle, Liuccio, had moved to Bologna by 1270, where Mondino was born about 1275. Little is known of his youth, but since his father was an apothecary and his uncle, who made him his heir, taught medicine, it seems probable that he early became interested in the subject of medicine. Mondino attended the University of Bologna, where he studied under Alderotti (Thaddeus of Florence), and received his doctorate in 1300. He probably joined the faculty of the college of medicine and philosophy shortly after his graduation, but the earliest inscription of his name that has been found there is 1321.

Mondino's chief work is his compendium of anatomy, *Anatomia Mundini*, completed in 1316, which made him, in Castiglione's words, "the first outstanding anatomist worthy of the name."[1] Mondino's book dominated anatomy for over two hundred years. The major reason for Mondino's great popularity was the simplicity, conciseness, and systematic arrangement of his book, which is divided into six parts: (1) an introduction to the whole body and a discussion of authorities; (2) the natural members including the liver, spleen, and other organs in the abdominal cavity; (3) the generative members; (4) the spiritual members, the heart, lungs, trachea, esophagus, and other organs of the thoracic cavity up to the mouth; (5) the animal members of the skull, brain, eyes, ears; and (6) the peripheral parts, bones, spinal column, extremities. This organization was not the result of any philosophical approach to the subject but rather derived from the necessity of dissecting the most perishable organs first.

There is some scholarly discussion over whether Mondino dissected human cadavers himself, even though he spoke of a female cadaver that he anatomized in January 1316, who had a womb "double as big as her." George Sarton[2] and Charles Singer[3] felt that Mondino must have done his own dissection, but Moritz Roth[4] was convinced that he utilized a dissector to perform the manual operations. Regardless of what Mondino himself did, it seems likely from the way in which his book was written that he intended it to be read aloud while others were doing the actual dissection. For example, in describing the chest, Mondino stated, "After the muscle, the bones. Now the bones of the chest are many and are not continuous in order that it may be expanded and contracted, since it has to be ever in motion. . . . The bones are of two kinds, namely the ribs and the bones of the thorax. . . ."[5]

Illustrations from the last part of the fourteenth century usually indicate a professor on an elevated platform reading from a book (probably that of Mondino), while an *ostensore* points to the part and a dissector, a barber or surgeon, performs the actual manual operation. Guy de Chauliac described the same sort of method in his *Chirurgia* when he talked about his master Bertruce, a student of Mondino.[6] The subjects for Mondino's dissections were apparently criminals, since he stated that anatomization begins by placing the body of "one who has died from beheading or hanging" in a supine position.

Mondino was not a particularly accurate observer of the actual results of his anatomies, perhaps because his purpose was not so much to enlarge knowledge through dissection as to memorize the works of the Arabic authorities. His book added very little to knowledge and instead repeated many old errors, thereby giving them new currency. He described the five-lobed liver (derived from dog anatomy), although he did say these were not always separate in man. Mondino reported black bile as coming from the spleen and being conducted to the stomach by a vein; his description of the heart was crude and also erroneous as was most of his physiology, which was that of Galen modified by Aristotelian or pseudo-Aristotelian notions. Surprisingly, his descriptions of the bones, muscles, nerves, veins, and arteries were also very inadequate, perhaps because physicians held that medicine should be concerned primarily with curing internal afflictions; consequently they gave their greatest attention to the viscera. Even though he performed anatomies on at least two women, his female anatomy seems to have been based almost entirely upon either that of animals or the erroneous notions of his predecessors; he described the womb as having seven chambers. He did give an interesting account of the sexual organs and tried to establish analogies between the male and female organs. He was also at some pains to emphasize the differences between the anatomy of the pig (as in Copho's *Anatomia porci*) and that of human beings.

Although Mondino regarded Galen as an almost infallible authority, he made errors that Galen did not. The trouble may have been that Mondino relied upon an abbreviated Latin translation of the *De juvamentis membrorum*, an incomplete Arabic version of the first nine books (of a total of seventeen) of Galen's *De usu partium*. This mixture of Arabic and Greek sources also helped create the confusion in terminology evident in Mondino's work. The sacrum, for example, is variously identified as *alchatim*, *allanis*, and *alhavius*. The pubic bone is called *os femoris* and *pecten*. On the other hand the same terms are used for different parts; *pomum granatum* can refer to either the thyroid cartilage or the xiphoid process, and *anchae* can mean the hips in general, the pelvic skeleton, the acetabulum, or the corpora quadrigemina of the brain. Much of Mondino's difficulty over terms was caused by the lack of standardization of anatomical nomenclature. Mondino himself seems to have introduced the words "matrix" and "mesentery" into anatomy.

In spite of the above criticism, Mondino should be regarded as the restorer of anatomy if only because his popular textbook and his experimental teaching were instrumental in preparing the revival of the subject. His text was the first book written on anatomy during the Middle Ages that was based on the dissection of the human cadaver; his efforts consolidated anatomy as a part of the medical program at Bologna and encouraged further study. His book also dominated the teaching of anatomy, and no real improvements were made upon it until 1521, when Berengario da Carpi wrote his famous commentary on Mondino.

Although he is best known for his *Anatomia*, Mondino wrote at least nine *consilia* dealing with such ailments as catarrh, fevers, stone, melancholic humors, and so forth. He also wrote a number of commentaries on the collection of classical writings known as the *Ars medicinae* including *Super libro prognosticorum Hippocratis*, *Super Hippocratis de regimine acutorum*, *Annotata in Galeni de morbo et accidenti*, and perhaps others. His commentary *Lectura super primo, secundo et quarto de juvamentis* is on part of Galen's *De usu partium*. Another commentary on the *Canones* of Mesue the Younger includes material from his *Anatomia*. Mondino also wrote treatises on weights and measures, human viscera, prescriptions and drugs, medical practice, and fevers.

NOTES

1. Arturo Castiglioni, *A History of Medicine*, trans. by E. B. Krumbhaar (New York, 1947), 341.
2. Sarton, *Introduction to the History of Science*, III, 1, 842.
3. Singer, *The Evolution of Anatomy*, 75–76.
4. Moritz Roth, *Andreas Vesalius Bruxellensis*, 20.
5. Mondino dei Luzzi, *Anothomia*, in Joannes Ketham, *Fasciculo di medicina*, trans. by Charles Singer, I, 80–81.
6. Guy de Chauliac, *La grande chirurgie*, trans. by E. Nicaise (Paris, 1890), 30–31.

BIBLIOGRAPHY

The first printed edition of the *Anatomia* appeared at Padua in 1476. Other editions in Latin appeared at Pavia, Bologna, Leipzig, Venice, Strasbourg, Paris, Milan, Geneva, Rostock, Lyons, and Marburg. All told there are approximately forty printed editions in Latin and other languages. Only a few of the editions include woodcuts or illustrations, but one or more appear in the Leipzig (1493), Venice (1494), Strasbourg (1513), Rostock (1514), Bologna (1521), and Marburg (1541) editions. A modern facsimile of the 1478 Pavia edition was edited by Ernest Wickersheimer, *Anatomies de Mondino dei Luzzi et de Guido de Vigevano* (Paris, 1926).

There were at least two early French translations, one by Richard Roussat (Paris, 1532), and another by an unknown translator (Paris, 1541). This last was erroneously labeled as the first French translation by LeRoy Crummer, who discovered it and published several interesting woodcuts from it. See Crummer, "La première traduction française de l'*Anatomie* de Mondini," in *Aesculape*, **20** (1930), 204–207. An Italian translation by Sebastian M. Romano was included in Joannes Ketham, *Fasciculo di medicina* (1493), and this was translated into English by Charles Singer in the reprinting of *Fasciculo di medicina* (Florence, 1924 and 1925). Another fifteenth-century Italian translation, with a photographic reproduction of a fourteenth-century MS of the *Anatomia*, was printed in Lino Sighinolfi, ed., *Mondino de Liucci Anatomia, Riprodotta da un Codice Bolognese del secolo XIV*[e]*; volgarizzata nel secolo XV* (Bologna, 1930).

Seven of Mondino's *consilia* were printed by Balduin Vonderlage in his dissertation, *Consilien des Mondino dei Luzzi aus Bologna* (Leipzig, 1922). Mondino's commentary on the *Canones* of Mesue, *Mesuë cum expositione Mondini super canones universales*, was printed at Venice in 1490, 1495, 1497, 1570, 1638, and Lyons in 1525. The following works have not been printed: *Practica de accidentibus morborum secundum Magistrum Mundinum de Liucius de Bononis; Tractatus de ponderibus secundum Magistrum Mundinum; De visceribus humani corporis; Super libro prognosticorum Hippocratis; Mundinus super Hippocratis de regimine acutorum; Annotata in Galeni de morbo et accidente; Super libro prognosticorum Hippocratis; Mundinus super Hippocratis de regimine acutorum; Annotata in Galeni de morbo et accidente; Super libro de pulsibus; Tractatus de dosis medicinae; De medicinis simplicibus; Practicae medicinae libri X; Consilia medicinalia; Consilium ad retentionem menstruorum*, and *De accidentibus febrium*.

For further information see Howard B. Adelmann, *Marcello Malpighi and the Evolution of Embryology*, 5 vols., I (Ithaca, 1966), 74–84; Vern L. Bullough, *The Development of Medicine as a Profession* (Basel–New York, 1966); Giovanni Fantuzzi, *Notizie degli Scrittori Bolognese*, 9 vols., VI (Bologna, 1782–1790), 41–46; Giovanni Martinotti, "L'insegnamento del'Anatomia in Bologna prima del secolo XIX," in *Studi e memorie per la storia dell'università di Bologna*, II (Bologna, 1911), 1–146; Moritz Roth, *Andreas Vesalius Bruxellensis* (Berlin, 1892); George Sarton, *Introduction to the History of Science*, 3 vols. in 5, III (Baltimore, 1927–1942), 1, 842–845; and Charles Singer, *The Evolution of Anatomy* (London, 1925), 75.

VERN L. BULLOUGH

MONGE, GASPARD (*b.* Beaune, France, 9 May 1746; *d.* Paris, France, 28 July 1818), *geometry, calculus, chemistry, theory of machines.*

Monge revived the study of certain branches of geometry, and his work was the starting point for the remarkable flowering of that subject during the nineteenth century. Beyond that, his investigations extended to other fields of mathematical analysis, in particular to the theory of partial differential equations, and to problems of physics, chemistry, and technology. A celebrated professor and peerless *chef d'école*, Monge assumed important administrative and political responsibilities during the Revolution and the Empire. He was thus one of the most original mathematicians of his age, while his civic activities represented the main concerns of the Revolution more fully than did those of any other among contemporary French scientists of comparable stature.

The elder son of Jacques Monge, a merchant originally of Haute-Savoie, and the former Jeanne Rousseaux, of Burgundian origin, Monge was a brilliant student at the Oratorian *collège* in Beaune. From 1762 to 1764 he completed his education at the Collège de la Trinité in Lyons, where he was placed in charge of a course in physics. After returning to Beaune in the summer of 1764, he sketched a plan of his native city. The high quality of his work attracted the attention of an officer at the École Royale du Génie at Mézières, and this event determined the course of his career.

Created in 1748, the École Royale du Génie at Mézières had great prestige, merited by the quality of the scientific and practical training that it offered. Admitted to the school at the beginning of 1765 in the very modest position of draftsman and technician, Monge was limited to preparing plans of fortifications and to making architectural models, tasks he found somewhat disappointing. But barely a year after his arrival he had an opportunity to display his mathematical abilities. The result was the start of a career worthy of his talents.

Monge was requested to solve a practical exercise in defilading—specifically, to establish a plan for a fortification capable of shielding a position from both the view and the firepower of the enemy no matter what his location. For the very complicated method previously employed he substituted a rapid graphical procedure inspired by the methods of what was soon to become descriptive geometry. This success led to his becoming *répétiteur* to the professor of mathematics, Charles Bossut. In January 1769 Monge succeeded the latter, even though he did not hold the rank of professor. The following year he succeeded the Abbé Nollet as instructor of experimental physics at the school. In this double assignment, devoted partially to practical ends, Monge showed himself to be an able mathematician and physicist, a talented draftsman, a skilled experimenter, and a first-class teacher. The influence he exerted until he left the school at the end of 1784 helped to initiate several brilliant careers of future engineering officers and to give the engineering corps as a whole a solid technical training and a marked appreciation for science. The administrators of the school recognized his ability and, after obtaining for him the official title of "royal professor of mathematics and physics" (1775), steadily increased his salary.

Parallel to this brilliant professional career, Monge very early commenced his personal work. His youthful investigations (1766–1772) were quite varied but exhibit several characteristics that marked his entire output: an acute sense of geometric reality; an interest in practical problems; great analytical ability; and the simultaneous examination of several aspects of a single problem: analytic, geometric, and practical.

This was the period in which Monge developed descriptive geometry. He systematized its basic principles and applied it to various graphical problems studied at the École du Génie—problems taken, for example, from fortification, architecture, and scaffolding. That Monge left only a few documents bearing on this work is not surprising, since he was essentially coordinating and rationalizing earlier knowledge, rather than producing really original material. Elements of descriptive geometry appeared very early in his teaching—to the degree that his familiarity with the graphical procedures currently in use and with the various branches of geometry allowed him to make the necessary synthesis. The documents from this period record the many investigations inspired by his readings in the rich collections of the library of the École du Génie. This research dealt with topics in infinitesimal calculus, infinitesimal geometry, analytic geometry, and the calculus of variations. His first important original work was "Mémoire sur les développées, les rayons de courbure et différents genres d'inflexions des courbes à double courbure." He published an extract from it in June 1769 in the *Journal encyclopédique*, and in October 1770 he finished a more complete version that he read before the Académie des Sciences in August 1771; the latter, however, was not published until 1785 (*Mémoires de mathématiques et de physique présentés à l'Académie . . . par divers sçavans . . .*, **10**, 511–550). By then some of the most important ideas in the memoir no longer seemed so original, because Monge had employed them in other works published in the intervening years. Nevertheless, this memoir is of exceptional interest, for it presents most of the new conceptions that Monge developed in his later works, as well as his very personal method of exposition, which combined pure geometry, analytic geometry, and infinitesimal calculus.

Wishing to make himself known and to have his work discussed, Monge sought out d'Alembert and Condorcet at the beginning of 1771. On the latter's advice, he later in the same year presented before the Paris Academy four memoirs corresponding to the main areas of his research. The first, which was not published, dealt with a problem to which he never returned: the extension of the calculus of variations to the study of extrema of double integrals. The second was the memoir on infinitesimal geometry mentioned above. The fourth treated a problem in combinatorial analysis related to a card trick.

In the third memoir Monge entered a field of study that was to hold his interest for many years: the theory of partial differential equations. In particular he undertook the parallel examination of certain equations of this type and of the families of corresponding surfaces. The geometric construction of a particular solution of the equations under consideration allowed him to determine the general nature of the arbitrary function involved in the solutions of a partial differential equation. Moreover, this finding enabled him to take a position on a question then being disputed by d'Alembert, Euler, and Daniel Bernoulli. Monge developed the ideas set forth in this memoir in two others sent to the Academy in 1772. The work presented in these papers was extended in four publications dating from 1776; two of these appeared in the *Mémoires* of the Academy of Turin and two in the *Mémoires* of the Paris Academy. In another paper (1774) Monge discussed the nature of the arbitrary functions involved in the integrals of finite difference equations. He also considered the equation of vibrating strings, a topic he later investigated more fully.

In May 1772 the Academy of Sciences elected Monge to be Bossut's correspondent. At this time he became friendly with Condorcet and Vandermonde. The latter's influence was probably responsible for two unpublished memoirs Monge wrote during this period, on the theory of determinants and on the knight's moves on a chessboard.

In 1775 Monge returned to infinitesimal geometry. Working on the theory of developable surfaces outlined by Euler in 1772, he applied it to the problem of shadows and penumbrae and treated several problems concerning ruled surfaces. A memoir composed in 1776 on Condorcet's prompting (and reworked in 1781 on the basis of a more thorough understanding) is of major importance, although not for its contributions to the practical problem of cuts and fills that served as its point of departure. Its great interest lies in its introduction of lines of curvature and congruences of straight lines.

Although in 1776 Monge was still interested in Lagrange's memoir on singular integrals, his predilection for mathematics was meanwhile slowly yielding to a preference for physics and chemistry. In 1774, while traveling in the Pyrenees, he had collaborated with the chemist Jean d'Arcet in making

altitude measurements with the aid of a barometer. Having some instruments at his disposal in Mézières and working with Vandermonde and Lavoisier during his stays in Paris, Monge carried out experiments on expansion, solution, the effects of a vacuum, and other phenomena; acquired an extensive knowledge of contemporary physics; and participated in the elaboration of certain theories, including the theory of caloric and triboelectricity.

In 1777 Monge married Catherine Huart. They had three daughters, the two elder of whom married two former members of the National Convention, N.-J. Marey and J. Eschassériaux: the two present branches of Monge's descendants are their issue.

During the period 1777–1780 Monge was interested primarily in physics and chemistry and arranged for a well-equipped chemistry laboratory to be set up at the École du Génie. Moreover, having for some time been responsible for supervising the operation of a forge belonging to his wife, he had become interested in metallurgy.

His election to the Academy of Sciences as *adjoint géomètre* in June 1780 altered Monge's life, obliging him to stay in Paris on a regular basis. Thus for some years he divided his time between the capital and Mézières. In Paris he participated in the Academy's projects and presented memoirs on physics, chemistry, and mathematics. He also substituted for Bossut in the latter's course in hydrodynamics (created by A.-R.-J. Turgot in 1775) and in this capacity trained young disciples such as S. F. Lacroix and M. R. de Prony. At Mézières, where he arranged for a substitute to give some of his courses—although he kept his title and salary—Monge conducted research in chemistry. In June–July 1783 he synthesized water. He then turned his attention to collecting stores of hydrogen and to the outer coverings of balloons. Finally, with J. F. Clouet he succeeded in liquefying sulfur dioxide.

In October 1783 Monge was named examiner of naval cadets, replacing Bézout. He attempted to reconcile his existing obligations with the long absences required by this new post, but it proved to be impossible. In December 1784 he had to give up his professorship at Mézières, thus leaving the school at which he had spent twenty of the most fruitful years of his career. From 1784 to 1792 Monge divided his time between his tours of inspection of naval schools and his stays in Paris, where he continued to participate in the activities of the Academy and to conduct research in mathematics, physics, and chemistry. A list of the subjects of his communications to the Academy attests to their variety: the composition of nitrous acid, the generation of curved surfaces, finite difference equations, and partial differential equations (1785); double refraction and the structure of Iceland spar, the composition of iron, steel, and cast iron, and the action of electric sparks on carbon dioxide gas (1786); capillary phenomena (1787); and the causes of certain meteorological phenomena; and a study in physiological optics (1789).

Meanwhile, with other members of the Academy, Monge assisted Lavoisier in certain experiments. For example, in February 1785 he participated in the analysis and synthesis of water. In fact, he was one of the first to accept Lavoisier's new chemical theory. After having collaborated with Vandermonde and Berthollet on a memoir on "iron considered in its different metallurgical states" (1786), he participated in several investigations of metallurgy in France. In 1788 he joined in the refutation, instigated by Lavoisier, of a treatise by the Irish chemist Kirwan, who was a partisan of the phlogiston theory. That Monge was among the founders of the *Annales de chimie* testifies to his standing in chemistry. During this period Monge's position as naval examiner obliged him to write a course in mathematics to replace Bézout's. Only one volume was published, *Traité élémentaire de statique* (1788).

When the Revolution began in 1789, Monge was among the most widely known of French scientists. A very active member of the Academy of Sciences, he had established a reputation in mathematics, physics, and chemistry. As an examiner of naval cadets he directed a branch of France's military schools, which were then virtually the only institutions offering a scientific education of any merit. This position also placed him in contact, in each port he visited, with bureaucracy that was soon to come under his administration. It also enabled him to visit iron mines, foundries, and factories, and thus to become an expert on metallurgical and technological questions. Furthermore, the important reform of teaching in the naval schools that he had effected in 1786 prepared him for the efforts to renew scientific and technical education that he undertook during the Revolution.

Although Monge was a resolute supporter of the Revolution from the outset, his political role remained discreet until August 1792. He joined several revolutionary societies and clubs but devoted most of his time to tours of inspection as examiner of naval cadets and to his functions as a member of the Academy, particularly to the work of the Academy's Commission on Weights and Measures.

After the fall of the monarchy on 10 August 1792, a government was created to carry on the very diffi-cult struggle imposed on the young republic by adherents of the *ancien régime*. On the designation of the Legislative Assembly, Monge accepted the post of minister of the navy, which he held for eight months. Although not outstanding, his work showed his desire to coordinate all efforts to assure the nation's survival and independence. His politics, however, were judged by some to be too moderate; and attacked from several sides and exhausted by the incessant struggle he had to wage, he resigned on 10 April 1793. Henceforth he never played more than a minor political role. A confirmed republican, he associated with Jacobins such as Pache and Hassenfratz; but he never allied himself with any faction or participated in any concrete political action. On the other hand, he was an ardent patriot, who placed all his energy, talent, and experience in the service of the nation, and he played a very important role in developing the manufacture of arms and munitions, and in establishing a new system of scientific and technical education.

Monge resumed his former activities for a short time; but after the suppression of the Academy of Sciences on 8 August 1793 his work came under the direct control of the political authorities, especially of the Committee of Public Safety. From the beginning of September 1793 until October 1794, he took part in the work of the Committee on Arms. He wrote, with Vandermonde and Berthollet, a work on the manufacture of forge and case-hardened steels, drew up numerous orders concerning arms manufacture for Lazare Carnot and C. L. Prieur, supervised Paris arms workshops, assembled technical literature on the making of cannons, gave "revolutionary courses" on this latter subject (February–March 1794), and wrote an important work on it. He also was involved in the extracting and refining of saltpeter and the construction and operation of the great powderworks of Paris. In addition, he participated in the development of military balloons.

Monge also engaged in tasks of a different sort. After the suppression of the Academy he joined the Société Philomatique; participated in the work of the Temporary Commission on Weights and Measures, which continued the projects of the Academy's commission; and took part in the activities of the Commission on the Arts, which was responsible for preserving the nation's artistic and cultural heritage. He was also active in the projects for educational reform then under discussion. His experience at the École de Mézières and in the naval schools explains the special interest that the renewal of scientific and technical instruction held for him. At the elementary level, he prepared for the department of Paris a plan for schools for artisans and workers that the Convention adopted on 15 September 1793 but rejected the next day. At a more advanced level, he was convinced of the value of creating a single national school for training civil and military engineers. Consequently, when he was appointed by the Convention (11 March 1794) to the commission responsible for establishing an École Centrale des Travaux Publics, he played an active role in its work. The memoir that Fourcroy prepared in September 1794 to guide the first steps of the future establishment ("Développements sur l'enseignement . . .") shows the influence of Monge's thinking, which derived from his experience at Mézières. Appointed instructor of descriptive geometry on 9 November 1794, Monge supervised the operation of the training school of the future *chefs de brigade*, or foremen, taught descriptive geometry in "revolutionary courses" designed to complete the training of the future students, and was one of the most active members of the governing council. After a two-month delay caused by political difficulties, the school—soon to be called the École Polytechnique—began to function normally in June 1795. Monge's lectures, devoted to the principles and applications of infinitesimal geometry, were printed on unbound sheets; these constituted a preliminary edition of his *Application de l'analyse à la géométrie*.

Monge was also one of the professors at the ephemeral École Normale de l'An III. From 20 January to 20 May 1795 this school brought together in Paris 1,200 students, who were to be trained to teach in the secondary schools then being planned. The lectures he gave, assisted by his former student S.-F. Lacroix and by J. Fournier, constituted the first public course in descriptive geometry. Like those of the other professors, the lectures were taken down by stenographers and published in installments in the *Journal des séances des écoles normales*.

Monge, who regretted the suppression of the Academy of Sciences, actively participated in the meetings held from December 1795 to March 1796 to prepare its rebirth as the first section of the Institut National, created by the Convention on 26 October 1795. But just when Monge's activities seemed to be returning to normal, events intervened that prevented this from happening.

Monge was named, along with his friend Berthollet, one of the six members of the Commission des Sciences et des Arts en Italie, set up by the Directory to select the paintings, sculptures, manuscripts, and valuable objects that the victorious army was to bring back. He left Paris on 23 May 1796. His mission took him to many cities in northern and central Italy, including Rome, and allowed him to become friendly with Bonaparte. At the end of October 1797 Monge returned to Paris, officially designated, with General Louis Berthier, to transmit to the Directory the text of the Treaty of Campoformio.

Immediately after returning, Monge resumed his former posts, as well as a new one, that of director of the École Polytechnique. But his stay in Paris was brief; at the beginning of February 1798 the Directory sent him back to Rome to conduct a political inquiry. While there, Monge took an active interest in the organization of the short-lived Republic of Rome. The following month, at the request of Bonaparte, he took part in the preparations for the Egyptian expedition. Although reluctant at first, he finally agreed to join the expedition. His boat left Italy on 26 May 1798, joining Bonaparte's squadron two weeks later. Monge arrived in Cairo on 21 July and was assigned various administrative and technical tasks. As president of the Institut d'Égypte, created on 21 August, he played an important role in the many scientific and technical projects undertaken by this body. He accompanied Bonaparte on a brief trip in the Suez region, on the disastrous Syrian expedition (February–June 1799), and, after another brief stay in Cairo, on his return voyage to France (17 August–16 October). During this period of three and a half years, in which he was for almost the whole time away from France, Monge's correspondence and communications to the Institut d'Égypte show that he was working on new chapters of his *Application de l'analyse à la géométrie*. Moreover, the observation of certain natural phenomena, such as mirages, and the study of certain techniques, including metallurgy and the cultivation of the vine, provided him with fruitful sources for thought. Meanwhile, at the request of his wife and without his knowledge, his *Géométrie descriptive* was published in 1799 by his friend and disciple J. N. Hachette, who limited himself to collecting Monge's École Normale lectures previously published in the *Séances*.

On his return to Paris, Monge resumed his duties as director of the École Polytechnique but relinquished them two months later when, following the *coup d'état* of 18 Brumaire, Bonaparte named him senator for life. By accepting this position Monge publicly attached himself to the Consulate. Although this decision may seem to contradict his republican convictions and revolutionary faith, it can be explained by his esteem for and admiration of Bonaparte and by his dissatisfaction with the defects and incompetence of the preceding regime. Dazzled by Napoleon, Monge later rallied to the Empire with the same facility and accepted all the honors and gifts the emperor bestowed upon him: grand officer of the

Legion of Honor in 1804, president of the Senate in 1806, count of Péluse in 1808, among others.

Monge had to divide his time among his family, his teaching of infinitesimal geometry at the École Polytechnique, and his obligations as a member of the Academy of Sciences and of the Conseil de Perfectionnement of the École Polytechnique, and his duties as a senator. Further tasks were soon added. He was founder of the Société d'Encouragement pour l'Industrie Nationale and vice-president of the commission responsible for supervising the preparation and publication of the material gathered on the Egyptian expedition, *Description de l'Égypte*. Even though his duties as senator took him away on several occasions from his courses at the École Polytechnique, he maintained his intense concern for the school. He kept careful watch over the progress of the students, followed their research, and paid close attention to the curriculum and the teaching.

Most of Monge's publications in this period were written for the students of the École Polytechnique. The wide success of the *Géométrie descriptive* was responsible for the rapid spread of this new branch of geometry both in France and abroad. It was reprinted several times; the edition of 1811 contained a supplement by Hachette; and the fourth, posthumous edition, published in 1820 by Barnabé Brisson, included four previously unpublished lectures on perspective and the theory of shadows.

In 1801 Monge published *Feuilles d'analyse appliquée à la géométrie*, an expanded version of his lectures on infinitesimal geometry of 1795. In 1802, working with Hachette, he prepared a brief exposition of analytic geometry that was designed to replace the few remarks on the subject contained in the *Feuilles*. Entitled *Application de l'algèbre à l'analyse*, it was published separately in 1805; in 1807 it became the first part of the final version of *Feuilles d'analyse*, now entitled *Application de l'analyse à la géométrie*. This larger work was republished in 1809 and again in 1850 by J. Liouville, who appended important supplements.

Aside from new editions of the *Traité élémentaire de statique*, revised by Hachette beginning with the fifth edition (1810), and some physical and technical observations made in Italy and Egypt and published in 1799, Monge's other publications during this period dealt almost exclusively with infinitesimal and analytic geometry. For the most part they were gradually incorporated into successive editions of his books. His production of original scientific work began to decline in 1805.

A decline likewise occurred in Monge's other activities. Suffering from arthritis, he stopped teaching at the École Polytechnique in 1809, arranging for Arago to substitute for him and then to replace him. Although he wrote a few more notes on mathematics and several official technical reports, his creative period had virtually come to an end. In November 1812, overwhelmed by the defeat of the Grande Armée, he suffered a first attack of apoplexy, from which he slowly recovered. At the end of 1813 he was sent to his senatorial district of Liège to organize its defenses but fled a few weeks later before the advancing allied armies. Absent from Paris at the moment of surrender, he did not participate in the session of 3 April 1814, in which the Senate voted the emperor's dethronement. He returned shortly afterward and resumed a more or less normal life. In 1815, during the Hundred Days, he renewed his contacts with Napoleon and even saw him several times after Waterloo and the abdication. In October 1815, fearing for his freedom, Monge left France for several months. A few days after his return to Paris, in March 1816, he was expelled from the Institut de France and harassed politically in other ways. Increasingly exhausted physically, spiritually, and intellectually, he found his last two years especially painful. Upon his death, despite government opposition, many current and former students at the École Polytechnique paid him tribute. Throughout the nineteenth century mathematicians acknowledged themselves as his disciples or heirs.

Scientific Work. Monge's scientific work encompasses mathematics (various branches of geometry and mathematical analysis), physics, mechanics, and the theory of machines. His principal contributions to these different fields will be discussed in succession, even though his mathematical work constitutes a coherent ensemble in which analytic developments were closely joined with material drawn from pure, descriptive, analytic, and infinitesimal geometry, and even though his investigations in physics, mechanics, and the theory of machines were also intimately linked.

Descriptive and Modern Geometry. Elaborated during the period 1766–1775, Monge's important contribution is known from his *Géométrie descriptive*, the text of his courses at the École Normale de l'An III (1795), and from the manuscript of his lectures given that year at the École Polytechnique. Before him various practitioners, artists, and geometers, including Albrecht Dürer, had applied certain aspects of this technique. Yet Monge should be considered the true creator of descriptive geometry, for it was he who elegantly and methodically converted the group of graphical procedures used by practitioners into a general uniform technique based on simple and rigorous geometric reasoning and methods. Within a few years this new discipline was being taught in French scientific and technical schools and had spread to several other Continental countries.

Monge viewed descriptive geometry as a powerful tool for discovery and demonstration in various branches of pure and infinitesimal geometry. His persuasive example rehabilitated the study and use of pure geometry, which had been partially abandoned because of the success of Cartesian geometry. Monge's systematic use of cylindrical projection and, more discreetly, that of central projection, opened the way to the parallel creation of projective and modern geometry, which was to be the work of his disciples, particularly J.-V. Poncelet. The definition of the orientation of plane areas and volumes, the use of the transformation by reciprocal polars, and the discreet introduction in certain of his writings of imaginary elements and of elements at infinity confirms the importance of his role in the genesis of modern geometry.

Analytic and Infinitesimal Geometry. Analytic and infinitesimal geometry overlap so closely in Monge's work that it is sometimes difficult to separate them. Whereas from 1771 to 1809 he wrote numerous memoirs on the infinitesimal geometry of space, it was not until 1795, in his lectures at the École Polytechnique, that he specifically developed analytic geometry.

Nevertheless, even in his earliest works, Monge sought to remedy the chief weaknesses of analytic geometry, although this discipline was then for him only an auxiliary of infinitesimal geometry. Rejecting the restrictive Cartesian point of view that was still dominant, he considered analytic geometry as an autonomous branch of mathematics, parallel to pure geometry and independent of it. Consonant with this approach, as early as 1772 and at the same time as Lagrange, Monge systematically introduced into the subject the elements defined by first-degree equations (straight lines and planes) that had previously not been part of it. He also solved the basic problems posed by this extension. Parallel with this endeavor, he sought, following Clairaut and Euler, to make up for the long delay in the development of three-dimensional analytic geometry. In addition Monge introduced an absolute symmetry into the use of the coordinate axes. He showed great analytic virtuosity in his calculations, some of which display, except for the symbolism, a skillful handling of determinants and of certain algorithms of vector calculus. His ability in this regard very early allowed him to establish the foundations of the geometry of the straight line (in Plücker's sense), which he systematized in 1795.

The first two editions (1795 and 1801) of Monge's course in "analysis applied to geometry" at the École Polytechnique contain as an introduction a brief statement of the principles and fundamental problems of this renewed analytic geometry, which was soon taught in upper-level French schools. With his disciple J. N. Hachette, Monge published in 1802 an important memoir, "Application de l'algèbre à la géométrie," which completed the preceding study, notably regarding the theory of change of coordinates and the theory of quadrics. In 1805 Monge collected these various contributions to analytic geometry in a booklet entitled *Application de l'algèbre à la géométrie,* which in 1807 became the first part of his great treatise *Application de l'analyse à la géométrie.* The many articles that Monge and his students devoted to individual problems of analytic geometry (change of coordinates, theory of conics and quadratics, among others) in the *Journal de l'École polytechnique* and in the *Correspondance sur l'École polytechnique* attest to the interest stimulated by the discipline's new orientation.

Throughout his career infinitesimal geometry remained Monge's favorite subject. Here his investigations were directed toward two main topics: families of surfaces defined by their mode of generation, which he examined in connection with the corresponding partial differential equations, and the direct study of the properties of surfaces and space curves. Since the first topic is discussed below, only the principal research relating to the second topic will be presented here. In 1769 Monge defined the evolutes of a space curve and showed that these curves are the geodesics of the developable envelope of the family of planes normal to the given curve. In 1774, after having returned to this question in a memoir presented in 1771, Monge completed the study of developable surfaces outlined by Euler. Concurrently utilizing geometric considerations and analytic arguments, he established the distinction between ruled surfaces and developable surfaces; gave simple criteria for judging, from its equation, whether a given surface is developable; applied these results to the theory of shadows and penumbrae; and solved various problems concerning surfaces. In particular, he determined by means of descriptive geometry the ruled surface passing through three given space curves. Still more important is the memoir on cuts and fills, of which Monge made two drafts (1776 and 1781). The point of departure was a technical problem: to move a certain quantity of earth, determining the trajectory of each molecule in such a way that the total work done is a minimum. Through repeated schematizations he derived the formulation of a question concerning the theory of surfaces that he examined very generally, introducing such important notions as the congruence of straight lines, line of curvature, normal, and focal surface. This memoir served as a starting point for several of Monge's later works, as well as for important investigations by Malus in geometrical optics and by Dupin in infinitesimal geometry.

Several memoirs written between 1783 and 1787 contain numerous studies of families of surfaces and some new results relating to the general theory of surfaces and to the properties of certain space curves.

In *Feuilles d'analyse appliquée à la géométrie* (1795 and 1801) Monge assembled, along with general considerations regarding the theory of surfaces and the geometric interpretation of partial differential equations, monographs on about twenty families of surfaces defined by their mode of generation. *Application de l'analyse à la géométrie* (1807) includes some supplementary material, notably attempts to find families of surfaces when one of the nappes of their focal surface is known. The manuscript of Monge's course for 1805–1806 also contains important additional findings (transformations by reciprocal polars, conoids, etc.). The richness and originality in Monge's lectures, qualities evident in this manuscript and confirmed by the testimony of former students, explain why so many French mathematicians can be considered his direct followers. Among them we may cite Tinseau and Meusnier at the École de Mézières, Lacroix, Fourier, and Hachette at the École Normale, and Lancret, Dupin, Livet, Brianchon, Malus, Poncelet, Chasles, Lamé, and still others at the École Polytechnique. Certain aspects of their writings show the direct influence of Monge, who thus emerges as a true *chef d'école*.

Mathematical Analysis. The theory of partial differential equations and that of ordinary differential equations occupies—often in close connection with infinitesimal geometry—an important place in Monge's work. Yet, despite his great mastery of the techniques of analysis and the importance and originality of certain of the new methods he introduced, his writings in this area are sometimes burdened by an excessive number of examples and are blemished by insufficiently rigorous argumentation.

As early as 1771 the memoirs presented to the Academy and the letters to Condorcet reflect two of the guiding ideas of Monge's work: the geometric determination of the arbitrary function involved in the general solution of a partial differential equation, and the equivalence established between the classification of families of surfaces according to their mode of generation and according to their partial differential equation. He returned to these questions several times between 1771 and 1774, developing many examples and extending his study to finite difference equations. Also, in the memoir of 1775 on developable surfaces he discussed the partial differential equation of developable surfaces and that of ruled surfaces.

From 1773 to 1786 Monge carried out new research in this area. In seven memoirs of varying importance he presented flawlessly demonstrated results, and a progressively elaborated outline of very fruitful new methods. His essentially geometric inspiration drew upon the ideas of his earliest papers and on the division, introduced by Lagrange, of the integral surfaces of a first-order partial differential equation into a complete integral, a general integral, and a singular integral. By means of his theory of characteristics Monge gave a geometric interpretation of the method of the variation of parameters. In addition he introduced such basic notions as characteristic curve, integral curve, characteristic developable, trajectory of characteristics, and characteristic cone. Monge was also interested in second-order partial differential equations.

In particular he created the theory of "Monge equations"—equations of the type

$$Ar + Bs + Ct + D = 0,$$

where A, B, C, D are functions of x, y, z, p, q, and where p, q, r, s, and t have the classical meanings—and solved the equation of minimal surfaces. Investigating the theory of partial differential equations from various points of view, Monge—despite some errors and a somewhat disorganized and insufficiently rigorous presentation—contributed exceptionally fruitful methods of approaching this topic. For example, he demonstrated the geometric significance of the total differential equations that do not satisfy the condition of integrability, thus anticipating J. F. Pfaff's treatment of the question in 1814–1815. Monge also introduced contact transformations, the use of which was generalized by Lie a century later. In addition he determined the partial differential equations of many families of surfaces and perfected methods of solving and studying various types of partial differential equations.

Monge resumed his research in this area in 1795–1796 and in 1803–1807, when he completed his courses in infinitesimal geometry at the École Polytechnique, with a view toward their publication. He perfected the theories sketched in 1783–1786, corrected or made certain arguments more precise, and studied the area of their application.

Mechanics, Theory of Machines, and Technology. From the time he came to Mézières, Monge was interested in the structure, functioning, and effects of machines; in the technical and industrial problems of fortification and construction; and in local industry, particularly metallurgy. He held that technical progress is a key factor governing the happiness of humanity and depends essentially on the rational application of theoretical science. His interest in physics, mechanics, and the theory of machines derived in part from his view that they are the principal factors of industrial progress and, therefore, of social progress.

Monge discussed the theory of machines in his course in descriptive geometry at the École Polytechnique (end of 1794). His ideas, employed by Hachette in *Traité élémentaire des machines* (1809), were derived from the principle that the function of every machine is to transform a motion of a given type into a motion of another type. Although this overly restrictive conception has been abandoned, it played an important role in the creation of the theory of machines in the nineteenth century.

Monge's *Traité élémentaire de statique* (1788) was a useful textbook, and its successive editions recorded the latest developments in the subject, for example the theory of couples introduced by Poinsot. The fifth edition (1810) included important material on the reduction of an arbitrary system of forces to two rectangular forces.

The unusual experience that Monge had acquired in metallurgy was frequently drawn upon by the revolutionary government and then by Napoleon.

Physics and Chemistry. Although the details regarding Monge's contributions to physics are poorly known, because he never published a major work in this field, his reputation among his contemporaries was solid. His main contributions concerned caloric theory, acoustics (theory of tones), electrostatics, and optics (theory of mirages).

In 1781 Monge was selected to be editor of the *Dictionnaire de physique* of the *Encyclopédie méthodique*. He did not complete this task, but he did write certain articles.

His most important research in chemistry dealt with the composition of water. As early as 1781 he effected the combination of oxygen and hydrogen in the eudiometer, and in June–July and October 1783 he achieved the synthesis of water—at the same time as Lavoisier and independently of him. Although Monge's apparatus was much simpler, the results of his measurements were more precise. On the other hand, his initial conclusions remained tied to the phlogiston theory, whereas Lavoisier's conclusions signaled the triumph of his new chemistry and the overthrow of the traditional conception of the elementary nature of water. Monge soon adhered to the new doctrine. In February 1785 he took part in the great experiment on the synthesis and analysis of water; he was subsequently an ardent propagandist for the new chemistry and actively participated in its development.

In the experimental realm, in 1784 Monge achieved, in collaboration with Clouet, the first liquefaction of a gas, sulfurous anhydride (sulfur dioxide). Finally, between 1786 and 1788 Monge investigated with Berthollet and Vandermonde the principles of metallurgy and the composition of irons, cast metals, and steels. This research enabled them to unite previous findings in these areas, to obtain precise theoretical knowledge by means of painstaking analyses, and to apply this knowledge to the improvement of various techniques.

BIBLIOGRAPHY

I. ORIGINAL WORKS. A partial list of Monge's works is given in Poggendorff, II, 184–186. More precise and more complete bibliographies are in L. de Launay, *Un grand français: Monge* ... (Paris, 1933), pp. 263–276, which includes a list of MSS and portraits; and in R. Taton, *L'oeuvre scientifique de Gaspard Monge* (Paris, 1951), pp. 377–393, which contains lists of MSS, scientific correspondence, and memoirs presented to the Académie des Sciences.

Works that were published separately are *Traité élémentaire de statique* (Paris, 1788; 8th ed., 1846), trans. into Russian, German, and English; *Avis aux ouvriers en fer sur la fabrication de l'acier* (Paris, 1794), written with Berthollet and Vandermonde; *Description de l'art de fabriquer les canons* ... (Paris, 1794); *Géométrie descriptive* ... (Paris, 1799), a collection in 1 vol. of the lectures given in 1795 at the École Normale de l'An III and published in the *Séances des écoles normales* ... (7th ed., Paris, 1847; repr. 1922), trans. into German, Italian, English, Spanish, and Russian; *Feuilles d'analyse appliquée à la géométrie* ... (Paris, 1801), a collection, with various additions, of lectures given at the École Polytechnique, which were published on separate sheets in 1795; *Application de l'algèbre à la géométrie* (Paris, 1805), written with Hachette; and *Application de l'analyse à la géométrie* (Paris, 1807), a new ed. of the *Feuilles d'analyse appliquée à la géométrie*, preceded, with special pagination, by *Application de l'algèbre à la géométrie* (new ed., 1809; 5th ed., 1850), J. Liouville, ed., with several appendixes, including Gauss's *Disquisitiones circa superficies curvas;* trans. into Russian, with commentary (Moscow, 1936).

II. SECONDARY LITERATURE. The most recent biography of Monge is P.-V. Aubry, *Monge, le savant ami de Napoléon: 1746–1818* (Paris, 1954). The most complete study of his scientific work is R. Taton, *L'oeuvre scientifique de Gaspard Monge* (Paris, 1951).

A few older monographs are still worth consulting, in particular the following, listed chronologically: C. Dupin, *Essai historique sur les services et les travaux scientifiques de Gaspard Monge* (Paris, 1819; repr. 1964); F. Arago, "Biographie de Gaspard Monge . . .," in *Oeuvres de François Arago, Notices biographiques*, II (Paris, 1853; repr. 1964), 426–592, trans. into German, English, and Russian; E. F. Jomard, *Souvenirs sur Gaspard Monge et ses rapports avec Napoléon . . .* (Paris, 1853); L. de Launay, *Un grand français: Monge, fondateur de l'École polytechnique* (Paris, 1933); and E. Cartan, *Gaspard Monge, sa vie, son oeuvre* (Paris, 1948).

A very complete bibliography of other works dealing with Monge is given in R. Taton, *L'oeuvre scientifique*, pp. 396–425. This list should be completed by some more recent studies, listed chronologically: C. Bronne, "La sénatorerie de Monge," in *Bulletin de la Société belge d'études napoléoniennes*, no. 9 (1953), 14–19; Y. Laissus, "Gaspard Monge et l'expédition d'Égypte (1798–1799)," in *Revue de synthèse*, **81** (1960), 309–336; R. Taton, "Quelques lettres scientifiques de Monge," in *84ᵉ Congrès des sociétés savantes. Dijon, Section des sciences* (Paris, 1960), pp. 81–86; J. Duray, "Le sénateur Monge au château de Seraing (près de Liège)," in *Bulletin de la Société belge d'études napoléoniennes*, no. 36 (1961), 5–17; A. Birembaut, "Deux lettres de Watt, père et fils, à Monge," in *Annales historiques de la Révolution française*, **35** (1963), 356–358; J. Booker, "Gaspard Monge and His Effect on Engineering Drawing and Technical Education," in *Transactions of the Newcomen Society*, **34** (1961–1962), 15–36; and R. Taton, "La première note mathématique de Gaspard Monge," in *Revue d'histoire des sciences*, **19** (1966), 143–149.

RENÉ TATON

MONIZ, EGAS. See **Egas Moniz, A. A. F.**

MONNET, ANTOINE-GRIMOALD (*b.* Champeix, Puy-de-Dôme, France, 1734; *d.* Paris, France, 23 May 1817), *chemistry, mineralogy*.

Little is known about Monnet's early life and education. He attended the chemistry lectures of G.-F. Rouelle at the Jardin du Roi in Paris (*ca.* 1754) and was for a time a pharmacist's assistant in Nantes. By 1767 papers on the analysis of mineral springs had attracted the attention of some scientists and of Malesherbes, who became Monnet's patron; and Monnet was able to secure a post with the Bureau du Commerce, then under the direction of Daniel Trudaine. Beginning in 1772, he also worked for Henri

Bertin, minister and secretary of state in charge of mining; in 1776 he was named France's first *inspecteur général des mines et minières du royaume*. Although his title and duties varied somewhat in later years, he survived many changes in the organization of the government corps of mining engineers and was finally retired in 1802.

His employment took Monnet to Alsace and the German states to study mining and metallurgy, and after 1772 his principal duty was to inspect and to suggest improvements in the French mining industry. Many of his published works were the result of these activities, and his post as mineralogist traveling at government expense was partly responsible for his appointment, in 1777, to direct the national geological survey earlier begun by Guettard and Lavoisier.

Monnet incorporated into his writings some of the findings of contemporary German and Swedish scientists, often before their treatises were available in French. Although French scientists considered his works useful, their judgments varied when they tried to assess Monnet's talents. Early in his career, he was pronounced a chemist of genuine ability by Macquer; but despite influential patronage, he failed in his attempts to become a member of the Académie Royale des Sciences. (He belonged to learned societies in Clermont-Ferrand, Rouen, Stockholm, and Turin.) After 1790 his persistent and violent adherence to the phlogiston theory and his personal eccentricities isolated him increasingly from the scientific community.

Monnet's first wife, by whom he had a son and a daughter, died in 1779. He married the writer Mariette Moreau in 1781. Monnet's brother was a mineralogist active in the Société Littéraire de Clermont-Ferrand.

BIBLIOGRAPHY

I. ORIGINAL WORKS. Monnet's publications are *Traité des eaux minérales* (Paris, 1768); *Traité de la vitriolisation & de l'alunation* (Amsterdam, 1769); *Exposition des mines, . . . à laquelle on a joint . . . une dissertation pratique sur le traitement des mines de cuivre, traduite de l'allemand, de M. Cancrinus* (London, 1772)—the major part of this work is a free rendering of A. F. Cronstedt, *Försök til mineralogie* (Stockholm, 1758), but is based on a German trans. of Cronstedt; *Traité de l'exploitation des mines* (Paris, 1773), based on an unidentified work published by the Council of Mines of Freiberg, Saxony; *Dissertation sur l'arsenic, qui a remporté le prix proposé par l'Académie Royale [de Berlin] pour l'année 1773* (Berlin, 1774); *Traité de la dissolution des métaux* (Paris, 1775); *Nouveau système de minéralogie* (Bouillon, 1779); *Mémoire historique et politique sur les mines de France* (Paris, 1790); and *Démonstration de la fausseté des principes des nouveaux chymistes* (Paris, 1798).

Monnet published articles in the *Journal de médecine, chirurgie, pharmacie, &c.; Observations sur la physique, sur l'histoire naturelle et sur les arts; Journal des mines; Mélanges de philosophie et de mathématiques de la Société royale de Turin pour les années 1766–1769* (*Miscellanea Taurinensia*, vol. IV); and *Mémoires de l'Académie royale des sciences* (Turin). He contributed maps to and was author of the text of *Atlas et description minéralogiques de la France, entrepris par ordre du roi ... première partie* (Paris, 1780); and 2nd ed., *Collection complète de toutes les parties de l'atlas minéralogique de la France, qui ont été faites jusqu'aujourd'hui* ([Paris, ca. 1799]); for an analysis, see the Lavoisier bibliographies cited below. Monnet was also translator of Ignaz von Born, *Voyage minéralogique fait en Hongrie et en Transilvanie* (Paris, 1780).

Approximately 20 vols. of papers are at the École des Mines, Paris; many were written after Monnet's retirement and are of varying reliability, showing evidence of increasing paranoia. Extracts from MS 4672, a volume of inaccurate copies of letters, have been published in *Nouvelle revue rétrospective*, **19** (1903), 289–298, 361–384; and **20** (1904), 1–24, 100–120, 169–192, 245–264, 445–446. Two travel journals, MSS 4688 and 8286, respectively, have been edited and published by Henry Mosnier, *Voyage de Monnet, inspecteur général des mines, dans la Haute-Loire et le Puy-de-Dôme, 1793–1794* (Le Puy, 1875); and "Les bains du Mont-Dore en 1786. Voyage en Auvergne de Monnet," in *Mémoires de l'Académie des sciences, belleslettres et arts de Clermont-Ferrand*, **29** (1887), 71–174. Important papers and letters are at the Archives Nationales, Paris, F¹⁴1313–1314; Bibliothèque Centrale du Muséum National d'Histoire Naturelle, Paris, MS 283; Bibliothèque Nationale, Paris, MSS fr. 11881, 12306; and Bibliothèque Municipale de Clermont-Ferrand, MSS 1339, 1390, 1400. One letter has been published by R. Rappaport, "The Early Disputes Between Lavoisier and Monnet, 1777–1781," in *British Journal for the History of Science*, **4** (1969), 233–244.

Letters by and about Monnet are in *Torbern Bergman's Foreign Correspondence*, G. Carlid and J. Nordström, eds., I (Stockholm, 1965).

II. SECONDARY LITERATURE. There is an anonymous eulogy of Monnet in *Annales des mines*, **2** (1817), 483–485. See also Louis Aguillon, "L'École des mines de Paris: notice historique," in *Annales des mines*, 8th ser., **15** (1889), 433–686; Denis I. Duveen and Herbert S. Klickstein, *A Bibliography of the Works of Antoine Laurent Lavoisier 1743–1794* (London, 1954); Denis I. Duveen, *Supplement to a Bibliography of the Works of Antoine Laurent Lavoisier 1743–1794* (London, 1965); and R. Rappaport, "The Geological Atlas of Guettard, Lavoisier, and Monnet: Conflicting Views of the Nature of Geology," in Cecil J. Schneer, ed., *Toward a History of Geology* (Cambridge, Mass., 1969).

RHODA RAPPAPORT

MONRO, ALEXANDER (Primus) (*b.* London, England, 8 September 1697; *d.* Edinburgh, Scotland, 10 July 1767), *anatomy.*

Monro was the only child of John Monro, military surgeon, and Jean Forbes, granddaughter of Duncan Forbes of Culloden. John Monro—who was the youngest son of Sir Alexander Monro, advocate, of Bearcroft, Stirlingshire—retired from the army in 1700 and took up private practice in Edinburgh. Alexander entered Edinburgh University in 1710, where he remained for three years, studying Latin, Greek, and philosophy. He also learned French, arithmetic, and bookkeeping under private teachers and received instruction in fencing, dancing, music, and painting. He did not graduate in arts, but, having decided on a medical career, was formally apprenticed to his father in 1713. He also attended such medical courses as were available locally, but these did not amount to much. He says "the dissection of a human body was shewed once in two or three years by Mr. Robert Elliot, and afterwards by Messrs. Adam Drummond and John Macgill, Surgeon-Apothecaries," who, he adds pointedly, "had the Title of Professors of Anatomy."

John Monro had studied at Leiden University under Archibald Pitcairne, whose idea of founding a medical school of repute in Edinburgh seems to have fired his imagination, and once his son's aptitude became apparent, he spared no efforts in preparing him to play a major role in the scheme. In 1717 Alexander was sent to London, where he studied physics under Whiston and Haukesbee and attended demonstrations by the great anatomist William Cheselden. With the encouragement of their master, Cheselden's students had formed a scientific society; and a paper read by Monro on "the bones in general" was a forerunner of his own important work on that subject. He also made a number of anatomical preparations, which he sent home and which were so admired by Adam Drummond, one of the professors of anatomy at Edinburgh, that he offered to resign in Monro's favor when he should return to Scotland. In the spring of 1718 he went to Paris, where he attended a course in anatomy by Bouquet and frequented the hospitals. He performed operations under the direction of Thibaut, was instructed in midwifery by Grégoire, in bandaging by Cesau, and in botany by Chomel. In the autumn of 1718 he went to Leiden, where he won the favorable attention of Boerhaave, his father's old fellow student. He returned to Edinburgh in 1719.

Monro had come to realize the value of the history of anatomy in the academic teaching of the subject, and with his customary thoroughness he enrolled as a student in Charles Mackie's newly inaugurated class of universal history. On 20 November 1719 he was admitted a fellow of the Royal College of Surgeons of Edinburgh, after passing the usual tests. On 29 January 1720, even though he was still only twenty-two years of age, the town council appointed him professor of anatomy. On Cheselden's recommendation he was elected a fellow of the Royal Society in 1723. In 1724 and 1725 there was a popular outcry against grave robbing in Edinburgh. Surgeons' Hall was beset, and there were threats to demolish it. In 1725 the town council accordingly provided Monro with an anatomy theatre and museum for his preparations within the comparative safety of the university precinct, and thereafter he undertook all the duties of a professor. One of these was to take his turn in delivering the public oration that inaugurated each session, and the subject of his first, delivered on 3 November 1725, was "De origine et utilitate anatomes," which he later incorporated into his course on the history of anatomy.

On 3 January 1725 Monro married Isabella MacDonald, daughter of Sir Donald MacDonald of Sleat (Isle of Skye). They had three sons and five daughters. Only one of his daughters survived infancy, and for her Monro wrote an "Essay on Female Conduct," which included a section on "The Laws of Nature, the Mosaical Institution and the Christian System." John, the eldest son, became an advocate; Donald, his second son, graduated M.D. (1753) and was physician to St. George's Hospital, London; and Alexander, the youngest, succeeded his father in the chair of anatomy at the University of Edinburgh. In 1726 Monro published his major work, *The Anatomy of the Humane Bones*. It had no illustrations, being intended as a commentary on actual demonstrations and dissections. Moreover, Monro knew that his old master Cheselden was preparing a set of accurate plates for his *Osteographia* (1733), made with the help of the improved camera obscura. The work is enlivened by Monro's acute and original comments based on close observation: for example, that different nationalities are distinguishable by the form of the cranium, that the nasal sinuses improve the power and tone of the voice, that a man's stature decreases as evening approaches, and that the bone at a healed fracture is stronger than before. In the second (1732) and later editions there is added "An Anatomical Treatise of the Nerves, an Account of the Reciprocal Motions of the Heart and a Description of the Human Lacteal Sac and Duct." Here he observes that the nerves consist of "a great many threads lying parallel to each other," and seems to anticipate Müller's law of specific nerve energies, noting that "when all light is excluded from the eyes an idea of light and colour may be excited in us by coughing, sneezing, rubbing or striking the eyeball." The work continued to be reprinted as late as 1828, by which time it had gone through nineteen English editions and appeared in several translations, the most notable being the large, illustrated French edition (1759) by Jean-Joseph Sue.

The Edinburgh Medical School had now a nucleus of medical professors, but there was still no hospital for clinical teaching. As early as 1721 John Monro had agitated for the establishment of a regular hospital in Edinburgh, and Alexander himself had published appeals for funds for the purpose, but it was not until 1725 that the matter was seriously pursued with the help of George Drummond, lord provost of Edinburgh. In 1729 a small hospital for the sick poor was opened, and it was from its case register that much of the material was derived for the *Medical Essays and Observations*, 6 vols. (1732–1744), edited by Monro for the Society for the Improvement of Medical Knowledge, of which he was secretary. The series owed much to the individual efforts of Monro, who contributed many of the papers, his most important being an "Essay on the Nutrition of Foetuses," in which he showed "that there is no Anastomosis, Inosculation or Continuation between the vessels of the Womb and those of the Secundines and that the Liquors are not carried from the Mother to the Foetus or from the Foetus to the Mother by continued Canals." The *Medical Essays* became a standard work of reference, went through five editions, and was translated into several languages.

The scope of this society was widened in 1737 at the suggestion of Monro's friend Colin Maclaurin, professor of mathematics, and it was renamed the Society for Improving Philosophy and Natural Knowledge, or the Philosophical Society, but Maclaurin's death and the rebellion of 1745 caused its decline. In 1752 it was revived and Monro was elected joint secretary with David Hume the philosopher, contributing six medical papers to their *Essays and Observations, Physical and Literary* (1754, 1756). This society became the Royal Society of Edinburgh in 1783. Monro belonged to several other societies: the Honorable Society of Improvers of the Knowledge of Agriculture in Scotland (disbanded in 1745); the Select Society, founded by Allan Ramsay the Younger; and the Edinburgh Society for Encouraging Arts, Sciences, Manufactures and Agriculture in Scotland, an offshoot of the Select Society. He was also a manager of the Royal Infirmary and a director of the Bank of Scotland. In addition he was a justice of the peace, a manager of the Orphans

Hospital and of the Scheme for the Widows of Ministers and Professors, although he was less active in these roles.

In politics Monro was a staunch Hanoverian but no bigot. After the battle of Prestonpans in 1745, which went against his cause, he impartially assisted the wounded of both armies. Upon the death of his friend Maclaurin (1745), he delivered before the university a memorial lecture that formed the basis of the memoir prefixed to Maclaurin's posthumously published *Account of Sir Isaac Newton's Philosophical Discoveries* (London, 1748). Monro actively fostered the career of his gifted youngest son, Alexander, with the parental concern characteristic of the family. For his benefit he wrote a "commentary" on his *Anatomy of the Human Bones* and in 1754 persuaded the town council to admit him as joint professor of anatomy with himself, although he had not yet graduated. After his son Alexander, Secundus as he was thenceforth designated, had taken his M.D. (1755), Monro Primus—to use the father's new epithet—was granted the degree of M.D., *honoris causa* (1 January 1756). The system of joint professorships was to provide emoluments for the retiring professor, but Monro Primus, having secured the succession for his son, continued to share the duties of the chair until 1758, after which he confined himself to his favorite clinical lectures in the new Royal Infirmary, which had been completed in 1741. The infirmary was designed by William Adam under the supervision of Monro and Lord Provost Drummond.

Monro Primus was of medium height, strongly built, and energetic, but subject to periodical inflammatory fevers. He continued to take an active part in university business until the end of 1765, although by 1762 he was beginning to feel the symptoms of cancer of the rectum, which caused his death on 10 July 1767 at his home in Covenant Close, Edinburgh. He was buried in Greyfriars Churchyard, Edinburgh. He had bought an estate at Auchenbowie, Stirlingshire, but his plan to retire there was thwarted by circumstances, although he often visited it and took a close interest in its management. He was a commissioner of supply and highroads for Stirlingshire and a benefactor of the local parish church. Earlier he had provided a country home at Carolside, Berwickshire, for his father in his declining years.

Monro was not ambitious as an author. His great work on the human bones was published rather as a teaching aid, and many of his important contributions to *Medical Essays and Observations* were anonymous. His lectures that exist in manuscript reveal his wide reading in their references to past and contemporary anatomical works. A section of them was published without his authority in *An Essay on Comparative Anatomy* (1744). In 1762 he published *An Expostulatory Epistle to William Hunter*, in which he rebuked his old pupil for some criticisms of himself included in Hunter's *Medical Commentaries* (1762), a work primarily directed against Monro Secundus, but there is little doubt that it was parental concern rather than personal pique that stirred him to the attack. His last publication, *An Account of the Inoculation of Smallpox in Scotland* (1765), was also due to external prompting. It contains the answers conscientiously gathered by Monro to a questionnaire sent to him by the Faculty of Medicine in Paris about the efficacy of inoculation, of which Monro himself was a strong advocate. After his death his course of lectures on the history of anatomy, which included his remarks on the usefulness of the study of the subject and the best method of teaching it, were plagiarized by William Northcote in *A Concise History of Anatomy* (1772).

Monro was not a great innovating genius (eighteenth-century anatomy indeed was marked more by advances in the field of description than by new discoveries), but his extraordinary industry, his wide reading, his accuracy of observation, and his open, original mind sometimes led him to correct conclusions that could only be verified by the more refined equipment of later times. He was a supreme teacher and demonstrator. A gifted technician, Monro improved methods of injecting minute vessels and preserving anatomical preparations. He had the manual dexterity of a master craftsman and was a cool and expert surgeon, in spite of a strong natural abhorrence of inflicting pain. His practice of lecturing informally in English was then a novelty, Latin being still the academic language, and he spoke from only the briefest notes. Oliver Goldsmith, who was a medical student at the University of Edinburgh (1752–1754), said he was "an able orator," explaining "things in their nature obscure in so easy a manner that the most unlearned might understand him." In 1720 his class numbered fifty-seven, but by 1749 he had 182 students, and by 1751 it had outgrown the anatomy theater and had to be taught at two separate meetings daily. His reputation attracted students from all parts of Europe, so that his father's dream of Edinburgh as a medical center rivaling Leiden began to come true. The advance guard of students from America also began to appear, and the influence of the Edinburgh Medical School was carried to the New World. The inspiration of Monro's teaching was frequently acknowledged in grateful dedications in the M.D. theses of his students, among whom were such distinguished names as William Hunter,

Robert Whytt, John Fothergill, Andrew Duncan, and, of course, his own son, Alexander Monro (Secundus).

BIBLIOGRAPHY

I. ORIGINAL WORKS. Note references in the text. Also Monro Secundus, ed., *The Works of Alexander Monro* (Edinburgh, 1781), with a life of A. Monro Primus by Donald Monro. This book contains the published works, including contributions to *Medical Essays and Observations*. The largest collection of his manuscript lectures and other unpublished material is in the Otago University Library, New Zealand; see W. J. Mullin, "The Monro Family and the Monro Collection of Books and MSS," in *New Zealand Medical Journal*, **35** (1936), 221. See also for MSS of his lectures *The Index Catalogue of the Library of the Surgeon General's Office*, IX (1888), 384. Monro's own carefully kept account book for his students' fees, 1720–1749, is in Edinburgh University Library (Dc.5.95). The short biography, "Alexander Monro, Primus," in *University of Edinburgh Journal*, **17** (1953), 77–105, although from an apparently holograph MS, may be wholly or partly the work of Monro's young friend, William Smellie, the printer, who published verbatim extracts from it in his "Life of the Celebrated Dr. Monro," in *Edinburgh Review*, **1** (1744), 302–306, 337–344.

II. SECONDARY LITERATURE. On Monro and his work see A. Duncan, Sr., *An Account of the Life and Writings of Alexander Monro, Senr.* (Edinburgh, 1780); D. J. Guthrie, "The Three Alexander Monros," in *Journal of the Royal College of Surgeons of Edinburgh*, **2** (1956), 24–34; J. A. Inglis, *The Monros of Auchenbowie* (Edinburgh, 1911); K. F. Russell, *British Anatomy, 1525–1800: a Bibliography* (Melbourne, 1963); S. W. Simon, "The Influence of the Three Monros on the Practice of Medicine and Surgery," in *Annals of Medical History*, **9** (1927), 244–266; and R. E. Wright-St. Clair, *Doctors Monro, a Medical Saga* (London, 1964).

C. P. FINLAYSON

MONRO, ALEXANDER (Secundus) (*b.* Edinburgh, Scotland, 10 March 1733; *d.* Edinburgh, 2 October 1817), *anatomy.*

The third and youngest son of Alexander Monro (Primus), Monro was educated first at James Mundell's private school, Edinburgh, and then at the University of Edinburgh. His name appears in his father's account book for his anatomy class in 1744, when he was only eleven years of age. In the following year he matriculated in the Faculty of Arts and studied Latin, Greek, philosophy, mathematics, physics, and history. Like the majority of arts students in the university at that time, he did not graduate, individual professors' certificates being then more highly valued than the official diploma. In 1750 he began the serious study of medicine under Andrew Plummer (chemistry), Charles Alston (botany), John Rutherford (practice of physic), Robert Whytt (institutes of medicine), and Robert Smith (midwifery).

His father encouraged his natural bent for medicine, making for him in 1750 a manuscript commentary on his *Anatomy of the Human Bones*, and entrusting him in 1753 with the teaching of the evening anatomy class necessitated by the growing numbers of students. After only one session of this arrangement Monro Primus petitioned the town council, the patrons of the university, to appoint his son joint professor of anatomy, and his request was backed by a certificate from the students of his son's evening class (they included Joseph Black) testifying to their satisfaction with his teaching. On 10 June 1754 the desired appointment was ratified, although Monro was still only twenty-one years of age. On 25 October 1755 he graduated M.D. with the thesis *De testibus et semine in variis animalibus*. Edinburgh M.D. theses were printed at this period, but most were essays based on secondary sources. Monro's thesis extended the knowledge of the seminiferous tubules by some original research. He injected the tubules with mercury and showed their connection with the epididymis, observing that semen has a close relationship with blood and lymph, although his later lectures show that his notions about the real nature of the substance were quite fanciful. Whereas his father considered that the spermatozoa alone formed the embryo, Monro Secundus taught that "these animalculae are no more essential to generation than the animals found in vinegar are to its acidity."

Soon after graduating he went to London, where he attended the lectures of William Hunter, an old student of Monro Primus. He then went on to Paris but had to return hastily to Edinburgh in 1757 to deputize for his father during an illness. He returned to the Continent later in the same year, spending several months in the home of the famous Berlin anatomist Meckel, with whom he performed the operation of paracentesis of the thorax. While there, he published his treatise *De venis lymphaticis valvulosis* (Berlin, 1757), in which he showed that the lymphatics were absorbents and distinct from the circulatory system. There was a counterclaim for priority in this discovery from William Hunter, which sparked off an acrimonious exchange of pamphlets. Monro Secundus replied to Hunter's claim in his *Observations, Anatomical and Physiological, Wherein Dr. Hunter's Claim to Some Discoveries Is Examined* (1758). Hunter retorted in *Medical Commentaries, Part I: Containing a Plain and Direct Answer to Professor*

Monro, Jun., Interspersed with Remarks on the Structure, Functions and Diseases of Several Parts of the Human Body (London, 1762–1764). Monro seems to have been ahead of Hunter in the matter of the lymphatics, but their mutual jealousy blinded them to the earlier discoveries of Friedrich Hoffman in this field.

Monro extended his attacks to include Hewson, his own former pupil and a colleague of Hunter, who in 1767 had recommended the operation of paracentesis of the thorax in traumatic pneumothorax and at the same time had published his own discovery of the existence of lacteals and lymphatics in non-mammalians. Monro asserted his own priority in both fields in *A State of Facts Concerning the First Proposal of Performing the Paracentesis of the Thorax and the Discovery of the Lymphatic Valvular Absorbent System of Oviparous Animals. In Answer to Mr. Hewson* (Edinburgh, 1770). There is no doubt that Monro had preceded Hewson in performing the operation of paracentesis of the thorax. Although he had earlier shown injections of the lymphatics and described them to his class, Hewson was the first to publish a full and accurate account of them in nonmammalian animals.

From Berlin, Monro went on to Leiden, where he met the anatomist B. S. Albinus, once a fellow student of Monro Primus and Peter Camper, professor of anatomy at Amsterdam. In January 1758, his father being again taken ill, Monro, now in his twenty-fifth year, had to cut short his European tour in order to conduct the anatomy class at Edinburgh. His father recovered and delivered the opening lecture of the session (1758–1759), but thereafter Monro Secundus undertook the main work of the chair and continued to do so for the next fifty years. On 1 May 1759 he became a fellow of the Royal College of Physicians of Edinburgh. His course started with a detailed history of anatomy and proceeded to anatomy itself, beginning with the bones; then came physiology, and finally the operations of surgery. His clear informal style of lecturing was even more effective than his father's. The official records of the Faculty of Medicine give him 228 students in 1808.

His earlier publications were largely polemical, and it was not until he had been teaching for twenty-five years that his three main contributions to medical literature appeared:

His *Observations on the Structure and Functions of the Nervous System* (Edinburgh, 1783; German ed., Leipzig, 1787) advanced the study of the subject by making several original discoveries, the most famous being of the foramen connecting the lateral and third ventricles of the brain, thereafter known as the "foramen of Monro."

The Structure and Physiology of Fishes Explained and Compared With Those of Man and Other Animals (Edinburgh, 1785) was the first important Edinburgh textbook on comparative anatomy, a subject that had been recently introduced to their London students by the Hunters.

A Description of All the Bursae Mucosae of the Human Body; Their Structure Explained and Compared With That of the Capsular Ligaments of the Joints, and of Those Sacs Which Line the Cavities of the Thorax and Abdomen: With Remarks on the Accidents and Diseases Which Affect Those Several Sacs, and on the Operations Necessary for Their Cure (London, 1788), trans. into German by J. C. Rosenmüller (Leipzig, 1799), was a practical manual for direct use in surgery. Although next to nothing was known of germ life at that time, Monro's acute observation and independent empirical judgment led him to the conclusion that the chief danger of infection in surgery of the joints lay in exposure to the air.

Monro published three lesser but original works:

In *Experiments on the Nervous System, With Opium and Metalline Substances; Made Chiefly With the View of Determining the Nature and Effects of Animal Electricity* (Edinburgh, 1793), he showed that stimulation of a nerve by Galvani's couple (tinfoil and silver) produced muscle contraction, but he failed to deduce the true nature of nervous energy, clinging to the old theory of nervous fluid. Still he did at least conclude that the nerves conducted "that matter by which the muscle is influenced more readily than the skin, flesh or blood vessels."

In *Observations on the Muscles and Particularly on the Effects of Their Oblique Fibres: With an Appendix, in Which the Pretension of Dr. Gilbert Blane, That He First Demonstrated the Same Effect to Be Produced by Oblique Muscles as by Straight Ones, With a Less Proportional Decurtation of Fibres is Proved to Be Quite Unfounded* (Edinburgh, 1794), his old combative spirit is shown not to be quite dead.

The third work was his *Three Treatises on the Brain, the Eye and the Ear* (Edinburgh, 1797).

Like his father, Monro Secundus was a sociable man. He was a member of the Harveian Society of Edinburgh, which cultivated conviviality as well as oratory, in both of which fields Monro shone brilliantly. He was joint secretary of the Philosophical Society of Edinburgh along with David Hume (1760–1763) and sole secretary (1763–1783) when it became the Royal Society of Edinburgh. He was also a district commissioner for cleansing, lighting, and watching the streets, a manager of the Royal Infirmary, and a member of the committee of defense for

Midlothian during the French invasion scare of 1794.

On 25 September 1762 Monro married Katherine Inglis, daughter of David Inglis, treasurer of the Bank of Scotland, and by her had three sons and two daughters. He lived first in a flat in Carmichael's Land in the Lawnmarket, Edinburgh. In 1766 he moved to a house with a garden in Nicolson Street, near the university, where he stayed until 1801, when he took up residence in the New Town, in St. Andrew Square. In 1773 he bought a property of 271 acres at Craiglockhart on the outskirts of the town, not as a residence but purely to indulge his passion for gardening.

In 1798 he persuaded the town council to appoint his elder son, Alexander, thereafter known as Monro Tertius, to be joint professor of anatomy with him. He himself continued to share the duties of the chair until 1808, when he retired at age seventy-five. He died of apoplexy on 2 October 1817, at age eighty-four. He had bequeathed his fine collection of anatomical and pathological specimens for the use of his son and his successors in the chair of anatomy.

Monro Secundus was a kindly man in family and social life but perhaps overjealous of his professional reputation. He used his powerful influence, for instance, to prevent until almost the end of his teaching career the establishment of a separate chair of surgery—a clear necessity as Monro, although officially professor of anatomy and surgery, was not himself a practicing surgeon. His medical ability had been proved in the most testing of situations, having to follow a great father and work with such colleagues as William Cullen, Joseph Black, Daniel Rutherford, James Gregory, and Andrew Duncan.

BIBLIOGRAPHY

I. ORIGINAL WORKS. Most are referred to in the text. Read also *Essays and Heads of Lectures on Anatomy, Physiology, and Surgery. With a Memoir of His Life . . . by His Son* (Edinburgh, 1840).

II. SECONDARY LITERATURE. On Monro and his work see A. Duncan, Senior, *An Account of the Life, Writings and Character of Alexander Monro, Secundus* (Edinburgh, 1818). Other relevant works are in the bibliography under Alexander Monro, Primus. See especially R. E. Wright-St. Clair, *Doctors Monro: a Medical Saga* (London, 1964).

C. P. FINLAYSON

MONTANARI, GEMINIANO (*b.* Modena, Italy, 1 June 1633; *d.* Padua, Italy, 13 October 1687), *astronomy, geophysics, biology, ballistics.*

When Montanari was ten, his father, Giovanni, died; and he and his brothers, who died very young, were educated by his mother, Margherita Zanasi. His adolescence may therefore have been somewhat unrestrained and turbulent. One of his last works, *L'astrologia convinta di falso*, contains many autobiographical notes which show that besides suffering several serious illnesses and severe falls, he was involved in brawls in which he both sustained and inflicted injuries. At the age of twenty he was sent to Florence to study law, a profession which would have enabled him to ease his family's financial problems. Montanari remained in Tuscany for three years, absorbed by many interests—but above all by a passion for a woman prominent in Tuscan society. The latter involvement led to trouble; and he was obliged to spend the last few months of this period at Grosseto, which was then in the middle of the swamps of the Maremma.

Fortunately Montanari was invited to go to Vienna and at Salzburg, he received a degree in both church and civil law. The epigraph on his tomb in the church of San Benedetto in Padua indicates that he also, probably at a different time, obtained degrees in philosophy and in medicine. In Vienna he practiced law and formed a friendship with Paolo del Buono (1625–1659), a young Florentine who had studied under Michelini at Pisa, where he had become imbued with the ideas and principles of Galileo. Del Buono was the director of the Imperial Mint and a correspondent of the Accademia del Cimento; and from him Montanari rapidly acquired a proficiency in mathematics and natural science, which until then he had considered merely a hobby. At the end of 1657 he accompanied Del Buono on a long trip to the mines which supplied the mint, visiting Styria, Bohemia, and Bergstetten, in the Carpathian Mountains of Upper Hungary (now Horni Mesto, Czechoslovakia). It appears that their research and inquiries aroused suspicions and accusations from which Del Buono fled to Poland, where he died at the age of thirty-four.

Montanari began the long and perilous journey back to Modena, where he entered the service of Duke Alfonso IV d'Este, and married a woman named Elisabetta. They had no children. She was an active and skillful collaborator in his work, including the construction of instruments and the polishing of lenses. After a few months Montanari tired of the ducal court and moved to Florence, where he became legal adviser to Prince Leopoldo de' Medici, who soon discovered his scientific abilities.

But in Florence too, Montanari's fiery character stirred up trouble; and when, at the beginning of

1661, the duke of Modena invited him to return to that city as court philosopher and mathematician, he accepted. The appointment was a brief one —Alfonso IV died in July 1662—but during this time he met Cornelio Malvasia, a Bolognese nobleman who commanded the duke's militia and who was passionately interested in astronomy. An active patron of talented scientists, in 1650 he had recommended to the Bolognese Senate G. D. Cassini, who had worked for him in the observatory that Malvasia had built in his house at Panzano, near Castelfranco Emilia. Now Malvasia became interested in Montanari, who had helped him to compile his volume of ephemerides covering 1661–1666 (Modena, 1662). Montanari left the court of Modena with him and went to Bologna and Panzano, where Malvasia died in March 1664 after having obtained the chair of mathematics at Bologna for his protégé.

Montanari began teaching at Bologna the following December, and the fourteen years that he spent there were the most productive years of his life. A. Fabroni, in the preface to his biography of Montanari, states that the extraordinary flowering of science in Bologna at the beginning of the eighteenth century had its beginning in Montanari's work. This flowering was of course attributable also to others, such as Cassini and Malpighi; but Montanari's influence must have been important, for he taught not only at the Archiginnasio but also at the many academies of natural philosophy. Soon after he arrived in Bologna, he founded such a school, which was modeled on the Florentine Accademia del Cimento and was called the Accademia della Traccia, or Accademia dei Filosofi (this was the precursor of the Accademia degli Inquieti, founded in 1690 by Eustachio Manfredi, which in 1712 became the Accademia delle Scienze dell'Istituto di Bologna).

Montanari also edited a volume of ephemerides and astronomical tables (1665). From 1669 he was concerned with Cassini's sundial in the church of San Petronio, and from the same year he published an annual almanac, in which he poked fun at judicial astrology because its predictions, rather than being deduced from the appearance of the heavens, were picked at random in the presence of friends.

The University of Bologna suffered a financial crisis in the late 1670's, during which the professors' salaries were greatly reduced and paid after long delays; Montanari decided to go to Padua, where a new chair of astronomy and meteorology was created for him, carrying a very high salary. But the Republic of Venice, not content to have him merely teaching, expected his advice and assistance on the control of rivers and the protection of the Venetian Lagoon, military fortifications and the training of the artillery, and especially the organization of the mint and all problems having to do with currency. This last, heavy duty occupied Montanari for the rest of his life and was detrimental to his health—he was obese and inclined to apoplexy. He gradually became almost blind and died suddenly of apoplexy in 1687.

The volume of Montanari's work was enormous. G. Venturi summarizes his achievements by saying that he was an astronomer in Modena, a physicist in Bologna, and an engineer in Venice. It could be said that in a relatively short life he continually added to his interests but he never abandoned old ones when he took up a new ones.

Montanari's major contribution to Malvasia's ephemerides (1662) consisted of a map of the moon thirty-eight centimeters in diameter, the largest at the time and one of the most exact and detailed. Its precision resulted from his use of a reticle, which he described in this work as a network of silver wires; it must certainly have been more sophisticated than those used, but not described, by Divini and Grimaldi. As for the richness of detail, Montanari probably engraved the map himself, thus saving it from the arbitrary simplification that often accompanied the transition from drawing to engraving, a fate that ten years earlier had befallen Grimaldi's similar map. The ephemerides also contains the description of an attempt to work a clock by means of a pendulum, a project with which Montanari was in all probability concerned.

It was in Bologna that Montanari showed his exceptional skill in inventing and making precision instruments. He constructed enormous objective lenses, that were greatly praised by Cassini; one of them, dated 1666, is preserved in Bologna. In 1674 he published a description of the "dioptric level," an instrument that gave extremely accurate levelings because the level was fitted onto a telescope. This telescope was also equipped with a distance-measuring reticle made from hairs arranged on the focal plane of the eyepiece.

In physics Montanari conducted experiments to obtain drops of tempered glass and to observe the curious way in which they shattered. He also made studies, much admired by Huygens, of the behavior of liquids in capillary tubes (1672–1678), which suggested a similarity of the ascent of water in capillary tubes and that of the sap in plant stems. Yet Montanari had already done some experimental biology; at Vienna in 1657 he had artificially incubated chicks, and at Udine in 1668 he had performed a blood transfusion between animals. It is likely that he had also taken part in similar experiments conducted in 1667 at Cassini's house in Bologna.

In 1673, in a note on the "tromba parlante," Montanari demonstrated that the principle of the megaphone, invented two years previously by Morland, could be reversed and used as an ear trumpet. With a pair of such instruments he was able to send and receive signals over distances of up to four miles.

Montanari was also interested in meteorological phenomena and was the first to use the term "atmospheric precipitation." In a work of 1675, published by C. Bonacini in 1934, he speaks of the barometer as a "meteoroscope," an instrument the variations of which can forecast weather conditions; and in 1671 he had used a barometer as an altimeter, first on the Asinelli tower in Bologna and then on Monte Cimone, the highest mountain in the Tuscan Apennines.

Montanari's greatest achievements, however, were in astronomy, particularly in his observations of the star Algol, which contributed to one of the earliest and most important chapters in the history of astrophysics, the study of the variable stars. He sent the results of his observations, which struck a fresh blow at the Aristotelian concept of the heavens' immutability, to the Royal Society in London and gave the first report on them in the paper "Sopra la sparizione d'alcune stelle et altre novità celesti," published in *Prose de' signori accademici Gelati* (1671; French version, 1672). In this paper he catalogued many stars of variable brightness, again drawing particular attention to Algol; having observed it when it was fairly bright, in 1667 he noticed that it was only of the fourth magnitude, in 1669 it was of the second magnitude, and in 1670 again fourth magnitude. Montanari seems not to have noticed the regularity of the phenomenon, but he was reasonably accurate in indicating the extremes of the variations. In fact Algol (β Persei) has a period, determined by Goodrike in 1782, of less than three days; but its magnitude varies from approximately 3.4 to 2.1.

Montanari failed to perceive either the regularity or the period of variation because the deterioration of his sight prevented him from making regular observations, as he stated in the same paper. But his considerations of these phenomena are extremely interesting, expressed as they were against the prevailing opinions of the time. He mentioned Boulliau's fairly accurate calculation, made in 1638, that it took 332 days for Mira Ceti to complete its cycle of appearances and disappearances (this strange behavior, but not the periodicity, had been noted in 1596 by David Fabricius), then stated that nothing was known about the causes of the appearance of new stars and of variations in the brightness of known stars, but offered the hypothesis that they might be phenomena analogous to sunspots.

At Padua, although his sight continued to fail, Montanari did not abandon astronomy—indeed, he made instruments for new observatories in Padua and in the Palazzo Corner in Venice.

Montanari contributed to the martial arts through his *Manualetto dei bombisti . . . con le tavole delle inclinazioni . . . secondo la dottrina di Galileo* (1680, 1682, 1690), a manual for gunners, which contains tables for firing based on the hypothesis that it is possible to ignore the resistance of air. His works on fortifications have never been published; and very little has been published of his valuable research in hydraulics, the results of which he passed on to his pupil D. Guglielmini. Perhaps influenced by Michelini, Montanari declared that to keep the lagoon surrounding Venice unpolluted and to prevent its silting up, it was necessary to divert directly into the sea the rivers that emptied into the lagoon. Fortunately his advice was heeded. A posthumous paper on the same topic, "Il mare Adriatico e sua corrente, et la naturalezza dei fiumi . . .," appeared in 1696 and was reprinted several times. Another, on civil engineering, has almost certainly been lost.

Montanari's final project, undertaken after he had become almost blind, was the compilation of two important works on money, which are still considered the precursors of modern ideas in this field: *Trattato del valore ed abuso delle monete* and "La zecca in consulta di stato."

His battles against astrology, in which he was passionately engaged all his life, are summarized in *L'astrologia convinta di falso . . .* (Venice, 1685), which aroused great interest and brought about the banning of this pseudoscience from the universities. He left unfinished a dialogue on a tornado which had devastated the Venetian hinterland in 1686; and it was completed and published in 1694 with the title *La forza d'Eolo . . .* by one of his students, Francesco Bianchini (1662–1729), who included a biography of his teacher in the introduction.

Montanari observed comets in 1664, 1665, 1680, 1681, and 1682; a solar eclipse on 2 July 1666; and several lunar eclipses: 29 September 1670, 18 September 1671, an unknown date in 1674, and in September 1681.

BIBLIOGRAPHY

I. ORIGINAL WORKS. Montanari's map of the moon and some of his poems are in Cornelio Malvasia, *Ephemerides novissimae motuum coelestium . . . ad longitudinem urbis Mutinae . . .* (Modena, 1662). His other works include *Cometes . . . observatus anno 1664 et 1665. Astronomico-physica dissertatio . . .* (Bologna, 1665); *Ephemeris Lans-*

bergiana ad longitudinem . . . Bononiae, ad annum 1666 . . . (Bologna, 1665); *Intorno diversi effetti de' liquidi in cannucce di vetro . . .* (Bologna, 1667); *Speculazioni fisiche . . . sopra gli effetti di que' vetri temprati che rotti in parte si risolvono tutti in polvere . . .* (Bologna, 1671); and "Sopra la sparizione di alcune stelle ed altre novità celesti discorso astronomico," in *Prose de' signori accademici gelati,* V. Zani, ed. (Bologna, 1671), 369–392.

He also wrote *La livella diottrica . . . per livellare col cannocchiale . . .* (Bologna, 1674; Venice, 1680); *Discorso sopra la tromba parlante . . . con dotte osservazioni della natura dell'eco e del suono* (Guastalla, 1678); *Manualetto dei bombisti . . . per ben maneggiare i mortari . . .* (Venice, 1680; Verona, 1682); *L'Astrologia convinta di falso col mezzo di nuove esperienze e ragioni fisico-astronomiche . . .* (Venice, 1685); *Le forze d'Eolo, dialogo fisico-matematico . . .,* F. Bianchini, ed. (Parma, 1694); and "Il mare Adriatico e sua corrente . . . et la naturalezza dei fiumi . . .," in *La Galleria di Minerva . . .* (Venice, 1696), 320. His tract on money, "La Zecca in Consulta di Stato, trattato mercantile ove si mostrano . . . le vere ragioni dell'aumentare giornalmente di valuta delle monete . . . co' modi di preservarne gli Stati," appeared first in C. Casanova, ed., *In Philippi Argelati tractatus de monetis Italiae appendix (seu pars VI)* (Milan, 1759), 3–70, and in A. Graziani, ed., *Economisti del Cinque e Seicento* (Bari, 1913), pp. 252 ff.

II. SECONDARY LITERATURE. See G. Albenga and F. Porro, "Montanari," in *Enciclopedia italiana,* XXIII (Rome, 1934), 720; C. Bonacini, "Una carta lunare di Geminiano Montanari," in *Nel primo centenario della fondazione dell'osservatorio geofisico dell'Università* (Modena, 1927), 1–14; "Sull'opera scientifica svolta a Modena da Geminiano Montanari," in *Annuario della R. Università di Modena,* 1933, Appendice (1935), 17–24; and "Nel terzo centenario della nascita di Geminiano Montanari," in *Atti e memorie. Accademia di scienze, lettere ed arti* (Modena), 4th ser., **4** (1934), 63–76; G. Campori, "Notizie e lettere inedite di Geminiano Montanari," in *Atti e memorie della Deputazione di storia patria di Modena e Parma,* **8** (1876), 65–96; P. Dore, "Origini e funzione dell'Istituto e dell'Accademia delle scienze di Bologna," in *Archiginnasio,* XXXV (Bologna, 1940), 192–214; A. Fabroni, *Vitae Italorum,* III (Pisa, 1779), 64–119; G. Horn-D'Arturo, "Montanari," in *Piccola enciclopedia astronomica,* II (Bologna, 1938; 2nd ed., 1960), 304–306; P. di Pietro, "Modena e la trasfusione del sangue," in *Bollettino dell'Ordine dei medici* (Modena) (1969), 123–128; P. Riccardi, *Biblioteca matematica italiana,* II (Modena, 1870; repr. Milan, 1952), col. 170–177; G. Targioni-Tozzetti, *Notizie degli aggrandimenti delle scienze fisiche accaduti in Toscana nel corso di anni 60 del secolo XVII* (Florence, 1780; repr. Bologna, 1967), I, 303–304; G. Tiraboschi, *Biblioteca modenese,* III (Modena, 1783; repr. Bologna, 1969), 254–279; G. Venturi, *Elogio di Geminiano Montanari recitato nel solenne aprimento delle scuole* (Modena, 1790); and Count Valerio Zani, ed., *Le memorie, imprese, ritratti e notizie dei signori accademici Gelati* (Bologna, 1672).

GIORGIO TABARRONI

MONTE, GUIDOBALDO, MARCHESE DEL (*b.* Pesaro, Italy, 11 January 1545; *d.* Montebaroccio, 6 January 1607), *mechanics, mathematics, astronomy.*

[He is known as Guidobaldo del Monte, although his signature reads Guidobaldo dal Monte. The form Guido Ubaldo (from the Latinized version) is often used, Ubaldo being taken incorrectly as the family name.]

Guidobaldo was born into a noble family in the territory of the dukes of Urbino. While at the University of Padua in 1564 he studied mathematics and befriended the poet Torquato Tasso. Later Guidobaldo served in campaigns against the Turks and in 1588 was appointed visitor general of the fortresses and cities of the grand duke of Tuscany. Soon afterward Guidobaldo retired to the family castle of Montebaroccio near Urbino, where he pursued his scientific studies until his death.

Guidobaldo was a prominent figure in the renaissance of the mathematical sciences. At Urbino he was a friend and pupil of Federico Commandino and an intimate of Bernardino Baldi, the mathematical historian. In 1588 Guidobaldo saw Commandino's Latin translation of Pappus through the press at Pesaro. The autograph transcript had initially been sent to the Venetian mathematician Barocius for publication; but Barocius, having refused to edit the work without making extensive changes, sent the manuscript to Guidobaldo, who published the text exactly as he found it. Concerning Pappus, Guidobaldo also corresponded with the Venetian senator Jacomo Contarini, who helped Guidobaldo secure an appointment at Padua for Galileo. Guidobaldo's correspondence with these and other friends is an important source for the history of the mathematics of the period.

Guidobaldo's first book, the *Liber mechanicorum* (1577), was regarded by contemporaries as the greatest work on statics since the Greeks. It was intended as a return to classical Archimedean models of rigorous mathematical proof and as a rejection of the "barbaric" medieval proofs of Jordanus de Nemore (revived by Tartaglia in his *Quesiti* of 1546), which mixed dynamic principles with mathematical analysis.

The *Liber* may be seen as a forceful argument that statics and dynamics are entirely separate sciences; hence no unified science of mechanics is possible. This attitude is evident in Guidobaldo's treatment of equilibrium in the simple machines, which he terms the case where the power sustains the weight. He stresses that a greater power is needed to move the weight than to sustain it and that the power which moves has a greater ratio to the weight moved than does the power which sustains to the weight sustained. Consequently, the same principle and proportions cannot hold good for both moving and sustaining.

Galileo overcame this objection to a unified mechanics by positing that an insensibly greater amount of power was needed to move, than to sustain, a given weight. Guidobaldo had scorned the use of *insensibilia* in mechanics, probably because they were not susceptible of precise mathematical definition. Like his contemporary Benedetti, Guidobaldo attacked Jordanus, Cardano, and Tartaglia for assuming that the lines of descent of heavy bodies were parallel rather than convergent to the center of the earth. The answer of both Tartaglia and Galileo to this demand for unreasonable exactitude in mechanics was that, at a great distance from the center, the difference between the parallel and convergent descents was insensible.

This extreme concern for precision led Guidobaldo to reject the valid inclined-plane theorem of Jordanus in favor of the erroneous theorem of Pappus. Pappus' premise that a definite amount of force was needed to move a body horizontally was in accord with the view of Guidobaldo that more power was required to move than to sustain the body. Moreover, Jordanus' theorem seemed vitiated by its neglect of the angle of convergence of the descents. By supposing against Pappus (whom he named) and Guidobaldo (whom he did not name) that an insensible amount of power was required to move a body horizontally, Galileo was able to apply the principle of virtual displacements to both static and dynamic cases and was able to frame useful principles of virtual work and inertia. Guidobaldo's quest for mathematical rigor may have barred such imaginative concepts from his mind.

The most fruitful section of the *Liber mechanicorum* deals with pulleys, reducing them to the lever. This analysis—which is far superior to that of Benedetti—was adopted by Galileo. In two subsequent mechanical works Guidobaldo developed other ideas of this first book. These works were the *Paraphrase of Archimedes: Equilibrium of Planes* (1588), a copy of which was sent to Galileo, and the posthumous *De cochlea* (1615).

Guidobaldo was Galileo's patron and friend for twenty years and was possibly the greatest single influence on the mechanics of Galileo. In addition to giving Galileo advice on statics, Guidobaldo discussed projectile motion with him, and both scientists reportedly conducted experiments together on the trajectories of cannonballs. In Guidobaldo's notebook (Paris MS 10246), written before 1607, it is asserted that projectiles follow parabolic paths; that this path is similar to the inverted parabola (actually a catenary) which is formed by the slack of a rope held horizon-

tally; and that an inked ball that is rolled sideways over a near perpendicular plane will mark out such a parabola. Remarkably the same two examples are cited by Galileo at the end of the *Two New Sciences*, although only as postscripts to his main proof—which is based on the law of free fall—of the parabolic trajectory.

Among Guidobaldo's nonmechanical works are three manuscript treatises on proportion and Euclid; two astronomical books, the *Planisphaeriorum* (1579) and the posthumous *Problematum astronomicorum* (1609); and the best Renaissance study of perspective (1600).

Guidobaldo helped to develop a number of mathematical instruments, including the proportional compass, the elliptical compass, and a device for dividing the circle into degrees, minutes, and seconds.

BIBLIOGRAPHY

I. Original Works. Guidobaldo's published works are *Liber mechanicorum* (Pesaro, 1577; repr. Venice, 1615); Italian trans. by Filippo Pigafetta, *Le mechanice* (Venice, 1581; repr. Venice, 1615); *Planisphaeriorum universalium theorica* (Pesaro, 1579; repr. Cologne, 1581); *De ecclesiastici kalendarii restitutione opusculum* (Pesaro, 1580); *In duos Archimedis aequeponderantium libros paraphrasis* (Pesaro, 1588); *Perspectivae libri sex* (Pesaro, 1600); *Problematum astronomicorum libri septem* (Venice, 1609); and *De cochlea libri quatuor* (Venice, 1615).

MS works of Guidobaldo are the *Meditatiunculae*, Bibliothèque Nationale (Paris), MS Lat. 10246; *In quintum Euclidis elementorum commentarius* and *De proportione composita opusculum*, Biblioteca Oliveriana (Pesaro), respectively MSS 630 and 631; and a treatise on the reform of the calendar, Biblioteca Vaticana, MS Vat. Lat. 7058. A collection of drawings of machines by Francesco di Giorgio Martini in the Biblioteca Marciana (Venice), MS Lat. VIII 87(3048), was formerly owned by Guidobaldo. The present location of the MS *In nonnulla Euclidis elementorum expositiones* (item 194 bis in the Boncompagni Sale Catalogue of 1898) is not known.

Guidobaldo's letters (some are copies) are scattered: Biblioteca Nazionale Centrale (Florence), MSS Galileo 15, 16, 88; Biblioteca Comunale "A. Saffi" (Forlì), MSS Autografi Piancastelli Nos. 755, 1508; Archivio di Stato (Mantua), Corrispondenza Estera, E.XXVIII, 3; Biblioteca Ambrosiana (Milan), MSS D.34 inf., J.231 inf., R.121 sup.; Bodleian Library (Oxford), MS Canon. Ital. 145; Bibliothèque Nationale (Paris), MS 7218 Lat.; Biblioteca Oliveriana (Pesaro), MSS 193 Ter.; 211/ii; 426; 1580 (MS 1538 = Tasso to Guidobaldo); Archivum Pontificiae Universitatis Gregorianae (Rome), Cassetta 1, MSS 529-530; Biblioteca Comunale degli Intronati (Siena), MS K.XI.52; Biblioteca Universitaria (Urbino), MS Carità Busta 47, Fasc. 6; and Biblioteca Nazionale Marciana (Venice), MS Ital. IV, 63 (Rari V.259).

Favaro has printed the Galileo correspondence in the *Opere* of Galileo, vol. X; and the two Marciana letters in *Due Lettere*. Rose, *Origins*, prints Ambrosiana MS J.231 inf., and Arrighi, *Un grande*, has six letters from Oliveriana MS 426, with the prefaces of MSS 630 and 631. Most of *Le mechanice* is translated in Drake and Drabkin, *Mechanics*. Important pages from Paris MS 10246 are in Libri, *Histoire*, IV, 369–398.

II. SECONDARY LITERATURE. A bibliog. is in Paul Lawrence Rose, "Materials for a Scientific Biography of Guidobaldo del Monte," in *Actes du XIIe congrès international d'histoire des sciences, Paris, 1968*, **12** (1971), 69–72. The earliest biography is the short note by Guidobaldo's friend Bernardino Baldi, *Cronica de' matematici* (Urbino, 1707), 145–147. Baldi's full *Vita* has disappeared. Giuseppe Mamiani, *Elogi storici di Federico Commandino, G. Ubaldo del Monte . . .* (Pesaro, 1828), is informative, although few references are given. The Guidobaldo section was earlier published in the *Giornale arcadico*, vols. IX, X (Senigallia, 1821). The 1828 ed. is reprinted in Mamiani, *Opuscoli scientifici* (Florence, 1845).

On Guidobaldo's mechanics see Antonio Favaro, "Due lettere inedite di Guidobaldo del Monte a Giacomo Contarini," in *Atti del Istituto veneto di scienze, lettere ed arti*, **59** (1899–1900), 303–312. Pierre Duhem, *Les origines de la statique*, I (Paris, 1905), 209–226, was very critical of Guidobaldo. Stillman Drake and I. E. Drabkin, *Mechanics in Sixteenth Century Italy* (Madison, Wis., 1969), 44–52 and *passim*, are more favorably disposed.

Guidobaldo's astronomical interests are illustrated in Gino Arrighi, "Un grande scienziato italiano; Guidobaldo dal Monte . . .," in *Atti dell' Accademia lucchese di scienze, lettere ed arti*, n.s. **12** (1965), 183–199.

For mathematical instruments see Paul Lawrence Rose, "The Origins of the Proportional Compass," in *Physis*, **10** (1968), 54–69, and "Renaissance Italian Methods of Drawing the Ellipse and Related Curves," in *Physis*, **12** (1970), 371–404.

See also Guillaume Libri, *Histoire des sciences mathématiques en Italie*, IV (Paris, 1841), 79–84, 369–398; and Antonio Favaro, "Galileo e Guidobaldo del Monte," (*Scampoli Galileani 146*), in *Atti dell' Accademia di scienze, lettere ed arti di Padova*, **30** (1914), 54–61.

PAUL LAWRENCE ROSE

MONTELIUS, GUSTAV OSCAR (*b.* Stockholm, Sweden, 9 September 1843; *d.* Stockholm, 4 November 1921), *archaeology.*

Montelius was strongly influenced by the great Scandinavian archaeologists Thomsen, Worsaae, and Nilsson, the creators of the scientific method of archaeology and the authors of the theory of three successive ages of Stone, Bronze, and Iron, of which they had demonstrated the stratigraphical validity in their work in the peat bogs and barrows of Denmark.

At the age of twenty Montelius joined the Swedish Archaeological Service and began working in the Swedish National Museum, where he remained for fifty years. In 1913, when he was seventy, he retired from the museum as director and state antiquary. Montelius traveled extensively; his reputation in his maturity and old age was international.

Montelius adopted the three-age system of Thomsen and Worsaae and expanded it into a four-age system comprising the Paleolithic, Neolithic, Bronze, and Iron. He was particularly interested in the Neolithic and Bronze ages, into which he introduced further subdivisions. He divided the Scandinavian Neolithic, for example, into four phases: the premegalithic (Neolithic I); the dolmen period (Montelius II); the passage grave period (Montelius III); and the long-stone cist period (Montelius IV). Montelius' work in subdividing epochs of the prehistoric past paralleled that of G. de Mortillet in France and his Neolithic subdivisions, although never widely adopted, were a model for the subdivisions of the Bronze age made by Déchelette in France and Fox in Britain.

Montelius believed firmly in the exact description and classification of prehistoric artifacts—indeed, he may be considered the founder of prehistoric taxonomy. He distinguished between open and closed finds and carefully classified prehistoric artifacts according to form, design, and ornament. He further taught the importance of studying the associations among these properly described and classified artifacts, and began to arrange them in sequences based upon changes in form, design, and ornament. This notion of typological sequence was developed by Worsaae; Montelius' refinement of it allowed him to establish a relative time sequence for Scandinavian artifacts.

Montelius next addressed himself to the problem of translating this relative chronology into an absolute one, and to the question of how new forms of implements and new customs came into existence in Scandinavia. Drawing upon the man-made chronologies of Egypt and Mesopotamia—going back to 3000 B.C.—he devoted himself to establishing links between the ancient East and Barbarian Europe; his *Bronze Age Chronology in Europe* was published in 1889. Between 1889 and 1891 Flinders Petrie was able, by cross-dating, to establish the absolute dates of Mycenaean Greece; Montelius then set out to develop these dated connections, although he realized that the opportunity to establish cross-dating diminished in proportion to geographical distance from the eastern Mediterranean. In 1892 Montelius published his own account of the relationship between Greek and Oriental chronology; in 1897 he extended this from Greece to Italy; in 1898 he developed the connections between Mediterranean chronology and that of Germany and Scandinavia; in 1900 he dealt with France and the Netherlands; and in 1908 with England and Scotland. By 1910 he had done all that it was possible to do with the methods of his time in correlating the undated prehistoric sequences of Barbarian Europe with the dated sequences of the eastern Mediterranean and Egypt. He thus established a historical chronology of prehistoric Europe that, however modified, served prehistory until the advent of geochronology and carbon-14 dating.

Montelius' popularizing work, *The Civilization of Sweden in Heathen Times* (1888), is a model of early *haute vulgarisation*. In the study of cultural origins he was, in the end, an advocate of the sort of modified diffusionism which was taken up after his death by Gordon Childe. Montelius applied his theories and tested them in relation to megalithic monuments; his *The Orient and Europe* (1894) is a classic statement of the theory of megalithic origins in the eastern Mediterranean.

BIBLIOGRAPHY

Montelius' chief works are discussed in the text; a *Festschrift* presented to him on the occasion of his seventieth birthday, *Opuscula archaeologica Oscari Montelio dicata* (Stockholm, 1913), contains a list of 346 of his writings.

GLYN DANIEL

MONTESQUIEU, CHARLES-LOUIS DE SECONDAT, BARON DE LA BRÈDE ET DE (*b*. La Brède, near Bordeaux, France, January 1689; *d*. Paris, France, 10 February 1755), *philosophy, political theory*.

Montesquieu was born into a noble family traditionally in the service of the king of Navarre. Since the seventeenth century a member of the family had been *président à mortier* of the Parlement of Guyenne, at Bordeaux.

After attending the Oratorian *collège* in Juilly (1700–1705) and studying law at Bordeaux (1705–1708), Charles-Louis de Secondat inherited from an uncle the name of Montesquieu and the office of *président à mortier*, which he held without enthusiasm and sold in 1726. Montesquieu was often received in Bordeaux society and became a member of the Académie de Bordeaux in 1716; traveled frequently to Paris, where he moved easily in high society. Famous for his *Lettres persanes* (1721) and elected to the Académie

Française (1728), he took a long trip through central Europe, Italy, and Germany and stayed for more than fifteen months in England (November 1729–May 1730), where he became a fellow of the Royal Society and a Mason. After his return to France he wrote his most important work, *L'esprit des lois,* which provoked a vigorous debate upon its publication in 1748.

Attracted to science in his youth, Montesquieu presented to the Académie de Bordeaux several reports on scientific memoirs submitted to it (1718–1720). In 1719 he commenced the compilation of a physical history of the earth in ancient and modern times, requesting scientists from all over Europe to send him papers on the subject. The project was never completed, but the topic long concerned Montesquieu. Several passages from *Mes pensées* and various memoirs on mines written during the period 1731–1751 are evidence of his continuing interest. On 20 November 1721 Montesquieu read before the Académie de Bordeaux his "Observations sur l'histoire naturelle." His remarks on insects, parasitic plants, and the anatomy of the frog show that he was well informed on the work of the Paris Académie des Sciences and accepted the primacy of observation, but that he remained much closer to the integral mechanism of Descartes than to the limited mechanism of Malebranche. Montesquieu denied the preexistence theory and interpreted the phenomena of vegetation purely mechanistically—including the formation of new tissues and of parasitic plants, such as mistletoe and mosses, which he considered to be vegetable excrescences rather than plants of a definite species. He was less interested in the notion of species than in the activity of nature, a position that led him to reject the intervention of Providence and to see the living world in a state of perpetual change, thus foreshadowing Diderot and recalling Lucretius. Similarly, the *Essai sur les causes qui peuvent affecter les esprits* outlines a psychophysiology with a clearly materialistic cast.

Montesquieu's most significant work was in the social and political sciences, of which he has been considered a founder. In *Considérations sur les causes de la grandeur des Romains, et de leur décadence* (1734) he rejected the moral and religious point of view in order to establish a historical science capable of discovering the real causes of major historical events. The goal of *L'esprit des lois* was to discover the scientific law of social institutions and phenomena, which, according to Montesquieu, depend neither on Providence nor on chance. Montesquieu's intention, in short, was to extend to human events his own mechanistic view of nature. This extension was effected without an unwarranted reduction of ethical, political, and social phenomena to physical factors. The analysis of political institutions led Montesquieu to link them with the *esprit général* of the societies that they govern, and analysis of this *esprit général* brought out the diversity of the factors that act on it. In addition to purely physical factors, such as climate and geography, there are also those pertaining to economics, demography, and ethical and religious traditions. (It may be remarked that Montesquieu studied religion as a social fact, without considering its truth or falsity.) The *esprit général* sustained the psychological principle proper to each type of government. Thus republican government rested on civic virtue, monarchy on honor, and despotism on fear. These moral foundations, without which governments could not remain what they are, can endure only so long as the various factors that determine the *esprit général* of the nation are appropriate. A healthy government should seek to maintain the vitality of its proper principle because the balance of physical, ethical, social, and political factors is never stable, and the government is always in danger of degenerating. That is why there is history. But knowledge of all the mediating factors and of their different combinations is bound to permit the rational explanation of even the most bizarre institutions and the most unexpected events.

This attempt to establish a science of social and political facts was based on the conviction that a rational order exists in seemingly diverse phenomena—a conviction especially evident in the writings of Malebranche, who influenced Montesquieu, and one shared by most scientists of the age. God, creator of this order and guarantor of its constancy and intelligibility, is also guarantor of the success of science. Montesquieu's originality consists in having applied this approach to human societies and institutions.

Not everything in *L'esprit des lois*, however, is original; the theory of climates, in particular, is very old. Montesquieu's writing often lacks scientific rigor: he selected the facts that suited his argument and rejected or misinterpreted those that did not. Moreover, he was far from possessing the knowledge necessary for the realization of his immense project. His purpose was not purely scientific: he wished to turn the French monarchy away from its despotic tendency and to introduce more humanity and reason into the laws. Although excessively moralistic and too involved in contemporary philosophical and political struggles to be a pure scientist, Montesquieu nevertheless offered an example of a scientific approach to political and social problems.

BIBLIOGRAPHY

I. ORIGINAL WORKS. Montesquieu's writings were collected as *Oeuvres complètes . . .*, Roger Caillois, ed., 2 vols. (Paris, 1949–1951). His major work is *L'esprit des lois*, J. Brethe de la Gressaye, ed., 4 vols. (Paris, 1950–1961).

II. SECONDARY LITERATURE. See L. Althusser, *Montesquieu, la politique et l'histoire* (Paris, 1969); S. Cotta, *Montesquieu e la scienza della società* (Turin, 1953); J. Ehrard, *L'idée de nature en France dans la première moitié du XVIIIe siècle*, 2 vols. (Paris, 1963), II, 493–515, 718–786, and *passim*; and R. Shackleton, *Montesquieu. A Critical Biography* (Oxford, 1961).

JACQUES ROGER

MONTGÉRY, JACQUES-PHILIPPE MÉRIGON DE (*b.* Paris, France, 25 July 1781; *d.* Paris, 9 September 1839), *military technology.*

Montgéry began his career as a seaman in the French navy in 1794. Commissioned midshipman second class in 1798, he rose to the rank of captain (1828). His commands included the gunboat *Enflammée* (1803) and the corvettes *Émulation* (1816–1818) and *Prudente* (1819–1820). In 1820 he made a military and naval tour of America. It was Montgéry's long-standing position as a member of the Conseil des Travaux de la Marine, however, that afforded him the opportunity to undertake his extensive scientific and military studies.

Montgéry was an analytical scientific chronicler and a prolific writer. He suggested the adoption of new weapons, including a flamethrower, the use of military railroads, and a rocket-firing submarine called *L'invisible*. A strong advocate of steamships, ironclads, mines, torpedoes, and rockets, he examined the *Steam Battery* and submarines of Robert Fulton and subsequently wrote extensively on the historical development of all phases of underwater warfare and exploration. He also wrote on Fulton's life and made elaborate critiques of his experiments.

Montgéry's investigations of pyrotechnics led him to do research into the war rockets of William Congreve and to the production of what may be the first documented history of rocketry, *Traité des fusées de guerre* (1825). Known throughout Europe, it became the standard work on the subject, appeared in serial form in several official journals, and was republished in 1841. Montgéry's coverage was exhaustive and analytical, particularly in his treatment of rocket physics.

Montgéry also wrote essays on the aeolipile designed by Hero of Alexandria (*circa* A.D. 60) and discussed in his *Pneumatica*; the origin of cannon shells; the development of whaling implements; and the rise of industrial education in England.

Montgéry's *Traité des fusées* earned him membership in the Royal Swedish Academy of Sciences (1825) and in other learned societies. He was also an officer of the Légion d'Honneur, Knight of Saint-Louis, and Knight of the Sword of Sweden. He never married.

BIBLIOGRAPHY

I. ORIGINAL WORKS. A bibliography of Montgéry's work is found in the *Catalogue général des Livres Imprimés de la Bibliothèque nationale,* **118** (1933), 417–419. *Traité des fusées de guerre* (Paris, 1825) was also printed in part or in whole in *Journal des sciences militaires,* **1** (1825), 260–286; *Bulletin des sciences militaires,* **1** (1824), 368–380; and *Annales maritimes et coloniales,* **26**, pt. 2 (1825), 565–741; and was republished in J. Corréard, ed., *Histoire des fusées de guerre,* I (Paris, 1841), 77–288. The work was reviewed at length in *Revue encyclopédique,* **28** (Dec. 1825), 699–711; and *Allgemeine Militär-Zeitung,* **1** (12 July 1826), 25–28; (5 July 1826), 20–23; (7 Mar. 1827), 148–151.

Other works include *Règles de pointage à bord des vaisseaux* (Paris, 1816, 1828); *Mémoire sur les mines flottantes* (Paris, 1819); *Mémoire sur les navires en fer* (Paris, 1824); *Notice sur la navigation et sous-marines* (Paris, n.d.); *Notice sur la vie et les travaux de Robert Fulton* (Paris, 1825); *Observations relatives aux ouvrages de M. Paixhans* (Paris, n.d.); and *Réflexions sur quelques institutions . . . sur . . . les progrès de l'industrie* (Paris, n.d.). Montgéry was also a regular contributor to the journals cited above.

II. SECONDARY LITERATURE. See Howard I. Chapelle, *Fulton's "Steam Battery": Blockship and Catamaran,* Museum of History and Technology Paper no. 39 (Washington, D.C., 1964), 147,149,150–152, 159; F. Forest and H. Noalhat, *Les bateaux sous-marins* (Paris, 1900), 21–23; H. J. Paixhans, *Nouvelle force maritime et application de cette force à quelques parties du service de l'armée de terre* (Paris, 1822), 6–7, 41, 136, 294; G. L. Pesce, *La navigation sous-marine* (Paris, 1906), 7, 15, 242–254; A. Pralon, *Les fusées de guerre* (Paris, 1883), 46–48; and [Louis Auguste Victor Vincent] Susane, *Les fusées de guerre* (Metz, 1863), 48–49.

FRANK H. WINTER

MONTGOLFIER, ÉTIENNE JACQUES DE[1] (*b.* Vidalon-les-Annonay, France, 6 January 1745; *d.* Serrières, France, 1 August 1799); **MONTGOLFIER, MICHEL JOSEPH DE**[2] (*b.* Vidalon-les-Annonay, 26 August 1740; *d.* Balaruc-les-Bains, France, 26 June 1810), *technology, aeronautics.*

The Montgolfier brothers were two of the sixteen children of Pierre Montgolfier, a paper manufacturer near Annonay, south of Lyons, and Anne Duret. Joseph de Montgolfier traveled widely in his youth, married in 1771, and settled in Vidalon, having founded his own paper factory fifty miles away at Voiron. He was a skillful and imaginative technologist, self-taught in mathematics and science. Étienne Jacques de Montgolfier excelled in mathematics at school in Paris and studied architecture under J. G. Soufflot; he practiced architecture until 1772, then returned to Annonay to direct his father's factory.

It is not known why Joseph and Étienne de Montgolfier first became interested in the problem of flight. At any rate, their early experiments were based upon the belief that a man could be raised by a balloon filled with a light gas. In 1782 they made small paper and silk model balloons filled with hydrogen; the balloons rose but the gas quickly escaped. They then found that air heated to about 80° R. (100° C.) became sufficiently rarefied to lift a balloon and did not diffuse. In November 1782 they made a balloon of forty-cubic-foot capacity, which reached a height of seventy feet; and on 5 June 1783 a paper and cloth globe thirty-five feet in diameter rose 6,000 feet above Annonay.

An incomplete account of the Montgolfiers' experiment convinced scientists in Paris that hydrogen had been used, and J. A. C. Charles began to develop a hydrogen balloon. Before Charles launched it on 27 August Étienne de Montgolfier himself arrived in Paris, where he constructed several hot-air balloons. The first human flight was made on 20 November 1783 by J. F. Pilatre de Rozier and the Marquis d'Arlandes in one of these "Montgolfières."

The Montgolfier brothers were elected as corresponding members of the Paris Académie des Sciences, and at its meeting on 15 November 1783 Étienne de Montgolfier discussed in mathematical terms the problem of navigating balloons. Joseph de Montgolfier was then in Lyons, where he described the brothers' discovery to the Lyons Academy and constructed a balloon of more than 100 feet in diameter, in which he and six others flew on 19 January 1784.

Joseph de Montgolfier may have witnessed Le Normand's parachute trials at Montpellier. He made a parachute of his own design and in March 1784 dropped a sheep from a tower at Avignon. After that the brothers withdrew from aeronautics. They had been helped in their efforts by F. P. A. Argand, and in October 1785 Joseph de Montgolfier visited London to support him in a patent case concerning his oil lamp.

After spending the winter of 1783–1784 in Paris, Étienne de Montgolfier returned to his father's factory, which produced high-quality paper and which in 1784 was given the appellation *manufacture royale*. He became the proprietor in 1787, and the factory remained his principal interest, apart from a brief excursion into local politics in 1790–1791.

Joseph de Montgolfier subsequently made several inventions, the most important of which was the hydraulic ram, a simple device for raising water, which was widely adopted. The machine consisted of two valves in an iron box (the "ram's head") which were automatically operated by the changing pressure of water flowing into it from a reservoir. When the valve leading to the waste pipe closed suddenly, that leading to the outlet pipe opened and a small volume of water was driven by its own momentum to a considerable height. The valves then recovered their original positions and the action was repeated. Argand helped to develop the ram, but in the *Journal des mines* for 1802–1803 Joseph de Montgolfier claimed that the invention was his own.

Never a very successful businessman, Joseph de Montgolfier retired from paper making after the French Revolution and moved to Paris, where in 1800 he was appointed demonstrator at the Conservatoire des Arts et Métiers. In 1801 he helped to found the Société d'Encouragement pour l'Industrie Nationale; he was elected to the Institut de France in 1807.

NOTES

1. He was named Étienne in the baptismal register, but Jacques Étienne in his death certificate. These documents, cited by Rostaing (see bibliography), are now in the Archives Départementales de l'Ardèche, Privas. The family was ennobled in December 1783 and only then acquired the right to use the prefix "de."
2. He was baptized Michel Joseph but was generally known as Joseph Michel.

BIBLIOGRAPHY

I. Original Works. Joseph de Montgolfier's *Discours prononcé à l'Académie des Sciences de Lyon* (Paris, 1784) was also printed by Saint-Fond (see below). Different versions of the hydraulic ram are described in several papers by Montgolfier: "Note sur le bélier hydraulique, et sur la manière d'en calculer les effets," in *Journal des mines*, **13** (1802–1803), 42–51; "Sur le bélier hydraulique," *ibid.*, **15** (1803–1804), 23–37; "Du bélier hydraulique et de son utilité," in *Bulletin de la Société d'encouragement pour l'industrie nationale*, **4** (1805), 170–181; "Mémoire sur la possibilité de substituer le bélier hydraulique à l'ancienne machine de Marly," *ibid.*, **7** (1808), 117–124, 136–152; and "Sur quelques perfectionnemens du bélier hydraulique," *ibid.*, **8** (1809), 215–220. Also by Joseph de Montgolfier is "Description et usage d'un calorimetre, ou appareil propre

à déterminer le degré de chaleur ainsi que l'économie qui résulte de l'emploi du combustible," *ibid.*, **4** (1805), 43–46; repr. in *Journal des mines*, **19** (1806), 67–72.

Many letters and other manuscripts concerning the Montgolfier family, formerly in the archives of the Château de Colombier le Cardinal (Ardèche), are now in the *Fonds Montgolfier* of the Musée de l'Air, Paris.

II. Secondary Literature. The earliest account of Joseph de Montgolfier is J. B. J. Delambre, "Notice sur la vie et les ouvrages de M. Montgolfier," in *Mémoires de la classe des sciences mathématiques et physiques de l'Institut de France ... Histoire* for 1810 (1814), xxvii–xliv; more detail is given by J. M. de Gerando, "Notice sur M. Joseph Montgolfier," in *Bulletin de la Société d'encouragement pour l'industrie nationale*, **13** (1814), 91–108; some information about his work in Paris is in R. Tresse, "La Conservatoire des Arts et Métiers et la Société d'encouragement pour l'industrie nationale au début du XIXe siècle," in *Revue d'histoire des sciences*, **5** (1952), 246–264.

There is a short account of Étienne Jacques de Montgolfier (with incorrect dates of birth and death) in Michaud's *Biographie universelle*, **29** (Paris, 1821), 570–571. A valuable study of the entire family is L. Rostaing, *La famille de Montgolfier, ses alliances, ses descendants* (Lyons, 1910).

The early balloon flights are described in B. Faujas de Saint-Fond, *Description des expériences de la machine aérostatique de MM. de Montgolfier, et de celles auxquelles cette découverte a donné lieu* (Paris, 1783; 2nd ed., 1784) and in his second volume, *Première suite de la description des expériences ...* (Paris, 1784). The *Première suite* includes Joseph de Montgolfier's "Mémoire lu à l'Académie de Lyon" (pp. 98–111) and Étienne de Montgolfier's "Mémoire sur les moyens mécaniques appliqués à la direction des machines aérostatiques, lu à l'Académie royale des sciences" (pp. 287–295).

Joseph de Montgolfier's parachute is described by C. A. Prieur, "Note historique sur l'invention et les premiers essais des parachutes," in *Annales de chimie*, **31** (1799), 269–273, with an extract from a letter by him. Le Normand's claim to priority is published by C. A. Prieur, "Réclamation relative à l'invention des parachutes," *ibid.*, **36** (1800), 94–99. For a guide to the extensive early literature of aeronautics, see G. Tissandier, *Bibliographie aéronautique* (Paris, 1887; repr., Amsterdam, 1971).

The relations between Argand and the Montgolfier brothers are discussed by M. Schröder, *The Argand Burner, Its Origin and Development in France and England, 1780–1800* (Odense, 1969), see index. Argand is named as one of the inventors of the hydraulic ram by Schröder (p. 57); the first published account of the ram, by "L. C." (probably Lazare Carnot), is "Sur une nouvelle espèce de machine hydraulique, par les CC. [Citoyens] Montgolfier et Argant," in *Bulletin des sciences par la Société philomathique*, no. 8 (1797), 58–60 with plate facing p. 72.

A final anonymous description of the ram is "Note sur le bélier hydraulique de feu M. Joseph Montgolfier," in *Bulletin de la Société d'encouragement pour l'industrie nationale*, **12** (1813), 10–11. Two other inventions are described posthumously by Desormes and Clément: "Description d'un procédé économique pour l'évaporation, imaginé par feu Joseph Montgolfier," in *Annales de chimie*, **76** (1810), 34–53, and "Fabrication du blanc de plomb (procédé de Montgolfier)," *ibid.*, **80** (1811), 326–329, repr. in *Bulletin de la Société d'encouragement pour l'industrie nationale*, **11** (1812), 16–17. A previously unpublished memoir by Joseph de Montgolfier, describing a device for raising water by the expansion of hot air, is printed, with a useful commentary and a misleading title, by C. Cabanes, "Joseph de Montgolfier: Inventeur du moteur à combustion interne," in *Nature* (Paris), **64**, pt. 1 (1936), 364–368, and *ibid.*, pt. 2, 252–255.

W. A. SMEATON

MONTGOMERY, EDMUND DUNCAN (*b.* Edinburgh, Scotland, 19 March 1835; *d.* Hempstead, Texas, 17 April 1911), *cell biology, philosophy.*

Montgomery was the illegitimate son of Duncan MacNeill, a famous Scottish jurist, and Isabella Montgomery. He received his early education in Paris and later in Frankfurt am Main. In 1852 Montgomery entered the University of Heidelberg as a medical student and in the same year met the sculptor Elisabet Ney. Her desire for intellectual and artistic success and her indifference toward the normal social standards mirrored Montgomery's philosophy of life, and they became close friends. The relationship in time was to be restrictive for Montgomery because it isolated him spatially, intellectually, and socially from fellow scientists. But he did continue his studies in Berlin (1855), Bonn (1856), and Würzburg (1857), and he later observed clinical practices at Prague (1858) and Vienna (1859). Although fully trained in the medical arts, there is doubt as to whether he received an official degree.

In 1860 Montgomery became a resident physician at the German Hospital in London. The following year he served as an attendant physician at Bermondsey Dispensary. In 1861–1862 he also served as demonstrator of morbid anatomy at St. Thomas' Hospital and in 1863 became a lecturer on that subject. Mostly for reasons of health Montgomery left London in 1863 for Madeira and set up private practice there. He was joined in November by Elisabet and was married to her by the British consul, although she later denied the legality of their relationship.

From 1864 to 1867 the couple worked and traveled in Italy, but to facilitate Elisabet's work as a sculptor, they became permanent residents of Munich in 1867. Although Munich society was liberal, the Montgomerys were socially ostracized and they moved

to the United States. Their two sons were born during a two-year stay in Thomasville, Georgia. Georgia was even less tolerant of their nonconformist behavior, and they left for Texas, arriving in Hempstead in March of 1873. Soon after his purchase of the Liendo plantation, their firstborn son died of diphtheria. They remained in Texas for the rest of their lives and Montgomery became a United States citizen in 1886. They both continued to travel widely in the United States and Europe.

During his student years (1852–1859), Montgomery encountered the divergent philosophies of materialism and idealism and participated in the blossoming of German experimental physiology. His work at St. Thomas' (1861–1863), at the London Zoological Gardens (summer of 1867), and at Munich (1869) culminated in a research publication, *On the Formation of So-Called Cells in Animal Bodies* (London, 1867), and a philosophical treatise, *Die Kant'sche Erkenntnisslehre widerlegt vom Standpunkt der Empirie* (Munich, 1871).

From 1873 to 1879 Montgomery performed intensive microscopical investigations of protozoans and multicellular organisms at his laboratory on his Texas plantation. From 1879 to 1892 his activities centered increasingly on synthesizing the results of his biological investigations and his philosophical viewpoints. He maintained an active correspondence with scientists and published occasional articles in American and European scientific and philosophic journals.

The years 1892–1911 were a time of great emotional stress aggravated by financial difficulties and the aberrant behavior of their surviving son. In 1907 Elisabet died and Montgomery suffered a paralytic stroke that obliged him to spend the rest of his life on his ranch. Yet he wrote three books that summarized his intellectual beliefs.

The Vitality and Organization of Protoplasm (Austin, 1904) was a statement of his biological researches. Believing mechanistic and vitalistic explanations of life to be in error, Montgomery felt that the vital properties of life resided in the protoplasm of living organisms. The vitality of this substance was due to the interdependencies of the chemical constituents of which it was composed, not to an aggregate of qualities of the atoms or to a vital spirit with which protoplasm might be imbued. This vitality was demonstrated by the ability of protoplasm to reconstitute itself from its elements, not by the activities carried out by living organisms.

Montgomery also disagreed with many cell theorists. He thought that cellular specialization was the result of "ontogenetic" differentiation of the protoplasm of the germ cell and not simply a division of labor in an aggregate of cells. For him this was an evolutionary development in which the resultant cells of the mature organism were not coequals of the original germ cell but lineal descendants with increased specialization. The inheritance of characteristics was effected through the protoplast of the germ cell, not through the nucleus, which structure he thought to be involved in oxidation. He disapproved of any theories of inheritance in which characteristics were carried to the germ cell or were attributed to vital properties of the process.

His biological researches as summarized in his book and articles show him to be a careful observer with original thoughts. Yet, at the same time, isolation from the scientific community partially explains misconceptions that appear in his writings and the lack of a broader acceptance of his work.

Montgomery's philosophy is characterized by an attempt to utilize biological observations as a basis for philosophical generalizations. He was neither a materialist nor an idealist but a monist, who strongly defended the concept of the unity and indivisibility of the living substance and thus of life as a whole. His book *Philosophical Problems in the Light of Vital Experience* (New York, 1907) presented these views in greater detail. His last book, *The Revelation of Present Experience* (Boston, 1910), was a philosophic treatise concerned with the function of the mind. Montgomery believed perception to be not reality but the subjective appearance of things in the mind of the viewer. The only reality was the substance and not its activities. Because of his unique approach to philosophy, Montgomery was not always understood. He gained a larger following among philosophers than biologists.

BIBLIOGRAPHY

I. ORIGINAL WORKS. Among Montgomery's significant works are *On the Formation of So-Called Cells in Animal Bodies* (London, 1867); *Die Kant'sche Erkenntnisslehre widerlegt vom Standpunkt der Empirie* (Munich, 1871); *The Vitality and Organization of Protoplasm* (Austin, Tex., 1904); *Philosophical Problems in the Light of Vital Experience* (New York, 1907); and *The Revelation of Present Experience* (Boston, 1910).

II. SECONDARY LITERATURE. See Morris Keeton, *The Philosophy of Edmund Montgomery* (Dallas, 1950), with bibliography, pp. 319–338; Vernon Loggins, *Two Romantics and Their Ideal Life* (New York, 1946); Ira Stephens, *The Hermit Philosopher of Liendo* (Dallas, 1951); and Bride Taylor, *Elisabet Ney, Sculptor* (New York, 1916).

LARRY T. SPENCER

MONTGOMERY, THOMAS HARRISON, JR. (*b.* New York, N.Y., 5 March 1873; *d.* Philadelphia, Pennsylvania, 19 March 1912), *zoology*.

In his brief life span of thirty-nine years Montgomery became one of the leaders in American zoology; he made substantial contributions in several fields and ranks as a major figure in one of them, cytology. He rose steadily in his profession and at his death he was professor and chairman of the department of zoology at the University of Pennsylvania.

Montgomery's background and early life were favorable for a scholarly career. His family, which settled in New Jersey in 1701, included paternal ancestors distinguished in religion, law, and business; one of them was "the first bishop of English consecration in the United States." Montgomery's maternal forebears included prominent physicians and scientists: his grandfather, Samuel George Morton, was one of the founders of anthropology and served a term as president of the Academy of Natural Sciences of Philadelphia. Montgomery's father, an insurance executive of scholarly bent, published a voluminous early history of the University of Pennsylvania, which made him an honorary doctor of letters. When Montgomery was nine years old, the family moved to a country home near West Chester, Pennsylvania; and there he developed the strong interest in natural history, particularly birds, that he maintained throughout his life.

After graduation from a private secondary school, Montgomery attended the University of Pennsylvania (1889–1891) and completed his studies at Berlin, taking his Ph.D. in 1894. At Berlin he met a group of scholars whose interest in the maturing science of cytology turned him toward the area in which he was to make his greatest contributions: the histologist F. E. Schultze; H. W. G. Waldeyer, who had published extensively on the structure of spermatozoa, on the differentiation of germ cells, and on cell division in the fertilized egg; and Oscar Hertwig, who had carried out pioneer investigations of fertilization and early development. Montgomery's doctoral thesis, however, dealt not with cytology but with a variety of lesser problems in phylogeny, taxonomy, and anatomy. The most extensive essay was on one of the nemerteans, a subject that interested him enough to continue work on the group for many years and to publish a series of ten papers.

After returning to the United States in 1895, Montgomery served for three years as an investigator at the Wistar Institute of Anatomy in Philadelphia. He spent the summer at marine laboratories, notably at Woods Hole, Massachusetts (1897), to which he returned nearly every summer. From 1897 to 1903 he taught zoology at Pennsylvania, serving for the last three years as assistant professor. After five years as professor at the University of Texas, Montgomery was recalled to Pennsylvania in 1908 to become professor and chairman of zoology, the post he held until his death. An arduous executive achievement during this tenure was the construction of a new laboratory building. Montgomery was a coeditor of the *Journal of Morphology* from 1908 until his death and was president of the American Society of Zoologists in 1910.

An unusually diligent researcher who published promptly, Montgomery produced more than eighty papers between 1894 and 1912. Like many biologists of his time, he was interested in certain older problems, such as animal behavior and taxonomy, while remaining active in cytology, a more modern, laboratory-oriented field. As classified by Conklin, sixteen of his papers were devoted mainly to taxonomy, five to animal distribution, eleven to ecology and behavior, sixteen to morphology, and eight to phylogeny—in addition to twenty-five papers in cytology, on which his reputation is based.

Montgomery made a fortunate choice of animals for cell studies, working mainly on the males of the Hemiptera-Heteroptera, or true bugs, which are represented in the United States by many common, easily collected species. They are peculiarly suitable for investigating the processes of meiosis and differentiation of the spermatozoon, because the successive stages are arranged in a series of follicles along the cylindrical lobes of the testis and culminate in the mature spermatozoa, in the follicle nearest the efferent duct. In 1898 Montgomery noted that in the premeiotic, spermatogonial metaphases in the bug testis, the chromosomes consist of a definite number of pairs, many of which are individually recognizable; for example, there are often exceptionally large or small pairs. In the later maturation divisions he found that the half number of chromosomes show the same size differences. Thus, for example, if there formerly was a single large pair there now would be one large chromosome. Although not all the individual chromosomes could be followed throughout the prophase of the first maturation division, certain exceptional chromosomes did remain condensed and hence continuously recognizable. These latter he called heterochromosomes, resulting from the property of heteropycnosis.

From these observations Montgomery concluded in 1901, "Through the germinal cycle the chromosomes preserve their individuality from generation to generation—that is, a particular chromosome of one generation is represented by a particular one of the preceding, so that the chromosomes are not produced anew in each generation." From this general conclusion he suggested that (1) the members of each chromosome pair are homologous and are of maternal and paternal origin respectively; (2) in each case the two are synaptic mates and conjugate to form a "bivalent" chromosome of the same size relative to the rest of the complement; (3) this pairing may be regarded as "the final step in the process of conjugation of the germ cells"; (4) the homologues separate at the reduction division to form the reduced number of "univalent" chromosomes; and (5) finally each spermatid receives a set of "semivalent" chromosomes, resulting from division of each univalent chromosome.

These conclusions, which contain the essentials of the chromosomal basis of biparental inheritance, were announced just prior to the rediscovery of Mendel's laws of segregation and recombination. Montgomery himself failed to see such a possible relationship to inheritance, concluding only that the broader significance of the basic process (synapsis and subsequent separation) was that it might lead to a "rejuvenation of the chromosomes." Despite what seems in retrospect an unimaginative and narrow interpretation, it appears undeniable that the speed with which Sutton, Wilson, and others subsequently established the correlation with the rediscovered laws of inheritance was due in large measure to Montgomery's masterly analysis—not the least aspect of which was its clarifying terminology.

Another facet of Montgomery's work was basic to the theory of sex determination. In certain species of bugs he noted that one chromosome, which he called the X chromosome, is single, as distinct from the paired "autosomes." Consequently the somatic, or diploid, chromosome number is odd, and during meiosis only half the spermatids receive the X chromosome. It remained for others to point out the obvious possibility that this chromosomal mechanism could be the basis of determination of sex. Instead, Montgomery assumed that the females of these species, like the males, had the uneven chromosome number; and he became engrossed with the puzzle of how the odd number could be preserved to the next generation. Realizing that random fertilization in such a situation should also produce two even-numbered chromosomal complements with respectively one more and one less than the X type, he was led to postulate a sort of selective fertilization to maintain the odd number.

Montgomery's other cytological contributions were not inconsiderable. In his 1901 paper he brought order to the rather chaotic views of the nucleolus by clearly distinguishing "chromatin nucleoli" (among which were the heterochromosomes) from the plasmosomes, or true nucleoli. His careful seriation of steps in the differentiation of the hemipteran spermatozoon (1911) was a model for many later studies, including R. H. Bowen's (1920). Noteworthy in the 1911 paper was Montgomery's confirmation of observations on fixed material by examining cells teased out in a physiological fluid. This degree of sophistication was not attained by other cytologists for nearly two decades.

BIBLIOGRAPHY

Montgomery's writings include "Comparative Cytological Studies With Especial Reference to the Morphology of the Nucleolus," in *Journal of Morphology,* **15** (1898), 204–265; "A Study of the Chromosomes of Germ Cells," in *Transactions of the American Philosophical Society,* **20** (1901), 154–236; and "The Spermatogenesis of an Hemipteron, *Euschistus,*" in *Journal of Morphology,* **22** (1911), 731–799.

On his life and work, see R. H. Bowen, "Studies on Insect Spermatogenesis. I.," in *Biological Bulletin. Marine Biological Laboratory, Woods Hole, Mass.,* **39** (1920), 316–362; and E. G. Conklin, "Professor Thomas Harrison Montgomery, Jr.," in *Science,* n.s. **38** (1913), 207–214, an excellent obituary; the complete bibliography prepared to accompany it, however, seems to have been omitted.

ARTHUR W. POLLISTER

MONTMOR, HENRI LOUIS HABERT DE (*b.* Paris [?], France, *ca.* 1600; *d.* Paris, 21 January 1679), *scientific patronage.*

Montmor's family, which originally came from Artois, moved to Paris in the sixteenth century. Its leading members were high government officials who grew rich in the king's service. Related to the greatest families in the kingdom, including the Lamoignons, the Bethunes, and the Phélypeaux, and a grandnephew of Guillaume Budé, he received an excellent education. When Montmor was twenty-five, his father obtained for him a position as *conseiller* in the Parlement of Paris; and on 6 April 1632 he was appointed *maître des requêtes.* His connections with two of his cousins, the brothers Philippe Habert, artillery commissioner and poet, and Germain Habert, *abbé* of Cerisy and likewise a poet, undoubtedly account for his having been well enough known to Valentin Conrart to have been included in the small group forming the Académie Française. He was elected to the latter in December 1634 and formally welcomed by his cousin Germain Habert on 2 January 1635. On 30 April 1635 the group met at the handsome

town house on the Rue Sainte-Avoye (now 79 Rue du Temple) that his father had constructed about 1623.

On 29 March 1637 Montmor married a cousin, Marie Henriette de Buade de Frontenac, whose brother Louis later became governor of New France. Between 1638 and 1659 they had fifteen children, most of whom died young. The eldest son, who also became *maître des requêtes,* suffered a bankruptcy of 600,000 *livres*—which, if Jean Chapelain's letter to François Bernier is to be believed, was the cause of the "fatal melancholy" that overtook Montmor beginning in 1669. On 7 September 1671 Chapelain wrote to Nikolaas Heinsius: "M. de Montmor's fate is deplorable. For a year he has lived only on milk and to his distress he is unable to leave this life . . ." (*Lettres de Jean Chapelain*, II, 752). He was obliged to sell his post and as a result "suffered such a great mental disturbance that he became almost insane" (*ibid.*, to Régnier de Graff, 28 August 1671). Yet he lived until the beginning of 1679, having survived his wife by more than two years.

Very few of Montmor's writings are extant. In the *Histoire de l'Académie françoise* Pellisson states that Montmor delivered an address to the Academy on 3 March 1635, "De l'utilité des conférences." Today he is of interest for his role as patron of the scientists and philosophers of his age. A fine scholar, Montmor assembled a very rich library, in which the correspondence of important contemporaries (for example, Gui Patin and Chapelain) had a major place, and he attracted to his residence on Rue Saint-Avoye both men of letters and scientists. A Cartesian throughout his life, he offered Descartes "the full use of a country house [Mesnil-Saint-Denis] worth 3,000 to 4,000 *livres* in rent" (A. Baillet, *La vie de Monsieur Descartes*, II, 462), which the latter declined.

No document proves conclusively that regular scientific meetings took place at Montmor's residence before 1653. Toward the middle of the century political agitation attracted more attention than did scientific activity, and Montmor did not escape this preoccupation. Although not really a rebel, he stood with the Parlement and princes against the king and court. When the disorders of the Fronde had died down, and after Descartes was dead, Montmor, while remaining a Cartesian, offered Gassendi, Descartes's great adversary, lodgings in his house. Gassendi moved into the second floor of the house in the Rue du Temple on 9 May 1653. He spent the month of August 1654 at Mesnil, where he made astronomical observations. Montmor encouraged him to write *La vie de Tycho Brahe,* and Gassendi dedicated it to his patron, whom he also made the executor of his will and to whom he left all his books, manuscripts, and the telescope Galileo had given him. When Gassendi died, on 24 October 1655, Montmor returned in haste from Mesnil to arrange his friend's funeral; Gassendi was buried in the Montmor chapel in the church of St.-Nicolas-des-Champs. Montmor collected his writings—with the help of François Henri, Samuel Sorbière, and Antoine de La Poterie—and wrote a preface to the six-volume Latin edition published at Lyons in 1658.

Gassendi's presence in Montmor's household certainly contributed to the development of the meetings held there by the cultivated men who had previously gathered around Mersenne, the brothers Pierre and Jacques Du Puy, the Abbé Picot, and François Le Pailleur and who, with several newcomers, now assembled on the Rue du Temple: Boulliau, Pascal, Roberval, Gérard Desargues, Carcavi, Jean Segrais, Gui Patin, Michel de Marolles, Balthazar de Monconys, and others. In a letter to his friend Regnault of Lyons, dated 4 August 1656, Monconys described a meeting in Montmor's house in which experiments on glass drops were conducted. Although Monconys spoke of an "assemblée" (of which he was not then a member), it is only from the end of 1657 that the weekly gatherings of what came to be called the Académie Montmor can be dated.

At Montmor's request, Sorbière prepared a plan for the organization of meetings in the form of nine articles. The goals of the meetings "will not be the vain exercise of the mind on useless subtleties; rather, one should always propose the clearest knowledge of the works of God and the advancement of the conveniences of life, in the arts and sciences that best serve to establish them." Sorbière was also charged with preparing the *Mémoires* of the assembly, but unfortunately they have been lost.

Among the members of the Académie Montmor were Chapelain, Sorbière, Montmor (named the "Modérateur"), Clerselier, Rohault, Pierre Huet, Roberval (until he was "uncivil," boorish, and rude to Montmor, who supported the opinions of Descartes), and Huygens (when he was in Paris). The latter's journal provides information on the weekly sessions and on those he met there; on 9 November 1660 he was introduced to Auzout, Frenicle de Bessy, Desargues, Pecquet, Rohault, La Poterie, Sorbière, and Boulliau. Oldenburg also visited the house in the Rue du Temple when he stayed in Paris.

The activities of the Académie Montmor during its first years included Chapelain's announcement of Huygens' discoveries (the pendulum clock, the first known satellite of Saturn, a diagram of his system of Saturn—planet and ring), Rohault's experiments on the magnet, Pecquet's dissections, and Thévenot's presentation of his tubes "made expressly to examine the ascension of water that mounts by itself beyond its level."

Two currents soon appeared within the Académie Montmor: the first, a tendency to seek natural causes, was associated with the philosophers, both Cartesians and Gassendists; the second, a preference for observation and experiment, was emphasized by Auzout, Petit, and Rohault, who complained of sterile discussions and prating that explained nothing.

The problem worsened in the following years, and on 3 April 1663 Sorbière delivered "Discours à l'ouverture de l'Académie des Physiciens qui s'assemblent tous les mardis chez Monsieur de Montmor," which he sent to Colbert. Although he began by honoring the "illustrious moderator" who "first aroused interest in Paris in the studies we cultivate" and by praising the early meetings and experiments, he soon turned to severe criticism of the disputes and interruptions; "people who have come here only to waste time and to acquire esteem"; and the mutual intolerance of the partisans of experiment and philosophy. Even though Montmor had provided his guests with "an infinity of machines and instruments with which he has stimulated his curiosity for thirty years," he could not furnish them with a forge and a laboratory or an observatory. That was not within the power of an individual but, rather, of a sovereign. This implicit appeal to the king for the creation of an institution under royal patronage explains why the Académie Montmor has been seen as a forerunner of the Académie Royale des Sciences.

In response to all the criticism, the Académie Montmor attempted to reform itself. Experiments were tried there with an air pump constructed according to Huygens' plans. Nevertheless, so Huygens wrote to Moray in March 1664, a widespread desire was felt to establish the academy on a new basis. On 12 June, he wrote to Moray that "the academy has ended forever *chez* M. de Montmor" but that another was being born from its ruins. Montmor, meanwhile, continued to receive scientists and to take an interest in philosophers. Experiments on blood transfusion were carried out by Jean-Baptiste Denis at his home in 1668; and when the human subject died, Montmor exerted his influence to save the experimenters from legal penalties. It was to Montmor that Henri Justel sent Hooke's *Micrographia*. He also received the first copy of the *Saggi dell'esperienze naturali fatte nell'Accademia del Cimento*, and on the advice of Chapelain, Louis de La Forge dedicated his *Traitté de l'esprit de l'homme*, which was inspired by Descartes's philosophy, to Montmor (as had Mersenne his *Harmonie universelle*). Montmor's continued attachment to Descartes is proved by the fact that he undertook the writing of a Latin poem on Cartesian physics with the Lucretian title *De rerum natura* and by the fact that he was among the faithful Cartesians who followed Descartes's bier to the church of Ste.-Geneviève-du-Mont on 25 June 1667.

BIBLIOGRAPHY

Information on Montmor's life may be found in Adrien Baillet, *La vie de Monsieur Descartes* (Paris, 1691), 266–267, 346–347, 462; Faustin Foiret, "L'hôtel de Montmor," in *La Cité, Bulletin trimestriel de la Société historique et archéologique du IVᵉ arrondissement de Paris*, **13** (1914), 309–339; "Habert, Henri Louis, de Montmor," in Moreri's *Dictionnaire ...* (1759); René Kerviler, "Henri-Louis Habert de Montmor, de l'Académie française et bibliophile (1600–1679)," in *Le bibliophile français*, VI (Paris, 1872), 198–208; Frédéric Lachèvre, *Bibliographie des recueils collectifs de poésies publiés de 1597 à 1700*, III (Paris, 1903), 455; Pellisson and d'Olivet, *Histoire de l'Académie françoise depuis son établissement jusqu'en 1652* (Paris, 1729), 81, 175, 276, 344; and Tallemant des Réaux, *Historiettes*, Antoine Adam, ed., 2 vols. (Paris, 1960–1961).

On Montmor's relations with Gassendi see, in addition to the classic works on Gassendi, Georges Bailhache and Marie-Antoinette Fleury, "Le testament, l'inventaire après décès, la sépulture et le monument funéraire de Gassendi," in *Tricentenaire de Pierre Gassendi, 1655–1955. Actes du Congrès Gassendi, 4–7 août 1955* (Paris, 1957), 19–68.

Information on the Académie Montmor is in *The Correspondence of Henry Oldenburg*, A. Rupert Hall and Marie Boas-Hall, eds., I–IV (Madison–Milwaukee, Wis., 1965–1971); F. Graverol, ed., *Sorberiana* (Toulouse, 1691), 28–29; *Lettres et Discours de Monsieur de Sorbière sur diverses Matières Curieuses* (Paris, 1660), 60, 181, 190, 193, 369, 631, 694, 701; *Lettres de Gui Patin*, J.-H. Réveillé-Parise, ed., II (Paris, 1846), 107, 211, 317–318; *Lettres de Jean Chapelain*, P. Tamizey de Larroque, ed., II (Paris, 1883), *passim;* Balthazar de Monconys, *Journal des voyages* (Lyons, 1666), 162–169; and *Oeuvres de Christiaan Huygens*, J. Volgraf, ed., I–V, XXII (The Hague, 1888–1950).

The following studies have made extensive use of the above sources: M. G. Bigourdan, *Les premières sociétés savantes de Paris au XVIIᵉ siècle et les origines de l'Académie des sciences* (Paris, 1919); Harcourt Brown, *Scientific Organizations in Seventeenth Century France (1620–1680)* (Baltimore, 1934), 64–134; and René Taton, *Les origines de l'Académie royale des sciences* (Paris, 1966), 47–54.

SUZANNE DELORME

MONTMORT, PIERRE RÉMOND DE (*b.* Paris, France, 27 October 1678; *d.* Paris, 7 October 1719), *probability*.

Montmort was the second of the three sons of François Rémond and Marguerite Ralle. On the advice of his father he studied law, but tired of it and ran away to England. He toured extensively there and in Germany, returning to France only in 1699, just before his father's death. He had a substantial inheritance, which he did not exploit frivolously.

Having recently read, and been much impressed by, the work of Nicolas Malebranche, Montmort began study under that philosopher. With Malebranche he mastered Cartesian physics and philosophy, and he and a young mathematician, François Nicole, taught themselves the new mathematics. When Montmort visited London again in 1700, it was to meet English scientists; he duly presented himself to Newton. On his return to Paris, his brother persuaded him to become a canon at Notre Dame de Paris. He was a good ecclesiastic until he bought an estate at Montmort and went to call on the grand lady of the neighborhood, the duchess of Angoulême. He fell in love with her niece, and in due course gave up his clerical office and married. It is said to have been an exceptionally happy household.

Montmort's book on probability, *Essay d'analyse sur les jeux de hazard*, which came out in 1708, made his reputation among scientists and led to a fruitful collaboration with Nikolaus I Bernoulli. The Royal Society of London elected Montmort fellow when he was visiting England in 1715 to watch the total eclipse of the sun in the company of the astronomer royal, Edmond Halley. The Académie Royale des Sciences made him an associate member the following year—he could not be granted full membership because he did not reside in Paris. He died during a smallpox epidemic in 1719.

It is not clear why Montmort undertook a systematic exposition of the theory of games of chance. Gaming was a common pastime among the lesser nobility whom he frequented, but it had not been treated mathematically since Christiaan Huygens' monograph of 1657. Although there had been isolated publications about individual games, and occasional attempts to come to grips with annuities, Jakob I Bernoulli's major work on probability, the *Ars conjectandi*, had not yet been published. Bernoulli's work was nearly complete at his death in 1705; two obituary notices give brief accounts of it. Montmort set out to follow what he took to be Bernoulli's plan.

One obituary gave a fair idea of Bernoulli's proof of the first limit theorem in probability, but Montmort, a lesser mathematician, was not able to reach a comparable result unaided. He therefore continued along the lines laid down by Huygens and made analyses of fashionable games of chance in order to solve problems in combinations and the summation of series. For example, he drew upon the game that he calls "treize," in which the thirteen cards of one suit are shuffled and then drawn one after the other. The player who is drawing wins the round if and only if a card is drawn in its own place, that is, if the nth card to be drawn is itself the card n. In the generalized game, the pack consists of m cards marked in serial order. The chance of winning is shown to be

$$\sum_{i=1}^{i=m} \frac{(-1)^{i-1}}{i!}.$$

A 1793 paper by Leibniz provided Montmort with a rough idea of the limit to which this tends as m increases, but Euler was the first to state it as $1 - e^{-1}$.

The greatest value of Montmort's book lay perhaps not in its solutions but in its systematic setting out of problems about games, which are shown to have important mathematical properties worthy of further work. The book aroused Nikolaus I Bernoulli's interest in particular and the 1713 edition includes the mathematical correspondence of the two men. This correspondence in turn provided an incentive for Nikolaus to publish the *Ars conjectandi* of his uncle Jakob I Bernoulli, thereby providing mathematics with a first step beyond mere combinatorial problems in probability.

The work of De Moivre is, to say the least, a continuation of the inquiries of Montmort. Montmort put the case more strongly—he accused De Moivre of stealing his ideas without acknowledgment. De Moivre's *De mensura sortis* appeared in 1711 and Montmort attacked it scathingly in the 1713 edition of his own *Essay*. Montmort's friends tried to soothe him, and largely succeeded. He tried to correspond with De Moivre, but the latter seldom replied. In 1717 Montmort told Brook Taylor that two years earlier he had sent ten theorems to De Moivre; he implied that De Moivre could be expected to publish them.

Taylor was doing his best work at this time. He and Montmort had struck up a close friendship in 1715, and corresponded about not only mathematics but also general questions of philosophy, Montmort mildly defending Cartesian principles against the sturdy Newtonian doctrines of Taylor. Montmort's only other mathematical publication, an essay on summing infinite series, has an appendix by Taylor. It is notable that in this period of vigorous strife between followers of Newton and Leibniz, Montmort was able to remain on the best of terms with both the Bernoullis and the Englishmen.

BIBLIOGRAPHY

I. ORIGINAL WORKS. Montmort's mathematical writings are *Essay d'analyse sur les jeux de hazard* (Paris, 1708),

2nd ed. revised and augmented with correspondence between Montmort and N. Bernoulli (Paris, 1713; 1714); and "De seriebus infinitis tractatus," in *Philosophical Transactions of the Royal Society*, **30** (1720), 633–675. Part of Montmort's correspondence with Taylor is in William Young, ed., Brook Taylor, *Contemplatio philosophica* (London, 1793).

II. SECONDARY LITERATURE. See "Éloge de M. de Montmort," in *Histoire de l'Académie royale des sciences pour l'année 1719* (1721), 83–93.

IAN HACKING

MONTUCLA, JEAN ÉTIENNE (*b.* Lyons, France, 5 September 1725; *d.* Versailles, France, 19 December 1799), *mathematics, history of mathematics.*

Montucla, the son of a merchant, attended the Jesuit *collège* in Lyons, where he received a thorough education in mathematics and ancient languages. Following the death of his father in 1741 and of his grandmother, who was caring for him, in 1745, he began legal studies at Toulouse. On their completion he went to Paris, drawn by the many opportunities for further training. Soon after his arrival there he undertook the study of the history of mathematics. His work on the quadrature of the circle (1754) brought him a corresponding membership in the Berlin Academy. In the same year he announced the forthcoming publication of what was to be his masterpiece, *Histoire des mathématiques.* The exchange of ideas in the literary circle that had formed around the bookseller and publisher Charles Antoine Jombert (1712–1784), which included Diderot, d'Alembert, and Lalande, was very valuable to him. Before the appearance of *Histoire des mathématiques*, Montucla published, in collaboration with the physician Pierre Joseph Morisot-Deslandes, a collection of sources on smallpox vaccination (1756).

From 1761 Montucla held several government posts. His first appointment was as secretary of the intendance of Dauphiné in Grenoble, where in 1763 he married Marie Françoise Romand. In 1764–1765 he was made royal astronomer and secretary to Turgot on a mission to Cayenne. After his return, Montucla became inspector of royal buildings (1766–1789) and, later, royal censor (1775). From this period date his new edition of Ozanam's *Récréations mathématiques* (1778) and his translation of Jonathan Carver's account of travels in North America (1784).

As a result of the Revolution, Montucla lost his posts and most of his wealth. He was again given public office in 1795—examination of the treaties deposited in the archives of the Ministry of Foreign

Affairs—but the salary was not sufficient to meet his expenses, so he also worked in an office of the national lottery. During these years Montucla, at the insistence of his friends, began to prepare an improved and much enlarged edition of *Histoire des mathématiques*. The first two volumes appeared in August 1799, four months before his death, just when he had been promised a pension of 2,400 francs.

Montucla's major work, the first classical history of mathematics, was a comprehensive and, relative to the state of contemporary scholarship, accurate description of the development of the subject in various countries. The account also included mechanics, astronomy, optics, and music, which were then considered subdivisions of mathematics; these branches *(mathématiques mixtes)* receive a thorough treatment in both editions, and only a third of the space is devoted to pure mathematics. The first volume of the two-volume edition of 1758 covers the beginnings, the Greeks (including the Byzantines), and the West until the start of the seventeenth century; the second volume is devoted entirely to the latter century. Montucla originally planned to take his work up to the middle of the eighteenth century in a third volume but could not do so, principally because of the abundance of material. In the second edition, extended to cover the whole of the eighteenth century, he was able to reach this goal. Much remained unfinished, however, since Montucla died during the printing of the third volume. Lalande, his friend from childhood, assisted by others, completed volumes III (pure mathematics, optics, mechanics) and IV (astronomy, mathematical geography, navigation) and published them in 1802.

Many authors before Montucla—beginning with Proclus and al-Nadīm—had written on the history of mathematics. Their accounts can be found in the citations of ancient authors, in the prefaces to many mathematical works of the sixteenth through eighteenth centuries, in university addresses (for example, that of Regiomontanus at Padua in 1464), and in two earlier books that, as their titles indicate, were devoted to the history of mathematics: G. I. Vossius' *De universae mathesios natura et constitutione* (1650) and J. C. Heilbronner's *Historia matheseos universae* (1742). All these early efforts constituted only a modest beginning, containing many errors and legends, and the latter two works give only a jumble of names, dates, and titles. Montucla was familiar with all this material and saw what was required: a comprehensive history of the development of mathematical ideas, such as had been called for by Bacon and Montmor. Inspired by them Montucla undertook the immense labor, the difficulty of which he recognized and which

he carried out with his own research in and mastery of the original texts.

Montucla had no successor until Moritz Cantor. The *Histoire des mathématiques* is, of course, obsolete—as, in many respects, is Cantor's *Vorlesungen*. Yet even today the expert can, with the requisite caution, go back to Montucla, especially with regard to the mathematics of the seventeenth century.

BIBLIOGRAPHY

I. ORIGINAL WORKS. Montucla's writings include *Histoire des recherches sur la quadrature du cercle* (Paris, 1754); *Recueil de pièces concernant l'inoculation de la petite vérole et propres à en prouver la sécurité et l'utilité* (Paris, 1756), written with Morisot-Deslandes; *Histoire des mathématiques*, 2 vols. (Paris, 1758; 2nd ed., 4 vols., Paris, 1799–1802); a new ed. of Ozanam's *Récréations mathématiques et physiques* (Paris, 1778); and a translation, from the 3rd English ed., of Jonathan Carver, *Voyages dans les parties intérieures de l'Amérique septentrionale, pendant les années 1766, 1767, et 1768* (Paris, 1784).

II. SECONDARY LITERATURE. See the following, listed chronologically: Auguste Savinien Le Blond, "Sur la vie et les ouvrages de Montucla. Extrait de la notice historique lue à la Société de Versailles, le 15 janvier 1800. Avec des additions par Jérôme de Lalande," in Montucla's *Histoire des mathématiques*, IV, 662–672; G. Sarton, "Montucla (1725–1799). His Life and Works," in *Osiris*, **1** (1936), 519–567, with a portrait, the title page of each of his works, two previously unpublished letters, and further bibliographical information; and Kurt Vogel, "L'historiographie mathématique avant Montucla," in *Actes du XIᵉ Congrès international d'histoire des sciences*. III, 179–184.

KURT VOGEL

MOORE, ELIAKIM HASTINGS (*b.* Marietta, Ohio, 26 January 1862; *d.* Chicago, Illinois, 30 December 1932), *mathematics*.

Moore was prominent among the small circle of men who greatly influenced the rapid development of American mathematics at the turn of the twentieth century. The son of David Hastings Moore, a Methodist minister, and Julia Sophia Carpenter, he had an impressive preparation for his future career. While still in high school he served one summer as an assistant to Ormond Stone, the director of the Cincinnati Observatory, who aroused his interest in mathematics. He later attended Yale University, from which he received the A.B. in 1883 as class valedictorian and the Ph.D. in 1885. The mathematician Hubert Anson Newton, his guiding spirit at Yale, then financed a year's study abroad for him at the universities of Göttingen and Berlin. He spent the summer of 1885 in Göttingen, where he studied the German language; and the winter of 1885–1886 in Berlin, where Kronecker and Weierstrass were lecturing. The work of Kronecker impressed him, as did the rigorous methods of Weierstrass and Klein, who was then at Leipzig.

In 1886 Moore returned to the United States to begin his career in mathematics. He accepted an instructorship at the academy of Northwestern University for 1886–1887. During the next two years he was a tutor at Yale. In 1889 he returned to Northwestern as an assistant professor and in 1891 was promoted to associate professor. When the University of Chicago first opened in the autumn of 1892, Moore was appointed professor and acting head of the mathematics department. In 1896, after successfully organizing the new department, he became its permanent chairman, a post he held until his partial retirement in 1931. Shortly before assuming his post at Chicago, he married a childhood playmate, Martha Morris Young, on 21 June 1892, in Columbus, Ohio. They had two sons, David and Eliakim.

During his career Moore became a leader at the University of Chicago and in mathematical associations. He helped shape the character of the university and gave it great distinction. With his faculty colleagues Oskar Bolza and Heinrich Maschke, he modified the methods of undergraduate instruction in mathematics. Casting aside textbooks, he stressed fundamentals and their graphical interpretations in his "laboratory courses." Although a gentle man, he sometimes displayed impatience as he strove for excellence in his classes. He became a teacher of teachers. Among his supervised Ph.D.'s were L. E. Dickson, O. Veblen, and G. D. Birkhoff.

Moore also advanced his profession outside the classroom. In 1894 he helped transform the New York Mathematical Society into the American Mathematical Society, of which he was vice-president from 1898 to 1900 and president from 1900 to 1902. A founder of the society's *Transactions* in 1899, he was chief editor until 1907. He served on the editorial boards of the *Rendiconti del Circolo matematico di Palermo* (1908–1932), the University of Chicago Science Series (chairman, 1914–1929), and the *Proceedings of the National Academy of Sciences* (1915–1920). With his encouragement in, 1916 H. E. Slaught saw through the formation of the Mathematical Association of America. In 1921 Moore was president of the American Association for the Advancement of Science.

Rigor and generalization characterized the mathematical research of Moore. His research fell principally into the areas of (1) geometry; (2) algebra, groups, and number theory; (3) the theory of functions; and (4) integral equations and general analysis. Among these he emphasized the second and fourth areas. In geometry he examined the postulational foundations of Hilbert, as well as the earlier works of Pasch and Peano. He skillfully analyzed the independence of the axioms of Hilbert and formulated a system of axioms for n-dimensional geometry, using points only as undefined elements instead of the points, lines, and planes of Hilbert in the three-dimensional case. During his investigation of the theory of abstract groups, he stated and proved for the first time the important theorem that every finite field is a Galois field (1893). He also discovered that every finite group G of linear transformations on n variables has a Hermitian invariant (1896–1898). His probe of the theory of functions produced a clarified treatment of transcendentally transcendental functions and a proof of Goursat's extension of the Cauchy integral theorem for a function $f(z)$ without the assumption of the continuity of the derivative $f'(z)$.

His work in the area of integral equations and general analysis sparkled most. He brought to culmination the study of improper definite integrals before the appearance of the more effective integration theories of Borel and Lebesgue. He diligently advanced general analysis, which for him meant the development of a theory of classes of functions on a general range. The contributions of Cantor, Russell, and Zermelo underlay his research here. While inventing a mathematical notation for his analytical system, he urged Florian Cajori to prepare his two-volume *History of Mathematical Notations* (1928–1929). Throughout his work in general analysis, Moore stressed fundamentals, as he sought to strengthen the foundations of mathematics. His research set a trend for precision in American mathematical literature at a time when vagueness and uncertainty were common.

Honors were bestowed upon Moore for his distinguished contributions to mathematics and education. The University of Göttingen awarded him an honorary Ph.D. in 1899, and the University of Wisconsin an LL.D. in 1904. Yale, Clark, Toronto, Kansas, and Northwestern subsequently granted him honorary doctorates in science or mathematics. In 1929 the University of Chicago established the Eliakim Hastings Moore distinguished service professorship, while he was still an active member of the faculty. Besides belonging to American, English, German, and Italian mathematical societies, he was a member of the American Academy of Arts and Sciences, the American Philosophical Society, and the National Academy of Sciences.

BIBLIOGRAPHY

I. ORIGINAL WORKS. Moore wrote *Introduction to a Form of General Analysis* (New Haven, 1910); and *General Analysis*, published posthumously in *Memoirs of American Philosophical Society*, **1** (1935).

His articles include "Extensions of Certain Theorems of Clifford and Cayley in the Geometry of n Dimensions," in *Transactions of the Connecticut Academy of Arts and Sciences*, **7** (1885), 1–18; "Note Concerning a Fundamental Theorem of Elliptic Functions, As Treated in Halphen's Traité," **1**, 39–41, in *Rendiconti del Circolo matematico di Palermo*, **4** (1890), 186–194; "A Doubly-Infinite System of Simple Groups," in *Bulletin of the New York Mathematical Society*, **3** (1893), 73–78; "A Doubly-Infinite System of Simple Groups," in *Mathematical Papers Read at the International Mathematical Congress in Chicago 1893* (New York, 1896), 208–242; "Concerning Transcendentally Transcendental Functions," in *Mathematische Annalen*, **48** (1897), 49–74; "On Certain Crinkly Curves," in *Transactions of the American Mathematical Society*, **1** (1900), 72–90; "A Simple Proof of the Fundamental Cauchy-Goursat Theorem," *ibid.*, 499–506; "The Undergraduate Curriculum," in *Bulletin of the American Mathematical Society*, **7** (1900), 14–24; "Concerning Harnack's Theory of Improper Definite Integrals," in *Transactions of the American Mathematical Society*, **2** (1901), 296–330; and "On the Theory of Improper Definite Integrals," *ibid.*, 459–475.

Subsequent articles are "Concerning Du Bois-Reymond's Two Relative Integrability Theorems," in *Annals of Mathematics*, 2nd ser., **2** (1901), 153–158; "A Definition of Abstract Groups," in *Transactions of the American Mathematical Society*, **3** (1902), 485–492; "On the Foundations of Mathematics," in *Bulletin of the American Mathematical Society*, **9** (1903), 402–424; also in *Science*, 2nd ser., **17** (1903), 401–416, his retiring address as president of the American Mathematical Society; "The Subgroups of the Generalized Finite Modular Group," in *Decennial Publications of the University of Chicago* (1903), 141–190; "On a Form of General Analysis with Application to Linear Differential and Integral Equations," in *Atti del IV Congresso internazionale dei matematici* (Rome, 6–11 Apr. 1908), II (1909), 98–114; "The Role of Postulational Methods in Mathematics" (address at Clark University, 20th Anniversary), in *Bulletin of the American Mathematical Society*, **16** (1909), 41; "On the Foundations of the Theory of Linear Integral Equations," *ibid.*, **18** (1912), 334–362; "On the Fundamental Functional Operation of a General Theory of Linear Integral Equations," in *Proceedings of the Fifth International Congress of Mathematicians* (Cambridge, 1912), I (1913), 230–255; "Definition of Limit in General Integral Analysis," in *Proceedings of the National Academy of Sciences of the United States of America*, **1** (1915), 628–632; "On Power Series in General Analysis," in *Mathematische Annalen*, **86** (1922), 30–39; and "A General Theory of Limits," in *American Journal of Mathematics*, **44** (1922), 102–121, written with H. L. Smith.

II. SECONDARY LITERATURE. Articles on Moore are G. A. Bliss, "Eliakim Hastings Moore," in *Bulletin of the American Mathematical Society*, **39** (1933), 831–838; and "The Scientific Work of Eliakim Hastings Moore," *ibid.*, **40** (1934), 501–514, with bibliography of Moore's publications; and G. A. Bliss and L. E. Dickson, "Eliakim Hastings Moore (1862–1932)," in *Biographical Memoirs. National Academy of Sciences*, **17** (1937), 83–102.

RONALD S. CALINGER

MOORE, JOSEPH HAINES (*b.* Wilmington, Ohio, 7 September 1878; *d.* Oakland, California, 15 March 1949), *astronomy.*

The only child of John Haines Moore and Mary Ann Haines, Moore graduated from Wilmington College in 1897. His field was classics, but during his senior year he became interested in astronomy. He then entered Johns Hopkins University, concentrating in physics, with minors in mathematics and astronomy, and received his Ph.D. in 1903. He immediately took a position as assistant to W. W. Campbell, director of the Lick Observatory; he passed through all the grades to astronomer (1923), was appointed assistant director in 1936, and director in 1942. Poor health forced him to relinquish the directorship in 1945 and move to a lower altitude, but he was engaged in teaching and research at the University of California at Berkeley until six months before his death. He was a member of the National Academy of Sciences, served as chairman of the astronomical section of the American Association for the Advancement of Science, and was twice president of the Astronomical Society of the Pacific. Moore was married in 1907 to Fredrica Chase, a computing assistant at the Lick Observatory. Modest and unassuming, he held to the Quaker philosophy all his life and was always regarded with deep affection by his colleagues and students.

Moore's principal scientific work was concerned with astronomical spectroscopy, in particular with the measurement of radial velocities of stars. From 1909 to 1913 he was in charge of the observatory's southern station at Santiago, Chile, and during this time some 2,700 stellar spectrograms were obtained there. As progressively more of Campbell's time was expended on other duties, Moore took over more of the spectrographic work of the observatory. In collaboration with Campbell he published (1918) the radial velocities of 125 bright-line nebulae, and he played the major role in producing (1928) the exhaustive discussion of the Mount Hamilton and Santiago radial-velocity measurements of all stars brighter than visual magnitude 5.51. Moore also made observations of fainter stars, and his "A General Catalogue of the Radial Velocities of Stars, Nebulae and Clusters" (1932) remained the standard work for two decades.

A by-product of radial-velocity studies was the discovery of spectroscopic binary stars. Moore discovered and calculated the orbits of many of these objects, and the results of this work were included in the third, fourth, and fifth catalogues of spectroscopic binaries, which he published in 1924, 1939, and 1948, respectively.

Moore took part in five eclipse expeditions, obtaining important spectroscopic information on the structure and composition of the solar corona. He led the Lick eclipse expeditions to Camptonville, California (1930) and to Fryeburg, Maine (1932).

Among Moore's other contributions were spectroscopic observations of novae, the companion of Sirius, the comet Pons-Winnecke, and the eclipsed moon. He also made spectroscopic determinations of the rotation periods of Saturn, Uranus, and Neptune (the last two in collaboration with D. H. Menzel); the result for Neptune, published in 1928, is still the accepted value.

BIBLIOGRAPHY

I. ORIGINAL WORKS. Moore's most important writings are "Methods of Measurement and Reduction of Spectrograms for the Determination of Radial Velocities," in *Publications of the Astronomical Society of the Pacific*, **19** (1907), 13–26; "The Spectrographic Velocities of the Bright-Line Nebulae," in *Publications of the Lick Observatory*, **13** (1918), 75–186, written with W. W. Campbell; "Third Catalogue of Spectroscopic Binary Stars," in *Lick Observatory Bulletin*, **11** (1924), 141–185; "Radial Velocities of Stars Brighter than Visual Magnitude 5.51 As Determined at Mount Hamilton and Santiago," in *Publications of the Lick Observatory*, **16** (1928), written with W. W. Campbell; "The Crocker Eclipse Expedition of the Lick Observatory to Camptonville, California, April 28, 1930," in *Publications of the Astronomical Society of the Pacific*, **42** (1930), 131–144; "The Lick Observatory Crocker Eclipse Expedition to Fryeburg, Maine, August 31, 1932," *ibid.*, **44** (1932), 341–352; "A General Catalogue of the Radial Velocities of Stars, Nebulae and Clusters," in *Publications of the Lick Observatory*, **18** (1932); "Fourth Catalogue of Spectroscopic Binary Stars," in *Lick Observatory Bulletin*, **18** (1936), 1–37; and "Fifth Catalogue of Spectroscopic Binary Stars," *ibid.*, **20** (1948), 1–31, written with F. J. Neubauer. Moore also wrote numerous shorter items and survey papers for the *Lick Observatory Bulletin* and the *Publications of the Astronomical Society of the Pacific*.

II. SECONDARY LITERATURE. For biographical informa-

tion see R. G. Aitken, "Joseph Haines Moore: 1878–1949 —A Tribute," in *Publications of the Astronomical Society of the Pacific*, **61** (1949), 125–128; R. G. Aitken, C. D. Shane, R. J. Trumpler and W. H. Wright, "Joseph Haines Moore, 1878–1949," in *Popular Astronomy*, **57** (1949), 372–375; and F. J. Neubauer, "J. H. Moore—A Good Neighbor," in *Sky and Telescope*, **8** (1949), 197–198.

BRIAN G. MARSDEN

MOORE, WILLIAM (*fl. ca.* 1806–1823), *rocketry.*

Moore's origin and education are unknown. His writings and position as a mathematical instructor at the Royal Military Academy at Woolwich, England, suggest that he was influenced by Charles Hutton, professor of mathematics at the academy from 1773 to 1807. Moore was chosen as an assistant mathematical master in October 1806, Hutton being one of the three examiners on the selection board. By August 1807, Moore had advanced to the post of mathematical master. In July 1823 he left the academy because of a staff reduction.

Moore's first published writing was "Observations on the Problem Respecting the Radius of Curvature," in Nicholson's *Journal of Natural Philosophy* (1808). In 1810 he was prompted to investigate the ballistics of rockets when the Royal Danish Academy of Sciences offered a prize for the best paper describing the motion of rockets. Moore examined hypothetical rocket motion, both with and without air resistance, but did not submit a paper.

His theories on rockets first appeared in Nicholson's *Journal* for 1810 and 1811. In 1813 Moore published his collected findings as *A Treatise on the Motion of Rockets*. The world's first mathematical treatise on rocket dynamics, it had many shortcomings; and Moore admitted that lack of data had hindered his calculations. Nonetheless, he correctly recognized and demonstrated that Newton's third law of motion explained the principle of rocket motion. Moore was the first to consider rocket performance in terms other than range and altitude, and he arrived at calculations for thrust and specific impulse. He also suggested the use of the ballistic pendulum for a more accurate determination of performance.

BIBLIOGRAPHY

I. ORIGINAL WORKS. Moore's principal writings are "Observations on the Problem Respecting the Radius of Curvature," in *Journal of Natural Philosophy, Chemistry, and the Arts*, 2nd ser., **21** (1808), 256–259; "On the Penetration of Balls Into Uniform Resisting Substances," in

Tilloch's *Philosophical Magazine*, **36** (1810), 325–334, and in *Emporium of Arts and Sciences*, **1** (July 1812), 277–289; "On the Destruction of An Enemy's Fleet at Sea by Artillery," in *Journal of Natural Philosophy*, **28** (1811), 81–93, also published in French in *Bibliothèque britannique*, **48** (1811), 365–379; *Treatise on the Doctrine of Fluxations* (London, 1811); and *A Treatise on the Motion of Rockets: To Which Is Added An Essay on Naval Gunnery* (London, 1813).

II. SECONDARY LITERATURE. A note on Moore appears in *Journal of Natural Philosophy*, **27** (1810), 318. See also Harry Harper, *Dawn of the Space Age* (London, 1946), p. 19; J. G. von Hoyer, *System der Brandraketen* (Leipzig, 1827), pp. 55–58; B. Allerslev Jensen, "Fra Leipzig til London," in *Dansk Artilleri-Tidsskrift*, **49** (June 1959), 61–79; Jacques-Philippe Mérigon de Montgéry, "Traité des fusées de guerre," in *Annales maritimes et coloniales*, **26**, pt. 2 (1825), 576–580; and H. D. Turner, "Sir William Congreve and the Development of the War Rocket," in *Research* (London), **19** (Aug. 1961), 326–328.

FRANK H. WINTER

MORAT, JEAN-PIERRE (*b.* St.-Sorlin, Saône-et-Loire, France, 18 April 1846; *d.* La Roche-Vineuse, near St.-Sorlin, 25 July 1920), *physiology*.

Morat contributed to physiological knowledge primarily by his studies of what is now called the autonomic nervous system; in particular, he and Albert Dastre showed in 1880 that stimulation of the cervical portion of the sympathetic nerve led to vasodilation in the gums and hard palate of the dog. His subsequent research emphasized the general significance of vasodilator nerves in the regulation of organic function.

Morat studied at Lyons in the early 1870's and then in Paris, where he worked in Claude Bernard's laboratory at the Museum of Natural History and in 1873 received his medical degree from the Faculty of Medicine.

From 1873 to 1876 Morat served as the *chef des travaux anatomiques* for the medical school at Lyons. A year after the founding of a new Faculty of Medicine at Lille in 1875, he became the *chargé de cours* for physiology and assistant professor of the subject in 1878. He returned to Lyons in 1882 as professor of physiology at the Faculty of Medicine and Pharmacy, which had been established in 1877. He became an associate member of the Société de Biologie in 1906 and a correspondent of the medical and surgical section of the Academy of Sciences in 1916.

In 1899 Morat received the Academy's Lacaze Prize for his research career, which was dominated especially by the ideas and techniques of Bichat, Bernard, and Chauveau. In 1877 he had won the Academy's Montyon Prize in experimental physiology for his first significant research, which concerned muscle physiology.[1]

This work was performed with J. J. H. Toussaint in Chauveau's laboratory and depended on both the graphical recording techniques developed by Chauveau and Marey and the use of Chauveau's unipolar electrode. It clarified the analogy which had been drawn between induced tetanus and the voluntary contraction of skeletal muscle by showing that the two were comparable only when the tremors composing tetanus were perfectly fused.

Morat and his later, more renowned, collaborator, Dastre, began their joint study of the vasodilator nerves (1876–1882) in Chauveau's laboratory. They were among the first to employ simultaneous graphical recordings of arterial and venous pressures to study vasomotor action. Chauveau and Marey had previously used a similar method to study other aspects of circulation.

At the beginning of their study of the vasomotor nerves, Morat and Dastre assumed the inverse of what they are best known for having discovered: the vasodilatory effect of excitation of the cervical portion of the sympathetic nerve. In their attempt (1878) to resolve the question of whether the sciatic nerve had vasodilator properties, they used the cervical sympathetic nerve as an exemplar of a vasoconstrictor. They argued that since excitation of the sciatic had the same effect on vascular pressures as excitation of the cervical sympathetic, then the sciatic, like cervical sympathetic, must be a vasoconstrictor.

Two years later, however, Morat and Dastre announced that the cervical sympathetic was a vasodilator.[2] The reason for the change is unclear; but it seems to have resulted from interpreting the recent studies of other researchers in the light of views they already held, which were based on those of Bernard. In Bernard's view, vasodilation resulted from nervous inhibition or paralysis of vasoconstrictor nerves. On this basis Dastre and Morat had supposed that if vasodilator nerves were present, they were most likely to be found related to ganglia (where the inhibitory action would be localized), especially those of the sympathetic. At about the same time that they were studying the sciatic nerve, work by others had shown that branches of the submaxillary nerve caused dilation in vessels of certain parts of the face and that the submaxillary nerve's dilator fibers did not originate in the brain. Their expectation that vasodilators were related to ganglia probably led Dastre and Morat to suppose that the submaxillary dilator fibers arose at the cervical ganglia of the sympathetic and, hence, to test the cervical sympathetic to see whether it caused dilation in the specified regions of the face, which it did.

Morat's research frequently returned to topics related to vasodilation or to other functions mediated by the sympathetic system. For example, he collaborated with Maurice Doyon in demonstrating (1891) that sympathetic nerve fibers have an effect opposite to that of the ciliary nerve: they accommodate the lens of the eye for nearby objects.

In their study of the consumption of sugar by resting muscle (1892), Morat and E. Dufort used Bernard's chemical test for blood sugar to treat a problem that Bernard's work had suggested and that Chauveau had explicitly raised: the role of glycogen in the various organs of the body. This work led to a study of nervous control over liver glycogenesis (1894), which showed that liver glycolysis can be stimulated without changing the flow of blood through hepatic vessels and, thus, independently of its vasomotor nerves.

In Morat's later studies of vasodilation he rejected Bichat's view that had dominated his early thought about the sympathetic system: that the sympathetic system was independent of the cerebrospinal system and was the sole regulator of visceral organ function. In 1894 Morat expressed the view that vasodilation was localized neither in the spinal nor in the sympathetic trunk but was a property of certain nervous elements which compose both these trunks.

In rejecting Bichat's distinction Morat made no reference to the histological results which had led Gaskell to a similar conclusion a decade earlier. Rather, Morat had come to regard metabolic and functional behaviors as concurrent activities, elicited at the same time by the same fiber. For this reason there was no longer any motive for ascribing all "organic" vasomotor functions to a distinct nervous structure, the sympathetic trunk.

Morat's last significant research, performed with M. Petzetakis just before the beginning of World War I, showed that cardiac fibrillation can result from a disequilibration between cardiac excitor and inhibitor nerves, and that the rhythms of auricles and ventricles are mutually related but not in a totally dependent fashion.

NOTES

1. The report of the commission awarding the Lacaze Prize appears in *Comptes rendus de l'Académie des sciences*, **129** (1899), 1140–1144. The Montyon commission report is *ibid.*, **84** (1877), 848–851.

2. Dastre and Morat claimed that this result of work begun in 1876 was first announced to the Société de Biologie in 1878; but there are no citations to Morat in the Society's 1878 *Mémoires et comptes rendus*, and the note he alluded to seems to be one of a series submitted in 1880 and published in 1881. The error may have been part of an effort to avoid a priority dispute with Jolyet and Laffont, whose study of dilation in the facial region, published in 1878, may in fact have led immediately to the finding by Dastre and Morat.

BIBLIOGRAPHY

I. ORIGINAL WORKS. Morat published about 75 scientific papers, more than half of which were written in collaboration with other physiologists. Papers published prior to 1900 are indexed in the Royal Society's *Catalogue of Scientific Papers*, X, 843–844; XII, 184, 519; XVII, 342–343; and XVIII, 278.

Among the most important are "Variations de l'état électrique des muscles dans différents modes de contraction . . .," in *Archives de physiologie normale*, 2nd ser., **4** (1877), 156–182, written with H. Toussaint; "Sur l'expérience du grand sympathique cervical," in *Comptes rendus . . . de l'Académie des sciences*, **91** (1880), 393–395, written with A. Dastre; "Sur la fonction vasodilatatrice du nerf grand sympathique," in *Archives de physiologie*, **9** (1882), 177–236, 337–382, written with A. Dastre; "Le grand sympathique nerf de l'accommodation pour la vision des objets éloignés," in *Comptes rendus . . . de l'Académie des sciences*, **112** (1891), 1327–1329, written with M. Doyon; "Les fonctions vaso-motrices des racines postérieures," in *Archives de physiologie*, 5th ser., **4** (1892), 689–698; "Nerfs et centres inhibiteurs," *ibid.*, **6** (1894), 7–18; "Les nerfs glyco-sécréteurs," *ibid.*, 371–380, written with E. Dufort; and "Le système nerveux et la nutrition. Les nerfs thermiques. [Les nerfs trophiques.]," in *Revue scientifique*, 4th ser., **4** (1895), 487–495; **5** (1896), 193–199, 234–241.

In addition to papers indexed in the Royal Society's *Catalogue of Scientific Papers*, Morat published the following: "Réserve adipeuse de nature hivernale dans les ganglions spinaux de la grenouille," in *Mémoires de la Société de biologie*, **53** (1901), 473–474; "La réforme des études médicales," in *Revue scientifique*, 5th ser., **5** (1906), 524–526; "Les racines du système nerveux: Le mot et la chose," in *Archives internationales de physiologie . . .*, **8** (1909), 75–103; "Les variations de la formule sanguine chez les morphinomanes et les héroïnomanes au cours de désintoxication rapide par la méthode de Sollier," in *Mémoires de la Société de biologie*, **66** (1909), 1025–1027, written with Chartier; and three articles written with M. Petzetakis: "Production de la fibrillation des oreillettes par voie nerveuse, au moyen de l'excitation du pneumogastrique," *ibid.*, **77** (1914), 222–224; "Fibrillation auriculaire et ventriculaire produite par voie nerveuse," *ibid.*, 377–379; and "Production expérimentale d'extrasystoles ventriculaires retrogrades, et de rythme inverse, par inversion de la conduction des excitations dans le coeur," in *Comptes rendus . . . de l'Académie des sciences*, **163** (1916), 969–971.

Morat also published with A. Dastre a book-length account of their study of the vasomotor system: *Recherches expérimentales sur le système nerveux vasomoteur* (Paris, 1884). With Maurice Doyon he wrote *Traité de physiologie*, 5 vols. (Paris, 1899–1918). Vol. II, Morat's treatment of the nervous system, was translated into English and published under the title *Physiology of the Nervous System* (London, 1906).

II. SECONDARY LITERATURE. The longest published account which I have been able to locate of Morat's life is a paragraph in *Biographisches Lexikon der hervorragenden Ärzte, 1800–1930*, II (Munich, 1962), 1065.

Background for Morat's work on vasodilation is in Donal Sheehan, "Discovery of the Autonomic Nervous System," in *Archives of Neurology and Psychiatry*, **35** (1936), 1081–1115, esp. 1102–1105; and E. A. Schafer, ed., *Textbook of Physiology*, II (London, 1898), 71, 130–136, 618, 626, 659–661.

MICHAEL GROSS

MORAY (or **MURREY** or **MURRAY**), **SIR ROBERT** (*b.* Scotland, 1608 [?]; *d.* London, England, 4 July 1673), *chemistry, metallurgy, mineralogy, natural history*.

Moray was the first president of the Royal Society of London and contributed significantly to its survival and growth during the early years. Little is known of his early life. He was born between 10 March 1608 and 10 March 1609 and was the elder of two sons. His grandfather was Robert Moray of Abercairney. His father, Sir Mungo Moray of Craigie, in Perthshire, married a daughter of George Halket of Pitfirran.

As a soldier, statesman, and diplomat, Moray played an important part in the politics of England, France, and Scotland. He served in the Scottish regiment which joined the French army under Colonel Hepburn in 1633, was Richelieu's agent in England during the Puritan Revolution, was knighted by Charles I on 10 January 1643, and became a colonel in the Scottish Foot Guards in April 1645. In the autumn of 1645 Moray went to London as political mediary for the Scots. He later served as royal secretary to Charles I and as confidential agent to the duke of Hamilton. While engaged by John Maitland (1616–1682), duke of Lauderdale, in 1648 to negotiate with the Prince of Wales, Moray befriended the future Charles II. In 1651 he was a justice clerk and privy councillor in Scotland.

Moray's political life has an indirect relationship to his importance in the history of science. His title, which lent prestige, and his close friendship with Charles II, which aided in obtaining a charter for the Royal Society, may have occasioned his election as first president of the Society. He was also religious,

a gentleman of high character, and was well-liked and respected by his colleagues. Furthermore, he was very enthusiastic about the group's scientific interests. Besides his terms as president, Moray served frequently on the council and on numerous committees and carried on a vast correspondence to procure scientific information. He was fluent in French, German, Dutch, and Italian and strengthened the international character of the Society through his powerful connections and many foreign correspondents. He often served as a liaison for men of science in England, Scotland, America, and on the Continent.

Moray's versatility and utilitarian view of science are reflected in his knowledge of trades and industrial processes, such as fishing, lumbering, mining, shipbuilding, windmills, watermills, magnetism, and mineralogy. Chronometry was a major interest; at times he offered advice to Huygens. When Alexander Bruce and Huygens argued over patent rights to the pendulum clock for use at sea, Moray, often a peacemaker when disputes arose, proposed that the patent be taken in the name of the Royal Society.

It appears that Moray earned some renown in chemistry, although no lasting influence can be detected. Anthony Wood recorded that Thomas Vaughan, who became eminent in medical chemistry, served in London under the patronage of "that noted Chymist Sir *Rob. Murrey* or *Moray* Kt." Metallurgy and pharmaceutical preparations were enduring interests throughout Moray's life; and although nothing is known of his formal education, he wrote to Bruce in 1657 that he was "so far advanced towards the gown as to be already about half an Apothecary" and "I was as long at the Anatomy school as the Chimicall."

Moray's direct contributions to science are difficult to assess, but his unabated interest in and work on behalf of the Royal Society and its scientific developments from 1660 until his death in 1673 were perhaps unequaled.

BIBLIOGRAPHY

I. ORIGINAL WORKS. According to Royal Society records (*Letter Books*, 16 and 26 Sept. 1665), Moray worked on a history of masonry. Sprat (see below), pp. 257–258, recorded the title, but the work is not preserved in the Archives of the Royal Society. Some of Moray's papers and letters are listed in Sir Arthur Church, *The Royal Society. Some Account of the "Classified Papers" in the Archives. With an Index of Authors* (Oxford, 1907). An MS catalog, also compiled by Church, "The Royal Society 'Classified Papers' in the Archives Titles and Authors" (1907) (Church MS) includes several references to Moray not in the printed volume. Other Royal Society archival sources include *The Letter Books* (LBC), *The Register Books* (RBC), *Boyle's Letters* (BL), and *Miscellaneous Manuscripts* (MM).

Among his writings are "Relation Concerning Barnacles" (RBC.1.19); "A Copie of the Letter Sent to Paris to Mr. de Monmort" (LBC.1.1); "An Account of Glass Dropps" (RBC.1.57); "Clarke, Dr. Observations on ye Humble & Sensible Plants in Mr. Chaffin's Garden in St. James' Parke, Made August 9, 1661. Present the Lord Brouncker, Sr. *Robert Murrey*, Dr. Wilkins, W(?) Evelin, Dr. Goddard, Dr. Henshaw, Dr. Clarke" [Read 21 Aug. 1661] (Church MS), "The Description of the Island Hirta" (RBC.1.97); "Account of the Sounding of the Depth of the Sea Between Portsmouth & the Isle of Wight," written with Brouncker [FRS] (Church MS); "Sr R, Moray's Letter to Sr Phil. Vernatti in Java, by Order of the R. Society" (LBC.1.79); "An Account of an Echo" (RBC. 1.263); "The Way How Malt is Made in Scotland" (RBC. 1.306); "Sr Robert Moray's Story of Persons Killed With Subterranean Damps" (RBC.1.319).

Additional writings are "Of the Minerall of Liege Yeilding Both Brimstone and Vitrioll and the Way of Extracting Them Out of it Used at Liege" (RBC.2.35); "The Measure of the Parts of a Gyant Child Borne in Scotland" (RBC.2.50); "An Account Englished Out of French of an Unusuall Way of Cutting the Stone of the Bladder Practiced by a Frenchman" (RBC.2.72); "Of a Spring Near Chertsey" (Church MS); "Of the Way Used Upon the Coast of Coromandell of Cooling of Drincks by Exposing Them to the Heat of the Sun" (RBC.2.50); Murray to Sir P. Vernatti, 21 Sept. 1664 (LBC.1.237); "On a Tumulus in Lord Seamore's Garden at Marlborough" (Church MS); "Directions for Observing the Conjunction of Mercury With the Sun" (Church MS); "Observations Made in Their Late Excursion Into ye Country," written with Sir P. Neil and Dr. Wren [FFRS] (Church MS); "Description in German With Drawing, of a Comet of January, 1663/4" [Read 9 March 1663 (1664); comm. by R. M.].

See also "An Extract of a Letter of Mr. Moray" (LBC. 1.280); "Eclipse as Observed by ——, on June 22, 1666," written with F. Willughby *et al.* [FFRS] (Church MS); "A Fair Copy of No. 13, With Diagram on a Folded Leaf" [Read 27 June 1666]; "Letter of 30 Jan 1667/8 to Him . . . From the Counsell of the Royal Society . . . Solliciting Contribution in Scotland for Building a Colledge" (LBC.2.160); "Calendarium ecclesiasticum et astronomicum, cum tabulis et figuris zodiaci." In the folding form, of the first half of the fifteenth century, on vellum. The *homo signorum* and the *homo venarum* appear to be deficient. Presented by Moray (Church MS); Murray to R. Boyle, 15 Jul. 1672 (BL4.75); "Experiments Propounded by Sir Robert Moray and Recommended to Dr. Power" (RBC.1.167); no origin, undated, to the grand duke of Tuscany (MM.3.119), credited to Moray; "Sounding Between Portsmouth & the Isle of Wight With the Wooden Globe & Lead," written with Brouncker (Church MS).

Some of the papers were published in the *Philosophical*

Transactions of the Royal Society without clear authorship; e.g., Moray suggested several experiments to Newton in "Some Experiments Propos'd in Relation to Mr. Newton's Theory of Light, Printed in Numb. 80; Together With the Observations Made Thereupon by the Author of That Theory; Communicated in a Letter of His From Cambridge, April 13. 1672," **7** (1672), 4059–4062. Although Moray is not cited as the author of the paper, Newton in a letter to Oldenburg indicates that he was (Rigaud, II, 324).

II. SECONDARY LITERATURE. The major source of information about Moray is Alexander Robertson, *The Life of Sir Robert Moray, Soldier, Statesman and Man of Science* (London, 1922); it does not include a bibliography of Moray's writings, but some of his work and scientific interests are discussed. Other biographical sketches, which add little, include D. C. Martin, "Sir Robert Moray, F.R.S. (1608?–1673)," in *Notes and Records. Royal Society of London*, tercentenary no., **15** (1960), 239–250; Agnes Mary Clerke, *Dictionary of National Biography*, XIII (1967–1968), 1298–1299, under "Murray." An obituary appeared in Thomas Birch, *History of the Royal Society of London*, 4 vols. (London, 1756–1757), III, 113–114. See also John Aubrey, *Brief Lives*, A. Clark, ed., 2 vols. (Oxford, 1898); *Bishop Burnet's History of His Own Time*, Osmund Airy, ed., 2 vols. (London, 1840), *passim*; Patrick Gordon, *A Shorte Abridgement of Britane's Distemper* (Aberdeen, 1844), pp. 5–6; L. C. Martin, ed., *The Works of Henry Vaughan*, 2 vols. (Oxford, 1914), *passim*; W. Shaw, *Knights of England* (London, 1906), *passim*; Thomas Sprat, *History of the Royal Society of London*, 2nd ed. (London, 1702), *passim*; T. Thomson, *History of the Royal Society From Its Institution to the End of the Eighteenth Century* (London, 1812), *passim*; C. R. Weld, *A History of the Royal Society With Memoirs of the Presidents*, 2 vols. (London, 1848), *passim*; Anthony Wood, *Athenae Oxonienses*, 3rd ed., 5 vols. (London, 1813–1820), *passim*; and Dudley Wright, *England's Masonic Pioneers* (London, 1925), *passim*.

Two helpful general articles are Marie Boas Hall, "Sources for the History of the Royal Society in the Seventeenth Century," in *History of Science*, **5** (1966), 62–76; and R. K. Bluhm, "A Guide to the Archives of the Royal Society and to Other Manuscripts in Its Possession," in *Notes and Records. Royal Society of London*, **12** (Aug. 1956), 21–39.

For additional information relating to Moray's scientific interests and his activities in the Royal Society, see the *Journal Books, Council Minutes, Minutes of Meetings of Committees*, and the *Kincardine Papers* (transcript, MS246) in the archives; *Oeuvres complètes de Christiaan Huygens*, 22 vols. (The Hague, 1888–1950), *passim*; S. P. Rigaud and S. J. Rigaud, eds., *Correspondence of Scientific Men of the Seventeenth Century*, 2 vols. (Oxford, 1841–1842), *passim*; and A. R. Hall and M. B. Hall, eds., *The Correspondence of Henry Oldenburg*, 8 vols. (Madison, Wis., 1965–   ), *passim*.

Most sources relating to his career in the French army are in the archives at Paris. For MS collections see

Robertson (above), pp. 201–203; sources of a political nature include Osmund Airy, ed., *Lauderdale Papers*, 3 vols. (Westminster, 1884–1885), *passim*; J. G. Fotheringham, ed., *The Diplomatic Correspondence of Jean de Montereul and the Brothers de Bellièvre*, 2 vols. (Edinburgh, 1898–1899), *passim*; and Samuel R. Gardiner, ed., *The Hamilton Papers; Being Selections From Original Letters in the Possession of His Grace the Duke of Hamilton and Brandon, Relating to the Years 1638–1650* (Westminster, 1880).

BARBARA ROSS

MORE, HENRY (*b.* Grantham, Lincolnshire, England, October 1614; *d.* Cambridge, England, 1 September 1687), *philosophy*, *theology*.

The youngest child of Alexander More, a fairly prosperous gentleman and several times mayor of Grantham, Henry More was educated at Grantham School, Eton, and Christ's College, Cambridge, from which he graduated B.A. in 1636. In 1639 he received the M.A., took orders, and was appointed a fellow of his college—which position he held, refusing preferment, all his life. More became doctor of divinity in 1660 and was elected fellow of the Royal Society on 25 May 1664. (He had been among the original fellows under the first charter but was omitted when the Society was refounded.)

In theology More was a moderate latitudinarian, known for piety and an almost saintly nature. He wrote extensively against sectarians and enthusiasts, for their uncharitable doctrinal wrangling and their depreciation of reason in religion, and against the Roman Catholic Church, on the usual contemporary grounds. He concerned himself particularly with the interpretation of prophetic and apocalyptic Scriptures.

In the history of philosophy More is counted among the Cambridge Platonists. His "Platonism" was rather vague and highly eclectic; its basic themes were those of the middle Platonists and Neoplatonists, and he found them in a great variety of ancient thinkers, including Democritus, Hermes Trismegistus, and Moses. The central point is the primacy of spirit over matter. Dissatisfaction with the scholastic fare of his undergraduate studies led More to turn briefly to the ascetic-mystical side of Neoplatonism: true knowledge requires spiritual purification, and devotion is more important than learning. Both doctrines were soon greatly moderated, as his bent for philosophy (including natural philosophy) reasserted itself. Under the influence of the *Theologia Germanica*, More came to emphasize moral goodness over asceticism; and the "spiritual purification" idea had little real effect on his mature writings, unless in a certain tendency

to overrate the rational perspicuity of arguments which have edifying conclusions.

A factor in More's return to philosophy was his discovery, sometime before 1647, of Descartes, whose writings seemed to show how to combine a scientific interest in nature with a primary concern for vindicating the reality of God and immortal human souls. This suited More admirably: his interest in the new experimental philosophy was genuine (he was the only fellow of the Royal Society among the Cambridge Platonists), but he conceived his main philosophical mission to be the refutation of mechanistic materialism.

Appropriately, More's first major work was *An Antidote Against Atheisme* (1652), one of the most prominent early responses to Thomas Hobbes. The first part of this three-part work is primarily an elaboration of the ontological argument as found in Descartes. The second part enumerates a great range of natural phenomena that can be understood only as showing a divine providence. This section provided the structure and core of John Ray's *Wisdom of God Manifested in the Works of Creation*, and thus considerably influenced the subsequent tradition of scientifically elaborated teleological arguments. Two points should be noted, however. First, relatively little of More's argumentation really depends on contemporary science; the majority of his examples had been, or could have been, used in antiquity. Second, the comparison with machinery (such as the watch) is not made. The emphasis is, rather, on the usefulness to man or other creatures of various features of nature, and on phenomena which show the working of immaterial substances, such as an unintelligent "spirit of nature" which can be invoked to account for botches in nature as well as for phenomena (such as gravity and the formation of animals) which cannot be explained mechanically. The relation between this "spirit of nature" and the intelligent Designer remains unclear, but just showing the reality of spiritual agents is what More really cares about. Thus it is perfectly in accord with his design when he devotes the third part of his treatise to stories of witches, hauntings, and so on. These direct empirical evidences of the activities of spirits should convince those on whom the arguments of the first two sections are lost.

More's opposition to mechanism eventually led him to a repudiation (in large part) of Descartes and a sad skirmish with Robert Boyle. In his early enthusiasm he had been instrumental in introducing Cartesian philosophy to England; but an unsatisfactory correspondence with Descartes, further reflection on his metaphysical principles, and observation of the path taken by Spinoza and other Cartesians convinced More that there were great dangers in Cartesianism. More was persuaded that to *be,* a thing must be *somewhere;* Descartes's identification of matter with extension thus seemed to exclude spirits (including God) from reality. Therefore, in *The Immortality of the Soul* (1659) and *Enchiridion metaphysicum* (1671) More argued at length that spirits are extended. The defining characteristic of body is not extension but impenetrability and physical divisibility ("discerpibility"); spirits, More deduced, are by definition "indiscerpible" and capable of penetrating themselves, other spirits, and matter. He adds that bodies are passive and spirits are capable of initiating activity. If spirits are extended, God in particular is (infinitely) extended. More does not flinch from this consequence but, listing a long series of properties predicable both of God and of space, concludes that absolute space is an attribute of the substance, God; it is the medium in which God acts upon bodies.

The Immortality of the Soul is actually an elaborate treatise on the nature, kinds, and habits of spirits—by far More's most systematic work—in which many doctrines of Descartes and others are criticized. It defies summary.

More consistently argued that gravity, magnetism, and various of Boyle's experimental results in hydrostatics could not be accounted for mechanistically. In the *Enchiridion metaphysicum* he treated the latter point in detail, attempting with physical as well as metaphysical arguments to refute Boyle's interpretation of his own experiments. Boyle found it necessary to demolish More's efforts, carefully adding that one could be a great scholar without being a good hydrostatician. He patiently corrected More's mistakes, pointed out that a mechanical explanation is one based on the laws of mechanics and need not (for instance) specify the cause of gravity, and suggested that the watchmaker version of the design argument is more effective than any that resort to such dubious entities as the spirit of nature. More was rather hurt but eager to maintain their friendship. Unlike Descartes, the Royal Society and its virtuosos were never even partially repudiated by More, who distinguished sharply between their "experimental philosophy" and the "mechanical philosophy" he combated.

The exchange with Boyle shows that More's grasp of the new natural philosophy was limited. His interest was genuine, but he was himself no virtuoso. His main contributions lay in introducing generations of students to Descartes, in lending to the Royal Society the prestige of his great reputation for learning

and piety, and (arguably) in his influence upon Newton. The nature and extent of that influence are hard to assess. It appears that More and Newton were well acquainted and perhaps close. More left Newton a funeral ring; a letter survives in which he good-humoredly reports to a friend that Newton stubbornly clings to a misinterpretation of a passage in the Apocalypse, which More thought he had corrected; Newton informs a correspondent that he had "engaged Dr More to be of" a "Philosophick Meeting" then proposed at Cambridge. E. A. Burtt and A. Koyré have argued powerfully that More influenced Newton's views on space and on such matters as the (immaterial) cause of gravity. Certainly there are interesting parallels; other evidence for or against direct influence is, unfortunately, scarce.

BIBLIOGRAPHY

I. ORIGINAL WORKS. *Philosophical Writings of Henry More,* Flora I. MacKinnon, ed. (New York, 1925), contains a useful selection, with intro., extensive notes, and a bibliography of works by and about More. For more recent bibliographical information see Aharon Lichtenstein, *Henry More: The Rational Theology of a Cambridge Platonist* (Cambridge, Mass., 1962).

II. SECONDARY LITERATURE. Marjorie Nicolson, ed., *Conway Letters* (New Haven, 1930), has biographical information as well as letters. More's views and their relation to those of Descartes and Newton are discussed by Edwin A. Burtt, *The Metaphysical Foundations of Modern Physical Science* (Garden City, N.Y., 1955), esp. 135–148; and Alexandre Koyré, *From the Closed World to the Infinite Universe* (Baltimore, 1957), esp. 110–154, 190. On More's relation to Hobbes, see Samuel I. Mintz, *The Hunting of Leviathan* (Cambridge, 1962), esp. 80–95; and on his relation to Boyle, see Robert A. Greene, "Henry More and Robert Boyle on the Spirit of Nature," in *Journal of the History of Ideas,* **23** (1962), 451–474. Also of interest are C. A. Staudenbaur, "Galileo, Ficino, and Henry More's *Psychathanasia,*" in *Journal of the History of Ideas,* **29** (1968), 565–578; and C. Webster, "Henry More and Descartes: Some New Sources," in *British Journal for the History of Science,* **4** (1969), 359–377.

WILLIAM H. AUSTIN

MORGAGNI, GIOVANNI BATTISTA (*b.* Forlì, Italy, 25 February 1682; *d.* Padua, Italy, 5 December 1771), *medicine, anatomy, pathological anatomy.*

Morgagni was the son of Fabrizio Morgagni and Maria Tornielli. After completing his early studies at Forlì, in 1698 he went to Bologna, where he attended the university, taking the degree in philosophy and medicine in 1701. His principal university teachers were Antonio Maria Valsalva and Ippolito Francesco Albertini, both former pupils of Malpighi, who trained him in Malpighi's methods and in the rational medicine that follows from them. Having received his degree, Morgagni remained in Bologna to work in the three hospitals of that city and carry out further anatomical studies with Valsalva.

Morgagni was admitted to the Accademia degli Inquieti in 1699 and became its head in 1704. He reformed the academy on the model of the Paris Académie Royale des Sciences and accepted an invitation to hold meetings in the mansion belonging to Luigi Ferdinandino Marsili, thus paving the way for its incorporation into the Istituto delle Scienze that was founded by Marsili in 1714. It was to the Inquieti that Morgagni in 1705 communicated his *Adversaria anatomica prima*, which he also dedicated to them. The *Adversaria* was published in Bologna in 1706 and earned Morgagni international fame as an anatomist.

At the beginning of 1707 Morgagni moved to Venice, where he stayed through May 1709. Venice offered him the opportunity to study chemistry with Gian Girolamo Zanichelli, to investigate the anatomical structure of the great fishes, and to secure a number of rare and choice books. He also conducted a number of dissections of human cadavers with Gian Domenico Santorini, who was at that time dissector and lector in anatomy at the Venetian medical college. In June 1709 Morgagni returned to Forlì, where he practiced medicine with great success. In September 1711 he was called to the second chair of theoretical medicine at Padua University; the chair had become vacant when Antonio Vallisnieri was promoted to the first chair, following the death of Domenico Guglielmini. Morgagni delivered his inaugural lecture, *Nova institutionum medicarum idea*, on 17 March 1712. He was appointed to the first chair of anatomy at Padua in September 1715 and began teaching that subject on 21 January 1716. He held this post until his death. Morgagni's teaching was always clear and gave the impression of a perpetually fresh mind.

The *Adversaria anatomica prima* is a series of researches on fine anatomy conducted according to the tradition established by Malpighi, although Morgagni showed greater caution in the use of the microscope and in making anatomical preparations. Morgagni's profoundly inquiring intellect is apparent in even this early work. Despite the modesty of its title—"Notes on Anatomy"—Morgagni's book actually records a whole succession of discoveries regarding minute organic mechanisms, including the glands of the trachea, of the male urethra, and of the female genitals. These represent new contributions to the mechanical interpretation of the structure of the organism, as do the descriptions contained in Morgagni's five subsequent *Adversaria* (1717–1719), *Epistolae anatomicae duae* (published in Leiden by Boerhaave in 1728), and *Epistolae anatomicae duodeviginti* on Valsalva's writings (1740).

Morgagni's most important work, however, is his *De sedibus et causis morborum per anatomen indagatis* of 1761. This book grew out of a concept of Malpighi, which Morgagni then developed into a major work. The concept may be stated simply as the notion that the organism can be considered as a mechanical complex. Life therefore represents the sum of the harmonious operation of organic machines, of which many of the most delicate and minute are discernible, hidden within the recesses of the organs, only through microscopic examination.

Like inorganic machines, organic machines are subject to deterioration and breakdowns that impair their operation. Such failures occur at the most minute levels, but, given the limits of technique and instrumentation, it is possible to investigate them only at the macroscopic level, by examining organic lesions on the dissecting table. These breakdowns give rise to functional impairments that produce disharmony in the economy of the organism; their clinical manifestations are proportional to their location and nature.

This thesis is implicit in the very title *De sedibus et causis morborum per anatomen indagatis*. In this book Morgagni reasons that a breakdown at some point of the mechanical complex of the organism must be both the seat and cause of a disease or, rather, of its clinical manifestations, which may be conceived of as functional impairments and investigated anatomically. Morgagni's conception of etiology also takes into account what he called "external" causes, including environmental and psychological factors, among them the occupational ones suggested to Morgagni by Ramazzini.

The parallels that exist between anatomical lesion and clinical symptom served Morgagni as the basis for his "historiae anatomico-medicae," the case studies from which he constructed the *De sedibus*. There had, to be sure, been earlier collections of case histories, in particular Théophile Bonet's *Sepulchretum* (1679), but Bonet's work was, as René Laënnec wrote of it, an "undigested and incoherent compilation," while the special merit of Morgagni's work lies in its synthesis of case materials with the insights provided by his own anatomical investigations. In his book Morgagni made careful evaluations of anatomic-medical histories drawn exhaustively from the existing literature. In addition, he describes a great number of previously unpublished cases, including both those that he had himself observed in sixty years of anatomical investigation and those collected by his immediate predecessors, especially Valsalva, whose posthumous papers Morgagni meticulously edited and commented upon. The case histories collected in the *De sedibus* therefore represent the work of an entire school of anatomists, beginning with Malpighi, then extending through his pupils Valsalva and Albertini to Morgagni himself.

Morgagni may thus be considered to be the founder of pathological anatomy. This work was, in turn, developed by Baillie, who classified organic lesions as types (1793); Auenbrugger and Laënnec, who recognized organic lesions in the living subject (1761 and 1819, respectively); Bichat, who found the pathological site to be in the tissue, rather than the organ (1800); and Virchow, who traced the pathology from the tissue to the cell (1858).

BIBLIOGRAPHY

I. Original Works. Morgagni's writings include *Adversaria anatomica prima* (Bologna, 1706); *Nova institutionum medicarum idea* (Padua, 1712); *Adversaria anatomica altera et tertia* (Padua, 1717); *Adversaria anatomica quarta, quinta et sexta* (Padua, 1719); *Epistolae anatomicae duae* (Leiden, 1728); *Epistolae anatomicae duodeviginti ad scripta pertinentes celeberrimi viri A. M. Valsalvae* (Venice, 1740); *De sedibus et causis morborum per anatomen indagatis* (Venice, 1761); *Opuscula miscellanea* (Venice, 1763); *Opera omnia* (Venice, 1764); and *Opera postuma* (Rome, 1964–1969), vol. I, *Le autobiografie*, and vols. II–IV, *Lezioni di medicina teorica*.

A bibliography is Renato Zanelli, "Catalogo ragionato delle edizioni Morgagnane in ordine cronologico," in *Le onoranze a G. B. Morgagni, Forlì, 24 maggio 1931–IX* (Siena, 1931), 137–147.

II. Secondary Literature. Bibliographies are Carlo Fiorentini, *Giovanni Battista Morgagni: Primo saggio di bibliografia sintetica* (Bologna, 1930); and Loris Premuda, "Versuch einer Bibliographie mit Anmerkungen über das Leben und die Werke von G. B. Morgagni," in Markwart Michler, ed. and trans., *Sitz und Ursachen der Krankheiten* (Bern–Stuttgart, 1967), 163–195.

More recent works include Luigi Belloni, "Aus dem Briefwechsel von G. B. Morgagni mit L. Schröck und J. F. Baier," in *Nova acta leopoldina*, **36** (1970), 107–139; "Lettere del 1761 fra D. Cotugno e G. B. Morgagni," in *Physis*, **12** (1970), 415–423; "Contributo all'epistolario Boerhaave-Morgagni. L'edizione delle Epistolae anatomicae duae, Leida 1728," *ibid.*, **13** (1971), 81–109; "L'epistolario Morgagni–Réaumur alla Biblioteca Civica di Forlì," in *Gesnerus*, **29** (1972), 225–254; "L'opera di Giambattista Morgagni: dalla strutturazione meccanica dell'or-

ganismo vivente all'anatomia patologica," in *Simposi clinici*, **9** (1972), I–VIII; and in *Morgagni*, **4** (1971), 71–80; and "G. B. Morgagni und die Bedeutung seines 'De sedibus et causis morborum per anatomen indagatis,' " in Erna Lesky and Adam Wandruzka, eds., *Gerard van Swieten und seine Zeit* (Vienna–Cologne–Graz, 1973), 128–136. See also Giuseppe Ongaro, "La biblioteca di Giambattista Morgagni," in *Quaderni per la storia dell'Università di Padova*, **3** (1970), 113–129.

Luigi Belloni

MORGAN, CONWY LLOYD (*b.* London, England, 6 February 1852; *d.* Hastings, England, 6 March 1936), *comparative psychology, philosophy*.

Lloyd Morgan, as he was usually called, was a pioneer of animal psychology and an outstanding contributor to the evolutionary understanding of animal behavior. He was the second son of James Arthur Morgan, a solicitor, and received his early education at the Royal Grammar School, Guildford. When he was seventeen he entered the School of Mines at the Royal College of Science in London, intending to become a mining engineer. His progress was brilliant and at the same time he studied philosophy and biology. After a spell of traveling in the Americas he worked under T. H. Huxley, who influenced him profoundly. From 1878 to 1883 he taught physical sciences, English literature, and constitutional history at the Diocesan College of Rondebosch, South Africa. On his return to England Lloyd Morgan took the chair of geology and zoology at University College, Bristol, and stayed there for the rest of his professional career. In 1887 he was elected principal of the college and when a university charter was granted in 1909 he became the first vice-chancellor, although he held the position for only a few months. On resigning from it he returned to his studies as professor of psychology and ethics. He retired in 1919. In 1899 he became the first fellow of the Royal Society to be elected for work in psychology. He was also the first president of the psychological section of the British Association (Edinburgh, 1921); in 1910 he received the honorary D.Sc. from Bristol University. He married Emily Charlotte Maddock, the daughter of a vicar, and had two sons.

Lloyd Morgan's academic activity comprised work in geology and general science, comparative psychology, and philosophy. His geological writings include *Water and Its Teachings* (1882) and *Facts Around Us* (1884). He also wrote introductions to books on the geology of the Bristol region. His chief accomplishments, however, lie in the area of comparative psychology. Lloyd Morgan extended the work of G. J. Romanes and, together with E. L. Thorndike of the United States, helped to establish modern animal psychology. He was one of the first psychologists to recognize the need for an experimental as well as an observational approach to learning. Instead of using casual, recorded observations (the "anecdotal method" of Romanes), Lloyd Morgan resorted to rigorously controlled experiments.

Like Romanes, Lloyd Morgan relied on the concept of continuity in evolution as a justification for comparative psychology. He argued that because mind evolved from a lower to a higher mental state, the existence of the latter means that all others below it in the evolutionary scale also exist. To fathom the minds of animals, therefore, it is necessary to proceed from the lowest and simplest to the highest and most complex forms, rather than assuming human mental processes for all animals. A dictum embodying this basic prerequisite, "a law of parsimony," is now known as "Lloyd Morgan's canon." It states that "in no case is an animal activity to be interpreted as the outcome of the exercise of a higher psychical faculty, if it can be fairly interpreted as the outcome of his exercise of one which stands lower in the psychological scale" (*An Introduction to Comparative Psychology*, p. 59). This was a salutary warning; like his insistence that new levels of adaptive response are not necessarily the sum of simpler processes, it is still useful to recall.

Lloyd Morgan's literary output was astonishing. His experimental work, although not extensive, was nonetheless characterized by precise observations and vivid accounts of behavior. He advanced extremely cautious interpretations concerning instinctive behavior and its relationship to intelligence, and these appeared in *Animal Life and Intelligence* (1890–1891), *Animal Sketches* (1891), *An Introduction to Comparative Psychology* (1895), and *Animal Behavior* (1900). A more detailed consideration is in *Instinct and Experience* (1912). No one has written with more sense about the animal mind than Lloyd Morgan and although there is some disharmony and ambivalence in his writings, his contribution to psychology, especially in the area of methodology, is nevertheless important.

During this same period Lloyd Morgan published books on general biology and psychology; his influence spread to the United States, where he lectured in the 1890's.

Following his retirement Lloyd Morgan became primarily concerned with general philosophy and metaphysical speculation. He developed the theory of "emergent evolution," which maintained that evolution is not a steady, continuous process and that during it new properties suddenly emerge at certain levels of complexity. He developed this theory in a number of works—*Emergent Evolution* (1923), *Life, Mind and Spirit* (1926), *Mind at the Crossways* (1929), *The Animal Mind* (1930), and *The Emergence of Novelty* (1933).

BIBLIOGRAPHY

I. ORIGINAL WORKS. Lloyd Morgan published a great number of articles in journals of psychology and philosophy and numerous books based upon them. His works include *Water and Its Teachings in Chemistry, Physics and Physiography. A Suggestive Handbook* (London, 1882); *Facts Around Us: Simple Readings in Inorganic Science; with Experiments* (London, 1884); *Springs of Conduct; an Essay in Evolution* (London, 1885); *Animal Biology. An Elementary Textbook* (London, 1887; 2nd ed., 1889); *Animal Life and Intelligence* (London, 1890–1891); *Animal Sketches* (London, n.d. [1891], 1893); *Psychology for Teachers* (London, [1894], new ed., 1906); *An Introduction to Comparative Psychology* (London, 1895; 2nd ed., 1904); *Habit and Instinct* (London, 1896); *Animal Behavior* [rev. version of *Animal Life and Intelligence*] (London, 1900); *The Interpretation of Nature* (Bristol, 1905); *Instinct and Experience* (London, 1912); *Eugenics and Environment* (London, 1919); *Emergent Evolution* (London, 1923); *Life, Mind, and Spirit* (London, 1926); *Mind at the Crossways* (London, 1929); and *The Emergence of Novelty* (London, 1933).

II. SECONDARY LITERATURE. On the development of Lloyd Morgan's thought, especially concerning philosophic topics, see C. Murchison, ed., *A History of Psychology in Autobiography*, II (Worcester, Mass., 1932), 237–264. The best obituary notices are G. C. G., "Professor C. Lloyd Morgan 1852–1936," in *British Journal of Psychology*, **27** (1936), 1–3, with portrait; J. H. Parsons, "Conwy Lloyd Morgan 1852–1936," in *Obituary Notices of Fellows of the Royal Society of London*, **2** (1936–1938), 25–27, with portrait; and *Dictionary of National Biography 1931–1940*. There is an excellent account of Lloyd Morgan's contributions to psychology and philosophy in L. S. Hearnshaw, *A Short History of British Psychology 1840–1940* (London, 1964), 96–100. Briefer assessments are E. G. Boring, *A History of Experimental Psychology*, 2nd ed. (New York, 1957), 472–476 and 497–498; R. Watson, *The Great Psychologists* (Philadelphia, 1963), 296–298; and R. J. Herrnstein and E. G. Boring, eds., *A Source Book in the History of Psychology* (Cambridge, Mass., 1965), 462–468, which incorporates pp. 47–59 of Lloyd Morgan's *An Introduction to Comparative Psychology*.

EDWIN CLARKE

MORGAN, HERBERT ROLLO (*b.* Medford, Minnesota, 21 March 1875; *d.* Washington, D.C., 11 June 1957), *astronomy*.

Morgan was the son of Henry D. and Olive Sabre Smith Morgan. He received the B.A. from the

University of Virginia in 1899 and the Ph.D. in 1901. On 25 May 1904 he married Fannie Evelyn Wallis; they had one daughter. Morgan was a member of the American Astronomical Society (vice-president 1940–1942), American Geophysical Union, International Astronomical Union, American Association for the Advancement of Science (vice-president 1935–1936), and the Washington Academy of Science. He was president of the Commission on Meridian Astronomy of the International Astronomical Union from 1938 to 1948 and associate editor of *Astronomical Journal* from 1942 to 1948. He received the Watson Medal of the National Academy of Sciences in 1952 for his achievements in fundamental astronomy.

As a child Morgan suffered from an asthmatic condition, and at the age of nine to avoid the rigors of Minnesota winters his mother took him to Tennessee. He obtained his early education in a country school there whenever his bouts with asthma allowed him to attend. This intermittent schooling was supplemented by instruction at home under the guidance of his mother. When Morgan entered the University of Virginia, his primary interests were mathematics and astronomy. After one year, however, he had to withdraw in order to support his mother, who was growing old. At the university he had met Ormond Stone, director of the Leander McCormick Observatory. Stone took an interest in Morgan and helped him to obtain a Vanderbilt fellowship at the observatory. Stone's was probably the most important single influence in directing Morgan's interest toward classical astronomy.

With the aid of the fellowship, Morgan resumed his studies in 1896 and went on to receive the Ph.D. in 1901. During his last year of graduate study he taught mathematics at Pantops Academy, Charlottesville, Virginia, until receiving an appointment as a calculator at the U.S. Naval Observatory in Washington from 1901 to 1905. In 1905 he accepted an appointment as professor of astronomy and mathematics at Pritchett College, Glasgow, Missouri, and director of the Morrison Observatory. In 1907 he returned to the U.S. Naval Observatory, where he remained for the rest of his career. He started as an assistant astronomer on the staff of the nine-inch transit circle and by 1913 was in charge. For the next thirty-one years Morgan carried out a series of fundamental observations of the sun, moon, planets, and selected stars with this instrument. The resulting catalogs are milestones in fundamental astronomy and demonstrate Morgan's outstanding ability to analyze observations.

Morgan's earliest scientific papers dealt with the orbits of comets and asteroids. As the precise observations obtained with the nine-inch transit circle ac-

cumulated, Morgan turned his attention to the analysis of these observations and those from other observatories to obtain information on some of the fundamental constants on which astronomy is built. These analyses led to an extensive series of papers dealing with the position and motion of the equinox, the elements of the principal planets and their variations, and the constants of nutation and aberration. Although he formally retired in 1944, Morgan continued to work voluntarily at the U.S. Naval Observatory on his research, from 1947 to 1950 as a research associate under the auspices of Yale University.

It was during this period that Morgan produced what may be considered his most important work, "Catalog of 5,268 Standard Stars, 1950.0 Based on the Normal System N30." The N30 catalog is probably the most accurate source of positions and proper motions available today. It proved so useful in the interpretation of problems involving both astrophysical and astrometric data that Morgan was besieged with requests to extend the N30 proper motion system to a larger group of stars. Until several months before his death, he was engaged in deriving the proper motions on the N30 system of several hundred O- and B-type stars.

BIBLIOGRAPHY

Morgan's writings include "Results of Observations with the Nine-Inch Transit Circle, 1903–1911," in *Publications of the United States Naval Observatory*, 2nd ser., **9**, pt. 1 (1920), 1–452; "Observations made with the Nine-Inch Transit Circle, 1912–1913," *ibid.*, pt. 4 (1918), 1–116; "Results of Observations with the Nine-Inch Transit Circle, 1913–1926: Observations of the Sun, Moon, and Planets: Catalogue of 9,989 Standard and Intermediary Stars: Miscellaneous Stars," *ibid.*, **13** (1933), 1–228; "Results of Observations on the Nine-Inch Transit Circle, 1932–1934: Positions and Proper Motions of 1117 Reference Stars in Declination −10° to −20°: Miscellaneous Stars," *ibid.*, **14**, pt. 2 (1938), 81–125; "Vertical Circle Observations made with the Five-Inch Alt-Azimuth Instrument, 1916–1933: Catalog of Declinations of Standard Stars: Declinations of the Sun, Mercury and Venus," *ibid.*, pt. 3 (1938), 127–216; "Proper Motions of 2916 Intermediary Stars, Mostly in Declination −5° to −30°," *ibid.*, pt. 4 (1938), 217–283; "Results of Observations made with the Nine-Inch Transit Circle, 1935–1945: Observations of the Sun and Planets: Catalog of 5446 Stars: Corrections to GC and FK3," *ibid.*, **15**, pt. 5 (1948), 115–390; and "Catalog of 5,268 Standard Stars, 1950.0 based on the Normal System N30," which is *Astronomical Papers of the American Ephemeris*, **13**, pt. 3 (1952).

RAYNOR L. DUNCOMBE

MORGAN, THOMAS HUNT (*b.* Lexington, Kentucky, 25 September 1866; *d.* Pasadena, California, 4 December 1945), *embryology, genetics.*

Although known best for his studies in heredity with the small vinegar fly *Drosophila melanogaster* (often called fruit fly), Morgan contributed significantly to descriptive and experimental embryology, cytology, and, to a lesser extent, evolutionary theory. In recognition of his work in establishing the chromosome theory of heredity (the idea that genes are located in a linear array on chromosomes), Morgan was awarded the Nobel Prize in medicine or physiology for 1933.

The son of Charlton Hunt Morgan and the former Ellen Key Howard, Morgan came from two prominent family lines. His father had been American consul at Messina, Sicily, in the early 1860's and had given assistance to Giuseppe Garibaldi and his Red Shirts. John Hunt Morgan, Charlton's brother, was a colonel and later general in the Confederate Army and leader of his own guerrilla band, "Morgan's Raiders." His mother's maternal grandfather was Francis Scott Key, composer of the national anthem.

As a boy Morgan spent much time roaming the hills and countryside of rural Kentucky. His visits to his mother's family in western Maryland, provided the opportunity for further explorations during summers, and particularly for collecting fossils. He also worked for two summers in the Kentucky mountains with the U.S. Geological Survey. All of these activities gave Morgan an ease and familiarity with natural history which he retained throughout his life.

Morgan entered the preparatory department of the State College of Kentucky in 1880 and, after two years, the college itself (now the University of Kentucky). In 1886 he received a B.S., *summa cum laude,* in zoology. While an undergraduate Morgan was particularly influenced toward science by one of his teachers, A. R. Crandall, a geologist, and an undergraduate friend, Joseph H. Kastle. Kastle graduated two years ahead of Morgan and went to Johns Hopkins University in 1884 to do graduate work in chemistry. Perhaps through Kastle's influence, and because his mother's family lived in and around Baltimore, Morgan was attracted to Hopkins for graduate work. The summer before he entered graduate school (1886), Morgan went to the Boston Society of Natural History's marine biological station at Annisquam, Massachusetts. This was his first experience in working with marine organisms, an interest he was to continue throughout his life, primarily in association with the Marine Biological Laboratory, Woods Hole, Massachusetts.

At Hopkins, Morgan took courses in general biology, anatomy, and physiology with H. Newell Martin, a former student of Michael Foster and assistant to T. H. Huxley; anatomy with William N. Howard; and morphology and embryology with William Keith Brooks. He concentrated on morphology with Brooks. In 1890 he completed his doctoral work, on sea spiders, and received his Ph.D. He stayed on at Hopkins for a postdoctoral year on a Bruce fellowship; and in the fall of 1891 he went to Bryn Mawr College, where he remained until 1904, when E. B. Wilson offered him the chair of experimental zoology at Columbia. He was a member of the Columbia zoology department from 1904 until 1928, when he resigned to found the division of biological sciences at California Institute of Technology. He remained at Cal Tech and was active in scientific and administrative work until his death, after a short illness, in 1945.

During his academic life Morgan was involved not only in research and teaching but also in numerous professional organizations and activities. He was a member of the Genetics Society of America, the American Morphological Society (president, 1900), the American Society of Naturalists (president, 1909), the Society for Experimental Biology and Medicine (president, 1910–1912), and the American Association for the Advancement of Science (president, 1930). He also served as president of the Sixth International Conference on Genetics held in Ithaca, New York, in 1932. He was a member of the American Philosophical Society and the National Academy of Sciences (president, 1927–1931); through the National Academy he was intimately involved with the function of the National Research Council, especially in its formative years between 1921 and 1940. In addition to the Nobel Prize, Morgan received numerous scientific honors, including the Darwin Medal (1924) and the Copley Medal (1939) of the Royal Society.

In 1904 Morgan married Lilian Vaughan Sampson, one of his former students at Bryn Mawr. Lilian Morgan was a cytologist of considerable skill who always maintained an active interest in her husband's work. After the four Morgan children were in school, she returned to the laboratory and made important contributions to the *Drosophila* work.

Morgan was known to his friends, colleagues, and students as a man of quick mind, incisive judgment, and sparkling humor. While rarely showing his inner feelings, he nonetheless enjoyed people immensely and was a personal friend as well as teacher to many of his students. Frequently he paid the salaries of laboratory assistants from his own funds; and he shared his Nobel Prize money with his lifelong assistants and co-workers C. B. Bridges and A. H.

Sturtevant, to provide for the education of their children.

Morgan has been described as down-to-earth, practical, and sensitive. He retained an alert inquisitiveness and excitement for new ideas throughout his life. An extremely hard worker, Morgan pursued his scientific interests enthusiastically and relentlessly. He seldom took vacations, and used only one sabbatical during his twenty-four years at Columbia (in the year 1920–1921, when he went to Stanford University, where he continued his work in heredity and embryology). Despite his busy schedule and concentration on work, however, Morgan always found a small part of every day to spend with his family.

Early Scientific Work. As a student of W. K. Brooks, Morgan was trained as a morphologist—one who sought to discover evolutionary (phylogenetic) relationships among organisms by studying their comparative anatomy, embryology, cytology, and, to some extent, physiology. Morphologists relied heavily on descriptive and comparative methods, drawing their conclusions by analogy and inference. Such conclusions necessarily were highly speculative, because they could not be tested in any direct way. Brooks had been a student of Louis Agassiz and later Alexander Agassiz, and was thoroughly grounded in comparative anatomy and embryology, two of the hallmarks of late nineteenth-century descriptive biology. Through detailed studies of early and later embryonic stages of various groups of marine organisms, Brooks sought to elucidate phylogenetic relationships which were not apparent simply from examining the adult forms. Marine organisms seemed particularly important to Brooks, because he felt they were the oldest and most basic types of animals, and thus demonstrated most clearly the fundamental principles of animal organization. Like most morphologists, he viewed his own special subdiscipline, embryology, less as a field in its own right than as a tool for studying evolutionary relationships.

According to Bateson, Brooks taught his students to see subjects such as heredity not as completed axioms but rather as unsolved problems for further investigation. Brooks elucidated for them the interrelationships among such disparate areas of biology as heredity, anatomy, embryology, cytology, and evolution. He had, according to Morgan, a wide-ranging and philosophical mind, which, if not always rigorous, was at least provocative.

Morgan's doctoral dissertation under Brooks involved a study of four species of marine invertebrates, the Pycnogonida (sea spiders), focusing largely, but not exclusively, on their comparative embryology. The purpose of this study was to determine whether the Pycnogonida belonged to the Arachnida (a group including spiders and scorpions) or to the Crustacea (including crabs, lobsters, and crayfish). Observing both large anatomical and smaller cellular changes during embryogenesis, Morgan found that the pattern of development more closely resembled that of the Arachnida than that of the Crustacea. He continued this line of work during the first several years after leaving Hopkins, extending his investigations of early embryology to other forms such as *Balanoglossus* and the ascidians (both primitive chordates). Morgan had, however, become increasingly dissatisfied with morphology during his graduate days; he objected to the subordination of disciplines such as embryology almost exclusively to phylogenetic and evolutionary problems. Increasingly, he saw embryology and other disciplines as having their own sets of problems for study; moreover, he felt that an experimental approach to problem-solving would make it possible to draw more firm and rigorous conclusions than the inferences and speculations that characterized morphology.

Several factors contributed to Morgan's growing disaffection with the morphological tradition. The first was perhaps his association with the physiologist H. Newell Martin (head of the biology department at Hopkins),[1] an emphatic and vocal exponent of the experimental method. Following Michael Foster's lead, he had introduced experimental teaching laboratories when he came to Hopkins; and he made it clear from the outset that he regarded physiology as the queen of the sciences, with morphology as its servant.[2] A second factor was Morgan's early acquaintance with Jacques Loeb. Both joined the faculty of Bryn Mawr in the same year (1891) and maintained a lifelong friendship. Loeb was a strong proponent of the mechanistic conception of life. He believed that (1) organisms function in accordance with the laws of physics and chemistry, so that to understand living phenomena, it is necessary to approach them from a physicochemical standpoint; and (2) only quantitative and experimental methods would allow biologists to get at the fundamental chemical and physical processes involved with life. These methods, in contrast with those of descriptive biologists, would yield rigorous and testable conclusions. Loeb believed that biologists should emulate the methods used in the physical sciences. Loeb's views no doubt strongly influenced Morgan at a time when the latter was beginning to turn away, on his own accord, from descriptive methods.

A third, and perhaps crucial, factor which may have caused Morgan to embrace the experimental approach was his association with Hans Driesch, his colleague in 1894–1895 at the zoological station in Naples. Driesch was at the time an enthusiastic proponent of experimental embryology (the school of *Entwicklungsmechanik*) and had performed some highly controversial experiments on sea urchin eggs. Morgan and Driesch collaborated on experimental studies of development in Ctenophora (published in 1895).[3] Not only was Driesch's influence important, but so was that of the zoological station itself. Morgan had visited the station first in 1890 and had become intrigued with the many possibilities that the institute offered for research on marine forms. During his ten months at Naples, he was excited by the work, the constant stream of visitors, the exchange of ideas, and the emphasis on new modes of thought, such as performing experiments in areas of biology, like embryology, previously approached only descriptively. He wrote in 1896: "No one can fail to be impressed [at the Naples Station] and to learn much in the clash of thought and criticism that must be present where such diverse elements come together."[4] By contrast, Morgan found the situation in America more parochial and less exciting: "Isolated as we are in America, from much of the newer current feeling, we are able at Naples as in no other laboratory in the world to get in touch with the best modern work."[5]

After he returned to the United States in 1895, Morgan's biological interests expanded in scope; and his research methods became largely experimental for the remainder of his life. Between 1895 and 1902 he focused on experimental embryology; between 1903 and 1910, on evolution, especially heredity and cytology in relation to sex determination; between 1910 and 1925, on problems of heredity in *Drosophila*; and from 1925 to 1945, on embryology and its relations to heredity and evolution. Yet in none of these periods was Morgan exclusively concerned with a single subject. The breadth of his interests was such that he always worked simultaneously on several problems, often of a divergent nature. At almost any point in his career he moved back and forth between the broad areas of evolution, heredity, and development with considerable ease and grasp of fundamental concepts.

Embryological Studies (1895–1902). Morgan's earliest work in experimental embryology largely concerned the factors influencing normal embryonic development. These studies were motivated by the controversy raging in the early 1890's between Driesch and the founder of the *Entwicklungsmechanik* school, Wilhelm Roux, on the question of whether the differentiation of embryonic cells is directed by internal (hereditary) or external (environmental) forces. Morgan studied

fertilization of egg fragments, both nucleated and nonnucleated, in the sea urchin and in amphioxus. Both types of fragments were able to undergo varying degrees of normal development and even to produce partial larvae. Morgan carried out other studies in which he removed cells from normally fertilized blastulae to produce embryos which, although modified, still developed along the major outlines of their normal course. Other experiments during the same period involved the effects of various salt solutions and of the force of gravity (or lack of it) on the course of development in the eggs of sea urchins, mollusks, and teleost fishes. Beginning in 1902 he published an extensive series of papers on normal and abnormal development in the frog's egg. Here, Morgan tested the effects of such factors as injury to the egg yolk; varying concentrations of lithium chloride; and injuries to the embryo at various stages, including repetition of Roux's experiment involving injury to the first blastomere. The results of all these experiments showed Morgan that despite the alterations in development which could be brought about by various physical constraints, the embryo still displayed a tendency to reach its prescribed goal. It became clear to him that environmental influences might shape the embryo's development within certain limits, but that the overriding factors determining the sequence of events in development must lie within the embryo itself: the interaction of embryonic tissues and of specific embryonic regions with each other.

Coupled with Morgan's interest in early embryonic development was a corresponding interest in the regeneration of lost or injured tissues (or organs) in adults. While still a student at Hopkins, he had studied regeneration in the earthworm; and in the late 1890's he pursued these studies in flatworms (*Planaria* and *Bipalium*); jellyfish (*Gonionemus*); bony fishes (teleosts); and ciliate protozoa (*Stentor*). In 1901 he published his first major book, *Regeneration*, a compendium of contemporary information on this subject. More than simply a review of the literature, *Regeneration* provided a foretaste of Morgan's writing and analytical skill. He saw that the events in regeneration (regrouping of cells in the wound area, despecialization, and renewed differentiation) were the other side of the coin from those of early embryonic development. In regeneration there was a return to the embryonic state. The same essential questions lay behind both processes: How could different components of a cell's hereditary information be signaled to turn on or off at different periods in its life? Morgan emphasized the relationship between the two processes (he was not alone in making the connection); he saw that any explanation for one must be able to account for the other.

As in most of his later writings, Morgan presented the problem of regeneration as one composed largely of questions—of unknowns—rather than of knowns. He made clear the gaps in contemporary knowledge, in terms of specific experiments or broad interpretations. Morgan sought an understanding of problems such as regeneration (or embryonic differentiation) in terms of underlying (and continuing) processes. He was not content to "explain" one event simply by describing the events or organizational relationships which might lead to it. For example, he felt that those who saw embryonic differentiation as the result of "formative stuffs" already organized in the cytoplasm of the unfertilized egg, or regeneration as simply the work of special cells which congregate at a wound site, really explained nothing. They simply pushed the causal factors back to a further point in the organism's life history.

It was important to Morgan to view such phenomena less as series of events than as processes. These processes were chemical and physical, and they followed regular laws—if only one could discover what they were. Development and regeneration were to some extent programmed events, but they were not simply the unfolding of preexisting structures. Specific interactions were programmed between structures that gave rise to new and qualitatively different structures. The job of the developmental biologist, he argued, was to seek the general laws governing these interactions. This discovery could not come about simply by describing anatomy—it required experimental analysis as well.

Study of Sex Determination (1903–1910). In the latter part of the nineteenth and the first years of the twentieth centuries there were two schools of thought on the problem of sex determination. One maintained that the causal factors were environmental: temperature, or amount of food available to the embryo or to the mother during development. This argument derived from the observation that changes in various environmental factors affected the sex ratio in many species, particularly insects. Another school, however, felt that sex was by and large determined at the moment of fertilization, or perhaps even before, by factors internal to the egg or sperm or both. This school emphasized the hereditary, as opposed to environmental, factors in determining sex differentiation.

After 1900 there were several attempts by those favoring the hereditary view to understand sex in terms of the newly discovered Mendelian principles. In 1903 Morgan published a review of the sex deter-

mination problem, criticizing all of the existing theories, including those based on Mendel's laws. His major argument was that there was relatively little evidence substantiating the claims of either the environmentalists or the hereditarians. Most of the current theories of sex determination tried to explain only the customary 1:1 sex ratio found in most species. Any theory of sex determination, however, had to account for a number of other phenomena, such as the process of parthenogenesis, either natural or artificially induced; the appearance of gynandromorphs, often observed in insects (in gynandromorphs, one half of the organism has male characteristics and the other half female characteristics); and sex reversals, as observed in fowl and other species, especially under the influence of hormonal changes.

In his analysis of the sex determination problem, Morgan displayed his deep-rooted embryological bias. He was unwilling to see sex as a primarily hereditary phenomenon, determined at the moment of fertilization, but, rather, he analyzed it as a developmental process, guided by natural laws; he was clearly an epigenesist. He found most of the environmentalists' experiments inconclusive, but this did not mean that sex could be explained by postulating hereditary units, such as Mendel's "factors," or by reference to visible cell structures, such as chromosomes. To Morgan, structures such as chromosomes were only indicators of underlying processes—they were not causal factors themselves. For this reason he was not initially sympathetic to C. E. McClung's suggestion in 1901 and 1902 that sex was determined by the disposition of the accessory (or X) chromosome. Before 1910 Morgan admitted only that the fertilized egg might inherit a predisposition toward maleness or femaleness. The realization of that sexual potential, however, was largely a result of the same developmental forces involved in differentiation, organogenesis, and regeneration.

Through his interest in sex determination, Morgan carried out important cytological studies on the movement and disposition of chromosomes during the formation of eggs of naturally parthenogenetic forms. Studying in detail two kinds of insects, the aphids and phylloxerans, Morgan was able to demonstrate conclusively that the production of parthenogenetic males was associated with the loss of a chromosome during development from a diploid egg. His papers on this subject, published in 1909 and 1910, show the beginning of Morgan's realization that chromosomes might actually be related to sex determination.[6] He did not conclude at the time, however, that the accessory chromosome (X) was a sex determiner. Morgan maintained that the real sex-determining process occurred *before* the actual loss of the chromosome; the latter was only an indication of this process, not the cause. He wrote in 1909: "The preliminaries of the sex determination for both sexes go on in the presence of all chromosomes . . . clearly I think the results show that changes of profound importance may take place without change in the number of chromosomes."[7]

Evidence had been accumulating since the 1870's that the chromosomes were somehow intimately involved with general hereditary processes. Morgan had remained skeptical of such conclusions, however, not only because the idea had been inferred from circumstantial evidence but also because of his bias against explaining phenomena in terms of preexisting structures. Yet shortly after 1910 increasing experimental evidence led him to change his mind and to accept the chromosomes as important hereditary structures. It was largely work on sex determination that brought Morgan to accept these new ideas. His own studies on chromosomes in aphids and phylloxerans suggested that more attention ought to be paid to the possible role of chromosomes in determining sex. At the same time, between 1901 and 1905, E. B. Wilson, Morgan's colleague at Columbia, and Nettie M. Stevens, at Bryn Mawr, amassed considerable evidence suggesting that the accessory (X) chromosome was responsible for sex determination. Although Morgan did not accept these findings unequivocally, Wilson's concern for the hereditary implications of these chromosome studies strongly influenced Morgan's ideas about sex determination. Morgan and Wilson had been close friends and colleagues for many years and Morgan had great respect for Wilson's judgment.

Evolution and Heredity (1903–1910). Morgan had become interested in the Darwinian theory of natural selection, through the influence of W. K. Brooks and through his own studies on regeneration. He reported that he constantly wondered how the regenerative power in higher organisms could have evolved by a mechanism such as natural selection. In 1903 Morgan published *Evolution and Adaptation* (dedicated to W. K. Brooks), a lengthy attack on the Darwinian theory of natural selection as it was interpreted around the turn of the century by the neo-Darwinians. Morgan believed that Darwin himself was an outstanding naturalist who approached his conclusions with caution, reasoning only within narrow bounds from the data itself. He felt, however, that many of Darwin's followers had become "ultra selectionists," investing natural selection with more powers than was legitimate. While maintaining that evolution was a fact, Morgan argued that the theory of the mechanism

by which evolution was brought about—natural selection—had many loopholes.

Morgan's many objections to natural selection have been discussed in detail in the secondary literature; but one major criticism deserves mention here. Morgan shared with many prominent biologists (especially embryologists) the view that the Darwinian theory (as stated by Darwin or modified in the 1890's by his followers) was incomplete because it lacked a concept of heredity. Although Darwin had emphasized that selection acts on slight individual variations (what some people at the time came to call "continuous variations"), more recent evidence had suggested that such variations were not usually heritable. It was a cardinal principle to Darwin and the neo-Darwinians that the only variations upon which selection could act were hereditary ones. Thus, Morgan and many of the less orthodox Darwinians came to believe that variations of evolutionary significance must be large-scale, or discontinuous, because these were the only ones which appeared to be inherited. Morgan maintained that in the face of this dilemma, the neo-Darwinians, rather than abandoning the idea of small, individual variations as the raw material for evolution, interpreted selection itself as the creative agent. Morgan believed that selection was only a negative factor, however, which sorted out the favorable from the unfavorable variations already present. It could not, as some neo-Darwinians believed, create new variations in the germ plasm.

Morgan's view of evolution was like his view of heredity and development, in that it was fashioned by a skepticism about single answers or mechanisms for which experimental proof was inconclusive. From his graduate days on, he felt that heredity was in some ways central to an understanding of all biological phenomena, especially development and evolution. Recognizing the lack of what seemed to be any coherent theory of heredity in the period before 1910, he was skeptical of any attempts to explain processes such as cell differentiation or the origin of species by analogies, inferences, or speculative hypotheses. A change in Morgan's ideas led him to the dramatic discoveries with *Drosophila*. A brief examination of his ideas on heredity, especially in relation to cytology and evolution between 1900 and 1910, will be useful in understanding this change.

Three concepts of heredity, representing several lines of reasoning and experimentation, had become well-known to most biologists by the first decade of the twentieth century. The first of these was the newly discovered Mendelian laws, based on data from plant-breeding experiments. The second was the chromosome theory of heredity, based on cytological studies of chromosome movement during gametogenesis in both animals and plants. Third was the publication of *The Mutation Theory*, a monumental treatise on heredity, variation, and evolution by the Dutch botanist Hugo de Vries.

Although by 1902 several workers had suggested the possible relationship between chromosome movements and the segregation of Mendel's alternate factors, there was no agreement that this relationship was anything more than coincidental. Morgan's objections to the Mendelian scheme can be summarized as follows:

1. If the Mendelian theory were correct, and if Mendelian "factors" (what Mendel more commonly called *Anlagen*, and what later became known as genes) were actually associated with chromosomes, then breeding results ought to show large groups of characteristics inherited together (as many groups as there were chromosome pairs). Because few "linkage groups" had been observed in the period before 1910 (Bateson and Punett in England had shown some in 1905 and 1906), the identification of Mendel's factors with chromosomes seemed less than likely.

2. The results of animal- and plant-breeding experiments showed that many characteristics in an offspring were a mixture of parental types, and not simple dominance or recessiveness. Thus, Mendel's "laws" might apply only to special, exceptional cases.

3. The Mendelian theory of dominance and recessiveness could not explain the normal 1:1 sex ratio. According to Mendel's scheme, the sex ratio would be 3:1 (if one sex factor were dominant over the other) or 1:2:1 (if incomplete dominance were involved). Since neither sex ratio occurred in nature, Mendel's laws provided no clear way to account for the important phenomenon of sex inheritance.

4. On methodological grounds, Mendel's laws called for too neat a set of categories among the offspring of any cross. Since such categories seldom occurred in nature, Morgan claimed that Mendelians often placed borderline organisms into whichever category was necessary to give the expected ratios.

5. On a more philosophical level, both the Mendelian and the chromosome theories seemed to be preformationist in character; they referred basic hereditary characteristics to preexisting particles or units in the cell. Morgan felt that, like all preformationist theories of the past, the Mendelian and chromosome doctrines simply pushed a basic problem back further in the life history of the organism.

6. In addition, the Mendelian and chromosome theories seemed to Morgan to be based too much on speculation, and too little on sound experimental evidence. They reminded him of the speculative theories—especially those of Ernst Haeckel and August Weismann—that attempted to explain all of biology that abounded during his student years. Morgan was inalterably opposed to speculation that could not be subjected to experimental tests.

Skeptical of both the Mendelian and the chromosome theories, Morgan was, however, an outspoken advocate of de Vries's mutation theory (published in a two-volume work between 1901 and 1903). De Vries proposed that large-scale heritable variations occurring in one generation could produce offspring that were of species different from their parents. De Vries's evidence was based largely on experiments with the evening primrose *(Oenothera lamarckiana)*. What he called "mutations" are now known to be the result not of actual changes in genetic material, but complex chromosome arrangements which are peculiar to *Oenothera*. Thus they did not produce species-level changes in a single generation, as de Vries claimed. Nevertheless, the mutation theory is historically important, for Morgan and others saw in it, as did de Vries himself, an answer to the perplexities of Mendelian heredity and Darwinian selection. It accounted for the origin of new variations which were definite enough to be of evolutionary significance (that is, would not be lost by swamping), and yet were also heritable. Furthermore, Morgan's acceptance of the mutation theory was influenced by the sound experimental evidence behind de Vries's work. De Vries had a large experimental garden where he grew his plants and made crosses under carefully controlled conditions. New mutants could be isolated and shown to breed true. Thus de Vries not only provided a new concept that made evolution conceivable; he also provided an experimental approach by which his conclusions could be tested.

Morgan's Work With Drosophila. Morgan appears to have begun breeding the fruit fly *Drosophila melanogaster* somewhere around 1908 or 1909. It is not clear how he came to use this organism, or where he obtained his original cultures. *Drosophila* seems to have been an organism favorable for laboratory studies, however, between 1900–1910. It was used in Castle's laboratory at the Bussey Institution (Harvard) as early as 1900–1901; by W. J. Moenkhaus at Indiana in 1903; by F. E. Lutz at the Carnegie Institution Laboratory (Cold Spring Harbor, New York, and after 1909, when Lutz was at the American Museum of Natural History); by Nettie Stevens at Bryn Mawr in 1906; and by Fernandus Payne and L. S. Quackenbush in the Columbia laboratory itself prior to 1909. Morgan's original purpose had been to test de Vries's mutation theory in animals. He exposed *Drosophila* cultures to radium in an attempt to induce the formation of new mutants, but he never obtained mutations of the magnitude which de Vries claimed for *Oenothera*.

In 1910 Morgan discovered a small, distinct variation in one male fly in one of his culture bottles. This fly had white, as opposed to the normal (wild-type) red, eye color. This variation did not make a new species, but Morgan thought he would try to breed the fly with its red-eyed sisters to see what would happen. All of the offspring (F_1) were red-eyed. Brother-sister matings among the F_1 generation produced a second generation (F_2) with some white-eyed flies—all of which, Morgan noticed with astonishment, were males. Further matings showed that while the white-eye condition almost always occurred in males, occasionally a white-eyed female would appear. Morgan noted that the white-eye and red-eye conditions behaved as typical Mendelian factors, with red being dominant over white.

The limitation of the white-eye condition largely, but not exclusively, to males presented a very curious problem. Morgan found that the only way he could explain this phenomenon was to assume that the red- and white-eye conditions were determined by Mendelian factors, and that these somehow associated with the element which determined sex in the cell. In his first paper on heredity in *Drosophila*, Morgan refrained from identifying the eye color with chromosomes in general, or the accessory chromosomes in particular.[8] Within a year, however, he concluded that such caution was unwarranted. The cytological studies on chromosomes and sex determination by Wilson and others, and his own work with *Drosophila*, convinced Morgan that chromosomes could in fact be the real bearers of Mendelian factors. Much to his credit, he rejected his skepticism about both the Mendelian and the chromosome theories when he saw from two independent lines of evidence (breeding experiments and cytology) that one could be treated in terms of the other.

Morgan called the white-eye condition sex-limited (later sex-linked), meaning that the genes for this character were carried on (linked to) the X chromosome. Sex-linked genes, if recessive to their wild-type alleles, will show up almost exclusively in males, who do not have a second X chromosome to mask genes on the first. Sex linkage was found to hold for all sexually reproducing organisms and accounted for many other perplexing hereditary patterns, including red-green color blindness and hemophilia in man. Morgan's *Drosophila* work showed for the first time the clear association of one or more hereditary characters with a specific chromosome.

Early in 1910 Morgan had taken into his laboratory several enthusiastic Columbia undergraduates: A. H. Sturtevant and Calvin B. Bridges, both juniors in the college and Hermann J. Muller, a graduate student of E. B. Wilson's. With Morgan these men quickly developed the *Drosophila* work into an intensively active project. As more breeding experiments were initiated, new mutants began to appear. Careful records were kept of the mutants, and their hereditary patterns were studied through various crosses and backcrosses. It would be impossible to describe or list all of the new findings which emerged from the *Drosophila* studies. A few major developments will illustrate the enormous breakthroughs which Morgan and his colleagues were able to make with this new experimental organism.

At first the relationship between Mendelian genes and chromosomes was purely inferential. While it was not possible to make that relationship more concrete (no one could "see" a gene on a chromosome), a means appeared by which the inference could be tested. In 1909 the Belgian cytologist F. A. Janssens had published a careful series of cytological observations of what he called chiasmatype formation (intertwining of chromosomes during meiosis).[9] Janssens believed he could show that occasionally homologous chromosome strands exchanged parts during chiasma. Morgan was familiar with Janssens' concept and applied it to the conception of genes as parts of chromosomes. He reasoned that the strength of linkage between any two factors must be related in some way to their distances apart on the chromosome. The farther apart any two genes, the more likely that a break could occur somewhere between them, and hence the more likely that the linkage relationship would be disturbed. During a conversation with Morgan in 1911, Sturtevant, then still an undergraduate, suddenly realized that the variations in strength of linkage could be used as a means of determining the relative spatial distances of genes on a chromosome. According to Sturtevant's own report, he went home that night and produced the first genetic map in *Drosophila* for the sex-linked genes y, w, z, m, and r. The order and relative spacing which Sturtevant determined at that time are essentially the same as those appearing on the recent standard map of *Drosophila's* X chromosome.

Following the initial success of this technique, positions were determined for many other genes. The *Drosophila* group depended upon the appearance of mutants to determine the existence and chromosomal location of specific genes. Thus the initial work of the group took two directions: the location of mutants and the maintenance of a stock for each mutant (or group of mutants), and the mapping of these mutant gene positions on the appropriate chromosomes. The success of the mapping technique added further weight to the inferred relationship between genes and chromosomes and at the same time provided an increasingly clear picture of the architecture of the germ plasm. The major outcome of the mapping work was the idea that genes are arranged in a linear fashion and occupy specific positions, or loci, on the chromosomes. While the direct and final proof of this relationship had to wait until proper cytological materials (the giant salivary glands of *Drosophila*) and techniques were developed by T. S. Painter and others in the 1930's, the mapping work firmly established the inference in the years between 1912 and 1915.

As the work progressed, other problems arose. Genes were discovered which, when combined in the homozygous condition, caused the embryo to die before birth (so-called lethal genes). Various traits proved to be determined by a number of alternative genes (alleles) at the same locus, which could be combined in various forms to give a series of phenotypes (multiple alleles). Because crossover frequencies did not always turn out as predicted, they arrived at the idea of crossover interference, in which segments of a homologous chromosome pair showed little or no crossing over, often as the result of alterations in chromosome structure which prevented normal intertwining during chiasma. A furor among orthodox Mendelians was aroused by Sturtevant's suggestion that the expression of a given gene was affected by its position on the chromosome (the "position effect"). Position effect became the target of one of the most persistent attacks on the Mendelian and chromosome theories to be launched in the twentieth century, by Richard Goldschmidt, for many years director of the Kaiser Wilhelm Institute for Biology in Berlin–Dahlem. Goldschmidt argued that the suggestion that a gene's effect could be modified by a change in its position along the chromosome (that is, by what genes were on either side of it) violated the basic Mendelian conception of the purity of the gametes. The necessity of invoking a hypothesis such as position effect was, to Goldschmidt, tantamount to an admission that the Mendelian and chromosome theories were not compatible, and that a new conception had to be substituted. Yet position effect and its cytological basis, as worked out in the 1930's by Muller, Prokofieva, Bridges, and others, proved to be a valid conception—a modification, if not a contradiction, of orthodox Mendelian theory.

Among the most important ideas to emerge from the *Drosophila* work was the balance concept of sex, developed largely by Bridges between 1913–1925

through an analysis of the cytological phenomenon of nondisjunction. Nondisjunction is a condition occurring during oogenesis, in which the X chromosomes fail to segregate, so that a haploid egg may end up with two X chromosomes. Bridges' work of 1916, in particular, showed clearly that sex was determined not simply by the inheritance of one or two X chromosomes but, rather, by the ratio of X chromosomes to autosomes (the other, nonsex chromosomes in the nucleus). According to this idea, organisms could inherit various degrees of sexuality based upon variations in this ratio. The genes governing male and female characteristics (such as production of testes or ovaries) are found in both sexes and apparently are not located exclusively on the sex chromosomes but throughout the genome. Which of these sets of genes express themselves is a result not simply of their presence or absence but, rather, of some complex and little-understood relationship between the sex chromosomes and autosomes.

The major early findings of the *Drosophila* group were summarized in an epoch-making book, *The Mechanism of Mendelian Heredity*, published by Morgan, Bridges, Sturtevant, and Muller in 1915. They presented evidence to suggest that genes were linearly arranged on chromosomes and that it was possible to regard the Mendelian laws as based on observable events taking place in cells. Most important, however, they demonstrated that heredity could be treated quantitatively and rigorously. For almost the first time since the advent of experimental embryology in the 1880's, a previously descriptive area of biology had proved itself accessible to quantitative and experimental methods. Through *The Mechanism of Mendelian Heredity*, the new science of genetics reached many teachers, students, and specialists in other areas.

All of the early work on *Drosophila* between 1910 and 1925 was carried out in the winter in Morgan's small laboratory space, called the "fly room," at Columbia, and during the summers at the Marine Biological Laboratory in Woods Hole, Massachusetts. Although Morgan was considerably older than his co-workers, there was a give-and-take atmosphere in the "fly room" that precluded formal barriers and rigid teacher-student distinctions. There was little consideration of priority in new ideas or discoveries at the time (although some did emerge in later years); and each was free to criticize anyone else openly, and sometimes vehemently. Sturtevant has described the relationship among the workers in the "fly room" as follows:

As each new result or new idea came along, it was discussed freely by the group. The published accounts do not always indicate the source of ideas. It was often not only impossible to say but was felt to be unimportant, who first had an idea. A few examples come to mind. The original chromosome map made use of a value represented by the number of recombinations divided by the number of parental types as a measure of distances; it was Muller who suggested the simpler and more convenient percentage, the recombinance formed of the whole population. The idea that "crossover reducers" might be due to inversions of sections was first suggested by Morgan, and this does not appear in my published account of the hypothesis. I first suggested to Muller that lethals might be used to give an objective measure of the frequency of mutation. These are isolated examples, but they represent what was going on all the time. I think we came out somewhere near even in this give and take, and it certainly accelerated the work.[10]

However, all was not idyllic within the *Drosophila* group. H. J. Muller, perhaps Morgan's most independent and brilliant student, felt that Morgan had a tendency to use his students' ideas without fully acknowledging them. While recognizing Morgan's unsurpassed abilities as a leader, his fiery and quick imagination, and his frequently penetrating insights, Muller claimed that Morgan was frequently confused about rather fundamental issues involved in the work—such as the theory of modifier genes, or the supposed swamping effect of dominant genes in a population. According to Muller, Morgan frequently had to be "straightened out" on such issues by hardheaded arguments with his students—mostly Muller and Sturtevant, with occasional help from E. B. Wilson. Sturtevant concurs with this evaluation at least with regard to the idea of natural selection, which he claims Morgan persisted in misunderstanding until as late as 1914 or 1915.

What is clear from an analysis of the reports of many people who worked in the "fly room" during the years 1911–1915, was that Morgan's primary role was that of leader and stimulator. He was constantly coming up with ideas—some wrong, others right—and throwing these out to the eager and brilliant group of young people whom he had working with him. That many of the most far-reaching ideas (such as a quantitative method of making chromosome maps, crossover interference, modifier genes) were first proposed by his students, not directly by Morgan, is also clear. His genius in the development of the *Drosophila* work may have rested more in bringing together the right group of people, in working together with them in a democratic and informal way, and in letting them alone, than in producing all the major ideas himself. In fact, it is clear from an analysis of Morgan's published work that he

frequently proposed ideas "off the top of his head" and was not always careful to work out their details or implications.

Morgan's laboratory became the training ground for a school of Mendelian genetics—one generation of which emphasized particularly the relationship between genes and chromosomes. Besides Bridges, Sturtevant, and Muller, Morgan's students or postdoctoral associates at Columbia included Alexander Weinstein, E. G. Anderson, H. H. Plough, Theodosius Dobzhansky, L. C. Dunn, Donald Lancefield, Curt Stern, and Otto Mohr. These workers, and many others, developed what has come to be called "classical genetics"—that is, genetics at the chromosome level.

Morgan's mind ranged freely over the broad areas of genetics, embryology, cytology, and evolution. Soon after the *Drosophila* work had gotten under way, he saw that the Mendelian concept could throw considerable light on the problem of natural selection. In 1916 Morgan published his second major work on evolution, *A Critique of the Theory of Evolution* (revised in 1925 as *Evolution and Genetics*), showing clearly his altered views about Darwinian selection. Although he had previously regarded de Vries's mutation theory as an alternative to natural selection, Mendelism now provided a mechanism for understanding the Darwinian theory itself. Mendelian variations (called also "mutations" by Morgan) were not as large or as drastic as those postulated by de Vries. Yet they were more distinct and discontinuous than the slight individual variations which Darwin had emphasized. Most important, they could be shown to be inherited in a definite pattern and were therefore subject to the effects of selection. The Mendelian theory filled the gap which Darwin had left open so long before.

Morgan found it more difficult to make explicit the relationships which he instinctively knew existed between the new science of heredity and the old problems of development (such as cell differentiation or regeneration). In 1934 Morgan attempted to make these connections in a book titled *Embryology and Genetics*. The work proved to be less an analysis of interrelated mechanisms and more a summary of efforts in the two separate fields. Morgan knew well that the time was not ripe for understanding such problems as how gene action could be controlled during development. Yet *Embryology and Genetics* served an important function of keeping before biologists the idea that ultimately any theory of heredity had to account for the problem of embryonic differentiation. Morgan wisely refrained from drawing conclusions or proposing hypotheses which could not be experimentally verified. One of the most important characteristics of his genius was the ability to restrict the number and kinds of questions which he asked at any one time. For example, by focusing primarily upon the relationships between the Mendelian theory and chromosome structure, he was able to work out the chromosome theory of heredity in great detail. In contrast, other workers, such as Richard Goldschmidt, tried to make those relationships more explicit than the evidence at the time would allow. Consequently, they were often drawn into realms of speculation where no concrete advances could be made.

Later Work (1925–1945). After the mid-1920's Morgan's interest shifted away from the specific *Drosophila* work. His new concerns took two forms. One was the attempt to summarize the conclusions deriving from his genetic studies. To this category belong those broader works relating heredity to development and evolution. His other interest turned him to some of the original problems of development and regeneration which had launched his career thirty-five years previously. During the summers at Woods Hole, and especially after his move to California in 1928, Morgan returned to studies of early embryonic development. The cleavage of eggs; the effects of centrifuging eggs before and after fertilization; the behavior of spindles in cell division; preorganization in the egg; self-sterility in ascidians; and the factors affecting normal and abnormal development were some of the problems in experimental embryology. They represented the type of biological work that Morgan was most interested in. Although he approached the *Drosophila* studies enthusiastically, the mathematics of mapping and many other highly technical problems were less interesting to him than working directly with living organisms. Morgan had the naturalist's love of whole organisms and of studying organisms in their natural environment. He was a good naturalist with a knowledge of many species.[11] His strong interest in laboratory and experimental work in no way detracted from his interest in whole systems. He was not in spirit a mechanist, although he recognized the value of studying systems in isolation to obtain rigorous and useful data.

Methodology in Science. Being a thorough experimentalist, Morgan saw that unbounded speculation was detrimental to the development of sound scientific ideas. He did not object to the formulation of hypotheses for he saw them as essential to developing new concepts and experimental ideas. For Morgan, however, the only acceptable hypotheses were those which suggested experimental tests.

Yet Morgan was not a mere empiricist—that is,

one who simply tries to amass large amounts of basically similar kinds of evidence before drawing a conclusion. As an experimentalist he drew conclusions most readily when several different types of data sources were available (for example, determining the existence of a chromosomal deletion from breeding data and from cytological examination of chromosome preparations). By 1909 considerable breeding data suggested that Mendel's laws had wide application. Yet Morgan remained skeptical because there was no evidence (in his mind) that Mendel's "factors" had any reality. What began to change his mind was not the finding that he could apply the Mendelian theory to yet another organism (*Drosophila*), but that he could test the Mendelian theory (studied by breeding experiments) with evidence from a wholly different area—cytology—in the observed behavior of chromosomes during gametogenesis. As soon as he saw that the white-eye mutation acted as if it were part of the X chromosome, he began to view the Mendelian theory in a completely different light.

That Morgan saw Mendel's "factors" as having a possible material basis in the chromosome does not imply that he automatically accepted the idea that genes were physical entities; nor was he primarily concerned with determining how much of the chromosome a mutant gene occupied whenever a new mutation was discovered. The physical existence of genes was unnecessary for the validity of the original Mendelian theory and for much of the *Drosophila* work. The Mendelian-chromosome theory was largely a formalism: it stood on its own as a consistent scheme without necessarily being tied to observable physical structures. Until cytological techniques materials were developed by Painter and others in the late 1920's, it was impossible to determine a point-by-point correspondence between genetic maps (determined by crossover frequencies) and chromosome structure (determined cytologically). Nevertheless, from the outset Morgan was never content to deal with a purely formalistic theory. In the preface to *The Mechanism of Mendelian Heredity*, he and his coauthors admitted that Mendel's theories could be viewed independently of chromosomes. But they hastened to point out that this was not the course they were going to follow:

> Why then, we are often asked, do you drag in the chromosomes? Our answer is that since the chromosomes furnish exactly the kind of mechanism that the Mendelian laws call for; and since there is an ever-increasing body of information that points clearly to the chromosomes as the bearers of the Mendelian factors, it would be folly to close one's eyes to so patent a relation.[12]

Preliminary evidence suggested that genes were real entities on chromosomes, even though it could not be proved conclusively.

As an experimentalist Morgan urged other biologists to employ the quantitative and rigorous methodology which had been so successful in experimental embryology and in his own work on heredity. For biology to attain the same level of development as the physical sciences, it was necessary to adopt the same standards. Yet Morgan did not believe that biology should be reduced simply to expressions of physical and chemical interactions. He believed too much in the naturalist's view of living systems. Reductionism was too simplistic for Morgan; he could never follow Loeb to the logical conclusions of the mechanistic conception of life. What Morgan did believe, however, was that biology should be placed on the same footing as the physical sciences: that is, that the criteria for evaluating ideas in biology should be the same as those in physics and chemistry (quantitative measurement, experimentation, and rigorous analysis).

The California Institute of Technology. In 1927 George Ellery Hale invited Morgan to come to the California Institute of Technology to establish its first division of biology. After weighing the matter for a short time, Morgan accepted with enthusiasm. Although he had doubts about his abilities as an administrator (he wrote to Hale that he was a "laboratory animal, who has tried most of his life to keep away from such entanglements"),[13] the opportunity of heading a new department seemed to far outweigh the possible administrative problems. This move offered several advantages to Morgan, who was then sixty-two. Because the Kerckhoff Laboratory had a generous endowment (from the Kerckhoff family) as well as assistance from the Rockefeller Foundation, Morgan was able from the start to attract a first-rate staff. At Caltech, Morgan developed a modern department based on the concept of biology as he thought it should be studied and taught, where the new experimentalism could play a predominant role. Moving to Caltech also provided Morgan with the opportunity of achieving on a permanent basis the kind of scientific interaction and cooperation which he found so productive first at Naples and later during summers at the Marine Biological Laboratory, Woods Hole. As he wrote to Hale: "The participation of a group of scientific men united in a common venture for the advancement of research fires my imagination to the kindling point."[14]

In the Caltech period Morgan's influence in genetics extended beyond the *Drosophila* work and the classical chromosome theory. Although he did not

pioneer in the newer biochemical and molecular genetics that began to emerge in the 1940's, he nourished that trend. Both George Beadle, as a National Research Council fellow in 1935, and Max Delbrück, as an international research fellow in biology of the Rockefeller Foundation in 1939, worked with Morgan's group at Caltech; both saw that the next logical questions arising out of the *Drosophila* work were those of gene function. It was their work on the relationships between genes and proteins in simple organisms, such as yeasts and bacteriophages, that prepared the way for the revolution in molecular genetics during the 1950's and 1960's.

Morgan's influence was central to the transformation of biology in general, and heredity and embryology in particular, from descriptive and highly speculative sciences arising from a morphological tradition, into ones based on quantitative and analytical methods. Beginning with embryology, and later moving into heredity, he brought first the experimental, and then the quantitative and analytical, approach to biological problems. Morgan's work on the chromosome theory of heredity alone would have earned him an important place in the history of modern biology. Yet in combination with his fundamental contributions to embryology, and his enthusiasm for a new methodology, he can be ranked as one of the most important biologists in the twentieth century.

NOTES

1. A. H. Sturtevant, "Thomas Hunt Morgan," p. 285.
2. D. M. McCullough, "W. K. Brooks' Role in the History of American Biology," in *Journal of the History of Biology*, **2** (1969), 411–438, esp. p. 420.
3. T. H. Morgan and Hans Driesch, "Zur Analysis der ersten Entwickelungsstadien des Ctenophoreneies. I. Von der Entwickelung einzelner Ctenophorenblastomeren. II. Von der Entwickelung ungefurchter Eier mit Protoplasmadefekten," in *Archiv für Entwicklungsmechanik der Organismen*, **2** (1895), 204–215, 216–224.
4. T. H. Morgan, "Impressions of the Naples Zoological Station," in *Science*, **3** (1896), 16–18.
5. *Ibid.*
6. T. H. Morgan, "A Biological and Cytological Study of Sex Determination in Phylloxerans and Aphids," in *Journal of Experimental Zoology*, **7** (1909), 239–352; "Chromosomes and Heredity," in *American Naturalist*, **44** (1910), 449–496.
7. T. H. Morgan, "A Biological and Cytological Study . . .," p. 263.
8. T. H. Morgan, "Sex-Limited Inheritance in *Drosophila*," in *Science*, **32** (1910), 120–122.
9. F. A. Janssens, "La théorie de la chiasmatypie," in *La Cellule*, **25** (1909), 389–411.
10. A. H. Sturtevant, *A History of Genetics* (New York, 1965), pp. 49–50.
11. A. H. Sturtevant, "Thomas Hunt Morgan," p. 297.

12. T. H. Morgan, A. H. Sturtevant, H. J. Muller, and C. B. Bridges, *The Mechanism of Mendelian Heredity*, p. viii.
13. Morgan to George Ellery Hale, 9 May 1927, G. E. Hale papers, California Institute of Technology Archives, microfilm roll 26, frame 29.
14. *Ibid.*

BIBLIOGRAPHY

I. ORIGINAL WORKS. A complete bibliography of Morgan's published writings can be found in Sturtevant's "Thomas Hunt Morgan" (see below). Among the more important books and articles are "The Relationships of the Sea-Spiders," in *Biological Lectures Delivered at the Marine Biological Laboratory of Woods Hole in the Summer Session of 1890* (Boston, 1891), pp. 142–167; "Regeneration: Old and New Interpretations," in *Biological Lectures Delivered . . . Summer Session of 1899* (Boston, 1900), pp. 185–208; *Regeneration* (New York, 1901); *Evolution and Adaptation* (New York, 1903); "Recent Theories in Regard to the Determination of Sex," in *Popular Science Monthly*, 64 (1903), 97–116; "The Assumed Purity of the Germ Cells in Mendelian Results," in *Science*, 22 (1905), 877–879; *Experimental Zoology* (New York, 1907); "A Biological and Cytological Study of Sex Determination in Phylloxerans and Aphids," in *Journal of Experimental Zoology*, 7 (1909), 293–352; "What Are 'Factors' in Mendelian Explanations?," in *American Breeders' Association Report*, 5 (1909), 365–368; "Chromosomes and Heredity," in *American Naturalist*, 44 (1910), 449–496; and "Sex-Limited Inheritance in *Drosophila*," in *Science*, 32 (1910), 120–122.

After 1910 there appeared "An Attempt to Analyze the Constitution of the Chromosomes on the Basis of Sex-Limited Inheritance in *Drosophila*," in *Journal of Experimental Zoology*, 11 (1911), 365–412; "Random Segregation Versus Coupling in Mendelian Inheritance," in *Science*, 34 (1911), 384; "The Explanation of a New Sex Ratio in *Drosophila*," *ibid.*, 36 (1912), 718–719; *Heredity and Sex* (New York, 1913); "Multiple Allelomorphs in Mice," in *American Naturalist*, 48 (1914), 449–458; *The Mechanism of Mendelian Heredity* (New York, 1915; reiss., New York, 1972), written with A. H. Sturtevant, H. J. Muller, and C. B. Bridges; *A Critique of the Theory of Evolution* (Princeton, 1916), rev. as *Evolution and Genetics* (Princeton, 1925); *Sex Linked Inheritance in Drosophila*, Carnegie Institution Publication no. 237 (Washington, D.C., 1916), written with C. B. Bridges; "The Theory of the Gene," in *American Naturalist*, 51 (1917), 513–544; "The Origin of Gynandromorphs," in *Contributions to the Genetics of Drosophila Melanogaster*, Carnegie Institution Publication no. 278 (Washington, D.C., 1919), 3–124, written with C. B. Bridges; *The Physical Basis of Heredity* (Philadelphia, 1919); "Chiasmatype and Crossing Over," in *American Naturalist*, 54 (1920), 193–219, written with E. B. Wilson; "The Evidence for the Linear Order of the Genes," in *Proceedings of the National Academy of Sciences of the United States of America*, 6 (1920), 162–164, written with A. H. Sturtevant and C. B. Bridges; "The Bearing of Mendelism on the Origin of Species," in *Scientific Monthly*,

16 (1923), 237–247; "The Modern Theory of Genetics and the Problem of Embryonic Development," in *Physiological Reviews*, 3 (1923), 603–627; *The Theory of the Gene* (New Haven, 1926); "The Relation of Physics to Biology," in *Science*, 65 (1927); *The Scientific Basis of Evolution* (New York, 1932); *Embryology and Genetics* (New York, 1934); and "The Conditions That Lead to Normal or Abnormal Development of *Ciona*," in *Biological Bulletin*, 88 (1945), 50–52.

There is no single collection of Morgan's letters, notebooks, or other unpub. materials. Numerous Morgan letters can be found, however, in the papers of Ross G. Harrison (Yale University), Edwin Grant Conklin (Princeton University), William Bateson (American Philosophical Society), and George Ellery Hale (Mount Wilson and Palomar Observatories Library, Pasadena). The American Philosophical Society Library, Philadelphia, is collecting the papers of important American geneticists; Morgan letters appear prominently in many of these collections.

II. SECONDARY LITERATURE. The fullest account of Morgan's life to date remains A. H. Sturtevant, "Thomas Hunt Morgan," in *Biographical Memoirs. National Academy of Sciences*, 33 (1959), 283–325. Selected writings about Morgan and his work include G. E. Allen, "Thomas Hunt Morgan and the Problem of Natural Selection," in *Journal of the History of Biology*, 1 (1968), 113–139; "T. H. Morgan and the Emergence of a New American Biology," in *Quarterly Review of Biology*, 44 (1969), 168–188; "T. H. Morgan and the Problem of Sex Determination," in *Proceedings of the American Philosophical Society*, 110 (1966), 48–57; "T. H. Morgan, Richard Goldschmidt and the Opposition to Mendelian Theory 1900–1940," in *Biological Bulletin*, 139 (1970), 412–413; and a slightly fuller treatment of this same material, "Richard Goldschmidt's Opposition to the Mendelian-Chromosome Theory," in *Folia Mendeliana*, 6 (1971), 299–303. See also Edward Manier, "The Experimental Method in Biology. T. H. Morgan and the Theory of the Gene," in *Synthese*, 20 (1969), 185–205; and A. H. Sturtevant, "The Fly Room," ch. 6 of *A History of Genetics* (New York, 1965). An analysis of the work of the *Drosophila* group from Muller's point of view is given in E. A. Carlson, "The Drosophila Group: the Transition From the Mendelian Unit to the Individual Gene," in *Journal of the History of Biology* (in press).

Background material on much of the development of Mendelian genetics after 1900 can be found in three general historical studies: E. A. Carlson, *The Gene, a Critical History* (Philadelphia, 1966); L. C. Dunn, *A Short History of Genetics* (New York, 1965); and Sturtevant's *History of Genetics*.

GARLAND E. ALLEN

MORICHINI, DOMENICO LINO (*b.* Civitantino, Aquila, Italy, 23 September 1773; *d.* Rome, Italy, 19 November 1836), *medicine, chemistry.*

The son of Anselmo Morichini and Domitilla Moratti, Morichini went to Rome for his university studies and remained there. In 1792 he graduated in philosophy and in medicine. The following year he was appointed assistant physician, and later head physician, at the Arcispedale di Santo Spirito. While holding important executive positions in public hygiene and health organizations and continuing to practice medicine throughout his lifetime, Morichini lectured in chemistry at the University of Rome from 1800. In fact, he introduced this new subject of instruction by presenting Lavoisier's doctrines instead of the phlogiston theory and by setting up an experimental chemistry laboratory.

In 1802 Morichini was appointed to make the chemical examination of fossil elephant teeth found in Rome. Treating them with concentrated sulfuric acid, he noted a lively effervescence due to the discharge of gas, which he recognized to consist of both carbon dioxide and fluorine. The latter, released especially from the tooth enamel, was recognizable because it corroded the glass of the vessel used in the experiment and because, when brought into contact with limewater, it formed lime fluoride "endowed with all the properties of natural fluorspar" (that is, CaF_2). Morichini subsequently found elemental fluorine in human teeth.

BIBLIOGRAPHY

I. ORIGINAL WORKS. Morichini's "Analisi chimica del dente fossile" is included in Carlo Lodovico Morozzo, "Sopra un dente fossile trovato nelle vicinanze di Roma," in *Memorie di matematica e di fisica della Società italiana delle scienze*, **10**, pt. 1 (1803), 166–170. Morichini returned to the subject in "Analisi dello smalto di un dente fossile di elefante e dei denti umani," *ibid.*, **12**, pt. 2 (1805), 73–88, 268–269. See also *Raccolta degli scritti editi ed inediti del Cav. Dott. Domenico Morichini* (Rome, 1852).

II. SECONDARY LITERATURE. See the anonymous "Memorie storiche del Cavalier Domenico Morichini," in *Raccolta degli scritti* (see above); and Luigi Belloni, "Il fluoro dentario scoperto a Roma nel 1802 da Domenico Morichini," in *Scritti in onore di Adalberto Pazzini* (Rome, 1968), 199–205.

LUIGI BELLONI

MORIN, JEAN-BAPTISTE (*b.* Villefranche, Beaujolais, France, 23 February 1583; *d.* Paris, France, 6 November 1656), *medicine, astronomy, astrology.*

Morin was a strange person but typical of his age in that he undertook very varied activities. He was sufficiently successful and intelligent to acquire a reputation in his own time, but he failed to demand of himself the thorough discipline that would have enabled him to produce truly scientific work. A medical doctor at first, he then took an interest in all the topics associated with hermetic literature. In order to penetrate the mysteries of nature he studied mining and astrology (he was later to draw up an astrological chart for the infant Louis XIV). His talents won him the support of influential people, and in 1630 he was professor of mathematics at the Collège Royal (now Collège de France), a position he held until his death.

A polemicist by disposition, he quickly sought to distinguish himself in the major debates most likely to bring him widest attention. In 1624 he published a defense of Aristotle in conjunction with the refutation of the theses of Antoine de Villon and of Étienne de Claves, both of which had been condemned by the Sorbonne. He opposed Galileo before and after the trial of 1633. He attacked Descartes in 1638, flattering himself that he had detected how bad his philosophy was from the moment that they had met, before Descartes's departure for Holland.

If Morin suffered injustice in the judgments reached by his contemporaries, especially Boulliau, he owed his poor reputation to the way in which he conducted his disputes. This fault is best illustrated in the matter of the determination of longitudes. During the very period when he was presenting himself as the champion of the immobility of the earth, Morin simultaneously wished to prove that he was capable of drawing inspiration from Kepler, of correcting the Rudolphine Tables, and of proposing a method for finding longitudes that would always be usable at sea and sufficiently precise for navigation. The only original thing about this method, which was based on the observation of the moon, was its claim of utilizing the movements of the moon relative to the stars as a universal clock and of generalizing this phenomenon to calculate the difference in hours between two positions on the earth. The method required new observational instruments, which could be used with sufficient precision on ships, the improvement of the mathematical solution of spherical triangles, and the possibility of a systematic checking of tables of lunar motion established for a given position. Morin glimpsed these three facets of the problem and made an important contribution to instrumental technique by utilizing telescopes for the sights and verniers for the measurement of angles; but he was incapable of mastering the complex problem of precision in a process involving both observation and computation. Ambition and the desire to obtain a pension from Richelieu made him deaf to all objections.

From 1626 to 1628 Morin undertook research in optics with the engineer Ferrier, in whom Descartes had placed his hopes. Shortly afterward his friendships with Peiresc and Gassendi helped him in observational astronomy. But the affair of the longitudes, with the prolonged debate (1634–1639) that put him in opposition to Étienne Pascal, Mydorge, and Beaugrand, alienated the scientific community, and he continued his work largely in isolation.

Morin's posthumously published *Astrologia gallica* reveals that he had interesting ideas concerning the theory of heat and the temperature of mixtures. Moreover, in the correspondence of Mersenne and Descartes references to Morin are not entirely negative. Despite his undoubted talents, Morin's philosophical and scientific choices were too often political ones and prevented him from producing the caliber of work of which we now see he was capable.

BIBLIOGRAPHY

I. ORIGINAL WORKS. For works of Morin see *Astronomicarum domorum cabala detecta* (Paris, 1623); *Refutation des thèses ... d'A. Villon et E. de Claves ... contre les doctrines d'Aristote* (Paris, 1624); *Famosi et antiqui problematis de telluris motu vel quiete hactenus optata solutio* (Paris, 1631); *Trigonometriae canonicae libri tres quibus planorum et sphaericorum triangulorum theoria ... adjungitur liber quartus pro calculi tabulis logarithmorum* (Paris, 1633); *Pro telluris quiete* (Paris, 1634); *Astronomia jam a fundamentis integre et exacte restituta ...* (Paris, 1640); *La science des longitudes ...* (Paris, 1647); and *Astrologia gallica ...* (The Hague, 1661), published posthumously under the auspices of Marie Louise of Gonzaga, queen of Poland, which also contains a Latin trans. of the anonymous *Vie de Morin* (1660), the French original of which is lost.

II. SECONDARY LITERATURE. For information about Morin see P. Bayle, *Dictionnaire historique et critique*, II, pt. 1 (Rotterdam, 1697), 602–612; M. Delambre, *Histoire de l'astronomie moderne*, II (Paris, 1821), 236–273; G. de Fouchy, "Sur la date de l'application des lunettes aux instruments d'observation ...," in *Mémoires de l'Académie royale des sciences pour l'année 1783* (1787), 385–392; L. Moreri, *Le grand dictionnaire historique*, VII (Paris, 1759), 786–788; and J. Montucla, *Histoire des mathématiques* (Paris, 1799), II, 336–1802; IV, 543–545.

PIERRE COSTABEL

MORISON, ROBERT (*b.* Dundee, Scotland, 1620; *d.* London, England, 11 November 1683), *botany.*

Morison was the son of John Morison and his wife, Anna Gray. He was educated at Aberdeen University, where he obtained the M.A. in 1638. He taught at that university until his career was interrupted by the Civil War. In 1644, after fighting against the Covenanters, he fled to France as a Royalist. Morison studied medicine at Paris and obtained an M.D. at Angers in 1648. Botany quickly became his main interest, an interest that led to his appointment as gardener to Gaston d'Orléans at Blois. He undertook extensive journeys to collect material for the gardens and probably contributed to the catalog of the Blois garden and was regarded as a suitable authority to revise the first English plant list, *Phytologia Britannica* (1650).

Charles II brought Morison back to England at the Restoration in 1660 as royal physician and botanist. In 1669 he became the first professor of botany at Oxford. His activities were closely related to the Oxford botanical garden, founded forty years earlier. Its gardener, Jacob Bobart the younger, became Morison's closest colleague. At Oxford, Morison's duties were not onerous, allowing him ample leisure for the compilation of his major botanical works.

Morison's first publication, *Praeludia botanica* (1669), was a composite volume containing an augmented list of the plants at Blois arranged according to the orthodox classification; critical animadversions on the taxonomic work of Jean and Gaspard Bauhin; and an intriguing dialogue announcing his dissatisfaction with current approaches to a plant classification. The latter stressed the need for a single, key criterion for determining the *nota generica*, or natural relationships, of plants. He revived Cesalpino's suggestion that classification should be based on fruit and seed characteristics.

This principle was first applied in Morison's monograph on umbelliferous plants (1672), which successfully isolated the Umbelliferae from other plants with similar inflorescence forms. The family was then subdivided into a series of genera that closely resembled later categories. Vegetative characteristics were consulted only for subsidiary taxonomic affinities.

Morison next endeavored to apply his taxonomic principles to the entire plant kingdom. Like so many similar enterprises this was destined for a fragmentary conclusion. He pursued the work with great enthusiasm, however, even obtaining substantial financial assistance from Oxford and private patrons to meet the cost of publishing his voluminous illustrated *Historia plantarum*. Part I, on trees, was thought to exist by contemporaries but was never published. Morison himself published part II (1680), and his colleague Bobart completed part III (1699). Bobart also assembled an herbarium of 5,000 plants organized to illustrate Morison's system. The published sections of the *Historia* include about 6,000 plants. Those in part II are described in considerable detail, and the illustrations are of higher quality than has usually been appreciated by modern commentators. The crucial system of classification was a poor application of Morison's original idea. His taxonomic principle was not followed consistently, vegetative criteria frequently being invoked to establish major divisions. Hence Morison's system had many of the defects which it was designed to counteract.

In reputation Morison was quickly eclipsed by his gifted contemporary John Ray. This decline in fortune was undoubtedly reinforced by the excessively critical tone of his writings and his false claims to originality. Thus even during his lifetime Morison was a relatively isolated figure, avoiding association with such major organizations as the Royal Society and the London College of Physicians. Certain major taxonomists, however, recognized the importance of his declared principles. Both Tournefort and Linnaeus regarded Morison as the "instaurator" of taxonomy. His pioneer attempt to apply a single, clear taxonomic criterion to the whole plant kingdom had the potential to rescue taxonomy from a state of strangled confusion resulting from the rapid accumulation of data.

BIBLIOGRAPHY

I. ORIGINAL WORKS. Morison's writings are *Hortus regius Blesensis auctus, praeludium botanicorum* (London, 1669), known as *Praeludia botanica; Plantarum umbelliferarum distributio nova* (Oxford, 1672); *Plantarum historiae universalis Oxoniensis pars secunda* (Oxford, 1680); and *Plantarum historiae universalis Oxoniensis pars tertia*, Jacob Bobart, ed. (Oxford, 1699), introduced with a biographical sketch of Morison by Archibald Pitcairne.

Morison also edited Paulo Boccone's *Icones et descriptiones rariorum plantarum . . .* (Oxford, 1674).

II. SECONDARY LITERATURE. See G. S. Boulger, "Robert Morison," in *Dictionary of National Biography*, XIII (1967–1968), 958–960; J. Reynolds Green, *A History of Botany in the United Kingdom* (London, 1914), 98–110; R. Pulteney, *Historical and Biographical Sketches of the Progress of Botany*, I (London, 1790), 289–327; and S. H. Vines, "Robert Morison and John Ray," in *Makers of British Botany*, F. W. Oliver, ed. (Cambridge, 1913), 8–43; and *An Account of the Morisonian Herbarium* (Oxford, 1914).

CHARLES WEBSTER

MORLAND, SAMUEL (*b.* Sulhamstead Bannister, Berkshire, England, 1625; *d.* Hammersmith, Middlesex [now London], England, 30 December 1695), *mathematics, technology.*

Morland was the son of Thomas Morland, rector of Sulhamstead Bannister, from which village Samuel Morland took his title when he was created baronet. He was educated at Winchester College from 1639 and at Magdalene College, Cambridge, from 1644. Elected a fellow of the college on 30 November 1649, he continued his studies of mathematics there until 1653.

From 1653 to the Restoration in 1660, Morland was deeply involved in politics. He was a supporter and associate of Oliver Cromwell, who employed him on two foreign embassies, to Sweden in 1653 and to the duke of Savoy in 1655, with the object of persuading him to grant amnesty to the Waldenses. Morland was finally successful and in 1658 he published a history of the Waldensian church.

Close association with the intrigues of Cromwell and John Thurloe and, in particular, knowledge of a plot to murder Charles II and his brother disgusted Morland with the Commonwealth cause; and he began working as an agent to promote the restoration of the monarchy. Despite serious charges brought against him, he was granted a full pardon by Charles II in 1660, knighted, and later in the same year was created a baronet. He was also appointed gentleman of the privy chamber, but he did not receive the financial help he had hoped for. From 1660 he devoted himself to experimental work with occasional support from the king, who named him "Master of Mechanicks" in 1681.

Morland was married five times and was survived by only one son, Samuel, who became the second and last baronet of the family. Morland became blind three years before his death and retired to Hammersmith, where he died on 30 December 1695.

Morland's studies of mathematics and his inventiveness led him to make two "arithmetick instruments," or hand calculators, with gear wheels operated by a stylus, for pedagogic use. His perpetual almanac was a concise form of pocket calendar, adapted for use on coin-sized disks, sundials and other instruments, and snuffboxes. A speaking trumpet, described in his treatise on the subject as a "*tuba stentoro-phonica*," was another of his inventions; with it he estimated that a conversation could be carried on at a distance of three-quarters of a mile. It has recently been established that Morland also invented the balance barometer and the diagonal barometer.

Morland's most important work was in the field of hydrostatics. There was much interest in the mid-seventeenth century in mechanical methods of raising water. Morland invented an apparatus using an airtight cistern from which air was expelled by a charge of gunpowder, the water below rising to fill the vacuum thus produced. The *London Gazette* for

30 July 1681 describes how at Windsor Castle, "Sir Samuel Morland, with the strength of eight men, forced the water (mingled with a Vessel of Red Wine to make it more visible) in a continuous stream, at the rate of above sixty Barrels an hour, from the Engine below at the Parkpale, up to the top of the Castle, and from thence into the Air above sixty Foot high."

Morland's efforts to raise water at Versailles led to the publication of *Élévation des eaux* in 1685, but in the manuscript version in the British Museum, written in 1683, there is an account of the use of steam power to raise water. Although he did not develop the steam engine, his experiment is one of the first to show the practical possibilities of steam power.

BIBLIOGRAPHY

I. ORIGINAL WORKS. A list of Samuel Morland's published works is given in app. 2 to the biography by H. W. Dickinson cited below. The main scientific works are *Tuba stentoro-phonica, an Instrument of Excellent use as Well at sea as at Land; Invented, and Variously Experimented, in the year 1670* ... (London, 1671); *The Description and Use of two Arithmetick Instruments. Together With a Short Treatise Explaining and Demonstrating the Ordinary Operations of Arithmetick. As Likewise A Perpetual Almanack, and Several Useful tables* (London, 1673); *Élévation des eaux par toute sorte de machines réduite à la mesure, au poids, à la balance par le moyen d'un nouveau piston & Corps de pompe d'un nouveau mouvement cyclo-elliptique* ... (Paris, 1685); *The Poor Man's Dyal With an Instrument to Set It. Made Applicable to Any Place in England, Scotland, Ireland, &c.* (London, 1689); and *Hydrostaticks: or Instructions Concerning Water-works, Collected out of the Papers of Sir Samuel Morland. Containing the Method Which he Made use of in This Curious art,* Joseph Morland, ed. (London, 1697). There is MS material at the British Museum, Lambeth Palace Library, and Cambridge University Library, all noted by Dickinson. Examples of Morland's calculating machines are at the Science Museum, London; Museum of the History of Science, Oxford; and the Museo di Storia della Scienza, Florence; a speaking trumpet is at Trinity College, Cambridge.

II. SECONDARY LITERATURE. See J. O. Halliwell, *A Brief Account of the Life, Writings, and Inventions of Sir Samuel Morland* (Cambridge, 1838); W. E. Knowles Middleton, "Sir Samuel Morland's Barometers," in *Archives internationales d'histoire des sciences,* **5** (1962), 343–351. H. W. Dickinson, *Sir Samuel Morland, Diplomat and Inventor 1625–1695* (Cambridge, 1970), published eighteen years after the author's death by the Newcomen Society, includes an iconography and a bibliography; and D. J. Bryden, "A Didactic Introduction to Arithmetic, Sir Charles Cotterell's 'Instrument for Arithmeticke' of 1667," in *History of Education,* **2** (1973), 5–18.

G. L'E. TURNER

MORLEY, EDWARD WILLIAMS (*b.* Newark, New Jersey, 29 January 1838; *d.* West Hartford, Connecticut, 24 February 1923), *chemistry, physics.*

Morley was the eldest of four children of Sardis Brewster Morley and Anna Clarissa Treat; his father was a Congregational minister. Morley's education was conducted under his parents' tutelage until he was nineteen, when the family moved to Williamstown, Massachusetts, so that the three boys could attend Williams College, the father's alma mater. With the intention of entering the ministry, Morley entered Andover Theological Seminary in 1861, after receiving the B.A. from Williams College in 1860. While pursuing his theological studies he completed work for the master's degree at Williams College in 1863. Having finished his theological studies in 1864, he served for a year on the Sanitary Commission at Fort Monroe, Virginia.

Morley resumed studies at Andover for another year before receiving an offer to teach at South Berkshire Academy, Marlboro, Massachusetts. There he became acquainted with Isabella Ashley Birdsall, whom he married on Christmas Eve 1868. In September of that year he had accepted an invitation to become minister at the Congregational Church in Twinsburg, Ohio, and was then invited to teach at Western Reserve College in nearby Hudson. In 1882, when the college was transferred to Cleveland and became Adelbert College of Western Reserve University, he was chosen to fill the chair of chemistry and natural history, a position he held until his retirement to West Hartford, Connecticut, in 1906. From 1873 to 1888 Morley also held the professorship of chemistry and toxicology at the Cleveland Medical School, a position which required him to travel back and forth between Cleveland and Hudson for many years. He died just three months after his wife and was buried in the family lot in Pittsfield, Massachusetts. The couple had no children.

Morley's scientific achievements fall into three rather well-defined periods, which are linked by a passionate concern for precise and accurate quantitative measurements, in the tradition of Berzelius and Stas, and by a keen interest in the theories of the structure of matter, especially as reflected in Prout's hypothesis. During his first period, while at Hudson, he employed and refined eudiometric methods for analyzing the oxygen content of the atmosphere to within .0025 percent. His purpose was to test the correctness of Loomis' hypothesis that cold waves were caused by the descent of air from high elevations at times of high barometric pressure rather than by horizontal currents moving from north to south. He reasoned that if Loomis' theory were correct, the oxygen content of air collected during a cold wave should be lower due to gravitational separation at high altitudes of molecules of different mass, which had been predicted by Dalton on the basis of his atomic theory. A careful correlation of meteorological records with precise determinations of the oxygen content of air revealed good agreement with Loomis' theory.

After spending three years constructing apparatus and equipping his laboratory at Western Reserve University in Cleveland, Morley undertook a painstakingly planned program to determine the atomic weight of oxygen relative to hydrogen taken as unity. His aim was to test the validity of Prout's hypothesis that the elements of the periodic table were built up from hydrogen or hydrogenlike units. First, he determined quantitatively the extent to which moisture could be removed from gases by drying with sulfuric acid and phosphorus pentoxide. He then made a careful study of the volume proportions in which oxygen and hydrogen unite. Finally, by two independent methods, one based on direct weighings of components and product and the other based on density determinations of oxygen and hydrogen, he found the atomic weight of oxygen to be 15.879, with an uncertainty of the order of one part in ten thousand. With this result Morley felt that he had laid Prout's hypothesis to rest. It was only during the last two decades of his life, after his retirement, that the full significance of exact atomic weight determinations by chemical methods was fully grasped: that they measure the weighted average of all the stable isotopes of the elements in question.

The final period of Morley's career overlaps the previous one and is characterized by extensive collaborative studies with A. A. Michelson, H. T. Eddy, W. A. Rogers, D. C. Miller, C. F. Brush, and J. P. Iddings. His famous ether-drift experiments with Michelson, and much of his work with the others, reflect a fascination with the sensitivity of the interferometer and measuring techniques based upon the wavelengths of light. They also suggest an interest in the rapidly developing field of spectroscopy because it seemed to hold out promise for a deeper understanding of the structure of matter, a promise which was being realized during the last decade and a half of his life. Even in retirement Morley kept active professionally. He constructed an analytical laboratory of his own and carried out an extensive series of exact analyses of rocks collected by J. P. Iddings in Java and the Celebes. In the latter years of his life Morley was honored with the Davy Medal of the Royal Society, the Elliot Cresson Medal of the Franklin Institute, and the Willard Gibbs Medal of the Chicago section of the American Chemical Society, principally for his careful atomic weight determinations.

BIBLIOGRAPHY

A bibliography of 55 papers was collected by F. W. Clarke in *Biographical Memoirs. National Academy of Sciences*, **21** (1927), 1–8. This bibliography was extended by Morley's biographer, H. R. Williams (see below). Morley's letters are preserved at the Library of Congress, and photostat copies are kept in the archives of Case Western Reserve University. Morley's notebooks are in the custody of Frank Hovorka, Hurlbut professor of chemistry at Case Western Reserve University.

A biography is Howard R. Williams, *Edward Williams Morley* (Easton, Pa., 1957).

ERNEST G. SPITTLER

MORO, ANTONIO-LAZZARO (*b*. San Vito del Friuli, Italy, 16 March 1687; *d*. San Vito del Friuli, 12 April 1764), *geology*.

Moro was the son of Bernardino and Felicita Mauro. Although his early education was marked by frequent changes of instructors whose academic preparation and instruction were poor, he distinguished himself in mathematics, music, languages, literature, natural sciences, and ecclesiastical studies. Upon completion of the latter and his ordination into the ministry, he was offered a post as professor of philosophy and rhetoric at the seminary in Feltre and shortly thereafter became its director. Following the death of the bishop of Feltre and because of his own poor health, Moro returned to Friuli, where he became chapelmaster of the cathedral at Portogruaro. Of his varied interests Moro's involvement was greatest in scientific studies, which he pursued with a Galilean conviction that the proper research methodology would inevitably, if gradually, reveal the secrets of nature.

In 1721 Vallisnieri had concluded a study of fossils with a categorical rejection of all theories on the subject, on the ground that none of them could hold up under analytical scrutiny. Moro agreed with this polemical judgment and decided to accept the challenge of the question left open by Vallisnieri. In 1740 he published his best-known work, *Dei crostacei e degli altri corpi marini che si trovano sui monti*, a study of the origin and development of fossiliferous deposits.

The logical order of Moro's work reflects an empirical spirit characteristic of the enlightened intellectual climate of eighteenth-century Europe. Despite its archaic language the book is a model of cogent reasoning. Moro first provides a survey of fossil occurrence, with regional and global distribution, based on personal and reported observations. Elaborating upon earlier indications of L. Marsili and Vallisnieri, he gives a stratigraphic compilation of various fossilized marine flora and fauna, with sequential indications that preceded by almost a century the chronological intuitions of William Smith and his French contemporaries, G. Cuvier and Alexandre Brongniart.

Moro divided prevailing opinions into two groups—neptunist and nonneptunist. After singling out the most popular current opinions—the theory of total submersion and the diluvial views of Burnet and J. Woodward—for reexamination, he finally rejected them as scientifically invalid. Moro's main objection to Burnet was that the British theologian, in *Sacred Theory of the Earth*, had contrived an elaborate antediluvian system in order to force proofs of conjectures established a priori as scientific conclusions.

The examination of Woodward's theories presented a greater challenge, since the noted British naturalist had made considerable and valid contributions to the fossil debate. Moro asserted that when Woodward attempted to construct a scientific theory upon two antithetical principles, one factual (direct observation of fossils) and one hypothetical (miraculous, divine causes of geological phenomena), he violated his stated objectives and thereby undermined his preliminary observations.

Like Burnet before him, Woodward espoused the notion of an aqueous abyss, to which he ascribed, among other functions, the process of supplying water to the rivers and streams of the earth. Moro denied such hydrologic function to an "imaginary abyss," pointing out that, among the scholars (P. Perrault, P. de la Hire, Mariotte, Purchot, J. Cassini, and, more recently, Vallisnieri, D. Corradi, and Giorgi) concerned with the origin and sources of the water on earth, Woodward alone disregarded or rejected the theory of natural precipitation as the initial source of groundwater. The most questionable theory, according to Moro, was Woodward's theory of global disintegration, which attributed to divine intervention the loss of gravity during diluvial submersion.

Because of his plutonism Moro categorically rejected the view that stratification was caused by aqueous agents, arguing that such a view was contradicted by the evidence of both chromatic and density differentiation among layers. Unlike the Plutonist views, which were characteristic largely of the eighteenth century, the theory of total submersion had persisted from ancient times (Plutarch, Strabo) and was espoused among moderns by Fracastoro and Leibniz; Vallisnieri had also been tempted by the notion until he found it unprovable. Moro's main objection to the theory was that it did not take into account the structural or dynamic aspects of mountain formation or land building, which were crucial to an understanding of the fossil problem.

Moro began his contribution to the fossil debate with a clear statement of his scientific credo: It is within nature that one must search for laws governing physical reality. But since nature seldom reveals efficient causes to man, one may use its constancy and uniformity and the stability of natural law to deduce from certain effects their dynamic causes, which are similar if not identical. The guiding principle and unifying theme of Moro's theory and proof was thus the Newtonian axiom that affirms this concept: "Effectuum naturalium ejusdem generis eadem sunt causae."

Moro noted that in order to understand his fossil theory, it was first necessary to determine the dynamic forces and physical laws involved in the formation of fossiliferous deposits. The refuted theories had been exclusively neptunist and Moro's attitudes were exclusively plutonic, attributing geomorphological development of the globe to igneous agents. On the basis of observations made by contemporary and classical scientists of volcanic mountains and islands, Moro established a chronological framework within which he synthesized and historicized the two aspects of his theory: the formation and development of the earth and fossil phenomena. Proceeding retrospectively, he quoted from a detailed report, made to Vallisnieri by a student, G. C. Condilli, of the volcanic island of Mea Kaumen, which surfaced in the Greek archipelago near Santorini in 1707 and which continued to rise, shift, and settle until it stabilized in 1711. This, Moro noted, was but the latest incident in a long history of volcanic island formation in the archipelago, accounts of which had been left by Strabo, Pliny, and Justinian.

Historical incidents of volcanological mountain formation similarly offered proof that these land masses were the result of igneous forces within the earth. Referring to reports by N. Madrisio and Agricola, Moro cited the example of the volcanic birth in 1538 of Monte Nuovo in the Bay of Naples. On the basis of these and other historical incidents, Moro concluded that (1) mountains and islands are volcanic in origin and (2) the presence of marine fossils on the surface of these landmasses justifies the belief that the newly formed surfaces were once submerged and, in the process of rising, brought marine organisms to the surface with other materials.

Although Vallisnieri, Steno, Woodward, and F. Colonna (Hooke and J. Ray are not mentioned) had already indicated that a necessary and essential relationship exists between mountain fossils and marine organisms, Moro defended the originality of his work on the ground that he had integrated the incidental, particular observations of his predecessors into a systematic and generalized theory that correctly placed the problem of fossil deposits in the broader framework of mountain formation and tectonics. He also indicated that the dynamic processes involved are igneous rather than aqueous.

Moro then passed from dynamic to structural geology, describing insular mountains as massive gneisses folded in numerous directions—concave, convex, perpendicular, oblique—all caused by the pressure of intense subterranean heat. Generalizing his plutonic theory to include mainland masses, Moro differentiated these masses into two types: primary mountains—massive orthogneisses pushed up from the center of the earth when that part of the surface of the earth was submerged by water, and secondary (or stratified) mountains—composed largely of paragneisses and formed on the surface of the earth. To corroborate his distinction between volcanic and sedimentary mountains, Moro quoted Marsili, who had similarly distinguished two types of ocean floor: essential (or original) crustal rock and accidental rock, composed of sands and mineral deposits carried back to sea by returning lava flows. If the essential bedrock of the sea is similar to the massive gneisses of primary mountains, Marsili noted, it is reasonable to conclude that the latter were once a part of the ocean floor and that they were thrust above the water when that portion of the crust was still uncovered by secondary deposits.

The divergent views of mountain formation held by Moro and Vallisnieri reflect, to a large extent, the basic tensions between plutonists and neptunists, who often agreed upon structural effects but disagreed upon the dynamic principles involved. While Vallisnieri considered mountain building to be the result of successive aqueous "inundations," Moro insisted that these "inundations" actually consisted of igneous materials, of which each successive crust is composed.

Moro attributed the striated and undulating patterns of marble to seismic action and ground shifts during the cooling and solidifying of the magma. The process of crystallogenesis, which Vallisnieri was unable to define to his satisfaction, also was interpreted by Moro as dependent upon intense heat.

The effects of volcanic action upon biological development were indicated in Moro's consideration of the problem of skeletal remains of extinct or exotic animals in areas that are no longer a natural habitat for such species. He refuted Woodward's diluvial explanations in favor of a surprisingly modern, naturalistic theory: that the areas of occurrence of extinct animal fossils were once their life-supporting environment. He insisted that the chronological aspect of the plutonic principle must always be kept in mind. Between volcanic eruptions, vast periods of time elapse. If the volcanic deposit is organically sterile, animal life will become extinct. As subsequent volcanic activity deposits additional strata, in which organic matter fosters the development of vegetation, the chain of being is reestablished.

Moro terminated his work with a chronological résumé of his system that is in effect a miniature composite biogeological history. Briefly, his summary is as follows: On the first day God created, among other things, the terraqueous globe surrounded by fresh water. There followed a division of the waters, without mountainous protrusions to disturb the uniform spheroid form. On the second day Moro's concept of an active Creator as the dynamic principle is abruptly replaced by natural actualism. The shift is so sudden that one suspects that the scriptural inclusion was but a token gesture made by Moro to insure permission from religious and civic authorities to publish his work. Moro makes it quite clear that the natural potential combustibility of the core of the earth was set in motion according to divine plan or will, not according to a divine act.

Once activated, igneous pressures push up the rocky surface of the submerged lithosphere, forming primary mountains. Volcanic matter may return to the sea, depositing salts, minerals, and bitumen into the fresh water and changing its chemical composition. Secondary mountains and landmasses are built up by the same volcanic activity, with the seabed rising also as a result of the deposition of strata.

Biology also was determined by physical conditions. Marine flora and fauna were not yet formed. As the accidental seabed was transformed by mineral deposits into life-supporting systems, marine vegetation appeared, followed by marine animals, the latter with their origin and habitat in the soft earth, sand, and clay of redeposited lava flows. As landmasses built up, marine biological processes and patterns were repeated on land, with the formation of vegetation preceding that of animal life. Crowning this chain of being is man, viewed, as all else in Moro's system, as a product of natural evolution rather than of divine creation. This audacious view of anthropogenesis by a clergyman was vehemently

MORO

MOROZOV

condemned by contemporary scripturalists. For Moro subsequent volcanic activity involved the uplift of part of the ocean floor with its flora and fauna. This in turn caused the formation of fossiliferous deposits in stratified mountains which preserved the fossils as a museum preserves evidences of human life, arts, and crafts. Superposed strata were for Moro indicative of chronological as well as environmental and cultural data.

The work provoked vehement reactions among European scientists, polarizing them into neptunists and plutonists. Among the former were Zolmann, who published his views in the *Philosophical Transactions of the Royal Society* in 1745, and Giuseppe Costantini, whose impassioned defense of the diluvial theory, *La verità del diluvio dimostrata* (1747), was so indiscriminate in its attack on Moro that it had the effects of confirming rather than disproving Moro's views. In 1749 G. C. Generelli added his support to Moro's theory in a paper read before the Academy of Sciences at Cremona. A German translation of the work, *Neue Untersuchung über die Abanderungen der Erde* (1751), was followed by a lengthy review by C. Delius in his *Anleitung zu der Bergbaukunst.* Moro was one of the authorities cited by Knorr (1755) and Desmarest. His scheme of periodization (primary, secondary) was amplified in Italy by Arduino and in Sweden by Bergman, who referred to Moro; by J. G. Lehmann and Pallas, in Germany and Russia, respectively; and the ultimate development was the establishment of the geologic column by A. G. Werner. Oddly enough, this work, so influential on German neptunism, made little impression on British volcanism. In 1767 E. King, in an article in the *Philosophical Transactions,* admitted that his geological theories had been anticipated by those of Moro, whose work he allegedly had discovered only after the publication of his own study. King's cursory reference to Moro disappeared altogether in J. Hutton's *Theory of the Earth,* which contains observations and conclusions similar to those made by Moro half a century earlier. Hutton's ideas were influenced by the still earlier plutonic geodynamics of Hooke, and his neglect of Moro was emphasized by J. Playfair in his *Illustration of the Huttonian Theory of the Earth* (1802).

Moro's work was most thoroughly analyzed and its importance emphasized by Hutton's principal successor, Lyell.

The modernity of Moro's views, the broad scope of knowledge that he brought to his investigations, and the breadth of the scientific fields that he examined and illuminated place him at the center of the intense intellectual activity of Italy's "second Renaissance."

BIBLIOGRAPHY

I. ORIGINAL WORKS. Moro's works include *Dei crostacei e degli altri corpi marini che si trovano sui monti,* 2 vols. (Venice, 1740); *Lettera, ossia dissertazione sopra la calata de' fulmini dalle nuvole* (Venice, 1750); and his MS "Due lettere latine sul sistema dei crostacei" (see below).

II. SECONDARY LITERATURE. See A. Altan, "Memorie biografiche della terra di Sanvito," in *Memorie storiche della terra di Sanvito al Tagliamento* (Venice, 1832), pp. 87–89, which also locates a number of Moro's MSS; G. Dandolo, *La caduta della Repubblica di Venezia, Appendice* (Venice, 1857), p. 70; G. Generelli, "Dissertazione de' crostacei, e dell'altre produzioni marine che sono ne'monti," in *Raccolta Milanese dell'anno 1757* (Milan, 1757), pp. 1–22; C. Lyell, *Principles of Geology* (London, 1830), pp. 42–47; F. di Manzano, *Cenni biografici dei letterati ed artisti friulani* (Udine, 1887), p. 135; Saccardo, "La botanica in Italia, materiali per la storia di questa scienza," in *Memorie del R. Istituto veneto di scienze, lettere ed arti,* **25**, no. 4 (1895), 76; **26**, no. 6 (1901), 76, 114; and P. Zecchini, *Vita di A. L. Moro* (Padua, 1865).

See also the article on Moro in *Biografia degli italiani illustri nelle scienze, lettere ed arti del secolo XVIII e dei contemporanei* (Venice, 1834–1845), pp. 304–305.

ROSE THOMASIAN

MOROZOV, GEORGY FEDOROVICH (*b.* St. Petersburg, Russia, 7 January 1867; *d.* Simferopol, U.S.S.R., 9 May 1920), *biogeography, ecology.*

Morozov's father, a cutter in a linen draper's shop who later became commissar of the administration of city property in St. Petersburg, planned a military career for his son. Morozov accordingly entered the Pavlovsk military academy in 1884, graduating as a second lieutenant of artillery two years later. He was then sent to the fortress of Daugavpils, in Latvia, where he became acquainted with a group of youthful students and began to broaden his own education. In particular he was influenced by a young woman revolutionary, O. N. Zandrok, who had been sent into exile for participating in the People's Will movement. Zandrok, for whom he clearly felt affection, fostered Morozov's sympathy for the peasant classes; when he decided to devote himself to studying science, it was therefore natural for him to select the agricultural sciences as being closest and most necessary to the people. He chose forestry as his specialty and spent his free time reading the works of Timiryazev, Gustavson, and the other professors at the Petrovskaya (now Timiryazev) Agricultural Academy and in attending lectures on Russian village economy.

When Zandrok's term of exile was up she returned to St. Petersburg. Morozov gave up his commission and accompanied her there, entering the St. Petersburg Forestry Institute in 1889. Morozov's father thought that he was mad and refused him financial aid; he broke with his family and was forced to live on the meager earnings that he made giving lessons. At the Forestry Institute Morozov's teachers included the botanist I. P. Borodin, the soil scientist P. A. Kostichev, and the zoologist N. A. Kholodkovsky. His scientific views were, however, more strongly influenced by the anatomist and social activist P. F. Lesgaft, whom he had met in the Zandrok household, Lesgaft having been introduced into the family circle by O. N. Zandrok's sister, Lidia Nikolaevna. When Lesgaft, who had been dismissed from the University of St. Petersburg for his radical social opinions, began to give an anatomy course in his own home, Morozov was his most eager auditor. From Lesgaft, a convinced evolutionist, Morozov learned to consider the mutual relationship of the form and function of an organism and to view the animal within its environment; he learned to think in broad terms and to see in each biological phenomenon the outcome of development under the influence of a complex chain of interrelationships in nature.

Morozov's student years were saddened by the death from diphtheria of O. N. Zandrok. He remained on good terms with her family, however, and after a period of shared mourning married her sister. He graduated from the Forestry Institute in 1894 and became an assistant forester and teacher at the school in the Khrenovk forest preserve in Voronezh gubernia, where he was faced with the complex problems of managing a forest on sandy soil in a dry climate. His first article, published in 1896, was "O borbe s zasukhoy pri kulture sosny" ("On the Struggle Against Drought in the Culture of Pine Trees").

In May 1896 Morozov received a commission to go abroad to study forest management in Germany and Switzerland for two years. He attended lectures on forestry at Munich University and at the Eberswalde Academy and met the leading German specialists in forest economy. Shortly after his return to Russia he was appointed director of the Kammeno-Steppe experimental forestry preserve in Voronezh gubernia, one of the preserves created by Dokuchaev in an attempt to prevent drought. (The drought of 1891 had led to a terrible famine in the steppe chernozem zone.)

It was Dokuchaev who had founded soil science in Russia, and in 1899 Morozov, who had completed a zealous study of Dokuchaev's works, published a paper of his own, "Pochvovedenie i lesovodstvo" ("Soil Science and Forestry"). In this, and in a series of other works, Morozov proposed the establishment

of forest management as a specific discipline with a theoretical basis in forestry and forest economy. Morozov's work became widely known, and in 1901 he was appointed professor of forestry at St. Petersburg University; from 1904 until 1919 he also edited the *Lesnoy zhurnal* ("Forest Journal"). He had always been an ardent advocate of women's education, and he participated actively in the creation of the first women's institution of higher learning devoted to agricultural sciences—the Stebutovsky Higher Women's Agricultural Courses—of which he was the director from 1905. He took part in congresses on forestry and lectured to foresters throughout Russia; he was head of the Forestry Institute until 1917.

Morozov began to suffer from a serious nervous disorder in 1904, and his health, undermined by the deprivations of his student years and by overwork, rapidly grew worse until in 1917 he was forced to leave St. Petersburg for the milder climate of the Crimea. His condition was aggravated by professional frustration; all about him he observed the senseless, irremediable despoliation of Russia's forests. Morozov's health did not improve in the Crimea; isolated from his work, his friends, and from a scientific environment, he had nothing to live for. He therefore joyfully accepted the offer to give a course in forest management when a new university was opened in Simferopol in 1918. Those who knew him at this time were struck by the contrast between his physical disability and the cheerfulness and enthusiasm that he brought to his work. He died two years later, at the age of fifty-three.

Morozov's work laid the theoretical bases for rational forest management. His theory of the forest as "a single complex organism with regular inter-connections among its parts and, like every other organism, distinguished by a definite stability" had a further general biological importance. Morozov showed that "a forest is not simply an accumulation of trees, but is itself a society, a community of trees that mutually influence each other, thus giving rise to a whole series of new phenomena that are not the properties of trees alone." He further stated that trees in a forest display an influence "not only on each other, but also on the soil and atmosphere . . . ." In one of his last articles, in 1920, he wrote, "The forest is not only a community of trees; it is also a community of a broader order, in which . . . plants are adapted to each other, as well as animals to plants and plants to animals; all this is influenced by the external environment . . . ." Morozov also showed the forest to be a geographical as well as a biological phenomenon. He made detailed investigations of the interrelationships of plants, animals, soils, and their geographical distribution; he may thus be considered to have been one of the founders of the modern studies of phytosociology, phytobiology, phytogeography, biogeography, and ecology.

Morozov was a firm Darwinist, maintaining that "the forest is not some sort of homogeneous thing in space, unchanging in time," but that "for every forest community, as for every living substance, there is a tendency toward development." He drew upon a wealth of ecological data to reach a theory of the transformation of species, showing that the replacement of species can be understood only in the dynamical context of climate, geography, soil, plant communities, the activities of man as they affect natural processes, and the complex interrelationships among all these factors. His theory of the types of forest plantation had considerable practical significance. He distinguished among types of plantations according to soil composition, climate, geological considerations, topography, the processes by which the soil had been formed, and distribution of plants. Morozov considered this concept of plantation type to be analogous to the botanical-geographical classification of vegetational zones.

BIBLIOGRAPHY

I. ORIGINAL WORKS. Morozov's major writings are "Pochvovedenie i lesovodstvo" ("Soil Management and Forest Management"), in *Pochvovedenie* (1899), no. 1; *Biologia nashikh lesnykh porod* ("Biology of Our Forest Species"; St. Petersburg, 1912); *Les kak rastitelnoe soobshchestvo* ("The Forest as a Plant Society"; St. Petersburg, 1913); "O biogeograficheskikh osnovaniakh lesovodstva" ("On the Biogeographical Bases of Forest Management"), in *Lesnoy zhurnal* (1914), no. 1; *Les kak yavlenie geograficheskoe* ("The Forest as a Geographical Phenomenon"; St. Petersburg, 1914); *Smena porod* ("The Replacement of Species"; St. Petersburg, 1914); *Uchenie o tipakh nasazhdeny* ("The Theory of Types of Plantation"; Petrograd, 1917; Moscow–Leningrad, 1931); *Uchenie o lese* ("Theory of the Forest"), 7th ed. (Moscow, 1949); and *Ocherki po lesokulturnomu delu* ("Sketches on Forest Matters"), 2nd ed. (Moscow–Leningrad, 1950).

II. SECONDARY LITERATURE. See I. G. Beylin, *G. F. Morozov—vydayushchysya lesovod i geograf* ("G. F. Morozov —Distinguished Forest Manager and Geographer"; Moscow, 1954); *Istoria estestvoznania v Rossii* ("History of the Natural Sciences in Russia"), III (Moscow, 1962); V. G. Nesterov, "G. F. Morozov," in *Vydayushchiesya deyateli otechestvennogo lesovodstva* ("Distinguished Workers in Forestry of Our Country"), no. 2 (Moscow–Leningrad, 1950); and V. N. Sukachev and S. I. Vanin, *G. F. Morozov kak ucheny i pedagog* ("G. F. Morozov as Scientist and Teacher"; Leningrad, 1947).

S. R. MIKULINSKY

MORSE, EDWARD SYLVESTER (*b.* Portland, Maine, 18 June 1838; *d.* Salem, Massachusetts, 20 December 1925), *zoology.*

Morse was the son of Jonathan Kimball Morse, a businessman, and Jane Seymour Beckett Morse, who claimed descent from Thomas à Becket and who was much interested in science. He collected shells when very young, even corresponding with such experts as A. A. Gould and Amos Binney, and showed a remarkable drawing ability.

Morse attended Bethel Academy and Bridgeton Academy, both in Maine, before going to Harvard as one of Louis Agassiz's special students at Lawrence Scientific School, where he had an assistantship from 1859 to 1862. He then went to the Essex Institute in Salem, Massachusetts; and when the Peabody Academy of Science (later Peabody Museum) was founded there in 1867, Morse became curator of its Radiata and Mollusca. From 1871 to 1874 he was professor of zoology at Bowdoin College, and from 1877 to 1880 was a professor at Tokyo University, before returning to the Peabody Academy as a highly effective director (emeritus from 1916).

Among many other honors Morse received an honorary Ph.D. from Bowdoin (1871) and a D.Sc. from Yale (1918); he was elected to the National Academy of Sciences in 1876. With Alpheus Hyatt, Alpheus Spring Packard, and Frederic Ward Putnam he founded the *American Naturalist* in 1867.

From his childhood interest in shells, Morse went on to considerable work with mollusks, including pioneering studies on land snails of Maine. He soon specialized in brachiopods, which were then considered mollusks. Through detailed studies on the anatomy and the larval development of this relict group, he proved them to be more closely affiliated with worms.

Having gone to Japan in 1877 to enlarge his brachiopod studies, Morse established one of the earliest marine stations, at Enoshima. Charmed by the country, he delved deeply into its architecture, archaeology, and midden pottery. The Boston Museum of Fine Arts bought his great collection.

Morse illustrated effectively all his own articles and some for others, most notably Gould's *Invertebrata of Massachusetts.*

BIBLIOGRAPHY

I. ORIGINAL WORKS. Morse's most significant publications on mollusks and brachiopods were "Observations on the Terrestrial Pulmonifera of Maine," in *Journal of the Portland Society of Natural History*, **1**, no. 1 (1864), 1–63; and "Systematic Position of the Brachiopoda," in *Memoirs of the Boston Society of Natural History*, **15** (1873), 315–

372. He also wrote many valuable shorter papers in these fields. The Peabody Museum at Salem has a full bibliography of his publications, in both science and Japanese studies.

II. SECONDARY LITERATURE. An account of Morse's life and interests, by L. O. Howard, is in *Biographical Memoirs. National Academy of Sciences*, **17**, 1–29; it includes a selected bibliography and citations to shorter memorials on Morse. A fine tribute by J. S. Kingsley appeared in *Proceedings of the American Academy of Arts and Sciences*, **61** (1925–1926), 549–555.

ELIZABETH NOBLE SHOR

MORSE, JEDIDIAH (*b.* Woodstock, Connecticut, 23 August 1761; *d.* New Haven, Connecticut, 9 June 1826), *geography*.

The son of Jedidiah Morse, holder of local offices and deacon of the Congregational Church, and Sarah Child, Morse was educated in the Academy of Woodstock. He entered Yale College in 1779, graduating in 1783. He remained in New Haven to study theology and supported himself by conducting a school for young girls. In 1785 he became pastor of the church at Norwich, Connecticut, but returned to Yale as tutor in 1786. During part of 1787 Morse was pastor of a church in Midway, Georgia, after which he returned to Yale. In 1789 he was installed as minister of the First Parish Church of Charlestown, Massachusetts, where he remained until 1819. In 1789 he married Elizabeth Ann Breese of New Jersey. Of their eleven children only three sons survived to maturity, one of whom was Samuel Finley Breese Morse, painter and inventor of the telegraph. Throughout his career at Charlestown Morse took a leading (and often inflexible) part in upholding orthodox Calvinist views in opposition to the growing liberal Unitarianism in New England. Morse was one of the founders of Andover Theological Seminary (1808) to train orthodox ministers, and of the Park Street Church in Boston (1809) to provide an orthodox center in that city. He moved to New Haven in 1820. He visited Indian tribes in the Northwest as a representative of the government and prepared a report of his investigation in 1822.

For use in his school in New Haven in 1784, Morse wrote *Geography Made Easy*, the first geography to be published in the United States. This was so well received that he extensively revised and extended the work and published in 1789 the famous *American Geography; or A View of the Present Situation of the United States of America*. It was an immediate success and the edition of 3,000 copies was soon sold. The book was quickly reprinted in Edinburgh, Dublin, and London, and translated into German and Dutch, but no benefit except scholarly recognition came to the author from the foreign editions. A second edition, published in 1793, *The American Universal Geography*, was much enlarged and a second volume added on "The Eastern Continent." Later editions included even more on foreign countries. Morse was immediately established as the "American Geographer" and as such he commanded the field for the next twenty-five years.

In the preparation of his books Morse sought the aid by consultation and correspondence of any who would contribute information. Elaborate questionnaires were circulated far and wide and produced information of varying reliability and importance. Many well-known people provided data. He submitted sections for criticism to men like Jeremy Belknap, who reviewed and corrected his work on New England. Morse's limited travels to the several states provided some firsthand information, but he was in no sense a field geographer.

The first edition of the *American Geographer*, and also later editions, contained much historical and political material as well as sections on the "Face of the Country" for the various states and regions. The latter contained paraphrases or direct quotations (not always acknowledged) from the work of Lewis Evans, Thomas Pownall, Robert Rogers, Jonathan Carver, John and William Bartram, Thomas Jefferson, Thomas Hutchins, Mark Catesby, Noah Webster, John Filson, Gilbert Imlay, Samuel Mitchell, and many others. They form an instructive summary of geomorphology and geology of the United States in 1789. Although his own interests were historical and political geography, Morse paid enough attention to topography in his travels to understand physical geography and geology as described by others. One of the greatest criticisms of his geographies was that their maps were small and inadequate.

BIBLIOGRAPHY

I. ORIGINAL WORKS. Morse's earliest geography was *Geography Made Easy* (1784). This went through 20 editions by 1819. His great work was *American Geography* (Elizabethtown, 1789; London, 1792, also Edinburgh and Dublin); the 2nd ed., in two vols. (now called *The American Universal Geography*), with the 2nd vol. on the eastern hemisphere (Boston, 1793), was followed by successive two-volume eds. to the 7th in 1819. *The American Gazetteer* (Boston, 1796) was followed by successive editions and abridgments; *The New Gazetteer of the Eastern Continent* (Charlestown, 1802), with Elijah Parish, was followed by several editions to 1823. His historical works, sermons, editorials and other theological works are listed in the

50-page typed bibliography in the Yale University Library; a copy is in the Clements Library, University of Michigan. The locations of the extraordinarily voluminous Morse papers and correspondence are given in detail by J. K. Morse, R. H. Brown, and W. R. Waterman.

II. SECONDARY LITERATURE. A biography by his son, R. C. Morse, remains unpublished. The only published biography is W. B. Sprague, *The Life of Jedidiah Morse, D.D.* (New York, 1874). It contains excerpts from letters and a long chapter of personal notes from Morse's three sons and from his other associates. The short biography by W. R. Waterman in the *Dictionary of American Biography* is an excellent summary. J. K. Morse, *Jedidiah Morse, a Champion of New England Orthodoxy* (New York, 1939), with elaborate bibliographies, is devoted entirely to Morse's career as a minister and strenuous advocate of orthodox Calvinism, without any mention of his geographical work. R. H. Brown, "The American Geographies of Jedidiah Morse," in *Annals of the Association of American Geographers*, **31** (1941), 145–217, is the definitive work on Morse as a geographer, his geographical associations, and sources. It contains Winfield Shires' "Geographical Works of Jedidiah Morse, a Brief Bibliography, ... adapted and simplified from a list of the works of Jedidiah Morse with notes, from the fifty typewritten pages in the Yale Library," 214–217.

GEORGE W. WHITE

MORTILLET, LOUIS-LAURENT GABRIEL DE (*b.* Meylan, Isère, France, 29 August 1821; *d.* St.-Germain-en-Laye, France, 25 September 1898), *archaeology, anthropology.*

Mortillet was educated at a Jesuit seminary in Chambéry and in Paris, where he became a revolutionary freethinker. He took part in the revolution of 1848 and was a fervent disciple of Ledru-Rollin. He was found guilty of violating the laws governing the press, and left France in 1849 for Switzerland and Savoy, where he engaged in scientific and archaeological work. His scientific work was concerned mainly with zoology (particularly the study of mollusks) and geology. He organized and classified the material in the museums of Geneva and Annecy. In addition to many scientific papers he was author of the *Guide de l'étranger en Savoie* (Chambéry, 1856), generally accepted as a model of its kind and an early demonstration of his flair for popularization. In Italy he directed works exploiting hydraulic lime and collaborated on the construction of railroads in Lombardy. Together with Stoppiani and Édouard Desor he explored the lakes of Lombardy and discovered the first Italian Neolithic settlement, at Isolino (Isola di San Giovanni), on Lake Varese, in 1863.

He edited the *Revue scientifique italienne*, published in French at Turin (1862–1863) as part of the political daily *Italie*; under his direction it became a complete and masterly summary of current scientific progress.

Mortillet returned to Paris in 1864, at a period when the study of prehistoric man through the interpretation of archaeological remains was in its infancy. Indeed, the word "prehistory" itself was not widely known until John Lubbock published his *Prehistoric Times* (1865): in Italy, Mortillet and his colleagues had used the term "antéhistoire." Lyell's *Antiquity of Man* and Huxley's *Man's Place in Nature*, both published in 1863, greatly affected Mortillet, and he decided to devote himself to the new and growing science of early man. In September 1864 he founded in Paris a new journal, *Matériaux pour l'histoire positive et philosophique de l'homme*, to discuss and summarize all new prehistoric discoveries. Salomon Reinach has described the founding and editing of *Matériaux* as one of the greatest services ever rendered to the development of prehistoric science in France. Mortillet edited it with vigor and distinction and in his first year exposed the forgeries of M. Meillet in the rock shelters of Poitou.

The first public recognition of prehistory at a scientific congress occurred at the meeting of the Italian Scientific Congress at La Spezia in 1865. Mortillet was invited by the president to give a survey of prehistory, and as a result it was decided to found an international congress of anthropology and prehistoric archaeology. Mortillet was secretary of the first two congresses, held in Neuchâtel in 1866 and in Paris the following year.

In 1867 Mortillet was appointed secretary of the committee charged with setting up an *Exposition des oeuvres caractérisant les diverses époques de l'histoire du travail* at the Paris universal exposition, and he prepared a guide, *Promenades préhistoriques à l'Exposition universelle* (Paris, 1867), for it. In his enthusiastic appraisal of prehistory as a new discipline Mortillet declared that prehistorians had already discovered three important facts, which he termed the *loi de progrès de l'humanité*, the *loi de développement similaire*, and the *haute antiquité de l'homme*.

In 1867 Mortillet joined the staff of the newly created Musée des Antiquités Nationales at St.-Germain-en-Laye and subsequently became its director. Largely responsible for saving the museum during the Franco-Prussian war, he directed it until 1885, when he became deputy to the national assembly from Seine-et-Oise. He held this post for four years, always voting with the extreme left.

The pressure of work at St.-Germain forced him to give up the editorship of *Matériaux* in 1872, but his keen journalistic sense and devotion to the need for publishing archaeological results in an easily accessible form led him in September 1872 to found a new journal, *Indicateur de l'archéologue*, which lasted only two years, and then *Homme*, published every two weeks from 1884 to 1887. In a spate of learned papers, published beginning in 1869, he dealt with such varied subjects as Paleolithic art, megalithic monuments and bronze axes, lake dwellings, and the archaeology of the Celts. His views on prehistory were set out in *Musée préhistorique* (Paris, 1881), written with his son Adrien, and in *Formation de la nation française* (Paris, 1897).

By the early 1870's Lubbock had expanded the basic three-age system of Thomsen and Worsaae into the four-age system of Paleolithic, Neolithic, Bronze, and Iron ages. Mortillet subdivided these ages into periods, and the periods into epochs. His "Tableau de la classification," published in *Musée préhistorique*, proposed a succession of fourteen epochs. This idea of successive epochs as well as its underlying theoretical structure represented an extension of the idea of stratigraphic geology to prehistory. It predominated until the mid-1920's, when the concept of culture was borrowed from anthropologists and anthropogeographers, and the prehistorian's role was seen to be the definition and description of cultures. Certain French archaeologists had already realized that Mortillet's fourteen epochs did not represent a true and universal succession. If the Thomsen-Worsaae three-age system was the foundation stone of modern prehistory, then Mortillet's idea of epochs was an important stepping-stone between the beginnings of classification in prehistory and the ideas of the second and third quarters of the twentieth century.

From the time of his decision to devote himself to prehistory Mortillet remained in the forefront of French archaeology. He became professor of prehistory at the school of anthropology in the École des Hautes-Études in Paris. In 1878 the French government established a commission charged with listing and classifying the megalithic monuments of France and Algeria. Henri-Martin was appointed the first president and Mortillet vice-president; on Henri-Martin's death, Mortillet became president. He retained his interest in the International Congress of Anthropology and Prehistoric Archaeology, which he had helped to found, and participated in subsequent meetings until 1880. Following the discovery in 1879 of the Altamira cave paintings and the controversy over the authenticity of Upper Paleolithic art, Mortillet wisely accepted their true nature. "This is not the art of a child," he declared, "It is the childhood of art."

BIBLIOGRAPHY

A listing of nearly 100 of Mortillet's papers may be found in Royal Society *Catalogue of Scientific Papers*, IV, 487; VI, 730; VIII, 443–444; X, 858; XII, 521; and XVII, 367–368. On his life and work, see E. Cartailhac's obituary in *Anthropologie*, **9** (1898), 601–612.

GLYN DANIEL

MORTON, JOHN (*b.* England, 18 July 1670–18 July 1671; *d.* Great Oxendon, England, 18 July 1726), *natural history.*

Morton, rector of Great Oxendon, wrote *The Natural History of Northamptonshire* (1712). In it he discusses the general geography, topography, natural history, and prehistory of the county. The work shows careful observation and the descriptions are generally good. Morton chose popular theoretical assumptions as bases for his commentary.

His observations on geology and paleontology are of interest. Although Morton knew John Ray, Martin Lister, and others who were especially concerned with geology and with fossils, he chose to follow the ideas of John Woodward. The latter believed that the biblical Deluge was responsible for geological features and for the presence of fossils, and Morton applied this assumption to his regional study. As Woodward had done, Morton interpreted the strata as having originated in water and as having settled out of the Flood waters according to the specific gravity of the matter of which they were composed. The remains of invertebrate sealife and the teeth and bones of land vertebrates destroyed by the Deluge settled out concurrently, also according to their specific gravity, and were entombed in the strata as fossils.

The botanical section of Morton's *Natural History* received significant attention from his contemporaries and is notable for its attempt to arrange the flora of Northamptonshire systematically. The arrangement is principally that of John Ray's *Synopsis methodica stirpium Britannicarum* (1690).

Morton was elected a member of the Royal Society in 1703. In 1705 a letter from him on fossils was published in the *Philosophical Transactions*. It is Morton's only other publication.

BIBLIOGRAPHY

Morton's two works are "Letter From the Reverend Mr. Morton Containing a Relation of River and Other Shells Digg'd up, Together With Various Vegetable Bodies, in a Bituminous Marshy Earth, Near Mears Ashby in Northamptonshire: With Some Reflections Thereupon:

As Also an Account of the Progress He Has Made in the Natural History of Northamptonshire," in *Philosophical Transactions of the Royal Society*, **25** (1705), 2210–2214; and *The Natural History of Northamptonshire; With Some Account of the Antiquities. To Which Is Annexed a Transcript of Doomsday-Book, so Far as It Relates to That County* (London, 1712).

A biographical notice is George Simonds Boulger, "John Morton," in *Dictionary of National Biography*, XIII, 1050–1051.

PATSY A. GERSTNER

MORTON, SAMUEL GEORGE (*b*. Philadelphia, Pennsylvania, 26 January 1799; *d*. Philadelphia, 15 May 1851), *anthropology*.

Morton was the last of nine children of George and Jane Cummings Morton (he a native of Ireland, she a birthright Friend). He was educated at the Quakers' Westtown School in Pennsylvania and at the Friends' School in Burlington, New Jersey, kept by John Gummere, mathematician and astronomer. An early interest in science was encouraged by his stepfather, Thomas Rogers, an amateur mineralogist. After a period as a merchant's clerk, he became a student of Dr. Joseph Parrish of Philadelphia and attended the University of Pennsylvania Medical School, graduating in 1800. With support from a wealthy Irish uncle, Morton studied medicine at Edinburgh University, where he also attended Robert Jameson's geology lectures, and received a second M.D. degree in 1823; his thesis was *De corporis dolore*. In 1827 he married Rebecca Pearsall of Philadelphia; they had eight children, seven of whom survived their father.

Morton was inclined to study and had time as well because, without influential connections, he acquired a practice slowly. His first medical paper, on the use of cornine to treat intermittent fevers, appeared in 1826; in another he recommended fresh air for pulmonary consumption. He was a physician to the Almshouse in 1829; taught after 1830 in the Philadelphia Association for Medical Instruction, which grew out of Parrish's private lectures; prepared an American edition of John Mackintosh's *Principles of Pathology* in 1836; was professor of anatomy in the Medical Department of Pennsylvania College (1839–1843); and in 1849 published *An Illustrated System of Human Anatomy*. He achieved this sound medical reputation while engaged in scientific research.

Richard Harlan, one of Parrish's assistants, directed Morton's scientific interests and saw that he was elected to the Academy of Natural Sciences of Philadelphia in 1820. The Academy was Morton's scientific home until his death. His papers were chiefly on geology and fossils; his description of fossil remains collected by Lewis and Clark, *Synopsis of the Organic Remains of the Cretaceous Group of the United States* (Philadelphia, 1834), marks him as a founder of invertebrate paleontology in the United States. As secretary of the Academy for many years, Morton maintained a wide scholarly correspondence. In 1849 he was elected president.

In 1830 Morton began collecting human craniums and eventually owned over 1,000 specimens. Never a field anthropologist, he depended on military and naval officers, consuls, physicians, missionaries, and naturalists for both skulls and identifications. He devised ingenious ways to measure and calculate the capacity of craniums and concluded that races are distinguished by their skulls as well as by color. His *Crania Americana* (1839), by its use of physical measurements, the classification and comparison of data, and its accurate drawings, was a landmark in anthropology. In an "Introductory Essay" of ninety-five pages Morton asserted that the American Indians are a separate race, not descendants of migrants from Asia. "We are left to the reasonable conclusion," he continued, "that each Race was adapted from the beginning to its peculiar local destination. In other words, it is assumed, that the physical characteristics which distinguish the different Races, are independent of external causes." The work was hailed in the *American Journal of Science* as "the most extensive and valuable contribution to the natural history of man, which has yet appeared on the American continent." In *Crania Aegyptiaca* (1844), based on 137 skulls collected by George R. Gliddon, United States consul at Cairo, Morton concluded that the ancient Egyptians were not Negroes and indicated that the races are of great antiquity. Morton's last important work on the subject, "Hybridity in Animals . . ." (*American Journal of Science*, 2nd ser., **3** [1847], 39–50, 203–212), rejected the argument of other anthropologists that the capacity of individuals of different races to produce fertile progeny is a proof of the unity of the human species.

Morton's conclusions were in conflict with the biblical version of creation, James Ussher's chronology, and widely accepted ideas, reinforced in the United States by ideals of the Enlightenment, that all men are descended from a single pair and that racial differences are the effects of environment. Morton preferred not to press the issue with his critics. His views received support in the scientific community from Louis Agassiz; approval of another kind came from Josiah C. Nott, of Mobile, Alabama, who used them enthusiastically to attack the orthodox clergy and to support notions of white superiority congenial to the American South. At the time of his death Morton was said to have been planning a comprehensive work to be called *Elements of Ethnology*.

BIBLIOGRAPHY

I. ORIGINAL WORKS. Most of Morton's scientific writings, in addition to works cited in the text, appeared in *American Journal of Science*, *Journal of the Academy of Natural Sciences of Philadelphia*, *Philadelphia Journal of the Medical and Physical Sciences*, and *Transactions of the American Philosophical Society*. A fairly complete bibliography is in Charles D. Meigs, *A Memoir of Samuel George Morton, M.D. . . .* (Philadelphia, 1851), 45–47. His books include *Crania Americana; or, a Comparative View of the Skulls of Various Aboriginal Nations of North and South America* (Philadelphia–London, 1839); and *Crania Aegyptiaca; or, Observations on Egyptian Ethnography* (Philadelphia–London, 1844), which first appeared as "Observations on Egyptian Ethnography, Derived from Anatomy, History, and the Monuments," in *Transactions of the American Philosophical Society*, n.s., **9** (1844), 93–159.

II. SECONDARY LITERATURE. Biographical data are recorded in memoirs prepared by medical colleagues after Morton's death: Charles D. Meigs, *A Memoir of Samuel George Morton, M.D.* (Philadelphia, 1851); William R. Grant, *Lecture Introductory to a Course on Anatomy and Physiology in the Medical Department of Pennsylvania College* (Philadelphia, 1852); and George B. Wood, "A Biographical Memoir of Samuel George Morton, M.D.," in *Transactions of the College of Physicians of Philadelphia*, n.s., **1** (1853), 372–388. A fuller sketch, with emphasis on Morton's ethnographic work, is by Henry S. Patterson, in Josiah C. Nott and George R. Gliddon, eds., *Types of Mankind* (Philadelphia, 1854), xvii–lvii. William Stanton, *The Leopard's Spots: Scientific Attitudes Toward Race in America, 1815–1859* (Chicago, 1960), 25–35, 39, 40–44, and *passim*, places Morton's work in its scientific and social background.

WHITFIELD J. BELL, JR.

MOSANDER, CARL GUSTAF

MOSANDER, CARL GUSTAF (*b*. Kalmar, Sweden, 10 September 1797; *d*. Ångsholm, Sweden, 15 October 1858), *chemistry, mineralogy*.

Mosander began his career as a pharmacist, at the age of fifteen becoming an apprentice at a Stockholm apothecary. Seven years later he began medical studies and, after serving as an army surgeon, received the M.D. in 1825. In 1824 he was appointed teacher of chemistry at the Caroline Institute and shortly thereafter was put in charge of the chemistry laboratory. He succeeded Berzelius as professor of chemistry and pharmacy in 1832, when the latter retired. He held this position until his death. For a time Mosander and his wife lived with Berzelius, who had befriended the couple. Berzelius was taught Dutch by Mrs. Mosander. A close friendship also developed between Friedrich Wöhler and Mosander, who was affectionately referred to as "Father Moses" in correspondence between Wöhler and Berzelius.

Among Mosander's responsibilities was the mineral collection at the Royal Swedish Academy of Sciences, which was helpful to his research on minerals containing rare earth elements. In 1839 he showed that ceria (isolated independently by Berzelius and by Martin Klaproth in 1803) was really a mixture of earths. When he treated the substance with dilute nitric acid, a yellow residue, true ceria (cerium oxide), remained; he named the dissolved component lanthana (from Greek *lanthanein*, "to escape notice").

Two years later Mosander showed that lanthana was really a mixture of a white substance, lanthana, and a brown earth named didymia (Greek, "two") because of its similarity to lanthana. Didymia was regarded as a pure earth until 1885, when Auer von Welsbach decomposed it into praseodymia and neodymia. Mosander also separated yttria (discovered by Gadolin in 1794) into yttria, erbia, and terbia (the oxides of yttrium, erbium, and terbium) in 1843. These names were derived from the Swedish town of Ytterby, where the mineral was discovered. In 1839 Axel Erdmann discovered lanthana in a new Norwegian mineral, which he named mosandrite.

BIBLIOGRAPHY

I. ORIGINAL WORKS. Many of Mosander's discoveries were communicated orally at meetings of chemists; Wöhler and Berzelius have commented on his reluctance to publish. A summary of his important work is his article, "On the New Metals, Lanthanum and Didymium, Which Are Associated With Cerium; and on Erbium and Terbium, New Metals Associated With Yttria," in *Philosophical Magazine*, **23** (1843), 241–254. A short portion of this paper was published as "Lanthanum and Didymium, Erbium and Terbium: A Classic of Chemistry," in *Chemistry*, **20** (Sept. 1946), 53–59.

II. SECONDARY LITERATURE. Biographical material on Mosander is rather scanty. A short article describing his work is J. Erik Jorpes, "Carl Gustaf Mosander," in *Acta chemica scandinavica*, **14** (1960), 1681–1683. A more informal treatment and a photograph can be found in Mary Elvira Weeks and Henry M. Leicester, *Discovery of the Elements*, 7th ed. (Easton, Pa., 1968), 671–678.

SHELDON J. KOPPERL

MOSELEY, HENRY GWYN JEFFREYS (*b.* Weymouth, Dorsetshire, England, 23 November 1887; *d.* Gelibolu, Gallipoli Peninsula, Turkey, 10 August 1915), *physics.*

Like his friends Julian Huxley and Charles Galton Darwin, Harry Moseley came from a family long distinguished for its contributions to science. His paternal grandfather, Canon Henry Moseley (1801–1872), F.R.S., the first professor of natural philosophy at Kings College, London, was an international authority on naval architecture. His maternal grandfather, John Gwyn Jeffreys (1809–1885), F.R.S., was the dean of England's conchologists. His father, Henry Nottidge Moseley (1844–1891), F.R.S., a protégé of Charles Darwin's, was the founder of a strong school of zoology at Oxford. Harry inherited a full share of his ancestors' energy, intelligence, and singleness of purpose.

H. N. Moseley died just before his son's fourth birthday. The family then moved to Chilworth, near Guildford, in Surrey, where Harry and his two older sisters received their elementary education. The elder sister died in childhood; the other, Margery, four years Harry's senior, was his constant companion, confidante, and collaborator in neighborhood bird's-nesting expeditions. Harry's mother and such old family friends as E. R. Lankester encouraged the children in their natural-historical interests, which they never discarded. Margery later published a paper about protozoa in the *Journal of the Royal Microscopical Society*, and Harry, who became an enthusiastic gardener, was to fill his last letters from Gallipoli with observations of the flora near his campsites. At the age of nine Harry was sent to Summer Fields near Oxford, a preparatory school that specialized in training King's Scholars, winners of scholarships to Eton. He and six of his fellow students won seven of the dozen scholarships available for 1901.

Although Edwardian Eton tended to produce over-cocky, undereducated sportsmen, those who preferred not to conform, to be "saps" like most King's Scholars, could obtain a thorough grounding in almost any respectable branch of learning. After passing through the required curriculum with a prize for Latin prose, Harry specialized under T. C. Porter, the discoverer of Porter's law of flicker and one of the first Englishmen to experiment with X rays. Harry fought with most of the stodgy science masters, but found Porter's unconventional approach—a minimum of books and a maximum of challenging experiments— exactly to his taste. Before leaving Eton he had begun quantitative analysis, had measured the freezing point of saline solutions of diverse concentrations, and had discovered, to his "astonishment," that helium, despite its lower boiling point, is denser than hydrogen. For the rest Harry shared quietly in Eton life. He won a place in the college boats, participated in college debates, and found nourishment for his natural patrician aloofness.

In 1906 Harry entered Trinity College, Oxford, on one of the few science scholarships then available in the university. He was the only important early contributor to atomic physics who attended Oxford, which he chose over Cambridge in order to be near his mother, who had returned there in 1902. He read for honors in physics, rowed for his college, and worked in the Balliol-Trinity laboratory where, among other things, he built a primitive Wilson cloud chamber. The official curriculum provided no opportunity for the kind of independent work to which Porter had exposed him; and partly from tension over his course of study he obtained a second-class degree in the bookish Oxford honors schools. Nonetheless with the help of testimonials gathered before the examinations and a visit to Rutherford, he obtained a demonstratorship in the physics department at the University of Manchester for the fall of 1910.

Harry found the students dense and provincial and taught them without enthusiasm. But he worked happily as much as sixteen hours a day on the research problem Rutherford had given him—to determine how many β particles are expelled in the disintegration of one atom of radium B (Pb^{214}) or radium C (Bi^{214}). No one at Manchester doubted that the answer would be one; but it was an important fact to establish, and gave the neophyte opportunity to master the techniques of high vacuums and radioactivity. Difficulty with the apparatus prevented completion of the work until 1912. Meanwhile Harry also collaborated on small projects that trained him to handle α particles and γ rays. These exercises, typical of Rutherford's laboratory, came to an end in the spring of 1912, along with Harry's teaching duties. In the fall he was to enjoy a fellowship established by a Manchester industrialist and the congenial obligation of devoting himself entirely to research.

As Moseley passed from being Rutherford's apprentice to independent journeyman, news of the success of Laue's experiment on the diffraction of X rays by crystals reached Manchester. Moseley decided to exercise his new independence in investigating how the wavelike properties of the rays, established by Laue, could be reconciled with the phenomena from which W. H. Bragg had persuasively deduced their particulate nature. Anticipating that he would need the help of a mathematical physicist, Moseley asked C. G. Darwin, then also between researches, to collaborate. They approached Rutherford for permission. The master refused, apparently on the ground that he knew nothing about the subject and consequently could not offer his usual paternal guidance. Moseley insisted, won, and went off to Leeds to W. L. Bragg, who had generously agreed to instruct him. It appears that Moseley's habit of having his own way and his Etonian experience with circumventing inconvenient masters made possible the researches that made his reputation.

To explain his diffraction patterns Laue assumed that the radiation striking the crystal contained precisely six groups of effective monochromatic rays. Darwin and Moseley rejected the assumption, which indeed was scarcely plausible, and concluded instead that only certain planes through the crystal—namely, those "rich" in atoms—gave rise to sensible interference. W. L. Bragg reached the same conclusion earlier and undertook to confirm it by reflecting X rays from the atom-rich cleavage surface of mica. He found, as he had anticipated, that in reflection the crystal did behave like a pile of semitransparent mirrors, causing interference of reflected radiation of wavelength λ incident upon the surface at glancing angle θ in accordance with the formula $n\lambda = 2d \sin \theta$, where n is the order of the interference and d the separation of the atom-rich planes. Moseley adopted Bragg's method with the important exception, typical of Rutherford's school, of substituting an ionization chamber for a photographic plate as detector of the reflected radiation. In their first research, in which the Braggs again anticipated them, Moseley and Darwin determined that the reflected radiation had the same penetrating power as the incident. They next undertook to measure the intensity of reflection I as a function of θ; their results, obtained with the sensitive ionization chamber, quickly became standard. The narrowness of their collimation, however, caused them to miss places where $I(\theta)$ had sharp peaks. The Braggs found the peaks, which Darwin and Moseley then examined carefully. All agreed in referring the maxima to monochromatic radiation characteristic of their platinum anticathodes and identical to the L rays earlier identified by Barkla.

On the publication of their paper in July 1913, the collaborators separated, Darwin to consider theoretical problems relating to $I(\theta)$ and Moseley to map the characteristic K and L spectra of the elements. It appears that Moseley aimed to test the doctrine of atomic number, then recently suggested by van den Broek of Amsterdam, and doubtless also independently invented at Manchester where, besides Moseley, Bohr, Russell, and Hevesy also worked in 1912. According to measurements made at the Cavendish Laboratory in 1911 by R. Whiddington, the minimum velocity w that a cathode ray requires to stimulate the emission of a K ray from a target of atomic weight A is $w = A \cdot 10^8$ cm/sec. The doctrine of atomic number, however, would suggest a dependence on Z, rather than on A; and apparently Moseley's initial intent was to discover, by examining those places in the periodic table where the sequence of weights inverts the chemical order, whether the frequency ν_K followed A or Z. Very likely he expected ν_K to grow roughly as Z^2; for assuming that the entire energy of Whiddington's electron goes into the K ray,

$$\nu_K \approx (m/2h) \, A^2 \cdot 10^{16} = 2.7Z^2 \cdot 10^{15} \text{ sec}^{-1},$$

where the approximation $Z = A/2$, derived from Rutherford's famous analysis of α scattering, has been used. By no means did Moseley expect the coefficient of Z^2 to be exactly constant independent of Z. Among other considerations, the atomic model of his friend Niels Bohr, which assumed that the population of the innermost ring changed with Z, ruled out any such regularity.

Moseley began his experiments in the fall of 1913, using a clever device that enabled him to bring different anticathodes into position without interrupting the vacuum in his X-ray tube. He photographically recorded the position of constructive interference and found the K rays to consist of a soft, intense line, which he called K_α, and a harder, weaker satellite K_β. The L rays appeared to be more complicated, a soft intense line L_α and several weaker companions. Measurements of Co and Ni immediately showed, as expected, that ν_{K_α} followed Z. In addition, and most unexpectedly, the frequencies for ten elements from Ca to Zn satisfied to a precision of 0.5 percent the astonishingly simple relation

$$\nu_{K_\alpha}/R = (3/4)(Z - 1)^2,$$

where R stands for the Rydberg frequency. Emboldened by this formula, and especially by the appearance of the Bohr-Balmer coefficient $3R/4$, Moseley guessed on very little evidence that

$$\nu_{L_\alpha}/R = (5/36)(Z - 7.4)^2.$$

These results were published in the *Philosophical Magazine* for December 1913, about one month after the photographic measurements began.

Moseley quickly perceived that if these formulas held exactly, they could be used to test the periodic table for completeness; he need only obtain ν_{K_α} and/or ν_{L_α} for the known elements and determine which values of Z (if any) were not represented. The task offered no difficulties of principle. The procurement of rare substances, however, presented a severe problem which could not be confronted with any particular advantage in Manchester. Since at this juncture (December 1913) Moseley considered that Rutherford had no more to teach him, he decided to resign his fellowship and to migrate to Oxford. There he could be near home and might build up local support for a possible candidacy for the professorship of experimental physics, then still held by its first incumbent, R. B. Clifton, whose overdue resignation was expected momentarily. Moseley obtained permission to work in a private capacity in the new electrical laboratory of Townsend, where he carried his examination of the elements into the fuzzy family of the rare earths.

Chemists then officially recognized thirteen "lanthanides" stretching from cerium to lutetium, the most recently accepted elemental earth, which had been independently isolated in 1906/1907 by Auer von Welsbach and Urbain. There were a great many other putative earths, including Auer's thulium II and Urbain's celtium; and it was this confusion that Moseley proposed to resolve with his X-ray machine. After hasty examination he announced with his usual confidence that three elements remained undiscovered between aluminum and gold. Two of these, numbers 43 and 75, corresponded to spaces the chemists had long recognized. The other, 61, lay in the middle of the lanthanides which, according to Moseley, began at cerium 58 and terminated with Auer's two thuliums, 69 and 70, and Urbain's ytterbium 71 and lutetium 72.

This assignment, which Moseley deduced without examining any samples of the heaviest earths, annoyed Urbain, as it left no room for celtium and established the second thulium of his rival Auer. In May 1914 Urbain brought his best specimens to Oxford, where the X rays revealed (to his mixed satisfaction) neither celtium nor thulium II nor any trace of element 72 and demonstrated that the known lanthanides terminated at lutetium, which Moseley had given a Z one unit too high. Elements 43 and 61 do not appear to exist naturally; number 75 was found among manganese ores as expected; and hafnium, which is not a rare earth, came to light in Copenhagen in the fall of 1922 after Urbain, in violation of one of Bohr's theories, had again tried to install celtium as element 72.

Moseley's formulas not only terminated what Urbain called the "romantic age of chemical discovery"; they also seemed to lift the veil guarding the atom's innermost recesses. Moseley himself argued that the factors

$$3R/4 = (1/1^2 - 1/2^2)R$$

and

$$5R/36 = (1/2^2 - 1/3^2)R$$

showed that Bohr's rules of behavior for the single electron of hydrogen also governed the deep-lying electrons of the heavy elements; in particular, according to Moseley, his formulas confirmed the principle of quantization of the angular momentum. The factor $(Z - 1)^2$ gave him more trouble; and, in the event, neither he nor Bohr was able to design a plausible model of X-ray emission that satisfied Bohr's principles and agreed even qualitatively with the K_α formula. Nonetheless Moseley expressed his confidence in a letter to *Nature*, for which he was roundly and unfairly cudgeled by F. A. Lindemann. In the fall of 1914 W. Kossel supplied a successful qualitative model of X-ray emission. No one, however, has managed to derive Moseley's formulas from Bohr's initial principles of atomic structure.

In June 1914 Moseley and his mother left England for a leisurely trip to Australia, where the British Association for the Advancement of Science was to meet in September. When news of the outbreak of war reached him, he determined to return home immediately upon concluding his obligations to the association—participation in a discussion on atomic structure and delivery of a paper on the rare earths. He practiced semaphore and Morse code aboard ship and upon arrival rushed to procure a commission in the Royal Engineers. Neither the solicitations of his family nor the initial refusal of the engineers deterred him from what he and his former classmates at Summer Fields and Eton considered their duty. His obstinacy eventually secured the commission, and after eight months' training he was shipped to the Dardanelles as signal officer of the thirty-eighth brigade of the new army. He participated in some minor skirmishes near Cape Helles before his unit went to reinforce the last desperate effort to reach the critical ridge of Sari Bair. He was killed in a furious counterattack led by Kemal Ataturk.

BIBLIOGRAPHY

I. ORIGINAL WORKS. Moseley's important papers are "The Number of β Particles Emitted in the Transformations of Radium," in *Proceedings of the Royal Society of London*, **87A** (1912), 230–255; "The Attainment of High Potentials by the Use of Radium," *ibid.*, **88A** (1913), 471–476; "The Reflexion of X Rays," in *Philosophical Magazine*, **26** (1913), 210–232, written with C. G. Darwin; "The High-Frequency Spectra of the Elements," *ibid.*, 1025–1034, and **27** (1914), 703–713. A full list of Moseley's published writings is in Poggendorff and in J. B. Birks, ed., *Rutherford at Manchester* (London, 1962), 349. Moseley's correspondence, scientific and personal, has been published in J. L. Heilbron, *H. G. J. Moseley. The Life and Letters of an English Physicist, 1887–1915* (Berkeley, 1974).

II. SECONDARY LITERATURE. For Moseley's career and work see the *Life and Letters;* Rutherford in *Proceedings of the Royal Society of London,* **93A** (1916), xxii–xxviii; C. G. Darwin, "Moseley and the Atomic Number of the Elements," 17–26 in the volume edited by Birks; and (for high-schoolers) B. Jaffe, *Moseley and the Numbering of the Elements* (New York, 1971).

J. L. HEILBRON

MOSS, WILLIAM LORENZO (*b.* Athens, Georgia, 23 August 1876; *d.* Athens, 12 August 1957), *medicine, pathology.*

Moss was the son of Elizabeth Luckie Moss and Rufus Lafayette Moss. After being educated privately and in local public schools, he enrolled in the University of Georgia and earned his B.S. in 1902. He proceeded to The Johns Hopkins University Medical School and received his M.D. three years later. Several years later he undertook further study on the continent. Moss spent his career teaching and doing research at Johns Hopkins, at the State Institute for the Study of Malignant Diseases in Buffalo, New York, and at Yale and Harvard Universities. In 1926 he became acting dean of the School of Public Health at Harvard, where he served for one year. Moss served as dean of the University of Georgia School of Medicine from 1931 to 1934, when he retired and returned to Athens.

Moss' most renowned contribution to medicine was a classification system of the four blood groups, which he designated by the roman numerals I through IV. He took as the basis of these blood groups the content of the serum, because in a small sample experiment he found that Landsteiner's classification, which was based on the agglutination (clumping) properties of serum and red blood cells, did not hold in all cases. Landsteiner's blood groups were labeled A, B, O, and AB. A study published in 1929 by Moss' colleague, James Kennedy, revealed that prior to 1921, ninety percent of the hospitals that were surveyed used the Moss system and that five years later seventy-eight percent continued to use it, although a committee of immunologists recommended use of a rival system that was proposed by Jansky in which the blood groups were labeled in reverse to Moss' system, although the system had the same basis. The three systems relate in this way:

Moss	Jansky	Landsteiner
I	IV	AB
II	III	A
III	II	B
IV	I	O

With the advent of World War II and the need to systematize large quantities of blood for use in transfusions, the Landsteiner system was adopted on a worldwide basis and remains in use at present.

Moss gathered information on blood groups among a wide variety of the population of Santo Domingo during scientific expeditions in 1920 and 1925. His other scientific trips were to Peru (1916), the Pacific Islands (1928), and New Guinea (1937).

Moss was a member of the small group who in the early twentieth century studied the immunization properties of the blood components, especially in relation to tuberculosis, diphtheria, and allergy reactions leading to the extreme effects in anaphylactic shock.

His honors include decoration by the French government for service in World War I in the French Medical Corps and membership in the Cosmos Club and Phi Beta Kappa.

In 1925 he married Marguerite E. Widle and they had three children: Marguerite, Elizabeth, and William Lorenzo II.

BIBLIOGRAPHY

I. ORIGINAL WORKS. Moss' widow in Athens and the library of the University of Georgia retain the personal papers and correspondence. Moss' works include "Studies in Opsonins," in *Johns Hopkins Hospital Bulletin,* **18** (1907), 237–245; "Traumatic Pneumothorax," in *Journal of the American Medical Association* (1908), 1971; "A Recent Visit to Some of the Medical Laboratories Abroad," in *Johns Hopkins Hospital Bulletin,* **19** (1908), 188–192; "Studies on Iso-Agglutinins and Isohemolysins," in *Transactions of the Association of American Physicians,* **19** (1909), 419–437; "The Relationship of Bovine to Human Tuberculosis," in *Johns Hopkins Hospital Bulletin,* **20** (1909), 39–49; and "Tuberculosis: A Plan of Study," *ibid.,* p. 87.

See also "Studien über Isoaglutinine und Isohämolysine," in *Folia serologica,* **5** (1910), 267–276; "A Cutaneous Anaphylactic Reaction as a Contra-Indication to the Administration of Antitoxin," in *Journal of the American Medical Association,* **55** (1910), 776–777; "Studies on Isoagglutinins and Isohemolysins," in *Johns Hopkins Hospital Bulletin,* **21** (1910), 63–70; "Subcutaneous Reaction of Rabbits to Horse Serum," in *Journal of Experimental Medicine,* **12** (1910), 562–574, written with J. W. Mason Knox and G. L. Brown; "Paroxysmal Hemoglobinuria: Blood Studies in Three Cases," in *Johns Hopkins Hospital Bulletin,* **22** (1911), 238–247; "Paroxysmale Hamoglobinurie. Blutstudien in drei Fallen," in *Folia serologica,* **7** (1911), 1117–1142; "Concerning the Much–Holzmann Reaction," in *Johns Hopkins Hospital Bulletin,* **22** (1911), 278–282, written with F. M. Barnes, Jr.; "Variations in the Leucocyte Count in Normal Rabbits, in Rabbits Following the Injection of Normal Horse Serum, and During a Cutaneous Anaphylactic Reaction," *ibid.,* 258–268, written with G. L. Brown; "Serum Treatment of Hemorrhagic Diseases," *ibid.*, 272–278, written with J. Gelien; "Diphtheria Bacillus Carriers," in *Transactions of the XV International Congress on Hygiene and Demography*, IV (1913), 156–170; "Diphtheria Bacillus-Carriers," in *Transactions of the International Congress of Medicine*, pt. 2, sec. 4 (1914), 75–79, written with G. Guthrie and J. Gelien; and "A Simple Method for the Treatment for the Indirect Transfusion of Blood," in *American Journal of the Medical Sciences*, **147** (1914), 698–703.

Other works are "An Attempt to Immunize Calves Against Tuberculosis by Feeding the Milk of Vaccinated Cows," in *Johns Hopkins Hospital Bulletin*, **26** (1915), 241–245; "A Simplified Method for Determining the Iso-Agglutinin Group in the Selection of Donors for Blood Transfusion," in *Journal of the American Medical Association*, **68** (1917), 1905–1906; "Diphtheria Bacillus Carriers; Second Communication," in *Johns Hopkins Hospital Bulletin*, **31** (1920), 388–403, and "The Effect of Diphtheria Antitoxin in Preventing Lodgement and Growth of Diphtheria Bacillus in the Nasal Passages Of Animals," *ibid.*, 381–388, both written with C. G. Guthrie and J. Gelien; "Experimental Inoculation of Human Throats with Virulent Diphtheria Bacilli," *ibid.*, **32** (1921), 369–378, written with C. G. Guthrie and B. C. Marshall; "Diphtheria Bacillus Carriers. A Report on Conditions Found in an Orphan Asylum," *ibid.*, 109–113, written with C. G. Guthrie and J. Gelien; "Experimental Inoculation of Human Throats with Virulent Diphtheria Bacilli," *ibid.*, 37–44, written with C. G. Guthrie and B. C. Marshall; "Yaws; An Analysis of 1,046 Cases in the Dominican Republic," *ibid.*, **33** (1922), 43–55, written with G. H. Bigelow; and "Hospitalization of Pneumonia Cases. Criticisms of the Recommendation of the Chicago Pneumonia Commission," in *Modern Hospital*, **25** (1926), 425–430.

Also see "Yaws; Results of Neosalvarsan Therapy After Five Years," in *American Journal of Tropical Medicine*, **20** (1926–1927), 365–384; "Malta Fever; Laboratory Infection in Humans," in *Transactions of the Association of American Physicians*, **43** (1928), 272–284, written with M. Castenada; "Blood Groups in Peru, Santo Domingo, Yucatan and Among Mexicans at Blue Ridge Prison Farm in Texas," in *Journal of Immunology*, **16** (1921), 159–174, written with J. A. Kennedy; and "From the South Seas," in *Harvard Alumni Bulletin* (1930), 532.

II. SECONDARY LITERATURE. Work done with data gathered by Moss includes William W. Howells, "Anthropometry and Blood Types in Fiji and the Solomon Islands Based Upon Data of Dr. William L. Moss," in *Anthropological Papers of the American Museum of Natural History*, **33**, pt. 4 (1933).

AUDREY B. DAVIS

MOSSO, ANGELO (*b.* Turin, Italy, 30 May 1846; *d.* Turin, 24 November 1910), *physiology, archaeology.*

Mosso was taken at a very early age to Chieri, where his father had a carpenter's shop and where he completed his elementary and part of his secondary schooling. He then went to Cuneo and Asti to attend the *liceo*, aided by a small scholarship given by the town of Chieri. In 1865 he enrolled in the medical school of the University of Turin. Two of Mosso's professors, the zoologist Filippo de Filippi and the botanist Moris, procured him a post as teacher of natural sciences in the *liceo* of Turin, so that he could support himself. His financial situation improved somewhat during his last two years at the university, when he became an intern at the Mauriziano Hospital in Turin and was given free board and lodging.

Mosso graduated *summa cum laude* on 25 July 1870. The board of examiners was so impressed by his experimental thesis on the growth of bones that it decided to have it printed. His work at the hospital decided his future, for it was there that he met Luigi Pagliari, who introduced him to Jacob Moleschott, then teaching physiology at Turin. At the end of his military service (which had prevented him from accepting an assistantship offered by Moleschott), Mosso obtained a scholarship, on Moleschott's recommendation, to the University of Florence, where for two years he worked in the laboratory of Moritz Schiff and wrote his first scientific papers. Next he went to Leipzig, where he studied under Ludwig (1873–1874), and learned to use machines for the graphic registration of physiological phenomena, an approach he later used extensively in his work. It was also at this time that Mosso first proposed his plethysmograph.

Refusing a number of assistantships offered him by German universities, Mosso returned to Italy after visiting Paris, where he met Bernard, Brown-Séquard, and Marey. (Marey stirred his interest in graphic registration machines yet again.) At Turin, Mosso entered Moleschott's institute and began fundamental studies on blood circulation; in 1875 he became professor of pharmacology (materia medica, as it was then called), and in 1879 he succeeded Moleschott, who had moved to Rome, as professor of physiology.

Under Mosso's leadership the physiology institute of the University of Turin became an extremely active center of research, especially in experimental physiology and biology, and attracted many foreign researchers. During this period Mosso founded *Archivio italiano di biologia* (1882), and established the Institute of Physiology in the Parco del Valentino (1893) and a station in the Alps (1895) for the study of human physiology at high altitudes.

In recognition of his scientific achievements Mosso was named a senator in 1904 but almost immediately contracted locomotor ataxia, which forced him to give up his physiological studies. Because of his illness, however, he dedicated himself to archaeology and conducted studies in the Roman Forum, in Crete, and in southern Italy. His last publications were all in this field, in which he acquired as great fame as he had in physiology. He died in 1910, following a more serious attack of his illness.

The importance of Mosso's physiological research lies in his emphasis on experimenting directly on man whenever possible, as well as on animals, so that his research was truly in human physiology. His scientific experiments were carried out with special equipment, which he devised to suit the requirements of the studies. He pursued two main lines of research, the analysis of motor functions and the relationship between physiological and psychic phenomena. On the first topic, Mosso carried out highly accurate studies on movements of both smooth and striated muscles, in relation to a great variety of physiological and pathological conditions, such as heat, cold, sleeping, waking, and hibernation. He also considered movement from a mechanical point of view and from that of heat production. On the second topic he studied the variations in the frequency and energy of cardiac systoles, the increase of blood flow into the brain, and the increase of blood pressure in situations that today would be described as those of intellectual or emotional stress.

Outstanding among the many machines that Mosso perfected for his physiological research is the plethysmograph, with which he measured slow changes in the volume of the blood vessels; as a result he was able to determine which part of the movement of the pulse was due to cardiac pulsation and which to contraction of the vessels' walls. With the ergograph and the ponograph, he completed very accurate studies on fatigue.

Mosso also studied respiration during sleep, pointing out the inversion of thoracic respiration; and human physiology at high altitude, demonstrating the phenomenon of acapnia, the difficulty of breathing due to absence or scarcity of carbon dioxide in the organism.

BIBLIOGRAPHY

I. ORIGINAL WORKS. Mosso wrote about 200 articles and books. His most important works are *Saggio di alcune ricerche fatte intorno all'accrescimento delle ossa* (Naples, 1870), his thesis for the M.D.; "Sopra alcuni sperimenti di trasfusione del sangue," in *Sperimentale*, **30** (1872), 369–375; "Sull'irritazione chimica dei nervi cardiaci," *ibid.*, 358–368; "Sopra un nuovo metodo per scrivere i movimenti dei vasi sanguigni dell'uomo," in *Atti dell'Accademia delle scienze (Turin)*, **11** (1875), 21–81; "Introduzione ad una serie di esperienze sui movimenti del cervello

nell'uomo," in *Archivio per le scienze mediche*, **1** (1876), 216–244; "Sul polso negativo e sui rapporti della respirazione addominale e toracica nell'uomo," *ibid.*, **2** (1878), 401–464; "Sulla circolazione del sangue nel cervello dell'uomo," in *Atti dell'Accademia nazionale dei Lincei. Memorie*, 3rd ser., **5** (1879–1880), 237–358; "Ricerche sulla fisiologia della fatica," in *Rendiconti dell'Accademia de medicina Torino*, **31** (1883), 667; *La paura* (Milan, 1884); *La respirazione dell'uomo sulle alte montagne* (Turin, 1884), a volume in honor of C. Sperino; "Le leggi della fatica studiate nei muscoli dell'uomo," in *Atti dell'Accademia nazionale dei Lincei. Memorie*, 4th ser., **5** (1888), 410–426; *La fatica* (Milan, 1891); *La temperatura del cervello* (Milan, 1894); "Descrizione di un miometro per studiare la tonicità dei muscoli nell'uomo," in *Memorie della Accademia delle scienze di Torino*, **46** (1896), 93–120; and *Fisiologia dell'uomo sulle Alpi* (Milan, 1897).

Major twentieth-century publications are "La fisiologia dell'apnea studiata nell'uomo," in *Memorie della Accademia delle scienze di Torino*, **53** (1902), 367–386; "Crani preistorici trovati nel foro romano," in *Notizie degli scavi* (Rome, 1906), fasc. 1, 46–54; *Escursioni nel Mediterraneo e gli scavi di Creta* (Milan, 1908); and *Le origini della civiltà mediterranea* (Milan, 1910).

II. SECONDARY LITERATURE. See *Angelo Mosso, la sua vita e le sue opere* (Milan, 1912), with a detailed bibliography of his writings; A. Botto Micca, "A. Mosso archeologo," in *Atti del XV Congresso italiano di storia della medicina* (Turin, 1957), 20; L. Ferretti, *A. Mosso, apostolo dello sport* (Milan, 1951); and A. Gallassi, "Angelo Mosso e la medicina sportiva," in *Atti del XV Congresso italiano di storia della medicina* (Turin, 1957), 22–25.

CARLO CASTELLANI

MOSSOTTI, OTTAVIANO FABRIZIO (*b.* Novara, Italy, 18 April 1791; *d.* Pisa, Italy, 20 March 1863), *physics*.

Mossotti came from a moderately well-to-do family. Little is known directly of his life. He attended the University of Milan, and spent ten years as an assistant at the Milan observatory before leaving to seek a position in England. Following four years without an appointment, Mossotti accepted the post of astronomer at the topographical bureau in Buenos Aires and also served as professor of physics at the university. He remained in Argentina for several years, returning to become a professor of mathematics at the Ionian University at Corfu, founded by Frederick North in 1824. In 1841 he became professor of mathematics, theoretical astronomy, and geodesy at the University of Pisa, where he remained until his death.

As is evident in his first work (1815), Mossotti's outlook and methods derived from that French group of analysts best exemplified by Laplace, Poisson, and Ampère. Like them, he believed that the proper way to explain all physical phenomena was by means of forces acting centrally at a distance between various fluids. Given such a force and its subject, the correct application of mathematics to the equilibrium situations of the fluids in all circumstances should, they believed, lead one to the observed phenomena. Poisson had been the first to subject Coulomb's magnetic and electrical fluids to extensive analysis, while Ampère had postulated a central force acting between the elements of galvanic circuits. While most scientists granted the general applicability of these forces and fluids, they were utilized fully only by the Continental "action-at-a-distance" group. Indeed, after Faraday's work of the 1830's and 1840's many refused to grant even the existence of the requisite fluids. Mossotti, however, held firmly to the outlook of Poisson and others, and much of his work derived from this belief.

Between 1815 and 1832 Mossotti concentrated on the question of which forces were responsible for cohesion and aggregation in liquids and solids. In accordance with the French tradition, Mossotti thought that these forces were best explained by means of a fluid distributed in an atmosphere about the particles of the ordinary matter that constituted all bodies. Mossotti's "ether" was subject to the two central forces of self-repulsion and attraction to "natural matter"—these two were the only electrical forces he imagined. In the absence of an external concentration of the electrical ether the molecules of a body were evenly surrounded by the electrical fluid, and the whole existed in stable equilibrium under the action of the two forces, with the self-repulsion of the ether atmospheres balancing the mutual attraction of the ether and the matter. Mossotti thought these two forces were sufficient to explain cohesion as well as a number of other phenomena, including the propagation of light in transparent bodies.

In the mid-1840's Mossotti read of Faraday's investigation of dielectric, or nonconducting, bodies. Until then it was believed that nonconductors were unlike conductors only in opposing the motion of electrical fluid. Faraday sought an explanation predicated upon the ability of an intervening medium to propagate electrical force from point to point between "charged" bodies. Faraday assumed that all dielectrics—solid and liquid as well as gaseous—were constituted so that their smallest parts were somehow "polarized" under electrical influence, each part transmitting the action to its neighbor by its "polarity." Although Faraday rejected the notion of an absolute electrical fluid, Mossotti ignored this rejection and accepted Faraday's assumption of

dielectric polarity, preferring to explain polarity by means of ether-bearing molecules.

Mossotti thought that all bodies were built of ether-matter molecules in which the ether acted as an electrical fluid. The difference between conductors and nonconductors resulted from a variation in the abilities of bodies to retain the ethereal atmosphere about a single molecule under electrical action. A conductor had no retentive strength, while a dielectric retained the ether, but in a condition of varying density about the molecule. Mossotti believed this conception to be in the tradition of Franklin's single electrical fluid.

When Mossotti's dielectric was placed near an element of ether, its molecules became polarized in the sense that the ether density about each particle varied from point to point. The variation resulted in a net force on the molecule because of the change in distance of the ether and matter from the external fluid. In Mossotti's notation, if ρ is the distance from a volume element $d\psi\,d\xi\,d\varsigma$ of the ether to the electricity, then $\mu\,d\psi\,d\xi\,d\varsigma/\rho^2$ represents the force produced on the electricity by $d\psi\,d\xi\,d\varsigma$. The function μ was positive if the density in $d\psi\,d\xi\,d\varsigma$ was greater than the equilibrium value, and negative if it was less, since a decrease in ether density yielded an attraction. Mossotti was thus able to show that, if k' represents the ratio of ether volume to total volume, then the force on a unit of electrical fluid is given by the negative coordinate derivatives of

$$Q = \iiint \left(\frac{d^1/\rho}{dx'} \alpha' + \frac{d^1/\rho}{dy'} \beta' + \frac{d^1/\rho}{dz'} \gamma' \right) k'\,dx'\,dy'\,dz'$$

integrating over the dielectric. The functions α', β', γ' are the "dipole moments" of a molecule, their form being $\alpha' = \iiint \mu\psi\,d\psi\,d\xi\,d\varsigma$, integrating over a molecule.

Mossotti made an extensive analysis of the internal conditions in a dielectric subject to electrical action. Employing the mathematics derived by Poisson in 1826 for the actions of magnetic molecules, he obtained expressions like $\frac{4}{3}\pi k'\alpha'$ for the force in a small element of the dielectric resulting from the distribution of the molecules therein. This result is the Clausius-Mossotti relation in its original form. In addition Mossotti showed that the action of a polarized dielectric can be fully represented by an imaginary distribution of ether on its boundary surfaces. By means of this equivalent surface distribution Mossotti demonstrated in 1846 that "[because of] the polarization of the atmospheres of its molecules the dielectric simply transmits the action between conducting bodies . . ." ("Sull'influenza . . ." [1850], p. 73).

Mossotti reached this last result—which he considered his most important—only after an extensive analysis. In Faraday's view such a transmission was an elementary proposition. The difference between Mossotti's and Faraday's work—and, eventually, between the proponents of mediated action and those of electrical matter—was a deep one, hinging on the acceptance or rejection of fluids acting directly at a distance. Thus, Mossotti felt called upon to explain why electrical fluid does not fly off the surface of a conductor under its self-repulsion; while Faraday considered the question unnecessary because he did not employ an electrical fluid like Mossotti's ether. Mossotti's success in accounting for dielectric behavior may be considered together with the impact of Faraday's work to illustrate the conceptual flux that characterized the study of electricity and magnetism from 1840 to 1870. Mossotti's work was not very influential theoretically; it remained in the Continental action-at-a-distance tradition and used none of Faraday's newer ideas on the distribution of force in space. However it was an important formal development in that it showed that one could explain dielectric behavior without abandoning the scheme of central forces and subtle fluids as Faraday had. During the late 1840's and early 1850's, electrical fluids came to be viewed with increasing distrust both because of Faraday's work and because they seemed to imply unacceptable behavior for the fluid *qua* fluid.

BIBLIOGRAPHY

I. ORIGINAL WORKS. Mossotti's writings include "Del movimento di un fluido elastico che sorte da un vase e della pressione che fa sulle pareti dello stesso," in *Memorie di matematica e di fisica della Società italiana delle scienze*, **17** (1815), 16–72; *Sur les forces qui régissent la constitution intérieure des corps, aperçu pour servir à la détermination de la cause et des lois de l'action moléculaire* (Turin, 1836), repr. in Richard Taylor, ed., *Scientific Memoirs*, I (London, 1837), 448; *Dell'azione delle forze moleculari nella produzione dei fenomeni della capillarità* (Milan, 1840), repr. in *Scientific Memoirs* (London, 1841); *Lezioni elementari di fisica matematica*, 2 vols. (Florence, 1843–1845); and "Sull'influenza che l'azione di un mezzo dielettrico ha sulla distribuzione dell'elettricità alla superficie di più corpi elettrici disseminati in esso," in *Memorie di matematica e di fisica della Società italiana delle scienze*, **24**, pt. 2 (1850), 49–74.

II. SECONDARY LITERATURE. On Mossotti and his work, see Salvatore de Benedetti, *Ottaviano Fabrizio Mossotti. Elogio pronunziatonella inaugurazione del monumento all'illustre scienziato li di 16 giugno 1867, e le interpretazioni del Mossotti ai versi astronomici della Divina Commedia* (Pisa, 1867).

Related works are Samuel Earnshaw, "On the Nature of the Molecular Forces Which Regulate the Constitution of the Luminiferous Ether," in *Transactions of the Cambridge Philosophical Society*, **7** (1839), 97–112; Michael Faraday, *Experimental Researches in Electricity*, I (London, 1839); George Green, *An Essay on the Application of Mathematical Analysis to the Theories of Electricity and Magnetism* (Nottingham, 1828), repr. in his *Mathematical Papers* (New York, 1970), 3–115; James Clerk Maxwell, *A Treatise on Electricity and Magnetism* (Cambridge, 1891); and William Thomson, *Reprint of Papers on Electrostatics and Magnetism* (London, 1872).

JED ZACHARY BUCHWALD

MOTTRAM, JAMES CECIL (*b.* Slody, Norfolk, England, 12 December 1879; *d.* London, England, 4 October 1945), *medicine, natural history.*

Mottram was the only son of James Alfred Mottram and Clara Ellen Swanzy. He qualified as a doctor in 1903 at University College Hospital, London. After research in Cambridge, he joined the Cancer Research Laboratories of the Middlesex Hospital Medical School in 1908. He remained there until 1919, except for service in the Royal Navy from 1916 to 1918. Mottram was director of the research department of the Radium Institute from 1919 to 1937 and then director of the research laboratories of Mount Vernon Hospital until his death in 1945. He married Rhoda Pritchard, and they had two sons and one daughter.

Mottram's first published work (1909) was on spectroscopic analysis of tissues for sodium and potassium, and he did some work on nutrition; but his professional life was mainly devoted to the study of cancer. This work can be broadly divided into three phases: (1) the effects of X rays and radium on the cells of normal and malignant tissues; (2) carcinogenesis; and (3) the development of methods of treating cancer. He was a competent experimenter who usually planned and executed his work alone, but he also collaborated easily. He was always particularly concerned with the practical applications of his discoveries, and much of his work in all fields appears to have been conceived as exploring the basic concepts likely to improve some known practical problem.

Mottram's most important discovery came early and was published in 1913. He showed that in both plant and animal tissues (the tips of bean shoots and ova of *Ascaris megalocephala*) cells are more vulnerable to damage by beta and gamma radiation when they are in process of division than in the resting stage, and that the metaphase is the most vulnerable stage. This damage results in profound nuclear changes affecting chromatin. Further work on radiation damage (published in 1926 in collaboration with G. M. Scott and S. Russ) showed that although there were no immediate changes apparent in cells subjected to beta rays from radium, subsequent examination of the tissue showed an absence of cells in active division. The final changes, which were profound enough to prevent the growth of a tumor, were interpreted as due to the incapacity of daughter cells to divide normally. In 1934 Mottram showed that if cells from bean roots were treated with X rays the chromosomes were fragmented and migration to the poles of the spindle was delayed, preventing normal cell division.

The practical applications of this work were not only in the treatment of tumors by exposure to radium but also careful measures to protect those working with X rays and radium. Mottram and Russ studied dosage in radium therapy (1916–1917) and Mottram and Clarke the leucocyte blood content of those handling radium for therapeutic purposes. Mottram served on the X-ray and radium protection committee, and he reorganized safety programs at the Radium Institute.

The most important paper on the part played by lymphocytes in carcinogenesis and immunity was published by Mottram and Russ in 1917–1918. Rats immune to Jensen's sarcoma showed a high content of lymphocytes in the spleen and accumulation of lymphocytes around a graft of sarcoma cells; if this accumulation were delayed, growth of the sarcoma occurred. Rats could be made immune by inoculation of sarcoma cells previously exposed to beta and gamma rays from radium, and immune rats could be made tumor-bearing by exposure to X rays. This work was used to test for radiation hazard by lymphocyte counts.

Mottram's only book on tumors (1942) examined the effect of blastogenic agents on populations of *Paramecium* and showed that fission time was prolonged and that abnormal individuals (often polyploids) were produced and spread through the population. These changes were related to an increase in viscosity of the protoplasm, which inhibited normal fission.

Mottram's contribution in World War I was his fundamental and applied work on the principles of camouflage. He was already interested in the coloration of animals, and the most useful part of his book *Controlled Natural Selection and Value Marking* (1914) was his discussion of the function of color and pattern in natural selection. The main theme of the book is that individuals differ in their value to society, as for example in age and sex, and this influences natural selection, which may result in the destruction of the less valuable; alternatively, natural selection may act not upon the individual but upon a group such as the family.

Zoologists had been aware for some time that a color pattern that broke the outline of an animal was protective. But Mottram, using plain and patterned objects against plain and patterned backgrounds for human vision, showed experimentally that if the pattern interrupts the margin of the object blurring of the outline occurs. Also the near presence or contact with the object of an area of tone similar to the object makes it less visible. Blending of patterns near the margin also masks an outline and even small details of pattern may be sufficiently important in concealment to have a survival value. This work (published 1915–1917) was of obvious value in Mottram's service at the Camouflage School during the war.

Mottram's research on fish was related to his hobby of fly-fishing. He published numerous articles in sporting journals—particularly *The Field, Salmon and Trout Magazine, Game and Gun Magazine,* and *Flyfisher's Journal*—ranging from personal anecdotes to papers on cultivating weed beds, breeding trout, breeding food for trout, pollution, and disease. The three books *Fly-fishing* (1915), *Sea Trout* (1925), and *Trout Fisheries* (1928) were based on these articles and included chapters designed to encourage the recreational fisherman to take a greater interest in ecology and in special techniques such as reading the age of fish from their scales. He served on the furunculosis committee of the Ministry of Agriculture and Fisheries, which studied the susceptibility of trout to this epizootic and the influence of temperature on its spread. The committee recommended legislation to aid in the control of the disease.

BIBLIOGRAPHY

I. ORIGINAL WORKS. Mottram's books are *Controlled Natural Selection and Value Marking* (London, 1914); *Fly-fishing: Some New Arts and Mysteries* (London, 1915; 2nd ed., actually only a new impression, London, 1921); *Sea Trout and Other Fishing Studies* (London, 1922); *Trout Fisheries: Their Care and Preservation* (London, 1928); *The Problem of Tumours. The Application of Blastogenic Agents to Ciliates. A Cytoplasmic Hypothesis* (London, 1942).

The medical papers are "A Method of Quantitative Analysis of the Tissues for Potassium and Sodium by Means of the Spectroscope," in *Archives of the Middlesex Hospital,* **15** (1909), 106–117; "On the Action of Beta and Gamma Rays of Radium on the Cell in Different States of Nuclear Division," *ibid.,* **30** (1913), 98–119; with G. M. Scott and S. Russ, "On the Effects of Beta Rays

From Radium Upon the Division and Growth of Cancer Cells," in *Proceedings of the Royal Society of London*, **100B** (1926), 326–335; "Some Effects of Cancer-Producing Agents on Chromosomes," in *British Journal of Experimental Pathology*, **15** (1934), 71–73; with S. Russ, "A Contribution to the Study of Dosage in Radium Therapy," in *Proceedings of the Royal Society of Medicine*, **10** (1916/ 1917), section electrotherapy, 121–140; with J. R. Clarke, "The Leucocytic Blood Content of Those Handling Radium for Therapeutic Purposes," *ibid*., **13** (1919/1920), 25–32; with S. Russ, "Observations and Experiments on the Susceptibility and Immunity of Rats Towards Jensen's Rat Sarcoma," in *Proceedings of the Royal Society of London*, **90B** (1917/1918), 1–33; "A Diurnal Variation in the Production of Tumours," in *Journal of Pathology and Bacteriology*, **57** (1945), 265–267.

Papers on camouflage are "Some Observations on Pattern-Blending With Reference to Obliterative Shading and Concealment of Outline," in *Proceedings of the Zoological Society of London* (1915), 679–692; "An Experimental Determination of the Factors Which Cause Patterns to Appear Conspicuous in Nature," *ibid*. (1916), 383–419; "Some Observations Upon Concealment by the Apparent Disruption of Surface in a Plane at Right-Angles to the Surface," *ibid*. (1917), 253–257.

II. SECONDARY LITERATURE. There is no bibliography of Mottram's papers, but they may be traced through *Index Medicus*, *Zoological Record*, and individual indices of periodicals mentioned in the text.

Three obituaries are worth noting: one by "S.R." in *Lancet* (1945), **2**, 581, with a photograph; R. J. Ludford, in *Nature*, **157** (1946), 399–400; and an anonymous notice in *Salmon and Trout Magazine*, no. 116 (1946), 16.

The furunculosis committee issued three reports: interim report (Edinburgh, 1930); second interim report (Edinburgh, 1933); final report (Edinburgh, 1935).

DIANA M. SIMPKINS

MOUCHEZ, ERNEST BARTHÉLÉMY (*b*. Madrid, Spain, 24 August 1821; *d*. Wissous, Seine-et-Oise, France, 25 June 1852), *cartography, astronomy*.

Mouchez studied at Versailles and then entered the École Navale to prepare for a career in the navy. He became an ensign in 1843, a post captain in 1868, and a rear admiral in 1878. In the meantime he was elected a member of the Bureau des Longitudes (1873) and of the astronomy section of the Académie des Sciences (1875, replacing L. Mathieu), and became director of the Paris observatory (26 June 1878).

As soon as he began his voyages, Mouchez started making important hydrographical studies along the coasts of Korea, China, and South America (sailing 320 kilometers up the Paraguay River). In 1862 he was sent by the minister of the navy to explore the Abrolhos Islands of Brazil, and he then explored 4,000 kilometers of coastline between the Amazon and the Río de la Plata. From 1867 to 1873 Mouchez charted the coast of Algeria during several expeditions. In all, he published about 140 maps and determined many geographical positions.

From the beginning Mouchez worked to improve surveying techniques and promoted the use by the navy of suitably adapted stationary observational instruments. In particular he employed a meridian telescope designed to determine lunar culminations and generalized the use of the theodolite in topographical surveying. By means of these modifications, he reduced the margin of error in the determination of longitudes from 30″ to 3″ or 4″.

In 1874 Mouchez was sent by the Académie des Sciences to St. Paul Island in the Indian Ocean to observe the transit of Venus on 9 December; he succeeded in making more than 400 extremely sharp exposures. In 1878 he succeeded Le Verrier as director of the Paris observatory. Dissatisfied both with its state of repair and with the quality of the work being done there, he tried in vain to persuade the authorities to build a branch of the observatory outside of Paris, in Versailles or in the forest of Verrières, and to construct lodgings for the staff nearby. Although he failed in this project, Mouchez improved the observatory of the Bureau des Longitudes in the park of Montsouris (at the southern edge of Paris), created a school of practical astronomy at the Paris observatory (1879), and founded the *Bulletin astronomique* (1884).

Arago had embarked on a program of improving Lalande's catalog of 50,000 stars with the aid of new, more precise measurements. Mouchez published the part observed up to 1875. Most notably, however, he enlisted the support of Sir David Gill, director of the Cape observatory, to bring about an international astronomical congress at Paris in 1887. It was there decided to produce photographically a large-scale general map of the heavens and to establish a catalog giving the position and brightness of all stars up to the eleventh magnitude. Two young astronomers at the Paris observatory, the brothers Prosper and Paul Henry, both of whom were also talented opticians, had just completed an astrograph and Mouchez had it adopted for this gigantic undertaking, which took more than fifty years. Four French observatories covered nearly half of the northern hemisphere, and eighteen other observatories participated.

BIBLIOGRAPHY

I. ORIGINAL WORKS. A list of Mouchez's books and other scientific publications can be found in the Royal

Society's *Catalogue of Scientific Papers*, IV, 498; VIII, 448; and X, 864; in Poggendorff, III, 940; and IV, 1034–1035; in *Catalogue général des livres imprimés de la Bibliothèque nationale*, CXX, cols. 533–538; and in *Notice sur les travaux scientifiques de M. Mouchez* (Paris, 1875).

On hydrography he wrote *Recherches sur la longitude de la côte orientale de l'Amérique du Sud* (Paris, 1866); *Rio de la Plata. Description et instructions nautiques* (Paris, 1873); *Instructions nautiques sur les côtes d'Algérie* (Paris, 1879); and *Instructions nautiques sur les côtes du Brésil* (Paris, 1890).

In astronomy, see *La photographie astronomique à l'Observatoire de Paris et la Carte du ciel* (Paris, 1887); and *Rapport annuel de l'Observatoire de Paris* for 1884–1891 (Paris, 1885–1892). He was also responsible for the publication of vols. **24–39** of *Annales de l'Observatoire de Paris*.

II. SECONDARY LITERATURE. Besides the *Notice sur les travaux scientifiques de M. Mouchez* (Paris, 1875), written at the time of his candidacy for the Académie des Sciences, there are only a few brief biographies: that in the *Dictionnaire universel des contemporains*, G. Vapereau, ed., 5th ed. (Paris, 1880), 1323; that in *Polybiblion*, 2nd ser., **36** (July-Dec. 1892), 78; the pamphlet containing the speeches given at his funeral (Paris, 1892); and an address delivered by B. Baillaud at the unveiling of his statue at Le Havre in 1921 (Paris, 1921).

JULIETTE TATON

MOULTON, FOREST RAY (*b.* Osceola County, Michigan, 29 April 1872; *d.* Wilmette, Illinois, 7 December 1952), *astronomy, mathematics.*

Forest Ray Moulton was the eldest of eight children born to Belah and Mary Smith Moulton. He was named Forest Ray because his poetic mother thought him a "perfect ray of light and happiness in that dense forest." He received his early education in a typical frontier school and at home. At the age of sixteen he taught in this same school, where one of the students was his brother Harold, who was later to become the first head of the Brookings Institute. At the age of eighteen he enrolled in Albion College, where he received his B.A. in 1894. Moulton received his Ph.D. in astronomy, *summa cum laude*, from the University of Chicago (1899). He also received honorary degrees from Albion College (1922), Drake University (1939), and the Case School of Applied Science (1940).

Moulton had a variety of careers. His academic life began at the University of Chicago with his appointment, while a graduate student, in 1896 as an assistant in astronomy, and it continued through his appointment as professor in 1912 until retirement in 1926. From 1927 to 1936 he was a director of the

Utilities Power and Light Corporation of Chicago. He was also a trustee of the Exposition Committee of Chicago's Century of Progress from 1920 to 1936, and its director of concessions from 1931 to 1933. From 1936 to 1940 he was executive secretary of the American Association for the Advancement of Science. During his tenure in this position, he edited more than twenty symposium volumes.

In 1898, while still a graduate student at Chicago, Moulton was invited by Thomas Crowder Chamberlin, then chairman of the geology department, to participate in an investigation of the earth's origin. Chamberlin's investigations on glacial movements had raised doubts that were relevant to the then existing theories. Kant had originally proposed his nebular hypothesis in 1755. Half a century later, and with no knowledge of Kant's theory, Laplace developed a similar theory. He suggested that the earth had originated in a vast mass of blazing gas, which had been thrown off by the sun and had liquefied into a molten sphere. According to this theory the earth was steadily cooling off from its original molten state. After the primordial sun, which was five and a half billion miles in diameter, had cast away the planets, it reached its present diameter and a rotational velocity of 270 miles per second. When Moulton imagined that all planets were returned to the sun, his calculations indicated that the sun would not have enough momentum to hurl off any rings of matter. Chamberlin and his group investigated everything that was written on the origin of the solar system. The most promising prospect was offered by that of nebular "knots," revealed in photographs of spiral nebulae, which could have served as collecting centers.

On 28 May 1900 there was an eclipse of the sun. Chamberlin and Moulton meticulously studied the photographs that illustrated the sun's eruptive nature. Their observation of great clouds of gaseous matter flaring out and away from the sun's surface led to the planetesimal hypothesis proposed in 1904. They proposed that the nebula quickly cooled and solidified, creating small chunks of matter, the planetesimals. Although today neither the Laplace-Kant nor the Moulton-Chamberlin hypothesis stands by itself, both provide a basis for current theories.

During World War I Moulton was assigned to do ballistics research at Fort Sill. Here he is said to have effectively doubled the range of artillery. His work was the forerunner of the efforts in World War II to get improved ballistics tables faster and more accurately, which was one of the links giving impetus to contemporary high speed electronic computing equipment.

In 1920, Moulton, one of the founders of the Society for Visual Education, gave the first radio address broadcast from the University of Chicago. As one of the pioneers of educational broadcasting, Moulton was heard weekly in Chicago from 1934 to 1936, and in Washington from 1938 to 1940.

Moulton was a fellow of the American Academy of Arts and Sciences, the American Physical Society, and the Royal Astronomical Society; President of Sigma Xi, and Honorary Foreign Associate of the British Association for the Advancement of Science. He was also an active member of many other professional societies.

In 1897 Moulton married Estelle Gillete. They had four children and were divorced in 1938. In 1939 he married Alicia Pratt of Winnetka, Illinois. They were divorced in 1951.

BIBLIOGRAPHY

I. ORIGINAL WORKS. No complete bibliog. of Moulton's publications has been published. His major bks. include *An Introduction to Celestial Mechanics* (London–New York, 1902, 1914, 1935); *Descriptive Astronomy* (Chicago, 1912, 1921, 1923); *Periodic Orbits* (Washington, 1920); *Differential Equations* (New York, 1930), written with D. Buchanan, T. Buck, F. Griffin, W. Longley, and W. MacMillan; and *New Methods in Exterior Ballistics* (Chicago, 1926). The last work is the beginning of a contemporary mathematical approach to the science of ballistics. For interesting and opposing reviews of this work see J. E. Rowe, *Bulletin of the American Mathematical Society*, **34** (1928), 229–332, and L. S. Dederick, *ibid.*, 667.

The first twenty vols. of the *Carnegie Institution of Washington Yearbooks* (1902–1921) provide a clear picture of the work of Moulton and Chamberlin on the planetesimal hypothesis. *Yearbook*, no. 2 (1903), 261–270, contains a report by T. C. Chamberlin, entitled "Fundamental Problems of Geology," in which he describes the progress of the investigators and collaborators, and their roles and status to date. *Yearbook*, no. 3 (1904), 255–256, contains a letter from Moulton to Chamberlin describing different hypotheses and their applications, pertinent observational data, and the laws derived from the data. Other vols. of the *Yearbook* and their relevant p. nos. are no. 1, 25–43; no. 3, 195–258; no. 4, 171–190; no. 5, 166–172; no. 6, 195; no. 7, 204–205; no. 8, 28–52, 224–225; no. 9, 48–222; no. 10, 45, 222–225; no. 11, 13–44, 264–266; no. 12, 52, 292, 297; no. 13, 45–46, 356–357, 376; no. 14, 36–37, 289, 368; no. 15, 358–362; no. 16, 307–319; no. 17, 297; no. 18, 39, 343–345, 349–351; no. 19, 21, 366–382, 386; and no. 20, 412–425. See also "The Development of the Planetesimal Hypothesis," in *Science*, n.s. **30** (1909), 642–645, written with T. C. Chamberlin; "An Attempt to Test the Nebular Hypothesis by an Appeal to the Laws of Dynamics," in *Astrophysical Journal*, **11** (1900), 103; and "Evolution of the Solar System," *ibid.*, **22** (1905), 166.

One of Moulton's more important papers from the standpoint of current research is "The Straight Line Solutions of the Problem of *n* Bodies," in *Annals of Mathematics*, **12** (1910–1911), 1–17. In this paper the number of straight line solutions is found for *n* arbitrary masses. This is the generalization of the problem solved by Lagrange for three bodies. Moulton also attacks what is a sort of converse of this problem by determining, when possible, *n* masses such that if they are placed at *n* arbitrarily collinear points, they will, under proper initial projection, always remain in a straight line. This paper was originally presented to the Chicago Section of the American Mathematical Society on 28 December 1900 (see *Bulletin of the American Mathematical Society*, **7** [1900–1901], 249–250).

II. SECONDARY LITERATURE. The anonymous "The Washington Moultons, Forest Ray, '94, and Harold Glenn, 1907," in *Io Triumphe* (March, 1947) (Albion College Alumni Magazine), is an excellent art. with portraits of both Forest and Harold. This art. also contains a photograph of the seven Moulton brothers and their sister on the occasion of the awarding of an M.A. to Mary Moulton by Wayne University in 1945. Other biographical arts. appear in *Current Biography* (1946), 421–423; *The National Cyclopaedia of American Biography*, XLIII (1946), 314–315; and A. J. Carlson, "Forest Ray Moulton: 1872–1952," in *Science*, **117** (1953), 545–546.

HENRY S. TROPP

MOUTARD, THÉODORE FLORENTIN (*b.* Soultz, Haut-Rhin, France, 27 July 1827; *d.* Paris, France, 13 March 1901), *geometry, engineering.*

Moutard was educated at the École Polytechnique from 1844 to 1846. Like many of his fellow students and alumni, he was both an engineer and a geometer. He was graduated from the École des Mines in 1849 and entered the engineering corps. He was discharged in 1852, because as a republican he refused to take the required loyalty oath after the coup d'état by Napoleon III. He was reinstated in 1870. The majority of his mathematical publications date from these years. In 1875 Moutard was appointed professor of mechanics at the École des Mines, but he retained his army rank and was named *ingénieur en chef* in 1878 and *inspecteur général* in 1886. He retired with the latter rank in 1897 but retained his position at the École des Mines. From 1883 he also served as an outside examiner at the École Polytechnique. He was one of the collaborators on *La grande encyclopédie.*

Moutard's mathematical work was primarily in the theory of algebraic surfaces, particularly anallagmatic surfaces, differential geometry, and partial differential equations. His broadest work was a memoir on elliptic functions, which was published as an appendix in Victor Poncelet's *Applications d'analyse et de géométrie.*

BIBLIOGRAPHY

I. ORIGINAL WORKS. The works by Moutard in Victor Poncelet, *Applications d'analyse et de géométrie*, 2 vols. (Paris, 1862–1864), are "Rapprochements divers entre les principales méthodes de la géométrie pure et celles de l'analyse algébrique" (I, 509–535); the work on elliptic functions, "Recherches analytiques sur les polygons simultanément inscrits et circonscrits à deux coniques" (I, 535–560), and a short note "Addition au IVᵉ cahier" (II, 363–364), on the principle of continuity. A bibliography of Moutard's papers in various journals can be found in Poggendorff, IV, 1037.

II. SECONDARY LITERATURE. An account of Moutard's life is in *La grande encyclopédie*, XXIV, 504. His work is also mentioned in Michel Chasles, *Rapport sur les progrès de la géométrie* (Paris, 1870).

ELAINE KOPPELMAN

MOUTON, GABRIEL (*b.* Lyons, France, 1618; *d.* Lyons, 28 September 1694), *mathematics, astronomy*.

Mouton became *vicaire perpétuel* of St. Paul's Church in Lyons in 1646, after taking holy orders and obtaining a doctorate in theology. He spent his whole life in his native city, fulfilling his clerical responsibilities and untroubled by any extraordinary events. During his leisure time he studied mathematics and astronomy and rapidly acquired a certain renown in the city. Jean Picard, who also was an *abbé*, held Mouton in high esteem and always visited him when in Lyons to work on the determination of the city's geographic position.

The book that made Mouton famous, *Observationes diametrorum solis et lunae apparentium* (1670), was the fruit of his astronomical observations and certain computational procedures he had developed. Lalande later stated: "This volume contains interesting memoirs on interpolations and on the project of a universal standard of measurement based on the pendulum."

Mouton was a pioneer in research on natural and practicable units of measurement. He had been struck by the difficulties and disagreements resulting from the great number of units of length, for example, which varied from province to province and from country to country. First he studied how the length of a pendulum with a frequency of one beat per second varies with latitude. He then proposed to deduce from these variations the length of the terrestrial meridian, a fraction of which was to be taken as the universal unit of length. Mouton selected the minute of the degree, which he called the *mille*. The divisions and subdivisions of this principal unit, all in decimal fractions, were called *centuria, decuria, virga, virgula, decima, centesima*, and *millesima*—or alternatively,

in the same order, *stadium, funiculus, virga, virgula, digitus, granum*, and *punctum*.

The *virgula geometrica* (geometric foot), for example, was 1/600,000 of the degree of meridian. In order to be able to determine the true length of this foot at any time, Mouton counted the number of oscillations of a simple pendulum of the same length over a span of thirty minutes and found it to be 3,959.2. These ideas were espoused by Picard shortly after the book appeared and a little later, in 1673, by Huygens. They were also favorably received by members of the Royal Society.

Although Mouton's proposals were seriously considered in theoretical terms in his own time, they led to no immediate practical results. Contemporary measuring procedures were too unsatisfactory to assure their valid and definitive application. It was not until 1790 that projects like Mouton's were taken up again. At a session of the Academy of Sciences on 14 April of that year, M. J. Brisson proposed that a new system be based on a natural standard. The Academy preferred to press for a geodesic survey, however, and decided to adopt one ten-millionth of the quadrant of the meridian of Paris as the standard for the meter.

In the *Observationes diametrorum* Mouton presented a very practical computational device for completing ordered tables of numbers when their law of formation is known. He used successive numerical differences, an idea previously employed by Briggs to establish his logarithmic tables.

When Leibniz went to London in January 1673, he took with him his *Dissertatio de arte combinatoria*. He summarized its contents to John Pell and, in particular, explained what he called "différences génératrices." Pell remarked that he had read something very similar in Mouton's book, which had appeared three years earlier. Leibniz had learned, during his stay in Paris, that the book was in preparation but did not know that it had been published. While visiting Oldenburg, Leibniz found Mouton's book and observed that Pell had been right; but he was able to prove that his own, more theoretical and general ideas and results had been reached independently of Mouton's.

A skillful calculator, Mouton produced ten-place tables of logarithmic sines and tangents for the first four degrees, with intervals of one second. He also determined, with astonishing accuracy, the apparent diameter of the sun at its apogee. A skilled experimentalist, he constructed an astronomical pendulum remarkable for its precision and the variety of its movements. It was long preserved at Lyons but was ultimately lost.

BIBLIOGRAPHY

I. ORIGINAL WORKS. Mouton's major work is *Observationes diametrorum solis et lunae apparentium, meridianarumque aliquot altitudinum, cum tabula declinationum solis; Dissertatio de dierum naturalium inaequalitate, . . .* (Lyons, 1670).

His trigonometric tables, which remained in MS, are now in the library of the Academy of Sciences. Esprit Pézénas, director of the observatory at Avignon, consulted this MS and used Mouton's method in preparing the new ed. of William Gardiner's *Tables of Logarithms* (to seven decimals) (Avignon, 1770).

II. SECONDARY LITERATURE. See the following (listed chronologically): J. B. Delambre, *Base du système métrique décimal ou mesure de l'arc de méridien compris entre les parallèles de Dunkerque et Barcelone, exécutée en 1792 et années suivantes par MM. Méchain et Delambre*, I (Paris, 1806), 11; *Biographie universelle ancienne et moderne*, XXIX (Paris, 1861), 485; Rudolf Wolf, *Geschichte der Astronomie* (Munich, 1877), 623; and Moritz Cantor, *Vorlesungen über Geschichte der Mathematik*, III (Leipzig, 1901), 76–77, 310, 389, and IV (Leipzig, 1908), 362, 440.

PIERRE SPEZIALI

MUḤYI 'L-DĪN AL-MAGHRIBĪ (Muḥyi 'l-Milla wa 'l-Dīn Yaḥyā ibn Muḥammad ibn Abi 'l-Shukr al-Maghribī al-Andalusī) (*fl.* Syria, and later Marāgha, *ca.* 1260–1265), *trigonometry, astronomy, astrology.*

Al-Maghribī was a Hispano-Muslim mathematician and astronomer, whose time and place of birth and death cannot be determined. Little is known about his life except that he was born in the Islamic West and flourished for a time in Syria and later in Marāgha, where he joined the astronomers of the Marāgha directed by Naṣīr al-Dīn al-Ṭūsī. He made observations in 1264–1265. It has been said that he was a guest of Hūlāgū Khân (Īl-khân of Persia, 1256–1265) and met Abu 'l Faraj (Bar Hebraeus, 1226–1286).

Suter and Brockelmann ascribe quite a long list of writings to al-Maghribī.

Trigonometry

1. *Kitāb shakl al-qaṭṭāʿ* ("Book on the Theorem of Menelaus").

2. *Ma yanfariʿu ʿan shakl al-qaṭṭāʿ* ("Consequences Deduced From *shakl al-qaṭṭāʿ*").

3. *Risāla fī kayfiyyat istikhrāj al-juyūb al-wāqiʿa fī 'l-dāʾira* ("Treatise on the Calculation of Sines").

Astronomy

4. *Khulāṣat al-Majisṭī* ("Essence of the *Almagest*"). It contains a new determination of the obliquity of the ecliptic made at Marāgha in 1264, 23; 30° (the real value in 1250 was 23; 32, 19°).

5. *Maqāla fī istikhrāj ta ʿdīl al-nahār wa sa ʿat al-mashriq wa 'l-dāʾir min al-falak* ("Treatise on Finding the Meridian, Ortive Amplitude, and Revolution of the Sphere").

6. *Muqaddamāt tataʿallaqu bī-ḥarakāt al-kawākib* ("Premises on the Motions of the Stars").

7. *Tasṭīḥ al-asṭurlāb* ("The Flattening of the Astrolabe").

Editions of the Greek classics; they are called recensions (sing. *taḥrīr*).

8. Euclid's *Elements.*

9. Apollonius' *Conics.*

10. Theodosius' *Spherics.*

11. Menelaus' *Spherics.*

He also wrote more than six books on astrology and a memoir on chronology.

Al-Maghribī's writings on trigonometry contain original developments. For example, two proofs are given of the sine theory for right-angled spherical triangles, and one of them is different from those given by Naṣīr al-Dīn al-Ṭūsī; this theorem is generalized for other triangles. He also worked in several other branches of trigonometry.

Ptolemy (A.D 150) used an ingenious method of interpolation in the calculation of chord 1°. This is of course approximately equivalent to chord 1°. The same method was used for sines in Islam. To find the exact value, one must solve a cubic equation. This was done later by the Persian astronomer al-Kāshī (*d.* 1429/1430). Al-Maghribī, and before him Abu 'l-Wafāʾ (940–997/998), tried to find the value of the sine of one-third of an arc. For that purpose Abu 'l-Wafāʾ laid down a preliminary theorem that the differences of sines of arcs having the same origin and equal differences become smaller as the arcs become larger.

Using this preliminary theorem, al-Maghribī calculated sin 1° in the following way (see Fig. 1):

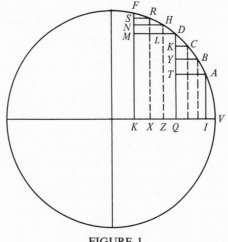

FIGURE 1

$VF = 1; 7, 30°$ and $\sin VF = FK = 1; 10, 40, 12, 34^p$

$AV = 0; 45°$ and $\sin AV = AI = 0; 44, 8, 21, 8, 38^p.$

The arc AF is divided into six equal parts and each part $= 0; 3, 45°$; therefore,

arc $DV +$ arc $DH = 1°$ and $\sin HV(=1°) = HZ.$

The perpendiculars AT, BY, and CK divide DT into three unequal parts: $TY > YK > DK$; $TD/3 > HL$; $DQ + TD/3 (=1; 2, 49, 43, 36, 9^p) > HZ(=\sin 1°)$. FM is divided into three unequal parts: $MN > NS > SF$; $DQ + FM/3 (=1; 2, 49, 42, 50, 40, 40^p) < NK = HZ(=\sin 1°)$. Then he found $\sin 1° = 1; 2, 49, 43, 24, 55^p$.

Al-Maghribī calculated $\sin 1°$ by using another method of interpolation based on the ratio of arcs greater than the ratios of sines. He found $\sin 1° = 1; 2, 49, 42, 17, 15, 12^p$ and said that the difference between two values of sines found by using different methods is $0; 0, 0, 0, 56^p$, which is correct to four places.

Using these methods, al-Maghribī calculated the ratio of the circumference to its diameter (that is, π).

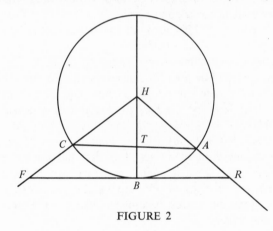

FIGURE 2

$$AC(=2AT) < \text{arc } ABC < RF$$

$$\sin AB(=3/4°) = AT = 0; 47, 7, 21, 7, 37^p$$

$$\Delta RFH \sim \Delta AHC, \quad RF/AC = BH/TH.$$

$$RF = 1; 34, 15, 11, 19, 25^p$$

$$\text{arc } ABC = \frac{AC + RF}{2} = 1; 34, 14, 16, 47, 19, 30^p.$$

The circumference $= 240$. Arc $AB = 6; 16, 59, 47, 18^p$, the diameter being 2^p. The diameter being 1^p, the circumference $= 3; 8, 29, 53, 34, 39^p < 3R + 1/7$, since $1/7 = 0; 8, 34, 17, 8, 34, 17^p$.

Al-Maghribī compared the latter and Archimedes' value, $3R + 1/7 <$ the circumference $< 3R + 10/71$, found by computing the lengths of inscribed and circumscribed regular polygons of ninety-six sides. Half of the difference between $10/71$ and $10/70$ is equal to $0; 8, 30, 40^p$.

Al-Maghribī determined two mean proportionals between two lines, that is, the duplication of the cube (the problem of Delos). In antiquity many solutions were produced for this problem. It was thought that in terms of solving this problem the mathematicians of Islam stood strangely apart from those of antiquity; but recently many examples have been discovered, thus altering this opinion. The following example of al-Maghribī's is of interest in this respect. He finds two values (see Fig. 3):

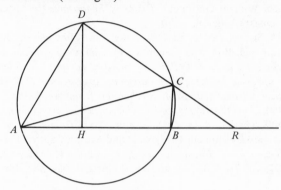

FIGURE 3

AB and BC are given and $AB > BC$, and $AB \perp BC$. AC are joined. Triangle ABC is circumscribed by a circle. The perpendicular DH is drawn so that DC must pass through point R.

$HR = AB$, $RH/DH = BA/DH$

$AH = BR$, $RH/HD = DH/HA$, since angle $D = 90°$

$BA/DH = DH/HA$

But

$$RH/DH = RB(=HA)/BC$$
$$BA/DH = DH/HA = HA/BC.$$

BIBLIOGRAPHY

The following works should be consulted: A. Aaboe, "Al-Kāshī's Iteration Method for Determination of sin 1°," in *Scripta mathematica*, **20** (1954), 24–29; and *Episodes From the Early History of Mathematics* (New Haven, 1964), 120; C. Brockelmann, *Geschichte der arabischen Literatur*, I (Leiden, 1943), 626, and supp. I (Leiden, 1937), 868–869; P. Brunet and A. Mieli, *Histoire des sciences d'antiquité* (Paris, 1935), 333–415; H. Bürger and K. Kohl, "Zur Geschichte des Transversalenzatzes," in *Abhandlungen zur Geschichte der Naturwissenschaften und der Medizin*, no. 7 (1924), 55–57, 67, 70, 71, 73–75, 89; Carra de Vaux, "Remaniement des sphériques de Théodose par Iahia ibn Muhammed ibn Abī Schukr Almaghrabī Alandalusī," in *Journal asiatique*, **17** (1891), 287–295; T. Heath, *A History of Greek Mathematics*, I (Oxford, 1921), 244–270; P. Luckey, "Der Lehrbrief über Kreis

Umfang (ar-Risāla al-Muhītīya) von Čamšid b. Mas'ūd al-Kāšī," in *Abhandlungen der Deutschen Akademie der Wissenschaften zu Berlin*, Math.-naturwiss. Kl., no. 5 (1950); and G. Sarton, *Introduction to the History of Science*, II, pt. 2 (Baltimore, 1931), 1015–1017.

H. Suter, *Die Mathematiker und Astronomen der Araber und ihre Werke* (Leipzig, 1900), 155; S. Tekeli, "Taqī al-Din's Work on Extracting the Chord 2° and sin 1°," in *Araştirma*, **3** (1965), 123–131; and "The Works on the Duplication of the Cube in the Islamic World," *ibid.*, **4** (1966), 87–105; F. Woepcke, "Sur une mesure de la circonférence du cercle due aux astronomes arabes et fondée sur un calcul d'Aboul Wafā," in *Journal asiatique*, **15** (1860), 281–320; and S. Zeki, *Asari bakiye*, I (Istanbul, 1913), 106–120.

S. Tekeli

MUIR, MATTHEW MONCRIEFF PATTISON (*b.* Glasgow, Scotland, 1 November 1848; *d.* Epsom, England, 2 September 1931), *chemistry*.

Muir was the son of a Glasgow merchant and received his elementary education in his native city. He began the study of chemistry at the University of Glasgow. In 1870 he entered the University of Tübingen in order to continue his studies, but the Franco-Prussian War forced his return home in 1871. He then served for two years as demonstrator in chemistry at Anderson College in Glasgow, and in 1873 he accepted a similar position at Owens College in Manchester.

In 1877 he was appointed to the praelectorship in chemistry at Gonville and Caius College at Cambridge, where he remained for the rest of his scientific career. He received an honorary M.A. in 1880, and in 1881 he became a fellow of the College. At the time of his death he was its senior fellow. By his 1873 marriage to Florence Haslam he had two sons, both of whom became clergymen. He retired from active teaching in 1908 and spent the remainder of his life at his home in Epsom, devoting himself to writing. Throughout his life he took an active part in politics.

Muir's laboratory investigations, which were carried out between 1876 and 1888, chiefly related to compounds of bismuth. He and his students published eighteen papers in this field. It is said that for a time his students called him Mr. Bismuth. He was not essentially interested in laboratory work, but rather preferred teaching and writing. His courses, especially those for medical students, were considered outstanding, and he excelled in encouraging weaker students, to whom his home was always open.

He closely followed the scientific literature and was therefore able to write a number of textbooks for the use of his students. His text *Principles of Chemistry* (1889) went through two editions, and his *Elements of Thermal Chemistry* (1885) was highly successful. He translated Ostwald's book on solutions (1891) and took part in a major revision of Watts' *Dictionary of Chemistry*. From the beginning of his career, his chief interest lay in the philosophical aspects of chemistry. In the 1880's he turned to historical studies, and in this field he made his greatest contributions. His historical writings began when he was asked to prepare a biographical work on famous chemists for a series on heroes of science. The book appeared in 1883 and so aroused his interest in the subject that for the rest of his life he devoted himself with increasing frequency to historical studies. In his later years Muir worked entirely in this field. Besides his biographical studies of famous chemists, he wrote on the chemical elements and alchemy. His chief historical work, which was published in 1907, was his *History of Chemical Theories and Laws*. He said that in this book he was trying to picture the steps in the development of major advances in chemistry without obscuring them by details. The book remains a classic in the history of chemistry.

BIBLIOGRAPHY

I. Original Works. Muir's original studies lay in the field of historical works. His books included *Heroes of Science: Chemists* (London, 1883); *The Alchemical Essence and the Chemical Element* (London, 1894); *History of Chemical Theories and Laws* (London and New York, 1907); *The Story of the Chemical Elements* (London, 1908); and *The Story of Alchemy and the Beginnings of Chemistry* (London, 1914).

II. Secondary Literature. The only substantial biography is R. S. Morrell, "M. M. Pattison Muir 1848–1931," in *Journal of the Chemical Society* (1932), 1330–1334.

Henry M. Leicester

MULDER, GERARDUS JOHANNES (*b.* Utrecht, Netherlands, 27 December 1802; *d.* Bennekom, Netherlands, 18 April 1880), *chemistry*.

Mulder studied medicine at the University of Utrecht (1819–1825), from which he graduated with a dissertation on the action of alkaloids of opium, *De opio ejusque principiis, actione inter se comparatis* (1825). He practiced medicine in Amsterdam and then in Rotterdam, where he also lectured at the Bataafsch Genootschap der Proefondervindelijke Wijsbegeerte and taught botany to student apothecaries. At the foundation of a medical school at

Rotterdam (1828), Mulder became lecturer in botany, chemistry, mathematics, and pharmacy. His attention was directed primarily to the practical training of his students. In 1840 Mulder succeeded N. C. de Fremery as professor of chemistry at the University of Utrecht. He applied for his retirement in 1868 and spent the rest of his life in Bennekom. Besides publishing on scientific subjects, Mulder took an active part in education, politics, and public health. The works of Faraday and Berzelius exerted a great influence on him; his *Leerboek voor Scheikundige Werktuigkunde* (1832–1835) was written in the spirit of Faraday's *Chemical Manipulation*. Mulder edited a Dutch translation by three of his students of Berzelius' textbook of chemistry as *Leerboek der Scheikunde* (6 vols., 1834–1845). His difficult character caused problems with some of his pupils and with other chemists.

From 1826 to 1865 Mulder edited five Dutch chemical journals (see bibliography), in which most of his work was published. He worked in physics and in both general and physical chemistry, the latter in combination with medicine, physiology, agriculture, and technology. Most of his work had a polemic character. His most important contributions are in the field of physiological chemistry and soil chemistry, in which he published two extensive works that attracted much attention in translation despite their many mistakes and erroneous speculations.

Studies on proteins led Mulder to his protein theory (1838): he supposed that all albuminous substances consist of a radical compound (protein) of carbon, hydrogen, nitrogen, and oxygen, in combination with varying amounts of sulfur and phosphorus. The differences among proteins resulted from multiplication of the protein units in conjunction with the two other elements. Thus, casein was formulated as

$$10 \text{ protein units} + S,$$

and serum albumin as

$$10 \text{ protein units} + SP_2.$$

In 1843 Mulder published the first volume of a treatise on physiological chemistry, which was translated into English as *The Chemistry of Vegetable and Animal Physiology* (1845–1849). At first both Liebig and Berzelius accepted Mulder's analysis of proteins; but Liebig soon opposed the theory vigorously, and a deep conflict with Mulder ensued. In 1839–1840 Mulder investigated humic and ulmic acids and humus substances and determined the amounts of geic acid (acidum geïcum), apocrenic acid (acidum apocrenicum or Quellsatzsäure), crenic acid (acidum crenicum or Quellsäure), and humic acids in fertile soils (1844). The structure of these various brown or black substances is unknown. They are a group of aromatic acids of high molecular weight, which can be extracted from peat, turf, and decaying vegetable matter in the soil. The difference between these acids is the oxygen content. In the decay of vegetable matter ulmic acid is formed. According to Mulder, this has the formula $C_{20}H_{14}O_6$ (in modern equivalents). In contact with air and water more oxygen is absorbed, which results in the successive formation of humic acid ($C_{20}H_{12}O_6$), geic acid ($C_{20}H_{12}O_7$), apocrenic acid ($C_{24}H_{12}O_{12}$), and crenic acid ($C_{12}H_{12}O_8$).

His studies on agricultural chemistry led to the treatise *De scheikunde der bouwbare aarde* (1860). Mulder confirmed Berzelius' suggestion that theine and caffeine are identical (1838) and was the first to analyze phytol correctly in his researches on chlorophyll. Among his other works are technical chemical publications on indigo (1833), wine (1855), and beer (1857), detailed research on the assaying method for analyzing silver in relation to the volumetric silver determination of Gay-Lussac (1857), and a study on drying oils (1865).

BIBLIOGRAPHY

I. ORIGINAL WORKS. Mulder's writings include *Dissertatio de opio ejusque principiis, actione inter se comparatis* (Utrecht, 1825); *Leerboek voor Scheikundige Werktuigkunde*, 2 vols. (Rotterdam, 1832–1835); *Proeve eener algemeene physiologische scheikunde*, 2 vols. (Rotterdam, 1843–1850), translated as *The Chemistry of Vegetable and Animal Physiology* (Edinburgh, 1845–1849); *De vraag van Liebig aan de zedelijkheid en de wetenschap getoetst* (Rotterdam, 1846), also in *Scheikundige onderzoekingen*, **3** (1846), 357–487, and translated as *Liebig's Question to Mulder Tested by Morality and Science* (London, 1846); "De essayeermethode van het zilver scheikundig onderzocht," which is *Scheikundige verhandelingen en onderzoekingen*, **1**, pt. 1 (1857); *De scheikunde der bouwbare aarde*, 4 vols. (Rotterdam, 1860); and "De scheikunde der droogende oliën en hare toepassing," which is *Scheikundige verhandelingen en onderzoekingen*, **4**, pt. 1 (1865). Journals edited by Mulder are *Bijdragen tot de natuurkundige wetenschappen*, 7 vols. (Amsterdam, 1826–1832), with H. C. van Hall and W. Vrolik; *Natuur- en scheikundig archief*, 6 vols. (Rotterdam, 1833–1838); *Bulletin des sciences physiques et naturelles en Néerlande*, 3 vols. (Leiden, 1838–1840), with F. A. W. Miquel and W. Wenckebach; *Scheikundige onderzoekingen, gedaan in het laboratorium der Utrechtsche hoogeschool*, 6 vols. (Utrecht, 1842–1851); and *Scheikundige verhandelingen en onderzoekingen*, 4 vols. (Utrecht, 1857–1865).

II. SECONDARY LITERATURE. See the biography by W. Labruyère, *G. J. Mulder (1802–1880)* (Leiden, 1938), with bibliography, pp. 113–130. See also E. Cohen, "Wat leeren ons de archieven omtrent Gerrit Jan Mulder?" which is *Verhandeling der K. akademie van wetenschappen. Afdeling Natuurkunde*, **19**, pt. 2 (1948). An autobiographical sketch of Mulder was published posthumously as *Levensschets. Door hemzelven geschreven en door drie zijner vrienden uitgegeven* (Rotterdam, 1881; 2nd ed. Utrecht, 1883). Mulder's correspondence with Berzelius was published as *Jac. Berzelius Bref*, H. G. Söderbaum, ed., V (Uppsala, 1916), *Briefväxling mellan Berselius och G. J. Mulder (1834–1837)*.

H. A. M. SNELDERS

MÜLLER, FRANZ (FERENC), BARON DE REICHENSTEIN (*b*. Nagyszeben, Transylvania [now Sibiu, Rumania], 1 July 1740; *d*. Vienna, Austria, 12 October 1825), *chemistry*.

Müller, the son of a treasury official, was educated in Nagyszeben and then studied law in Vienna. By then he had become interested in chemistry and mineralogy and went to Selmecbánya (Schemnitz, in Hungary), where a short time earlier one of the world's first mining academies had been opened. There he studied mining and metallurgy under N. J. Jacquin. After completing his studies in 1768, Müller entered the service of the state saltworks in Transylvania; later he was active in mining in southern Hungary. From 1775 to 1778 he was director of the state mines in the Tirol; and from 1778 to 1802 he directed all mining operations in Transylvania from his office in Nagyszeben. In 1802 Müller moved to Vienna to head the council that had jurisdiction over minting and mining in Austria and Hungary. He held this position until 1818. On his retirement he received the Order of St. Stephen and the title of baron.

Müller discovered the chemical element tellurium in 1784 at Nagyszeben. For several years sylvanite, an auriferous mineral from Transylvania, had been causing problems because its processing always yielded less gold than expected. Anton von Ruprecht, a former schoolmate of Müller's and professor of chemistry at the Selmecbánya Mining Academy, analyzed the ore in 1782 and published his finding that it contained antimony as well as gold. Müller did not share this view, asserting in print that the substance involved was bismuth. Ruprecht responded by stating the reasons it could not be bismuth. In his next publication Müller admitted his error and announced that a new, previously unrecognized semimetal was present in the ore; he also enumerated its characteristic chemical reactions (*Physikalische Arbeiten der einträchtigen Freunde in Wien*, **1**, no. 2 [1783], 63).

Müller, however, did not name the new element.

Instead, he sent a sample of the ore to Torbern Bergman at Uppsala, wishing to confirm his conclusion by submitting the substance for examination to the most famous analyst of the century. Bergman reported in a letter that he was starting to work on the matter, but he died soon after. Ten years later the Berlin chemist Martin Klaproth asked Müller to send him a sample. He carried out an analysis, confirmed Müller's finding, and gave a lecture on the subject at the Berlin Academy, where he proposed that the previously unnamed element be called tellurium.

Müller also contributed to mineralogy. He discovered a variety of tourmaline and a variety of opal that is also called Müller glass.

BIBLIOGRAPHY

Müller's publications are listed in Poggendorff, II, 231.

Secondary sources include R. Jagnaux, *Histoire de la chimie*, I (Paris, 1891), 500–504; F. Szabadváry, *Az elemek nyomában* ("In the Traces of Elements"; Budapest, 1961), 142–148; and M. E. Weeks, *Discovery of the Elements* (1956), 303–304, also in *Journal of Chemical Education*, **12** (1935), 403.

F. SZABADVÁRY

MÜLLER, FRITZ (JOHANN FRIEDRICH THEODOR) (*b*. Windischholzhausen, Thuringia, Germany, 31 March 1822; *d*. Blumenau, Brazil, 21 May 1897), *natural history*.

Although described by Blandford in *Nature* (1897) as "one of the greatest and most original naturalists" of the nineteenth century, Müller's reputation has always been overshadowed by those of his illustrious scientific contemporaries. His innate modesty, complete indifference to fame, and physical isolation in southern Brazil further contributed to obscure the significance of his work. His book, *Für Darwin* (1864), however, was a fundamental contribution to evolutionary biology at a critical moment during its infancy; and his name has been immortalized in scientific literature with the term "Müllerian mimicry."

Müller was born in a small village outside Erfurt. His father, Johann Friedrich Müller, was a minister, and his mother was the daughter of the distinguished Erfurt chemist and pharmacist J. B. Trommsdorff. Both parents had a strong interest in natural history, and his father in particular greatly influenced Fritz and his younger brother Hermann, who became a well-known botanist at Lippstadt.

Müller's early formal education began at the village school of Mühlberg and continued at the Erfurt

Gymnasium (1835–1840), where his extraordinary linguistic ability—he learned Italian, Russian, Syriac, Arabic, English, and later Portuguese—became evident. After studying pharmacy for one year at Naumburg, he began advanced work at the University of Berlin, where he studied mathematics and the natural sciences. His anatomy professor was Johannes Müller. He spent the following academic year (1842–1843) at the University of Greifswald, then returned to Berlin, where he completed the Ph.D. on 14 December 1844. His dissertation, "De hirudinibus circa Berolinum hucusque observatis," dealt with the leeches found near Berlin. He continued work at Berlin for his advanced teaching certificate (Ober-lehrerexamen) before returning to the Gymnasium at Erfurt for his teaching period as a probationary candidate (1845). Later that year, however, he decided to study medicine, with the intention of becoming a ship's surgeon and seeing the world, especially the tropics, where he hoped to study zoology.

Returning to the University of Greifswald (1845–1849), Müller completed all the work for his medical degree except for the state certification examination (Staatsexamen). The Ministry of Education would not allow him to take the examination because he had sided with the democrats in the Revolution of 1848 and had refused to take a religious oath recognizing the established church and orthodox religious views. (Müller believed in free love, and Katherine Töllner bore three of their ten children out of wedlock.) In 1849, unable to obtain his degree, Müller in October became a private tutor at Roloffs-hagen (near Grimmen). He eventually received honorary medical degrees from Bonn in 1868 and from Tübingen in 1877. Prussian religious intolerance finally led Müller to abandon his homeland in 1852 and sail to Blumenau, Brazil, on the Itajai River near the coast between Río de Janeiro and Buenos Aires. Most of his important scientific work was done in South America, where he spent the rest of his life.

Despite his superb education, Müller lived there as a farmer until 1856, when he was appointed mathematics teacher at the provincial lyceum at Desterro (now Florianópolis), Santa Catarina Island. Various conflicts—particularly with the Jesuits—led to the termination of his employment in 1867, and he returned to Blumenau, where he worked as a civil servant for the provincial government until 1876. Müller was then appointed traveling naturalist for the National Museum in Río de Janeiro, a post which he lost (including the pension) in 1891 when he refused to move to Río de Janeiro. His last years in Blumenau were marred by a variety of misfortunes—imprisonment and trial by rebels, and the death of both his

wife and his daughter—although he resumed his work before his death.

Müller's scientific contributions ranged from anatomical work on Coelenterata, Annelida, and especially Crustacea to entomology, emphasizing mimicry, and to botany, particularly in his later years. After moving to Desterro, he began to study the marine invertebrates of the Brazilian coastal waters. Darwin's Origin of Species (1859) led Müller to test those evolutionary ideas by applying them to the Crustacea. He traced the genealogies of various groups, hoping to uncover affinities and the origins of fundamental (primitive) forms. While Darwin offered general propositions, Müller provided a specific test case in the development of the Crustacea. His verdict was rendered in favor of Darwin's views: "In one thing, I hope, I have succeeded,—in convincing unprejudiced readers, that Darwin's theory furnishes the key of intelligibility for the developmental history of the Crustacea" and "many other facts [are] inexplicable without it" (Für Darwin, 1869 translation, p. 141). Publication of such enthusiastic, sympathetic views led to a lengthy correspondence with Darwin, who provided the financial backing for the English translation of Für Darwin in 1869, frequently sent Müller's letters to journals for publication, and quoted him extensively in his own work.

During the 1870's and 1880's Müller published many articles on entomology, the most famous of which discussed mimetic phenomena. In 1862 the English naturalist Henry Walter Bates had first published his own observations concerning examples of relatively scarce, palatable, and defenseless species of insects (primarily) which closely resembled other species which were plentiful and relatively unpalatable or were protected in some other manner. He thought such situations arose through the process of evolution by means of natural selection; that is, those mimics which most closely resembled the protected species would be rejected by predators and therefore survive, but those which varied greatly in appearance from the protected species would be eliminated in the struggle for existence. Bates, however, did not explain why two or more distasteful but unrelated species resembled one another.

In a series of articles beginning in 1878, Müller explained that predators must learn through warning characteristics which species are palatable, and that in this process some of the prey population must be sacrificed. If there are two or more similar, unpalatable species, then predators will be educated faster by the warning characteristics, the similar species will be better protected, fewer deaths will result, and the losses will be absorbed by a larger group. These views were quickly adopted and expanded by other evolutionists, including A. R. Wallace and E. B. Poulton, and form an important part of contemporary literature in evolutionary biology.

Müller's botanical work dealt mainly with the fertilization of plants, with discussions of hybridization and sterility, including self-sterility. Darwin cited this work frequently in his book *The Effects of Cross and Self Fertilisation in the Vegetable Kingdom* (1876).

Altogether, Müller published almost 250 articles in which he demonstrated extraordinary powers of observation, while his book *Für Darwin* and his articles on mimicry reflect his considerable ability to formulate perceptive conclusions. In general, however, he was content to allow others to build upon his smaller, albeit valuable, contributions.

BIBLIOGRAPHY

I. ORIGINAL WORKS. All of Müller's works were conveniently collected by his nephew, Dr. Alfred Möller, *Fritz Müller. Werke, Briefe und Leben*, 3 vols. in 4 plus atlas (Jena, 1915–1921). His works are in vol. I (in two pts., plus an atlas of plates [1915]). *Für Darwin* (Leipzig, 1864) was trans. into English as *Facts and Arguments for Darwin* (London, 1869; repr., 1968) and into French. The rich and extensive correspondence, including letters to Charles Darwin and many German biologists, is in vol. II (1921); and his biography is in vol. III (1920), with a valuable map of his excursions. MS letters and additions to *Für Darwin* are in the Darwin Papers, University Library, Cambridge.

Important early articles on mimicry are "Ueber die Vortheile der Mimicry bei Schmetterlingen," in *Zoologischer Anzeiger*, **1** (1878), 54–55; a note on a remarkable case of mimicry of *Eueides pavana* with *Acraea thalia* referred to in *Proceedings of the Entomological Society of London* (1879), ii; and particularly "Ituna and Thyridia; a Remarkable Case of Mimicry in Butterflies," *ibid.*, pp. xx–xxviii, discussion pp. xxviii–xxix—the article first appeared in *Kosmos*, **5** (1879), 100–108. The latter two articles were trans. by R. Meldola. English trans. of some other entomological articles appear in George B. Longstaff, *Butterfly-Hunting in Many Lands. Notes of a Field Naturalist. To Which Are Added Translations of Papers by Fritz Müller on the Scentorgans of Butterflies and Moths: With a Note by E. B. Poulton, D.Sc., F.R.S.* (London–Bombay–Calcutta, 1912). Numerous letters exchanged by Darwin and Müller appear in both Francis Darwin, ed., *The Life and Letters of Charles Darwin*, 3 vols. (London, 1887); and Francis Darwin and A. C. Seward, eds., *More Letters of Charles Darwin*, 2 vols. (New York, 1903).

II. SECONDARY LITERATURE. The best biography of Müller is Alfred Möller's *Leben* (vol. III of the *Works*). He also lists some obituaries on p. 163, two of which are F. Ludwig, "Ueber das Leben und die botanische Thätigkeit Dr. Fritz Müller's," in *Botanisches Centralblatt*, **71** (1897), 291–302, 347–363, 401–408, plus 4 plates, (100

articles are listed on pp. 404–408); and W. F. H. B. [Walter F. H. Blandford], "Fritz Müller," in *Nature*, **56** (1897), 546–548. Blandford's observations on mimicry are quite interesting, as are those of Roland Trimen, "President's Address. Mimicry in Insects," in *Proceedings of the Entomological Society of London* (1897), lxxiv–xcvii. Also on mimicry, see Mary Alice Evans, "Mimicry and the Darwinian Heritage," in *Journal of the History of Ideas*, **26** (1965), 211–220. For additional references on mimicry, see H. Lewis McKinney, "Henry Walter Bates," *Dictionary of Scientific Biography*, I, 504. For Müller's work on botany, see the article by F. Ludwig cited above.

H. LEWIS MCKINNEY

MÜLLER, GEORG ELIAS (*b.* Grimma, Germany, 20 July 1850; *d.* Göttingen, Germany, 23 December 1934), *psychology.*

Müller was the son of Oberpfarrer Müller and Rosalie Zehme. At the *Fürstenschule* in Grimma, where his father was a professor of religion, Müller became intellectually awakened by Goethe's *Faust* and by romantic poetry, an enthusiasm from which he was rescued by studying Lessing. He briefly attended the Gymnasium at Leipzig, and on leaving there he determined to accept in philosophy only what could be proved by strict logic, a resolve from which he never wavered.

He spent the next two years, successively, at the universities of Leipzig and Berlin. During this time he was much concerned with whether science or history should be the propaedeutic to philosophy. During a year in the Franco-Prussian War, he decided in favor of science. Müller then returned to Leipzig but went on to Göttingen to study psychology and philosophy under Lotze. Lotze's influence is shown in Müller's 1873 doctoral dissertation, *Zur Theorie der sinnlichen Aufmerksamkeit*, a nonexperimental but exhaustive study of sensory attention which was soon cited extensively.

While at Leipzig, Müller had heard Fechner lecture, and he continued a somewhat belligerent scientific correspondence with him from Rötha, where he had a job as a tutor. This correspondence resulted in his *Grundlegung der Psychophysik*, which Müller presented as his *Habilitationsschrift* at Göttingen. He became *Dozent* there in 1876. The work was published in 1878, and its meticulous discussion of Weber's law and many innovations in psychophysical method became the chief reason for Fechner's own *Revision der Hauptpunkte der Psychophysik* (1882).

Müller remained at Göttingen as *Dozent* for four years, then spent a year as professor of philosophy at Czernowitz. He succeeded Lotze at Göttingen in 1881.

Remaining at Göttingen for the rest of his life, he became an institution, much like Wundt at Leipzig. His laboratory vied with Wundt's as the best in Germany for psychological research. Müller was methodological, austere, and had a mania for impartiality. His work was characterized by a fierce insistence on order, so much so that he refused to partake in seminars, regarding them as too improvised to be of value.

Müller's work can be classified as being in three areas: psychophysics, learning, and vision.

Psychophysics. Beyond the work already mentioned, Müller's contributions in psychophysics comprised articles on method and the muscle basis of weight judgments. He and L. J. Martin published jointly in 1899 *Zur Analyse der Unterschiedsempfindlichkeit*, which, after Fechner's *Elemente der Psychophysik*, is the classical study of the psychophysics of lifted weights, the most thoroughly investigated psychophysical function. In 1903 there appeared the definitive handbook on psychophysics, the *Gesichtspunkte und Tatsachen der psychophysischen Methodik*. This book did not present anything very new, but it was a thorough summing-up of the entire field and what, in Müller's view, psychophysics had accomplished up to that time.

Learning. In 1885 Ebbinghaus published his classic work on the learning and memory of nonsense syllables. In 1887 Müller made the problem his own. Where Ebbinghaus was original, Müller was thorough. He carefully extended Ebbinghaus' findings, and he and Schumann invented the memory drum for more accurate presentations; most interestingly, they recorded introspections while the learning was going on. This innovation contradicted the feeling one gets from Ebbinghaus that learning is a mechanical and automatic process occurring through mere contiguity. During learning, subjects are active, not passive, using groupings and rhythms, finding meanings even in nonsense materials, and, in general, consciously organizing material. And the preparatory set or *Anlage* of the subject is a determining factor in memory.

These emphases are entirely absent from Ebbinghaus' work and anticipated those of the Würzburg laboratory under Külpe, once Müller's student. Another student at this time was Adolph Jost, whose work with Müller led to Jost's law—when two associations are of equal strength, a repetition is more strengthening to that which occurred first. This work led to the theory of the advantage of distributed practice; and with another student, Alfons Pilzecker, Müller published a joint monograph in 1900 showing the significance of reaction times as indicators of the strength of associations.

Müller summarized his work in learning in the encyclopedic, three-volume *Zur Analyse der Gedächtnistätigkeit und des Vorstellungsverlaufes* (1911–1917).

Vision. Müller's first work dealing with vision presented the hypothesis that cortical gray is the zero point from which all color sensations diverge. This work was an attempt to solve the paradox of color mixture inherent in Hering's theory of three reversible photochemical substances which in equilibrium should, but do not, result in visual silence. After occasional publications in this area over the years, Müller published his lengthy *Über die Farbenempfindungen: Psychophysische Untersuchungen* in 1930, reviewing and evaluating the entire field.

From 1907 to 1918, David Katz worked with Müller, and he published his important work in surface and volumic colors, a landmark in experimental phenomenology, during this time. Edgar Rubin, working in Müller's laboratory, printed his own phenomenological analysis of visual perceptions into figure, ground, and contour, instead of into the more conventional sensory ultimates.

Müller's position at the beginnings of phenomenology and Gestalt psychology was extremely important, if complex. One of his last works was his 1923 *Komplextheorie und Gestalttheorie*, a work on methodology in perception that criticized the more strident claims to newness on the part of Gestalt psychology.

Much more than Wundt, Müller's approach and work set the ideal pattern for experimental psychology. It was Müller who established the precedent that psychology had to be separated from philosophy if it was to become a rigorous science. Titchener, although Wundt's student, always turned to Müller for criticism and guidance. Among German psychologists of the period, Müller is usually ranked second to Wundt partly because of the large numbers of American students whom Wundt managed to attract, partly because of Müller's austerity and occasional absentminded ungraciousness to visitors, and partly because Müller, unlike Wundt, never wrote popular or systematic books. But at the present day Wundt's influence is difficult to find because it is so diffuse; whereas the emphases, problems, and particularly the tough-minded experimentalism represented by Müller are at the heart of contemporary experimental psychology.

BIBLIOGRAPHY

I. ORIGINAL WORKS. Müller's major works are *Zur Theorie der sinnlichen Aufmerksamkeit* (Leipzig, 1873); *Zur Grundlegung der Psychophysik* (Berlin, 1878); "Ueber die psychologischen Grundlagen für die Vergleichung der gehobenen Gewichte," in *Pflüger's Archiv für die gesamte Physiologie des Menschen und der Tiere*, **47**, 37–112, written with F. Schumann; "Theorie der Muskelcontraction," in *Nachtrichten von der Gesellschaft der Wissenschaften zu Göttingen* (1889); "Experimentelle Beiträge zu Untersuchungen des Gedächtnisses," in *Zeitschrift für Psychologie und Physiologie der Sinnesorgane*, **6** (1893), 81–190, 257–339, written with F. Schumann; with L. J. Martin, *Zur Analyse der Unterschiedsempfindlichkeit* (Leipzig, 1899); with A. Pilzecker, *Experimentelle Beiträge zur Lehre vom Gedächtnis* (Leipzig, 1900); *Zur Analyse der Gedächtnistätigkeit und des Vorstellungsverlaufes* (Leipzig, 1911–1917), also published in *Zeitschrift für Psychologie*, vols. 5, 8, 9; *Komplextheorie und Gestalttheorie: ein Beitrag zur Wahrnehmungspsychologie* (Göttingen, 1923); and *Über die Farbenempfindungen: psychophysische Untersuchungen* (Göttingen, 1930).

II. SECONDARY LITERATURE. The only biographical source for Müller's early life is two letters from him to E. G. Boring, which are now in the Boring Papers of the Harvard archives. These letters are excerpted in Boring's obituary of Müller, in *American Journal of Psychology*, **47** (1935), 344–348; see also E. G. Boring, *A History of Experimental Psychology* (New York, 1929), 361–373, which contains a more complete bibliog.; for his personality see the obituary by his student D. Katz, in *Psychological Bulletin*, **32** (1935), 377–380; and for a description of the Göttingen Laboratory in 1892, see O. Krohn, in *American Journal of Psychology*, **5** (1893), 282–284.

E. B. Titchener discusses Müller's work throughout his own publications, but see particularly his *Lectures on the Elementary Psychology of Feeling and Attention* (New York, 1908), esp. 188–206, 356–359; *Experimental Psychology*, II (New York, 1905), 2, esp. 300–313; and for Müller on introspection, see "Prolegomena to a Study of Introspection," in *American Journal of Psychology*, **23** (1912), 490–494.

See also O. Klemm, *A History of Psychology* (New York, (1914), esp. 257–262, 296; H. Münsterberg, *Professor G. E. Müller's "Berichtigung"* (Boston, 1893); and reviews of Müller's books by: J. A. Bergstrom, in *American Journal of Psychology*, **6** (1894), 301–303; F. Angell, *ibid.* **11** (1899), 266–271; J. W. Baird, in *Psychological Bulletin*, **13** (1916), 373–375; and K. Koffka, *ibid.* **19** (1922), 572–576.

W. Köhler's reply to Müller's 1923 criticism of Gestalt psychology can be found in *Psychologische Forschung*, **6** (1925), 358–416; and Müller's rejoinder, in *Zeitschrift für Psychologie*, **99** (1926), 1–15.

JULIAN JAYNES

MÜLLER, GUSTAV (*b.* Schweidnitz, Germany [now Świdnica, Poland], 7 May 1851; *d.* Potsdam, Germany, 7 July 1925), *astronomy, astrophysics.*

Müller's father, a merchant, died when Gustav was only six years old. Müller was educated at a private school and then at the Gymnasium of his native city. After passing the final secondary school examination in 1870, he began the study of mathematics and natural science at Leipzig. From 1872 he continued his studies in Berlin, where the lectures of Wilhelm Foerster induced him to give up his original plans of becoming a teacher and to dedicate himself to astronomy. His other professors included Helmholtz, Weierstrass, and Ernst Kummer. Even before completing his studies Müller took part in the calculations made for the Berlin *Astronomisches Jahrbuch* and in Auwers' new reduction of Bradley's observations. He also assisted Hermann Vogel in his spectroscopic work and in 1877 followed him to the newly created astrophysical observatory at Potsdam. The work done there in spectrophotometry provided the decisive impetus for Müller's enduring interest in photometry. In 1877 he earned his doctorate with *Untersuchungen über Mikrometerschrauben*. He became an observer in 1882, chief observer in 1888, and professor in 1891.

Müller's contributions to the development of astrophysics, especially to the gathering of primary data, were distinguished less by bold innovations than by a clear grasp of the needs of an organically growing science and by the persevering and precise execution of the vast programs of research required by such growth. His photometric studies began in 1877 with investigations of the luminosities of the planets and of the absorption of starlight in the earth's atmosphere. He published extensive results in 1883 and 1893. His absorption tables for Potsdam were used for decades.

Müller's most important photometric project was the *Photometrische Durchmusterung des nördlichen Himmels*—the *Potsdamer Durchmusterung*—which he planned and, for the most part, carried out himself. Observations were begun in 1886, in collaboration with Paul Kempf. Utilizing an astrometer that he had constructed in accordance with the principle described in 1861 by Zöllner, he ascertained the luminosities of more than 14,000 stars in the Northern sky listed in the *Bonner Durchmusterung* (*BD*) to a magnitude of 7.5. The work devoted to this undertaking lasted for several decades. Partial results appeared in 1894, 1899, 1903, and 1906; the general catalog appeared in 1907. The *Potsdamer Durchmusterung* furnished, with the *Harvard Photometry* of Pickering and his coworkers, the most exact photometric information on stars then available; and it is still an indispensable standard work. Moreover, through its consistent use of Pogson's scale it played a decisive role in the general adoption of this scale.

In 1909 Müller began with E. Kron a further series of zonal observations of the luminosities and colors of the *BD* stars from magnitude 7.6 to 9.5. However,

World War I hindered the progress of this undertaking, and Müller was unable to publish a compendium of the results.

Müller's proposal at the 1900 meeting of the Astronomische Gesellschaft that a complete catalog of the variable stars be produced led to the *Geschichte und Literatur des Lichtwechsels der bis Ende 1915 als sicher veränderlich anerkannten Sterne (GuL)*. This three-volume work (1918–1922), which exercised an extremely positive influence on variable-star research, was continued by R. Prager, who published two volumes of a new edition in 1934 and 1936; the third volume, prepared by H. Schneller, appeared in 1952.

Müller's work in the field of spectroscopy includes his contribution to Vogel's *Spektroskopische Beobachtungen der Sterne* (1883) and his determination with Kempf (1886) of the absolute wavelengths of 300 lines of the solar spectrum.

Müller also produced a series of works that contributed to increasing the precision of observations and to improving reduction elements. This series included an investigation of the influence of temperature on the refraction of light in various types of glass (1885).

Müller participated in many of the great scientific expeditions sponsored by the Potsdam observatory. He led the 1882 expedition to the United States to observe the transit of Venus and participated in the expeditions to Russia to observe the total solar eclipses of 1887 and 1900. He also assisted in absorption studies conducted in Tenerife.

Müller exercised important functions in the organization of scientific research; from 1896 to 1924 he was secretary of the Astronomische Gesellschaft. Following the death of the second director of the Potsdam observatory, Karl Schwarzschild, he directed the institution from 1917 to 1921. During this time the Einstein Foundation was created and the Einstein Tower for solar physics was constructed. Admitted to the Prussian Academy of Sciences in 1918, Müller became chairman of the commission on the *Geschichte des Fixsternhimmels* ("history of the fixed stars"). Although not active in popularizing astronomy, he wrote the well-known monograph *Die Photometrie der Gestirne* (1897).

BIBLIOGRAPHY

A complete bibliography of Müller's 107 published works, compiled by his son Rolf, is in *Vierteljahrsschrift der Astronomischen Gesellschaft*, **60** (1925), 174–177. See also H. Ludendorff's obituary, *ibid.*, 158–174; and his notice on Müller, in *Astronomische Nachrichten*, **225** (1925), cols. 199–200.

DIETER B. HERRMANN

MULLER, HERMANN JOSEPH (*b.* New York, N.Y., 21 December 1890; *d.* Indianapolis, Indiana, 5 April 1967), *genetics, evolution, eugenics.*

Muller's grandfather came to the United States from Germany following the revolution of 1848. His father, for whom he was named, was to train in the law, but instead had to take over the family business of manufacturing bronze artworks. He died when Muller was nine years old, leaving his widow, Frances Lyons, a modest income. Even as a child, Muller was interested in evolution and the sciences; as a student at Morris High School, he founded a science club. Upon graduation, Muller entered Columbia College, where in his sophomore year he decided to make genetics his major study, after reading R. H. Lock's *Heredity, Variation, and Evolution.*

At Columbia, Muller attended Edmund B. Wilson's course, which, through its emphasis on the chromosome theory of heredity, shaped his genetic view of biological problems. He received the B.A. in 1910, then enrolled in Cornell Medical School and the Columbia University department of physiology. His master's thesis (1912) concerned the transmission of nerve impulses. His interest in genetics was unabated, however, and he remained in daily contact with two of his classmates, Alfred H. Sturtevant and Calvin B. Bridges, who were working at Columbia with Thomas Hunt Morgan. In 1912 Muller himself was accepted by Morgan as a graduate student; he rapidly established a reputation for imaginative theorizing and ingenious experimental design. His dissertation, on crossing-over, contributed the new concepts of coincidence and interference in the resolution of genetic maps and established the law of linear linkage. After taking the Ph.D. in 1916, Muller accepted an invitation from Julian Huxley to teach at Rice Institute. His own research at this time comprised studies of the complex relationship of gene and character in which he isolated and mapped the modifier genes that control the quantitative expression of inherited characteristics. From these investigations Muller was led to recognize the significance of the individual gene.

Muller analyzed mutations to conclude that the concept should be confined to variations arising in the individual gene. Upon his return to Columbia (1918–1920), he produced his most important theoretical work. Since genes, unlike all other cellular components, can reproduce the alterations arising in them (indeed, this property of self-replication is their unique feature), Muller argued that all other cellular components must be ultimately produced by genes; he theorized that life must have begun with the appearance of self-replicating molecules, or "naked genes," which he thought similar to viruses.

From 1921 until 1932 Muller worked at the University of Texas, where he became full professor. During this period he studied mutation frequency and designed complex genetic stocks to detect the most commonly occurring lethal mutations (which kill unless protected by a normal allele). In 1926 Muller induced mutations by exposing *Drosophila* to X rays. He reported his findings in an article entitled "Artificial Transmutation of the Gene," which was published in *Science* in 1927. This work won Muller an international reputation, stimulated a number of other workers to take up the subject, and became the basis for the study of radiation genetics.

In 1932 Muller went to Berlin, where he spent a year as a Guggenheim fellow working in Oskar Vogt's Brain Research Institute. He did research with N. W. Timofeev-Ressovsky on mutation, evaluating and criticizing physical models (among them the "target theory"), and exploring the structure of the gene. As Hitler achieved increasing power, Muller, a staunch supporter of socialist causes, decided to leave Germany. He accepted an invitation from N. I. Vavilov to do research in the Soviet Union, which he regarded as an experimental society that would support genetics and eugenics.

Muller worked in Leningrad and Moscow at the Academy of Sciences from 1933 until 1937. He was chiefly concerned with radiation genetics, cytogenetics, and gene structure. By 1935 he was embroiled in the growing controversy about the work of Lysenko, which he could not support. Muller himself hoped to win Soviet sponsorship for basic genetics and for the program of positive eugenics that he presented in his book *Out of the Night* (New York, 1935). Lysenko won Stalin's backing, and Muller left the Soviet Union, after volunteering to serve in the Spanish Civil War.

In 1938 Muller received an appointment to the University of Edinburgh, where he analyzed the chromosomal basis of embryonic death from radiation damage. With the outbreak of World War II, he returned to the United States. He thought that it would be difficult to continue scientific research in Great Britain and since he and his second wife, Dorothea Kantorowicz, were part Jewish, he was also concerned with their own safety. He first went to Amherst College, where he continued his genetic studies, and then, in 1945, he secured a permanent post at Indiana University, where he remained until his death.

In 1946 Muller was awarded the Nobel Prize in physiology or medicine. He took advantage of the concomitant fame to publicize his campaign against the medical, industrial, and military abuse of radiation.

He also publicly criticized the doctrines of Lysenko and resigned from the Soviet Academy of Sciences in 1947. In his later years Muller also worked for the reform of the teaching of biology in secondary schools (he advocated a strong genetic and evolutionary viewpoint) and set out a positive eugenic program, based on what he called "germinal choice," whereby the semen of unusually healthy and gifted men would be frozen for use by later generations. Although his social views were the subject of considerable public controversy, they were prompted by his genuine scientific concern about the accumulating load of human spontaneous mutations produced by the relaxation of natural selection through modern culture and technology.

Muller was a member of a number of scientific societies, including the National Academy of Sciences. He was a fellow of the Royal Society, and served as president of several genetic societies and congresses.

BIBLIOGRAPHY

I. ORIGINAL WORKS. Muller published 372 works, of which a complete bibliography is given by Pontecorvo (below). His published and manuscript articles, correspondence, notebooks, and other scholarly documents are in the Lilly Library of Indiana University in Bloomington. His most famous publication is "Artificial Transmutation of the Gene," in *Science*, **66** (1927), 84–87.

II. SECONDARY LITERATURE. On Muller and his work see E. A. Carlson, "The Legacy of Hermann Joseph Muller: 1890–1967," in *Canadian Journal of Genetics and Cytology*, **9**, no. 3 (1967), 437–448; "H. J. Muller," in *Genetics*, **70** (1972), 1–30; G. Pontecorvo, "Hermann Joseph Muller 1890–1967," in *Biographical Memoirs of Fellows of the Royal Society*, **14** (1968), 349–389, with complete bibliography; and T. M. Sonneborn, "H. J. Muller, Crusader for Human Betterment," in *Science*, **162** (1968), 772–776.

ELOF AXEL CARLSON

MÜLLER, JOHANN. See **Regiomontanus**.

MÜLLER, JOHANN HEINRICH JACOB (*b.* Kassel, Germany, 30 April 1809; *d.* Freiburg im Breisgau, Germany, 3 October 1875), *physics*.

Müller's father originally studied law, but gave it up to become, in 1807, a painter to the court of the prince of Waldeck. Johann Müller—as he unfortunately called himself in publications, thus creating confusion in bibliographies—inherited his father's talent and excelled in illustrating his books. He spent his early years in Frankfurt am Main and Darmstadt, then, in 1829, enrolled in the University of Bonn to study mathematics and physics. His teachers included Karl von Münchow and Heinrich Plücker. In 1832 he entered Giessen University, where he attended lectures on chemistry, physics, and mathematics given by Heinrich Buff, Liebig, and Hermann Umpfenbach. He received the Ph.D. in 1833 with a thesis on the optics of crystals. In 1837 he became a teacher at the Giessen Realschule and was eventually, in 1844, appointed professor of physics and technology at the University of Freiburg.

Early in his career Müller developed a systematic concept of physics which was partially determined by his didactic talent. He wrote a number of synopses (see Bibliography) before his appointment at Freiburg and from 1842 he edited his work *Lehrbuch der Physik und Meteorologie*. The subsequent enlargements of this work, which remained well-known until the 1930's, constituted Müller's principal activity for the rest of his life.

When the University of Freiburg ended the mandatory study of physics in 1836 Müller attempted to attract students by improving the instruction. He purchased and built many improved instruments for the laboratory and asked Lerch to draw large-scale illustrations for his lectures. During the university's summer term Müller lectured on statics of solids, fluids, and aeriform bodies; acoustics; heat; electricity; and magnetism. His winter lectures comprised wave mechanics and optics, his preferred subjects. He also introduced experimental practice in physics and in 1850 the first doctorate was awarded.

Müller conducted research into optics, magnetism, and light and heat radiation. Applying George Airy's theory to crystal optics, Müller calculated the isochromatic curves of plates of crystals with one parallel optical axis; he also calculated the black hyperbolic beams in the system of lemniscates of crystals with two axes. In 1849 he experimentally found, independently of Joule, the limits of intensity of the magnetism (m) of iron, which according to Siméon Poisson, Heinrich Lenz, and Carl Jacobi should have been proportional to the magnetizing force (p). Müller's findings were more precise than Joule's results, and he calculated $p \propto$ an m for a constant diameter of the rod, a relation subsequently used with success.

From 1846 Müller studied Fraunhofer lines, an investigation that led him to explore ultraviolet radiation by fluorescence; with the chemist Lambert

Babo, he was able to measure, in 1855, the first Fraunhofer lines beyond the violet end of the spectrum. He then examined the *Thermische Wirkungen des Sonnenspectrums* ("infrared spectrum") by drawing upon the work of Rudolph Franz, who first measured the infrared spectrum quantitatively by heat transmission (1856). This process, known as "diathermancy," plus the analysis of the spectrum with rocksalt and the use of a linear thermopile to determine the spectral energy, permitted Müller to draw a curve of the intensity of radiation by heat effect. This was the first such curve ever to be drawn. Müller thus proved, contrary to Antoine Masson and Jules Jamin, that the maximum of heat energy lies in the dark region. He also found the wavelength of the rays on the extreme end of the spectrum to be 0.0048 mm. Although it was impossible to take a curve in the diffraction of heat because of the energy distribution by diffraction, Müller construed the curve geometrically from the prismatic spectrum and concluded that the heat spectrum is three times as extensive as the visible one.

Müller's most significant textbook, the *Lehrbuch*, first appeared as *Pouillet's Lehrbuch der Physik und Meteorologie*, a "free adaptation" of the 1837 edition of C. S. Pouillet's *Éléments de physique expérimentale et de météorologie*. Müller's innovations included numerous woodcuts inserted directly into the text, whereas Pouillet had inserted copper-plate engravings after the text. The illustrations of the apparatus were particularly useful for the mechanician. The book was initially styled for the nonphysics major. He supplied the derivations of mathematical formulas and stressed mechanical theorems. Müller incorporated Gauss's works on magnetism for the first time and recast the chapters on galvanism, light, and meteorology. Each of the seven editions that were published during his lifetime underwent considerable emendation. A third volume, *Lehrbuch der Kosmischen Physik*, based upon Müller's own observations was added in 1856. A supplement, *Die medizinische Physik*, edited by A. Fick, also appeared in the same year. The rapid evolution in physics was characteristically reflected by the "Reports on the Most Recent Developments in Physics," edited by Müller in 1849.

Liebig's letters of 1844 induced Müller to edit *Physikalische Briefe für Gebildete aller Stände*, a new edition of Euler's *Letters to a German Princess*. Müller subsequently added a third and fourth part; there, in his own letters on physics, he was emphatic that natural sciences taught objective truth, the limits of man's intellectual power, and tolerance. Müller encouraged the criticism of traditional preoccupations. He read many papers before the Naturforschende

Gesellschaft zu Freiburg im Breisgau and helped to extend the society's activity into physics.

BIBLIOGRAPHY

I. ORIGINAL WORKS. MS documents on Müller's employment at Freiburg are in the university archive. A letter to an unknown person, 3 April 1843, is in the Germanisches Nationalmuseum, Nuremberg, Germany; 6 letters to Karl Mohr, 30 December 1838, 1 January 1848, 30 April 1848, 4 August 1862, 1 April 1868, and 17 April 1868, are at the University of Bonn. The Staatsbibliothek Preussischer Kulturbesitz, Berlin, contains one letter to an unknown person, 15 October 1843, one letter to Peter Riess, 30 September 1856, and one letter to an unknown person (perhaps Steeg), 9 September 1873.

Müller's dissertation was *Erklärung der isochromatischen Curven, welche einaxige parallel mit der Axe geschnittene Krystalle im homogenen polarisirten Lichte zeigen* (Darmstadt, 1833); his main synopses are *Kurze Darstellung des Galvanismus* (Darmstadt, 1836); *Elemente der ebenen Geometrie* (Darmstadt, 1838); *Elemente der ebenen Trigonometrie* (Darmstadt, 1838); *Elemente der sphärischen Trigonometrie* (Darmstadt, 1840); *Pouillet's Lehrbuch der Physik und Meteorologie, für deutsche Verhältnisse frei bearbeitet*, 2 vols. (Brunswick, 1842–1844); a second ed. (Brunswick, 1844–1845), with subtitle *Lehrbuch der Physik und Meteorologie*, includes about 1,000 woodcuts; the eleventh and final ed., 13 pts. in 5 vols., was published in Brunswick in 1926–1935; extended by the third volume, *Lehrbuch der Kosmischen Physik* (Brunswick, 1856), and by a supplement edited by A. Fick, *Die medizinische Physik* (Brunswick, 1856).

Subsequent writings are *Grundzüge der Krystallographie* (Brunswick, 1845); *Grundriss der Physik und Meteorologie. Für Lyceen, Gymnasien, Gewerbe- und Realschulen, sowie zum Selbstunterrichte* (Brunswick, 1846); *Mathematischer Supplementband zum Grundriss der Physik und Meteorologie* (Brunswick, 1860); *Physikalische Briefe für Gebildete aller Stände von Leonhard Euler und Dr. Johann Müller*, edited by Müller, contains a third part, *Die neuesten Ergebnisse und Bereicherungen der Physik in Briefform behandelnd* (Stuttgart, 1847–1848), and a fourth part (Stuttgart, 1854) edited by Müller; *Bericht über die neuesten Fortschritte der Physik, in ihrem Zusammenhange dargestellt*, 2 vols. (Brunswick, 1849–1851), with an English trans. in *Report of the Board of Regents of the Smithsonian Institution*, (1856), 311–423; (1857), 357–456; (1858), 333–431; (1859), 372–415; *Die constructive Zeichnungslehre, oder die Lehre vom Grund- und Aufriss*, 2 parts (Brunswick, 1865); *Die Schule der Physik. Eine Anleitung zum ersten Unterricht in der Naturlehre* (Brunswick, 1874); Müller was an editor of *Berichte über die Verhandlungen der Gesellschaft für Beförderung der Naturwissenschaften zu Freiburg im Breisgau* (from vol. 2 on entitled *Berichte über die Verhandlungen der naturforschenden Gesellschaft . . .*, ed. by Müller et al.), of which vol. 1 (1855) contains a number of his papers.

Papers cited in the article are "Berechnung der hyperbolischen dunkeln Büschel, welche die farbigen Ringe zweiaxiger Krystalle durchschneiden," in *Annalen der Physik* **120** (1838), 273–291; "Fraunhofer'sche Linien auf einem Papierschirm," *ibid.*, **145** (1846), 93–115; "Anwendung der stroboskopischen Scheibe zur Versinnlichung der Grundgesetze der Wellenlehre," *ibid.*, **143** (1846), 271–272; "Entwickelung der Gesetze des Elektromagnetismus," repr. from *Bericht über die neuesten Fortschritte*, **1**, 494–538, with a defense of his statement on saturation of magnetism (Brunswick, 1850); "Photographirte Spectren," in *Annalen der Physik* **173** (1856), 135–138; "Die Photographie des Spectrums," *ibid.*, **185** (1860), 151–157; *Programm, wodurch zur Feier des Geburtsfestes Seiner Königlichen Hoheit . . . Grossherzogs Friedrich . . . einladet der gegenwärtige Prorector Dr. J. Müller* (Freiburg im Breisgau, 1858), which contains a sketch of the *Geschichte . . . des physikalischen Kabinets* of Freiburg University; "Untersuchungen über die thermischen Wirkungen des Sonnenspectrums," repr. in *Annalen der Physik* **181** (1858), 337–359, 543–547; and "Rutherfurd's Photographie des Spectrums," *ibid.*, **202** (1865), 435–440. For a bibliography of Müller's papers see *Annalen der Physik, Namenregister und Sachregister 1875*; and Poggendorff (not always exact), II, 228–229; III, 944; VI, 1799. A bibliography of his books is given in W. Heinsius, **10** (1849), III, 124; British Museum, *Catalogue of Printed Books*; *Catalogue Général de la Bibliothèque Nationale, Paris*.

II. SECONDARY LITERATURE. The only biographical sketch is Emil Warburg, *Gedächtnisrede auf Johann Heinrich Jacob Müller bei dessen academischer Todtenfeier am 16. Juli 1877* (Freiburg im Breisgau, 1877), repr. in large part in Friedrich von Weech, ed., *Badische Biographien*, III (Karlsruhe, 1881), 114–121; on Müller's activities at Freiburg see Hans Kangro, "Die Geschichte der Physik an der Universität Freiburg," MS copy (1954) deposited at Freiburg University, pp. 77–89.

HANS KANGRO

MÜLLER, JOHANNES PETER (*b.* Coblenz, Germany, 14 July 1801; *d.* Berlin, Germany, 28 April 1858), *physiology, anatomy, zoology.*

Müller introduced a new era of biological research in Germany and pioneered the use of experimental methods in medicine. He overcame the inclination to natural-philosophical speculation widespread in German universities during his youth, and inculcated respect for careful observation and physiological experimentation. He required of empirical research that it be carried out "with seriousness of purpose and thoughtfulness, with incorruptible love of truth and perseverance." Anatomy and physiology, pathological anatomy and histology, embryology and zoology—in all these fields he made numerous fundamental discoveries. Almost all German scientists who achieved fame after the middle of the nineteenth century considered themselves his students or adopted his methods or views. Their remarks reveal his preeminent position in medical and biological research. Helmholtz, one of his most brilliant students, termed Müller a "man of the first rank" and stated that his acquaintance with him had "definitively altered his intellectual standards."

Life. Müller came from a family of winegrowers in the Moselle Valley. His father learned shoemaking and moved to Coblenz, where he became fairly well-to-do. Müller distinguished himself as a student through his unusual gifts, methodical and assiduous work habits, and craving for knowledge. From the works of Aristotle to Goethe's scientific writings, he devoured all the books he could obtain. His most striking trait was evident from childhood: a powerful ambition that drove him to be first, on the playing field as in the classroom. In the winter semester of 1819–1820 he entered the University of Bonn, which, founded in 1818, prided itself on being open to the latest intellectual currents. The Ministry of Education in Berlin had selected the professors chiefly according to their opinions of Schelling's *Naturphilosophie*. Almost all the members of the Faculty of Medicine were adherents of the latter. Some embraced the Romantic belief in supernatural cures; others endorsed Mesmer's animal magnetism.

During his second year at Bonn, Müller's father died; and henceforth he had to appeal to his family, friends, native city, and the state for support. He then attracted the attention of Philipp Jakob Rehfues, curator of the University of Bonn, who assisted his academic career. Rehfues applied, on Müller's behalf, to the authorities in Berlin—he could only give the grounds for such requests, not grant them himself—for stipends, travel allowances, and printing subsidies; later, money for vacations, remission of a loan, and a new microscope; and, finally, an increase in salary. Nevertheless Müller had financial problems even after he had become famous, since he unhesitatingly spent money for scientific purposes, for printing, and for books and instruments.

Müller received his medical degree in December 1822 and went to Berlin to continue his studies for another year and a half. In Berlin he came under the influence of Carl Rudolphi, Germany's most distinguished anatomist. Rudolphi sought to lead scientific research out of the "turbid mire of mysticism" and endow it with an exact method. Müller credited Rudolphi with having enabled him to escape the dangers of natural-philosophical speculation and to cease adorning his writings with the fashionable

vocabulary of electrical, magnetic, and chemical polarities, and positive and negative forces. In 1824 Müller passed the state medical examination in Berlin and then returned to Bonn, where in the same year he qualified as lecturer in physiology and comparative anatomy. A year later the Faculty of Medicine assigned him to lecture on general pathology as well. In 1826, not yet twenty-five years old, he became extraordinary professor; and in 1830 he was appointed full professor at an annual salary of 1,000 talers. In April 1827, after a long engagement, Müller married Nanny Zeiller of Coblenz; they had a daughter, Maria, and a son, Max.

The recognition that Müller enjoyed in the scientific world resulted in an offer from the University of Freiburg in 1832. He turned it down, even though it would have considerably improved his financial situation. He knew that Rudolphi was deathly sick and probably assumed that he would succeed him. Rudolphi died at the end of 1832. Since the Berlin Faculty of Medicine first offered the post to the Heidelberg anatomist Friedrich Tiedemann—who, however, did not accept it—Müller decided on a most unusual step for a German professor. In a letter to the Prussian minister of education, he proposed himself for the position and described the tasks that the holder of the Berlin chair of anatomy ought to fulfill. He must survey human, comparative, and pathological anatomy and must have done distinguished work in physiology, the foundation of all medicine. He must be familiar with microscopic observation, with experimental techniques in physiology, and with studying problems from an embryological perspective. Furthermore, he must be able to attract and encourage talented students. All this was necessary if Berlin were to take its rightful place in the international competition for scientific predominance. He convinced the minister of the brilliance of his own attainments, and during the Easter season of 1833 he assumed the Berlin professorship of anatomy and physiology.

At Berlin, Müller lost interest in experimental physiology. The appearance of the last section of his two-volume *Handbuch der Physiologie des Menschen* in 1840 more or less marks this shift. Henceforth he devoted himself almost exclusively to comparative anatomy and zoology, especially to research on marine animals—down to the protozoans. In the last years of his life he also contributed to paleontology through his publications on fossil fish and echinoderms. He gathered the material for these studies on numerous expeditions in the North Sea and in the Mediterranean.

By 1834 Müller had become a member of the Prussian Academy of Sciences. In 1841 and in 1853 he received offers from the University of Munich, both of which he declined. He was elected rector for the years 1838–1839 and 1847–1848. This position burdened him with many difficulties during the Revolution of 1848. As rector he was caught between those students who longed for a new German Reich and those who demanded reforms in the university and in the state. At the same time, he stood between the government and the student body. Considering himself a loyal servant of the state, he did not contemplate a revolutionary change in the form of government and could not grasp the thinking of the students, who were filled with new ideals. Furthermore, he was dominated by the fear that the university, and with it the irreplaceable treasures of his anatomical collection, might go up in flames.

At the end of 1857 Müller complained of insomnia, with which he had been afflicted for years. He is reported to have wandered through backstreets in Berlin, driven by inexplicable anxiety. On the morning of 28 April 1858 his wife found Müller dead in his bed. Since he had forbidden an autopsy, the cause of death remains unknown.

In his lifetime Müller experienced several periods of depression, which, like his periods of intense productivity, are traceable to a manic-depressive condition. The first depression, lasting for about five months, occurred in the summer of 1827. He was unable to work and ceased lecturing. The minister of education, when informed of Müller's condition, granted him a leave of absence and provided him with money for a trip. In 1840 Müller again became depressed, but he did not suffer as much as the previous time. This depression may have been precipitated by his realization that he was no longer the leader in physiological research. He lacked a thorough knowledge of chemistry and physics, which was becoming a necessity in an age that had set out to investigate causal relationships among vital phenomena.

The depression that Müller experienced at the end of his year as rector in 1848 was far more serious. Incapable of working, he obtained an indefinite leave of absence, gave up his residence in Berlin, and fled with his family to Coblenz; but, unable to find peace in his native city, he traveled on to Bonn. In a state of extreme despair, he finally sought refuge in Belgium, at Ostend. He did not lecture during the winter semester of 1848–1849, returning to Berlin only at the end of March 1849. The end of his life was also marked by depression. He was obsessed by the fear that his field of research was exhausted and that his productivity was ended. Many of his contemporaries suspected that his sudden death was a suicide, a hypothesis that accorded with the clinical record of his depression. Ernst Haeckel, his last close student, had no doubt that he had ended his life with an overdose of morphine.

Physiology. Müller's first publication and the doctoral dissertation based on it, *De phoronomia animalium* (1822), dealt with locomotion in animals. The investigation began with the movements of arthropods but continued in a comparative physiological manner, involving other classes of animals. He couched his excellent observations in terms of the doctrines of *Naturphilosophie*, which he had fully assimilated.

In 1820 the Bonn Faculty of Medicine posed its first prize question: Does the fetus breathe in the mother's womb? Müller entered the competition and sought to clarify the problem through experiments on live animals. Experiments on pregnant cats were not successful. He was first able to demonstrate that the fetus breathes in an experiment on a ewe. Observing the umbilical cord, he ascertained that bright red blood flows to the fetus through the umbilical vein and that dark blood flows back to the placenta through the umbilical artery. Fetal respiration is one of the few problems that Müller solved through vivisection on warm-blooded animals. Later he had harsh words for this crude, "knife-happy" type of experimentation.

In 1826 Müller published an extensive work that attracted the attention of the scientific world: *Zur vergleichenden Physiologie des Gesichtssinnes des Menschen und der Tiere nebst einem Versuch über die Bewegungen der Augen und über den menschlichen Blick*. The book, in nine parts, reported on Müller's various studies and interests. It opened with his inaugural lecture, "Von dem Bedürfnis der Physiologie nach einer philosophischen Naturbetrachtung," in which he outlined his views on science at the time of his habilitation. The succeeding sections offered a wealth of new findings on human and animal vision, brilliant investigations into the compound eyes of insects and crabs, and truly perceptive analyses of human sight. Moreover, the book recorded the young physiologist's most important achievement, the discovery that each sensory system responds to various stimuli only in a fixed, characteristic way—or, as Müller stated, with the energy specific to itself: the eye always with a sensation of light, the ear always with a sensation of sound, and so forth. This "law of specific nerve energies" led to the insight that man does not perceive the processes of the external world but only the alterations they produce in his sensory systems: "In intercourse with the external world we continually sense ourselves." This statement had important implications for epistemology.

Later, in the *Handbuch der Physiologie* (4th ed., I, 534), Müller maintained that all stimuli acting on the nerves have the same effect, whether they be mechanical, chemical, thermal, or galvanoelectric; each nerve can react only with its "specific energy." The reaction is determined by the properties of the stimulated organic substance, not by the quality of the stimulus. Müller conducted many experiments on isolated nerve-muscle preparations. Those on frog legs, employing galvanic electricity, were designed to determine the general conditions under which muscle contraction occurs. He utilized both changes in the galvanic stimulus and the effect of closing and opening the electric circuit. These experiments, along with those of Humboldt and Johann Wilhelm Ritter, constituted the first advances in electrophysiology. Matteucci's research in this field led Müller to encourage his student Emil du Bois-Reymond to enter it.

Müller's second book, *Über die phantastischen Gesichtserscheinungen* (1826), is still of interest. In it he showed that the sensory system of the eye not only reacts to external optical stimuli but also can be excited by interior stimuli arising from organic malfunction, lingering mental images, or the play of the imagination. He himself found it easy to make luminous images of people and things appear suddenly, move about, and disappear whenever he closed his eyes and concentrated on his darkened field of vision. With such self-observation and self-experimentation, supplemented with reports of earlier and contemporary authors—including Goethe, who in his scientific research likewise commenced from subjective experience—Müller demonstrated that optical perceptions can arise without an adequate external stimulus. When the stimulus is mistakenly assumed to have originated outside the body, the result—depending on the situation—is the reporting of religious or magical visions, or the seeing of ghosts.

Embryology. In the following years Müller's research made him the most celebrated member of the Bonn Faculty of Medicine. During a period of extraordinary productivity he investigated problems of physiology, embryology, and comparative anatomy and was usually busy with several investigations at once. In 1830, under the title *De glandularum secernentium structura penitiori earumque prima formatione*, he published his studies on the emergence and structure of the glands; in the course of this research he employed anatomical preparations, injections, and especially the microscope. The book considerably fostered the advance of embryology and histology. In it he demonstrated that glands are invaginations of the covering membranes that are closed at one end and that blood vessels do not open into the glandular ducts but lie like capillaries in the walls of these ducts.

Simultaneously, Müller studied the origin of the omentum and its relation to the peritoneal sac (1830) in the human embryo and the embryonic development of the sexual organs in man and other vertebrates. In his *Bildungsgeschichte der Genitalien* he clarified the very complicated relationships between the initial form of the kidneys and their ducts, on the one hand, and the sexual organs, on the other. He discovered that the embryonic duct (described by Heinrich Rathke) now called "Müller's duct" forms the Fallopian tubes, uterus, and vagina: only rudiments of it are found in the male.

Neurophysiology and Neurology. Müller was responsible for a remarkable advance in neurophysiology: confirmation of the Bell-Magendie law by means of a simple experiment performed on the frog. In 1822 Magendie had reported experiments indicating that the anterior roots of the spinal nerves conduct motor impulses outward, while posterior roots transmit sensations from the periphery to the central nervous system. Bell thereupon interpreted, in this sense, experiments that he had published in 1811, claiming priority of discovery. Unfortunately, in remarks made shortly afterward, Magendie partially retracted his findings. Since the research of several others had further complicated the situation, in 1831 Müller took up this important subject. At first he experimented on rabbits, but the work was difficult and yielded ambiguous results. Consequently he continued his investigation on frogs, the use of which in the laboratory had almost entirely ceased. In the frog the spinal cord was far easier to remove, the relationships between the nerve roots were much more apparent, and the results unambiguous and always reproducible. Cutting through the posterior roots leading to a hind leg, he found that the limb became insensible but was not paralyzed. When he cut through the anterior roots, however, he observed that the limb was paralyzed but not rendered insensible. The simplicity, conclusiveness, and memorableness of the experiment—which has been repeated countless times in physiology courses—made a marked impression on Müller's contemporaries. To be sure, Müller, who was driven by ambition throughout his life, did not hesitate to make his experiment widely known. In that very year (1831) he reproduced it in Paris for Cuvier and Humboldt and, in Heidelberg, for Tiedemann. He also had his friend Anders Retzius perform the experiment in Stockholm.

Closely related to the demonstration of the Bell-Magendie law were Müller's efforts to determine the sensory and motor portions of the cranial nerves. He established experimentally that the first and second branches of the trigeminal nerve are sensory and that the third branch contains, in addition to sensory fibers, motor fibers for the jaw muscles. He also asserted, again on the basis of his own research, that the glossopharyngeal and vagus nerves are of the mixed type. In opposition to Magendie, however, Müller held that the hypoglossal nerve is of the motor type. This research led to the first comprehensive scientific conception of the nervous system as a unit. At the same time he postulated motor and sensory fibers for the autonomic nervous system; otherwise, it would be incapable of governing the intestinal functions under its control. Its motor function was demonstrated, he contended, by the fact that when a caustic is lightly applied to the celiac ganglion in the opened abdominal cavity of a rabbit the peristaltic movements of the intestine become far stronger.

In 1833 Müller studied the phenomenon of reflection, by which he meant the involuntary transition—occurring in the spinal cord or brain—of excitation from the centripetally conducting nerves to the centrifugally conducting ones. He took up this subject independently of Marshall Hall, who, shortly before Müller presented his results, had published *On the Reflex Function of the Medulla Oblongata and Medulla Spinalis. . . .* That the stimulation of an afferent or sensory nerve can provoke involuntary movements had already been asserted by Descartes. Müller provided the experimental proof that no communication exists between the afferent and efferent fibers, even though they are in the same nerve. Only the spinal cord or brain, he held, can mediate between the site of stimulation and the effector organ. According to Müller, the sensory organ, which receives the stimulus, can lie in the skin, the mucous membrane, or a muscle. As soon as the stimulus has reached the spinal cord, the impulse goes directly to the appropriate motor nerves—it does not pass up through the entire spinal cord: "The easiest path for the current or vibration of the nervous principle is from the posterior root of a nerve to its anterior root or to the anterior roots of several neighboring nerves." He thought that the simplest type of reflex movement was the quick jerk with which one withdraws an injured limb when the skin has been burned. He also described coughing, sneezing, hiccuping, vomiting, and ejaculation as reflex arcs located along the spinal cord and medulla oblongata, thereby contributing a fundamental new insight into the study of such phenomena.

To elucidate reflex action, physiology no longer had to fall back upon the old concept of "sympathies," as Boerhaave had been constrained to do. Even Procháska, professor of anatomy and physiology at Prague and later at Vienna, who had observed the reflex mechanism in 1784, still spoke of the *consensus nervorum* or the "polar interaction of the organs."

Hall preceded Müller by some months in the publication of his *Reflex Function*, but he diminished the practical value of his observations by assuming the existence of a special "excitomotor" nervous system—leading only to the spinal cord—that supposedly carried stimuli to the central nervous system. With his reflex theory Müller was able to explain many processes in the human organism and was also able to demonstrate his ideas on animals—an achievement that his era, so fond of experimentation, considered of no less importance.

Handbuch der Physiologie. While at Bonn, Müller had planned to write a handbook of human physiology. The first section appeared in 1833, shortly before he moved to Berlin; the last section of the second volume was published in 1840. The work became a milestone in the history of European medicine. In Germany it established a fruitful interaction between physiology and clinical practice. Beyond a critical examination of the established knowledge of the subject, it furnished a wealth of new findings derived from his own work. Among the many topics in which Müller was able to draw upon the results of his own research, or upon his verification of the work of others, were the composition and coagulation of the blood, the origin of fibrin, the nature of lymph, the occurrence of the retinal image, the origin of the voice in the human and animal larynx, the propagation of sound in the tympanic cavity, the process of secretion, the nerves of the erectile sexual organs, and the function of the sympathetic nerve and other elements of the nervous system.

Müller's *Handbuch der Physiologie* was a powerful stimulus to physiological research and one of the sources of the mechanistic conception of the life processes that prevailed in the second half of the nineteenth century. Yet the book's fundamental tendency was vitalistic. For Müller, the cause and supreme organizer of life phenomena—the vital force (*Lebenskraft*)—acted in accord with the law of rational adaptation to function and had nothing in common with the forces of physics and chemistry. He attributed to this vital force the peculiar nature of the physiology experiment, which sets it apart from every other type. In the chemical experiment, both the reagents and the substance under consideration enter into the final product; in the result of a physiology experiment, however, the applied stimulus is by no means a more important component than is living nature: the result is determined solely by the vital energies of the organism. In whatever manner a muscle is stimulated, it always reacts with a contraction. A stimulus, however, can only provoke something fundamentally different from itself. This vitalistic tendency explains why Müller took a very critical view of the validity of physiological experimentation. Consequently, he underestimated the importance of Magendie, who must be considered the true creator of the techniques of experimental physiology.

The Soul. Müller's *Handbuch der Physiologie* contains an extensive section on the soul (II, 505–588). This emphasis is understandable, in the light of his initial adherence to the ideas of *Naturphilosophie*. Starting from the philosophy and psychology of Aristotle, Giordano Bruno, Spinoza, Schelling, Hegel, and especially Herbart, he approached the questions of the identity of the psychic principle and the vital principle, the divisibility of the soul, and the seat of the soul. He arrived at the following alternative: The soul, which utilizes the organization of the brain in its activity, is either foreign to the physical body, not a force of organic nature, and only temporarily united with the body; or else it is inherent in all matter, a force of matter itself. Müller appears to have inclined more to the panpsychic conception when he wrote:

> The relationship of the psychic forces to matter differs from that of other physical forces to matter solely because the spiritual forces appear only in organic and especially animal bodies, [whereas] the general physical forces, which are also called imponderables [light, electricity], are much more commonly active and widespread in nature. Since, however, the organic bodies take root in inorganic nature and draw their nourishment from it, . . . it remains uncertain whether or not the rudiments [*Anlage*] of psychic activities, like the common physical forces, is present in all matter and attains expression in a definite manner through the existing structures [brain and nervous system] [*Handbuch*, II, 553].

This panpsychism accounts for the fact that Müller considered the brain to be the seat of the soul but still suspected that it "might perhaps be more widespread in the organism." To support this supposition, he pointed out that lower animals like polyps and worms are divisible; and that therefore among such lower creatures, and thus in organic matter in general, the life principle and psychic principle can be separated.

Pathological Anatomy. At Berlin, Müller displayed a new interest in pathological anatomy as a result of his access to the holdings of the Anatomisch-zootomische Museum, which had come under his direction when he assumed his professorship. The surgeons of Berlin had contributed many operation preparations, tumors, and deformities. Through studying these specimens Müller realized that the traditional description of the external form of tumors could lead to no further advance. It had to be supplanted by the chemical analysis and microscopic examination of the pathological elements and by the study of their development. He saw the desirability of establishing a system able to distinguish between benign and malignant growths.

At the end of 1837 Müller's student Theodor Schwann began working on his new cell theory, according to which the cells were the ultimate constituents of the animal body. On this basis Müller investigated pathological tumors, observing the similarity between the development of embryonic tissue and the formation of tumors from cells and showing that elements of normal tissue could be detected in the tumors. In 1838 he published the first, and only, part of his *Über den feineren Bau und die Formen der krankhaften Geschwülste*. The publication of this work fostered the use of the microscope in the study of pathological formations. Müller thus founded pathological histology as an independent field and provided physicians with diagnostic procedures that are now used in daily clinical work. Several decades later his brilliant student Rudolf Virchow—to whom, in 1856, Müller entrusted the lectures on pathological anatomy at Berlin—greatly expanded research on pathological growths.

Zoology. After 1840 Müller devoted himself primarily to comparative anatomy and zoology, and his research in these fields made him the most respected scientist of his day. Collecting, describing, and classifying were now virtually the only methods he employed. He accomplished little of interest in physiological experimentation, which was by then drawing increasingly on the methods of physics and chemistry.

As early as 1832 Müller published a systematic classification of the amphibians and reptiles. In 1834 he turned his attention to the Cyclostomata, members of the most primitive class of vertebrates. In broadly conceived comparative anatomical studies, completed in 1842, he examined their skeleton and musculature, sensory organs and nervous system, and vessels and intestines. His considerations ranged from the muscles of the Cyclostomata to human trunk musculature and to the homology of the cranial and spinal nerves.

Müller placed the Cyclostomata among the fishes. He was thus led to study the sharks (which he called Plagiostomi) and the rays; he published the results of his research jointly with his student Jakob Henle as *Systematische Beschreibung der Plagiostomen* (1841). A further product of this investigation was "Über den glatten Hai des Aristoteles" (1842). In *Historia animalium*, Aristotle had reported that the embryos of the "so-called smooth shark" are attached to the uterus of the mother by a placenta, as is the case among mammals. Rondelet had described such a shark in 1555 and Steno had observed one in 1673 off the coast of Tuscany, but it had not been referred to in more recent times. Müller was the first who was able to corroborate the earlier testimony.

In conjunction with the study of the shark, Müller constructed a natural system of the fishes based on work as painstaking as it was perceptive. He also devoted attention to the systematics of the songbirds, employing the vocal apparatus as his chief criterion of classification.

In the introduction to his account of the Cyclostomata Müller emphasized that the animals most apt to provoke the curiosity of the scientist are those "standing on the border of a class." This was doubly true of the Cyclostomata because they stood at the border of the fishes and at that "of the vertebrates in general." This curiosity led him to study the lancelet, especially the *Branchiostoma lanceolatum*. The latter could serve, Müller stated, as the simplest model of the basic plan of the vertebrate subphylum. A flexible member which serves as an axial skeleton, the *Chorda dorsalis,* extends through the animal's body. This same skeleton is also found in the embryos of birds and mammals. The lancelet had been described in 1774, but Müller was the first to recognize its great systematic importance. In 1841, with Retzius at Stockholm—who had been his close friend since the Berlin scientific congress of 1828—he studied this primitive animal in Bohuslan, Sweden, and on the Felsen Islands near Göteborg and in the same year sent a description of it to the Prussian Academy of Sciences. This research, to which later work could add but little, became of great importance for knowledge of general vertebrate structure.

In his zoological research, Müller at first was satisfied to rely on the material in the collections available to him or that had been sent to him, but beginning in 1845 he traveled to the seashore to examine its animal life, especially the microscopic forms, *in situ*. During vacations he made many trips to the coasts of the North Sea and the Baltic, Adriatic, and Ligurian seas. He was rewarded with many unexpected results. In carefully executed studies, some of them lasting for years, Müller explored the echinoderms and sea slugs. Through observation and comparison he was able to elucidate their complex metamorphoses. He recognized the connection, bordering on the fantastic, between the double-ray larvae of the echinoderms, which are microscopic,

transparent plankton animals, and the squat, five-ray, sexually mature animals of the same phylum. Thus, from the bilaterally symmetric larva that he named *Pluteus paradoxus* he was able to derive the radially symmetric sea urchin. In short, Müller not only opened this field, with its wealth of forms, to research but also penetrated its secrets conceptually. It is characteristic of the way he worked that he never attempted to clarify the development of the echinoderms through experimentation, which might have led him to his goal more quickly.

These studies, which revealed the extraordinary creative powers of nature in a unique manner, received greater recognition than any of Müller's previous achievements. He was awarded the Copley Medal of the Royal Society and the Prix Cuvier of the Académie des Sciences. His last research was devoted to the single-celled marine animals the Radiolaria and the Foraminifera. Haeckel continued this work.

Research Methods. Müller began his scientific career with vivisection in order to demonstrate that the fetus breathes in the uterus. He also utilized vivisection later when he was convinced that it could elucidate a question. Yet in setting forth his views on the study of living nature in his Bonn inaugural lecture, he stressed the technical difficulties of physiological experimentation and dissociated himself from the fondness for experiment characteristic of Magendie's school. Müller's scientific ideal was not Magendie or brilliant experimentalists like Haller or Spallanzani, but Cuvier, who devoted himself to the description and comparison of the forms and species of living creatures.

In the same inaugural lecture Müller spoke against the speculative interpretation of biological processes. Accordingly, he criticized the ideas of *Naturphilosophie*, the temptations of which he had escaped through Rudolphi's influence. He advocated a physiology that united "exact empirical training" in all the methods suited to the investigation of living nature with a philosophical penetration of the data. Such a union, he claimed, would uncover the *Urphänomene*, the ideas underlying everything in the universe.

As he grew older, Müller expressed his methodology in much more modest terms in the *Handbuch der Physiologie*. He remained convinced that a strictly empirical approach to physiology could not solve the ultimate questions of life, but he conceded that philosophy could not yield results usable in an empirical science. Only a union of the two paths to knowledge, which he termed "critically evaluated experience" ("denkende Erfahrung"), could lead to scientific truth, although he added that there would always be something unsolved. He no longer expressed the hope of penetrating to the *Urphänomene*. At Berlin, holding that the researcher's principal instrument was "conceptual empiricism," not experiment, Müller increasingly shifted his attention from functional to morphological issues. While his students sought to elucidate vital phenomena with the methods of physics and chemistry, he was satisfied to describe them. In opposition to this new generation of scientists, he remained a vitalist throughout his life, never doubting the existence of the "vital force."

BIBLIOGRAPHY

I. ORIGINAL WORKS. A complete list of Müller's 267 writings is in *Abhandlungen der K. Preussischen Akademie der Wissenschaften* for 1859 (1860), 157–175; it was reprinted in Koller's biography (see below), pp. 241–260.

His works include *De phoronomia animalium* (Bonn, 1822); *De respiratione foetus* (Leipzig, 1823); *Von dem Bedürfnis der Physiologie nach einer philosophischen Naturbetrachtung* (Bonn, 1825), his inaugural lecture, repr. in Müller's *Zur vergleichenden Physiologie* and in Adolf Meyer-Abich, *Biologie der Goethezeit* (Stuttgart, 1949), 256–281; *Über die phantastischen Gesichtserscheinungen* (Coblenz, 1826), repr. in vol. XXXII of *Klassiker der Medizin* (Leipzig, 1927) and in Ulrich Ebbecke, *Johannes Müller* (see below), 77–187; *Zur vergleichenden Physiologie des Gesichtssinnes des Menschen und der Tiere nebst einem Versuch über die Bewegungen der Augen und über den menschlichen Blick* (Leipzig, 1826); *Bildungsgeschichte der Genitalien aus anatomischen Untersuchungen an Embryonen des Menschen und der Tiere* (Düsseldorf, 1830); *De glandularum secernentium structura penitiori earumque prima formatione in homine atque animalibus* (Leipzig, 1830); and "Über den Ursprung der Netze und ihr Verhältnis zum Peritonealsacke beim Menschen, aus anatomischen Untersuchungen an Embryonen," in *Archiv für Anatomie und Physiologie* (1840), 395–411.

See also "Bestätigung des Bell'schen Lehrsatzes, dass die doppelten Wurzeln der Rückenmarksnerven verschiedene Funktionen haben, durch neue und entscheidende Experimente," in *Notizen aus dem Gebiete der Natur- und Heilkunde*, **30** (1831), 113–117; *Handbuch der Physiologie des Menschen für Vorlesungen*, 2 vols. (I, Coblenz, 1833–1834; 4th ed., 1841–1844; II, Coblenz, 1837–1840), also trans. into English by Baly, 2 vols. (London, 1840–1843) and into French by Jourdan, 2 vols. (Paris, 1845; 2nd ed., 1851); "Vergleichenden Anatomie der Myxinoiden (Cyclostomen)," in *Abhandlungen der K. Preussischen Akademie der Wissenschaften*, Phys. Kl., for 1834, 1837–1839, 1843 (1836–1845); *Über den feineren Bau und die Formen der krankhaften Geschwülste* (Berlin, 1838); *Systematische Beschreibung der Plagiostomen* (Berlin, 1841), written with Jakob Henle; "Über den glatten Hai des Aristoteles und über die Verschiedenheiten unter den Haifischen und Rochen in der Entwicklung des Eies," in *Abhandlungen der K. Preussischen Akademie der Wissenschaften*, Phys. Kl., for 1840 (1842), 187–257; and "Über den Bau und die Lebenerscheinungen des *Branchiostoma lubricum* Costa, *Amphioxus lanceolatus* Yarrell," *ibid.*, for 1842 (1844), 79–116.

Müller's many publications on echinoderms began with his description of a sea lily—"Über den Bau des *Pentacrinus caput* Medusae," in *Abhandlungen der K. Preussischen Akademie der Wissenschaften*, Phys. Kl., for 1841 (1843), 177–248—and was followed by eight papers on larvae, metamorphoses, and the structure of echinoderms, *ibid.*, for 1846, 1848, 1850–1854 (1848–1855).

II. SECONDARY LITERATURE. Although the writings of du Bois-Reymond and Virchow on their teacher are limited by the thinking of their generation and do not always do justice to Müller, they are nevertheless indispensable: Emil du Bois-Reymond, "Gedächtnisrede auf Johannes Müller," in *Abhandlungen der K. Preussischen Akademie der Wissenschaften*, for 1859 (1860), 25–191, repr. with additional material in du Bois-Reymond's *Reden*, 2nd ed., I (Leipzig, 1912), 135–317; and Rudolf Virchow, *Johannes Müller. Gedächtnisrede* (Berlin, 1858).

Among the more recent literature, see Wulf Emmo Ankel, "Branchiostoma ist ein Wirbeltier—eine 130 Jahre alte Erkenntnis," in *Natur und Museum*, no. 101 (1971), 321–339; Ulrich Ebbecke, *Johannes Müller, der grosse rheinische Physiologe* (Hannover, 1951), which includes a reprint of Müller's *Über die phantastischen Gesichtserscheinungen*; Wilhelm Haberling, *Johannes Müller. Das Leben des rheinischen Naturforschers* (Leipzig, 1924), a detailed biography with letters from Müller to his family, friends, and colleagues; Gottfried Koller, *Das Leben des Biologen Johannes Müller* (Stuttgart, 1958), with a bibliography of secondary literature, pp. 261–263; Walther Riese and George E. Arrington, Jr., "The History of Johannes Müller's Doctrine of the Specific Energies of the Senses," in *Bulletin of the History of Medicine*, **37** (1963), 179–183; Robert Rössle, "Die pathologische Anatomie des Johannes Müller. Nach einem aufgefundenen Kollegheft aus dem Jahre 1834," in *Sudhoffs Archiv für Geschichte der Medizin und Naturwissenschaften*, **22** (1919), 24–47; Johannes Steudel, *Le physiologiste Johannes Müller*, Conférences du Palais de la Découverte, D85 (Paris, 1963); and Manfred Stürzbecher, "Auf dem Briefwechsel des Physiologen Johannes Müller mit dem preussischen Kulturministerium," in *Janus*, **49** (1960), 273–284.

JOHANNES STEUDEL

MÜLLER, OTTO FREDERIK (*b.* Copenhagen, Denmark, 2 March 1730; *d.* Copenhagen, 26 December 1784), *botany, zoology*.

The son of a court trumpeter, Müller was educated from the age of ten by his mother's family at the grammar school of Ribe, Jutland. Five years later he was sent to the University of Copenhagen, where he earned his living by teaching music while studying theology and law. In 1750 he enrolled in Borch's College and wrote two short theological theses (1751, 1753) while there. Three years later he was appointed tutor to Sigismund Schulin, the son of an influential noble family; for nearly twenty years he lived with this family on their estate, Frederiksdal (northern Zealand), and traveled with them to Germany, Switzerland, Italy, France, and the Netherlands. In this way Müller met many outstanding scientists and became a member of the Academia Caesarea Leopoldina (1764), the Royal Swedish Academy of Sciences (1769), and the Norwegian Society of Sciences (1770). In 1771–1773 he was secretary to the Danish Ministry for Norway; but his marriage on 26 May 1773 to a wealthy widow, Anna Carlsen, née Paludan (1735–1787), daughter of a Norwegian bishop, made Müller financially independent, so that he was able to devote the last thirteen or fourteen years of his life to science. In 1774 he became a corresponding member of the Paris Academy of Sciences and the Berlin Society of Friends of Natural Science, and two years later he became a member of the Royal Danish Academy of Sciences and of the Academy of Sciences of the Institute of Bologna.

During Müller's years as a tutor, his pupil's mother interested him in the flora and fauna of the estate, procuring microscopes and other equipment for his growing absorption in biological studies. Because of his theological training Müller examined nature in terms of natural theology, considering it his task to investigate and point out the wisdom of the Creator everywhere in nature. The mainsprings of his scientific research were his love of beauty and his discovery that previous systematists had largely neglected to take microorganisms into account. Even the smallest puddle was full of organisms, and his unique powers of observation enabled Müller to demonstrate their adaptations. Thus he stands as the foremost representative of the Linnaean period in Danish natural history. He established the classification of several groups of animals—including Hydrachnellae, Entomostraca and Infusoria—completely disregarded by Linnaeus. He pursued his zoological studies and became one of the first field naturalists, using surprisingly modern methods long before the development of experimental biology.

At the age of thirty-four Müller published his first zoological work, a systematic study written entirely in the Linnaean spirit, *Fauna insectorum Fridrichsdalina* (1764). The description of 858 "insects" found at the estate of Frederiksdal—including spiders, wood lice and centipedes—contains several errors. Two years later there appeared *Flora Fridrichsdalina* (1766), a description of 1,100 species intended to represent most of the Danish flora. But Müller's main work in systematics consisted of studying animal groups that were very little known before he identified them: the Hydrachnida, the Tardigrada, the Entomostraca, and the Infusoria. Among his works on these groups he lived to see only one published, *Hydrachnae, quas in aquis Daniae palustribus detexit* (1781). The other fundamental writings—"Von dem Bärthierchen" (1785), *Entomostraca, seu Insecta testacea* (1785), and *Animalcula infusoria* (1786)—were printed after his death. Müller applied the term "Entomostraca" to the small, often minute crustaceans: many genera belonging to this group—including *Daphnia*, *Cyclops caligus*, and *Argulus*—were first defined by him, and he formulated a systematic classification and created Danish names for the various groups. His classic paper was for many years accepted as the best study of the Infusoria, which he placed near the order Acarina, where it is still placed by most authors. Illustrated with fifty plates, his work on Infusoria describes algae, bacteria, and many other microorganisms as well as some protozoans.

It was not only on microscopic animals that Müller did significant and fundamental studies. His main work concerning mollusks and worms, *Vermium terrestrium et fluviatilium* (1773–1774), in which he first described a large number of new species of freshwater and terrestrial mollusks, also presented his primary system on the Infusoria. Neither did Müller limit his interests to invertebrate taxonomy; in *Von Würmern des süssen und salzigen Wassers* (1771) he clearly demonstrated the propagation of naiads. He wrote on annelids (1771), on the moth (1779), and on helminths (1779). In this field of studies his contemporaries rightly called him the Danish Linnaeus.

Besides his systematic works Müller wrote several entomological papers in Réaumur's style, for instance, on the propagation of the daphnids. For the collection of sea animals he invented a special dredge; and with his brother, Christian Frederik Müller (1744–1814), who was responsible for some of the illustrations in Müller's books, he published an anonymous account of a journey from Norway (1778).

In 1776 Müller published *Zoologiae Danicae prodromus*, an excellent survey of the fauna of Norway and Denmark. It was the first manual on this topic and was for many years the most comprehensive. It was planned as the beginning of a large illustrated fauna, but only one volume appeared before his death; the following volumes—the last published in 1806—prepared by Abildgaard, Rathke, and others, never reached the standard of the *Flora Danica* begun by Georg Christian Oeder.

Müller also wrote a number of botanical studies dealing especially with fungi and other groups, but they were little known during his lifetime. They presented findings and views pointing far beyond what was known then—for instance, in his "Ueber die Feld-Lilie" (1766).

Besides his systematic and exact studies Müller was also occupied with the philosophy of biology, advancing his "monadic" theory, a view that all living things are composed of minute elements—monads—that are set free by putrefaction and reunited in propagation. This belief indicates that he was an adherent of the preformation hypothesis.

BIBLIOGRAPHY

I. Original Works. A full list of Müller's writings is in H. Ehrencron-Müller, *Forfatterlexikon*, VI (Copenhagen, 1929), 17–22.

Among his works are *Fauna insectorum Fridrichsdalina* . . . (Copenhagen–Leipzig, 1764); *Flora Fridrichsdalina* . . . (Strasbourg, 1766; 1767); *Von Würmern des süssen und salzigen Wassers* (Copenhagen, 1771); *Vermium terrestrium et fluviatilium* . . ., 2 vols. (Copenhagen–Leipzig, 1773–1774); *Zoologiae Danicae prodromus* (Copenhagen, 1776); *Zoologiae Danicae seu animalium Daniae et Norvegiae rariorum ac minus notorum icones*, 2 vols. (Copenhagen, 1777–1780); *Rejse igiennem Övre-Tillemarken til Christianssand og tilbage 1775* (Copenhagen, 1778), published anonymously; *Hydrachnae, quas in aquis . . . palustribus detexit . . .* (Leipzig, 1781); *Zoologia Danica eller Danmarks og Norges sieldne og ubekiente Dyrs Historie* (Copenhagen, 1781), also trans. into German (Leipzig–Dessau, 1782); *Entomostraca seu insecta testacea, quae in aquis Daniae et Norvegiae reperit . . .* (Copenhagen, 1785); *Animalcula infusoria, fluviatilia et marina . . .* (Copenhagen, 1786); and *Zoologia Danica seu animalium Daniae et Norvegiae rariorum ac minus notorum descriptiones et historia*, 4 vols. (Copenhagen, 1788–1806).

His diary, which remains unpublished, is in the Royal Library, Copenhagen, Add. 4° no. 710.

II. Secondary Literature. See Jean Anker, *Otto Friderich Müller* (Copenhagen, 1943), of which only the 1st vol., covering 1730–1767, has been published (because of the author's death); V. Meisen, *Prominent Danish Scientists* (Copenhagen, 1932), 60–64; and Jens Worm, *Lexicon over laerde Maend*, II (Copenhagen, 1773), 88–91, and III (Copenhagen, 1784), 548–549.

E. Snorrason

MÜLLER, PAUL (*b*. Olten, Solothurn, Switzerland, 12 January 1899; *d*. Basel, Switzerland, 13 October 1965), *chemistry*.

Müller's earliest years were spent in Lenzburg, in the canton of Aargau; but when he was nearly five, his father, an employee of the Swiss Federal Railroads, was transferred to Basel, where the boy received his elementary education. His interest in chemistry was stimulated in 1916, when he was employed as a laboratory assistant in the chemical factory of Dreyfus and Company. In 1917 he became a chemical assistant in the research laboratories of Lonza A. G., where he remained for a year. The experience thus gained convinced Müller that his future lay in chemistry, and he therefore entered the University of Basel in 1919 to work with F. Fichter and Hans Rupe. He received his doctorate in April 1925, with a thesis on the chemical and electrochemical oxidation of *m*-xylidine and its derivatives. His minor subjects were physical chemistry and botany. In May 1925 he became a research chemist in the dye factory of J. R. Geigy A.G., where he remained for the rest of his active career, rising to the post of deputy head of pest control research.

Because of his interest in botany Müller began a study of plant pigments and natural tanning agents. His work on the preservation and disinfection of animal skins led him to utilize biological studies, and he soon turned his attention to pesticides. He discovered a mercury-free seed dressing, which was of value for Swiss farmers.

In 1935 Müller began to study contact insecticides and drew up a set of criteria to guide him in his search for an ideal agent. These included great toxicity for insects, rapid toxic action, no or slight toxicity for plants and warm-blooded animals, no odor, long-lasting action, and low price. He did not consider stability and decomposability.

Müller first studied the action of a great many different types of compounds on a variety of insects. He believed that besides its practical value, this work was of philosophical interest in bringing together biologists and chemists. He soon concluded that it would be possible to discover safe insecticides, since the absorption of toxic substances by insects was entirely different physiologically from their absorption by warm-blooded animals. His attention was drawn to the group of chlorinated derivatives of phenyl ethane. In September 1939 he observed that in its action on flies 4,4′-dichloro-diphenyl-trichloro-ethane satisfied nearly all of his criteria, and he soon found that it was equally effective against other types of insects. The compound had first been prepared in 1873 by Othmar Zeidler, who had published a brief description of the substance in *Berichte der Deutschen chemischen Gesellschaft* (**7** [1874], 1181), but with no indication that it had any physiological action.

Müller called the substance DDT, and the basic Swiss patent was secured in March 1940. He described his work on this and other insecticides in papers published in the *Helvetica chimica acta* in 1944 and 1946. In the second of these papers he reported the investigation of a large number of compounds related to DDT, none of which proved as effective as the original. Müller was unable to find any general relations between structure and insecticidal action and noted, "A chemical compound is an individual whose characteristic action can be understood only from its totality, and the molecule means more in this case than the sum of its atoms."

The first commercial preparation of DDT appeared on the market at the beginning of 1942, and its value was immediately recognized. Müller noted rather proudly that in spite of many attempts by the combatants in World War II to obtain a better insecticide, none had improved on his DDT. Since much of the war was fought in tropical areas, the value of DDT in destroying disease-bearing insects was obvious. The early work seemed to indicate that the substance was completely safe for humans. After the war it was widely used in the Mediterranean area to eradicate malaria-bearing mosquitoes, and the incidence of this disease was greatly reduced. Honors quickly came to Müller, culminating in his receipt of the Nobel Prize in physiology or medicine in 1948. In 1963 he was awarded an honorary doctorate by the University of Thessaloniki because of the value of DDT in the Mediterranean region. In 1961 Müller retired from the Geigy Company and established a private laboratory at his home in Oberswil, where he continued his investigations until his death.

In establishing his criteria for the properties of an ideal insecticide, Müller had not considered the possibility of the accumulation of the agent in various biological species until it reached dangerous proportions. He was not unaware of this possibility, however, for in concluding his 1946 article he wrote, "Pyrethrum and rotenone, like all natural insecticides, are completely destroyed in a short time by light and oxidation, as opposed to the synthetic contact insecticides which have been shown to be very stable. Nature must and will behave in this way, for what a catastrophe would result if the natural insecticide poisons were stable. Nature plans for life and not for death!" Such considerations, disregarded at first, were gradually recognized in the years immediately following his death. As the use of DDT increased, it became apparent that the stability of the compound caused it to accumulate to a harmful degree in some animal species. Far-reaching ecological changes could be foreseen, and numerous controversies arose as doubts were expressed concerning the long-range safety of DDT. It was apparent that the contact insecticides of the DDT type were not the complete answer in the search for an ideal agent of this sort.

BIBLIOGRAPHY

The basic papers describing Müller's investigations are "Über Konstitution und toxische Wirkung von natürlichen und neuen synthetischen insektentötenden Stoffen," in *Helvetica chimica acta*, **27** (1944), 892–928, written with P. Läuger and H. Martin; and "Über Zusammenhänge zwischen Konstitution und insektizider Wirkung. I," *ibid.*, **29** (1946), 1560–1580. An account of his discovery of DDT is given by Müller in "Dichlorodiphenyltrichloroäthan und neuere Inzekticide," in *Les Prix Nobel en 1948* (Stockholm, 1949), 122–132. His autobiography is on pp. 75–76 of this work.

An obituary in *Nature*, **208** (1965), 1043–1044, gives information on the latter part of Müller's life.

HENRY LEICESTER

MÜLLER-BRESLAU, HEINRICH (FRANZ BERNHARD) (*b*. Breslau, Germany [now Wrocław, Poland], 13 May 1851; *d*. Berlin, Germany, 23 April 1925), *theory of structures.*

The son of a merchant, Müller (after the 1870's he styled himself Müller-Breslau) grew up in Breslau. In 1869, upon graduation from the Realgymnasium, he joined the Prussian army engineers and saw action in the Franco-Prussian War. After the war he gave up plans for a military career in order to become a civil engineer. Müller then moved to Berlin and embarked upon an informal program of study consisting of courses in engineering at the Gewerbeakademie and of lectures in mathematics at the university. Without graduating he began practicing as an independent consulting engineer at Berlin in 1875, specializing in the design of iron structures, chiefly bridges. At the same time he prepared his first major book, *Theorie und Berechnung der eisernen Bogenbrücken* (1880) and a series of articles on problems of statically indeterminate structures. In 1883 Müller-Breslau was appointed professor of bridge design at the Polytechnic Institute of Hannover. The steady flow of his publications and some notable designs rapidly established his reputation, and in 1888 he was appointed to the chair of structural engineering at the Berlin-Charlottenburg Institute of Technology. Here he worked as a teacher, researcher, and consultant for the rest of his life, serving in 1895–1896 and 1910–1911 as rector.

Müller-Breslau has been termed the founder of modern structural engineering in Germany. Among the more significant designs credited to him are the Volga bridge at Kazan, Russia, and the new cathedral in Berlin. He also participated in the construction of Count Ferdinand von Zeppelin's airships, designed large aircraft hangars, and contributed to the introduction of cantilever wings on airplanes.

Müller-Breslau exerted even greater influence through his publications, notably his books. His numerous monographs deal with specific problems in the theory of structures, such as cantilevers, arches, lattice structures, earth pressure on retaining walls, and buckling of straight bars. He did not present methods or theories of fundamental novelty; his strength was the refinement and elaboration of earlier methods, presented in systematic and unified form. In *Die neueren Methoden der Festigkeitslehre und der Statik der Baukonstruktionen* (1886) he consistently based the solution of statically indeterminate structural systems upon the strain energy methods of L. F. Menabrea and C. A. Castigliano. The last three decades of Müller-Breslau's life were devoted chiefly to his magnum opus, *Die graphische Statik der Baukonstruktionen*. A three-volume handbook (1887, 1892, 1908), it came to be internationally regarded as the definitive presentation of the graphical methods of structural design.

BIBLIOGRAPHY

I. ORIGINAL WORKS. A bibliography of Müller-Breslau's most important publications is given by H. Reissner in *Zeitschrift für angewandte Mathematik und Mechanik*, **5** (1925), 277–278. Besides some 35 research papers it lists the following books: *Theorie und Berechnung der eisernen Bogenbrücken* (Berlin, 1880); *Die neueren Methoden der Festigkeitslehre und der Statik der Baukonstruktionen* (Leipzig, 1886); *Die graphische Statik der Baukonstruktionen*, 3 vols. (Leipzig, 1887–1908); and *Erddruck auf Stützmauern* (Stuttgart, 1906).

II. SECONDARY LITERATURE. Biographical information on Müller-Breslau can be found in Karl Bernhard, "Müller-Breslau," in *Bautechnik*, **3** (1925), 261–262; A. Hertwig, "Rede, gehalten bei der Gedenkfeier für Müller-Breslau am 25. Juni 1925," in *Stahlbau*, **20** (1951), 53–54; H. Müller-Breslau, Jr., "Heinrich Müller-Breslau," in H. Boost *et al.*, *Festschrift Heinrich Müller-Breslau* (Leipzig, 1912), v–viii; Poggendorff, VI, 1802; H. Reissner, "H. Müller-Breslau," in *Zeitschrift für angewandte Mathematik und Mechanik*, **1** (1921), 159–160, and **5** (1925), 277–278; and Stephen P. Timoshenko, *History of Strength of Materials* (New York, 1953), *passim*.

OTTO MAYR

MUNCKE, GEORG WILHELM (*b*. Hillingsfeld, near Hameln, Germany, 28 November 1772; *d*. Grosskmehlen, Germany, 17 October 1847), *physics*.

Muncke served as an overseer at the Georgianum in Hannover. In 1810 he became professor of physics at the University of Marburg, where he stayed until 1817, when he went to the University of Heidelberg to take up the professorship that he held until his death.

Muncke's chief importance lies in his critical attitude toward much of the scientific speculation of his time, and in particular in his opposition to Kant's dynamical theory of matter. He attributed the wide influence of *Naturphilosophie* in German science to Kant's "mystical play with unknown forces," and to the elaboration of Kant's ideas by Fichte, Schelling, Ritter, Steffens, Oken, and Hegel. Muncke was himself an advocate of the atomic theory of matter and his views are explicitly stated in his books *System der atomistischen Physik* (1809) and *Handbuch der Naturlehre* (1829–1830).

Muncke also collaborated with Brandes, Gmelin, Horner, Pfaff, and Littrow in preparing the edition of Johann Gehler's *Physikalisches Wörterbuch* published in Leipzig in eleven volumes (1825–1845). This work constitutes one of the best records of the state of the natural sciences in the first quarter of the nineteenth century; Muncke's contribution consists of descriptions of individual physical subjects and an excellent, objective general discussion of current physical theories and knowledge.

Muncke's own experimental results were trivial. He published a series of observations on the expansion and boiling of water, and he determined the densities of water, alcohol, and ether (1816). He adhered to the theory that the earth has four magnetic poles, and he explained Brownian movement as the passage of light and heat rays through the liquid medium.

BIBLIOGRAPHY

Muncke's works are *System der atomistischen Physik* (Hannover, 1809); *Anfangsgründe der Naturlehre*, 2 vols. (Heidelberg, 1819–1820); *Handbuch der Naturlehre*, 2 vols. (Heidelberg, 1829–1830); *Physicalische Abhandlungen. Ein Versuch zur Erweiterung der Naturkunde* (Giessen, 1816); "Hypothesen zur Erklärung einiger räthselhafter Naturphänomene," in *Journal für Chemie und Physik*, **25** (1819), 17–28; "Versuche über den Elektromagnetismus zur Begründung einer genügenden Erklärung desselben," in *Annalen der Physik*, **70** (1822), 141–174, **71** (1822), 20–38, 411–435; and "Ueber Robert Brown's microscopische Beobachtungen," *ibid.*, **17** (1829), 159–176.

Bibliographies of Muncke are given in the Royal Society *Catalogue of Scientific Papers*, IV, 543–544; and Poggendorff, II, 238–239.

H. A. M. SNELDERS

MUNIER-CHALMAS, ERNEST CHARLES PHILIPPE AUGUSTE (*b.* Tournus, France, 7 April 1843; *d.* Saint-Simon, near Aix-les-Bains, France, 8 August 1903), *paleontology, stratigraphy.*

Although he received only an inferior early education, Munier-Chalmas was able, through a combination of intelligence and willpower, to teach himself geology so successfully that he eventually became a professor of that subject at the Sorbonne. After holding a number of menial jobs, Munier-Chalmas in 1863 was made an assistant in the Sorbonne's geology laboratory. He worked under the supervision of Edmond Hébert and, as a result of his diligence in his task of self-education, became Hébert's closest collaborator, accompanying him on geological trips throughout France, northern Italy, Austria, and Hungary. Having attained the master's degree, Munier-Chalmas was able to begin teaching at the École Normale in 1882, but his doctoral thesis, on the Jurassic, Cretaceous, and Cenozoic deposits of the Vicentin, presented in 1891, was never published. He succeeded Hébert in the chair of geology at the Sorbonne in 1891 and was elected to the Académie des Sciences in 1903.

Munier-Chalmas's paleontological skills complemented Hébert's stratigraphical ones, and their collaboration was mutually profitable. His own paleontological work included his investigations of the Brachiopoda, Cephalopoda, Gastropoda, Foraminifera, and Calcareous Algae. He was also concerned with classification and nomenclature, and established a number of new genera, comprising *Toucasia, Matheronia,* and *Heterodiceras.* One of his findings—that the shapes of the shells of some groups of ammonites clearly indicate sexual dimorphism, while those of other groups do not—led to a number of taxonomic changes and reclassifications.

In stratigraphy, Munier-Chalmas's chief contribution concerned the Cenozoic of the Paris Basin. "Note sur la nomenclature des terrains sédimentaires," published in 1893 and written with Lapparent (who had earlier supervised the surveying of that region) is his chief work. He also collaborated with Paul Henri Fischer, to whom he supplied much data for his *Manuel de conchyliologie* (1880–1887).

Munier-Chalmas was not particularly successful as a teacher; he was unable to communicate his ideas to large audiences, and he was continually hampered by

an awareness of his own educational deficiencies. His influence, however, is clear in the works of his students—the more so that he was reluctant to publish his findings himself. Nevertheless, he had published more than sixty papers before 1900, including nine in the single year of 1892.

BIBLIOGRAPHY

I. ORIGINAL WORKS. Munier-Chalmas's publications include "Prodrome d'une classification des Rudistes," in *Journal de conchyliologie*, 3rd ser., **13** (1873), 71–75; "Matériaux pour servir à la description du terrain Crétacé supérieur en France," "Description du bassin d'Uchaux," and "Appendice paléontologique (Fossiles du bassin d'Uchaux)," in *Annales de la Société géologique*, **6**, pt. 2 (1875), 1–132, all written with E. Hébert; "Mollusques nouveaux des terrains paléozoïques des environs de Rennes," in *Journal de conchyliologie*, 3rd ser., **16** (1876), 102–109; "Diagnosis generis novi Molluscorum Cephalopodorum fossilium," ibid., 3rd ser., **20** (1880), 183–184; *Étude du Tithonique, du Crétacé et du Tertiaire du Vicentin* (Paris, 1891); "Note sur la nomenclature des terrains sédimentaires," in *Bulletin de la Société géologique de France*, 3rd ser., **21** (1893), 438–488, written with A. de Lapparent; and "Note préliminaire sur les assises montiennes du bassin de Paris," ibid., 3rd ser., **25** (1897), 82–91.

II. SECONDARY LITERATURE. Munier-Chalmas's *Étude du Tithonique . . .* is reviewed by A. Andreae in *Neues Jahrbuch für Mineralogie, Geologie und Paläontologie*, pt. 1 (1894), 156–160. See also G. F. Dollfus, "Nécrologie de E. Munier-Chalmas," in *Journal de conchyliologie*, **52** (1904), 100–106.

ALBERT V. CAROZZI

MUNĪŚVARA VIŚVARŪPA (*b.* Benares, India, 17 March 1603), *astronomy, mathematics.*

The member of a noted family of astronomers who originated at Dadhigrāma on the Payoṣṇī River in Vidarbha with Cintāmaṇi, a Brahmana of the Devarātragotra, in the middle of the fifteenth century, and continued with successive generations represented by Rāma (who was patronized by a king of Vidarbha), Trimalla, and Ballāla, Munīśvara was a grandson of Ballāla, born after the latter had moved the family to Benares. Ballāla had had five sons: Rāma, who wrote a commentary on the *Sudhārasasāraṇī* of Ananta (*fl.* 1525); Kṛṣṇa (*fl.* 1600–1625); Govinda, whose son Nārāyaṇa wrote commentaries on the *Grahalāghava* of Gaṇeśa (*b.* 1507) and, in 1678, on the *Jātakapaddhati* of Keśava (*fl.* 1496); Raṅganātha, who finished his commentary on the *Sūryasiddhānta,* the *Gūḍhārthaprakāśa,* in 1603; and Mahādeva. Munīśvara was the son of Raṅganātha and the pupil of Kṛṣṇa, who traces his *guruparamparā*, or lineage of teachers, back through Viṣṇu (*fl. ca.* 1575–1600) and Nṛsiṃha (*b.* 1548) to the great Gaṇeśa himself.

Although thus tracing his intellectual genealogy back to the school of Gaṇeśa and Keśava (see essay in Supplement), Munīśvara followed his uncle's example of studying the works of Bhāskara II (*b.* 1115); as Kṛṣṇa had written a commentary, the *Bījāṅkura*, on Bhāskara's *Bījagaṇita*, Munīśvara continued the task by commenting on the *Līlāvatī* in the *Nisṛṣṭārthadūtī* and on the two parts of the *Siddhāntaśiromaṇi* in the immense *Marīcī*, begun in 1635 and finished in 1638.

In the 1640's and 1650's Munīśvara's family entered into a scientific controversy with another Benares family of astronomers whose intellectual genealogy was traced back to Gaṇeśa. This second family had originated in Golagrāma in Mahārāṣṭra at about the same time that Cintāmaṇi appeared in Dadhigrāma; its representatives contemporary with Munīśvara were the three brothers Divākara (*b.* 1606), Kamalākara (*fl.* 1658), and Raṅganātha. They generally favored the *Saurapakṣa* (see essay in Supplement). And, in this connection, it should be noted that Munīśvara's greatest work, the *Siddhāntasārvabhauma*, which was completed in 1646 and on which he wrote a commentary, the *Āśayaprakāśinī*, in 1650, is fundamentally *Saura* in character; there is, however, a strong admixture of material from the *Brāhmapakṣa* (see essay in Supplement), reflecting his intense study of Bhāskara II's *Siddhāntaśiromaṇi* and of the *Siddhāntasundara* of Jñānarāja (*fl.* 1503). He also demonstrates some knowledge of Islamic astronomy, although much less acceptance of it than is shown by Kamalākara. It is around their respective attitudes toward Islamic astronomy that the controversy between the two families principally turned. Despite his negative attitude, however, the author of the *Siddhāntasārvabhauma* seems to have enjoyed the patronage of Shāh Jahān (reigned 1628–1658).

Munīśvara also composed a *Pāṭīsāra* on mathematics, of which the earliest manuscript, still in Benares, was copied in 1654.

BIBLIOGRAPHY

I. ORIGINAL WORKS. Only one of Munīśvara's works has been published in full. Of the *Marīcī* the part relating to the *Golādhyāya* was edited by Dattātreya Āpṭe as Ānandāśrama Sanskrit Series 122, 2 vols. (Poona, 1943–1952). Of the part relating to the *Gaṇitādhyāya*, the first chapter only was edited by Muralīdhara Jhā (Benares, 1917) and the rest by Kedāradatta Jośī in vols. II and III of his ed. of the *Grahagaṇitādhyāya* (Benares, 1964).

Muralīdhara Ṭhakkura edited 2 vols. containing the first two chs. and a part of the third of the *Siddhāntasārvabhauma* with the *Āśayaprakāśinī* as Saraswati Bhavana Texts 41 (Benares, 1932–1935); no more has appeared.

II. SECONDARY LITERATURE. There are notices on Munīśvara in S. Dvivedin, *Gaṇakataraṅgiṇī* (Benares, 1933), repr. from *The Pandit*, n.s. **14** (1892), 91–94; Ś. B. Dīkṣita, *Bhāratīya Jyotiḥśāstra* (Poona, 1896, 1931), 286–287; and M. M. Patkar in *Poona Orientalist*, **3** (1938), 170–171.

DAVID PINGREE

MUÑJĀLA (*fl.* India, 932), *astronomy.*

A Brahmana of the Bhāradvājagotra, in 932 Muñjāla composed a *Bṛhanmānasa* which was known to al-Bīrūnī (*India*, translated by E. C. Sachau, 2 vols. [London, 1910], I, 157), who claims that a commentary on it was written by Utpala (*fl.* 966–968). We now have only fragments of the *Bṛhanmānasa*; but the second treatise of Muñjāla mentioned by al-Bīrūnī, the *Laghumānasa*, is extant. It was composed after the lost work at a place called Prakāśa; the earliest commentary on it, by Praśastidhara of Kashmir, was written in 958.

The *Laghumānasa* is a rather eclectic work (see essay in Supplement), although it possesses elements derived from the two schools of Āryabhaṭa I (*b.* 476) and some original insights into lunar theory. Besides the commentary of Praśastidhara mentioned above there are others by Sūryadeva Yajvan of Kerala (*b.* 1191), Parameśvara (*ca.* 1380–1460), and Yallaya (*fl.* 1482). All three of these later commentators lived in southern India, where Muñjāla's work maintained some influence although it had been forgotten in the northwest since the eleventh century.

BIBLIOGRAPHY

The *Laghumānasa* was edited with Parameśvara's *vyākhyā* by Dattātreya Āpṭe as Ānandāśrama Sanskrit Series 123 (Poona, 1952), and with an English trans. and commentary by N. K. Majumdar (Calcutta, 1951). Majumdar had previously published a short note on it, "Laghumānasam of Muñjāla," in *Journal of the Department of Letters, University of Calcutta*, **14** (1927), art. 8.

DAVID PINGREE

MÜNSTER, SEBASTIAN (*b.* Nieder-Ingelheim, Germany, 1489; *d.* Basel, Switzerland, 26 May 1552), *geography.*

Münster began his studies at Heidelberg and entered the Minorite order at the age of sixteen.

Early in his career he became fascinated with Hebrew and Greek and mastered both. His first printed work was a Hebrew edition of the Psalms (Basel, 1516). During the first part of his life his primary concern was with the publication of Hebrew texts, dictionaries, and grammars; and on the strength of his important contributions he was elected to the chair of Hebrew at Basel in 1527. Münster moved to Basel in 1529, having become a Protestant in the same year, married, and spent most of the rest of his life there, except for extensive travels in Germany and Switzerland.

Münster's first major contribution to geography dates from 1540, the year of the publication of his Latin translation of Ptolemy's *Geography*, illustrated with maps of his own design. Having addressed an appeal in 1528 "to all lovers of the joyful art of geography to help him in a true and correct description of the German nation," he spent fifteen years collecting up-to-date information on Germany and adjacent lands and in 1544 published his most important work, *Cosmographei*, "a description of the whole world and everything in it." This book set a new standard in the field, diverging widely from such earlier works as Gregor Reisch's *Margarita philosophica* (1496) and following both a regional and an encyclopedic approach. The work ran to 660 pages in the first edition and to nearly twice as many in later editions; its most valuable parts are those dealing with Germany and Central Europe, as well as the illustrations and maps, the latter drawn by Münster himself. Besides the *Cosmographei* Münster is noted for his common-sense approach to geography: when he asked his German colleagues for information about their districts, he provided them with detailed directions, including a simple plane-table survey, the first of its kind. The *Cosmographei* was among the most popular treatises of the sixteenth and seventeenth centuries: forty-six editions, in six languages, were published prior to 1650.

Although Münster was celebrated in his lifetime as a Hebraic scholar, his influence was most widely felt through his understanding of the interests of the reading public: he was not at all reluctant to include some choice miraculous happenings in his otherwise sober and factual narrative. *Cosmographei* may still be consulted with profit by those interested in the humanist world view in the Reformation.

BIBLIOGRAPHY

An outstanding facs. of the 1550 Basel ed. of the *Cosmographei* was published by Theatrum Orbis Terrarum (Amsterdam, 1967), with 910 woodcuts and intro. by Ruthardt Oehme.

For many years the standard source on the life and works of Münster was Victor Hantzsch, "Sebastian Münster—Leben, Werk, wissenschaftliche Bedeutung," which is *Abhandlungen der K. Sächsischen Gesellschaft der Wissenschaften*, Phil.-hist. kl., **18**, no. 3 (1898). A more recent biography is Karl Heinz Burmeister, *Sebastian Münster: Versuch eines biographischen Gesamtbildes*, Basler Beiträge zur Geschichtswissenschaft no. 91 (Basel, 1963). The most up-to-date bibliography is Karl Heinz Burmeister, *Sebastian Münster—eine Bibliographie* (Wiesbaden, 1964).

GEORGE KISH

MURALT, JOHANNES VON (*b.* Zürich, Switzerland, 18 February 1645; *d.* Zürich, 12 January 1733), *surgery, medicine, anatomy.*

Muralt was a member of the old noble de Muralto family, which had been driven from its seat in Locarno in 1555 upon its conversion to Protestantism. The refugees were eventually invested with citizenship in the Reformed Swiss cities of Bern and Zürich, and found new prosperity. Some of Muralt's ancestors were physicians and diplomats; his father, Johann Melchior Muralt, was a merchant.

Muralt was educated at the Zürich Carolinum. When he was twenty he published his *Schola mutorum ac surdorum*, then set out on his academic travels, which took him to Basel, Leiden, London, Oxford, Paris, and Montpellier. He studied anatomy, surgery, and obstetrics with a number of famous teachers, among them Franciscus Sylvius. He returned to Switzerland to take the M.D. at the University of Basel in 1671 with a dissertation "De morbis parturientium et accidentibus, quae partum insequuntur." The following year he settled in Zürich, where he married Regula Escher; they had many children, including the distinguished physician Johann Conrad Muralt.

The Zürich surgeons' guild challenged Muralt's right to practice in that city, and he encountered widespread disapproval for conducting public animal dissections. His success as a physician overcame all opposition, however, and after five years of argument the Zürich Bürgerrat authorized him to dissect the bodies of executed criminals and of hospital patients who had died of rare diseases. Muralt was admitted to the Academia Caesario-Leopoldina Naturae Curiosorum (with the name "Aretaeus") in 1681; forgetting their old feud, the surgeons also made him an honorary member of their guild.

In 1686 Muralt gave a course of lectures at the surgeons' guildhall, "Zum Schwarzen Garten." His audience was composed of surgeons, their apprentices, medical students, and laymen; the lectures themselves were the first on anatomical subjects to be given in the vernacular. Once a week, for an entire year, Muralt displayed dissected bodies (chiefly animal) and discussed the anatomy, physiology, and pathology of the organs. He expounded the theory of diseases and outlined medical and surgical treatment, including precise directions for the use of medicinal plants and detailed instructions for military surgeons.

In 1688 Muralt was named archiater of Zürich, with duties that comprised devising sanitary measures to protect the city against infectious diseases, advising the municipal marriage court, inspecting apothecaries, supervising the training of midwives, and treating internal diseases in the city's hospital. Ex officio, Muralt also performed all operations for fractures, the stone, and cataracts. In 1691 he was appointed professor of natural sciences at the cathedral school and also became canon of its chapter. He made use of this multitude of offices to transform Zürich into an important center for the study of anatomy and surgery.

Muralt's considerable achievement was largely based upon his surgical skill. He developed new procedures and set them forth systematically in his writings. His work is, however, more notable for the quantity and range of his material than for the depth of his knowledge. His twenty-one titles on anatomy, medicine, and physiology, as well as his thirteen separate publications on mineralogy, zoology, and botany, are marred by repetitiousness. Many of his printed works represent a collection of what are, in effect, his laboratory notes on experiments, natural objects, or the course of a disease (for example, the 174 "Observationes" that he published in *Miscellanea curiosa medico-physica Academiae naturae curiosorum*); others, among them the *Anatomisches Collegium* of 1687, record his lectures more or less verbatim. His principle work on natural history was *Systema physicae experimentalis . . .* (1705–1714); a manuscript regional pharmacopoeia has also been preserved. The last of his writings, *Kurtze und Grundlich Beschreibung der ansteckenden Pest* (1721) remains of interest for its suggestion of the "animal" nature of the plague contagium.

In general, Muralt was a keen observer and a poor critic. He was occasionally prey to superstition, and elements of popular medical beliefs are apparent in his theory of disease. But if some of his therapeutic measures derive from the operations of magic, Muralt was nevertheless an effective physician and a tireless popularizer and communicator of genuinely scientific knowledge.

BIBLIOGRAPHY

I. ORIGINAL WORKS. Muralt's writings include *Vademecum anatomicum sive clavis medicinae* (Zurich, 1677); *Anatomisches Collegium* (Nuremberg, 1687); *Curationes medicae observationibus et experimentis anatomicis mixtae* (Amsterdam, 1688); *Kinder- und Hebammenbüchlein* (Zurich, 1689; Basel, 1697); *Chirurgische Schriften* (Basel, 1691); *Hippocrates Helveticus oder der Eydgenössische Stadt- Land- und Hauss-Artzt* (Basel, 1692); *Systema physicae experimentalis*, 4 vols. (Zurich, 1705–1714), of which the fourth part, *Botanologia seu Helvetiae paradisus*, was trans. into German as *Eydgenössischer Lust-Garte* (Zurich, 1715); *Schriften von der Wund-Artzney* (Basel, 1711); *Kriegs- und Soldaten-Diaet* (Zurich, 1712); and *Sichere Anleitung wider den dissmal grassirenden Rothen Schaden* (Zurich, 1712).

II. SECONDARY LITERATURE. On Muralt and his work, see C. Brunner, *Die Verwundeten in den Kriegen der alten Eidgenossenschaft* (Tübingen, 1903); and *Aus den Briefen hervorragender Schweizer Ärzte des 17. Jahrhunderts* (Basel, 1919), written with W. von Muralt; E. Eidenbenz, "Dr. Leonhard von Muralts 'Pharmocopoea domestica,'" in *Schweizerische Apothekerzeitung*, **60** (1922), 393–399; J. Finsler, *Bemerkungen aus dem Leben des Johannes von Muralt* (Zurich, 1833); H. Koller, "Das anatomische Institut der Universität Zürich in seiner geschichtlichen Entwicklung," in *Zürcher medizingeschichtliche Abhandlungen*, **11** (1926); K. Meyer-Ahrens, "Die Arztfamilie von Muralt, insbesondere Joh. v. Muralt, Arzt in Zürich," in *Schweizerische Zeitschrift für Heilkunde*, **1** (1862), 268–289, 423–436, and **2** (1863), 25–47; O. Obschlager, "Der Zürcher Stadtarzt Joh. von Muralt und der medizinische Aberglaube seiner Zeit," M.D. dissertation, University of Zurich (1926); G. Sticker, *Abhandlungen aus der Seuchengeschichte und Seuchenlehre*, vol. I *Die Pest* (Giessen, 1910); and G. A. Wehrli, "Die Bader, Barbiere und Wundärzte im alten Zürich," in *Mitteilungen der Antiquarischen Gesellschaft Zürich*, **30**, pt. 3 (1927), 99.

JÖRN HENNING WOLF

MURCHISON, RODERICK IMPEY (*b.* Tarradale, Ross and Cromarty, Scotland, 19 February 1792; *d.* London, England, 22 October 1871), *geology.*

Murchison was born into a long-established family of Highland landowners. His father, Kenneth Murchison, died when the boy was only four; and after his childhood he never lived in Scotland. He was educated at the military college at Great Marlow and in 1808 saw active service briefly in the Peninsular War. In 1815 he married Charlotte Hugonin and soon afterward resigned his commission. From 1816 to 1818 Murchison traveled in Italy and under his wife's influence showed signs of artistic interests, but on his return he sold his family estate and for several years devoted himself chiefly to fox hunting. A chance acquaintance with Humphry Davy turned his attention toward science, however, and in 1824 he settled in London and attended lectures at the Royal Institution. Encouraged by his wife, Murchison soon focused his interests on geology, chiefly through the influence of William Buckland; he was elected a fellow of the Geological Society of London in 1825 and of the Royal Society in 1826. With the advantages of a private income, he was able thereafter to devote himself entirely to science.

Taking as a model the stratigraphical handbook of W. D. Conybeare and W. Phillips (1822), Murchison began the long series of geological studies which brought him worldwide fame and recognition. Almost every summer, for over twenty years, he undertook long and often arduous journeys in search of new successions of strata which would help to bring order to the reconstruction of the history of the earth. He entered geology during the first great period of stratigraphical research, and stratigraphy remained his chief area of interest. He was not a theoretician and generally delegated the paleontological parts of his work to others, but he was an excellent observer with a flair for grasping the major features of an area from a few rapid traverses.

Some of his earliest work convinced Murchison of the superiority of fossils over lithology as criteria of geological age: in 1826 he showed that the fauna and flora of the isolated coalfield of Brora in northeastern Scotland indicated it to be of the same age as the English Oolites (that is, Jurassic), although the rock types resembled the Coal Measures (that is, Carboniferous). In 1828 he accompanied Charles Lyell through the celebrated volcanic districts of the Massif Central into northern Italy, and their joint papers suggest that Murchison was at this time much influenced by Lyell's theoretical views. His subsequent work in the Alpine region, some of it in the company of Adam Sedgwick, included an attempt to show the continuity of the Secondary and Tertiary strata; but, at the same time, firsthand experience of the vast scale of folding and faulting in the Alps led Murchison toward an increasing catastrophist emphasis on the role of occasional episodes of drastic disturbance in the crust of the earth.

During these first years of research Murchison's travels brought him into contact with most of the leading geologists on the Continent, and his position as secretary (from 1827) of the Geological Society made him equally well known in Britain. In 1831 he was elected president of the Geological Society (he held office until 1833, and again from 1841 to 1843), and in the same year began his most important research.

At this time the major features of the stratigraphical succession had been clarified down to the Old Red Sandstone underlying the Carboniferous rocks, but below that was what Murchison called "interminable grauwacke"—rocks containing few fossils, in which no uniform sequence had been detected. It was widely doubted whether the method of correlation by fossils would even be applicable to these ancient Transition strata, yet in them—if anywhere—lay the possibility of finding evidence for the origin of life itself. Acting on a hint of Buckland's, Murchison was fortunate to find in the Welsh borderland an area in which there was a conformable sequence downward from the Old Red Sandstone into Transition strata with abundant fossils. He gave a preliminary report of his work at the first meeting (1831) of the British Association for the Advancement of Science; and in 1835, after further fieldwork, he named the strata Silurian after the Silures, a Romano-British tribe that had lived in the region.

The Silurian constituted a major system of strata with a highly distinctive fauna, notable for an abundance of invertebrates and for the complete absence, except in the youngest strata, of any remains of vertebrates or land plants. It thus seemed to Murchison to mark a major period in the progressive history of life on earth. Even before he had completed his great monographic account *The Silurian System* (1839), its validity had been rapidly recognized by geologists in many other parts of the world. The striking uniformity of the Silurian fauna, in contrast with the highly differentiated faunal provinces of the present day, was taken by Murchison to underline the limitations of Lyell's uniformitarian approach, and was attributed by him to the greater climatic uniformity of the globe in Silurian times, a result of the greater influence of conducted heat from the still incandescent interior of the earth.

Murchison was well aware of the vast economic implications of his delineation of a Silurian system. If the Silurian period had truly predated the establishment of terrestrial vegetation, the recognition of Silurian fossils in any part of the world would reliably indicate a base line beneath which it was pointless to search for coal: this would save much useless expenditure and also help to assess more accurately the possible reserves of undiscovered coal. A report by Henry de la Beche of coal plants in the "grauwacke" of Devonshire (1834) therefore seemed to Murchison to be a very serious anomaly, and he devoted several years to an attempt to explain it away. He and Sedgwick discovered first that the fossil plants were in fact in strata of Coal Measure age overlying the true "grauwacke"; and later, in 1839, following a suggestion of William Lonsdale's, they concluded that even these older strata were not pre-Silurian, as they had originally thought, but were the lateral equivalents of the Old Red Sandstone. This definition of a Devonian system was at first criticized as being based purely on paleontological criteria and not on any plain evidence of superposition; but Murchison and Sedgwick soon showed that the distinctive Devonian invertebrate fauna occurred in Westphalia in the expected position immediately below the Carboniferous strata. The following year (1840) Murchison resolved the matter by discovering in European Russia a sequence of undisturbed strata in which the Devonian was clearly underlain by Silurian and overlain by Carboniferous, and in which Devonian invertebrates were interbedded with Old Red Sandstone fish. This established the temporal equivalence of the Devonian and Old Red Sandstone despite their contrasting lithology and fauna.

A second expedition to Russia in 1841 took Murchison as far as the Urals and confirmed this Paleozoic sequence. At the same time it showed him how undisturbed and unaltered sediments could change their appearance radically when traced laterally into a region of mountain-building, and this convinced him of the validity of Lyell's hypothesis of metamorphism. He also found a vast development of Paleozoic strata overlying the Carboniferous and named them Permian after the Perm region near the Urals.

In 1839 Murchison's financial position had greatly improved, and he had moved into a grander house, which thereafter became a fashionable salon of the London intelligentsia. His enhanced social position, coupled with the many distinctions conferred on him for his work in Russia, unfortunately made him increasingly conscious of social prestige and increasingly arrogant and intolerant of opposition in scientific matters.

Murchison's capacity for transforming scientific controversies into paramilitary "campaigns" against opponents had already been evident in his treatment of de la Beche over the Devonian problem. It was now shown much more seriously in his controversy with Sedgwick over the base of the Silurian. In the same year that Murchison had first investigated the Transition strata, Sedgwick had begun to unravel still older strata in Wales; and when Murchison first established the Silurian, Sedgwick had suggested the name Cambrian system (after the Latin name for Wales) for the older rocks. During their only joint fieldwork in Wales (in 1834) Murchison had assured Sedgwick that the latter's Upper Cambrian lay below his own Lower Silurian strata, although, as expected,

there was a faunal gradation between the two. But when Murchison later realized that the fossils of the Upper Cambrian Bala series were indistinguishable from his own Lower Silurian Caradoc series, he boldly proclaimed their identity and annexed the Upper Cambrian into his Silurian system.

Sedgwick protested that the Cambrian had been clearly defined by reference to an undisputed succession of strata in northern Wales and that it was wrong to alter the meaning of the term just because its upper part contained Silurian fossils. But Murchison continued to annex more and more of the Cambrian into his Lower Silurian, until the two terms were virtually synonymous. Sedgwick claimed that this unjustified annexation was designed to cover two major mistakes of Murchison's. He had misinterpreted the Lower Silurian succession in its type area and had therefore believed that these strata were younger than the Upper Cambrian when in fact they were of the same age; and—an even more serious mistake—he had wrongly incorporated some Upper Silurian strata (May Hill sandstone) into the Lower Silurian Caradoc series, despite their very different faunas, thus giving the Silurian fauna a spurious uniformity down into Sedgwick's Cambrian.

But there was even more to the controversy than technical mistakes and a priority dispute over stratigraphical nomenclature. Each geologist, as a firm believer in a progressionist interpretation of the fossil record, ardently desired the distinction of showing that his own system contained the evidence for the origin of life on earth. Thus, when Murchison wrote his *Geology of Russia* (1845), he asserted that the "unequivocal base-line of palaeozoic existence" was to be seen in the Lower Silurian strata, within which there was a "gradual decrement and disappearance of fossils" toward the base. Furthermore, in Scandinavia (where he had traveled in 1844) these strata were immediately underlain by "Azoic" crystalline schists, in which Murchison believed that it was "hopeless to expect" to find fossils. This was not because they had been metamorphosed (although he agreed that they resembled the metamorphic rocks of later periods) but because they had been formed under conditions too hot to support life. He therefore argued, against Lyell, that geology provided "undeniable proofs of a beginning" to life on earth. His desire to have sole credit for providing these "proofs" is shown by his obstinate insistence that the Silurian fauna was the earliest. Thus when Joachim Barrande first described a distinctive "primordial" fauna (the Cambrian of modern geology) below the previously known Lower Silurian faunas, Murchison did not allow it as a possible paleontological basis for Sedgwick's

Cambrian but incorporated it too into his Silurian.

In 1846 Murchison was knighted and served as president of the British Association for the Advancement of Science; and in 1849 his work was recognized by the award of the Royal Society's Copley Medal. He later published an updated and more popular version of his work as *Siluria* (1854), expressly in order to deliver a "knock-down blow" (the aggressive metaphor is characteristic) to those, like Lyell, who still denied the reality of organic progression. The book also contained an assessment of the world's probable resources of gold, designed to reassure those who feared that the recent Australian gold rush presaged a slump in that metal's monetary value. In 1855 he succeeded de la Beche as director general of the Geological Survey of Great Britain (thus becoming a professional scientist for the first time), and in 1856 he was appointed to a royal commission to report on the nation's coal reserves.

From the 1840's Murchison became increasingly rigid and intolerant of scientific innovation. He opposed the glacial theory of Louis Agassiz and continued to assert that icebergs alone had been responsible for the transport of erratic blocks ("drift") long after most other geologists had accepted at least a modified glacialism: under his influence the Geological Survey's maps long continued to use the term "drift" for glacial and postglacial deposits. Murchison's last major fieldwork, in 1858–1860, was devoted to arguing that the Moine schists of the northwestern Highlands were Silurian sediments, although he had always favored relatively catastrophist interpretations of mountain tectonics and had been convinced a decade earlier of the reality of large-scale thrusting in the Alps. He was totally opposed to Darwin's evolutionary theory.

Murchison retired temporarily from the council of the Geological Society in 1863 and was therefore eligible to be awarded the Wollaston Medal the following year. He was created a baronet in 1866. He had earlier been one of the founders of the Royal Geographical Society and was for many years its president. Indeed, despite his post with the Geological Survey, he was better known as a geographer than as a geologist in his later years, being prominent in the support of David Livingstone's and other expeditions. The Murchison Falls of the Nile in Uganda are named after him.

BIBLIOGRAPHY

The following are the more important of Murchison's published works: "On the Coal-Field of Brora in Sutherlandshire, and on Some Other Stratified Deposits in the North of Scotland," in *Transactions of the Geological Society of London*, 2nd ser., **2**, pt. 2 (1829), 293–326; "A Sketch of the Structure of the Eastern Alps . . .," *ibid.*, **3**, pt. 2 (1832), 301–420, written with Adam Sedgwick; *The Silurian System, Founded on Geological Researches in the Counties of Salop, Hereford, Radnor, Montgomery, Caermarthen, Brecon, Pembroke, Monmouth, Gloucester, Worcester, and Stafford; With Descriptions of the Coal-Fields and Overlying Formations* (London, 1839); "Classification of the Older Rocks of Devonshire and Cornwall," in *Philosophical Magazine*, **14** (1839), 242–260, written with Adam Sedgwick; "On the Classification and Distribution of the Older or Palaeozoic Rocks of the North of Germany and of Belgium, as Compared With Formations of the Same Age in the British Isle," in *Transactions of the Geological Society of London*, 2nd ser., **6**, pt. 2 (1842), 221–302, written with Adam Sedgwick; and *The Geology of Russia in Europe and the Ural Mountains*, 2 vols. (London–Paris, 1845), written with Édouard de Verneuil and Alexander von Keyserling—Murchison wrote the stratigraphy in vol. I.

See also "On the Palaeozoic Deposits of Scandinavia and the Baltic Provinces of Russia, and Their Relations to Azoic or More Ancient Crystalline Rocks; With an Account of Some Great Features of Dislocation and Metamorphism Along Their Northern Frontiers," in *Quarterly Journal of the Geological Society of London*, **1** (1845), 467–494; "On the Meaning Originally Attached to the Term 'Cambrian System,' and on the Evidences Since Obtained of Its Being Geologically Synonymous With the Previously Established Term 'Lower Silurian,'" *ibid.*, **3** (1847), 165–179; "On the Geological Structure of the Alps, Apennines and Carpathians, More Especially to Prove a Transition From Secondary to Tertiary Rocks, and the Development of Eocene Deposits in Southern Europe," *ibid.*, **5** (1849), 157–312; *Siluria. The History of the Oldest Known Rocks Containing Organic Remains, With a Brief Sketch of the Distribution of Gold Over the Earth* (London, 1854); and "On the Succession of the Older Rocks in the Northernmost Counties of Scotland; With Some Observations on the Orkney and Shetland Islands," in *Quarterly Journal of the Geological Society of London*, **15** (1859), 353–418.

Murchison's field notebooks and a collection of his scientific correspondence are in the library of the Geological Society of London. Material in the Institute of Geological Sciences, London (formerly Geological Survey), is described by John C. Thackray, "Essential Source-Material of Roderick Murchison," in *Journal of the Society for the Bibliography of Natural History*, **6**, pt. 3 (1972), 162–170.

Some excerpts from Murchison's journals and letters are published in the only full-length biography, Archibald Geikie, *Life of Sir Roderick Murchison . . . Based on His Journals and Letters With Notices of His Scientific Contemporaries and a Sketch of the Rise and Growth of Palaeozoic Geology in Britain*, 2 vols. (London, 1875), which also includes a fairly full list of Murchison's publications.

M. J. S. RUDWICK

MURPHY, JAMES BUMGARDNER (*b.* Morganton, North Carolina, 4 August 1884; *d.* Bar Harbor, Maine, 24 August 1950), *biology.*

Murphy was the son of Patrick Livingston Murphy, a pioneer in modern psychiatric therapy and director of the state mental hospital at Morganton. He received the B.S. from the University of North Carolina in 1905 and the M.D. in 1909 from the Johns Hopkins University, where his surgical finesse was appreciated by Harvey Cushing, who became his good friend. From 1910 to 1950, the year of his retirement and of his death, he pursued research on cancer and related physiological problems as a scientist and later as administrator at the Rockefeller Institute in New York City.

Brought to the Institute in 1910 by the noted cancer researcher and his first collaborator, Peyton Rous, Murphy soon demonstrated a skill in developing methods to answer the ill-defined and unlimited questions concerning the origin and growth of malignant tissues. In showing that the frozen and dried tissue extract of the spindle-cell chicken sarcoma (Chicken Tumor I) could be used to transmit this form of cancer, he produced one of the earliest successful applications of the process known as lyophilization, now commonly used in biological research. Later he perfected the technique of growing a chicken tumor virus in fertilized eggs, a method of fundamental importance to virus research.

In 1923 Murphy was placed in charge of the department of cancer research, succeeding Rous, who had turned to other research interests. Thus Murphy began to play a significant role in determining the direction of cancer research for over a quarter of a century at the Rockefeller Institute.

Two lectures presented by Murphy as Thayer lecturer at Johns Hopkins in 1935 summarized the four main lines of cancer research, for which he had helped to lay the foundation, in the first half of the twentieth century. These areas, which were explored independently, included the discovery that certain tumors in mice could be transplanted, that specific chemical substances produced malignancies after an animal was repeatedly exposed to them, that certain cancers occurred more frequently in individuals whose ancestors had expressed the same disease, and that chicken tumors were transplantable and were equivalent to cancer in mammals. He emphasized that the data gathered to test the inheritance factor were useful in examining the possibility that cancer was an infectious disease transmitted by a parasite; he later became more skeptical of this mode of transmission as an explanation of the origin of cancer. By 1942 Murphy had reduced the main lines of research to the first three of these areas and pointed out how study of chemical carcinogens was on the rise.

A skilled administrator, Murphy wisely marshaled public support for cancer research and stressed the need for increasing public awareness of the early signs of treatable cancers, especially breast and uterine tumors. He encouraged the formation of the Woman's Field Army, which campaigned for women to seek medical aid when suspicious symptoms in these areas first developed. As a member of the board of the American Society for Control of Cancer, which became the American Cancer Society in 1929, he sought to change public opinion from one of shame toward cancer victims to sympathy for them and interest in their care.

Murphy contributed his knowledge and talents to a broad range of activities in the field of cancer research. He lectured extensively and was a member of the National Academy of Sciences, National Research Council, American Society for Cancer Research, of which he was president from 1921 to 1922, American Society of Experimental Pathology, and a number of foreign scientific societies. He was on the editorial board of the journal *Cancer Research*, and served as a delegate to several international congresses devoted to cancer studies. He received numerous medals and awards, and honorary doctorates from the University of Louvain, the University of North Carolina, and Oglethorpe University.

At his death, Murphy was survived by his wife, Ray Slater Murphy, and his two sons.

BIBLIOGRAPHY

Murphy published over 130 papers between 1907 and 1950. Over three-quarters of these were collaborative papers published in association with visitors and staff at the Rockefeller Institute, including F. Duran-Reynals, Arthur W. M. Ellis, Fred Gates, R. G. Hussey, Karl Landsteiner, Douglas A. MacFayden, J. Maisin, John J. Morton, Waro Nakahara, Peyton Rous, H. D. Taylor, W. H. Tytler, and especially Ernest Sturm, his last assistant and colleague for 31 years.

His more significant papers include a series published between 1911 and 1914 describing transplanted chicken tumors. Most appear in the *Journal of Experimental Medicine;* "The Lymphocyte in Resistance to Tissue Grafting, Malignant Disease, and Tuberculosis Infection. An Experimental Study," in Rockefeller Institute *Monographs,* no. 21 (1926); "Experimental Approach to the Cancer Problem. I. Four Important Phases of Cancer Research. II. Avian Tumors in Relation to the General Problem of Malignancy," in *Bulletin of the Johns Hopkins Hospital,* **56** (1935), 1–31, two lectures of the Thayer lectureship; "An Analysis of the Trends in Cancer Research," in *Journal of the American Medical Association,*

120 (1942), 107–111, Barnard Hospital lecture; and "The Cancer Control Movement," in *North Carolina Medical Journal*, **5** (Apr. 1944), 121–125.

A series of papers produced in the last decade of his life on the development of experimental leukemia and its relationship to basic physiological processes, written with Ernest Sturm, include "The Transmission of an Induced Lymphatic Leukemia and Lymphosarcoma in the Rat," in *Cancer Research*, **1** (1941), 379–383; "The Effect of Sodium Pentobarbital, Paradichlorbenzene, Amyl Acetate, and Sovasol on Induced Resistance to a Transplanted Leukemia of the Rat," *ibid.*, **3** (1943), 173–175; "The Adrenals and Susceptibility to Transplanted Leukemia of Rats," in *Science*, **98** (1943), 568–569; "The Effect of Adrenalectomy on the Susceptibility of Rats to a Transplantable Leukemia," in *Cancer Research*, **4** (1944), 384–388; "Effect of Adrenal Cortical and Pituitary Adrenotropic Hormones on Transplanted Leukemia in Rats," in *Science*, **99** (1944), 303; "The Inhibiting Effect of Ethyl Urethane on the Development of Lymphatic Leukemia in Rats," in *Cancer Research*, **7** (1947), 417–420; "The Effect of Diethylstilbestrol on the Incidence of Leukemia in Male Mice of the Rockefeller Institute Leukemia Strain (R.I.L.)," *ibid.*, **9** (1949), 88–89; and "The Effect of Adrenal Grafting on Transplanted Lymphatic Leukemia in Rats," *ibid.*, **10** (1950), 191–193.

For brief biographies of Murphy see *National Cyclopedia of American Biography*, XXXVIII, 69; an obituary in *Journal of the American Medical Association*, **144** (14 Oct. 1950), 562, and a longer biography by C. C. Little in *Biographical Memoirs of the National Academy of Sciences*, **34** (1960), 183–203, which contains a bibliography arranged chronologically.

For a discussion of his work at the Rockefeller Institute see George W. Corner, *A History of the Rockefeller Institute 1901–1953. Origins and Growth* (New York, 1964), *passim*. Personal business papers and correspondence are held by the Rockefeller University and Murphy's family.

AUDREY B. DAVIS

MURRAY, GEORGE ROBERT MILNE (*b.* Arbroath, Scotland, 11 November 1858; *d.* Stonehaven, Scotland, 16 December 1911), *botany*.

Murray was one of eight children born to George and Helen Margaret Murray. He was educated in Arbroath until 1875, when he spent a year in Strasbourg studying under Anton de Bary. In 1876 he became an assistant in the botany department of the British Museum, where he was put in charge of the cryptogamic collections. He spent the rest of his career in this department, becoming Keeper in 1895. His early research was in mycology, and was of sufficient taxonomic interest to result in his election as fellow of the Linnean Society in 1878, before he was twenty-one, and an invitation to write an article on fungi for the *Encyclopaedia Britannica* in 1879. The natural history departments of the British Museum moved to South Kensington in 1881, and Murray was responsible for the transfer of the cryptogams, reorganization of the herbarium, and later development of the section.

Murray always maintained his links with Scotland and worked there during vacations, investigating salmon disease and collecting diatoms and pelagic algae from the sea and the lochs while on board the Fishery Board's vessel *Garland*. New techniques in trawling for phytoplankton by pumping water through fine silk nets allowed him to study seasonal variations in forms; he taught these methods to captains of trawlers, who then collected for him in the course of their normal business. His work on the reproduction of diatoms by asexual spore formation was published in 1897. Working with *Biddulphia* spp., *Chaetoceros* spp., and *Coscinodiscus concinnus*, he showed that small specimens growing inside the shells of adult forms were not only a means of rejuvenating those individuals, but might divide into two, four, or eight new individuals, which would eventually be released and grow to full size.

Murray was associated with several expeditions, generally sponsored by the museum. In 1886 he visited the West Indies as a naturalist attached to the solar eclipse expedition, and in 1888 he sorted the algae and fungi from the expedition to Fernando de Noronha, and wrote those sections of the report. He was secretary to the West Indies exploration committee from 1891, and in 1897 he returned there on the *Para* to visit Barbados, Haiti, Jamaica, and Panama, collecting particularly *Coccosphaera*, a hitherto little-known unicellular alga. He differentiated the species, and showed how the cover of overlapping calcareous scales, arranged in a definite order, provide defensive armor while still allowing for growth, an evolutionary advance on the structure of diatoms.

In 1898 he organized an expedition under the Royal Geographic Society in the *Oceana* to collect material in an area off the coast of Ireland where the sea bed dropped steeply. He was also scientific director of the *Discovery* expedition of 1901, but sailed only as far as Cape Town. He organized the ship's stores and apparatus, and edited *The Antarctic Manual* for the expedition, writing a brief section, "Notes on Botany and How to Collect Specimens."

In 1884 he married Helen Welsh; they had one son and one daughter. He was elected fellow of the Royal Society in 1897. In 1905 he retired because of ill health and returned to Scotland.

Massee named the new fungal species *Schizophyllum murrayi* after Murray.

BIBLIOGRAPHY

I. ORIGINAL WORKS. Murray published approximately forty papers on cryptogams and oceanography, in which he described new species, surveyed distribution, and listed specimens in the British Museum collections. Many of these papers appeared in *Journal of Botany, British and Foreign*. His reports on the work of the botany department from 1895 to 1903 appeared in *Journal of Botany*. His other works include the section on fungi in A. Henfrey, ed., *An Elementary Course of Botany*, 3rd ed. (London, 1878), 455–472; 4th ed. (London, 1884), 428–449; *A Handbook of Cryptogamic Botany* (London, 1889), written with A. W. Bennett; two articles, "Algae" and "Fungi," in *The natural history of the Island of Ferdinand de Noronha, based on the Collections made by the . . . Expedition of 1887* (London, 1890), 75–81, extracted from *Journal of the Linnean Society*, Botany, **26** (1888), 1–95, and *ibid.*, Zoology, **20** (1888), 473–570; *Phycological Memoirs*, pts. I–III (London, 1892–1895), edited by Murray; *Introduction to the Study of Seaweeds* (London, 1895); "Report of Observations on Plant Plankton," in *Edinburgh Fisheries Board Report*, **15** (1897), pt. 3, 212–218; *Report of the Lords Commissioners of H.M. Treasury of the Departmental Committee on the Botanical Work and Collections at the British Museum and at Kew . . . 1901*, questions 1–198 (London, 1901), 1–13; and *The Antarctic Manual* (London, 1901), edited by Murray.

His scientific papers may be traced through the Royal Society *Catalogue of Scientific Papers*, XVII, 429–430. Papers mentioned in the text are "On the Reproduction of Some Marine Diatoms," in *Proceedings of the Royal Society of Edinburgh*, **21** (1897), 207–218; and "On the Nature of the Coccospheres and Rhabdospheres," in *Philosophical Transactions of the Royal Society*, **190B** (1898), 427–441, plus 2 plates, written with V. H. Blackman.

II. SECONDARY LITERATURE. The most useful obituary is James Britten, in *Journal of Botany*, **50** (1912), 73–75. There is also an obituary by K.F. and W.C., in *Proceedings of the Royal Society*, **B86** (1913), xxi–xxiii; and the entry by G. S. Boulger, in Sidney Lee, ed., *Dictionary of National Biography*, supp. 1901–1911 (Oxford, 1912), 667–668.

DIANA M. SIMPKINS

MURRAY, JOHN (*b.* Cobourg, Ontario, Canada, 3 March 1841; *d.* Kirkliston, Scotland, 16 March 1914), *oceanography, marine geology.*

As editor (after C. Wyville Thomson's death) of the fifty-volume *Report on the Scientific Results of the Voyage of H.M.S. Challenger During the Years 1872–1876* (London, 1880–1895; reprinted New York, 1966) and coauthor (with Johan Hjort) of *The Depths of the Ocean* (London, 1912), Murray presided over the organization of oceanography as a separate science. His most significant personal contribution was the mapping and classification of the sediments on the ocean bottom.

Raised "on the plains of Canada which lie between the great lakes of Erie, Huron, and Ontario" (J. L. Graham, p. 173), to which his parents, Robert and Elizabeth (Macfarlane) Murray, migrated in 1834, John Murray first saw the ocean when he sailed to their native Scotland at age seventeen. This voyage and his first glimpse of the rise and fall of the tide along the Scottish coast was the beginning of his lifelong interest in the ocean. His maternal grandfather, for whom he founded a natural history museum at Bridge of Allan, Stirlingshire, sent him to Stirling High School and the University of Edinburgh, where he studied medicine with John Goodsir and his successor, William Turner. In 1868 he sailed on the whaler *Jan Mayen* from Peterhead to Spitzbergen and the Arctic, returning with a large collection of marine organisms and observations on currents, temperatures, and sea ice. Murray then returned to Edinburgh to enter the physical laboratory of P. G. Tait. Marine biology was left for vacations, when Murray, Laurence Pullar, and the anatomist Morison Watson would hire a fishing boat from which to dredge along the rugged Scottish coast.

Murray's days as a gentleman-student (he took no examination or degree) ended in 1872. Tait and Sir William Thomson (who in a chance encounter with Murray aboard his yacht, was impressed by Murray's knowledge of the sea) recommended him to C. Wyville Thomson, regius professor of natural history at Edinburgh and scientific director of the voyage of circumnavigation which the Royal Society was organizing for the British navy. Murray spent the next three and a half years aboard H.M.S. *Challenger*. At thirty-one he was the oldest of Thomson's four scientific assistants. Less clearly bent on a scientific career than the two younger naturalists, Henry N. Moseley and Rudolph von Willemoes-Suhm (the fourth assistant, John Y. Buchanan, was a chemist), Murray took over, perhaps by default, the newest of the *Challenger* expedition's scientific quests: investigating the deposits on the sea bottom.

Of the major sedimentary types, only globigerina ooze had been named prior to Murray's work aboard *Challenger*, and there was no agreement whether the organisms whose calcareous skeletons made up this deposit lived at the surface or the bottom. By his careful towing of fine nets to catch living specimens, Murray proved that they were surface dwellers, confirming the earlier view of J. W. Bailey. Murray also collected the surface-living forms whose skeletons made up the other major organic sediment types, which he named radiolarian, diatom, and pteropod oozes. The most widespread deposit was a brownish, largely inorganic mud. Murray named it red clay, showed that it originated mainly from volcanic dust, and deduced that it covered those parts of the deep ocean where calcareous skeletons were so few that they had almost all dissolved, an explanation that still stands. Murray's work with the sediments he collected demonstrated conclusively the surprising slowness of deposition over much of the ocean. Murray increased considerably the collection of pelagic animals by towing at depths the nets previously used only at the surface. He also took charge of the small collection of vertebrates.

Murray combined exceptional organizing skill with a strong desire to stake out new scientific territory. When Thomson's scientific staff was disbanded in 1877 shortly after the return of the *Challenger*, Murray stayed on to help Thomson set up, in Edinburgh, the Challenger Expedition Commission, charged with preparing a report in five years. With Thomson and Alexander Agassiz, Murray sorted into groups the contents of 600 cases of specimens, each group to be the subject of a specialist's monograph. Thomson's health soon gave way under the combined pressures of teaching, public lecturing, and accounting personally to the British Treasury for the *Challenger Report*. He died early in 1882 as the grant expired; printing had barely begun.

Pressed by the Royal Society, the Treasury appointed Murray as Thomson's successor with another five-year grant, increased by 20 percent. Murray distributed those specimens which remained in Edinburgh, hounded his dilatory authors, and saw their contributions through the press. When the Treasury tried to halt the project in 1889, with the *Report* still unfinished after a year's extension to his original five, Murray fought back. He saved the *Report*, but the Treasury paid him only a small lump sum for the editorial work from 1889 to 1895; he thus must have been put to considerable personal expense. Among the final volumes of the *Challenger Report*, which might otherwise have failed of publication, were Murray's masterly two-volume *Summary* (1895) and the volume on *Deep-Sea Deposits* (1891), written with Alphonse Renard of the University of Ghent.

Murray did not neglect his own researches, even during the years he traveled around Europe to prod his authors and edited the thousands of manuscript pages they sent him. Cruises in *Knight Errant* (1880) and *Triton* (1882) enabled him and his *Challenger* shipmate, Commander Thomas Tizard, to confirm, by their discovery of the Wyville Thomson ridge, Thomson's proposed solution to the problem of faunal distribution at the bottom of the Faroe-Shetland channel.

Murray's study of coral reefs led him to challenge Charles Darwin's widely accepted notion that they were universally built up on subsiding island bases. Murray suggested instead that reef building could begin when deposition brought a submerged base close enough to the surface for corals to grow, so that uplift rather than subsidence could be the dominant mechanism in some localities. In Murray's view the reef grew seaward on a talus of dead shells, while the retardation of coral growth away from the sea and the solvent action of seawater on the dead coral accounted for the formation of lagoons. Although his views have not stood up, Murray stimulated much contemporary debate, especially after the eighth duke of Argyll charged that only Darwin's great name had prevented the replacement of his theory by Murray's. Murray stimulated the long series of reef explorations by his friend Alexander Agassiz, and with another friend, Robert Irvine, Murray studied the deposition of carbonate and silicate by organisms and the composition of manganese nodules. In 1886, working from a few samples of rocks and deep-ocean sediments, Murray deduced that the Antarctic ice sheet must be underlain by continental rocks. He was one of the strongest advocates of the renewal of polar exploration which began about 1900. His 1888 estimates of the proportion of the ocean floor at different depths, based on rope and wire soundings, have not been much altered by the incalculably greater number of soundings provided since the 1920's by the sonic fathometer.

Murray and Renard's 1891 volume, *Deep Sea Deposits*, in the *Challenger Report*, was the first treatment of its subject for the entire ocean. Murray and Renard classified and named the major sediment types, delineated their provinces, and provided their successors with most of their subsequent research problems, including the origin of glauconite and manganese nodules. From his comparison of marine sediments with the sedimentary rocks found on land, Murray came to a firm belief that the ocean basins have been a persistent feature of the surface of the earth throughout geologic time. To the International Congress of Zoology meeting in Leiden in 1895, Murray gave the classic statement of the relations between the physical conditions of life and the faunal and floral provinces of the ocean.

In spite of his commitments to the *Challenger Report* and his own researches for it, Murray also found time to use his organizational skills in other areas. From 1883 to 1894 he dredged on the east and west coasts of Scotland in *Medusa*, a specially equipped steam yacht. He founded marine stations at Granton and Millport; the latter is still in operation. Murray was also a founder of the short-lived meteorological observatory atop Ben Nevis. He served as a scientific member of the Fishery Board for Scotland, and he represented the British government at the 1899 Stockholm conference, which founded the International Council for the Exploration of the Sea. After the *Challenger Report* was completed in 1895, Murray organized a survey of the freshwater lochs of Scotland with Frederick Pullar, carrying it to completion (6 vols., 1910) after the latter's drowning.

Murray was able to continue his scientific career after the dissolution of the Challenger Expedition Commission in 1889 because of the independence provided by his marriage (1889) to Isabel Henderson, the only daughter of a Glasgow shipowner. His fortune was further increased by his development of phosphate mining on Christmas Island, in the Indian Ocean. Murray discovered the island's rich deposits when a small specimen was sent to him by a *Challenger* shipmate. He persuaded the British government to annex the island in 1887 and to grant him a lease in 1891. Phosphate exploitation began in earnest about 1900; Murray used his substantial profits to support both a new "Challenger Office" at his home outside Edinburgh and the four-month cruise of the Norwegian fisheries' vessel *Michael Sars* in 1910. The general account by Murray and Johan Hjort of his voyage became the leading textbook of oceanography for three decades after its publication in 1912, and the small volume *The Ocean*, written by Murray himself and published in 1913, served as a popular introduction to the subject. Murray died in an automobile accident in 1914, leaving most of his mining fortune to subsidize oceanographic research.

BIBLIOGRAPHY

I. ORIGINAL WORKS. A complete list of Sir John Murray's scientific writings is given in *Proceedings of the Royal Society of Edinburgh*, **35** (1914–1915), 313–317. Murray's major works are his coral-reef theory, "On the Structure and Origin of Coral Reefs and Islands," *ibid.*, **10** (1880), 505–518, and the volume on *Deep Sea Deposits* (Edinburgh, 1891), in *Challenger Reports*, written with A. Renard. Of primary biographical material, the most important items are the bound volume of outgoing letters and the corrected copy of Murray's autobiography (in the form of an obituary booklet); both are in the Mineralogical Library of the British Museum (Natural History). The 126 letters to Alexander Agassiz in the Library of the Museum of Comparative Zoology, Harvard University, and the typescript narrative of the Christmas Island phosphate industry in the possession of the Murray family, are also important. Additional material is in the Public Record Office and the Royal Society.

II. SECONDARY LITERATURE. There is no biography of Murray. In its absence one must turn to the general histories of oceanography: Margaret Deacon, *Scientists and the Sea 1650–1900* (London, 1971), and Susan Schlee, *To the Edge of an Unfamiliar World* (New York, 1973), and to the obituary articles: G. R. Agassiz, in *Proceedings of the American Academy of Arts and Sciences*, **52** (1917), 853–859; J. Graham Kerr, in *Proceedings of the Royal Society of Edinburgh*, **35** (1914–1915), 305–317; Robert C. Mossman, in *Symons's Meteorological Magazine*, **49** (1914), 45–47; and Sir Arthur Shipley, in *Proceedings of the Royal Society*, **89B** (1915–1916), vi–xv, and in *Cornhill Magazine*, **34** (1914), 627–636. The latter is reprinted in Shipley's *Studies in Insect Life and Other Essays* (London, 1917). There are reminiscences by Murray himself in J. Lascelles Graham, "*Old Boys*" *and Their Stories of the High School of Stirling* (Stirling, 1900); other reminiscences are included in Hugh R. Mill, *An Autobiography* (London, 1951), 43–44; Laurence Pullar, *Lengthening Shadows* (privately printed, 1910), *passim*; and A. L. Turner, *Sir William Turner* (Edinburgh, 1919), 496. A recent summary is William N. Boog Watson, "Sir John Murray—A Chronic Student," in *University of Edinburgh Journal*, **23** (1967), 123–138.

HAROLD L. BURSTYN

MŪSĀ IBN MUḤAMMAD IBN MAḤMŪD AL-RŪMĪ QĀḌĪZĀDE. See **Qāḍī Zāda al-Rūmī.**

MŪSĀ IBN SHĀKIR, SONS OF. See **Banū Mūsā.**

MUSHET, DAVID (*b.* Dalkeith, Scotland, 2 October 1772; *d.* Monmouth, Wales, 7 June 1847), *metallurgy.*

Mushet was the son of William Muschet, an iron founder, and Margaret Cochrane. The family name, the origins of which have been traced to the Norman period, appears in various forms, including Mushett. Educated at Dalkeith Grammar School, Mushet frequented his father's and other foundries in the Glasgow area, although his first job (1792) was as an accountant at the Clyde ironworks at Tollcross, near Glasgow, where he began experiments with iron in 1793. Working after business hours, he used the firm's reverberatory furnace and other facilities until he was summarily denied access to them in 1798. His first three papers, published in 1798 in Tilloch's *Philosophical Magazine,* were the product of this period.

Mushet stayed with Clyde until 1800, continuing his research in his own laboratory and reporting the results in thirteen more papers. From 1801 to 1805 he was associated in partnership with William Dixon and Walter Neilson (the father of J. B. Neilson, the inventor of the hot-blast stove) at the Calder Ironworks. During this period he discovered, in the parish of Old Monkland, some ten miles east of Glasgow, the blackband ironstone formation (1801). This discovery, later to put Scotland in a favorable competitive position vis-à-vis England and Wales, brought no advantage to Mushet because its full utilization had to await the introduction of the hot blast (1828–1830), first tried out at the Clyde and Calder Ironworks. Because of the "speculative habits of one partner and the constitutional nervousness of another," Mushet abandoned his interests in Calder and in the blackband leases and left Scotland. Another group of ten papers was published during this period.

From 1805 to 1810 Mushet was associated with the ironworks at Alfreton, Derbyshire. Not much is known of his activities there, apart from his publication of six papers and, apparently, the writing of articles on the blast furnace and blowing engine for Rees's *Cyclopaedia* and on iron for the 1824 supplement to the fourth, fifth, and sixth editions of the *Encyclopaedia Britannica*.

In 1810 Mushet moved to Coleford, in the Forest of Dean. He published nothing during his first six years there, being occupied with a partnership in the Whitecliff Ironworks until he became "dissatisfied with his partners" and withdrew. Between 1816 and 1823 he published eight more papers in *Philosophical Magazine*; but subsequently—apart from three studies on the alloying of copper with iron (1835)—seems to have confined himself to his experiments, to consultation with neighboring ironmasters, and, presumably, to the training of his son Robert. He was also active during the early 1830's in a controversy over the right of the Free Miners of the Forest of Dean to transfer their rights to "foreigners" like himself, that is, those who had not worked a year and a day in the iron mines.

Mushet was granted five patents: one (2,447 of 1800) in the Clyde period, three (3,944 of 1815; 4,248 of 1818, and 4,697 of 1822) from the middle period at Coleford, and one in 1835 (6,908). The technical value of the processes described, especially in the patent of 1800, was the subject of controversy in the trade press of the 1870's, and Robert Forester Mushet proved an aggressive defender of his father.

The publication of Mushet's collected papers in 1840 was initiated by his son David, and Mushet appended considerable material in the form of illustrative notes to the originals. He notes, for example, that in 1798, as is claimed in the 1800 patent, he had asserted that carbon in a gaseous state passes into iron by the mouth or through the pores of the crucible to form steel. His later note states: "This opinion I have long considered the effort of a young mind eager to account for the whole phenomena before it, without that knowledge of the subject which long experience and observation confer" (*Papers*, p. 33). This disclaimer was overlooked in the later arguments, particularly by J. S. Jeans.

In a field in which scientific research had to wage a long battle with the empiricism of the ironmaster, it is not surprising that Mushet's acknowledged contributions to the development of the iron and steel industry were less spectacular than those of his son. It is, indeed, strange that eight years after the publication of the *Papers*, the Institution of Civil Engineers, of which Mushet had been an associate, expressed the hope that his family would collate the papers of one "whose researches were carried on with such indefatigable industry and perseverance and yet of whose labor so little is really known" (*Proceedings, Institution of Civil Engineers*, **7** [1848], 12).

Samuel Smiles credits Mushet with the successful application of the hot-blast stove to anthracite in iron smelting and states that Heath developed his patent cast steel from Mushet's experiments on the "beneficial effects of oxide of manganese on steel." Mushet's work on ferromanganese (1817) may have given Robert Forester Mushet the hint that led to his involvement with the Bessemer process.

BIBLIOGRAPHY

I. ORIGINAL WORKS. Mushet's papers were collected by his son David as *Papers on Iron and Steel* (London, 1840). Three other papers are "Blast" and "Blowing Machine," in Abraham Rees, ed., *The Cyclopaedia or Universal Dictionary of the Arts, Sciences, and Literature* (London, 1819) (the *Papers*, p. xix, states that the volume was in the hands of a committee appointed by the iron trade in 1807 "on occasion of the proposed tax on iron"), and "Ironmaking," in *Supplement to the Fourth, Fifth and Sixth Editions* of the *Encyclopaedia Britannica* (London, 1824), 114–127.

II. SECONDARY LITERATURE. See F. W. Baty, *Forest of Dean* (London, 1952), 98; *Dictionary of National Biography*, repr. ed., XIII, 1326–1327; Henry Hamilton, *The Industrial Revolution in Scotland* (London, 1932; repr. 1966), 179; C. E. Hart, *The Free Miners* (Gloucester, 1953), 136, 272, 290, 506; J. S. Jeans, *Steel* (London, 1880), 23; Fred M. Osborn, *The Story of the Mushets* (London, 1952); H. S. Osborn, *The Metallurgy of Iron and Steel* (Philadelphia, 1869), esp. 124–142, which frequently confuses the work of

Mushet and his son Robert; John Percy, *Metallurgy (Iron and Steel)* (London, 1875), 424–425; and Samuel Smiles, *Industrial Biography* (London, 1863), 141–148.

Philip W. Bishop

MUSHKETOV, IVAN VASILIEVICH (*b.* Alekseevskaya, Voronezh, Russia, 21 January 1850; *d.* St. Petersburg, Russia, 23 January 1902), *geology, geography.*

Mushketov was born to a family of modest means. After the death of his father, Vasily Kuzmich, in 1864, he continued his education at the Gymnasium at Novocherkassk, supporting himself by tutoring children of wealthy parents. While attending the Gymnasium he acquired an interest in natural history, inspired by his teacher, S. F. Nomikosov, that determined his life as a scientist. Recommended by the Gymnasium authorities on the basis of his progress in ancient languages, in 1867 he entered the department of history and philology of St. Petersburg University. He quickly realized his mistake, however, and transferred to the St. Petersburg Mining Institute, where he studied mineralogy and petrography under P. V. Eremeev.

While still a student Mushketov published his first scientific work, a description of volynite. Immediately after graduating from the Mining Institute in 1872 he was sent to the Urals to study deposits of precious stones. Here he continued his work in mineralogy, discovered several arsenical minerals, and journeyed along the Chusovaya River. In 1873 he was assigned to Turkistan and began his many years of research in central Asia. The following year Mushketov worked in the Karatau Mountains and the western spur of the Tien Shan, also investigating the Badamsky Mountains and the plain of the Syr Darya River between Tashkent and Samarkand. In 1875 he traveled from Tashkent through the central Tien Shan to Kuldja; climbed the Talass Ala-Tau, Terskei Ala-Tau, Kungei Ala-Tau, and Zailissky Ala-Tau ranges; traversed the Kirghiz Range, went around the high mountain lakes Son Kul and Issyk Kul; and visited the Dzungarian Ala-Tau. In 1876 he published *Kratky otchet o geologicheskom puteshestvii po Turkestanu v 1875 g.* ("A Short Account of a Geological Trip Through Turkistan in 1875").

In 1876 Mushketov reported to the St. Petersburg Mineralogical Society and the Russian Geographical Society on the scientific results of his trips. For these communications the two societies elected Mushketov a member, and the Geographical Society gave him a silver medal. The Mining Institute invited Mushketov

to teach; but in order to do so he had to present a dissertation, and the material on central Asia was too extensive and required more work. In December 1877 he defended his dissertation, "Materialy dlya izuchenia geognosticheskogo stroenia i rudnykh bogatstv Zlatoustovskogo gornogo okruga v yuzhnom Urale" ("Material for the Study of the Geognostic Structure and Ore Resources of the Zlatoust Mountain Region in the Southern Urals"), which contained extensive material on mineralogy and descriptions of ore deposits. He was then appointed adjunct professor, and from 1896 professor, of geology, geognosy, and ore deposits.

In the summer of 1877 Mushketov returned to central Asia, completing a trip from Fergana across the Alai and Trans-Alai ranges to the Pamir, studying the relations between the Tien Shan and the Pamir. In 1878 he investigated the region where the Fergana and the Alai ranges meet, and in 1879 he participated in an expedition to the Turan lowlands.

In 1880 Mushketov made his last trip to central Asia, to study glaciers, and climbed Zeravshan glacier, previously considered inaccessible. Part of the results of these investigations appeared in publications of the Russian Geographical Society and the St. Petersburg Mineralogical Society. These articles brought him a gold medal from the Russian Geographical Society and a prize from the Academy of Sciences. He was also elected an honorary member of the Vienna Geographical Society. In 1884 Mushketov and G. D. Romanovsky published *Geologicheskaya karta Turkestanskogo kraya* ("A Geological Map of the Turkistan Region"), the first summarizing work on the geology of the region.

In 1886 there appeared the first volume of Mushketov's *Turkestan,* which contained a description of the geological structure of that territory. This was widely recognized as a basic work and was awarded a prize by the Academy of Sciences and the St. Petersburg Mineralogical Society. Unfortunately, Mushketov did not finish working out all the material; and the second volume, containing journals of the trip, was published posthumously. The first volume was reprinted in 1915 by his students and for many years served as the basic source on the geology of central Asia.

After completing his expeditions in central Asia, Mushketov undertook diverse projects in various regions of Russia. In 1881 he traveled to the Caucasus to study mineral sources and ore deposits, as well as the Elbrus glacier. During this trip he participated in the fifth Congress of Archaeologists in Tiflis, where he presented a report on nephrite from the tombs at Samarkand.

In 1882 Mushketov became senior geologist of the Geological Committee of Russia. The following year, on instructions from the Committee, he studied the Lipetsk mineral waters and suggested measures to increase their flow. In 1884–1885 he investigated the geological structure of the Kalmuck steppe region along the lower Volga and inspected the Caucasian mineral waters and salt lakes of the Crimea. In 1886 he organized a geological study of the Transcaspian region for his students V. A. Obruchev and K. I. Bogdanovich and established a research program for them.

Mushketov published the results of this work in 1891—"Kratky ocherk geologicheskogo stroenia Zakaspyskoy oblasti" ("A Short Account of the Geological Structure of the Transcaspian Region")—in *Zapiski Imperatorskogo mineralogicheskogo obshchestva*; a supplementary geological map was based on the data of Obruchev and Bogdanovich.

In 1887 a government commission headed by Mushketov was organized to study the causes and consequences of the powerful earthquake that had struck the town of Verny (now Alma-Ata) that year. This work led to his lasting interest in earthquakes. The preliminary data from the investigation were published by Mushketov in a series of articles as early as 1888; and in "Vernenskoe zemletryasenie 28 maya 1887 g." ("The Verny Earthquake of 28 May 1887"), which appeared in 1890, he analyzed the causes of the earthquake and of seismic phenomena in general.

In 1888, at Mushketov's initiative, a seismic commission was organized in the Russian Geographical Society. To collect information on earthquakes it compiled a list of questions, which it sent to all seismically active regions. In a supplement to the list Mushketov wrote an explanatory note on earthquakes, methods of observing them, and the reasons for them. On the basis of the material thus compiled and processed by Mushketov, *Materialy dlya izuchenia zemletryaseny Rossii* ("Materials for the Study of Earthquakes in Russia") was published (1891, 1899).

During this time A. P. Orlov began to compile "Katalog zemletryaseny Rossyskoy imperii" ("Catalog of Earthquakes in the Russian Empire") but died without finishing the work. Mushketov expanded and published this catalog (1893), which became the most valuable source of information on earthquakes in Russia.

In 1900 Mushketov became a member of the Permanent Central Seismic Commission of the Academy of the Sciences, as a representative of the Geological Committee. In the same year he investigated the severe earthquake at Akhalkaliki in the Caucasus.

In 1888–1891 Mushketov published his two-volume *Fizicheskaya geologia* ("Physical Geology"). In 1892 he studied the upper reaches of the Don, with the aim of organizing hydrological research. He worked in the lower Volga region and in the Kirghiz steppe in 1894 and investigated the salt lakes of the Crimea. He revisited the Crimean lakes in 1895 and also studied the plain of the Teberda and Chkhalta rivers and the glaciers of the Caucasus. In his account of this trip (1896), Mushketov described the rocks he had seen and suggested that the gradual formation of the main Caucasus range had been accompanied by dislocations caused by horizontal pressure.

In the region where he worked, Mushketov discovered fifteen previously unknown glaciers. In 1895 Mushketov was elected to the International Commission for the Study of Glaciers. As director of glaciological studies in Russia he attracted a large group of young scientists. Also in 1895 Mushketov published *Kratky kurs petrografii* ("A Short Course in Petrography").

In 1900, having investigated the aftereffects of the Akhalkaliki earthquake, Mushketov traveled to Transbaikalia as consultant on a projected new railroad and then to Paris to take part in the eighth session of the International Geological Congress.

To explain the complex orography and tectonics of central Asia, Mushketov considered it necessary to study its geological history, believing that "every contemporary phenomenon can be fully explained and understood only by the study of its history . . ." (*Kratky otchet o geologicheskom puteshestvii po Turkestanu . . .*, p. 24). Such an approach to the study of the geological structure of central Asia distinguishes Mushketov from his predecessors, who understood its tectonics only through purely external, morphological signs.

On the basis of his own observation and study of its geological history, Mushketov offered a scheme for the geological structure of central Asia which showed that the Tien Shan and Pamir-Alai consist of folded arcs that extend to the northeast and northwest but are bent toward the south by tangential pressure from the north.

Mushketov also distinguished the stratigraphic relations of the formations in the region and described many deposits of useful minerals. He worked out the particular details of the glaciers of central Asia, arguing that the mountain glaciers were retreating; he described the central Asiatic loess; and he provided a classification of quicksands.

Mushketov believed the earth to be so complex that it can be studied only through the aggregate efforts of many sciences. Physical geology, to which his major work is devoted, examines tectonic and erosional processes. He felt, however, that to study processes it is necessary first to understand the position of the earth in space, the hypotheses concerning its origins, and its physical properties, and then to grasp the interplay of tectonic processes, volcanic and seismic phenomena, the record of surface features, and development of the phenomena of denudation. The book is organized according to this plan. The second volume is devoted to a description of the geological activity of the atmosphere, water, and ice.

Mushketov was an adherent of the Kant-Laplace nebular hypothesis, the generally accepted cosmogony of the time. He considered the internal heat of the earth a remnant of the previous molten state. But the idea of a molten state and thin crust was contradicted, as Mushketov stressed, by the phenomena of precession and nutation; yet in the assertion of a solid earth or thick crust, volcanic phenomena remained inexplicable. He saw the solidification of the earth as proceeding both from the center to the periphery and from the periphery to the center. Thus he considered the present structure of the earth to comprise a hard crust and nucleus, with an intermediate belt, possibly of olivine composition.

On the causes of tectonic processes, Mushketov started from the then widely accepted contraction hypothesis. "The main reasons for dislocation and plasticity," he asserted, "are found in the gradual tightening or shrinking of the crust as a consequence of the decreasing volume of the nucleus due to cooling and the loss of volcanic material" (*Fizicheskaya geologia,* vol. 1, p. 599). The contraction of the crust as a consequence of the cooling of the earth was, in Mushketov's opinion, the main cause of seismic phenomena. The statistics of earthquakes and data on the geological structure of various areas led him to distinguish five seismically active regions in Russia: the Caucasus, Turkistan, Transbaikalia, Altai, and Kamchatka.

In the Mining Institute Mushketov taught geology and physical geography for twenty-five years. He also taught in the Institute of Communications Engineers, in the Higher Courses for Women, and in the Historical-Philological Institute, as well as giving many public lectures. Among his students were V. A. Obruchev, K. I. Bogdanovich, and L. I. Lutugin.

Mushketov was president of the physical geography section of the Russian Geographical Society, a member of the St. Petersburg Mineralogical Society, a member of the Council of the St. Petersburg Biological Laboratory, and a representative of Russia at the International Commission for Research on Glaciers.

His work was especially influential in the study of the geology of central Asia, tectonics, seismology, and glaciology.

BIBLIOGRAPHY

I. Original Works. His works include "Volynit" ("Volynite"), in *Zapiski Imperatorskogo mineralogicheskogo obshchestva,* 2nd ser., **7** (1872), 320–329; *Kratky otchet o geologicheskom puteshestvii po Turkestanu v 1875 g.* ("A Short Account of a Geological Journey Through Turkistan in 1875"; St. Petersburg, 1876); "Geologicheskie issledovania v Kalmytskoy stepi v 1885 g." ("Geological Research in the Kalmuck Steppe in 1885"), in *Izvestiya Geologicheskogo komiteta,* **5** (1886), 203–233; *Turkestan,* 2 vols. (St. Petersburg, 1886–1906); *Fizicheskaya geologia* ("Physical Geology"), 2 vols. (St. Petersburg, 1888–1891); "Vernenskoe zemletryasenie 28 maya 1887 g." ("The Verny Earthquake of 28 May 1887"), in *Trudy Geologicheskogo komiteta,* **10**, no. 1 (1890), 1–154; *Zemletryasenia, ikh kharakter i sposoby nablyudenia. . . .* ("Earthquakes, Their Character and Methods of Observing Them. . . ."; St. Petersburg, 1890); "Kratky ocherk geologicheskogo stroenia Zakaspyskoy oblasti" ("A Short Sketch of the Geological Structure of the Transcaspian Region"), in *Zapiski Imperatorskogo mineralogicheskogo obshchestva,* **28** (1891), 391–429; and "Katalog zemletryaseny Rossyskoy imperii" ("Catalog of Earthquakes in the Russian Empire"), in *Zapiski Russkogo geograficheskogo obshchestva,* **26** (1893), a completion of the work begun by A. P. Orlov.

II. Secondary Literature. See D. N. Anuchin, "I. V. Mushketov i ego nauchnye trudy" ("I. V. Mushketov and His Scientific Work"), in *Zemlevedenie,* **1**, 9, no. 1 (1902), 113–133; B. A. Fedorovich, "I. V. Mushketov kak geograf" ("I. V. Mushketov as a Geographer"), in *Izvestiya Akademii nauk SSSR,* Geog. ser., no. 1 (1952), 63–67; A. P. Karpinsky, "Pamyati I. V. Mushketova" ("Memories of I. V. Mushketov"), in *Gornyi zhurnal,* **1**, no. 2 (1902), 203–207; V. A. Obruchez, "Ivan Vasilievich Mushketov," in *Lyudi russkoy nauki* ("People of Russian Science"; Moscow, 1962), 54–62; and L. A. Vayner, *Ivan Vasilevich Mushketov i ego rol v poznanii geologii Sredney Azii* ("Ivan Vasilievich Mushketov and His Role in the Knowledge of the Geology of Central Asia"; Tashkent, 1954).

Irina V. Batyushkova

MUSSCHENBROEK, PETRUS VAN (*b.* Leiden, Netherlands, 14 March 1692; *d.* Leiden, 19 September 1761), *physics*.

Musschenbroek belonged to a well-known family of brass founders and instrument makers who were originally from near Tournai in Hainaut and who settled at Leiden in the latter part of the sixteenth century. His grandfather, Joost Adriaensz (1614–1693), manufactured lamps, especially church lamps, and was also a gauger of weights and measures. He was succeeded in his craft by his sons Samuel (1639–1681) and Johan (1660–1707). In accordance with the spirit of the times, they turned their skill to the making of scientific apparatus such as air pumps, microscopes, and telescopes. Christiaan Huygens mentions one of them as a maker of microscopes (letters of 1678 and 1683, *Oeuvres complètes,* VIII, 64, 422; see also *ibid.*, XXII, 762). Swammerdam used a microscope made by Samuel (Boerhaave, in his preface to the *Biblia naturae,* 1737); and the anatomist Regnier de Graaf employed anatomical injection spouts also made by him. Leeuwenhoek's aquatic microscope (letter to the Royal Society of 12 January 1689) was made by Johan. Many of Johan's instruments are still preserved; the extant instrument made by Samuel is an air pump of 1675.

In 1685 Johan married Maria van der Straeten; they had two sons, Jan (1687–1748) and Petrus. Jan, who succeeded his father in the workshop, obtained a good education at the Latin school and studied under Boerhaave. He was offered teaching positions but preferred to remain an instrument maker. This may well have been due to his friendship and collaboration with 'sGravesande, who based his physics lectures on experiments and had many of his instruments constructed by Jan. They can be studied in 'sGravesande's *Physices elementa mathematica experimentis confirmata* (Leiden, 1720–1721; 2nd ed., 1742); some seventy-five of them still exist. The popularity of this book brought numerous orders to Jan from universities and amateurs; many of his instruments were imitated, for instance, by George Adams for the cabinet of George III of England. His workshop on the Rapenburg (now no. 66) was famous. Albrecht von Haller, who visited him between 1725 and 1727, especially admired Jan's magic lantern. Apart from catalogs of his works—as many as 200 items—he published only a description of new air pumps and of "agreeable and instructive" experiments to be performed with them (1736).

Petrus, not yet fifteen when his father died, owed his further education to his brother. He studied at the University of Leiden and in 1715 received his doctorate in medicine. He then made a study trip to London, where he met Desaguliers, then famous as lecturer and demonstrator of scientific experiments, who visited Holland in 1730. Back in Leiden he practiced medicine and shared with his brother both the friendship and the philosophy of 'sGravesande. In 1719 Petrus received his doctorate in philosophy and accepted a professorate in mathematics and philosophy at Duisburg, where in 1721 he also became extraordinary

professor of medicine. From 1723 to 1740 he occupied the chair of natural philosophy and mathematics at Utrecht, in 1732 also holding the chair of astronomy. Here he lectured on experimental philosophy, presenting views like those of 'sGravesande and Newton and often using apparatus made by his brother.

Musschenbroek became increasingly famous, especially because of his lecture notes collected in ever larger volumes; the *Epitome elementorum physico-mathematicorum conscripta in usus academico* (Leiden, 1726), *Elementa physicae* (Leiden, 1734), *Institutiones physicae* (Leiden, 1748), and the posthumous two-volume *Introductio ad philosophiam naturalem*, edited by J. Lulofs (Leiden, 1762), were widely used and translated into Dutch, English, French, and German. He refused offers of academic chairs at Copenhagen in 1731 and at Göttingen in 1737; but at the end of 1739 he accepted a chair at Leiden, where he taught from 1740 until his death. In 1742, after the death of 'sGravesande, Musschenbroek became his logical successor in the teaching of experimental physics. The excellence of his lectures maintained the reputation that Leiden had acquired under Boerhaave and 'sGravesande, and students interested in experimentation came from all parts of Europe. One of them was Jean-Antoine Nollet (in 1736), who became the leading exponent of this school in France.

Primarily a lecturer and author, Musschenbroek tended more to supervise than to become involved in the construction of apparatus. He devised many of his experiments, in the process consulting records of other experimenters, among them those of the Accademia del Cimento. Musschenbroek translated their accounts into Latin, adding reports concerning his own work (1731). Many of his instruments were made by his brother Jan; but those of other craftsmen —for instance, Jan Paauw—were also employed. The Musschenbroeks never made barometers or thermometers; these were supplied by Gabriel Daniel Fahrenheit in Amsterdam and by others.

The experiments can be studied in Musschenbroek's books, which contain many fine illustrations; they deal with the mechanics of rigid bodies, air pressure, heat, cohesion, capillarity, phosphorescence, magnetism, and electricity. Many of these experiments have become classics in elementary instruction. One of the better-known apparatuses is the pyrometer (the name was given by Musschenbroek), first described in the *Tentamina* of 1731; it consists of a horizontal metal bar fixed at one end and connected at the other end to wheelwork that shows the expansion of the bar when it is heated. It was originally used without a thermometer, which was not mentioned until the

Introductio of 1762. Musschenbroek's best-known experiment is that with the Leyden jar, discussed below.

Underlying Musschenbroek's lectures demonstrated with experiments was the experimental philosophy. This philosophy, which he proclaimed in Holland along with Boerhaave and 'sGravesande, was set forth in their books and in academic lectures such as Musschenbroek's inaugural address at Utrecht, *Oratio de certo methodo philosophiae* (Leiden, 1723). The principal source of inspiration was Newton; but Galileo, Torricelli, Huygens, Réaumur, and others were important to this school. Since the mind, Musschenbroek states in his *Elementa physicae* (1734), has no innate idea of what bodies and their qualities are, we can obtain knowledge about them only by observation and experiments. But we must be extremely careful, use good instruments, and take into consideration all circumstances—atmospheric pressure, temperature, locality, and weather. Thus we can discover the laws that govern the behavior of bodies, provided the results of experiments, repeated over and over again, are the same, and specific causes are admitted only when the phenomena investigated leave no doubt. The stress is therefore on induction; but deduction, for example, by means of mathematics, is admissible, as Newton had shown, provided such deductions are constantly tested by experiment. The success of such reasoning on the basis of careful experimentation finds its guarantee in the infinite wisdom of the Supreme Being. This philosophy inspired the founding of many amateur societies in Holland and abroad for experimental study.

Musschenbroek is generally credited with originating the Leyden jar. He knew that a charged conductor surrounded by air loses its charge very rapidly, especially in a rainy climate like that of Holland. He had a gun barrel suspended by two silk lines and the barrel charged by means of a rapidly rotating glass globe rubbed by hand. A brass wire from the barrel led a few inches through a cork into a bottle and extended into water in the bottle. Thus the water was charged. Musschenbroek's assistant, Andreas Cunaeus, accidentally took hold of the bottle, thus giving it the necessary outer coating. Then he touched the wire with his other hand—and received a fearful shock. He had unintentionally experienced the effect of a true capacitor.

This accident occurred in January 1746. Musschenbroek reported the experiment to Réaumur, who showed the letter to Nollet. Musschenbroek's other collaborator, Jean Nicolas Sebastien Allamand (who later wrote a biography of 'sGravesande), wrote directly to Nollet. The latter, quite excited about this "Leiden experiment," reported to the Académie des Sciences at its April meeting. Nollet continued to write on and repeat the "expérience nouvelle mais terrible" in a sensational way. Thus the *bouteille de Leyde* became widely known during 1746. Musschenbroek first described it in the *Institutiones physicae* of 1748.

As to the priority of the experiment, in 1744 Georg Matthias Bose in Wittenberg had published the drawing of "fire" from electrified water in a glass, an experiment that Musschenbroek knew and wanted to repeat. Early in 1745 Allamand had received a terrible shock in the same way that Cunaeus did the following year, and he had reported on it in the *Philosophical Transactions* of 1746. And on 4 October 1745 J. G. von Kleist, dean of the cathedral at Kammin (now Kamień Pomorski), made a similar experiment. This was reported to other Germans interested in electricity and was published by J. G. Krüger in his *Geschichte der Erde* (Halle, 1746), but it passed unnoticed for a long time. Yet it was Musschenbroek's communication which, through Nollet, made the capacitor known, so that there were soon improvements in its construction, and Benjamin Franklin analyzed the experiments on "M. Musschenbroek's wonderful bottle" in his third and fourth letters to Peter Collinson (1747, 1748). In them he established that the charge is not in the wire or the water, but in the glass. He also corresponded with Musschenbroek and in 1761 visited him in Leiden.

Musschenbroek married Adriana van de Water (*d.* 1732) in 1724 and Helena Alstorphius in 1738. A son, Jan Willem (1729–1807), wrote the family history.

BIBLIOGRAPHY

I. ORIGINAL WORKS. There is no modern critical bibliography of the Musschenbroeks' works. For a preliminary listing see D. Bierens De Haan, *Bibliographie néerlandaise historique-scientifique* (Rome, 1883; repr. Nieuwkoop, 1960), 202–204. Petrus' main literary production consists of a gradual extension of his Utrecht lecture notes published first in the already mentioned *Epitome* of 1726. These include *Beginsels der natuurkunde* (Leiden, 1736; 2nd ed., 1739); *Essai de physique . . . avec une description de nouvelles sortes de machines pneumatiques et un recueil d'expériences par Mr. J. Musschenbroek*, translated by P. Massuet, 2 vols. (Leiden, 1736–1739; 2nd ed., 1751); *The Elements of Natural Philosophy*, translated by J. Colson, 2 vols. (London, 1744); *Grundlehren der Naturwissenschaft nach der zweiten lateinischen Ausgabe*, translated by J. C. Gottsched (Leipzig, 1747); and *Cours de physique expérimentale et mathématique*, translated by Sigault de la Fond, 3 vols. (Paris, 1769), with a preface by J. Lulofs, a colleague of Musschenbroek's at Leiden, and a description of the relation of these different books to each other.

See also *Disputatio medica inauguralis de aeris praesentia in humoribus animalibus* (Leiden, 1715; 2nd ed., 1749); *Oratio de certo methodo philosophiae* (Leiden, 1723), his inaugural address at Utrecht—on its influence on the spread of Newtonianism in France see Brunet, below; *Physicae experimentales et geometricae, de magnete, tuborum capillarium vitreorumque speculorum attractione magnitudine terrae, cohaerentia corporum firmorum dissertationes ut et ephemerides meteorologicae ultrajectinae* (*anni 1728*) (Leiden, 1729; Vienna–Prague–Trieste, 1754); *Tentamina experimentorum naturalium captorum in Accademia del Cimento . . . quibus commentarios, nova experientia, et orationem de methodo instituendi experimenta physica additit P. v. M.*, 2 vols. (Leiden, 1731; Vienna–Prague–Trieste, 1756), French version in *Collection académique* (Dijon–Auxerre, 1755); *Oratio de mente humana semet ignorante* (Leiden, 1740), his inaugural address at Leiden; *Oratio de sapientia divina* (Leiden–Vienna, 1744); *Institutiones logicae, praecipue comprehentes artem argumentandi* (Leiden, 1746; Venice, 1763); and *Compendium physicae experimentales conscripta in usus academicos*, J. Lulofs, ed. (Leiden, 1762). Jan Musschenbroek's writings are *Liste de diverses machines de physique, de mathématique, d'anatomie et de chirurgie* (Leiden, 1736); and *Description de nouvelles sortes de machines pneumatiques tant doubles que simples* (Leiden, 1738), also published in Dutch.

The only extant instrument of Samuel Musschenbroek, the air pump of 1675, was made for Professor Burchard de Volder and is in the Leiden Museum of Science, which also has a considerable number of Johan's instruments, identifiable by the trademark of Samuel and Johan, an oriental lamp. The collection of Johan's instruments includes the aquatic and other microscopes, as well as air pumps. The instruments gathered by Jan for 'sGravesande have been to a great extent preserved at Leiden. Many other instruments made by Jan may still exist, but they cannot be identified with certainty because he seldom used the family trademark (see the books by Rooseboom, Crommelin, and van der Star). Many of Jan's models are illustrated, however, in the *Physices elementa* of 1720–1721 and 1742. The university museum at Utrecht has an air pump and two microscopes by Jan, the first pyrometer made by Petrus, and three cylinders of Petrus' friction meter. Instruments made by the Musschenbroeks and their imitations exist elsewhere—for instance, in the cabinet of George III. The *Catalogus van Mathematische, Physische, Astronomische, Chirurgische, en andere Instrumenten te Bekomen in de Fabricq van Mr. J. H. Onderdewyngaart Canzius te Delft* (1804) lists a number of Jan's apparatuses, with reference to the pictures in 'sGravesande.

Another catalog that mentions instruments of Musschenbroek is *Collectio exquisitissima Instrumentorum in Primis ad Physicam experimentalem Pertinentium, quibus, dom vivebat, Usus fuit Celeberrimus Petrus van Musschenbroek . . . quorum Auctio fiet . . . ad Diem 15 Martii et Seqq. 1762* (Leiden, 1762).

In the university library at Leiden there is much MS material by Petrus and some by Jan. They are listed in J. Geel, *Catalogus librorum manuscriptorum qui inde ab 1741 bibliotheca Lugduno Batavae accesserunt* (Leiden, 1852), 221–223. The municipal archives of Utrecht contain Petrus' handwritten copy of the list of instruments he was authorized to buy for the Theatrum Physicum and the observatory at Utrecht.

II. SECONDARY LITERATURE. No full-length modern biography of the Musschenbroeks exists. A concise sketch of their lives, based partially on the MS history by Jan Willem van Musschenbroek (Petrus' son), together with a description of their extant instruments, can be found in M. Rooseboom, *Bydrage tot de geschiedenis der instrumentmakerskunst in de Noordelyke Nederlanden tot omstreekts 1840* (Leiden, 1950); supplemented by C. A. Crommelin, *Descriptive Catalogue of the Physical Instruments in the National Museum of the History of Science at Leyden* (Leiden, 1951); "Leidsche leden van het geslacht Musschenbroek," in *Leidsch Jaarboekje* (1939), 135–149; and "Huizen der Leidsche van Musschenbroeks," *ibid.* (1945), 127–133; and P. van der Star, *Descriptive Catalogue of the Simple Microscopes in the National Museum of the History of Science at Leyden* (Leiden, 1953). See also H. J. M. Bos, *Mechanical Instruments in the Utrecht University Museum* (Utrecht, 1968), where 22 of the *ca.* 100 mentioned instruments are copies of instruments described in Musschenbroek's books; and E. J. Dijksterhuis, "Uit het Utrechts verleden der fysica," in *Nederlands tijdschrift voor natuurkunde*, **22** (1956), 163–180; and A. Savérien, *Histoire des philosophes*, VI (Paris, 1768); A. N. Condorcet, "Éloge de Musschenbroek," in *Oeuvres*, II (1847), 125–127; and F. Boerne, *Nachrichten von den vornehmsten Leben und Schriften jetz lebender berühmter Aertze und Naturforscher*, I (Wolfenbüttel, 1749), 529–541.

On Musschenbroek's influence on the spread of Newtonianism see P. Brunet, *Les physiciens hollandais et la méthode expérimentale en France au XVIII siècle* (Paris, 1928), 68–100; and his *L'introduction des théories de Newton en France au XVIIIᵉ siècle* (Paris, 1931), 124, 326. The invention of the Leyden jar is discussed in C. Dorsman and C. A. Crommelin, "The Invention of the Leyden Jar," in *Janus*, **46** (1957), 275–280; F. M. Feldhaus, *Die Erfindung der elektrischen Verstärkungsflasche durch E. J. von Kleist* (Heidelberg, 1903); and J. L. Heilbron, "G. M. Bose: The Prime Mover in the Invention of the Leyden Jar?" *Isis*, **57** (1966), 264–267. The original publications on this subject are G. M. Bose, *Tentamina electrica in academiis regiis Londensi et Parisina primum habita omni studio repitata . . .* (Wittenberg, 1744), 64; *Tentamina electrica tandem aliquando hydraulicae chymiae et vegetabilibus utilia* (Wittenberg, 1747), 36–37; J. A. Nollet, "Observations sur quelques nouveaux phénomènes d'électricité," in *Histoire de l'Académie des sciences* for 1746, 1–33; and "Recherches sur la communication de l'électricité," *ibid.*, 447. See also J. Priestley, *The History and Present State of Electricity* (London, 1767); P. F. Mottelay, *Bibliographical History of Electricity and Magnetism* (London, 1922); and I. B. Cohen, *Benjamin Franklin's Experiments* (Cambridge, Mass., 1941).

D. J. STRUIK

MYDORGE, CLAUDE (*b*. Paris, France, 1585; *d*. Paris, July 1647), *mathematics, physics.*

Mydorge belonged to one of France's richest and most illustrious families. His father, Jean Mydorge, *seigneur* of Maillarde, was *conseiller* at the Parlement of Paris and judge of the Grande Chambre; his mother's maiden name was Lamoignon. He decided to pursue a legal career and was, first, *conseiller* at the Châtelet, then treasurer of the *généralité* of Amiens. In 1613 he married the sister of M. de la Haye, the French ambassador at Constantinople. His duties as treasurer left him sufficient time to devote himself to his passion, mathematics.

About 1625 Mydorge met Descartes and became one of his most faithful friends. In 1627, to aid Descartes in his search for an explanation of vision, Mydorge had parabolic, hyperbolic, oval, and elliptic lenses made for him. He also determined and drew their shapes with great precision. He subsequently had many lenses and burning glasses made. It was said that altogether he spent more than 100,000 écus for this purpose.

After a thorough study of Descartes's *Dioptrique*, Mydorge at first criticized the book on various points but later completely adopted his friend's theories. Fermat, however, in 1638, wrote to Mersenne to refute the *Dioptrique*. On 1 March 1638 (see *Oeuvres de Descartes*, C. Adam and P. Tannery, eds., II, *Correspondance*, 15–23) Descartes sent a long letter to Mydorge—he knew that the latter had openly taken his side in the dispute—in which he provided him with the seven documents relating to the case and asked him to be judge and intermediary. He also asked Mydorge to make a copy of the letter and send the original to Fermat's friends Étienne Pascal and Roberval. (It should be noted that Fermat's correspondence indicates that Pascal and Roberval were in no way his friends.) Through the good offices of Mydorge and Mersenne, Descartes and Fermat were reconciled.

Mydorge was held in high regard by other famous contemporaries; for instance, on 2 March 1633 Peiresc wrote from Aix to Gassendi, who was then at Digne: "If you have any special observations by M. Mydorge, you would do me a great favor by communicating them to me" (see Galileo Galilei, *Opere* [Edizione nazionale], XVIII [Florence, 1966], 430).

Mydorge's work in geometry was directed to the study of conic sections. In 1631 he published a two-volume work on the subject, which was enlarged to four volumes in 1639. The four volumes were reprinted several times under the title *De sectionibus conicis*. A further portion of the work, in manuscript, is lost. It seems that two English friends of the

Mydorge family, William Cavendish, duke of Newcastle, and Thomas Wriothesley, earl of Southampton, took it to England, where apparently it disappeared.

In his study of conic sections Mydorge continued the work of Apollonius, whose methods of proof he refined and simplified. Among the ways of describing an ellipse, for example, two from volume II may be cited. According to the first definition, an ellipse is the geometric locus of a point of a straight line the extremities of which move along two fixed straight lines. (This definition had already been demonstrated by Stevin, who attributed it to Ubaldi; actually, it goes back to antiquity, as Proclus indicates in his commentaries on Euclid.) According to the second definition, the ellipse can be deduced from a circle by extending all its ordinates in a constant relationship. In the same book Mydorge asserts that if from a given point in the plane of a conic section radii to the points of the curve are drawn and extended in a given relationship, then their extremities will be on a new conic section similar to the first. This statement constitutes the beginnings of an extremely fruitful method of deforming figures; it was successfully used by La Hire and Newton, and later by Poncelet and, especially, by Chasles, who named it *déformation homographique*.

Mydorge posed and solved the following problem in volume III: "On a given cone place a given conic section"—a problem that Apollonius had solved only for a right cone. Mydorge was also interested in geometric methods used in approximate construction, such as that of the regular heptagon. Another problem that Mydorge solved by approximation—although he did not clearly indicate his method—was that of transforming a square into an equivalent regular polygon possessing an arbitrary number of sides.

Mydorge's works on conic sections contain hundreds of problems published for the first time, as well as a multitude of ingenious and original methods that later geometers frequently used, usually without citing their source. The collection of Mydorge's manuscripts held by the Académie des Sciences contains more than 1,000 geometric problems. Finally, it should be noted that the term "parameter" of a conic section was introduced by Mydorge.

A friend of Descartes and an eminent geometer, Mydorge was also well versed in optics. He possessed a lively curiosity and was open to all the new ideas of his age. Like Fermat, he belonged to that elite group of seventeenth-century scientists who pursued science as amateurs but nevertheless made contributions of the greatest importance to one or more fields of knowledge.

BIBLIOGRAPHY

I. ORIGINAL WORKS. Mydorge's first major writing, *Examen du livre des Récréations mathématiques* (Paris, 1630; repr. 1643), with notes by D. Henrion, is a commentary on *Récréations mathématiques* (Pont-à-Mousson, 1624), published under the pseudonym H. Van Etten (actually Leurechon).

The second was *Prodromi catoptricorum et dioptricorum, sive conicorum operis . . . libri duo* (Paris, 1631), enlarged to *Conicorum operis . . . libri quattuor* (Paris, 1639, 1641, 1660), also issued as *De sectionibus conicis, libri quattuor* (Paris, 1644), which Mersenne inserted in his *Universae geometriae, mixtaeque mathematicae synopsis . . .* (Paris, 1644).

A selection of the geometry problems preserved in Paris was published by C. Henry in *Bullettino di bibliografia e di storia delle scienze matematiche e fisiche*, **14** and **16**. Mydorge's son assembled three short treatises from his father's MSS—*De la lumière*, *De l'ombre*, and *De la sciotérique*—but all trace of them has been lost.

II. SECONDARY LITERATURE. See the following, listed chronologically: C. G. Jöcher, *Allgemeines Gelehrten-Lexicon*, III (Leipzig, 1751), 787; *Biographie universelle*, XXIX (Paris, 1860), 666; *La grande encyclopédie*, XXIV (Paris, 1899), 657; M. Chasles, *Aperçu historique sur l'origine et le développement des méthodes en géométrie* (Paris, 1889), 88–89; and M. Cantor, *Vorlesungen über Geschichte der Mathematik*, II (Leipzig, 1913), 673–674, 768–769.

PIERRE SPEZIALI

MYLON, CLAUDE (*b.* Paris, France, *ca.* 1618; *d.* Paris, *ca.* 1660), *mathematics.*

Mylon's place in the history of science derives from the service he provided in facilitating communication among more learned men in the decade from 1650 to 1660. He was the third son of Benoist Mylon, counselor to Louis XIII and Controller-General of Finance; he himself was admitted to the bar as an advocate before Parlement in 1641, even though he lacked two years of being twenty-five, the legal age of majority.

As early as 1645 Mylon had become concerned with mathematics, making written notes of new Cartesian mathematical problems. He was also in contact with Mersenne, Debeaune, and Roberval, and when Schooten passed through Paris he was able to transmit a considerable amount of new information to him. Mylon also served as secretary to the "Académie Parisienne," a continuation of the Mersenne group, under the direction of F. le Pailleur, which in 1654 received Pascal's famous "Adresse." Mylon achieved a certain importance when the death of Pailleur, in November 1654, left the papers of the society at his disposal; it was thus he who told Schooten (who told Huygens) of Fermat's and Pascal's problems and solutions concerning games of chance. He also forwarded to Holland Fermat's and Frenicle's problems in number theory. In 1655 Huygens, who was making his first trip to France, visited Mylon; the following year he suggested the "commerce scientifique" that provides the chief documentation of Mylon's career.

Mylon maintained a number of rather delicate relationships with other mathematicians. He had access to Pascal in his retirement (although to a lesser degree than did Carcavi), and while his affection for Conrart threatened his friendship with Roberval, the latter continued to make use of him as an intermediary. He was less happy in his two attempts at personal achievement: in 1658 he hazarded his own solution to the quadrature of the cubic curves known as the "perles de M. Sluse" and in January 1659, in the wake of the debate provoked by Pascal, he proposed to prove Wren's solution of the length of the cycloid. These efforts stand as a monument to his inadequacies as a mathematician, and it is with them that all mention of Mylon by Huygens stops. No publication by him is known.

BIBLIOGRAPHY

On Mylon and his work, see J.-B. du Hamel, *Astronomia physica, . . . Accessere P. Petiti observationes. . . .* (Paris, 1660), 12, which includes an account of Pierre Petit's pamphlet on the observation made by Mylon and Roberval of the solar eclipse of 8 Apr. 1652.

See also C. Adam and P. Tannery, eds., *Oeuvres de Descartes*, IV (Paris, 1901), 232, 397, which deals with the problem of the "trois bâtons" and Roberval's "Aristarchus."

See L. Brunschvicg, P. Boutroux, and F. Gazier, eds., *Oeuvres de Blaise Pascal*, IX (Paris, 1914), 151–156; the letter referred to here (Mylon to Pascal, 27 Dec. 1658) is at the Bibliothèque Nationale, Paris, Res. V 859, with a demonstration by Mylon of "the equality of the cycloid and its partner."

There are numerous references to Mylon in Huygens' correspondence, as well as letters from him, in *Oeuvres complètes de Christiaan Huygens*, 22 vols. (The Hague, 1888–1950); see esp. I, 517, for Roberval's demonstration on the surface of spherical triangles; II, 8–25, for Frenicle's results on compatible numbers; "Propositio Domini Wren Angli. Demonstrata a Claudio Mylon die 26 Januarii 1659," II, 335; and "La quadrature des perles de M. Sluse par Claude Mylon. En juin 1658," II, 337. Mylon's role in the problem of games of chance is discussed in "Avertissement," XIV, 4–9. See also *The Correspondence of H. Oldenburg*, I (London, 1965), 225.

PIERRE COSTABEL

NAEGELI, CARL WILHELM VON (*b.* Kilchberg, near Zurich, Switzerland, 27 March 1817; *d.* Munich, Germany, 10 May 1891), *botany, microscopy.*

The son of a physician, Naegeli was educated at a private school, the Zurich Gymnasium, and Zurich University. His enthusiasm for science was stimulated by Oken's lectures on zoology, and in 1839 he gave up medicine at Zurich to study botany under Alphonse de Candolle at Geneva. In 1840 he received the doctorate for his study of Swiss *Circia*, a work marked by the same precision and detail as his later studies. There followed a summer semester in Berlin when he studied Hegel's philosophy. Hegel had been dead eleven years, but his writings were still much admired. Although in retrospect Naegeli claimed that he had found nothing useful in Hegelianism, his work is characterized by a Hegelian search for universal concepts which at times seems pedantic and misdirected.

In the autumn of 1842 Naegeli left Berlin for Jena, where he worked with Schleiden. Together they published the new, and short-lived, journal *Zeitschrift für wissenschaftliche Botanik.* Naegeli's eighteen months in Jena were highly productive. From 1845 to 1852 he worked in Zurich, first as *Privatdozent,* then as assistant professor. There his collaboration with Carl Cramer in plant physiology research began in 1850. This work was continued when he became full professor at Freiburg im Breisgau in 1852. Finally in 1857 he accepted the chair of botany in the University of Munich. There, in 1890, he celebrated the fiftieth anniversary of his degree.

When Naegeli arrived in Jena, Schleiden had just published his famous *Grundzüge der wissenschaftlichen Botanik*, which begins with a lengthy critique of the philosophy of science and goes on to enunciate the Schleiden-Schwann theory of free cell formation, the analogy of cryptogamous spores with phanerogamous pollen, and the assertion that the embryo in phanerogams is the transformed tip of the pollen tube. Like Schleiden, Naegeli began with a philosophical essay, "Über die gegenwärtige Aufgabe der Naturgeschichte, insbesondere der Botanik," in which he eschewed compilations of empirical data, since science is concerned not with the changing characteristics of individuals but with the unchanging laws relevant to all individuals. When he sought to practice science in harmony with this definition he ran into difficulties. His early studies of cell division (1844, 1846) appeared to show two types of cell formation—free cell formation and division of preexisting cells. At first he found the latter process in all cells of algae and diatoms and in all spore mother and pollen mother cells of lower and higher plants. Two years later he altered this

decision, making a simple distinction between reproductive tissues, in which free cell formation rules, and vegetative tissues, in which cell division rules. Meanwhile a more decisive stand in favor of cell division had been taken by Unger.

These studies of cell formation illustrate Naegeli's striving for general laws, the strong influence of Schleiden on him, and his eye for detail. Thus he realized that in cell division the wall formed between the two daughter cells is the result, not the cause, of cell division. The latter he recognized as the function of the whole protoplast. These studies also gave valuable support to Robert Brown's assertion of the invariable presence of a single nucleus in every cell, and it is to his and Mohl's credit that the protoplasmic lining of the cell (Naegeli's *Schleimschicht*) was recognized as the living substance.

Naegeli's failure in 1846 to limit correctly the application of Schleiden's theory of cell formation must be balanced against his brilliant achievement in 1845, when he studied apical growth. This work culminated thirteen years later in his researches into the formation of tissues in the stems and roots of vascular plants, which constituted a major contribution to plant anatomy. For his study of apical growth he began with simple cases—from the Bryophyta—and in his thorough manner he traced back the various tissues and organs in a cell lineage to the apical cell. The regular way in which this cell cuts off daughter cells in either one, two, or three rows gave Naegeli an example of the operation of laws which he could represent mathematically and which for him pointed the way to absolute concepts of the sort characteristic of science proper. It was no accident that he used the phrase *wissenschaftliche Botanik* in the title of two of his series of papers, nor was it uncharacteristic for him to represent apical cell division in terms of equations. This was the realization of Schleiden's hope that the development of plants would one day be expressed by mathematical laws. Naegeli's success in thus tracing cell lineages had a profound impact on the botanists of his time.

Extending these studies to the vascular cryptogams and the angiosperms, Naegeli arrived at the important distinction between formative tissues (*Bildungsgewebe*), which he divided into cambia and meristems, and structural tissues (*Dauergewebe*) no longer actively multiplying. In the stems and roots of plants was a strain of cells (cambial and meristematic) which remained untouched by differentiation and whose origin could be traced back to the original "foundation cell" or zygote. Unfortunately he did not draw the same conclusion from these findings as did Weismann from his study of the Coelenterata.

Naegeli's conception of an hereditary and a nutritive component in every cell derived instead from the facts of sexual reproduction.

In 1844 Naegeli discovered the antherozoids of ferns and in 1850 those of the Rhizocarps. He also discovered the protonema and archegonia in *Ricciocarpus*, but it was left for Hofmeister to arrive at the correct analogies between these organs and those of the phanerogams. It seems that Naegeli was too much under Schleiden's influence. How else could he have rejected the discovery of antherozoids in *Fucus* by Decaisne and Thuret in 1849?

Naegeli made a major contribution to the field of cell ultrastructure when he published his detailed study of starch grains in 1858. Here he arrived at his micellar theory, according to which such amorphous substances as starch and cellulose consist of building blocks, which he later termed "micelles," packed in crystalline array. Each micelle was an aggregate of up to nine thousand molecules ("atoms" in Naegeli's terminology) of starch. Water could penetrate between the micelles, and new micelles could form in the interstices between old micelles. The swelling property of starch grains and their growth by intussusception were thus based on a molecular-aggregate model, which he also applied to the cellulose of the cell wall. Three years later (1861) he reported on the anisotropy of starch grains and of cell walls from observations with the polarimeter, which he took as supporting his assumption of crystalline ultrastructure. Other botanists, notably Strasburger, put a different interpretation upon this anisotropy.

Nevertheless, Naegeli's micellar theory stimulated studies of ultrastructure and initiated a tradition of the study of botanical ultrastructure in Germany and Switzerland, a tradition continued by Hermann Ambronn in Jena and Alfred Frey-Wyssling at the Polytechnic in Zurich. Naegeli's work also fostered a belief in micellar aggregates at the expense of the macromolecular concept; a lengthy debate ensued in the 1920's and 1930's between the concept of a long chain polymer and an aggregate or micell of several shorter chains.

In his search for general laws, Naegeli used his micellar theory, which was based on carbohydrate products, to arrive at a molecular-aggregate model of the hereditary substance, its expression, growth, and modification. This inspired piece of deductive thinking appeared in his famous *Mechanisch-physiologische Theorie der Abstammungslehre* (1884), where the important distinction is made between the nutritive trophoplasm and the hereditary idioplasm—the egg being rich in trophoplasm, the spermatozoon almost completely without it. Since paternal and maternal characteristics are transmitted approximately equally, they must be carried by the idioplasm and not by the trophoplasm. Other biologists, notably Weismann and Nussbaum, developed this idea in relation to current work in cytology. Whereas Naegeli made his idioplasm a continuous web of fibers which penetrated cell walls, Weismann limited it to the chromosomes in each cell. Oscar Hertwig, on the other hand, who was much influenced by Naegeli, did not restrict the idioplasm to the chromosomes but to the nuclear substance as a whole.

Naegeli's micellar theory can be seen as the fulfillment of his aim to put Schwann's crystal model of cell growth on a sound footing. The studies he published on the cell wall of *Caulerpa* in 1844 mark the beginning of this work which culminated in his grand synthesis of 1884.

Despite Naegeli's creation of molecular models, he never made a complete break with the vitalistic and teleological ideas so popular among German-speaking biologists of his youth. Consequently natural selection was for him only a pruning device, evolution being the result of an internal perfecting principle. To the end of his days he believed in the spontaneous generation of cells and that, in view of the time required for complexity to be achieved, simple organisms must be younger than complex ones. His search for discontinuities between species and between the plant and animal kingdoms was consistent with his desire for absolute concepts. It was to Naegeli—who had denied the existence of antherozoa in *Fucus*, of genuine species of microorganisms responsible for infectious diseases, and of Darwin's role for natural selection—that Gregor Mendel sent his "Versuche über Pflanzenhybriden." Naegeli, who believed he himself knew how hybrids behaved from his study of crosses in the genus *Hieracium*, regarded Mendel's hybrid ratios and demonstration of complete reversion as of purely empirical significance, irrelevant to genuine species.

As one of the nineteenth century's foremost botanists and influential theoreticians, Naegeli deserves sympathetic evaluation as both an innovator and a victim of the biological thinking to which he contributed so much. Where he failed so conspicuously his famous pupil Carl Correns succeeded. Correns was one of the three rediscoverers of Mendel's laws.

BIBLIOGRAPHY

I. ORIGINAL WORKS. A complete list of Naegeli's publications will be found in S. Schwendener's obituary notice (see below). With Schwendener he wrote the very popular *Das Mikroskop; Theorie und Anwendung desselben*,

2 vols. (Leipzig, 1867), English trans. by F. Crisp (London, 1887; 2nd ed., London, 1892). Naegeli introduced the term *Micell* in the 2nd German ed. of 1877. With A. Peters he wrote *Die Hieracien Mittel Europas. Monographische Bearbeitung der Piloselloiden mit besonderer Berücksichtigung der mitteleuropaischen Sippen*, 2 vols. (Munich, 1885–1889). Naegeli's final statements on heredity, growth, and ultrastructure will be found in *Mechanisch-physiologische Theorie der Abstammungslehre* (Munich–Leipzig, 1884).

The majority of his earlier cytological papers appeared in the short-lived journal which he and Schleiden edited, *Zeitschrift für wissenschaftliche Botanik* (Jena, 1844–1847). The most important papers from this journal were translated into English by Arthur Henfrey and published in the Ray Society's *Reports and Papers on Botany* (London, 1846, 1849). Naegeli's studies of starch grains, his micellar theory, and his work with C. Cramer were published in the series *Pflanzenphysiologische Untersuchungen von C. Naegeli und C. Cramer*, nos. 1–4 (Zurich, 1855–1858). A selection from Naegeli's contributions was published by Albert Frey in *Die Micellartheorie . . . Auszüge aus den grundlegenden Originalarbeiten Nägelis, Zusammenfassung und kurze Geschichte der Micellartheorie,* in Ostwald's *Klassiker der exakten Wissenschaften,* no. 227 (Leipzig, 1908).

Forty-two papers presented by Naegeli to the Bavarian Academy are in *Botanische Mitteilungen aus den Sitzungsberichten der k. b. Akademie der Wissenschaft in München,* III (Munich, 1863–1881). Extracts from Naegeli's letters to Mendel were published by Hugo Iltis in his *Life of Mendel* (London, 1932; repr. 1966).

II. SECONDARY LITERATURE. A long list of obituary notices is given in the Royal Society *Catalogue of Scientific Papers*, 17 (1891), 443. Readily available is D. H. Scott's notice in *Nature*, 44 (1891), 580–583.

The only biographical notice which includes a full bibliography is that by S. Schwendener in *Bericht der deutschen botanischen Gesellschaft*, 9 (1891), (26)–(42). Most accounts of Naegeli's life rely on C. Cramer, *Leben und Wirken von Carl Wilhelm Nägeli* (Zurich, 1896; first published in the *Neue Zürcher Zeitung*, 16 May 1891). For a critical account of Naegeli's botanical work see Sidney Vines's obituary notice in the *Proceedings of the Royal Society*, 51 (1892), 27–36. The work of Naegeli and Schwendener is included in A. Frey-Wyssling's paper, "Frühgeschichte und Ergebnisse der submikroskopischen Morphologie," in *Mikroskopie,* 19 (1964), 2–12. Naegeli's micellar theory has been analyzed in depth by J. S. Wilkie. His summary of this work appeared in *Nature*, 209 (1961), 1145–1150, and his detailed papers are "Nägeli's Work on the Fine Structure of Living Matter," nos. I, II, IIIa, IIIb, in *Annals of Science,* 16 (1960), 11–42, 171–207, 209–239, and *ibid.*, 17 (1961), 27–62.

Naegeli's philosophical position and his attitude to Mendel are discussed in J. S. Wilkie's commentary to the paper by Bentley Glass, "The Establishment of Modern Genetical Theory as an Example of the Interaction of Different Models, Techniques, and Inferences," in A. C. Crombie, ed., *Scientific Change, Symposium on the History of Science, . . . Oxford* (London, 1963), 521–541, commentary on 597–603. Naegeli's attitude to Mendel has also been discussed by A. Weinstein, "The Reception of Mendel's Paper by His Contemporaries," in *Proceedings of the Tenth International Congress of the History of Science* (Ithaca, 1962; Paris, 1964), 997–1001, and in R. C. Olby and P. Gautrey, "Eleven References to Mendel Before 1900," in *Annals of Science,* 24 (1968), 7–20. C. C. Gillispie has compared the speculative ideas of Naegeli and Weismann in *The Edge of Objectivity: An Essay in the History of Scientific Ideas* (Princeton–London, 1960), 322–328.

ROBERT OLBY

IBN AL-NAFĪS, ʿALĀʾ AL-DĪN ABU ʾL-ḤASAN ʿALĪ IBN ABI ʾL-ḤAZM AL-QURASHĪ (or AL-QARASHĪ) (*b.* al-Qurashiyya, near Damascus, thirteenth century; *d.* Cairo, 17 December 1288), *medicine.*

Ibn al-Nafīs' *nisba*, al-Qurashī, is from his birthplace or, according to other authorities, from Qarash, a village beyond the River Oxus from which his family originally came. He studied medicine in Damascus, at the great Nūrī Hospital (al-Bīmāristān al-Nūrī al-Kabīr) founded by the Turkish prince Nūr al-Dīn Maḥmūd ibn Zankī (Nureddin) in the twelfth century. Among his teachers was Muhadhdhab al-Dīn ʿAbd al-Raḥīm ibn ʿAlī al-Dakhwār (*d.* 1230), founder of al-Dakhwāriyya Medical School at Damascus, and among his students at Damascus was Abu ʾl-Faraj ibn Yaʿqūb ibn Isḥāq al-Masīḥī ibn al-Quff Amīn al-Dawla al-Karakī (1233–1286), who at one time was Ibn Abī Uṣaybiʿa's student.

The hospital in which Ibn al-Nafīs practiced and taught in Egypt is not known with certainty. Eventually he became *raʾīs al-aṭibbāʾ* (chief of physicians), possibly appointed by the Mamlūk ruler al-Ẓāhir Baybars al-Bunduqdārī (reigned 1260–1277), for whom Ibn al-Nafīs worked in the capacity of personal physician; this post was not merely honorific but conferred disciplinary powers over medical practitioners. His name does not anywhere appear in connection with the al-Bīmāristān al-Nāṣirī, founded in 1171 by Ṣalāḥ al-Dīn al-Ayyūbī (or Saladin, who reigned from 1169 to 1193), where Ibn Abī Uṣaybiʿa (*d.* 1270) was an oculist during the one year (1236–1237) he spent in Egypt. Toward the end of his life Ibn al-Nafīs bequeathed his house and library to the newly founded Dār al-Shifāʾ (House of Recovery), also called Qalāwūn Hospital or al-Manṣūrī Hospital, founded in 1284 by the Mamlūk al-Manṣūr Sayf al-Dīn Qalāwūn al-Alfī (reigned from 1279 to 1290), during whose time Ibn al-Nafīs died in

602

Cairo—he had then reached the age of about eighty lunar years—on 21 Dhu 'l-Qaʿda 687 or 17 December 1288.

In addition to being a physician Ibn al-Nafīs lectured on *fiqh* (jurisprudence) at al-Masrūriyya School in Cairo. The inclusion of his name in the *Ṭabaqāt al-Shāfiʿiyyīn al-Kubrā* ("Great Classes of Shāfiʿī Scholars") of Tāj al-Dīn al-Subkī (*d.* 1370) indicates his eminence in religious law. He wrote his *Kitāb al-Shāmil fi 'l-Ṣināʿa al-Ṭibbiyya* ("Comprehensive Book on the Art of Medicine") when he was in his thirties. It was said to consist of 300 volumes of notes, of which he published only eighty. This voluminous work was thought to have been lost until 1952, when one large but fragmentary volume was cataloged among the Cambridge University Library Islamic manuscripts. Much earlier, the Bodleian Library cataloged four manuscripts of this work, without identifying the author. In 1960 three autograph manuscripts (MS Z276) were found in Lane Medical Library, Stanford University, of which one is referred to by the author as the thirty-third *mujallad* (volume). The two other manuscripts are its forty-second and forty-third volumes, the latter dated 641/1243–1244. Another manuscript of the same book is extant in al-Mutḥaf al-ʿIrāqī, Baghdad; and al-Ziriklī mentions one manuscript in Damascus (not in the Ẓāhiriyya collection) without specifying any particular library.

The *Kitāb al-Shāmil*, so far unpublished, contains an interesting section on surgical technique and throws new light on Ibn al-Nafīs as a surgeon. In it he defines three stages for each operation—*al-iʿṭāʾ* (the presentation for diagnosis, upon which a patient entrusts a surgeon with his body and life), *al-ʿamal* (the operative procedure), and *al-ḥifẓ* (preservation, that is, postoperative care)—and gives detailed descriptions of the duties of surgeons and the relationships among patients, surgeons, and nurses. He discusses each stage in detail, touching upon such subjects as the decubitus of the patient and the posture, bodily movement, and manipulation of instruments of the surgeon in the course of carrying out his duties. Ibn al-Nafīs illustrates his points with examples of specific operations.

Ibn al-Nafīs' book *Sharḥ Ṭabīʿat al-Insān li-Buqrāṭ* ("Commentary on Hippocrates' *Nature of Man*") was housed in a private library at Damascus owned by Aḥmad ʿUbayd and in 1933 was owned by professor A. S. Yahuda in London. (The medical manuscripts that were in the Yahuda collection are now in the National Library of Medicine, Bethesda, Maryland; the *Sharḥ Ṭabīʿat al-Insān li-Buqrāṭ* is MS A69.) It has an *ijāza* (license) written and signed by Ibn al-Nafīs stating that a physician named Shams al-Dawla Abu 'l-Faḍl ibn Abi 'l-Ḥasan al-Masīḥī had studied the entire book under him. Perhaps one of Ibn al-Nafīs' earliest books is *Sharḥ Tashrīḥ al-Qānūn* ("Commentary on Anatomy in Books I and III of Ibn Sīnā's *Kitāb al-Qānūn*"), of which a copy was written forty-seven lunar years before his death, and is presently at the University of California, Los Angeles (MS Ar. 80). In this book he gives the earliest known account of the pulmonary blood circulation. His major work, *Sharḥ al-Qānūn* ("Commentary on *Kitāb al-Qānūn*") is in four books: "A Commentary on Generalities"; "A Commentary on Materia Medica and Compound Drugs"; "A Commentary on Head-to-Toe Diseases"; and "A Commentary on Diseases Which Are Not Specific to Certain Organs." In the first of these books, the "Commentary on Generalities," Ibn al-Nafīs repeats his account of the lesser circulations of the blood:

> . . . This is the right cavity of the two cavities of the heart. When the blood in this cavity has become thin, it must be transferred into the left cavity, where the pneuma is generated. But there is no passage between these two cavities, the substance of the heart there being impermeable. It neither contains a visible passage, as some people have thought, nor does it contain an invisible passage which would permit the passage of blood, as Galen thought. The pores of the heart there are compact and the substance of the heart is thick. It must, therefore, be that when the blood has become thin, it is passed into the arterial vein [pulmonary artery] to the lung, in order to be dispersed inside the substance of the lung, and to mix with the air. The finest parts of the blood are then strained, passing into the venous artery [pulmonary vein] reaching the left of the two cavities of the heart, after mixing with the air and becoming fit for the generation of pneuma . . . .

According to one manuscript of *Sharḥ Tashrīḥ al-Qānūn* (MS Ar. 80), the *terminus ante quem* of Ibn al-Nafīs' discovery of the lesser circulation can be fixed at 1242, three centuries before those published by Servetus (1553) and Colombo (1559). The determination by Iskandar of discussions of the lesser circulation in commentaries on book I of the *Kitāb al-Qānūn* of Sadīd al-Dīn Muḥammad ibn Masʿūd al-Kāzarūnī (completed in 1344) and ʿAlī ibn ʿAbdallāh Zayn al-ʿArab al-Miṣrī (written in 1350), who used Ibn al-Nafīs' *Sharḥ Tashrīḥ al-Qānūn* and his *Sharḥ al-Qānūn,* may serve to reopen the widely debated question of whether the Latin West had access to Ibn al-Nafīs' description of the lesser circulation. It is believed that Andrea Alpago of Belluno (*d.* 1520) may have transmitted Ibn al-Nafīs' work orally or in hitherto unpublished writings.

Alpago lived in the Middle East (mainly in Syria) for thirty years, collecting, translating, and editing the writings of Arab physicians. He made a Latin translation (Venice, 1547) of the commentary on compound drugs that is a part of Ibn al-Nafīs' *Sharḥ al-Qānūn*. In a section (fds. 24v–30r) entitled "Consideratio sexta de pulsibus ex libro Sirasi arabico," Alpago gives some interesting statements on the Galenic doctrine related to the heart and arterial system, together with Ibn al-Nafīs' criticism.

Ibn al-Nafīs' *Kitāb al-Mūjiz* or *Mūjiz al-Qānūn* ("Epitome of *Kitāb al-Qānūn*") is a concise book divided into four sections corresponding to the four books of the *Sharḥ al-Qānūn*, except that in *Kitāb al-Mūjiz* he does not deal with anatomy or with the lesser circulation. The popularity of *Kitāb al-Mūjiz* led many physicians to write commentaries on it and to translate it into other languages. Two Turkish translations are known, one by Muṣliḥ al-Dīn Muṣṭafā ibn Shaʿbān al-Surūrī (*d.* 1464) and the other by Aḥmad Kamāl, a physician in Adrianople. There is a Hebrew translation entitled *Sefer-ha-Mūjiz*. The author of *Kitāb Tadhkirat al-Suwaydī*, ʿIzz al-Dīn Abū Isḥāq Ibrāhīm ibn Muḥammad ibn Ṭarkhān al-Suwaydī (*d.* 1291), also wrote a commentary on *Kitāb al-Mūjiz*. Other commentaries, still preserved in manuscript, were written by Jalāl al-Dīn Muḥammad ibn ʿAbd al-Raḥmān al-Qazwīnī (*d.* 1308), Muẓaffar al-Dīn Abu ʾl-Thanāʾ Maḥmūd ibn Aḥmad al-ʿAyntābī ibn al-Amshāṭī (*d.* 1496), and Shihāb al-Dīn Muḥammad al-Ījī al-Bulbulī. Three major commentaries, widely used until recently, are *Kitāb al-Mughnī fī Sharḥ al-Mūjiz*, by Sadīd al-Dīn al-Kāzarūnī; *Kitāb Ḥall al-Mūjiz* ("Key to *Kitāb al-Mūjiz*") by Jamāl al-Dīn Muḥammad ibn Muḥammad al-Āqṣarāʾī (*d.* 1378); and *Kitāb al-Nafīsī*, also known as *Sharḥ Mūjiz Ibn al-Nafīs*, by Burhān al-Dīn Nafīs ibn ʿAwaḍ al-Kirmānī (written in 1437). Among many marginal commentaries to the *Kitāb al-Nafīsī* are *Ḥāshiya ʿAlā Sharḥ Nafīs Ibn ʿAwaḍ al-Kirmānī ʿAlā Mūjiz Ibn al-Nafīs* ("Marginal Commentaries on the Commentary of Nafīs ibn ʿAwaḍ al-Kirmānī on *Kitāb al-Mūjiz* of Ibn al-Nafīs") by Ghars al-Dīn Ibrāhīm al-Ḥalabī (*d.* 1563) and *Ḥall al-Nafīsī* ("Key to *Kitāb al-Nafīsī*"), which was begun by Muḥammad ʿAbd al-Ḥalīm and posthumously completed by his son, Muḥammad ʿAbd al-Ḥayy, who published the whole work in 1872. Ibn al-Nafīs wrote out his *Sharḥ Fuṣūl Buqrāṭ* ("Commentary on Hippocrates' *Aphorisms*") more than once, each time to meet certain requests made to him by physicians. An introductory note to a lithographed edition of this book (dated 1892) repeats the statement that he made in his *Sharḥ Tashrīḥ al-Qānūn* and *Sharḥ al-Qānūn*—that he decided to ". . . throw light on and stand by true opinions, and forsake those which are false and erase their traces. . . ." This statement seems to suggest that he rebelled against the authority of books, a view substantiated by his rejection of Galen's concept of invisible pores in the interventricular septum, his notion of blood flow, and his belief that arterial blood was produced in the left ventricle.

Other books written by Ibn al-Nafīs are: *Sharḥ Abīdhīmyā li-Buqrāṭ* ("Commentary on Hippocrates' *Epidemics*"); *Sharḥ Masāʾil Ḥunayn* ("Commentary on Ḥunayn [ibn Isḥāq's] *Questions*"); *al-Muhadhdhab fi ʾl-Kuḥl* ("Polished Book on Ophthalmology"); and *Bughyat al-Ṭālibīn wa Ḥujjat al-Mutaṭabbibīn* ("Reference Book for Physicians"). He also wrote on logic and theology, including such books as his commentary on Ibn Sīnā's *Kitāb al-Hidāya* ("Guidance"), and *Fāḍil Ibn Nāṭiq* (also entitled *al-Risāla al-Kāmiliyya fi ʾl-Sīra al-Nabawiyya*), a counterpart to Ibn Ṭufayl's (*d.* 1185) *Ḥayy Ibn Yaqẓān*. Ibn Ṭufayl's purpose was to show the discovery of philosophical truths by an individual who had been created by spontaneous generation on a desert island, while that of Ibn al-Nafīs was to show the discovery by independent reasoning (under similar conditions) of the main principles of Islamic religion and natural sciences.

Ibn al-Nafīs was reputed to have recorded his own experiences, observations, and deductions rather than using reference books. His religion (Islam) and his mercy toward animals, he tells us, prevented him from practicing anatomy. His major contribution—the discovery of the lesser circulation—was nonetheless a physiological one and would probably have been more adequately documented had he resorted to animal dissection. His experimental approach to physiology is evident in his *Sharḥ Tashrīḥ al-Qānūn*: ". . . In determining the use of each organ we shall rely necessarily on verified examinations and straightforward research, disregarding whether our opinions will agree or disagree with those of our predecessors."

BIBLIOGRAPHY

I. ORIGINAL WORKS. Ibn al-Nafīs' books are *Manāfiʿ al-Aʿḍāʾ al-Insāniyya* (Dār al-Kutub al-Miṣriyya, MS 209, III, *majāmīʿ*); *al-Muhadhdhab fiʾl-Kuḥl* (Vatican, MS Arabo 1307); *Mūjiz al-Qānūn* (Calcutta, 1244/1828, 1261/1845; Lucknow, 1288/1871, 1302/1884, 1324/1906); *Kitāb al-Shāmil fiʾl-Ṣināʿa al-Ṭibbiyya* (incomplete autograph copy, Lane Medical Library, Stanford University, MS Z276; al-Mutḥaf al-ʿIrāqī, Baghdad, MS 1271; Cambridge

University Library, MS Or. 1546 (10); Bodleian Library, MSS Pocock 248 and 290–292); *Sharḥ Abīdhimyā li-Buqrāṭ* (Aya Sofya, MS 3642, fols. 1-200a; Dār al-Kutub al-Miṣriyya, MS 583 Ṭibb Ṭal'at); *Sharḥ Fuṣūl Buqrāṭ* (Teheran [?], 1310/1892; Aya Sofya, MSS 3554, fols. 35b–137b, 3644, fols. 1–109b; Dār al-Kutub al-Miṣriyya, MS 1448 Ṭibb; Forschungsbibliothek, Gotha, MSS 1897–1898; Deutsche Staatsbibliothek, Berlin, MS 6224); *Sharḥ Masāʾil Ḥunayn* (Leiden University Library, MS Or. 49, II, fols. 101b–174a); *Sharḥ Ṭabīʿat al-Insān li-Buqrāṭ* (National Library of Medicine, Bethesda, Md., MS A69; MS owned by Aḥmad ʿUbayd, Damascus and later by A. S. Yahuda, London); *Sharḥ Taqdimat al-Maʿrifa li-Buqrāṭ* (Forschungsbibliothek, Gotha, MS 1899; Leiden University Library, MS Or. 49, I, fols. 1–98; Bodleian Library, MS Marsh 81); *Sharḥ al-Qānūn* (Wellcome Historical Medical Library, London, WMS. Or. 51; and incomplete in WMS. Or. 154); and *Sharḥ Tashrīḥ al-Qānūn* (University of California, Los Angeles, MSS Ar. 80, and Ar. 102, I, pp. 1–298; Bibliothèque Nationale, Paris, MS 2939; Al-Ẓāhiriyya Library, Damascus, MS 3145 Ṭibb XX). See also M. Meyerhof and J. Schacht, *The Theologus Autodidactus of Ibn al-Nafīs*, ed. with intro., trans., and notes (Oxford, 1968).

Other works directly related to Ibn al-Nafīs' writings are al-Āqṣarāʾī, *Ḥall al-Mūjiz* (Lucknow, 1325/1907; Urdu trans., 2 vols., Lucknow, 1325–1326/1907–1908); al-Kāzarūnī, *Kitāb al-Mughnī fī Sharḥ al-Mūjiz* (Calcutta, 1244/1828, 1832; Lucknow, 1295/1878, 1307/1890, 1894); al-Kirmānī's *Kitāb al-Nafīsī* (Lucknow, 1282/1865); ʿAbd al-Ḥalīm and ʿAbd al-Ḥayy, *Ḥall al-Nafīsī* (Cawnpore, 1288/1872; Lucknow, 1302/1885); al-Kāzarūnī, *Sharḥ al-Qānūn* (*al-Kulliyyāt*) (Wellcome Historical Medical Library, WMS. Or. 89); Zayn al-ʿArab al-Miṣrī, *Sharḥ al-Qānūn* (Wellcome Historical Medical Library, WMS. Or. 119); and Ibn Rushd, . . . *Avicenna . . . libellus de removendes nocumentis quae accidunt in regimine sanitatis* . . ., A. Alpago, trans. (Venice, 1547).

II. SECONDARY LITERATURE. General works are Ibn Abī Uṣaybiʿa, *ʿUyūn al-Anbāʾ* (al-Ẓāhiriyya Library, MS 4883, I, ʿāmm, fol. 104)—the concise account at the end of this manuscript seems to have been written by a later author, not by Ibn Abī Uṣaybiʿa himself, and does not appear in the Būlāq ed., 2 vols. (1882–1884); Ibn Faḍlallāh al-ʿUmarī, *Masālik al-Abṣār* . . . (Dār al-Kutub al-Miṣriyya, MS 8 mīm, Maʿārif ʿāmma, VIII, 119a); al-Ṣafadī, *Kitāb al-Wāfī bi'l-Wafayāt* (British Museum, MS Or. 6587, fols. 20v–21v); Abū ʿAbdallāh Muḥammad ibn Aḥmad al-Dhahabī, *Tārīkh al-Islām* (Bodleian Library, MS Laud Or. 279, fol. 170a); ʿAbdallāh ibn Asʿad al-Yāfiʿī, *Mirʾāt al-Janān*, IV (Hyderabad, 1920–1921), 207; Tāj al-Dīn al-Subkī, *Ṭabaqāt al-Shāfiʿiyyīn al-Kubrā*, V (Cairo, 1906–1907), 129; J. Uri, *Bibliothecae Bodleianae codicum manuscriptorum orientalium* (Oxford, 1787), pt. 1, 130; A. Nicoll and E. B. Pusey, *Bibliothecae Bodleianae* . . ., (Oxford, 1821–1835), pt. 2, 586; L. Leclerc, *Histoire de la médecine arabe*, II (Paris, 1876), 207–209; W. Pertsch, *Die arabischen Handschriften der herzoglichen Bibliothek zu Gotha* (Gotha, 1878–1892), III, 444–446; W. Ahlwardt, *Verzeichniss der*

arabischen Handschriften (Berlin, 1887–1899), V, 496; *The Encyclopaedia of Islam* (Leiden–London, 1913–1938), supp., 94–95; *ibid.*, new ed. (Leiden–London, 1960–1971), III, 897–898; G. Sarton, *Introduction to the History of Science* (Baltimore, 1927–1948), II, 1099–1101; A. Issa, *Histoire des bimaristans (hôpitaux) à l'époque islamique* (Cairo, 1928); and *Tārīkh al-Bīmāristānāt fī 'l-Islām* (Damascus, 1939).

See also C. A. Wood, "The Lost Manuscript on Ophthalmology by the Thirteenth-Century Surgeon Ibn al-Nafīs," in *Journal of the American Medical Association*, **104** (1935), 2122–2123; C. Brockelmann, *Geschichte der arabischen Litteratur* (Leiden, 1943–1949), I, 649, and supp. (Leiden, 1937–1942), I, 899; I. al-Baghdādī, *Īḍāḥ al-Maknūn* . . . (Istanbul, 1945), I, 188; and *Hadiyyat al-ʿĀrifīn* . . . (Istanbul, 1951), I, 714; J. ʿAwwād, *Jawla fī Dūr al-Kutub al-Amrīkiyya* (Baghdad, 1951), 46; A. J. Arberry, *A Second Supplementary Hand-List of the Muḥammadan Manuscripts in the University and Colleges of Cambridge* (Cambridge, 1952), 57; Kh. al-Ziriklī, *al-Aʿlām* . . ., 2nd ed. (Cairo, 1954–1959), V, 78, and pl. 740; J. Schacht, "Ibn al-Nafīs et son *Theologus Autodidactus*," in *Homenaje a Millás-Vallicrosa*, II (Barcelona, 1956), 325–345; ʿU. R. Kaḥḥāla, *Muʿjam al-Muʾallifīn* . . . (Damascus, 1957–1961), VII, 58; Ṣ. al-Munajjid, "Maṣādir Jadīda ʿAn Tārīkh al-Ṭibb ʿInd al-ʿArab," in *Majallat Maʿhad al-Makhṭūṭāt al-ʿArabiyya*ʾ, 5, no. 2 (1959), 270; M. J. L. Young, "Some Observations on the Use of Arabic as a Scientific Language as Exemplified in the *Mūjiz al-Qānūn* of Ibn al-Nafīs (*d.* 1288)," in *Abr-Nahrain*, **1** (1959–1960), 68–72; N. Heer, "Thalāthat Mujalladāt Min Kitāb al-Shāmil lʾ Ibn al-Nafīs," in *Majallat Maʿhad al-Makhṭūṭāt al-ʿArabiyya*, **6** (1960), 203–210; S. K. Hamarneh, *Index of Manuscripts on Medicine, Pharmacy, and Allied Sciences in the Ẓāhiriyah Library* (Damascus, 1969), 476–481, and pl. 7; M. Ullmann, *Die Medizin im Islam*, which is pt. 1, supp. VI, of *Handbuch der Orientalistik* (Leiden–Cologne, 1970), 172–176.

On blood circulation see M. Tatawi, *Der Lungenkreislauf nach el-Koraschi*, inaugural diss. (Freiburg, 1924); M. Meyerhof, "M. El-Tatawi: Der lungenkreislauf nach el-Koraschi," in *Mitteilungen zur Geschichte der Medizin und Naturwissenschaften*, **30** (1931), 55–57; "La découverte de la circulation pulmonaire par Ibn an-Nafīs, médecin arabe du Caire (xiiie siècle)," in *Bulletin de l'Institut d'Égypte*, **16** (1934), 33–46; "Ibn an-Nafīs und seine Theorie des Lungenkreislaufs," in *Quellen und Studien zur Geschichte der Naturwissenschaften und Medizin*, **4** (1935), 37–88, and 1–22 (Arabic text); and "Ibn An-Nafîs (XIIIth cent.) and His Theory of the Lesser Circulation," in *Isis*, **23** (1935), 100–120; S. Ḥaddād and A. Khairallah, "A Forgotten Chapter in the History of the Circulation of the Blood," in *Annals of Surgery*, **104** (1936), 1–8; S. Ḥaddād, "Who Is the Discoverer of the Lesser Circulation?" in *al-Muqtaṭaf*, **89** (1936), 264–271; and "Arabian Contributions to Medicine," in *Annals of Medical History*, **3** (1941), 60–72; O. Temkin, "Was Servetus Influenced by Ibn an-Nafīs?" in *Bulletin of the History of Medicine*, **8** (1940), 731–734; T. Bannurah, "Enthüllungen in der

Geschichte der Medizin, Ibn al-Nafīs oder Serveto?" in *Münchener medizinische Wochenschrift*, **88** (1941), 1088 ff.; L. Binet and A. Herpin, "Sur la découverte de la circulation pulmonaire," in *Bulletin de l'Académie nationale de médecine*, 3rd ser., **132**, nos. 31–32 (1948), 542–549.

See also A. Chéhadé, *Ibn al-Nafīs et la découverte de la circulation pulmonaire*, M.D. dissertation (Faculté de Médecine, Paris, 1951), no. 1143; *Ibn al-Nafīs et la découverte de la circulation pulmonaire* (Damascus, 1955); and "Ibn al-Nafīs et la découverte de la circulation pulmonaire," in *Maroc médical*, **35** (1956), 1013–1016; C. D. O'Malley, *Michael Servetus, A Translation of His Geographical, Medical, and Astrological Writings With Introductions and Notes* (Philadelphia, 1953), 195–200; and "A Latin Translation of Ibn Nafis (1547) Related to the Problem of the Circulation of the Blood," in *Journal of the History of Medicine and Allied Sciences*, **12**, no. 2 (1957), 248–253; E. E. Bittar, "A Study of Ibn Nafis," in *Bulletin of the History of Medicine*, **29** (1955), 352–368, 429–447; and "The Influence of Ibn Nafis: A Linkage in Medical History," in *University of Michigan Medical Bulletin*, **22** (1956), 274–278; G. Wiet, "Ibn al-Nafīs et la circulation pulmonaire," in *Journal Asiatique*, **244** (1956), 95–100; E. D. Coppola, "The Discovery of the Pulmonary Circulation: A New Approach," in *Bulletin of the History of Medicine*, **31** (1957), 44–77; and J. Schacht, "Ibn an-Nafīs, Servetus and Colombo," in *al-Andalus*, **22** (1957), 317–336.

Also of value are L. G. Wilson, "The Problem of the Discovery of the Pulmonary Circulation," in *Journal of the History of Medicine*, **17** (1962), 229–244; R. E. Siegel, "The Influence of Galen's Doctrine of Pulmonary Blood-flow on the Development of Modern Concepts of Circulation," in *Sudhoffs Archiv für Geschichte der Medizin und der Naturwissenschaften*, **46** (1962), 311–332; A. Z. Iskandar, *A Catalogue of Arabic Manuscripts on Medicine and Science in the Wellcome Historical Medical Library* (London, 1967), 38–42, 47–50; and E. Lagrange, "Réflexions sur l'historique de la découverte de la circulation sanguine," in *Episteme*, **3** (1969), 31–44.

ALBERT Z. ISKANDAR

NAGAOKA, HANTARO (*b.* Nagasaki, Japan, 15 August 1865; *d.* Tokyo, Japan, 11 December 1950), *physics*.

Nagaoka graduated from the department of physics of the University of Tokyo in 1887 and entered the graduate school, where he began experimental research in magnetostriction under the British physicist C. G. Knott, who was in Japan between 1883 and 1891. After receiving a doctorate, Nagaoka studied at the universities of Berlin, Munich, and Vienna from 1893 to 1896. He was especially impressed by Boltzmann's course on the kinetic theory of gases at the University of Munich. In 1900 Nagaoka was stimulated to study atomic structure to explain radioactivity by the lecture of the Curies at the first international congress of physics in Paris, where he had been invited to deliver a paper on magnetostriction.

From 1901 to 1925 Nagaoka, a leading professor of physics at the University of Tokyo, was primarily responsible for promoting the advancement of physics in Japan. In addition to studying magnetostriction, he did work in atomic structure, geophysics, mathematical physics, spectroscopy, and radio waves. The present Japanese tradition of experimental and theoretical physics has been formed almost entirely by Nagaoka and his successors. These include his pupils Kotaro Honda, Jun Ishiwara, Shoji Nishikawa, and Yoshio Nishina and his protégé Hideki Yukawa. For his efforts the Japanese government awarded him the National Cultural Prize in 1937.

Nagaoka is known for his Saturnian atomic model, published in 1904. His criticism of Lord Kelvin's Aepinus atom, proposed in the paper "Aepinus Atomized" (*Philosophical Magazine*, 6th ser., **3** [1902], 257–283), was essential for the formation of his model. Rejecting the interpenetrability of two kinds of electricity, which had been supposed by Kelvin, Nagaoka arranged electrons outside the central positive charge. Thus his model consists of a number of electrons of equal mass, arranged uniformly in a ring, and a positively charged sphere of large mass at the center of the ring. This material view of electricity played the most important role in Nagaoka's theory of the structure of matter, which was based partly on Boltzmann's atomistic influence and partly on the reflection of unsophisticated scientific thought in Japan during the early Meiji period. He obtained the equations of motion of the ring in his model according to Maxwell's work on the stability of the motion of Saturn's rings, which he had read in Germany. In 1904–1905 Nagaoka dealt with band spectra, dispersion of light, and mutual action of atoms, based on the assumption of a Saturnian atom. Having renounced his model, he started spectroscopic experiments to investigate the actual arrangement of electrons in the atom in 1908.

BIBLIOGRAPHY

Nagaoka's paper on the Saturnian atomic model is in *Proceedings of the Tokyo Mathematico-Physical Society*, 2nd ser., **2** (1904), 92–107; and *Philosophical Magazine*, 6th ser., **7** (1904), 445–455.

Anniversary Volume Dedicated to Professor Nagaoka by His Friends and Pupils on the Completion of Twenty-Five Years of His Professorship (Tokyo, 1925) contains a bibliography of his works. The origin of his model is discussed in Eri Yagi, "On Nagaoka's Saturnian Atomic Model," in *Japanese Studies in the History of Science* (1964), no. 3, 29–47. Nagaoka's life and work are fully discussed in connection with the development of physics in Japan in Kiyomobu Itakura, Tosaka Kimura, and Eri Yagi, *A Biography of Hantaro Nagaoka* (Tokyo, 1973), written in Japanese.

ERI YAGI

NĀGEŚA (*fl.* Gujarat, India, *ca.* 1630), *astronomy.*

Nāgeśa was born into a family of learned Brāhmaṇas of the Gārgyagotra, who resided at Khecaramaṇḍala in Gujarat. His father, Śiva, and his grandfather, Keśava, are otherwise unknown to us; but his son, Śiva, was the author of a *Saṅkrāntipaṭala* on the entry of the sun into the signs of the zodiac. Nāgeśa's principal astronomical work is an unpublished *Grahaprabodha* in thirty-seven verses, which gives instructions for computing the true longitudes of the sun, the moon, and the planets according to the parameters of the *Gaṇeśapakṣa* founded by Gaṇeśa in 1520 (see essay in Supplement); its epoch is 5 March 1619. In 1663 Nāgeśa's pupil, Yādava, wrote a set of tables based on the *Grahaprabodha* (see D. Pingree, *Sanskrit Astronomical Tables in the United States* [Philadelphia, 1968], 63a–64b, and *Sanskrit Astronomical Tables in England* [Madras, 1973], 149).

Nāgeśa also wrote a *Nirṇayatattva* in 102 verses which describe the computation of the *tithis* in a synodic month. Based on the *Nirṇayasindhu*, which was composed by Kamalākara Bhaṭṭa in 1612, the *Nirṇayatattva* uses as an example the year 1629–1630. A *Parvādhikāra* on the syzygies is also attributed to Nāgeśa.

BIBLIOGRAPHY

Aside from the articles mentioned above, see Ś. B. Dīkṣita, *Bhāratīya Jyotiḥśāstra* (Poona, 1896; repr. Poona, 1931), 285–286, and D. Pingree, "On the Classification of Indian Planetary Tables," in *Journal for the History of Astronomy*, **1** (1970), 95–108, esp. 99–100.

DAVID PINGREE

AL-NAIRĪZĪ. See al-Nayrīzī.

NAIRNE, EDWARD (*b.* Sandwich [?], England, 1726; *d.* London, England, 1 September 1806), *mathematics, optics, physics.*

Nairne achieved an international reputation as one of the foremost makers of mathematical, optical, and philosophical instruments of the eighteenth century. He became free of the Spectaclemakers Company in 1748 and established his business in London at 20 Cornhill, not far from the shop of Matthew Loft, to whom he had been apprenticed in 1741. Nairne took Thomas Blunt, his own former apprentice, into partnership in 1774, and the firm, which in 1791 was moved to 22 Cornhill, continued as Nairne and Blunt until the latter's death in 1822.

In 1771 Nairne contributed to the *Philosophical Transactions of the Royal Society* the first of many papers on experiments in optics, pneumatics, and, most notably, electricity. He was elected a fellow of the Royal Society in 1776.

In 1772 Nairne invented an improved form of electrostatic machine using a cylindrical glass vessel as the generator. Its quick acceptance in England and on the Continent did much to enhance his reputation. The regular production from Nairne's shop included microscopes, telescopes, navigating and surveying instruments, electrical machines, vacuum pumps, and measuring equipment required by the new philosophical laboratories.

Franklin seems to have had a long acquaintance with Nairne and his work. In 1758 Nairne made a set of artificial magnets for him, and the swelling and shrinking of the mahogany case led to a later correspondence between them on a possible design for a hygrometer. After the Harvard College fire of 1764, Nairne was one of the makers commissioned, on Franklin's recommendation, to replace the lost instruments.

Nairne also reported on his experiments on the specific gravity and freezing point of seawater, desiccation by means of a vacuum, and the adaptation of the mercury barometer for use at sea.

BIBLIOGRAPHY

I. ORIGINAL WORKS. Nairne's papers published in the *Philosophical Transactions of the Royal Society* include "Description of a New Constructed Equatorial Telescope," **61** (1771), 223–225; "Water From Sea Ice," **66** (1776), 249–256; "Experiments With the Air-pump," **67** (1777), 614–648; and "Experiments on Electricity," **68** (1778), 823–860. Other works are *Description of a Pocket Microscope* (n.p., 1771); *Directions for Using the Electrical Machine as Made and Sold by E. Nairne* (London, 1773); *Directions for the Use of the Octant* (n.d.).

Many of Nairne's instruments survive and some may be seen in the collections of the Adler Planetarium, Chicago; Conservatoire National des Arts et Métiers, Paris; Harvard University; the museums of the history of science at Oxford and Florence; National Maritime Museum, Greenwich; Naval Museum, Madrid; Science

Museum, London; and the Smithsonian Institution, Washington.

II. SECONDARY LITERATURE. See Maria Luisa Bonelli, *Catalogo degli strumenti dei Museo di storia della scienza* (Florence, 1954), 92, 131, 194, 200, 208, 210, 251–252, 254, 256; I. Bernard Cohen, *Some Early Tools of American Science* (Cambridge, Mass., 1950), 166, 169; Maurice Daumas, *Les instruments scientifiques au XVII et XVIII siècles* (Paris, 1953), 316–317; Nicholas Goodison, *English Barometers, 1680–1860* (New York, 1968), 52–53, 123, 168–170, 257; W. E. Knowles Middleton, *The History of the Barometer* (Baltimore, 1964), 163; Leslie Stephen and Sidney Lee, eds., *Dictionary of National Biography*, XIV, 25–26; E. G. R. Taylor, *The Mathematical Practitioners of Hanoverian England* (London, 1966), 50, 53, 62–63, 66, 214; Carl Van Doren, ed., *Benjamin Franklin's Autobiographical Writings* (New York, 1945), 490–494; and David P. Wheatland, *The Apparatus of Science at Harvard, 1765–1800* (Cambridge, Mass., 1968), 22–23, 79, 155–161.

RODERICK S. WEBSTER

NAJĪB AL-DĪN. See **al-Samarqandī, Najīb al-Dīn.**

NAMETKIN, SERGEY SEMENOVICH (*b.* Kazan, Russia, 3 July 1876; *d.* Moscow, U.S.S.R., 5 August 1950), *chemistry.*

Nametkin's parents died when he was ten; he graduated from a Gymnasium in Moscow, earning his living as a private tutor. From 1896 to 1902 he studied and then taught at Moscow University. From 1910 he was assistant professor and, from 1911, when he was awarded his M.Sc., professor of organic chemistry at the Higher Women's Courses, which in 1917 became the Second Moscow University (of which he was rector from 1919 to 1924), and then the Moscow Institute of Fine Chemical Technology. In 1938 he returned to Moscow University, where he was head of the organic chemistry department until 1950. From 1927 to 1950 he was professor of organic chemistry and petrochemistry in the petroleum department of the Moscow Mining Academy; the department was reorganized as the Moscow Petroleum Institute.

In 1917 Nametkin was awarded the degree of D.Sc.; from 1932 he was a corresponding member, and from 1939 a member, of the Academy of Sciences of the U.S.S.R. From 1939 to 1950 he was director of the Institute of Fossil Fuels, and then of the Petroleum Institute of the Soviet Academy of Sciences, which was created from the former.

Nametkin's scientific work concentrated on the nitration of saturated hydrocarbons, the chemistry of terpenes, stereochemistry, the chemistry and technology of petroleum, and the synthesis of growth stimulators and perfumes.

Having examined in his thesis the effect of dilute nitric acid on monocyclic and bicyclic hydrocarbons, Nametkin developed a logical scheme of the resulting transformations: if hydrogen at a tertiary carbon atom reacts, then a tertiary nitric compound is immediately formed; in other cases intermediate isonitroso compounds are formed, which subsequently either isomerize into stable nitric compounds or are decomposed into nitrous oxide and a ketone or an aldehyde. The latter is easily oxidized into carboxylic acid.

Nametkin's many investigations in the chemistry of terpenes, particularly the study of the hydration of α-methylcamphene with the formation of 4-methylisoborneol, led him to an important generalization—the discovery of the camphene rearrangement of the second type; this has been called the Nametkin rearrangement and has led to the clarification of phenomena in the chemistry of camphor and camphene that were not explained by the Wagner-Meerwein rearrangement.

Nametkin studied the composition of petroleum and natural gases of the Soviet Union; investigated the chemical nature of petroleum paraffins and ceresins; showed the presence in them of a significant quantity of hydrocarbons with branched structure; discovered a new type of transformation of ethylene hydrocarbons—the hydro-dehydropolymerization reaction—as a result of which hydrogenated lower-polymers and highly unsaturated higher-polymers are formed in the presence of acid catalysts; showed that thiophanes constitute a significant part of the sulfur compounds of petroleum; conducted systematic research on the desulfurization of shale gasolines and on the chemistry of the cracking process with simultaneous partial oxidation, developed a method for the analysis of cracking gasolines. Nametkin published more than 300 works on organic and petroleum chemistry.

BIBLIOGRAPHY

I. ORIGINAL WORKS. Many of Nametkin's writings were brought together in *Izbrannye trudy* ("Selected Works"; Moscow–Leningrad, 1949); and almost all are in *Sobranie trudov* ("Collected Works"), 3 vols. (Moscow–Leningrad, 1954–1956), with a sketch of his life and works and a bibliography in vol. I. Among his works are *K voprosu o deystvii azotnoy kisloty na uglevodorody predelnogo kharaktera* ("On the Action of Nitric Acid on Saturated Hydrocarbons"; Moscow, 1911), his master's thesis;

Issledovania iz oblasti bitsiklicheskikh soedineny ("Research on Bicyclic Compounds"; Moscow, 1916), his doctoral thesis; and *Khimia nefti* ("The Chemistry of Petroleum"; Moscow–Leningrad, 1955).

II. SECONDARY LITERATURE. See V. M. Rodionov, A. K. Ruzhentseva, A. S. Nekrasov, and N. N. Melnikov, "Akademik Sergey Semenovich Nametkin," in *Zhurnal obshchey khimii*, **21** (1951), 2101–2146; P. I. Sanin, "Sergey Semenovich Nametkin (k devyanostoletiyu so dnya rozhdenia)" ("Sergey Semenovich Nametikin [on the Ninetieth Anniversary of His Birth]"), in *Neftekhimia*, **6** (1966), 649–658; *Sergey Semenovich Nametkin*, in the series *Materialy k bibliografii uchenykh SSSR* ("Material for a Bibliography of Scientists of the U.S.S.R."; Moscow–Leningrad, 1946); A. V. Topchiev, S. R. Sergienko, and P. I. Sanin, "Trudy vydayushchegosya sovetskogo uchenogo S. S. Nametkina v oblasti khimicheskoy nauki i neftyanoy promyshlennosti" ("Works of the Distinguished Soviet Scientist S. S. Nametkin in Chemistry and the Petroleum Industry"), in *Izvestia Akademii nauk SSSR*, Otd. tekhn. nauk (1951), no. 1, 3–21; and G. D. Vovchenko and A. F. Platé, "Akademik Sergey Semenovich Nametkin (k godovshchine so dnya smerti)" ("Academician S. S. Nametkin [on the Anniversary of His Death]"), in *Vestnik Moskovskogo . . . universiteta* (1951), no. 10, 89–94.

A. PLATÉ

NANSEN, FRIDTJOF (*b.* Fröen, Norway, 10 October 1861; *d.* Oslo, Norway, 13 May 1930), *anatomy*.

For a detailed study of his life and work, see Supplement.

NAPIER, JOHN (*b.* Edinburgh, Scotland, 1550; *d.* Edinburgh, 4 April 1617), *mathematics*.

The eighth laird of Merchiston, John Napier was the son of Sir Archibald Napier by his first wife, Janet Bothwell, daughter of an Edinburgh burgess. At the age of thirteen he went to St. Salvator's College, St. Andrews, where he lodged with John Rutherford, the college principal. Little is known of his life at this time save that he gained some impetus toward theological studies during the brief period at St. Andrews. His mother's brother, Adam Bothwell, bishop of Orkney, recommended that he continue his studies abroad and it seems likely that he did so, although no explicit evidence exists as to his domicile, or the nature of his studies. At all events, by 1571 he had returned to Scotland and, in 1572, he married Elizabeth, daughter of Sir James Stirling, and took up residence in a castle at Gartnes (completed in 1574). On the death of his father in 1608, he moved to

Merchiston Castle, near Edinburgh, where he lived for the rest of his life. In 1579 his wife died and he subsequently married Agnes Chisholm of Cromlix, Perthshire. There were two children by the first marriage, a son, Archibald, who in 1627 was raised to the peerage by the title of Lord Napier, and a daughter, Joanne. By the second marriage there were ten children; the best known of these is the second son, Robert, his father's literary executor.

Napier lived the full and energetic life of a sixteenth-century Scottish landowner, participating vigorously in local and national affairs. He embraced with great fervor the opinions of the Protestant party, and the political activities of his papist father-in-law, Sir James Chisholm, involved him in continuous embarrassment. There were quarrels with his half brothers over the inheritance and disputes with tenants and neighboring landlords over land tenure and rights. In all these matters, Napier seems to have shown himself forthright and determined in the pursuit of his aims, but nonetheless just and reasonable in his demands and willing to accept a fair settlement. As a landowner, Napier gave more than the usual attention to agriculture and to the improvement of his crops and his cattle. He seems to have experimented with the use of manures and to have discovered the value of common salt for this purpose, a monopoly for this mode of tillage being granted to his eldest son, Archibald, in 1698. A monopoly was granted to Napier also for the invention of a hydraulic screw and revolving axle to keep the level of water down in coal pits (1597). In 1599 Sir John Skene mentioned that he had consulted Napier, "a gentleman of singular judgement and learning, especially in mathematic sciences," with reference to the proper methods to be used in measuring lands.

In sixteenth-century Scotland, intellectual interest centered on religion, theology, and politics rather than on science and mathematics and Napier's first literary work arose out of the fears entertained in Scotland of an invasion by Philip II of Spain. *A Plaine Discovery of the Whole Revelation of Saint John* occupied him for about five years before its publication in 1593. In this tract Napier urged the Scottish king, James VI (the future James I of England), to see that "justice be done against the enemies of Gods church" and implored him to "purge his house, family and court of all Papists, Atheists and Newtrals." Through this publication, Napier gained a considerable reputation as a scholar and theologian and it was translated into Dutch, French, and German, going through several editions in each language. It is possible that, in later life, his authority as a divine saved him from persecution as a warlock, for there are many stories told suggesting that, locally, he was suspected of being in league with the powers of darkness. Not content with opposing popery by the pen, Napier also invented various engines of war for the defense of his faith and his country. In a document preserved in the Bacon Collection at Lambeth Palace, Napier outlines four inventions, two varieties of burning mirrors for setting fire to enemy ships at a distance, a piece of artillery for destroying everything round the arc of a circle, and an armored chariot so constructed that its occupants could fire in all directions. It is not known whether any of these machines were ever constructed.

Although documentary evidence exists to substantiate the active part Napier played in public affairs in this tumultuous age, it is more difficult to trace the development of his mathematical work, which seems to have begun in early life and persisted, through solitary and indefatigable labors, to the very end, when he made contact with Henry Briggs. Some material was, apparently, assembled soon after his first marriage in 1572 and may have been prompted by knowledge he had gleaned during his travels abroad. This treatise, dealing mainly with arithmetic and algebra, survived in manuscript form and was transcribed, after Napier's death, by his son Robert for the benefit of Briggs. It was published in 1839 by a descendant, Mark Napier, who gave to it the title *De arte logistica*. From this work, it appears that Napier had investigated imaginary roots of equations, a subject he refers to as a great algebraic secret.

There is evidence that Napier began to work on logarithms about 1590; the work culminated in the publication of two Latin treatises, known respectively as the *Descriptio* (1614) and the *Constructio* (1619). The *Descriptio* bears evidence of having been written all at one time and contains, besides the tables, a brief general account of their nature and use. An English translation of this work was made by Edward Wright but was published only after Wright's death by his son, Samuel Wright (1616). Napier approved the translation, both in substance and in form. The *Constructio* was brought out by Robert Napier, after the death of his father, and consists of material which Napier had written many years before. The object of the *Constructio* was to explain fully the way in which the tables had been calculated and the reasoning on which they were based. In the *Constructio* the phrase "artificial numbers" is used instead of "logarithms," the word "logarithm" being apparently of later invention. Napier offered no explanation for the choice but Briggs, in the *Arithmetica logarithmica* (1624), explains that the name came from their inventor because they exhibit numbers which preserve always the same ratio to one another.

Although it is as the inventor of logarithms that Napier is known in the history of mathematics, the two works mentioned above contain other material of lesser importance but nonetheless noteworthy. In the course of illustrating the use and application of logarithms Napier made frequent use of trigonometric theorems and the contribution he made to the development and systematization of spherical trigonometry has been rated highly. Napier's rules (called the Napier analogies) for the right-angled spherical triangle were published in the *Descriptio* (Bk. II, Ch. 4). He expressed them in logarithmic form and exhibited their character in relation to the star pentagon with five right angles. Another achievement was the effective use he made of decimal notation (which he had learnt of from Stevin) in conjunction with the decimal point. Although he was not the first to use a decimal separatrix in this way, the publicity that he gave to it and to the new notation helped to establish its use as standard practice. In 1617 Napier's intense concern for the practicalities of computation led him to publish another book, the *Rabdologiae*, which contains a number of elementary calculating devices, including the rods known as "Napier's bones." These rods, which in essence constitute a mechanical multiplication table, had a considerable vogue for many years after his death. Each rod is engraved with a table of multiples of a particular digit, the tens and units being separated by an oblique stroke. To obtain the product 267×8, the rods 2, 6, 7 are assembled and the result is read off from the entries in the eighth row; thus ⬛⬛⬛ gives 2,136. Book II is a practical treatment of mensuration formulas. Book III, the method of the promptuary, deals with a more complicated system of multiplication by engraved rods and strips, which has been called the first attempt at the invention of a calculating machine. The concluding section deals with a mechanical method of multiplication that was based on an "areal abacus" consisting of a checkerboard with counters, in which numbers were expressed in the binary scale.

Until recently the historical background of the invention of logarithms has remained something of an enigma. At the Napier tercentenary celebrations, Lord Moulton referred to Napier's invention as a "bolt from the blue" and suggested that nothing had led up to it, foreshadowed it, or heralded its arrival. Notwithstanding, Joost Bürgi, a maker of watches and astronomical instruments, had turned his attention to the problem about the same time and developed a system of logarithms entirely independently. Many Continental historians have accorded him priority in the actual invention, although he certainly did not have it in the publication of his *Arithmetische und geometrische Progress-Tabulen* (1620).

After the revival of learning in western Europe some of the first advances made were in trigonometry, which was developed as an independent field of study, largely in the interests of astronomy but also for surveying, mapmaking, and navigation. Much time was spent in calculating extensive tables of sines and tangents. Trigonometric tables were appearing in all parts of Europe, and stress was laid on the development of formulas, analogous to

$$\sin A \sin B = \tfrac{1}{2}(\cos \overline{A - B} - \cos \overline{A + B}),$$

which could, by converting the product of sines into sums and differences, reduce the computational difficulties. This conversion process was known as prosthaphaeresis. Formulas generated in this way were much used in astronomical calculations and were linked with the names of Longomontanus and Wittich, who both worked as assistants to Tycho Brahe. It is said that word of these developments came to Napier through a fellow countryman, John Craig, who accompanied James VI to Norway in 1590 to meet his bride, Anne of Denmark. The party landed near Tycho Brahe's observatory at Hven and was entertained by the astronomer. Although the construction of Napier's logarithms clearly owes nothing to prosthaphaeresis, the aim—that of substituting addition and subtraction for multiplication and division in trigonometrical calculations—was the same, and if Napier was already working on the problem, he may well have been stimulated to further efforts by the information he received through Craig. There is evidence in a letter written by Kepler in 1624 that he had received an intimation of Napier's work as early as 1594. This information presumably came through Tycho Brahe and Craig.

Napier's own account of his purpose in undertaking the work is printed in the author's preface to the *Descriptio* and is reprinted with slight modification in Wright's translation. Napier says that there is nothing more troublesome to mathematical practice than the "multiplications, divisions, square and cubical extractions of great numbers" and that these operations involve a tedious expenditure of time, as well as being subject to "slippery errors." By means of the tables all these operations could be replaced by simple addition and subtraction.

As presented, Napier's canon is specifically associated with trigonometric usage, in the sense that it gives logarithms of natural sines (from the tables of Erasmus Reinhold). The sine of an arc was not, at that time, given as a ratio but as the length of the semichord of a circle of given radius, subtending a specified angle at the center. In tabulating such sines, it was customary to choose a large number for the radius of the circle (or whole sine); Napier's choice of 10^7 gave him seven significant figures before introducing fractions.

The theory of arithmetic and geometric progressions, which played a central role in Napier's constructions, was of course available from ancient times (Napier quotes Euclid). The correspondence between the terms of an arithmetic and a geometric progression had been explored in detail by many sixteenth-century mathematicians; and Stifel in *Arithmetica integra* (1544) had enunciated clearly the basic laws—but without the index notation—corresponding to

$$a^m a^n = a^{m+n}, \qquad (a^m)^n = a^{mn}.$$

But, in all this work, only the relation between discrete sets of numbers was implied. In Napier's geometric model the correspondence between the terms of an arithmetic and a geometric progression was founded on the idea of continuously moving points and involved concepts of time, motion, and instantaneous speed. Although such notions had played a prominent part in the discussions of the fourteenth-century philosophers of the Merton school (most notably Swineshead in his *Liber calculationum*), there is nothing to suggest that any of this work directly influenced Napier.

Most historical accounts of Napier's logarithms have suffered considerably through translation into modern symbolism. Napier himself used virtually no notation, and his explanatory detail is almost wholly verbal. Without any of the tools of modern analysis for handling continuous functions, his propositions inevitably remained on an intuitive basis. He had, nonetheless, a remarkably clear idea of a functional relation between two continuous variables.

Briefly, two points move along parallel straight lines, the first moving arithmetically through equal distances in equal times and the second moving geometrically toward a fixed point, cutting off proportional parts of the whole line and then of subsequent remainders, also in equal times.

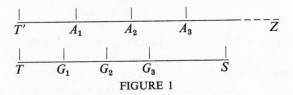

FIGURE 1

If the first point moves through the spaces $T'A_1$, A_1A_2, A_2A_3, $\cdots$, in equal times, then

$$T'A_1 = A_1A_2 = A_2A_3 = \cdots.$$

If the second point moves toward a fixed point S and is at T, G_1, G_2, G_3, $\cdots$, when the first point is at T', A_1, A_2, A_3, $\cdots$, then the spaces TG_1, G_1G_2, G_2G_3, $\cdots$, are also covered in equal times. But since the second point moves geometrically,

$$TG_1/TS = G_1G_2/G_1S = G_2G_3/G_2S = \cdots.$$

It follows that the velocity of the second point is everywhere proportional to its distance from S.

The definition of the logarithm follows: Two points start from T' and T respectively, at the same instant and with the same velocities, the first point moving uniformly and the second point moving so that its velocity is everywhere proportional to its distance from S; if the points reach L and G respectively, at the same instant, the number that measures the line $T'L$ is defined as the logarithm of GS (GS is the sine and TS, the whole sine, or radius).

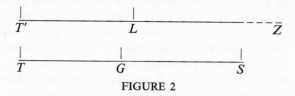

FIGURE 2

From the definition, it follows that the logarithm of the whole sine (10^7) is 0 and that the logarithm of n, where $n > 10^7$, is less than 0. In modern notation, if $T'L = y$, $y_0 = 0$, $GS = x$, $TS = x_0 = r = 10^7$, $dx/dt = -kx$, $dy/dt = kr$, $dy/dx = -r/x$, $\log_e(x/r) = -y/r$, or $\log_{1/e}(x/r) = y/r$. It remained to apply this structure in the calculation of the canon. Without any machinery for handling continuous functions it was necessary for Napier to calculate bounds, between which the logarithm must lie. His entire method depends upon these bounds, together with the corresponding bounds for the difference of the logarithms of two sines.

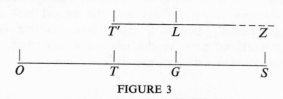

FIGURE 3

If the point O lies on ST produced such that $OS/TS = TS/SG$, then the spaces OT and TG are covered in equal times. But, since $OS > TS > GS$, the velocity at $O >$ the velocity at $T >$ the velocity at G. It follows that $OT > T'L > TG$, and $OS - TS > \log SG > TS - GS$. If $TS = r$, $GS = x$, we have

$$\frac{r-x}{x} > \frac{\log x}{r} > \frac{r-x}{r};$$

the corresponding bounds for the difference between two logarithms are given by

$$\frac{x_1 - x_2}{x_2} > \frac{\log x_2 - \log x_1}{r} > \frac{x_1 - x_2}{x_1}.$$

Napier then calculates in a series of tables the values of

$$10^7 \left(1 - \frac{1}{10^7}\right)^n, \quad n = 0, 1, 2, 3, \cdots, 100;$$

$$10^7 \left(1 - \frac{1}{10^5}\right)^n, \quad n = 0, 1, 2, \cdots, 50;$$

and finally,

$$10^7 \left(1 - \frac{5}{10^4}\right)^n \left(1 - \frac{1}{10^2}\right)^m, \quad n = 0, 1, 2, \cdots, 20;$$

$$m = 0, 1, 2, \cdots, 68.$$

The terms in each progression were obtained by successive subtraction, the last figure in the first table giving the starting point for the second. The final figure in the last table gave a value very little less than $10^7/2$, so that Napier had available a very large number of geometric means distributed over the interval 10^7, $10^7/2$. Using his inequalities, he was able to derive bounds for the logarithms of these numbers and, by taking an arithmetic mean between the bounds, to obtain an accuracy of seven significant figures. By interpolation, he tabulated the values of the logarithms of the sines (and tangents) of angles, taken at one-minute intervals, extending the tables to cover angles between 0 and 90 degrees.

Napier did not think in terms of a base, in the modern sense of the word, although since $\left(1 - \frac{1}{10^7}\right)^{10^7}$ is very nearly $\lim_{n\to\infty} \left(1 - \frac{1}{n}\right)^n$, it is clear that we have virtually a system of logarithms to base $1/e$. In Napier's system, the familiar rules for the logarithms of products, quotients, and exponents did not hold because of the choice of the whole sine (10^7), rather than 1, as the logarithm whose number was zero. Napier's tables were also awkward to use in working with ordinary numbers, rather than sines or tangents.

The calculation of the canon was a tremendous task and occupied Napier personally for over twenty years. Although not entirely free from error the calculations were essentially sound and formed the basis for all subsequent logarithm tables for nearly a century. The publication in 1614 received immediate recognition. Henry Briggs, then Gresham professor of geometry in the City of London, was enthusiastic and visited Napier at Merchiston in the summers of 1615 and 1616. During discussions that took place there the idea emerged of changing the system so that 0 should become the logarithm of unity and 10^{10} that of the whole sine. Briggs in the preface to *Arithmetica logarithmica* (1624) clearly attributes this suggestion to Napier and apparently believed that Napier had become convinced of the desirability of making this change, even before the publication of the *Descriptio*. Because of failing health, however, Napier did not have the energy to embark on this task, and it was left to Briggs to recalculate the tables, adapting them to use with a decimal base. The first 1,000 logarithms of the new canon were published after Napier's death by Briggs, without place or date (but at London before 6 December 1617), as *Logarithmorum chilias prima*. The earliest publication of Napier's logarithms on the Continent was in 1618, when Benjamin Ursinus included an excerpt from the canon, shortened by two places, in his *Cursus mathematici practici*. Through this work Kepler became aware of the importance of Napier's discovery and expressed his enthusiasm in a letter to Napier dated 28 July 1619, printed in the dedication of his *Ephemerides* (1620).

In matters of priority in the invention of logarithms the only serious claims have been made on behalf of Joost Bürgi. Many German historians have accorded him priority in the actual invention on the grounds that his tables had been computed about 1600, although they were not published until 1620. Since Napier's own work extended over a long period of time, both must be accorded full credit as independent inventors. The tables were quite differently conceived, and neither author owed anything to the other. Napier enjoyed the right of priority in publication.

BIBLIOGRAPHY

I. ORIGINAL WORKS. Napier's works are *A Plaine Discovery of the Whole Revelation of Saint John* (Edinburgh, 1593); *Mirifici logarithmorum canonis descriptio, ejusque usus,* . . . (Edinburgh, 1614); *Rabdologiae, seu numerationis per virgulas libri duo* (Edinburgh, 1617); *Mirifici logarithmorum canonis constructio; et eorum ad naturales ipsorum numeros habitudines* (Edinburgh, 1619); *De arte logistica*, Mark Napier, ed. (Edinburgh, 1839); *A Description of the Admirable Table of Logarithmes*: . . ., translated by Edward Wright, published by Samuel Wright (London, 1616). *The Construction of the Wonderful Canon of Logarithms* (Edinburgh, 1889), W. R. Macdonald's trans. of the *Constructio*, contains an excellent catalog of all the editions of Napier's works and their translations into French, Dutch, Italian, and German. Details are also included of the location of these works at that date. Further details and descriptions are included in R. A. Sampson, ed., "Bibliography of Books Exhibited at the Napier Tercentenary Celebrations, July 1914," in C. G.

Knott, ed., *Napier Tercentenary Memorial Volume* (London, 1915).

II. SECONDARY LITERATURE. Such information as is available about Napier's life and work has been fairly well documented by his descendants. Mark Napier, *Memoirs of John Napier of Merchiston; His Lineage, Life and Times* (Edinburgh, 1834), based on careful research of the private papers of the Napier family, is the source of most modern accounts. The tercentenary of the publication of the *Descriptio* was celebrated by an international congress, organized by the Royal Society of Edinburgh. The papers communicated to this congress were published in the *Napier Tercentenary Memorial Volume* (see above) and supply much detail on the historical background to Napier's work. E. M. Horsburgh, ed., *Modern Instruments and Methods of Calculation: A Handbook of the Napier Tercentenary Exhibition* (London, 1914), is also useful. Of the various reconstructions of Napier's work, Lord Moulton's, in the *Tercentenary Memorial Volume*, pp. 1–24, is the most imaginative; E. W. Hobson, *John Napier and the Invention of Logarithms* (Cambridge, 1914), is the most useful.

Still valuable on the early history of logarithms are J. W. L. Glaisher's articles, "Logarithms," in *Encyclopaedia Britannica*, 11th ed. (1910), XVI, 868–877; and "On Early Tables of Logarithms and Early History of Logarithms," in *Quarterly Journal of Pure and Applied Mathematics*, **48** (1920), 151–192. Florian Cajori, "History of the Exponential and Logarithmic Concepts," in *American Mathematical Monthly*, **20** (1913), 5–14, 35–47, 75–84, 107–117, 148–151, 173–182, 205–210, is also useful. A more recent discussion of the development of the concept of logarithm is that of D. T. Whiteside, "Patterns of Mathematical Thought in the Later Seventeenth Century," in *Archive for History of Exact Sciences*, **1** (1961), 214–231.

MARGARET E. BARON

NĀRĀYAṆA (*fl.* India, 1356), *mathematics.*

Nārāyaṇa, the son of Nṛsiṃha (or Narasiṃha), was one of the most renowned Indian mathematicians of the medieval period. His *Gaṇitakaumudī*, on arithmetic and geometry, was composed in 1356; in it he refers to his *Bījagaṇitāvataṃsa*, on algebra (see Supplement). The *Karmapradīpikā*, a commentary on the *Līlāvatī* of Bhāskara II (*b.* 1115), is found in several south Indian libraries attributed to Nārāyaṇa; but the author, a follower of Āryabhaṭa I (*b.* 476), may be the Kerala astronomer and mathematician Mādhava of Saṅgamagrāma (*ca.* 1340–1425).

The *Gaṇitakaumudī* consists of rules *(sūtras)* and examples *(udāharaṇas)*, which in the only edition, the two-volume one of P. Dvivedi (Benares, 1936–1942), are given separate numberings that do not coincide with the division of the work into chapters *(vyavahāras).* In fact, the edition is based on a single manuscript which was evidently corrupt and perhaps incomplete. We do not really know in detail the contents of the *Gaṇitakaumudī.* The *Bījagaṇitāvataṃsa* is preserved in a unique and incomplete manuscript at Benares; only the first part has been edited, by K. S. Shukla as a supplement to *Ṛtam* (**1**, pt. 2 [1969–1970]).

BIBLIOGRAPHY

Various rules from the *Gaṇitakaumudī* are discussed by B. Datta and A. N. Singh, *History of Hindu Mathematics,* 2 vols. (Lahore, 1935–1938), *passim;* and the section of that work devoted to magic squares is analyzed by S. Cammann, "Islamic and Indian Magic Squares," in *History of Religions,* **8** (1968–1969), 181–209, 271–299, esp. 274 ff. The algebra of the *Bījagaṇitāvataṃsa* has been commented on by B. Datta, "Nārāyaṇa's Method for Finding Approximate Value of a Surd," in *Bulletin of the Calcutta Mathematical Society,* **23** (1931), 187–194. See also R. Garver, "Concerning Two Square-Root Methods," *ibid.,* **23** (1932), 99–102; and "The Algebra of Nārāyaṇa," in *Isis,* **19** (1933), 472–485.

DAVID PINGREE

AL-NASAWĪ, ABU 'L-ḤASAN, 'ALĪ IBN AḤMAD

(*fl.* Baghdad, 1029–1044), *arithmetic, geometry.*

Arabic biographers do not mention al-Nasawī, who has been known to the scholarly world since 1863, when F. Woepcke made a brief study of his *al-Muqniʿ fī 'l-Ḥisāb al-Hindī* (Leiden, MS 1021). The introduction to this text shows that al-Nasawī wrote, in Persian, a book on Indian arithmetic for presentation to Magd al-Dawla, the Buwayhid ruler in Khurasan who was dethroned in 1029 or 1030. The book was presented to Sharaf al-Mulūk, vizier of Jalāl al-Dawla, ruler in Baghdad. The vizier ordered al-Nasawī to write in Arabic in order to be more precise and concise, and the result was *al-Muqniʿ.* Al-Nasawī seems to have settled in Baghdad; another book by him, *Tajrīd Uqlīdis* (Salar-Jang, MS 3142) was dedicated in highly flattering words to al-Murtadā (965–1044), an influential Shīʿite leader in Baghdad. Nothing else can be said about his life except that al-Nasawī refers to Nasā, in Khurasan, where he probably was born.

Al-Nasawī has been considered a forerunner in the use of the decimal concept because he used the rules $\sqrt{n} = \sqrt{nk^2}/k$ and $\sqrt[3]{n} = \sqrt[3]{nk^3}/k$, where k is taken as a power of 10. If k is taken as 10 or 100, the root is found correct to one or two decimal places.

There is now reason to believe that al-Nasawī cannot be credited with priority in this respect. The two rules were known to earlier writers on Hindu-Arabic arithmetic. The first appeared in the *Paṭīgaṇita* of Śrīdharācārya (750–850). Like others, al-Nasawī rather mechanically converted the decimal part of the root thus obtained to the sexagesimal scale and suggested taking k as a power of sixty, without showing signs of understanding the decimal value of the fraction. Their concern was simply to transform the fractional part of the root to minutes, seconds, and thirds. Only al-Uqlīdisī (tenth century), the discoverer of decimal fractions, retained some roots in the decimal form.

In *al-Muqniʿ,* al-Nasawī presents Indian arithmetic of integers and common fractions and applies its schemes to the sexagesimal scale. In the introduction he criticizes earlier works as too brief or too long. He states that Kūshyār ibn Labbān (*ca.* 971–1029) had written an arithmetic for astronomers, and Abū Ḥanīfa al-Dīnawarī (*d.* 895) had written one for businessmen; but Kūshyār's proved to be rather like a business arithmetic and Abū Ḥanīfa's more like a book for astronomers. Kūshyār's work, *Uṣūl Ḥisāb al-Hind,* which is extant, shows that al-Nasawī's remark was unfair. He adopted Kūshyār's schemes on integers and, like him, failed to understand the principle of "borrowing" in subtraction. To subtract 4,859 from 53,536, the Indian scheme goes as follows:

Arrange the two numbers as 53536
4859.

Subtract 4 from the digit above it; since 3 is less than 4, borrow 1 from 5, to turn 3 into 13, and subtract. And so on. Both Kūshyār and al-Nasawī would subtract 4 from 53, obtain 49, subtract 8 from 95, and so on. Only finger-reckoners agree with them in this.

In discussing subtraction of fractional quantities, al-Nasawī enunciated the rule $(n_1 + f_1) - (n_2 + f_2) = (n_1 - n_2) + (f_1 - f_2)$, where n_1 and n_2 are integers and f_1 and f_2 are fractions. He did not notice the case when $f_2 > f_1$ and the principle of "borrowing" should be used.

Al-Nasawī gave Kūshyār's method of extracting the cube root and, like him, used the approximation $\sqrt[3]{n} = p + \dfrac{r}{3p^2 + 1}$, where p^3 is the greatest cube in n and $r = n - p^3$. Arabic works of about the same period used the better rule

$$\sqrt[3]{n} = p + \frac{r}{3p^2 + 3p + 1}.$$

Later works called $3p^2 + 3p + 1$ the conventional denominator.

Al-Muqniʿ differs from Kūshyār's *Uṣūl* in that it explains the Indian system of common fractions, expresses the sexagesimal scale in Indian numerals, and applies the Indian schemes of operation to numbers expressed in this scale. But al-Nasawī could claim no priority for these features, since others, such as al-Uqlīdisī, had already done the same thing.

Three other works by al-Nasawī, all geometrical, are extant. One of them is *al-Ishbāʿ*, in which he discusses the theorem of Menelaus. One is a corrected version of Archimedes' *Lemmata* as translated into Arabic by Thābit ibn Qurra, which was later revised by Naṣīr al-Dīn al-Ṭūsī. The last is *Tajrīd Uqlīdis* ("An Abstract From Euclid"). In the introduction, al-Nasawī points out that Euclid's *Elements* is necessary for one who wants to study geometry for its own sake, but his *Tajrīd* is written to serve two purposes: it will be enough for those who want to learn geometry in order to be able to understand Ptolemy's *Almagest*, and it will serve as an introduction to Euclid's *Elements*. A comparison of the *Tajrīd* with the *Elements*, however, shows that al-Nasawī's work is a copy of books I–VI, on plane geometry and geometrical algebra, and book XI, on solid geometry, with some constructions omitted and some proofs altered.

BIBLIOGRAPHY

I. Original Works. Al-Nasawī's writings include "On the Construction of a Circle That Bears a Given Ratio to Another Given Circle, and on the Construction of All Rectilinear Figures and the Way in Which Artisans Use Them," cited by al-Ṭūsī in *Maʾkhūdhāt Arshimīdis*, no. 10 of his *Rasāʾil*, II (Hyderabad-Deccan, 1940); *al-Ishbāʿ*, trans. by E. Wiedemann in his *Studien zur Astronomie der Araber* (Erlangen, 1926), 80–85—see also H. Burger and K. Kohl, *Geschichte des Transversalensätze* (Erlangen, 1924), 53–55; *Kitāb al-lāmiʿ fī amthilat al-Zīj al-jāmiʿ* ("Illustrative Examples of the Twenty-Five Chapters of the *Zīj al-jāmiʿ* of Kūshyār"), in Ḥājjī Khalīfa, *Kashf* (Istanbul, 1941), col. 970; and *Risāla fī maʿrifat al-taqwīm waʾl-asṭurlāb* ("A Treatise on Chronology and the Astrolabe"), Columbia University Library, MS Or. 45, op. 7.

II. Secondary Literature. See H. Suter, "Über des Rechenbuch des Ali ben Ahmed el-Nasawi," in *Bibliotheca mathematica*, 2nd ser., **7** (1906), 113–119; and F. Woepcke, "Mémoires sur la propagation des chiffres indiens," in *Journal asiatique*, 6th ser., **1** (1863), 492 ff.

See also Kūshyār ibn Labbān, *Uṣūl Ḥisāb al-Hind*, in M. Levey and M. Petruck, *Principles of Hindu Reckoning* (Madison, Wis., 1965), 55–83.

A. S. Saidan

NAṢĪR AL-DĪN AL-ṬŪSĪ. See **al-Ṭūsī, Naṣīr al-Dīn.**

NASMYTH, JAMES (*b*. Edinburgh, Scotland, 19 August 1808; *d*. London, England, 7 May 1890), *engineering, astronomy.*

Although best known for his steam hammer, Nasmyth also did much to improve the design of machine tools in general. His mechanical skills were used to help William Lassell build a very fine Newtonian reflector, and he published astronomical observations of some interest.

Nasmyth was the youngest son of Alexander Nasmyth, a portrait and landscape painter, and Barbara Foulis. Leaving the high school in Edinburgh, in 1820, he was educated privately—and not at all well—but he acquired some knowledge of chemistry, mathematics, and natural philosophy. Through his skill in model engineering, he met John Leslie, who gave him admittance to his classes at Edinburgh University. In 1821 he attended the Edinburgh School of Arts. In 1829 he found employment as personal assistant to Henry Maudslay in his works in London, and in 1834 he established his own business in Manchester. So successful was he there, and in many later enterprises, that by 1856 he was able to retire with a large fortune.

The steam hammer was Nasmyth's most successful invention. Power hammers had previously been worked by steam, but in an imprecise and relatively uncontrolled manner, actuated by levers or cams. Nasmyth produced his design in November 1839 with a view to its being used for the forging of a thirty-inch-diameter paddle shaft in prospect for the steamship *Great Britain*, then on the stocks at Bristol. (The shaft was forged, but not actually used, since the ship was eventually screw-driven.) His first solution was a single-acting hammer, operating by gravity, the steam merely lifting the hammer for each successive drop. Acceptance of his design was at first slow; and the first steam hammer to be built, in 1842 at the ironworks founded by Adolphe and Eugène Schneider at Creuzot, was copied without Nasmyth's knowledge from his private "scheme-book" design. James Watt is said to have anticipated the idea. The steam hammer, with many improvements, soon became perhaps the most dramatic symbol of steam power, particularly as it made possible the forging of very large guns for the British navy.

Nasmyth also designed a milling machine, a planing or shaping machine, and a steam pile driver. After his early retirement, he took up astronomy, creating something of a stir when he announced that the solar surface was patterned like willow leaves (1862). A book on the moon, written jointly with James Carpenter, was well illustrated.

BIBLIOGRAPHY

I. ORIGINAL WORKS. Nasmyth's book on the moon is *The Moon Considered as a Planet, a World, and a Satellite* (London, 1874; 4th ed., London, 1903), written with James Carpenter; his paper on the sun is "On the Structure of the Luminous Envelope of the Sun," in *Manchester Philosophical Society Memoirs*, **1** (1862), 407–411. For his astronomical work, all of minor importance, see Agnes Clerke, *History of Astronomy During the Nineteenth Century*, 3rd ed. (London, 1893), 103, 204, 313, 326, 352. Apart from his autobiography, Nasmyth published nothing on the steam hammer except his patent (No. 9382, 9 June 1842).

II. SECONDARY LITERATURE. The literature is very extensive, but the main biographical source is Nasmyth's autobiography, edited by Samuel Smiles (London, 1883; Cambridge, 1931). See also Thomas Baker, *Elements of Mechanism. With Remarks on Tools and Machines by J. Nasmyth*, 2nd ed. (London, 1858).

J. D. NORTH

NATALIS, STEPHANUS. See **Nöel, Étienne.**

NATANSON, WŁADYSŁAW (*b*. Warsaw, Poland, 18 June 1864; *d*. Cracow, Poland, 26 February 1937), *physics.*

Natanson, a son of Ludwik Natanson and Natalia Epstein, came from a distinguished literary and scientific family. His father, a physician, wrote papers on medicine and edited a medical journal. While attending school in Warsaw from 1874 to 1882, he wrote his first memoirs, collaborating with his older brother Edward. In 1882 he began to study mathematics and physics at the University of St. Petersburg. During vacations, in a laboratory in the family home in Warsaw, Władysław and Edward carried out experiments on the dissociation of nitrogen tetroxide—one of the first experimental confirmations of the law of mass action. In 1886 Natanson completed his studies at St. Petersburg and went to England, where he worked for a time in the Cavendish Laboratory, then directed by J. J. Thomson. In 1887 he received a master's degree in science after presenting "Über die kinetische Theorie unvollkommener Gase" at the University of Dorpat, where the physics department

was directed by A. von Oettingen. Here too in 1888 he presented his thesis, "Über die kinetische Theorie der Jouleschen Erscheinung," and was awarded a doctorate. In 1891 Natanson received the *veniam legendi* at the Jagiellonian University in Cracow and became a professor there, occupying the chair of theoretical physics until his retirement in 1935. In 1911 he married Elżbieta Baranowska.

A member of the physical societies of London, Berlin, and Paris, Natanson was a founder and first president (1920) of the Polish Physical Society. From 1893 he was a corresponding member, and from 1900 a member, of the Academy of Sciences at Cracow (later the Polish Academy of Sciences). In 1925 he was elected vice-president of the International Union of Pure and Applied Physics. Rector of the Jagiellonian University in 1922, Natanson received an honorary Ph.D. from that university in 1930.

After the experiments on the dissociation of nitrogen tetroxide that he had carried out with his brother, Natanson worked on the kinetic theory of gases. His "Über die kinetische Theorie unvollkommener Gase" contains, for example, a proof that the aggregate of molecules of a gas, however great, underlies both Maxwell's law of distribution and the law of the equipartition of energy—a statement important for the theory of Brownian movement, although the paper was not seen then in this light. Beginning in 1891 Natanson published several papers on thermodynamics. The most important are "On the Laws of Irreversible Phenomena" (1896) and "Sur les propriétés thermocinétiques des potentiels thermodynamiques" (1897). Considering the thermodynamics of his time to be mere thermostatics, Natanson sought a way to achieve genuine thermodynamics, examining the function of energy dissipation and introducing a generalization of Hamilton's principle. For postulating this principle of many applications and general scope (sometimes called Natanson's thermokinetic principle), Natanson is considered a pioneer in the thermodynamics of irreversible processes.

Natanson later worked on the hydrodynamics of viscous liquids and on such related phenomena as the double refraction of light in moving viscous liquids. Inspired by Lorentz' works, he published several papers on the optical properties of matter. In "On the Elliptic Polarization of Light Transmitted Through an Absorbing Naturally-Active Medium" (1908) Natanson gave a theory of Cotton's phenomenon and a rule governing it (known in the French literature as the *règle de Natanson*). In 1929–1933 he worked on Fermat's principle in relation to wave mechanics.

Natanson published five volumes of lectures and essays on scientists, writers, and philosophers, as well as on intellectual and religious trends. He was also an author and a coauthor of university and secondary school textbooks.

BIBLIOGRAPHY

I. ORIGINAL WORKS. German, English, and French versions of Natanson's works are in Wiedemann's *Annalen der Physik und Chemie* (1885–1891); *Philosophical Magazine* (1890–1933); and *Bulletin international de l'Académie polonaise des sciences et des lettres de Cracovie* (1891–1933). Lists of his publications are in the articles by Weyssenhoff and Klecki (see below).

His articles include "Über die Dissoziation des Untersalpetersäuredampfes," in *Annalen der Physik und Chemie*, **24** (1885), 454, and **27** (1886), 606, written with E. Natanson; "Über die kinetische Theorie unvollkommener Gase," *ibid.*, **33** (1888), 683; "On the Laws of Irreversible Phenomena," in *Philosophical Magazine*, **41** (1896), 385; "Sur les propriétés thermocinétiques des potentiels thermodynamiques," in *Bulletin de l'Académie des sciences de Cracovie* (1897), 247; "On the Elliptic Polarization of Light Transmitted Through an Absorbing Naturally-Active Medium," *ibid.* (1908), 764; and "Fermat's Principle," in *Philosophical Magazine*, **16** (1933), 178. Natanson's autobiography was published in *Postępy fizyki*, **9** (1958), 115.

II. SECONDARY LITERATURE. See the following, listed chronologically: J. W. Weyssenhoff, in *Acta physica polonica*, **6** (1937), 295, an obituary in English and Polish with a bibliography of Natanson's works; L. Klecki, in *Prace matematyczno-fizyczne*, **46** (1939), 1, an obituary in French with a bibliography without titles; and articles by J. W. Weyssenhoff, A. Piekara, and L. Infeld, in *Postępy fizyki*, **9** (1958).

See also Armin Teske, "Sur un travail de Ladislas Natanson de 1888," in *Actes du VIIIᵉ Congrès international d'histoire des sciences*, II (Florence, 1958), 123; and K. Gumiński, "O pracach termodynamicznych Władysława Natansona" ("Władysław Natanson's Works on Thermodynamics"), in *Postępy fizyki*, **17** (1966), 101.

ANDRZEJ A. TESKE

NATHORST, ALFRED GABRIEL (*b.* Väderbrunn, Södermanland, Sweden, 7 November 1850; *d.* Stockholm, Sweden, 20 January 1921), *paleobotany, geology, exploration.*

His parents, Hjalmar Otto Nathorst and Maria Charlotta af Georgii, moved in 1861 to Alnarp, in Skåne, where his father had been appointed professor at the Institute of Agriculture. Nathorst was educated at Malmö and entered the University of Lund in 1868. In 1871 he enrolled at the University of Uppsala but returned to Lund, where he took his doctorate in 1874. He was docent of geology from 1874 to 1879. In 1873 he became a member of the staff of the Geological Survey of Sweden serving until 1884. He was then given the post of professor and director of the newly created Department of Archegoniates and Fossil Plants at the Swedish Museum of Natural History in Stockholm. Nathorst held this position until he resigned in 1917.

Nathorst showed an early inclination for the outdoors and natural science, particularly botany. In Lund, he turned to geology under the influence of N. P. Angelin, a pioneer in Swedish paleontology and stratigraphic geology. Nathorst's first published paper (1869) was a detailed study of a Cambrian sequence in Skåne. As an officer in the Geological Survey, Nathorst made many important contributions to the knowledge of the geology of south Sweden. He discovered and described (1871) the remains of glacial plants in a freshwater clay in Skåne. This paper was the first in a series of contributions to the study of vegetational history in Sweden in postglacial times.

Nathorst's paleobotanical investigations of the Rhaeto-Liassic flora of Skåne resulted in a number of publications beginning in 1875. Since all but one of these papers are in Swedish, they failed to win the recognition they deserved. His international reputation as a paleobotanist is based instead on his monographs of the Tertiary floras of Japan (1882, 1888) and of the Paleozoic and Mesozoic floras of the Arctic. He was not speculative, and he treated his material from a strictly morphological and taxonomic point of view. Nathorst himself assembled part of the collections that he studied.

In 1871 Nathorst took part in an expedition to Spitsbergen. He led several expeditions to Svalbard and Greenland to study the geography, geology, and biology of the Arctic. Nathorst also attempted to elucidate experimentally the origin of fossil trails and tracks (1881, 1886). Although temperamental he won friendship and respect in international circles. His enormous capacity for work explains in part the great extent and importance of his scientific output.

BIBLIOGRAPHY

Nathorst's most important works were "Zur fossilen Flora Japans," in *Palaeontologische Abhandlungen*, **4**, pt. 3 (1888), 195–250; *Zur fossilen Flora der Polarländer*, 2 vols. in 5 pts. (Stockholm, 1894–1920); and "Beiträge zur Geologie der Bären-Insel, Spitzbergens und des König-Karl-Landes," in *Bulletin of the Geological Institute of Uppsala*, **10** (1910), 257–416. The most exhaustive biography of Nathorst is by T. G. Halle, in *Geologiska föreningens i Stockholm förhandlingar*, **43** (1921), 241–280, with bibliography, 281–311. See also the obituary by A. C. Seward in *Botanical Gazette* (Chicago), **71** (1921), 464–465.

GERHARD REGNÉLL

NAUDIN, CHARLES (*b.* Autun, France, 14 August 1815; *d.* Villa Thuret, near Antibes, France, 19 March 1899), *horticulture, experimental botany.*

Naudin was the son of a petty entrepreneur whose financial successes were rare. His childhood and youth were thus marked by frequent moves and numerous schools but also by an extraordinary determination to prepare for a medical, and then a scientific, career. After receiving the baccalaureate in science at Montpellier in 1837, he moved on to Paris. Working as bookkeeper, tutor, private secretary, and gardener, he earned his doctorate in 1842 and awaited an opening in the French educational system. He occupied minor posts until 1846, when, recommended by his lifelong friend and supporter, the botanist Joseph Decaisne, he joined the herbarium staff at the Muséum d'Histoire Naturelle and became professor of zoology at the Collège Chaptal. Almost immediately Naudin was obliged to resign these posts and to seek his livelihood elsewhere in Paris and in the provinces. He had been struck by a severe nervous disorder which left him totally deaf and in constant pain; his public career, so arduously earned, had to be abandoned. He finally settled at Collioure, in 1869, and established a private experimental garden devoted especially to problems of acclimatization and earned his living by the sale of seeds and specimens. In 1878 he became the first director of the experimental garden at Antibes given to the state by the family of the horti-culturist Gustave Thuret. Thus, not until age sixty-three did Naudin find financial security and suitable institutional support. His plaint rings true: "Happy is the professor who enjoys an assured income and whom the government provides with assistance and collaborators."

Throughout these years of insecurity and frequent isolation, Naudin pursued a remarkably varied program of research and horticultural promotion. His primary interests focused on acclimatization and economic botany and on the relation of hybridization to the formation of new biological species. The gardens at Collioure and Antibes were directed toward the introduction into France and her colonies, notably Algeria, of foreign plants of potential eco-nomic value. Naudin demonstrated exceptional skill as horticulturist and arboriculturist, and the garden at Antibes soon became a primary means of communi-cation among French botanists and agronomists and their foreign colleagues. Naudin himself paid particular attention to the economic potential of the Australian import *Eucalyptus* for dry and saline areas of southern France.

By far Naudin's most celebrated scientific work was done on problems of plant hybridization. His research began in 1854 and continued for two decades. Decaisne had suggested hybridization as a seemingly fruitful approach to the issue of species stability; Linnaeus' famous experiments (1759) with speedwell and goats-beard had suggested that man might indeed modify nature's creations. Working primarily with *Datura* species, Naudin pursued this suggestion and arrived at results of interest to the history of both the study of inheritance and of evolution theory. He ascertained that the first generation of hybrids was relatively homogeneous in appearance and that reciprocal crosses produced identical results. From this first generation of hybrids he then produced a second and thereby established that second-generation hybrids display extraordinary diversity; "disjunction" of all the species' characters seems to occur, with new and unexpected combinations appearing in the offspring. His contemporary Gregor Mendel also recognized these phenomena, but, unlike Naudin, he marshaled the data from the second generation and sought its explanation in the statistical distribution of hereditary factors. Naudin overlooked this crucial step and could only emphasize the seemingly chaotic distribu-tion of characters in second-generation hybrids, a phenomenon now called segregation.

Hybridization proved effective for Naudin in the limited production of new species. His faith in evolution was real but constrained. He held that the present diversity of specific forms had been produced from a reduced number of aboriginal forms. Hybridization was the primary agency of change, not natural selection or environmental action. The ancestral or primary forms were of basic importance; all other species were secondary productions and might or might not exhibit permanence. Naudin's scheme, remarkably consonant with the century-old conclusions of Linnaeus, thus reveal his belief in the reality of species transformation as well as his res-ervations regarding proposed evolutionary mech-anisms. Hybridization, the object of Naudin's most prolonged and assiduous investigations, thus provided a seemingly plausible alternative mechanism. At the same time it ensured the creation of but one more explanation of evolutionary change in those confused years between 1859 and 1900, when the phenomena of inheritance were brought by Darwin to the center of attention of natural history and left there unresolved.

BIBLIOGRAPHY

I. ORIGINAL WORKS. Naudin published voluminously and widely. The principal listing of his scattered writings is the Royal Society *Catalogue of Scientific Papers*, IV, 575–576; VIII, 483; X, 901; XVII, 459. These lists are nonetheless incomplete. His major papers on hybridization are "Réflexions sur l'hybridation dans les végétaux," in *Revue horticole*, 4th ser., **4** (1855), 351–354; "Sur les plantes hybrides," *ibid.*, **10** (1861), 396–399; "Nouvelles recherches sur l'hybridité dans les végétaux," in *Annales des sciences naturelles*, Botanique, 4th ser., **19** (1863), 180–203, which offers only the "Conclusions" to Naudin's foremost contribution to the study of heredity, published under the same title in *Nouvelles archives du Muséum d'histoire naturelle*, **1** (1865), 25–176; and "De l'hybridité considérée comme cause de la variabilité dans les végétaux," in *Comptes rendus . . . de l'Académie des sciences*, **59** (1864), 837–845.

Other publications include "Les espèces affines et la théorie de l'évolution," in *Bulletin. Société botanique de France*, **21** (1874), 240–272; *Le jardin du cultivateur* (Paris, 1857); *Manuel de l'amateur des jardins, traité général d'horticulture*, 4 vols. (Paris, 1862–1871), written with Joseph Decaisne; *Mémoire sur les eucalyptus introduits dans la région méditerranéenne* (Paris, 1883), also published in *Annales des sciences naturelles*, Botanique, 5th ser., **16** (1883), 337–430.

II. SECONDARY LITERATURE. The principal account of Naudin's life is Marcelin Berthelot, *Notice historique sur la vie et les travaux de M. Naudin, lue à l'Académie des sciences le 17 décembre 1900* (Paris, 1900); see also E. Bornet's brief notice in *Comptes rendus . . . de l'Académie des sciences*, **128** (1899), 127–128. The only comprehensive study of Naudin's scientific inquiries, especially those dealing with plant hybridization, is Louis Blaringham, "La notion de l'espèce et la disjonction des hybrides d'après Charles Naudin (1852–1875)," in *Progressus rei botanicae*, **4** (1913), 27–108. Shorter accounts are H. F. Roberts, *Plant Hybridization Before Mendel* (Princeton, 1929), 129–136; R. C. Olby, *Origins of Mendelism* (London, 1966), 62–66; Jean F. Leroy, "Naudin, Spencer et Darwin dans l'histoire des théories de l'hérédité," *Actes du XIᵉ Congrès international d'histoire des sciences*, V (Warsaw–Krakow, 1968), 64–69; and A. E. Gaisinovich, *Zarozhdenie genetiki* ("The Origin of Genetics"; Moscow, 1967), 54–71.

WILLIAM COLEMAN

NAUMANN, ALEXANDER (*b.* Eudorf, near Alsfeld, Prussia, 31 July 1837; *d.* Giessen, Germany, 16 March 1922), *chemistry*.

The son of a Protestant minister, Naumann attended the Gymnasium in Darmstadt and then studied chemistry and mathematics at the University of Giessen. After graduating in 1858 he became an assistant at the technical school in Darmstadt and in 1860–1861 was an assistant in the chemistry institute of the University of Tübingen. He moved to Giessen in 1862 and taught mathematics in the Gymnasium there. Naumann qualified as a lecturer in chemistry in 1864 at the University of Giessen. While continuing to teach at the Gymnasium, he lectured and conducted research at the university. He became associate professor in 1869 and, in 1882, full professor and director of the chemistry laboratory, where he remained active until his retirement in 1913.

Naumann began his scientific work in organic chemistry with an investigation of the chlorination of butyric acid and studies of the esters of benzoic acid. In his *Habilitationsschrift*, which dealt with the bromination of acetyl chloride, his interest in the study of the reaction mechanism was already evident. From this time on, he dedicated himself to physical chemistry, especially thermochemistry. During the 1860's the thermodynamic knowledge recently acquired in physics was slowly penetrating the field of chemistry, and the results of Naumann's tireless work contributed significantly to preparing the way for later important discoveries in chemical thermodynamics.

In an essay (1867) that can be considered a contribution toward Guldberg and Waage's law of mass action, Naumann expressed the view that only those molecules which possess energy higher than the critical energy can react with each other. At a constant temperature molecules form and disintegrate, thus producing an equilibrium. With increasing temperature the number of molecular collisions increases while the reaction velocity increases at an ever greater rate.

In his investigation in 1878 of the dissociation process $N_2O_4 \rightleftharpoons 2NO_2$ Naumann demonstrated the validity of the law of mass action, which had already been formulated. Many of his papers dealt with the equilibrium ratios between water vapor and various crystal hydrates, as well as determinations of vapor densities and heats of decomposition.

Naumann's scientific activity diminished drastically after his appointment as full professor at Giessen. Perhaps the legacy of his predecessors at the chemistry laboratory, Liebig and Heinrich Will, both great organic chemists, proved too heavy a burden. Moreover, his responsibility for teaching primarily organic chemistry diverted him from the field in which he had originally done creative work—without providing a substitute. As a result he devoted himself to university administration and took an interest in politics.

BIBLIOGRAPHY

Naumann's most important books are *Grundriss der Thermochemie* (Brunswick, 1869); and *Lehr- und Handbuch der Thermochemie* (Brunswick, 1882). Many of his other publications are listed in Poggendorff, III, 958–959; IV, 1059; V, 895. An obituary is *Akademische Rede zur Jahresfeier der Hessischen Ludwigs Universität* (Giessen, 1922), 43.

F. SZABADVÁRY

NAUMANN, KARL FRIEDRICH (*b.* Dresden, Germany, 30 May 1797; *d.* Dresden, 26 November 1873), *mineralogy, geology.*

Naumann discovered tetartohedrism in the isometric, tetragonal, and hexagonal crystal systems and was the first to observe hemimorphism. His *Lehrbuch der Geognosie* (1850–1854) was the most authoritative work on petrography in the mid-nineteenth century and served as a standard textbook for decades.

Naumann's father, Johann Gottlieb, was a noted composer of church music. In 1816 Naumann went to the mining academy at Freiberg to study mineralogy under Werner. After Werner's death in 1817, Naumann continued his education at Leipzig and at Jena, where he received his doctorate in 1819. During 1821 and 1822 he traveled in Norway observing its geology and collecting minerals. In 1823 he became a *Privatdozent* at Jena, in 1824 a *Dozent* at Leipzig, and in 1826 he was named professor of crystallography at Freiberg. His first book, *Beiträge zur Kenntnis Norwegens* (1824), described his observations in Norway. In 1825 he published his *Grundriss der Krystallographie,* in which he introduced the concept of a "crystal series," that is, the aggregate of all crystal forms that can be developed from a basic form in accordance with Weiss's law of zones (the law of rational intercepts). In this work also Naumann examined Mohs's 1822 suggestion that crystal systems might exist in which the crystallographic axes are not mutually perpendicular and successfully identified the present monoclinic system. His *Lehrbuch der reinen und angewandten Krystallographie* (1830) was even more important in that Naumann introduced a novel method for the designation and treatment of crystal forms, which greatly simplified and coordinated those of Weiss and Mohs and which was adopted almost immediately by German crystallographers. Naumann also analyzed the tetragonal system in this work and commenced an examination of the incomplete symmetry of some crystals, which led to many published descriptions of tetartohedrism and hemimorphism.

Although Naumann continued to write on crystallography, his central interest turned to geognosy. In 1835 he was named professor of geognosy at Freiberg, and in 1842 he became professor of mineralogy and geognosy at Leipzig. His 1846 *Elemente der Mineralogie,* which successfully coordinated the

systems of Mohs and Berzelius, went to fifteen editions, seven of them posthumous.

Naumann's most important work was his *Lehrbuch der Geognosie.* In it he differentiated rocks primarily according to their origin, which he determined from their texture, for example, crystalline, clastic, and hyaline. He supported the theory that most gneisses and schists had been formed from sedimentary rocks but admitted that some gneisses had been produced by the deformation of igneous rocks. The first text to devote considerable space to tectonics, his *Lehrbuch* contained all of the scientific information known about earthquakes at that time. Naumann held that certain earthquakes occurred independently of any volcanic activity and might therefore be termed "plutonic." This view was in opposition to that of Humboldt, who believed earthquakes and volcanoes to be merely different manifestations of the same causes.

Late in life, Naumann's proficiency in mathematics led him to the study of symmetry in plants and conch shells. In 1872 he retired from his chair at Leipzig and returned to Dresden, where he died the following year. He was a corresponding member of the academies of Berlin, Munich, St. Petersburg, and Paris, of the Royal Society of London and of the American Philosophical Society, and he received the Wollaston Medal of the Geological Society of London in 1865.

BIBLIOGRAPHY

I. ORIGINAL WORKS. Naumann's principal works are *Beiträge zur Kenntnis Norwegens,* 2 vols. (Leipzig, 1824); *De granite juxta calcem transitorium posito* (Jena, 1823); *De hexagonali crystallinarium formarum systemate* (Leipzig, 1824); *Grundriss der Krystallographie* (Leipzig, 1825); *Entwurf der Lithurgik oder ökonomischen Mineralogie* (Leipzig, 1826); *Lehrbuch der Mineralogie* (Leipzig, 1828); *Lehrbuch der reinen und angewandten Krystallographie,* 2 vols. (Leipzig, 1830); *Geognostische Beschreibung des Königreiches Sachsen,* 5 vols. (Dresden–Leipzig, 1834–1844), written with B. von Cotta; *Anfangsgründe der Krystallographie* (Dresden–Leipzig, 1841); *Elemente der Mineralogie* (Leipzig, 1846); *Lehrbuch der Geognosie,* 2 vols. (Leipzig, 1850–1854); *Elemente der theoretischen Krystallographie* (Leipzig, 1856); *Geognostische Beschreibung des Kohlenbassins von Flöha* (Leipzig, 1864); and *Geognostische Karte des erzgebirgschen Bassins* (Leipzig, 1866). He published about 100 scientific articles; see Royal Society *Catalogue of Scientific Papers,* IV, 576–578; VIII, 484.

II. SECONDARY LITERATURE. See *Allgemeine Deutsche Biographie,* XXIII, 316–319; H. B. Geinetz, "Zur Erinnerung an Dr. Carl Friedrich Naumann," in *Neues Jahrbuch für Mineralogie, Geologie und Paläontologie* for 1874, p. 147; and Franz von Kobell, "Nekrolog auf Dr. K. F. Naumann," in *Sitzungsberichte der Bayerischen Akademie der Wissenschaften zu München,* Math.-phys. Kl., for 1874, pp. 81–84.

JOHN G. BURKE

AMERICAN COUNCIL OF LEARNED SOCIETIES

Dictionary
of Scientific
Biography

cSs